# A New History of Jazz

# A NEW HISTORY OF JAZZ

## JAZZ

*Alyn Shipton*

**continuum**
LONDON • NEW YORK

*For Catherine and Don*

**Continuum**
The Tower Building, 11 York Road, London, SE1 7NX
370 Lexington Avenue, New York, NY 10017–6503

© Alyn Shipton 2001

First published 2001, by arrangement with Bayou Press Ltd
Published in paperback with corrections 2002

**British Library Cataloguing-in-Publication Data**
A catalogue record for this book is available from the British Library.

ISBN 0–8264–4754–6 (hardback)
0–8264–6338–X (paperback)

**Library of Congress Cataloging-in-Publication Data**
Shipton, Alyn.
    A new history of jazz/Alyn Shipton.
      p. cm.
    Includes bibliographical references and index.
    ISBN 0–8264–4754–6 (hardback)—0–8264–6338–X (paperback)
    1. Jazz—History and criticism. I. Title.
ML3506 .S47 2001
781.65′09—dc21

                                              2001017177

Typeset by YHT Ltd, London
Printed and bound in Great Britain by MPG Books Ltd,
Bodmin, Cornwall

# Contents

CONTENTS

# Preface and acknowledgments

No book, least of all one as large as this, can be achieved without the help, support and enthusiasm of others, and first and foremost I owe a debt to my parents for introducing me to the sounds of jazz at a very early age. Many of the ideas I propose about the origins of jazz, particularly the connections with the black theatre and vaudeville, arise out of conversations with John Chilton, Paul Oliver and Howard Rye, all of whom have been diligent and constructive reviewers of this book as it took shape. I am grateful to all three of them for suggesting (and often providing) literature and recordings to prompt new lines of enquiry for all of the areas I have covered. I should also like to thank Robert Walser for his extremely perceptive suggestions arising from his reading of early drafts of the manuscript.

In the New Orleans section, I have drawn heavily on my long association with Danny Barker, and also my friendship with Bill Russell. Through Dick Allen, Mike Casimir, Lars Edegran, Norman Emberson, and Trevor Richards, I have had the good fortune to meet, listen to, and occasionally play alongside a number of the founding fathers of New Orleans and swing era jazz. Working a number of times with Kid Thomas Valentine in the 1970s and 1980s was an insight into the world of pre-Armstrong trumpet, as were my many conversations with Doc Cheatham about how Freddie Keppard and Joe Oliver sounded in 1920s Chicago. In the early jazz section I have also attempted to rethink the position of Bunk Johnson, whose reputation has suffered somewhat in the wake of Donald M. Marquis's investigations into Buddy Bolden. I discussed Bunk at length with his one-time pianist Don Ewell, and as a consequence of his strong conviction that Bunk was a much-underrated brilliant and talented musician, together with the insights of others who knew him well, I have taken the view that his work still has plenty to teach us about early jazz trumpeting.

I am grateful to Tony Russell and Jenny Mulherin, editor and publisher respectively of Marshall Cavendish's *Jazz Greats* partwork series, for giving me the chance to investigate the careers of numerous jazz musicians in detail, and to have the opportunity of compiling CD collections of their work, with access to the splendid sound resources of John R. T. Davies and Ted Kendall. A number of the chapters in this book have their origins in research done for this series.

Several other sections of the book arise out of research done for BBC radio documentaries, and I am grateful to my producers, Felix Carey, Terry Carter, Derek Drescher, Gabriel Gilson, and Oliver Jones for allowing me to investigate many areas of jazz in such depth, and to supplement questions intended for radio use with others of my own. In particular, the Ornette Coleman section arises from background research on a series to celebrate his seventieth birthday, the Coltrane chapter from a radio documentary investigation of *Ascension*, the AACM material from a series on its thirty-fifth birthday, and the jazz-rock and world music sections from research carried out as background for programmes presented by Barbara Thompson and John Surman. Other research was carried out in conjunction with that for programmes on British traditional jazz, on Central Avenue in Los Angeles, and on the lives of Cab Calloway, Doc Cheatham, Dizzy Gillespie, Bud Powell, Shorty Rogers, and Fats Waller.

Thanks to Steve Voce for providing out-of-the-way discographical information, copies of rare liner notes, and access to his voluminous address book.

I am grateful to the following for their time and help, many of whom I have interviewed in the course of twenty years of jazz journalism and broadcasting: Rashied Ali, Don Alias, Fred Anderson, George Avakian, Benny Bailey, Blue Lu Barker, Danny Barker, Sylvia Barker, Bob Belden, Louie Bellson, Dave Bennett, Paul Bley, Anthony Braxton, Ari Brown, Ray Brown, Clora Bryant, Ian Carr, William Carter (and other members of the San Francisco Traditional Jazz Foundation), Al Casey, Doc Cheatham, Buck Clayton, Denardo Coleman, Ornette Coleman, Buddy Collette, Ravi Coltrane, Bob Cranshaw, Michael Cuscuna, Wild Bill Davison, Harry Dial, Bill Dillard, Bill Doggett, Dave Douglas, Teddy Edwards, Nancy Miller Elliott, Don Ewell, Malachi Favors, Tommy Flanagan, Elizabeth Forbes, Von Freeman, Gary Giddins, Ira Gitler, Benny Golson, Claire P. Gordon, Al Grey, Johnny Griffin, Trilok Gurtu, Charlie Haden, Roy Haynes, Jimmy Heath, Bob Helm, Andrew Hill, Milt Hinton, Dave Holland, Illinois

Jacquet, Joseph Jarman, Leroy Jenkins, Cousin Joe, Jonah Jones, Diana Krall, Joachim Kuhn, Dame Cleo Laine, Oliver Lake, Pete La Roca (Sims), Gene Lees, John Lewis, Abbey Lincoln, John Litweiler, Jimmy McGriff, Jackie McLean, Pops Mahomed, Howard Mandel, Wynton Marsalis, Hugh Masekela, John Mayer, Pat Metheny, Grover Mitchell, Roscoe Mitchell, Sonny Morris, Snub Mosley, Famadou Don Moye, Chuck Nessa, Oscar Peterson, Lewis Porter, Roy Porter, Sammy Price, Dewey Redman, Roswell Rudd, George Russell, Shorty Rogers, Bill Russell, John Scofield, Gunther Schuller, Archie Shepp, Horace Silver, Evelyn McGhee Stone, Jesse Stone, Dr. Billy Taylor, Buddy Tate, Clark Terry, McCoy Tyner, Peter Vacher, Rudy Van Gelder, Nana Vasconcelos, Cedar Walton, Gerald Wiggins, Bob Wilber, Gerald Wilson, Jimmy Woode.

This is not primarily an illustrated book, but I have sought to find pictures of some of the musicians who are most important to the narrative. For these I have been reliant on the help of my old friend Peter Symes, who has been an entertaining companion among the press corps at dozens of concerts and festivals over the years. Photographs in the plate section come from Peter's collection, and from Ray Avery, Danny Barker, The Cab Calloway Collection at Boston University, Mike Doyle, Derek Drescher, Nancy Miller Elliott, Claire P. Gordon, Randi Hultin, Don Hunstein, Jan Persson, Charles Peterson (by courtesy of Don Peterson), and my own collection.

Finally, this book would not have been possible without the commitment and support of everyone at Continuum, my publisher and long-term colleague Janet Joyce, managing editor Sandra Margolies, copy-editor Alan Worth, proof-reader Karolin Thomas, and indexer Jan Worrall.

# Rethinking Jazz History

Of all the musical forms to emerge during the twentieth century, jazz was by far the most significant. In the early years of the century it spread first throughout the United States of America like wildfire, and then quickly to the rest of the world, where its combination of syncopation, unusual pitching, vocal tones, and raw energy touched the hearts and minds of people across the entire spectrum of social and racial backgrounds. Its message was universal, and it stood for something new, something revolutionary, something risqué that overturned the old orders of art music and folk music alike.

The first references to it in print come from the West Coast of the United States, where the San Francisco *Bulletin* of March 1913 used the term to describe a dance music full of vigor and "pep." By the time it came into general use, the word "jazz" was mainly used to describe the syncopated bands from New Orleans that played in pre-1920s Chicago and then New York, but it carried with it scatological connotations that the related forms "ragtime" and "blues" did not. As a consequence, jazz gained a disreputable image that has never entirely disappeared – and when the word came to be applied to define the "Roaring Twenties" as the "Jazz Age" it stood for decadence, late nights, illegal booze, licentious dancing, and a host of dubious pleasures indulged in by societies the world over who were recovering from the trauma of the Great War.

Because the music had African-American origins, the question of race also was bound up in it from the start, and to a white public it symbolized something "other," something daring and exotic, while, simultaneously, to a black public it was a unifying force, an aspiration, that the pioneer composer and bandleader Will Marion Cook hoped would be "a great school of music [to] enrich musical literature."

Yet despite its relatively recent origins in the same century as that which brought the "information age," the documenting of the history of jazz has been a haphazard process. A lot of what we think we know about jazz is the result of a small body of information being passed on from one generation of historians to another, much of it being accepted uncritically by each succeeding generation. During the half century or so from the first serious attempts to document jazz to the point where the whole of the music's first hundred years can be surveyed, the assumptions that underlie what might be regarded as the mythology of the emergence of jazz have seldom been tested rigorously.

Some vital questions are still unanswered: first, how did a completely new direction in popular music emerge so rapidly? And why and how did this music spread so widely in the first two decades of the century?

Another conundrum in trying to understand how jazz began is a consequence of historians being slow to ask the musicians who actually created the music what went on. Few of the first generation of jazz players were born earlier than the 1880s. Many of the most significant were not born until the start of the twentieth century itself. Despite this, and the fact that the first scholarly historians of jazz, writing in the late 1930s, had direct access to a wide range of pioneers, the origins of jazz remain remarkably obscure. Oral history was in its infancy; much of the early investigation of jazz was done by record collectors who were at one remove from the creators of the music. But above all it was not seen as anything more than a branch of ephemeral popular music for a long period of its early development. It did not begin to be debated in terms of an art form until discussions of Duke Ellington's music began, on both sides of the Atlantic, in the critical press of the mid-1930s, and it took another few years for any serious historical investigation to begin, which was often conducted by enthusiastic amateurs with a point to prove, rather than by academics.[1]

The mythology of jazz is not restricted to its origins. A long-running debate about the critical reaction to jazz, and whether this took hold in Europe or the United States in the first instance, has tended to occlude the extraordinary rapidity with which jazz spread around the world. The American perspective tends only to recognize the gipsy guitarist Django Reinhardt as the first non-American to play jazz successfully. But this would be to ignore the wealth of accomplished musicians in Europe, Asia, and South America who adopted jazz early and laid the foundations for it to become a fully international music in the second half of the century.

Movements such as bebop in the 1940s have been tied to ideas of political and racial revolution, rather than analyzed to see just how genuinely revolutionary the *musical* events themselves actually were. Dividing lines drawn for purposes other than strictly musical debate have hijacked our perception of history. History book after history book compartmentalizes this period as one of revolt by African-American musicians, which leaves unanswered the question as to why several of the first generation of bebop musicians (pianist Al Haig, drummer Stan Levey, trumpeter Johnny Carisi, to name a few) were white, and why a significant amount of innovation took place far away from the after-hours clubs of New York. Also, if the modern jazz of the 1940s was truly a political development, why was it not more widely espoused? Why was this revolutionary music less attractive to many African-Americans than rhythm and blues which emerged at the same time and quickly eclipsed jazz in terms of popularity?

Few histories have attempted to examine the genuine political revolution of the 1960s among African-American jazz musicians, which led to a number of umbrella organizations being set up in Chicago, St. Louis, Los Angeles, and, to a lesser extent, New York, to foster and encourage the arts as a unifying social force. Just how effective were BAG, the AACM, and their successors such as the Art Ensemble of Chicago? And how did these revolutionary movements align themselves with the longer-term develop-ment of jazz during the final 30 years of the twentieth century?

Underlying all of this is a complex question of definition: just what does the word "jazz" actually mean? It is easy to see how, with a plethora of different styles claiming to be jazz, and all kinds of cross-overs into world music, rock, blues, and other forms, it is so difficult to define the music today. Yet in many ways this definitional question has been omnipresent throughout jazz history. Writers discussing the 1920s have been quick to point out that what was often called jazz at that time was, in their view, no such thing. This began with Hugues Panassié in 1934, when he produced this critique of Jack Hylton's British band and Paul Whiteman's American orchestra:

> An orchestra like Hylton's ... may seem to be playing jazz. Everything helps deceive the inexperienced listener. The make-up is that of a jazz band; tunes used are the same ones used by real jazz musicians ... but there isn't any swing. ... Similarly Paul Whiteman, who once had a band that could really swing, concerns himself now with "what the public wants." He

specializes in what strikes me as empty, pompous performances – nicknamed "symphonic jazz."[2]

And, in 1946, Rudi Blesh made much the same point about both attempts to "swing" the classics, and about the jazz-influenced compositions of George Gershwin:

> Jazz is not a mere "jazzy" rendition, say, of a Beethoven minuet. For this is only a manner of playing with no real transformation of the material. Even less jazz, is the Gershwin *Rhapsody in Blue* that treats certain jazz harmonies and certain jazz instrumental traits in a symphonic manner. And the music of Whiteman and the various "jazz symphonists" misses the mark by employing jazz material in a completely non-jazz manner.[3]

Even though one of these writers defined jazz mainly in terms of its rhythmic qualities – whether syncopation developed into "swing" – and the other in terms of a more obscure "transformation" brought about by a complex mixture of elements, Panassié and Blesh sought to bring an intangible quality into the definition. This became harder still to pin down as time went on. Panassié's search for "swing" is irrelevant to much jazz from the 1960s onwards, for example.

The fundamental idea of definition behind both schools of criticism is that there is an element of "transformation" present in a jazz performance; in other words, that partly through arrangement of the music, but mainly through individual or collective improvisation, the "performer . . . creates the musical substance he lets us hear." The extraordinary range of jazz – from fully improvised to almost completely notated performances – means that this focus on the role of the performer in defining the music is problematic, as are Panassié's clumsy attempts to define swing. When he asserted that it was based on binary rhythm with no triplets, he inadvertently excluded from his definition of jazz much of the music he was passionate about, were his assertion to be rigidly applied as some kind of formulaic test. But the points he and other such critics made are, nonetheless, significant. There is an intangible quality – call it heat, spirit, heart, adrenaline, or indeed swing – that separates the inspired performance from the mundane, and which frustrates any attempt to arrive at a clear and universally applicable definition of jazz. Consequently, unlike many other forms of music, there is no clear consensus. The definition of jazz depends on the listener's perception of whether the kind of ingredients I have mentioned above are present: Is there sufficient rhythmic momentum or "swing" for a dance band, playing written arrangements, to be perceived as playing jazz? Is there enough rhythmic or harmonic invention in a solo for it to qualify as jazz improvisation?

Nevertheless, some attempt needs to be made after a century of the music's existence to reconcile what passed for jazz in the public's eyes with the narrower definition that satisfied various critics as being the genuine article. Do we need to look again, for example, at Paul Whiteman, a musician who described himself as "King of Jazz," and who was certainly perceived as such by the public, but who has generally been derided by critics as having had little to do with "pure" jazz?

To define a word according to its widespread use by the public might have been acceptable to most lexicographers from Dr. Johnson onwards, but in jazz it has continued to cause problems. During the "Jazz Age" of the 1920s, for instance, the term "jazz band" was applied widely to ensembles that had very little to do with the syncopated and improvised music of King Oliver, Louis Armstrong, and the Original Dixieland Jazz Band. In one extreme example, during the 1926 general strike in Britain, groups of marching musicians playing little more than kazoos, and dressed in outlandish costumes to lend support to the strikers, were known as "jazz bands," implying a direct link between comic presentation and lightweight or non-existent musical content, and similar ensembles bore the name in the North of England well into the 1970s. In another international example, pop music groups in Zaire and Tanzania in the 1960s were nicknamed "jazz bands," employing a mixture of Western and traditional instruments to accompany vocals in Linguala and, later, Swahili. This music had little to do with jazz, but the term was appropriated because somehow the image of a jolly, improvising small group transferred itself across time and attached itself to this new and emergent tradition.[4]

In what follows, I have attempted to examine what was being described as jazz throughout its history, and I have taken a very broad view of how jazz should now be defined. As a starting point, the definition offered by the *New Grove Dictionary of Jazz* is a workable one: "A music created mainly by black Americans in the early 20th century through an amalgamation of elements drawn from European-American and tribal African musics."

\* \* \*

Jazz began as a collectively improvised music, with syncopated rhythms over a strong underlying pulse, involving the use of some notes in both its melodies and harmonies that are flattened to a degree smaller than a semitone. These notes, which have come to be known as "blue" notes, and their accompanying syncopated rhythms, are the most obvious elements of what the *Grove* definition calls "tribal African musics." In most jazz literature they are referred to as "African retentions," that is survivals from the indigenous music of West Africa which was transplanted into the United States and kept alive among the African-American population during and after the era of slavery.

Among African-Americans, the West African notions of pitch and of rhythm brought to the American continent became subject to the twin processes known as acculturation and enculturation, the first being the evolution of a new culture from the meeting of two existing ones, and the second being the passing on to one generation from another the cultural values of a society. In the latter half of the nineteenth century and the first years of the twentieth, African survivals became inextricably intertwined with the musical traditions of white Americans: the instrumentation and structures of brass and military bands, the hymns and psalms of the Christian Church, the Hispanic rhythms brought to the New World by Spanish colonists, and the folk songs, shanties, or work songs sung by manual laborers.

There is a consensus among historians that by the end of the nineteenth century, three distinct forms of African-American music had started to emerge: ragtime, blues, and jazz. All of them shared a similar patrimony: the cross-fertilization of African musics to different degrees with various European forms. Furthermore, jazz itself is generally held to have emerged from the music of the city of New Orleans, where customs with African connections, including a weekly dance for slaves, had been well-documented in the nineteenth century, and where a licensed red-light district, Storyville, encouraged the widespread use of syncopated music for the entertainment of its clients. When Storyville closed in 1917, its jazz musicians traveled North to Chicago, and thence to New York, bringing jazz first to the United States and subsequently to the world at large.

This, at any rate, is the opening thesis of most extant jazz histories, but does it go far enough? What, for example, was going on elsewhere in the United States, away from New Orleans?

The outline presented above is broadly uncontestable. There are few precedents in Western music displaying the basic ingredients of jazz, notably polyrhythmic and polytonal ensembles, a strong accompanying rhythm that emphasizes what (in European music) are regarded as the "weaker" second and fourth beats of a four-beat measure, the microtonal flattening of certain pitches of the scale, and collective improvisation over a regularly repeated pattern. These are intrinsically African contributions to the mix.[5]

The use of sound recordings to pin down the specifics of these African antecedents and to demonstrate precisely which elements might have been imported into North America in the eighteenth and early nineteenth centuries started with isolated examples of ethnomusicological observation, several decades after jazz began to be identified by name as a distinct genre. An early example is the series of field recordings made in Dahomey, as well as in Trinidad and Brazil, by Melville Herskovits in the early 1930s.[6] His African recordings illustrate some rhythmic and tonal similarities with early jazz, but fall short of being able to tell us to what extent the aural traditions had mutated over time. We can only speculate as to how faithfully these discs portray the music of Africa as it had been more than a century earlier.

In comparing discs of early jazz in the United States with African field recordings, to demonstrate the nature of African retentions, a second question also goes unanswered; namely the degree of acculturation involved. In other words, to what extent is jazz an intrinsically American form, comprising not just African retentions, but many more ingredients (such as eighteenth- and nineteenth-century British and French popular songs and dances or the work songs and shanties of sailors) that became part of the mix. These cross-currents in nineteenth-century African-American music are most clearly documented in the areas of minstrelsy and pre-blues song, and from this it is proven that source material as varied as Irish reels, hornpipes, Appalachian mountain songs, and jigs were contributing factors to the repertoire of "songsters," African-American singers of the post-Reconstruction era. Their music is preserved in written form from the late nineteenth century and a considerable amount was recorded in the 1920s.[7]

Undoubtedly, African influences alone were hugely important in defining the initial characteristics of jazz,[8] but what is known about the songster repertoire implies that many other ingredients were also significant. It is therefore reasonable to suppose that jazz is a syncretic music from a wider range of sources than have traditionally been explored. The argument of most jazz texts was aptly summarized by British historian Paul Oliver in his own attempt to examine African retentions in the blues, through fieldwork in West Africa during the 1960s:

> These emphasise the drumming that was long a tourist attraction
> in Congo Square, New Orleans, and the conclusions that may be
> drawn as to the influence of African derived music on military

brass and parade music, when jazz began to emerge as a musical
form of distinctive character at the close of the nineteenth
century. For their arguments, the studies made by Herskovits in
Dahomey or the West Indies, of Harold Courlander in Haiti, or
Father Jones in Ghana amply supported the contention that the
rhythmic character of New Orleans jazz, the multi-lineal structure
of its instrumentation and the melodic-rhythmic nature of jazz
improvisation were essentially "African" in origin. These
contentions could be borne out and can be explained readily
enough in terms of enculturation and acculturation.[9]

So, if we are to enrich this summary, and examine what survives from the
era before sound recordings, what do we have to go on?

First, in the late nineteenth century, a few folk-song and dance
collectors started to turn their attentions to the music of black Americans.
The result of their efforts is that some notated music survives, especially
among Christianized communities, where the words (and sometimes music)
of spirituals were written down and published on a fairly widespread basis.
Such contemporaneous documentation offers a series of snapshots of African
retentions, preserving a melodic and rhythmic catalog of fragments of the
music. The most significant components of this informal catalog are the
indications that, by the mid-nineteenth century, syncopation was present
along with melodies that remained in use until they appeared again in
recordings half a century or so later. One of the earliest notated examples of
syncopation – the technique of moving the emphasis of a phrase away from
the main beats of the measure – is to be found in *Briggs' Banjo Instructor*,
published in 1855 and containing music "which the author learned when in
the South from the negroes, which have never before been published." The
writer, Thomas Briggs, was a famous white banjoist who gave hints at a
more subtle layer of syncopation to be found in banjo playing through the
additional emphasis given to certain notes by using the fingers to pick the
notes.[10]

Further evidence exists relating to the social role of music within rural
communities, and the syncretic nature of this background was aptly
summarized, as early as 1917, by one of the most respected folk-song
collectors, Henry F. Gilbert:

> The folksongs of a race, often born in sorrow and cherished with
> love through hundreds of years, become at length an integral part

of the race consciousness and are well-nigh inseparable from it. America is not merely an association of persons but also a mixture of race consciousnesses.[11]

In addition to the documentation of rural music, both in the form of notation and travelogue, several oral histories, recounted by the generation born between 1880 and 1915, make it evident that many of the elements which went to make up jazz were also present in many urban areas of the United States, and that a significant number of musicians, both black and white, adopted what they believed to be "jazz," with little or no first-hand exposure to New Orleans musicians.[12]

One reason musicians far away from the supposed birthplace of jazz — New Orleans — were able to assimilate elements of the new music is that jazz emerged at a time when the means of transmitting popular music to its public was undergoing the most complete revolution in history. Within a very few years, piano rolls, mechanical music-boxes, and the first sound recordings all appeared, coincident with an explosion in music publishing for the masses. All these means helped to disseminate musical ideas at an unprecedented rate.

Another reason was that, by the early years of the twentieth century, an independent channel of communication had opened up, which existed among those who performed for a living. This was the elaborate network of theaters that had grown up across the United States. Some African-Americans worked alongside white performers as novelty or specialty acts on the national, commercial Keith or Orpheum theater circuits, but the new century saw the beginnings of a network intended solely to feature black performers, a loose-knit organization that acted as a conduit for musical ideas which, consequently, spread very rapidly through an itinerant population of singers, musicians, and dancers. (Less formally, and at a level of organization below that of the theaters, a plethora of tent and medicine shows traveled across the country, and many fledgling jazz musicians were influenced by, or even traveled with, such entertainments.)

The first steps towards creating a formal umbrella organization for these theaters were taken by the Barasso brothers in Memphis in 1907, and by 1909 they had set up a network of 40 venues known as the Theater Owners' Booking Agency (T.O.B.A.).[13] Because of a widespread view that the T.O.B.A. was not established until the 1920s, there has been a tacit assumption amongst scholars that little of importance happened before that date. However, plenty of oral histories and biographies of pioneer jazz and blues musicians stress the importance of T.O.B.A. and are thoroughly infused with the smell of greasepaint and the drama of the footlights. "It was a very interesting training ground," wrote pianist Sammy Price, who began his own career as a teenage dancer.

> It was like a *Who's Who in America* — or Black America — because if they were anybody in Black entertainment, they travelled the T.O.B.A. From George Williams and Bessie Brown to Bert Williams, Ma Rainey, and Trixie Smith, they were all there.[14]

From early in the twentieth century, the newspapers that catered for African-American readers, such as the *New York Age*, listed the itineraries of touring show troupes which criss-crossed the country taking new musical styles with them. From these papers alone, it is possible to discern just how well developed a network there was, from slightly before the T.O.B.A. was set up, and during its main period of growth and expansion across the country.[15]

This theatrical network soon had another social structure erected alongside it: outside what Jelly Roll Morton called the "organization-minded" society of New Orleans, where there were musicians' societies in the nineteenth century, new musicians' clubs and associations began to spring up in other cities across the United States, bringing together instrumentalists who wished to further their careers in popular music. For example, by 1910, the Clef Club was established for black musicians in New York with a conscious focus on forms of popular music alongside the classics. Its history was relatively well documented in the local press of the day, and its president, James Reese Europe, was a schooled musician who epitomized the dilemma, aptly summarized by Samuel Charters and Leonard Kunstadt, between "a career as an unsuccessful serious musician or a career as a popular entertainer, playing music that the public expected Negro musicians to play."[16]

This is the final link in the chain. It was clear that by 1910 there was such a thing as music which "the public expected Negro musicians to play." What then was this music and where can we find out more about it?

First, the lyrics of popular songs had, for almost a century-and-a-half, been printed in so-called "songsters" — collections of varying size ranging from eight-page "chapbooks" to sophisticated anthologies containing several hundred sets of words. These provide a useful archive of the subject matter and scope of popular songs in the United States.

Unfortunately, very few songsters contained notated music, but the final decades of the nineteenth century saw these collections supplanted rapidly by cheaply printed sheet music, which made the widespread distribution of both the words and music of popular songs possible for the first time. Collections of such sheet music allow us the opportunity to examine both words and music from the period when jazz, ragtime, and blues began to make their presence felt.

Even before sound recording, the small number of folk-song scholars who began to collect African-American melodies created a further body of melodic information in the form of notation. This started in the early 1800s, but the first significant published collection, by William Allen, Charles Ware, and Lucy McKim Garrison, is *Slave Songs of the United States*, from 1867.

Composers from the classical world, in search of source material, explored similar territory, starting with Frederick Delius's sojourn on a Florida plantation in the 1880s, followed by Antonin Dvořák's work at the National Conservatory of Music, in New York, between 1891 and 1895, and continuing with his pupils William Arms Fisher, Rubin Goldmark, and others. One significant traveling collector of song, among the first to transcribe African-American music for use in concert orchestral works, was Henry F. Gilbert. His *Negro Episode* was performed in New York in 1896, and is an adaptation of pieces he had heard on field trips. He incorporated five Creole themes into his subsequent symphonic poem *The Dance in Place Congo* (written in 1908, but banned from public performance in Boston as "niggah music," so that it was not performed until the Metropolitan Opera Company played it as a ballet in 1918). His work preserves much of the melodic and rhythmic character of African-American music of the 1890s.[17]

Such folk-song collectors preserved music that was actually being performed across the United States by African-Americans, but this does not necessarily tell us about the kinds of music that black performers were "expected to play" according to the social and cultural mores of the time. In the immediate post-Civil War era, there was a schism between what was performed informally within black communities and what was performed on stage for audiences, both black and white. Following the war, in the climate of emancipation, black troupes of minstrels began to sing and play minstrel songs in public that had hitherto been performed by white musicians in blackface; and there were also traveling troupes of black concert performers, most notably the Fisk Jubilee Singers, much of whose sheet music has survived intact. This group of student fundraisers for Nashville's

Fisk University went on the road in 1871, singing programs of concert songs, heavily leavened with gospel and slave-song material, including *O brother don't stay away* and *Go down Moses*. Between 1871, when the Fisk Jubilee Singers began to tour, and the turn of the century, the repertoire that black musicians were "expected to perform" crystallized, and it fell between the Fisk Singers' formal concert-hall versions of slave and gospel songs and the comic stereotypes of black performers in blackface acting out minstrel songs.

The notated songs from the Fisk repertoire offer firm and tangible evidence of some of the melodic and harmonic elements that went into jazz, alongside the rhythm of the drums, the polytonality of the ensemble, and the use of altered pitches. The large number of press reports and reviews of the singers show that these ingredients of jazz have, at least, an authentic lineage in mainstream nineteenth-century popular entertainment, which is the antithesis of the view proposed by some jazz historians, namely that the new music was somehow a spontaneous reaction to emancipation.[18] And recognizing this, the search for a definition comes full circle, because just as Panassié and Blesh were searching for an indefinable quality that made jazz special, its roots in theaters and traveling shows firmly bring the concept of popularity into jazz definition.

Jazz has only been a truly popular music a few times in its history, but its history is inextricably bound up with the development of popular music as a whole.

# PART I
# Origins

CHAPTER 1

# Precursors

## The Music of the Plantations

In the winter, when they were clad in their long capots of
blanket, with the hood drawn over the head, they looked
like a monastery of monks in the field; their shoes, called
"quantiers," were pieces of raw-hide, cut so as to lace
comfortably over foot and ankle. These were the first
cargos, the African *bruts*, as they were called.

Grace King, *New Orleans: The Place and the People*, 1895

Slavery, colonialism, and exploitation are significant and uncomfortable
elements in the development of African-American music. Romantic,
evocative descriptions of slaves in the fields, such as the one above, conceal
harsh and unpalatable truths about the buying and selling of human lives and
the conditions under which people were forced to live and work. The first
generation of jazz musicians were all born at a time when slavery and all that
it stood for was well within living memory, and reminders of that era were
omnipresent in the early years of the music. Even the most successful would
look back in later life with, at best, a matter-of-factness about this
unpleasant era of America's past. "My grandfather kept us informed of what
had happened to the family in its creative stage," recalled pianist, arranger,
and territory bandleader Jesse Stone, born in 1901, who was, in his old age,
a wealthy man as the result of his compositions like *Shake, Rattle and Roll*. He
told me:

We were slaves, and we were owned by the Stone family from

which we took our name. The way we got from Tennessee to Kansas was that, after slavery was abolished, one of the Stones gave my grandfather a wedding present. He bought him 600 acres of land in Kansas at 75 cents an acre, and that's how we got to where I was born in Atchison. All the rest of my family were born in Tennessee, and they were all musicians, including my cousins, the Browns, Caters, and Stones. I started on violin, and then kept switching from instrument to instrument.[1]

Music was deeply ingrained among those whose families had lived on the plantations during and after slavery. But so too were experiences of the exploitation and abuse of slaves by their white owners. Trumpeter Doc Cheatham, whose family came from the same area of Tennessee as Stone, remembered: "I guess back in those far off days there was a lot of hanky panky going on, between the Indians, the black folks, the white folks."[2] Cheatham said it would need a book to tell the story straight about his own family's complex origins, which included a native North American grandfather on his father's side.

Some families knew their background; others simply knew it was confused, and there were some who did not find out the whole truth for many years, or even a generation or two. For example, it was not until he reached the age of 42, in 1959, that Dizzy Gillespie, from Cheraw, South Carolina, discovered that the white slave owner who bought his grandmother (herself the daughter of a Nigerian chief) at auction had been his own grandfather. He laughed it off to a newspaper reporter: "I said, 'Just call me your majesty.' My . . . grandfather was a white man, and this white man there now calls me 'cousin.' "[3]

In the early years of the twentieth century, although slavery had long been abolished, not every aspect of it had disappeared from poor rural communities, and plantation owners operated a micro-economy which allowed them to dispense with money and control the price of goods. One musician who experienced this at first hand was "Cousin Joe" Pleasant (also known as Pleasant Joseph), a blues and jazz singer born in 1907 (later famous for his 1940s recordings with clarinetist Sidney Bechet), who grew up in the fields of rural Louisiana. As a boy of seven or eight, he joined his extended family in the rice fields, rising at three o'clock in the morning to be out in the fields as the sun came up, in order to avoid the searing main heat of the day.

> We didn't get paid in money on that plantation. . . . They'd give you a book with coupons in it, and in this book they had coupons for five cents, ten cents, twenty-five cents, fifty cents, and a dollar. . . . They had a company store on that plantation, they sold everything from soup to nuts in that store. You could buy anything . . . just give them a coupon.

Yet despite these conditions of carefully controlled hardship, where everyone aspired to work in the sugar refinery, which paid its workers in real money, there was one omnipresent feature:

> Only one person had to start singing and the whole bunch would fall in line. Now, these in this section might be singing spirituals, and these, in this section, might be singing the blues. Or just humming, not singing any particular words. Just a tune.[4]

Among the musicians of this early generation of jazz players, the connection that Henry F. Gilbert identified in 1917 between folk music and race consciousness was made even more powerful by the experience of plantation life. If we sift grains of detail from nineteenth-century writing about plantations and the era of slavery, a clear picture emerges of this highly significant section of the background from which jazz itself developed.

In the 1830s, the English actress Fannie Anne Kemble kept a journal of life on her husband's Georgia plantation, writing of the "wild and unaccountable" music she heard sung by slaves. Particularly striking was the call-and-response pattern of a work song: "The way in which the chorus strikes in with the burden between each phrase of the melody chanted by a single voice is very curious and effective."[5] In this and other early accounts, work songs and religious songs, or spirituals, are mentioned frequently, in a setting that was often portrayed outside the South as the music of a picturesque rural idyll, despite the social reality that it was a music created by a people deprived of the most basic human rights.

Because of its seminal importance to the development of jazz, the area in and around New Orleans is of particular interest in respect of nineteenth-century sources, and before examining what went on in other areas of the United States, this is a good place to begin examining African-American music. "The Negroes made their own segregations on the plantations," wrote Grace King in her 1895 history of New Orleans. She goes on to describe further how, after arriving from Africa, the fit and well, and those who were from common regions were drawn together:

> They are described as singing in unison in the fields; incoherent, unintelligible words, in one recurring monotonous, short strain of harmony, eddying around a minor chord, as they may in fact be heard in any field or street gang today.

One major element stands out in King's account of Louisiana plantation workers during and after slavery, in contrast to accounts of other plantations in the Carolinas or other parts of the South. It is that the prevailing European influences were French and Spanish, not English or American, and that this brought about a rather different process of acculturation in the areas surrounding New Orleans than elsewhere in the United States. For a start, it is surprising to discover her transcription of a field song is in French:

> *Di temps Missié d'Artaguette,*
> *Hé! Ho! Hé!*
> *C'était, c'était bon temps!*
> *Yé té menin monde à la baguette,*
> *Hé! Ho! Hé!*
> *Pas Nègres, pas rubans,*
> *Pas diamants*
> *Pour dochans,*
> *Hé! Ho! Hé!*[6]

The song commemorates a notion of an ideal world still run by the French commandant Monsieur d'Artaguette, who was comptroller of the town of Mobile during the lifetime of New Orleans's founding father Bienville, in the eighteenth century. The world may have been "led with a stick" (*à la baguette*), but it was a time when common white Americans (*dochans* or *des gens*) did not have "Negroes, ribbons or diamonds." In other words, Creole, French-speaking African-Americans were expressing nostalgic regret for the paternalistic colonial regime of France, in contrast to the latter-day "laxer régime," as Grace King puts it, of the Americans who took over New Orleans, and who came themselves to be slave owners.

For the music historian, King's subsequent comment is most significant:

> They improvised their songs as they went along, as children do; picking up any little circumstance in the life about them, and

setting it afloat on the rill of music that seemed to be ever running through the virgin forest of their brain. And their language, known only through the ear, became itself a fluent doggerel of harmony.

She categorizes the subject-matter of the nineteenth-century Creole work songs (implying that some were also in English), covering specific events such as Master Cateyane's Circus in Congo Square, or the Battle of New Orleans, as well as "biting sarcasms about the free quadroons and mulattoes whom they called 'mules.' "

Away from the plantations, slaves in the New Orleans area congregated once a week in the city itself, during the first half of the nineteenth century, to dance and celebrate. These events, which took place in Congo Square, were already a thing of the past by 1895, but were, nevertheless, well within the memories of "people who are yet living." King's text offers an account of what went on there. In addition to describing the hundreds, occasionally thousands, of black dancers "in their gay, picturesque finery," dancing the Bamboula or Calinda, she describes the street entertainments and food stalls set up round and about for white onlookers.

Earlier chroniclers (Benjamin Henry B. Latrobe, William Wells Brown, and George W. Cable, himself quoting Krehbel and Lafcadio Hearn) describe the drumming that went on, the penetrating sound of a species of lute, and the crowd dancing in circles or rings, leading to a state of ecstatic excitement. The drumming, and the setting up of simultaneous or overlaid "polyrhythms," is, beyond doubt, an ingredient of early jazz, although to go looking for examples among early recordings would be misleading. Apart from a handful of discs from 1913–14 by James Reese Europe, which feature the masterly playing of Buddy Gilmore, stretching acoustic technology to the limits on pieces like *Castle House Rag*, the sound of the drums was seldom well-recorded (or in many cases recorded at all) until the mid-1920s, and, as a consequence, there is little aural evidence of the rhythmic excitement described in print by many witnesses.

Many chroniclers link the trance-like condition of Congo Square dancers with the sinister counterpart of the dancing tradition – the practice of voodoo – which was firmly embedded in New Orleans culture, and traceable back to the early eighteenth century. King suggests links to Santo Domingo slaves and describes the ecstatic state induced through collective supplication to the serpent deity Damballa or Da:

Among the African slave, under any applications or assumptions of Christianity, there was always voudou superstition. . . . There was the same secrecy of place and meeting, the altar, serpent, and the official king and queen; the latter with much profusion of red in her dress, the oath to the serpent; a string of barbarous epithets and penalties, the suppliants to the serpent coming up, one by one, with their prayers, always and ever for love or revenge, the king with his hand on the serpent, receiving from it the trembling of the body which he communicates to the queen and which she passes on to all in the room; the trembling increasing to movement, to contortions of the body, convulsions, frenzy, ecstasies, the queen ever leading; the low humming sound rising louder and louder; the dancers whirling around, faster and faster, screaming, waving their red handkerchiefs, tearing off their garments, biting their flesh, falling down delirious, exhausted, pell mell, blind, inebriated, in the hot dense darkness.[7]

Voodoo remained an underlying element in New Orleans culture, and some aspects of it remain to the present day. William Russell's oral-history interviews from the 1950s and 1960s with New Orleans pioneers at Tulane University include material on voodoo, including the legend of Marie Laveau, the Voodoo Queen, but the superstition attached to the cult also allowed one or two more skeptical musicians to have a little fun and games at the expense of their non-Southern counterparts, as guitarist Danny Barker recalled. While on the road in the 1930s he would regale his fellow lodgers at rooming houses with sombre tales of New Orleans:

After I had told a few of these tales I would gradually find that everybody knew my name – "Dan this," "Dan that," "Dan, tell so-and-so about that killing," "Dan, is that true about the Hoodoo in New Orleans?"

But most of the time I'd catch the owner watching me out of the corner of his eye, with the expression: I wonder if he knows about that Hoodoo and good luck potions or charms?

While touring with Cab Calloway I carried a large black candle which had burned down to about four inches. It was two inches in diameter. Also three pieces of lodestone which had a hairy fuzzy substance on them. I had a lot of fun with them. I'd leave them in my room on the dresser or table where the landlady or maid could see them. I would place them in front of a small postcard sized photo of St. John the Conqueror. I'd also put a small book called *The Sixth and Seventh Book of Moses* there, until this was stolen. When I left these Voodoo gimmicks about, I knew that when I returned to the lodgings I would have to answer many questions.[8]

Most modern historians agree with Grace King's assertion that voodoo has links with the island of Santo Domingo, and that when the Haitian Revolution took place in 1804, Louisiana received many immigrants from the area who brought with them their conjunction of West African belief and colonial Catholicism. This association continued as Louisiana imported slaves from the West Indies in general, and Haiti in particular.

Voodoo offered the oppressed African-American population a form of insulation, a psychological buffer against the humiliations of slavery. The voodoo religion occupied just as significant a place in the hopes and aspirations of many of the slave population as Christianity did, and these parallels gave voodoo a significant place in the background to early jazz and blues that extended far beyond Louisiana. The ecstatic element of the slave and voodoo dances described by nineteenth-century historians was carried forward into the atmosphere of early jazz dances in New Orleans and Chicago.[9]

The final element of King's description of New Orleans's musical traditions refers back to another well-documented area of music during the era of slavery, in which slaves performed for their white masters. In many places this was instrumental music, but in New Orleans, according to King, there was a strong vocal tradition, underpinned with the "poetry and inspiration of the dance." She states:

> Under the *ancien régime*, it was a favourite after-dinner entertainment to have the slaves come in and sing, rewarding them with glasses of wine and silver pieces . . . and it is a pleasure to own the conviction, whether it can be maintained or not, with reason, that America will one day do homage for music of a fine and original type, to some representative of Louisiana's colored population.

King is explicitly referring to Creole songs, but this is a very early statement by any white writer identifying a strand of music that is specifically African-

American, and crediting it as "fine and original."

We can therefore infer from Grace King that, in Louisiana and particularly in terms of plantation music, African-Americans sang work songs that repeated short strains of melody in unison. These involved improvisation, and flattened or minor pitches. French songs were drawn into the cultural mix, expressing a dislike of white Americans and involving subject-matter that also touched on the complexities of racial interbreeding that had produced a caste system of *gens de couleur*. This music was often accompanied by percussionists playing explicitly African-derived rhythms, as well as collective dances or acts of worship that involved the achievement of an ecstatic state. By 1895 there was a discernible and distinctive character about the African-American music that was performed for white listeners.

Some historians of jazz have seen the emergence of jazz in the post-slavery era as a revolutionary act, a collective musical response to the appalling and inhumane treatment of people who had been treated as chattels and investments rather than human beings. Such treatment was exacerbated in the Southern states, where "slave codes" did not admit the granting of any human rights to slaves. Under the Civil Code, setting out the legal relationship between master and slave in Louisiana, an individual slave "can do nothing, possess nothing, nor acquire anything, but what must belong to his master."[10]

The development of jazz now seems a slower and less revolutionary business than it once did, involving a much wider range of influences, but the conditions likely to nurture a new musical form, born out of hardship, certainly existed.

In a remarkably perceptive analysis of the complex racial issues that surround the perspective of late nineteenth-century African-Americans in Louisiana, Grace King points out that the prevailing world picture imposed on slaves and their descendants was that of Catholic continental Europe:

> Crudely put, to the black Christian, God was a white man, the devil black; the Virgin Mary, the Saviour, the saints and angels, all belonged to the race of the master and mistress; white, divinized; black diabolized. Is it necessary to follow, except in imagination, the infinite hope, the infinite struggle contained in the inference?

The development of Creole society – the population of mixed Hispanic, or French and African, origin – in and around New Orleans was, therefore, built on a structure in which the aspiration to be white played a major part.

This point is not made in order to make any kind of assertion of racial superiority, but to attempt to understand that while much emphasis has been given by historians of jazz to the specifically African ingredients that were brought into and retained in the acculturated mix, during the 1890s Creole society in New Orleans was at pains to distance itself from all things African and to identify with all things white, especially if this could be tied to an idealized perception of the original colonists. It led many Creoles to "base aristocratic pretensions upon their French and Spanish antecedents," according to King, an experience borne out by pioneer pianist and composer Jelly Roll Morton, who told Alan Lomax: "It was my godmother, Eulalie Echo, helped to name me the christened name of Ferdinand, which was named after the king of Spain."[11]

At a broader level, King's observation raises the question about how much jazz development was based within the socially ambitious section of black society that in many areas of the United States became a relatively prosperous middle class during the early part of the twentieth century. As will become apparent later, this element of society was crucial in fostering ragtime, and formed the background for some of those who subsequently became the most influential figures in jazz, such as Fletcher Henderson. In New Orleans, in particular, such a middle class existed within the Creole society of *gens de couleur* throughout the last quarter of the nineteenth century. Many of the most significant musicians, bandleaders, composers, and publishers in the early years of jazz, such as Isadore Barbarin, John Robichaux, Armand J. Piron, and Lorenzo Tio Jr., came from this section of New Orleans society, which was fully involved in the city's classical and operatic traditions.

Within the city limits, this middle-class Creole society was predominantly located in the *vieux carré* ("French Quarter") of New Orleans, the "downtown" section of the city, while, "uptown," across Canal Street to the West, a newer, tougher American city grew up, with a black underclass that had an altogether more rough-and-ready approach to music, which had much in common with the music of the surrounding rural plantation areas.

It seems that this "uptown" population continued many of the more explicitly African elements of plantation music, from the drumming and dancing traditions of Congo Square to an extrovert and raucous approach to instrumental music. So marked was the difference that some uptown musicians feigned the inability to read music to emphasize the differences between themselves and their well-schooled downtown Creole counterparts.[12] What New Orleans had, however, was a symbiotic relationship between, on the one hand, the Creole traditions, where musicians of mixed race aspired towards European virtues, and, on the other, the uptown African traditions that deliberately retained elements of African rhythms and pitching; and it is from the interrelationships between these two groups that early jazz grew up within that city.

How, then, does this picture of the music of Louisiana plantations, and the balance between uptown and downtown New Orleans, differ from what went on elsewhere in the United States? And were there aspects of plantation music away from the hothouse atmosphere of New Orleans that had an impact on jazz as significant as those in and around Louisiana?

Across the United States there were, generally, three distinct types of plantation music: first, secular collective songs associated with work and with social dance; second, religious collective songs which shared many of the elements of dance with their secular counterparts and which involved an ecstatic component; and, finally, non-vocal music often connected with dance, but which included performing European forms of music on instruments such as the violin and banjo for slave masters and, subsequently, for employers.

From editions of slave songs that were notated and collected during the nineteenth century, one very significant element appears, to do with pitch:

> Tones are frequently employed which we have no musical characters to represent. ... The tones are variable in pitch, ranging through an entire octave on different occasions, according to the inspiration of the singer.[13]

This kind of flexible tonality – accommodating around seventeen discernible variations in pitch within an octave – seems to be a constant element in plantation music in many parts of North America, and is consistent both with Grace King's observations and with what has survived into twentieth-century African-American music. Other aspects of African music that were either barely discernible or widely adopted in many areas were summarized by Richard Alan Waterman as follows:

> Polymeter is usually absent, except by implication, and there is a dearth of African-type musical instruments. Metronism, however, is present in all Negro sacred and secular styles, as is the importance of percussion (wherever percussion instruments or effects are not proscribed by circumstances) and the overlapping call-and-response pattern.[14]

Many scholars have given great weight to the importance of call-and-response in African-American music, especially in respect of its adoption within gospel and early jazz. Yet it would be mistaken to believe that call-and-response is an exclusively African feature, and it is perhaps too tempting to draw parallels between African work songs and the singers on American plantations in the nineteenth century, or between the role of a West African *griot* and the lead singer in a gospel group. Similar patterns were present in work songs, such as sea shanties, as early as 1493, as described by Friar Felix Fabri: "Work at sea is very heavy and is only carried on by a concert between one who sings out orders and the labourers who sing in response."[15]

Nautical songs – for turning the capstan, hauling the sheets, and swinging up sails and topmasts – seem to have perpetuated the call-and-response tradition well into the twentieth century, suggesting that the crews who transported immigrants (both black and white, willing and unwilling) to North America might have also had a hand in the confluence of musical influences in the new continent. This suggests that the call-and-response technique is as closely linked to class – to the working person – as it is to a particular racial or cultural tradition.

Furthermore, when we reach the discussion of jazz itself, the collective ensemble polyphony of the earliest bands to make recordings relegates the idea of call-and-response to a relatively insignificant role, save for the fondness of those musicians for solo "breaks." The concept became more important within the context of larger ensembles, where different sections of a band could respond to one another, or to a soloist.

The elements specifically characterized by Waterman existed within nineteenth-century African-American music across much of North America, and were not restricted to states south of the Carolinas.

Yet the most detailed picture we have of a rural community during the era of slavery and shortly afterwards does come from that region, in the form of Charles Joyner's painstaking account of All Saints Parish in South Carolina. It would be misleading to adopt this as a paradigm for a continent, but it does offer some observations which contrast with what we have already seen of Louisiana.

First, there was a simple linguistic difference. In South Carolina the prevailing language among whites was English, and the prevailing language among the African-American population was Gullah. In purely linguistic terms, this was a "Creole" language, in other words a product of the colonial milieu, which in this case was an amalgam of the languages of white and black settlers. Yet it was more than that. Gullah was a synthetic language, a new creation, based on an amalgam of Wolof and English, summarized as follows by Charles Joyner:

> If there were forces at work on the plantations to discourage retention of their native languages, there were also circumstances that had an opposite effect. While the social dominance of the masters served as a strong incentive to learn English, the numerical dominance of the blacks facilitated their retention of African patterns of speech. While they lacked a common linguistic heritage, through trial and error, Africans increasingly became aware of common elements in their diverse tongues. . . . Out of these opposing tendencies – to learn English and to retain African speech patterns – they created a new language: Gullah.[16]

It is tempting to use this linguistic model as a metaphor for the development of African-American music. The same tension exists between adopting the instrumentation and some (but not all) of the tonality of European music, and retaining African rhythms and microtonal variations in pitch. Gullah is not an original African language, any more than it is a pure form of English; it is, essentially, a new, syncretic creation, and it makes sense to think of jazz in the same terms, although, whereas Gullah was restricted to the Georgia Sea Islands and the area of South Carolina around All Saints Parish, jazz was to become far more widespread.

One kind of music in particular conforms to this idea. It is the string band of banjo or mandolin, and violin. Whereas Grace King specifically describes New Orleans slave owners being entertained by singing, it seems to have been common practice elsewhere in the South for slaves to perform in string bands for their masters. Charles Joyner's detailed depiction of All Saints Parish lists the musicians who played banjo, fiddle, and even fife and drum. He has unearthed accounts that show that not only did such musicians entertain their masters, but also they were in demand to play for gatherings of slaves themselves, accompanying dances such as a "half walk-round, half break-down."

String bands were portable, flexible, and musically adaptable. In the early years of the twentieth century, there are documented examples of all three major forms of emergent African-American music – ragtime, blues, and jazz – being performed by ensembles that contain banjos, guitars or mandolins, and violins. In early sound recordings, the percussive attack of the banjo was more easily captured than drums or bass instruments, and a clear impression of syncopation and the beginnings of "swing" or jazz rhythm is discernible in recordings of banjo rags from the late 1890s.

Even more significant is that in some of the earliest recordings by a full African-American string band, the London recordings by Dan Kildare and Ciro's Club Coon Orchestra from 1916, many of the elements of jazz are actually present. On *My Foxtrot Wedding Day*, the opening banjo solo contains some skilfully inserted nursery rhyme quotes; there is consistently inventive interplay between the solo banjos (or banjo and banjoline), and a strong sense of underlying syncopated rhythm from the drums. The tearaway tempo and lilting swing of *My Mother's Rosary* brings a strong jazz feeling to an old Irish melody, and all these elements combine in *Yaaka Hula Hickey Dula*, a song later recorded by jazz musicians such as Bunk Johnson and Kid Ory. All in all, Ciro's Club Coon Orchestra, a contingent of traveling musicians from New York's Clef Club, give a strong hint that jazz rhythms and the mixture of improvisation and ragtime themes was much more advanced by 1916 than historians have generally supposed.[17]

This suggests that string ensembles derived from plantation music are every bit as significant in the early history of jazz as the singing and percussion-playing that have hitherto preoccupied jazz historians, given the geographically widespread nature of such groups, and their direct links with the musical forms that emerged. This can be borne out further because, since the 1940s, a small number of scholars has explored the connections between the banjo music of the plantations and the rhythmic character of ragtime and early jazz, notably Hans Nathan, who linked the irregular accentuation of minstrel banjo tunes notated during the 1840s and 1850s to the rhythms of ragtime.

One problem confronting anyone trying to determine the African-American contribution to banjo music from the minstrel repertoire is that it was predominantly preserved by white musicians, in the form of notated examples and (eventually) recordings. Yet copious acknowledgement on the part of song collectors and performers to black musicians from whom they collected their repertoire suggests an authentic origin amongst black Americans.[18]

So why were string bands so important, and what was it about their universality that made them an important stepping stone towards jazz?

In the nineteenth century, black performers who sang, played, and danced for other African-Americans, either at a local level or as itinerant musicians, were called "songsters" and "musicianers." The former group were entertainers, who both sang and made up songs, while the latter were instrumentalists, especially including (according to Howard Odum in 1911) "the individual who claims to be expert with the banjo or fiddle." The term "musicianers" was still in use in the 1990s; for example, the New Orleans singer Blue Lu Barker used it to describe to me the instrumentalists who had played on her 1930s recordings.[19]

The concept of a "musicianer" goes back well over a century earlier to plantation music, supplying what Paul Oliver describes as: "the regular beat that provided the pulse for the dance, and the cross-rhythms of vocal and instrumental that inspired the shuffles, shimmies, hip-shakes and shoulder rolls."[20]

Oliver is specifically describing dance within an African-American community, but he also makes the point that during Reconstruction and afterwards, the practice continued of black musicians playing for "the white balls in the big plantation houses . . . [where] they performed the tunes for the quadrilles and cotillions, set dances and barn dances of the white rural communities."

Here was the opportunity for the kind of syncretism that took place linguistically with the development of "Gullah." The very same musicians who played improvised or quickly invented spur-of-the-moment songs for their own communities were familiar with the formal repertoire of European dances. The same process of musical cross-fertilization that Jelly Roll Morton describes in New Orleans when he was a young man was going on in plantations across the South:

> The *Tiger Rag*, for example, I happened to transform from an old quadrille, which was originally in many different tempos. First there was an introduction, "Everybody get your partners!" and the people would be rushing around the hall getting their partners. After a five-minute lapse of time the next strain would be the waltz strain . . . and then another strain that comes right beside the waltz strain in mazooka time. . . . We had two other strains in two-four time.[21]

The string band was a ubiquitous ensemble in this formative period; it was not tied to either the black or white community, yet there was universal acceptance of skilled African-American performers who were in demand to perform for both audiences. The music such ensembles played varied from the overtly "African" in nature, according to descriptions from the time, to the formal European dances of the whites. It was both logical and natural that as ragtime and blues emerged, such ensembles should play both styles, and with a long tradition of aural assimilation, it did not matter whether the music played was predominantly folk-based, or more formally composed: both could be accommodated within the string-playing tradition.

Within New Orleans, string bands flourished in the late nineteenth century, and well into the twentieth. Samuel Charters lists several in his index of African-American New Orleans musicians, making the point that many of the formal brass bands also had counterpart string orchestras that furnished music for "dances in the smaller halls."[22] Generally, jazz historians have placed emphasis on the brass-band tradition because of the obvious instrumental links with early jazz bands, but since many of the same musicians were playing in string groups, tackling a similar repertoire, and belonging to a more widespread Southern tradition among African-Americans, string bands were every bit as significant as their louder, brassier counterparts.

New Orleans string groups, extant before the turn of the century, include the Big Four, the Excelsior, the Tio and Doublet (or Dublais) Orchestra, and the Union String Band. By 1911, the white ensemble known as the Six And Seven Eighths Band was in existence (a group which went on to record in the 1940s), and there was an informal tradition of string groups perpetuated by young musicians who grew up in the early years of the twentieth century.

Both Danny Barker and "Cousin Joe" Pleasant (born in 1909 and 1907 respectively) recall playing in a New Orleans children's string band called the Bouzan Kings, which existed into the early 1920s. Barker, writing about playing with the band in the bars and joints of the former Storyville area immediately after its official closure, powerfully expressed the race-consciousness which lay behind their performances, and which may be interpreted as underlying the late nineteenth-century traditions of string bands performing separately for both black and white audiences:

> In the Negro joints we were relaxed, at home; but in the white joints we were all eyes and ears, and anything could happen. In the colored joints the smiles were pleasant, but in the white joints you saw all kinds of expression. The Southern white supremos would enjoy our music; they got a big kick out of us kids. But every time without fail, there were descriptive slurs. We were used to hearing them as far back as we could remember. The

comments bounced off our ears in torrents, especially when our white audience was boozed up.[23]

Their contemporary, clarinetist Joe Darensbourg (born in 1906), grew up some distance away in Baton Rouge, but his memory chimes with theirs in respect of the music that he heard there as a child, because at every social function:

> Usually they would hire a band. Most of the time it was string bands ... [they] usually had a mandolin, guitar, bass and a violin in there. Sometimes you'd see an accordion or a banjo. ... To me, those are your first jazz bands. Hell, none of those fellows could read notes. Maybe the violin player could spell a little. It was improvising, that's mostly all they did. They was natural musicians; whatever they could hear or come to their mind, they would play it.[24]

String groups remained popular in rural areas across the South and became the natural accompanists for some of the earliest field recordings of blues singers in the early 1920s, just as they are remembered as playing ragtime, formal European dances, and jazz tunes in more urban settings. Territory bandleader and violinist George Morrison played violin in a string band in Boulder, Colorado, around 1915, and he recalled the typical repertoire of such bands, including waltzes, two-steps, and well-known songs and ballads, but he added, significantly: "We'd also play pieces like *Darktown Strutters' Ball* – pretty fast and lively. We played that as a jazz number."[25]

## Ragtime and Syncopated Music

> The ragtime piano was played all over in bars, cabarets and sporting houses. From what I have heard from the older men who played in New York in 1890 and 1900, there was a kind of ragtime played then. W. C. Handy told me the same.
> James P. Johnson, from *Conversations with James P. Johnson*
> by Tom Davin

Unlike the speculative nature of much of our modern understanding of plantation music, ragtime is well-documented in almost every respect. Sheet music, press reports, lengthy biographies of principal figures, and early recordings on cylinder and disc, complemented by piano rolls and music boxes, give a comprehensive account of this musical style which emerged during the 1890s and lived on into the 1920s as an active genre. We can also be confident that ragtime emerged as a fully fledged form some twenty years before the consolidation of what was eventually termed "jazz." The word "jazz" or "jass" only starts to appear frequently in the press from about 1917, so ragtime (although in many ways an overlapping form) might be viewed as a paradigm – the first original African-American style to emerge as a genre in its own right.

Both as solo music for piano or banjo and as an ensemble music, ragtime incorporated the syncopated character already noted in connection with mid-nineteenth-century minstrel tunes. Essentially, syncopation involves an alteration in the duration and accenting of notes that creates uneven patterns over a regular underlying beat. It can be fairly efficiently notated, but in performance, players have a great degree of license as to how vigorously they choose to syncopate.

The term "ragtime" is derived from the "ragged" or syncopated rhythms of the music. Initially it was mainly a piano-based genre, and is reckoned to have coalesced as a recognizable style at around the time of the 1893 World's Columbian Exposition in Chicago (otherwise known as the Chicago World's Fair), where many significant African-American pianists gathered together and played what was remembered as a new type of syncopated music. The fair was also a venue for African drumming and dancing of the Congo Square variety, but while this was not by any means a new form of music, there is little or no evidence of a homogeneous style resembling ragtime existing for any great period before the Exposition, as composer and bandleader Will Marion Cook wrote in 1918: "As far back as 1875 Negroes in questionable resorts along the Mississippi had commenced to evolve this musical figure, but at the World's Fair in Chicago, ragtime got a running start."[26]

The popularity of ragtime within a matter of months of that event led to its jaunty rhythms being incorporated into a style of popular dance known as the cake-walk, which became more obviously syncopated as a result.

Within two decades, ragtime was being recognized as a truly original American form of music – the kind of syncretic creation described in relation to Gullah. In a review of a 1912 Clef Club concert, the *New York Age* declared: "syncopation is truly a native product – a style of music of which the Negro is the originator, but which is generally popular with all Americans."[27]

In the years that followed the Colombian Exposition, ragtime rapidly became a recognizable and distinctive style, its development taking place in the Midwest, principally at Sedalia, St. Louis, and Indianapolis. Early in its history, ragtime players and composers formed alliances with publishers, who distributed their pieces to a world in which the piano was an increasingly popular form of home entertainment. John Stark, who published the works of ragtime's most famous composer, Scott Joplin, as well as James Scott, Artie Matthews, and the white composer Joseph Lamb, was the most important figure in obtaining widespread popular acceptance for the genre through sheet music distribution and marketing.

Ragtime made the transition easily from piano to string ensemble, and also to larger groups with brass or military band instrumentation, such as Sousa's band. In time, a specific instrumentation for orchestrated ragtime emerged, with violin, clarinet, trumpet, trombone, cello, piano, double bass, and drums. Published arrangements existed for such bands, but as we know from clarinetist Barney Bigard, whose uncle Emile played in the Magnolia Orchestra and later Kid Ory's Ragtime Band in New Orleans in the early 1910s, the style became well-established enough for ensembles to play by ear:

> When a new tune came out usually the violinist who had more musical knowledge than the others, would go and buy the sheet music and call a rehearsal. The violin would play the straight lead for them and keep on until the trumpet player got it. When the trumpet player had it down, the rest of them would fall in with their parts. A lot of people talk about those early "New Orleans" bands, or "Dixieland" bands, but they forget most of those bands had a violinist as the leader. Those early bands didn't sound anything like the jazz bands that you hear today.[28]

Pieces written for this type of ensemble retained the highly syncopated character of piano ragtime, but as ragtime songs became popular (especially in touring shows) transferring the onus from pianist to vocalist, the element of syncopation declined, so that a piece like Irving Berlin's *Alexander's Ragtime Band*, from 1911, is relatively free of it.

In its original piano-based form, and in its ensemble incarnation, ragtime had an impact on early jazz, the former providing many of the characteristics of solo piano jazz, and the latter, as Bigard has suggested, going a long way to define the instrumentation of what would become known as the first jazz bands.

Ragtime was also one of the main types of music played by a larger type of ensemble known as the "syncopated orchestra," which flourished from around 1910 until the start of the 1920s. These bands, and the literature surrounding them, have not been thoroughly explored by many jazz historians, with the result that their crucial role in providing a foundation for jazz, and particularly the jazz big band of the mid-1920s, has not been fully recognized. Furthermore, since such orchestras were based in New York and traveled to Europe during and after the First World War, they played an equally crucial role in disseminating the music that became jazz. Because they were run by musicians who were well-covered in the press, these orchestras offer a documentary basis for many of the ideas that underpinned African-American thinking about music in the years leading up to 1920.

From as early as 1910, syncopated orchestras of up to 50 musicians mixed a diet of light classics with instrumental ragtime. Such pieces as Joe Weatherley's *Grizzly Bear* or Ford Dabney's *Minor Strain* were played in 1910 Clef Club concerts, and other popular works included W. H. Tyers's *Panama Rag*.[29] From 1913, James Reese Europe and Ford Dabney took black musicians into areas where organized groups of African-American players had barely worked before – Europe into the armed forces with his "Hellfighters" band, and Dabney into the theaters of Broadway.

Significantly, and well away from the musical melting-pot of New Orleans, a musical philosophy began to coalesce around the leaders of the syncopated orchestras in New York. Their unofficial spokesman became Will Marion Cook, who wrote in 1918:

> 1898 marked the starting and quick growth of the so-called "ragtime" . . . [it] swept the Americas, next Europe, and today the craze has not diminished. . . . "Ragtime" offered unique rhythm, curious groupings of words and melodies which gave the zest of unexpectedness.

Cook then turns his attention to comedian George W. Walker, the former partner of the well-known entertainer Bert Williams, pointing out that Walker encouraged the theaters that employed him to support his popular comedy act with African-American music and players. Through Walker, and others like him who could communicate through the theater network to a wide public across the United States, came the germ of a whole movement:

> The colored American is finding himself. He has thrown aside
> puerile imitations of the white man. . . . From the Russian he has
> learned to get his inspiration from within: that his inexhaustible
> wealth of folklore legends and songs furnish him with material for
> compositions that will establish a great school of music and enrich
> musical literature.[30]

In Cook's writing is the same glimmer of middle-class aspiration already
noted among the New Orleans Creoles, except that, whereas the *gens de
couleur* aspired towards the values of the old white South, or at any rate the
imported continental European tastes for opera and the classics, Cook's
sights were set on something new and uniquely African-American:

> Negro music is on the ascendancy. However the height it is to
> reach within the next few years depends largely on the efforts of
> our colored musicians in the United States to bring this distinctive
> type of American music prominently before the public.

In Cook's eyes, there was as yet no distinction between sub-genres of
African-American music, between ragtime, blues, and jazz. His vision was
for a single, but distinct, brand of music that would develop from "the
upward flight" of "Negro music." His own inclination was towards the light
classics of Coleridge Taylor or J. Rosamond Johnson (who was head of the
Music School Settlement in Harlem), yet the philosophy he expressed can be
seen as underpinning the entire genesis of jazz.

As the term jazz began to creep into public consciousness, from 1916 or
so, the syncopated orchestras incorporated "jazz" into their programs. The
use of the term itself by the black press to describe the playing of a black
orchestra is significant, showing that it was by no means restricted to the
white Dixielanders, like Johnny Stein's band and the Original Dixieland Jazz
Band, who were first described as jazz bands in 1916 and 1917. When he
was murdered in 1919, by one of the drummers in his band, James Reese
Europe was recognized as having done much to popularize the music: "The
jazz craze was started in earnest," ran his obituary. "Lieut. James Reese
Europe was responsible for this style of music becoming immensely popular,
and for this reason he was nicknamed 'the Jazz King.' "[31]

After his death, in July 1919, when his Hellfighters band, "All Star

Wizards of Jazz and Syncopation," appeared under Gene Mikell's direction at Carnegie Hall, the press notices recalled his successful tour playing "jazz" in France the previous year. The program included standards such as *Beale Street Blues* and *Ole Miss*, and the personnel included trombonist "Jazz" Rijos.

The majority of jazz histories draw attention to the Original Dixieland Jazz Band, a white New Orleans ensemble arriving in London in April 1919 and "bringing jazz to Europe." In reality the syncopated orchestras had got there first. Not only had James Europe's Hellfighters played "jazz" on their 1918 tour, but so had the Negro orchestra formed at Camp Dix in July 1918 by Will Vodery. This band performed for President Poincaré at Verdun, immediately after the war, who declared "it was the first colored band he had heard and its music was astounding." In sets that resembled a variety performance, jazz was the centerpiece of the "olio" or interval, there was a syncopated "saxophone quartet" and a "Jazz Band" that played after the formal concert for dancing.[32]

Ragtime allows a clear view of the social and organizational structures that were in place as jazz developed, many of which were carried straight into the fledgling jazz environment. In particular, ragtime demonstrated how popular music publishing was to develop: sheet music was widely distributed, piano rolls were cut, and sound recordings of rags were made before 1900, offering a prototype for the ways in which jazz was to be disseminated. It is possible, however, to extend the analogy much further. Not only did ragtime open up the channels of distribution to the customer that jazz was to exploit, but it made use of the network of touring shows and theaters to communicate between musicians. Equally, if one examines what went on in Sedalia, where ragtime developed very rapidly in the years after the 1893 Chicago Exposition, it had many of the same ingredients as New Orleans during the earliest years of jazz.

In his study of Scott Joplin's life and work, Edward A. Berlin has drawn attention to the emergent black middle class in Sedalia, the institutions it established, and the George R. Smith College, which opened in 1894 to offer Bachelor of Arts courses and a range of other adult education. George R. Smith College became a center for musical education, and ran its own ensembles and choirs for African-Americans.[33] (Similar educational establishments were to play a significant part in jazz development just over a quarter of a century later, when, for example, Wilberforce University in Ohio became the base for Horace Henderson's band, Alabama State College launched its Collegians who became Erskine Hawkins's band, and the Johnson C. Smith University in Charlotte S.C. provided a home base for

Taylor's Dixie Serenaders, which launched the careers of Skeets Tolbert and several other well-known players.)

By 1896, Sedalia had African-American newspapers, churches, sporting, and fraternal organizations, and, like many other towns, a black brass band. This was known as the Queen City Cornet Band. Edward Berlin has also traced many other African-American musical organizations there from an orchestra to gospel quartets, jubilee singers, and informal tent shows. This Midwestern town is almost a microcosm of descriptions of contemporary New Orleans, albeit without the prevailing continental European traditions. The African-American middle class of Sedalia mirrored the organizational and social structures of their Southern Creole counterparts, and just as New Orleans had its red-light zone, so did Sedalia, with its Main Street honky-tonks offering to cater for the usual vices from gambling to sex, to the accompaniment of piano ragtime thrown in for good measure.

Scott Joplin, and the school of ragtime pianists to whom he was mentor (notably Arthur Marshall, Louis Chauvin, and Scott Hayden), played in the black social clubs of Sedalia, the Maple Leaf, and the 400, but they also worked in brothels. Thus, in just the same way as jazz was emerging in 1890s New Orleans, in the symbiosis between downtown Creole and uptown African-American, between upwardly mobile aspiration and African retention, with its piano incarnation being played in the brothels of Storyville in an ironic juxtaposition between the refined technical and musical abilities of the players and the basic instincts of their clientele, ragtime emerged in the Midwest in remarkably similar circumstances. It was played by musicians who aspired to the educational opportunities offered by Smith College (Joplin himself was briefly a pupil there), in due course it took advantage of the burgeoning popular music publishing industry through the Sedalia music shop proprietor John Stark, and it performed a social function that balanced uneasily between the entertainment of respectable black society in its own social clubs, and the entertainment of white, paying customers in the town's vice districts.

Contemporary accounts suggest that ragtime and its associated dance, the cake-walk, were widely popular in Sedalia, but the same papers condemn the "piano thumping" of Main Street, implicitly suggesting that one reason for the music's popularity was its connection with low-life notoriety. In the years that followed, these links would be turned into a morally (and racially) based argument against ragtime, from critics such as the *Musical Courier*'s Walter Kenilworth:

> The American "ragtime" or "rag time" evolved music is symbolic
> of the primitive morality and perceptible moral limitations of the
> Negro type. With the latter, sexual restraint is almost unknown,
> and the widest latitude of moral uncertainty is conceded.[34]

It was only a few years after the appearance of such pieces that jazz itself was to be decried in very similar terms.

In the years following his period in Sedalia, Joplin moved to St. Louis, which became the regional center for ragtime in the Midwest up until about 1907. It was from here that he and his publisher, John Stark, distributed a large number of Joplin's compositions, and also pioneered the idea of a composer of popular music receiving royalties for his work.

Joplin's St. Louis period offers some further insights as to the ways in which his musical ideas and those of other ragtimers were disseminated. As in Sedalia, the center of activity was again the city's red light area, extending about eight blocks above Market Street, where many ragtime pianists played in brothels such as "Mother" Johnson's, where Tom Turpin was principal attraction. But such dives were not the only outlet for Joplin's work and, in 1903, he went on tour with his own "opera company," playing his "grand opera," *Guest of Honor*. He was no stranger to the touring theater circuit, having been a member of the touring Texarkana Minstrels as early as 1891, and in many ways this show (its lost score and apparently incomplete tour giving it an air of mystery) conformed to the usual type of itinerary undertaken by a traveling black production. Edward Berlin's detective work shows that it visited (or planned to visit) locations throughout Nebraska, Kansas, Iowa, Missouri, and Illinois.

Although the music for *Guest of Honor* is lost, it was written at a stage in Joplin's development when his characteristic style of ragtime was well-developed, so the tour demonstrates one way in which Joplin disseminated his music first-hand to theater audiences. Joplin also had many close friends who were well-connected in the black theater world, in particular Sam Patterson and William N. Spiller.

Spiller became leader of what cornetist Rex Stewart called "one of the first big-time colored acts in show business," the "Musical Spillers."[35] This ensemble became a six- or seven-piece group of multi-instrumentalists, singers, and dancers. From 1907 they are documented as playing ragtime, their principal feature being a xylophone version of Tom Turpin's *St. Louis Rag*. Initially known as the "Musical Bumpers," they are referred to as "The Five Spillers" from April 1907 onwards. They were the dedicatees of

Joplin's 1908 *Pineapple Rag.*[36]

Their skills were honed from 1912 onwards by the remarkable talents of Spiller's wife Isabele, who trained the members of the troupe in everything from solfeggio to instrumental technique. She accompanied the ensemble to England in November 1912, where they presented "original ragtime music." From Isabele's own account, we know that she was instructed in the correct method of playing ragtime by Scott Joplin himself: "It was fascinating to me because it was the first time I had ever heard a composer explain in detail what he wanted done."[37]

As early as 1912, they were including a saxophone "choir" among their instrumental talents, similar to recording ensembles like the Brown Brothers, or Wilber Sweatman's Jass Band (which recorded in 1917). By the 1920s, with clarinetist Willie Lewis taking a similar solo role to Sweatman's, Rex Stewart (who joined them in 1921) recalled Isabele training the ensemble how to tackle elaborate dances while blowing their saxophones. She made the bass saxophonist do weight-training to cope with the physical demands of doing dance steps while playing such a cumbersome and heavy horn.[38]

Despite the fact that they were a particularly high-profile and long-lasting act, William Spiller's troupe typified the kind of versatile groups of entertainers that worked the vaudeville circuit in the early years of the century. We know from Isabele that around 1913–16 a typical program mixed the classics and ragtime pieces, the *Raymond Overture* followed by *Pineapple Rag* for example, and this kind of programing was the norm. Ragtime was undoubtedly disseminated fast and widely by such touring groups, and they took the addition of such a new style in their stride.

Why not, then, when jazz appeared, just add that new fad as well? Certainly in the case of the Spillers, this is exactly what happened, and by late 1917 they were billed as a "Jass Band."[39] Four years or so later, Rex Stewart was blowing improvised choruses with the same group, by then calling itself "The World's Greatest Ragtime Orchestra," from the moment he joined them.

Musicians trained in the Spillers' particular blend of African-American music and show-business included several significant future jazz players. In addition to Stewart and Lewis, the group's alumni included trumpeters Walter Bennett and Russell Smith (who both, like Stewart, later joined Fletcher Henderson's jazz orchestra), composer and bandleader Noble Sissle, and pioneer trumpeter Crickett Smith, who was featured with James Reese Europe's syncopated orchestra.

The Spillers are a significant ensemble, however, from another point of view also, since William Spiller was involved in one of the growing number of associations of black musicians that sprung up around North America. In Spiller's case, this was the Colored Vaudeville Benevolent Association (C.V.B.A.) which was a fraternal organization similar to the present-day Musicians' Benevolent Fund, but which also undertook a social and promotional role for its members. This, and similarly powerful local associations (including black locals of the American Federation of Musicians), created a highly organized framework in which black musicians operated, and jazz developed at precisely the time when this communication network had become sufficiently established to spread the word about a new musical style.

As I have said, ragtime developed first as a piano music, although one theory of its origin is that it began when pianists tried to imitate the African-American dances of the kinds of string ensemble discussed above under plantation music – indeed Joplin had "banjo imitation" printed on some of his published pieces. From ragtime, two principal characteristics were absorbed into jazz.

The first is the idea of multi-part compositions, made up of several "strains" in contrasting keys, connected by "bridge" passages. Such a structure is not unique to ragtime, and many of the military marches that made their way into jazz via the brass-band repertoire are similarly constructed, but virtually all ragtime pieces follow this principle, and several of them became the basis for jazz improvisation – by solo pianists and instrumental ensembles – with little modification. The "Society" orchestras of New Orleans, such as those led by John Robichaux and Armand J. Piron, played multi-part orchestrated rags, with a little gentle opportunity for improvisation, and Piron's 1923 recordings show how such a band sounded, the majority of its pieces little altered in style from that of surviving sheet music from around ten years earlier.

The second characteristic is more specific, and is to do solely with the piano form of the music, in which there is a rhythmic apposition between a player's left and right hands. The left hand provides a regular pulse, generally with a bass note on the first and third beats of a measure (the "on" beats), and a chord on the second and fourth (the "off" beats). The right hand provides the melodic content of the rag, frequently made up from a sequence of short, formulaic phrases. These right-hand phrases are often syncopated, and the intrinsic drama, or tension, of a rag comes from the way the performer plays off the steady rhythms of one hand against the decorative syncopations of the other.

Ragtime scholars have identified several styles or "schools" of ragtime, but overall these components are common to all of them, whether from the Midwest, the "East Coast" (the area around Baltimore), or New York. In just the same way as the improvised "hot" choruses of jazz crept into the ensemble ragtime of the Musical Spillers, there was a slow, almost imperceptible transition from piano ragtime into jazz. This is discussed more fully later, but, in essence, it took place in and around New York, and was complete by 1923, when the young Fats Waller cut his first discs in the "stride" style of jazz piano.

Waller, and his mentors James P. Johnson and Willie "The Lion" Smith, along with players from outside New York like Eubie Blake, started with the fundamental components of piano ragtime and took them one degree further. The left-hand "oompah" was intensified, and then often broken up as the emphasis of the beat was temporarily moved from the on beat to the off beat for a couple of measures. The right-hand syncopations gave way to a number of stand-alone, formulaic patterns that could be strung together in varying sequences and formed the basis of a new vocabulary for improvisation. In the transition from piano ragtime to stride we have a very clear example of the mutation of one African-American sub-genre into another.

## Blues and Vaudeville

> The best blues singer was Bessie Smith. She could really sing the blues. The rest of them sang, but not like Bessie Smith. She had her own style. And she was one of the popularest blues singers there was, living.
>
> Freddie Moore, from *Voices of the Jazz Age* by Chip Deffaa

Another of the elements of mythology that has crept into the study of early jazz is the idea that jazz is an offshoot of the blues, and that the two genres are joined at the hip like Siamese twins. As Paul Oliver demonstrated, in an analysis of several histories of jazz and blues, this idea seems to have been self-perpetuating among writers on the subject, and, therefore, giving "a shaky argument the impression of a firm foundation." Yet, looking deeply at the ideas presented by these writers, he summarizes a confusing mass of contradiction drawn from their books:

it is not possible to find a consensus among jazz historians on these matters: blues began, variously, before the Civil War, during the War, after Emancipation, during Reconstruction, after Reconstruction, in the 1880s, the 1890s. Blues was African in origin, it was not African in character, it was a rural music, it was a city music, it was part of the pre-history of jazz, it was an influence on the formation of jazz, it was part of a convergence phenomenon in the shaping of jazz, it was assimilated by jazz after its marching phase, it was played with ragtime before jazz bands played jazz . . ..[40]

Setting aside the views of earlier writers on jazz history, it would be true to say that, for the most part, blues has a history independent of jazz, although, from early in the twentieth century, jazz musicians could and did play alongside blues singers. The use of the term blues to define an African-American song form, derived from late nineteenth-century ballads and hollers, plus elements of spiritual and gospel music, dates from the early twentieth century, although there is evidence of the word being used for a much longer period to denote the melancholy state of mind that underlies a vast number of blues lyrics. The form seems to have developed in many areas of the South of the United States, although not necessarily those that overlap geographically with the early history of jazz. New Orleans, for example, produced a tiny number of pioneer blues singers, and no distinctive local variant of the style until the middle of the twentieth century.

Because blues undoubtedly began as a rural music, its origins are haphazardly documented, and the majority of scholars have focused their efforts on the period from 1920 onwards when blues began to be recorded on a significant scale.[41] References to it, however, appear in the press earlier than references to jazz, and in the period that jazz was emerging, two crucial relationships were established that did have a direct bearing on the development of jazz.

The first relationship is straightforwardly musical, and relates to the harmonic structure of blues forms, principally a standard twelve-measure chord sequence which underpinned the vast majority of blues lyrics.

$$I, I, I, I / IV, IV, I, I / V, V, I, I$$

Example 1: The harmonic structure of the twelve-measure blues sequence

This structure was adopted early by ragtime composers (for example on the anonymous *Dirty Dozens*, a reference both to a common African-American word-game of derogatory remarks, and also to the chord sequence), and from there slid easily into jazz, becoming one of the most commonly used bases for jazz improvisation. In addition, the blues chord sequence went hand-in-glove with melodies that employed "blue notes," a flattening of the third and seventh of the scale by less than a semitone.

The second relationship is to do with the emergent performance traditions of blues and, in particular, the ways in which the first generation of "classic" female blues singers worked on the same theatrical network already described in connection with ragtime, and brought about a cross-fertilization of musical influences with those jazz musicians who accompanied them, both solo pianists or guitarists, and ensemble players.

One of the earliest musicians to notate a twelve-measure blues was the cornetist W. C. Handy (1873–1958). His *Memphis Blues* (originally written in 1909 and published in 1912) and *St. Louis Blues* (1914) both became popular sheet-music publications in the form of multi-thematic ragtime compositions that conclude with a repeated twelve-measure strain using the blues sequence. Handy wrote that he had first heard the blues being sung "on a plantation in Mississippi," and, hearing the singer, had been "seized with a desire to play and sing, imitating his style."[42] Handy clearly viewed his earliest composition as ragtime, not least because this was the predominant African-American genre to be published in sheet music in the early 1900s, but in his account, he sets out why his piece was different from the run-of-the-mill multi-theme ragtime composition:

> To have composed a number, however joyous, with sixteen bars to a strain I would have been following in the steps of other writers of ragtime, but this composition carries twelve measures to a strain – typical "blues" – which makes me somewhat proud to know that I have added another form to musical composition and to the world.[43]

Handy was not, of course, "adding" a new form to the world's music, but he was one of the earliest composers to transcribe the blues he had heard being played and sung in the South, and subsequently to notate and publish it. He was also one of the first musicians to articulate in print what it was about this "entrancing" music that made it both musically distinct from other forms and endowed with a character that "represented . . . sorrows rather than joys." In his writings of the period, Handy identified that it was the twelve-measure harmonic sequence which underpinned the lyrics that gave the majority of blues an underlying similarity, a recognizable family resemblance with one another.

A considerable amount of the effort of blues scholars has gone into the documentation and analysis of blues lyrics, words which represent a cross-section of the social, political, regional, and cultural experiences of African-Americans.[44] Less effort has gone into the analysis of musical structure, of the variations in chord sequences, harmonies, and melodic lines. Blues lyrics are, however, vitally important in understanding the social milieu in which the music developed, and underline the fact that blues is, predominantly, a form of song. In this it has quite distinct characteristics from those of the instrumentally based ragtime and jazz genres. Although there have been many jazz singers, what defines them as such is their improvisatory ability, and the degree to which they can adapt jazz instrumental practice to vocal performance.

Conversely, the musical relationship between early jazz and blues reinforces the verbal qualities of blues, because, although "jazz bands" were used to accompany blues singers, their instrumental support generally played a subservient role to singers such as the first female blues singer to make records, Mamie Smith (1883–1946). At the same time, it seems that those instrumentalists most highly regarded by their peers as blues players incorporated elements of the sound of the human voice into their playing.

Smith recorded *Crazy Blues* with her Jazz Hounds in 1920, and it promptly sold a large number of copies.[45] Before the year was out, the New York press was reporting that she and her band were commanding "the largest figure ever paid colored artists by colored management . . . she is making the biggest reputation ever scored by a colored woman in the phonograph records."[46]

In common with tent-show singers like Ma Rainey, Smith used the backdrop of a jazz band to add variety to the sound of her songs, and the jazz musicians she used were experienced in playing the twelve-bar musical form of the blues.

Her saxophonist, Garvin Bushell, recorded his experiences in print, and made it clear that in common with other pioneer jazz musicians he regarded "the blues" as a way of playing – a stylistic approach to performance. He pointed out that, in contrast to the aspiring values of New York's black middle class, typified by James Reese Europe or Will Marion Cook, who followed the concert music of composers like J. Rosamond Johnson, blues and jazz catered for "the lower class" and were mainly heard in low-life or "gutbucket" cabarets, prior to the success of Mamie Smith on record. Bushell proposes an unorthodox patrimony for blues harmonies (but one entirely in keeping with the syncretic background to jazz and blues suggested earlier), suggesting they are drawn from Irish songs and native North American pitch systems as much as from African-American music: "The real blues used a special melodic line together with a way of playing that combined Irish cadences and Indian quarter-tones, together with the Negro's repetition of melody."[47]

Yet it was the overall approach or attitude of an individual musician, the fact that "gutbucket" players tackled their solos with the maximum of expression and feeling, that defined for Bushell how successfully a jazz musician played the blues.

> What you hear on those early Mamie Smith sides was the prevailing style around Harlem at that time. Harlem was a melting pot and many styles from different parts of the country were introduced by musicians who came to live there. . . . The clarinet style I played was something I just concocted there in New York. Dope Andrews was also a New Yorker . . . his was more or less the New York trombone style – also similar to what they played in the circus bands.

Bushell reserved his real admiration for Smith's trumpeter, Johnny Dunn: "He came from Memphis and he played the blues so it moved you, but not as soulfully as those blues players out of Louisiana."

Dunn's drive, his use of double time, dynamics, and the "wa-wa" plunger mute further marked him out for Bushell as an effective blues player.[48]

Trumpeter Doc Cheatham, growing up in Nashville, reacted in much the same way to hearing the jazz bands that accompanied touring blues singers. Occasionally (playing saxophone, rather than the trumpet on which he subsequently specialized), he joined in the pit bands for Bessie Smith, Ethel Waters, Ida Cox, and Clara Smith as they played the Bijou theater for a few nights each. The jazz player who impressed him most was trumpeter Joe Smith (1902–37). Smith toured with both Ethel Waters and Mamie Smith in the early 1920s, while Cheatham was a still a teenager. "He really thrilled me with his plunger playing," wrote Cheatham.[49] This idea of modifying the trumpet's sound, of "talking" with a mute, seems to have been an essential element in the way early jazz players tackled the blues.

In addition to adopting the chord structures and vocal nuances of blues into their instrumental playing, a large number of musicians who eventually became jazz musicians began their working lives by accompanying blues singers. In doing so, many became involved in the network of black theaters across the United States, but others worked on the parallel networks of touring tent and medicine shows, circus bands (some of which were mixed-race groups), or traveling minstrel troupes.

To base any assumptions on how these musicians might have sounded on recorded evidence, either in their role as accompanists or (as Garvin Bushell recalls) playing energetic dance numbers between the vocalist's appearances, is probably only to hear part of the story. For a start, the blues discs cut by Mamie Smith were not examples of how her band normally sounded, but the work of an intermediary called Perry Bradford (1893–1970), who acted as producer for the recordings. Bradford's role in the recording industry as a whole, and his championing of African-American artists, will be discussed shortly, but as musical director for Mamie Smith his participation was clear-cut. "Perry Bradford used to direct those sessions with Mamie," wrote Garvin Bushell.

> He'd stand on a big platform and make motions for what he wanted the instruments to do, moving his hands up for high notes, down for low ones. We knew little about recording in those days. . . . If we'd just used common sense, we would have done things much different.[50]

Bradford's background was in the black theater, to which he had graduated from being a sporting-house pianist, after serving an apprenticeship in traveling minstrel shows. His long experience in stagecraft was what he brought to the studio, with mixed results. Undoubtedly, he was attempting to shape a performance to fit the playing length of a disc well before the more famous jazz musicians who are usually credited with pioneering the idea, Jelly Roll Morton or Duke Ellington, refined that art. Yet he was using a set of presentational values that were more to do with recreating a stage show than giving his musicians space to play in their natural style on disc. Consequently, there is a stilted air about many of his recordings which is at odds with the recollections of the band's actual sound by the musicians involved and one suspects that Mamie Smith's acclaimed live shows were in themselves rather more free-flowing than her recorded cameos.

Bradford's importance was in using the experience he had garnered on the touring circuits to pioneer a role for African-American musicians on disc. His instincts told him that it would be the blues that would break through to a mass audience, a perception that he acquired at first hand during the period that blues was being developed into a distinctive form in its own right, following his debut with "Allen's New Orleans Minstrels" in 1906. He saw the effect singers like Ma Rainey had on crowds all over the country, and later, when he arrived in New York, he sought to overcome the perception mentioned by Garvin Bushell that blues was "low-life" music, by devising a blues-based revue called *Made in Harlem*, which opened at the Lincoln Theater in 1918.

Not for nothing was Bradford nicknamed "Mule," as in the years following this show he stubbornly kept up a relentless pressure on the companies that controlled the record industry to allow black artists to make discs. Bradford wrote:

> I tramped the pavements of Broadway with the belief that the country was waiting for the sound of the voice of a Negro singing the blues with a Negro jazz combination playing for him or her.[51]

After rejections from Columbia and Victor, he was successful in February 1920, when Fred Hager, the recording manager of Okeh records, agreed to record Mamie Smith – although, ironically, this was partly because the white singer Sophie Tucker had canceled a studio date. The Russian-born Tucker had been billed as early as 1906 as a "coon shouter," appearing in blackface, and in much the same way as theatrical presentations of African-Americans in minstrelsy had featured whites in blackface, white character singers such as Tucker got to record some time before those whom they imitated.[52]

It was a critical time in the fortunes of the phonograph industry, which was undergoing both a technical and commercial shakedown in the aftermath of the World War I. Okeh was initially part of the General Phonograph Corporation, an agency of the German Lindström company, making discs of the kind devised by Edison that had grooves cut vertically rather than laterally. In 1920 they abandoned "hill and dale" discs and began to make records that used lateral grooves, as did the market leaders, Victor and Columbia. Hager's decision to record an African-American artist singing the blues involved him, as Bradford put it, "taking a chance with his position." Although various African-Americans had already recorded – from comedian Bert Williams to the syncopated orchestra of James Reese Europe – Okeh's discs were the first attempt by any record company to reflect the mainstream of black musical entertainment. They were extremely successful.

As the major companies hesitated in following Hager's lead (they were, after all, making considerable profits from the music of white jazz bands, following the Original Dixieland Jazz Band's debut both for Columbia and for Victor in 1917), Okeh proved that there was a larger and hitherto untapped market for recordings within the African-American community. Their Colored Catalog was launched in 1921, and paved the way for other "race" record series, both from the major companies and from smaller independents including Black Swan records, the first African-American owned and managed label to record vernacular music.[53] Until June 1921, when Kid Ory's band made its first discs on the West Coast, the only black jazz bands to record did so in these race series as the accompanists to blues singers, underlining the *status quo* of a performing relationship that had grown up over the previous two decades.[54]

So what had gone on in the period from 1900 to 1920? What had happened to create a public taste among African-Americans that produced a ready market by 1920 for the first "race" records? How had blues managed to develop in parallel with jazz during this time, without either genre swamping or overtaking the other?

The simplest explanation is to take the view that jazz was a predominantly instrumental music, and blues was predominantly vocal. Their intersection was a practical one – jazz musicians could supply accompaniments to blues singers, whether in the form of full bands or as solo pianists or guitarists. As noted already, in the discussion of string bands, it was a relatively simple matter for musicians already skilled in various different genres to adapt their string ensemble playing at will, and accompanying blues singers was a skill not far removed from that of playing for African-American dancing. In effect, this separation of skills, between singer and accompanist (or "musicianer"), between the performer of previously written lyrics and, often, a spontaneously improvised accompaniment, is what prevented fuller long-term interbreeding between jazz and blues, and preserved each as a distinct genre. Blues was a form in which improvisation was restricted to the sequence of words, lines, or stanzas recalled by a singer's memory, and ways of fitting these to relatively standard melodic lines; whereas the accompanying musicians were often employing their improvisatory skills to supply the entire musical backdrop for the singer.

Yet that is not the whole story, since something slightly more complex, and certainly more interesting, than this straightforward division had been going on in theaters and tent shows across the United States, leading to one genuine hybrid form, a type of vaudeville song. It was hybrid both in terms of its provenance and its performance practice. This genre of singing, which Perry Bradford exploited, is what became known as the "classic" blues.[55] Generally, the name is applied to the work of female vocalists such as Bessie Smith, Ma Rainey, Ida Cox, and Mamie Smith. Their songs were not restricted to the ubiquitous twelve-measure format of the most basic blues, with its three-line stanzas. Instead, they took in material from the songster repertoire and from African-American musical theater, which was developing fast in the wake of the nineteenth-century minstrel era. Minstrel shows still continued well into the first two decades of the twentieth century, but perpetuated an older style of music rather than developing a new one.

Several blues singers cut their teeth in the large number of African-American minstrel shows of the early twentieth century, while others had a more overtly theatrical apprenticeship. Their blend of experience, plus the instrumental background of their accompanists, helped to create a type of vaudeville number that combined the 16-measure or 32-measure structure of a ragtime or popular song with the flattened pitches and soulful delivery of the blues. This was often prefaced by "verses" in quatrains leading up to the main part of the song. To understand the nature of this hybrid, and the way that it became a vehicle for emergent jazz and blues musicians to work together, it is helpful to look in turn at three separate elements that contributed to the "classic" blues. These are:

1. the first full-length works for the African-American musical theater;
2. the backgrounds of the classic blues singers themselves; and
3. what we know of the jazz musicians who accompanied them.

### African-American Musicals

In the nineteenth century a number of types of song, based on African-American material to varying degrees, had achieved a more than local popularity. Chief among them was the "coon song," generally performed by white singers, such as Sophie Tucker, in blackface make-up, and built around ideas that modern society would consider reprehensible: a contempt for blackness reinforced by a stereotypical representation of Africans as primitive.

At the very tail end of the nineteenth century, a group of New York composers and songwriters began to challenge this orthodoxy, with subtle modifications of the genre. These were Will Marion Cook (already mentioned in connection with syncopated orchestras), Paul Laurence Dunbar, J. Rosamond Johnson, and Joe Jordan. In addition to writing individual songs, they began to compile complete entertainments, some resembling revue and others moving toward the more operatic idea of complete stories in song and dance, so that by 1903–5, for a brief period, a number of shows with all-black casts appeared on Broadway.

These shows and their content have been studied in detail by Thomas L. Riis, who concludes that they contain a number of elements which subsequently materialized in both jazz and blues. In particular, he sees the replacement of crude stereotypes with ideas drawn from the black heritage. Riis suggests that it was J. Rosamond Johnson, in particular, who "removed the dialect text entirely and reshaped the four-measure phrases of Tin Pan Alley songs with a more African-American musical gesture."[56]

Riis observes that, by introducing an element of call-and-response, by exorcizing coon-song linguistic cliché and by bringing fresh harmonic components to their songs, Johnson and the others initiated a revolution that created a genre which was syncretic, to be sure, but which incorporated several specifically African-American characteristics in an entirely new way.

By far the most significant of his observations concerns the inclusion in several Cook and Johnson songs of syncopation and blue notes – or at least the use of piano harmonies that involved neighboring semitones being sounded together to create a simulation of the microtonal flattening effect of genuine blue notes. In Cook and Dunbar's 1900 song *Lover's Lane*, for example, Riis finds not only syncopated dotted rhythms drawn from ragtime, but the sophisticated use of these rhythms being repeated at various pitches over underlying harmonies that contain augmented-sixth chords – a precursor of the kinds of substitute harmonies found in much later jazz compositions.

The most subtle part of his investigation concerns the 1902 musical-theater production by Dunbar and Cook called *In Dahomey*. This was one of a series of vehicles they wrote for comedians and dancers Bert Williams and George Walker, starting with *Clorindy, or the Origins of the Cakewalk*, in 1898. *In Dahomey* concerned themes of social status, high caste, and royalty amid the black community, and a contrast between the social mores of an African state ruled over by King Eat-em-all and the joyous celebration of African-Americans marking the public holiday of "Emancipation Day." The lyrics of this last song contain plenty of the kind of double meaning and political symbolism defined by Henry Louis Gates Jr. as "Signifyin(g)," but for jazz historians it also presents several fascinating references to components that were to be absorbed into the new music. The next section of this chapter considers brass bands and street parades more fully, but what better description is there of a New Orleans street parade and its dancing, marching followers known as its second line?

> On Emancipation Day
> All you white fo'ks clear de way,
> Brass ban' playin' several tunes,
> Darkies eyes look jes' like moons,
> Marshal of de day astruttin'
> Lord but he is gay.
> Coons dress up lak masqueraders.
> Porters arm'd lak rude invaders,
> When dey hear dem ragtime tunes,
> White fo'ks try to pass fo' coons
> On Emancipation Day.[57]

This show ran for around four years, including several months in England in 1903. Its primary theatrical importance is that it was the most successful and high-profile of the Williams and Walker collaborations. Later there were to be other such influential stage partnerships such as Miller and Lyles, for example, who toured in shows by Eubie Blake and Noble Sissle, and later, by Fats Waller and James P. Johnson. But in the early years of the twentieth century Williams and Walker became hugely important role models for black performers, not least as patrons of composers, songwriters, and performers, in the ways suggested (in the section above, concerning syncopated orchestras) by Will Marion Cook. Even though Bert Williams usually performed in blackface, he managed to impart (as his biographer Ann Charters put it) "a rare humanity to a degrading racial caricature." His influence as a stage performer, and subsequently as a recording artist, was second to none on the generation who developed jazz and brought blues to the stage circuit.

The songwriting revolution of Cook, Dunbar, Johnson, and Jordan, and the Williams and Walker collaborations, ending in 1908 with *In Bandanna*

*Land*, underpinned much of the development of the classic blues singers and their repertoire. The shows toured widely within the United States, on the very network of theaters that acted as a communications thoroughfare for African-American performers, and brought a dominant style of performance practice and a repertoire that was beginning to explore syncopation and blue-note harmonies to a very wide public indeed.

## The Classic Blues Singers

Most of the generation of female singers known as the "classic" blues singers garnered at least some of their experience on the touring theater circuit in the early years of the twentieth century. However, there were other kinds of traveling production in which many singers also worked: tent or medicine shows, minstrel troupes, and circuses. Although more haphazard in organization than the embryonic African-American theater circuit, these touring entertainments were important in bringing singers into contact with instrumentalists who were to establish the kind of "jazz-band" accompaniments that in due course found their way onto disc.

Since Mamie Smith was a pioneer of recording the blues with such accompaniment, what was her own background? Although some blues critics find her less emotionally involved with her material than singers who recorded a little later, was her career in any way a paradigm for that of a classic blues singer?

She was born in Cincinnati in 1883, and as she entered her teens she began her apprenticeship on the touring circuit in a dance troupe called the Four Dancing Mitchells. Before she entered her twenties, she had become a chorus dancer in the Smart Set, part of J. Homer Tutt and Salem Tutt-Whitney's theater company. She went on to sing in the kind of low-life New York cabarets described earlier by Garvin Bushell.

Those three segments of her career alone have much in common with other female blues singers of the period. Above all, she worked in exactly the kind of milieu in which jazz and blues began to intermingle – often for pragmatic rather than aesthetic reasons. When fellow blues singer Victoria Spivey, for example, heard Mamie Smith in the City Auditorium in Houston, Texas, it was obvious that there were more than simply musical reasons why she sang with a little instrumental group:

I looked at her dress. Nothing but sequins and rhinestones, plus a

velvet cape with fur on it. We all went wild, and then she sang –
she tore the house apart. Between numbers while the band was
playing she would make a complete change in about a minute, and
was back in record time for her next selection.[58]

The instrumental variety of the band would hold the attention of the
audience while Mamie changed her costume, thus creating the impression of
more of a show than the audience actually heard from the singer herself.

Mamie Smith was not alone in working with this kind of accompaniment. Lucille Hegamin, for example, who was one of the first blues singers
to follow Smith into the studio, began in a traveling theater company from
her native Georgia. She recalled, "before the words 'jazz' and 'blues' came
to be used . . . I sang nearly all the popular ballads and ragtime tunes of the
day."[59]

Hegamin, like so many touring artistes, was "stranded" when her show
ran out of work in Peoria, Illinois. This is a phenomenon recorded in
memoir after memoir of musicians who traveled in the United States at that
stage, whose companies clung together in ever more remote areas until
there was simply no more money or work to keep them going. Gathering
what resources she had, Hegamin made her way the 150 or so miles to
Chicago, and her account of what happened next gives an interesting insight
into the aspirations of a singer from the period 1910–20. She became a
"cabaret artist . . . and never had to work theaters, and I sang everything
from blues to popular songs in a jazz style." She makes it clear that there was
a hierarchy of venues – and that the cafés and cabarets where she sang were
vastly preferable to being just one of many acts on a theater bill or, even
worse, a traveling show. Around 1915 she sang at the Elite No. 2 in
Chicago, a cabaret where New Orleans pianist Tony Jackson was her
accompanist, and she remembered his infinite capacity to improvise behind
her vocals. Here, then, is proof of a vaudeville-trained singer working
alongside a musician who had absorbed the raw materials of jazz, and the
two of them putting their respective experience together in front of a
sophisticated northern audience.

Despite their short-lived fame from early records, neither of these
singers was as important or influential as Ma Rainey or Bessie Smith, the two
most celebrated classic blues singers. Both of them owed their success every
bit as much to a reputation built up by live appearances on touring circuits as
they did to recordings, and both of them have a convincing emotional punch
to their work, making most other singers sound light-weight by comparison.

Ma Rainey, born Gertrude Pridgett in Columbus, Georgia, in 1886, left home at eighteen to go on the road with the man who became her husband, Will Rainey. They traveled the theater circuit together, but she went on to work in tent and minstrel shows, initially with the Rabbit's Foot Minstrels, and, ultimately, her own troupe. She also worked in circuses from time to time, such as the Tolliver Circus between 1914 and 1916, most probably appearing in the so-called "After Show," a musical event that took place on an improvised stage in the ring after the main circus acts were over.

Music played a large part in all tent and traveling productions, from the brass bands that would go out and about to "ballyhoo" for the show, to the actual accompanists for the circus and musical acts that were featured on the bill. Ma Rainey's accompanists as she toured the Southern states were generally a rough-and-ready form of prototype jazz band or (more in keeping with the blues side of her work) a jug band, and both forms of accompaniment survived into her 1920s recording career, although it was a small jazz band that backed her very first session in December 1923. This included pianist Lovie Austin and the New Orleans trumpeter Tommy Ladnier. Like Hegamin, Rainey performed her songs to an instrumental accompaniment that included elements of improvisation.

What is most significant about Rainey, however, is that she was interviewed by a pioneering scholar of American song, John Work, who established that (in her view) she had learned her first blues as early as 1902 in Missouri, when a girl came to the tent where Ma was appearing and sang a "strange and poignant" song about a man who had left her.[60] Rainey is just as specific in her recollections as W. C. Handy was in his articles and autobiography, that it was in the early years of the twentieth century that she first encountered the form, distinguished by its twelve-measure structure. This, and the absence of similar recollections dated any earlier, suggests to me that we can regard the twelve-measure, ubiquitous form of the blues as originating in the twentieth century, rather than the nineteenth. The blues became a central and fundamental part of Rainey's repertoire, so much so that when she came to record for Paramount in the 1920s this was almost all they asked her to sing, although accounts suggest that her live shows contained a much wider repertoire of minstrel and vaudeville songs.[61]

Bessie Smith's recorded repertoire, by contrast, included a greater proportion of multi-thematic vaudeville songs. Pieces like *Alexander's Ragtime Band, Cake Walkin' Babies*, and *A Good Man Is Hard to Find* sit easily alongside her twelve-measure blues recordings. She had honed her abilities in performing such songs on the touring theater and minstrel-show circuits, much like Ma Rainey, having started her career in the same company in 1912. Up until Smith began her career, there was often a separation between the performer and the meaning of the lyrics that were being performed. Many of the earliest female blues singers to have recorded, sound (to modern ears) relatively uninvolved and detached from their songs of unrequited love, hardship, and social realism, despite the fact that the words themselves touched a chord with the buying public.

It was Smith's unparalleled ability to use her vocal technique to express the content of her songs with both emotional power and clear meaning that made her so significant in early jazz. It has already been noted that the most celebrated of the jazz players to accompany blues singers were those who adopted some measure of vocal quality into their playing. Smith's work gave them a lexicon of vocal effects upon which they could draw – from her lowering of the pitch to emphasize particular parts of a phrase, to the robust growling sound with which she delivered some of her lines. Smith came into contact with the emergent generation of jazz musicians from 1912 onwards, through her work as a touring singer, but the nature of her influence during that period can be assessed, to some extent, by examining the records she came to make in the following decade. Her 1928 record of *Empty Bed Blues*, for example, finds her exchanging phrases with trombonist Charlie Green for over six minutes, across two sides of a 78 r.p.m. disc, and several lines of her vocal employ a rasping, growling tone for occasional emphasis of its plentiful *double-entendres*, while Green responds with a mixture of vocalized instrumental growls, smears, and slurs.

Bessie Smith's ability to bend the meaning of a song to her will, and to inhabit the world she was singing about, gave jazz musicians a powerful message, and few who heard her forgot it. The strength with which she delivered her songs was an object lesson in how to inject passion and drama into a performance, and, in due course, through vocalized effects and other devices culled from Smith, jazz players were able to enrich their art. Teddy Wilson, who accompanied her as late as 1933, recalled:

> I was always impressed by her tremendous power. She had the dynamic range of an opera singer and the same control and power of voice, from the softest pianissimo, and a tremendous pulse in her singing.[62]

The same qualities were noticed by saxophonist Bud Freeman, whose first encounter with her was almost ruined by an intoxicated Bix Beiderbecke, who flung all his money at her in a gesture of appreciation. Freeman recalled: "Her phrasing was exquisite, and she was making something religious out of a popular song . . . she had the most fantastic voice I was ever to hear."[63]

Another side of Smith's persona was described by guitarist Danny Barker: "Bessie Smith was a shouter: she would scream, holler! Primitive. Old feelings about 'When her man done her wrong . . .' or 'Once I lived the life of a millionaire. . . .' That kind of thing. Highly dramatic."[64]

Teddy Wilson's fellow pianist, Art Hodes, heard Smith in 1920s Chicago, and Hodes's description of her is a perfect summary of all that she had learned of stagecraft from her time on the touring-theater circuit:

> Now comes the big hush. Just the piano going. It's the blues. . . .
> There she is. Resplendent is the word, the only one that can
> describe her. Of course, she ain't beautiful, though she is to me.
> A white, shimmering evening gown, a great big woman, and she
> completely dominates the stage and the whole house, when she
> sings *The Yellow Dog Blues*. Ah! I don't know, she just reaches
> out and grabs and holds me. There's no explaining her singing,
> her voice. She don't need a mike; she don't use one. Everyone
> can hear her. This gal sings from the heart. She never lets me get
> away from her once. As she sings, she walks slowly round the
> stage, her head sort of bowed. From where I'm sitting I'm not
> even sure she has her eyes open. On and on, number after
> number, the same hush, the same deafening applause. We won't
> let her stop. . . . You just know you're listening to the greatest
> blues singer you ever heard.[65]

The significance to jazz history of Mamie and Bessie Smith, Lucille Hegamin, Ma Rainey, and the other classic blues singers, all of whom, incidentally, were female, is that their work became the principal meeting-ground between what was going on in jazz and in blues. They shared a vaudeville touring background. Their work grew out of the narrative, multi-part minstrel song and added the plaintive, emotional appeal of the blues, and – notably in the work of Bessie Smith – provided the opportunity for cross-fertilization of ideas with their accompanists, who, more often than not, tended otherwise to be players who specialized in ragtime or jazz.

## The Blues Accompanists

Many a jazz musician started out as an accompanist on the vaudeville circuit. Some, indeed, like the Harlem stride pianist Luckey Roberts, could trace their careers back to the world of George Walker and Bert Williams. A 1920s newspaper report about Roberts's sideline in supplying up-to-date jazz records to Edward, Prince of Wales, in Britain, made it clear that as Alex Rogers's songwriting partner and Bert Williams's former accompanist, he could trace his jazz credentials back to the time when he "carried the orchestral burdens of many musical comedies."[66] On a revue like the 1920 *This and That*, at the Lafayette Theater in Harlem, Roberts set several songs by Rogers, music that was praised in the press of the time as "very tuneful . . . with real song hits in the show," although:

> the intrinsic value of some of the most beautiful numbers is lost due to mediocre rendition, but in justice to the writers, the numbers compare favourably with any musical production on Broadway.[67]

Other accompanists, like Roberts's fellow Harlem pianist James P. Johnson, had worked in all manner of stage productions, composed ragtime and popular songs, and fronted a band. Johnson was already playing the piano when he moved with his parents from Jersey City to New York in 1908, aged fourteen. The music he had heard as a child in Jersey City was not ragtime, which he did not remember hearing until he got to New York, but was based on the dances of rural communities, these tunes having become part of the repertoire of African-American urban pianists by the early years of the twentieth century. He recalled: "Most East Coast playing was based on cotillion dance tunes, stomps, drags, and set dances like my *Mule Walk Stomp* . . . they were all country tunes."[68]

Arriving in New York brought about a change in Johnson's perception of the role of a pianist. He observed that the city's public was used to hearing classical pianists playing in a variety of public settings, and that "the ragtime player had to live up to that standard. They had to get orchestral effects, sound harmonies, chords and all the techniques of European concert pianists."

Attempting to acquire such skills himself, Johnson, in common with a small group of Harlem pianists already mentioned for having progressed ragtime towards jazz, perfected a strengthening of solo piano technique that was ideal for accompanying singers:

> New York developed the orchestral piano – full, round, big, widespread chords and tenths – a heavy bass moving against the right hand. The other boys from the South and West at that time played in smaller dimensions – like thirds played in unison. We wouldn't dare do that because the public was used to better playing. We didn't have any instruments then except maybe a drummer, so we had to use a solid bass and solid swing to get the most colorful effects.[69]

At eighteen, Johnson dropped out of school and became a full-time pianist, first in Charlie Ett's bar in Far Rockaway, Queens, and then in Manhattan, on 27th Street between 8th and 9th Avenues, the city's Red Light district. There he accompanied singers, but, in 1912, "blues had not yet come into popularity by that time – they weren't known or sung by New York entertainers." Instead, the vocal repertoire was the familiar vaudeville song mixture that was to become part of the "classic" blues singers' stock-in-trade; ragtime songs like *Hiawatha*, *Red Wing*, or *Big Chief Battleaxe*. Using his full, orchestral technique, Johnson was the sole accompanist for the singers who appeared at Dan Williams's sporting-house. In common with players like Luckey Roberts (whose naturally harmonically dense style was aided by the ability of his huge hands to stretch an interval of a fourteenth, almost two octaves) and Eubie Blake, Johnson trained himself to be able to play any song in any key, so as always to pick the most appropriate key for the pitch of a singer's voice.

Johnson had been composing ragtime almost since his arrival in New York, but he also turned his hand to popular songs, and his *Mamma's and Pappa's Blues* was later adapted by Perry Bradford as the basis for Mamie Smith's first recording, *Crazy Blues*. In due course, Johnson cut piano rolls of his own compositions, by his own account, the first African-American pianist to do so. Most famous among his pieces was *The Charleston*, a good example of a musical idea conceived to satisfy dancers. Indeed, Johnson had the dance rhythms of the Southern port of Charleston itself in mind; rhythms he had heard danced by "the working seamen who sailed to and from the South to New York."[70] Yet he was not so fortunate in making gramophone records, since although he made a test pressing of his *Caprice Rag* for the Okeh company, it was never issued, leaving Mamie Smith to pioneer that firm's "race" catalog.

Nevertheless, Johnson's skills were so much in demand that when the 15th Infantry Regiment mounted a blues-singing contest in January 1922, newspaper reports made much of the fact that he was the automatic choice of accompanist:

> Lt. Vodery [subsequently bandleader Will Vodery] has enlisted the help of James H. [sic] (Jimmie) Johnson, the well-known accompanist, at present distinguished by his connection with the QRS record company. Mr. Johnson, aided by members of his Syncopated Jazz Orchestra will accompany the competing blues singers.[71]

The eventual winner of the competition was "The Southern Nightingale," Trixie Smith, who sang her own *Trixie Blues* to triumph over Lucille Hegamin performing Spencer Williams's *Arkansas Blues*. Although Johnson had spent the majority of his career in Jersey City or New York, rather than out on the road in the South, it is clear that his skills were complementary to those bred on the touring circuit, because, as the *New York Age* reported: "Trixie Smith was practically unknown to New York audiences, but she is well-known to audiences on the T.O.B.A. circuit, as she is one of its strongest attractions."[72]

Johnson himself drew "enthusiastic appreciation" from the "mammoth audience" both for his efforts as accompanist, and also for the instrumental numbers played by his "orchestra of syncopated jazz artists." He exemplifies the constructive way in which the genres of ragtime, blues, and jazz could interrelate, and, in particular, the way that jazz musicians composed and performed an appropriate repertoire for "classic" blues singers – many of their so-called "blues" songs actually being no such thing, but conventional vaudeville songs with references to blues in the lyrics. It is notable that the other songwriters whose pieces were performed on the contest were both jazz pianists and composers: Spencer and Clarence Williams.

Among Johnson's many recordings of blues accompaniments, one pair of performances stands out: his February 1927 session with Bessie Smith that produced both *Preachin' the Blues* and *Backwater Blues*. Both credited to Bessie herself as composer, they represent an intriguing contrast of the repertoire of the "classic" blues singer, as the first is a 32-measure popular song and the second a twelve-measure blues. Johnson's facility is such that he adds a

58

variety of rain-like effects to the second piece, a sad commentary on a
backwater tributary of the Mississippi being flooded to save the levees, but
his forte is in providing a steady, rhythmically fluid backdrop to both songs.
Each is a perfect example of a jazz accompaniment of great finesse, sitting in
a compatible way with a blues vocal, and, as Edward Brooks comments in
his study of Smith's songs:

> his seemingly endless pianistic attributes must be mentioned; his
> superb dynamic control, one moment pounding away triple forte,
> and the next fingering a delicate trill pianissimo (occasionally
> doing both simultaneously); the fact that he rarely plays exactly
> on the pulse and the exceptional independence of his two hands.[73]

One of the most prolific blues accompanists to record was the pianist and
bandleader Fletcher Henderson, who had started his musical career in New
York as a song-plugger for the African-American publishing firm run by Pace
and Handy. When these two entrepreneurs decided to form a record
company, Black Swan, it was Henderson who became their house pianist,
supplying back-up chording for many a blues singer in a style that seemed
starkly anachronistic in contrast to the forward-looking ideas he was to
pioneer with his band. The band was not formed as a regular unit until
1924, by which time Henderson had made numerous discs as an
accompanist, many of them demonstrating that although he was a technically
proficient pianist, he was not a natural jazz player with the kind of rhythmic
freedom demonstrated, for example, by Johnson. Indeed, he sounds stilted
and ill-at-ease on even his best-known early recordings with Bessie Smith,
from 1923.

Henderson's importance as an accompanist is that he was the most high-
profile pianist to employ jazz players (mostly drawn from his orchestra) to
work alongside him in the studio bands accompanying blues singers. The
trend had been started by producer Perry Bradford in his recordings of
Mamie Smith, and, as noted above, her cornetist, Johnnie Dunn, was justly
celebrated, first for his work in Smith's Jazz Hounds, and later with Florence
Mills, with whom he appeared on stage in the *Plantation Revue*. The *New York
Age* praised Dunn's *Bugle Call Blues*, saying "[his] eccentric work with a
cornet cannot be beaten."[74] But Henderson's consistent supply of
impressive instrumental accompanists, alongside his own rather plodding
piano, strengthened the links on record between blues singing and jazz
playing – capturing for posterity a stage in the development of both musics

that had been an everyday aspect of touring-show life for the previous two decades.

Garvin Bushell worked for Henderson in 1921, on recordings by Edith Wilson. He recalled:

> Fletcher was in charge of the record dates. He might pick the numbers in the office, present them to the vocalists, then we'd have rehearsal and get it together. Often there were two pieces of music, one for the piano and one for the trumpet (or violin) . . . since we couldn't use a bass drum or a bass, the rhythm tended to get ragged. Also, we'd be in awkward positions and scattered all over the place, which made it hard to keep together. But when Fletcher was in charge it usually was a little more organized, and we'd have good musicians who were concerned about what they were playing.[75]

Three years later, cornetist Joe Smith and trombonist Charlie Green worked with Henderson on Bessie Smith's *Weeping Willow Blues*, from September 26, 1924. It was the first recording Bessie had made with a cornet in her back-up band, the two horns adding instrumental punctuations to the vocals and interpolating four-measure interludes between each vocal chorus. Both brass players use mutes, and Joe Smith, in particular, demonstrates the skill so admired by Doc Cheatham of using the plunger to match the vocal nuances of Bessie Smith's voice, as well as imitating the sound of a railroad engine's wailing whistle.

It is highly likely that such a line-up comes close to the reality of the accompaniment a singer like Smith would have had on the touring circuit, in those theaters affluent enough to afford a backing band rather than a solo pianist. (Some singers traveled with their own small band; others appeared with house orchestras. In the late 1920s, Smith toured with another of her recording partners, pianist Fred Longshaw, described in the *Pittsburgh Courier* as an "artist of the ivories who is one of the best in his line we've heard in many a moon."[76] At other stages of her career she fronted a small band of her own.)

In two typical examples of house bands that accompanied singers, Doc Cheatham remembers his local black theater in Nashville employing a three-piece band, and his contemporary, drummer Freddie Moore, worked in similar circumstances in Alabama for several years leading into the 1920s:

> Way back in the 'teens, I played for all of them: Sarah Martin,
> Butterbeans and Susie, Ida Cox, Ma Rainey ... Bessie Smith, all
> the old-timers. In the Gaiety Theater, Fourteenth Street and
> Third Avenue in Birmingham.[77]

Nevertheless, the role of the accompanying musician was limited on the theater circuit to the kind of cameo preserved on *Weeping Willow Blues*, as Sammy Price, remembering his own T.O.B.A. days, recalled:

> During those years, singers were the principals. You don't think
> Coleman Hawkins could have taken his tenor saxophone and gone
> out on stage and stood in front of Butterbeans and Susie and been
> the star? He was just another musician in the background. Maybe
> they'd let him play a number. Maybe. Or he'd have an
> opportunity to play when the chorus girls were featured. Then
> you could really do your thing and play as hard as you wanted to,
> which would be an inspiration to the chorus girls.[78]

As his band became more celebrated and famous, Henderson continued to bring his best musicians into the studios to provide varied instrumental backings for the singers he accompanied. There were more sides with Green and Smith, and with cornetist Tommy Ladnier. There were appearances by Buster Bailey on clarinet, by arranger Don Redman on alto saxophone, and by a small band that included both Coleman Hawkins on clarinet, and trombonist Jimmy Harrison, which fell naturally into a relaxed, spontaneous polyphony closer to New Orleans Dixieland than the highly arranged style of Henderson's own group. And there was one outstanding masterpiece – the appearance of Henderson's star cornetist Louis Armstrong on Bessie Smith's *Careless Love Blues*, from May 1925. Armstrong's role in developing the jazz solo will be discussed in the next chapter, but on this track he uses his cornet to produce an intricate, harmonically sophisticated additional melody line that perfectly complements Bessie Smith, as if he were an additional vocalist. There is no better example of the degree to which the vocal qualities of blues transferred themselves to the instrumental jazz playing of the singers' accompanists.

This disc is also evidence of the kind of "transformation" of the basic raw material of a song that critics like Hugues Panassié looked for to determine a "true" jazz performance. Moreover, the significance of this interrelationship between voice and instrument was also perceived at the time by another French author, André Schaeffner, as being an essential component in creating the syncretic music of African-Americans, when he wrote, in 1926: "the choice of timbres and intonation implies a vocal experience that carries its results well into the domain of instruments."[79]

His circle of French intellectuals recognized far earlier than any other group of critics the genuine emergence of a tradition that had its origins jointly in African and European music. The composer Darius Milhaud is cited by Schaeffner as expressing a fascination for the "mixture of glissando and vibrato" to be heard in this kind of performance, and both men were drawn to the co-existence of primitivism and sophistication, or "barbarism given legitimacy," as Schaeffner put it. For those with a classical music background, like Milhaud, the singer's traditional role was to emulate an instrument: aspiring, for example, to the kind of coloratura brilliance of Mozart's Queen of Night in *The Magic Flute*. Now the roles were reversed, and jazz instrumentalists became *imitatrices de la voix* – (imitators of the voice).

Jazz players themselves were not unaware of what was going on, some observing that the vocal–instrumental relationship was a two-way street. Garvin Bushell, for example, wrote of Ethel Waters that, "She syncopated. Her style was influenced by the horns she'd heard, and by church singing."

Certainly, until the early 1920s, when jug-band or string-band players who were familiar with providing blues accompaniments, such as Lonnie Johnson or Joe McCoy, began to play and record *as jazz musicians*, in small groups up and down the country, I think the main blues influence on jazz, from shortly before World War I, was that of the sophisticated female classic blues singers. As a consequence of their work, in Schaeffner's words, jazz players arrived at "an exact instrumental translation of what Negroes obtained in their singing."

## Brass Bands

Suddenly, from round the corner marched these colored men. Oh, they walked so tall and stiff. Bright buttons down the front of their uniforms, red caps on their heads with a round button right in the front. As they came closer I saw them playing flashy, shiny instruments that bounced the bright sunshine right in my eyes. Horns all raised up high,

blasting so very loud. Some long ones sliding in and out. Big
fat ones going Umph, Umph. Banjos played fast, drums rat-
a-tatting, and a huge round drum that boomed-boomed as it
went by.

Clyde E. B. Bernhardt, from *I Remember*, as told to Sheldon Harris

The quotation above could be a description of any street parade by a New
Orleans brass band, at almost any time from the beginning to the end of the
twentieth century. In fact it is a description of a marching band in Salisbury,
North Carolina, in 1909. Although most historians' attention has been
focused on the well-documented brass-band tradition of New Orleans, such
ensembles existed at the beginning of the twentieth century in African-
American communities in many parts of the United States. In the period
following Reconstruction, the vogue for brass bands was not just the
preserve of white Americans, and in urban centers and rural communities
alike, African-American brass bands flourished. Not all of these acquired the
syncopated, improvising characteristics of the Crescent City groups, but
they did provide a disciplined environment in which aspiring young
musicians were trained alongside more accomplished older players, and in
which a variety of brass, woodwind, and percussion skills were developed.
There was also a degree of common repertoire, and Sousa marches, well-
known funeral dirges, and popular hymns were learned, with varying
degrees of precision, across the nation.

This variance was entirely to do with the degree to which the band
relied on printed sheet music or on playing by ear. In urban communities
where there was either a long tradition of freedmen or an emergent African-
American middle class, printed scores were the norm, and bandmasters
encouraged musical literacy. In many such urban areas, driven by both a
political and social incentive, the black communities had established social
clubs or benevolent societies. As early as 1878, in one of the first bands to
be documented, James M. Trotter commented on the "very intelligent class
of young men, studious and of excellent moral character"[80] who were in the
St. Bernard Brass Band in New Orleans. But these qualities were to become
the norm anywhere in the country where benevolent societies sponsored
bands. In St. Louis, for example, within the next two decades, the Odd
Fellows established a brass band that became the launch-pad for the careers
of many future jazz musicians, such as Shirley Clay, R. Q. Dickerson,
Dewey Jackson, Emmett Mathews, Irving "Mouse" Randolph, and Gene
Sedric. Taught by a Mr. Langford, and managed by Major McElroy, who

instituted an instrument loan scheme, the band members wore smart uniforms and played for public parades.[81]

In sharp contrast to this well-heeled urban ensemble which prided itself on playing published arrangements, rural communities relied on less-sophisticated training. When Frederick Ramsey Jr. was recording and interviewing members of country brass bands in Alabama in the 1950s, he talked to men whose training in the groups went back to the turn of the century. One recalled that their leader would learn a new tune, then,

> after he got it prompt in his mind, then he'll pick up his horn. Then he'll try to play it, you see? That's the way it was. They first start playing spirituals . . . got them at the church. They go way back. . . . Sometimes us' leader . . . us' captain . . . set down and play a new piece. He'll jump out there on it. . . . Some people plays by note, and they can't jump on them notes . . . .[82]

Ramsey suggests, plausibly, that the shared experience of the community and their collective folk memory of singing spirituals and hymns together in church provided a core repertoire for bands that played by ear. But in the evolution of the brass band within the African-American population, the church was more important than simply as a supplier of melodies. In many areas, the black churches were central to community music-making. Pianist Sammy Price wrote about his early years in rural Texas:

> Black families scorned any music that wasn't church music because the structure of black families was very religious at that time. There were very few marching bands that I can recall. People usually marched with drums. Well, before I left Waco they did have some marching bands, but around 1912, 1913 there were very few. . . . The simple reason was that black folk couldn't get their hands on any instruments, and those that did played church music.[83]

Price's view was that in the strictly segregated society of the early 1900s the majority of the respectable African-American community eschewed songs about drinking, trouble with women, and secular life – these subjects could lead to trouble in a white-dominated world. But within the church, as long as the subject-matter was appropriate, then there was a chance to use music to escape such problems, and it was also where what musical education that was on offer could be found. This was certainly also the experience of his contemporary, Buck Clayton, who grew up in the Midwest, but whose father, Simeon, came, like Price, from rural Texas.

Simeon Clayton was not only an accomplished singer, but, having learned the cornet in his native Rockwall, Texas, ran the band at his new local church in Parsons, Kansas. Buck recalled:

> Dad's chapel orchestra practiced at my home every Sunday afternoon. Some of the members would leave their instruments at my home until the following week when they would rehearse again, so I had access to all kinds of instruments. Sometimes I would play trombone, saxophone, cornet or anything I felt like playing because of these instruments lying all around my house.[84]

Both Buck Clayton's parents were members of the Brown Chapel African Methodist Episcopal Church, and they took a similar view to that of Sammy Price about secular music. "Mom used to say that jazz was for low-life people," wrote Clayton, remembering her abhorrence of "little what we call 'bucket of blood' places where you go in and never know if you're going to come out alive or not."

Even as jazz grew popular during Clayton's teenage years in the 1920s, there was no place for it at his home. The family's phonograph records were predominantly classical, with a few of Bert Williams's comic discs as well, and Clayton's musical education at first consisted entirely of classical piano lessons, followed by cornet lessons from his father. Yet what he recalled most vividly from his childhood was the music of his local "holy roller" church. There he found

> people who worship with such spirit and enthusiasm that the music they create makes you want to dance whether you're religious or not. Many Sunday nights I used to . . . swing with the Holy Rollers, who used to play tambourines, trombones or anything else that could be used for rhythm. The songs they played and sang were natural swingers, such as *When the Saints Go Marching In*. The Holy Rollers had more pep than our ordinary churches.[85]

Many miles away from Parsons, in Cheraw, South Carolina, less than a dozen years later, and in a rural African-American world that was musically isolated from external change by the absence of phonographs and no more than a handful of radio sets, another man who was to become a prominent jazz trumpeter, the young Dizzy Gillespie, grew up amid similar influences. His father, too, ran the local band and had a houseful of instruments, yet Dizzy's own earliest musical memories were of the rhythmic hand-clapping and singing from the Sanctified Church a few doors away from his family home.

Not surprisingly, many of the rhythmic, dance-like elements of church worship like this found their way into the instrumental and band music fostered by churches. In Louisiana, in particular, this manifested itself in the tradition of musical funerals, something which was by no means confined to the well-known setting of New Orleans. Clarinetist Joe Darensbourg, for example, grew up the best part of 100 miles away in Baton Rouge, and remembered that in the period from 1910 to 1920

> Two or three times a week you seen a funeral parade. If a cat amounted to anything or if he had any quality about him, he had a band playing at his funeral. ... I couldn't hardly miss them because they passed right in front of my house. They would go maybe two miles to the cemetery and it look like it would take them near three hours to do it. The one tune they would play was *Nearer My God to Thee*, with the drums beating "boom, boom, boom." Everybody marching, just like that, with the horses right along with them. Needless to say, we kids would make a second line and follow the parade all the way.[86]

According to Darensbourg, every small town in Louisiana had its own band, and the majority played not only for church events and funerals but, increasingly, for social functions as well, as the century went on.

This region and its music has been thoroughly investigated in the research of Austin M. Sonnier, who has not only produced personnel listings for bands in the settlements of the Louisiana lowlands such as Cade, Crowley, Jeanerette, Lake Charles, Laplace, Loreauville, New Iberia, Opelousas, and Parks, but whose interviews in the 1970s with musicians of the generation born before 1900 suggest that many of the elements of jazz – rhythmic syncopation, swing, melodic improvisation – were present in these

66

bands. He believes that in such tightly knit rural communities, the musical bond that grew up in their ensembles, with knowledge being passed from generation to generation, fostered music that, while it was parallel in many ways, had very little close connection to New Orleans itself. Consequently, he argues, it was not the supposed founding father of the music, cornetist Buddy Bolden, who "was responsible for this birth and evolution of jazz that took place so far from the city," but an independent tradition born of rural band experience.[87]

Even so, it is probably a mistake to look too far into the brass-band tradition for evidence of "jazz" being played very early in the twentieth century. Apart from attempting to identify aspects of music that was never recorded from language that, because both the music and the terms to describe it were in transition, carries a range of possible definitions, such speculation would miss a larger more central point. Not only did the brass-band tradition share an instrumentation that was to be carried forward into jazz, both in small groups and big bands, but it had at its heart a tradition of teaching and mentoring of young players that was to be a cornerstone of jazz across the United States. The continuous survival of the tradition within New Orleans allows us the additional luxury of being able to learn something further about repertoire and style, but the widespread nature of brass bands across the nation, and the collective values of their musicians and instructors, suggests that they had as much to do with the rapid spread of jazz in America as the theatrical networks so far discussed.

This shared resource of technique allowed players from many parts of the United States to grasp rapidly the nascent jazz ideas of pioneer New Orleans players such as Joe Oliver, Freddie Keppard, Louis Armstrong, and Natty Dominique, who were themselves brass-band trained. Musicians who had come through the syncopated orchestras of Will Marion Cook or James Reese Europe had garnered comparable experience, and if we delve into the careers of a vast number of early big-band players, we find more examples of this shared background.

This is swing trumpeter Bill Coleman (born 1904), recalling events of his childhood in Centerville, Kentucky, that took place around 1910:

> My father played the snare drum in the hometown band, my uncle Ernest played tuba, and on rehearsal nights he would pass by our house blowing with pride on his bass tuba. The "get-together" or rehearsal took place in the summer on the front lawn of my uncle John Coleman's house. ... Uncle John played

67

cornet. Everyone was welcome to listen to the rehearsal and I am certain I never missed one.[88]

And this is Ellingtonian cornetist Rex Stewart (born 1907), from Washington D.C.:

> My first adventure in music began when a policeman by the name of Johnson . . . formed a kids' military band of about 25 pieces. I was nearly ten years old and, as Mr. Johnson went to AME Zion and sang in Grandfather's choir, it was natural for him to tell my mother he wanted me to be in his band . . . each kid had individual instruction, then sections would play together, and twice a week the entire band would rehearse while Pop would supervize, playing bass drum.[89]

And in rural Louisiana it was the same story for many young players, as Joe Darensbourg (born 1906) remembered:

> Donaldson was where the Claiborne Williams band came from. They didn't play any jazz, but it was a great band. All young kids. Williams was a fine teacher and he used to take those kids and turn them into one of the best marching bands, maybe thirty or forty pieces.[90]

Such examples are plentiful among the first generations of musicians to play jazz.

Moving beyond town or benevolent society groups to institutions devoted to the education of African-Americans, there were other bands that paralleled this kind of community-based music. At Tuskegee College in Alabama, Captain Dry ran the marching band in which pianist Teddy Wilson played reed instruments in the early 1920s, and the college's brass coach, Philmore "Shorty" Hall, later taught Dizzy Gillespie and his cousin Norman Powe in the band at the very similarly organized Laurinburg Institute in North Carolina. Elsewhere in the Carolinas, the Jenkins Orphanage band in Charleston produced generations of band players from around 1900 onwards, many of whom went on to have significant careers in jazz, including trumpeters Jabbo Smith and Cat Anderson.

So what was the repertoire played by African-American brass or military-style bands that fed directly into the jazz tradition?

Certainly there was a conscious emulation of the brass-band music popularized by such nationally famous bandmasters as John Philip Sousa and Arthur Pryor, and performed by hundreds of amateur white bands all over the United States – marches, concert overtures, and light classics. And in the programs of those bands from the early 1900s was also an element of ragtime: arrangements of cake-walks, rag-influenced popular songs such as those of Irving Berlin, and, in some instances, transcriptions of piano rags by the likes of Tom Turpin or J. Bodewalt Lampe. To put the large number of African-American bands that existed in perspective, there was, at the end of the nineteenth century, a national American craze for brass-band music, which saw comparable bands of white musicians widely established. W. H. Dana, the author of *Pepper's Guide*, an 1878 manual for would-be arrangers and band directors, published in Philadelphia, the heartland of band territory, noted: "A town without its brass band is as much in need of sympathy as a church without a choir. The spirit of a place is recognized in its band."

In the history of jazz, the best-documented and most musically active band community was in New Orleans. In his analysis of the music of New Orleans brass bands, William J. Schafer notes that in the years 1901–3, there were well-established concert series where such Sousa-derived music, as described above, could be heard, played by the likes of T. P. Brooke's Chicago Marine Band, Braun's Naval Brigade Band, Boehler's First Regiment Band, and Armand Veazey's Military Band.

At the same time, the most highly organized African-American bands, the Excelsior and Onward (known as the "Old" Onward to distinguish it from later successors), which had been in existence for some years, read stock arrangements of similar tunes – as trumpeter Peter Bocage confirmed: "now that was all old-time musicians . . . nothing strictly but marches you understand."[91]

What then took place, in the early years of the twentieth century, was a coming-together of this well-schooled reading tradition with the kind of musically illiterate, ear-trained bands that had grown up both in rural Louisiana and in the rough "uptown" population of the city itself. William J. Schafer wrote:

> Bandsmen in small black brass bands inhabited the musical landscape from which the other groups grew. They borrowed tunes like *High Society* or *My Maryland* from the repertoire of music-reading bands. They learned standard marches like *Our*

*Director* or *National Emblem*. They patterned themselves on the brass band as it was generally known, using the same instruments and instrumental balance.[92]

Just as the Alabamian bandsmen, interviewed in the 1950s by Frederick Ramsey Jr., recalled a cascading process of instruction by which the lead trumpeter passed on the gist of each piece to the other musicians, so many first generation New Orleans players described the process by which their bands learned – a close parallel to the ragtime bands discussed earlier in this chapter by Barney Bigard.

The coaches of the bands that read music well were men like Theodore Bacquet, James Humphrey, George Moret, and William Nickerson, but they had their equivalents among the less-literate musicians. And, in those other areas of the United States where documentation exists to prove it, we know that there were parallels. The Jenkins Orphanage band in Charleston, S.C., for example, played a comparable repertoire of standard tunes and marches, and the institution's young musicians learned by a similar cascade process, at the hands of instructors like Gene Mikell (who went on to James Reese Europe's Military Band and the New York Clef Club). In his researches into the Jenkins band, historian and author John Chilton is cautious about suggesting that anything approaching jazz was played, especially during the first decade of the twentieth century, but he detects, from eyewitness reports and his interviews with survivors, that in that period there was the beginning of a rhythmic loosening, of polyrhythmic syncopation, that would subsequently pave the way for melodic improvisation.[93]

Similar reports and interviews confirm how, in the intensely musical atmosphere of New Orleans, little by little, the ear-trained musicians added something more of their own to brass-band arrangements, and spiced up the rhythm as well. A number of the brass bands had musicians within their ranks who also played in string bands, where a similar process was also taking place, and many brass and woodwind players also worked in small dance or ragtime orchestras. A large section of the city's musical population (and this went for the white bands led by musicians such as drummer Jack Laine as well) found that as they moved into the twentieth century, their music was at a crossroads. On the one side, looking back, were classical traditions, formal brass-band playing, the social dances of the 1890s, the European-influenced instrumental techniques of the downtown Creole community, and on the other, looking forward, were the ragtime pianists of the red-light district, the songs of African-American musical plays and vaudeville, the rhythms and quarter-tones of the self-taught musicians of the African-influenced uptown community, and the equally instinctive music that came from the rural hinterland in the form of blues songs and band music. As the music moved forward and became jazz, it brought with it more than a little of the past.

CHAPTER 2

# Classic Jazz

## New Orleans

> On Saturdays we used to play ball in the street and we
> would hear a parade coming. That's really my first
> interest in music: as a kid watching the brass bands. We'd
> hear the parade coming down the street and, well, that
> was the end of the game. We would try to follow the band
> as far as our folks would let us.
>
> Barney Bigard, from *With Louis and the Duke*

In the last decades of the nineteenth century it was hard to avoid music in the city of New Orleans for too long. Sounds hung in the air, whether in the benign cool of winter or the hot humidity of summer, mingling with the sights and sounds of this fascinating cosmopolitan city. The town has already been mentioned in the opening chapter, but it is unique in North America, combining French and Spanish colonial influences – cultural, linguistic, and architectural – with the internationalism of a major port. Unlike most ports that traded with Europe and South America, New Orleans was built 107 miles inland, on a broad sweeping bend of the Mississippi River. Sufficiently upstream to be above the complexities of the river's delta, but far enough downstream to allow navigation by sail from the sea without being prevented by strong river currents, it became a gateway to the North, with river trade possible to places as far afield as St. Paul, Minnesota.

It was founded in 1718 by Jean Baptiste Le Moyne, Sieur de Bienville, who was the governor of the French colony of Louisiana. In 1722, it became the capital of the colony, and was laid out on the grid pattern of many colonial cities with a large square, the Place des Armes (now Jackson Square), facing the river, just as the great squares of European cities like Bordeaux or Lisbon face out to their trading routes. In 1763, the part of Louisiana to the east of the city was ceded to the British, but Louis XV had secretly transferred the city itself and the westerly part of the colony to his cousin, the King of Spain. Under Spanish rule, and the aegis of Governor Almonaster y Rojas, much of the "French Quarter," as we know it today, was constructed, including the cathedral and the classically inspired Pontalba buildings on Jackson Square.

With the Louisiana purchase of 1803, the city passed into American hands, and trade was gradually built up, especially after the advent of steam navigation, which made the unruly Mississippi more consistently navigable from 1812. At one point in the mid-nineteenth century, the export trade passing through New Orleans exceeded that of New York, and, commensurate with a town of its size and importance, not only commodities but also elements of European culture were imported there. The French Quarter was the scene of numerous American operatic premieres in the nineteenth century.

Following the transfer of ownership to America, newer settlements grew up on the outskirts of the original city, including the uptown area across Canal Street from the French Quarter, and in the heart of this new commercial district, James Caldwell, an American impresario, set up an English-language opera company in 1824, first at the Camp Street Theater and then at the St. Charles Theater, establishing a strong vernacular operatic tradition to which he later added the Italian repertoire. Beyond the banks, trading halls, and commercial centers of the uptown section close to Canal Street was a poorer residential district that was to become the heart of the African-American population.

Because of its site on the river bank, in an area much given to high rainfall, flash floods, and poor drainage, the first 200 years of New Orleans's history were dogged by natural disasters as well as serious fires that swept devastatingly through the predominantly wooden buildings. There were also problems in keeping a city that was largely below sea level clear of water in time of flood, but still maintaining a good supply of fresh water in periods of drought. To combat sudden rises in river level, a high retaining wall, known as the levee, was built along the dockside to hold back the Mississippi. Only a foot or two below the streets was the water table, so the city established other customs, including the principle of interring its dead in tombs built above ground level. In common with other parts of Louisiana, funerary rites were established that not only involved the construction of overground vaults, with all manner of decorative architectural features, but also included the accompaniment of burials with music, with solemn hymns as the cortège made its way from the city center to one of the cemeteries, and festive music to celebrate the life of the deceased on the return to the wake. Parade bands accompanied funerals from very early in the nineteenth century, such events being noted by Benjamin Henry Latrobe in 1819.

From the beginning of its history, the population of New Orleans was a jumbled mixture of backgrounds and races. There were French, Spanish, British, and American whites and their families, slaves, and descendants. There were Creoles who were the product of interbreeding among all these groups, and there were new white, Creole, and black immigrants from Europe, Cuba, Santo Domingo, and many Caribbean islands. A majority of these latter groups aligned with the Creole community, making it the most numerically dominant in the early nineteenth century. Further white immigrants, many from Italy, Germany, and Ireland, added to the mix as that century wore on, again altering the balance. By the mid-nineteenth century, the social distinctions between white, Creole, and African-American had settled into a complex caste system which, paradoxically, also allowed a degree of informal intermingling.

Gradually, as the twentieth century dawned, many of the musical elements discussed in the last chapter, all of which were present in New Orleans, coalesced to become jazz. One major reason for this is that, with its mixed patrimony, New Orleans seems to have used music to observe and celebrate a larger number of high days and holidays than any other American city.

In July, for example, hard on the heels of the usual American Independence celebrations of the fourth, everything stopped again ten days later for Bastille Day.

> The thoroughfares are arched with the colours of the French Republic, the tricolor flutters from the carheads, the Marseillaise is the national hymn of the hour and patriotism is again speaking French to commemorate the fete of the old mother country of Louisiana.[1]

And the author of this 1895 eyewitness description immediately goes on to note the music that accompanied the festivities of the French-speaking population:

Moreau Gottschalk's *Danse Negre* falls upon the ear. . . . It is a Creole pianist who is playing the *Danse Negre* now. All the Creole pianists play Gottschalk's pieces, one can hear them at any time in the Creole portion of the city . . . his Danses, Berceuses and Meditations.

Earlier in the year, the start of Lent would have been marked by the Mardi Gras celebrations, paralleling the festivities of the Hispanic Catholic world, and not observed on such a scale anywhere else in the United States. In French and Spanish times, the New Orleans festivities were somewhat *ad hoc*, but once the city came fully under American rule, the events were organized into the lavish social calendar of balls and street parades that persists to the present.

In addition to the music that accompanied such major festive events in the city's social calendar, the African-American, Creole, and white communities all made music of their own, for picnics, weddings, funerals, and weekly dances. Accounts are plentiful of everything from French and Spanish songs being sung to guitars in the Vieux Carré to the string bands and society orchestras that accompanied outdoor social events.

Many accounts of music in New Orleans at the end of the nineteenth century present this apparently idyllic setting itself as the major reason for jazz to have developed. There was, such writers suggest, simply so much going on in a festive riot of music and dance, that the city became a sort of musical hot-house that forced the cross-pollenation of syncopation and blue notes, leading to the flowering of collective polyphonic improvisation.[2]

But was there a pollenating agent? Was there a specific event or sequence of events that accelerated the symbiotic relationship between African-American and Creole that led to jazz?

The answer lies in the murky post-Reconstruction politics of Louisiana, where the votes of black and mixed-race adults, as well as their rights to freedom and education, became bargaining chips in a protracted battle for control of the state between the heirs of the old Southern Confederacy and the newer radical Republicans. In late 1862, the post-Civil War Union military government had framed and introduced a new constitution for the state which enshrined the principles of permanently abolishing slavery, introducing universal suffrage for Negroes, and providing free education. With minor changes this was agreed and formally adopted by the first elected government of Louisiana in 1864, but little or nothing was actually done as the old Confederate officials progressively regained their influence.

They were opposed by an increasingly radical Republican opposition, who knew they would have to depend on the black vote to achieve power.

It took the massacre of 200 people, precipitated when the police opened fire on a procession of African-Americans in 1866, to initiate a second stage of Reconstruction, during which the federal authorities applied pressure on the state to introduce universal suffrage, save for those whites who had been active in trying to bring about secession from the Union. This was done, slavery was abolished, and Louisiana was formally readmitted to the Union in July 1868, with the majority of its African-American and Creole population able to vote – at least in principle. However, in practice, the state's problems were far from over, and for almost a decade a sense of farce crept into local politics alongside widespread corruption, where, following a schism in the Republican party between those radicals who believed in the voting rights of African-Americans and those who threw in their lot with the old white-dominated Confederate lobby, two legislatures were established, and at one point two rival candidates were simultaneously returned to the U.S. Senate. In due course, there was once again federal intervention, and a Democrat, Governor Francis T. Nicholls, a representative of the White League, who opposed universal suffrage, set up a single state government in 1877.

Now, with the firm establishment of a long-term Democratic government backed by federal authorities, it was no longer necessary for the radical Republicans to support the black vote as a passport to political power, and African-Americans were systematically disenfranchised from 1877 onwards. Although there remained limited provision of free education, the political independence of Louisiana's black and Creole population was progressively eroded, culminating in amendments to the state legislature that took away many civil rights from the downtown Creole population of New Orleans in 1894, and finally disenfranchised the majority of non-whites in 1898. While the city's Creole society of the 1890s kept up its European associations, its linguistic ties with France, its operatic and social traditions, together with an atmosphere of *fin-de-siècle* decadence, in which the keeping of mistresses and the establishing of brothels in or close to the French Quarter of New Orleans continued apace, it was being undermined by political change to the extent that, by 1900, over 100,000 previously enfranchised citizens had lost the right to vote. Suddenly, the social independence of the Creole community vanished, and they found that in the eyes of the state and the law, they were treated as African-Americans. This conjunction of the two communities was a major factor in creating the social conditions from which jazz was to emerge.

One man who was an eyewitness to the birth of jazz in New Orleans, and who became expert on it, was Roy Carew, later a friend and confidante of Jelly Roll Morton and of jazz historian William Russell. He set down his experiences of living in the city's white community from 1904–19 in a series of letters to Ken Hulsizer in 1952, which were collected and published by the writer Walter C. Allen.[3] Carew is blunt about the racial climate as the twentieth century began:

> In New Orleans you were classed as white or black, regardless of shade up to octoroons; babies with less than one eighth coloured blood were registered by the doctors as white. "Creoles" were American descendants of white French or Spanish emigrants, in the opinion of the white population. The Creoles with Negro blood or vice versa doubtless had their own classification, but the whites paid no attention to them.

The Creoles "with Negro blood," who now found themselves on a level basis with the African-Americans from whom they had for so long been at such pains to distance themselves, attempted to maintain a separation by emphasizing their differences. Wrote drummer Baby Dodds:

> Canal Street was the dividing line, and the people from the different sections didn't mix. The musicians mixed only if you were good enough. But at one time the Creole fellows thought the uptown musicians weren't good enough to play with them, because most of the uptown musicians didn't read music. Everybody in the French part of town read music. Then, too, the Creole people in New Orleans were very high strung. Most of them had a little better education and it seems as though they had a little more money.[4]

Nowhere in musical life was that distinction greater than in the marching brass bands. Before the social changes of the end of the century, light-skinned Creoles had played regularly in some of the city's white bands (according to the researches of Samuel B. Charters), but after the passing of Legislative Code no. 111, in 1894, many were forced to move uptown and to play in the same environment as the less-schooled African-Americans. Maintaining a high standard of musicianship became a badge of status for the Creoles.

Danny Barker, for example, who grew up in the years leading into the 1920s, had childhood memories of his Creole grandfather, Isidore Barbarin, discussing in minute detail the attributes of the various cornetists who played in the Onward Brass Band, and making a sharp distinction between those educated musicians who read music perfectly, and those who played by "routine," in other words largely by ear. In the brass bands, string groups, and society orchestras of the African-American and Creole communities, a hierarchy emerged. The most celebrated bands were those that preserved the Creole values of legitimate technique, mainly playing from sheet music, with good intonation and control: the Columbia, the Excelsior, the Onward, the Pacific, and the Tuxedo. Across the river in Algiers was Henry Allen Sr.'s band, and out on the Magnolia Plantation Professor James Humphrey brought a sense of Creole discipline to the Eclipse Brass Band. Uptown musicians were involved in the Camelia (from 1917) and the Eureka (from 1920). We can infer from Austin Sonnier's research in the Louisiana lowlands that the majority of African-American musicians from out-of-town had more in common with the uptown players, the "ratty" bands that played by ear.

As Barker recalled, at the top of the pile were the best brass bands, notably the Creole-dominated Onward, which included members of the Alexander, Barbarin, Bocage, and Tio families, and was under the leadership of Manuel Perez.

> He looked like a Mexican or Spaniard and was the idol of the downtown Creole colored people. To them, nobody could master the cornet like Mr. Perez. When this brass band played a march, dirge or hymn it was played to perfection – no blunders. The personnel of the Onward stayed intact as a highly polished musical organization for many years, and that was also the case with the great Excelsior Brass Band. Many of these marching musicians only played in brass bands, never in dance or jazz bands. . . . The Onward name was famous, stood for class, the greatest.[5]

To young children like Barker, the names of the musicians in the brass bands became as significant as those of star football or baseball players. These became idols because, as Barker was often to tell me, playing music was a passport to a way of life that ultimately offered an escape from the menial jobs that were the lot of the African-American population. All sections of society, white or black, turned out to hear brass bands as they passed, especially as the new, intangible, elements of swing and improvisation began to be added to the mix. Roy Carew, working in the offices of a typewriter company recalls:

> In 1912 the head salesman of the Remington company where I was working came back to New Orleans after a couple of years up north. One day, shortly after his return, a band was parading up Baronne Street, a few doors from our offices on Gravier Street. The salesman jumped up and called a friend who had come from the north with him, saying "Come here, Listen to this! That's music you won't hear anywhere else in the United States."[6]

The typical New Orleans brass band had a smaller instrumentation than might have been the case elsewhere in the United States, among either black or white ensembles. The local fashion was to have three cornets, two trombones (at the turn of the century these were generally valve trombones), alto, baritone and bass horn (or tuba), a clarinet or two, snare drum, and bass drum.[7] Despite not being numerically strong, such bands developed a distinctive sound, which not only embodied great spirit, according to ear-witnesses, but could achieve a surprising volume, as Roy Carew recalled:

> I remember that about 1909 in Grand Rapids, Michigan, I was listening to the 40-piece Kiltie Band, and after a bit of listening I told my niece who was with me that there were outfits a quarter of the size in New Orleans that could produce a bigger volume of music.[8]

Whereas Carew turned out elsewhere to be a very informative witness of many aspects of Storyville and early jazz musicians, he does not add much more to the brass-band story, saying: "If I were watching a parade and a good outfit went by with Eagle Band or Superior Band printed on the bass drum, I never had the urge to run out and ask who was playing cornet." But from the generation of jazz musicians who were just growing up as jazz began, we can be sure of the names of the players who made the biggest impression. Trumpeter Lee Collins, for instance, recalls the annual carriage drivers' parade:

The carriage drivers hired the Onward Brass Band, Tig Chambers and, in fact, all the great brass bands to play for these parades. The musicians would include Joe Oliver, Bunk Johnson, Tig, Buddy Petit, Sidney Bechet, and lots more. All the kids followed these parades as far as we could go. New Orleans did not have many paved streets then, so it was easy to get stuck in the mud if you weren't careful. In the summer, when it was hot and dry and sultry, the dust whipped into your face and you could smell the dead in the cemetery. At night the big New Orleans mosquitoes sang "cousin" around your ears.[9]

There were white brass bands as well as Creole or African-American groups. Clarinetist Johnny Fischer, trombonist Happy Schilling, and drummer "Papa" Jack Laine all ran brass bands as well as smaller dance units well before World War I. Laine, who directed several small groups under the umbrella name of his Reliance Band, is generally credited in the city with being the father of Dixieland, or white New Orleans jazz. His various line-ups were, it seems, the first white dance bands to play something approaching jazz, and because he quit the music business when the war broke out, it must, therefore, be the case that in the years before 1917, white musicians were already closely mirroring what was going on in the African-American and Creole communities. We can learn something of how their music might have sounded from the playing of several instrumentalists, from Laine's various groups, who went to Chicago in 1915 starting with trombonist Tom Brown, and, in due course, leading to the Original Dixieland Jazz Band, whose work is discussed in the next section of this chapter.

The changes that led to jazz, and the introduction of "routine" playing, which, as Barker says, established the "now 'classic' jazz pattern: melody then variations on a theme," began in the smaller dance groups of the city some time before the new style became apparent in the brass bands. In particular, they seem to have taken hold as players in the ubiquitous string bands of African-American music made the transition to a different kind of instrumentation.

I have already discussed the instrumentation of both string bands and the ensembles that played orchestrated ragtime, and it was the latter grouping that eventually crystallized into the first New Orleans jazz bands, in both the black and white sections of society. Among the Creole musicians, drummer and violinist John Robichaux (1886–1939) was the most significant figure, playing bass drum in the Excelsior Brass Band, but also leading his own society orchestra from 1893 to 1939, for which he made copious ragtime-influenced arrangements, a substantial number of which survive. His band was occasionally enlarged to orchestral proportions, but generally consisted of violin, one or two trumpets, clarinet, trombone, piano, guitar, double bass, and drums. The instrumentation was similar to the band led by his contemporary, the violinist, composer, and publisher Armand J. Piron, which made a number of recordings in New York during the early 1920s. Roy Carew confirms Robichaux's importance: "Robichaux's outfit was the top Negro band in New Orleans in my time ... the only one I heard mentioned."[10] And further confirmation comes from what might be thought of as the unlikely source of bandleader Paul Whiteman, who wrote in his autobiography of the importance of the bands of Robichaux and Piron, and the conviction of both men that "the great American noise [jazz] started along the waterfront among natural Negro musicians, and developed into the heart and soul of New Orleans."[11]

The playing experience of one African-American musician, the trombonist Hamp Benson, took him from string bands into just such society groups in the very early years of the century:

> I, Hamilton Benson, called Hamp Benson, was born in 1885 at 752 Tchoupitoulas Street, New Orleans, La. My four brothers all played musical instruments. In 1901, I started playing bass. My brother taught me. The first band I played with was a three-piece combination: Russell Williams, guitar, Johnny Bradley, mandolin, and I played bass. We played in the Red Light District from 1901 to 1903. Johnny Bradley went visiting to Osiko, Miss., and was found dead on the railroad track. That broke up the combination.
>
> After that, in 1903, another combination was made: Jim Williams, violin; Andrew Kimball, cornet; Russell Williams, guitar. We stayed together two years, to 1905. Due to Jim Williams' work as a call boy at the Round House, this combo broke up. A barber, John Hynes on Julius St. near Condolet, had a band named Hill City Band. Andrew Kimball and I joined his four pieces: trombone – John Hynes (manager); Charlie McCurtis [McCurdy] – clarinet; Charlie Pierson – guitar and Cato on drums. The later part of 1906, John Robchaw [Robichaux] had the leading band down there [and] took Kimball from our band. Two months later I joined Tom Brown's band, playing valve

trombone which I had been practicing all this time. I also had a slide trombone and the numbers I could play on it I would. Maybe it only be one or two numbers a night, but at last I could play the slide well enough to leave the valve at home. That is the way I started playing the slide.[12]

Benson typifies the transition from playing in string groups to society or dance bands. The Tom Brown with whom Benson worked was a Creole mandolin player, who had initially led a string trio at the Arlington Annex, a nightclub on Basin and Iberville Streets, before expanding his group into a larger "society" ensemble in the years after 1905. The club was owned by a colorful character called Tom Anderson, nicknamed the "King of the Tenderloin," who had a finger in most of the rackets operating in the city's red-light areas, but also employed a number of the bands that were active during the transition from ragtime to early jazz. Before moving on to examine the venues such as Anderson's, where the music that became jazz was played, one name comes up in almost every account of the city's music as being instrumental in bringing about that transition.

This was the legendary cornetist Charles "Buddy" Bolden, who had himself moved from string bands to dance or ragtime groups. If Manuel Perez and the Creoles listed above by Danny Barker and Lee Collins epitomized the skilled downtown players, then the rough-hewn Bolden was their uptown counterpart. Apparently a powerful lead cornetist, famous for his sheer volume, Bolden played largely by ear and was credited by many of those who heard him as being the first to bring the explicitly African qualities of flattened blue notes, vocalized tones, and "hot" syncopation into the ragtime setting – in other words, he was seen as the progenitor of improvisation in jazz. However, he was institutionalized in 1907, while still in his twenties, his erratic behavior causing him to be committed for the rest of his life to the Louisiana State Asylum for the Insane, at Jackson, where he died in 1931, having never made a recording of his influential style. And so the word "legendary" is used advisedly.

Because Bolden was apparently a pioneer of jazz before anyone knew what jazz was, and because he was an African-American from the area of New Orleans where few such turn-of-the-century lives were documented in any substantial detail, not many contemporary references to him survive, and his career emerges into a hazy light only occasionally from the tangential and patchy records of the period. The colossus of jazz history which he became is largely on account of his folkloric importance to the generations that followed him. Principal among those who spun the Bolden legend was trumpeter Willie Geary "Bunk" Johnson, himself a pioneer trumpeter who was widely interviewed by the enthusiastic jazz researchers of the late 1930s and early 1940s as a key figure in what became the "revival" of New Orleans jazz discussed in Chapter 11. Research into Johnson's birth date, by Lawrence Gushee and others, indicates that he probably lied about his own age and about many of his associations – almost certainly including the claim that he had played with Bolden, who was not noted for hiring a second cornetist – as a way of furthering his own career after his rediscovery and early recordings.

In Johnson's vivid word picture, Bolden comes to life as a strong, magnetic character with vast appetites for alcohol and women, who was adored both by his string of mistresses and by the general public. He was a barber and the author-cum-editor of a scandalsheet called *The Cricket*. His cornet was so powerful that it would "call his children home," stealing audiences away from other bands by the sheer charisma of his playing, especially in the outdoor setting of Johnson Park, where he could outplay the band in the neighboring Lincoln Park and capture its audience. It was said that his ringing tones could be heard "fourteen miles away on a clear night," yet he could play his set piece, *Carnival of Venice*, so sweetly it would bring tears to the eyes.

This account was embroidered by many others, notably by Danny Barker, at one time a guitarist in Bunk Johnson's band and a friend of Jelly Roll Morton (who also set down his memories of Bolden), so he was, therefore, a confidant of the two men on whose recollections the traditional portrait of the cornetist is largely based. Barker collected everything he knew about the legend into his stories of *Buddy Bolden and the Last Days of Storyville*, posthumously published in 1998 and first brought to public attention in an edited version which appeared, under the aegis of Martin Williams, in the *Evergreen Review* in 1961. Within the setting of a fictional oral history interview with "Mr. Dude Bottley," the imaginary brother of Bolden's one-time Master of Ceremonies, Barker weaves a convincing and complex portrait of the great cornetist, vividly describing everything from his repertoire and how it sounded, to the banter among his musicians, such as banjoist Lorenzo Staulz and trombonist Frankie Dusen. Yet compelling as Barker's portrait is, it is as problematic as anything other than folklore, because the detailed documentary researches of Donald M. Marquis show that few of the "facts" about Bolden can be substantiated. For example, he almost certainly was not a barber, and he did not edit a scandalsheet.

Nevertheless, he does seem to have been an influential and popular cornetist. His band included several pioneers of what became jazz, and, overall, Marquis uncovered sufficient evidence to confirm that Bolden was indeed in the vanguard of those who began to develop jazz, before the tragic downfall of his alcohol-induced insanity. There is a moment of genuine pathos as Marquis describes the moment in his search for the facts when he opened the court ledger no. 25 to find the record of Bolden's committal, where, in a bundle of brittle, dusty documents, the copperplate hand of the day records the one-time cornet "king" and flamboyant instrumentalist as "destitute, dirty, incoherent and listed as a laborer."[13]

If Bolden had not existed, someone would have had to invent him. He is the single figure on whose career the transition into jazz can be pegged. His life is the first of many examples in jazz history where folklore and the sharing of stories among jazz musicians have become larger than the truth, as the Chinese whispers of time have exaggerated and distorted the original tale.

We know for certain that Bolden played in the public parks in the Garden District, the section of uptown New Orleans that stretches along the streetcar lines that run west and then north to Carrollton. From oral history accounts we can also get a sense of where else the music that became jazz was played. Bolden was, as Jelly Roll Morton put it:

> a light brownskin boy from uptown. He drink all the whiskey he could find, never wore a collar and tie, had his shirt busted open so all the girls to see that red flannel undershirt, always having a ball – Buddy Bolden was the most powerful trumpet in history. ... Buddy played at most of the rough places like the Masonic Hall on Perdido and Rampart, at the Globe Hall in the Downtown section on St. Peter and St. Claude, and occasionally in Jackson Hall, a much nicer place on the corner of Jackson and Franklin.[14]

Rampart Street, where the Masonic or Oddfellows' Hall was situated, was the unofficial boundary between the respectable part of the city, which extended towards the river to the south, and the Tenderloin vice district, which covered a number of blocks to the north. The demarcation was even clearer to the east of Canal Street, where the railroad lines ran into the southern terminus on Basin Street (one block away and parallel to Rampart), dividing the main French Quarter from the raunchier neighbourhood that was, literally, on "the other side of the tracks." This neighborhood, the District as it was popularly known, otherwise called "Storyville," had legalized prostitution until it was closed by the Navy in 1917. In addition to the cribs of the prostitutes, there were bars, tonks, and brothels, and it seems that many of the city's jazz musicians worked there.

However, it is important not to get too rosy-eyed about Storyville and the birth of jazz. For a start, venues came and went with some rapidity. Few were stable and long-lasting, and few had music on a regular basis. Also, the majority of the city's musicians were unable to make a living from music alone, and even the most highly regarded Creole players had other occupations. Isidore Barbarin was an undertaker, Papa Bechet (Sidney's father) a shoemaker, clarinetist "Big Eye" Louis Nelson a butcher, bassist Albert Glenny a painter, Manuel Perez a cigarmaker, clarinetist Alphonse Picou a tinsmith, and publisher and violinist A. J. Piron a barber.[15]

Even as semi-professional musicians, there was still a gulf between the Creoles and their downtown counterparts. The researches of Alan Lomax in the 1940s show that downtown musicians were used to being paid $2.50 each time they appeared with a band such as the Olympia, whereas uptown musicians at the Big 25, one of the few Storyville venues to have nightly music, played for $1.25 a night, but had to work a seven-day week. Privilege had its price, but it did not necessarily mean regular work – even John Robichaux's prestigious groups tended to work only at weekends: "The bands didn't have too many steady jobs in those days," recalled his guitarist from 1905–11, Bud Scott. "It was a question of playing anywhere that they had an offer."[16] Also, it seems unlikely that even with a constant influx of foreign sailors and customers with money to burn, Storyville could actually have supported a substantial enough number of bars and tonks for many to be able to employ entire bands of musicians. Regular activity boiled down to a small number of places for white or black customers respectively. Roy Carew remembered:

> Anyone who lived in New Orleans from 1904 to 1919 would know about the place. The legal limits were three blocks by five, but during my time there, nearly one half could be ignored as containing nothing of interest or value. . . . The gambling houses where real gambling went on were located at the city boundaries . . . nobody who wanted to gamble went to Storyville. As to music, there wasn't as much as many books would lead you to believe. As I recollect, there were only three places where

"bands" played regularly during my time – 101 Ranch, Tuxedo and a third place at the corner of Iberville and North Liberty. I never counted the men, but I don't believe the musicians numbered more than eight in each place. The first two had white bands and the third band was Negro. . . . There were a couple of places in Storyville that would have music on special days (Mardi Gras and other holidays) but not with regularity. "Fewclothes" place was one of these. I never saw or heard of but one string trio, and that was in Tom Anderson's bar at Customhouse and Basin, where a trio played irregularly. During the later years, probably about 1915, a cabaret was opened in the back of Touro's bar room at Basin and Bienville, with a piano and a couple of other instruments. . . . All these places I mention played to white patrons; I don't know of any Negro dance halls in the District.[17]

In fact, as we know from many musicians' reminiscences and from the researches of Dr. Edmond Souchon and Al Rose for their *Family Album*, there were some "Negro dance halls," and there were also bars or saloons where African-American and Creole musicians gathered to play, such as the Eagle Saloon on Rampart and Gravier, where the Eagle Band of Bolden's former trombonist, Frankie Dusen, was based. But it would be a mistake to think that these venues were all throbbing to music every night of the week. Danny Barker produced a splendid anecdotal account of witnessing a dance during his childhood, at the Animule Hall,[18] again a folkloric synthesis of the real life Globe, Geddes, Veterans, Frans Amis, Economy, and Hope Halls and their like, other names such as Longshoreman's Hall and Screwmen's Hall revealing their normal use as the base of trade and friendly associations, who held dances on weekends and holidays. In the dances held at these halls, the ecstatic elements from Grace King's description of a voodoo dance in the last chapter certainly seem to have been present. When the band played a slow drag, as Danny Barker described it: "some of the patrons would get so carried away by these blues that their crying and wailing could be heard above the band."

The very irregularity of such events gave rise to another New Orleans custom, the ballyhoo, or advance advertisement for a dance. Not only did this often involve the band playing on the outdoor balcony of a hall immediately before the event, but touring the neighborhood earlier in the day on a truck. Sometimes two trucks would come across each other on the street, and their wheels would be bound together until one band or the other had triumphed in a battle of music. The practice gave at least one new word to the language, describing the trombonist's practice of playing the slide over the rear of the truck as "tailgate" trombone. Many musicians, playing from 1910 well into the 1920s, recall such battles, and they are colorful additions to the memoirs of Baby Dodds, Lee Collins, and Danny Barker.

Similar ballyhoos – though seldom involving a band battle – took place away from New Orleans on the entire touring-theater network, as well as for tent and circus shows, where it was the custom for itinerant troupes across the United States to send out their bands to advertise the evening performance.

In New Orleans itself, as the better uptown musicians and the Creoles began to work more and more frequently together in the years following Bolden's hospitalization, the elements of jazz grew apace. Small six-piece dance bands such as those of Frankie Dusen or Kid Ory brought together the best of uptown and downtown. Dusen and another survivor of Bolden's group, guitarist Brock Mumford, played with Bunk Johnson on cornet, and later with Sidney Bechet on clarinet and Baby Dodds on drums. Kid Ory's band, described as "soft-playing" by Barney Bigard, whose uncle Emile played violin in the group, had more future jazz stars in its line-up: Mutt Carey, cornet; Johnny Dodds, clarinet; and Pops Foster, bass.

In Ory's ensemble in particular, the schooled, Creole violin of Bigard blended with the forthright cornet of Carey (whose brother Jack was the celebrated trombonist credited with creating the tigerish roars on *Tiger Rag*), and the vocal-toned, bluesy, uptown clarinet of Dodds. There is doubt as to how effective Johnny Dodds ever became at reading music – his brother Baby Dodds said that he and Johnny were exceptions among uptown players, being able to read, but Barney Bigard, who later came to know Dodds in Chicago, doubted his reading ability. Yet, reader or not, his soulful playing epitomized what Schaeffer called the "imitation of the voice."

From 1906 or thereabouts, cornetist Freddie Keppard organized his Olympia band, which quickly became one of the most highly regarded local bands, until he left to play in Los Angeles in 1914, whereupon the mantle was taken up by the "young" Olympia which included Sidney Bechet, trumpeter Buddy Petit, and trombonist Ernest Kelly. Other major musicians born in the last decades of the nineteenth century, who were significant members of the New Orleans generation that promoted the change from ragtime to jazz, included cornetists Peter Bocage, Oscar "Papa" Celestin, Sidney Desvigne, Chris Kelly, Punch Miller, Joe Oliver, and Kid Rena;

trombonists Honore Dutrey, George Filhe, and Roy Palmer; clarinetists George Bacquet, "Big Eye" Louis Nelson, Jimmie Noone, Alphonse Picou, and Lorenzo Tio Jr.; pianists Richard M. Jones, Manuel Manetta (also a multi-instrumentalist), and Clarence Williams; guitarists Johnny St. Cyr and Bud Scott; bassists Wellman Braud, Ed Garland, Albert Glenny, Bill Johnson, Henry Kimball, and John Lindsay (who also played trombone); and drummers Louis Cottrell Sr., Tubby Hall, and Zutty Singleton. By 1920, a younger generation of players, born after 1900, was also emerging, and one name above all others began to be mentioned after 1918, when he first started appearing with Kid Ory's band – a talented young trumpeter called Louis Armstrong.

Armstrong's contribution will be discussed in the sixth section of this chapter, but what was it that all these New Orleans pioneers actually did? What were the changes they were bringing about to create jazz?

For a start, within the instrumentation of the ragtime orchestra there was a gradual shift from the violin to the cornet or trumpet to carry the main melody, focusing the melodic lines of the ensemble on the brightest-sounding, most powerful instrument, in common with the brass-band tradition. It is possible to hear exactly what a dramatic difference this made on A. J. Piron's recording of *Lou'siana Swing*, from February 18, 1924. Opening in the clipped, syncopated ragtime style, with a firm two beats to each measure from the tuba and trombone, plus a few solo instrumental breaks, a bridge passage leads to the final melodic strain. In this, Piron's violin leads the first of three choruses, playing the melody while Lorenzo Tio Jr.'s clarinet weaves a delicate lower register obbligato. Peter Bocage takes over for the next chorus on cornet, gently syncopating the melody as violin, alto sax, and clarinet play counter-melodies. Then, on the final run through, the cornet plays a much freer version of the lead, with John Lindsay's trombone playing a contrapuntal "tailgate" bass line. As Lindsay plays approximately four regular beats to each measure, sometimes slightly anticipating and sometimes retarding the beat, Bocage moves the rhythmic emphasis around, creating a shimmering sense of motion. Suddenly the band has slid from playing a rhythmically restricted two-beat ragtime into a much freer, looser jazz style, and although the disc was made some fifteen to twenty years after this transition first took place, it is a dramatic illustration of it.

This freeing-up of the trumpet or cornet part, without mutes, growls, or vocal tones, was the most noticeable way in which an element of improvisation began to be introduced to a performance, becoming the first building-block for the other members of a collective front line to improvise freely around the lead. The most proficient trumpeters would punch out a clear, relatively unsyncopated version of a melody, and then apply the kind of alteration in rhythmic emphasis demonstrated by Bocage. Baby Dodds's description of Willie Hightower's playing catches the idea well: "He'd play one chorus nice and then he would chop it up and play it jazzy."[19] Notwithstanding his *braggadocio* about Bolden, it is clear that Bunk Johnson was another early exponent of this new, looser style of lead. His fellow trumpeter, Lee Collins, who claimed to have learned much from Johnson, wrote: "Bunk was way ahead when it came to jazz – I'm talking about hot phrasing, not trick tone or trick effects."[20] Johnson himself was interviewed by Bill Russell for a set of oral history discs in May 1943, and even if Johnson's claims to be recreating Bolden's style are dubious, his whistled ragtime figures and diminished runs on Bolden's *Making Runs*, or his trumpet illustrations of playing lead on the famous New Orleans song *Make Me a Pallet on the Floor*, are excellent examples of how to move the emphasis of the beat around while stating a melody, giving some impression at least of how his own style sounded in the days before recording reached the Crescent City.

Lorenzo Tio Jr.'s liquid obbligato on *Lou'siana Swing* is an equally important illustration of the Creole clarinet style: pure-toned, accurately pitched, and highly melodic, with a decorative filigree quality as finely wrought as the ironwork of the balconies on Royal Street. His pupil, Barney Bigard, described the way Tio patiently explained to him how to master the idea of jazz timing, anchoring his playing in a lilting two beats to the measure, even if the band was actually playing four or six: " 'When you get to playing in a jazz band, kind of think in two-four all the way, then you'll have it,' he told me . . . it took me forever but I finally got it down."[21]

With little recorded evidence to go on, it is hard to assess the role of the rhythm section in early New Orleans jazz. Baby Dodds made it clear that the majority of drummers were using just snare and bass drum, and transferring brass-band techniques to these, while the "guitar carried only rhythm in the bands." The tentative examples of drumming that made it onto record before the mid-1920s do nothing to conjure up the polyrhythmic texture of African percussion – there is no magical evocation of Congo Square in early recorded jazz. Instead, this polyrhythmic character is present in the front line – the trumpet, clarinet, saxophone, and trombone. No better example exists of this than the single, glorious example of Freddie Keppard's playing in full flood which he cut in September 1926 with his Jazz Cardinals: *Stock*

*Yards Strut*. (Although Keppard made other discs, including a handful with Doc Cook, few of these recordings, also made late in his short life, match up to the many descriptions of his prowess as a trumpet "king.")

On this tune, he punches out a jaunty lead, with trombonist Eddie Vincent (his colleague from the Original Creole Orchestra which went to Los Angeles in 1914) and clarinetist Johnny Dodds providing the other front-line parts. The lame piano and percussion accompaniment is almost irrelevant; indeed, when the band creates a series of breaks for Dodds's clarinet, it is Keppard and Vincent who place the stops in the right places, both pianist and drummer getting it wrong. In his own first break, Keppard slightly anticipates the beat, an obvious example of the subtle and magisterial way he moves the rhythmic emphasis around throughout the piece. With a range of devices to carry the listener's interest from one chorus to the next, ranging from a repeated high note towards the start, to long-held notes that are released with a burst of energy as the next chorus begins, Keppard provides the entire rhythmic momentum for the piece, with Vincent and Dodds placing their notes in such a way that they are sometimes with him and sometimes pulling against him – exactly the same sensation as Bocage and Lindsay create with Piron's band.

Obviously, it remains a matter of conjecture how early Keppard was playing in this way, but he left New Orleans in 1914 and spent much of the remainder of his career elsewhere – mainly in Chicago – so there is a strong chance his style had coalesced before he left his home town. Jelly Roll Morton, for example, had no doubts as to Keppard's talent as far back as 1907. He told Alan Lomax: "He had the best ear, the best tone, and the most marvelous execution I ever heard and there was no end to his ideas: he could play one chorus eight to ten different ways."[22]

In this one disc by Keppard we have a powerful indication of the way the jazz front line moved away from ragtime, changing the ebb and flow of the beat, and anchoring this with the overall two-four sensation described by Bigard. Another early example of New Orleans players achieving this effect is on a recording of a blues made out on the West Coast in June 1921 by the first African-American band of musicians from the city to make out-and-out jazz records: Kid Ory's Original Creole Jazz Band. Their *Society Blues* shows clearly how trumpet, trombone, and clarinet could create their own momentum, even at a relatively slow tempo, with a minimum of explicit support from a rhythm section.

As well as the introduction of jazz ideas to the ensemble, there was further impetus to the development of the music in what, in many respects, was to become an entirely separate form of jazz – solo piano. Many pianists were employed in the District, in the plentiful bars and tonks, and in the brothels themselves. Compared to a full band, a solo pianist was relatively inexpensive, could play the latest Tin Pan Alley hit songs or popular local favorites, and provide instant entertainment for the clientèle. Jelly Roll Morton described how he added a touch of Spanish rhythm to the blues, and with his quick ear he no doubt imitated many of the sounds of the bands of the city. He also recalled numerous pianists whose playing he heard at first hand in the District, of whom the most accomplished was Tony Jackson.

Jackson is important to the development of jazz for two reasons. First, he was a consummate improviser and melodist (he has already been mentioned in respect of his improvised accompaniments to classic blues singer Lucille Hegamin, and he wrote the enduring standard *Pretty Baby*), and second, he went on the road early, traveling from Louisville, Kentucky, to Chicago between 1904 and 1911, and then working mainly in Chicago from 1912, spreading musical ideas from New Orleans through the entertainment world. To those who heard him, before his death in 1921, he provided a memorable experience: "I asked another listener outside of Antonia Gonzales' place, 'Who in the world is that?'" wrote Roy Carew in his Storyville reminiscences. "I got the reply 'That's Tony Jackson; he knows a thousand songs.'"[23]

Carew's friend Jelly Roll Morton praised Jackson's all-round ability:

> He was the outstanding favorite of New Orleans. I have never known any pianists to come from any section of the world that could leave New Orleans victorious. Tony was considered among all who knew him the greatest single-handed entertainer in the world.[24]

Morton's own recreations of Jackson's style tell us a little of how he might have sounded – a robust ragtime-styled player on up-tempo pieces, but also a splendid lilting ballad interpreter, who sang in a high tenor register like the much later New Orleans entertainer Fats Pichon. Slinky sensuous ballads (in the manner of Morton's reading of *Pretty Baby*) would have made Jackson popular with the clientèle in the District's sporting houses where he worked until 1904 – Gipsy Shaefer's, Hilma Burt's, Lulu White's, and Countess Willie Piazza's. Their customers would be far more likely to proffer tips to a player who had managed to combine memorable melodies with a genuinely sensuous, slow two-beat rhythm than to someone playing nothing but tearaway ragtime. (When Jackson did play ragtime, it was to accompany his speciality, the "naked dance" – in Morton's recollection a Joplinesque stomp played while one of the whores danced in the nude for the customers.)

There is a further sense of Jackson's prowess as a composer and player of ballads in Bunk Johnson's 1943 recording (on piano) of Jackson's song *Baby I'd Love to Steal You*, played to demonstrate how Jackson worked out the song after hours in the Wine Room behind the Big 25 in the District.[25] Jackson and his fellow players in Storyville in the early 1900s had the same advantage that Scott Joplin and the ragtime "ticklers" had enjoyed in the red-light district of New Sedalia a decade before. They could use their nightly experience of playing for clients whose minds were elsewhere to try out new compositions, and hone them until they were right. It is highly likely that a significant part of the transition from ragtime to jazz took place in front of an audience who had little or no idea, and less interest, in what was going on.

Jelly Roll Morton was, in the opinion of many fellow musicians, employed in the District because he was light-skinned and Spanish-looking: Louis Armstrong wrote:

> Jelly Roll with lighter skin than the average piano players got the job because they did not want a Black piano player for the job. He claimed he was from an Indian or Spanish race. No Cullud at all. He was a big Bragadossa. Lots of big talk. . . . Jelly Roll made so much money in tips he had a diamond inserted in one of his teeth. No matter how much his diamond sparkled he still had to eat in the kitchen, the same as we Blacks.[26]

When times got rough in the District, early in the twentieth century, Morton tried his hand at bandleading, but before long, he, like Jackson, had set off on the road. Initially, from 1906 or so, he worked as a part-time pianist and part-time pool shark along the Gulf Coast, but in time he was living the life of an itinerant musician, either working solo or in a vaudeville act called McCabe's Troubadours. In the period in which ragtime was making its slow transition into jazz, Morton was to be found in Kansas City, St. Louis, Chicago, Detroit, and California; and later in Canada, Wyoming, and Colorado. After 1906, he seldom visited his home town for long, leaving for good the following year, and yet the sound of its music remained clear in his mind. Many of the New Orleans musicians who started playing in bands elsewhere in the country encountered Morton during that time, and he was not slow to tell them, along with any other musicians he met, how he thought they could improve their playing.

James P. Johnson, still wearing short pants, heard him at Barron Wilkins's club in New York in 1911:

> He had just arrived from the West and he was red hot. The place was on fire! We heard him play his *Jelly Roll Blues*. I remember that he was dressed in full-back clothes and wore a light brown melton overcoat, with a three-hole hat to match. He had two girls with him.[27]

Morton's sartorial elegance (he used to travel with several suits and change them a number of times a day when he arrived in a new place, to give the impression of wealth) and his fondness for women were legendary. ("Where he came from," commented cornetist Rex Stewart, "jelly roll didn't refer to cake.")

By 1911, Morton had made the acquaintance of many of the great ragtime pianists of the Midwest and East. Through the vaudeville network, and through competing in contests such as the one in St. Louis that he described when he recorded his recollections for Alan Lomax at the Library of Congress, in which he triumphed over local competition by playing Suppé's *Poet and Peasant* overture at least partly from memory, Morton would have heard the ragtime styles that were in vogue. Yet it is significant that Johnson recalls Morton playing his own *Jelly Roll Blues*, rather than a current rag by another composer. Given the chance, and his fondness for his own work, it is likely Morton would most often have played his own pieces, and in doing so demonstrated to those who heard him the kind of looser, jazzier feeling from New Orleans which his best work embodies. For him, as for other pianists on the variety circuit, in Gunther Schuller's memorable phrase: "going from ragtime to jazz was not so much a historical process as an everyday occurrence and necessity, depending primarily on where the next dollar might come from."[28]

In his various writings on Morton, Schuller has generally advanced the proposition that, because of the compositional maturity of his writing and arranging by the time he came to record frequently in the 1920s, Morton's ideas must have crystallized considerably earlier.[29] Indeed, Morton himself said that by writing out parts for a band in St. Louis as early as 1912, he was able to get a pick-up band of locals to play "some pretty fair jazz." This is a thoroughly credible idea. It was only six or seven years later that Jesse

Stone, leading his first territory band in Kansas, found he had to do the same, notating parts that sounded like jazz improvisations for musicians who had yet to understand the idea or the idiom.[30] And, as Morton was to point out in his Library of Congress recordings, and to indicate in markings on his holograph scores, jazz piano, properly played, imitates a band.

So was Morton, along with other New Orleans piano "professors" who took to the touring variety circuit like Tony Jackson or Sam Davis ("one of the greatest manipulators I guess I've ever heard in the history of the world"),[31] already disseminating jazz ideas from 1906 or 1907? Certainly Morton used the words "jazz" and "ragtime" with considerable care. In an analysis of Morton's work and its relationship to ragtime, James Dapogny concludes:

> while ragtime was still a powerful, living tradition, Morton used the lessons learned from ragtime to develop a distinctly new piano style, making syncopation a pervasive part of the music's fabric. He had done this before 1907, when he left New Orleans for the last time.[32]

And in Dapogny's list of the attributes he feels Morton brought to the music are the following:

> He had departed from notated ragtime conventions, he had integrated the jazz-blues scale into his music . . .; had developed composed, rather than improvised, variations on melodies and devised new ways of relating ideas from different strains . . .; had developed a riff-like compositional phrase structure . . .; had created new approaches to melody and new ways for the pianist's left hand to operate; and had made a place in composed music for varied kinds and amounts of improvisation.[33]

This makes a compelling case for some of the earliest jazz ideas spreading through the United States by a very different route from the conventionally accepted "up-the-river-to-Chicago" method, and earlier in time by a decade or so. Within the African-American entertainment community, it is likely that a very large number of "show people" had come into contact with New Orleans jazz well before the events described in the next section concerning the Original Dixieland Jazz Band. And what makes an even more compelling argument for the rapid spread of jazz and its adoption by musicians in many parts of the United States is the traveling undertaken by another group of New Orleans pioneers who formed Freddie Keppard's Original Creole Orchestra. This band went to Los Angeles at the behest of bassist Bill Johnson in 1914, and subsequently traveled the Orpheum theater circuit, during which it visited Chicago and New York. If Morton brought a piano reduction of ensemble jazz to the country's theaters, then Keppard is likely to have brought to the same venues plenty of the instrumental fire and rhythmic excitement preserved in his disc of *Stock Yards Strut*.

Morton's ensemble recordings, and his talent as a composer and arranger, will be discussed later, but his other great talent was as a proselytizer. Those who encountered him on the touring circuit did not forget it. Andy Kirk remembers Morton substituting in one of George Morrison's bands in Denver around 1920 or 1921, and the musicians being told: "That's a good piece, but you ain't saying nothin'. Man, you gotta stomp it!" A couple of years later he ran into Joe Darensbourg in Cairo, Illinois: "Jelly Roll was a helluva name in those days and he could play, yessir." And Marshal Royal, then a child prodigy on violin, was introduced to Morton in Los Angeles at Reb Spikes's Music store by his father, a veteran of the variety circuit: "Jelly Roll was quite a pompous type of fellow, almost arrogant in his manners, but you had to respect him for what he had accomplished."[34]

We have a vivid portrait of Morton, with his diamond tooth, his dandified clothing, and his opinionated conversation, from two of the finest writers among the early generation of jazz musicians, Rex Stewart and Danny Barker. Stewart wrote:

> Morton was a rather tall, well-built, apricot-colored person, with features that reminded me of a Spanish grandee who had become a bit jaded with life. His eyes were the most fascinating as they darted from face to face, emphasizing those sometimes disputatious monologues. . . . He exemplified everything that I had ever heard about the glamorous piano players of the bordellos, where they reigned supreme. He started his upward climb from there, winding up as a respectable innovator and creator of jazz (although he didn't invent the music as he claimed).[35]

This boastful tendency of Morton's (aggravated by a press correspondence in 1938 in which he claimed to be the inventor of jazz and "World's greatest hot tune writer") has often worked against him, and tended to occlude his talent. Danny Barker explained it to me by saying: "Jelly Roll felt that he was the greatest jazz pianist and composer, and he was just not concerned with any other talent but his own – that is his own piano playing and composing."[36]

It is clear that by the 1930s, Morton's sense of timing and close affinities to ragtime seemed dated to the up-and-coming swing players, and it is their perception of him that has clung to much of his work as a pianist and composer. He should, however, be revalued in terms not only of his 1920s band recordings, but his role as one of the first true ambassadors of jazz.

## The Original Dixieland Jazz Band

> We only called the music "jazz" after someone in the
> audience one night in Chicago kept hollering at us to "Jazz it
> up!", and it seemed to fit our music. No, I never heard the
> word in New Orleans. I found out later it was a foul word in
> Chicago, but I guess we purified it.
> Nick LaRocca, interviewed by Brian A. L. Rust, *Storyville* No. 9

Up until this point, jazz has been discussed mainly in terms of its origins as a syncretic music, and of the considerable African-American contribution to its early development. Rhythmically and tonally, African-American musicians created most of the framework in which jazz could develop, and their entertainment networks provided conduits along which the earliest forms of the music traveled to many parts of the United States and beyond. However, as noted in the previous section, there was a lively musical scene among the white population of New Orleans, and musicians like Johnny Fischer, Happy Schilling, and Jack Laine were all playing music well before the outbreak of World War I that had plenty in common with that of their Creole and African-American counterparts. Their working lives followed a similar pattern: picnics, dances, house parties, and festivals such as Mardi Gras, plus work in the clubs or bars of the District that employed white musicians as well as catering for white patrons.

Equally, only a small number of the emergent white musicians, playing a prototype of jazz, could sustain themselves by music alone – many had comparable jobs to those of their Creole counterparts. Among the best-known, trombonist Tom Brown and his bassist brother Steve were tinsmiths, the clarinetist Gus Mueller was a plumber, and so on. In due course, several pioneer white New Orleans musicians were to have a major role in taking jazz forward – Steve Brown, for example, was a prodigiously talented double bassist, who bucked the trend to adopt the tuba, and succeeded in being audible on recordings in the very early 1920s, subsequently anticipating many of the technical innovations of 1930s bass players. But such talented instrumentalists aside, there is relatively little evidence that the white musicians of New Orleans were true innovators, participants in what was being created through the symbiosis between Creole and African-American, and, therefore, directly responsible for the consolidation of the constituent parts of the music itself. However, through the medium of the phonograph, the white New Orleans musicians of the Original Dixieland Jazz Band were to make the running in disseminating the music to the world, and in enshrining for posterity the name by which it would be known, however inappropriate.

In 1917, the recording business was white-owned and white-dominated. As Pekka Gronow and Ilpo Saunio point out in their history of the industry, by that time very few attempts had been made to record African-American music, in comparison to the plethora of discs catering for immigrant groups from "Albanians to Icelanders" – a wealth of ethnic traditions which are detailed in Richard K. Spottswood's voluminous discography of pre-1942 recordings. The handful of notable exceptions include discs by Bert Williams (including such pieces as *Nobody*, from 1913), and several by James Reese Europe's syncopated orchestra. Sporadic recording of this kind had begun as early as 1891 when George W. Johnson started recording "coon songs" on cylinders, continuing until around 1903 when he died. But these were minority efforts, ignoring a huge potential market, as Gronow and Saunio make clear:

> Although there were millions of Negroes in the United States, black music had not been recorded more than occasionally, and when it had it was mostly in "refined" versions for a white audience. There were several reasons for this. The Negroes, mostly poor, did not constitute a significant market, and doing business with blacks was not thought proper, due to the long tradition of racial segregation. In 1916, the *Chicago Defender*, a weekly newspaper that had a quarter of a million readers in black communities, appealed to record companies to have "records of

the race's great artists placed on the market," but at the time nothing came of it.[37]

This economic decision by the record industry has prevented us from using sound recording reliably to determine the early history of jazz. It was not until some time after Kid Ory's West Coast debut on disc, in 1921,[38] that African-American and Creole jazz musicians began to record with any regularity, or that white-owned companies woke up to the potential of the "race" market, and that African-American companies, like the publisher Pace and Handy, or the recording firm Black Swan, began to challenge the exclusively white ownership of the industry. In Marxist terms, this meant that, just as plantation dwellers like Cousin Joe Pleasant were obliged to use tickets or tokens to subsist entirely within a white-owned and white-controlled economy, African-American musicians owned the tools of their trade, but they did not have any control over what they produced. As Frank Kofsky eloquently put it:

> The artistry of the jazz musician operates primarily to enrich not its possessor, but those white executives who own and/or manage the means of production and distribution within the political economy of jazz; and the decisions of such owners and managers, particularly those involved in the recording industry, are absolutely crucial in determining both the total amount of employment for black musicians and which specific musicians will be granted access to it.[39]

This is the background against which the first jazz recordings came to be made. And, just as with Buddy Bolden, to explain the inexplicable, a mythology and folklore grew up about why it was that white musicians came first to record what was in essence black music.

Central to this is the idea that Freddie Keppard was asked to make records with his Original Creole Orchestra some time before the Original Dixieland Jazz Band, and that he turned the proposal down. Unlikely as it may seem for such an extrovert and flamboyant player, according to the legend he covered his valves with a handkerchief to prevent other players "stealing his stuff" and, in a move that seems remarkably prescient about the manner in which recorded music would become common property, he was similarly protective about making his repertoire public by issuing it on record. "He wasn't gonna let the other fellows hear his records and catch his stuff," said guitarist Johnny St. Cyr.[40] Other commentators, some of whom knew Keppard well enough to dispute that version of events, said that his decision was purely financial, and that Victor – who apparently made the approach – did not offer him enough money. "The Creole Band was not poor, they were not stranded and financially they were doing well," wrote Danny Barker, of a conversation he had with George Bacquet, the clarinetist in Keppard's group. "Freddie had read about the huge sums of money paid to Caruso for recordings and believed his music on record would earn something approaching this amount."[41]

On another occasion, Bacquet told a *Down Beat* correspondent that the issue hinged on Victor refusing to pay Keppard for a test session that was to precede the actual recording date.[42] Whatever the truth about Keppard's failure to be the first jazz musician to enter the record business, this vitally important step was taken by the Original Dixieland Jazz Band in New York shortly after they had enjoyed a successful period in Chicago, well away from their home town of New Orleans. Ironically, they followed in Keppard's footsteps there as well.

Chicago has always been proud of its position as America's "second city." Founded as a trading post on Lake Michigan in the seventeenth century, and built close to the site of Fort Dearborn, Chicago became a fully fledged city in the state of Illinois in 1837. Today's city was created after a disastrous fire in 1871 flattened many of the original buildings, and a new town sprang up on the southwest shore of the lake. Water transport, and more particularly railways, created the city's wealth. It was the center of transportation for the whole of the upper Mississippi area, and the gateway to the Midwest and Canada for much of the rest of the country.

The town that grew up with its manufacturing industry and stockyards, along the windswept shores of Lake Michigan, quickly acquired the nickname of the "windy city," (although this had as much to do with its filibustering style of politics as its climate) and in winter the extreme northern conditions meant several months of sub-zero temperatures. The music that flourished there was played outdoors in the city's many parks and open spaces in summer, and in a motley collection of indoor venues for the rest of the year, from vast clubs and ballrooms to small backstreet dives. The city was divided into several areas, but historically the most important for jazz were the Loop – the old central commercial district bounded by the elevated railway that encircles it, with plentiful hotels and restaurants – and the South Side, where the main black population was centered, between 22nd and 95th Street.

After an influx of ragtime pianists for the 1893 World's Columbian Exposition, Chicago had established itself as a base for ragtime, and this explains why, in the early 1900s, visiting New Orleans players like Tony Jackson and Jelly Roll Morton became such local celebrities. When the young Russian-born pianist Art Hodes, barely into long trousers, first heard Jackson at a barbecue joint on State and 48th Street, he recalled how "the blues just flowed out of him." In 1914, Morton established a New Orleans band at the Elite Club at 3445 State Street. Morton's band was celebrated until the Original Creole Band opened in February the following year at the Grand Theater, where Freddie Keppard's virtuoso playing apparently wooed the crowds away from Morton.

White jazz – or at any rate proto-jazz – in Chicago began with the arrival in the city in May 1915 of a ragtime band led by trombonist Tom Brown from New Orleans. The group opened at Lamb's Café, at North Clark and West Randolph, at the recommendation (among others) of Charlie Mack, a white vaudeville artist who specialized in demeaning blackface impersonations of rural African-Americans and who was to become famous in the 1920s as one of the "Two Black Crows." It was Mack who papered the house at Lamb's by bringing in the entire cast of his own show at the Shubert Theater to create a publicity buzz for the band, after the group's raucous sounds had drawn little enthusiasm from its audiences and derogatory shouts from the string orchestra that played opposite it of "jazz" or "jass." This was a scatological term for sexual congress that seems to have had its origins in the San Francisco area where the word also meant "pep" or "enthusiasm."

Buoyed up by the attention created by Mack and the resultant gossip, "Brown's Band from Dixieland" began to attract substantial crowds, and soon started billing itself (using this new word with a *frisson* of daring) as "Brown's Dixieland Jass Band, Direct from New Orleans, Best Dance Music in Chicago."[43] Their residency ran until the end of August, when the club closed, and after a few desultory engagements and an abortive trip to New York, the band folded. Yet, from that brief engagement, Tom Brown's legacy to jazz was to give the new music the name that would eventually be taken up on a national basis. The word "jazz" was applied to African-American and white ensembles a little earlier on the West Coast, but these had no impact on national consciousness in the way Brown's use of the word did. Within a few months, other Chicago establishments were emulating the success of Lamb's, by presenting bands from "Dixie," playing "jass" or "jazz."

There was – as so often in the history of this music – a political motive

behind this. Chicago's rapid growth since the 1870s had given it something
of the reputation for a town on the make, where all kinds of money-making
enterprises, legal and illegal, were developed hand-in-glove with its
expansion of population. One fast-growing area was that of organized
prostitution, together with the supply of plentiful cheap alcohol. The city
authorities felt compelled to be seen to be clamping down on such illicit
activities, but at the same time were not unaware of the money that was
being made from them, and which could, consequently, be made from other
types of entertainment that did not attract too much disapproval from the
reform lobby. The growing craze for social dances that followed on from the
cake-walk to become the one-step or two-step, involving a certain amount
of inevitable physical contact between the participants, were a vexed
question: some reformers disapproved of them on principle as immoral and
a mere step (or two) away from prostitution; others took the view that if
dancers and musicians were kept reasonably separate from one another, and
if the dance hall was efficiently managed, this was a great deal preferable to
the illicit alternatives.

In his history of Chicago jazz, William H. Kenney points out how, from
1916 onwards, the city council tried to "respond to the contrary pressures
from leisure time entrepreneurs and urban reformers. Music turned out to
be one important medium for compromise between these two contrasting
pressure groups."[44] By granting licenses to dance halls and cabarets that
allowed them to present music, and, indeed, singling out instrumental music
as an acceptable form of entertainment, the council assured itself a share of
the revenue to be made from what one of its advisers called "noisy ragtime
[and] the jangle of the jazz band," while moving to suppress prostitution or
drunkenness. The raunchy new name given to the "jass" music played by
Brown's band and others like it carried the suggestion of licentious behavior,
but, when all was said and done, came down to being little more than rather
noisy, extrovert dance music. By putting on such music, promoters could
present something apparently quite daring, but without the risk of censure
from the city fathers.

It was the loud, slapstick, comedic character of the music of the early
white Dixieland groups that was its most noticeable feature – in many
respects as two-dimensional a representation of the new African-American
music as blackface white singers were of what lay behind the old minstrelsy
traditions. This brashness was a particularly high-profile component in the
work of the quintet that started life as "Stein's Band from Dixie," and, after
some changes of both personnel and venue, became the Original Dixieland

Jazz Band, playing at the Casino Gardens. Like many other musicians from Louisiana, this "Dixie" group had not heard the term "jass" or "jazz" used to describe their music until they arrived in Chicago, but they readily adopted the word in their name, despite its scatological connections, just as Tom Brown had done before them. The band included two musicians who had worked for Papa Laine in New Orleans – trombonist Eddie Edwards and clarinetist Larry Shields (who replaced another Laine alumnus, Alcide "Yellow" Nunez). On piano was a New Orleans ragtimer called Henry Ragas, and on drums (replacing the group's original leader, Johnny Stein) was Tony Sbarbaro, but the most significant character in the group was its cornetist Nick LaRocca. He was to become a shameless self-publicist, as devoted in later life to pressing his claims to be the originator of jazz as Jelly Roll Morton became in the late 1930s, yet based on a far smaller and less broadly based body of work, and consistently ignoring any African-American contribution to the genesis of jazz. However, in 1916 he knew that he could benefit by playing up the *risqué*, the bizarre, and the unusual in his music to draw attention to it.

The illustrated letterhead which came to be used by the band ("Original Dixieland Jazz Band: The Creators of Jazz") is a revealing insight into the group's self-image. Sbarbaro's giant bass drum booms as he waves castanets and bells above his head. Edwards and Shields point to left and right respectively, while LaRocca sits atop the back of his chair, feet on the seat, aiming his cornet at the ceiling. Ragas appears simultaneously to be dancing a kind of Charleston and pressing his nose to the keyboard, while a terpsichorean couple spin round the dance-floor. In its subsequent publicity photographs, the band members wore hats with large letters on them, spelling out the word "D-I-X-I-E." The whole impression is of a group of lighthearted good-time entertainers fraught with the nervous anxiety of comedians whose jokes might fall flat if the momentum is allowed to slacken for a second.

Challenged on the funny hats and the stage antics, LaRocca was quick to justify them:

> We had to play up over the heads of the dancers, for if we played at them or down to the floor, we wouldn't have been heard in a large ballroom. . . . We used the top hats to show who we were, that's all. As for the dancing I did, I was always supposed to be a good dancer, and when I started doing it on the stand, and it brought rounds of applause, I kept on doing it.[45]

Initially, the band courted controversy in the Chicago press, which made much of its cacophonous din, its "blatant scream," and reports using language like this began to draw crowds. Much as Brown's band had benefited from the attention of Charlie Mack, it was another white variety performer who specialized in blackface, Al Jolson, who took a hand in the success of the Original Dixieland Jazz Band. Early in 1916, the Lithuanian-born Jolson had been starring in the show *Robinson Crusoe Jr.* (famous for the song *Where did Robinson Crusoe Go, with Friday on Saturday Night?*), and he had already created his tragi-comic blackface character Gus in several earlier stage productions. In common with numerous other high-profile stars, he dropped into the Casino Gardens to check out the new craze for "jass," and ended up suggesting to his manager that the band should be booked into a venue in New York.

Leaving behind the burgeoning (if short-lived) Chicagoan vogue for five-piece bands from Dixie, the O.D.J.B. (as it became known) moved to New York, and on January 15, 1917, opened in one of the seven dance areas in the new Reisenweber's Restaurant near Columbus Circle in Manhattan. This was a racially segregated venue catering for white audiences, and initially the band played only a couple of numbers or so between sets by a resident dance orchestra. For almost two weeks they were spectacularly unsuccessful. Then they were moved to the venue's new "400" club room, to play on their own as the main attraction. At first, audiences remained hostile, but when the management urged the public to dance, the band's incipient failure transformed into success, and within a few days the room was packed, lines stretched down Eighth Avenue, and the musicians began to earn amounts unprecedented for ragtime or "jass" performers, sharing $1000 per week between the players – a small fortune in 1917.

At the end of the month, on January 30, the band made its first recordings for Columbia, but the firm's executives disliked the music, and shelved the masters, so that the first discs by the group to be issued were recorded almost a month later for the competing Victor company, on February 26. Victor rushed out the results, and *Dixie Jazz Band One-Step* and *Livery Stable Blues* were released as the two sides of disc number 18255, priced at a mere 75 cents, on March 5, 1917.

The rooster calls and braying donkey of *Livery Stable Blues*, combined with Sbarbaro's fondness for woodblocks and other percussion effects, including a dramatic cymbal crash at the end of most main phrases, caught the imagination of the public. While the horrors of the First World War still raged in Europe, New Yorkers could amuse themselves with the jolly,

103

garrulous sounds of the O.D.J.B., most numbers consisting of continuous full-band ensembles with little variety between each repetition of a chorus, breakneck tempos, cloppity drums, and the occasional animal imitation thrown in. With the push of the Victor Talking Machine Company behind it, the first disc sold well not just in New York, but elsewhere in North America also, and subsequently throughout the world. It eventually notched up several hundred thousand copies (according to some reports, over a million, a figure which has almost certainly been achieved over time).[46] Not surprisingly, the press went to town, and the band's work was described in tones of shock and horror: "The musical riot that breaks forth from clarinet, trombone, cornet, piano, drum and variants of tin pan instruments resembles nothing so much as a chorus of hunting hounds on the scent with an occasional explosion in the subway thrown in for good measure."[47]

LaRocca played this attention for all it was worth, but he also worked hard at building up a core repertoire of original compositions, the majority of which continue to be performed by Dixieland groups at the start of the twenty-first century. Among his compositions are *Dixie Jazz Band One-Step*, *Skeleton Jangle*, and *Barnyard Blues*, and the entire band copyrighted *Tiger Rag*, despite Jelly Roll Morton's subsequent claim that he had much to do with its creation. At the heart of LaRocca's pieces was his own robust lead cornet, around which the band's front-line ensemble could be built: "I cut the material," he said, "Shields put the lace on it and Edwards sewed it up."[48] Among other white Dixielanders, LaRocca's angular, somewhat stilted, lead playing had its admirers; for example, cornetist Bix Beiderbecke, who wrote in November 1922 to LaRocca to tell him: "All I knew was that you were the best lead in the country."[49]

What was lacking, however, from LaRocca's lead was the kind of infinite variety which Morton found, for example, in Freddie Keppard's ability to play endless variations on a single chord sequence. In a piece like *At the Jazz Band Ball*, recorded in March 1918, the O.D.J.B. works its way through an ABBB structure twice. There is almost no variation between the first run through the sequence and the second – even the instrumental breaks for clarinet and cornet are identical. Equally, on *Indiana* **[CD track 1]**, the band's very first recording for Columbia (eventually released in the wake of Victor's success with the band), the alternation between one verse and two choruses is consistent, and every time through the sequence, its treatment remains virtually unaltered. There was, it seems, a great deal less improvisation going on than collectively memorized arrangements that varied little from one performance to another.

Significantly, one justification offered for the breathless tempi of the majority of the band's recordings was that they had to be played fast to fit the three-minute playing time of a 78 r.p.m. disc, or have a chorus cut from the arrangement, which the band refused to do, thereby suggesting that they tended to play each piece the same way at every performance.[50] Even when there was less time pressure, and when the tempo relaxes a little, such as on the band's English recordings from 1919 and 1920, which were on larger twelve-inch discs with a four-minute duration, there is little variety between choruses. A typical piece like *Look at 'Em Doing It*, from the London recording session of May 1919, sounds like a dogged ragtime pianist plugging carefully and relentlessly through the sheet music for a song. The AABBB structure is repeated twice, with no added inspiration or variation.

It is easy to be dismissive of the O.D.J.B. with the benefit of hindsight, or with some inkling of what the band's African-American counterparts might have sounded like had they been given the chance to make the first jazz records. (Piano-roll firms, for example, caught on much earlier to the marketing potential of presenting music by black players like James P. Johnson. His May 1917 Universal roll of *Steeplechase Rag* – a transitional piece on the cusp of moving from ragtime to jazz – is a more accomplished composition, a more complex structure, and a more dramatically executed performance than anything the O.D.J.B. managed to produce over the next five years.) Nevertheless, it is indisputable that the band had an enormous impact, and its discs contained music like nothing that the majority of those who purchased them had ever heard before. To the record-buying public – which at the time principally meant white America – the O.D.J.B. *was* jazz. Mezz Mezzrow wrote:

> They were fast and energetic and they had a gang of novelty effects the public went wild about, jangling cowbells, honking automobile horns, barnyard imitations, noises that sounded like anything but music. ... When I was just a kid, in Pontiac Reformatory, I was hit hard by the Dixieland Jazz Band's recording of *Livery Stable Blues*, but what really got me was the clarinet playing of Larry Shields and Nick LaRocca's trumpet that sounded kind of interesting.[51]

This ability to "hit hard" with sheer novelty was also true when European audiences heard the group in Britain in 1919, and it had a subsequent influence on many English players.

In the United States, the numerous five-piece bands, established in the wake of the O.D.J.B. to play the new music, such as the Original Memphis Five (despite its name a New York group), similarly cast themselves in the mold of jolly, extrovert entertainers. Theirs was music without the profound emotional depth of Bessie Smith, the nostalgic nuance of Morton's piano, the gritty power of Sidney Bechet, or the heartfelt joy of Louis Armstrong; and it would not be until the explosion in 1923 of African-American jazz on recordings, mainly cut in and around Chicago, that such things would begin to become available to the public.

Before that happened, the music of the O.D.J.B. and its imitators successfully exploited the phonograph record to disseminate a new style. Before 1917, no other radically new genre had used this technology in such a way, but following the release of *Dixie Jazz Band One-Step* and *Livery Stable Blues*, recording was to become, and remain, a vital aspect of jazz history. Even though the amount of improvisation in the Original Dixieland Jazz Band's performances was relatively small, their music was at least partially spontaneous, and recording was the only medium that could capture it effectively. As the role of the improviser increased in the 1920s, so too would the importance of recording as the means of preserving and disseminating spur-of-the-moment creations.

Equally importantly, for part of the 1920s, the sound of the O.D.J.B. with its collective polyphonic front line briefly became the definition of jazz in the public mind. Although bands exist to the present day that play in a manner directly descended from the O.D.J.B., this kind of collective front-line playing lasted little more than a decade as a current jazz style, in which genuine innovation was taking place. We can think of this polyphonic interweaving of clarinet, trumpet, and trombone, with occasional second trumpets or cornets and additional reed instruments, as being the epitome of what has come to be known as "classic" jazz. By the late 1930s it was already beginning to be "revived" with considerable nostalgia as the prevailing fashions in jazz moved ever onwards.

## Jazz on the Move

Freddie [Keppard]'s cornet was powerful and to the point; the way he led the ensemble, breathing at the right breaks and carrying the lead all the time, there never was any letdown. He kept the band paced better than a jockey does a racehorse.

Mezz Mezzrow, from *Really the Blues*

Some time before Tom Brown's band had traveled from "Dixie" to Chicago and helped to christen the music it played as "jass," numerous other players from New Orleans had followed in the footsteps of Jelly Roll Morton and Tony Jackson onto the variety or vaudeville circuit. In the same way that a band like the Musical Spillers carried new musical fashions round the theaters, or Ma Rainey added blues to the act she did in the touring minstrel shows and circuses, Creole and African-American musicians were taking their music to audiences across the United States.

As I have already mentioned, Freddie Keppard and the Original Creole Orchestra were one of the earliest bands to have carried the musical developments of New Orleans on to the Pantages, Orpheum, and Keith variety circuits from 1914, although prior to that, the band's members had already garnered some considerable experience of the black entertainment networks. Clarinetist George Bacquet, for example, had toured extensively in the South as the century began:

> I got started as early as 1902. Went on tour with P. T. Wright's Nashville Students' Minstrels. They toured the Dixie circuit – had a special train arrangement carrying a sleeper and a baggage car. There were two bands, a great big one and a small 10-piece orchestra. I played E-flat clarinet in the big band, B-flat clarinet in the 10-piece orchestra. We came back to New Orleans around 1905.[52]

Bacquet went on to play in John Robichaux's band, during which he had his first experience of hearing Buddy Bolden's "plenty tough" band at Oddfellows Hall, after which he claimed to have started to play in a less "legitimate" fashion himself. One trick (later adopted by Sidney Bechet) that Bacquet used in order to win battles of music for Robichaux was to dismantle his clarinet whilst playing, ending up with just the mouthpiece. So it was not just the O.D.J.B. who used tricks and antics to please crowds, and no doubt this stunt became very popular on the theater circuit.

It was not stunts, however, but sheer musicianship that got the Original Creole Orchestra its first big break after bassist Bill Johnson had lured his fellow players to Los Angeles in May 1914. George Bacquet himself was an accomplished Creole clarinetist, and a pupil of Papa Luis Tio, who had taught several New Orleans players to play in the prevailing decorative French style. (Bacquet did not go on to make many recordings, but a tantalizing glimpse of his filigree work is to be found in the brief clarinet solo on Jelly Roll Morton's *Burnin' the Iceberg*, from July 9, 1929.) According to Bacquet, Keppard's band had specialized in playing to ballyhoo prizefights before leaving for the West, and its first work in California was to do the same – initially playing just for tips at Jack Doyle's Arena.

> This arena took up a whole square block and was packed. After every bout we played, and when we played the then popular number *In Mandalay*, Freddie Keppard, our cornetist, stood up with his egg mute and old derby hat on the bell of the instrument. The crowd stood up as one man, and shouted for us to get in the ring, and screamed and screamed. That was just before the main bout. When we got down, Mr. Carl Walker (Mr. Alec Pantages' manager) stepped up asking for our card, and asked if Mr. Pantages would send for us, would we come do the theater?[53]

The musical prowess of the band was such that this story of the musicians that upstaged a popular prizefight made the local press, and the *Los Angeles Times* printed cartoons of Bacquet and Keppard. After an audition for Mr. Pantages, the band was invited to appear in his network of theaters, where the conventions of the day involved musicians creating an act to play a cameo scene or two with music, rather than just appearing in a concert setting. So when the Original Creole Orchestra eventually set out on the Pantages circuit, in Bacquet's words: "we formed a plantation act with a comedian doing the character of 'Old Man Mose.' " Reviews tell of this "old darkey" singing *Old Black Joe* and then dancing to the band's instrumental playing before falling back exhausted.[54]

Once out on the theatrical network, the band traveled widely, in due course appearing in Chicago at the Grand, and then moving, in late 1915, to the Winter Garden, and eventually the Columbia and American Theaters in New York. Subsequently, it traveled for 26 weeks with Shubert's Town Topics Company. However, in New York, in 1916, the band lost Bacquet, who stayed to appear in a new vaudeville act called *Irresistible Rag*, featuring his solo clarinet, before moving to Philadelphia to join the Lafayette Players at the Dunbar Theater. Meanwhile, Keppard, Johnson, and the others took the rest of their band to Boston. Already, by the time the Original Dixieland

Jazz Band arrived in New York, the sounds of early Creole and African-American New Orleans jazz had been heard widely across the United States.

It is significant that the West Coast saw the launch of the Original Creole Band's career, as California had attracted numerous African-American entertainers in the late nineteenth century, and many musicians from the South settled either in the Bay Area or Los Angeles in the first decades of the twentieth century. I have already noted that the term "jass" or "jazz" appeared in San Francisco before Tom Brown's band adopted it, and Tom Stoddard's research into the region's music suggests that it was in common use by 1913 or 1914 to describe the music of African-Americans in the Barbary Coast area of San Francisco, and of the city's white groups, like the one led by drummer Art Hickman.

The Original Creole Band itself did not use the term "jazz" to describe its music – Bacquet, in common with many older New Orleans players, tended to use the word "ragtime" – and the first African-American ensemble to use the name appears to be the San Francisco group led by pianist Sid LeProtti: his So Different Jazz Band, which adopted its name around 1914, and appears as such in billings that survive from April 1917 from a trip to Honolulu.

LeProtti and his colleague Reb Spikes, eventually a music store proprietor and publisher, were pioneers of jazz on the West Coast. Spikes recalled: "When I [first] visited San Francisco I think they just called the music ragtime. I wasn't playing music then . . . it was called jazz music [by] 1914 when I came back to San Francisco, because we were called a jazz band then."[55]

Both men acknowledge that well before Keppard and Bacquet arrived in California, it was New Orleans bassist Bill Johnson and his first Creole Band (with trumpeter Ernest Coycault) who had had an influence in changing what the black West Coast musicians played from ragtime to something approaching jazz. From their comments and a press advertisement that appeared in the *Oakland Sunshine* in December 1907, we can be confident that Johnson's impact on local players happened very early in the century.

"Will Johnson came here in 1907, playing bass with his Creole band," recalled Spikes, and LeProtti added:

> They were the first New Orleans jazz band I ever heard of. He went East from New Orleans and then came out here. Will Johnson was quite a character . . . he played bass fiddle with a

glove on it, and we was kind of amazed out here in the West to
see a man pick a bass.

Johnson's light four-to-a-measure beat was a marked contrast to the heavy
two-beat of ragtime – most ragtime bassists tending to bow the instrument
in the manner of a tuba on the first and third beats of every measure. Just as
Lorenzo Tio would explain the concept of "split time" to Barney Bigard,
showing how New Orleans melody players could anchor their phrasing with
a sense of two to the measure, Johnson demonstrated how employing a
swinging four beats in the rhythm section could be used to produce the sense
of ebb and flow between front line and rhythm section – the tension
between four and two beats per bar – that became essential to the rhythmic
momentum of New Orleans jazz. "I listened," recalled LeProtti. "And I says
to the fellas, 'You know that old heavy two-beat we play – you know we've
got to get that four beats like them boys.' "[56]
    In the period from Johnson's arrival in 1907 to Keppard's in 1914, Le
Protti and Reb Spikes came into contact with several other Louisiana
musicians, including Jelly Roll Morton, whose playing was described by
Spikes (who initially met him in Tulsa, Oklahoma in 1911) as "the greatest I
ever heard." The communication network of black "show people" seems to
have worked efficiently during this period in spreading the ideas that would
coalesce into jazz very widely indeed. When LeProtti's band was
conscripted *en masse* in 1917, it was posted to Nogales, Arizona, where
one of the band's concerts was reviewed the following year. It seems that,
whereas the music was new to the indigenous population (remote from the
innovations of Chicago, New York, and California), and equally foreign to
the journalist who reviewed the event, "the black infantrymen were
thoroughly familiar with the music and were a most receptive audience."[57]
Here is evidence as to just how efficient the touring network had been in
creating an audience for the music among African-Americans.
    Back in New Orleans, after Freddie Keppard's departure, his place in
various local groups was taken by Joe Oliver, by 1914 a 29-year-old
trumpeter, who had served his apprenticeship in various brass bands as well
as the Eagle and Olympia dance bands. The comings and goings of Oliver's
fellow musicians demonstrate that it was not just the big names like Jackson,
Morton, and Keppard who took New Orleans ideas out onto the touring
networks, but other players like bassist Ed Garland, who went to Chicago in
1914, or clarinetist Johnny Dodds, who spent a year around 1917 touring
with Billy Mack's Merrymakers. In due course, Oliver himself answered a

call from Bill Johnson to come to Chicago, and later he worked alongside Kid Ory and Jelly Roll Morton in California. While he was there, he established the core personnel of what would become his own regular band in Chicago from 1922, which is discussed in the next section.

The drummer who joined Oliver on the West Coast and subsequently worked with him in Chicago was Baby Dodds, who arrived by way of an extraordinary musical institution – the orchestra led by pianist Fate Marable on various Mississippi steamers of the Streckfus line, which plied between St. Louis and New Orleans, as well as venturing further afield to St. Paul to the North, and up the Ohio River to Pittsburgh in the East.

Marable was, according to Dodds, "a very light-colored man with red hair," and he had begun his career as a ragtime pianist and calliope player on the steamer "*J.S.*" in 1907. From 1907 until the 1940s, he was the unchallenged supremo of the calliope – a kind of steam organ mounted on the superstructure of a steamship, and traditionally played to announce the boat's arrival in port. Others who tried their hand at this instrument found it unforgiving and unmanageable, and pianist Jess Stacy, who grew up on the riverside in Missouri and worked for a short while as a calliope player, recalled that it was frequently possible to burn one's fingers quite severely on the hot copper keys. Marable's own mastery had not come easily, and on one memorable occasion in 1907, Captain Streckfus forced the seventeen-year-old pianist to play the instrument for an entire day at Bayou Sara, Louisiana, while the captain listened from a distance to his protegé's gradual improvement as he went about his business in town. Such tough lessons paid off, and Marable's prowess was such that at one river festival in Cairo, Illinois, the President of the United States emerged to dance to his playing as he performed *Turkey in the Straw*.

As well as playing the calliope, Marable initially provided piano accompaniment for ragtime violinist Emil Flindt (who doubled on trumpet and banjo). By 1908, the band had enlarged to include cornet and drums, and the four-piece group (in which the other three players were white) remained stable for some time. In a fragment of a memoir that he wrote about himself (in the third person), Marable recalled that it was on voyages south to New Orleans "where Fate got his idea of the New Orleans swing – jazz in those days."[58]

He also recognized that there was an entirely different quality to the music being played by black musicians, and in due course, abandoning his white colleagues, he organized a larger all-black band of his own called the Kentucky Jazz Band, which in two separate memoirs he dated as beginning in 1917. His fellow players had been recruited from his home town of Paducah, Kentucky, a riverside settlement where the Streckfus boats often put in for repair, and where his mother was a music teacher. In an illuminating comment, Marable made it clear that these musicians had some way to go to be able to play the way he wanted: "The Paducah boys played fine, but they couldn't play jazz the way the New Orleans fellows played it. I knew if I wanted to play real jazz I had to have New Orleans musicians."[59]

During his frequent summer voyages there, Marable set about recruiting a band of predominantly New Orleans players, earning his floating orchestra the nickname "the conservatory" among those who benefited from his strict musicianship and discipline. This band's all-round musical excellence had an extraordinarily widespread influence on musicians throughout the regions navigable from St. Louis and New Orleans, and there are plentiful accounts of Marable and his musicians playing for, sitting in with, advising, and getting to know musicians in locations as varied as "The Hill" (the musical heart of the black section of Pittsburgh, where players like Earl Hines and Roy Eldridge grew up), the riverside towns of Davenport and Cape Girardeau (where white musicians like Bix Beiderbecke and Jess Stacy got to know them), and St. Louis itself, where a thriving black music scene grew up around players like Charlie Creath and Dewey Jackson.[60]

Only two tantalizing glimpses of Marable's band were ever committed to disc, and this did not happen until as late as 1924. The recordings reveal a ten-piece ensemble that played tightly written dance pieces, with scored ensemble passages, plus solos and breaks that generally have the air of being composed rather than improvised. From comments made by most of the members of his band to have been interviewed or who set down their memoirs, Marable's group was probably playing this way six or seven years earlier, shortly after it was formed. He was a stickler for good sight-reading, working hard on the talented improvisers he recruited to ensure they could read the band's material. "During our Intermissions – He would help me out with my 'reading music,' " remembered Louis Armstrong, who joined him in 1919.

> I learned a whole lots of reading music Real Quick. – Fate Marable was a good Band leader – And very Strict on us when it came to playing that music Right. He is Absolutely responsible for a lot of youngsters Successes. Anybody who ever worked under Fate's Directions can gladly verify this.[61]

Yet at the same time as Marable wanted his musicians to read arrangements and become well-schooled players, he went out of his way to recruit musicians who could play improvised jazz. Among them were trumpeters Joe Howard, Louis Armstrong, Henry "Red" Allen, Amos White, and Sidney Desvigne; reed players Johnny Dodds, Sam Dutrey, and David Jones (who doubled on mellophone); trombonist Bebe Ridgeley; guitarist Johnny St. Cyr; bassists Pops Foster and Henry Kimball, and drummers Baby Dodds and Zutty Singleton. Paradoxically, despite having been recruited because of their New Orleans background, and because Fate apparently wanted "to play real jazz," very few of them got the chance to play anything approaching the kind of loose, improvised polyphonic sounds of, say, the O.D.J.B.

Baby Dodds remembered Louis Armstrong as the only one who played any improvised solos while he was in the band, and that unlike Joe Oliver's group, which was "a real jazz band," Marable's orchestra was different: "we played some semi-classics and numbers like that."[62] This suggests two things: first that Marable created a largish dance orchestra that was markedly similar in terms of instrumentation and approach to the syncopated orchestras of New York. It played a mixed repertoire of light classics and popular tunes, and involved a large number of New Orleans's best musicians from around 1917 onwards. Second, what Marable looked for from his New Orleans recruits was a *way of playing*, a rhythmic and interpretational freedom that imbued his arrangements with the character and spirit he had heard on his first visit to the Crescent City. These were characteristics he sought to instil in the musicians he later recruited from the shipping line's base in St. Louis, including drummer Harry Dial, who recalled: "you could not work for the man for any length of time and not become a better instrumentalist. He discovered a player's faults immediately and knew what to tell you to do to overcome them, or at least to improve."[63]

From Dial, we get a sense of what it was about Marable that was so influential: he would recruit a player even if that musician did not yet possess all the qualities Marable was after, and he allowed everyone to play to their strengths. Baby Dodds had featured his characteristic shimmy dancing while he played drums on the band's written arrangements. Louis Armstrong was given his head to improvise solos as he learned to read music, as was Tommy Ladnier, whose work with a Harmon mute (emulating his mentor King Oliver) caused great jealousy from his fellow brass players.

Marable's influence did not go away as the locus of jazz development gradually shifted from New Orleans to the north and east. He was the physical embodiment of a conduit for new ideas, spreading his music through a wide geographical area, and he was a widely respected leader and talent scout from the early 1900s until the 1940s. Because of his astute hiring abilities, he became a byword among musicians as a stepping-stone in any career, and this extended way beyond the early 1920s. Many swing players of the 1930s and 1940s graduated from his ranks, of whom the most famous was bassist Jimmy Blanton.

His band's influence on the "classic jazz" of 1920s Chicago may have been restricted to the qualities of musicianship he instilled in many of his bandsmen who went on to make their names there. But in the longer term, his ability to meld the rhythmic and improvisational talents of individual players to the needs of a large band playing written arrangements was an even more significant harbinger for the future.

## Chicago and King Oliver

> For my money there never was or will be a better place than Chicago in the twenties. Young musicians had the best possible opportunity for learning about this music because we had most of the great jazz musicians living among us.
>
> Bud Freeman, from *Crazeology*

So far in this chapter, it is evident that jazz development was taking place in many parts of the United States prior to 1920. However, as the new decade began, for a few years the main center in which the music moved forward became the lakeside city of Chicago. Two historical events established the town as a major center for jazz during the 1920s.

The first was a major demographic shift, known as the "Great Migration," in which 50,000 African-Americans from the Southern states arrived in Chicago in the years leading up to 1920. Such a mass relocation, spurred on by the wartime economic boom of armament production and the need for unskilled labor in manufacturing and packing, meant that the new arrivals brought musical tastes and awareness with them, and almost overnight Chicago acquired a knowledgeable and enthusiastic audience for jazz and the early forms of blues.

This black population settled mainly on the South Side, whereas the north of the city remained predominantly white. Although segregation was not as overt as in the Southern states, deep-seated prejudice and racial tensions existed, and in 1919 there were savage race riots, partially arising from the inadequate provision of housing for the newly arrived Southern workers. As the 1920s began, the continued influx of African-Americans was joined by post-war European immigrants, and the city's cosmopolitan character encompassed over 40 languages as communities of Germans, Irish, Czechs, Italians, Poles, and Yiddish-speaking Jews were established. These groups, too, contained strong musical traditions, and a number of the most talented instrumentalists in jazz were to come from such immigrant backgrounds. There was a cross-fertilization of European concepts of instrumental excellence with African-American rhythms and pitches which mirrored much that had happened prior to the 1920s in the cosmopolitan society of New Orleans. Surprisingly, despite the enormous musical influence of the black community, even as late as the 1940 census African-Americans accounted for slightly less than 10 percent of the city's total population.[64]

The second major event was the introduction of Prohibition in 1919, under which it became illegal to sell or supply alcohol. As soon as an amendment to the United States Constitution introduced this ban, opportunities arose for organized crime on an unprecedented scale. Mayor Thompson's *laissez-faire* administration and the energetic expansion of Al Capone's criminal empire went hand-in-glove. Soon, Chicago was the hub of a web of booze syndicates, speakeasies, and large clubs in which alcohol was freely available. The rough, violent tactics of the crime bosses went alongside the creation of dozens of jobs for musicians and entertainers in the dance halls, clubs, and bars controlled by Capone and his rivals, including the Apex, the Arcadia Ballroom, the Cellar, the Coliseum, the Dreamland, the Royal (later Lincoln) Gardens, the Nest, the Plantation, and the Rainbow Gardens. Many of these venues had been established immediately prior to Prohibition, during the city council's war on prostitution and drink, and had created a ready market for social dancing.

In a remarkable paradox, the very moment that Chicago fell to the lawless rule of the crime bosses, it gave birth to a golden age of musical creativity. The coincidental arrival of an audience for jazz, with circumstances where crime bosses sought actively to promote the music as a means to sell illegal liquor, attracted the finest musicians in the United States to the city.

These exceptional circumstances had much more to do with drawing many New Orleans musicians to Chicago than did the closure of Storyville in their home city in 1917. Down South, several of the music venues in the former District continued to flourish, and a number of dance halls still operated, but whereas Chicago was, as saxophonist Bud Freeman put it, "the fastest-growing city in the world, bustling and crass . . . still raw, still a young giant with belching steel mills,"[65] New Orleans was entering a period of gradual decline.

Also, since Tony Jackson's arrival, Chicago had provided a platform for several New Orleans musicians, and many had become well-known in the city, white and black, before the Prohibition era began. One of the best-known was the black violinist Charlie Elgar. He had a string-band background in New Orleans and had studied in Milwaukee before arriving in Chicago in 1913. His five-piece band grew gradually until it was a nine-piece orchestra by 1921, and he later added more musicians. Like Fate Marable, Elgar played "legitimate" ballroom music, but accommodated more jazz-orientated players, including Freddie Keppard, from time to time at his long-term engagement at the Dreamland, a roller-skating rink-cum-ballroom operated by Paddy Harmon.[66] Harmon later employed a similar large band led by Charles "Doc" Cook, and this adds weight to the idea that such large groups were well-established by the late 1910s and continued through the 1920s, independently of, but interacting with, smaller, collectively improvising groups playing in the polyphonic manner of the O.D.J.B., and, more importantly, of cornetist Joe "King" Oliver's Creole Jazz Band.

Certainly, the most influential among the African-American and Creole arrivals from New Orleans was Oliver, a large, striking-looking man with a scar over his left eye which made it protrude in a distinctive fashion. As I have mentioned, he had been sought out to come to Chicago by the ubiquitous Bill Johnson to open at a new club called the Royal Gardens early in 1918. Oliver worked there, in Johnson's band, but he also appeared at the Dreamland Café with a group led by the Creole clarinetist Laurence Duhé. Oliver alternated nightly between the two groups.

In Duhé's band, Oliver played for a time alongside another clarinetist, Sidney Bechet, who enjoyed a reputation as one of the most talented younger reed players from New Orleans, and who would go on to become one of the first significant solo improvisers in jazz, first in Europe and then in New York, where he was to make his first influential recordings within a few weeks of Oliver's own in 1923.

In Bill Johnson's 1918 group, the clarinetist was another important Creole musician, Jimmie Noone, and Bechet also joined this band for a short period that fall. More significantly, Johnson briefly brought his old friend Freddie Keppard into the line-up alongside Oliver.[67] A few years later, Oliver's reputation would be enhanced by the two-cornet partnership he established with Louis Armstrong, but his work with Keppard seems not to have had so significant an impact on the public, although he became increasingly well-known as time went on.

For three years, Oliver worked steadily, generally playing his two jobs a night, and becoming recognized as one of the best cornetists in Chicago. His speciality was using a variety of mutes to create a range of effects, and his skill was such that he could imitate a range of sounds, including a crying baby. Many musicians admired his deftness with a tiny cup mute, later formalized into a metal mute with the cup attached to the end of a sliding stem, and patented, to Oliver's chagrin, by Paddy Harmon, the owner of the Dreamland, as a "Harmon" mute.[68] Clarinetist Barney Bigard believed it was this particular ability that won Oliver the accolade of "King" in his home town. When Doc Cheatham arrived in the city a year or two later, he became such an admirer of Oliver's playing that he persuaded the King's valet to give him one of Oliver's discarded mutes – a tiny brass straight mute which Cheatham used regularly until the end of of his long life.

By 1920, Oliver was doubling under his own name at the Dreamland and a State Street club called the Pekin Cabaret. His band was a prototype of his Creole Jazz Band of a few years later, including Johnny Dodds on clarinet and Lil Hardin on piano, but in 1921 his somewhat troubled residency at the Pekin, a club that remained open until 6 a.m. every morning, with frequent outbreaks of violence, led Oliver to forsake Chicago temporarily for the period in California mentioned above.

In June 1922, Oliver returned to Chicago, and at the Royal Gardens, now renamed after former President Lincoln, he embarked on his most famous period as a leader, and, for a brief period, consolidated the New Orleans small-group polyphonal style as the most influential in jazz. This began when, in July, he summoned Louis Armstrong – whom he had made a special trip to hear playing with Marable, and whose career he had nurtured since New Orleans days – to join his band on second cornet. The public flocked to hear the Creole Jazz Band, with Oliver and Armstrong on cornets, Johnny Dodds on clarinet, Honoré Dutrey on trombone, Baby Dodds on drums, Lil Hardin on piano, and Bill Johnson doubling banjo and double bass. (Later, Bud Scott joined on banjo, and Johnson played only bass.) Their biggest impact was among other musicians. "The Lincoln Gardens was a nightclub, about the largest I've ever seen, a big square place that held several hundred people," wrote Bud Freeman, one of the crowd of young white musicians who was drawn to hear the band, and who first visited it as a seventeen-year-old in 1923. "It was very dark inside and always jammed ... strictly a black club, but they didn't keep us out. The bouncers and the waiters knew us."[69]

Freeman goes on to describe the uninhibited dancing, and the fact that the evening's music began with stock orchestrations of general popular music, not strictly jazz. The crowds that attended were there to dance rather than listen, and the floor monitor who controlled activities on the dance-floor would work with Oliver to determine the length of each piece, and when to change tempo or tune, to keep the patrons dancing. The band's drummer, Baby Dodds, reckoned the hall held about 600 people, and would often become so crowded that it was impossible to dance. He remembered:

> One couldn't help but dance to that band. The music was so wonderful that they had to do something, even if there was only room to bounce around. It was a dance band that liked to play anything. We didn't choose any one number to play well. We had the sort of band that, when we played a number, we all put our hearts in it.[70]

As well as the dancers, musicians, white and black, young and old, gathered to hear the sensational interplay between the magisterial Oliver and the young and brilliant Armstrong. As the evening went on they abandoned their stock arrangements and played ragtime-influenced pieces with several parts or strains, and they also played a healthy number of pieces based on the blues. "When the band played slow tempos, the [dancers'] bodies seemed to be glued together as though they were trying to move through each other," wrote Freeman.

On several of the band's livelier pieces, the cornetists took unison breaks that came as second nature to both men after their apprenticeship in New Orleans parade bands, but which thrilled the Chicago crowds, many of whom had never heard this exciting style before. Although Armstrong was to emerge within a couple of years from the shadow of his mentor, he was initially content to play a subsidiary role to Oliver. The extent to which this was the case is perhaps more apparent on record than it was on the band's live appearances. Armstrong related that Oliver was already beyond his prime by 1922, and was unable to play as strongly as his protégé, being forced to stand close to the acoustical recording horn when they cut their first discs, while Armstrong was "standing back in the door playing second trumpet," unwilling to dominate his mentor. In the flesh, the crowd at the Lincoln would shout for Oliver to "Let the youngster blow!" and Armstrong would take several choruses on the blues.[71]

Had the Oliver band simply continued to play its regular sessions at the Lincoln Gardens, it is unlikely that it would have had the considerable impact on the development of jazz that it did. It was the medium of recording that changed everything, and while Oliver's band was not the first African-American New Orleans group to record, it soon became the most influential. Kid Ory's 1921 discs for an obscure West Coast label had barely achieved the kind of distribution to have any lasting effect on jazz. White bands still dominated the market, and in 1922 the prevailing influence in Chicago, both on disc and in the flesh, was an extremely accomplished Dixieland band, half of whom were from Louisiana, called the New Orleans Rhythm Kings, that played at a North Side club called Friar's Inn. Their clarinetist, Leon Roppolo, was not only an excellent ensemble player in the manner of the O.D.J.B.'s Larry Shields, but clearly an interesting and inventive soloist as well, until his career was cut short a mere three years later by mental illness and drug addiction which confined him to an asylum. George Brunies, the band's trombonist, was a lusty tailgate player in the true New Orleans fashion, and continued to bring his swing and energy to Dixieland bands for several decades; and, as already mentioned, the group's sometime bassist Steve Brown was in the vanguard of players on the double bass. (Other bass players who played with the group included Arnold Locoyano and Chink Martin, who was to become a fine string bassist, but was recorded on tuba.)

Not only was this band popular with the public, but it had begun to inspire a new generation of local teenage musicians to try to play jazz. Bud Freeman wrote:

> Soon after our gang heard that first record of the New Orleans Rhythm Kings, I borrowed a pair of long pants and went with the McPartlands to Friar's Inn to hear them. . . . We didn't call this music jazz. I haven't the faintest idea where the name came from. We didn't use any musical categories. We just knew this was a new sound, and we got on and began to understand it through the records of the New Orleans Rhythm Kings. Bill Grimm, a student of the University of Chicago, took us out to the Lincoln Gardens to hear King Oliver's Creole Jazz Band. After that we never went

back to the New Orleans Rhythm Kings because when we heard the King Oliver Band, we knew we were hearing the real thing for the first time.[72]

When Oliver's band made its first discs in April 1923, it caused something of a sensation, and other jazz musicians wore out the records, learning the parts note-for-note. The young, white Chicagoan players whom Freeman knew, like Jimmy McPartland, Art Hodes, Eddie Condon, and Dave Tough (many of them alumni of the city's Austin High School), all heard Oliver's band at this stage and recall a group that sounded many times more impressive in the flesh than on its records, hamstrung as it was by the acoustic technology of the time.

The band's earliest discs were cut at Richmond, Indiana, for the Gennett label, a subsidiary of a piano firm whose studios (next to a railroad track and with uncertain atmospheric conditions) appear to have been a wholly unlikely place in which to make records. Subsequent sessions in Chicago itself, for the Paramount and Okeh labels, were not much more accommodating, but there is a distinct development in the music. This is most noticeable in the six numbers that were made in different versions for different labels. Most obvious, perhaps, is *Dippermouth Blues*, initially made for Gennett in April 1923, and then re-recorded for Okeh in June **[CD track 3]**. Both versions follow the same overall arrangement, with stops for the clarinet, an ensemble chorus led by Armstrong, and then Oliver's extended muted solo, ending (first by accident, to allow Oliver time to put down his mute, and subsequently by design) in a shout of "Oh, play that thing!" Oliver's set-piece solo broadly follows the same pattern, and indicates that he, in common with many soloists, had a routine worked out in advance that could be relied on every time he played the piece.

Between the April and June performances, a number of things happened. On the later disc the tempo is increased, and the band plays with more swagger and confidence. Perhaps this is due in part to familiarity with the recording process, and perhaps also to the fact that Baby Dodds uses more of his drum set, and relies less on his clopping woodblocks. In particular, behind Armstrong's solo he supplies a syncopated snare drum off-beat (on the second and fourth beats of each measure) that propels the trumpet forward. Armstrong's solo itself is more formed and ends in an upward flourish that has signs of the flair he was subsequently to display on his own discs.

Despite the foggy quality of acoustic recording, the second *Dippermouth*

*Blues* is a masterly piece of ensemble jazz. The arrangement fits the playing time of the record well, there is contrast between the clarinet, ensemble, and solo-cornet choruses, and there is rhythmic variety too. Compared to the way in which the Original Dixieland Jazz Band had been boxed in to the repetitive form of its arrangements, this is loose, flowing jazz that remains quite highly arranged, yet which has plenty of freedom, ebb, and flow in the manner in which the arrangement is played.

In case there should be any doubt about the impact the records had, the Okeh label saw to it that they were marketed aggressively. Oliver's band took to the streets on a wagon decked with hoardings advertising *Dippermouth Blues* soon after its release in August 1923, and the *Chicago Defender* reported that this and *Sobbin' Blues*, recorded a day apart, were "remarkable, and dealers all over the country are having very big sales of them." A subsequent issue noted that the discs' popularity had swelled crowds at the Lincoln Gardens; and in New York one paper praised these "barbaric indigo dance-tunes played with a gusto and muchado that leaves very little doubt as to their African origin."[73] As the band's recording career went on, it was billed as "the razziest, jazziest band you ever heard,"[74] and both its traditional repertoire, such as versions of old marches like *High Society*, and new original pieces by the band, such as *Snake Rag*, were equally praised. Yet, by the end of 1923, the band had broken up. Partly driven apart by Oliver's practice of bringing in freelance musicians to supplement or replace his regular personnel on recordings, and partly because of deep-seated New Orleans suspicion over the band's finances, Johnson, the Dodds brothers, and Dutrey quit.

When Oliver's new line-up took to the road in 1924, he added an extra front-line reed player (something he had already done on discs) and a bass saxophone, moving closer to the larger dance-band line-up favored by Fate Marable. As the 1920s went on, Oliver added further instrumentalists in a gradual move that reflected the fashion for fronting larger forces. Whereas some of the Creole Jazz Band's output from 1923 is, unquestionably, collectively improvised, small-group jazz, with a strong polyphonic character in the front line, the presence of two cornets in harmony or unison for much of the time, as well as the way in which Oliver used the two cornets in a microcosm of the brass-band setting to play breaks and lead ensemble passages, suggest that, to some extent, he always thought in terms of larger ensembles, and of a high proportion of pre-arranged or composed material. Back in the 1918 period, he had generally worked in a larger band setting with Duhé, whose line-up included three reeds (himself, Bechet, and

J. Pollard, with Pollard later replaced by Willie Humphrey). Hence, Oliver's importance to establishing a model for "classic" jazz on record, although dramatic, was short-lived. Few other bands were to employ two cornets in the same way (one notable exception being George Mitchell and Natty Dominique in Johnny Dodds' recording groups), and most other polyphonic improvising groups of the 1920s preferred a single cornet or trumpet lead. Once Armstrong left Oliver in mid-1924, first to play with Ollie Powers in Chicago and then to work in Fletcher Henderson's band in New York, he was gradually to become the dominant influence on jazz-cornet playing, but his greatest impact on Chicago happened after his return there in November 1925.

Before that, Jelly Roll Morton re-enters the story of the development of classic jazz, both leading his own groups and playing in one of the earliest mixed-race recording sessions with the New Orleans Rhythm Kings.

## Chicago and Jelly Roll Morton

We had a sketch of his tunes – a guide sheet in other words – and we went from there. . . . We ran over each piece a few times 'til we had it, then we cut it. . . . It was his lead but my improvisations.

Barney Bigard, from *With Louis and the Duke*

Oliver's Creole Jazz Band had proved that it was possible to transfer the main attributes of a regular working band to disc, and, through recordings, to reach out to a far wider public, in due course influencing not only other Chicago-based musicians but also players in many parts of the United States. By contrast, Jelly Roll Morton, for reasons I will outline shortly, had no regular working band, but, by focusing his energies on recording and publishing, managed to exert an even wider influence, becoming a best-selling recording artist and leading the way in tailoring jazz performance to the new medium. Although some of Morton's finest recordings took place after Armstrong had begun his trail-blazing work as a soloist, overall, his 1920s Chicago sessions illustrate the heights that polyphonic ensemble jazz could reach, with an emphasis that is almost always on the band rather than the soloist.

Morton's debut on disc took place around June 1923, leading a sextet under his own name (mis-spelled on the label as "Marton") that displayed several of the characteristics he was to refine over the following four years or so, in spite of some relentless and obtrusive woodblock percussion. In particular, these concern the transfer of pianistic and compositional devices to the band format.

In *Big Foot Ham*, for example, a lively ragtime-inspired piece, the second strain includes instrumental breaks by trombone, then trombone and cornet in unison, and then clarinet, which are skilful instrumental voicings of figures transferred directly from his piano arrangement of the piece, which he copyrighted shortly after this recording, and subsequently recorded as a solo approximately a year later.[75] Discographers are divided as to the personnel on this disc, but the cornetist (who may be Natty Dominique or Bernie Young) and the trombonist (who is generally presumed to be Roy Palmer) play with considerable drive, particularly as the band clusters round the growling lead cornet on the final chorus. Significantly though, Morton uses the alto sax to take a lead role in the penultimate chorus, playing a simple repeated figure, and he uses a similar device early on the band's other disc, *Muddy Water Blues*. Here, as he was often to do later, Morton employed the saxophone as a tonal contrast with brass and clarinet, and his thinking has more in common with generic practice in later large-band arrangements than with the simple polyphony of the O.D.J.B. In his tonal vocabulary, the full-ensemble, polyphonic style was just one of a range of effects he was able to call upon, and he produced dramatic contrasts in tone and timbre between sections of a piece by varying the instrumental forces involved.

Equally, the opportunity for improvisation was relatively limited, even more so than in Oliver's band. I have already referred to Morton having written out instrumental parts back in 1912. On the majority of Morton's early ensemble records it is clear that he similarly worked out and then notated, or dictated, the arrangement in considerable detail, leaving his instrumentalists a certain amount of liberty to interpret nuances of his compositions, or to take relatively limited solos over highly arranged backdrops. He granted the greatest interpretational freedom to himself, often playing delightful variations on his melodies behind the solos and ensemble passages he had written for his sidemen.

This approach to band recording was a practice he continued throughout his career, something borne out for me when the late Bill Russell gave me the opportunity to examine the original autograph set of band parts for Morton's 1939 Bluebird recordings, for which virtually every detail was notated in his characteristic, slightly spiky hand. (On these latter-day discs, only Albert Nicholas, confident in his own ability to reproduce the traditional clarinet choruses in *High Society*, played anything markedly different from the written chart.)[76] Although he is most likely to have dictated his requirements, rather than written them out, Morton's tightly arranged style is particularly noticeable in his session with the New Orleans Rhythm Kings from July 1923, in which the group was expanded to become a ten-piece band, comparable in many respects to Marable's instrumentation.

On its own discs from 1922 and early 1923, this band (initially using the name Friar's Society Orchestra, and employing an eight-piece Dixieland line-up of trumpet, trombone, clarinet, saxophone, piano, banjo, bass, and drums) had already produced a number of assured performances that are less stilted and have a more fluent, swinging rhythm than anything that had gone on record before. It is easy to discern from the band's playing why it was an important influence on up-and-coming Chicagoan musicians, prior to Oliver's discs. In particular, the use of the banjo in the rhythm section creates an urgent sense of forward motion, notably behind Leon Roppolo's clarinet solo on *Tiger Rag*. Also, in common with the African-American bands already mentioned, much of the ensemble's propulsion comes not just from the rhythm section, but also from the melody instruments of the front line, most notably the somewhat frantic trombone of George Brunies, who manages to play a new note on almost every beat of the opening chorus of a quintet version of *Weary Blues*.

The band's regular pianists, Elmer Schoebel and Mel Stitzel, were both composers, the former jointly responsible, mainly with trumpeter Paul Mares and Roppolo, for a considerable part of the band's repertoire, much of which, like LaRocca's pieces, continues to be played by Dixieland bands the world over. These compositions include *Oriental*, *Bugle Call Blues*, *Farewell Blues*, and *Tin Roof Blues*, and the band's recorded versions of them stand out from earlier discs not just because of their rhythmic zest, but also because they contain several examples of solo playing. With few exceptions, the Original Dixieland Jazz Band's discs are played throughout by the full ensemble, whereas the New Orleans Rhythm Kings regularly used solo choruses by trombone, trumpet, or clarinet to great effect.

This group of tunes by members of the New Orleans Rhythm Kings is important for another reason. These were among the first jazz compositions to be published and marketed as precisely that – sometimes with written hints that the band's recordings of each piece should be listened to before playing from the music, in order to catch the nuances of jazz phrasing and timing. This was the brainchild of the brothers Lester and Walter Melrose, who introduced the band to the Gennett record company, and then made sure that their Chicago-based publishing firm promptly brought out sheet music of the majority of the band's recorded numbers. The New Orleans Rhythm Kings also recorded Morton's *Wolverine Blues* some four months before they teamed up with the composer, and it appears that this disc was not made as a result of any personal contact between Morton and the band's members, but because of the working arrangement between the Melrose Brothers (who had published Morton's piece in February 1923) and Gennett. This informal partnership was to become typical of the white-owned control of both the publishing and recording media characterized above by Frank Kofsky, and it is particularly significant that from 1923 onwards, the Melrose brothers relied heavily on African-American composers to supply them with new song copyrights. They were able to use this flow of new material, and the musicians who created it, as calling-cards with increasingly more presitigous record companies to ensure that the compositions they published were as effectively disseminated by this new medium as was possible.[77]

Owing to this commercial association, Walter Melrose was instrumental in bringing Morton to Gennett's Richmond studios, both to record a solo selection of the pianist's compositions that had been, or were shortly to be, published by his firm, and to cut a small number of additional pieces with the augmented version of the New Orleans Rhythm Kings. Despite the additional reed players, the enlarged band is seldom unwieldy, and the overall impression is of an efficiently rehearsed group playing well-crafted arrangements. In common with the discs he made a month earlier with his own sextet, the band sides owe a lot to the way he approached composing for the piano. We know, for example, that on his piano pieces he occasionally specified band instruments to play particular elements of a composition (James Dapogny's edition of Morton's complete keyboard music includes reproductions of holographs in which such instructions exist)[78] and he seems to have had a clear idea of how to go about transferring *Mr. Jelly Lord* and *London Blues* from the keyboard to instrumental forces.

In the former, a couple of Morton's favorite devices stand out: the use of eight repeated notes in a dotted-quaver pattern between choruses, which drives the ensemble on into the next section of the piece, and a double-time section, in which most of the band speeds up, while clarinet and piano continue to play at the original speed. In *London Blues*, as well as Roppolo's well-executed breaks, another trademark Morton device is the way he re-introduces the rest of the ensemble during the final measures of his piano-solo chorus. Together with considerable invention, and variety in the use of breaks, and a genuine feel for the orchestral qualities of the line-up, Morton manages to smooth out his soloists' occasionally corny phrasing, to calm the more agitated aspects of the New Orleans Rhythm Kings' accustomed style, and to create a sense of both relaxation and swing that goes far beyond the band's own already high standards. We know from trumpeter Paul Mares that the majority of this band were not skilled readers,[79] but Morton's methods of dictation must have been employed in achieving his effect, and they were described in detail by the clarinetist in his 1926 recording band, Omer Simeon.

Simeon himself was a gifted reader, and went on to play in the big bands of Earl Hines and Jimmie Lunceford, as well as returning to the small-group format with Kid Ory and Wilbur De Paris in the 1940s and 1950s. However, he recalled that with Morton:

> we used to spend maybe three hours rehearsing four sides and in that time, he'd give us the effects he wanted, like the background behind a solo – he would run that over on the piano with one finger and the guys would get together and harmonize it.[80]

This is a world away from the heady concept, advanced in so many jazz histories, of instinctive musicians freely improvising together,[81] and in the case of the New Orleans Rhythm Kings, there is some irony that this was a band of white musicians, not all able to read instrumental parts, being directed by a highly literate and sophisticated Creole musician and, in a further irony, a Creole who had to feign being Latin American in order to be able to stay at a segregated hotel in downtown Richmond at the time of the recordings.[82] Because of the consistently high standards of Morton's 1926–7 Red Hot Peppers discs, and the assumption that the "classic jazz" New Orleans front line consisted of just cornet, trombone, and clarinet, his early band records have tended to be sidelined in jazz criticism. Even such a diligent researcher and musicologist as Gunther Schuller tells us (in connection with Morton's June 1923 sides) that:

> Morton departs from the typical New Orleans format of a three-man front line by adding a saxophone. Although the saxophone had begun to be used extensively in jazz by 1920, many of the

New Orleans-trained musicians were still opposed to it. Morton experimented with putting the saxophone into the New Orleans ensemble conception from time to time with mixed success.[83]

But this is, at least in part, another jazz myth. Photographic and anecdotal evidence from 1915 or so onwards shows us that many New Orleans bands had larger instrumental forces than the "three-man" front line, and routinely added saxophones. Duhé and Oliver, for example, both employed additional reeds, and Oliver's October 5, 1923 recording session for Gennett has C-melody saxophonist Stump Evans drafted into the line-up of the Creole Jazz Band. There is a strong case to be made for assuming that numerous Creole and African-American bands with New Orleans connections never used the orthodoxy of O.D.J.B. instrumentation, and consistently aspired towards larger forces; that Marable's expanded line-up was by no means an exception; and that Morton's recordings demonstrate from the outset how the strong individual sound of the saxophone could be used both within and in opposition to the polyphonic front line of cornet, trombone, and clarinet. (It is no accident that later revivalist bands of musicians who had had some degree of direct contact with early New Orleans players, like Muggsy Spanier's Ragtimers, or members of Bob Crosby's Bobcats, routinely added a tenor saxophone to the polyphonic front line.)

In many ways, Morton adapted the saxophone to the role formerly taken by the violin in the ragtime orchestra, although he was not above employing violinists himself, as on his 1926 recording of *Someday Sweetheart*, which combines two violins with bass clarinet. His early discs, as much as his later ones, show a new kind of imagination at work – a performer who structured his recordings as compositional entities; extensions of, and complementary to, his written pieces.

Yet it is also the case that Morton's most brilliant work with his 1926–7 Red Hot Peppers did much to enshrine the concept of the classic three-piece front line of cornet, clarinet, and trombone, because of the perfect match between his compositional ideas and the forces he employed to perform them. This band only existed within the recording studio, in the same way as Louis Armstrong's Hot Five and Seven (discussed below). But whereas Armstrong's recordings took jazz forward by comprehensively defining the idea of the jazz soloist, Morton's consolidated the concept of the ensemble, and in the mid-1920s that ensemble still bore a close relationship to the instrumental forces of the early ragtime orchestra. Also, Morton's work inside the studios was curiously unconnected with changes of style and fashion in the outside world, because he seldom led a band of his own in Chicago after his return there in 1922, although he periodically took groups of musicians out on the road as well as organizing recording sessions.

The main reason for this is that his habitual dabbling in pool-sharking, pimping, club management, and a dozen other mildly illegal activities that had hitherto gone hand-in-glove with his bandleading were closed to him in Chicago because the city was in thrall to the bosses of far larger-scale crime. Morton's character would have put him on a direct collision course with the mob had he gone about things in his normal way, and his loud-mouthed personality was outspoken enough in any case that word went out, in Alan Lomax's words, that it was "unhealthy" for other musicians to work with Morton in the city's speakeasies and clubs. So he was compelled to make his living from other aspects of music: as a song-plugger for his own material at the Melrose Brothers' music store, as a composer who was able to earn a considerable amount from royalties on popular pieces like *Wolverine Blues*, and as a bandleader for record sessions, many of which continued to be fixed up by his publishers (who took the credit for introducing him to Victor in 1926). Chicago nightlife's loss was to be posterity's gain.

His first session with the Red Hot Peppers, on September 15, 1926, produced three pieces, *Black Bottom Stomp*, *Smoke-House Blues* and *The Chant*, and these are the most successful examples of New Orleans ensemble jazz to have been recorded up until that point. For a start, there is a perfect balance between front line and rhythm section, with John Lindsay's bass and Andrew Hilaire's drums both clearly audible in the mix, allowing us to hear something that matches up to descriptions of how earlier bands are supposed to have sounded in the flesh, but which is seldom apparent from recordings. In particular, Lindsay's slapped bass on *Black Bottom Stomp* alternates between two and four beats to the measure, stepping up to four whenever an increase in momentum or tension is required, and demonstrating the inherent tension between two and four mentioned in the earlier discussions of Bill Johnson's playing and of Bigard's concept of "split time."

Second, although considerable elements of the pieces are obviously fully arranged, with soloists backed by different combinations of rhythm instruments, or playing short melodies in unison or close harmony; from time to time in each number there is a chorus or so of collective ensemble jazz – again used, as on Morton's 1923 discs, as one of a range of tonal effects, but so sparingly and cleverly applied that this appears to be what each performance is aiming at. The forceful lead cornet of George Mitchell is countered by the ornate clarinet of Omer Simeon and the gruff trombone of Kid Ory, who was, even then, tending toward the tailgate minimalism of his 1940s recordings.

*The Chant* was written by the New Orleans Rhythm Kings' sometime pianist and regular Melrose composer Mel Stitzel, and it was also recorded just seven weeks after Morton's version by Fletcher Henderson in an arrangement by Don Redman. The difference is striking. The Henderson arrangement, albeit for larger forces, is taken more slowly, and misses out on the glorious range of inventive detail that Morton supplies. Redman, by and large, simply harmonizes the melody of each of the successive strains for brass or reed sections (including a three-clarinet "choir") with soloists superimposing their work over these linear harmonies. Even in Henderson's most unusual chorus for banjo and organ duo (Charlie Dixon and Fats Waller) the same principle applies, whereas Morton not only comes up with greater tonal variety throughout, but alternates unaccompanied brass and reeds with the full band in the introduction, adds dynamic flares in the second section of the piece, and ensemble stops with a Latin-tinged rhythm in the third. Before the disc is a minute through, his combination of the unexpected and the inexorable is compelling. I also suspect that, even if he did not compose the subsequent solos note for note, he suggested the motific ideas for each soloist – the two clarinet solos, especially, are so markedly different (the first full of florid Creole decoration, the second based on a repeated descending bluesy phrase) that it seems obvious there was a compositional input of some kind, and this equates with the kind of instructions we know he generally gave to his soloists.

Morton's titles were shrewdly chosen. Even a band as accomplished as this might not have succeeded commercially had the material supplied by Morton himself or his publishers and song-pushers not struck a chord with the public. The very first piece the Red Hot Peppers recorded, Morton's own *Black Bottom Stomp*, was adapted from a two-part tune he had written the previous year called *Queen of Spades*, and re-titled for this session to cash in on a national craze for the "black bottom" dance, a fashion which had been slowly growing for a year or two, but which blossomed in the six months after the recording. At the height of the fad, the following April, *McClure's Magazine* published a feature on "the dance that set America wiggling," and gave credit for its national introduction to Perry Bradford. He told the *Pittsburgh Courier*:

> My folks live in a little Negro settlement named Darktown, just outside of Atlanta. Darktown is probably the dancing capital of the American Negro. The people dance in the open air and

indoors, at picnics and house parties, and in the church, most of all. Every prayer meeting of the African Methodist Church ends in a sort of Black Bottom circle dance, with the dancers clapping their hands and crooning and the preacher calling out the steps.[84]

Bradford wrote down a melody and lyrics, based on this dance and a song he heard sung in his home town, and introduced it as *Black Bottom* in a New York revue called *Dinah* in 1923, featuring dancer Ethel Ridley. By the time of Morton's recording, the craze had reached Chicago, and by 1927, vaudeville and "classic blues" singer Clara Smith was on the road with her 25-piece "Black Bottom Revue." Around the time of Morton's disc, several other musicians cashed in on the title: violinist Joe Venuti and guitarist Eddie Lang cut *Black and Blue Bottom* just a fortnight after Morton's recording; Red Nichols made two versions of Morton's piece in October and November 1926; across the Atlantic, English pianist Harry Bidgood cut a version of Bradford's *Black Bottom*, in January 1927; and, the same month, American trumpeter Arthur Briggs recorded the piece in Berlin; in February 1927, Fats Waller cut organ solos of both *Blue Black Bottom* and the unissued *Black Bottom is the Latest Fad*.

These were by no means the only musicians to cash in on the craze in 1926–7, but Morton's disc did well for Victor, and he followed up his first session with several more for the company, reaching a point where his group was billed as Victor's best-selling "hot" band.[85] Victor's publicists enjoyed themselves with the good-natured hokum on some of the discs, notably the sound effects on Morton's programmatic titles like *Steamboat Stomp* or *Sidewalk Blues*, and a typical press piece described the coupling of two titles from the December 1926 session by the band as follows:

> Jelly Roll Morton's Red Hot Peppers, whose name is extremely descriptive, have just recorded a stomp entitled *Grandpa's Spells*, played in a manner which would indicate that Grandpa was a gay old bird with a foot as active as that of a 20-year-old high stepper. With it is recorded *Cannonball Blues* by the same organization, and it is as blue as a Monday washtub.[86]

Much analysis has been devoted to Morton's Red Hot Peppers recordings.[87] Their key importance is as the culmination of his technique of combining improvised passages with formal arrangement and composition, and matching this to the medium of the phonograph record. The first three sessions, with Lindsay on double bass, have the lightest, most modern-sounding rhythm, although Baby Dodds supplied some propulsive and well-recorded drumming on the fourth session, which replaced Lindsay with Quinn Wilson's anachronistic tuba.

By mid-1927, the moment had passed, and Morton's polyphonic ensembles themselves were beginning to sound anachronistic. He was not to create such assured music in a studio again until 1939, when Victor's Bluebird subsidiary allowed him to reassemble a New Orleans-style band which simultaneously looked back to his 1920s successes and forward to the New Orleans revival which began shortly after his death in 1941.

The conventional view of Morton has been as a paradoxical figure. To quote Schuller: "His emphasis on composition and well-rehearsed, co-ordinated performances was unique and antithetical to the primarily extemporised polyphonic New Orleans style."[88] But is this really the case? We know, for example, that the O.D.J.B. discs were primarily exercises in collective memory for carefully plotted routines. We know, too, by comparing his 1923 recordings of the same tunes for different companies, that over a period of several months, King Oliver consistently played broadly similar arrangements of multi-thematic pieces. We know that Fate Marable, in the "floating conservatory," emphasized exactly the same qualities of composition, co-ordination, and occasional extemporization that Schuller regards as antithetical. If we look in detail at the jazz played by white Dixielanders, like Red Nichols, in New York during the same period, we will find a very similar mix of written arrangement and improvised solo or occasional ensemble.

The Red Hot Peppers discs are as close as we get in early recorded jazz to the New Orleans polyphonic style, and, in my view, they are successful not because they are antithetical to it but because they embody it. New Orleans jazz at its best, apart from the "ratty" or "routine" music so despised by Danny Barker's Creole relatives, has generally tended to rely far more heavily than has generally been supposed on pre-arrangement, and it has this in common with most of the jazz played by medium- to large-sized ensembles everywhere else in the United States in the 1920s. Small improvising bands did exist on a considerable scale in 1920s Chicago, many of them playing at neighborhood joints on the south side, and, in due course, several found their way onto record. But Morton's sidemen, by and large, were working in large, prestigious orchestras. Simeon, for example, was in Charlie Elgar's sizeable band. Trumpeter George Mitchell, banjoist Johnny

St. Cyr, and drummer Andrew Hilaire were members of Doc Cook's big band at the Dreamland. The paradox, then, such as it is, is that musicians used to working in large orchestras, playing a high percentage of written arrangements, should have been responsible for such a definitive collection of discs in the polyphonic New Orleans style. Nevertheless, it is no surprise that in the late 1920s, after moving to New York, Morton, like many of his contemporaries including Oliver, was, to some extent, seduced by the prospect of transferring his thinking to even larger ensembles, with an even greater element of written material.

## Chicago and Louis Armstrong

At that time Louis Armstrong could have been elected
Mayor of the South Side; he was loved. I can still see him
being carried clear across the dance floor of that huge Savoy
Ballroom by his cheering fans.

Art Hodes, from *Hot Man*

Although there were plenty of opportunities for individual members of Jelly Roll Morton's recording bands to take solos, none of his sidemen, even such distinctive players as Johnny Dodds or Omer Simeon, produced recorded performances that eclipsed the overall artistic success of Morton's ensemble work. It took the return of Louis Armstrong from New York to create the first substantial body of recordings in jazz history to contain extended virtuoso solos.

In his work with Oliver, both on record and in live performance, Armstrong had retained a deference for his mentor, and in a total of just four solo choruses in approximately 40 different discs by the Creole Jazz Band, there is little more than a glimpse of the talent that was to emerge over the next couple of years. His solo career began in earnest while he was in New York in 1924–5, in live appearances and recordings with Fletcher Henderson's band, and on a series of freelance recording dates. Two aspects of Armstrong's work emerged clearly in this latter group of discs – first, his ensemble playing with Clarence Williams's Blue Five, and second, his instrumental blues accompaniments for such singers as Bessie Smith.

With Williams he demonstrated his talent for leading a collective polyphonic front line, and in doing so brought an element of improvisation into the phrasing and timing of the lead itself that had not yet been achieved on record by other players. In general, the most inspiring solos on these sides are by other musicians, notably the New Orleans clarinetist and soprano saxophonist Sidney Bechet, whose energetic blend of inspirational ideas with formulaic fingering patterns that fell naturally over the keys of his instrument moved forward the art of reed playing dramatically, by integrating aspects of the decorative Creole style with the more heartfelt, bluesy idiom of the uptown players from his home town. In the handful of discs he cut before Armstrong's arrival in New York, Bechet's playing dominates Williams's bands – a piece like Williams's and Fats Waller's composition *Wild Cat Blues* [**CD track 5**] showing how effortlessly Bechet could interpret a ragtime-based melodic line and infuse it with syncopated heat and energy. Bechet's finest hour as a soloist was to come a decade or so later, but it is clear that by the mid-1920s his style was already mature and well developed within and beyond the polyphonic ensemble.

Armstrong's novel contribution to the Williams recordings (and a sister set of discs by the Red Onion Jazz Babies in which Lil Armstrong replaced Williams at the piano) is his inventive variations on the melody as he leads the ensemble. On *Mandy Make up Your Mind*, his muted lead is firm and authoritative, and he anticipates or delays elements of the tune with far more subtlety than, for example, Keppard on his disc of *Stock Yards Strut*, discussed earlier. Yet just like Keppard's recording, the main rhythmic momentum of *Mandy Make up Your Mind* comes from the front-line instruments, exemplified when Williams on piano and Buddy Christian on banjo threaten to race away with the tempo in the opening chorus, leading up to Eva Taylor's vocal. Somehow, Armstrong manages the almost impossible feat of continuing to provide a swinging, forceful lead while actually holding the excessive zeal of his rhythm section in check. He is equally in control during Bechet's extraordinary solo on the bass sarrusophone, one of an unusual family of instruments, and one which, in this register, sounds a strange and unattractive hybrid between baritone saxophone, euphonium, and bassoon. As Bechet makes a series of low, grunting noises, Armstrong delicately paraphrases the melody in the background, keeping the entire performance on an even keel. Armstrong's talent as a lead player is equally well demonstrated on other sides made under Williams's aegis, including the powerful *Cake-Walking Babies from Home* and the evocative *Texas Moaner Blues*.

This small body of work by Armstrong with Williams is the demarcation line in small-group polyphonic jazz between lead trumpeters who essentially derived their ideas from the timing and mannerisms of instrumental ragtime, and something altogether looser and more rhythmically daring. What Armstrong brought to small-group jazz was a sense of swing; a relaxed, yet even more dramatic and original way of interpreting a melody than that of trumpeters like Keppard and Oliver, both of whom were light years more inventive than players like Nick LaRocca, whose doggedly repeated ragtimey lead had precious little light and shade in it.

Although Williams himself was not a pianist in the Morton class, he was a resourceful songwriter, and he had the knack of putting together small groups that showed a consistent and imaginative exploration of the small-group New Orleans style, continuing to do so even when it became anachronistic. However, despite the efforts of such jazz historians as Charters and Kunstadt to emphasize the rich variety of music in Williams's output,[89] his most significant work is still considered to be his discs with Armstrong and, to a lesser extent, Bechet.

In particular, this is because these recordings were one of the ways in which Armstrong exerted considerable influence over those of his contemporaries who aspired to play in similar ensembles. Ironically, this style was shortly to be comprehensively outmoded by Armstrong himself in his Chicago recordings, albeit using comparably sized forces, so in the longer term, the other two aspects of his 1924–5 work in New York – with blues singers and in Henderson's big band – are more important. This is true both of his own development, and the long-term development of jazz itself, as, through a combination of unerring instinct and trial and error, he can be heard developing many of the basic principles of constructing and improvising a solo.

I have already touched on how Armstrong's discs with blues singers allow us the opportunity to hear his instrument mirroring the human voice. More than that, Armstrong's playing took on emotional strength from the lyrics and vaudeville personae of the singers he accompanied. His discs, with Bessie Smith, Ma Rainey, Trixie Smith, Alberta Hunter, and others, combine flamboyant and bravura cornet interjections with a sensitive display of human feeling; the first time in jazz that a soloist used this new musical language to explore emotions in any depth. A perfect example is Bessie Smith's *St. Louis Blues* [**CD track 2**] from January 14, 1925.

On this recording, Smith and Armstrong are accompanied by Smith's regular pianist Fred Longshaw on an organ – probably a reed organ or harmonium. Apart from providing a vague air of sanctity, this instrument comes as close as possible to creating a completely neutral background. It offers harmonic support, but no rhythm or momentum, just a gentle series of chord changes. This has the effect of throwing trumpet and voice into sharp relief, intensifying the conversational and dramatic aspects of their performance. Smith's voice is at its most powerful as she throws her emotional weight behind a blues that is all too often sung in a jazz context as something of a superficial romp. There is nothing lightweight about Smith's interpretation, but her evocation of sadness and despair is matched from the beginning of the piece by Armstrong. His interjections between the vocal phrases ("filling up the windows," as Buck Clayton was later to describe his similar work with Billie Holiday) is both an emphatic and assertive commentary on the lyrics and a lament which is sufficiently powerful in its own right that, as Richard Hadlock put it, "Armstrong commands so much attention that the listener might momentarily lose touch with the continuity of the blues song as interpreted by Bessie Smith."[90]

Up until this point, only Sidney Bechet, in a performance with Will Marion Cook during his 1919 visit to London that was glowingly reviewed by the conductor Ernst-Alexandre Ansermet, had indicated that jazz solos might be thought of in terms of art: "admirable for their richness of invention, force of accent, and daring in novelty and the unexpected."[91] Armstrong's contribution to the discs by several classic blues singers gave an even stronger set of signals that this was possible, although this was not something remarked upon by writers at the time.

Nevertheless, his contributions to Bessie Smith's discs would certainly have brought his work to a very substantial listening public. By the spring of 1925, when the two musicians recorded together, Smith was reputedly "the highest-paid Negro entertainer in the theatrical world."[92] Press notices from around the time she recorded with Armstrong demonstrate her popularity. "In Bessie Smith," ran one report, "the T.O.B.A. has one of the biggest drawing cards of the season. Safe to say, she's a huge box-office success." The "hundreds of letters, both out-of-town and local," that poured into theaters asking for her to be held over were also reported, while other news items confirm her reputation as "one of the greatest Blues singers," and she also displayed the badges of success, being "bedecked with costly diamonds and gems of priceless value" when she was attacked by a knife-wielding robber during her appearance in Chatanooga just a few weeks after recording with Armstrong.[93] With her records being energetically promoted by Columbia, using slogans like "wherever blues are sung, there you will hear the name of Bessie Smith, best loved of all the Race's great blues singers,"[94] there was no doubt that Armstrong's playing found its way into a very large number of homes.

He was also widely heard through his recordings, live appearances, and tours with Fletcher Henderson. In the winter of 1924–5, the band held forth at the Roseland Ballroom in New York, where it played opposite the white musicians of Sam Lanin's Orchestra, but in the spring, Henderson, in Armstrong's words,

> booked the band for a long road tour through New England and down into the mining towns of Pennsylvania. We stayed out all summer. We had the largest colored band on the road in the North, and we had a big welcome wherever we went. I now played a feature trumpet.[95]

Despite this, Armstrong's name appears in relatively few of the press notices about the band. Typically, journalists concentrated on the band's arranger, Don Redman, and on soloists who were already well-known in New York, and the other big cities on the Eastern circuit: Pittsburgh and Philadelphia. For example, one piece from the summer of 1925 runs:

> Donald Redmond [sic], a Pittsburgh boy and director of the orchestra, has promised special arrangements and several new numbers not yet introduced to the public. Redmond is quite phenomenal in his abilities as an arranger, and is employed by many of New York's popular orchestras. Included in this number are Vincent Lopez, Paul Specht and one or two other hotel orchestras. Redmond is known throughout the country as a most versatile musician, being able to play practically every American-made instrument with equal success. ... Joe Smith, another Pittsburgher, who was cornet soloist with Sizzle [sic] and Blake and their "Chocolate Dandies" is a member.[96]

In 1924, Smith had been replaced by Armstrong in Henderson's band, but before his return to the fold, alongside Armstrong the next year, Smith's name had become recognizable to the public through his fairly regular moves from one band (or revue) to another. Redman had worked hard to create a convincing style of jazz big-band arranging within Henderson's ranks.

Initially, Armstrong, who despite his musical prowess was otherwise quite shy (describing himself on arrival as "a wee bit Frightened etc."[97]), was given the third trumpet chair (for which not all Henderson's arrangements had parts), and he was required to take the occasional solo.

But, as he said, he soon became the band's featured soloist on a significant percentage of its discs and during its regular public appearances. Although at this stage in his career he did not command vast amounts of attention from the press or the general public, he made a swift and dramatic impact on his fellow musicians. His successor with Henderson – Rex Stewart – wrote graphically of the effect Armstrong had on other trumpeters who clustered around the opposite bandstand at the Roseland or the Savoy to hear Louis play, and whose adulation extended to trying to dress, walk, and talk like their idol.[98]

I shall deal with the effect this had on the subsequent evolution of the large ensemble in Chapter 4, but there are striking parallels between Armstrong's experiences with Henderson and his earlier work with Marable. In both cases he was required as a soloist to bring his unique qualities of swing and improvisation to a band playing arrangements that were largely crafted in the fashion of the day. The difference is that, because Henderson made recordings, we can hear a wide range of examples showing just how these qualities differed from the prevailing style of the rest of the band. It became Don Redman's challenge to find ways of incorporating Armstrong's solos into what still seems to modern ears a very pedestrian style of arrangement.

The Henderson band's celebrated reworking of *Dippermouth Blues* into *Sugar Foot Stomp* is one obvious example, but this mainly shows Armstrong adopting Oliver's mannerisms on his pre-set choruses and transferring them to a broader setting. More indicative of Armstrong's effect on the band is the startling contrast between the lumpy two-beat of the ensemble and the swinging four-to-a-measure feel of Armstrong's solo (emphasized by Kaiser Marshall's off-beat cymbals) on *I Miss My Swiss*, cut by a contingent from Henderson's band under the name Southern Serenaders in August 1925. This short solo, and similar muted examples, such as the full band's *Tell Me Dreamy Eyes* from the previous October, show Armstrong basing his ideas on familiar thematic fragments from the melody of the piece, and radically reconstructing them in terms both of melodic contour and rhythm.

Redman's arrangements tend to carry the melody on either brass or reeds, with the other section used in apposition to add banjo-like syncopated figures behind the tune, often with neatly executed stops at the end of a chorus. In both recordings I have mentioned, Armstrong follows such arranged sections by playing solos against a less dense background, supported by no more than a simple rhythm from banjo, tuba, and drums. His improvisations cut across this regular accompaniment, and shift the rhythmic and tonal emphasis around (much as he did in his lead parts with Clarence Williams). Often, he deftly inserts little bravura flourishes, such as the demi-semiquaver upward run that ends the sixteenth bar of his solo on *I Miss My Swiss*, that is dashed off with nonchalant ease.

The need to accommodate such free-flowing solos made a gradual impression on big-band arrangers, and Armstrong's presence in Henderson's band sparked a gradual move toward greater opportunities for other soloists to take a role comparable to that pioneered by the cornetist. In his discs with Henderson, Armstrong drew together the rhythmic and melodic freedom he demonstrated so dramatically on his contemporaneous small-group and blues recordings, and he united this with a clear sense of compositional construction in his solos. These were the qualities he was to develop to unprecedented heights on his return to Chicago and the beginning of his own recording contract for the Okeh company.

The discs that Armstrong made, from November 1925 until December 1928, with his Hot Five, Hot Seven, and Savoy Ballroom Five, became extremely influential all over the world. They confirmed that Armstrong had successfully combined emotional depth, rhythmic innovation, and a liberating sense of solo freedom into a heady and original mixture. He pushed at the boundaries of the cornet's range. Even in his hottest solos, he explored a lyricism that might, in part, have come from his love for light classics and opera (indeed he regularly played a selection from *Cavalleria Rusticana* as his solo feature with Erskine Tate's band during this period).[99] Overall, he brought a new set of aesthetic qualities into jazz, a sense that there could be considerable artistic worth in music conceived as popular entertainment.

Yet his activities in the recording studio, and their sublime results, had little to do with his everyday working life at a series of Chicago theaters or black-and-tan cabarets. Principal among these, he was the featured soloist with his wife Lil's band at the Dreamland, then with Erskine Tate's large orchestra at the Vendome Theater, and (after doubling between locations for a spell), ultimately, with Carroll Dickerson's band at the Sunset and the Savoy Dance Hall. In all these groups Armstrong played, as he had begun to do with Marable and continued with Henderson, as a soloist within a large, predominantly arranged, ensemble. The cabaret bands generally accompanied floor shows with occasional instrumental interludes, whereas Tate's orchestra played for silent films, plus a few pieces between each showing, including features for Armstrong, who began to use the brighter-toned trumpet for these appearances. By the end of the 1920s, when he began leading his own big bands in New York, and subsequently on tour, he was simply continuing a way of playing that he had begun much earlier.

From his handful of late 1920s large-band recordings made in Chicago, one example, *Chicago Breakdown* (a Jelly Roll Morton composition originally titled *Stratford Hunch*), cut under Armstrong's own leadership in May 1927, exemplifies some aspects of his solo playing that were transferred directly into the Hot Five and Hot Seven small group discs. As well as the way his trumpet is obvious in the ensembles, these include a stop chorus that follows Earl Hines's assured piano, and Armstrong's subsequent solo with guitar accompaniment.

In the other such large-band recordings he made, from 1926 onwards, we can hear Armstrong continuing to draw together the three components of his New York work: paraphrasing the melody as he played lead (and, in due course, substituting new melodies of his own based on the underlying chords), incorporating vocal nuances into his solos, and using his solo choruses to inject swing and momentum into even the most mundane arrangement. These discs (with Tate in May 1926 and with Dickerson in July 1928) offer snapshots of Armstrong's quotidien routine, and are stepping-stones to his substantial and instrumentally brilliant series of big-band discs from the 1930s.

There is no doubt that once he had returned from New York, through his solo appearances, and also the promotional efforts of, first, Lil Armstrong and then (after she and Armstrong separated) journalist and bandleader Dave Peyton, the name of Louis Armstrong became very well known around Chicago. "I wasn't in Tate's Orchestra 2 weeks before I was makin' records with them for the Vocalion Recording Company," wrote Armstrong, "I became quite a figure at the Vendome, especially with the girls."[100]

Trumpeter Doc Cheatham told me how, shortly after his arrival in Chicago to play with trombonist Albert Wynn, in 1926, he was hired to deputize for Armstrong at the Vendome. He knew the trumpeter was "the talk of the town," and he had been along himself to hear Armstrong playing what had become a popular featured solo on *Poor Little Rich Girl*. "The people were screaming and hollering for Louis," he recalled. "As I stood up they screamed 'Louis! Louis!' When they got a good look at me, the screaming died away to nothing."[101]

Armstrong's growing fame as an individual musician was boosted inside and outside Chicago by the recordings he began to make under his own name. These started with a small-group instrumentation that used the New

Orleans formula of cornet (or trumpet), clarinet, and trombone, with a rhythm section of piano and banjo. Occasionally, Armstrong added the virtuoso guitarist Lonnie Johnson, and later he brought in tuba and drums to make his Hot Five into his Hot Seven. As I have said, these discs mark his transformation into the first heavyweight soloist in jazz. In them he achieved some of his best and most inspirational playing, at the very time his personal life was in turmoil – splitting up from Lil and taking up with a new girlfriend, Alpha Smith. Yet, at least to start with, Lil had been an important element in Armstrong's success. She promoted his career, hired him to play with her own eight-piece group, and co-wrote many of the pieces he played. Materially, they were successful as well. Armstrong wrote:

> Lil and I were making real good money between us and we began to do what we wanted. I never had any time to be at home except just for a few hours' sleep. I met myself coming and going. I guess it was about that time, and because of that, that Lil and I first started to drift apart.[102]

For his recordings, Armstrong was clear in his own mind that by recruiting colleagues from his home town, plus Lil, who had worked with all of them, he would be able to rely on their collective experience. He recalled:

> The minute Mr. Fern [sic] (President of the Okeh Company) gave me the go sign I hit the phone and called the Musicians' Union, and asked permission to hire Kid Ory, Johnny St. Cyr, and Johnny Dodds (who was already in Chicago playing at Kelly's Stable). ... We began to really get into the groove, the New Orleans groove.[103]

There are several pieces in the band's output that do incorporate the polyphonic New Orleans ensemble style. However, as its recording career went on there were fewer and fewer such examples, since the discs increasingly became a setting for Armstrong's virtuoso solos, which increased in drama, confidence, and daring from session to session, and were only matched for inventiveness by the contribution of pianist Earl Hines, who replaced Lil Armstrong from early 1928.

From the very inception of the group there are obvious signs of Armstrong's thinking having been conditioned by his work with larger forces. His definition of "New Orleans groove" is perhaps closer to

Marable's concept of a "way of playing" than to what Schuller termed the "primarily extemporised polyphonic New Orleans style." Certainly, the band seldom, if ever, achieves the unity of purpose, balance, and cohesion achieved by Morton with his Red Hot Peppers. This had something to do with the way the repertoire was created. Many of the numbers Armstrong recorded were written by himself and Lil. "I used to sit on the back steps of Lil's house and write five or six songs a day . . . just lead sheets . . . and Lil would put the other parts to them, cornet, clarinet, trombone etc."[104] In the studio the routines appear to have been hurriedly transmitted to the others, and even in the surviving issued discs from the first few sessions there are examples of Armstrong himself hitting fluffed notes, or occasionally messing up the chord sequence.

These arrangements frequently use the other horns to create backdrops for Armstrong's solo playing, just as a big-band arranger might use entire sections, and several of the pieces are structured so that the solos are played over repetitions of the same chord sequence, using rhythm-section stops, occasional breaks, or repeated off-beats to create contrasts between choruses, rather than introducing new harmonic sequences like the multi-strain rags of Oliver or the O.D.J.B., or Morton's even more complex arrangements.

These traits were apparent early on in the life of the new recording group. For example, *Cornet Chop Suey*, from February 26, 1926, is a bravura cornet solo in which (apart from a stodgy chorus-length piano solo from Lil Armstrong) the rest of the band are mere passengers as Armstrong creates all the movement and life of the piece. In *Oriental Strut*, from the same date, the minor vamps of the opening, and a subsequent chorus in which the trombone boldly underpins the supporting harmonies, give Armstrong the opportunity to lead the ensemble with what is in effect a solo, and after his subsequent cornet breaks, he leads the out-choruses in a similarly dominant manner, using a flared high note (in the traditional style demonstrated by Keppard) to usher in the final run through the sequence.

The most complete early example of large-band thinking transferred to the Hot Five comes in *Skid-dat-de-dat* (November 1926), where for a great part of the piece the clarinet and trombone simply hold long notes behind the cornet. They return to this form of accompaniment even after their own solo breaks, and the constantly changing texture – achieved by alternating short sequences of clarinet, Armstrong's wordless "scat" singing, trombone, clarinet, more scat, and so on – is reminiscent of the contrasts of a typical big-band arrangement of the period. A further contrast between the other soloists and the trumpet is the daring harmonic invention that Armstrong brings to his breaks, not being restricted to the prevailing key, but setting up concepts of bitonality that would sit happily in the experimental jazz of the 1940s.

As the series went on, Armstrong's confidence and abilities grew, so that he began creating masterful and memorable solos of great beauty and invention at almost every session. His lead playing grew more flexible, his melodic paraphrases more audacious, and his solos departed further and further from the written tune. His tone developed warmth and roundness, and he devised countless minor tonal variations from a broad vibrato, with which he frequently ended his longer notes or phrases, to upward moving rips and smears. The vocal qualities of his playing are obvious in slower pieces like *Wild Man Blues* (May 1927), and his invention reached its height in pieces like *Potato Head Blues* (also May 1927), *Struttin' With Some Barbecue* and *Hotter Than That* (both December 1927).

In *Potato Head Blues*, it is the series of inspired breaks that Armstrong plays over a sequence of stops that transform the piece into something exceptional, just as the way he trades vocal phrases with Lonnie Johnson's guitar on *Hotter Than That*, before capping everything with a series of audacious trumpet high notes, achieves a similar transformation. If one subscribes to the definition of jazz favored by Hugues Panassié in the 1930s that it was the presence of a magical quality of "swing," impossible to define, then these two records are sublime examples of it. They capture what the French pianist Stéphane Mougin (quoted by Panassié) put into words in his description of "swing," namely: "One must feel the musician to be completely at ease; you must feel him to be free from any constraint, even though his rhythm, his time, is marvellously exact and marked. In other words, such playing seems to be a divine gift."[105]

Armstrong had begun to sing on record early in the series, and although his natural range was still a convincing tenor, from the outset there were signs of the gravely tone that was later to become his trademark. *Heebie Jeebies*, on which he abandoned the lyrics for nonsense scat syllables, became his first substantial hit, selling some tens of thousands.

Earl Hines was the pianist with Tate and Dickerson, eventually becoming Armstrong's own big-band musical director at the Sunset. He was not only a skilled ensemble musician (his leading talents were admired by many of his subsequent colleagues including Dizzy Gillespie), but he brought to Armstrong's recording groups sufficient originality and panache as a pianist to complement the trumpeter's innovations as a soloist. The high-water mark of their work together was a 1928 duo performance of Oliver's *Weather Bird*, in which they swapped ideas with great fluency, neither falling into rigid structures of breaks and solos nor trading consistent numbers of bars. It shows an instinctive mutual understanding of the direction in which they were both taking jazz – where imaginative solo improvisation would be the yardstick of a successful performance.

One disc above all others from the Hot Five output points to the direction in which jazz was to go. *West End Blues* **[CD track 7]**, from June 1928, draws together everything in Armstrong's work up to this point, and consolidates his contribution to early jazz. He opens with a magnificent solo cadenza, states the blues melody, shares a vocal chorus with the clarinet, and, after Hines's imaginative piano solo, rounds off with impressively held high notes and a dramatic ending. It is tempting to describe this as simply a magnificent solo vehicle for Armstrong, but the disc is more than that. It demonstrates a way of using the old New Orleans line-up to create a new kind of music. The ensemble is subservient to a series of changing textures, the soloists are given space to develop their ideas, and yet there is a consistency and unity about the whole that makes it profound and moving.

The year 1928 was Armstrong's last full one in Chicago before he moved to New York, and began the phase in his career that elevated him from a supreme jazz performer to a popular entertainer. Away from the studio, Hines and Armstrong had already split up, as Hines worked with New Orleans clarinetist Jimmie Noone at the Apex Club, and Armstrong fronted his own big band at the Savoy. Until the Savoy ran into financial difficulties, in early 1929, this was where Armstrong consolidated his local reputation with the public. He was, as he put it, "getting to be a 'big man' on the South Side." As many of Armstrong's contemporaries began to make the move to New York, and Chicago jazz entered its final flourish before the onset of the Depression, *West End Blues* sounded the death-knell for the pioneering ensemble style of classic jazz, until it was self-consciously revived a decade later.

## Red Nichols, Bix Beiderbecke, and the Austin High School Gang

Now in the opinion of our group, Red Nichols was a synthetic player. He was a clever musician and made a lot of

records, but he was a very mechanical player. He copied
every line he had ever learned in jazz from Bix.

Bud Freeman, from *Crazeology*

Ogden, Utah, is not a placename that appears often in American musical
history. However, it was there that Ernest Loring Nichols (nicknamed
"Red" in common with others of his complexion and hair-coloring) was
born and grew up. The most prolifically recorded cornetist of the 1920s,
Red Nichols came to epitomize New York small-group jazz in the pre-
Depression years. For much of that decade, he was certainly better known
to the white record-buying public than Louis Armstrong, and although there
are no touches of genius among his recordings that compare to the discs I
have singled out in the last section, he was a good brass technician with a
clean execution and clear, ringing, tone.

Because he liked to plan his performances, even penciling out sketches
of his solos so that he left little to chance, Nichols's work is short on the
spontaneity and swing of many of the African-American small groups to
have recorded in the same period. Yet he worked hard to rectify this: first,
for example, by hiring many of the most technically accomplished players
in and around New York (such as the Dorsey brothers, violinist Joe Venuti,
multi-instrumentalist Adrian Rollini, and guitarist Eddie Lang) to bring
high instrumental standards to his discs, and subsequently (from 1929 or
so) adding some of the best of the young, white Chicagoan musicians who
had learned from Oliver and Armstrong (including Eddie Condon and
Gene Krupa) to inject the vital ingredients of life and fire. Together with
his long-term colleague, trombonist Miff Mole, Nichols produced dozens
of miniature examples of the energetic dance music of the "Jazz Age," and
he was also an occasional member of many larger ensembles, such as the
California Ramblers, which committed to disc a substantial body of big-
band arrangements, played by a pool of talented and adaptable musicians.
Despite being dismissed by such pioneer jazz critics as Rudi Blesh as
"stylized and restricted,"[106] the large and consistent body of work by
Nichols and Mole stands favorably alongside that of other white groups of
the period, notably the bands that involved cornetist Bix Beiderbecke
(whose own shimmering and beautiful playing was not consistently
matched by his recording colleagues), and those of the white Chicagoans,
whose rugged swing often made up in enthusiasm what they lacked in
finesse.

Given his family background, there was little doubt that Nichols would follow a musical profession, since his father taught music at the local college and was proficient on just about every instrument. As the son of so prodigiously versatile a musician, Nichols started lessons early, playing in the family band as well as a local brass group. He also studied piano and violin, and acquired the skills that were to make him into a fine all-round studio musician. He could sight read difficult parts, had a sense of dynamics and how to shape a performance, and he was instrumentally talented – all the elements needed to become a bandleader in his own right.

As he entered his teens, he played with several local musicians in Utah before going to the Culver Military Academy at the age of fourteen. By this time, in late 1919, he had already started listening to jazz records and tried to emulate the playing of the Original Dixieland Jazz Band, a style much disapproved of by his father. Although he had gone to the Academy on a music scholarship, Nichols was sent home the following summer and resumed playing in and around Ogden. His work included playing in pit bands at the town's theater, and this was also a skill he was to exploit in later life.

As his seventeenth birthday approached, he got one of those chances that is the stuff of legend, and which shows strong parallels with the African-American touring networks discussed earlier. A traveling band came to town, heard him, and offered him the opportunity to travel to Piqua, Ohio. The band was led by Ray Stilson, for whom Nichols played both cornet and violin, and both men went on to join a co-operative band called the Syncopating Five. This band had been a quintet when it began, but was a seven-piece by the time Nichols joined. We have little hard evidence as to the group's repertoire, or how it was performed. It is likely that it was a syncopated dance band, influenced (as many white bands had been throughout the United States) by the O.D.J.B.

They cut three privately recorded sides in November 1922, at the Gennett studios in Richmond, Indiana, where Oliver was later to record and where Bix Beiderbecke would also make his first recordings. The titles they recorded included a couple of up-tempo dance numbers: *Toot Toot Tootsie (Goodbye)* and *Chicago*. Although many critics (and other musicians) saw Nichols as deriving his style and playing from the records of Beiderbecke, he actually began his own recording career with these discs fifteen months before Beiderbecke's earliest session with the Wolverines. Nevertheless, the tables would in due course be turned, as Beiderbecke eventually did become a major influence on Nichols's approach to both lead and solo playing.

The Syncopating Seven, as the band became known, criss-crossed the country, in due course appointing the musically adept Nichols as their director, and changing their name to the Royal Palms Orchestra in order to secure a booking at a classy hotel in Atlantic City. From there they went back to the Midwest, and Nichols eventually left, in due course joining Johnny Johnson, with whose band he went to New York in 1923.[107]

At this point, New York had still only played a series of bit parts rather than a major role in jazz history. It was undergoing only modest population growth, having grown dramatically in the years before 1920, when there had been a big influx of African-American population to the city's northerly area of Harlem, but throughout the 1920s it was in the relatively stable political hands of the Tammany Hall Democrats, and so it had little in common with the turbulent population changes and organized crime of Chicago. Musically, in the African-American world, it had given rise to a local school of jazz piano – the "stride" style discussed in the next chapter – and it had played host to the Syncopated Orchestras of Will Marion Cook and James Reese Europe, in which numerous early jazz ideas developed. It also launched the recording career of the O.D.J.B. and a host of direct imitators, of which the most famous was the Original Memphis Five. Bands such as the Alabama Five, the Georgia Five, the Rio Five, and the St. Louis Five (collectively known for obvious reasons as "fives")[108] worked both in midtown theaters, and in dance halls and roadhouses in the outer areas of the city – Brooklyn, Coney Island, or Long Island. There was a growing trend among these predominantly white, educated musicians to use smooth arrangements and well-rehearsed ensembles to temper the aspects of jazz that had whipped up so much criticism in the press, such as its "mixture of acrobatics and cacophony," or its "concatenation of sounds . . . that has struck a section of New York . . . giddy."[109] But compared to New Orleans or Chicago, New York had yet to carve out a definitive local style of jazz.

Within a relatively short time of his arrival, Red Nichols became one of the core of musicians who managed to create a distinctive New York sound. It lacked the hard drive of much Chicagoan jazz, the earthy qualities of the "routine" New Orleans players, and the ethereal lyricism that was to become the preserve of Bix Beiderbecke, but it had jaunty syncopation, danceable rhythms, and a degree of control and sophistication that caught on with a public more used to waltzing to string orchestras, or – for those who wanted more excitement – the orchestrated big-band jazz of Paul Whiteman (discussed in Chapter 4). Furthermore, the New York style of the 1920s was predominantly that of white musicians. Unlike Chicago, which had its wealth of clubs, speakeasies, cabarets, and dance halls that were operated hand-in-glove with the mob, where the new music flourished in groups of every size, New York had a more diffuse live-jazz scene; many of the players who were to create the local style in small groups on record worked the rest of the time in the less jazz-friendly environment of theater orchestras, pit bands, and hotel dance groups. They relied on the medium of the phonograph record for their jazz playing to reach its widest public.

In 1924, Nichols took over Johnny Johnson's band for a spell, before joining "society" bandleader Sam Lanin. This band played at the Roseland Ballroom, and in late 1924 this meant they were featured opposite Fletcher Henderson, just at the very time that his personnel included Louis Armstrong and Coleman Hawkins. Lanin's group played its arrangements with brisk precision, to the extent that even Henderson and his musical director, Don Redman, were impressed, and sought out the charts they heard, only to discover that to put them off the scent, Lanin had marked fake titles at the head of his instrumental parts.

There is little indication in his playing that Nichols ever absorbed much from Armstrong beyond the ability to create a sophisticated melodic paraphrase in his lead and solo work. His concept of swing went little beyond dotted rhythms, and when he tackled a piece from the Armstrong/ Oliver repertoire, such as *Buddy's Habits* (December 20, 1926), his approach to the melody was polite, rather than inspired, leaving the heat of the chase to clarinetist Jimmy Dorsey and trombonist Miff Mole. The intricacy of the arrangement, and the precision with which it is played, is revealing of the personality of a man who apparently once said: "King Oliver's records were full of mistakes. So were ours, but *we* tried to correct them!"[110]

Nevertheless, following his tenure with Lanin, Nichols became a sought-after session man, and a player whom most large-band leaders were keen to hire. It was in an orchestra organized by saxophonist Russ Gorman for the *Earl Carroll Vanities of 1925* that Nichols met Miff Mole, a veteran of the Original Memphis Five, and the two men began a fruitful musical partnership that in due course culminated in dozens of small-group jazz recordings, under a huge variety of band names. Nichols's talent for organizing and arranging studio bands, and playing a mixture of precise lead trumpet and neatly executed solos dovetailed with the earthier personality of Mole's trombone playing. Mole was the first virtuoso trombonist in jazz, and liberated his instrument from the stilted tailgate style of players like the Original Dixieland Jazz Band's Eddie Edwards to become a fluent solo voice with a freedom subsequently matched by other white players, such as Jack Teagarden or African-Americans such as Henderson's Jimmy Harrison.

Mole became the link between the early New York tradition of the "Fives" and the city's coterie of floating session players of the mid-1920s, and along the way he also recorded with Bix Beiderbecke and members of the Wolverines in October 1924 as part of a pick-up band called the Sioux City Six, thereby establishing an additional link with the white-jazz tradition that had grown up in the Midwest.

In the spring of 1925, Nichols recorded alongside many of New York's star white jazzmen in the California Ramblers (a group which had its own roadhouse at Pelham Bay, and which drew a succession of recording groups from its large pool of personnel), but he was also in demand for theater orchestras where his experience made him a valuable addition to a band. Among those he worked with was the group nominally led by Don Voorhees, but in reality put together and directed by Nichols. It was the pit band in a show called *Rain or Shine*, and the line-up included several musicians who shaped the sound of New York jazz along with Nichols: Joe Venuti on violin, Eddie Lang on guitar, Jimmy Dorsey on clarinet, Joe Tarto on bass and tuba, and a relatively unknown figure called Dudley Fosdick on mellophone. Tarto recalled that Fosdick was "the greatest mellophone player during that period. Nobody ever followed him."[111] Playing the valved mellophone, in a range slightly higher than the trombone, Fosdick delighted in playing close harmony duets with Miff Mole, some of which found their way onto record in Mole's various sessions.

The *Rain or Shine* band was the first of a number of pit orchestras led by Nichols where crowds turned up to listen to the band every bit as much as to see the stage show. The group was visually exciting because Tarto had a tuba specially made that stood eight feet tall, which, as well as catching the stage lights as it moved, projected its sound out of the pit into the auditorium very successfully.

The distinct style of Red Nichols's recording bands started to emerge in late 1925, most of his groups involving himself and Mole, plus Jimmy Dorsey on clarinet and alto, Eddie Lang or Dick McDonough on guitar, Arthur Schutt on piano, and Vic Berton on drums. The earliest such discs came out under the name of singer Cliff "Ukulele Ike" Edwards and His Hot Combination, and more followed as the Red Heads, We Three, Jay C. Flippen and His Gang, and the Charleston Chasers. But the two most significant sessions were on December 8, 1926, when the first date was cut by "Red Nichols and His Five Pennies," and a few weeks later on January 26, 1927, when "Miff Mole's Molers" had their debut.

Before long, Nichols's discs were selling as many as 100,000 each, whereas the earliest Bix Beiderbecke discs managed only three or four thousand each.

The consequence of this was that, at the time, Nichols was more widely known to the general public than Beiderbecke. His discs exerted a huge influence on other musicians, African-American or white, both in the United States and overseas. Teddy Wilson, for example, recalled that Speed Webb's Midwestern-territory band, an African-American group in which he played from 1929 to 1931, had learned numerous Nichols arrangements from recordings. In Britain, according to critic Albert McCarthy, local jazz musicians learned arrangements from these discs as well, helped by the presence in London, for some months in the late 1920s, of a number of Nichols's New York associates, including Adrian and Arthur Rollini, Chelsea Quealey, and Fud Livingston.[112] And in some ways his reputation lasted into the 1950s, when Danny Kaye starred as Nichols (with the cornetist himself recreating his solos) in the biographical motion picture, *The Five Pennies* (1959), suggesting that he was seen at the time as a suitable subject for a movie, despite the far more dramatic account of Beiderbecke's short-lived, self-destructive career in Dorothy Baker's novel *Young Man with a Horn* (1938).

Comparatively, Nichols's life was unremarkable – there is nothing particularly glitzy about someone who made his living playing on dozens of recording sessions, or in pit bands – and it lacked the poignant drama of Beiderbecke's, in the same way that his own playing was workman-like rather than imbued with Beiderbecke's qualities of inspiration.

Leon "Bix" Beiderbecke grew up in a middle-class family in Davenport, Iowa, where he heard the bands on passing riverboats – no doubt including Marable's, because legend has it that he met the young Louis Armstrong during his time in the "floating academy." He was a self-taught cornetist and pianist, and although his formal education seems to have been a series of disastrous escapades with frequent episodes of truancy and misbehavior, he developed a keen interest in twentieth-century classical music. "He had a love of the great composers of the day such as Ravel, Holst, Schoenberg and Debussy," wrote saxophonist Bud Freeman, who met him in 1925 and was treated by Bix to an impromptu piano recital of Debussy and Eastwood Lane compositions. "It was Bix who got [drummer] Dave Tough and me into listening to them. They gave us a much better feeling for jazz."[113]

It seems a controversial idea that this group of European composers should have made any impression on Freeman and Tough's Chicagoan crowd, several of whom Beiderbecke first encountered as early as 1921, when he sneaked out of Lake Forest Military Academy to hear jazz in the clubs and speakeasies of the Windy City, where he subsequently joined the band with whom he first recorded, the Wolverines. Despite Freeman's pronouncements, I find little evidence of European classical influence on the recorded work of Beiderbecke's colleagues, but there is plenty on his own playing (just as it appears from the recollections of those who knew him that, particularly in terms of literature and the visual arts, he was well-acquainted with several areas of European intellectual culture in his general conversation).[114] In his mature solos, the choice of notes veers less towards the flattened tones of the African-American blues scale than to whole-tone scales or ninth and thirteenth intervals, played with a clear, bell-like cornet tone. He also adopted an unhurried timing that frequently placed key notes or accents slightly behind the beat. This created an air of relaxation, which he could stir into excitement by dropping the occasional phrase precisely on the beat, or by the odd dramatic flurry or rip into the higher register above his normal middle range. A good example of all these elements working together can be found in his lead chorus and solo on *Riverboat Shuffle*, recorded with Frank Trumbauer's Orchestra in May 1927 (rather than the less-developed version of the piece he made with the Wolverines three years earlier), where Hoagy Carmichael's tune has some of its rough edges smoothed off, and the solo itself is sufficiently relaxed to give the impression that Beiderbecke is somehow creating space around it, playing tricks with the time to sound less urgent than his supporting rhythm section.

Such a potent combination of unusual note-selection, timbre, and timing came to make an impact on many other trumpeters or cornetists including Bunny Berigan, Sterling Bose, Jimmy McPartland, Red Nichols, and Andy Secrest, as well as slightly younger players like Bobby Hackett and Yank Lawson. Many critics and musicologists have gone so far as to describe Beiderbecke as "the greatest white jazz musician of the twenties,"[115] and it certainly seems to be the case that he was one of the very few players whose ideas were not restricted to one geographical area of development, but were equally influential in the Midwest, Chicago, and New York, in due course spreading to Europe, and being adopted by such young brass players as Norman Payne in Fred Elizalde's English Orchestra.

The way in which this influence came to be felt was a somewhat haphazard process. Clearly, from all the oral history accounts we have, Beiderbecke made a tremendous impression on everyone who heard him in the flesh from the beginning of 1924 onwards, when he began working throughout the Midwest with the Chicago-based Wolverines. Eddie

Condon, for example, initially heard him playing piano: "For the first time I realized that music isn't all the same," he wrote. "Some people play it so differently from others that it becomes an entirely new set of sounds." When he finally heard Beiderbecke's cornet, "The sound came out like a girl saying yes."[116]

Bud Freeman also first heard him on piano, and gushed compliments, to which Beiderbecke's reaction was typical, spending the next few minutes introducing Freeman to Hoagy Carmichael's music rather than dwelling on his own. Beiderbecke seems to have been an indefatigable enthusiast for everything that was going on in jazz, and for the work of a huge range of musicians, black or white. He took Freeman to hear Bessie Smith, he escorted Condon round Chicago's nightspots, and he introduced many others to a wider range of music than they were accustomed to.

Yet, while it is obvious that such qualities as his enthusiasm, personal charm touched with reticence, and considerable talent account for his influence on those who heard him first-hand, it is harder for modern ears to accept the significance of his earliest records. His first tranche of recordings, made with the Wolverines between February and October 1924, seem patchy at best, and generally undistinguished. This is a view apparently shared, just four years after the discs were recorded, by Beiderbecke himself, who, according to his biographers, found the recordings "crude, musically simple minded, one-dimensional, and without depth."[117] Nevertheless, despite a high reliance on the routines and repertoire of the O.D.J.B. (unsurprising, given Beiderbecke's early enthusiasm for LaRocca's lead playing), even the band's earliest discs contain obvious examples of improvised solo playing between the arranged sections, and it was this, particularly the indications of Beiderbecke's own ability to shape his ideas into a coherent and logically organized solo chorus, that was so influential to the listeners of the time.

There is a gentle singing quality to Beiderbecke's lead on his first record, *Fidgety Feet* (February 18, 1924), and an unexceptional but well-shaped cornet solo on his second number from the same date, *Jazz Me Blues*. These discs were made eight months before Armstrong began recording with Clarence Williams, so at this point Armstrong had only been heard on record with Oliver (although Beiderbecke was familiar with his playing in the flesh). To the few thousand listeners, and especially the musicians among them, who heard Beiderbecke's first discs, they exerted an influence almost as potent as that of Armstrong's was soon to become. On the Wolverines' subsequent sessions, the stabilizing trombone of Al Gandee is absent, and despite some neatly arranged passages on numbers such as *Copenhagen* or *Tiger Rag*, there is a tendency for lengthy wandering reed solos alongside Beiderbecke's more thoughtful contributions, played with a particularly distinctive tone, although the acoustic technology of the time allows us to hear only a hint of what was eloquently described by one contemporary as like "shooting bullets at a bell."[118]

It was not until Beiderbecke reached the ranks of Jean Goldkette's big band in late 1924 that the modern listener can hear with any clarity his fresh ideas and confident personality in his first recorded cornet solo with the group, *I Didn't Know*. Just as Armstrong's playing matured during the time he was a featured soloist with Henderson, Beiderbecke's made a similar leap forward in the larger band of Goldkette, with the difference that he was never entirely comfortable as a big-band ensemble player, apparently never mastering the art of sight-reading, and for the most part relying on his quick ear and ability as a soloist, while those around him diligently played their parts from the sheet music.

The apparent mediocrity, to modern ears, of many of the Wolverines' recordings does not square with what his fellow musicians tell us of the effect the discs had at the time. Perhaps Jimmy McPartland was biased (he took Beiderbecke's job with the Wolverines when the cornetist joined Goldkette), but he said:

> There came out some new records on Gennett by the Wolverines. When we heard Bix on those we did another flip. How could it be so good? . . . What beautiful tone, sense of melody, great drive, poise, everything! He just played lovely jazz and knew how to lead a band.[119]

Hoagy Carmichael felt the same:

> The Wolverines sounded better to me than the New Orleans Rhythm Kings. Theirs was a stronger rhythm, and the licks that Jimmy Hartwell, George Johnson, and Bix played were precise and beautiful. Bix's breaks were not as wild as Armstrong's, but they were hot and he selected each musical note with care.[120]

It was these same Wolverine sides that led to the direct influence of Beiderbecke on Red Nichols.

On a large-band record by George Olsen, in June 1924, the arranger had transcribed Bix's solo from *Jazz Me Blues* note-for-note for Nichols to play. Nichols heard people saying that it was "just like Bix," and, on hearing about the Davenport cornetist, made a trek to hear him in person, playing with the Wolverines. They fast became friends, often playing alongside one another, and when Beiderbecke arrived in New York in the early fall of 1924, shortly before the Wolverines broke up, he stayed with Nichols, whom he introduced to a level of carousing, boozing, and decadence he had seldom experienced before. The signs were already present of the incipient alcoholism that was to lead to Beiderbecke's early death, and even at this stage (according to Ralph Berton, brother of the cornetist's regular drummer, Vic Berton), he was showing signs that he was plagued with self-doubt, particularly concerning his piano playing. All these negative factors eventually came together to put an end to Beiderbecke's career, after he suffered a major breakdown during his stay with Paul Whiteman's big band (following bronchial illness in late 1928, a subsequent collapse in early 1929, and, shortly afterwards, a violent physical assault upon his person). He died from pneumonia in 1931, his system and spirit beaten by alcoholism and the jobbing life of a freelance musician during the Depression. His early death, and the glimpses of genius in the lyrical and romantic sounds of his recorded legacy, created the most potent legend in jazz history since that of Buddy Bolden.

Beiderbecke's importance to jazz as a whole, and 1920s classic jazz in particular, can be discerned from his finest small-group records, which appeared well over two years after the last Wolverines session, when he played under the leadership of C-melody saxophonist Frankie Trumbauer, a fellow member of Goldkette's and Paul Whiteman's big bands. On these recordings, the cornetist produced some dazzling, shimmering cornet solos of great lyrical beauty, within arrangements that were perfectly designed to display his introspective talent, and a lead style that achieved as much by understatement as it did by gentle rhythmic emphasis.

The two finest examples of this both date from the early part of 1927: *Singin' the Blues* [CD track 6] and *I'm Coming Virginia*. The former is set in a minimal arrangement by Bill Challis, whose musical career interlocked with Beiderbecke's, and who played to the strengths of the musicians involved in this small-group recording, just as he had learned to do by writing for them within the larger ranks of Jean Goldkette's band. The Goldkette Orchestra will be discussed in Chapter 4, but it had an influential effect on many musicians, including Fletcher Henderson's band, which was resoundingly trounced when Goldkette's group played opposite it at the Roseland

Ballroom in New York in October 1926. Not only was Challis able to write for brass and reed sections in such a way that they were able to swing naturally and without sounding forced, but he built on the band's instinctive way of using its soloists. "They'd leave open a space for the cornet and saxophone and Bix and Trumbauer would fill it in like you wouldn't believe," he said.[121] And this was precisely how he tackled *Singin' the Blues*.

Challis told interviewers that in his writing he was influenced by Beiderbecke: "I'd listen to a couple of things of Bix's and put them in an arrangement," he said;[122] and he also took the trouble to transcribe Beiderbecke's handful of finished piano compositions into publishable sheet-music editions, thereby preserving at least some of Beiderbecke's interest in combining jazz and impressionism, in a form that others could play and analyze. If he did not share Beiderbecke's taste for booze and high living, the two men were clearly close friends, and together they explored the European and contemporary American classical repertoire for the piano.

After a short introductory ensemble, Challis's arrangement of *Singin' the Blues* (itself a former O.D.J.B. interlude) starts with an eloquent C-melody chorus by Trumbauer, whose clean lines are underpinned by Lang's counter-melodies. From the saxophonist's strong melodic statement, balanced by deftly executed and tricky-to-play runs or fills, it is obvious how he became a powerful influence on the generation of saxophonists that followed him, including Lester Young, who favored a similar light tone and vibrato-less sound with flawless and rapid fingering patterns. Jimmy Dorsey's neatly phrased clarinet solo towards the end displays comparable virtues, but neither has the lyricism, poise, and timing of Beiderbecke. The cornetist's phrases have the same hint of the inevitable as Armstrong's, and although some of his figures nonchalantly include unusual intervals, these are so un-selfconscious that they never occlude the clarity of his melodic line. The solo became a set piece, as beloved by brass players as Armstrong's best work with his Hot Five or Hot Seven. Rex Stewart, for example, who always talked of his debt to Armstrong, made a chillingly accurate recreation of Beiderbecke's solo when Fletcher Henderson's band recorded Challis's full-band arrangement of the piece in 1931.

The lyrical qualities in *Singin' the Blues* are taken further in Irving Riskin's arrangement of *I'm Coming Virginia*, recorded three months later. Beiderbecke's solo is a masterly paraphrase of the melody, and he continues his ideas with authority and poise over the final arranged ensemble, ending with a coda that leaves just his cornet and Eddie Lang's guitar trading phrases.

Beiderbecke made more small-group discs, under his own name and Trumbauer's, but the bulk of his remaining recordings were made from within the ranks of Goldkette's or Whiteman's large orchestras.

In the majority of his work his solos were placed in an arranged setting – from the worked-out routines of the Wolverines to the elaborate charts of Paul Whiteman. In his small-band discs, the polyphonic choruses were often planned in detail, and in *I'm Coming Virginia*, for example, the close-harmony section writing of Riskin dominates any freedom the ensemble might have. This is true even of pieces based on a collective recreation of the O.D.J.B.'s repertoire, such as Trumbauer's February 1927 *Clarinet Marmalade*, which has a close-harmony section in the center, and a similarly tightly written final chorus.

Beiderbecke, therefore, like Armstrong, made his main impact as a solo improviser within a context that was far from spontaneous, free-flowing, collective improvisation, but which had been carefully planned and structured by composers and arrangers.

So, too, did many of the colleagues who recorded with him, or with Nichols and Mole in New York, although few matched the creative improvisational genius of Beiderbecke's moments of solo glory – even those, like Nichols, who brought the composer's pencil to bear on the shape and content of their solos. However, one coterie of players connected with Beiderbecke, namely Adrian Rollini, Joe Venuti, and Eddie Lang, did manage to create a style of hard-swinging chamber jazz in a series of duos, trios, and quartets, where the informal intimacy of their groups encouraged a degree of spontaneity absent from their work with larger forces.

In part, this was the consequence of the long friendship between Venuti and Lang (born Salvatore Massaro) who had been at school together in Philadelphia. Their work is a natural and creative extension of the turn-of-the-century string-band tradition, and relies on an extraordinary degree of rapport, in which the lead switches effortlessly between violin and guitar, and in which Lang brilliantly combines melodic and chordal playing. Lang was one of the first guitarists to exploit electrical recording technology to use single-string guitar solos played close to the microphone that could be heard clearly over the rest of the band, just as the guitar's melodic lead in a string band was carried over the accompaniment of the other chordal instruments. Lang's obvious indebtedness to African-American string bands is demonstrated in the race records he made under the alias Blind Willie Dunn as duos with his fellow guitarist Lonnie Johnson – his pseudonym chosen, no doubt, to suggest to purchasers that he was African-American, not Italian-American. Lang had also been a part of the successful novelty band The Mound City Blue Blowers, who played a somewhat primitive, if robust, kind of jazz using home-made instruments such as the kazoo, and who visited London in 1924–5.

Following their arrival in New York in 1925, Venuti and Lang joined the floating pool of session players that were part of the Nichols–Mole circle, but they also made many discs in their own right, particularly a series under Venuti's name.

A piece like *Beatin' the Dog*, recorded in June 1927 by Joe Venuti's Blue Four, is a perfect example of their output and of the way Venuti and Lang instinctively understood each other. (This is testimony perhaps to their shared musical heritage, inherited from their Italian forbears; a tradition of jazz – and, in particular, string playing – that continues into the twenty-first century in the work of such players as guitarists Bucky and John Pizzarelli.) On this disc their intuitive relationship is combined with the prodigious talents of Adrian Rollini on bass saxophone. Only a handful of players in jazz have harnessed this unwieldy and gruff instrument sufficiently effectively to make any impact on the music's history, and Rollini remains its outstanding exponent. Here, as on so many of his other small-group discs, he provides an authoritative opening statement, recedes into the background of the ensemble to provide a flexible, syncopated bass line, combining the mobility of the double bass with the throaty punch of a tuba, and then emerges for a hard-driving solo that demonstrates his complete freedom from the physical limitations of his normally cumbersome instrument. On the third chorus, which includes a sequence of breaks for violin, Rollini anticipates the resumption of the rhythm at the end of each break, and then launches into his own solo at the end of the chorus.

Venuti's contribution is equally important – his violin playing is a considerable departure from the ragtimey style of New Orleans players like A. J. Piron, or Chicagoan bandleaders like Carroll Dickerson. He is an assertive lead player, in the same way as a cornetist or clarinetist might be, and also an inventive soloist, using the resources of his instrument to bring into his improvisational language its unique characteristics: high-note harmonics, double- or (his speciality) quadruple-topping simultaneous notes, and sliding glissandi. This kind of playing was to be a formative influence on many jazz violinists, notably Europeans such as Stephane Grappelli and Svend Asmussen, although there were several emergent African-American players who were making similar attempts to bring jazz vocabulary to the fiddle, including Stuff Smith, Eddie South, and Fiddler Williams.[123]

Rollini's work as a soloist on bass saxophone was equally effective away from these Venuti and Lang small groups, in the more formal arranged setting of discs by Beiderbecke, Trumbauer, and Nichols. In particular, he is responsible for adding a sense of individuality and swing to many of Nichols's discs that would otherwise have been stilted and unremarkable. His innate sense of rhythmic and melodic freedom is the more extraordinary, given that Rollini had been relentlessly pushed by his parents, and hailed as a child prodigy. His father, Baron Ferdinando Rollini, was an artist and engraver who was on social terms with classical musicians like Gigli and Caruso, and not only arranged piano lessons for his son from the age of three-and-a-half with the high-profile teacher Madame Negri, but had him performing in public to considerable acclaim the following year.[124]

Fortunately Adrian Rollini's talent and constitution withstood this early fame, and a good example of his accomplishments is *Cornfed* by Red Nichols and His Five Pennies, from June 1927. Not helped by an unusually heavy guitar accompaniment from Lang, described in the immortal phrase by fellow guitarist Marty Grosz as "a bit lumpy, like a guy running along with a pie in his pants,"[125] Rollini casts inhibition to the wind. He opens by trading phrases with Vic Berton's tympani, and in the first full ensemble (as well as the penultimate ensemble), he provides a counterpart to the largely unison phrasing of trumpet, trombone, and alto. Later, he adds a series of four-bar interludes and breaks, before settling in to supply the bass line for the subsequent solos by Jimmy Dorsey on alto and Nichols himself on cornet, finally reappearing as a soloist in the coda. His playing is a jazzy catalyst for the whole performance, and during the years he specialized on bass saxophone, in the 1920s, before moving to the vibraphone, on which he was less inspirational, Rollini managed to galvanize countless New York small-group recordings into life, as well as larger orchestras such as the California Ramblers or his own short-lived big band.

Within Nichols's output, Rollini's best work is to be found in his moody opening chorus on *Mean Dog Blues* (June 26, 1927); his assertive breaks, contrasting with his sensitive accompaniment to Pee Wee Russell on the gently paced *Riverboat Shuffle* (August 15, 1927); his mobile solo from *Eccentric* (cut on the same day); and his short, but free-flowing solo on Miff Mole's Molers' version of *Original Dixieland One-Step*.

Despite the presence of Rollini and the idiosyncratic Russell, making some of his first discs in New York after moving there from his native St. Louis, the tough Chicagoan school of white musicians, who were the regular associates of Eddie Condon, were highly critical of Nichols's discs. They found them over-arranged, jerkily syncopated rather than swinging, and, above all – notwithstanding Nichols's protestations to the contrary – derivative of the man they thought of as "their" discovery: Bix Beiderbecke.

Although he remained critical of Nichols, Eddie Condon was among the first of the influx of Chicagoans who came to New York in the late 1920s to work with him. Nichols was a wise enough musician to recognize that to stay in touch with contemporary tastes his bands needed the grittier sound and driving swing of these Windy City players, and, in 1929, Benny Goodman, Bud Freeman, and drummer Gene Krupa became regular members of Nichols's line-ups, Krupa staying almost two years.

The number of freelance record dates available to Nichols (and to all bandleaders) declined dramatically after October 1929 with the onset of the Depression. However, the New York entertainment business continued to operate – albeit on a reduced scale – despite the rapid downturn in the recording industry. In the months leading up to the Wall Street Crash, Nichols made a short film of the Five Pennies for Vitaphone, and then organized the musicians for a revue called *Almanac* by John Murray Anderson. It opened in July, in Boston, and then ran from August to October in New York.

The pit band included Pee Wee Russell and another strong soloist, Fud Livingston, who moved with Nichols, when *Almanac* folded, to a residency at the Hollywood Restaurant on Broadway and 48th Street, where Condon, Krupa, and pianist Joe Sullivan joined the line-up. Condon recalled that the band had to accompany a cabaret by three Greek dancers. The two males hurled their female colleague into the air as the act finished. "I heard Pee Wee's clarinet quaver as she sailed through the air," wrote Condon. "We all had the feeling that if we missed a cue she'd either keep going or fall on her face."[126]

The arrival of Condon and his colleagues brought first-hand experience of Chicago's white small-group jazz to New York, at more or less the same time as the major exodus of African-American musicians like Oliver, Morton, and Armstrong from Chicago enriched other aspects of New York's musical life. Ideologically, Condon's contemporaries fell into two groups. The first included Goodman and Krupa, who would go on to shape the larger ensembles of the swing era, and the second was made up of those like Condon himself, who remained true to the Austin High School tradition of informal small-group improvisation. In his eyes, the problem with Nichols's discs was that "the music is planned. Jazz can't be scored."[127] Perhaps it is principally due to Condon's powers of persuasion that many jazz historians from Blesh and Panassié onwards have believed this to be true of all classic jazz, despite abundant evidence to the contrary.

So far, I have referred to the Austin High School Gang in passing. The name derives from a group of school friends who attended Austin, which was near Washington Boulevard and Central Avenue in Chicago, in the early 1920s. Cornetist Jimmy McPartland recalled:

> Every day after school, Frank Teschemacher and Bud Freeman, Jim Lannigan, my brother Dick, myself and a few others used to go to a little place called the Spoon and Straw. It was just an ice-cream parlour . . . but they had a Victrola there, and we used to sit around listening to a bunch of records laid on the table . . . this went along for two or three months; we'd go in there every day, and one day they had some new Gennett records on the table. They were by the New Orleans Rhythm Kings and I believe the first tune we played was *Farewell Blues*. Boy – when we heard that – I'll tell you we went out of our mind. Everybody flipped. It was wonderful.[128]

Spurred on by this, the boys acquired instruments, and started their own band. They learned their repertoire by painstakingly copying recordings of the New Orleans Rhythm Kings. Before long, their influences widened, as did the circle of musicians itself, which soon included drummers Dave Tough and Gene Krupa, clarinetist Benny Goodman, guitarist Eddie Condon, and pianist Joe Sullivan. It became possible for them to hear the bands they idolized in person, and, in due course – as related earlier by Bud Freeman – to discover King Oliver and Louis Armstrong, as well as many of the other influential African-Americans in Chicago. Nevertheless, the Gang represent one of the first – if not *the* first – discrete movements in jazz to have drawn its initial inspiration from phonograph recordings.

The earliest discs by members of the Gang are distinctly patchy. Two sessions, from December 1927, by McKenzie and Condon's Chicagoans have plenty of elemental drive, but they suffer from intonation problems. Curiously, the up-tempo pieces *China Boy* and *Nobody's Sweetheart* both start with choruses in which the three melody instruments (McPartland's cornet, Teschemacher's clarinet, and Freeman's tenor sax) play the tune in unison (with occasional patches of simple close harmony), which creates the effect of the numbers being just as "arranged" as the Nichols recordings Condon so disliked, something exacerbated by the neat introduction and central ensemble passage on the second disc. The strengths of the band are its invigorating freshness, the rocking rhythm of Condon's guitar, Sullivan's piano, and Krupa's drums, with resounding tom-tom off-beats on the final sections of each piece. Lannigan's syncopated slapped bass superimposes a nervous tic over this, but is more or less an accessory to the band's infectious momentum.

Lannigan becomes a more integral part of the rhythm section on the recordings he made on tuba, such as those with a band called the Chicago Rhythm Kings about four months after the McKenzie and Condon discs. A piece like *There'll Be Some Changes Made* (April 6, 1928) is an excellent example of the Austin High style at its best. Muggsy Spanier provides a direct, uncomplicated lead, Frank Teschemacher's clarinet weaves a spiky obbligato around it, and, amid the same cohesive rhythm section, Gene Krupa's off-beat tom-tom accents once again spur the band forward.

When Muggsy Spanier became a figurehead of the first attempts to "revive" this kind of traditional or "classic" jazz in the late 1930s, it was this punchy, unfussy style of Dixieland jazz that he recreated with most success, simply continuing to play in the manner he had established in the 1920s.

I will return to the subject of the revival in Chapter 11, but it is worth noting, in passing, that throughout the 1930s, classic jazz continued to be played and recorded – although not at a particularly high-profile level. New Orleans-born trumpeter Wingy Manone is a good example – he led a convincing bluesy small band on record in Chicago, in 1930, called the Cellar Boys (remarkable also for including some of the first jazz accordion playing ever to be recorded). He went on to make numerous discs in New York in the 1930s that kept his energetic style of small-band jazz alive. So, too, did his home-town counterparts Louis Prima and Sharkey Bonano. The latter's New Orleans recordings from the 1920s (with Monk Hazel) and 1930s (under his own name) were followed up by a sequence of New York studio sessions similar to those of Manone, involving several of the same musicians.

Bonano was an exceptionally gifted trumpeter, and his playing on a piece like Monk Hazel's *Sizzlin' the Blues*, from December 1928, not only demonstrates his effortless mastery of diminished scales and complex breaks, but also shows him trading phrases with guitarist Joe Cupero, much as Armstrong had done on *Hotter than That*. In Bonano's work there is a degree of controlled relaxation absent from the more exuberant and less technically assured Austin High School players. He belonged to a tradition of white New Orleans players, all of whom, to some extent, shared his ability to match excitement with relaxation, including the trumpeters Johnny Bayersdorffer, Johnny Wiggs (also known as John Hyman), Johnny DeDroit, and the clarinetist Tony Parenti, the latter two both making records in New York as well as in their home town.

As the 1930s moved on, both the Austin players who remained in Chicago and those who had relocated to New York gradually added levels of additional sophistication to their work. In the case of pianist Elmer Schoebel, who recorded with his Friar's Society Orchestra in Chicago in 1929, this involved adding the kind of urbane arrangement Bill Challis had been providing for Beiderbecke and Trumbauer. His *Prince of Wails* (September 1929) is a neatly arranged chart, and contains one of Frank Teschemacher's most nimble and assured solos, less rugged than his first recordings, yet still full of bluesy feeling.

Condon, by contrast, continued to prefer the informal studio jam session, with hastily scribbled routines and often a mixture of African-American and white players, in which he relied on the talents of his individual soloists to provide the spark of sophistication I have mentioned. These sessions were often hit or miss in terms of overall success, but his best efforts came close to proving his dictum that jazz should not be arranged or scored. As Condon's distinctive style emerged during the 1930s, it developed into an encapsulation on record (later to be repeated in concert) of an after-hours jam, with little more than an opening or closing ensemble, and a string of solos, which at their best picked up and developed ideas from one player to the next like a kind of musical relay race. A perfect example is the informal blues *Home Cooking*, from November 1933, in which Pee Wee Russell's croaky clarinet and Floyd O'Brien's muted trombone carry the solo honours, between ensembles dominated by the fiery trumpet of Max Kaminsky.

In discs like this, and those of Bud Freeman's Summa Cum Laude Orchestra, from a few years later, classic jazz remained alive, creating a link between the inspirational musicians of the 1920s and those who sought to revive older styles during the 1940s and 1950s. As time went on, the degree of planning and arrangement, that is so obvious a feature of the earliest jazz on record, diminished. By the late 1930s, the polyphonic opening and closing choruses of, say, Condon's *Meet Me Tonight in Dreamland* (April 30, 1938) or Freeman's *Copenhagen* (March 25, 1940) are genuinely improvised – except not quite. What happened was that – particularly given that the Austin High School Gang's original inspiration came from recordings – the music took on a self-referential quality. By continuing to play in an established style, rather than seeking new stylistic territory, this group of players consolidated its style into something relatively predictable. In 1924, when Don Redman produced his arrangement of *Copenhagen* for Fletcher Henderson, it was at the cutting edge of jazz. By 1940, when Freeman recorded it, his way of approaching the tune had become so much a *lingua franca* among musicians that no arrangement was needed, and the players went through a different kind of collective memory exercise from that of the O.D.J.B. In recreating a familiar piece with slightly different forces, the performance is undoubtedly new, but it simultaneously refers to a recording well-known to everyone present. This disc, and others like it, mark the transition of classic jazz from a new style of music into something akin to folk music, with a tradition largely shared through the medium of recordings.

## The Chicago Small Groups

> Chicago was once the hottest café town in the United States, famous for sizzling music, torrid night life, a great little spot for the great little guys. But that's history now. Night by night it gets tougher for the cabarets.
>
> *Variety*, March 28, 1928

For most of the 1920s, Chicago boomed. Cabarets, clubs, cafés, theaters — all seemed to prosper, supported by a public hungry for entertainment and dance, and doing well for their owners, many of whom were involved in organized crime. But, as the date of the above quote from *Variety* suggests, the beginning of the end came for this flourishing environment for classic jazz somewhat earlier than the Wall Street crash, which had such a devastating effect on American life throughout the nation the following year.

Chicago principally fell victim to a federal clampdown against liquor consumption. In addition, the clubs underwent systematic attention from urban reformers who disliked the racially integrated nature of several of the jazz cafés. There was also a bizarre war of attrition between crime bosses as they saw the bottom gradually dropping out of the club business, and sought to eliminate their competitors, in the most extreme cases by fire-bombing venues such as the Café De Paris and the Plantation (hitting the latter while King Oliver's band was actually on stage). Mayor Dever's regime encouraged mass police raids against illegal alcohol in 1926, and by the time his successor Big Bill Thompson came to office the following year, the federal campaign against liquor had gathered such momentum that the city was powerless to stop it, eventually losing most of the key venues where jazz had been heard, either to the padlocks of the Feds or the infighting between the crime bosses. As William Howland Kenney put it, "the most famous South Side cabarets became increasingly notorious as gangland properties, cutting themselves off from legitimate businessmen in both the black and white communities."[129]

As a consequence, there was a slow exodus of leading jazz musicians, including King Oliver and Jelly Roll Morton, who made their way to New York. For many, their desire to leave was accelerated when the white local of the American Federation of Musicians, headed by James C. Petrillo, began to impose a color bar, declaring which venues would be open to African-American musicians, and which would only employ white players.[130] However, some big African-American names in the jazz world remained, mainly at the two large clubs catering for white audiences. Earl Hines began his decade-long run at the first of these, the Grand Terrace, late in 1928, protected partly by the strongest of gangland connections. Its counterpart the Sunset remained open into the mid-1930s, and in 1929 the bands of Charlie Elgar and Boyd Atkins were among those who worked there. Downtown at the Savoy Ballroom, Louis Armstrong was featured in 1929, before his move to New York to star in *Hot Chocolates* at Connie's Inn and on Broadway. Other well-known names on the Chicago scene hung on too, like clarinetist Jimmie Noone, who moved from the Apex Club, where he had played for much of the 1920s, to various other venues, until he eventually followed the tide to New York in 1931.

In the years leading up to this exodus, before the authorities moved to close the bulk of the clubs, Chicago had an extraordinarily diverse range of African-American groups playing jazz through the mid-1920s. The better-known bands, like those of Doc Cook, Jimmie Noone, Tiny Parham, and Albert Wynn, played in some of the larger venues, like the Plantation, the Apex, or the Dreamland. But there were numerous other groups as well, playing in far less salubrious surroundings, from middling-sized speakeasies to the dozens of "living room and dining room cabarets [that] lined South State Street between 43rd and 55th Streets."[131] This diversity is reflected in recordings made at the time as well. On the one hand, the informal musical life of the South Side speak-easy was reflected in the good-natured hokum of groups like Jimmie O'Bryant's Washboard Band, which appeared alongside blues singers and other loose-knit jazz groups, such as Lovie Austin's on Mayo Williams's Paramount series of race records. On the other, the sounds to be heard in the larger clubs were represented on a range of other record labels, including Jimmie Noone on Vocalion, Jabbo Smith on Brunswick, and Tiny Parham on Victor (after making the switch from Paramount).

Whereas Oliver, Morton, and even Armstrong's first recording groups had retained strong New Orleans connections, in many of the city's groups Southern players mingled with home-grown musicians, demonstrating the same kind of mixed influences and cross-currents as had been taking place out on the road in the network of African-American theaters. Whatever rivalry there might have been among gangland bosses and clubowners, there was comradeship among African-American musicians. Doc Cheatham, arriving from the South via the T.O.B.A., joined New Orleans trombonist Albert Wynn's band, and he told me: "As I got known in Chicago, I found all the musicians I met to be equally friendly and relaxed towards one another, which was a big contrast to what I found a few years later in New York."[132] In this "friendly and relaxed" atmosphere, a number of individual musicians stood out.

The bluesy clarinet of Johnny Dodds has already been mentioned in connection with Oliver and Armstrong, but he made numerous discs under his own name, with bands of all sizes from a duo (with Tiny Parham on piano), up to a seven-piece jazz band. He also appeared in a recording group in 1926 known variously as the New Orleans Wanderers or the New Orleans Bootblacks, which captured on disc some excellent examples of collective improvisation within some neatly worked-out head arrangements.

Another clarinetist from New Orleans, who I have mentioned in passing, is Jimmie Noone. He contributed to recordings by King Oliver and Doc Cook, but his principal legacy from this period in Chicago is a long series of discs, begun in May 1928, with his Apex Club orchestra, a band unusual in the recorded jazz of the time because its front line consisted of Noone and alto saxophonist Joe Poston. Whereas Dodds had a powerful, throbbing bluesy tone, Noone had a clear, delicate, almost classical timbre, and he also had the dazzling speed of articulation of other Creole players like Barney Bigard and Albert Nicholas. Some of his up-tempo playing, which darts all over the clarinet and moves effortlessly from one register to another, was a clear influence on Benny Goodman, and Gunther Schuller has pointed out the neat fit between Noone's playing on King Oliver's *Camp Meeting Blues* and Goodman's characteristic phrasing and tone.[133] To my mind, another connection arises out of the trumpetless front line of Noone's

Apex Club Orchestra. Because he took the lead on the bulk of the band's discs, Noone gave Goodman a model for his own small-group playing, so that in both his trio and quartet there are clear signs of the Noone influence.

The best-known example of Noone's work with his own band is *Apex Blues*, from July 23, 1928, built around a simple little riff shared between alto and clarinet. As the piece progresses, after a characteristically mobile piano solo from Hines, Noone takes center stage, with a gentle solo that has guitar punctuations from Bud Scott. The clarinet runs easily into the lower register, each note clearly articulated, and in the second chorus he produces decorative Creole trills and runs before leading the head arrangement to a close. The whole piece shows off the skills of a player used to leading from the clarinet and able to stamp his personality on a piece even at a medium-slow tempo, and using the warm middle and low register of the instrument, rather than moving straight to the shrill upper notes.

Right at the end of the decade, another New Orleans clarinetist recorded under his own name in Chicago with a group that included Earl Hines. This was Omer Simeon, who had been a member of Morton's Red Hot Peppers, and was to become a member of Hines's Grand Terrace Orchestra. In his trio and quartet sides with Hines, his playing combines the bluesiness of Dodds with the facility of Noone, and the up-tempo piece *Beau Koo Jack*, from September 11, 1929, is an interesting insight into how a briskly articulated ragtimey melody similar to *Shreveport Stomp*, which Simeon had recorded with Morton, is utterly transformed into something more modern-sounding by the fluid, audacious piano of Hines.

Of all the freelance musicians in Chicago, Simeon was one of the most prodigious, and he recorded with many of the city's leading figures during the 1920s "golden age," in the process proving himself to be an all-round musician and a virtuoso clarinetist. Among those he worked with were the New Orleans pianist Richard M. Jones, who organized many sessions for Okeh Records, and two of the leading trumpeters in Chicago at the time, Jabbo Smith and Reuben Reeves.

Jabbo Smith was one of the most unorthodox players and mercurial characters in jazz. His playing with his Rhythm Aces in 1929, several of them with Simeon on clarinet, reveals a man with dazzling, audacious imagination. *Jazz Battle*, the band's very first disc from January that year, has extraordinary chromatic runs and octave leaps in the final choruses, giving some hint of the brilliance of a trumpeter whom his contemporaries felt was one the few real rivals to Louis Armstrong. Smith had been educated at Jenkins's Orphanage in Charleston, had played in New York, and arrived in

Chicago in November 1928, when the traveling production of the revue *Keep Shufflin'*, in which he was playing, went broke after its financial backer was murdered. He had originally appeared in the New York premiere of the show at Daly's 63rd Street Theater on Broadway, with its co-composers Fats Waller and James P. Johnson, with whom he also recorded.

He gigged around Chicago, playing at a speakeasy called the Bookstore, and appearing as a regular "guest" at the Sunset, while waiting the inordinately long time the local musicians' union required for his transfer to come through. He began recording with Ikey Robinson, the banjoist, and was then signed up to record under his own name for Brunswick with his Rhythm Aces, a little group that was modeled on Armstrong's Hot Five. Despite what is now recognized as original and remarkable playing, the records did not sell well, and Smith drifted off to Milwaukee where he spent much of his life, working in and out of music, and occasionally making comebacks, which ranged from a brilliantly original big band in New York in 1938, to his triumph in the 1970s and 1980s in the off-Broadway musical play *One Mo' Time*. Those of us who heard him on a solo visit to London, in 1979, could hardly believe this legend of the 1920s had sprung back to life, and that despite a limited technique from years of neglecting his trumpet, he could still surprise the crowd with the audacious ideas in his playing.

Perhaps it is the same sense of carefree abandon that makes Smith's 1929 records so attractive today. They have a slightly shambolic, spontaneous feel about them with a charm closely related to that of Smith's personality, something also captured in his quirky vocal to *Till Times Get Better*. (He wrote witty and sometimes profound lyrics to several of his own songs, occasionally with slightly unusual structures that emphasize the words.) His 1929 discs are also packed with a questing, restless way of running rapidly over the trumpet by way of passing harmonies and unorthodox rhythms that prefigured much of what Roy Eldridge and Dizzy Gillespie were to do in the late 1930s. Indeed, it was Smith's speed of execution that so marked him out from his contemporaries, and I can think of few, if any, other players until well into the 1930s who could match his accuracy at the highest extreme of his range and his speed of thought on *Jazz Battle* or *Decatur Street Tutti*. This second disc also offers an interesting comparison between Smith's singing and his playing. In the scat vocal, he introduces a kind of sobbing sound over the descending harmonies towards the end of the chorus, and in his trumpet playing he manages to produce exactly the same kind of sound – a close match between human voice and instrument that takes us back once again to Scheaffner's observations. If he had remained in Chicago, or spent more time in New York in the 1930s furthering his career, it is possible that Smith would be a less shadowy presence in jazz history. The brilliance of his 1920s discs clearly rubbed off on other players, and those who tangled with him in his heyday never forgot it. "Jabbo Smith caught me one night and turned me every which way but loose," recalled Roy Eldridge, who was to become one of the most innovative trumpeters of the 1930s. "He wore me out before the night was through. He knew a lot of music and he knew changes. . . . Jabbo Smith didn't have Louis' sound, but he was faster."[134]

The other trumpeter with whom Omer Simeon recorded, Reuben "River" Reeves, from Evansville, Indiana, did show much more of "Louis' sound" in his playing, and a piece such as his *Low Down Rhythm*, with the Hollywood Shufflers from 1929, includes a powerful solo and some searing high notes on the final chorus that are firmly modeled in the Armstrong manner. Some of Reeves's other discs from that same year look forward to the devices Armstrong would habitually use in his 1930s big bands, such as the opening, declamatory chorus, and final buoyant solo over sustained notes of *Blue Sweets*, but even though Reeves arrived at a setting for his work that prefigured Armstrong, his playing, however accomplished, remained derivative. Reeves was the featured trumpeter with Dave Peyton's band at the Regal Theater in Chicago, where, as Danny Barker related, "many in the Chicago area believed Reeves to be greater than Armstrong."[135] The resulting battle, when Peyton's band opened for Armstrong and featured Reeves at his hottest and highest, was a knockout victory for the New Orleans trumpeter.

Among Armstrong's New Orleans compatriots, another trumpeter, "Punch" Miller, stood out as combining original ideas about speed and phrasing with Armstrong's overall approach. In several recordings with Tiny Parham he contributed fiery choruses, but his playing is at its best in the little band led by trombonist Albert Wynn which recorded in 1928. Wynn himself was an energetic trombonist who played some impressive, fast-moving figures, but Miller stands out on their recording of *She's Crying for Me*, with some perfectly executed breaks and a flamboyant lead in the final chorus. He spent much of his life in touring vaudeville and carnival shows, but re-emerged during the New Orleans revival, first on Rudi Blesh's 1947 New York radio show, *This Is Jazz*, and then back in New Orleans itself, where his final recordings mix some of his 1920s flamboyance with a particularly poignant approach to blues playing. Some hints of this blues-playing skill were apparent in the 1920s, and show up in Miller's up-tempo appearances with Tiny Parham, notably on *Fat Man Blues*, which includes several of his most characteristic phrases, as well as a mobile tuba solo from Quinn Wilson that mimics the traditional New Orleans street-parade tune *Joe Avery's Piece*.

The best moments of Chicago's huge legacy of recorded jazz from the 1920s tend to occur in the kind of small-band recordings I have mentioned. The larger orchestras, Doc Cook's, Erskine Tate's, Carroll Dickerson's, Charlie Elgar's, and so on, often acted as a framework for the most inspirational soloists, with relatively simple scoring for the brass and reeds. In Doc Cook's Dreamland Orchestra, for example, many of the charts involved little more than simple unison figures for each section. A piece like *Spanish Mama* has this kind of writing, and the variety comes from the way that Cook alternates the reeds (basically the Apex Club front line of clarinetist Jimmie Noone and altoist Joe Poston) with the brass, led by an on-form Freddie Keppard. The drama in this arrangement comes from Fred Garland's trombone solo and from Keppard's lead on the full-band choruses. But, stylistically, it is not far away from the two-part melodic writing of orchestrated ragtime arrangements, and for the development of a more sophisticated approach to writing for larger forces in the 1920s it is necessary to look elsewhere – to the West Coast first of all, and then to New York.

# CHAPTER 3

# Piano Jazz: Stride and Boogie-Woogie

> The higher class fellows who played things from the big shows looked down on this music. Nobody thought of writing it down. It was supposed to be the lower type of music, but now it is considered all right. I don't quite get that part of it.
>
> Eubie Blake, quoted in *Rudi Blesh, Combo USA*

Piano jazz has a story that can be traced independently from that of instrumental ensemble jazz. From time to time, through a particularly influential soloist or accompanist, such as Jelly Roll Morton or Earl Hines, the two genres intertwined, but in dating, geography, and style, there are strong arguments for considering piano jazz separately from the main currents of the music's development.

In Chapter 1, I looked at the origins of piano jazz within the earlier and related genre of ragtime, which was immensely popular across the United States for a period of about 25 years. At the end of the nineteenth century, and in the first two decades of the twentieth, the piano was the pre-eminent medium of home entertainment, before it was overtaken by the phonograph. There was an astonishingly high rate of production of inexpensive, mass-produced instruments, and at the height of the industry, in 1910, 350,000 instruments were manufactured in the United States. In other words, one in every 252 Americans bought a new piano that year.[1] With a similarly high output throughout the following decade, and with plenty of serviceable older instruments in operation, there were few who had no access to a piano. In addition, there was a parallel vogue for reed organs or harmoniums, which greatly increased the number of keyboard instruments in circulation. Through widely available sheet music, and through player-piano rolls (a widespread form of entertainment; almost 50 percent of the instruments made in the year of 1919 alone were equipped to play back this type of paper-roll recording), the popular repertoire was readily available to a huge section of the population.

Although domestic ownership of pianos was higher among white Americans, plenty of African-American homes had one, particularly in large urban centers, and in the poorest or more rural areas, there were instruments in churches, bars, and tonks. James P. Johnson recalled:

> In the years before World War One, there was a piano in almost every home, colored or white. The piano makers had a slogan: "What is a home without a piano?" It was like having a radio or TV today. Phonographs were feeble and scratchy. Most people who had pianos couldn't play them, so a piano player was important socially.[2]

Johnson highlights the paradox that, despite such widespread ownership, only a relatively small number of Americans ever became reasonably proficient on their instruments. Within the African-American population, as Johnson put it, "a piano player was important socially."

Many promising pianists who went on to become celebrated jazz musicians began their careers on keyboards belonging to neighbors or friends, but often their blandishments cajoled proud parents into making sufficient sacrifices to buy an instrument for the family home. A good example was Eubie Blake, whose impromptu performance as a child on a reed organ in Eisenbrandt's store in Baltimore saw the salesman turn up on the doorstep a day or two later offering the instrument for a dollar down and 25 cents a week, until the 75-dollar price (plus interest) had been covered. "My mother didn't have the dollar to give him, [as] we were very poor," remembered Blake, "so the man left the organ and said he'd just collect the twenty-five cents every week. You can imagine how long [it] took."[3]

Blake's career consolidates several of the themes explored in Chapter 1. He was the eleventh child of parents who had been born into slavery. He began his professional life during the 1890s, and through playing ragtime in the tonks of Baltimore he became one of the central figures in the local cadre of piano "professors." He went on the road in 1901 in a medicine show. Several years later, he became involved with the syncopated orchestra of James Reese Europe, and with his songwriting and performing partner Noble Sissle he wrote and performed in stage shows for the vaudeville and touring-theater circuits, including the immensely successful vehicle for the comedians Miller and Lyles, *Shuffle Along*, which brought African-American theater back to Broadway in 1921 after a gap of a decade and a half.

Most importantly, Blake was both a significant ragtime and early jazz composer, initially writing formal rag compositions, but subsequently turning his hand to popular songs, many of which, such as *I'm Just Wild About Harry* and *Memories of You*, became standards for jazz improvisation. In his compositions, as in those of several other ragtime composers, there was, over time, a gradual diminution of syncopation and more emphasis on memorable tunes. Born in 1883, just over fourteen years after Scott Joplin, Blake continued to perform into his nineties, keeping the traditions of the ragtime era alive well into the second half of the twentieth century.

In his final years, there was a sense that he was celebrated more because of his longevity than his accomplishments. He died just a few days after his hundredth birthday. (On the anniversary he quipped that if he'd known he was going to live so long he would have taken better care of himself.) Yet his musical achievements were considerable, and he deserves to be re-examined as a significant link in the chain of events that led to the emergence of piano jazz. When I met him and heard him perform in 1976, he was still an impressive pianist, with a genuine sense of jazz timing in his solo breaks and right-hand figures, but who never quite seemed to have loosened his left hand from the stiff beat of 1890s ragtime. Hearing him led me to examine his output of compositions, and in particular his 1899 piece *Charleston Rag*. (This was originally titled *Sounds of Africa* but was not published until 1919, when it acquired its new title to link it to the fashionable Charleston dance.)

This piece contains a number of ideas that would become central to the jazz performance tradition, and which are, for the most part, not found in the Midwestern ragtime style of Scott Joplin and his Sedalia or St. Louis associates described earlier. These innovations included frequent suspensions or "turnabouts" of the regular left-hand alternation of bass note and chord, numerous (and often abrupt) key changes, plus an almost conversational melodic interchange between registers. However, the most noticeable feature is Blake's use, in his first theme, of a descending left-hand figure which incorporates the sixteenth-note pattern of boogie-woogie – something more often associated with the blues and the blues-inflected piano style that was to develop to maturity in 1920s Chicago. In Blake's piece, the boogie pattern is not employed in a twelve-bar setting, but occurs in eight-measure sections, each alternating with a more conventional ragtime passage.

At the time Blake composed *Charleston Rag*, he had not learned to write his music down. He memorized the piece, he said, by playing it night after night in cabarets.[4] He also memorized music written by other ragtime composers, including that of William Turk, a man born in 1866 or thereabouts, who was the father-figure for Baltimore's ragtime players, and also that of Jess Pickett, a gambler and pimp described by Blake as a "gentleman of leisure."

The boogie-woogie left-hand patterns of *Charleston Rag* came from Turk. Blake believed he had developed this walking bass style because his vast stomach got in the way of the more conventional striding left hand, but whatever the actual cause, he had become accustomed to pounding out sixteen bass notes to the measure by the time Blake heard him, describing him as having a "left hand like God."

From Pickett's rag *The Dream*, which was still in Blake's repertoire in the late 1970s, some 80 years after he first heard it, he learned how to incorporate several other ideas into his music which were subsequently to become the stock-in-trade of the jazz player. Such devices include Latin rhythms, left-hand ostinato figures that run for several measures, suspensions of time with dramatic pauses lasting up to a measure in length, and growling onomatopoeic left-hand runs, whose mean and dirty quality apparently led Pickett's piece to be nicknamed the *Bull Dyke's Dream* because of its popularity among the lesbians who worked in the Baltimore sporting houses where the composer played.

Blake's extraordinary musical memory helped him adopt other pianistic devices he heard during his career, not least the ornamental flurries and frills of the nineteenth-century classical repertoire, which he began to be taught formally as a small child by his neighbor Mrs. Marshall, who had him familiar with the basic Czerny keyboard exercises well before his first ventures into ragtime. He also remembered hearing famous classical concert pianists in the flesh, and recalled how, in 1909, Rachmaninov's apparently simple opening to *The Stars and Stripes Forever* had given way to a devastating display of descending left-hand octaves in the second section of the piece – an effect that Blake could reproduce well into his old age. Into his own music he poured the sounds he had heard around him, not – as his description might suggest – in late nineteenth-century New Orleans, but hundreds of miles away in Baltimore: "I heard syncopation in the Negro bands coming back from funerals and, of course, in the shouting in the church."[5]

Blake performed in several other American cities during his time on the touring vaudeville circuit, and he was to become a major influence on many up-and-coming young musicians who became the first generation to play jazz. Among them was Duke Ellington, who heard Blake on a visit to his home town of Washington D.C., a city which bred a distinguished line of pianists of its own, including Ellington himself, and Claude Hopkins.[6]

From as early as 1906, Blake worked regularly in Atlantic City, which was to become a major center for jazz. Musicians, both African-American and white, sought work there during its extended summer season, and it became a place where players from all over the country could hear one another and exchange ideas, as well as (within the boundaries of the racial divide) sharing practical experience on the bandstand. "The top entertainers and all our working people from New York City, Newark, Philadelphia, Baltimore and Washington would hunt jobs in Atlantic City," wrote Willie "The Lion" Smith. "Everybody wanted to go there because A[tlantic] C[ity] moved fast."[7]

Just as, in the first decade of the twentieth century, St. Louis had been a clearing-house for the ideas of the Midwestern ragtimers discussed in Chapter 1, in the years leading up to World War I, Atlantic City became one of the main locations, if not *the* place, where the seeds of the transition from ragtime to stride piano were sown. Blake himself worked at several of the city's main venues: Ben Allen's Grotto Café, the Middlesex Club, the Goldfield, and the Boat House. And there were more, as recalled by "The Lion," including: Charlie Reynolds's Philadelphia House, Welloff's New World, The Pekin, the Elephant Café, and Kelly's Café. In yet another of the paradoxes that surround the genesis of this music, and with striking parallels to New Sedalia and Storyville, the greatest creativity took place in the seamiest area of town. As Blake put it:

> Atlantic City had big-time bawdyhouses in the District on North
> Carolina Avenue between Arctic and Baltic. Money flowed there.
> But only in the summer. On September 6 you could shoot a gun
> right down the street and not hit a soul.[8]

It was there that Blake heard One-Leg Willie Joseph from Boston, a man he regarded as the most accomplished of all the early pianists he heard, and whose glittering conservatory career was curtailed because he was African-American. Joseph was apparently one of the first to introduce one of the main types of accompanimental variation adopted by many stride pianists. This involved repetitive left-hand figures in which four-note patterns of quarter-notes are repeated in place of the striding, oompah crotchets of ragtime, or the walking bass of boogie-woogie. The bass notes still occur on the first and third beats of each measure, but instead of a chord on the second and fourth, the three intermediate quaver beats each carry a single note, usually an alternation of two tones from the chord that would otherwise be played. Blake incorporated this configuration into some of his own pieces, including *Betty Washboard Rag*, and it was particularly popular with Willie "The Lion" Smith who used it in several of his compositions, of which the most famous is *Echoes of Spring*.[9]

Other musicians Blake encountered included Bobby Lee and Luckey Roberts from Philadelphia (although Roberts moved around 1910 to New York), and from New York itself came a contingent of first-rate players that included "The Lion" and James P. Johnson.

Johnson's observations about Atlantic City (and the surrounding area, including Egg Harbor, where he won a piano contest) confirm its importance as a meeting-place of styles. When he arrived there in 1914, Johnson was immersed in the keyboard music being developed by the New York school of ragtimers. Some of them, with whom James P. was already familiar, like Charlie Johnson, were already playing summer seasons in Atlantic City, but he also met players from elsewhere. He encountered Blake for the first time, and quickly learned his test piece *Troublesome Ivories*. In addition he recalled:

> There was a pianist there who played quadrilles, sets, rags, etc.
> From him I first heard the walking Texas or boogie woogie bass.
> The boogie woogie was a cotillion step for which a lot of music
> was composed.[10]

Willie "The Lion" Smith had similar memories:

> There was still one more piano player in A.C. who impressed me
> a lot. He was known as Kitchen Tom. No one to my knowledge
> ever knew his regular name. Tom was from somewhere down
> South, and was the first one I ever heard using what has become
> known as the "walking" or "boogie bass."[11]

So we can assume that ideas that have frequently been ascribed to one area or region of the United States may well have reached a broader public, and, more importantly, were taken up by musicians from other areas, through the annual summer influx of entertainers to Atlantic City. This was not just a matter of technique, but of the source material on which piano compositions or performances were based. The players that arrived in Atlantic City brought with them all kinds of source material. From the New York contingent alone, these included country dances – the cotillions, stomps, drags, and set dances recalled by Johnson – to classical pieces, and from Midwestern rags to "early New Orleans tunes."[12]

As Labor Day arrived and each summer season drew to a close, for the rest of the year the center of early development in piano jazz was undoubtedly New York. Blake ended up there, along with Roberts, Johnson, Smith, and many other inventive and original players, just as the transition from piano ragtime to jazz was beginning in earnest, leading, by the dawn of the 1920s – as I noted in Chapter 1 – to the creation of the first fully identifiable jazz-solo style known as stride. Whereas it is also possible to trace a parallel transition from ragtime to jazz in the compositions and playing of Jelly Roll Morton, his peripatetic life meant that he was very much an individual and not part of a school or movement as the stride players were. The New Orleans bassist George "Pops" Foster put it succinctly when he said that the New York stride players, like James P. Johnson, were soon perceived as more "up-to-date" than Morton.

Blake's breadth of experience is a paradigm for the elements that combined into stride, and his importance to the genre by the early 1920s was neatly summed up by clarinetist Garvin Bushell, who wrote:

> Being in big-time vaudeville with Noble Sissle, Eubie Blake was way above the rest of us then. You'd never find him in the cabarets; the people he hung out with were Victor Herbert and Jerome Kern. James P. and Willie "The Lion" were just performing musicians, but Eubie was a composer and considered a great pianist in those days.[13]

Blake continued to be highly regarded well into the 1930s, both for his playing as a soloist, and for his directing of bands and shows, including (in 1934) taking to the road once more with *Shuffle Along*, during which he was hailed in the press as a "musical genius."[14]

Because the piano was universally available, and versatile, it was used in every form of musical entertainment, often to the exclusion of any other instruments, and so the new style that emerged drew strongly on the varied experience of players like Blake who, to recap, had reached his position of eminence by playing solo ragtime in clubs, bars, and tonks, accompanying singers, touring the medicine show and theater circuits, and playing in pit bands or other kinds of ensemble settings. I have already quoted James P. Johnson's view that audience expectations were a vital part of developing the full sound of New York stride piano, but equally important in shaping the genre was the wide range of employment open to pianists. In addition to the list of activities in which Blake had already excelled, there was also the opportunity to make piano rolls or sound recordings.

Of the pre-eminent pianists who worked in New York as stride emerged, it is significant that Blake, Johnson, and Luckey Roberts all had theater experience: writing, rehearsing, accompanying, and playing memorable, distinctive show tunes. Experience of taking to the road with shows added to their array of pianistic skills through much the same kind of cross-fertilization of ideas as in the clubs and joints of Atlantic City. Johnson, for example, collected numerous stylistic tips during a tour with the show *Smart Set*, in 1918–19. In Toledo, Ohio, he encountered Johnny Waters (a man who also influenced the novelty pianist Roy Bargy) who taught him ways of tackling very slow blues and of using left-hand tenths. Back in New York, Johnson introduced many of these techniques to the local scene. (And, in a two-way traffic of ideas, his own playing left an indelible impression on the young Art Tatum, who heard him during this visit to Toledo.)[15]

Perhaps the most colorful of the three was Philadelphia-born Roberts, who had begun his stage career by the time he was five – singing, dancing, and jumping out of bamboo trees in a touring revue, then traveling to Europe and becoming a vaudeville accompanist before reaching his teens. He went on to compose musical plays and revues.[16] The younger generation of pianists that followed, such as Fats Waller and Count Basie, also went out on the touring vaudeville circuit, the latter pair both accompanying the same singer, Katie Crippen, at different times in the early 1920s. In due course, Waller also became a successful show composer.

It was no accident that many of the most effective accompanists on the theater and club circuit became outstanding solo pianists, having frequently had to provide vocalists with support equivalent to that of a whole band, and incorporating what Johnson called "orchestral effects" into their playing. As Willie "The Lion" Smith confirmed, providing backing for singers developed the pianists' technique in other ways as well:

You had to be a fast thinker to handle them. First, it was

necessary to be able to play in any key, run the chords as we called it, because the entertainers worked in them all. A singer might change into any key on the piano at any time.[17]

Such musical resources were essential for the pianists who migrated to the numerous clubs and cabarets of Harlem, which briefly became New York's focal point for African-American entertainment. In the years leading up to 1918, these venues tended to be in the northern section of the area, and included the Rock (or "Garden of Joy") on 140th Street, Livia's, and the 101 Ranch, both on 139th Street. As the 1920s dawned, more clubs were established further south, including The Orient, Jerry Preston's and Leroy's on 135th Street, and the Band Box on 131st.

When stride was first developing, these cabarets were predominantly for African-American clientèle. The writer Rudolf Fisher, who was also a doctor and amateur musician, wrote a penetrating memoir of several nightclubs as they were in the early 1920s, notably the Garden of Joy, where, during the summer, its secular sounds would mingle with the singing from the local Abyssinian Baptist Church summer camp, so that "night after night there would arise the mingled strains of blues and spirituals."[18] To Fisher's regret, by the late 1920s most of these cabarets were excluding black patrons in favor of white customers from downtown, who made their way to Harlem "to see how Negroes acted."

As African-American audiences were squeezed out of their neighborhood cabarets by the financial imperative of wealthy white customers paying for what they thought of as a kind of exotic entertainment, stride pianists were drawn further into their own community, and focused their energies on the fiercely competitive parallel world of the Harlem "rent party," noisy affairs where pianists were the sole entertainment. The experience of the cabaret world, particularly playing in any key, was an obvious asset for those musicians who came to dominate these events.

Rent parties were by no means restricted to New York, and took place in other urban centers (notably Chicago), but the densely populated Harlem became synonymous with the term. In essence, a rent party was a neighborhood shindig, where apartment tenants, who were short of the money to pay their rent, charged their neighbors and friends admission to eat, drink, and listen to music, with the idea that the ticket price covered both the shortfall in the rent plus the money to feed and water the guests, plus paying a first-rate pianist to provide the music.

Because of failed property speculation in the early years of the twentieth century, Harlem's tenements and apartment blocks were crammed with up to five times their intended population, the majority of whom were African-American. Even though some tenants were squeezed up five to a room, it was a common occurrence to get behind with the rent.

As a consequence, the rent party became so popular that in the early 1920s it provided a full-time living for many pianists, and for every player who was paid to attend, a coterie of hangers-on and musical challengers usually turned up as well, so that there was both a bounteous supply of music and a cut-throat competitive atmosphere. It is hardly surprising that in such a hot-house environment, the Harlem stride-piano style developed very rapidly, its main advances taking place between 1917, when many of its principal practitioners were still cutting ragtime piano rolls, and about 1923, by which time both rolls and phonograph recordings had moved into territory that was unequivocally jazz.

According to Garvin Bushell, James P. Johnson, who became the "Dean" of Harlem pianists, owed much of his style to an unrecorded but formidable player known as Abba Labba. Others who contributed to the development of stride piano included Jack the Bear, Lippy Boyette, Russell Brooks, Willie Gant, Bob Hawkins, "Beetle" Henderson, Joe Turner, and Corky Williams. The music that was developed by this group of players took ragtime forward, as detailed in Chapter 1, by adding rhythmic variation to the left-hand "oompah" pattern, and by introducing a series of formulaic display patterns into right-hand improvisation. The style is usefully defined by one of its latter-day practitioners, Henry A. Francis, as follows:

> A truly solo idiom; it is entirely self-sufficient and requires no rhythmic or harmonic assistance. In fact the addition of rhythm instruments usually obscures the impish strut of solo stride piano. The style generates a very full, orchestral sound, as the oscillating left hand activates simultaneously both the low and middle registers, while the right hand operates in the upper registers.[19]

As rent parties developed into competitive "cutting contests" in which the most virtuoso or bravura performer would emerge triumphant, this very element of flamboyance became an integral ingredient of stride. A successful pianist not only had to play difficult, written compositions brilliantly, note for note, as the ragtimers did, but had to be equally competent to add his or her own variations in a similar style. Considerable acclaim was afforded to those who managed to integrate familiar fingering patterns and recognizable motifs into their solos, especially if they could do so in the context of one of the demanding "set-piece" compositions that defined the genre, such as James P. Johnson's *Carolina Shout*. The unadorned piece is difficult enough, as demonstrated in the composer's 1921 piano roll for QRS, but in Johnson's own subsequent recorded versions and, more importantly, in those recordings of the piece made by other pianists, the generic vocabulary of stride creeps in, nowhere more convincingly than in Fats Waller's May 13, 1941, disc, where the final chorus superimposes an amalgam of many of Waller's favorite devices over Johnson's basic structure.

In the areas where stride is most closely related to ragtime, its characteristics show a clear and straightforward extension of the earlier genre, particularly in the left hand, where this was largely built around two ideas.

First, the "broken" or "backward tenth," in which the left hand strikes intervals of a tenth at slightly different times, so that while the little finger carries a strong bass line, the thumb (playing the upper note) sets up a counter-melody to the main tune. This is clearly demonstrated in the very first piano roll cut by Fats Waller in March 1923, *Got to Cool My Doggies Now*. By the time Waller recorded his *Handful of Keys* in 1929, an equivalent set piece to Johnson's *Carolina Shout*, he had mastered the idea of integrating left-hand broken tenths into his main theme, so that on the first and third beats of each bar his thumb strikes the upper note a fraction after his little finger has hit the bass harmony. In addition to creating an unusually full sound, this also adds to the sense of motion in the piece, as Humphrey Lyttelton observed: "what gives the listener his sense of the direction in which the bass harmonies are moving is not the root notes of the chords but notes in effect a third above – the E in the case of a C chord."[20]

Second, is the idea of reversing or "turning about" the oompah rhythm, so that – in the simplest type of example – for a few beats, here or there, the bass note is placed on the second and fourth beat of the measure, and the accompanying chord on the first or third. The subsequent resumption of normal rhythm propels a piece forward with the intensity of a cork leaving a champagne bottle. Few better demonstrations exist of the range of left-hand variations that are possible within the style than James P. Johnson's *Riffs*, which he recorded for Okeh on January 29, 1929.

Of all the stride pianists to record, the most accomplished exponent of the style was Fats Waller. Born in 1904, his short life was lived in the fast lane, until his death from pneumonia in 1943. He was an impressive figure, standing five feet eleven inches tall, weighing 285 pounds, and with vast hands, each of which could stretch well over an octave-and-a-half on the keyboard. Famous as much for his gargantuan appetite (for food, drink, and female company) as for his musical abilities, Waller's success as a popular entertainer and singer tended to mask his brilliance as a pianist and organist, let alone as the composer of dozens of tunes, many of which became hit songs. Nothing better demonstrates the way in which his louche lifestyle contrasted with the refinement of his musical achievements than the story that his own son, when asked at school what his father did for a living, paused for a moment and then said: "He drinks gin."[21]

Waller's initial public success was not at the piano at all. He became the first great jazz organist, using the instrument he had begun playing as a consequence of his lay preacher father's religious work to extend improvisational ideas in jazz. He used imaginative combinations of pipes (or registrations) within an atmospheric style that combined the sacred world of spirituals and gospel with the secular charms of the darkened movie-house. He was still at school when he began work as organist at the Lincoln Theater, and in his early teens when James P. Johnson took him under his wing, and brought him along (still wearing short pants) to replace Willie "The Lion" Smith as house pianist at Leroy's Harlem cabaret.

Playing stride piano, Waller not only demonstrated a technical command of the style and an immediately identifiable touch that imbued all levels of dynamic, from the quietest tinkle to the loudest fortissimo, with innate confidence, but his melodic imagination and improvisational abilities made even the most routine application of stride formulae sound challenging and fresh. He was also one of the most rhythmically subtle of players, and from the late 1920s until his death, his mere presence in the studio was an almost certain guarantee of swing, relentless momentum, and joyful zest. During his career, he made over 400 recordings, but at the heart of his output is a series of piano solos, of which the fifteen different pieces recorded in 1929, four sequels from 1934, his *London Suite* from 1939, and a final five pieces from 1941 definitively cover almost every aspect of stride.

In them, he also adopted many of the techniques of a style that has traditionally been frowned upon by jazz critics – "novelty piano." As James P. Johnson's biographer Scott E. Brown says about the main progenitors of this genre: "the music of [Zez] Confrey, Roy Bargy (Paul Whiteman's pianist), Billy Mayerl, and others bore little resemblance to ethnically black music."[22] Nevertheless, these pianists harnessed an impressive array of technically difficult embellishments to a light ragtime style, albeit without the rhythmic emphasis or harmonic inflections of jazz. But if their work had taken only a little from the African-American tradition, it was liberally plundered in return by African-American pianists, who wished to expand the boundaries of stride technique. The novelty repertoire included several devices that were admired and adopted by the New York stride players, so that Johnson, for example, produced his own novelty pieces such as *High Brown*, *Jingles*, and *Jungle Nymphs*.

Waller produced few such compositions of his own (the light-hearted blues *Numb Fumblin'* is his principal foray into the genre), but in much of his work he happily adopted such aspects of the novelty pianists' vocabulary as stating a melody with his left hand, while adding bravura decorations with his right, as he did in *Love Me or Leave Me*, playing extended right-hand tremolos above a melodic or chordal statement (in the same piece), using out-of-tempo themes and extended cadenzas, as in "Chelsea" from his *London Suite*, not to mention the oriental pastiche of "Limehouse" and the classical parody of "Whitechapel." Under Johnson's influence, Waller had developed a sound classical technique, and he was one of the first jazz pianists to make attempts to "swing the classics," as well as producing a skilful parody of the nineteenth-century romantic style in his final recording of his own *Honeysuckle Rose*.

A consummate pianist, Waller drew all the various elements of his technique together in his best stride compositions. Of these, *Handful of Keys* is his masterpiece. It is a multi-section composition, following in the tradition of Joplin, Blake, and Morton, and it draws its main thematic material from the piano exercise books – an upward scale in the first chorus, repeated an octave higher in the second, and a series of broken chords in the lead-up to the final section. This last part of the piece involves repeated right-hand chords that work rather in the manner of big-band riffs over the inexorable progress of Waller's powerful left hand. All in all, this is perhaps the most developed example of the pure stride-piano style by any pianist, and Waller's 1929 recording includes many of the set-piece right-hand patterns that characterized the genre. His more subtle composition *Smashing Thirds* runs it close, with closely harmonized upward scales in the third chorus, and a counter-balancing downward figure in the left hand that appears later, during the sixth and seventh choruses. Of his other pieces for piano, *Alligator Crawl* makes use of left-hand boogie-woogie figures, as Blake had done in *Charleston Rag*, whereas *Viper's Drag* alternates passages of pure stride with slower sections built over a sinister left-hand ostinato.

All these pieces are conceived as piano solos. They were not written, or played, as band vehicles, and they demonstrate the degree to which stride was a stand-alone solo genre. From its high noon of Waller's 1929 recordings, and despite its affinities with ragtime, stride remained central to the jazz-piano tradition until the mid-1930s, Waller himself keeping the style alive a little longer on the back of his successful career as a popular entertainer. This even inspired some younger musicians to take up the style as it fell into decline, and Ralph Sutton, for example, growing up during the 1930s in a small town in the Midwest, learned the rudiments of stride from hearing Waller's discs on a weekly broadcast from WIL in St. Louis called *Harlem Rhythm*.

Billed by the late 1930s as "the most versatile artist in radio today,"[23] Waller's "several accomplishments to achieve stardom" (including witty vocals and merciless lampooning of flimsy pop songs and ballads) occluded the fact that his piano style was increasingly outmoded, and by the time of his final 1941 solo discs was already becoming an anachronism.

Paradoxically, despite all that I have said about stride being a predominantly solo style, through Waller's lengthy series of small-group recordings with his Rhythm, which began in 1934, he also became the most successful of the New York school at integrating with a band. His protégé, Bill Basie (who had shared the organ stool at Harlem's Lincoln Theater), took forward Waller's methods of ensemble piano well into the 1980s, retaining those aspects of stride that added impetus to a rhythm section, and using set-piece patterns for his occasional solo displays within the ensemble. By contrast, James P. Johnson tended to subjugate his own playing to the needs of an ensemble, only rarely demonstrating his keyboard prowess in his band recordings, whereas Willie "The Lion" Smith and his Cubs tended to produce lightly orchestrated versions of Smith's solo repertoire.

The other most significant jazz-piano soloist of the 1920s shared Waller's ability to blend what was essentially a solo style with an ensemble. This was Earl Hines, who developed his mature "trumpet style" in Chicago. Some elements of Hines's playing reflect the accentuated right-hand technique of other Chicagoan pianists such as Zinky Cohn and Cassino Simpson, neither of whom approached Hines's virtuoso flair. His fellow pianist Teddy Wilson aptly summed up Hines's brilliance both as a soloist and as a band player:

> I enjoy him in both roles. He has a beautifully powerful rhythmic approach to the keyboard and his rhythms are more eccentric than those of Art Tatum or Fats Waller. When I say eccentric, I mean getting away from a straight 4/4 rhythm. He would play a lot of

what we call accent on the "and" beat. This is the beat that comes *between* the 4/4 quarter note beats, and Hines accented it by starting a note between the 4/4 beats. He would do this with great authority and attack.[24]

Hines was born, in a suburb of Pittsburgh, into a musical family. His father, Joseph, was a cornetist, his mother played the organ, and his sister Nancy was a pianist, who went on to lead her own bands. Hines started serious study of the piano when he was only nine, and he left high school to go straight into the band of a local baritone singer called Lois Deppe, who recognized Hines's talent, and organized jobs for him that involved bandleading and directing as well as simply accompanying at the piano.

After a tour with Deppe in 1923, Hines moved to Chicago late the following year. He quickly found work with some of the city's leading bandleaders including Carroll Dickerson and Erskine Tate, who provided backing for Louis Armstrong. Consequently, Hines became a regular accompanist for Armstrong, joining his studio recording bands whenever possible, and cutting several influential discs with Armstrong's Hot Five. His playing was nicknamed the "trumpet" piano style, since his right-hand phrases to some extent mimicked the melodies of the trumpet in early jazz bands, and, to emphasize their melodic content, he played them in octaves. This technique made Hines's melodies stand out more effectively than those of any other band pianist of the day. The most graphic illustration of the style in action, also demonstrating that Hines's overall improvisational capabilities were very advanced for the time, is his 1928 duet with Armstrong *Weather Bird*, discussed briefly in the previous chapter.

Not only is Hines's left-hand rhythmic support far more open-ended than the playing of the New York stride school, but in the opening chorus, in which he accompanies Armstrong, he demonstrates the ability, described by Teddy Wilson, to place accents on the eighth notes between the main quarter notes of a measure. Subsequently, he moves the emphasis of the beat around, creating a dramatic sense of movement. As his own solo sections open up, he uses the whole range of the keyboard, but the most noticeable feature is his right-hand doubled octaves – the epitome of his "trumpet" technique – as he echoes the phrases of Armstrong. As well as being a new way of approaching solo playing, the octaves intensified the sound of the piano, so that, transferred to a band setting, even unamplified in a large dance hall, Hines stood a chance of being heard.

This innovation by Hines was gradually adopted by other pianists, but few managed it as efficiently as he had done. For a brief period, Teddy Wilson had the opportunity to play alongside Hines, and he related what, from a fellow pianist's point of view, he observed about his technique:

> What always amazed me about Earl was that, no matter how loudly he played, he never lost his touch; he never really banged the piano. He would always come at that keyboard and play each note with complete control and intention, no matter how loud, whereas many players, when they get carried away with emotion and want to achieve . . . high volume, stiffen and begin to hit the piano and consequently lose the rhythm. But Hines never did and never lost his touch, although he could carry the volume up to the point where he might break a string on the piano![25]

It seems that Hines was physically well-equipped for the piano, with extremely flexible hands and wrists, and he was naturally able to achieve a level of playing that took considerable practice and long experience for others.

No doubt it was because Hines developed his style in isolation, away from a group of fellow pianists, that his preoccupations were rather different from those of the stride school (although Hines was sufficiently technically adept to play in a stride style when he felt like it). Whereas they built a technique solidly based on the classics and ragtime to employ the full resources of the keyboard, complex fingering patterns, and dense harmonies, Hines saw his instrument as a means to a different end. Again, Teddy Wilson, who was familiar with the New York players as he was with Hines, defined the difference:

> Comparing Fats Waller with Hines, we find that his was not so much a horn style as a pianistic one: lots of chords and intervals such as right hand thirds. . . . With Hines what was most important was the single line – a horn can only make one note at a time.[26]

In this respect, Hines pointed the way forward for jazz piano – harmonically sophisticated and rhythmically provocative in its role as accompanist, but emulating the fluent, single-line melodic improvisations of a saxophone or trumpet as a solo voice.

Stylistically, Hines developed relatively little over the years. He reached his mature approach by the late 1920s, and although he followed the general trend of the 1930s and 1940s by adopting a more relaxed approach to rhythm, and playing less on top of the beat, the main change in his work was that its characteristics became more pronounced. His habit of beginning a phrase on an off-center eighth-note beat developed into ever greater interruptions to the regular meter, his arpeggios seemed to consume even more of the keyboard, and his passing harmonies suggested a greater chordal variety than was actually present. Overall, however, it was the continuous sense of melodic line that marked out his approach, and which influenced the next generation of pianists. He was also to become a figure of admiration among the musicians who developed the modern jazz of the 1940s, many of whom passed through the ranks of the big band he began leading in 1928, and which came to full flower in the late 1930s. According to Dizzy Gillespie, who was one of Hines's more high-profile alumni, what they most liked about him was his endless ability to improvise, as well as his ability to translate new ideas to his ensemble, using little more than sketches, hand signals, and hastily demonstrated riffs to create full-band performances.[27]

Hines was born in late 1903, and Fats Waller six months later, during the following year. The musician who combined many of their ideas and created the final jumping-off point for many modern jazz pianists was Art Tatum. Although he was born a mere five years later than Waller, in 1909, the pace of change was so rapid that Tatum regarded Waller as a major influence, and acknowledged him as such in many interviews (more so than James P. Johnson whom he had heard in Toledo). Tatum also admired a little-known pianist called Lee Sims, and it is clear from his close friend Teddy Wilson, and from various other accounts, that, in addition, Tatum owed a considerable debt to Hines. Saxophonist Eddie Barefield, for example, who also got to know Tatum in Toledo, said: "His favourite jazz piano player was Earl Hines – used to buy all of Earl's records and he would improvise on 'em. Yeah, he'd play with the record, but he'd improvise over what Earl was doing."[28]

By the time Tatum arrived in New York in 1932, as accompanist to the singer Adelaide Hall, he had developed the stride style epitomized by Waller by combining it with a more linear approach to right-hand figures, that owed much to Hines, but which he took further in the form of dazzlingly fast runs and arpeggios. Not everything Tatum did could be easily mastered, and only the most technically proficient pianists could attempt to play in anything approaching his style. Teddy Wilson was taught the fingering patterns for some of the most difficult runs by Tatum himself, and the jazz piano historian Billy Taylor told me that among his circle of younger New York players, only Clyde Hart could instantly get the hang of how such complex figures were put together.[29] One reason for this was that, like stride itself, Tatum's derivative from it was essentially a solo style, and it made technical demands on the player no less strenuous than those of the classical and romantic keyboard repertoire.

Whereas I have suggested that some stride pianists were not particularly successful in integrating with a group, Tatum took a totally different tack. To be sure, many of his discs were made with a trio, which added bass and guitar to his piano, and he also made a number of small-band discs, but musicians who played in these ensembles (including guitarist Al Casey and bassist Truck Parham) have told me that they always felt completely subservient, and that their job was always to accompany him, by simply fleshing out, tonally and harmonically, what he was doing at the keyboard. Apart from the odd occasion when he clearly wanted to provide a sympathetic backing for another improviser, such as his own band's record session of January 21, 1941, which provides some openings for trumpeter Joe Thomas and clarinetist Edmond Hall, Tatum was not an ideal accompanist – the same sense of subservience mentioned by Casey and Parham overcame almost all those who played with him. However, what set him apart was that, in at least part of his solo repertoire, he was actually playing piano reductions of pieces he had heard played by bands, thereby turning the process of integration with a group on its head.

His first solo recording, *Tiger Rag*, from 1933 **[CD track 8]**, owes its provenance not to the Original Dixieland Jazz Band, but to the far more complex version of the piece recorded by Duke Ellington in 1929. The arrangement is not absolutely identical, and from the impressionistic introduction through to the final cadence many of the figures are pianistic, built around Tatum's characteristic fingering patterns. Nevertheless, his sweeping runs capture from the Ellington recording the essence of Barney Bigard's fluent clarinet dashes through both registers of the instrument, and the riff patterns which he uses are clearly based on, first, the clipped brass phrases that open part two of Ellington's double-sided disc, and, second, the reed section riffs that conclude it. It might be a little far-fetched to suggest – as the Tatum scholar Felicity Howlett does – that he "becomes the Ellington band"[30] but he undoubtedly drew on his familiarity with this recording to shape his piano performance.

Tatum was not alone in this, as Fats Waller's final solo recording (made in 1941) of Ellington's *Ring Dem Bells* also conjures up the ghostly presence of the full orchestra by making creative use of the space between phrases at a moderate tempo. But Tatum's bravura performance at breakneck speed is far more of a technical triumph. It brought his skills to a national audience in the United States, and established a standard by which all subsequent jazz pianists have been judged.

In particular, Tatum's nimble runs of single notes, and the way in which he occasionally broke down the momentum of his stride accompaniment for something more impressionistic and sparse, often including passing chords and chromatic interjections, would inspire the bebop pianists of the 1940s. His work included occasional examples of devices that have generally been identified with the subsequent innovations of musicians like Thelonious Monk and Dizzy Gillespie. As bassist Charles Mingus put it, well before the 1940s Tatum had been "making minor ninths and going through a cycle of fourths on a song like *I Can't Get Started* . . . sometimes so fast you weren't even conscious of it."[31] Even so, in the all-consuming sweep of his playing, Tatum made no attempt to modify his established style to become a bebopper himself, and his playing was too dense, too pianistic, and too much of a solo technique for it to transfer unaltered into modern jazz. Instead, the most advanced of the bebop pianists, Bud Powell, while remaining hugely indebted to Tatum, also drew on the work of several ensemble pianists of the swing era who had worked at creating a self-consciously sparser style, which pared away much of the density of stride, and which was adaptable into both solo and ensemble work.

The most high-profile of these was Teddy Wilson, who had learned at first-hand from both Tatum and Hines. Wilson was also significant in that, as a member of Benny Goodman's Trio (with whom he began recording in 1935), and subsequent Quartet, he was in one of the first racially integrated bands to appear before audiences across the United States. Neither of these Goodman small groups employed a double bass, so Wilson maintained a highly rhythmic left-hand style, which created a sense of continuity between his mentors – Waller, Hines, and Tatum – and those younger pianists who were, in turn, influenced by him.

Wilson recorded relatively few solos, but a piece like *Breaking in a Pair of Shoes*, from January 1936, is an excellent demonstration of his pared-down approach. Most of the ingredients of a standard stride performance are there, from the decorative out-of-tempo introduction, to the phrasing of the opening chorus, which employs familiar stride motifs in the right hand, and a largely oompah left-hand pattern, except that this is economical in its use of tenths, and, from time to time, for a couple of measures or so, places a full chord on each beat with a slight change of inversion. The overall effect is rather like a Waller solo that has been on a successful slimming diet – elegant, poised, and without a note out of place.

Wilson's main innovation, however, was the way he focused his right-hand playing into single-note melodic lines. Although resorting to the odd phrase in octaves, his right hand neither has the volcanic quality of Hines, nor the sweeping breadth of Tatum's. Instead there is a logical, inexorable development of ideas, which resembles the style of a swing saxophonist or trumpeter even more closely than Hines. The touch is closer to Tatum's, which is not surprising given that Wilson wrote:

> I use a finger technique inspired by Tatum (whose finger technique was unsurpassed) and I combine that . . . with the melodic ideas and touch of Hines's octave playing, and, since I can stretch a tenth in the left hand, I use the stride bass I got from Fats Waller.[32]

Few pianists have written more explicitly and directly about their influences, or explained them as succinctly as Wilson. Yet what he describes is exactly the same process of synthesis of ideas that Eubie Blake, Willie "The Lion" Smith, and James P. Johnson experienced in Atlantic City. He supports my contention that jazz piano developed as a distinct entity, in parallel to ensemble jazz, each new generation of pianists selectively drawing on the innovations and characteristics of the last.

Among the pianists who came after those surveyed in this chapter, both Thelonious Monk (born 1917) and Bud Powell (born 1924) began their careers by absorbing the stride style. Powell's father, Richard, was himself a stride pianist and recalled: "Nobody had ever seen a jazz musician that young, or heard one play like Bud. He was a l'il old chubby fellow, and by the time he was ten, he could play everything he'd heard by Fats Waller and Art Tatum."[33]

Certainly, by the late 1930s Powell was playing stride in some of the established venues in New York, and he was not quite out of his teens when he joined Cootie Williams in 1944. The degree to which he could emulate the approach of Art Tatum is obvious from his May 1951 recordings of *It Could Happen to You*, where, particularly on the second, and originally unissued, take, he spatters the performance with Tatumesque runs and chord clusters. Despite the originality of his own contributions to bebop, Powell was clearly steeped in the whole piano tradition, and, to pick an example at random, his August 1957 recording of Jesse Stone's *Idaho* includes an uncannily accurate recreation of Teddy Wilson's style.

Wilson's single-line melodies were particularly influential on the pianists of Powell's generation, who took jazz piano forward into the modern era; but there was another swing player who made a similarly important contribution. This was Billy Kyle, born a couple of years later than Wilson, in 1914, and who was pianist with Lucky Millinder and later John Kirby's small group, before joining Louis Armstrong, with whom he remained until his death in 1966.

Kyle was strongly influenced by Earl Hines, and was given encouragement by the older man when Hines's band passed through Philadelphia, where Kyle grew up. But he was less physically suited to the piano than Hines, saying: "With my rather less elastic hands, I found I couldn't play all those rapid succession of octaves that Earl goes in for."[34]

The consequence of this was that Kyle worked round his physical limitations, and developed a single-note right-hand style that was in many ways comparable to Wilson's. Unable to base this directly on the model of another pianist, he identified a different influence, writing in 1939:

> My present style of playing came from a saxophone player who was working with me in 1934, and who gave me the idea of using the piano in the manner of a melody instrument, brass or reed. The main idea of improvisation in swing music is to create a new melody line in your improvisation, and naturally the saxophone, clarinets, trumpets and trombones all do this in a sequence of single notes. I adopted this technique on the piano, and incidentally I was doing it long before I heard anyone else trying it.[35]

What made Kyle's playing entirely different from Wilson's, and paved the way for players like Powell, was the use of his left hand. Kyle may have felt that this hand suffered from a similar physical inhibition to his right, when it came to stretching tenths and creating the familiar oompah bass of stride, because, for the most part, he ignored such a concept of playing entirely. Instead, to back up his right-hand melodies, he created an incredibly varied mixture of occasional chords, tremolos, repeated single notes, off-center punctuating discords, and – most characteristic of all – a slight anticipation of the first beat of a measure, in which two notes, the interval of a second apart, are struck almost together, but with the lower coming fractionally earlier. He created the impression that no harmony was ever truly resolved, and each measure looked forward to the one that followed. This made for a feeling of considerable tension, which he could build and maintain throughout a chorus, and which is perfectly demonstrated on his May 1939 trio recording for Decca, *Finishing up a Date*.

Kyle had solved the problem of how a pianist could accompany the kind of complex melodic lines that would be developed by the bebop players from the style he and Wilson had created, without resorting to the increasingly anachronistic conventions of stride. Kyle himself never made the transition to modern jazz, but pianists who took a similar approach, notably Kenny Kersey and Clyde Hart, provided the stylistic bridge between stride and bebop.

Stride was not, however, the only popular jazz piano style in the period from the 1920s to the 1940s. If it was the *lingua franca* of the Harlem rent party, its Chicago counterpart was the rough-edged, blues-based style of boogie-woogie, which reached its zenith a little later than stride, during World War II. Some stride players took such exception to what they saw as a simplistic variation on the twelve-measure blues that they refused to play it – Fats Waller even including a clause in his contracts that expressly stated he would not perform any kind of boogie-woogie. But not even Waller could ignore the popularity of the style, and demonstrated his nonchalant mastery of a rolling boogie left hand in his recording of *Alligator Crawl*, a piece originally called *Charleston Stomp* (which may explain its use of the device, as a direct emulation of Eubie Blake's *Charleston Rag*).[36]

Despite his personal taste, Waller often found himself billed alongside pianists who specialized in the genre. For example, during his 1939 residency at Chicago's Panther Room, he alternated sets with the formidable team of Albert Ammons, Pete Johnson, and Meade "Lux" Lewis at three pianos, who called themselves the "Boogie Woogies."[37] Their playing offered a lively cross-section of the various patterns that made up the style, which had emerged onto the national stage during the 1920s, and taken its name from Clarence "Pinetop" Smith's December 1928 recording of *Pinetop's Boogie Woogie*.

Boogie-woogie piano goes back much further than that, however. We know from Blake that William Turk had been playing left-hand patterns that were absorbed into the style in the early years of the twentieth century, and that other Eastern-school pianists, such as James P. Johnson and Willie "The Lion" Smith, also heard "Texas" or "Southern" bass patterns in use in Atlantic City in 1914 or thereabouts. So where did these come from?

Like most other styles in jazz, boogie-woogie is a synthesis of different elements, in this case mainly drawn from piano accompaniments that were developed to back blues singers on the various touring circuits, and also from a rough-and-ready type of African-American solo piano, played for entertainment and dancing in the lumber, turpentine, and railroad camps of the Southern states: Texas, Louisiana, Mississippi, Alabama, Arkansas, Georgia, and Florida. This piano style was predominantly blues-based as well, as one of its rural practitioners, Buster Pickens, explained:

> Up and down the Santa Fe tracks in those days was known as the barrelhouse joints. These places were located in the area where the mill was in, and you played all night long in those days. They danced all night long. And the blues was what they wanted; they didn't want anything else. They wanted them low. You didn't have to be fancy at all – just bear down![38]

Barrelhouse was the generic term for a bar, café, or restaurant that provided food, drink, and, once a week or so, dancing as well, for isolated rural communities and labor camps. There was, frequently, illicit back-room gambling too, and, according to those who played the circuit, like Little Brother Montgomery and Danny Barker, often there were girls on hand. As Peter Silvester says in his history of the genre, the pioneer pianists "provided a brash musical backdrop for the gambling, drinking, whoring and dancing that were the popular forms of entertainment in many of the isolated communities near the work places."[39] With the requirements of this kind of setting to provide an escape from the grind of daily life, the pianists who played the circuit produced an almost endless flow of variation on the basic blues harmonic sequence.

Montgomery, a master of the style from Kentwood, Louisiana, did not come to record until 1930, but he is an important witness to the emergence of boogie-woogie. He was born in 1906, and he grew up in a barrelhouse "juke joint" run by his father. As a consequence, from around 1911, when his father first installed a piano, he heard most of the itinerant players who passed through, and it is clear from his comments that by the early 1910s an early form of the boogie-woogie style had crystallized. In his own memoirs and in those of Danny Barker, who toured the juke joints of Mississippi with him in the mid-1920s and later wrote down Montgomery's dictated account of his experiences, we have lists of names of these obscure players whose work went unrecorded, but which was clearly influential in shaping an entire genre.

Montgomery was a child prodigy, able to play by ear and remember what he heard from an early age. His own playing was influenced by his uncle, Gunzy Montgomery, and the pianists he recalled hearing in his childhood included Vanderbilt Anderson, Leon Bromfield, Friday Ford, Son Framion, Loomis Gibson, Blind Homer, Blind Jud, Bob Martin, Gus Pevsner, and Sudan Washington. The most impressive were Jelly Roll Morton (who passed through around 1913) and Tony Jackson's cousin, Tommy Jackson, both of whom were more versatile, but Montgomery's own favorite remained Cooney Vaughn (or Vaughan), whom he described as "the greatest pianist he had ever heard."[40] By the age of eleven, in 1917, Montgomery was on the road himself, working the Santa Fe circuit as a juke-joint pianist, although soon afterwards he also played at various cabarets in New Orleans, and was a sufficiently accomplished band pianist to play in a number of pioneer jazz groups.

By and large, boogie-woogie seems not to have cross-fertilized with ensemble jazz in New Orleans; and Montgomery, whose subsequent playing credits included work with Kid Ory and Lee Collins in Chicago, seems to have been a rare exception as a player who could cross over into the more varied repertoire of jazz. Danny Barker told me that boogie-woogie piano, in keeping with its rural background and juke-joint provenance, remained very much a neighborhood entertainment in New Orleans, for those who lived back of town, in the sixth and seventh wards. He heard the style there as a boy, and wrote this memoir of it being nicknamed "the horses" after the galloping left hand.

> In New Orleans around 1918, there had been a boy named Wilfred Atkins, whose mother, aunts and uncles taught at their own small private school. Wilfred had a disfigured eye and so was named "Buck Eye Wilfred". He was a neighborhood celebrity in the Seventh Ward, and played at all social affairs — parties, weddings, divorces and in bar-rooms. He could be found in any affair in that neighborhood. He was a fair piano player, and when the affairs heated up, the older folks would start to shout: "Wilfred, play the horses." Then he would start to play boogie woogie with a continuous, monotonous, medium rhythmical beat. He would tire, but would not stop. He would just raise his right hand for three or four minutes while he continued to play with his left hand, then he would rest his left hand. ... The folks would dance, barely moving — you'd just hear feet shuffling and the bass boogie beat.[41]

When Barker talked to Jelly Roll Morton about his memories of the boogie-woogie style, at the time they played together in 1930s New York, Morton was disparaging about the role it had played in New Orleans, before he went on the road. He was equally harsh in his Library of Congress interviews, making only passing references to it, and indicating that it was a rural and untutored genre: "Why shouldn't I hold my own with fellows who only know one tune?" he asked Alan Lomax.[42]

However, within the limitations of the genre, a fascinating range of variation developed. This is principally to do with the left hand, which is used to create a kind of rhythmic perpetual motion underneath right-hand patterns that frequently include complex cross-rhythms. The basic rolling left hand, using alternating octaves on each eighth note is the best known device, but other frequently used variants range from eighth-note or quarter-note chords to single-note ostinatos.

Little Brother Montgomery recalled his own development in mastering these various patterns, starting with the single-note walking bass:

> When I first tried to play it I was only around the age of nine so I used to only play a walking bass with one finger then, but after I got up around twelve or fourteen I could double up and I could play with all of my hand. . . . I was playin' what you call boogie woogies ever since I was twelve or fourteen years old but then we called it *Dud Low Joe*.[43]

Montgomery's speciality was a very slow form of blues, known as the "44s" in which the left hand began by slightly anticipating the first beat of each measure by rolling up to the bass note with a slur. In subsequent choruses, the left hand rolled up to each beat in turn. In some of these choruses, the bass part was played in intervals of a tenth, the left hand rolling on each beat between the fundamental and the tenth above it in an entirely different manner from the way the same interval was used in stride. Montgomery taught the technique to a clothes presser and amateur pianist in Vicksburg, Mississippi, called Lee "Pork Chops" Green, who in turn taught it to the Arkansas pianist Roosevelt Sykes. In due course, Sykes introduced it to Chicago, where it became a staple of the city's boogie-woogie pianists. When I heard both Sykes and Montgomery in the mid-1970s, they were both still using this slow, effective type of blues piano in their repertoire.

The *Vicksburg Blues* was Montgomery's showcase example of the 44s, which he recorded three times in the early 1930s. In each, the slow, rolling left-hand sets what seems at first an impossibly slow tempo. Hearing it today has the same electrifying effect as when the teenage Danny Barker first heard it floating out of the window of a New Orleans cabaret in 1926:

> What I heard excited me because I'd never heard a blues played so slowly, so sad and so complicated before. . . . What I was hearing on the piano that night was a tempo which was precise – on time, in time, but slower than a funeral march.[44]

Montgomery showed Barker how to accompany him on banjo, playing just the first beat of each measure and keeping up a slow tremolo for the remainder of the bar.

Such slow blues pieces were just one small part of the arsenal of variations within the twelve-measure structure developed by the boogie players. Playing initially for a rural audience of working people, and later for the African-American population in Northern cities, principally on Chicago's South Side, the pianists' work in all its variety was richly invested with semantic value. As a solo instrumental form of blues, let alone a frequently used form of accompaniment to singers, boogie-woogie had a direct semantic relationship with the subject-matter of blues lyrics, and the meaning of this music would have been readily understood by listeners directly familiar with the themes of everyday life, heartache, imprisonment, love, pain, poverty, and racial tension, frequently expressed in such lyrics. But beyond that, boogie offers a series of musical tropes that achieve what Albert Murray has called a "telling effect." These "tell a story," using musical devices to create what Samuel A. Floyd Jr. terms the Call–Response trope, building up in the informed listener a sense of what the player "feels and assumes," in other words, creating a Signifyin(g) effect, a range of metaphorical meanings that stretch well beyond what is superficially apparent.[45]

A powerful illustration of this comes where, in similar vein to "the horses," boogie-woogie has been used to create onomatopoeic pieces, to do with trains. An early example was Lemuel Fowler's *Express Train Blues*, from 1925, but the most famous piece of this type was *Honky Tonk Train Blues*, by Meade "Lux" Lewis, first recorded in 1927. Lewis's sound-portrait of a train ride, from his rolling warm-up to the series of choruses built over the charging, inexorable railroad rhythm of his left hand, with occasional chime whistles, the clacketty sounds of level crossings, the rattle of passing bridges and tunnels, and the final slowing down to a stop, would have been instantly familiar to all who heard it. Indeed, it is possible for all listeners to decode the piece at that simplistic level, but at a far more fundamental level the piece plugged directly into the experience of those African-Americans who had taken part in the Great Migration from the South to Chicago, and of their extended families who either remained in the South or who were crowded into the urban North. The very title of the piece was a reference to the "honky tonk" excursion trains, consisting entirely of "Jim Crow" cars, that were organized to take migrants back to visit their families in the South. Non-stop entertainment, often with a boogie-woogie pianist, was provided, thus adding an additional layer of meaning to the piece. It had resonances, too, of the élite group of African-American Pullman porters, who – as they plied the country – were as effective a conduit for news, intelligence, ideas, and music as the show business networks I have discussed already. As Stanley Crouch put it:

> The story goes in as many directions as the country goes. Tracks and tracks and tracks and tracks. You could step out of the Atlantic Ocean and get on the big train. You could step off the Pacific Coast and take a ride on the big train. Coming up from the South to Chicago, the big train put the riverboat in its place.[46]

At the time the boogie-woogie pianists were making their presence felt in Chicago, the railroad routes that led there, every bit as much as the city itself, were already integral to African-American consciousness. Danny Barker set out how this was perceived in 1920s New Orleans:

> Chicago was considered to be the safest place near New Orleans; all other places between those two points were looked upon just as visiting points ... and the trip there was a direct one, preferably by way of the Illinois Central Railroad. ... I had the idea when I was a youngster that getting off a Chicago-bound train (or being put off) before it reached its destination was like a ship's captain in mid-ocean, putting someone on a small raft to drift without provisions (naturally thousands of sharks surrounded the craft). ... I hear people tell of the wonderful city of Chicago in detail. The end of the telling is always of the porter hollering, "Kankakee and Hammond, Indiana; you are almost there – at the gates of heaven." No more mean white folks. Every stop of the train to Chi was bad territory and to be avoided.[47]

Additionally, there was something in the feel of Chicago itself that further fueled the fashion for this variant of boogie-woogie, perhaps most obviously the rhythms of the elevated railroad or "El" which ran alongside so many of the city's buildings at first or second-floor height. Amid its constant noise, the rumbling of trains and clicking of points, the forceful, rhythmic piano style echoed its clatter.

Meade "Lux" Lewis (who got his curious nickname by imitating the mannerisms of a comic strip character, the "Duke of Luxembourg") owed at least part of his skill at recreating railroad noises at the keyboard to the fact that "Big Bertha" freight locomotives on the New York Central roared past the windows of his home on South La Salle. His childhood friend Albert Ammons was one of the host of other pianists who adopted the train motif in his playing, recording *Sixth Avenue Express* in 1941 as a duet with Pete Johnson.

One of the most vivid and effective employments of train devices in this repertoire comes from the obscure Alton, Illinois, pianist Wesley Wallace. His *Number 29* combines the musical tropes of boogie-woogie with a spoken narrative, relating the story of a hobo riding freight train 29 from Cairo to East St. Louis, how the train gathered speed too fast for him to climb down, and his fall head-over-heels from the train as it dashed along. In this performance, irony and hyperbole combine in the spoken commentary, but words and music together create an allegorical picture that represents far more than a single hobo riding the freight train until "I got up and waved my hand, told her goodbye."

In New York, the stride pianists reflected the world of the rent party in their performances. Fats Waller, for example, both recorded and made a film short of *The Joint Is Jumpin'*, depicting the mayhem of an apartment shindig that gets so far out of hand that the police are called. Again, this operates on several levels, but what all listeners would find amusing, boisterous, and humorous took on a different layer of meaning within the urban African-American cultural base of the time. The performance is a Signifyin(g) musical event. The same applies to the parallel world of the Chicago rent party with its boogie-woogie backdrop.

Certainly, the impact of Alabama-born Clarence "Pine Top" Smith (1904–29) on his 1928 recreation on disc of a characteristic rent-party piece, *Pine Top's Boogie Woogie*, was important. So was the evocation of this world in the playing of other musicians like Cripple Clarence Lofton (1887–1957), who dominated the rent-party scene from about 1917, and "Cow Cow" Davenport (1894–1955), who arrived in the city in 1925 from the touring-theater circuit. Indeed, both Smith and Davenport had toured in vaudeville, and while this no doubt equipped both men to play a wider range of material than boogie-woogie alone, it had also allowed them to develop a spoken patter that went hand-in-glove with their playing, and which was an integral part of the persona their audiences expected of them.

It is a straightforward matter to assess stride pianists in the conventional musicological and critical terms of technical virtuosity, because of their style's explicit links with the classical tradition. By contrast, boogie-woogie has fewer parallels with the European approach to piano. It has neither the harmonic nor melodic variety of stride, nor does it have equivalent opportunities for displaying classical qualities of touch, timing, and complexity. The historian, record producer, and sometime *avant-garde* percussionist Bill Russell neatly described how, despite being "rhythmically more simple than some types of African music, it is still more complex and polyrhythmic than the conventional jazz piano style."[48] Its principal exponents combined considerable technical mastery of repetitive patterns and complex cross-rhythms with the ability to pack emotion and meaning into their playing. Meade "Lux" Lewis, Albert Ammons, and the Kansas City-based Pete Johnson excelled at these qualities, producing programmatic sound-pictures in their playing, and combining this with buoyant energy and the power of the blues.

One of the most effective of all boogie-woogie pianists at expressing blues feeling was Jimmy Yancey, as demonstrated in his legacy of recordings from 1939 to 1940. Even at a brisk clip, such as on *Yancey Stomp*, he manages to keep a sense of melancholy running through the piece by occasional use of flattened thirds and sevenths, but at medium or slow tempo he excels. His *State Street Special* is taken at a stately tempo, but it uses a considerable variety of left-hand patterns to create variety and – when he slows, suspends, or interrupts the regular ostinato – builds up considerable tension which is released both by transferring a more rapid sequence of patterns to the right hand, or by subsequently resuming his original left-hand figures.

Not all Yancey's blues-inflected pieces followed the conventional twelve-bar sequence, and his *Slow and Easy Blues* is based on a sixteen-measure structure. Nevertheless, this piece, with its skipping left-hand figure, also demonstrates Yancey's ability to suggest Hispanic or Creole rhythms in his compositions, many of which were written years before he came to record them. In later life he made his living as groundskeeper for the White Sox baseball team at Comiskey Park, and during his major period as a professional performer, he had not been a pianist, but a child dancer (even, he told Art Hodes, dancing "for the King and Queen of England in my time").[49]

Yancey was typical of several of the major names in boogie-woogie, in that he was seldom a full-time professional musician for long, and largely relied on other jobs. Whereas the best-known of the stride players in New York were involved in show-business, touring revues, providing backing for singers, making records, and so on, only a few of their boogie-woogie counterparts were versatile enough to follow such a path, as for the most part their music was, as Hodes put it:

> from a time when people spoke simply and plainly. They understood one another. No explanations needed. . . . This is (for want of a better word) black folk music. You hang out and listen and take it in and you dig the different moods and feelings of a people.[50]

Boogie-woogie compressed this expression of moods and feelings into a remarkably rigid stylistic framework, and only a few pianists experimented with any kind of fusion or integration with other styles. A piece such as J. H. Shayne's *Mr. Freddie Rag* stands out as a rare example of fusing boogie with the earlier fashion for ragtime in his home town of St. Louis.

When their music slipped out of fashion, many boogie pianists disappeared into obscurity. The subtle and harmonically sophisticated Montana Taylor gave up playing in 1936 for several years and settled in Cleveland. The same city became home around the same time to Cow Cow Davenport for some years, after he temporarily retired from touring, a broken man. Others who faded from view included Clarence Lofton, Turner Parrish, and Charles Spand.

The trio of Ammons, Johnson, and Lewis suffered no such fate, and were celebrated in Chicago and later in 1940s New York, as well as being recorded for major labels alone and together. All three, but particularly Ammons and Johnson, also successfully made the transition to being effective ensemble pianists.

Johnson's *Piney Brown Blues*, from 1940, with his Fly Cats and blues shouter Joe Turner, is a magnificent example of ensemble blues, but what Gunther Schuller describes as Johnson's "astonishing piano embellishments" are taken directly from the vocabulary of slow boogie-woogie. His "dense web of blue-note tremoloes, trills and runs, mostly in sixty-fourth notes"[51] is an urgent, rococo counterpart to Turner's anguished singing, and through it all, Hot Lips Page weaves some virile muted trumpet. Johnson made several other band discs, many with Turner as vocalist, and in the majority he found an equally effective way to integrate his dense right-hand patterns with an ensemble which itself assumed the role of a boogie pianist's left hand.

This was also Ammons's great strength, and his *Boogie Woogie Stomp*, from February 1936, cut with his Rhythm Kings, became the template for transferring up-tempo boogie pieces into the jazz-ensemble repertoire. In addition to integrating his surging left hand with Ike Perkins on guitar, Israel Crosby on bass, and Jimmy Hoskins on drums, Ammons created space for his soloists: clarinetist Delbert Bright and Louisiana trumpeter Guy Kelly. It is Kelly, in particular, who demonstrated how a floating, laid-back New Orleans-style jazz trumpet could hover over the pulsating rhythm (an effect subsequently widely imitated, not least by Harry James in his 1939 trio discs with Pete Johnson or Ammons himself). Kelly and Bright combine on the final choruses to play simple riff patterns, a prototype of what happened when boogie-woogie was drawn into the repertoire of the popular swing orchestras of the late 1930s and 1940s.

For the most part this process was gradual, though occasionally it was sudden and overt. Texan boogie pianist Sammy Price, for example, who contributed piano backing to dozens of jazz and blues discs for Decca in the late 1930s and early 1940s, recorded a band arrangement of *Cow Cow Blues* in March 1940. "Later," wrote Price, "Bob Crosby took the whole arrangement, note for note, and didn't say a word to me. Well, I didn't care because I wasn't greedy, I was making money and I had gained recognition."[52]

Nevertheless, it is a supreme irony that just as many of the pianists who developed the style were leaving music, or retreating to obscurity, swing orchestras discovered the genre and popularized it to an unprecedented degree. Most effective were African-American bands, from King Oliver (who recorded *Boogie Woogie* in 1930) to Erskine Hawkins (who cut Avery Parrish's feature *After Hours* a decade later), and Count Basie mastered the genre. As Lewis A. Erenberg points out, Basie's incorporation of train imagery into his boogie-woogie orchestral arrangements was as significantly loaded with meaning for its audience as the piano-based pieces I discussed earlier. Although he was a stride player first and foremost, Basie spent long enough in Kansas City and the Midwest to become thoroughly immersed in the boogie style. Erenberg says: "The boogies (*Boogie Woogie, House Rent Boogie, Red Bank Boogie, Basie Boogie*) . . . filled with folk references and shout licks and choruses, touched on the realities of the depression for blacks, solidified the group around them, yet pointed to a better future."[53]

In parallel with this, and also capitalizing on the boisterous feel-good factor of up-tempo boogie-woogie, many white swing orchestras also added boogie pieces to their books of arrangements. Among others, Ben Pollack (1937), Les Brown, Bob Crosby, and Tommy Dorsey (1938), Harry James and Bob Zurke (1939), Frankie Trumbauer and Will Bradley (1940), Woody Herman (1940 and 1941), and Gene Krupa (1941) all recorded boogie-woogie numbers, and the transfer of a Southern folk form of African-American piano blues to mainstream American entertainment was complete. But that is getting ahead of the story, and of the rise of the big bands, which is covered in the following chapter.

CHAPTER 4

# The Rise of the Big Bands

## Paul Whiteman: The King of Jazz

The more I worked with jazz, the surer I was that its
authentic vitality would take root and develop on what I
called a symphonic basis.

Paul Whiteman, from *Jazz*, 1926

Few famous bandleaders have been the cause of more critical controversy
than Paul Whiteman. To many Americans in the 1920s and 1930s, this
avuncular, rotund figure, waving a baton, and with a wry grin under his
pencil moustache, personified jazz. By no means everything his band played
could be called jazz – from arrangements of the light classics to settings for
singers – but particularly in the period from 1927 onwards, his big band
included in its ranks many of those who have come to be regarded as the
finest white soloists in the history of the music, from Bix Beiderbecke and
Jack Teagarden to Frank Trumbauer and Jimmy Dorsey. Furthermore, his
ambition to bring jazz into conjunction with European symphonic music
resulted in the composition of George Gershwin's *Rhapsody in Blue*, which,
while not jazz itself, draws heavily on aspects of it, and is one of the most
enduring and universally popular pieces of American concert music of the
twentieth century.

Whiteman was beloved by his musicians, whom he treated fairly and
generously. They nicknamed him "Pops" or "Fatho," and the majority of
them shared saxophonist Arthur Rollini's view that he was "truly a great
man with a quick wit. But he was also a gentle man."[1] The son of the head
of musical education for Denver's public-school system, Whiteman was an

accomplished violinist and arranger, and his credentials for a career in music were impeccable. Nonetheless, this background also gave him the values and the aspirations of the white middle class to which he belonged, and when he discovered the fledgling jazz scene on the West Coast during a spell as a viola player in the San Francisco Symphony Orchestra, in 1914–15, he wrote: "The great American noise, jazz, was then just drifting out of the shanties and tango belt to begin its ascent into the ballrooms of the cultured." [2]

There is strong evidence to suggest that it was as a consequence of this aspiration that Whiteman held for jazz – to bring it out of the roughneck shanties and brothels of San Francisco's Barbary Coast into the mainstream of popular entertainment – that the whole craft of the big-band arranger was initiated.

Yet, until a revaluation of sorts began in the 1970s, spearheaded by the British writer Max Harrison, the majority of jazz critics gave him little credit for his achievements, including those who grudgingly acknowledged his early success, like Hugues Panassié, in the 1934 comment I quoted earlier: "Paul Whiteman, who once had a band that could really swing, concerns himself now with 'what the public wants.' He specializes in what strikes me as empty, pompous performances – nicknamed 'symphonic jazz.' "[3]

Taking his output as a whole, rather than looking for the many examples of spirited jazz it contains, other critics have been even harsher on Whiteman than Panassié was, and their focus on the vast, lumbering orchestras of his later years as a leader has tended to create a view of his work that ignores both the considerable innovations he made in the early 1920s, and his more zesty jazz-orientated discs of the late 1920s. Even in these, despite a rhythm section driven along by the buoyant bass of Steve Brown, and some uncompromising jazz solos from the likes of Bix Beiderbecke, critics still found little good to say. The British author Albert McCarthy, for example, wrote in 1971: "While the Whiteman band was, as a group, incapable of turning out an authentic jazz performance, it could at least provide a setting for a jazz soloist that was not totally inept."[4]

To my mind, it produced a number of extremely effective jazz discs, and an example like *From Monday On* (February 1928), notwithstanding the light-hearted vaudeville vocals by Bing Crosby and the Rhythm Boys, or a half-chorus of slightly stilted string playing, is far from inept, and, as well as including an outstanding Beiderbecke solo, is as good an example of big-band ensemble jazz as one is likely to hear from the period.

Nevertheless, it is undoubtedly on account of such vocally – not to say theatrically – centered pieces that even such a recent writer as the historian

Frank Tirro ignores the vaudeville connections of so much other early jazz, or the musically diverse programs of New York's Clef Club concerts, and complains of the "endless supply of popular singers, semiclassical arrangers and composers, [and] vaudeville tricksters" that Whiteman, "whose claim to the title 'King of Jazz' does not go undisputed among jazz connoisseurs, paraded before his public."[5]

This uncharitable view of Whiteman reached its zenith in the 1950s, Barry Ulanov writing that Whiteman "needed the subsidiary reputations of his musicians and singers to maintain his holding-company position as 'King of Jazz,'" but he nevertheless acknowledged the unique chord that Gershwin's *Rhapsody in Blue* touched in the American sensibility, and that it was this which filled out "the gigantic shadows cast by the Fatho's gargantuan figure."[6] Rudi Blesh was more forthright still:

> Whiteman never played jazz, not even when his bands employed men like Beiderbecke and Teagarden. Beginning in the early 1920s, he has played inferior music which "dates" immediately. He merely added to the confusion of the various decadent, inferior imitations of the Negro music.[7]

He went on to point out that much critical writing of the 1920s and 1930s did not refer at all to jazz, but to "Whiteman's sort of product." Finally, Blesh berates the tendency (as he sees it) encouraged by Whiteman towards "more harmony, more instruments, more technique."

Such a viewpoint assumes that the prototypical jazz ensemble was the five- to seven-piece Dixieland group epitomized by the O.D.J.B. or New Orleans Rhythm Kings, and it ignores the considerable evidence mentioned already, and in the next section of this chapter, that in parallel with such small groups, there were large jazz ensembles extant from very early in the music's history, ranging from the syncopated orchestras of Europe and Cook to the first "territory bands" and the floating conservatory of Marable. Fate Marable's band was, as we know from Louis Armstrong, using written arrangements as the mainstay of its performances by 1919, and had done so for some years. On the other hand, there is little evidence that any kind of consensus existed as to how such large ensembles should go about organizing their performances into a prevailing style.

My contention is that Whiteman played the leading role in influencing the kind of arrangements played by such bands of ten pieces or more – white and African-American – during the early 1920s, by supplying a functional and effective pattern for composers and arrangers to follow. The *manner* in which his band actually played these charts is more open to doubt. He originally employed no improvising soloists, and the phrasing of his ensemble was often stilted. Nevertheless, his concept of brass and reed sections, and how to voice the parts they played, was the important aspect of his innovation. He was successful because he developed his approach at the very time when big bands were making the transition from the instrumentation and ragtime-derived ensemble approach of the syncopated orchestras to the modern style of big band typified by Fletcher Henderson, and subsequently Duke Ellington.

Whiteman was nothing if not an astute observer and manipulator of popular taste, and his own account of his personal discovery of jazz is laden with the kind of language that demonstrates in equal measure what it was that attracted him to the music, and how he would subsequently create a romanticized view of it, in order to sell his own brand of jazz to his public.

> We first met – jazz and I – at a dance hall dive on the Barbary Coast. It screeched and bellowed at me from a trick platform in the middle of a smoke-hazed, beer-fumed room. And it hit me hard. Raucous? Yes. Crude – undoubtedly. Unmusical – sure as you live. But rhythmic, catching as the small-pox and spirit-lifting.[8]

He goes on to recount the account of an eyewitness who heard Tom Brown's New Orleans band:

> He was halted first by the perspiring grotesque energy of the four players. They shook, they pranced, they twisted their lean legs and arms, they swayed like madmen to a fantastic measure, wrung from a trombone, clarinet, cornet and drum.

Brown's band was, of course, made up of white Dixielanders, but contemporary accounts suggest it got close to the authentic sounds of African-Americans, one 1915 Chicagoan paper saying: "The Brown organization is said to be one of the few made up of white men which is capable of playing Negro music with the proper verve and tempo."[9]

As a symphonic player himself, bound by the conventions of the classical concert platform, such wild abandon obviously attracted Whiteman. He knew also that playing up the daring and controversial aspects of the new music would add a *frisson* of excitement to his own attempts to play it, and in his book on the subject, he includes a chapter documenting the pernicious effect jazz is supposed to have had on 1920s Americans. Harsh diatribes came from many quarters, and Whiteman quotes Dr. Florence H. Richards, medical director of a Philadelphia girls' school, who saw jazz as being "as harmful and degrading to civilized races as it always has been among the savages from whom we borrowed it."[10]

Despite quoting this blatantly racist description of African-Americans as "savages," it seems that throughout his career Whiteman was actually very highly regarded by many African-American musicians, not least because he unfailingly credited them as the source of his music – acknowledging A. J. Piron and John Robichaux, among others, in his writing. The black press, too, was generally kind to Whiteman, because, as a piece in the *New York Amsterdam News* put it, in a preview of his appearance at Harlem's Savoy ballroom in 1933: "Whiteman long ago established an *entente cordiale* between himself and Negro orchestra leaders, when he unhesitatingly paid tribute to the Harlem boys."[11]

That *entente cordiale* was further strengthened by Whiteman's very clear understanding of how jazz worked. In 1926, he wrote a description of the challenge facing the arranger that would not be out of place on many a jazz education course in the twenty-first century:

> Jazz seems to me to be, as nearly as I can express it, a musical treatment consisting largely in question and answer, sound and echo. It is what I call unacademic counterpoint. It includes rhythmic, harmonic and melodic invention. To rag a melody, one threw the rhythm out of joint, making syncopations. Jazz goes further, "marking" the broken rhythm unmistakeably. The great act in a jazz orchestra is a counterbalancing of the instrumentation, a realization of tone values and their placement.[12]

As a former symphony-section player, Whiteman couched his description in conventional orchestral terms, but together with the man he took on in 1919 as joint arranger, Ferde Grofé, who had acquired similar background experience in the Los Angeles Symphony Orchestra, he began systematically to establish consistent roles for brass, reed, and rhythm sections, and to feature these in a series of best-selling recordings, so that his approach became the norm throughout the 1920s.

Both Grofé and Whiteman emerged from the San Francisco entertainment world that flourished during World War I. Fortunately, during the Depression, the Works Progress Administration commissioned a history of San Francisco that documented this period of West Coast American music in some detail, and from it we learn that Grofé began his arranging career in the band led by drummer Art Hickman.

As I mentioned in Chapter 2, Hickman's band had been described in the San Francisco *Bulletin* as early as March 1913 as playing music that contained "jazz" or "pep." This was at a time when it was playing for a baseball training-camp at Boyes Hot Springs, and soon afterwards it moved into the St. Francis Hotel in San Francisco, to play at the Rose Room (a venue immortalized in Hickman's song of the same name).[13] Grofé, meanwhile, had been employed as a pianist at two Barbary Coast venues, Thalia and the Old Hippodrome, and he later recalled how the extraordinary *melée* of different music he heard there, including European folk tunes, African-American dances, and sailors' shanties, all formed the backdrop for his subsequent symphonic pieces such as the famous *Grand Canyon Suite*. The W.P.A. history then takes up the story:

> When Grofé left the Barbary Coast to play the piano with Hickman's band at the St. Francis Hotel, the two arranged music that was different and sparkling. Other orchestra leaders who played in San Francisco – Paul Whiteman, Rudy Seiger, and Paul Ash – became conspicuous exponents of this new music.[14]

Like Grofé, Hickman had picked up some of his ideas in the dives of the seamy Barbary Coast area, in particular at a club that featured African-American entertainers, called Purcell's. As the W.P.A. chronicler vividly described it:

> Along the Barbary Coast, the underworld whirled in fantastic steps to the rhythmic tunes of banging pianos, banjos, tom-toms, and blaring brass horns. . . . Assisted by honky tonk pianos ringing out *Frankie and Johnny*, gamblers fleeced their victims with inscrutible calm.

Hickman's predecessor, Herman Heller, brought the banjo from the Barbary Coast to the more refined surroundings of the Rose Room, and Hickman went one better, adding saxophones to his ensemble. The men he brought in were Bert Ralton and Clyde Doerr, members of a vaudeville team that was evidently one of a number of white equivalents to such African-American saxophone acts as the Musical Spillers, or the members of Wilbur Sweatman's Jass Band (which made some records in 1917). Hickman and Grofé wrote arrangements that used the saxophones playing together in harmony as a kind of "choir," against the melodic lines of the brass, and the effect proved immensely popular with the public, both at the St. Francis, and across the continent at New York's Biltmore Hotel, where the band traveled to play a residency in 1919.

Using saxophones in a large ensemble was not new – and some jazz historians have gone too far in suggesting that the Biltmore residency itself was where the "boom for the saxophone began."[15] Self-contained saxophone ensembles popular from 1907 onwards include the "American Saxophone Band," The Brown Brothers Sextet, and the various-sized ensembles led by the virtuoso Rudy Wiedoeft. The syncopated orchestras of James Europe, Will Vodery, and Will Marion Cook had been using saxophone "choirs" as an element of their concerts for some time, and W. C. Handy's blues and ragtime recordings made in New York by his Orchestra of Memphis, during September 1917, include a full saxophone section. However, Handy's scoring makes little or no independent use of the saxophones, who are for the most part given parts in unison with the strings (three violins and a cello). It is probable that Handy's use of his thirteen musicians is a pointer to how other unrecorded bands of similar size went about deploying their forces in the pre-Hickman period. The Memphis Orchestra's arrangements are directly derived from Joplin-style orchestrated ragtime of the *Red Backed Book* variety, although there is a little jazz license taken here and there, for example when the trombonist adds slurs and introductory glissandi to the cello part on *The Snaky Blues*.

Elsewhere in the United States, pictures from around 1915 taken in New Orleans show that Happy Schilling's white dance orchestra employed a saxophone section of Fred Dantagnan, Jack Piptone, and Don Sanderson.[16] In the next section of this chapter I shall investigate the first territory bands from the Midwest and Southwest in more detail, but typical among them was that of violinist and guitarist George Morrison, who progressively added saxophonists to his African-American band in Denver during the period from 1918 onwards, to the extent that he had a four-man section by 1920. He recalled that his group worked from unwritten "head" arrangements: "The other players played mostly straight, but I improvised." Yet he also made it clear that when his musicians got together to work out their new tunes, they had a model in mind, as he told Gunther Schuller: "You know at that time I was so very fond of the Art Hickman band."[17]

Hickman and Grofé were the first to arrive at a paradigmatic treatment for the way the saxophones would work together in the ensemble, and this was helped along by playing the written scores with greater precision than the majority of their predecessors.

Here was what Whiteman seized on as his opportunity. Initially, while still holding down his job with the symphony, Whiteman had led a seven-piece dance band, which he claims was "playing jazz in San Francisco prior to World War One,"[18] in other words, before April 1917. Once he had left the orchestra, and after a brief wartime spell in the navy, Whiteman followed Hickman's example, and brought saxophones into an enlarged version of his dance band, which he took to southern California in 1919, to cash in on the reputation he had achieved in San Francisco. As he established himself in Pasadena, and later the Alexandria district of Los Angeles, where he became popular with those who worked in the silent-movie industry, he transferred his musicians from a cooperative to a salaried basis, thereby laying the foundations for his subsequent vast business empire. He wrote:

> For quite a while I did the arrangements and orchestrations, as well as conducting, but it was too much for one man, so we took on Ferde Grofé, talented symphony player and composer. Now the two of us [could] work out our ideas together.[19]

With new arrangements that built on Grofé's pioneering work with Hickman, allied to Whiteman's exacting musical standards and flair for showmanship, the band went to Atlantic City and thence to New York, where it remained based at the time of its first recordings in 1920.

Partly as a consequence of these recordings, but also because of its fashionable and high-profile residency at the Palais Royal on Broadway, where it played for the likes of such well-heeled socialites as the Vanderbilts, Drexel Biddles, and Goulds, the band rapidly became very popular. Whiteman's own avuncular persona combined the role of society bandleader with the idea that he was the epitome of something new, daring, and exotic. On the back of this, Whiteman was soon a wealthy man, in due course moving into an estate at Pelham on the borders of Westchester County, and indulging his taste for fast cars and high living.

In some respects the band's popularity was a lucky accident of timing. For several years the self-same vogue for dancing that the Chicago city fathers had encouraged, around the time that Tom Brown's band opened at

Lamb's Cafe in 1915, had been spreading outwards from Chicago and New York. It had been helped along by the extraordinary enthusiasm with which the same white, upper social echelons who flocked to Whiteman at the Palais Royal had taken up the various dances promoted by the dance team of Vernon and Irene Castle, New York's leading exponents of steps ranging from the hesitation waltz to the foxtrot. The majority of these dances, particularly after the end of World War I, mixed what Ronald M. Radano memorably called "patrician sophistication with sexual suggestiveness and lack of restraint,"[20] to the extent that by 1920 they had become a national phenomenon. Although James Reese Europe's syncopated orchestra had provided backing for the Castles, thereby linking African-American music with the dances in the public mind, Whiteman arrived in New York at the precise moment to exploit the craze, with music that was designed to sell his idea of jazz to the white public.

In terms of recordings, prior to 1921 when Ralph Peer launched Okeh's "Race" series of discs, targeted specifically at African-Americans, the market for discs was still predominantly white, but it was a large and insatiable market, in particular for music to satisfy the dance craze, to the extent that the major companies, Victor and Columbia, were turning out as many one-steps, two-steps, foxtrots, waltzes, and tangos as possible. There had been some shortage of raw materials, such as shellac, during the war, even in the United States, and it was not until 1920 that record production was finally able to grow to meet the public's demand. That year, 100 million records were sold across the country, and approximately one million of those were the Paul Whiteman Band's recording of *Whispering*, backed by *Japanese Sandman*.

Anti-trust legislation and the court ruling to set aside the lateral-cut patent broke the main record companies' monopoly in 1919, and brought several competitors to Victor and Columbia onto the scene in the early 1920s. The market consequently fell back somewhat, but Whiteman's disc of *Three O'Clock in the Morning*, made in 1923, achieved an overall total by 1928 of 1,723,034 copies, which was at that time a staggering quantity for a single performance by one artist.[21]

It is small wonder then that Whiteman's band became so influential. To its white record-buying audience, it became the epitome of jazz, but it was not long before a critical controversy arose as to whether the word "jazz" could accurately be applied to Whiteman's work. The arguments were eloquently summarized by the dancer and critic Roger Pryor Dodge in 1929, when he wrote of his doubt as to whether Whiteman should be "considered as belonging to the ranks of jazz at all." What Dodge believed as a prerequisite for jazz was a strong element of the primitive. His passionate writing described: "the savage rhythms that had shaped or been shaped by the ancestral dances of the tribe, and these formed in time a definite playing style; and in recognising this style, we recognize jazz."[22]

To Dodge, jazz that sought to eliminate or overly contextualize the primitive was not worthy of the name:

> It is a musical form produced by the primitive innate musical instinct of the Negro and those lower members of the white race who have not yet lost their feeling for the primitive. ... It is disliked by those who know it only in its diluted form and who, often under the impression that they are defending it, desire to bring about its fusion or confusion with the windbag symphony or the trick programme-closing rhapsody.[23]

The problem is that, even though this dates from the 1920s, Dodge already had the benefit of hindsight. By 1929, when this was written, it was all too obvious that Whiteman's work did not have the inspirational qualities of Armstrong, Bechet, or Morton, nor did he have the consistent ability to imbue every single one of his big-band discs with the kind of spirit that Henderson and Ellington were by then achieving. It was also obvious that ever since his first recording, *Wang Wang Blues*, made in September 1920, which had overtones of the O.D.J.B., Whiteman had quite deliberately distanced himself from the "savage rhythms" of Dixieland, and the polyphonic front line of the small band. Nevertheless, Dodge, in his passion for the primitive, overlooks the degree to which, between 1920 and 1924, Whiteman attained a level of ensemble cohesion and precision unmatched by other bands of the period, and by coupling this to the organizational principles he had worked out with Grofé, laid the foundation for Henderson's and Ellington's subsequent achievements.

The writer Gilbert Seldes spotted this aspect of Whiteman's importance in 1924 in his book *Seven Lively Arts*, which also proposed the notion that one of the essential qualities in popular art is transience, and that a desire for freshness, the new, and the original is a defining characteristic of jazz, and – in a wider sense – the whole of popular music. He says: "Although nearly every Negro jazz band is better than nearly every white band, no Negro band has yet come up to the level of the best white ones, and the leader of the best of all, by a little joke, is called Whiteman."[24]

It was not until after 1924, and his "Experiment in Modern Music" concert at the Aeolian Hall in New York, when Gershwin's *Rhapsody in Blue* was premiered, that Whiteman ceased to make the running in large-band jazz. From then on, as he drifted for three or four years towards larger ensembles and symphonic pastiche, and until he re-stocked his band with outstanding jazz soloists and arrangers in the late 1920s, many arrangers and musicians, white and African-American, took up the baton of developing his earlier ideas and ran further with it, most notably Don Redman in his writing for the Fletcher Henderson Orchestra. However, up until 1924, Whiteman (mainly through the work of Grofé) established many devices, even trivial ones, that were imitated by other arrangers, and, as Max Harrison has pointed out in his detailed analysis of Whiteman's work, he also included a level of in-jokes and sophisticated musical commentary that only a few initiates among his listeners would have understood.[25]

*The Man I Love* quoted Wagner's *Tristan and Isolde*, *Nobody's Sweetheart Now* involved a wry allusion to Stravinsky's *Petrushka*; while other classical devices were, in Whiteman's early years, used to create a deliberate contrast with jazzy syncopation, as in the paraphrase of Rachmaninov during the introduction to *Hot Lips*. More to the point, in terms of the general development of big-band arranging, other bands imitated what had come to be recognized through his recordings as Whiteman hallmarks, including the slide whistle on *Whispering* (King Oliver's *Sobbin' Blues*), the oriental pastiche of *Japanese Sandman* (Ellington's *Arabian Lover*), and the "classical" piano of *When Day Is Done* (Louis Armstrong's *You're Next*). Even if many of these techniques were in common use, and Whiteman was merely following them as other arrangers later did, the fact that he was among the first to record them consolidated his influence.

Such specifics aside, Whiteman and Grofé showed, from the time of their earliest collaborations, ways of handling large brass and reed sections that nobody else had yet mastered. They gradually moved away from the ragtime orchestra concept of simultaneous unison statements of theme and counter-melody, which Handy's orchestra exemplified, and began to use antiphonal responses between the sections. Apart from the occasional inclusion of some tailgate trombone, they also steered the band's sound away from the Dixieland of the O.D.J.B. or its numerous imitators, the "Fives," and it is worth recalling that Handy had also used the trombone in a similar way to engender some jazz movement and feeling in his large ensemble. As Max Harrison says of Whiteman:

The overall sound of his earliest tracks ... was close to that of jazz bands which recorded a few years later, particularly in the disposition of brass and reed parts. ... During the four years between *Stairway to Paradise* [1922] and *Song of India*, for example, great advances were made in orchestral technique. The band's sound was now as personal, as instantly recognisable, as Ellington's later became, and had a far more consistent identity than Henderson ever attained on disc.[26]

At the same time as he was creating this aural identity for his band, Whiteman was equally successful in obtaining high-profile work and publicity, which is what did so much to cement his connection with jazz in the public imagination. In 1921 he played New York's Palace Theater, he appeared at the Globe on Broadway the next year in *George White's Scandals of 1922*, and topped that with a tour to England in 1923, in the revue *Brighter London*. On his return he began to be billed as the "King of Jazz," and this was the backdrop against which he commissioned George Gershwin to write *Rhapsody in Blue*, for the composer to perform using Ferde Grofé's orchestration for the band at the Aeolian Hall.

Whiteman was not a man to do things by halves. He demonstrated repeatedly in his career how he would pursue a single-minded ambition, such as to command the biggest band, the largest fees, or the most high-profile publicity, and he was generally successful in his aims. As we know, from the first time he heard jazz he claimed to have wanted to "develop" its "authentic vitality" on a "symphonic basis," and given his orchestral background plus (it is reasonable to suggest) his own father's significant role in music education, he nurtured this plan to bring jazz to the concert hall. When he eventually decided that it was time to lift his orchestra out of Broadway and onto the concert platform to present his "Experiment in Modern Music," he enlisted such prominent patrons and publicly advertised guests that their names alone comprehensively underlined the seriousness of his ambitions. They included Walter Damrosch, Leopold Godowsky, Jascha Heifetz, Fritz Kreisler, John McCormack, Sergei Rachmaninov, and Igor Stravinsky. The works he performed included pieces by Zez Confrey, Victor Herbert, and Irving Berlin, as well as Gershwin, and he was to follow this up in successive years with a string of further semi-symphonic performances of pieces by composers as varied as William Grant Still and Duke Ellington.

Much as jazz critics have rushed to condemn Whiteman's efforts, it seems to me that he not only took a hand in creating Gershwin's most enduring orchestral piece, but also initiated a public taste for jazz-inflected concert works, leading ultimately to such pieces as Stravinsky's 1945 *Ebony Concerto* for Woody Herman, and Benny Goodman's 1947 commissions of clarinet concerti from Aaron Copland and Paul Hindemith.

The program of the Experiment in Modern Music itself included over two dozen items, of which *Rhapsody in Blue* came near the end. Perhaps what has given rise to the bitterest critical furore over the years was the fact that Whiteman chose to open the evening by treating his audience to an exaggerated caricature of the O.D.J.B.'s *Livery Stable Blues*, about which he subsequently wrote: "When they laughed and seemed pleased with *Livery Stable Blues*, the crude jazz of the past, I had for a moment the panicky feeling that they hadn't realized the attempt at burlesque – that they were ignorantly applauding the thing on its merits."[27]

His intention was to show how many "million miles apart" such crude jazz was from the artistic subtlety of his new commissions, such as Gershwin's piece. And, of course, in the long term, he was right. In overall terms of American music (which was very specifically the context in which Whiteman compared the two) the sweeping musical landscape of *Rhapsody in Blue*, with its programmatic compilation of the sounds of 1920s urban America, of trains and bustling cities, coupled with echoes of the music of eastern European immigrants cheek-by-jowl with that of African-Americans, was of a totally different order from the knockabout fun of the O.D.J.B. It was about as different as the O.D.J.B.'s music itself was from the sublime statements of Armstrong, or the inspired ensembles of Morton's Red Hot Peppers. But fueled by Roger Pryor Dodge's views, published in 1939 in the influential book *Jazzmen*, critics have tended to take the view that Whiteman's comments show just how remote he was from "real" jazz, or what Dodge calls "the style which encourages musicians to improvise in jazz."

It seems absurd to believe that the vaudeville impressions of farm animals within the ragtime-inflected ensemble setting of the O.D.J.B. are in some way more profound music than *Rhapsody in Blue*, yet, for ten years before *Jazzmen* was published, Dodge had consistently advanced the view that "Whiteman, Gershwin, Berlin, and others are exponents of frivolous art,"[28] while simultaneously proposing that bands such as the O.D.J.B., because of their "primitive" qualities, were anything but frivolous. Other critics and jazz historians have followed his lead in assessing Whiteman, seldom, it seems, questioning whether the O.D.J.B. was actually representative of a long-term trend in jazz. Yet by the end of the 1920s, the five- or six-piece Dixieland band of this type would forever be an anachronism, and large bands taking their cue from the innovations of Whiteman and Grofé would continue to figure in the forefront of jazz development for several more decades.

Before leaving the subject of *Rhapsody in Blue*, it is worth making a couple more observations. First, because Whiteman's band was limited in size, Grofé's orchestration made exceptional technical demands on the musicians. The three reed players were required to double on a total of seventeen instruments, setting a standard for versatility and excellence which has continued into the jazz big bands of the twenty-first century, and which has few parallels in any other form of music. Even the twenty-first-century jazz *avant-garde* has been affected by the virtuoso doubling pioneered by Whiteman, and, in conversations with me, both Roscoe Mitchell and Anthony Braxton have cited the versatile reed players of such 1920s big bands, surrounded by their forests of instruments, as motivation for their own efforts to master all the woodwinds.

Second, because of his desire to bring his music into the concert hall, and because of the corresponding instrumental brilliance of his musicians, Whiteman, in Max Harrison's words "led some part of the audience for American popular music to listen instead of to dance."[29] In this he anticipated the subsequent endeavors of many jazz musicians from Benny Goodman and Stan Kenton to John Lewis and the Modern Jazz Quartet.

Although Whiteman's efforts alone did not elevate *Rhapsody in Blue* to its position of continuing popularity, they certainly helped. He recorded the piece, played it on concerts (including a European tour in 1926 to Paris, Berlin, Vienna, and London, where unsuccessful attempts were made to record it again in a live performance at the Royal Albert Hall), and in 1930 he included it in the movie *King of Jazz*. He was unshakable in his conviction that Gershwin was America's foremost composer, and his own prodigious success as a recording artist ensured that the piece sold extremely well on disc. The conductor Michael Tilson Thomas recalled:

Both my father and uncle knew George Gershwin, and as they were hearing it first being played, they knew that this piece was a great breakthough. And of course in the recordings that were made it swept the United States. My mother's family in Philadelphia told me how they rushed to the record stores to get it, and of the huge excitement when it first came out.[30]

Whiteman's championing of Gershwin continued – and it was a two-way process, the composer joining the Whiteman band on stage at the Roxy Theater in New York for two weeks in 1930 to accompany showings of *King of Jazz*. It is a convincing argument that it was Gershwin's long-term formal contact with Whiteman, every bit as much as his informal contact with the pianists of the Harlem rent-party circuit, that helped bring jazz rhythms into the mainstream of popular music. In Richard Crawford's words, Gershwin "learned from jazz musicians a more aggressive swinging beat, which by the mid-1930s had pervaded popular song ... from the swing beat, popular song gained both variety of rhythmic detail and coherence."[31] This led, in Gershwin's own case, to the composition of numerous songs which became staples of the jazz repertoire, as vehicles for solo and ensemble improvisation. Most significant was *I Got Rhythm* (1930), whose underlying chord sequence (the "rhythm changes") has underpinned dozens of related jazz numbers by other tunesmiths. But equally significant are others that date from the year of the Experiment in Modern Music onwards, including *Oh! Lady Be Good* (1924), *Fascinating Rhythm* (1924), *Someone to Watch Over Me* (1926), *Embraceable You* (1930), *Summertime* (1935), and *Nice Work If You Can Get It* (1937).

Whiteman's own work of the late 1920s was not so innovative as the best of that which dates from 1920–4, but his more jazz-orientated efforts from that later era, involving the Dorsey brothers, Beiderbecke, and the Teagarden brothers, contain plenty of evidence that Whiteman retained his early enthusiasm for jazz, and within the constraints of a big commercial dance band and broadcasting unit, could still turn his hand occasionally to creating some convincing jazz, using arrangements – mainly by Bill Challis – that remained demanding for the instrumentalists and ingenious to the listener.

Finally, despite all that I have said about the importance of Grofé and Whiteman on the development of the big band, it is nevertheless true that there is much from Whiteman's early career that is only tangentially connected to jazz, from flimsy popular songs and dances on the one hand, to pompous attempts at combining the classical and jazz worlds that lack the common touch and melodic creativity of Gershwin on the other. Nor was the early band awash with improvising soloists of the quality that Whiteman systematically employed in the late 1920s, which therefore put more emphasis on his arrangers, and the versatility of such skilled section players as saxophonists Ross Gorman, Chester Hazlett, and Charles Strickfadden in interpreting what they wrote. But Whiteman's colossal popularity should be borne in mind, as should the degree to which this colored the public perception of what jazz was, during a critically important time in the music's development. Nobody has better summed up the ambivalent and paradoxical role of early 1920s Whiteman better than Max Harrison in his 1970 essay on the subject: "The best aspects of his music were helping produce a climate sympathetic to jazz while the worst were responsible for the misrepresentation from which it has suffered ever since."[32]

# Territory Bands

> We played against some of the biggest bands in the business and we played them down, because we had such a versatile band. . . . We could do at least ten or twelve weeks of shows without doing the same thing over.
>
> Jesse Stone, in Nathan W. Pearson Jr., *Going to Kansas City*

The innovations of Art Hickman, Paul Whiteman, and Ferde Grofé helped to create a vocabulary for large jazz bands, playing something quite different from the Dixieland or "classic jazz" style. In their wake, music publishers employed staff arrangers to produce literally hundreds of dance-band arrangements crafted along similar lines by such writers as Archie Bleyer, Jimmy Dale, Arthur Lange, Jack Mason, Walter Paul, and Frank Skinner. The charts by these highly proficient arrangers were bought by would-be successful bands across the nation, both white and African-American, from the mid-1920s onwards. However, at least as important in shaping the type of big-band jazz that came to maturity in the middle-to-late 1920s was the loose-knit collection of traveling orchestras, most of them African-American, known as "territory bands." In terms of the geographical spread of jazz, and of launching the careers of many provincial musicians who subsequently became famous, these bands were equally significant.

Earlier historians have seen these bands as an adjunct to jazz history, a sideshow to the developments in New Orleans, Chicago, and New York. I prefer to take the view that they exemplify both the rapid expansion of jazz across North America, and the creation of ensemble music with quite distinct and original characteristics, which sprang up virtually simultaneously in many different locations. There remains an element of speculation as to the precise nature of these characteristics, and exactly when they emerged, because they were at best sporadically recorded. A few lucky orchestras got to make discs in the early-to-mid-1920s, but the majority of such bands to record did so in the late 1920s and early 1930s, by which time their innovations were no longer new, or their originality had been diluted by the influence of frequently recorded Eastern bands like those of Fletcher Henderson or Duke Ellington.

Nevertheless, we can be sure that the territory bands bred a number of individuals whose very independence from the better-known urban centers of the music had a very important role in shaping new directions in the development of jazz and popular music. Bennie Moten's band from Kansas City, Missouri, for example, grew from a trio to a sextet between 1918 and 1922, and made its first recordings the following year. Alphonso Trent became leader of his band in Dallas in 1923. Elsewhere in Texas, the white bandleader Peck Kelley was fronting his Bad Boys in Houston by 1921, if not before.

These bands were followed by others, such as those of Troy Floyd, George E. Lee, and T. Holder, and together they provided launch-pads for the careers not only of their leaders, but of numerous well-known musicians. Count Basie, for instance, may have begun as a stride pianist in the Harlem style, and worked the vaudeville circuits in 1924–5, but it was his experience in the territories from 1927 with Walter Page, Bennie Moten, and his own fledgling groups that launched his unique contribution to big-band jazz.

Among Basie's immediate associates, trombonist, guitarist, and arranger Eddie Durham learned his craft in the bands of the Southwest, and brought what he learned not only to Basie's band but also to Jimmie Lunceford's and to the all-female International Sweethearts of Rhythm. And the list goes on: Andy Kirk's career and that of his famous pianist-arranger Mary Lou Williams began in the Southwest, as did that of Jesse Stone, who went on to have as much to do with shaping rock and roll in the 1940s and 1950s as he had with creating big-band jazz in the 1920s. The most obvious example of a territory band musician who altered the entire course of jazz – although from the late 1930s rather than the early 1920s – is Charlie Parker, whose first significant playing experience was with Buster Smith and George E. Lee, and whose pioneer recordings were made in Jay McShann's Kansas City-based orchestra.

Criss-crossing the small towns and cities of the South, Southwest, and Midwest, territory bands brought jazz to local communities. If there was a theater, a dance hall, even a tobacco warehouse that would hold a band and the huge audiences such groups attracted, then the show was on. Although many important regional bands never recorded, those that did offer a fascinating glimpse of a provincial jazz world that vanished forever in the late 1940s.

Even the name "territory band" has something of a frontier atmosphere about it. Far from the urban centers of the United States, where much jazz development took place – such as New York, Chicago, and New Orleans – the territories were farming land, cattle country, or wilder, untamed expanses of plain or mountain. Amid the endless horizons of farmland in the Midwest, or the forested slopes of the mountainous states to the north and west, there were plenty of small towns and settlements where trading routes met, where railroads branched across country, or where the great river routes had their confluences. It was in these rural centers that the territory bands found their public.

As travel became easier during the late teens and early 1920s, with the advent of the mass-produced motor car, and as the network of roads began to improve, the "Jazz Age" reached the outlying districts of the territories. "There was a change in society going on," the pioneer territory bandleader Jesse Stone told me.

> World War I was over, and the period we called the "Roaring Twenties" was beginning, and it took hold because, since the changes that took place in wartime, women were now working. They had more freedom, they were smoking, buying cars, and driving them. Some of the women working in factories had a lot of money, and slowly but surely, the United States was getting entertainment conscious. In fact, in Kansas, people were hungry for entertainment.[33]

I have already discussed the growth of the dance craze from its origins in Chicago and New York, on the back of which Paul Whiteman launched his successful recording career. Out in the territories, the vogue for dance had its effect as well. From the end of World War I, popular songs and dances were disseminated aurally to some extent through vaudeville and traveling variety troupes, by sporadic live performances by touring orchestras from the big cities of the north and east, and by the spread of sheet music and the player piano as well as via the phonograph. This meant that gradually a demand built up, in even the most outlying areas, for home-grown entertainment, and above all for live music to dance to. In due course, broadcasting also played a significant part in reaching a far-flung rural audience, but as the 1920s began, as Gunther Schuller has pointed out, the demand may have existed, but the supply was another thing altogether. "Many smaller communities still could not afford a permanent dance hall, even less a permanent orchestra to provide the music," he wrote. "So the traveling territory bands came into existence in full force."[34]

Each orchestra or band needed to be based in a city that had access to a reasonable playing circuit of these smaller communities. If a band went the rounds too often, it would become stale and audiences would not turn out in sufficient numbers. Yet, conversely, a band needed a relative measure of exclusivity on its patch to build up a following.

This was equally true in areas not generally thought of in terms of territory bands, such as the well-developed Eastern industrial belt. Keyboard player and arranger Bill Doggett, who worked there in many touring groups, told me that in the mining district of Pennsylvania, a well-populated area with dozens of small-to-medium-sized communities, the Philadelphia-based Frankie Fairfax Orchestra, in which he was the pianist in the mid-1930s, "played out" the available circuit by touring just too often. When Fairfax took a short break and then went back with a different line-up, people turned up in force.[35] So, to avoid this kind of over-exposure, as well as having access to rural districts, the ideal central base for a touring orchestra was a city with a large-enough urban population to support a band in residence for a few weeks at a time, between forays onto the road.

Establishing this *modus operandi* actually took place very early in jazz history, and yet again demonstrates the independence of this significant slice of jazz development from what went on in New Orleans, Chicago, or New York.

The earliest traveling bands were formed in the period before 1920, when there was little in the way of available jazz recordings. Some itinerant groups, like Fate Marable's riverboat orchestras, traveled between the centers where jazz was being developed, and absorbed the current fashions, as well as employing several of the players who created them. But in the Midwest the story was quite different, and in the rural farming areas, or the regional commercial centers, national fashions were slow to arrive. "When I put together my first band of ten musicians," recalled Jesse Stone, "I had never seen or heard a similarly sized ensemble."[36] So, influenced by not more than a handful of best-selling discs, and by what sheet music he could get hold of, the seventeen-year-old Stone, whose career began somewhat earlier than has been recognized, played a mixture of ragtime, popular songs (from published editions), and his own compositions.[37] By the time that influential African-American bands such as King Oliver's began to record in 1923, many territory bands such as Stone's were already well on their way, mapping out a musical policy by trial and error, and playing at their next engagement what had gone over well with the public wherever they had played last.

Consequently, right from the start, many of these bands stood slightly outside the main jazz tradition, or appeared continually to ignore developments that caught on swiftly in the fashion-conscious environments of Chicago and New York. So, for example, when tubas and banjos were gradually replaced in the late 1920s and early 1930s by double basses and guitars, this happened in the big cities well before it caught on in the territories.

Often, the entire musical direction of a territory band was the result of an accidental meeting, or a coincidental influence. Jesse Stone, for example, playing in and around his home town of Atchison, Kansas, heard at second hand some of the jazz sounds being developed hundreds of miles away in New York in the syncopated orchestra of James Reese Europe. This happened when saxophonist Theodore Thyus, an ex-serviceman who had played in Europe's military band in World War I, returned to the area. Not long after his arrival, Thyus formed a trio, and Stone got to work with it when the first regular pianist died suddenly from gangrene, which set in after having the corns on his feet trimmed. According to Stone, he more or less invented his own entire style by absorbing what he learned from Thyus about rhythm, timing, and ensemble sound into his repertoire of ragtime and popular songs.

As I pointed out earlier, Europe's Orchestra, like that of Will Marion Cook, included a few "jazz" numbers in its programs of military band concert music, and Stone caught on quickly to the explanations of this new vogue. Soon (and from his own account, this was before 1918 was out), Stone was writing complete jazz arrangements for his players, including all their apparently "improvised" solos, since his musicians (largely friends from the local high school) had no instinctive grasp of this kind of music, and even less of improvisation. "Some of them didn't even know how to read music," he told me, "so I had to sing to them, so they could learn the stuff I wanted them to play."[38]

To his credit, Stone succeeded in creating an influential group, which seems from the outset to have had a sound of its own. Among his early band members were saxophonists Jack Washington, who went on to join Count

Basie, and Coleman Hawkins, a St. Joseph resident, who had newly taken up tenor saxophone after first learning cello and then C-melody sax. When Stone's Blue Serenaders finally came to record in 1927 (with Washington still in the line-up), the group retained plenty of its originality on *Boot to Boot* and *Starvation Blues*. Its distinct difference from Chicagoan or New York fashion depended on yet another ingredient from those aspects of timing and voicing Stone had learned from Thyus; something that was neatly summarized by Gunther Schuller:

> The utter freedom and relaxation of the phrasing . . . the melodic lines richly spiced with blue notes, the earthy, almost rough rhythmic feeling – all exemplify a vocally orientated musical style that could only emanate from the blues.[39]

I have already discussed the influence of the blues on individual instrumentalists, but Stone's band epitomizes a common feature of territory bands, and particularly those with Kansas City connections, in which blues feeling was created not by a single soloist but by an entire band, and absorbed into the vocabulary of the ensemble, both in terms of the underlying arrangement, and the way in which the musicians collectively approached playing it.

Like many first generation jazz bandleaders, Stone (born in 1901) had a classical music training on violin and piano. As I mentioned in Chapter 1, his forefathers had been slaves, but they were also musicians who had played for their white owners. Stone's own parents, from the first generation after emancipation, became professional musicians and entertainers, and so he received a valuable musical training from his family. In part, this may account for his extraordinary blues sensibility – he went on to become a significant blues singer himself as "Charles Calhoun," and he produced blues-inflected recording sessions for musicians as different as Louis Jordan and Big Joe Turner. Stone recalled:

> During the years of slavery and those decades that followed . . . each of the three families from whom I am descended was asked to organize a musical entertainment at the end of the week. This would include music, singing games, dancing, poetry, juggling, conjuring and so on. Don't forget, things like the radio and discs weren't invented until many years later! There were no external sources of inspiration, so [when I started playing] I had to follow

my own ideas. A lot came from the fact I had a strong left hand on the piano, which was tremendously helpful in allowing me to play different rhythmic figures. ... My grandmother had learned to read music and to sing, thanks to her masters, during the time of slavery. She passed on what she knew to her children, including my own father, who, with the assistance of my mother, did the same for me.[40]

As he began to play ragtime and dance music, he was able to apply this practical training and three generations of experience to create for his band the sounds he was able to hear in his head. No doubt, in spite of the fact he had not consciously heard another ten-piece band playing "jazz," as a consequence of his parents' work and his own childhood apprenticeship as a dancer and violinist on the African-American theater circuit, he would have encountered some of the bands who were pioneering aspects of the new music, and he undoubtedly also absorbed these influences.

Stone's musicians began by rehearsing in the local pool hall in Atchison, and taking what paid jobs they could find. One outlet was obviously the network of variety theaters, and Stone's first professional work as a bandleader included retracing the steps of his childhood career and playing the few such venues within practical traveling distance of Atchison. Although his band began by playing vaudeville, and his musicians performed a complete show lasting from 45 minutes to an hour-and-a-half, with dancing, revue skits, songs, and jokes, Stone's path to fronting the most popular band in the Midwest, in the early 1920s, was not to come from staying within the theatrical environment, but by finding different venues where his musicians could play for dancing – school halls, Masonic halls, and the like. Nevertheless, there remained a strongly theatrical element in his performances, and this seems to have been a common factor in the work of many territory bands.

The process of finding new and different venues began when a high-school friend, Cecil Self, began to act as the band's manager. Today, the concept of the manager is so entrenched in the music business that it seems almost impossible that, back at the start of the 1920s, this was an innovation. "I didn't know what a manager was at that particular time," said Stone.

He convinced me that he could get us a lot of work, and he had us playing for parties and dances in little small towns around Atchison. In due course, he booked us to play in St. Joseph,

Missouri, which is about thirty miles north of Atchison, and is more of a small city. We were to play two nights, a Friday and Saturday, but it rained and nobody showed up, and so there was no money, and we were stranded. We couldn't escape right away, and Cecil went off and left us.

We stayed in a black hotel, with eighteen of us in one room, where we were allowed to stay for nothing, because we practiced in the ballroom, and this brought in a lot of outsiders to whom the owner could sell drinks. So she fed us and accommodated us. The band was so big, it wasn't easy to book, so we had to take odd jobs to try and get the money to get home to Atchison. We carried bags, shined shoes, but we weren't making any headway. In the end I walked into town to try and find some work for the band, when I happened across a storefront with a lot of what looked like electrical equipment inside. I went in, and they told me that this was a radio station. I'd never heard of such a thing, but they explained to me how it could broadcast sound over the air. "You need a band," I told them, and so they hired the whole band to play for the sum of five dollars. We took the job, and opened up in the place. Soon the station began to get calls, not too many, because this was the first and only one in the area, and not that many people had radios, and they were mostly wealthy people. But as we played during the course of two or three days, the calls increased and they got letters, too.[41]

This took place in the very early 1920s, making Stone's band one of the first jazz orchestras ever to broadcast. The result of its radio appearances was that it was heard by a local entrepreneur called Frank Rock, who took on the band's management in earnest. Rock's methods became a paradigm for the management of a territory band.

To the bandleader's astonishment, he advanced Stone hundreds of dollars to buy better instruments and clothes, and to have photographs taken of the band wearing new tuxedos, as well as to acquire transportation.

"He'd never booked a band before in his life," Stone told me.

But he called up agents in New York, pretending to have an interest in booking a New York band. He took note of what they did, and then he did the same himself. He hired an advance man to go and put up bills and sell tickets before we reached the places we were going to play. He bought us three cars – that's one truck and two sedans. He asked me how we preferred to travel, and when I told him we'd prefer cars, that's what he got us.

He'd go out and rent halls on the circuit we were going to play. In most of the towns there were no dancehalls, just school gyms or lodge halls, so he booked us into those, until we were engaged some thirty days ahead. Then we started out from St. Joseph. At first there were no more than three or four people at the places we played. And it seemed like it was the same day after day. I think we had at most twenty people at the best of all the dates during the first month. In the meantime, Mr. Rock was advancing us fifty dollars apiece per week, and all our expenses. At first he didn't give me anything, because he reckoned I was part of the business, but as the month drew on and we weren't making anything, I finally asked him and "Pow! Pow! Pow!" he snapped his fingers and handed me one hundred dollars. And after I stopped being squeamish about asking, he'd pay me whenever I wanted . . . .

I couldn't understand it, because there were no crowds. It seemed like nobody wanted to hear us. But then he turned us right around, and we went back and played in exactly the same places, and you couldn't get into any of the halls, they were so crowded. He had used the first circuit like an advertisement, to create stories in the papers and so on. After three months, we had the Northern Territories sewed up. We became, without question, the best and most popular band in the Midwest.[42]

Stone's band set a pattern which was similar to that taken up by other groups working out of the main large towns in the Midwest and Southwest. Many of their experiences coincided with Stone's. For example, almost every touring musician remembers being "stranded," when a band ran out of work, or did not get paid. Saxophonist Buddy Tate told me how he got stranded with a contingent of Bennie Moten's band who went on the road from Kansas City under Count Basie's leadership around 1934:

It got so bad, musicians were creeping away in the night and not coming back. One night, very late, I heard Rush [Jimmy Rushing] creeping off. I said: "Where are you going?"
He said: "To the drugstore."

I said: "There ain't no drugstore open this time of night!"
That time he stayed, but a few nights later he crept off.[43]

Andy Kirk's memories of his early days on the road with George Morrison and T. Holder involved traveling in a fleet of automobiles, like those Frank Rock bought for Stone. Kirk played bass and tuba, and bought a Model-T Ford truck to transport his bulky instruments. As the Morrison band's fame grew, he found himself one of a fleet of Model-T drivers, who drove the musicians, their wives, girlfriends, and hangers-on as far afield as Mexico. The same applied to Alphonso Trent's Texas-based territory band, who "dressed in silk shirts and drove around in Cadillac touring cars."[44]

Even New York bands who took to the road, such as Fletcher Henderson's, preferred this method of transport, as it was quicker and more comfortable than using a bus, for those bands who could afford it. For Henderson's musicians, the slickest, newest, and largest automobiles signified the band's commercial success, although their legendary lateness for engagements led to some high-speed chases, and a high incidence of accidents – Henderson himself was involved in one of the more dramatic crashes. Later, some white orchestras such as Benny Goodman's 1930s band occasionally took to the road by automobile, rather than by bus, and Goodman paid saxophonist Art Rollini extra to transport the band's primitive public-address system in the trunk of his roadster.

Traveling this way led to higher risks for some musicians, and saxophonist Chu Berry was one of the more famous fatal casualties of a road accident as he and other members of Cab Calloway's band hurried from gig to gig by car, in an effort to improve the conditions they experienced on the band bus in regions where they were unable to use their habitual Pullman train. Only the highest-paid orchestras such as Calloway's could afford to charter a train for traveling, where the band's railroad coaches were moved overnight after they had finished playing to the next town. By careful planning, the band could cover hundreds of miles between engagements, and Calloway could accommodate his musicians, his supporting singers, and dancers from the Cotton Club revue, and, on occasion, his automobile, so that he was able to get out and about when the band's coaches were shunted into a siding while they played a single theater for a few days at a time. But such traveling (exemplified by Calloway's film short, *Rail Rhythm*) was a rarity, and the majority of groups were confined to buses.

Band buses themselves were, at their best, similar to the Greyhound fleet which plied all over the United States. However, many bands were unable to afford even this level of transportation, and musicians tell horrifying tales of ramshackle vehicles press-ganged into unreliable service. In his declining years, based in Georgia during the early 1930s, King Oliver's big band became one such orchestra, criss-crossing the South in ever more unsuitable buses, and on one occasion having to burn the tires to keep warm overnight, when the bus conked out on a lonely mountain range.

Fats Waller's touring band of the mid-1930s christened their bus "Old Methuselah," and when I spoke to Waller's drummer, Harry Dial, he recalled having to jump out to make it light enough to climb some of the steeper hills they encountered, and then a mad scramble to get back aboard as they crested the hill and started careering down the other side.

Many African-American musicians used the bus as a place of sanctuary, temporarily immune from racial privations that increased as bands traveled further south, where segregated washrooms, restaurants, and gas stations that would not serve them led to many problems. Doc Cheatham recalled touring with Marion Hardy's Alabamians and, in areas where there were few black hotels, using the bus to sleep on, wearing his pajamas on the bus and (along with the entire band) pulling on his stage clothes for the brief time they were off the bus and working in a dance hall or theater.

Returning to Stone's formative experiences, a small number of other territory bands also used the new medium of radio to make themselves heard, notably Alphonso Trent, who led one of the first African-American territory bands to appear regularly on the air, in broadcasts from the Adolphus Hotel, Dallas, over station WFAA. These appearances were initially far more significant in spreading the group's popularity than its recordings, as Trent did not begin recording until late in 1928. What we can be sure of, however, from this recorded evidence, is that his band had an entirely original approach, exuding a self-confidence that owes little to Northern or Eastern models. Even on a standard such as *After You've Gone*, from March 5, 1930, the arrangement includes deft key changes (taking some remarkably difficult keys in its stride) and there is a sense of compositional form about the section writing, which suggests the piece was thought of as an entity rather than a succession of separate choruses. The solos, notably Snub Mosley's eccentric trombone, fit the prevailing mood of the arrangement, rather than standing out from it.

Radio was also influential in areas some way away from the heartland of the territories, such as the various bands in which pianist Jimmie Gunn worked in the Carolinas. He first broadcast regularly from Charlotte in the late 1920s in Taylor's Dixie Orchestra, and subsequently made less frequent broadcasts under his own name in the mid-1930s.

Just as Stone had done, several bands were able to use the network of black theaters to give themselves a viable touring itinerary, and one such band, the Synco Jazzers led by saxophonist John Williams, played on this circuit from Nashville to St. Louis. There were, however, pitfalls involved in theatrical work, according to trumpeter Doc Cheatham, who joined them on one tour (around 1926), and remembered that although the band was entirely made up of African-American musicians, they were nevertheless required to play in blackface for their theater shows. He told me, ruefully, that in the dim theater lighting, smothered in burnt cork, Williams became almost invisible as he struggled to direct the band.[45]

By the mid-1920s, the following cities had established themselves as the "hubs" of the territory-band business: Milwaukee, Omaha, Indianapolis, Cincinnati, St. Louis, Kansas City, Denver, Oklahoma City, Tulsa, Little Rock, Birmingham, Atlanta, and Charlotte. In Texas, which had a rather different circuit, Dallas and San Antonio became the focus for touring groups, while isolated at the tip of Florida, Ross's Deluxe Syncopators worked out of Miami. Similarly geographically isolated, there were good touring bands based in Los Angeles, which served California and the Pacific Northwest, but for the most part these did not have any direct influence on the territory bands of the South, Southwest, and Midwest.

Although it never reached the exalted heights of Kansas City in the history of territory bands, St. Louis lived up to its reputation of colonial days as the "gateway to the West," and it became the base for an early generation of touring orchestras, as well as being the place where Jesse Stone made his first recordings in 1927. Its position on the confluence of the Mississippi and Missouri rivers gave it a head-start over those towns where development was dependent on the road or rail network, and it was also the most easterly of the Missouri towns where bands were based. Although St. Louis had been a significant center for ragtime, by the 1920s that earlier genre was not so entrenched in the local culture there as it still was further west, and the city's public — and therefore its musicians — were open to the newer sounds of jazz and the blues. From 1920 or thereabouts, many bands were following Fate Marable's example, and using St. Louis as a base for river tours, as well as forays into the hinterland.

Chief among them were those of trumpeters Charlie Creath and Dewey Jackson. Creath was a long-term associate of Fate Marable, playing aboard riverboats with New Orleans musicians like Louis Armstrong and Henry "Red" Allen. But he also led numerous bands in and around the city, occasionally fielding several outfits on the same night at venues like the Plantation, Jazzland, and the Arcadia. Jackson played with Andrew Preer's band – a forerunner of the Missourians (the band that eventually became Cab Calloway's orchestra), before leading his own Jazz Ambassadors on riverboats and at St. Louis's Castle Ballroom.

In the 1920s, cornetist Oliver Cobb was a serious rival to Jackson and Creath, especially after his popular Rhythm Kings recorded some rather risqué songs. Unfortunately, his death by drowning in 1931 ended his chances of leading the region's major territory band, which is what his former line-up became under the leadership of Eddie Johnson. Renaming the band the St. Louis Crackerjacks, Johnson took the band out on the road, as well as providing support for visiting stars like Fats Waller (whom the group accompanied on a road tour through Ohio, Kentucky, and Indiana). Johnson was a canny leader, and one brilliant piece of showmanship he applied was to learn from records the hit songs of other leading bands of the day. Then, whenever his men were in a "battle of music," the Crackerjacks led off with the other band's hits – giving the audience the impression that it was the other band who were imitating the Crackerjacks. This ruse won many a contest.

The other principal St. Louis band, founded somewhat later, was the Jeter-Pillars Orchestra, formed by two ex-members of Alphonso Trent's Texan touring band. However, rather than going on the road, they tended to remain in the city, playing at the Plantation, where they become more a "second generation" group of former territory band players than the genuine article.

St. Louis had a direct connection by water to New Orleans, and Marable in particular exploited this to create a musical channel of communication between St. Louis and Louisiana. Kansas City, Missouri, had a less direct umbilical link, being over one hundred miles west of St. Louis on the Missouri River. Yet, because it also had an influential position in the road and rail networks, and because of its political climate under the wide-open Pendergast regime, Kansas City had a greater effect than any other city on territory band life. It was also something of a ragtime center, and the composer and pianist James Scott, one of the few ragtimers to write pieces that were on a par with those of Joplin, was the organist and musical director at the city's Panama Theater. It seems that through his presence and that of a number of other significant ragtime musicians, the style remained popular there, even when it began to wane elsewhere, and there is evidence of a lingering ragtime influence in some of the early jazz recordings from

Kansas by bands such as Bennie Moten's.

It was to Kansas City that Jesse Stone moved from the outlying towns of St. Joseph and Atchison – first continuing to lead his own band and later helping other leaders including George E. Lee, Thamon Hayes, and Bennie Moten to run theirs, as well as providing arrangements for them. Yet – and this seems to have been typical – as a consequence of being stranded on the road from time to time, Stone also worked out of the territory band centers of St. Louis; Muskogee and Tulsa, Oklahoma; or Gulliver and Dallas in Texas. Nevertheless, he continued to return to Kansas City, and only finally left the area for Chicago in the 1930s. Before that, as he toured the states to the north and west of Kansas City during the 1920s, Stone witnessed big ballrooms being built to accommodate the audiences that bands such as his had created. He said of his Blue Serenaders:

> We were booked exclusively on the right bank of the Mississippi, because all the other orchestras were trying to travel towards New York. Because of the politics of this, and the fact we were the first of the bands to tour the area, we met with very little competition. The pay was good, and I was taking home seven hundred dollars a week. This lasted for two and a half years.[46]

It was in Kansas that Stone's one-time sideman, the trombonist Thamon Hayes, formed his Kansas City Rockets in 1932, which, Stone told me, briefly became the outstanding band of the time, just as his own line-up had been in the 1920s.

Whereas Stone eventually left the world of jazz to focus on rhythm and blues, record producing, and composing, during the time he was in Kansas City several other bandleaders were established there whose careers remained firmly inside the world of jazz.

Musically, the most important was pianist Bennie Moten, not least because his stylistic development from 1923 until his death in 1935 is well-documented by recordings. Whereas his first discs show a rhythmic stiffness and a debt to ragtime, despite a reliance on the harmonic structure of the blues, he went on to define the loose, blues-influenced style, with a four–four pulse, which became the predominant local jazz genre, and underpinned the work of later Kansas City bands like those of Count Basie and Jay McShann. Moten's work is discussed in more detail below in terms of its relationship with Basie's music, but in addition to the rhythmic development I have mentioned, his later discs make use of the repetitive phrases or riffs that were to become a hallmark of Basie's first nationally successful band.

Another of Stone's contemporaries was Andy Kirk, who gravitated to Kansas after taking over T. Holder's band while operating on a circuit between Tulsa and Oklahoma City. Kirk played for a management company called Northeastern, for whom his was the only African-American band. When, spurred by Kirk's success with white and mixed audiences, Northeastern added George E. Lee's band to their roster, Lee returned the favor by tipping off Kirk that the Pla-Mor Ballroom in Kansas City was looking for a band to rival Cab Calloway in popularity. A few phone calls were made, and the Pla-Mor's manager drove 360 miles to Tulsa to hear Kirk, and engaged him on the spot.

Kirk's candid account of his residency at the Pla-Mor in Kansas City gives a good idea of a territory band's repertoire, proving that such bands were no more able than Paul Whiteman's to depend on just one style of music to make their living.[47] They played waltzes and ballads as well as hot jazz, and their jazz numbers were presented with all the hokum of a variety show. Their popular version of *Casey Jones*, for example, involved the band dressing up as railroad engineers, and Kirk blowing out clouds of smoke through the bell of his sousaphone.

Even though there were several white orchestras in Kansas City, such as the Coon-Sanders Nighthawks, a popular broadcasting band, Kirk believed that it was the influx of African-American territory bands that made Kansas City's reputation as a jazz center, to the extent that some aspiring white jazz players actually applied to join the black Local (branch) of the American Federation of Musicians. He pointed out that with one or two exceptions there were virtually no well-rehearsed white bands, and the black groups constituted a "Hall of Fame." They were (in his words): "Bennie Moten, George E. Lee, Paul Banks, Clarence Love, Thamon Hayes, Harlan Leonard and Jap Allen – a young band that at one time included Ben Webster and Clyde Hart."[48]

Few of the Midwest bands ever traveled as far as the Carolinas, Georgia, and Alabama. The Southeast developed its own territory-band traditions, exemplified by Taylor's Dixie Orchestra and Jimmie Gunn's band from Charlotte, North Carolina. Musically, both bands had some unusual characteristics, and they shared an ability to work a Caribbean flavor into their arrangements. A series of dotted-rhythm stops behind the saxophone solo on Taylor's 1931 *Wabash Blues* is so relaxed and loosely timed as to take on a Latin feel, while Gunn's 1936 *Operator Special* has a similar loping atmosphere, both numbers benefiting from the interaction between Harry Prather's bass (actually a tuba on the earlier side) and Jimmie Gunn's piano. Gunn was a central figure in this area, a schoolteacher and amateur musician who took over a band made up of local students at the African-American university in Charlotte. He toured widely through North and South Carolina, but resisted invitations to go further afield so as to keep his day job. Among the musicians who went on from Gunn's band to achieve fame in New York was saxophonist Skeets Tolbert.

Despite its name, another band from this region, the Carolina Cotton Pickers, was actually an Alabama band, but it toured on a similar circuit to Gunn, absorbing into the personnel a number of players from the famous Jenkins Orphanage band at Charleston, South Carolina, who had learned their craft as traveling musicians from a very early age. These, plus the band of J. Neal Montgomery (active from 1921 in the Atlanta area) and the aging King Oliver (who eventually settled in Savannah, Georgia) made up the principal touring contingent in the Southeast during the late 1920s and into the 1930s.

The North Texas bands based in Dallas enjoyed a pretty free interchange of musicians with the Oklahoma and Kansas bands, often touring the same circuit and, for reasons of simple geography, all passing through staging posts like Wichita or Tulsa. Walter Page's band, which was for some time based in Oklahoma City, was a bridge between these two traditions, as was Andy Kirk's band, during the period he was based in Oklahoma. Kirk's progress is interesting in that he moved further and further east during his career, beginning with the Denver band of George Morrison and then moving to Dallas to join T. Holder, the band he brought to Oklahoma before moving first to Kansas City and then New York.

The other key Texan bands were those of Alphonso Trent and of Troy Floyd. The latter was based in San Antonio, as was the somewhat shadowy figure of the drummer Boots Douglas, who recorded in 1937 with his band Boots and His Buddies, and who worked in the city's Turner's Park. Also based in San Antonio was the expatriate New Orleans band of Don Albert, who employed many musicians who subsequently became significant in the traditional New Orleans revival, such as clarinetist Louis Cottrell and trumpeter Alvin Alcorn.

Last of the main territory-band locations was the city of Omaha, Nebraska, where several groups were based. Red Perkins led one, famous for its versatility as most of its musicians doubled on many instruments (a tradition drawn directly from vaudeville groups like the Musical Spillers).

Trumpeter Lloyd Hunter led another of the city's longest-lived groups from 1923, whose 1931 recordings demonstrate it to have been the equal of many a better-known Eastern group. But, reputedly, the best of all was the big band led by New Orleans-born Nat Towles. Famous as the best band never to record (apart from a few accomplished sides made by a number of his musicians under Horace Henderson's leadership and some obscure 1943 discs made by a later, different line-up), this was avowed by all that heard it as the greatest of all the territory bands.

Perhaps it is fitting that the sound of the finest territory band should remain unpreserved on wax, shellac, wire, or tape, keeping alive a romantic legendary idea of its sound, in keeping with this vanished tradition of jazz history.

## Fletcher Henderson

Fletcher was never accepted by blacks as much as Duke. I
don't think the blacks of Harlem bought many of his
records: they were too sophisticated, not racy enough, and
sounded like a white band.

Garvin Bushell, from *Jazz from the Beginning*

A scholarly-looking, middle-class chemistry graduate, with a penchant for baseball, Fletcher Henderson was the living antithesis of those primitive qualities held in such high regard by early jazz critics like Roger Pryor Dodge. Although he grew up in the South, at Cuthbert, Georgia, Henderson had little to do with the stereotypical image of the African-American laborer picking cotton, which was still the state's dominant rural industry during his childhood. Instead he came from a well-educated family, who had high aspirations for him, and sent him to Atlanta University. As a pianist, he became an adept sight-reader as a child, with a good sense of relative pitch and a broad classical repertoire – all qualities instilled in him by a demanding father – but as a young adult, Henderson had to learn how to play jazz and blues, neither of which came naturally to him. His nickname, "Smack," came both from his ability with the baseball bat as a youngster, and his lifelong habit of smacking his lips between sentences.

I have already discussed his early career as a song-plugger and accompanist to blues and vaudeville singers, in which role he made great

232

strides in introducing jazz musicians to the back-up bands that he directed on numerous early New York recordings from 1921 onwards. He even tried to bring Louis Armstrong to New York in 1922, after hearing the cornetist during a tour with Ethel Waters that took Henderson to the South. This particular innovation would have to wait another two years. Nevertheless, he was sufficiently successful in this role as a freelance musical director that, despite the stylistic shortcomings in his playing, in October 1923 he was billed in the press as: "one of the best-known of race record artistes . . . whose recordings are now procurable on Victor, Columbia, Vocalion, Okeh, and Paramount records, and who is unquestionably one of the best-informed among contemporary 'blues' specialists."[49]

In the longer term, however, Henderson's importance lay in his role as a bandleader, and the way that, in the mid-1920s, he and his colleagues Don Redman and, later, Benny Carter took forward the innovations of Hickman, Grofé, and Whiteman to establish a paradigm for big-band arranging that lasted for the next twenty years. By 1925, Henderson's orchestra was the leading African-American big band in New York, and, through its extensive touring, it also established itself on a national basis. It maintained this position until the end of the 1920s, and Henderson's bands of the early 1930s were also highly regarded, although by that period there was stiff competition from Duke Ellington and Cab Calloway, among others.

Paradoxically, although he arranged some of his band's very earliest discs himself, Henderson's own significance as an arranger came much later on, in the 1930s, when he was writing for other leaders such as Benny Goodman. Nevertheless, the work of his 1920s band was a very significant step on the way towards this later writing, which, by paring back his craft to its essentials, became the foundation of the universal sound of the swing era, in a way that the more subtle and varied writing of Duke Ellington, for example, did not. Not just Goodman's, but other 1930s swing orchestras built their style on what Leonard Feather described as Henderson's "pitting of reed against brass section, and the use of forthright, swinging block-voiced passages."[50]

To some extent, the historical importance of his first regular band occurred almost in spite of his own efforts. In contrast to the thrusting, dominant personality of Paul Whiteman, the withdrawn, diffident Fletcher Henderson was a mass of contradictions. Despite Garvin Bushell's account of Henderson's professional competence as an accompanist, his overall character seems to have been far more lackadaisical, so that it took the urging of his fellow musicians on a recording session to coerce him into attending the audition that got his band its first residency at the Club Alabam.[51] His reliable abilities in shaping a performance in the studio were not matched by his retiring personality, and in his earliest days as a leader, he preferred to direct his band from the keyboard, leaving another musician, violinist Allie Ross, to "conduct" the band on its club appearances. As time went on, possibly as a result of injuries he sustained in a 1928 motor accident, Henderson showed even more alarming signs of vagueness or lack of leadership, as the entrepreneur John Hammond found out in the early 1930s when he booked the band for a recording on which only five of the thirteen musicians showed up, and a subsequent theater engagement he organized was plagued by numerous infringements of the band's contract by its members.[52]

Danny Barker was a witness to Henderson's withdrawn character off the bandstand, and remembered him implacably playing pool at New York's Rhythm Club, ignoring everything around him from spontaneous jam sessions to the barbed comments of his fellow players with a single-minded calm.[53] Other musicians recalled him with a mixture of emotions. Rex Stewart, despite criticizing his uncompetitive temperament, saw him as a fatherly figure who packed him off from New York in his late teens to avoid the pitfalls of alcohol and infighting; Garvin Bushell recalled a leader too "cowardly" to stand up to any promoters who short-changed him; and the recollections of several of his musicians dwell on the chaotic side of his organization which more than once saw them driving hundreds of miles to New York after a dance, only to drive virtually the whole distance back the next night because of a failure of communication with the band's agent. On the other hand, there is almost complete unanimity that Henderson's band was, on its day, without equal in mid-1920s New York. His musical skills, and his ability to attract and retain highly proficient players and writers, were what gave the band its edge. When it eventually took to the road, it was welcomed by fans and musicians alike, as trumpeter Bill Coleman said when he first heard the band in Cincinnati; "it was like having heaven sent to us."[54]

The orchestra's combination of clever writing with an astute choice of musicians gradually brought together disciplined ensemble playing, increasingly more confident improvised solos, and a growing concept of rhythmic drive. Together, these elements sparked a considerable leap forward in the way all large ensembles approached their music.

Essentially, what Henderson achieved was a logical development from Whiteman's style of arrangement. Whiteman and Grofé had worked out how to use a saxophone section effectively, and to give it a role which contrasted to that of the brass, as well as using a variety of instruments to create great tonal variety. Henderson's band, through its first significant arranger Don Redman, went further in integrating the role of the sections. In his work, the ragtime-based approach of the syncopated orchestras of New York was progressively combined with the blues-inflected solos and looser rhythm of players who hailed from the South or from the territories. I have already discussed the most obvious example of this combination at work, in the recordings that Louis Armstrong made with Henderson in 1924–5.

To start with, however, Henderson's band had little in common with what was going on outside New York. Whereas his blues accompaniments were somewhat a-rhythmic, or "watery" in Gunther Schuller's term, his first band recordings reveal a somewhat tense, occasionally frenetic, ensemble, with little of the relaxed swing of the better King Oliver recordings, or of A. J. Piron's New Orleans Orchestra. Henderson epitomized the African-American New York fashion of the time recalled by his colleague and friend Garvin Bushell: "New York 'jazz' then was nearer the ragtime style and had less blues. . . . Up North we leaned to ragtime conception – a lot of notes."[55]

When he began to make regular band recordings, from March 1923 onwards, Henderson had no regular working group of his own outside the studios. Along with the majority of his session musicians, he was working with another leader, the violinist "Shrimp" Jones, at a Harlem club. Not surprisingly, therefore, his first band discs were a mirror of the various styles prevailing in New York, and rather than displaying a cohesive identity, they reflected competent impressions of everything from the Whiteman dance-band style to something close to the liveliness of a Dixieland band.

In a perceptive speculation about the kind of music Henderson and his New York associates would actually have been listening to themselves, Gunther Schuller points out that the influence of white groups such as the Original Memphis Five, the O.D.J.B., and the California Ramblers (along with the ubiquitous Whiteman) would have been every bit as significant as African-American bands of the time, further reinforcement of my comments in Chapter 2 about the initial dominance of white bands on the New York scene.[56] As if to confirm that Henderson was searching for an identity in his first months as a leader, rather as he worked as a freelance blues accompanist for the labels mentioned in the press piece quoted above, he made full-band recordings for an equally broad spread of labels, using a variety of band names: Henderson's Dance Players, Henderson's Hot Six, Seven Brown Babies, Fletcher Henderson and His Sawin' Six, Henderson's Club Alabam' Orchestra, and, most often of all, just Fletcher Henderson and Orchestra.

It is surprising that although several of his players had accompanied some of the same blues singers as Henderson himself, their first discs show they had absorbed little of the timing, pitching, and phrasing of those they backed up. This is even odder when the breadth of their collective experience is taken into account. The trumpet-playing brothers Joe and Russell Smith were steeped in African-American show-business, having both worked in various revues in New York. In addition, Russell had been a member of the Musical Spillers, whereas Joe, whose pure, open tone and skill in playing a range of muted trick effects was already a local legend, had gone out on the vaudeville circuit with some high-profile blues singers. So, too, had saxophonists Ernest Elliott and Coleman Hawkins (the latter, in addition to touring with Mamie Smith, was the only member of Henderson's 1923 band to have any territory-band experience, which he had gathered with Jesse Stone).

However, on Henderson's discs these experienced musicians put the sound of the blues to one side, and melded with the style of their colleagues who had mainly played in a number of Eastern big bands: saxophonist and arranger Don Redman had been in Pittsburgh with Billy Paige, whereas trumpeter Elmer Chambers (a veteran of the Atlantic City summer seasons) and banjoist Charlie Dixon were in cities as varied as Boston, Detroit, and New York with Sam Wooding. Dixon then moved to "Shrimp" Jones's band, where he met drummer Kaiser Marshall and, in due course, most of the others I have mentioned. Even Puerto Rican tuba player Ralph Escudero was steeped in the Eastern tradition, having worked regularly at the Clef Club and toured with Sissle and Blake in *Shuffle Along*.

In due course, as well as contracting "Shrimp" Jones's sidemen for his own record sessions, Henderson took over from Jones as leader of the band at the 65 West 192nd Street cabaret where it played.

It took a move down town and the cohesive effects of a regular job for six months or so at the Club Alabam, from late in 1923, for Henderson's band to begin to develop a sound of its own. The club was beneath a theater at 216 West 44th Street, and for much of the time the band backed singer Edith Wilson in the "Club Alabam Revue."[57] It was Coleman Hawkins's refusal to move down from the bandstand to back Wilson in the floor show without extra payment that indirectly led to the entire group leaving the club in June 1924, but within a couple of weeks the band had found a new home, and on July 16, 1924 it opened at the Roseland Ballroom, also in midtown, at 1658 Broadway, near 51st Street, where it played exclusively for dancing. For its first nine-week season opposite Sam Lanin, one of New York's finest white dance bands who played alternate sets from the hall's other bandstand, Henderson's orchestra continued with virtually the same personnel mentioned above, plus trombonist Charlie Green, an experienced soloist from Red Perkins's territory band in Omaha, Nebraska. When it was re-booked for the fall, it was joined by Louis Armstrong on cornet, and the process of change accelerated, during which the band arrived at a distinct identity, and a stylistic model for subsequent African-American big bands.

Both at the Club Alabam and at the Roseland, Henderson was playing for a white clientèle, and although the latter establishment had employed a number of African-American bands, including A. J. Piron's, it actually went so far as to deter its orchestras from playing jazz, insisting on a mixture of waltzes, tangos, foxtrots, and two-steps — although, more and more, jazz crept into the repertoire as Henderson's popularity grew.[58] If there are similarities, therefore, between some of Henderson's earliest recordings and the output of white bands such as Paul Whiteman's or the California Ramblers, this reflects the tastes of the clientèle for whom he was regularly performing, every bit as much as the fact that it was these large white bands who had first begun to establish a *modus operandi* for their arrangers. Henderson's band *looked* the part of a stereotypical African-American jazz band, but what the Roseland and their audience required to hear from them at first was not necessarily stereotypical jazz. They are a representative case of what Kathy J. Ogren pinponts as a "contrived tradition." In other words: "the persistence among whites of stereotypes about black entertainment may have trapped both blacks and whites in roles that were not 'authentic' but staged."[59]

On disc, both with blues singers and leading his own band, Henderson's efforts were mainly directed at a black audience, and undoubtedly this duality between the expectations of two very different groups of listeners added to the stylistically diverse nature of his earliest discs.

Certainly before Armstrong's arrival, despite what I described in Chapter 2 as a rather pedestrian approach overall, there are signs that Henderson and Don Redman were trying out a number of different methods of tackling arranging. The use of trumpets playing "wah-wah" figures together came from Whiteman, as did the idea of clarinet duos or trios, although Redman was to make this very much a trademark device of his own. He even made an explicit nod in the direction of the California

Ramblers and Adrian Rollini by including a bass saxophone on a few pieces, such as *Charleston Crazy* or *Somebody Stole My Gal*, where tenorist Coleman Hawkins, rapidly emerging as the band's most convincing soloist, doubled on the larger horn. A piece like *Dicty Blues*, recorded for three different labels and featuring Hawkins in his more conventional role, shows that, despite being dependent on written charts, the band was prepared to vary the way it tackled an individual piece from one recording to another far more than, say, King Oliver's Creole Jazz Band did on its different versions of a single, memorized tune. Henderson's orchestra experimented with quite marked changes of tempo and a complete recasting of the sequence of solos.

Nevertheless, prior to Armstrong's arrival, the band's phrasing was still jerky and somewhat stilted, and Hawkins's solos were played very much on the beat, often emphasizing this by employing a technique of the period known as "slap-tonguing," which added a percussive thump to the production of each note. However much Hawkins later denied it, the arrival of Armstrong with his fluent grasp of how to construct a solo chorus, and his rhythmic freedom based on the New Orleans tension between two and four beats to the measure, radically altered the saxophonist's solo playing. Between Armstrong's debut with the band in 1924 and the end of the decade, Hawkins was to become the pre-eminent voice on the jazz saxophone, and Armstrong had an equally decisive effect on the arranging of Don Redman.

Redman was, like Henderson, a well-educated, middle-class musician. In his case he had honed his skills at college in West Virginia, where he acquired a music degree. A talented multi-instrumentalist, he took on the main arranging duties for the band until his departure to McKinney's Cotton Pickers in Detroit in 1927. (He also became a prolific freelance arranger, writing for both African-American and white bandleaders, including Paul Whiteman.) With Armstrong's arrival, Redman began to shine, in due course finding a confident voice of his own, and gradually allowing his compositional instincts to dictate what he did, rather than echoing the fashions of the day. In October 1924, he produced an arrangement of *Copenhagen* which pointed firmly to the future – a consistent rhythmic underpinning with a dazzling variety of ensemble and solo turns above it, alternating section, soloist, trio, and ensemble in a brilliantly creative sequence. It exemplified Redman's ability to achieve something that Whiteman and Grofé had not: to create space for improvised solos within the context of a composed setting. He often restricted these to four or eight measures, thereby ensuring that the mood of the surrounding ensemble was retained, but he nevertheless ensured that the overall sound of the band became dependent on its soloists. In addition, the melodic lines of his ensemble passages had some of the feel and phrasing of improvised solos about them. It was this potent combination of distinctive individual voices within an increasingly coherent and consistent framework that became the Henderson band's lasting contribution to big-band jazz.

I have already mentioned Redman's reworking of Oliver's *Dippermouth Blues* into *Sugar Foot Stomp* in Chapter 2, and even if the apocryphal story is true that this piece was helped along by Armstrong bringing a sheet-music sketch with him from Chicago, the arrangement is clearly Redman's and holds several pointers to the way he was to develop his arranging between 1924 and 1927. The chart contrasts dramatically with King Oliver's accomplished recording of June 23, 1923, with its driving collective polyphony, the punchy shared lead of Oliver and Armstrong, and Dodds's carefree clarinet weaving its way through the ensemble before soaring over the stops of the third and fourth choruses. As a performance, Oliver's is the more convincing and balanced, its fullness of sound contrasting with the relatively linear way Redman treats the piece at this transitional stage in his writing.

Through repetition in live performance, and on account of his recordings, Oliver's muted solo had become an integral part of the composition and was treated as such by Redman; but otherwise, apart from the main melodic contour, he leaves little else from the original in his version. The tempo is slower, over a two-beat rhythm, with the opening melody carried by the saxophones as the brass section adds strangely accordion-like punctuations. In the next chorus the brass take the lead, their clipped phrases more or less in unison, although Charlie Green ventures a little tentative counterpoint below them while, instead of Dodds's breaks, there follows a clarinet trio spread over two choruses punctuated by the ensemble. A similar ensemble phrase wraps up Green's trombone solo, which in itself is swaggering and confident, ushering in Armstrong's recreation of Oliver's muted set piece. The final four ensemble choruses alternate sustained notes with agitated four–four playing.

Yet tucked inside this arrangement are most of the devices that, within a year or two, Redman would have expanded into the basis of his compositional language. Allowing Green's solo to work its way towards a prearranged ending was one technique he was to repeat often, particularly with the band's subsequent, more technically advanced, trombonists Jimmy

Harrison and Benny Morton. Over time, the idea of a reed section carrying a lead punctuated by brass (or *vice versa*) became ever more complex, as the rhythms of one section began to work in apposition to the melodic phrasing of the other. This was taken to extremes in *Whiteman Stomp* (May 1927), a devastatingly difficult chart in which Redman wrote figures in three–four or three–eight time for one section to play against phrases in two–four or four–four for the other. The clarinet trio – not, as I have said, a Redman innovation, but something he developed – would often form the core of a complex arrangement, such as *Henderson Stomp* (November 1926). Equally, the relatively simple backdrop he created for Armstrong's solo would transform into the block chording played by brass and reeds together behind Tommy Ladnier on *Rocky Mountain Blues* (January 1927).

After Armstrong's departure, and before Redman himself left, although the Henderson band was still playing plenty of stock arrangements for white clientèle at the Roseland, it became more jazz-orientated, not least because of extended road tours of the kind mentioned in Chapter 2, where it played for plenty of African-American audiences, in addition to well-heeled whites. As Armstrong's replacement, Rex Stewart, put it:

> Now we had become regular attractions in swank places such as Castle Farms in Cincinnati, the Palais Royale in Buffalo, the Graystone Ballroom in Detroit, and many other big time spots including country clubs. Of course, in between the weekly engagements there would be the one-nighters, and we ran up and down the scale of clientele from a tobacco barn to a beautiful ballroom. One night we'd dine in splendor when we played a high-class hotel and the very next evening, a mere hundred miles or so away, we'd be lucky to fill the inner man with hot dogs.[60]

Its recordings demonstrate how rapidly, through playing for this varied diet of different audiences, it transformed itself into the leading big band of the period, and eclipsed the established large bands in Chicago led by Doc Cook, Carroll Dickerson, and Erskine Tate. Furthermore, regular broadcasts from the Roseland ensured that even its regular appearances there were heard not just by the hall's white dance patrons but by a growing cross-section of society. A recording like the celebrated *Stampede*, from May 1926 **[CD track 4]**, is a good illustration of the band's prowess, and demonstrates how Redman's writing had built on the basis of pieces like *Copenhagen* to become open enough for the band's own soloists to be an integral ingredient in the arrangement.

After an introductory flourish that wiggles through all the sections, Rex Stewart's cornet stamps an immediate imprint on *Stampede*. Following an ensemble chorus, Coleman Hawkins also takes a forceful solo accompanied by ensemble flares that urge him on. Then Joe Smith produces a smooth, clear-toned passage, before one of Redman's trademark clarinet trios ushers in more fiery cornet from Stewart. This is a good early example of an arrangement that deliberately contrasts two different players of the same instrument, with Smith's elegant, poised cornet contrasting with the pugnacious drama of Stewart's. The device was to be one featured later by several other big bands including Count Basie's, with the battling trumpets of Harry "Sweets" Edison and Buck Clayton, or the tenor saxophones of Lester Young and Herschel Evans, and, notably, by Duke Ellington, where Rex Stewart himself was to become one of the most distinctive Ducal brass players, alongside Cootie Williams, Harold "Shorty" Baker, or Ray Nance.

By the time Redman left, in June 1927, the transformation of Henderson's band from its origins in the world of the syncopated orchestra to a leading force in jazz was complete. Six months after Redman's departure, the *New York Age* described the band unequivocally as "the best-known aggregation of colored musicians on the stage today."[61]

This was in an article about a relatively rare instance of the band playing in a stage show or revue, in this case directed by choreographer Leonard Harper, although for its own portions of the program, as it had a few weeks previously at the Capitol Theater, Henderson's band played "featured numbers," of the kind that "had a lot to do with the success of the Roseland Dance Hall on Broadway."

Unlike many other bands of the period, including Sam Wooding's, which was playing in such revues as *Creole Revels* at the Lafayette, or the ensembles led in New York and Chicago by Fess Williams, whose extra personnel included tap-dancing Indians,[62] Henderson's group did not carry its own revue, or its own specialist vocalists. (Such vocals as it required were provided by the musicians themselves.) It focused on playing as a band, more often than not for dancing, and including in its programs many of the waltzes and two-steps that remained popular with dance patrons. It epitomized what Kathy J. Ogren has called the "participatory dynamic" between the musicians and those on the dance-floor, and its regular re-bookings at the Roseland, plus its road tours that took in dances for African-American audiences, are evidence that the band "perfected their sound through interaction with dancers."[63]

Among large New York jazz groups, many of whom more regularly backed shows in theaters and cabarets, this marked it out as unusual, and so did the fact that its crop of distinguished improvising soloists, which now included trombonists Jimmy Harrison and Benny Morton, plus clarinetist Buster Bailey, were just as prepared to produce their finest work on the sweeter waltzes or ballads as on the more overtly jazz numbers. Rex Stewart recalled the "thirty-five or so special and lovely waltz arrangements in the book," also singling out Russell Smith's delicate ballad high-register playing on pieces like *Dear on a Night like This*, which was way above the range of most trumpeters of the time.[64] Stewart also believed that the band seldom captured its true sound on disc – not least because few of these more romantic pieces were ever recorded, with the record companies' insistence on "blues and hot stuff."

From early on at the Roseland, Henderson had begun to earn substantial sums, not perhaps in the league of Whiteman, but certainly more than the average African-American band. The press reported his band's earnings as in excess of $1200 per week,[65] a very considerable amount for 1925, and this was further increased with recording income, all of which was reflected in the apparel and lifestyle of his musicians. Tailored suits, silk shirts, and handmade shoes were *de rigueur*, to the extent that Louis Armstrong's old-fashioned appearance was a considerable source of mirth when he arrived from Chicago, still wearing his best Southern clothes. Rex Stewart described the band's automobiles:

> Those were the days of running up and down those bad roads at 75 and 80 miles an hour. We traveled by auto, Smack leading the pack in his ever-present Packard, buying a new one every year. Jimmy Harrison drove a Pontiac; Joe Smith ... enjoyed his Willys Saint Clair roadster; Kaiser Marshall had a Buick which unfortunately was involved in an accident and didn't last long. .... Don Redman also had bad luck. He bought a brand new Cadillac and only owned it a few hours as I recall.[66]

It was one of Henderson's Packards that he turned over during a road tour to Kentucky, and although he shrugged off his injuries at the time, it may well have contributed to his eventual partial paralysis and premature death aged just 55.

Until the very end of the 1920s, the band appeared regularly at the Roseland, and for the most part it took Redman's departure in its stride.

Henderson himself began to produce arrangements, and he also commissioned pieces from other writers including John Nesbitt of McKinney's Cotton Pickers (the Detroit band Redman had gone to join) and Bill Challis, the white arranger for Jean Goldkette's band.

Henderson's own charts included a treatment of Jelly Roll Morton's *King Porter Stomp*, which he recorded on March 14, 1928. The band made a dramatically improved version four years later, but in essence, Henderson's 1928 arrangement was the basis for the disc eventually cut by Benny Goodman, and it shows Henderson (influenced, apparently, by Coleman Hawkins, who outlined the guts of the head arrangement) beginning to simplify some of Redman's ideas. If Redman had a fault, it was that in his more ambitious pieces he tended to pack too much into an arrangement, and some of his intricate figures were unnecessarily convoluted for a functional dance band. In *Rocky Mountain Blues*, for example, despite Ladnier's assured solo, there is a constant exchange of ideas between the orchestra and piano which prevents a build-up of momentum throughout the piece. In *I Need Lovin'*, the rhythm is interrupted first by passages of off-beat chords from the full ensemble, then a novelty piano solo from Henderson himself, and – just as the piece is settling into an easy swing – a modulation and the return of the off-beat emphasis. Henderson, in his own work, instinctively withdrew from anything this fussy and complex.

His thinking was no doubt colored by the charts he acquired from others. Nesbitt's brilliantly mobile *Chinatown* (recorded somewhat later, in October 1930) replaces the tuba with the double bass, and John Kirby's propulsive playing, often in octaves with Henderson's left hand, notably in the final 32 measures, creates a sense of forward motion that allows the soloists, particularly Coleman Hawkins, to take off effectively (even though Rex Stewart, who contributes a fizzing firework of a solo himself, was dissatisfied with the result).

For different reasons, the influence of Bill Challis is also interesting. Henderson first encountered him when the white Jean Goldkette Orchestra, complete with Bix Beiderbecke, Frank Trumbauer, Eddie Lang, and Joe Venuti, opened on the opposite bandstand at the Roseland, on October 6, 1926. By then, no other band was considered serious competition for Henderson's, particularly as a hot-jazz orchestra, and certainly not, as Rex Stewart put it, "a Johnny-come-lately white band from out in the sticks." However, playing a set of Challis's new arrangements, the Goldkette band comprehensively outplayed Henderson. "Their arrangements were too imaginative and their rhythm too strong," wrote Stewart.[67]

Impressed with Challis's charts, which *Orchestra World* described at the time as "nothing short of marvelous," Henderson swapped some arrangements there and then with Goldkette's band. But in the subsequent months, he got to know Challis himself, when the Henderson Orchestra were playing at Connie's Inn in Harlem, and Challis would stop by as he drove home to Greenwich, Connecticut, from a job in midtown. "Fletcher and I became good friends," Challis told Gene Lees. "He began to commission some arrangements from me. I wrote a lot for that band. They paid me well ... it was a great band."[68]

Not many African-American bands of the time were commissioning charts from white musicians, let alone paying handsomely for them, and there is a distinction here between the stock arrangements by the likes of Mel Stitzel which Henderson bought to keep up a flow of fresh music for the Roseland, and work which he commissioned *ab initio* from Challis or the bandleader and trombonist Russ Morgan. The Goldkette band had made a lasting impression on Henderson, and his musicians admired what they heard, from Beiderbecke's shimmering cornet to the deft writing of Challis. Some years later, Henderson was to record items of repertoire associated with Beiderbecke, including *Singin' The Blues* with Rex Stewart recreating the cornet solo, but as early as 1928, when his band recorded Challis's version of *D Natural Blues*, it took on some of the Goldkette sound, from the Bixian phrasing of the opening ensembles to the texture of the reed writing with its natty trombone counter-melodies in the middle of the piece. There were lessons here about block-chord writing (particularly in the long notes of the reed "choir") which would filter into Henderson's paradigm for swing-era arranging.

The other man who made a real difference to Henderson's own eventual output as an arranger was the alto saxophonist who filled Redman's role in the band for the fall of 1928 and again for some months in 1930, Benny Carter. Because Carter followed Redman, and his work is less startlingly "compositional," he has generally been viewed as a less significant component in the development of swing arranging. Gunther Schuller, for example, felt that Carter went too far in introducing numerous short solos into many of his pieces, to the extent that "neither they nor the interspersed ensemble passages can create a meaningful single conception. One is cancelled out by the other. The danger of this procedure is obvious today, but in 1929 it took a visionary like Ellington to see it."[69]

I will discuss the fusion of conception with execution in Ellington's work later, but to my mind Schuller misses the point that, fussy strings of solos or not, Carter's charts generally have a consistent sense of rhythm and swing that is allowed to run throughout the piece, uninterrupted by Redman's characteristic bridge passages, modulations, or suspensions of the beat.

An arrangement like Carter's *Come On, Baby*, for example, from December 1928, makes use of a riff borrowed from Jelly Roll Morton's *Georgia Swing* in its opening chorus, but then continues to build rhythmic momentum throughout, as does *Blazin'*, from May 1929, a piece built on the simple chord sequence of the old standard *Ja-Da*. And when it comes to tackling a number firmly associated with Paul Whiteman's band, the *Wang Wang Blues*, Carter firmly moves it into Henderson territory by putting an improvising solo trumpet over the saxophone section as they play the melody, and then throws in a number of Redman devices, including spread chords played by all the voices in the section, yet without sacrificing forward momentum.

Carter had learned his craft in the band led in Wilberforce, Ohio, by Henderson's brother Horace, and in early 1928 he spent some months in the orchestra of one of Henderson's New York rivals, Charlie Johnson. The hallmarks of his arranging style are to be heard in his first recorded chart, *Charleston Is the Best Dance, After All*, which Johnson's Paradise Orchestra cut in January 1928. In the opening chorus, the brass take the lead with a clipped version of the melody over saxophone chords, swapping the lead with Carter's alto in the channel. The second chorus includes a slightly messy saxophone choir in which Carter's beautifully shaped lead, with changes in dynamic and emphasis, stands out, giving a clue to his thinking about the way a section should phrase together. Jabbo Smith's solo trumpet and Charlie Irvis's trombone both have solos, and Carter's few bars on alto reveal his debt to Frank Trumbauer, whom he acknowledged as an influence. The way the ensemble picks up from the trombone solo with a spread chord is a characteristic Carter device, as is the syncopated phrasing of the out-chorus.

The major contrast with Redman is that Carter's score sounds full of imaginative detail, but was relatively easy to play. When he moved to Henderson's band, Carter was to produce charts that were equally straightforward, allowing the band to focus on its phrasing and interpretation, and the soloists to make the most of their few bars of glory. This was a lesson he had learned the hard way with Charlie Johnson. His fellow saxophonist in Johnson's band, Benny Waters, recalled:

Benny Carter made an arrangement on *Santag*. ... It was a

number we never learned properly. We never did learn to play it! It was the hardest song, the hardest music I've ever seen in my life. Benny was crowding all his knowledge into one song, something hard and different. We tried it, rehearsed it, but it never came out right.[70]

Carter's charts for Henderson do not display such complexity. They do, however, show that he shared Henderson's interest in the Goldkette band and its soloists, his own playing frequently recalling Trumbauer, of whom he said: "He had something I thought was unique, and at that time I tried to emulate it . . . his sound, his manner of playing, and his phrasing."[71]

Carter did not stay long with Henderson. After leading his own groups, and briefly joining drummer Chick Webb, he once again followed in Don Redman's footsteps and took his place in McKinney's Cotton Pickers. Nevertheless, before he left Henderson, he wrote several arrangements which were to point directly towards Henderson's own mature writing style, of which *Keep a Song in Your Soul* is perhaps the best. Recorded in December 1930, it is underpinned by a medium tempo, four-to-the-bar rhythm (John Kirby's tuba struggling manfully to be as rhythmically flexible as his double bass), but its clever use of block chording for brass and reeds that cuts across the basic tempo would be a cornerstone of Henderson's own technique.

Carter's departure coincided with a low point in the Henderson band's fortunes. A disastrous attempt to feature the band in a revue called *Horseshoes*, in 1929, had led to the departure of several key musicians, and the band Henderson led in the 1930–1 season involved him recruiting several new players. From that time onwards, Henderson undertook a growing amount of writing for the band, his misfortune precipitating him into action with the pencil, although as a leader he was increasingly indifferent or inept, sometimes starting the band on broadcasts before it was ready to play, and also accepting competing engagements on the same night from different agents. Nevertheless, his writing for his band from the early 1930s completed Henderson's own progression to an arranger of distinction, and to the point where he would be one of the architects of the sound of Benny Goodman's Orchestra and other swing-era bands.

At the same time the permanent transition in the rhythm section, from tuba and banjo to double bass and guitar, following the fashion set by arrivals from Chicago like Luis Russell, opened up the band's sound, as did the growing maturity of its soloists – Stewart (subsequently replaced by Henry

Allen and then Roy Eldridge), trombonist Claude Jones, and, above all, Coleman Hawkins, of whom Benny Carter said: "He had almost no-one to pattern his style after, so he was really, as I consider, a great creator."[72]

In April 1931, the band made a fresh version of *Sugar Foot Stomp*, in which Henderson himself revised the old Redman chart, opening out its final section and allowing Benny Morton to paraphrase the Oliver cornet solo after Stewart had first run through it. Like John Nesbitt's *Chinatown*, this is a sensational example of the band playing flawlessly at speed, packed with excitement and pent-up power. This is one high-profile exception to the point made by many of Henderson's musicians, that the band seldom performed on record with the brilliance it managed in live performance. Hawkins said so fairly bluntly in an oral history for Riverside Records. Benny Carter, characteristically, tried to work out why, saying: "The band was engaged in a number of band battles, and the band always played better when they were sort of challenged, you might say."[73]

And Rex Stewart put it down to a different type of challenge:

> When the musicians reached the point of almost complete collapse from a hard trip, lack of food, sleep, etc. a small ember of pride in performance would spread. Within minutes, the flame of creative improvisation would be soaring to new heights – a "money" band, playing, blowing just for the love of it all.[74]

And by "money" band he meant one on whom you could bet that it would play well, whatever the circumstances.

There are plenty of examples of Henderson's late flowering as an arranger for his own group, but a piece like *Harlem Madness*, from March 1934, demonstrates his achievements, as well as featuring Buster Bailey in a role that illustrates exactly how Benny Goodman was to sound in dozens of similar arrangements that Henderson later produced. It opens with a Coleman Hawkins solo over simple punchy riffs that open into an ensemble statement on the middle eight bars, Henderson's own piano solo has a dialogue with the orchestra, just as Jess Stacy would with Goodman's band, and Bailey's chorus floats over more straightforward riffs and block chords. An indifferent vocal from Charles Holland gives way to an out-chorus that is a textbook example of swing-dance-band arranging, the saxes, and, for a short period, Coleman Hawkins alone, take the melodic lead, punctuated by stabbing brass chords and occasional flares, while Vic Engle, on drums, emphasizes the off-beat.

I very much doubt that Henderson would have arrived at this style were it not for Redman, Carter, Challis, and, indeed, his own brother, who wrote several pieces for the band. The period from this recording to the point in 1939 when he joined Benny Goodman as staff arranger, was one of slow decline in Henderson's fortunes as a bandleader. Despite some rewarding discs with Henry Allen, Chu Berry, and Roy Eldridge, all making their mark as soloists, he was no longer fronting New York's leading band. But his main achievement between 1923 and 1934 was to create the foundations of an enduring style for large jazz orchestras, and to build an act that was very hard indeed to follow.

## A Change in the Rhythm Section

> There were other bass players around, but they played with the West Indian gig bands and the Negro show orchestras. They played the bass fiddle dignified and not with the barrelhouse beat. There were dozens of bands in New York City and all used sousaphones.
>
> Danny Barker, from *A Life in Jazz*

The change that took place in the Fletcher Henderson Orchestra when John Kirby introduced the double bass to the rhythm section was remarkable. Within a short time the band shed any remaining sense of being stilted or playing in a ragtime two–four style – a stylistic development every bit as significant as that which had taken place in the writing and arranging for this same orchestra. It seems from the accounts of Danny Barker and other eye-witnesses, as much as from recorded evidence, that 1930 was the watershed; the moment that several large orchestras in the big urban centers of Chicago and New York more or less simultaneously threw out their tubas and replaced them with double basses, just as they progressively replaced the percussive clang of the banjo with the smoother sound of the guitar.

Although I have looked at contributions to the development of jazz from all over the United States, this general movement towards the string bass was definitely one that supports the traditional orthodoxy about New Orleans as the fount of jazz. Virtually all the first significant double bassists hailed from there, underlining my earlier point about the significance of the string-playing tradition, and several of them were recorded during the mid-1920s, mainly in smaller-sized bands. Amongst the Crescent City expatriates in Chicago, I have already singled out John Lindsay's exemplary bass playing in Jelly Roll Morton's *Black Bottom Stomp* of September 1926. Less than two years later, the globe-trotting pioneer of this style of bass playing, Bill Johnson, recorded *Bull Fiddle Blues* with Johnny Dodds's Washboard Band, involving a lengthy solo.

In essence, when playing in two–four, the style exemplified by these players involved underpinning the first and third beats of each bar, usually employing the tonic and fifth of the relevant chord; whereas in four–four, the player ran simple arpeggios up and down the chord, sometimes with a little syncopation added. Johnson made little or no attempt to alter his general approach for his solo, playing straight through it in a similar manner to his ensemble style.

From photographs taken in New Orleans in the 1920s, it looks as if from the start of the decade the double bass was a regular part of many medium- to large-sized jazz groups in the city. African-American players included Chester Zardis, who had worked with Buddy Petit as early as 1920; Jimmy Johnson (one of Bolden's former associates, and bassist in the famous Bolden photograph), who played with Manuel Perez in the Pythian Roof Orchestra around 1925; and August Lanoix with the Black Diamond Orchestra of the Dejan brothers in 1928; while white players included Chink Martin with the New Orleans Harmony Kings, and Joe Kinneman with Stalebread Lacoume's band.[75] This well-established local tradition is demonstrated on disc as well, for example, by Sidney Brown's forceful playing with Sam Morgan's Jazz Band in April and November 1927. This band, although a little larger than the conventional Dixieland band (it had nine pieces), nevertheless played a loose-limbed form of collective improvisation rather than fully arranged charts. On its discs, Brown, like Lindsay and Johnson, used the technique of "slapping" the string against the fingerboard in order to underpin each note with a percussive thump or loud click.

This physically demanding style amplified the sound of the instrument so that it could be heard above the rest of the band in a dance hall, and also made it easier to record. The player's right hand drew the string vertically away from, or across, the fingerboard, allowing it to "slap" back against the wood. Even the most proficient players, with right-hand finger tips hardened from long hours of playing, sometimes found it necessary to apply adhesive tape to their fingers to prevent cuts and blisters from this repetitive action, not least during several sets lasting an entire evening, and on into the small hours. In order that the slap fell exactly on the beat, this style involved a degree of anticipation in the initiation of each note, and less-experienced players sometimes overdid things, pushing the band to speed up. Another method that some bassists employed was to pluck the string normally, but to slap the flat of the hand across all the strings on the off-beat, creating an alternation between a sounded note and a percussive tone.

The emphatic sound of a slapped bass was helpful in delineating breaks and stops, Sidney Brown, for example, adding an emphatic off-beat to Morgan's recording of *Mobile Stomp*, and underlining the solo breaks in *Bogolousa Strut*. A similar range of emphasis can be heard in Al Morgan's playing on *Duet Stomp*, with the Jones and Collins Astoria Hot Eight, recorded in New Orleans in 1929. Morgan also mastered another technique of Crescent City bass players, which was to use the bow to emulate the more legato sound of a tuba, and he did this on the recording of *Damp Weather* by the same band. A very similar technique was used by the anonymous bassist on Tony Parenti's December 1928 New Orleans recording of *You Made Me Like It Baby*, alternating choruses of bowed long notes with percussive slapping, notably behind the baritone saxophone solo. Parenti's band, and other white groups, like that led by drummer Monk Hazel, were also using guitars rather than banjos by 1928. In Parenti's group, his combination of guitar and double bass gave a light lift to the rhythm that looked forward to the swing style of the 1930s.

To a New Orleans musician like the young Danny Barker, who had played guitar and banjo with Lee Collins in the Astoria band, it seemed incredible when he arrived in New York in 1930 that the flexible, rhythmic, approach to double-bass playing which had developed in his home town had not caught on there. It seems equally extraordinary to me that with all the positive rhythmic benefits of the double bass, only a handful of big bands anywhere in the United States were using the instrument on a regular basis before the 1920s were out, and that almost all the recorded examples I have cited from New Orleans or Chicago are small-group sessions.

Among African-American big-band players, there were just two key practitioners, both New Orleans musicians who had migrated to New York: Wellman Braud (with Duke Ellington at the Kentucky Club, and then the Cotton Club) and Pops Foster (who played with Luis Russell at the Nest, the Saratoga, and the Savoy Ballroom). As Danny Barker put it: "In 1930, Pops Foster and Wellman Braud were the only two string bass players in New York City. . . . The bandleaders in New York were finally convinced that the bass fiddle belonged and sounded better in the band than the tuba."[76]

I shall come back shortly to discuss the evidence of this progression on recordings, but there was one outstanding exponent of double-bass playing on record, from a year or so earlier than Braud made his debut on disc with Ellington, who deserves attention. This was another New Orleans player, the white bassist Steve Brown, with Jean Goldkette's band.

Goldkette himself was a French-born former concert pianist who managed a large entertainment empire from his base in Detroit. Not only did he run dance halls there, such as the Graystone, but he also ran amusement arcades. (He allegedly once refused Bix Beiderbecke a raise in salary because he claimed he would simply get the money back again through his own gaming machines.) Although he was a shrewd organizer and manager, Goldkette did not front the Victor Recording Orchestra that bore his name on tour and in the studio, leaving the musical direction to Frank Trumbauer and the arrangements to Bill Challis. More significantly, he left the choice of recorded repertoire to the Victor company's Eddie King, who had an antipathy to jazz. Challis said:

> I think they picked out the *stinking-est* tunes for us. We didn't really get any good tunes to do. The best one, I think, was *Sunday*. ... Eddie King picked out the tunes for us. We got a couple of waltzes. And then they gave us singers. ... but they weren't for our band. We had an exceptionally good dance band. And it was far ahead of its time.[77]

As a consequence of King's stewardship, which, to be fair, did produce high-volume sales of some of those "stinking-est" tunes, very little of the Goldkette band's recorded legacy is out-and-out jazz, and the majority of critics have pored over it for the few bars of solo playing by Bix Beiderbecke that surface here and there, or for the brief moments by Joe Venuti and Eddie Lang that bring a sense of unfettered jazz improvisation and timing to what are otherwise rather routine dance-band performances. Understandably, it irked Bill Challis that relatively few of his jazzier charts came to be recorded, and we have only a set of rather blurry aural snapshots of how this fine band must have actually sounded when it turned its hand to jazz.

I first became interested in re-examining its recordings after a conversation with cornetist Wild Bill Davison in the late 1980s, when he told me that the band's bassist Steve Brown was the "first great virtuoso of the string bass, doing things that no-one else did until Jimmy Blanton in the 1940s."[78] Davison had first heard Brown in Chicago with the New Orleans Rhythm Kings, but later encountered him again with Goldkette's band at the Graystone in Detroit, during a time when Davison was playing relatively nearby at the city's Pirate Ship Cafe, run by the notorious Epstein Brothers, Detroit's equivalent to Al Capone. Davison recalled Brown playing solos in front of the band, in which he was featured for an entire number, and that he used considerable showmanship as well as slap-bass technique.

The originality of this was striking, and extremely unusual for the mid-1920s, as Goldkette's saxophonist Doc Ryker recalled:

> At that time, most bands were using tuba. It was much stiffer, more metronomic. But Steve introduced an entirely different sort of idea. In some ways he was the real star of that band. He'd get out in front and do a feature and everybody – all the dancers – would stop and watch.[79]

His playing was one of the exceptional ingredients in a band that, as we know from its 1926 appearance opposite Fletcher Henderson, was capable of winning a battle of music against the stiffest opposition. Once the Goldkette Orchestra had come to the notice of African-American players, it became influential: Benny Carter citing Frank Trumbauer's light saxophone style as an influence, Rex Stewart admiring Bix Beiderbecke, and bassists everywhere admiring Brown. As Milt Hinton (later Cab Calloway's bassist, but playing tuba in Tiny Parham's Chicagoan big band in the late 1920s) told Richard M. Sudhalter:

> Steve Brown was the one everybody listened to. . . . You could hear him loud and clear, even from outside [the Midway Gardens in Chicago]. What a beat that man had! He was doing things, cross-rhythms and stuff, that I've never *yet* heard anybody else do. He was the best and we all knew it.[80]

Hinton also attested to the fact that Brown was a favorite of Ellington's new bassist, Wellman Braud, who joined Ellington while Brown was still a member of the Goldkette band, and who continued to listen to him after Brown (and a number of Goldkette's sidemen) joined Paul Whiteman.

On his earliest records with the Goldkette band, made from January 1926 onwards, Brown tended to use his bow in imitation of a tuba, playing a thoughtful, but uneventful, two–four on most pieces, even when Joe Venuti and Eddie Lang (who continued to record with the band after leaving its regular touring personnel) played four–four interludes on pieces like the

October 12, 1926, *Hushabye*. His pizzicato style appeared behind the vocal on *Sunday*, made three days later. But the first real hint of his abilities came in January 1927; he provides a solid four–four behind the brass section on *I'm Looking Over a Four Leaf Clover*, giving Beiderbecke the platform on which to add his own improvised flurries to the written parts of the other trumpets, and there is evidence of Brown's overall skills on Bill Challis's chart of *Hoosier Sweetheart*. On it, he moves to an agile, bowed four–four beat behind the saxophone solo, and then provides a syncopated slapped rhythm behind Joe Venuti's violin solo.

However, the finest example of Brown's band playing from this period is to be heard on *My Pretty Girl*, made in February 1927. Here, Brown's slapped bass provides a solid, driving pulse with some heavy syncopation on the central ensemble section, and brilliantly underpins both the saxophone soloist and the final ensemble. It took some time before any other band was able to demonstrate such accomplished rhythm-section playing on record. In the flesh, its accomplishments were likely to have been greater still, since what we hear on disc is only part of the total sound, as the band's trombonist Spiegle Willcox confirmed: "Drummers had to hold back in order not to jump the cutter out of the track. I don't remember we had drums on those 78s with Goldkette. I think all Chauncey Morehouse did was hold a cymbal and come in on the end."[81]

Comparing the Goldkette band in early 1927 with almost all its large-band rivals from the same period, no other rhythm section – African-American or white – gets close to this combination of lightness and swing. The band's high-profile appearances at the Roseland Ballroom and similar venues, as well as its recordings, undoubtedly signaled the beginning of a change in favor of the double bass among African-American and white bands alike.

I suspect that the influence and historical importance of the Jean Goldkette Victor Orchestra would have been even greater had it remained together beyond September 1927, when economic pressures forced Goldkette to break up the group. Keeping a band of this size on the road was expensive, although road tours were potentially more lucrative than employing the band at the Graystone. As other, less costly, bands worked there for him, including the fledgling Casa Loma Orchestra and McKinney's Cotton Pickers, Goldkette's Victor band earned its keep on a touring network of ballrooms and colleges in New England and the East Coast, with occasional forays as far as St. Louis, until it proved just too costly to keep going. Those who heard it were thoroughly impressed with the band's jazz-playing abilities, and, in particular, the way that Challis's arrangements used clever section writing to aid Brown and the rhythm section in fitting their innovations perfectly with the creative, forward-looking improvisations of Trumbauer and Beiderbecke. Artie Shaw, for example, made a pilgrimage from his New Haven home to the Ritz in Bridgeport, Connecticut, where he recalled being "open-mouthed" at the band's abilities.[82]

After the break-up, the majority of the Goldkette players moved to Paul Whiteman. Challis had done this just before Goldkette's band folded, and he was followed soon afterwards by Trumbauer and Beiderbecke, when the new, but short-lived, band they had joined, fronted by Adrian Rollini, ran out of work. As I have mentioned, this migration effectively stocked Whiteman's band with improvising jazz musicians. Within the orchestra's vast stylistic breadth and mixed output of everything from dances to Broadway shows, and advertising broadcasts to vaudeville engagements, there were some opportunities for Challis to flex his muscles in writing for 27 musicians, and for his soloists to play the occasional jazz chorus. In the same way as Brown had been used in the Goldkette band to lift the rhythm section in brief vignettes behind Venuti and Lang, he was now employed to do the same with Whiteman, the difference made more marked by the fact that the band also employed a tuba. The chorus Brown shared with Beiderbecke on the February 1928 recording of *Dardanella* still leaps out of the arrangement with remarkable life and vigor. There is a similar moment on *Lonely Melody*, made a month earlier, and here Brown also provides a syncopated slapped background for an ensemble reed chorus, but he is not allowed to sustain his invention through a whole recorded performance.

It was the same story for most of the stellar jazz musicians in Whiteman's band: Trumbauer, Beiderbecke, Jimmy Dorsey, and, later, Jack and Charlie Teagarden, or Bunny Berigan. Their jazz opportunities were mostly limited to cameos or vignettes, although these could make a big impression on those who heard them in concert, as no less than Louis Armstrong found when he heard Beiderbecke playing "those pretty notes" during his solo chorus on *From Monday On*, during a Whiteman band concert at the Chicago Theater.[83] As long as Steve Brown was restricted to similar walk-on parts, he was not to capitalize on his innovations as a bassist, or to develop the art of providing hard-swinging support for a big band that builds progressively throughout an entire performance. For whatever reason, Brown never did make this next step, and after less than a year with Whiteman he withdrew to Detroit, only making occasional appearances on disc from 1929 onwards.

The man who was the most conspicuously successful at developing Brown's innovations and building them into a vital ingredient of every performance was the African-American bassist George "Pops" Foster. Although Foster had played tuba in the mid-1920s in Dewey Jackson's band in St. Louis (appearing on four of Jackson's records), he had begun his career as a cellist and played double bass in many pioneer New Orleans bands, as well as in Fate Marable's floating conservatory, and in Kid Ory's band on the West Coast. This background brought him into direct contact with pioneers of the New Orleans bass style, like Bill Johnson and John Lindsay. I doubt whether Foster was particularly aware of Steve Brown (unlike his contemporary Wellman Braud), but he must have learned his craft in the Crescent City at the same time as Brown. It is highly likely that the two musicians – one white, one African-American – were subject to the same initial influences as they grew up during the 1890s, hearing Creole ragtime bass players like Jimmy Johnson and Billy Marrero. Danny Barker often told me that "Mr. Billy" taught many of the outstanding bassists to come from New Orleans, and was considered "the greatest bass violinist."

Foster, who is known to have been a pupil of Marrero, arrived in New York in February 1929 to play in the band led by Panamanian pianist Luis Russell, who had fairly recently been in Chicago with King Oliver. Oliver's late-1920s group had grown since the time of the Creole Jazz Band, and it had become a nine-piece unit, with a second trumpeter, trombone, and two reeds, plus a four-piece rhythm section, although, in the fashion of the day, this employed a tuba.

Russell brought with him several of Oliver's sidemen, including New Orleans drummer Paul Barbarin and banjoist Will Johnson, when he transferred to New York in 1927. He became a leader in his own right at the Roseland (where he briefly replaced Fletcher Henderson), and after moving to the Saratoga Club, where he settled in for a long residency, he hankered after the sounds he had experienced some years earlier when a lottery win had bought him and his family a lengthy trip to New Orleans. He had stayed there from 1919 to 1924, immersing himself in the city's musical life. As his clarinetist Albert Nicholas said:

> We hadn't gone long into 1929 when Russell sent to St. Louis for
> Pops Foster. The tuba was going out, and Russell wanted that
> string bass. Foster made the string bass popular . . . they should
> give that man a medal for that. There was only Braud . . . playing
> it and one or two that no-one took notice of, but Foster

popularised it. John Kirby, coming up then, was one who took lessons from Pops.[84]

Foster himself was no doubt familiar to Russell from the early 1920s in New Orleans. As soon as the bassist arrived, he immediately slotted into the rhythm section to produce the most effective and hard-swinging team of accompanists in New York. Foster himself recalled how he flouted the Musicians' Union transfer scheme, designed to protect the jobs of the city's own musicians: "I arrived on a Tuesday and went to work on Friday. You were supposed to wait six months but they had to let me work because they didn't have no bass players who played my style in New York."[85]

In his biography of Henry "Red" Allen (who was also a member of Russell's band), John Chilton dates this arrival as February 12, 1929, so it was less than a month after this that Foster demonstrated his skills on his first recording alongside his Russell band colleagues, backing up none other than Louis Armstrong.

Armstrong had made a flying visit from Chicago to appear for two nights at Harlem's Savoy with Russell, for which the trumpeter was offered "a big fat figure."[86] But a live engagement alone does not explain the chemistry that took place between band and soloist. Possibly because of a high contingent of New Orleans musicians, and possibly also because Russell was a minimalist arranger, sketching out a few riffs here and there, and merely drafting the overall shape of a performance, *Mahogany Hall Stomp*, which Armstrong recorded on March 5, 1929, is a masterpiece. Along with Foster, Russell, and Barbarin in the rhythm section were Eddie Condon on banjo, and Lonnie Johnson (veteran of such Hot Five sides as *Hotter Than That*) on guitar.

As the performace begins, at a medium tempo, Foster uses his bow as Steve Brown did to create a light, tuba-like, two–four beat, with Condon and Johnson chugging away four-to-the-bar. Then Johnson takes a single-string guitar solo, accompanied by just Condon, before Armstrong enters accompanied by Foster's slapped bass. Behind the muted trumpet, Foster's first percussive notes are not clear, but soon he is producing arpeggios with relentless rhythmic momentum, slapping out a crisp four-beat rhythm, with guitar and banjo (and an almost inaudible piano) floating above his solid foundation. It was a new departure on record for Armstrong to play over such a firm and swinging rhythm, and it drew a fine performance from him, the rock-steady backing allowing him to place his notes with more than usual variation across, behind, and ahead of the beat.

The pattern was to be repeated again that December in a momentous recording of *St. Louis Blues* where Armstrong's simple, high-register riffs ride over a series of ever more exciting out-choruses. Nobody has ever described this epoch-making disc better than the late poet Philip Larkin in his *Daily Telegraph* jazz column in 1968:

> Louis Armstrong's 1929 *St. Louis Blues* is the hottest record ever made. Starting *in medias res*, with eight bars of the lolloping tangana release, it soon resolves into a genial uptempo polyphony. . . . Louis leads the ensemble in four blistering choruses of solid riffing. By the third chorus the whole building seems to be moving.[87]

Few of Armstrong's other large-band discs from the early 1930s were to achieve this level of ensemble swing, power, and momentum (despite several of them including John Lindsay on double bass) until he began regularly to front the Russell band in 1935.

The year 1929 was a significant one for Armstrong, not just because of this new element in his recording career, but because of his successful appearance in Fats Waller and Andy Razaf's revue *Hot Chocolates*. He had opened in June at the Hudson Theater on Broadway, as well as at Connie's Inn in Harlem, singing the hit song *Ain't Misbehavin'*, which marked the beginning of his career as a popular entertainer. From that moment onwards, he was to balance his instrumental genius with his role as an avuncular, frequently comic, and occasionally romantic singer.

He began to develop a formula for his recordings in which he briefly stated the melody of the piece, cruised through a vocal, either in his light tenor range, or his increasingly familiar gravely growl, and then ended with a couple of choruses of trumpet improvisation. There are a few exceptions, but in general, the most artistically successful of all these formulaic discs were the ones with Russell's orchestra. In them, his empathy with what the band's one-time trombonist Snub Mosley described to me as "the 'clique' of New Orleans musicians in the group" allowed him an extraordinary range of expression.[88] The repertoire he recorded with Russell extended from ballads such as *I'm In the Mood for Love* or *Thanks a Million*, to comic songs like *Old Man Mose*, or medium-tempo romps like *I'm Shooting High* or *I Hope Gabriel Likes My Music* (in which various members of the band are introduced by name). But most noticeable are the up-tempo swingers, where Russell's band was unparalleled in its rhythmic support for Armstrong. Even some stilted reed section work fails to undermine the momentum in the remake of *Mahogany Hall Stomp* from May 18, 1936, in which Foster pushes the beat, plays across it, syncopates, inverts his arpeggio figures, and yet remains locked solidly to Barbarin's drumming. Finest of all is *Swing That Music*, from the same date, in which Armstrong's high-note pyrotechnics are matched only by the vigor of Foster's performance, which Humphrey Lyttelton once described as sounding like a man chopping down trees.

Russell's ability to pare away fussy arrangements to a core that left plenty of freedom for his soloists, and the way he allowed his rhythm team to build momentum and tension was refreshingly new in 1929, and in his own discs from that year, or those his band made as accompanists to Henry "Red" Allen, there are plenty of examples of exhilarating rhythmic playing. The best example of Foster's work is on *Jersey Lightning*, from September 1929, where, in addition to some driving solo breaks (notable for their accurate intonation as much as for their rhythmic intensity), he almost single-handedly supports successive choruses of solos by Red Allen, trombonist J. C. Higginbotham, and the entire ensemble.

Although Wellman Braud was, by this time, well-established in the Duke Ellington orchestra, and had made great changes to the sound of its rhythm section, Ellington's band seldom achieved the effortless momentum and drive of Russell's. Nor did many other bands until the arrival of Count Basie's orchestra in New York on Christmas eve, 1936. A small number of discs make the point about the magic ingredient that Foster brought into the Russell recipe.

First, consider how the Russell band sounded without Foster. A good example is the session of July 15, 1930, when brass bassist Ernest "Bass" Hill temporarily replaced Foster in Henry "Red" Allen's recording band of Russell sidemen. The up-tempo *Singing Pretty Songs* lacks the incisive bite of Foster's bass, the tuba failing to create any definition at speed, and leaving the rhythmic momentum to drums and banjo. Although on *Patrol Wagon Blues* and *Roamin'*, Allen produces a solo of great beauty, the band seems held back by the stentorian tuba, and it lacks Foster's characteristic lift, exemplified by the similarly paced *Feeling Drowsy*, made exactly a year before. In that, the bassist's support seems to spur on the trumpeter, as well as drawing above-average performances from altoist Charlie Holmes and trombonist J. C. Higginbotham.

Second – how did Foster sound in a more arranged setting, without Russell's open-ended approach? When a group of Russell sidemen joined Jelly Roll Morton in November 1929, Foster was among them, and although he fell naturally into the Lindsay role, Morton's multi-part compositions and the ragtime contours of his melodies were already sounding dated. Foster works manfully to swing his way through pieces like *Sweet Peter*, but the arrangement, with its bridge passages, piano interludes, and modulations, boxes him in, and he lacks the opportunity to build his performance gradually over several choruses. He was more successful with Fats Waller, Jack Teagarden, and a host of Russell colleagues in a session the following month that produced *Ridin' But Walkin'* and *Won't You Get Off It, Please?*, where Waller's own liking for forthright rhythmic momentum chimed perfectly with Foster's.

By the time Armstrong began working with the band regularly in 1935 (an association that continued for over a decade), Russell's orchestra had become very experienced, but, above all, as well as backing Tiny Bradshaw on the Loew's theater circuit, and doing regular turns at the Apollo or the Lafayette, it had become a favorite band for dancers, working regularly at the Savoy in Harlem, and sister dance halls in Pittsburgh and the Midwest. In such settings, the driving momentum of Russell's rhythm was popular with dancers, as numerous press reports confirm.[89] His band set the trend for rhythm sections that would have just as significant an effect on the swing era as the arrangements of Fletcher Henderson.

So what about Wellman Braud? So far, in this survey of larger bands, I have put much of the jigsaw in place, but I have deliberately left a gap around the subject of Duke Ellington. It is now time to fill in those extra pieces, not just in terms of his bassist, but his entire orchestra and the questions it raised about the complex relationship within jazz between entertainment and art.

## Early Ellington

If you're what people usually call a "serious" composer,
what you have done is a theme and variations, and you
publish it as part of an opus – or a big piece of work. But if
you're a swing musician, you may not publish it at all; just
play it, making it a little different each time according to the
way you feel, letting it grow as you work on it.

Duke Ellington, in *TOPS Magazine*, 1938

The last two months of 1926 marked the moment when Duke Ellington's music came of age. His debut on the Vocalion record label that November put a marker down that a new jazz voice of maturity and imagination had arrived, with original and creative ideas about how to use a large jazz band, and which raised the question Ellington himself posed about the balance in his work between the "serious composer" and the "swing musician." Both the discs he made, *East St. Louis Toodle-o* and *Birmingham Breakdown*, hinted at that fusion of "conception and execution" that Gunther Schuller found wanting in Benny Carter's early work. The dark, brooding, minor theme of the former, over which Bubber Miley's trumpet growls menacingly, is one of the most memorable and dramatic openings in jazz, not simply up until that point, but within the entire twentieth century.

Late 1926 was also the start of Ellington's regular and long-lived association with the agent, publisher, and sometime songwriter Irving Mills, who was to play a major part in deciding that Ellington would be presented to the world as an artist every bit as much as an entertainer.

By this time, Ellington was already 27 years old, and had been active on the New York music scene for some years, establishing himself as a talented stride pianist who accompanied several blues singers on disc. As a bandleader he had played, since 1924, at the Kentucky Club (and its forerunner the Hollywood Club) on West 49th Street in Manhattan. His recording career as a leader also stretched back to 1924, although his early discs include very little that pointed to his future artistic and commercial success.

Edward Kennedy Ellington was an urbane, middle-class African-American from Washington, D.C., who had a musical family, and had taken piano lessons, but he was largely an autodidact when it came to composition and bandleading. He had acquired his name "Duke" while working as a teenage soda jerk at the Poodle Dog Cafe in Washington, where his pride in his appearance gave him something of a regal air, which he retained throughout his life. In 1919, he won a scholarship to study art when he graduated from high school, and although he chose a musical career instead, he retained a painterly eye on the world around him. In addition to his immaculate appearance, his verbal skill, wit, and overall manner gave him an air of sophistication that transferred across into his music, and chimed well with Mills's ambition to promote him as an artist, rather than a mere dance-band leader.

As a boy, Ellington had more direct contact with the African-American musical world than did Fletcher Henderson, although he came from a similarly comfortable social background – his father was a butler who later worked for the U.S. Navy both as a caterer and as a draughtsman. The young Ellington was a regular attendee at Washington's Howard Theater, where he witnessed many touring vaudeville acts performing a wide range of music. He also came into contact with visiting pianists like Eubie Blake, Luckey Roberts, and James P. Johnson, as well as others who hailed from his home town like Claude Hopkins. He grew up with a coterie of close colleagues with whom he made music, and who were to become part of his professional musical world – they included his school friends trumpeter Arthur Whetsol and saxophonist Otto Hardwick, as well as drummer Sonny Greer, who played some of Ellington's earliest cabaret jobs. He also met his future colleague, trombonist and composer Juan Tizol, in a touring band that came to Washington.

He began working as a pianist and bandleader in Washington in the early 1920s, and after an abortive attempt to move to New York in early 1923, finally relocated there later that same year with his fellow members of the "Washingtonians" band, first working at Barron Wilkins's Club in Harlem and eventually moving to the Hollywood, which in due course was renamed the Kentucky Club. The leadership and arranging duties for the band fairly swiftly transferred to Ellington.

Nevertheless, the recorded evidence of Ellington's earliest discs, from 1924, suggests that, as Henderson also did at first, he looked towards the Whiteman/Grofé approach to orchestration as a model. Indeed, Ellington admired Whiteman, and in his notes for his autobiography he was more explicit about this than in the finally published book, saying:

> Paul Whiteman was known as the "King of Jazz" and no one as yet has come anywhere near carrying that title with more certainty and dignity. . . . There are those who have come onto the scene, grabbed the money and ran off to plush boring life of boredom. But nobody held onto their band always adding interesting musicians to the payroll with no regard to their behaviour.[90]

In later life, Ellington's words might just as effectively have applied to himself, as he similarly maintained a band packed with individual "interesting musicians," but back in the 1920s, demonstrating a degree of mutual admiration, Whiteman was a frequent attendee at the Kentucky Club to hear Ellington's fledgling band.

Ellington also admired Fletcher Henderson, and his musical development from 1924 to 1926 was almost a microcosm of Henderson's over a
slightly longer period. Certainly, Ellington drafted Don Redman into his
recording line-up on at least one occasion, and adopted some of Redman's
ideas about linear writing for sections, as well as ways of handling breaks and
part-writing.

However, one or two details of Ellington's pre-1926 recordings do offer
glimpses that an original mind was already at work, and of areas that he
would develop into his own musical language; one that was distinctly
African-American. The very first piece he recorded is a case in point. Called
*Choo Choo*, it had plenty of the traits of "novelty" music about it, but
beneath the effects was the beginning of Ellington's long-running love affair
with portraying trains in music. Later, there would be his compositions
*Daybreak Express* and *Happy Go Lucky Local*, both of which develop this
particular trope with a "telling effect" comparable to that already discussed
in terms of boogie-woogie piano. Also present in the piece was a theatricality,
a sense of drama and occasion, which Ellington was to package, as effectively
as Jelly Roll Morton did, into the running time of a 78 r.p.m. disc.

In June 1926, he made a disc called *Li'l Farina*, named after a comic film
character. Even more than *Choo Choo*, this is an indicator of Ellington's later
methods and, in particular, his talent for collating and assembling varied
source material into a new conception. Throughout his career he was to
produce effective settings for melodic ideas suggested or composed by his
band members, but he was equally adept at corralling tunes and rhythms
from other areas of his life to suit his compositional purpose. *Li'l Farina*
combines ideas drawn from the jazz world with quotations from popular
songs and African-American musical theater. There is just as explicit a
selection of sources and ironic references here as in the in-jokes I have
referred to in Whiteman's output, and I sense Ellington flexing his
intellectual muscles in the way he craftily quotes lines from Will Marion
Cook's song *Bon Bon Buddy* and Ethelbert Nevin's *Mighty Lak a Rose*, both of
which refer to a small boy such as Li'l Farina himself.

In a telling analysis of the musical material that has gone into this piece,
Ellington's biographer Mark Tucker also identifies the influences of Louis
Armstrong on the soloing of trumpeter Bubber Miley and trombonist Joe
Nanton (who also prototype their own characteristic growling style), of Don
Redman in some of the riffs and voicings, and of Whiteman and Grofé in the
sweeter, more melodic part of the piece. Overall, Tucker summarizes the
importance of *Li'l Farina* as follows:

262

> [It] forms a map of influences: Louis Armstrong, Don Redman, Fletcher Henderson, Paul Whiteman, black musical theatre, popular song, New Orleans, "jungle" brass. Where in all this is Ellington?
>
> He stands behind the scenes, plotting the sequence of events and directing the abrupt changes of mood from dramatic to hot, from sweet to stomping. The Ellington sound is taking shape . . . .[91]

Tucker goes on to point out that such embryonic pieces do not yet measure up to the mature work of other bandleaders of the same period: Morton, Oliver, and Henderson. But what was being set in motion was a career that would dramatically outlast the others, that of a man who would become one of the principal architects not only of big-band jazz, but also of twentieth-century African-American music as a whole.

In due course, it is probable that Ellington's talent for assembling compositions full of light and shade, with dramatic and colorful contrasts between sections of individual pieces, and also from one piece to another, all creating a sympathetic setting for the distinctive voices of a growing collection of striking instrumental soloists, would have gradually become widely recognized; but the process was accelerated by the strategy of Irving Mills, which he subsequently summarized as making Ellington's "importance as an artist the primary consideration."[92]

Six years or so earlier, when Frank Rock had begun to manage the affairs of Jesse Stone's Blues Serenaders, the concept of the jazz-band manager was in its infancy. By 1926, it was a sufficiently established career to be the logical next step for Irving Mills, a white entrepreneur who had already become a successful song-plugger, dance-band singer, lyricist, and publisher (the last in partnership with his brother Jack). The brothers specialized in publishing music by African-Americans, and were to build their business largely on the music of Ellington (and a number of comparably high-profile figures including Fats Waller), just as their counterparts, the Melrose brothers, had done with the compositions of Morton and Oliver. Once the Mills brothers took on Ellington's publishing, their press releases did not hold back in stressing their own importance:

> In accounting for his success, Ellington insists that all his remarkable rhythms and harmonies would not be before so wide a public today, were it not for Irving Mills of Jack Mills Inc., New York music publishers. This firm . . . has enabled him to reach the broad pinnacled heights of success.[93]

Not only did Irving Mills become Ellington's publisher, but from late 1926 he took a hand in recommending titles for Ellington's new compositions (apparently suggesting that the names of strong potential African-American markets for "race" records like East St. Louis or Birmingham were mentioned). Soon afterwards, he became Ellington's manager, encouraging him to record more of his own music and fewer pieces by other composers. At the most fundamental level, Mills was obviously driven by the profit motive, through boosting Ellington's sheet-music sales, but as Mark Tucker suggests, Mills "must have realized the band was more distinctive when it performed Ellington's own music than when it played arrangements of Tin Pan Alley tunes."[94]

Under the direction of Mills, the band began to record regularly (for the obscure Cameo and Harmony labels, and the major Victor, Okeh, and Columbia companies, as well as for Brunswick and Vocalion). It acquired growing amounts of press attention, and in due course migrated from the Kentucky Club, near Times Square, to the Cotton Club, in the heart of Harlem, at Lenox and 142nd Street. From the very week that it opened there, on December 4, 1927, in the context of a revue that featured numerous popular local acts, from singers like Edith Wilson to the "stylish clothes and warm personality" of master of ceremonies Jimmy Ferguson (who was later renamed "Baron Lee" by Mills), the band began to be mentioned in its own right in press reviews. *Variety*, a paper that had not previously devoted much attention to African-American bands, after noting that "Harlem has reclaimed its own after Times Square accepted them for several seasons," commented: "Ellington's jazzique is just too bad."[95]

There is a view – expressed among others by Gunther Schuller – that in the mid-1920s, downtown New York venues preferred sweeter, dance-orientated music (of the kind the Roseland management encouraged Henderson to play), whereas uptown Harlem clubs and cabarets, many of them catering to an African-American public, preferred something rougher and more syncopated. Judging by contemporary press reports, I think this may have been what the club owners wanted the public to believe, but it is a little over-simplistic. The prevailing taste throughout the city, for all kinds of audiences, covered both genres. Henderson and other downtown bands slipped in numerous jazz tunes among what Rex Stewart called their "musical and beautiful" waltzes and ballads. Equally, Charlie Johnson's orchestra at Smalls's Paradise in Harlem – a typical uptown band – played stock arrangements every night for dancers between floor shows like the *Kitchen Mechanics*. On Sundays, the owner, Ed Smalls, catered for an exclusively African-American clientèle, and, according to the band's saxophonist Benny Waters, they wanted plenty of sweet dance numbers, too.

However, there is no doubt that from the outset the Cotton Club aimed to lure in well-heeled white customers from downtown by giving them the impression that its entertainment reflected the rougher, more syncopated, *risqué* end of the music, supposedly popular with African-Americans. This was a somewhat artificial notion, but it was helped by the appearance of Carl Van Vechten's 1926 novel *Nigger Heaven*, and a small tranche of other plays and books of the time, which portrayed the nightlife in this northern district of New York as exotic, full of fast living, illicit liquor, and jazz clubs with racially mixed clientèle. There were, in reality, very few such clubs; a *Variety* reporter found little or no evidence of them when he went in search of this kind of nightlife for a piece published in February 1926. And, as we know from the experiences of the Harlem pianists, much of the area was far from exotic, being overcrowded, with poverty close at hand.

However, a number of club owners spotted an opportunity, and created what became known as "Black and Tans," clubs that lived up to Van Vechten's image of the area, even though, as the *Variety* article pointed out: "The Black and Tans are staged for the whites, like Paris is staged for the Americans."[96] In these venues, designed to make an evening uptown a memorable event, well worth the exorbitant sums they charged, there were bands and floor-shows, and the main ones were at Smalls's Paradise, Connie's Inn, and the Cotton Club.

Billed as "The Aristocrat of Harlem," the Cotton Club was run by the racketeer Owney Madden (a former contract killer, implicated in the murder of Ellington's earlier employer Barron Wilkins), and it had thinly veiled gangland connections. Mills, who made a point of ensuring that Ellington's men wore expensive band uniforms, and who also briefly underwrote the salaries of additional musicians as the band was expanded, was publicly to protest that he was "out thousands of dollars before anything ever developed," but the club was bankrolled by the gangster George "Big Frenchy" DeMange, and it is unlikely that its receipts alone were the measure by which the Mob decided on its business viability. Mills was soon sufficiently confident that the Mob was making an adequate return that he formed his own production company to manage the club's acts, with the intention of interweaving his business empire so closely to its fortunes that he would be hard to replace, should its owners decide to "make a change."

Although occasionally an African-American sporting star or wealthy show-business personality would make a discreet appearance in the audience, the club's high prices alone ensured that it drew a predominantly white crowd, in deference to whom its African-American female dancers were "light-skinned." As Kathy J. Ogren put it, "white patrons enjoyed themselves by watching blacks be 'primitive' – without sharing their enjoyment with black patrons."[97] Advertisements run in the New York press in 1929 showed lines of smart automobiles queuing outside the club, under the legend: "Join the crowds after the theater, all Broadway comes to Harlem. An eyeful of beauty! An earful of dance-compelling music! A mouthful of tasty food! Altogether a fine frolic for you!"

Mills saw to it that from early in Ellington's initial run, which lasted, on and off, until 1931, his Cotton Club sets were broadcast regularly, either between 6.00 and 6.30 p.m., or from midnight to 1 a.m. Press reviews of the broadcasts confirm my comments about the range of styles that were popular, and show Ellington "and his heated jazzopators" leaning "more to the sweet type of syncopation" in the early evenings, but being "dirty" late at night and "slipping in a real wicked ditty off and on."[98] This duality continued in his performances at the club, as well as in his appearances at various New York theaters, including runs at the Ziegfield, or supporting Maurice Chevalier at the Fulton, and it became a feature of Ellington's first film short in 1929, *Black and Tan*, built around the "half tender, half savage"[99] composition *Black and Tan Fantasy*.

With two floor-shows a night, each containing a variety of song-and-dance pieces, many of which emphasized the primitive "African" or "jungle" atmosphere that the club wished to project to its clientèle, plus the requirements of those who came to dance before and after the revue, the Ellington band was required to tackle a broad spectrum of music. It was, by all accounts, an efficient dance band, but, from early in its life at the club, it also played floor-show material that was never intended for the general public to dance to. In this respect it was unlike Fletcher Henderson's band at the Roseland ballroom. Ellington wrote and arranged music that was quite different in character from straightforward dance-band fare, and, as Irving Mills said, "this was obviously more than the mere launching of a dance orchestra or show band."[100]

Consequently, the period 1928–31 saw Ellington's orchestra consolidating a body of work unlike anything that had yet happened in jazz, with over 150 recordings made during 64 studio sessions, plus two movie appearances. Helped along by Mills's press contacts, by the well-organized publication of piano reductions and stock band arrangements of many of his pieces, and prolific recordings, as well as by promotion to white audiences at the Cotton Club and downtown theaters as "The King of Jungle Syncopation,"[101] Ellington began to personify an image of jazz that combined his own considerable sophistication with the primitive rhythms and growling horns of the "jungle." This is nowhere better exemplified than in the famous poster for the film *Black and Tan* that has the suave and sophisticated Ellington, in his conductor's evening-dress tailcoat, separated by a piano keyboard from his musicians, who are depicted as blackface caricatures playing trumpets, trombones, and a prominently featured banjo. This symbolizes a set of contradictions at the very heart of his music.

Ellington's compositions were being performed for white audiences in the center of an African-American district of New York. At the same time as Ellington's work was being packaged for that audience as "jungle" music, helped along by Bubber Miley and Joe Nanton's growling brass and Greer's "African" drumming, Mills was presenting him to a wider public as a sophisticated composer, and exploiting publishing and recording rights to the full, in a complex interrelationship between their various roles as bandleader and agent, composer and publisher, African-American creator and white entrepreneur. It was one and the same Irving Mills that sent out press releases saying "Come on! Get hot! Get happy! Harlem's jazz king, blaring, crooning, burning up the stage with his red hot rhythms, moaning saxophones, wailing cornets, laughing trombones, screaming clarinets," who also appeared deadpan in front of a Paramount Pictorial newsreel camera, talking of "one who seems to be set entirely apart from all other composers and musicians . . . the creator of a new vogue of music." He also had Ellington's *Creole Rhapsody* billed on screen as "modern music at its best. . . . Duke Ellington's latest symphonic poem."[102] In addition to this "entertainer/composer" duality, and to the "tender/savage" contrast in Ellington's music itself, there were equally complex relationships in much of his work between the improvised and the composed, and between the "borrowed" and the original, because of his habit of using melodic material introduced to him by his sidemen.

Furthermore, Ellington's craft, which was developed during his Cotton Club years, by face-to-face contact and informal lessons from the veteran African-American conductors and composers Will Vodery and Will Marion Cook, led him to tailor almost all his compositions with great flair to fit the medium of the phonograph record, in such profusion that we can think in terms of the recordings *being* his body of work. In this respect, Ellington fits perfectly Krin Gabbard's analogy, based on Andrew Sarris's writing about cinema, of the bandleader as a kind of film director, "a serious artist imprinting a unique vision on his films in spite of the arbitrary demands of studio bosses, star egos and the production code."[103]

For "films" read "recordings," and for the second phrase, read "record company personnel, the race records catalogue, and the physical limits of the 78 r.p.m. disc." The testimony of his musicians, plus contemporary press reports and criticism, confirm Ellington's growing sense of personal vision, although, in typically paradoxical fashion, it was one that depended just as heavily on the individual musical voices of his musicians as on his own writing. As he said: "I think all writing is much more interesting when it is more personalized, when it is individual or personally tailored to the musicians going to do the playing."[104]

The majority of the pieces he wrote, arranged, and recorded between 1929 and 1931 depend on his use of "personalized" settings for his major players, Bubber Miley, Joe Nanton, Barney Bigard, and so on, in which their own solo voices are subsumed within his compositional framework, while simultaneously being essential to it.

Both Ellington's body of work, and the methods he used have become central to the jazz-performance tradition from 1928 through to the start of the twenty-first century. Nevertheless, because his *oeuvre* is embodied primarily in soundrecordings, it raises the fundamental issue, expressed by the literary critic Jed Rasula, of whether a recording is "a conduit, an acoustic window, giving access to how the music really sounded – or is it an obstacle?"[105]

To my mind, while accepting Rasula's point that "the material constraints of recording have interceded in various ways in the development of jazz," in Ellington's case this intercession seems to have been entirely positive. Prolific recording activity offered him the chance to make several attempts at producing definitive versions of his key works. In the same way as his nightly experience of fronting a band that could play new material back to him developed his maturity and range as a composer, so did his work in the studio, and there are fascinating differences of nuance between different versions of the same piece, such as the frequently recorded *Black and Tan Fantasy*.

From early in his career, Ellington demonstrated that he was an extremely accomplished pianist, either playing solo, or accompanying others. This was a marked contrast to Henderson, whose abilities as a pianist were outshone by his bandleading and arranging. To the same extent, Don Redman was little more than a journeyman reed player, focusing on writing and bandleading. But good pianist that he was, and originator of a unique piano style, this was not Ellington's priority.

The orchestra became his instrument to the extent that on its recordings he could experiment with what Andre Hodeir and Gunther Schuller term "the timbral colourings, tonal effects and unusual voicings that became the hallmark of his style."[106] Furthermore, for the best part of two decades, until he embarked on his later large scale works, Ellington was most successful as a miniaturist, so even though a very small number of his pieces spilled onto two or more sides of a disc, he generally worked within structures that fitted the time constraints of a "single" 78 r.p.m. recording.

In essence, it was his conceptual approach, his compositional attitude, which his colleague Billy Strayhorn was later to term the "Ellington effect," that underpinned Ellington's lasting contribution to jazz.

Paul Whiteman had expanded his orchestra to symphonic size and commissioned fully composed works from Gershwin, but in doing so moved away from the first principles of jazz that had so excited him when he initially heard the music. Henderson and Redman were graphically reminded of the importance of those principles by the presence of Louis Armstrong, and absorbed them into the art of arranging popular songs by other composers, or pieces of their own that mirrored the form and style of such songs. Ellington, by contrast, managed to write original music – or fashion it from material brought to him by his band members – that was not wholly dependent on twelve-, sixteen-, and 32-measure song structures, or on recognizable lyrics, and arrange it in such a way that it fused the idiosyncratic improvisational voices of his soloists with a compositional framework.

In doing so, he made an irrevocable break with the idea of collective improvisation. Although much early jazz was a lot less dependent on this kind of extemporization than previous jazz historians have been prepared to admit, a new era opened with Ellington's late-1920s work. From that time onwards, within the context of large ensembles (and a growing number of small groups), improvisation would mainly be limited to individual soloists within an arranged or composed framework. Gunther Schuller identified this turning point, saying: "Although one may bemoan the demise of collective improvisation, with its unpredictable excitement, it is obvious that Ellington, had he retained this course, would never have attained his later creative heights."[107]

Before moving on to traverse the foothills of these creative heights, it is worth looking a little further at the individual voices who made up

Ellington's resource of soloists, and who made his break with collective improvisation possible.

Initially, the most distinctive instrumental voices in his band were his brass players. His school friend Arthur Whetsol had a beautiful, mellow, clear trumpet tone that epitomized the "sweet type of syncopation" described in press reviews. Although Whetsol spent time out of music in the mid-1920s, returning to Washington to attend medical school, he came back to the band for eight years from 1929. During his absence his role was taken by Louis Metcalf, who played a high, bright lead, and was a specialist in using a mute. Metcalf remained in the line-up for some time after Whetsol's return, but his place was then taken by the slightly more extrovert Freddie Jenkins from 1929 until 1934.

If these trumpeters were the "half tender" end of the brass spectrum, their "half savage" equivalents were trumpeter Bubber Miley and trombonist Joe Nanton. Miley, although born in South Carolina, had grown up in New York, and his first influence was Mamie Smith's trumpeter Johnny Dunn. In 1921, he had replaced Dunn in the band that accompanied Smith on the vaudeville circuit, apparently producing a fair approximation of Dunn's somewhat stilted lead phrasing and wa-wa muted solos. But as Garvin Bushell, who was also in Mamie Smith's band recalled, Miley underwent a transformation when the tour reached Chicago, and he heard King Oliver in the flesh.

> The trumpets and clarinets in the East had a better legitimate quality, but the sound of Oliver's band touched you more. It was less cultivated but more expressive of how the people felt. . . . [Bubber] had never growled or used the half-cocked silver mute. It was in Chicago after hearing Oliver, that Bubber changed his style and began using his hand over the tin mute.[108]

From then on, Miley's playing style became increasingly personalized. He used the straight mute and plunger mute in conjunction to produce a vocalized growling sound, and he caught the nuances of blues singers, becoming precisely what Schaeffner called an "imitatrice de la voix." There is a hair's breadth between some of his vocalized choruses and the growling, wordless anguish of Bessie Smith or Ma Rainey at their most expressive.

Ellington's use of the contrast between Miley's deliberately primitive sound and the legitimate tone and phrasing of Whetsol or Metcalf went much further than Henderson's apposition of Joe Smith and Rex Stewart. Whereas Henderson's soloists prefigured the kind of battle between sidemen that Count Basie later developed to a fine art, Ellington was more interested in constant tonal and timbral contrasts, often within the span of a single chorus. To be sure, there were times when he capitalized on his sidemen's competitive instincts, but from very early in his recorded output he thought about each of his brass players in terms of an orchestral color. The opening of his February 1927 disc *New Orleans Low-down* is a perfect example of Metcalf's legitimate phrasing of the melody contrasting with Miley's gut-bucket comments on it, within the space of relatively few measures.

The extrovert trombonist Joe "Tricky Sam" Nanton brought a similar vocalized quality into the band to that of Miley, and between them they invested the Ellington sound with much of its very personal character. Nanton exuded confidence, and his swaggering chorus on *East St. Louis Toodle-o* was the first of many exuberant appearances.

When Miley left the band in 1929, his long-term replacement was Cootie Williams, who assimilated Miley's muted and growling effects into what was already a formidably accomplished open-trumpet style. Over the next decade he became one of the most distinctive and distinguished trumpet soloists in jazz, not least because he was able to imply a broad range of emotion in his playing. Rex Stewart (who later sat alongside him in the Ellington brass section) described the first time he heard Williams's initial entry on *East St. Louis Toodle-o* as "a sound which could be likened to a baboon cursing his mate," and his subsequent solo as "slyly insinuating promises of sensual adventures to come."[109]

To begin with, the reed section had no such distinctive soloists. Otto Hardwick was a competent player on most reed instruments, but he lacked bite and either personal character or original ideas in his solos. This lack of an individual clarinet or saxophone voice in the line-up underwent a dramatic reversal when, for a time in 1924–5, Sidney Bechet became a member of the reed section, although no recordings of this are known to survive. Ellington liked both the combative spirit that led Bechet to engage in cutting contests with Miley, and also the distinctive woody sound of his clarinet and his broad, powerful soprano saxophone. Bechet's pugnacious personality and a lackadaisical approach to time-keeping led him to part company with Ellington's band, but he made a long-term impact on Ellington's music. At one level, some of Bechet's characteristic angular phrasing and rhapsodic melody lines found their way into Ellington's vocabulary – not surprisingly, given Ellington's magpie tendencies with thematic material – but at another more fundamental level the band was to take on certain aspects of his individual sound, starting with his Creole clarinet style: "They had an entirely different character, these New Orleans players," said Ellington.

> During the heyday of the clarinet they began to sound like whistles, they lost the wood and the timbre, but most of these New Orleans cats have that wood sound. And the guy who had the most wood I ever heard on clarinet was Bechet. Which I love, and I think is the greatest, there ain't nothing like wood when playing a clarinet.[110]

To start with, after Bechet's departure, Ellington hired clarinetist Rudy Jackson, who had recorded with King Oliver, but then, as Bechet's biographer John Chilton observed:

> Duke later found that it took two skilled musicians to fulfil the role in his arrangements that Bechet had undertaken during his brief stay in the band. The two players were Johnny Hodges on alto saxophone and Barney Bigard on clarinet.[111]

Both these players joined in 1928, and this duly gave the Ellington reed section an equivalent depth of personality to that of the brass, even drawing out a more personal style from Hardwick and his junior colleague, the band's alto and baritone saxophonist Harry Carney.

The Bostonian Hodges was directly influenced by Bechet, and the effect of informal lessons he had from the older man can be immediately heard on the few discs Hodges made with Ellington on which he played soprano rather than alto saxophone – even as late as 1940, when he introduced *Blue Goose* with some Bechet-like soaring phrases. Hodges also combined a beautiful lyric style on alto that owed plenty to Bechet's melodic approach with an unparalleled ability to inject swing and movement into more up-tempo pieces. Bigard, meanwhile, shared Bechet's New Orleans patrimony, and both men had learned aspects of their technique from Lorenzo Tio Jr.

Bigard had been an adequate soloist in King Oliver's mid-1920s band in Chicago, but his move to Ellington drew him out, and he became one of the most fluent, eloquent, and decorative clarinetists in jazz, his rococo lines adding movement, charm, and color to Ellington's arrangements. On one of

Bigard's earliest recordings with the band, *Take It Easy* (made in March 1928 at a time when Miley was temporarily absent, giving a clearly uneasy Whetsol the job of playing the growling parts), the clarinetist makes his presence felt with some characteristically flowing interjections, under which the band's other New Orleans member, bassist Wellman Braud reacts with a hint of the kind of bass playing I have discussed in terms of Pops Foster and Steve Brown. Braud had done something similar behind Rudy Jackson's solo on *Washington Wobble*, but as yet he was still being used in a cameo role as a slap bassist, and it took a little longer for him regularly to play pizzicato or slap bass throughout entire pieces. Nevertheless, creating a supple New Orleans feel in conjunction with Bigard's solos, or supporting extrovert final choruses where Bigard's clarinet weaved in and out of the arranged brass with just a hint of collective polyphony, Braud's double bass added yet another distinctive sound to Ellington's palette. On a piece such as *Double Check Stomp*, recorded in 1930, Braud's slapped bass provides a continuous momentum for the band, and he takes a brief series of solo breaks, in a style directly comparable to that of Pops Foster with Luis Russell. Yet the infectious dance-hall swing of the Russell band was not, for the most part, the sound Ellington sought after; he was far more interested in combining timbre, texture, atmosphere, and creative soloing into the framework of his band, and as early as mid-1928 his orchestra not only had a greater collection of individual solo voices than most of its competitors, but undoubtedly made far more enterprising use of them.

Among his considerable body of recordings from the Cotton Club period, a small number of pieces can be singled out as indicative of the "Ellington Effect."

First, *Black and Tan Fantasy*, across its various versions, begins and ends with a paraphrase of a funeral march (echoing Chopin's B flat minor piano sonata), although with two blues choruses by Miley's growling trumpet forming a centerpiece (on which he was replaced for one session by Jabbo Smith). To Ellington's uptown white audience, this piece fitted his "jungle" style by being what the African-American writer Ralph Ellison called "immensely danceable and listenable music." To the much wider African-American public who heard it on the radio, or in various recorded versions for different "race" labels, there was something deeper and more significant at stake. Within its "listenable" setting were all kinds of echoes of quotidian life in the African-American community: the dance hall, the choir, the bar-room, the pulpit, the graveyard. Miley's trumpet coupled the vocal blues with nuances of the preacher, and, overall, the arrangement locked into a complex web of cultural connotations that made each performance a Signifyin(g) event. Some of its range of meaning was eloquently captured by Ellison:

> We were reminded not only of how fleeting all human life must be, but with its blues-based tension between content and manner, it warned us not only to look at the darker side of life, but also to remember the enduring necessity for humor, technical mastery, and creative excellence.[112]

The contemporaneous *Creole Love Call* is by no means so successful in its execution, and the sloppy ensemble work in the penultimate clarinet trio chorus shows by what a huge margin the Ellington band lacked the instrumental precision of Henderson's. But what it may have lacked in technical excellence, it more than compensated for in feeling and meaning, and Ellington's inspired idea of using Adelaide Hall's wordless singing as an additional instrumental color is a dramatic demonstration of the vocal qualities in his instrumental soloists Bubber Miley and Rudy Jackson. Hall adds growls and smears to the end of her first vocal, and, tonally, these match the muted trumpet, just as Jackson catches the shrillness of her higher register. Few better examples exist of the transfer of vocal blues technique to instrumentalists, and again I am inclined to think this conveyed a greater than usual level of meaning to the record-buying audience.

Although Ellington made a break with polyphonic collective improvisation, he did not lose touch with those aspects of the New Orleans-style line-up that appealed to him, and in several pieces he scaled down his reeds and brass to just three or four individual instruments. In *Mood Indigo*, for example, he contrived to create a new and original sound by experimenting with the voicings of clarinet, trumpet, and trombone. Whereas in the traditional order of things, the clarinet would take the upper part, the trombone the lower, with the trumpet in the middle, he assigned the highest notes to muted trumpet, the central part to a muted high-register trombone, and the lowest notes to a clarinet in its deep *chalumeau* register. This created an appealing and unusual effect, helping to make the piece one of his most popular.

Equally, on *Saratoga Swing*, a front line of just alto, clarinet, and trumpet retains the informality of New Orleans bands, accompanied by the rhythm section in a manner that prefigures both the small swing groups of the following decade, and, notably, the similar-sized bands drawn from

Ellington's late 1930s orchestra that recorded under the leadership of Johnny Hodges, Rex Stewart, or Cootie Williams. In addition, within full-band arrangements, Ellington often produced tonal contrasts between a small "group within a group" and his entire line-up.

The few tracks I have singled out – and there are plenty of other worthy contenders for attention from Ellington's earliest years, including *Black Beauty*, *Creole Rhapsody*, *The Mooche*, *Ring Dem Bells*, *Saturday Night Function*, and *Stevedore Stomp* – are indicative of the huge variety in his work. To some extent, this variety was a necessary element of his survival at the top of his profession as the Depression took hold. With Irving Mills's support, promoting the band's club, theater, and recording appearances, and ensuring that there were also regular broadcasts, Ellington weathered this difficult economic climate well, but he did so by skilfully mixing his more commercial output with the more original of his compositions. As the critic R. D. Darrell said in one of the very earliest critical essays on Ellington, published in 1932:

> As a purveyor and composer of music that must be danced to (if he is to earn his living), Ellington's composition is narrowly limited by dance exigencies while he is allowed a wide range of experimentation in the way of instrumentation and performance . . . what is remarkable is that working within constricted walls he has yet been able to give free rein to his creative imagination and racial urge for expression.[113]

Perhaps the best example of this ability to fit his style to works that caught the popular imagination, and which became part of the *lingua franca* of the "Jazz Age," was *It Don't Mean a Thing If It Ain't Got That Swing* **[CD track 13]**, recorded in February 1932. The title came from a saying of Bubber Miley's, who had by this time left the band, and who died a few months later, having already made his significant contribution to Ellington's work.

The piece itself rolls together a number of Ellingtonian devices – Ivie Anderson's wordless scatting in the introduction which pits voice against instruments, the opening statement of the theme by Nanton's muted trombone interrupted by full-band punctuations, the neat but absorbing obbligatos that Carney and Bigard play behind Anderson's main vocal, and the lengthy alto solo by Johnny Hodges that alternates with orchestrated passages, before the final reprise of the vocal. Many of Ellington's listening public will have got no further in appreciating the piece than recognizing and remembering the catchy, repetitive lyric, but it is typical of him that he cushions this in a full-blown jazz setting, so that there is every bit as much of interest for the more dedicated student of jazz.

Although Darrell published the article quoted above in the American magazine *Disques*, in June 1932, it followed a series of his equally perceptive reviews, in the *Phonograph Monthly Review*, from 1927 onwards that noted Ellington's growing compositional skill. However, it was not until some months after the appearance of the *Disques* article, around the time of the Ellington band's first visit to Europe in 1933, that other writers took up many of these ideas and began publicly to debate the art-versus-entertainment issue in Ellington's music.

The English composer, bandleader, and critic, Spike Hughes was particularly vocal in this exchange of views, although he was character-istically paradoxical in disliking both extremes of Ellington's work. He had little good to say about the Cotton Club itself, hating the floor-show and expressing his "infuriation" and "outrage" at Ellington's band being used to accompany singers and dancers, or to play random chords as the spotlight picked out minor celebrities in the audience. On a visit to New York, he soon decided that, rather than go to the club, he preferred to stay at home and concentrate on the more focused musical content in the band's broadcasts. However (and somewhat surprisingly in view of the American recordings of his own pieces such as *Nocturne*, *Arabesque*, and the *Donegal Cradle Song*), Hughes found Ellington's 1935 extended work, *Reminiscing in Tempo* — which was a genuine attempt at a different level of composition from Tin Pan Alley fare — "a long, rambling monstrosity." The entrepreneur and writer John Hammond also took against this piece, and it seems odd, in retrospect, that these commentators, who were not over-enamored of the commercial and nightclub end of Ellington's work should so dislike music that was deliberately quite different. But, perhaps in the wake of Paul Whiteman's attempts to gentrify jazz for the concert hall, many writers on jazz harbored suspicions about *any* music that veered in this direction. When the English composer Constant Lambert described Ellington's work as "the standard by which we may judge not only other jazz composers, but also those high-brow composers, whether American or European, who indulge in what is roughly known as 'symphonic jazz,'"[114] alarm bells began to ring.

This controversy was not limited to critics, and raged among the more vocal musicians of the period as well. In particular, a 1933 piece in Ellington's more reflective, atmospheric style, dedicated to Mrs. Constant

Lambert, and titled *Rude Interlude* on account of her persistent references to *"Rude" Indigo*, stirred up the opinions at the Rhythm Club. Cornetist Rex Stewart recalled:

> Some of the guys said it was great. Others said it was just a bunch of noise. Chick Webb and Jelly Roll Morton almost broke up their friendship over *Rude Interlude*. Chick argued that the tune was unmusical and didn't swing, but Jelly Roll was equally positive that it was a beautiful mood piece, and stated publicly that Duke was on the right track because he wasn't afraid to experiment. When I heard the record I wanted to puke, it was so distasteful to me.[115]

As a consequence of such discord, and prompted by the views of American critics like Darrell and Roger Pryor Dodge, or British writers like Hughes, and the French commentator Hugues Panassié, a critical consensus was reached, which focused on celebrating Ellington's work as a writer of short, atmospheric pieces ideally suited to a phonograph record, and which never strayed too far from a concept of jazz that was closely identified with the growling brass and rolling tom-toms of the "jungle" recordings, or the bluesy overtones of Miley, Nanton, and Hodges. It took the gradual acceptance of Ellington's continued attempts, from the 1940s onwards, to write longer pieces, for critical attitudes to change.

Some confusion arose among the early writers, owing to the band's habit of playing many pieces without music (pieces they must have played dozens if not hundreds of times at the Cotton Club), as to whether this constituted improvisation (considered to be a vital ingredient in jazz) or not. Wilder Hobson wrote, in *Fortune* magazine, that "his band of fourteen can *fake* (improvise) as adroitly as the early five-piece combinations," but as we know, not all those five-piece bands improvised as much as had been supposed, and Hobson subsequently contradicted himself by then revealing that Ellington was in the habit of dictating parts to his men at rehearsals after the Cotton Club shows, thereby giving the lie to the idea of "faking." Hugues Panassié noted that the majority of *solos* in the band's concerts were quite different from those on the records, but he also observed that in the case of some particularly successful efforts, the soloists did stick closely to what they had recorded – an early example of a recording group becoming the "prisoner" of its recorded arrangements, as the public expected to hear the band adhering as nearly as possible to the familiar sounds of its discs.

However, Panassié pronounced himself "astonished" that in successive sets Ellington performed different arrangements of the same piece. "The *Mood Indigo* of the first concert," he wrote of the band's Paris appearances in July 1933, "scarcely resembled that of the second, where the melody was stated *pianissimo* by an extraordinary brass sextet."[116]

From the accounts of his sidemen, we know that Ellington's stage shows rattled by at a brisk pace, with one tune giving way to the next, and a constant re-shuffling of the band book and the way pieces were tackled. Such flexibility meant, as Rex Stewart pointed out, "Everybody memorized their parts. In this band you had to."[117] So in retrospect it is no surprise to find that the same song was presented in different versions, any more than it is to confirm that Ellington's range of interest covered material that varied from buoyant danceable tunes to the reflective, deeply personal, and through-composed score of the lengthy *Reminiscing in Tempo*.

By the mid-1930s, Ellington had refined the art of writing material that built on the characters of his key soloists, which now included Rex Stewart and trombonist Lawrence Brown, and pieces like *Clarinet Lament* (for Bigard) and *Echoes of Harlem* (for Cootie Williams) had been added to his repertoire. His experiences in Europe had convinced him that, to some discerning audiences at least, "I have kinda said something, maybe our music does mean something."[118]

It was this combination of music that communicated an immediate sense of meaning to the listener and that prompted his musicians to play at the limits of their creative powers which underpinned Ellington's appeal. Other African-American bands, including Cab Calloway's, may have had a bigger, more voluble audience, and the white swing bands of the 1930s also commanded a vast public, but Ellington was recognized by both the listening public and other musicians as something exceptional, and other bands who tried to interpret his material, or borrow aspects of his sound, found themselves sounding pale in imitation.

As the 1930s went on, he brought into place the elements for what was undoubtedly his finest swing-era band. In addition, his orchestra was now playing with a unity and precision even greater than that of the Henderson band in its heyday. In a brief experiment with two basses, Braud left, to be replaced by Billy Taylor and Hayes Alvis, giving a more modern sound to the rhythm section in which Fred Guy had substituted guitar for banjo. And in 1939, the remarkably accomplished bassist Jimmy Blanton joined, followed by Ellington's first-ever heavyweight tenor saxophone soloist, Ben Webster.

Blanton was not single-handedly responsible for the changes that were to take place in jazz-bass playing in the late 1930s and early 1940s, but he drew together many of the individual elements pioneered by players in other bands. Fletcher Henderson's late 1930s bassist, Israel Crosby, for example, had demonstrated how a moving bass pattern or obbligato could be used to underpin an entire performance in *Blues in C Sharp Minor*, recorded with Teddy Wilson in 1936. Cab Calloway's bassist, Milt Hinton, had shown that a single player could combine a range of styles, from flexible, mobile bass lines played with a light pizzicato to the determined slapping of *Pluckin' the Bass* (1939), and his bowed feature from 1941, *Ebony Silhouette*, showed a better *arco* technique than Blanton's. But Blanton had the rare ability to produce bass lines that combined harmonic precision with melodic creativity, and although he remains best known for his duos with Ellington, such as *Pitter Panther Patter* and *Mr. J. B. Blues*, his most enduring contribution to jazz was to bring about a transformation of the rhythm section of the big band. The momentum was focused on the bass, rather than drums, piano, or guitar, as it had been in Braud's powerful efforts on pieces such as *Double Check Stomp*, but with a far more supple, subtle, and flexible feeling.

When the band began to record for Victor, in March 1940, Blanton immediately stamped his personality on it in a piece called *Jack the Bear*. Starting with a bass solo, offset by the band, he moves into playing walking bass, and then echoes the opening orchestral phrases of the bridge section, before settling into a firm pulse that continues until he closes with yet another solo.

Owing to an unofficial recording made later that same year in a ballroom at Fargo, North Dakota, by the jazz enthusiasts Dick Burris and Jack Towers, it is possible to eavesdrop on Ellington's band in performance, playing for a rural dancing audience, and from it to understand more fully the way the rhythm section worked. Ellington himself was absent for the opening set, and the band relied on guitarist Fred Guy, Blanton, and drummer Sonny Greer to provide all its rhythmic momentum. In particular, the interplay between Blanton and Greer, in this set and the one that follows, with Ellington at the piano, foreshadows the way that jazz rhythm sections of the mid-1940s would work, leaving the piano free to be a solo or accompanying instrument, and also shifting the underlying pulse from being the responsibility of the drummer to that of the double bassist. (According to Rex Stewart, Greer was often in danger of dragging against Blanton's mobile beat, but he was urged back to life by the trumpet section encouraging him with shouts of approval.)

By 1940, Ellington's broadcasts, stage shows, films, and recordings had made him a big star, and his weekly earnings from public appearances were rated the fifth highest of all African-American orchestras, behind those of Cab Calloway, Louis Armstrong, Fats Waller, and Chick Webb (who died in 1939, but whose band was now led by Ella Fitzgerald). Each of these entertainers could command a guarantee of $7000 per week, and Ellington's 1940 band broke the house record at the Regal in Chicago with a gross of $10,000.[119] For most of the 1930s, Ellington had no longer been appearing just for a white, well-heeled audience backing the show at the Cotton Club, but playing across the country for both African-American and white audiences, with his discs and broadcasts reaching a large cross-section of the general public. The Fargo recordings prove that he could communicate brilliantly with a dance audience on its own terms, but the discs also show that he had consolidated his ability to combine a high level of artistic achievement with popular presentation. Pieces from his recorded repertoire, such as *Clarinet Lament* and *Boy Meets Horn*, were played exquisitely for the dance-hall public, and the date also shows an early stage in the gestation of his arrangement of *Sidewalks of New York*, which he formally recorded some seven weeks later, much improved by his try-outs on the road.

This 1940 version of the Ellington band was among his most successful line-ups, because, along with the popular dance beat and the excellent instrumental execution, Ellington conveyed deep levels of meaning to his audience, similar to those he had achieved in early pieces like *Black and Tan Fantasy*.

Examples from the commercial recordings that demonstrate this include *Bojangles*, *Dusk*, and *Harlem Airshaft*. The first has sharp, stabbing ensemble chords that instantly conjure up the famous dancer's percussive tap routines, the second uses the voicings of *Mood Indigo* to create an atmospheric mood, with bluesy overtones in Rex Stewart's muted solo, while the third is an ebullient romp, with several successive riff-based sections. Although it was initially conceived with a different title, Ellington once described *Harlem Airshaft* in terms of the noises that might be heard in the inner well that let a limited amount of light and air into a block of walk-up apartments. Scholars of his music, such as Mark Tucker and Eddie Lambert, have seen only scant connections in the piece with some of the more fanciful aspects of this description, such as the smells of coffee, fish, and turkey, or the noises of dogs, but the number undoubtedly made a connection in the public mind with the sounds of "praying, fighting, smoking," and "jitterbugs ... jumping up and down, always all over you."[120] The importance of this piece (and others from the same immediate period) as a Signifyin(g) event should not be underestimated.

However, when Ellington soon afterwards set out consciously to pick up many of these ideas and incorporate them into a major 45-minute tone-poem, *Black, Brown and Beige*, which he premiered at Carnegie Hall in January 1943 as a "tone parallel to the history of the Negro in America," he received a luke-warm critical reaction, which led him to shelve the complete work until 1965, otherwise only ever performing excerpts. Much of the response in the press revolved around the degree to which it was possible to comprehend an extended jazz composition in one sitting. In the same program, Ellington had included several of his current dance numbers; pieces like *Jack the Bear*, *Cottontail*, and *Bojangles*, as well as earlier standards from his book, such as *Rockin' in Rhythm* and *Black and Tan Fantasy*. These, plus short "concertos" for various of his soloists, were exactly what the audience had been expecting: a distillation of Ellington's recorded repertoire, presented for the concert stage. They had not bargained on a three-movement work lasting 45 minutes, and made up of many disparate elements, albeit linked here and there by thematic, motific, or rhythmic material, but without many recognizable or familiar melodies. In general, the writers for the national press felt he was "saying musically the same thing he had said earlier in the evening, only this time he took forty-five minutes to do it."[121]

*Black, Brown and Beige* is at the heart of the entertainment-versus-art debate about Ellington. Its apologists say that it shows many signs of Ellington's ability to think on a broad canvas, and that there are links, overt and disguised, between sections of the piece that show it was conceived as a whole and is not just a sequence of dance materials strung together. On the other hand, apart from Joe Nanton's extraordinary vocal sounds on the trombone in the opening movement (his plunger mute creating "ya" and "wa" openings to his phrases that sound entirely human), from Johnny Hodges's extraordinarily tender solo on the *Come Sunday* theme of *Black*, and from Betty Roché's vocal on the *Mauve* section of *Brown*, the piece has few arresting moments. Most professional critics, whether familiar with jazz or not, should have been able to make sense of the form and content of the piece at one hearing, and the fact that they could not, and that today it still takes several hearings on record for its shape and content to become obvious, suggests it was only a partial success.

Ellington fought shy of producing music that ran to such length for some years, and, subsequently, when introducing excerpts from *Black, Brown and*

*Beige*, he generally added some wry allusion to its duration. In due course, with his later suites and the sacred concerts, he mastered some aspects of extended writing, but by 1943, he had not yet done so. This may well have been exacerbated by the audience for which he was performing. The concert-hall crowds in New York (and a follow-up event in Boston) who heard the piece were not as attuned to the African-American tropes in his writing as were his dance-hall, record, or radio audiences, and were, perhaps, least likely to pick up many of the inferences in *Black, Brown and Beige*. It was to take another decade or more for Ellington to reach an ideal balance of meaning and musical content in his longer concert works, but by the mid-1940s he had gone further than most jazz bandleaders and composers in balancing these two ingredients in his shorter, orthodox pieces for his conventional jazz audience.

## Out of the Territories

> Conductors usually weren't conducting the music; they
> were an image in front of the band; they just put a lot of
> motion into the scene, introduced numbers and acted as
> emcees. They were clowns more or less.
>
> Garvin Bushell, from *Jazz from the Beginning*

Several of the main African-American bands of the 1920s and 1930s had a front man, or conductor, whose name became well-known to the public, irrespective of musical ability. Some were energetic dancers, like Tiny Bradshaw or Bardu Ali (who fronted drummer Chick Webb's band). Others, like Cab Calloway, did both a song and dance act. Some, like Lucky Millinder, despite no musical training, waved a baton with considerable conducting skill, combined with energetic and athletic movements around the stage. And finally, there were those like Jimmie Lunceford or Andy Kirk who had been serious instrumentalists, but who turned to conducting, and whose best work was often the summation of hours of backstage rehearsal and planning.

Once Duke Ellington had established himself at the Cotton Club, Irving Mills began to take a keen interest in expanding his business to manage other bands, a number of which he promoted on the basis of their front man, rather than – as he had with Ellington – the intrinsically musical content of their work. In due course he added Cab Calloway's orchestra to his roster, and later set up his own Mills Blue Rhythm Orchestra, which was first fronted by Baron Lee, and later Lucky Millinder.

Calloway began fronting a former territory group called the Missourians, which became his own band in 1930, and it is the first of three African-American bands I will look at in detail who brought ideas and musicians from the territories into the New York mainstream, and helped to bring about the conditions that launched the swing era. The others are those led by Jimmie Lunceford and Count Basie, the first arriving in New York for a season at the Cotton Club in 1934, and the second opening at the Roseland in late 1936.

Swing is the name usually given to the large-band style that emerged during the early 1930s, and consequently the "swing era" is the period from approximately 1934 until the end of World War II. The style consolidated many of the elements in jazz played by ensembles of ten players or more that I have charted with Whiteman, Henderson, Goldkette, Russell, and Ellington. It is a fallacy to suggest, as some historians have done,[122] that, barring a few early exceptions, the 1930s saw the *beginning* of large-band jazz. As we know, there were ensembles of more than eight players almost from the inception of the music, and groups grew ever larger during the late 1920s. However, what took place in the 1930s was a convergence of approach among big bands, that took in urban centers and the territories alike, although it is my view that many of the ideas that coalesced into "swing" had been developing for some years in different parts of the United States on the territory and touring networks.

In particular, there was a general fashion for rhythm sections to abandon the two–four of 1920s jazz, following the trend begun by Russell and Ellington to add guitars and double basses in place of banjos and tubas, and moving towards an even four–four pulse, generated as much by smooth interaction between guitar and bass as by drums and piano. This rhythmic platform remained the norm until the early 1940s, when the first stirrings of modern jazz encouraged drummers to start breaking up the even flow with unpredictable punctuations, at the same time removing the role of the bass and snare-drum as the basis of time-keeping, and transferring this to the cymbals. Most swing bands, while encouraging the use of cymbals – in particular the opposed pair operated by a pedal, and known as the hi-hat – still expected the drummer to provide a foundation for the band with the bass drum, and the models of this style of playing were Chick Webb, among African-American bandleaders, and Gene Krupa among his white counterparts.

On top of this rhythmic stability, bands relied on arrangements that made great use of repeated phrases or riffs, in the manner of Henderson's *King Porter Stomp* arrangement, which I mentioned earlier. As reed and brass sections worked together to play riffs, virtually every band developed (among its ensemble players) a team of principal soloists, who took forward the work of Louis Armstrong and of Henderson and Ellington's various individual voices into a more general context. The most high-profile band in which all these elements coalesced very early in the 1930s was the orchestra led by vocalist Cab Calloway.

## Cab Calloway

With his zoot suit, floppy long hair, wide grin, and cries of "Hi-de-ho," Cab Calloway was one of the larger-than-life characters on the jazz scene of the 1930s. His singing was powerful and dramatic, with a repertoire of songs that contained none-too-thinly veiled references to the Harlem drug culture of the time, featuring Minnie the Moocher and Smoky Joe. His stage act was famous for its energy and verve, and through his broadcasts and recordings he acquired a big national following. By the late 1930s, he was leading the most highly paid of all African-American bands, and his line-up included some of the most significant names in jazz. Musicians who worked with him at various times included trumpeters Reuben Reeves, Mario Bauza, Shad Collins, Dizzy Gillespie, and Jonah Jones; trombonists Tyree Glenn and Quentin Jackson; saxophonists Ben Webster and Chu Berry; bassists Al Morgan and Milt Hinton; and drummer Cozy Cole.

Calloway's singing occupied the majority of his earlier discs, but as the 1930s went on, he began to make regular space for his sidemen to record a fair percentage of sides on which he did not appear, and these instrumental recordings of his band (as well as its slick backings for Calloway himself) reveal it to have been extremely accomplished. Calloway's own act changed little from the moment he first recorded as a singer, but the 1930s saw his band progressively encompass all the main stylistic changes to take place within the African-American jazz world. This was at the level of innovation – it was no mere reflection of contemporary fashions. In his first wave of changes, he shed his original rhythm section, notably bringing in New Orleans double bassist Al Morgan, who played in a similar forthright style to Pops Foster and injected the same bouncy four–four feel to Calloway's band that Foster had brought to Luis Russell's. Simultaneously, he replaced some of his brass players, adding Doc Cheatham to play lead, who had experience of the precision required by Sam Wooding's band and McKinney's Cotton Pickers, and, in due course, he added some fine reed soloists as well, in particular his successive tenorists Ben Webster and Chu Berry.

The Calloway band's huge popularity made it one of the main agents that shaped the sound of the decade. Although it worked for long stretches at the Cotton Club, during which it would regularly be broadcasting and recording, it also toured for several months every year, taking its music to a vast cross-section of the American public. At the club, and in its recordings, the band was principally aiming at white audiences and record-buyers, but through its provincial appearances and broadcasts, it also reached out effectively to the African-American public. At dances for African-American crowds, there would be areas roped off for white patrons, but Calloway could whip his loyal audience into a frenzy: "The black crowds we played for in the South and Northeast could be quite rowdy," saxophonist Garvin Bushell recalled.[123]

Among the more memorable gigs that Bushell played during his time with the band was an outdoor session at the racetrack in New Orleans, where a vast crowd of 11,000 – African-American and white – turned out, prefiguring the large-scale Jazz and Heritage Festivals on the same site from 1972 onwards. Nevertheless, from the outset, Calloway's orchestra was particularly popular in the Midwest. This was because, unlike the Eastern sophisticated sounds of Fletcher Henderson, or the slick well-rehearsed McKinney's Cotton Pickers, the band's initial musical style came straight from the territories, where the Missourians had begun life as Wilson Robinson's Syncopators in St. Louis, before preceding Duke Ellington as the resident group at the Cotton Club in Harlem. The band's forthright style remained a firm favorite in the regions, where its musicians had started out. However, its main claim to fame, before Calloway's arrival, was winning contests at the Savoy Ballroom by playing its extrovert version of *Tiger Rag*, where its punchy brass and steady rhythm won out over most other local competition.

Although well before Calloway began to front them the Missourians had migrated from their home territory to work mainly in and around New York in the late 1920s, the line-up still retained several experienced Midwesterners who stayed in the line-up under the new leader and whose playing was the foundation of the band's lively style. These included trumpeter R. Q. Dickerson and saxophonist Thornton Blue from St. Louis, trumpeter Lammar Wright and trombonist De Priest Wheeler from Kansas

City, and the band's arranger Foots Thomas, who was from Oklahoma, but who had also worked in Kansas City before coming to New York.

Before Calloway joined the Missourians, the band made a small number of records that showed distinct stylistic affinities with the territory band of Jesse Stone. Indeed, *Ozark Mountain Blues*, one of its best recordings, is based on its Savoy success *Tiger Rag*, and has marked similarities with Stone's *Boot to Boot*, being written over the same chord sequence and following the main contours of the arrangement. In Calloway's own first records, his band still conveys the raw, vibrant energy of a group whose key members were used to playing for dancers in the Midwest.

The band's inaugural recording session with Calloway, in July 1930, included a version of *St. Louis Blues* that compares interestingly with Louis Armstrong's from the previous December. The rhythm romps along in four–four, although it lacks the innate drive of Pops Foster and Paul Barbarin, but the overall shape of the chart is similar, right down to the pattern of the closing riffs. The Missourians match the opening trumpet and trombone solos of Henry Allen and J. C. Higginbotham on the Armstrong disc with some forceful growl-muted playing from R. Q. Dickerson and DePriest Wheeler, both looking back stylistically to the muted effects made famous by King Oliver. The most startling contrast is the way that Calloway's extraordinary vocal is used to dominate his version, just as Armstrong's sublime trumpet is the central feature of his. Holding a long note on the word "Blues" for several measures is an arresting idea, and Calloway follows it with much of his repertoire of vocal tricks – scatting, mumbling nonsense, and soaring into his highest register for the blues choruses themselves. This is not blues singing as such, but vaudeville singing of the highest order, and in live performance it was matched by Calloway's ability to throw himself energetically round the stage as he sang, like a tumbler or acrobat. No doubt his stage interpretation of his first big hit, *St. James Infirmary*, was as energetic visually as it sounds vocally.

The mixture of a punchy band, which retained a unified, Midwestern ensemble approach, coupled with Calloway's extrovert act, distilled from his own formative period on the touring circuit, won him a popular following around the country. It was also a surefire success in a "battle of music." Bassist Gene Ramey, as a member of Jay McShann's equally musically competent band from Kansas City, told historian Albert McCarthy how the secret weapon of Calloway himself would wipe out the opposition:

When Calloway came on for the second set, he made a

remarkably spectacular entry, leaping over chairs, turning somersaults, and indulging in all manner of non-musical showmanship, all the while singing ... in his most eccentric manner.[124]

No band could follow that, and Calloway was proved right in his own dictum that, however good a band was, its live audiences "can't be held and entertained in the complete sense by sound alone. There must be something for the eyes to see."[125]

When he took over the Missourians in 1930, very few other big bands were fronted by a singer – the majority featured a vocalist or two for the occasional number. The same remained true as the decade went on, and in the mid-1930s, with the exception of Calloway's sister Blanche, who was also a bandleader-cum-vocalist, most bands featured singers who were either specialists, like Pha Terrell and June Richmond with Andy Kirk, or drawn from the ranks of the band, like Sy Oliver and Trummy Young with Jimmie Lunceford.

Calloway's orchestra was taken on by Irving Mills to replace Duke Ellington's as resident band at the Cotton Club at the end of January 1931, and according to the band's trumpeter Doc Cheatham, there was always a plentiful supply of money from the Mob to ensure its success. The Cotton Club residency cemented Calloway's reputation, helped by the fact that he inherited Ellington's nightly broadcast slot, live from the club. Broadcasting had done a vast amount to enhance Duke Ellington's reputation, but he did not exploit it as brilliantly as Calloway. "Cab wasn't a star who was made by records, and didn't really like to make recordings," Milt Hinton, who became his bassist in 1936, told me.

Radio was what made him and every night you could hear him coast-to-coast hi-di-ho-ing. He didn't really need records to make him famous, and wherever we went with the band, people flocked to hear him, like they would a rock star today, because of his fame from broadcasting.[126]

Calloway's band seldom went short of work, and during a Cotton Club season it worked from seven-thirty in the evening until four the next morning, fitting in recording sessions approximately once a month during the daytime. If it was playing a theater, the band would have to be there at 8.30 a.m., before the first show, and work through five or six full performances a day, well into the night. There was little time for the musicians to sleep or eat, and backstage resembled an army transit camp, with cots slung in the dressing-rooms for the musicians to catch some rest in their occasional breaks, and an array of little stoves going full tilt to cook meals between sets. In addition, Calloway and his band appeared in a number of film shorts (which led, during the decade that followed, to spots in some full-length movies), bringing his frenetic stage personality to an even wider cinema audience.

This prolific activity paid off, and Calloway's national popularity grew still further. His radio exposure led to a constant demand for new arrangements: "Cab already had famous writers and arrangers producing material for the band, like Harold Arlen, Cole Porter and Irving Mills," said Doc Cheatham.

> But the radio drew hordes of little guys that were trying to make it as songwriters, and they'd come and wait backstage every night, or they'd come to a theater where we were playing and stand out there all day hoping to sell Cab their new tunes.[127]

The consequence of this was that Calloway had the pick of arrangers to choose from, and this is another reason why his band was such an effective style-setter, together with the fact that, because he was a singer himself, he commissioned not just arrangements but also original songs. During the 1930s and early 1940s, in contrast to Ellington, who supplied the bulk of arrangements for his own band, Calloway employed a stellar list of writers, including Edgar Battle, Earl Bostic, Benny Carter, Andy Gibson, Dizzy Gillespie, Buster Harding, Will Hudson, Don Redman, Jesse Stone, Harry White, and Chappie Willett, as well as the band's original arranger, Walter "Foots" Thomas (of these, only Will Hudson was white). Benny Carter's title, *The Lone Arranger*, was a deliberately ironic reference to the rate at which the band "ate up charts." Not everything Calloway commissioned was state-of-the-art, by any means, but Carter's *Lonesome Nights* and Don Redman's futuristic *Cupid's Nightmare* rank with the very finest big-band writing of all, and the band's formidable musicianship, schooled by its constant hours of playing every day, allowed it to sight-read the most complex charts almost instantly.

This is no doubt why, when Dizzy Gillespie was in its line-up, from 1939–41, he was able to develop so effectively both his own writing and the improvisational ideas that would feed into bebop, because even if not all of his colleagues were sympathetic to what he was doing, he nevertheless knew they would be able to play what he wanted, and to understand what he was aiming at technically. His 1939 charts, *Pickin the Cabbage* and *Paradiddle*, both contain stylistic innovations. The former has complex chords involving elevenths and thirteenths, as well as a theme that runs over an ostinato for bass and baritone sax which destabilizes the underlying beat – a clear four-four is only allowed to establish itself in the middle, or "bridge," section, in just the way that Gillespie's later pieces, like *Night in Tunisia* or *Salt Peanuts*, would alternate complex ostinatos with straight-ahead rhythm. *Paradiddle* – a drum feature for Cozy Cole – includes some innovative chording as well, notably in a section immediately after the introduction, where the trumpet parts descend in parallel intervals of a "flatted fifth," one of the main stylistic devices of the decade that followed these recordings. Even after he left the band, Gillespie turned up on occasion with new charts and asked the band to run them down at rehearsal so he could hear how they sounded.[128]

Throughout the 1930s, Calloway's band made the running in jazz in two distinct ways. First, at the height of the Depression, it recorded more frequently than anyone in jazz, save Duke Ellington and the white Casa Loma Orchestra, and a number of its charts stand out as examples of its proficiency and excellence, setting a standard for most of New York's other bands. Second, Calloway himself created a body of vocal work that combined his brilliant diction and powerful delivery with an urban legend – his Harlem low-life characters, about whom he sang lyrics full of jive talk. These songs had a superficial level of meaning to many of his listeners, unfamiliar with the street slang about reefers or vipers, but who were drawn to his irrepressible *bonhomie*. They also contained a far more powerful set of coded information to those aware of, and able to interpret, his subject-matter. There is more about this aspect of Calloway's work, and the way these songs constitute a collection of "telling events," in Chapter 10, but here the focus is on the most innovative or significant arrangements recorded by his band.

For a start the band could control its playing at speeds so fast and furious that most other swing orchestras of the day would have come unstuck almost at once. *Some of These Days*, recorded in December 1930, was, as Gunther Schuller has pointed out,[129] a leading candidate for the fastest jazz tempo recorded up until that date, and included some brisk unison saxophone lines, and strutting, staccato solos from trombone and reeds. Notable among these is Thornton Blue's clarinet, whose spiky, almost twittering, sound is a complete contrast to the prevailing fluency of New Orleans players such as

Barney Bigard (with Ellington) or Albert Nicholas (with Luis Russell).

The following year Reuben Reeves's high-note trumpet was featured on *Bugle Call Rag*, in very much the manner that Armstrong soared over the Luis Russell band, but in this case Calloway offers a running commentary on his playing, rather as Fats Waller was to do in his small-group recordings with trumpeters Herman Autrey and Bill Coleman a few years later. This piece was one of a number of standards adapted by the band's arranger Foots Thomas to the forthright, hard-swinging style of the Missourians, and others included *Farewell Blues*, *Nobody's Sweetheart*, and *Between the Devil and the Deep Blue Sea*. But like all the best swing orchestras, Calloway's looked within its own ranks for some of its finest and most original numbers.

As well as Foots Thomas's major contributions to the band's book, and those of his mid-1930s saxophone section-mate, Eddie Barefield, trumpeter Edwin Swayze wrote the lively *Father's Got His Glasses On* and the romping *Jitterbug*, both including ironic references to the band's trombonist Harry "Father" White. White himself produced some stirring settings for Calloway, including the gospel-tinged *Harlem Camp Meeting*, which rolled Ellingtonian effects, such as Swayze's growling trumpet and Arville Harris's fluent clarinet, together with a Hendersonian clarinet trio, but all in a manner that was completely subservient to the needs of Calloway's "scat preaching" vocal. White also arranged Calloway's own *Scat Song*, from 1933, which alternated brief solos for members of the band, and, equally, brief passages of arranged ensemble, with intricate nonsense lyrics. Supported by Al Morgan's propulsive bass and Morris White's accented off-beats on guitar, the band achieves a bouncing swing that looks forward to the sounds Count Basie would bring to New York in 1936–7.

Ironically, White's most effective arrangement had a direct connection with Basie, as his composition *Evening* was included in Basie's first set of discs as a leader, with Jones-Smith Inc., in December 1936. However, Calloway's chilling version of this piece from September 1933, with its slightly operatic diction and instrumental effects, including bowed bass, celeste, and Doc Cheatham's eloquent muted trumpet, manages to be far more dramatic. The piece demonstrates that the band was prepared to attempt to be every bit as atmospheric as Ellington's, and on this number and Calloway's *Minnie the Moocher* sequence of songs, either written by himself and Irving Mills, or by such regular contributors to his library as Harold Arlen and Ted Koehler, who wrote *Kicking the Gong Around*, it succeeded admirably. With growling trumpets, minor themes, and call-and-response vocals, Calloway's songs of the opium den were just as much a signature of his band as the "jungle" numbers were of Ellington's.

Although most of the musicians Calloway inherited from the Missourians were competent – and sometimes distinguished – soloists, as the 1930s went on the majority were replaced, not least, as the band's subsequent guitarist Danny Barker told me, to break up the "clique" of former Midwestern players in the band, and create a group entirely under the thumb, or at any rate the baton, of Calloway himself.[130]

The advantage of this was that more and more capable and significant soloists joined the ranks, bringing with them playing experience and attitudes gained with the other leading bands of the day, such as those of Chick Webb, Lucky Millinder, Eddie South, Teddy Hill, Fletcher Henderson, and Benny Carter. The high point was reached in 1939–40, with Dizzy Gillespie and Mario Bauza, plus founder member Lammar Wright in the trumpet section, Claude Jones and Keg Johnson (alongside one original Missourian De Priest Wheeler) in the trombones, altoists Hilton Jefferson and Jerry Blake, tenorist Chu Berry, and the old stalwarts Foots Thomas and Andrew Brown in the saxes, Benny Payne on piano, Milt Hinton on double bass, Danny Barker on guitar, and Cozy Cole on drums.

During this period, Berry was the most accomplished soloist of them all. A few years earlier, he had made his reputation with the big band led by Teddy Hill, in which he had starred with trumpeter Roy Eldridge, and, as Danny Barker recalled, the two of them would go "on the rampage" in the smaller clubs of Harlem after hours, sitting in with all and sundry. On the strength of this and his discs with Hill and the latter-day Fletcher Henderson band, Berry had been recognized as a formidable improviser, and he was given considerable space on Calloway's recordings. He was also allowed to appear as a freelance on dates with the likes of Lionel Hampton and Wingy Manone – Calloway overcoming his innate dislike of seeing "his" sidemen featured on somebody else's recordings.

Berry made two discs with Calloway's orchestra that are among his finest recorded solos: *Ghost of a Chance* and *Lonesome Nights*. Although he had fallen under the influence of Coleman Hawkins as a young man, Berry developed a lighter tone, and had less of a tendency to work his way through the inner harmonies of a tune in his improvisations, preferring to retain a sense of lyricism and melodic line. Andy Gibson's arrangement of *Ghost of a Chance* uses the tonal backing of the entire orchestra as a backdrop for an extended lyric solo by Berry that lasted through the full duration of the recording. Even as late as 1940, this was not an opportunity afforded to many sidemen in a big band – only Ellington's "concerti" for his various star soloists compared with it. Bassist Milt Hinton believed that it was at Berry's encouragement that Calloway turned over a growing proportion of his recordings to his soloists: "Chu Berry made a great turnabout in that band. He got Chu in there after Ben Webster left, and Chu Berry told Cab one day at the Cotton Club, 'You've got all these great guys – you should really let the guys play sometimes.' "[131]

And, for the reasons I have already mentioned, Calloway believed more in the power of broadcasts and live appearances than in recording, so he was happy to "Make one side, and feature the guys on the other," as Hinton put it. Berry's lengthy solo on Benny Carter's *Lonesome Nights* is a good example of this, but among the others to be featured were Hinton on *Pluckin' the Bass* (which also had solo interludes for Dizzy Gillespie and Chu Berry) and *Ebony Silhouette*; and Cozy Cole on *Paradiddle*, *Ratamacue*, and *Crescendo in Drums*. In 1941, arranger Buster Harding wrote a feature for the band's new trumpet soloist Jonah Jones, called *Jonah Joins the Cab*, that broke with precedent, and Jones was not only given a substantial amount of disc space, but on live appearances he was invited to join Calloway in the footlights for his extended feature which climbed chromatically through the keys in each successive chorus; the first sideman to be so honored.

Supporting the entire band was a rhythm section that was the equal of any other band of the period. It was also more versatile than most, and when the band's Cuban trumpeter, Mario Bauza, suggested to Calloway that the band should include a few Cuban or Latin numbers, the rhythm team took this easily in their stride. Very few other African-American big bands of the period managed as authentic a Latin sound as Calloway's orchestra on *Chilli Con Conga* of October 1939, and this kind of piece (plus Bauza's enthusiasm) was one of the factors in triggering Dizzy Gillespie's great interest in developing Afro-Cuban jazz the following decade.

One or two other bands of the 1930s approached Calloway's mixture of popular vocal success and high musical content. Fats Waller, for example, toured from time to time with an enlarged version of his small group, the Rhythm, and his big band used his engaging vocals and virtuoso piano playing as the center of his act. In addition to his sidemen, he employed an extra pianist, Hank Duncan, to play the warm-up sets before he came on stage, and then to engage in a pianistic "cutting-contest" which Fats almost always won, except for the odd occasion when Duncan rose more magnificently than usual to the challenge. There were no added singers or dancers: "We were the show," recalled his drummer Harry Dial. "But then Fats was a show all by himself."[132]

Among other groups with featured vocalists, the drummer Chick Webb's orchestra stands out, featuring Louis Jordan's novelty vocals on sides like *Gee, But You're Swell*, and the clear-toned singing of Ella Fitzgerald on an increasing number of discs and broadcasts as the 1930s wore on. His musicians disliked *A-tisket A-tasket*, which became one of Fitzgerald's first big hits, but Webb had a knack of knowing what would succeed with his audience, not least from his long seasons of playing at the Savoy Ballroom in New York and (from 1934) Harlem's Apollo Theater, both of which were always accurate barometers of African-American public taste. Although Webb's success was eventually built on his successful recordings with Fitzgerald, his orchestra was a capable dance band, and his musicians enjoyed playing the charts that were out-and-out instrumentals. When Garvin Bushell made the change to join Webb from Calloway's band, he wrote:

> Musically it was much more pleasurable with Webb than with Cab. The arrangements were better and featured the band more. The sections had a better quality of sound. And in order to feature Webb, we had to play some uptempo tunes.[133]

Bushell, of course, was writing from the point of view of an improvising musician who enjoyed playing jazz whenever possible. It is true that however excellent Calloway's band was, on the majority of its recordings there was only a small amount of solo space, although broadcasts suggest that on regular gigs at venues such as the Meadowbrook Inn in New Jersey, or the Club Zanzibar in Manhattan, the band's sidemen were given more opportunity to play solos.

Calloway's band also worked for much of the time until the mid-1940s with a supporting revue – the kind of acts that were featured at the Cotton Club. When the band went on the road there were usually song-and-dance teams, comedians, and a female chorus-line, as well as the band itself. The links with the black show-business of the touring networks were never too far from Calloway's popular act.

At first, Irving Mills's other principal African-American band was a little different. For the initial two years of its life, from early 1930, the Mills Blue Rhythm Band (originally called by various names including Mills Blue Rhythm Boys) had no revue of its own, and although it was directed from the keyboard by Edgar Hayes, and employed former Chicagoan bandleader Carroll Dickerson on violin, it did not even feature a front man, until Baron Lee took on the role for a year in 1932. Unlike Calloway, he did not sing, and the band itself remained mainly an instrumental unit. That is not to say it did not appear in vaudeville, but when it did so, it was usually an individual act among many. So, for example, the band was billed in several of choreographer Leonard Harper's revues at the Lafayette Theater in Harlem during 1931, supporting various acts including the dancer Bill "Bojangles" Robinson, the one-legged entertainer Peg Leg Bates, and the singers Jazzlips Richardson and Ada Brown. Later the same year, the band was billed at the Howard Theater in Washington under the slogan "Direct from the Cotton Club – The Orchestra that Replaces Duke Ellington and Cab Calloway," as a headlining act alongside Butterbeans and Susie.[134]

When Baron Lee began to front the band in 1932–3, Mills beefed it up with a small-scale revue of its own, including singer Ida Henderson, dancer Florence Hill, and the entertainers Richards and De Leo. He also drummed up interest by billing it as "a Duke Ellington Unit."[135] Mills had a simple plan – he offered the Blue Rhythm Band to venues that wanted to book Calloway and Ellington. "Book this now, you get Duke Ellington next month," recalled Danny Barker, who was in the band in 1933.

> We played theaters, did split weeks; second rate theaters in towns like Erie, Chester, and York, Pennsylvania – not the major cities. There was a demand still for vaudeville. We did four days in one place and three days in another.[136]

A key element in the band's early musical success was its pianist Edgar Hayes, who was nevertheless reviewed in the press as favorably for his stylish clothes and warm personality as for his "phenomenal" piano playing. Trumpeters Wardell Jones and Shelton Hemphill contributed to the band book, just as Calloway's sidemen did to his – indeed, Harry White played and arranged for the Blue Rhythm Orchestra before he moved to join Calloway.

Mills, however, was not too deeply interested in the musical qualities of this band. He wanted to use it to help him book his main acts, and on the way, he also wanted to profit from it in any way possible. More than half the numbers the band recorded in 1931–2 were co-written by Mills, and he was the publisher of virtually the entire repertoire, thereby taking a profit on both mechanical copyright and publishing rights. He also set up freelance recording sessions for several of the band's sidemen, more often than not on his own record label. In 1936, the Reverend Adam Clayton Powell wrote a dismissive article about Mills's tactics in the *New York Amsterdam News* in which he pointed out that all Mills's orchestras were "musical share-croppers," that they were "laying by" the musical equivalent of cotton for "Massa Mills."[137] It took another few years before Duke Ellington severed his relationship with Mills because of his agent's profiteering, no doubt taking his time because Mills had been so fundamental to his initial success. Calloway also stuck with his agent, despite evidence that Mills was retaining an unjustifiably high percentage of the band's earnings. One reason they stayed with Mills was, as John Hammond pointed out in his autobiography, "he was a man who saved black talent in the 1930s when there was no one else who cared whether it worked or not."[138]

Because he owned the Blue Rhythm Orchestra outright, and well before Powell published his warning shot across the bows, Mills took no chances with Baron Lee, and in May 1933 he fired his frontman.

> Baron Lee former head of the combo is being dropped because, Mills contends, his name has meant nothing, and that the Blue Rhythm part of the handle has dominated all marquees, hence no leader's name will be coupled with the trade name.[139]

Unfortunately, Mills almost immediately tried to change the band's name as well, and after disastrous attempts to sell the "Musical Playboys," and a flirtation with Eddie Mallory as leader, Mills realized he could not sacrifice all public recognition, and reinstated the Blue Rhythm Orchestra tag, bringing in the entertaining frontman Lucky Millinder, whom he had employed to direct minor groups at the Cotton Club. This was a master stroke, and from 1933 until 1937 Millinder led for Mills a group which, although it was always second-string to Calloway and Ellington, could, on its day, be one of the most scintillating and exciting of all the New York-based African-American big bands.

Millinder was a vocalist of sorts, his husky-toned voice suggesting a lifetime in smoky clubs and after-hours joints, but he was undoubtedly a talented band director and an energetic stage presence, even if his critics saw him as a "minor league Calloway."[140] In late 1934, the band added trumpeter Henry "Red" Allen, clarinetist Buster Bailey, and trombonist J. C. Higginbotham to the line-up, the first two, recent members of Fletcher Henderson's band, and the last, a former colleague of Allen's with Luis Russell. This combination of solo strength with Edgar Hayes's already tightly disciplined group led to some tremendous recordings, and (in common with many of Mills's most successful groups) very popular broadcasts over the

NBC network. Millinder's forte was to create a kind of musical mayhem, urging on his men with his terse vocals and shouts of encouragement, and, on a disc such as Allen's feature *Ride, Red, Ride*, to combine this with several changes in tempo and a blistering climax for the soloist. The underlying feel of the band could sound dated in comparison to Ellington or Calloway, not least because the rhythm section often remained in two–four for much of a performance, only opening up into four beats for the closing choruses, but Millinder's volatile soloists could be relied on to overcome this by stamping their powerful personalities on broadcasts and recordings alike.

In its early days, the Blue Rhythm Orchestra was somewhat schizophrenic in its style, veering from imitation of the white Casa Loma band to authentic Midwestern-flavored remakes of Calloway's best-known pieces. The band of 1935–7 was more consistent, and some excellent examples of its playing survive on disc, including *Yes! Yes!* from December 1935, Henry Allen's feature *Algiers Stomp* from the following year, and the energetic *Blue Rhythm Fantasy*, with Charlie Shavers in the trumpet section, from February 1937. When I asked him how the public perceived Millinder in comparison to his main rivals, Danny Barker, who had joined the band by the time this last example was recorded, said: "I think he was a threat for a while to all those bands. Irving Mills handled it cleverly: kept him working, but in another direction."[141]

Certainly, both Barker and Harry "Sweets" Edison, who replaced Henry Allen in 1937, confirmed that Millinder's band was capable of beating Basie's band in a "Battle of Music," and before Mills ceased to manage the band in late 1937, the Blue Rhythm Orchestra was featured in venue after venue in similar events, where "two bands knock it out on the stage."[142]

After leaving the Mills Artists agency, Millinder abandoned his former colleagues in New York, leaving them to find other work. Hayes launched his own orchestra, Shavers, and pianist Billy Kyle, joined John Kirby's small group, and Danny Barker moved to Benny Carter's band. Millinder himself set up a replacement line-up in Philadelphia with local musicians Frankie Fairfax and Bill Doggett, but he seldom recaptured the heights of the mid-1930s. Nevertheless, during the period he worked for Mills, his band, albeit on a more modest level than Calloway's and Ellington's, shows something more of the effect Irving Mills had on shaping the sound of the African-American bands that were most influential in launching the swing era.

## *Jimmie Lunceford*

Jimmie Lunceford's band began life in the 1920s as a college group, and when he eventually became famous he retained several of his personnel from that initial period. In stark contrast to Cab Calloway's streetwise education and experience in a touring-theater troupe, which led him to front a former territory band, Lunceford's was one of a number of jazz orchestras that started life in and around a college campus, his career becoming a paradigm for talented African-Americans who chose education and music, rather than sport, as an escape route from manual labor and poverty. The band's exceptional musical standards had more than a little to do with the collective educational and social aspirations of his mainly middle-class musicians: "The only salvation for a Negro in America when I was born, in 1910, was education," declared Sy Oliver, who was to become the band's principal arranger. "There are several strata in Negro society. The educated Negro is at one pole, the uneducated at another. A different life, a different world."[143]

Lunceford's band was an amalgam of ex-students from Memphis and Nashville, and Oliver taught and directed bands at Ohio State University, Columbus. Other examples of African-American bands that followed this course include Chappie Willett's college band from West Virginia; Taylor's Dixie Orchestra from the Johnson C. Smith University in Charlotte, N.C.; Horace Henderson's Collegians from Wilberforce, Ohio; and Erskine Hawkins's Orchestra, which began as the 'Bama State Collegians; but Lunceford's was the best-known and highest-profile of all.

The long-term affiliation between Lunceford's players developed an almost telepathic understanding among them, helped by Jimmy Crawford's rhythmic control at the drums, and altoist Willie Smith's long hours of rehearsal with the reed section. Other, less disciplined, musicians nicknamed them the "performing seals," but not without a tinge of envy at the miraculous standard the band achieved in its records and broadcasts. Through its meticulous and well-drilled presentation, the Jimmie Lunceford Orchestra of the 1930s made phenomenal musicianship and exemplary execution sound easy, and it combined this with a level of showmanship that came entirely from within the ranks of the band, rather than from an accompanying entourage of singers and dancers.

James Melvin Lunceford was born in 1902, in Fulton, Missouri, but he spent his early childhood in Warren, Ohio, not far from Cleveland. His father was a choirmaster, and music featured early in Lunceford's life, but it became a passion when he went to school in Denver, Colorado, where the town's director of music for schools was Wilberforce Whiteman (Paul Whiteman's father).

Lunceford's future alto saxophonist Willie Smith was also at school in Denver at this time. There is no evidence that the young Lunceford knew either Smith or another contemporary, Andy Kirk, during his first months there, but he quickly established himself as one of the city's most promising young musicians, playing several instruments. He eventually recorded on alto sax and flute, but he had also mastered the rest of the saxophone family, plus trombone and guitar.

While he was still in Denver, Lunceford got himself a job with George Morrison's territory band, during which he encountered Kirk, who later commented that "even then he was showing signs of the professor and strict bandleader he was to become."[144] Certainly, he had a touch of the academic about him, and he went on to study at two very different institutions: City College, New York (where he was able to spend his time off playing in the jazz orchestras led by Wilber Sweatman and Elmer Snowden), and Fisk University, Nashville, where he eventually graduated with a Bachelor of Music degree in 1926.

Lunceford ended up as a music instructor at Manassa High School, Memphis, and he formed a fledgling jazz orchestra there, which he called the Chickasaw Syncopators, playing locally as well as for summer seasons out of town. He had kept in touch with several of his old Fisk associates, and in 1929 brought Willie Smith, pianist Edwin Wilcox, and trombonist Henry Wells into his band, combining these university friends with his own former students to form a fully professional outfit and touring the territories.

Although broadcasts over WREC, from Memphis, established something of a local following for the group, this did little to create an audience on their increasingly ambitious road tours, far beyond the reach of their radio work. On a winter 1929 trip to Cleveland, never the most hospitable of climates after November, pianist Edwin Wilcox recalled the band went cold and hungry. They fared little better in Buffalo, New York, in a similarly cold climate, but this time there were some benefits. Trumpeter Jonah Jones was in town, and he temporarily joined the trumpet section. But more importantly, the Chickasaw Syncopators (still jointly run at this point by Lunceford, Smith, and Wilcox) found the man who was to become their star tenor sax player for almost twenty years, Joe Thomas. "Joe had a lot of personality and a lot of tricks on the horn," recalled Wilcox.

He had a way of slopping over notes, too, instead of making all the notes in a run. Willie Smith wouldn't settle for that kind of stuff. He would turn his back on you, refuse to listen if you played that way. . . . Joe was a good tenor player when we first got him, but sitting alongside a man like that he naturally got better, for Willie was a perfectionist.[145]

After the Buffalo tour, the band handed over sole leadership to Lunceford, who got them booked into the Lafayette Theater in New York. Although it had by this time appeared on a few recordings, it was the move to New York that established this former collegiate territory band as a strong individual presence in the big league of swing orchestras.

The conventional view is that the Lunceford band really came into its own a few years after its arrival there, during the period 1934–9, when trumpeter Sy Oliver became its principal arranger. But there are good reasons for supposing that, just as with the Missourians, its most distinctive characteristics were formed well away from New York. A disc recorded in 1933 as a test, but not released for almost 30 years, *Flaming Reeds and Screaming Brass*, by Edwin Wilcox, has ample evidence of the band's disciplined reed and brass playing and of strikingly unusual writing for the saxophones, a year prior to Oliver's arrival.

In my view, its originality stemmed from it having possibly developed independently from other New York groups (and in relative isolation from other territory bands as well) in Tennessee. Wilcox, for example, always maintained that the basis of its style was formed by its core of ex-Fisk musicians. "It started between Willie Smith and myself," he wrote. "We didn't really hear other bands that gave us ideas. It was what we wanted to do. The melodic quality I had came from studying classical piano."[146]

Just as Wilcox was sure that he was the origin of the band's melodic approach to section work, he was equally convinced that the band's natural precision was a consequence of Willie Smith's discipline. Yet when Sy Oliver joined, he took a different view. He was cynical about the influence of the ex-Fisk musicians, but he was in awe of Lunceford.

It was different because of Lunceford. If he hadn't contributed a thing musically it wouldn't have made a bit of difference. It was that influence that counted. Until I met Jimmie, I'd never met anybody of whom I felt any intellectual fear. I'd never met anybody who impressed me as much. The musicians don't all

realise it, but that man raised them. He changed their lives. . . .
You could not be around him without learning – about life, that's
something he taught us. There was a certain *esprit de corps* existed
in that band, and he achieved the whole thing by saying absolutely
nothing.[147]

Oliver was hired when the band was on the road in Columbus, where he
was still teaching arranging and composition at Ohio State University, in
between spells on the road with the bands of Zack Whyte and Alphonso
Trent. He was an ideal fit with the college-based, middle-class background
of Lunceford's band, and he soon rehashed some of his old arrangements for
Whyte to fit his new band.

Before long, Oliver was writing material that gave the band an even
more individual sound. A good example is his 1934 version of Ellington and
Miley's *Black and Tan Fantasy*. Oliver does away entirely with Ellington's
brooding introduction, supplying entirely new riffs behind his own growling
trumpet. Similarly, he creates a series of dense passing chords behind Willie
Smith's playing of the first bridge passage on clarinet. The orchestra holds its
dynamics in check behind Eddie Tomkins's muted trumpet, and the whole
thing has a feeling of sophistication, no less attractive than the overtly
primitive "jungle" atmosphere of Ellington's various versions, but wholly
without the dynamic tension between the primitive and the sophisticated
that suffuses Ellington's recordings.

Oliver's whole trick was to present throughout his entire arrangements
an aura of the chic, the suave, and the cool (in the most modern sense of the
word). Indeed this is a form of Signifyin(g). The message is bound up with
the immaculate appearance of the band, with the idea of never raising one's
voice, of looking at the world through half-closed, knowing eyes. If you
were to hear Oliver's 1935 arrangement of *Four or Five Times* immediately
after Don Redman's 1928 version for McKinney's Cotton Pickers (a band
that was widely regarded before Lunceford's as the ultimate in
sophistication), there is no comparison. Redman's version sounds rushed,
and slightly unintentionally comic, with its witty close-harmony vocal
quartet, and its beautifully played chart somehow seeming crude in contrast
to Oliver's relaxed two-beat arrangement, complete with his own half-
spoken, half-sung vocal, which shifts out of its laid-back persona only for the
falsetto effect at the end.

Above all, Oliver succeeded because of his complete self-belief. He *knew*
he was writing better, more sophisticated arrangements than almost anybody

else, and that with Lunceford he had a uniquely skilled group of musicians to play them. The contrast was all too obvious when he finally left to join Tommy Dorsey:

> Things just grew and happened naturally in Lunceford's [band].
> . . . I had to write *down* for Dorsey's guys, because this was before
> the days when you couldn't tell the difference between a Negro
> and a white musician. There was a polarization in performance
> then – their approach to music and to swing was completely
> different. But even so, it wasn't just white musicians, because I
> don't think there ever was another band that phrased like
> Lunceford's.[148]

He was disenchanted with one aspect of his Lunceford colleagues' work, however, which goes back to Hugues Panassié's observations about Ellington:

> One of the problems we had when the records became popular
> was that the guys wouldn't learn to play the same solo. We'd go
> in a dancehall where everybody knew all the solos off the records,
> and when they started playing something different, people would
> be disappointed.[149]

Matching their live appearances as precisely as possible to the expectations created by their discs subsequently became a major aspect of the band's discipline, and saxophonist Benny Waters, who joined ages after Sy Oliver had moved to Tommy Dorsey's organization, told me he was still asked to play the old solos note for note, almost ten years after the discs were first cut.

But Lunceford's discipline, Smith's sax playing, and Oliver's arrangements were not the entire formula that began to give the band an extraordinary level of success. They became one of the first groups in the United States to put on an entire show from within the ranks of the orchestra, instead of relying on the kind of traveling revue that accompanied the bands of Cab Calloway or Lucky Millinder. Playing to the musicians' strengths, according to trombonist and arranger Eddie Durham, who was in the line up during 1936–7, their show involved accurate parodies of Louis Armstrong, Guy Lombardo, and Paul Whiteman.

This was not a new idea and, indeed, in the 1920s, Sam Wooding had used band members to supply his "acts" after the *Chocolate Kiddies* revue broke up, and he was unable to find a ready supply of black entertainers to provide replacements in the far corners of Europe where he was working. But Lunceford's motive was different from the outset: he wanted to create the best economic package for touring, with minimum additional overheads, and this endeared him to Irving Mills, who became his agent from 1934 onwards.

One of the band's most popular and enduring discs is a recorded illustration of the band's stage act – and of Sy Oliver's subtly swinging style of arrangement. This is the January 1939 *Tain't What You Do* **[CD track 16]**, jointly written by Oliver and trombonist Trummy Young, which featured Young as the principal singer, and a chorus of the band members as back-up vocalists. It includes a characteristic device of Oliver's, the slow build, beginning with just drums and a saxophone riff, to which the full band is gradually added, displaying the precision of its section playing. In the vocal the chorus sing out the repetitive "Tain't What You Do," with Young replying – creating evocations of "call-and-response" from the dawn of African-American music, but re-packaged into a typically sophisticated arrangement. As the instrumentalists re-enter after the vocal, the piece ends with question-and-answer phrases bouncing around the reed and brass sections, the saxes playing a series of riffs similar to the phrases of the chorus singers, while the brass strike shrill chords off them like sparks off an anvil.

The breakthrough to the major league of bands had been cemented when Mills booked Lunceford into the Cotton Club in the spring of 1934. Oliver's charts, backed up by contrasting yet resourceful arrangements by Wilcox, Durham, and Lunceford himself, created a unique sound for the band that immediately differentiated it from the other orchestras of the era. This was not just a question of its overall polish and sophistication, nor the precision and unanimity with which the sections phrased – although several of the band's members have spoken of the way they seemed to think together, so close was their control of breath and fingers – but because the band could turn its skills to a huge range of material. As Sy Oliver expressed it: "Ellington, Basie, any fine band of established character has a certain sameness about anything they play. Darn near every number Lunceford did was different from the one which preceded it and the one which followed it."[150]

In addition to Oliver's medium-tempo, relaxed pieces, there were driving up-tempo numbers arranged by Oliver, such as *Blue Blazes*; by Wilcox, including his version of Lunceford's tune *Rhythm Is Our Business*; or by Lunceford himself (often arranged by Eddie Durham), such as *Harlem Shout*, which featured Paul Webster's dramatic high notes, and the famous *Lunceford Special*. All of these confirmed the band's success.

Yet in the big-band business success was a relative term. As I have already mentioned, Cab Calloway was the highest-earning leader of the period, and treated his men accordingly. His band's one-nighters were spaced between long bookings at theaters or clubs, and like Ellington's orchestra, the band traveled by private train to avoid racial problems on the road. Furthermore, although he sold plenty of discs, Calloway's real money was made from live appearances, and the manipulation of his fame by a shrewd grasp of the power of radio. Lunceford, by contrast, believed in the power of the record. He put effort, energy, and his best arrangers into creating a series of miniature recorded masterpieces. Yet his treatment of his band was almost inhumane. "We do a couple of hundred one-nighters a year, fifteen to twenty weeks of theatres, maybe one four-week location and two weeks of vacation. In all we cover about forty thousand miles a year," said Lunceford himself.[151]

The inexorable touring was, he argued, the best way of bringing the band face to face with the public who bought its records, hence ensuring continued high levels of sales. One by one, his musicians began to find it all too much. Sy Oliver, for example, had long nurtured plans to put himself through law school, and only abandoned them when Lunceford achieved initial success very rapidly. He decided to quit the band in the fall of 1939, initially with the idea of going to college once more, but almost immediately reconsidering when Tommy Dorsey offered him $5000 a year more than he'd been making with Lunceford. Dorsey may have been a martinet, and his musicians may have lacked the instinctive, relaxed swing of Lunceford's, but he appreciated Oliver's talent and imposed a less irksome touring regime on his band.

Despite the arrival of new talents in his band, including the young white arranger, Roger Segure, Lunceford found it increasingly difficult to keep his routine going, and there was a series of awkward meetings in which his men demanded more money. As the 1940s began, the attrition caused by Lunceford, and his manager Harold Oxley's policy of relentless touring, combined with the draft to rob the band of many key talents, and, before long, a majority of his principal soloists – Bill Moore, Snooky Young, Gerald Wilson, Elmer Crumbley, Ted Buckner, and Moses Allen – had all left. Although their replacements were generally good, the band began to lose its inherent cohesion, and things came to a head when Willie Smith accepted an offer to join white trumpeter Charlie Spivak's band (Smith subsequently worked for sixteen years with Harry James). Industrial action by ASCAP, the composers' union, and the first of a series of American Federation of Musicians' bans on making records further damaged the band.

Lunceford's intake of replacement sidemen contained some genuinely important musicians, and those who heard the band in person during the record ban were impressed by the likes of New Orleans reedman Omer Simeon, King Oliver's veteran altoist Benny Waters, and the strong bassist Truck Parham. "I was so thrilled I sat through several shows," wrote critic George Simon on first encountering Lunceford's new line-up.[152] He also liked the work of trumpeter Freddie Webster, no doubt on the boppish arrangements provided by Tadd Dameron, which started to move the band into more daring and original territory.

But however musically advanced the band was on occasion, Lunceford was unwilling or unable to invest in enough new charts to keep it sounding fresh. It is probable that he had turned a major financial interest in the band over to Oxley, who did not see the need to buy new arrangements. It was mainly over this issue that the old stalwart Jimmy Crawford left.

In 1946, Lunceford finally severed the links with Oxley and signed up with the William Morris agency, which was already handling young talents like Billy Eckstine and Dizzy Gillespie, and a number of old sidemen, including Trummy Young, rejoined the ranks. But it was too little too late. The bebop bands of Eckstine and Gillespie had acquired a new level of technical prowess that outstripped the precision and drive that had always been Lunceford's hallmark.

In the unlikely location of Seaside, Oregon, Lunceford collapsed in 1947 while signing autographs. There were various conspiracy theories among the musicians as to what had caused Lunceford's sudden and premature death, but his bassist Truck Parham told me that it was the result of food poisoning from hurriedly eating a suspect portion of chili at a roadside diner, and that the payroll for the band was stolen from him while he was waiting for medical assistance. He died in the ambulance as it rushed him to hospital and his band was stranded. Omer Simeon used his last few dollars to reach Los Angeles, where his childhood friend Kid Ory loaned him the fare back to New York. Others were not so fortunate and it was a few weeks before everyone was back in New York to re-group under the leadership of Joe Thomas and Edwin Wilcox. The band struggled on for a while, but without Lunceford its days were numbered, and Wilcox led a pale shadow of the group until finally calling it a day.

## Count Basie

The key to Lunceford's success had been the intricate match of the writing of his arrangers with the technical perfection of his players, the peerless interpretation of complex charts that few other bands could have handled with comparable skill and authority. By contrast, when Count Basie's band arrived in New York, by way of Chicago, at the end of 1936, it had little more than a handful of arrangements, but it was long-practiced in the art of playing for listeners and dancers all through the night in Kansas City, using impromptu "head" arrangements built on the blues, or the 32-measure structure of common popular songs. Indeed, it was not until the band recorded some of its head arrangements the following year, and these were transcribed from the discs by trumpeter Buck Clayton, that many of its best-known tunes existed on paper at all.

Basie himself had grown up in New Jersey, where he was born in 1904, and initially he joined the ranks of the Harlem pianists. He was a close friend of Fats Waller, whom he followed on the vaudeville circuit with the singer Katie Krippen, and with whom he shared an interest in playing the theater organ at Harlem's Lincoln Theater. "That was a very personal part of my life that belonged to me," recalled Basie. "I got a few lessons from Fats, private things, where I just liked to sit down at the keys and piddle around with it a bit."[153] The organ and his vaudeville experience would both come in useful in the next stage of his career, when he worked his way around the theater circuit to Kansas City as accompanist to singer Gonzelle White, and became the organist at the Eblon Theater there.

From discs Katie Krippen had made before he joined her troupe, it is clear that she was much more of a revue actress than a blues singer, but in his years on the road, Basie obviously garnered plenty of experience as a blues accompanist, both with White and (after he got to Kansas) for Edith North Johnson, also known as Hattie North, with whom he cut a record *Lovin' That Man Blues*, in 1929. His playing for her is not unlike that of James P. Johnson's for Bessie Smith. He maintains a sense of motion by strongly placed left-hand chords, and he provides plenty of filigree detail of the kind beloved by stride pianists behind the vocal, while his own solo clearly shows the ragtime roots of his style.

At the end of the 1920s, Basie was also playing regularly in the Blue Devils, a band led by bassist Walter Page in Oklahoma, but following the Wall Street crash in 1929, employment began to run scarce in the territories. Kansas City's nightlife, encouraged by the Pendergast regime who controlled the city, was less decimated than most by the onset of the Depression, and Basie moved back to join the city's leading band, led by Bennie Moten. This band was unique for the territories in that (as mentioned earlier) it had established an active recording career in the early 1920s, and had sold substantial quantities of its best discs, including the 1924 *South*. This recording activity still continued, only now Basie took Moten's place at the piano, leaving the leader free to conduct. By the time Basie joined, Moten's band had already employed trumpeter Lammar Wright, before he went on to the Missourians and Cab Calloway, and fellow trumpeter Paul Webster, who subsequently joined Lunceford. In the reed section was a veteran of Jesse Stone's orchestra, Jack Washington.

Basie, therefore, came into the world of ensemble playing among the cream of territory-band players, and not (as his stride colleagues in New York had done) in the world of East Coast musicians, who, as we know from Fletcher Henderson's early line-up, fought shy of bringing the blues into their work. There was plenty of blues feeling in Moten's sound, but there was yet another more significant factor, in terms of its long-term effect on Basie: "I found out a lot of things about tempos, that band was a great tempo-town band," he said. "Bennie knew just where to put a lot of things, and he taught me quite a few things by just listening to him."[154]

Throughout his subsequent career, often by experimenting at the piano for a few bars before inviting the band to join in, Basie had the knack for choosing exactly the right tempo for a piece – where to "put" it, as he said – from the extraordinarily slow pace he chose for Neal Hefti's 1950s number *Li'l Darlin'* to the many medium-tempo bounce tunes his band played throughout its career, always catching precisely the right speed for dancers.

The late-1920s Moten orchestra had a very well-developed sense of orchestral color. Some of the charts approached Ellington's for their creative use of timbre, and a piece like *Band Box Shuffle*, from Basie's first session with the band in 1929, used some interesting effects, including Eddie Durham's primitive amplified guitar and the accordion of Moten's nephew Ira, nicknamed "Buster." The line-up was strengthened a few months later when Walter Page broke up his Blue Devils and joined Moten, and the band toured widely, including a visit to the East Coast.

Basie used his time in the Moten band to learn more than an appreciation of tempi. His piano playing lost the ragtimey James P. Johnson influence noticeable on his Edith North Johnson accompaniment, and his solos within the band shed some of the ornate qualities in his earliest records, to move towards the spare, economical style that was to become his trademark –

what the pianist Dick Wellstood once alluded to as the "skeleton" of stride.

There was another subtle shift in the sound of the band between 1929, at the time Basie joined it, and December 1932 when, on a disastrous road tour, and badly in need of funds, Moten managed to bail out his men by organizing a visit to Victor's Camden, N.J., studios. There they cut a number of celebrated discs including *Blue Room*. On this, there is the most marked opportunity to hear how the rhythmic "feel" of the band had altered, something painstakingly engineered by Basie and trombonist Eddie Durham, who between them had set to and modernized a majority of the band's arrangements, but without sacrificing the sense of variety and color in its playing. On *Blue Room*, Basie is unequivocally playing in four–four, matched by the bass of Walter Page. In particular, his left hand moves away from the stride two-beat of his earlier work, and underpins the four-to-the-bar rhythm in figures closer to a boogie-woogie bass line. As the rhythm section romps along under an ever more impressive-sounding series of simple brass and reed riffs, the entire ensemble could well be the late-1930s Basie band. The sense of movement, of relaxed drive, is a distinct progression from the urgent four-beat of Pops Foster and Paul Barbarin in Luis Russell's band, and in achieving it, Basie and Page are helped by drummer Willie McWashington's consistent emphasis on the "off" beat – the second and fourth in every measure.

There are no recordings to chart the next stage of Basie's progress – from leading his own first band at the Cherry Blossom in Kansas City, to brief, but largely unsuccessful, forays out on the road as the Depression bit hard in 1933. At the Cherry Blossom, tenorist Lester Young and drummer Jo Jones, both to be long-term Basie associates, joined his line-up, and both were back in the fold as he began broadcasting in 1936 with his Barons of Rhythm from the Reno Club, also in Kansas City.

Under the Pendergast regime, the city had plenty of opportunities for a musician to play, even if the pay was not always magnificent in the Depression years: "Over fifty venues operated, ranging from shebeens to the grandest ballrooms," wrote Basie's biographer Chris Sheridan.

> Many became landmarks that ... were immortalized in blues, songs and jazz originals – Twelfth Street, with the Century Theatre, Vanity Fair, Amos'n'Andy's, the Spinning Wheel, the Sunset, Lone Star, Reno and nearly a dozen others, gave its name to *Twelfth Street Rag*. Vine Street was similarly immortalised – more than once – and boasted, *inter alia*, the aforementioned

Eblon Theatre, the Kentucky Club, and the Cherry Blossom.[155]

And in such a plethora of clubs, the musical work itself was very varied, as one of Basie's rivals, pianist Jay McShann recalled:

> It was sort of like a melting pot of jazz, because you got musicians from everywhere, from the North, East, South, and West. And when cats came in . . . they'd hear different musicians. They'd hear sounds they'd never heard before, and they'd say: "Hey! Did you hear this guy over here?"
>
> "No, I haven't heard him, but did you hear such and such a guy?"
>
> Because everybody was coming up with something different. See, Kansas City musicians had to play everything. In other words, if you didn't swing in Kansas City, you hadn't said nothing. Then if you couldn't play a pop tune beautiful pretty, sweet music, like *Stardust* and stuff like that, you hadn't said anything. Then if you couldn't play boogie-woogie, you hadn't said anything. And if you couldn't play the blues, you hadn't said anything. See, in Kansas City you didn't just do one thing – you had to do the whole bit.[156]

Many of the clubs in Kansas City employed little more than a pianist, and relied on the innate competitive instincts of the city's musicians to supplement the hired help with a host of instrumentalists eager to play. In his autobiography, trumpeter Buck Clayton tells how his first attempts to jam with pianist Pete Johnson at the Sunset Club drew a horde of other trumpeters eager to hear and battle against the new arrival in town. And similar jam sessions acquired legendary status, including the many involving Basie's tenor saxophonist Lester Young, whose original approach to the instrument – his light, high tone, and feathery phrasing, coupled with a steely punch when needed – made him one of the most frequent victors in after-hours musical jousts. All the musicians in Basie's band were experienced hands at playing for such jam sessions, and both his own and the other rhythm sections in the city – notably Jay McShann's, with bassist Gene Ramey and drummer Gus Johnson, or Andy Kirk's built around pianist Mary Lou Williams – adopted a similar relaxed four–four style that allowed them to provide sympathetic backing for battling soloists for long stretches at a time.

During his period at the Reno, Basie assembled most of the band that, following the enthusiastic intervention of the entrepreneur John Hammond, was to go to New York in late 1936. Hammond had heard Basie's band on its broadcasts from the club, and immediately spotted that it was doing something new.

That something was born out of expediency, because the band played every night from around ten in the evening until four the next morning, and it would have been impossible to write new arrangements at the rate that would be needed to feed it with new material. In Kansas City, there was no money to pay external arrangers, as the wealthiest New York bands did, because each of Basie's musicians was only drawing $14 a week, having collectively agreed to take a cut of 25 cents each to add trumpeter Buck Clayton to the line-up. So Basie built his repertoire of spontaneous "head" arrangements, which involved starting a blues or a 32-bar chord sequence from the piano, and signaling to each section the riffs they were to play by giving them an outline of what he wanted. Other members of the band brought in thematic material for riffs, and there were a few charts, but not anything approaching the usual library for a fourteen-piece band, as Basie's was to become. Buck Clayton recalled:

> We did not have music to most of the things we played. They were made up from playing so long with each other. We did, however, have some arrangements that were held over from the Bennie Moten band, made by Basie and Eddie Durham, but they were old and the pages had turned yellow and the corners were dog-eared or lop-eared. But they were swinging just the same.[157]

Through Hammond's efforts, Basie was booked into New York's Roseland Ballroom, with enough jobs en route to help pay the way. Hammond also hoped to sign Basie to Columbia Records, for whom he was a talent scout and something of a freelance producer. But his competitor, Jack Kapp at Decca, sent a representative to Kansas City and pipped Hammond at the post, signing Basie to a stingy, but watertight, contract for which he got no royalties and a cash total of $750 for a dozen sides, recorded after his arrival in New York.

Nevertheless, the first discs Basie made with a quintet under his own leadership, cut in Chicago en route for New York, were actually done for Hammond, but the band was called Jones-Smith Incorporated (after drummer Jo Jones and trumpeter Carl Smith who played on the session), to avoid contractual problems, and Columbia's files were subtly amended to give the impression that the recording date had been prior to Basie's Decca agreement. The particular thing these sides do show – and perhaps illustrate better than the entire band would have done – is the way the musicians worked together to play riffs on the blues. For example, *Boogie Woogie* has Smith backing up Lester Young's solo by playing unison parts with Basie's right hand, just as Young subsequently underlines the piano harmonies during Smith's solo.

The quintet recordings from Chicago were a minor triumph, as well as being Lester Young's debut on record, introducing his radically different approach from the prevailing Coleman Hawkins orthodoxy, which, through his well-known recordings with Fletcher Henderson, had influenced just about every other significant player on the instrument.

In virtually all other respects, the Chicago stage of the band's journey east was a disaster. The relatively unknown Carl Smith played trumpet on the quintet discs because Buck Clayton had damaged his lip during their regular sets at the Grand Terrace. As the only competent sight-reader in the band, Clayton was trying to lead the brass section through the unfamiliar charts that accompanied the club's floor-show, and the strain had told. Basie's band was almost without rival in playing its distinctive brand of bluesy head arrangements for dancing, but its scant experience of playing from written arrangements was a real problem, especially in view of the kind of entertainment the Grand Terrace presented, as its usual bandleader Earl Hines explained:

> [It] housed eighteen girls in the chorus line, eight parade girls, then we had around eight or ten acts in the club. I learned how to produce a show from that. . . . This was something that very few people, specially other bandleaders, have gone into – all they know is [how to] stand in front of the band and direct the band and that's it. In other words, if I opened up with a nice band number, I'd follow that with a single tap dancer, then I'd follow that with a girl team or a boy team of dancing acts, then I'd follow that with a comedian. Then we'd go into what I'd call the second number, which was a beautifully staged number. Then we'd follow that with a very good dance act, before the person that we'd be featuring in the club, say for instance Bojangles, or Ethel Waters. Then we'd do the finale for the first portion of the show.[158]

To a band like Hines's, or Henderson's, or even Ellington's (which backed similar shows at the Cotton Club), this kind of show-business was second nature. If ever there was an illustration of the variety of genres such bands played in their everyday lives as well as jazz, this was it. By contrast, Basie's band, experienced in providing dance music in the territories and the clubs of Kansas City, was one of the first big bands to arrive in the East that *specialized* in playing jazz, and very little else. "We did get through the chorus girls' music, but when we got to the difficult music it was a catastrophe," recalled Clayton. "We abused that show every night we were there."[159]

The main reason for this was that some of the musicians in the line-up, who had no problem using their ears to latch on to every riff or counter-riff as it was set up, simply could not read music adequately, and Basie's first job on finally reaching New York was to replace these non-readers, as well as a few significant players who were habitually out of tune – something that was cruelly pointed out in the band's first reviews. Nevertheless, once it reached New York, the band started to record, and its bluesy discs, particularly those with Jimmy Rushing's vocals in the true Kansas City blues-shouting style, began to win them a big following and better, more lucrative bookings.

Although 1920s groups such as Mamie Smith's Jazz Hounds or Ma Rainey's Georgia Jazz Band had provided jazz-inflected backings for blues singers, the Kansas City shouting tradition (of which other notable exponents were Big Joe Turner and the Texas-born trumpeter Hot Lips Page) was a far more even match of singer and accompanist. Rushing even brought a blues feeling to conventional ballads and popular songs, like *Evening* or the politically charged *It's the Same Old South*, but his real strength was yelling out the blues, over the robust backing of the entire band on pieces like *Sent for You Yesterday*, *Good Morning Blues*, or the boogie-woogie *I May Be Wrong*. In these sides, Rushing successfully brought all the weight of meaning of his store of traditional blues lyrics into conjunction with a band whose soloists were masters of blues expression, turning virtually every performance into a Signifyin(g) event. The discs were widely available on juke-boxes all around the cities where the band played, and Buck Clayton and Lester Young would amuse themselves by putting their own records on in any bar they happened to visit.

One set of recordings of which the band was unaware at the time was a collection of its radio broadcasts on WBAE Mutual from Pittsburgh, that featured its original guitarist, Claude Williams, who doubled on violin. In Basie's pursuit of new players to improve his band, he was shortly to replace

Williams with guitarist Freddie Green, but a version of *Lady Be Good*, broadcast from the Chatterbox Room of the William Penn Hotel during that Pittsburgh season, is a rare glimpse of Williams playing a hard-swinging violin solo with the band. Had Williams stayed in the line-up, he might have won as much fame as Lester Young, Herschel Evans, or Buck Clayton, because he functioned as a proper jazz improviser, and his solos followed in the territory-band tradition established by violinist Stuff Smith in Alphonso Trent's orchestra, rather than the simply adorned melodies preferred by such Chicagoan violinist-leaders as Carroll Dickerson and Erskine Tate.

Basie's instincts told him that, however good Williams might have been as a violinist, he was not up to the mark as a guitarist, as his rather woolly rhythm playing on a piece like the January 1937 recording of *Swinging at the Daisy Chain* demonstrates. What the band needed most to support its brass and reed soloists was a rhythm section as dependable and swinging as that which Bennie Moten had had on his recording of *Blue Room*.

John Hammond – always out to help Basie – had his eye on a suitable replacement. He teamed up his prospect, Freddie Green, with a contingent of Basie sidemen, plus Benny Goodman, to record with Teddy Wilson and Billie Holiday on January 25, 1937, and on a series of famous discs including *Why Was I Born?* this line-up proved that Green's rhythm playing was a perfect fit with that of Walter Page and Jo Jones. Hammond also introduced Basie to Green, who auditioned at the Roseland, and joined the band in February 1937, around the time of the Chatterbox broadcasts from Pittsburgh, which were to be Williams's valedictory recordings with the Basie orchestra.

With Green's arrival, Basie's redefinition of the four-to-the-measure swinging rhythm section was complete. The change that had begun with Moten's *Blue Room* came full circle, and although Jimmie Blanton's subsequent work with Ellington and Milt Hinton's with Calloway were to have more effect on the way bebop musicians were to go about approaching a rhythm section's work in the following decade, Basie set the standard for the swing era, consolidating all the rhythmic change pioneered in the late 1920s with the adoption of the double bass by Jean Goldkette, Luis Russell, and Duke Ellington.

In true Kansas City style, where musicians had to accommodate any size of group swelled (or not) by sitters-in, his rhythm section was just as adept at playing for a small group as it was for the full band, and, from time to time, Basie gathered a septet from his band and recorded with it as the "Kansas City Seven." (Indeed, Basie was wont to tell his sidemen that his big band should swing as if they were "playing like five pieces,"[160] and he retained a fondness for working in a smaller line-up throughout his career.) With just such a group, in September 1939, he recorded a remarkable small-band disc that not only displays Freddie Green's deft contribution to the rhythm section – their collective control of dynamics, coupled with Basie's sparse, pared-down piano – but is also a magnificent example of the light, airy, swinging tenor sax of Lester Young. *Lester Leaps In* **[CD track 10]**, like so many examples of the Bassie band's core repertoire, is built on a simple series of riffs, but it opens up to allow Young an extended opportunity to develop his ideas, with occasional breaks or stops from the rhythm beneath the inexorable flow of his inspired playing.

Green's presence seemed to lift the rhythm section, and one obvious element of it that propelled the band forward, without actually pushing at the tempo itself, was his technique of changing the inversion of a chord on almost every beat, so that even if the same harmony was being held for an entire measure or series of measures, he played a different configuration of the chord. But this wasn't all, as I discovered from drummer Louie Bellson, who was to play alongside Green in a later version of the band:

> Freddie Green to me was one of the greatest rhythm players I ever heard in my life, because he had a certain stroke with the right hand, that really was a great marriage to the right hand of a drummer, to the right hand of a bass player, and the right hand of a pianist. It was something that you had to watch, because his stroke was not straight up and down, more *this* way – from the top of the fretboard and back – moving forward about three or four inches and back again, with a light pulsation on [beats] two and four. . . . [He] was just loud enough so you could feel it . . . because he blended so perfectly with the bass, the piano, and the drums that if you talk about four guys that were married, that Basie rhythm section – that was it![161]

Green's perfect blend with Basie, Page, and Jones created the bedrock for the band to pile on a superstructure of exciting riffs, for the sections to play across each other, and for soloists to play over all of that. Basie's band had what was generally agreed to be the most out-and-out swinging rhythm section of all. Because Jimmy Rushing was so heavily featured in the band's records and live appearances, using his repertoire based on his aural memory of dozens of blues lyrics, the twelve-bar blues was never far away, and the endless variations on it gave Basie's band a character unlike most of the other East Coast bands, something it shared with the groups it had left behind back in the territories, like Jay McShann's.

As 1937 wore on, Basie's band prospered, and he grew more famous, particularly in the middle of the year when Billie Holiday joined the band as an additional vocalist. He was more comfortable now in playing for variety, his improved sight-readers mastering what was required of them in meeting the conventional role of the big band on the East Coast variety circuit. At the Howard in Washington, for example, he appeared with a "troupe of eleven acrobats and fourteen dancing girls," and at the Apollo, New York, choreographer Leonard Harper's "sixteen lovely Harperettes" danced with what the press called "the most prominent 'up and coming' colored band in America."[162] Part of Basie's growing success was due to his astute management by Willard Alexander – first at MCA and later at the William Morris Agency – who remained Basie's manager for most of his career. Just as Irving Mills was responsible for Ellington and Calloway's success, and Joe Glaser took Louis Armstrong's career in hand, Alexander proved that the role of the manager was a vital one at the height of the swing era, as Benny Goodman – also a client of Alexander's – discovered to his cost when he failed to follow him to the Morris agency and found himself without a mentor at MCA, losing work and profile as a result. From Frank Rock's first efforts on behalf of Jesse Stone, the role of the manager had come a long way in less than twenty years.

Musically, two parallel developments went on in the band during its first year in the East. First, Basie began increasingly to exploit the musical contrasts between his tenor saxophonists Herschel Evans and Lester Young, drawing something of the atmosphere of an after-hours Kansas City jam session into their "battles," and taking this idea further than Henderson or Ellington. "It wasn't a malicious thing, it was a thing that was fun," said Basie (who was nevertheless not above stirring things up a little, by planting rumors in each man's mind about what the other thought of him). "They each had their so-called 'fan clubs': Lester had his and Herschel had his. It used to be quite a thing and I think the band was sort of built around the rhythm section and those tenors."[163]

Once Harry "Sweets" Edison joined the trumpets late in the year (having caught Basie's eye when the Lucky Millinder band, of which Sweets was a member, trounced Basie in a "Battle of Music" in Baltimore), he and Buck Clayton's contrasting styles were also played off against each other. This kind of "battling" – reducing a contest between bands to one between the members of an individual group, was to become the mainstay of Norman Granz's Jazz At The Philharmonic concerts from the late 1940s onwards, preserving this aspect of the swing era at least, at a time when much other jazz had moved beyond the bebop revolution.

Second, Basie used Clayton and trombonist Eddie Durham, who joined from the Lunceford band during July, to do exactly what Durham and Basie himself had done for Moten years before – to refine the rough-and-ready head arrangements of the Kansas days into far more thoroughly worked-through charts, that tightened them up for repeated performance so that they could be reproduced reasonably precisely each time they were played, yet without losing the sense of bluesy, bouncy spontaneity that was such a part of the band's appeal. As Basie's biographer Chris Sheridan has observed, Durham, in particular, managed this well, and in a piece like *John's Idea*, which survives in a broadcast from November 3, 1937, there is no doubt that the performance of his own arrangement is a spectacular improvement on the commercially recorded version from the previous July.

Basie's band survived the draft and personnel changes, and carried on virtually in its original form until 1950, when economics forced him to scale down to an octet. For ten years, from the late 1930s, the rhythm section maintained its pre-eminence in the swing style, having established a template for its work so comprehensive that temporary replacements found it easy to fall into place, and the same was true of the brass and reeds.

Harry "Sweets" Edison somehow stayed right through, but other trumpeters came and went, including Joe Newman and Snooky Young (who were both to return in the 1950s), Karl George, and Emmett Berry. In the reeds, tenorist Buddy Tate replaced Herschel Evans, who died from a heart complaint, and subsequent tenorists who replaced either Tate or Lester Young to keep the "battling tenors" tradition alive in the band were Illinois Jacquet, Don Byas, Lucky Thompson, Paul Gonsalves, and Wardell Gray.

One curiosity from the period when Lester Young was absent from the band, the early 1940s, was a single recording session on which Coleman Hawkins appeared as a guest. It was cut when the tenorist arrived in Chicago while Basie was working there in April 1941, and the two sides they made create an uncanny evocation of Basie's former tenor star, the late Herschel Evans. As Hawkins's biographer John Chilton points out,[164] it is more than mere association, and – perhaps in tribute to a man who was known to idolize him – Hawkins quite deliberately includes some of Evans's most characteristic phrasing on *9.20 Special* **[CD track 14]**, which is otherwise a spirited example of the mature Basie orchestra's match of first-rate

315

execution, effortless swing, and bluesy timbre.

These were qualities much admired by Benny Goodman – not simply on account of John Hammond's advocacy, but because Goodman genuinely enjoyed the heat of the jam session, and the Basie rhythm section's sound. Not only did Basie appear at Goodman's famous Carnegie Hall concert in January 1938, but he was also a frequent member of Goodman's sextet in the recording studio, and on one session in October 1940, Goodman actually assembled a line-up made up almost entirely of Basie's men plus himself and Charlie Christian, which produced one of Lester Young's most remarkable solos on *I Never Knew*. Through this kind of advocacy for his talents and those of his musicians, from the time of his arrival in the East in 1936, Basie played a highly significant part in influencing not just Goodman's band, but almost all the white orchestras who became part of the social and musical phenomenon of swing.

## The Swing Era

It is undoubtedly the only time in its history when jazz was
completely in phase with the social environment, and
when it both captured and reflected the broadest musical
common-denominator of popular taste in the nation.
            Gunther Schuller, from *The Swing Era*

As the 1930s began, the Depression was continuing to bite, and record sales fell away, as did the opportunities for jazz groups to work, especially given the trend for larger orchestras. In New York, the bands of Ellington and Calloway survived, not least because they habitually played for the well-heeled section of white society that attended the Cotton Club, and because they enjoyed the backing of organized crime, which helped them to continue to tour, record, and broadcast. Louis Armstrong, similarly, did lengthy tours of "one-nighters," seasoned with full weeks in the main theaters that remained open, plus a modicum of recording. Claude Hopkins, Chick Webb, and a handful of other big bands made a secure living at the Savoy Ballroom. This was one of the most upmarket "dime-a-dance" venues, where (male) patrons bought a book of ten tickets for a dollar, and peeled them off a dime at a time for the privilege of a few twirls round the floor with one of the ten resident female dancers, to the backing of one or other of two resident bands. Recalling the "happy atmosphere" of this Harlem haven of entertainment, trumpeter Bill Dillard, who played there with the orchestras of Luis Russell and Teddy Hill, told me:

> The dances varied from jitterbugs to slow numbers but it was a dime ticket for every dance. . . . Along the perimeter of the dance-floor they had tables that would seat four people, that were out there for people who just came to listen to the music and watch the lindy-hopping.[165]

Elsewhere in the United States there were similar dance halls, but only in the largest urban centers could these run to one full-scale big band, let alone two, and the majority hired smaller groups. Outside the big cities, some musicians made a living playing in such venues, yet as more and more of them closed, turf wars sprang up over who should work in those that remained.

In Chicago's northern Gold Coast district, for instance, where nobody had particularly cared about playing during the 1920s, while there was plenty of work in the Loop and on the South Side, there was suddenly a scramble for jobs. Drummer Harry Dial, who played with saxophonist Jerome Pasquall and pianist Alex Hill in this neighborhood of Art Deco and Victorian town-houses, watched other African-American bands getting squeezed out by white players, backed by their powerful Union, until theirs was the only black group left in the area: "The white local never sent their delegate to check on the jobs in that section until places all over town started closing like crazy because of no business."[166]

According to Dial, of the plethora of clubs, cabarets, and theaters that had flourished all over Chicago during the 1920s, only a handful were left for African-Americans, who were challenged not just by their white counterparts scrabbling for work, but by the availability of the new technology of the talking picture:

> the only spots open to us were on the South Side, with the exception of one or two small places in Cicero, the Grand Terrace . . . the Chin Chow and Savoy Ballroom, both located in the Regal Theater building, the Golden Lily and Eldorado Cafe on 55th Street, and that was it. All the theaters had installed the Vitaphone by this time.[167]

With the notable exception of Earl Hines, who had the financial backing of the Mob at the Grand Terrace, the majority of Chicago's remaining large groups broke up. Elsewhere, McKinney's Cotton Pickers in Detroit made a final visit to the studio in 1931, and although the band struggled on until the 1940s, it never recaptured its former level of success. Out in the territories, several famous orchestras disbanded, including those of Alphonso Trent and Troy Floyd, which both finished in 1932. The lights still burned brightly in Kansas City, but across the nation the picture grew more and more dismal.

There were aftershocks of the Depression in the record business as well. Disc sales plummeted from an all-time high, in 1929, of 150 million units to less than 10 percent of that figure in 1933. In 1930 and 1931, there were still plenty of freelance studio opportunities for those musicians who were versatile and adaptable, but these began to dry up rapidly as the industry faced up to the consequences of recession and cut back new recording activity to the bone. The Radio Corporation of America (RCA) took over Victor, who retained the largest market-share, and Consolidated Film Laboratories snapped up most of Victor's competitors, including Vocalion and Brunswick. The English Decca company, which had weathered the financial storm in Europe, began to invest in the United States, leasing material from Gennett, and setting up recording sessions of its own. Other labels that had specialized in jazz and blues vanished, including Paramount, whose metal masters were scrapped when it went out of business in 1932.[168] One immediate consequence of this restructuring of the industry was the focusing of recording on the main cities, with virtually no more forays into the territories. For much of the 1930s, American jazz discs were cut mainly in New York, Camden, N.J., Chicago, and Los Angeles.

In due course, a chain of events began that turned things around. First, Prohibition was repealed on December 5, 1933, and this encouraged some clubs to remain open, others to reopen, and even a few new ones to be set up, not least because the recently elected government was keen to realize taxation revenue from alcohol sales, turning what had been a costly measure to police into a source of funds. By 1935, with the New Deal in place, student work programs up and running, and an increasing number of potentially jobless young people electing to remain in high school, there were signs of a new market among younger customers.

The record industry was desperate to exploit any such new business it could find, not least because it was losing ground to radio broadcasting. As a consequence, the firms focused on trying to produce "hit" records that would sell in high volume, and they also pursued markets with the greatest number of potential purchasers. Discs that would be popular on the nation's juke-boxes – somewhere around 250,000 of them – were one obvious strategy, but there were further initiatives aimed at capturing complete market sectors. To revitalize sales to African-American consumers, Victor, for example, plunged into the "race record" area by launching its Bluebird subsidiary in 1933, and a year later, the English Decca company began financing its own American Decca "race" series.

In February 1935, on a radio show called *Make-Believe Ballroom*, Martin Block became New York's first disc jockey, and in his commercially sponsored show he played records on air, instead of presenting live bands in the studio, as had happened up until that point. Within a few months, his listeners numbered millions, and it became possible for repeated airplay on radio to create a hit record. The conditions were in place for the music of large jazz orchestras to reach a huge public, and to be backed by commercial sponsors, radio stations, and record companies alike. A major section of the public to whom they broke through was the high-school and college sector, and the bands that succeeded were white, well-presented, and rehearsed, playing a style of swing that had developed out of Fletcher Henderson's approach to arranging. Foremost among them was the orchestra led by the Chicagoan clarinetist Benny Goodman.

In 1920s Chicago, Goodman, who was born in 1909, had made a reputation for himself as a teenage prodigy. Cornetist Jimmy McPartland, one of the Austin High School gang, first heard Goodman as "a little kid clarinet player . . . aged thirteen at the most,"[169] but was astonished by the boy's formidable technical skill on his instrument. Although he grew up in a large family, who had little money, Goodman had started playing clarinet at the age of ten in Kehelah Jacob Synagogue boys' band, and then went on to a similar band at the Hull House settlement, as well as taking lessons from the distinguished classical teacher Franz Schoepp. He heard the soulful sounds of Klezmer music in his synagogue band, he tackled the standard march repertoire at Hull House, but above all he learned the benefits of a sound technique and constant practice, and he applied these throughout his life, to the extent of undergoing a radical revision of his embouchure in the late 1940s, in pursuit of greater technical command (although many critics felt he sacrificed power and emotion in his sound as a consequence of aiming at a purer tone).

By the time Goodman met McPartland, and other would-be jazz musicians a year or two older than he was, such as pianist Art Hodes, who was also involved with Hull House, he had fallen under the influence of jazz himself, and had learned to emulate the discs of the O.D.J.B., of a recording group of white New Yorkers known as Bailey's Lucky Seven, and of the vaudevillean clarinetist Ted Lewis. At thirteen, Goodman was playing regularly around Chicago, and many of the gigs he played were for the audience that would later become his biggest, and most loyal, following: college students. He and McPartland played for a band led by Murph Podolsky, and McPartland recalled:

> Guys from the University of Chicago and North-western University would call up one of us for a band, and we came to be quite a team round those different dances in Chicago. Both Benny and I would earn from 80 to 100 dollars a week, and still go to school. They paid good money those college boys.[170]

This was an extraordinary amount of money for a thirteen-year-old to be earning in the 1920s, and the lure of being a well-paid professional musician was too strong to keep Goodman in education. The following year he left high school to become a full-time clarinetist, and as his playing developed, he absorbed into his style elements of many of the most individual jazz musicians who were active in Chicago at the time. These included white clarinetists such as Leon Roppolo and Frank Teschemacher, but also New Orleans players such as Johnny Dodds and Jimmie Noone. Goodman's flowing phrasing and fruity lower register emulated Noone, but his powerful blues feeling and his ability to bend notes and insert rasping, vocal tones for a sense of urgency and human feeling came from Dodds. When he played the lead or melody of a tune, although there were clear affinities with Noone, his influences were not confined to other players of his own instrument, as he also adopted some aspects of the relaxed phrasing and timing of Bix Beiderbecke, whom he met in 1923, and also of Louis Armstrong, whole phrases from whose solos would occasionally turn up in the middle of one of Goodman's. Well before he was out of his teens, Goodman showed all the signs that he was becoming the consummate clarinetist in jazz. He had it all: phrasing, tone, timing, and imagination, and until the emergence of Artie Shaw as a bandleader in 1936, he was unrivaled.

From 1925 to 1929, he spent several long periods in the band of the former New Orleans Rhythm Kings drummer Ben Pollack, first in Los Angeles, then back in Chicago, and eventually in New York. Pollack's band was an important one in white jazz of the late twenties and, in many respects, was as significant as Jean Goldkette's band had been. For a start, just as Goldkette had provided a significant platform for Bill Challis's arrangements, Pollack employed three figures who were to make their own significant contributions to the art of jazz arrangement: Fud Livingston, Glenn Miller, and Gil Rodin. Furthermore, just as Goldkette had employed such luminaries as Tommy Dorsey, Bix Beiderbecke, and Frank Trumbauer, Pollack was an equally astute talent-spotter, and, as well as Goodman, his list of star sidemen included, at various times, trumpeters Harry James, Yank Lawson, and Charlie Teagarden, trombonist Jack Teagarden (as well as Glenn Miller), and reed players Irving Fazola, Matty Matlock, and Eddie Miller. Goodman recorded his first solos with Pollack, but by the time he left this group, which by then had a high-profile and well-paid residency at New York's Park Central Hotel, his own prolific freelance career was under way. Both in his early work around Chicago with the likes of Murph Podolsky, and with Pollack, Goodman played plenty of music that was not jazz. The bands in which he worked, just like those of Whiteman and Henderson, provided programs that included waltzes, ballads, and "sweet" numbers, and Goodman would undoubtedly have regarded this repertoire as a natural, indeed essential, ingredient of well-paid dance-band work. Indeed, he took some convincing that it was possible to play impromptu jazz of the kind at which he excelled in the informality of after-hours jam sessions, within the context of a commercially viable band, although Pollack's group played and recorded sufficient jazz numbers to show that it could perform them with considerable flair. As his mentor John Hammond said: "[Goodman] had the idea that real improvised jazz was uncommercial and that you had to have a compromise to sell any records."[171]

Ironically, Pollack made this kind of compromise more frequently in the recordings he made under his own name than in the various sessions he (and the ubiquitous Irving Mills) organized for his musicians under various pseudonyms. His January 22, 1929 session, for example, by "Ben's Bad Boys," features a conventional Dixieland line-up, and it renders the old Paul Whiteman standard *Wang Wang Blues* in an unaffected, sincere manner, with a long, soulful clarinet solo from Goodman, accompanied by some deft single-string guitar figures from Dick Morgan. A solo apiece for Goodman, McPartland, and Jack Teagarden, however, provide what jazz interest there is on a comparable offering from Pollack's complete Park Central Orchestra, *Buy, Buy for Baby*, made just over three months earlier, and which is dominated by a saccharine string section and a simpering vocal from Belle Mann. The consequence of this recording policy was that Pollack led a band full of first-rate jazz soloists, but he held their jazz talents in check on many of his recordings. Rather as in Paul Whiteman's contemporaneous band, members of his line-up contributed the odd hot chorus on discs of otherwise unexceptional charts, rather than recording the complete jazz arrangements by Miller, Rodin, and Livingston that the band played on some of its live engagements, and which made it, in the eyes of its members, the natural successor to the, by then, defunct Jean Goldkette band.[172]

However, the reason Pollack's orchestra, like Goldkette's band before it, followed this policy was down to an industry-wide perception of the market in the late 1920s and early 1930s: "According to record company wisdom, black record buyers required hot, sensually uninhibited music," wrote Richard B. Sudhalter,

> [these were] jazz and blues performances, often containing sexually explicit or at least highly suggestive material. White customers, by contrast, were thought to prefer their records respectable, more sedate. The racist implications of these policies aside, they had immediate and lasting effect: where Henderson, Russell or any of the hot black bands were expected to roll out their hottest numbers for records, their white counterparts were under orders to keep things strictly vanilla.[173]

This view is borne out in Rex Stewart's observation that Fletcher Henderson was seldom allowed to record his "prettier" numbers from the Roseland, and it is also in line with Bill Challis's ire at the Goldkette band being given the "stinkingest" numbers to record, instead of his out-and-out jazz charts that were so popular on live dates.

As the record industry slowly began to rebuild itself from 1934, and despite the fact that, initially, he conformed to the conventional views of what the market "wanted," it was principally Benny Goodman who came to challenge this orthodoxy by producing fiery, jazzy discs played by a white band for a predominantly white public. In a small number of late 1920s record dates under his own name, mainly organized by the music publisher Walter Melrose, Goodman had cut some out-and-out jazz sides, including versions of Jelly Roll Morton's *Wolverine Blues* and *Jungle Blues*. He was also a participant in a raucous Dixieland parody, *Shirt Tail Stomp*, which ended up selling quite well. At that time, as a freelance, with a regular job in Pollack's band, Goodman had no qualms about playing some relatively uninhibited jazz on disc, but when it came to the point when he was ready to start out as a leader himself, in 1933–4, his experience told him that compromise was needed. Ultimately, he ended up dropping this intention, and began recording pieces that were predominantly jazz, but it is unlikely he would have done so without the urging of his friend and, later, brother-in-law John Hammond.

I have already mentioned Hammond's name several times, so who was he, and how did he fit in to the development of jazz?

Eighteen months younger than Goodman, Hammond's background could hardly be a greater contrast to that of the clarinetist. Whereas Goodman grew up among the poorest section of Chicago's Jewish immigrant community, Hammond was born into a wealthy New York family and attended Yale, although he dropped out before graduating. He had discovered jazz as a thirteen-year-old boy when he was on a visit to London and heard a group of white Americans, the Georgians, which included clarinetist Jimmy Dorsey, playing for a tea dance at the famous Lyon's Corner House near Piccadilly Circus. On his return, in common with several of the well-heeled section of society from which he came, he discovered the attractions of the African-American show-business world of Harlem black-and-tans, and he became a knowledgeable (if opinionated) jazz enthusiast, writing articles on the subject from 1931 for the British magazines *Gramophone* and *Melody Maker*, and later for several American magazines. He also had a strong liberal conscience (no doubt inherited from his mother, a member of the Vanderbilt family, who espoused many good causes), and he held strong and unflinching views about breaking down racial barriers in the record industry. A private income allowed Hammond to follow his preferred choice of occupation, and in 1933 he persuaded the English Columbia company that he should start to produce jazz records for them. Goodman was one of the four musicians he nominated as his potential bandleaders, along with Fletcher Henderson, Benny Carter, and Joe Venuti.

As a consequence, within the course of five studio dates in the last few weeks of 1933, Goodman led a nine-piece band through ten simple arrangements, many of which had the after-hours jam session feeling Hammond loved, including some first-rate trombone solos by Jack Teagarden and the first recorded vocals by Billie Holiday – another of Hammond's enthusiasms, whose work is discussed in detail in Chapter 10. As well as Holiday, Hammond, who was largely responsible for the selection of musicians, also hired an African-American trumpeter, Shirley Clay, for some of the sessions, underlining his commitment to racial integration at the very outset of his working relationship with Goodman. (According to

Hammond himself, in a 1969 lecture given at a symposium in Indiana, at first Goodman was very worried that leading an integrated band on discs would cause him problems in maintaining his freelance career in white studio bands, but Hammond worked on him to overcome this objection, and there were ultimately no such limitations on Goodman's radio and recording schedule.)

The discs are generally attractive, with some of the hallmarks of Goodman's future, popular sound, including his sprightly solo over the brass on *Dr. Heckle and Mr. Jibe*, and his soulful blues playing on *Texas Tea Party*. Another piece, *Tappin' the Barrel*, involves the kind of four-bar exchanges between the leader's clarinet and the brass and reed sections that would be a frequent feature of Goodman's later records with his big band, but there is speculation as to who actually made this neat and well-crafted arrangement: possibly Deane Kincaide, possibly Lyle "Spud" Murphy – both of whom would later become regular contributors to the Goodman book.[174] The two sides recorded at the very first session in October – *Ain'tcha Glad* and *I Gotta Right to Sing the Blues*, both of which featured Jack Teagarden – were issued not only in Britain, but also as the two sides of a single by the American Columbia company (which at that stage had an arm's-length relationship with its British namesake), and they made something of an impression on the market. The disc's 5000-copy sale was more than respectable in the depressed conditions of the time, and it got well reviewed. It opened doors for Hammond to become a producer on a wider scale, making records for American companies as well as for his British clients, and it put Benny Goodman's name in front of the jazz public, not least when *Metronome* voted it record of the month in November 1933.

During the first six months of 1934, Goodman fronted another couple of record sessions, and freelanced around New York, although his sole dependable gig was a weekly radio show in which he played fourth saxophone in a large orchestra. At this point, he finally decided to organize his own band, so he assembled charts, rehearsed, and, in June, auditioned with the intention of landing the job of playing in a new midtown venture, Billy Rose's Music Hall. He was successful, and the engagement lasted three months, during which Goodman got a taste of leadership, indeed demonstrating that he had considerable skill in musical direction (although his ability to deal straightforwardly with his musicians was always somewhat suspect, owing to his remote personality and total absorption in matters musical). Most importantly, he was able to make records with his full big band that benefited from the cohesion of a regular working unit, and pieces like Will Hudson's *Nitwit Serenade* give an impression of how he sought to define the group's style. Significantly for the band's future sound, this chart leans heavily on Fletcher Henderson's recording of *Sugar Foot Stomp*, with parts of the trumpet and trombone solos directly transcribed from it.

In October, the Mob decided to change the entertainment policy at the Music Hall, and the band was fired from its regular job. That might have been the end of the story but, within weeks, Goodman narrowly won the audition to appear on a new nationwide network radio show called *Let's Dance*. This began in December, and gave the band six months of regular work, plus the all-important opportunity to commission a substantial number of new arrangements.

In this show, several ingredients came together that explain Goodman's ultimate success in reaching out to the new youth audience.

First, having been won round completely to Hammond's point of view, he knew exactly how he wanted his band to sound. He said:

> I was interested only in jazz. I wanted to create a tight, small-band quality, and I wanted every one of my boys to be a soloist. The band had to have a driving beat, a rhythmic brass section, and a sax section that would be smooth but with lots of punch.[175]

Second, to kickstart the library of arrangements, John Hammond approached Fletcher Henderson on Goodman's behalf and offered him $37.50 per chart to write for the band. Henderson's own orchestra had just broken up temporarily and so he accepted the deal, starting off by handing Goodman several of his existing charts (including a revised *King Porter Stomp*). Before long, Goodman was relying on Henderson (who was often helped out by his brother Horace) to provide three arrangements or so a week, and these formed a substantial proportion of the band book, together with pieces from Murphy, Kincaide, and Fud Livingston, as well as African-American writers such as Benny Carter and Edgar Sampson. The template for the band's sound, however, was Henderson's, in the simplified version of the ideas he had worked out with Don Redman the previous decade. In addition to the numerous examples of his charts that Goodman recorded in the 1930s, a 1999 disc by clarinetist Bob Wilber offers further proof of the way Henderson shaped the band's identity, as it includes several more of the pieces he wrote for Goodman, but which were never recorded at the time.[176]

Third, Goodman rehearsed the band with unusual precision. His methods were intended to get the charts so completely into his musicians' heads that they were not bound to the printed page and could think more about *how* they played, not *what* they played. He called it "digging out" the music, and the results are evident in some of the band's recordings. A disc like *Blue Skies*, made just after *Let's Dance* ended its run, is played with meticulous section work, subtle dynamics, and a relaxed swing behind Bunny Berigan's trumpet, with Gene Krupa's tom-toms underlining passages of ensemble, and Goodman floating over four-bar sections of the final chorus. Horace Henderson's up-tempo treatment of *Dear Old Southland*, from the same date, driven along by Krupa's drumming, shows how effective the band was at speed, with natty brass phrases behind the tenor solo, subtle sax-section long notes behind the piano solo, and exceptionally well-crafted section playing. Goodman's group lacked the mechanistic quality of the Casa Loma Orchestra of the same period, and his band showed more verve than any other large white orchestra of the period. Indeed, it attacked the charts more precisely than Henderson's own band had done, although at this stage his soloists – with the exception of Berigan and Goodman himself – were still not anywhere near as imaginative or flamboyant, and, overall, there was less freedom, less ebb and flow, than in Henderson's own interpretations.

Finally, Goodman had won his audition for Rose's Music Hall with the help of the singer Helen Ward, and she now joined the band. She was a crucial ingredient of the radio show, not just because she soon became popular with listeners, but because her natural, unaffected personality helped create the club-like atmosphere that the producer Josef Bonime was after. From time to time she even took a turn on the dance-floor with members of the studio audience, between her featured numbers. At this stage, Goodman's band was one of the few who had a full-time girl singer, and he realized that she would appeal to his growing audience of college students because, as one critic pointed out: "she cleverly combined a 'girl-next-door' personality with an astute grasp of the musical demand of Goodman's arrangements."[177]

Even though Goodman was well aware of Ward's potential appeal, the overall effect of *Let's Dance* was not immediately obvious to him. Because the band was working regularly in New York, he had little perception of how its music was received by listeners to the 50 or so regional stations across the United States to whom the music was networked. But, just as Cab Calloway's hi-de-ho-ing was well-known to audiences across the nation from his Cotton Club relays, Goodman's swing repertoire gradually became familiar, predominantly to young listeners, in many different locations. Lewis A. Erenberg has analyzed the reception of swing as it was reflected in several college and campus publications, and concludes that, as the movement gradually spread, and became identified with youth culture, "the eastern seaboard, the West Coast, and big Midwestern cities, with numerous colleges, and many blacks, Jews and Italians, continued to lead the way."[178] Radio became an essential backdrop to the activities of youth – dating, dancing, studying, and even going to sleep at night. Goodman's appearance on *Let's Dance* was broadcast at 12.30 to 1 a.m. in the East, but, because of the time difference, in California it was on between 9.30 and 10 p.m., where it captured an even wider share of the youth audience as they socialized, did their homework, or listened to bedside radio sets. What appealed to them was something unique that Goodman's well-drilled, youthful band and his own brilliance as a clarinetist communicated, admirably summed up by his biographer James Lincoln Collier:

> The lilting optimism, the clever arrangements, young soloists, Goodman's own playing . . . made the band sound fresh and new. The music it made was different from the hot stuff of the 1920s – by no means entirely different, but different enough to sound to audiences modern and up-to-date. This was the new music, and young people wanted to follow it where it was going.[179]

So what did this music have about it that made it popular for this young audience? What did it mean to them? Perhaps the most eloquent expression of this comes from John Hammond, who believed:

> It expresses America so clearly that its readiest recognition here has come from the masses, particularly youth. While the intelligentsia has been busy trying to water our scrawny cultural tree with European art and literary movements, this thing has come to maturity unnoticed. . . . In a tongue-tied nation, just growing into long pants and consuming its last frontier, art had to be a ready business, too, without highfalutin' airs. And it is an art that no one has had to graft onto the tree; nobody would be more incredulous upon hearing that this is art than the throngs of jitterbugs and the hot musicians themselves.[180]

The hot jazz played for the white consumer by Goodman's band was on the point of breaking through to the American public *en masse* in a way that even the "Jazz Age" syncopations of the 1920s had not. As Hammond said, the "hot" tones, insistent rhythm, and deep underlying feeling of this kind of jazz symbolized America itself. In the 1920s, Irving Mills had claimed Duke Ellington's music as art; but what Hammond recognized was something different – a movement in which the art was at one with popular culture on a far wider scale. Nevertheless, to some extent this movement shared with 1920s jazz the *frisson* of daring; the flavor of eroticism that had made it attractive to a wide audience from the time Stein's "jass" band – with all the risqué overtones of its name – hit Chicago. As Krin Gabbard observes:

> many white Americans embraced swing because it contained elements associated with African-American spontaneity, trans-gressiveness, and most importantly, sexuality. These elements were clearly implied even when the music was played by an entirely white band.[181]

However, not all the nation was quite prepared for an uncompromising diet of swing. Lewis A. Erenberg's analysis of where the music first caught on explains what happened when *Let's Dance* came to an end, and the Goodman band set off from New York on a sinuous tour that would take it to the West Coast. According to him, in the mid-1930s, away from the East and West Coasts, it was still largely the case that the "culturally conservative Midwest preferred ballads and novelties,"[182] and this was the country the band had to cross on its way to the West. The band's reception at a dime-a-dance hall in Denver, where, in the kind of compromise Goodman was all too familiar with from his time with Pollack, sections of the band ended up playing waltz selections to appease the management and patrons alike, was so disheart-ening that Goodman almost called it a day, and only his agent Willard Alexander and his more persuasive sidemen were able to convince him to continue.

West of the Rockies, things picked up dramatically, as the Californian youth audience created by the broadcasts began to turn out in force. Traditionally, the band's opening on August 21, 1935 at its ultimate destination, the Palomar Ballroom in Los Angeles, is reckoned to have been where the band was so rapturously acclaimed, as it unleashed its Henderson arrangements, that the "swing era" was truly born. In fact, the first realization that something was afoot came some days earlier in northern California, at a ballroom in Oakland, when huge advertisements for a forthcoming appearance by Guy Lombardo initially convinced Goodman that he had turned up on the wrong night. He recalled:

> It was impossible to believe that so many people had come to hear us. I called for *King Porter Stomp*, one of Fletcher's real killers. That number started off with Bunny Berigan playing a trumpet solo, the saxophones and rhythm behind him. Before he'd played four bars, there was such a yelling and stomping and carrying on in that hall that I thought a riot had broken out. When I went into my solo, the noise was even louder. Finally the truth got through to me: *We* were causing the riot.[183]

This was a foreshadowing of the reception at the Palomar, where the audience stood stony-faced through a set or two of the band's slushiest commercial arrangements, and then went wild for the jazz charts, continuing to do so during a lengthy run, which was eventually extended to a couple of months.

The Palomar engagement was obviously a breakthrough for Goodman, and the brilliance and confidence with which the band recorded during this visit to the West suggest that it was truly inspired by its sudden surge of popularity. Jimmy Mundy's arrangement of *Madhouse*, from a September 27, 1935 session in Hollywood, has a swagger and lift about it that the band had barely achieved up until this point. This was due to more than the effect of *Let's Dance*. The local disc jockey Al Jarvis, who had a similar radio show to that of Martin Block in New York, had been playing many of Goodman's records on air, and their popularity was reflected in strong regional sales. More than that, there was a healthy and well-developed audience for jazz in Los Angeles, which had built up ever since Bill Johnson's arrival with his New Orleans band early in the century. Bands like those of Kid Ory and Paul Howard had kept jazz alive through the 1920s, and Frank Sebastian's New Cotton Club in Culver City had opened in 1927 and defied the Depression to survive right through the 1930s. There Les Hite led a first-rate African-American band, playing nightly to up to 1200 patrons, many of whom were leading lights of the emergent movie industry. Guest stars at the club included many of the country's leading musicians including Louis Armstrong.

In the city's Central Avenue district, African-American entertainment was promoted to wealthy white customers in a manner similar to 1920s Harlem, with the important distinction that audiences at Central Avenue's flagship club, the Alabam, and many others were racially integrated from the outset. Curtis Mosby led the band there, and other acts to be featured included Edythe Turnham, Lorenzo Flennoy, and Leon Herriford.

All this had done much to build up a knowledgeable and enthusiastic public for jazz in Los Angeles. What Goodman's band and Helen Ward's vocals managed to do was to meet the demands of this market and those of the emergent youth culture more completely than any of their competitors. Here in the West, and on their return to New York via Chicago, they capitalized on this success. Later, at New York's Paramount Theater, where the management took the decision to present individual bands rather than full variety shows, Goodman appeared in the spring of 1937 to several packed houses a day of young listeners, many of whom had cut school to hear him, and he demonstrated the depth of his popularity with this age group by a first week gross of $58,000. Many audiences at this and other theaters around the country took to dancing in the aisles, often doing the gyratory lindy-hop or "jitterbug" – energetic dances which had begun in the Harlem dance halls of the 1920s. Although Goodman himself expressed disapproval of such antics getting in the way of his musical program, jitterbugging youngsters jumping from their seats to dance in the nation's theaters remains the enduring image of the youth culture spawned by his band's popularity. John Hammond also frowned on the effect of the jitterbug, aware of the danger that the mass popularity of the music would – as indeed became the case – dilute the very ingredients that had made it successful in the first place:

> The jitterbug millions, lurching along on their new Children's Crusade, have scared a lot of people away from hot jazz. Jitterbug taste is not the arbiter of hot music. Equally guilty of planting misconceptions about hot jazz are the cultists who have well nigh separated jazz from the recognition it should have as music.[184]

Over the next three years, as he gained the nickname "King of Swing," Goodman's band was extremely successful. It appeared in band battles opposite Chick Webb at the Savoy. It made a series of popular records, including *Don't Be That Way*; *Sing, Sing, Sing, Roll 'Em*; *Life Goes to a Party*; and *And the Angels Sing*. It toured widely, broadcast on a long-running radio show sponsored by Camel cigarettes, and appeared in movies. Its star musicians included trumpeters Harry James and Ziggy Elman, saxophonist Vido Musso, and pianist Jess Stacy; and when Helen Ward left, after recording such hits as the best-selling *These Foolish Things*, her successors included Martha Tilton and, later, Helen Forrest and Peggy Lee. At the heart of the rhythm section was the flamboyant style of Gene Krupa. Although Krupa lacked the finesse of many African-American swing drummers, his extrovert solos and gutsy ensemble playing appealed to Goodman, who similarly overlooked Musso's shortcomings as a sight-reader, because of his muscular solo style which was ideal for the band's young audience. According to Musso's fellow tenorist, Arthur Rollini, other members of the sax section – Bud Freeman and Dick Clark – were dismissed because their premature baldness went against Goodman's desire to market a young-looking band.[185]

Goodman himself combined his extraordinary musical talents, which remained the envy of a generation of musicians, with a personality that was capable of making such hiring-and-firing decisions for petty as well as businesslike reasons. His hostile stare – the "ray" – was a sign of displeasure that more than once led to dismissal for quite minor misdemeanors, and he was frequently unthinking and selfish towards his band members. Nevertheless, the success of his musical policy was unarguable. At the height of the youth cult, the band provoked scenes that were barely seen again until the onset of Beatlemania in the 1960s. Pianist Teddy Wilson observed:

> I remember once in Philadelphia, after a performance by the Goodman band, there were the usual wild demonstrations with people jumping up and down and tearing up seats, eating the lunches they had brought with them. And people in line outside because they couldn't get in. The manager was tearing his hair and the kids in the audience were giving a bigger performance than the band on the stage![186]

In more genteel surroundings than this teenage mayhem, Goodman's orchestra also formed the centerpiece of a landmark concert at Carnegie Hall on January 16, 1938, which integrated African-American and white musicians on the same stage, including members of the Basie and Ellington bands.

Goodman's work in integrated ensembles had begun in earnest in the summer of 1935, before the epic trip west to the Palomar, when John Hammond heard him jamming with pianist Teddy Wilson at a private party given by the singer Mildred Bailey and her husband, xylophonist and vibes player Red Norvo, and urged Victor to record something similar, adding Gene Krupa to make up a trio. (Wilson had actually just been signed to Brunswick by Hammond, who produced the pianist's long-running series of discs with Billie Holiday, and the reason Goodman appeared on the first of these was on account of a "swap" arranged between the record companies, to allow "their" stars to appear on one another's labels without financial penalty. His later appearances on Wilson's discs took place after the pianist had joined the Goodman organization.) The trio line-up was similar to Jelly Roll Morton's of the 1920s, but the music, even a version of *Someday Sweetheart* which Morton claimed to have written before the Spikes brothers copyrighted it, was decidedly more up to date. Wilson's piano on *After You've Gone*, with Goodman's clarinet darting around the melody, is far more fluent than even Earl Hines's 1920s accompaniments to Armstrong, and he brings a similar sense of movement to the ballad *Body and Soul*, which Goodman plays mainly in his middle register with a beautiful, woody tone. The masterpiece of this first trio session is a version of Oscar Hammerstein II and Jerome Kern's song *Who?*, in which the melody is barely stated directly, but it becomes the basis for dazzling solos by Wilson, Goodman, and Krupa (on brushes), all of which convey a scintillating sense of jam-session excitement, and the feeling that even in the formal setting of a recording studio the players have recaptured the joy of playing for one another that Hammond heard at the Norvos' party.

It was one thing playing in an integrated band on record: there had been plenty of examples of this in the 1920s, including a famous 1929 Fats Waller session with Eddie Condon that was hurriedly arranged after several nights on the tiles, and Louis Armstrong's equally celebrated *Knockin' a Jug* get-together with Jack Teagarden, Eddie Lang, and Joe Sullivan the same year. There was also a long tradition of white musicians sitting in informally with African-American bands and vice versa; not only on disc, but after hours or in a relaxed club setting. But to present a formal concert was quite another thing, and Goodman flouted convention when, with the encouragement of Hammond, the writer Helen Oakley, and jazz buff "Squirrel" Ashcraft, Wilson appeared in public with the trio in Chicago the following Easter. As it turned out the expected conservative backlash did not materialize, and Wilson joined the entourage, making appearances with the trio (but not the big band) at every engagement.

Later in the summer of 1936, Goodman added Lionel Hampton, whom he had heard playing in Los Angeles, to the trio, making it a quartet, and bringing an additional level of improvisatory challenge into the group. When

I attended one of the last reunions of Wilson, Hampton, and Goodman at Carnegie Hall in 1981, the vibraphonist was still able to provoke both the others into better and better playing in reaction to his own combative solos. Hampton had grown up in 1920s Chicago, and had become something of a local legend on the West Coast, mastering vibes and drums (he was billed as "the world's fastest drummer") and also developing a quaint, but effective, two-fingered piano style emulating his vibraphone mallets. One side effect of his association with Goodman was that he led a long series of freelance studio dates, on which he demonstrated time and time again his ability to produce remarkable impromptu jam sessions on record with various combinations of musicians, all of whom were simultaneously united and challenged by his formidable improvisatory ability. These qualities positively leap out of the grooves of many of his discs with the Goodman quartet, such as his dazzling introduction, subsequent solo, and breaks on *Dinah*, from his second session with the group in August 1936.

Goodman's quartet set a trend for other swing bands to feature small groups drawn from their full line-ups. White leaders such as Tommy Dorsey, Artie Shaw, and Bob Crosby all featured them (the Clambake Seven, Gramercy Five, and Bobcats, respectively), and so did African-Americans like Cab Calloway, whose Cab Jivers became a popular addition to his stage shows. In every case, such groups added pep, dynamism, and the sheer excitement of small-group jazz to their parent orchestra, and conveyed this to the youthful fans of the music who bought their discs. Goodman's small-group records sold extremely well, and the decision to contrast his trio or quartet with the big band was commercially astute. Moreover, it is important not to underestimate their social importance, as Teddy Wilson wrote:

> Credit must go to Goodman for having introduced for the first time public performances by an interracial small jazz group. . . . The Goodman innovation was significant. It should be remembered that, in those days, Negro people were excluded from practically every area of white activity in the higher income levels, except in show business.[187]

There were to be privations on the road; incidents of prejudice that Goodman was sometimes able to withstand and of which he was occasionally unaware, and, for the most part, Hampton and Wilson were compelled to seek separate accommodation from their fellows, being unable to stay in white hotels. Wilson took this quite stoically, remembering that his grandparents had been slaves, and that things had come a long way since then, but he was grateful to Goodman for stipulating that, wherever the band appeared, the small group, complete with its African-American musicians, would appear as well. He was always aware that Goodman had taken a gamble with his career in creating an integrated small group against the advice of almost everyone but Hammond, and Wilson remained eternally grateful for it.

Subsequently, other leaders went further, Artie Shaw touring with Billie Holiday and then adding trumpeters Hot Lips Page and Roy Eldridge to the line-up of his full band. Gene Krupa also hired Eldridge after leaving Goodman to start his own band, but in both cases the trumpeter found the experience of constant minor racial harassment, as a result of being a black sideman with a white orchestra, an unhappy one, despite creating such memorable recordings as Krupa's *Let Me off Uptown* **[CD track 15]** with singer Anita O'Day. In retrospect, it was a shrewd move of Goodman's to feature Wilson and Hampton only in his small group where they enjoyed a measure of star status and some degree of insulation from the reprehensible prejudices of the period.

Although there are plenty of fine moments on his big-band recordings, overall Goodman's small-group discs contain a far greater proportion of the spontaneous, unfettered jazz improvisation at which he excelled. They mirrored much of what was going on in the smaller clubs that opened up in the wake of Prohibition, particularly those in Harlem and on New York's 52nd Street. To some extent, John Hammond was responsible for keeping Goodman's ears open to what was going on. Certainly he introduced Goodman to many of Count Basie's musicians after their arrival in New York, and featured several of them with him on the Teddy Wilson small-group recordings he produced for Brunswick. From 1938, Goodman's own groups also occasionally included Fletcher Henderson's former bassist, John Kirby, at a time when Kirby's own small band with Charlie Shavers, Buster Bailey, and Russell Procope was becoming one of the most influential of all swing sextets. Kirby's band was to have a particular bearing on the music of the following decade, by providing a model for some of the first groups to play the modern jazz style of bebop.

In due course, Goodman's own 1939 sextet was to have an equally important influence, because of the presence of another musician brought into his orbit by Hammond, the guitarist Charlie Christian.

Hammond had been tipped off about this young guitarist from

Oklahoma City by Mary Lou Williams, and he traveled to hear him. What he found was a revelation: a guitarist using amplification to give him the ability to run long lines, like a saxophone or brass player, at a volume which allowed him to play alongside such instruments, and combined with harmonic sophistication, imaginative ideas, and a virtuoso technique. The best American acoustic guitarists of the 1930s, such as George Van Eps (formerly with Goodman's orchestra), Carl Kress, or Fats Waller's teenage protégé Al Casey, tended to play chordal solos that could be heard in an ensemble, and only to use single-string melodic lines when playing unaccompanied, or close to the microphone in the recording studio. (Casey's *Buck Jumpin'*, with Waller, is a good example of this; a piece that would have been impossible to play live in most venues because of the disparity in volume between his solo guitar and the accompanying band.)

A few brave pioneers had tried amplifying their guitars – trombonist Eddie Durham doubled on the instrument with Bennie Moten and Count Basie, Floyd Smith used a form of Hawaiian guitar with Andy Kirk's band – but no individual player in jazz before Christian had worked out a comprehensive technique on the electric instrument. (There is, however, a view that musicians in the Western swing tradition – a hybrid of jazz and country music local to Christian's home in the Southwest – were responsible for a large component of his style.)

Hammond purloined Goodman's budget for paying expenses to guests on his radio show and flew Christian to Los Angeles where the band was recording. The story goes that Goodman virtually ignored the young guitarist when he arrived, but was flabbergasted at his playing when Hammond smuggled him onto the bandstand to play with the quintet that same evening at the Victor Hugo Hotel in Beverley Hills. Christian subsequently became a member of the Goodman small group (occasionally also recording with the full orchestra) for the remainder of his short life, snuffed out in 1942 by tuberculosis when he was 25.[188] During Christian's time in what was now a sextet, Goodman brought in other African-American stars to join the band in the studio, including Fletcher Henderson, Count Basie, trumpeter Cootie Williams (who also played as a featured soloist with the big band), pianist Kenny Kersey, and drummers Jo Jones and J. C. Heard. On some of their discs it is obvious that Goodman found Christian's playing as potent a stimulus to his own improvisation as Lionel Hampton's, but just as impressive is Christian's ability to create lengthy solos over simple, relaxed backing, as he does on his very first recording with the group, *Flying Home* **[CD track 11]**. This disc also demonstrates how Christian's solo voice could blend with the clarinet and vibes to play the opening and closing thematic riffs of the arrangement, as well as providing the first extended solo, in which he throws out a string of melodic ideas, many of which are caught and re-used in Hampton's vibraphone solo which follows. On this early recording from his short career, Christian starts almost every phrase of his solo on the second beat of a measure and chops up the majority of his lines into two-measure phrases, as if in response to an "on-beat" riff from the clarinet. But his ideas flow from one phrase to the next, and it would not be long before he was constructing solos that ran over bar-lines and created long, seamless linear phrases, with no necessity (as a wind instrument would have) to stop for breath. When in New York, he became a frequent sitter-in at after-hours clubs, notably Minton's in Harlem, where some unofficial recordings were made that preserve some of these long, flowing solos. He played them in company with several of the bebop musicians discussed in Chapter 7, but he neither lived long enough nor developed quite far enough to become a bebopper himself. Instead, he demonstrated new ways of phrasing and building a solo that would be enthusiastically developed by other musicians of his generation whose lives were not cut so tragically short.

As the 1940s began, Benny Goodman did not recapture the level of popular adulation and acclaim he enjoyed throughout the late 1930s. But neither did he stand still musically. He commissioned challenging new arrangements from such writers as Eddie Sauter whose *Clarinet à la King* is a kind of mini-concerto for Goodman that borrows just as heavily from contemporary classical ideas as it does from jazz. Another Sauter composition, *Superman*, arranged to feature Cootie Williams, uses sections of varying length, and moves motifs around ahead of the meter, creating an effect very unlike the usual metrical precision of a well-oiled swing band. Both these pieces are progenitors of the kind of "Third Stream" classical cross-over music that composers like Gunther Schuller and William Russo would write in the 1950s and 1960s. Another innovative writer for the 1940s band was pianist Mel Powell, who eventually left jazz to become a full-time composer and teacher of composition.

In the late 1940s, Goodman even flirted with the emerging genre of bebop, in a sextet with Swedish clarinetist Stan Hasselgard and saxophonist Wardell Gray, and also, briefly, with a modern-jazz big band, for whom one of the main arrangers was Chico O'Farrill, a pioneer of Afro-Cuban jazz, and later a collaborator with Dizzy Gillespie. But these were short-lived ventures for Goodman. From the end of the 1940s onwards he reverted to a style close to his popular playing of the 1930s, and led a series of bands that revisited that repertoire, in parallel with a burgeoning career as a classical recitalist.

Goodman's was by no means the only large white swing orchestra of the 1930s, but his decision to feature an undiluted jazz style, rather than make the kind of compromise familiar from Ben Pollack's band, gave him a march on his competitors. Principal among these were the Dorsey brothers, Jimmy and Tommy, who had both established their reputations in the 1920s, as Goodman himself had done. Indeed, Jimmy was widely regarded as the most technically proficient clarinetist in jazz prior to Goodman, and on alto saxophone he remained unsurpassed for speed, accuracy, and versatility well into the 1930s, as he demonstrated on such features as his 1932 disc *Oodles of Noodles*, cut with a studio band co-led with his brother in 1932. His brilliant playing of the theme is so deft and evenly timed that at times he sounds like a more-than-usually speedy piano-accordionist flying over the keyboard.

Both brothers grew up in Shenandoah, Pennsylvania, where their father, Thomas F. Dorsey, was the director of the local Elmore Band and taught music for a living. Consequently, the Dorsey boys began lessons on the traditional brass band "starter" instrument, the cornet. Jimmy (born in 1904) was in the Elmore band from the age of seven, and Tommy (born in 1905) joined him just a year or two later. Over time, both boys became not just capable of playing a number of instruments, but dazzlingly proficient on them. Tommy remained a fine cornetist well after he became one of the most gifted trombonists in jazz, while Jimmy mastered all the reeds, and remained equally capable of producing fine performances on cornet as well. (A good example, from quite late in his career, is the February 1933 *Hey! Young Fella* by the Joe Venuti–Eddie Lang Blue Five, on which he plays a fluid muted swing solo sandwiched between equally proficient examples of his clarinet, with the bonus of a florid coda on alto sax.) Symphony orchestras held no dread for him, and he was always puzzled when his jazz-playing colleagues, like the young reed player Bud Freeman, found it hard to adapt. Freeman was so terrified when he first deputized for Jimmy in a symphony orchestra that he spent the evening frozen with fear and collected a $90 fee for not playing a single note on his clarinet.[189]

In Tommy's case the perfectionism drilled into him by his father led to a complex personality. His own shortcomings were taken out on those around him. He could be fiercely loyal to musicians whose ability he respected, but he more often than not lost his temper and fired players irrationally and quickly. At his memorial service, former colleagues were staggered to discover just how many sidemen had passed through the ranks of his bands over the years.

Tommy's instrumental perfectionism was coupled with a burning desire to succeed. "He'd never trained himself to lose," recalled his former trumpeter Max Kaminsky, remembering Tommy's dramatic outbursts of temper when he was beaten in a battle of bands. Kaminsky also believed that, in much the same way, it was the sheer technical difficulty Dorsey set himself in some of his trombone solos that made him a martinet, as he vented his frustration on those around him every time he failed to meet his own almost impossible standards:

> The concentration and control needed to play in that high register was a terrific strain on him, and sometimes Tommy couldn't rise to it and he'd get mad . . . his temperament was so volcanic and his rages so explosive that you could almost smell the sulphur and brimstone.[190]

Kaminsky was writing about the 1930s, but Tommy Dorsey's professional career in music began before either his playing or his temper had reached the exalted heights of that period. Before they were into their twenties, Jimmy and Tommy decided to work together to play jazz, first attempting to lead their own bands, the Novelty Six and the Wild Canaries, before working in the Scranton Sirens, led by Billy Lustig. For the most part they played together right through the 1920s, working their way through several bands and ending up with Paul Whiteman, during the time when he re-stocked his orchestra with improvising jazz players. On the way, they were in a number of significant and influential bands including the California Ramblers and Jean Goldkette's band, as well as jointly becoming two of the most prolific freelance recording artists in jazz history.

Jimmy made numerous records with his Goldkette colleagues, including some with Bix Beiderbecke. Through these and his other discs from the same period, a whole generation of jazz reed players was influenced by Jimmy's technical innovations, such as the rapid alternation of different fingerings for the same note, to give a variety of tone. This became an important element in the jazz technique of players like Lester Young, who always cited Jimmy as an early influence. It is possible Jimmy's career would have taken an even more influential turn in 1925, had he not left Goldkette to join his brother in a reunion of the Scranton Sirens. His replacement in Goldkette's band was Frankie Trumbauer, who went on to form his own effective recording partnership with Beiderbecke, and Dorsey only appeared on a handful of these influential discs. However, I should not give the impression that Jimmy Dorsey's playing was simply a matter of technical proficiency. To a greater extent than the majority of his white contemporaries in the larger bands of the late 1920s, he was capable of injecting considerable feeling and emotion into his playing, as he demonstrated on a long clarinet solo recorded in 1929 called *Praying the Blues*, which begins as a slow, mournful lament with some artfully bent notes, before opening up into an up-tempo romp in which his playing is every bit as robust and powerful as that of his New Orleans contemporaries.

By contrast, although he was capable of rough-edged, hard-swinging playing when necessary, Tommy never regarded himself as primarily a jazz player, and in later years happily stood aside when he and Jack Teagarden both won a trombonists' poll, to let Teagarden play the hot jazz solos. Yet his ability was highly regarded by others, and as well as playing on many of Beiderbecke's discs, he also participated in several interracial recording sessions, including the famous Jack Bland Rhythmakers of 1932, alongside trumpeter Henry "Red" Allen, and the New Orleans rhythm section of Pops Foster and drummer Zutty Singleton. He cut his best trumpet records in the late 1920s, including a splendid solo on *My Melancholy Baby*, which he recorded with his brother in April 1928, and on which he also played trombone.

In the spring of 1934, following several jointly led record dates, Jimmy and Tommy put together a regular big band of their own to work outside the studios as the Dorsey Brothers' Orchestra. It lasted for eighteen months, until a more than usually violent altercation between them over the speed at which they should play various pieces dissolved their partnership. Jimmy became the leader of the band that survived from the rift, leaving Tommy to form his own orchestra which he eventually did by taking over a band that had been led by pianist Joe Haymes.

However, in its short life, the Dorsey Brothers' Orchestra made some interesting attempts to vary the mold of how a swing band should sound, although more often than not this veered towards the kinds of compromise familiar from Ben Pollack. This is hardly surprising, since the brothers' chief arranger was the ex-Pollack trombonist Glenn Miller, who was already trying his hand at achieving a unique and distinctive sound. (Miller continued to experiment with the palette of a big band, particularly after forming his own bands, initially in 1937 and then from 1938 to 1942, when he enlisted in the U.S. Army Air Force and formed his final jazz-inflected dance band, which lasted until his disappearance in a flight over the English Channel in

December 1944. His use of the clarinet as a lead voice in the reed section was a hallmark of his later ensembles, although some of his most successful discs owed a lot to other arrangers, including Joe Garland, whose version of his own composition *In the Mood* had been recorded by Edgar Hayes almost eighteen months before Miller's hit arrangement.) With the Dorsey Brothers' Orchestra, Miller achieved his unorthodox sound by trying a non-standard instrumentation, and instead of the usual line-up of three trumpets, two trombones, and three saxophones, his charts were written for a topsy-turvy line-up of one trumpet, three trombones, and three saxes. Because the majority of the instruments were pitched in a similar range, it lacked the clear distinction among the sections of a more conventional jazz orchestra, but it allowed Miller to write some convincing attempts at "big band Dixieland," of which the February 1935 *Weary Blues* is a good example, despite the occasionally overwhelming sound of the massed trombones. The commercial appeal of this kind of chart was not lost on the band's singer, Bob Crosby (who was continually criticized by Tommy Dorsey during his time in the band for not being as good as his brother Bing). When Bob took over the remnants of Ben Pollack's band in 1935, such arranged Dixieland was already a major element of its style and continued to be so under his leadership.

This was not the only ingredient of the Dorsey Brothers' band. Early on, it made a number of fairly straightforward jazz discs, albeit some of them, such as *Milenburg Joys* and *St. Louis Blues*, with a slightly anachronistic feel for 1934. A surviving airshot of a complete set by the band includes quite a high proportion of instrumentals, but the vast majority of its commercial recordings were undistinguished ballad discs with Bob Crosby or Kay Weber. The band's musical policy was very much influenced by the conventional thinking of the time, that white audiences preferred such anodyne music to the hotter kind of jazz Benny Goodman was now playing, and, hardly surprisingly given the degree to which Goodman proved him to be right, John Hammond delivered this judgment on the group in the issue of *Down Beat* that was published shortly after it broke up:

> It has always been a mystery to me that the brothers Dorsey didn't take advantage of their golden opportunities to start a band which would have both musicianship and simple guts. At last part of the blame for the actual result may possibly lie at the door of their manager Tommy Rockwell, who is a demon for "knowing what the public wants."[191]

The most dominant soloist in the band had been Jimmy, on clarinet and alto sax, and Miller's arrangements less often featured Tommy's own serene, high-note ballad playing. The Dorsey Brothers' Orchestra left a legacy of discs that show the degree to which it was a transitional band, moving from arranged Dixieland towards a white swing-band style that would complement Goodman's work.

It was Tommy Dorsey whose new orchestra more quickly moved in this direction. Jimmy followed a more commercial dance-band path, but from the outset Tommy ensured he had a coterie of hot-jazz players as the core of his band, and featured them in his small group, the Clambake Seven. This was generally more of a Dixieland band than the kind of sophisticated swing small groups led by Goodman, but it included several excellent soloists, including trumpeters Max Kaminsky and Pee Wee Irwin, clarinetist Johnny Mince, tenorist Bud Freeman, and drummer Dave Tough. The big band – which took a while to shed a Dixieland feel in its jazzier numbers – transferred some of the small group's energy into its best performances, such as *Hawaiian War Chant*, from November 1938, which contrasted dramatically with the romantic ballads on which Dorsey built his personal reputation, like his theme-tune *I'm Getting Sentimental Over You*. At its best, more often than not through the writing of arranger Paul Weston, Dorsey's late 1930s band brought both elements together – in his smooth trombone, pleasant vocals, and outstanding jazz solos. This blend is best exemplified by *Marie*, from January 1937, where Dorsey's high-note introduction and Jack Leonard's lazy vocal lead up to an explosive trumpet solo by Bunny Berigan, which in turn ushers in hot solos from Dorsey and Bud Freeman.

To a public largely unaware of his reputation as a martinet, Tommy Dorsey adopted the nickname "The Sentimental Gentleman of Swing." His temper was as legendary as his bursts of quite genuine and unaffected generosity. Max Kaminsky recalled him taking the entire band out for meals at a time when Dorsey had very little money, and away from the bandstand he could be charming and amusing company. On it, he insisted on punctuality from his men, who would be heavily fined or sacked if they transgressed. He was also particular about the band uniforms, in which he invested equal proportions of pride and money. There were blue uniforms for matinees and brown uniforms for the evenings. Pianist Joe Bushkin turned up late and hungover for one matinee still wearing the night before's brown suit. As he slid onto the piano stool Dorsey stopped the band and announced acidly: "You used to play for us . . . ." Later there was a fight between Bushkin and drummer Buddy Rich in the parking lot. Tommy rushed out to try to stop it. For a moment Bushkin thought Dorsey was trying to help him until he heard his shouts of: "Take the jackets off! The jackets! We got another set to play!"[192]

In 1939, Dorsey recruited arranger Sy Oliver from Jimmie Lunceford's orchestra to inject new life and vigor into the band. The idea was not simply to replace one or two charts with new ones, but to re-engineer the entire sound of the band's jazz numbers to something more contemporary. This was an inspired move, although I have already quoted Oliver's observation that he had to write "down" for Dorsey's musicians because he found them less able to cope with his writing than Lunceford's sidemen. However competent they were as readers, Dorsey's instrumentalists had a different grasp of phrasing, and less innate sense of how to extract "swing" from Oliver's writing. Furthermore, as white musicians, they were obviously less attuned to the many levels of meaning that Oliver conveyed to his African-American listeners – that ineffable sense of "cool" to which I referred. Nevertheless, with Oliver's help, Dorsey recruited new sidemen capable of playing the new, technically demanding charts, and very quickly the band's sound changed entirely (and entirely for the better). "When I joined the band, it was of a Dixieland persuasion and literally couldn't play my arrangements," recalled Oliver. "A year later there were only two men that were in it when I joined. We wound up with Buddy Rich . . . and that was a swinging band. One of the best I ever worked with."[193]

Oliver produced a wider stylistic range of pieces than he had for Lunceford, and displayed even more facility as a writer, imbuing Dorsey's band with a new self-confidence that was perfectly in tune with the national mood at the dawn of the 1940s. There were four-square swingers like *Stomp it Off* (1939), which featured Dorsey's lip trills and Johnny Mince's neat clarinet; there were virtuoso high-tempo pieces that mounted a challenge for some of the most rapid tempos recorded up to that time, like Buddy Rich's drum features *Quiet, Please* (1940) and *Swing High* (1941), augmented by Ziggy Elman's powerful trumpet; and, finally, there were the relaxed two-beat, slinky vocals featuring Oliver himself that had made his name with Lunceford, such as *Swingin' on Nothing* (1941). To my mind, Oliver's success in remodeling this band make it one of the hidden secrets of the swing era, not adequately praised in the literature of jazz for its outstanding achievements. Indeed, so encyclopedic a listener as Gunther Schuller has observed that he had "never encountered as dramatic an overnight impact on any orchestra by just one individual as in the case of Sy Oliver with Tommy Dorsey's Orchestra."[194] From very soon after Oliver's arrival in 1939, a large proportion of its work until and after the 1942 recording ban is exceptional, as well as consistent (in a band not noted for this due to the rapid turnover of personnel, on account of its leader's character), and this applies even on those sides where Dorsey's string section (added in 1942) can be heard.

One reason for the strings was that in 1940, within six months or so of Oliver's arrival, Dorsey hired a singer who rapidly shot to stardom. Frank Sinatra made virtually all his best early discs with the band, and he later attributed his relaxed ballad-singing style to emulating the smooth sounds of Tommy's trombone, although the brilliantly written romantic settings for his vocals, by Axel Stordahl, helped greatly. It was these discs that sold in the greatest numbers, though the band played all its jazzier Oliver charts on its many theatrical appearances in front of Sinatra's growing army of fans. As Gunther Schuller has observed, Sinatra's success, and the rise of the dominant vocalist, was ultimately to be one of the major factors responsible for the demise of the swing big bands, but in the early 1940s the combination was a potent one, linking the public taste for hot jazz played by a large band with the best romantic vocalist of the age.

If the Dorsey Brothers' Orchestra was unconventional in its instrumentation, then it is also true that the other major figure of late 1930s swing, Artie Shaw, began his bandleading career with an equally unorthodox line-up on April 7, 1936. The event was a benefit concert at the Imperial Theater in New York, where Shaw's was one of a number of small groups chosen to appear between sets from Bob Crosby's big band, the Casa Loma Orchestra, and Tommy Dorsey's Clambake Seven. It was organized by Joe Helbock, who owned the Onyx Club on 52nd Street; and Shaw – who was then playing first alto with the CBS radio orchestra – suggested an idea prompted by the classical clarinet quintets he had been playing in his time off:

> I thought just for kicks that I'd write a piece for clarinet and string quartet, plus a small rhythm section. Nobody had ever done that sort of jazz chamber-music thing. So I asked some of the guys at CBS and NBC if they'd run it down with me during rehearsal breaks.[195]

It turns out that that other indefatigable experimenter, Glenn Miller, had tried a similar strings-plus-rhythm idea in 1935, but whereas that was a sidestep on the way to the smooth sound of Miller's own eventual orchestra,

Shaw's group had a measure of immediate success as a direct result of its unexpectedly enthusiastic reception at the concert. The agent Tommy Rockwell, who had represented Louis Armstrong as well as the Dorsey Brothers, took on a slightly enlarged version of the band, which contained three brass, two reeds, rhythm, and a string quartet. He managed to get the group booked round the country, though with mixed success. Swing with strings was not to the taste of those young audiences who were, as we have seen, at the very point of turning away from such kinds of musical compromise towards less adulterated large-band jazz.

Shaw nevertheless began to make records with this group, and these discs are worthy of some serious re-examination. The conventional view is that expressed by Gunther Schuller – namely that the strings brought a "soggy, syrupy" quality to the arrangements, and that Shaw himself was little more than a competent Benny Goodman imitator who had not yet developed his own virtuoso style on clarinet.[196] While it is undeniable that some of the arrangements are both "soggy" and "syrupy," it is by no means true of them all, and in some cases the quartet is used very effectively to supply additional harmonies to those carried by the trombone and tenor, while in others they play quite rapid passages, well-suited to the innate mobility of strings.

*It Ain't Right*, for example, from August 1936, uses quiet bridge passages from the strings to create dramatic contrasts with noisier surrounding sections from reeds and brass, and the strings also supply effective backing to Peg La Centra's vocal, as well as subtle and understated harmonies behind a fiery solo from Shaw himself. This solo has a clear, flowing melodic line, and plenty of interesting ideas in the phrasing, but above all it shows off Shaw's distinctively "clean" attack in the upper register, plus some dramatic moments of vocal tone that attest to the time he had spent in the early 1930s listening to African-American players in Harlem, as well as sitting in with Willie "The Lion" Smith. The Lion was complimentary about his blues playing from those early days, and his comments suggest that – contrary to the established view – Shaw had begun to develop an original voice well before he left the world of radio bands and society orchestras to lead his own group.

The strings also set the scene for the surging energy of Shaw's December 1936 solo feature *Streamline*. Made with just his rhythm section and string quartet, this includes some pacey solos from bassist Ben Ginsberg, guitarist Tony Gottuso, and drummer George Wettling, but the star is Shaw. His speed and accuracy on the clarinet rival Jimmy Dorsey's, and he plays an extraordinarily plaintive break, as he re-enters after the drums, which seems to roll personal pain and anguish together with echoes of Klezmer. (Shaw – born Arthur Arshawsky – shared a Jewish heritage with Benny Goodman.)

Nevertheless, despite such artistic triumphs, by early 1937 it was obvious to Shaw – always a stern self-critic and searcher for improvement – that his band with strings was not a commercial success, and he broke it up to form a conventional swing band: Artie Shaw and his New Music. For his previous group, he had written the majority of the string arrangements himself, and he now turned his hand to producing charts for his new line-up which tackled the "great American songbook" – the music of Kern, Porter, Youmans, Berlin, and so on. However, in its earliest recordings his new band also tackled some pretty standard swing-band fare, although these were already marked out by two things: a hard-swinging rhythm section, with drummer Cliff Leeman; and Shaw's, by now, even more exceptional clarinet-playing.[197] On one early disc by this band, *Ubangi*, from April 29, 1937, Shaw produces a dazzling closing cadenza, which includes a *Rhapsody in Blue*-style glissando through his instrument's entire range. His own composition, *Hold Your Hats*, from the same session, follows a block-written opening for brass and reeds, not unlike his string charts, with a clarinet solo that shows Shaw's exceptional skills in the clarinet's very highest register. This is attention-grabbing playing very different from Goodman's use of the lower or *chalumeau* register, and yet Shaw retains his clear, velvety tone, even in this extreme range. He had worked hard to develop tonal consistency throughout his instrument's registers, and he experimented in developing his own fingering system to give him accuracy and power at the top end, playing notes that had barely been required of clarinetists before that time, who had had no need to cut through massed brass and reed sections, particularly when unamplified in vast auditoriums.

There are signs in several of the discs he made later in 1937 of the difference between Shaw's approach and Goodman's. Goodman's band was essentially a "hot" orchestra, whereas Shaw's was more varied. The assured clarinet playing of Shaw's theme statements in *Night and Day* and *I Surrender Dear* show some of the qualities that had made him a highly regarded lead alto player in his radio days – above all his sensitive feeling for a melody. His solos generally have a reflective, lyric quality about them that many of Goodman's do not. This lyricism was the main ingredient of Shaw's first major hit, *Begin the Beguine*, made at his inaugural session for the Victor label's Bluebird subsidiary, in July 1938. Jerry Gray's arrangement features Shaw's warm statement of the melody at the start and towards the finish, and although there are several of them, he makes only short cameo appearances elsewhere. But, overall, the tune is never far away. As a formula, this is an ideal dance arrangement; smooth, romantic, but with just enough jazz feeling in Shaw's periodic solo appearances to lift it well above the mundane. Backed by a boisterous version of *Indian Love Call*, it sold in huge quantities, and marked Shaw's move into the major league of white swing bandleaders. Ironically, the same session saw the only appearance on record of Billie Holiday during her time as the band's vocalist.

Holiday was not the first African-American vocalist to sing with an all-white orchestra, since by 1938 both Ivie Anderson and June Richmond had done so already, but her nine months or so with Shaw's band was certainly much higher-profile. There were warning signs from Holiday's previous eleven months with Count Basie's band that her enormous talent came at a price – Willard Alexander, Basie's manager at the MCA agency, told *Down Beat* that, despite John Hammond's frequent intercessions on her behalf, she had been fired for inconsistency. "Billie sang fine when she felt like it," he said.[198] Part of this inconsistency was, no doubt, due to her dislike of life on the road, but it was probably equally to do with expectations – both from the public and from a band used to Jimmy Rushing's forthright blues shouting – of what she was to sing. She was not an out-and-out blues singer, and her whimsical timing, delicate voice, and subtlety were not attributes likely to prosper over the robust roar of the Basie band. Equally, her methods of altering melodic line, pitch, and rhythm were also not likely to find favor with that element of Shaw's audience that had become accustomed to the pop ballads sung by his vocalists Peg La Centra, Dolores O'Neil, and Anita Bradley, who all adhered more closely to the written melody.

Just how well Billie Holiday *could* sing with Shaw is demonstrated on her sole extant recording with the band, *Any Old Time*, a song he wrote for her during a temporary lay-off on a road tour in upstate New York. The melody is a characteristic Shaw ballad, which has a clear, linear structure, similar to the way he tended to shape a solo, and Holiday rephrases it magnificently, backed by the plush sound of the orchestra. It is altogether a sophisticated package, and as *Metronome* said of her live appearances with the band at the time, "her lilting vocals jibe beautifully with the Shaw style." Holiday's ever-faithful fan, John Hammond, wrote in *Down Beat* that "the combination of Artie and Billie makes me feel that Benny is going to have to watch out for himself." Yet, when it came to long arduous road tours, many of them in the segregated South, once again Holiday was not consistent, for many of the same reasons as with Basie, but exacerbated by the racial problem.

I suspect that many of the African-American public might have shared the view of her period with Shaw expressed by another *Down Beat* critic who felt her best, intrinsically African-American qualities sat unhappily with the "white man's jazz" of Shaw's band, and that she was "as incongruous as a diamond set in a rosette of old canteloup rinds with coffee grounds."[199] On record, her best qualities came out in the company of small groups, less formally arranged than Shaw's big band, and typified by her record dates with Teddy Wilson. The ideal setting for her work was to be provided a little later in her career by Barney Josephson, who presented her at the Cafe Society, with dramatic lighting, intimate accompaniments, and a close contact with her audience.

In the end, despite Shaw's personal affection for Holiday, his determined championing of the liberal cause, and his genuine enthusiasm for her music, he was compelled by his management and record company to add a white singer, Helen Forrest, for some public appearances and broadcasts, and Holiday's role became less and less prominent. An altercation as to whether she could use the main entrance to the Lincoln Hotel for a season at the Blue Room there finally led to her leaving the band, not on the best of terms. Shaw was not to give up on championing the interracial cause, but his first attempt to do so was not the unqualified success that Goodman had managed with his trio and quartet.

By contrast, the commercial and artistic success of Shaw's full band, particularly in its instrumental recordings, was considerable. Shaw's arrangements, and those of his former first violinist Jerry Gray, were more complex and modernistic than the Henderson-influenced charts of Goodman. For example, a piece like Shaw's composition *Nightmare*, at one time the band's theme tune, which was recorded in a definitive version in September 1938 and used a sinister four-note minor vamp running throughout its entire length, creates a far more futuristic landscape than most swing arrangements, not least because of its almost total lack of harmonic movement. Compared to the plentiful Goodman recordings of charts by the Henderson brothers, Murphy, Kincaide, and Sampson, there were relatively few such standard swing charts in the Shaw band's recorded repertoire, although Gray's lively arrangement of Cole Porter's *What Is This Thing Called Love?* had plenty of contemporary trappings added to it, including a short sequence where the leader's clarinet played to the accompaniment of Leeman's tom-toms – a regular Goodman device – but Shaw's conventionally backed opening solo is a masterpiece of melodic paraphrase and invention that is uniquely his.

It would be unfair to give the impression that Shaw's band could not play in the "hot" manner of Goodman, and on its own "flagwavers" it could hold its own against any of the competition of the time – the best example being Teddy McRae's up-tempo composition *Traffic Jam*, which featured the dynamic drumming of Buddy Rich, Leeman's replacement. (Shaw talked Rich into leaving him in 1939, believing that the drummer played too much for himself and not enough for the band. Rich's move to Dorsey's orchestra coincided with Sy Oliver's, and did much to enhance the success of Oliver's writing for Dorsey.) Nevertheless, it is revealing that in a 1939 *Time* magazine survey of campuses, Shaw's more unorthodox arrangements and his lack of straightforward dance standards seem to have counted against him with the youth market on which Goodman had so successfully capitalized. College students preferred the more danceable charts of Dorsey and Goodman, as well as non-jazz society dance bands like those of Kay Kyser and Hal Kemp. "Only the intelligentsia know Shaw well," ran the report.[200]

However, *Begin the Beguine* had ensured Shaw's overall commercial success, and he began to be greeted with the same kind of fervor and frenzy as Goodman – the more so in Shaw's case because his film-star looks made him the object of much personal adulation. He was mobbed in public, fans jumped on stages, and – as with Goodman – they jitterbugged and went crazy in the theaters where the band played. Always a sensitive and intelligent man, Shaw found this period of popular acclaim in 1938–9 a great strain, and in the spring of 1939 he collapsed on stage at the Palomar in Los Angeles with what appeared to be a serious illness. After his recovery, he returned to New York, but on November 18, 1939, he walked out on his band at the Pennsylvania Hotel, saying he was going "on vacation." Tenorist Georgie Auld tried to keep the group together, but without Shaw the flame died and went out.

The signs had been there for some time that all was not well for Shaw in his role as a superstar. In Hollywood, he had worked on a movie whose banality appalled him – he refused to speak fake "hep" talk on the basis that the millions of listeners to his radio shows knew perfectly well that he did not speak in such a manner. On live gigs he resented the repeated intrusions of those insensitive jitterbugs who leaped onto the stage and threatened his safety, and that of his instrument, and he railed against them in the press. He was also highly critical of the music industry itself, hating the idea that he was just "giving the public what they want" rather than being able to bring the spontaneity he so loved about jazz into his day-to-day appearances. In his public pronouncements, Shaw epitomized the "art versus commerce" debate about jazz, although, paradoxically, his own most successful records, such as *Begin the Beguine*, veered very close to commercial ballad recordings with relatively slender jazz content. After walking out on his band, he went to Mexico on an extended vacation. Had he not been tied to his RCA recording contract, he might well have disappeared from the jazz and popular music arena there and then.

As it was, in the spring of 1940, Shaw returned to the studios on the West Coast, and he assembled a large studio band which was to form a template for several of his subsequent big bands – a full jazz orchestra line-up plus strings, thereby drawing together the two styles of band he had led up until that point. He commissioned charts from the African-American composer William Grant Still, and the outstanding success from these recordings was a piece which became his biggest hit to date – a setting of *Frenesi*, which Shaw believed was a Mexican folk tune but which he later found, to his (substantial) cost, was actually a current composition by Alberto Dominguez. Shaw's own supremely melodic clarinet is the centerpiece, set in a simple string arrangement, and leaning easily on the rhythm section. In addition, Dick Clark on tenor and Manny Klein on muted trumpet take some cameo solos, and there are some memorable touches to the setting, including the use of flute and piano to create some lighter moments in contrast to the full band.

Once again, Shaw had achieved mainstream popular music success with something a little out of the ordinary, certainly no more orthodox than his first band with strings. The rest of the sides he recorded at the same time as *Frenesi*, with more arrangements by Still, were something of a curate's egg, but the effect of his sudden and largely unexpected hit was to prompt him to form another full-time band, which he led from the spring of 1940 for almost a year. This band also recorded a major triumph, and in characteristic Shaw fashion, this too was not a romping swing number, but a measured version of Hoagy Carmichael's *Stardust*, with distinctive solos from trumpeter Billy Butterfield and trombonist Jack Jenney framing a dramatically elegant chorus from Shaw himself, that combined great tonal beauty with the inevitability of phrasing of the finest jazz soloists, paraphrasing the melody in a way that created a new structure, but keeping the original firmly in view. The setting, with strings, brass, and reed sections playing a relatively unexceptional background, was nothing special, but the three jazz solos elevated it to something remarkable. Shaw's own contribution was hailed by his fellow clarinetist Buddy De Franco as "the greatest clarinet solo of all time."[201] The disc is unquestionably a jazz

349

record, but within it, improvisation is limited to the solos, and like much of Shaw's output it prompts yet another examination of where the definition of jazz should start and finish.

Similar questions of definition are raised by Shaw's small group, the Gramercy Five, which began as an offshoot of his 1940–1 band. It sat, stylistically, somewhere between Dorsey's Dixieland-influenced Clambake Seven and Goodman's more swing-flavored groups. Its most distinctive element was that pianist Johnny Guarnieri played harpsichord, which gave the rhythm a jangly, staccato texture, although his carefully picked out right-hand solo lines sounded like a rather strange and stilted breed of acoustic guitar, contrasting with the fluency and smoothness of Al Hendrickson's genuine electric guitar. A piece such as *Special Delivery Stomp* included some riffs borrowed directly from Goodman's sextet repertoire, but the group was better and more original at the more relaxed tempo of its best-selling *Summit Ridge Drive*, which offered Shaw and trumpeter Billy Butterfield a chance to show off their blues playing. Nevertheless, and despite considerable popularity, the jazz potential of Shaw's small group was held in check by the gimmick of the harpsichord, and its soloists seldom reached the high levels they managed in other contexts.

Shaw's most unusual recordings from 1940–1, with his big band, include his own *Concerto for Clarinet*, and two pieces by the composer Paul Jordan that are classically orientated, *Evensong* and *Suite No. 8*. They all prefigure to some extent the "Third Stream" movement of the 1950s, but they were out on a limb in terms of the swing era. The band's most conventional output, and some of its most enduring discs, were those made with the African-American trumpeter Oran "Hot Lips" Page, who followed Billie Holiday as the only non-white member of Shaw's touring entourage. In another interracial experiment from the same period, Shaw's rhythm section and strings made a small number of fairly undistinguished recordings with the front line of trumpeter Henry "Red" Allen's band, altoist Benny Carter, and singer Lena Horne in June 1941.

The entry of the United States into World War II at the end of that year, following the attack on Pearl Harbor, precipitated a further growth in the popularity of swing. Across the nation, the munitions industry geared itself up, pumping money not only into making weaponry, but also into the pockets of workers, so that the economy, already substantially recovered from the Depression as a result of the New Deal, picked up further. Particularly in view of the fact that for many listeners their music symbolized modern America, there was a ready market for the music of big bands, and soon after Shaw enlisted in early 1942, at a time when his existing discs were being widely played on forces' radio, he found himself ranked Chief Petty Officer, and leading a Navy band which became known as the Rangers. This band, with such old stalwarts as trumpeter Max Kaminsky and drummer Dave Tough, was nominally a marching band, but it achieved considerable success playing as a regular dance band for American troops, and touring the Pacific theater of war, until Shaw was invalided out of the service in late 1943, following persistent migraines brought about by the strains of leading a larger-than-usual orchestra short of replacement strings and reeds while under the constant threat of attack, surviving, as he put it, "any number of air raids and damp spells in fox holes."[202]

Shaw was one of around three dozen well-known bandleaders who served in forces' bands during the war. (Claude Thornhill, another such musician, was briefly in Shaw's band until he was moved to a band of his own.) However, Shaw drew a far greater amount of press attention than his former rivals, owing both to the high profile of the Rangers, and to the fact that his well-publicized personal life, with several marriages to some of America's most glamorous women (of whom the most recent was Jerome Kern's daughter, Elizabeth), made good copy. There was, reportedly, some resentment among those on active service, who suffered considerable privations in the Pacific, that quite so much attention was devoted to Shaw. However, partly because many of the other best-known names, such as Glenn Miller, were still in the United States (it was not until 1944 that he was posted to Europe), and partly because Shaw's reputation was made substantially before the outbreak of war, his war service in the Pacific was extremely well-publicized, and, according to his own account and those of his sidemen, such as Kaminsky, the band was rapturously received wherever it went. Kaminsky memorably compared a concert on a U.S. aircraft-carrier, where the band descended on an airplane lift into the bowels of the ship to be greeted by a wildly excited audience, to arriving on stage via the lift at New York's Paramount Theater at the height of the jitterbug craze.

Ironically, in view of his protestations about art versus commercialism, it was Shaw's most commercially orientated successes – the romantic, sentimental charm of *Begin the Beguine*, *Frenesi*, and *Stardust* – that fueled this popularity. As Lewis A. Erenberg points out, "as swing became enmeshed in national purpose, it became more bureaucratic and sentimental." More significantly, he adds that Glenn Miller, both the best-known and the most sentimentally inclined of all the wartime service bandleaders presented a "whitened and corporate" version of swing.[203]

Shaw himself retained his liberal conscience, and in his first band from the period that followed his spell in the Navy, he drew together some of the best aspects of his earlier groups. This 1944–5 orchestra, with another prominently featured African-American – time Roy Eldridge – in the starring role previously occupied by Hot Lips Page, combined the trumpeter's solos and Shaw's nimble clarinet with some challenging section writing, on pieces such as Jimmy Mundy's *Lady Day*, or on Buster Harding's *Little Jazz* (which starred only Eldridge as a soloist). Away from the music itself, Eldridge's experiences were often less than happy, and he was reduced to tears by the management of one major venue who refused to admit him on the grounds that he could not possibly be playing with a white orchestra.

During the war itself, there could hardly have been a greater contrast between the fortunes of those white bandleaders who enlisted and were given bands to direct, and their African-American counterparts. "Such famous musicians as Artie Shaw and Glenn Miller received recognition for going into the service," wrote altoist Marshal Royal.

> But it didn't happen to me or any other black musician. In World War II, everyone that enlisted in the Navy as a musician was sent to Camp Roberts Smalls for assignment. This was at the Great Lakes Naval Station, just South of Chicago, and was something new, the Navy's first grouping of black musicians.[204]

The Navy set up a number of separate bands for African-American musicians. The one at Great Lakes included such talented swing players as trumpeters Clark Terry and Gerald Wilson, and altoist Willie Smith from the Lunceford band. Royal also played there alongside Vernon Alley and Jerome Richardson, as well as a contingent of Los Angeles jazz players, such as altoist Buddy Collette. However, no African-Americans were promoted to the rank of Chief Petty Officer, which equated to that of a bandleader, and on his subsequent posting to a pre-flight school in California, where he saw out the war, Royal effectively led one of the base's two dance bands, but it was "conducted" by a white "Chief."

Nevertheless, over time the recruitment of several African-American orchestras into the services, following the example of James Reese Europe's World War I "Hellfighters" band, created an environment in which many future jazz musicians were to prosper during their enforced periods in the military in the 1940s, 50s, and 60s. The discipline recalled by Royal, which involved starting the day by playing for flag-raising at 8.00 a.m., rehearsing for three hours each morning, and the same again in the afternoon, consolidated instrumental technique to a remarkable degree. Many eventual *avant-garde* players, such as Albert Ayler and Roscoe Mitchell, developed their underlying instrumental prowess through the relentless practice regimes of service bands, and Mitchell told me how this became a melting-pot of musical influences in the 1950s:

> When I was in the Army, we had a jazz group modeled on the Jazz Messengers. It was at that time I first heard Ornette Coleman, although I didn't immediately get what he was doing. I was posted to Heidelberg, and that's where I encountered Albert Ayler, in another Army band that had been in France. Again, when I heard him playing, after hours, I didn't really understand what he was doing, but his enormous sound made you pay attention. At one of those sessions he was playing the blues. After the first few choruses he really started to stretch the boundaries, although much of what he was doing didn't make much sense to me until after I got back home.[205]

The African-American service bands that were revitalized during World War II swiftly became a lasting conduit for ideas, technique, and news for musicians, that took on something of the same importance as the theatrical networks of the early years of the twentieth century.

The war years saw other swing bands come and go. Two of the most high-profile leaders were Gene Krupa and Harry James, both of whom launched bands of their own in the late 1930s. Krupa's benefited from the presence of strong soloists (including Eldridge), and it survived after the leader was forced to disband during a messy court case in 1943–4. The re-formed band continued until the 1950s. James's band lasted even longer, sustained by its leader's brash style, regular high-paying residencies in Las Vegas, and several movie appearances. It was the most commercially successful of the bands spawned by Goodman's, and in the early 1940s James provoked scenes that outdid his former boss's ability to whip up a frenzy among his young fans. For the opening day of his Paramount Theater engagement in April 1943, over 7500 enthusiasts had formed a line outside the venue by 9.00 a.m., and as well as some broken windows in the surrounding streets, jitterbugging dancers even ended up on stage along with the band. The papers described the month-long run at the theater as

"James's 30-day riot," and the band easily smashed Goodman's attendance record of 1937 with 163,000 paying customers grossing $105,000 in the first week. James was taken ill during the run from the sheer pressure of playing up to seven shows a day, but his rapturous reception at the Paramount was a barometer of his national popularity in 1943. Although the A.F.M. ban on recording had begun by this time, the discs he had made beforehand grossed over three-and-a-half million dollars in the first six months of the year.[206]

Part of the secret of James's appeal was the very reason he was not liked by many jazz critics – he was a musical chameleon, whose broad range of output appealed to a huge variety of listeners way beyond jazz and swing enthusiasts. His fellow trumpeters were in awe of his brilliant playing technique, something he demonstrated in somewhat questionable taste in his 1940 recordings of set pieces, such as *Carnival of Venice* and *Flight of the Bumble Bee*, both of which he re-recorded in even more popular versions the following year. His wide-toned ballad playing on *By the Sleepy Lagoon* and *Estrellita*, in 1942, earned him huge sales, and such cross-over hits tended to obscure in the public mind the more jazz-orientated end of his output, such as *Jeffries' Blues* and *Sharp as a Tack*, from 1941.

He retained an admiration for the Basie band, and with altoist Willie Smith and tenorist Corky Corcoran in his later line-ups, he produced some effective remakes of Basie material. Yet, apart from his schmaltzy ballads, and later hits like *Three Coins in a Fountain*, there was never a convincingly original James sound. His instrumental genius allowed him to earn (and lose) a fortune, but he was not the kind of innovative bandleader who sought to stamp his personality on the entire sound of his band, nor did he use arrangers who crafted such a sound for him, and the charts he played in the 1950s by Neal Hefti and Ernie Wilkins mirror their more original contributions to the post-war Basie book. James's high-profile second marriage to film star Betty Grable gave him an entrée into the Hollywood high life, and this propelled him to a level of fame few other bandleaders achieved, with the possible exception of Artie Shaw, who ruefully summed up James's career by saying that "after trading his genuine musical talent for a tawdry parade of hollow perks, [James] finds he has made a bad bargain."[207]

After leaving Paul Whiteman in 1938, trombonist Jack Teagarden fronted his own big band from the following year, finally giving his own considerable instrumental talents the chance to blossom, after many years of minor cameo appearances in Whiteman's large orchestra. This group lasted until he went bankrupt in 1940, filing for $43,863 of debts.[208] To pay them off, despite the ominous warning that fronting a band might be a way of adding to his liabilities rather than reducing them, he continued to lead a band until he was declared bankrupt for the second time in 1946. As a consequence of the draft and disagreements over musical and traveling policy, Teagarden's line-up underwent almost constant change, and he failed to create a body of work that did his instrumental talent justice – something he only managed to do after joining Louis Armstrong's small group in the late 1940s.

Yet none of these bands added much in terms of innovation to the swing template established by Goodman, refined by Dorsey, smoothed out by Miller, and simultaneously challenged and reinforced by Shaw.

Those African-American bandleaders who kept their big bands going during the war did plenty of entertaining for the armed forces – indeed the Billy Eckstine band found that it depended on the allowances of gasoline that came with such work for its means of getting round the country for other engagements. Cab Calloway and Duke Ellington continued broadcasting and touring, as did Count Basie, and Earl Hines finally left Chicago's Grand Terrace to go on the road. In several of these bands the first stirrings began of what was to become modern jazz, which I will discuss in Chapters 6 and 7, but until after the war was over, the majority remained well within the boundaries of the swing style that had been set in the late 1930s.

There was, however, one major development within African-American music that was a departure from precedent, which was the success of the all-female International Sweethearts of Rhythm. This was not the first all-girl jazz group. Back in the 1920s, Leona Henderson had led her Twelve Vampires, and there had also been a similar group in the 1930s called the Harlem Playgirls. But neither of these made the impact of the Sweethearts, who were formed out of a school band from Piney Woods, Mississippi, when they first appeared at the Howard Theater in Washington, and the Apollo, New York, during 1940. The following year, based near Washington, they were trained by Eddie Durham and later by Jesse Stone, with the intention of becoming a big-league swing orchestra. To a large extent they succeeded, although the ban on recording in 1942, imposed by the American Federation of Musicians, has denied us the chance to hear how the band sounded in its formative stage. Nevertheless, it did come to record some vigorous examples of its style later in the decade, including an RCA session that produced *Don't Get Twisted*. The International Sweethearts did not make great changes to the sound of jazz, but they were the most high-profile of a growing number of all-female bands in the latter part of the swing era, and they also drew together a number of first-rate soloists, such as saxophonist Vi Burnside and trumpeter Tiny Davis. Their British counterpart was Ivy Benson, who toured her all-girl band round the variety circuit, and also broadcast regularly, with a period as BBC Dance Band. During the war, Benson took advantage of the fact that many of her male counterparts had been conscripted, but she used this to create a high-profile role for female instrumentalists playing swing that continued for some time after the war was over.[209]

When the war ended, America fairly swiftly turned its back on swing, and big-band jazz ceased to be the dominant popular music of the day. Musically, other genres like country and western or rhythm and blues overtook it, perhaps because the small groups that played them were less affected by the economics of the period. There was a post-war cut-back in the amount of money individuals were prepared to spend on entertainment, and this combined with several other factors to accelerate the end of the swing big bands. Albert McCarthy summed up the combination of elements that brought this about as follows:

> Faced with adverse trends in the general economic situation, and changing social patterns, spiralling travelling costs, the closedown of many ballrooms, recording strikes, the emergence of the vocalists in their own right, and the challenge of TV, not to mention developments within jazz that led to it becoming an increasingly esoteric music, bandleaders might well have thought the fates were conspiring against them.[210]

However, at least one element in the demise of swing as a popular form was a severe wound that the industry inflicted on itself. I have already mentioned the recording ban of 1942, but there was a parallel industrial dispute between the radio networks in the United States and the umbrella organization for music publishers, ASCAP, that had begun the year before. ASCAP demanded annual provision against royalties from the combined radio networks of $9,000,000, and the radio stations refused, thus opening a door for an alternative organization, BMI (Broadcast Music International) to represent composers and publishers. BMI represented a high proportion of country and blues composers, and because this music could be broadcast with no restrictions, it supplanted that written by the more established jazz and popular-song composers who belonged to ASCAP. When the problem was settled, late in 1941, a new group of songwriters had become firmly established within radio, and the balance of music that was broadcast across the United States had changed irrevocably, adding Latin American styles as well as country and blues to the mix.

To my mind, there is another even simpler explanation for the demise of swing. At the end of any war, the public wished to sweep away its collective pain and move on. In Britain, for example, the government of Winston Churchill, which had done so much to unite and motivate the people during the long conflict, was swiftly set aside in the landslide victory for Clement Atlee's Labour Party. What had been a unifying bond among people in adversity was done away with as soon as the conditions changed to peace. Swing bands were as much a symbol of America's war as Churchill's bowler hat and victory salute were symbols of Britain's. And the public voted the swing bands out just as if they were a government seeking re-election.

For some, the change had come earlier. Artie Shaw said of the moment he had been playing in a theater in Providence, Rhode Island, in 1941: "With the whole world in flames, playing *Star Dust* seemed pretty pointless."[211] But for a while, playing *Star Dust* had helped unite a nation in adversity. By the end of the 1940s, he had formed and broken up a number more bands. His final band, before he abandoned playing the clarinet for good, was a small group, a version of the Gramercy Five, that played a short season in New York in 1954, and which made some valedictory recordings in June 1954, in Hollywood. Some of its harmonic voicings show an awareness of bebop, but despite the customary brilliance of Shaw's own playing, by 1954, overall, the group was an anachronism. A major shift had occurred in jazz, and it was one that had been driven at least in part by similar such small swing bands in the setting of New York's 52nd Street a decade earlier.

# CHAPTER 5

# International Jazz to World War II

So far, jazz has been discussed entirely in terms of its origins within the United States of America. Many histories of jazz take the view that so few significant developments happened outside North America in the early years of jazz that the rest of the world barely got a look in until the emergence of Django Reinhardt, the Belgian-born French gipsy guitarist, in the 1930s. Yet in the same way that the precursors of jazz spread their ideas far and wide through the United States, the music spread rapidly elsewhere in the world from the very early years of the twentieth century. The first ambassadors of jazz carried it to Europe, to Asia, to South America, and to Africa. By the 1930s there were professional musicians in many countries of the world who were adept at playing jazz, although they had never been to America, and had learned their craft from the early ambassadors or from records. Today jazz is being shaped just as much by musicians from Norway and Brazil or from the South African townships and the bustling cities of Japan as it is by Americans.

## Origins of International Jazz

It is hard to define the precise moment when the jazz message started to be carried from the United States to other countries of the world. Certainly the process began long before the Original Dixieland Jazz Band carried their riotous tunes, like *Ostrich Walk* and *Barnyard Blues*, to admiring audiences in Britain in 1919. Instead, just as ragtime, blues, and vaudeville songs had spread through the turn-of-the-century network of black theaters in the United States, the international current had started well before World War I, with dozens of African-American entertainers who came to Europe in the early 1900s to ply their trade on the variety, theater, and vaudeville circuits.

The most significant early example was the arrival in Edwardian London on May 16, 1903, of *In Dahomey*, in which Bert Williams, George Walker, and a cast of singers and dancers introduced the cake-walk to Britain in a run of 251 performances at the Shaftesbury Theatre, before setting off on a short tour. Posters showing dancers on a giant wedding cake proclaimed the message at each provincial city where the show opened: "Don't forget to see the real cake walk when it comes to your town." The significance of this musical play as a document in the development of African-American music was discussed earlier, but it achieved sufficient celebrity through its "vitality, quaint comedians, catchy music and . . . unique environment" to be shipped, lock, stock, and barrel, to Buckingham Palace for a Royal Command Performance.[1]

A few years after the visit by Williams and Walker, the Musical Spillers came to London in 1912. Programs confirm that, in their performances, ensemble ragtime, probably with some measure of improvised solos, was heard on the European side of the Atlantic, along with light classics and dance routines, and there is a strong chance that, by this time, they were playing the blues as well.

At Ciro's Club in London's West End, World War I soldiers on home leave could hear Dan Kildare and his Clef Club Orchestra (which recorded as Ciro's Club Coon Orchestra), and the African-American string band referred to in Chapter 1, who cut several discs in London which include many elements of early jazz. And, in France, after the United States had joined the fray, wartime troops were entertained by the "Hellfighters" band of James Reese Europe. By 1918, this offshoot of his New York syncopated orchestra was playing jazz for the troops. The comparable band of Europe's fellow African-American Will Vodery, as already noted, played for the French President Poincaré during victory celebrations in Verdun, and featured a six-piece jazz band drawn from its ranks during the "olio," or interval, in its programs, as well as afterwards when the carpets were rolled back for dancing.[2]

Through bands like these, plus the Original Dixieland Jazz Band, and also the Southern Syncopated Orchestra of Will Marion Cook, which came to London in 1919 and played for King George V before setting off to tour in Europe, the sounds of early jazz reached audiences far from the United

States within a very short time of the music having coalesced into a recognizable form in its own right.

# Britain

Because Britain shared a language with the United States, and because many African-American musicians had "played the halls" (in other words, worked in Britain's established network of provincial musical theaters, known as music halls) before World War I, it was natural that Britain should become a primary destination for Americans seeking work overseas, and this applied to both black and white performers. It was logical that Will Marion Cook's Southern Syncopated Orchestra (including clarinetist Sidney Bechet among its personnel) would launch its European tour in England, every bit as much as that the first overseas destination of the Original Dixieland Jazz Band would be London, where it soon settled at the Hammersmith Palais. Yet, within a very short time, European musicians on both sides of the English Channel were working alongside their American counterparts, and were well on the way to becoming accomplished jazz players in their own right. The London-based pianist, Billy Jones, who joined the Original Dixieland Jazz Band in 1920 to replace J. Russell Robinson, and played a relatively unsophisticated two-handed ragtime, went on to communicate what he had learned to the many British jazz groups he subsequently joined.

Trombonist Ted Heath, who later became a significant swing bandleader, left the Queen's Hall Roof Garden Orchestra in London to travel to Austria in 1922 as a member of Will Marion Cook's band, picking up invaluable jazz expertise on the way.[3]

Throughout the 1920s, numerous African-American musicians came to work in Europe, from children's novelty groups such as the Jenkins' Orphanage band from Charleston, S.C., to professional outfits. These ranged from bandleaders like Benny Peyton and Sam Wooding, who imported entire orchestras, to soloists like Arthur Briggs or Valaida Snow, who worked with a mixture of local players and footloose Americans. Not all of these visited Britain, but before the country's labor laws were revised in 1935 to prevent visiting American bands appearing in circumstances which were deemed to be taking work away from British musicians, the entire Cab Calloway and Duke Ellington Orchestras had played in London, and even after the ban was imposed, Teddy Hill's band appeared in 1937, in the context of a stage revue. Individual soloists, including Louis Armstrong and Fats Waller, toured the variety theater circuit in the 1930s.

In the wake of the Original Dixieland Jazz Band, white big bands appeared in Britain as well, Art Hickman in 1920 and 1921, and Paul Whiteman in 1923 (returning to Europe in 1926). British publications such as the *Melody Maker* (issued from January 1926 onwards) began to write about jazz in an increasingly knowledgeable way, and visits of American bands were supported by the availability of 78 r.p.m. discs by a much wider range of artists.

As the 1920s and 1930s wore on, Britain developed a number of significant home-grown jazz musicians, and these were joined by Caribbean immigrants, some of whom, like Rudolph Dunbar, came by way of the American jazz scene, and others of whom, like trumpeters Leslie "Jiver" Hutchinson and Leslie Thompson, were part of the steady flow of migrants direct from the British Caribbean islands. Most importantly for the development of its native and Caribbean musicians, Britain became the temporary home to a number of American jazz pioneers, who acted as mentors to the fledgling local players. In the 1920s, one of the earliest of these visitors to make recordings was Edmund Thornton Jenkins, a clarinetist and son of the founder of the Jenkins Orphanage band in Charleston, S.C., who first came to London in 1914 to study at the Royal Academy of Music. His playing on discs, such as *Come Along* (from 1921), shows strong links with orchestrated ragtime, but the recordings have a jazz feeling about them that suggest, in the words of his biographer, Jeffrey P. Green, that in some respects the "jazz idiom was already well-developed" before Jenkins left America in 1914.[4]

Jenkins – who subsequently aspired towards becoming a classical composer – became part of the black intellectual and cultural circle in London in the period leading up to and including the early 1920s. By contrast, at exactly the same time, Sidney Bechet was becoming firmly enmeshed in the capital's seamier side. He had arrived with the Southern Syncopated Orchestra, with whom he played at numerous high-profile venues, including a Buckingham Palace garden party for the Prince of Wales. (For the future Edward VIII, later Duke of Windsor, jazz became a passion, leading him and his fashionable set to many nightclubs in London and Paris where the music was played, and where he was wont to sit in on drums. He and his fast-living European friends had a lot to do with establishing jazz as a chic pastime during the inter-war period.)

For Bechet, such elevated surroundings were not to last, and after a series of increasingly acrimonious crises that beset the Southern Syncopated Orchestra, he acquired his trademark straight soprano saxophone (having specialized only on clarinet up to that point) and moved to a small band led by drummer Benny Peyton, called the Jazz Kings. This band took the place of the Original Dixieland Jazz Band at the Hammersmith Palais and before long was doubling at a club in Tottenham Court Road called Rector's. A favorite hang-out of the smart set, this club was described in a police report as "frequented by wealthy kept women and wealthy men who are associated with them," and in the more prosaic language of a fellow London musician, this added up to "mugs and birds," those with money to burn and loose women who were keen to assist in the process, thereby establishing a link of sorts between the risqué associations of the word "jazz" and its early footholds in Europe.[5]

From there, Bechet became increasingly enmeshed in gambling and the unsavory after-hours world of late-night London during the two years before he was imprisoned and deported, following an affray in September 1922. But from late 1919 until that point, he was a monumentally important influence on jazz in Britain. The glowing reviews began as a result of his clarinet feature on *Characteristic Blues* with the Southern Syncopated Orchestra. Not only was there the often-quoted article by conductor Ernst-Alexandre Ansermet in the *Revue Romande* (October 19, 1919), which praised his "richness of invention, force of accent . . . daring in novelty and the unexpected." In addition, there were laudatory comments in publications as varied as national newspapers including the *Daily Herald* and *The People*, to the local *Cambridge Review*, or Empire papers such as Cape Town's *Clarion*. Many dwelt on this tubby figure's mixture of instrumental power and personal charm, especially when he sat cross-legged on the floor and played current popular songs.

At the Hammersmith Palais, Bechet would have been heard by many thousands of dancers as he played there over a period of several months; but, even more significantly in terms of his influence, and as he was to do throughout his career, he took pupils to whom he taught something of his skills, which were acclaimed by his colleague Benny Peyton as belonging to "the most original and possibly the greatest of the known clarionet players . . . in the world." After his deportation to the United States, Bechet again returned to Europe (as he was to do several times in his life until his eventual move to France in the late 1940s) and remained a consistently powerful influence on European jazz.

African-American musicians who based themselves in Britian during the period of Bechet's visit, and who undertook tours to Europe in which they helped spread the sounds of early jazz, include the Five Jazzin' Devils, who visited Oslo in 1921; Gordon Stretton, who traveled to Paris; and Mope Desmond (father of the jazz pianist and singer Cab Kaye), who worked in Belgium before he was killed in a British railway accident in 1922. A number of other important early jazz soloists came to London in 1923, the year after Bechet was deported. These include James P. Johnson whose band, including violinist and clarinetist Darnell Howard and bassist Wellman Braud, appeared in the revue *Plantation Days* as part of an entertainment called *The Rainbow* at London's Empire Theatre. Although there was considerable opposition in certain social and political quarters to "the employment of black people in a cabaret show," the visit went ahead at the insistence of the impresario C. B. Cochrane, and the revue ran for six weeks in the West End of London.

Johnson and his musicians entered into similar black social circles to those of Edmund Jenkins, and played for the organization called the Coterie of Friends, which united distinguished black visitors to London with the local population. Guests at the event in which Johnson performed included other entertainers and the West Indian cricket team. There is some evidence that, following their London run, Johnson and his band performed elsewhere in Europe before returning to the United States. Their visit brought the sounds of East Coast large-band jazz to Britain, as well as Johnson's distinctive brand of stride piano.[6]

From May to September the same year, cornetist Johnny Dunn was featured in Will Vodery's band for the revue *Dover Street to Dixie*, a show that featured the singers Florence Mills and Edith Wilson. However, the band did not tour, and only appeared in one theater, the London Pavilion, during its stay, having, in consequence, a limited impact on local musicians, who initially tended to follow a rather different set of influences.

During the time Bechet was in London, various British bands set themselves up in imitation of American groups, but perhaps because Bechet's daunting virtuoso playing was seen as something exotic and foreign, or perhaps for straightforward reasons of racial identification, these generally looked to the Original Dixieland Jazz Band rather than the Jazz Kings for inspiration. Prominent among those imitators who went on to transform a passing fad into the beginnings of an identifiable national style was Lew Davis, who heard the O.D.J.B. and took up trombone, eventually joining the brothers Sid and Harry Roy in a quintet called the Lyricals. These three musicians, plus Lew's saxophonist brother Ben, became significant figures in pre-war British jazz. Furthermore, Lew Davis was instrumental in taking jazz to Scandinavia and the low countries as early as 1921, when he toured Norway and Belgium with Laurie Huntingdon's Dixie Five; an early example of a non-American band introducing jazz to new territories.

Another British convert was saxophonist Harry Gold, who went on to lead his Pieces of Eight throughout the twentieth century, until his retirement in 2000, at the age of 93. He wrote:

> I persuaded my father to take me to hear the O.D.J.B. Their effect was electric. Then and there I resolved to be a musician. The sound has never left me and although I have many of their recordings, the records do not affect me in the same way. I suppose that is the difference between recorded music and live performance.[7]

Gold went on to join Drayson Marsh's London Dance Band, a quintet broadly modeled on the O.D.J.B., which then changed its name to the Metronomes and began winning amateur jazz-band contests from 1924, indicating that by the early 1920s there were sufficient numbers of home-grown jazz or "hot dance" musicians in Britain to sustain such competitions.

Gold also entered a milieu which became synonymous with those who aspired to play jazz in Britain, the unofficial musicians' employment exchange which took place in the open air in London's Archer Street. Those hoping to be hired to play in a band – any band – grouped round the barber's shop on the opposite side of the road to the Orchestral Association which had its headquarters there. The better-known or, at any rate, better-established musicians congregated outside the Association building itself, and anyone looking for, say, a drummer or a guitarist for that night would first trawl through this sea of familiar faces before perhaps venturing over the road to the hopefuls if nobody was available. Many young musicians (including Gold) got their early opportunities from contacts made in Archer Street, and the place continued to function until well after World War II as the main contact point for the capital's musical community. Consequently, it was there that each new fad caught on and was discussed, before being tried out by players, from Dixieland to swing to bebop. For the most part, the jobs on offer tended to be mundane commercial dance work, but for three decades from the early 1920s, the common aspiration of most of those who congregated there was to play jazz.

However, the first British band to make a significant body of recordings with a consistently high jazz content was the group led by the Philippine-born Fred Elizalde, who began playing jazz in California in 1923, read law at Cambridge in the mid-1920s, and after forming an undergraduate ensemble, brought a fully professional band into the Savoy Hotel in London, in 1927, which he progressively packed with several of New York's finest white jazz musicians, alongside a carefully chosen group of local players. Elizalde was from a wealthy family with wide-ranging business interests from mining to broadcasting, and in a life that seems to have sprung directly from the pages of a novel by Powell or Huxley, he fought (on the fascist side) in the Spanish Civil War, spent World War II in a French chateau, wrote no fewer than three operas to libretti by Lorca, and, before becoming an eminent classical recitalist and conductor in his home country, led an international Olympic rifle-shooting team. In 1920s Britain, perhaps looking ahead to his eventual career as head of the Philippine Broadcasting Company, he became a pioneer of radio himself, with relays from the Savoy which were only stopped when, despite winning a *Melody Maker* poll, listeners complained that his music was too hard to dance to.

Among his sidemen were the Americans Fud Livingston, Chelsea Quealey, and the brothers Adrian and Arthur Rollini. Elizalde wrote some of the group's pieces himself, but perhaps their most impressive recording is *Singapore Sorrows* (March 12, 1929), an arrangement by Livingston which owes the more otiose elements of its orchestration to Paul Whiteman's symphonic jazz ideas, but which has some genuinely strong jazz soloing from Americans Adrian Rollini on bass saxophone, Bobby Davis on clarinet, the Australian-born Frank Coughlan on trombone, and the 17-year-old Londoner Norman Payne on trumpet, who manages an uncanny evocation of Bix Beiderbecke.

Until the arrival in Britain of Ellington and Armstrong, Elizalde's Orchestra was the dominant stylistic influence on Britain's own bands. "The band," wrote Arthur Rollini, "was truly superb, resembling Paul Whiteman's great orchestra in the USA," and he believed that Payne's solos "in Bix's tradition still stand up today [1987]." As he had had first-hand experience both of Whiteman's band and of the Ramblers, in which his brother played alongside Beiderbecke, his assessment is a valuable one.[8]

Certainly, the Whiteman influence also lay behind the jazzier end of the repertoire of the British dance bands led by Jack Payne and Jack Hylton, and it featured strongly in the solo playing of musicians like trumpeter Jack Jackson and clarinetist Jack Miranda, who had worked with Elizalde and went on to these other large orchestras. In its columns, the *Melody Maker* offered transcriptions of Whiteman discs, including the Bix Beiderbecke solo on *Sweet Sue*.[9] Other white American musicians who worked in Britain with local players included trumpeters Frank Guarente and Sylvester Ahola, and clarinetist Danny Polo. British recording groups such as those led by Bert Firman (notably the Rhythmic Eight) benefited hugely from the influence of such visitors. Gradually, however, as the 1930s began, the impact of African-American musicians became more noticeable in British jazz, not least because the Wall Street crash in 1929 had eventually forced virtually all of Elizalde's white American associates to return home.

The most significant United States influence of the early 1930s was that of the complete orchestras that came to Britain, up until the time that an agreement between the British Ministry of Labour and the Musicians' Union banned such bands from appearing, a measure that lasted until it was progressively repealed from the mid-1950s. One band which visited before and after the Wall Street crash, with a remarkable array of talented players in its ranks, was the itinerant orchestra led by Noble Sissle, who based himself in Europe between 1927 and 1933, and recruited players who had gained their experience with orchestras such as Fletcher Henderson's. His September 1929 British recordings feature some exemplary clarinet playing by Buster Bailey (notably on *Miranda*), and his 1930 line-up included trumpeters Arthur Briggs and Tommy Ladnier.

One of the few white bands to visit after 1929 was Ted Lewis and his orchestra, with a line-up that included Jimmy Dorsey and Chicagoan cornetist Muggsy Spanier. Dorsey's playing, and particularly his fleet-fingered alto saxophone work, made a great impact on local players, who sought to emulate his style, and who still talked of his influence well into the 1950s.[10]

However, the greatest media attention was drawn to the 1933 appearance of Duke Ellington's Cotton Club Orchestra, which cut a number of records during its stay. After Ellington's visit, arrangements based on those of his band began to be recorded by British groups, notably that of Billy Cotton (initially a drummer, who became a leading impresario and television entertainer). In addition to having recordings transcribed, Cotton, whose band worked for some time in the Lancashire seaside town of Southport, would collect copies of arrangements used by the bands on American ships docking in nearby Liverpool after the transatlantic run; and amid an output of light dance music, on his occasional more fully fledged jazz discs, he was among the first non-Americans to record pieces like *Sophisticated Lady* (1933). A collection of London musicians called the Madame Tussaud's Dance Orchestra made equally creditable discs of

Ellington small-band material (including *Rockin' in Rhythm*) the same year.

In the discussion of Ellington's music in the British musical press, a leading advocate of the band's work was the *Melody Maker* columnist "Mike" – the pseudonym of double bassist, composer, and author Spike Hughes. Having taught himself the art of arranging, Hughes played as a freelance bassist in various bands, including Jack Hylton's, and made a series of recordings with his own groups for the English Decca label. Several of his compositions, such as *Six Bells Stampede*, were recorded by other groups, and his own arrangements showed considerable flair – in particular a set of pieces which he recorded in New York in 1933 with his All American Orchestra (originally called his "Negro Orchestra"), which included such soloists as Henry "Red" Allen and Coleman Hawkins. The atmospheric qualities of Hughes's writing in pieces such as *Donegal Cradle Song*, *Arabesque*, and *Nocturne* show an assimilation of Ellingtonian technique, but also a strikingly original mind at work. Unfortunately for jazz, Hughes did not continue his jazz-playing career beyond the mid-1930s.

Louis Armstrong's influence, from his first visit to the United Kingdom in 1932 and his second in 1933–4, was equally important as Ellington's, and his impressive power and strength as a soloist inspired many local players in Britain, none more so than Nat Gonella, whose playing and singing with Lew Stone's band, and then his own Georgians, was directly modeled on that of Armstrong.

Armstrong had an equally significant effect on the community of Caribbean musicians living and working in London, in particular Leslie Thompson, the trumpeter who was to play lead in the European big band that backed Armstrong in 1934. Thompson also met and got to know members of the Ellington and Calloway orchestras on their visits to Britain. The musicians were pleased to meet, as Thompson put it, "another coloured fellow who played trumpet and lived in England."[11] Firm friendships were established, despite the fact that the Calloway orchestra had been less successful than it should have been, owing in part to hostility from the British pit bands in the theaters where Calloway performed, but also to attacks from the press. "There are British bands that play better stuff than Cab Calloway and are just as proficient musically," thundered the *Melody Maker* in March 1934, and Calloway's lead trumpeter Doc Cheatham told me:

> It was a surprise when we opened up in London and the minute they announced Cab Calloway, all the musicians in the pit band

blew loud discords and started making funny sounds on their horns ... he didn't go down well in England and I don't think people appreciated the fantastic band he'd brought with him.[12]

Nevertheless, musicians like Thompson admired Calloway's well-drilled orchestra and excellent soloists: "My own West Indian background probably gave me a greater appreciation and understanding of what these fellows were doing and allowed me to become part of it."[13]

Getting to know Calloway's band socially was another thing entirely from Thompson's more valuable first-hand experience at working with Armstrong night after night, and he was quick to appreciate that, however brilliant some players in Europe were, there was still, in 1934, a substantial way to go. He wrote:

> There was a difference between American jazz and what was played over here. While our jazz had shades of urge about it, it erred more towards melody and counterpoint. But the American jazz had all that and something else that kept you tapping your feet whether you wanted to or not. And here was the number one man in the field bringing it right to your own doorstep! Fantastic![14]

Thompson's experience paid off, and he went on to form his own band. Subsequently taken over by the dancer Ken "Snakehips" Johnson, this predominantly West Indian orchestra became one of the most hard-hitting and authentic-sounding jazz bands in Britain, and on a disc like *Snakehips Swing* (September 1938, on which Thompson was replaced in the trumpet section by fellow West Indians Dave Wilkins and Leslie "Jiver" Hutchinson), it has the cohesion, collective ensemble, and solo strength found in many of its better American counterparts. Moreover, its rhythm section is entirely without the layer of inhibition that pervades many British recordings of the period.

If contemporary reports are to be believed, such inhibitions also vanished when musicians of all backgrounds got together to play informally. During the 1930s, London musicians had an after-hours scene of their own, which, while it may not have had the illicit charm of the speakeasies of Chicago or New York, encouraged jam sessions and cutting contests. In clubs like the Nest or the Bag O'Nails in Kingly Street, visiting Americans were encouraged to pit their wits against the locals, and it was in this environment, as well as the recording studios, that Britain's two most distinguished long-term visitors of the 1930s – Coleman Hawkins and Benny Carter – had their greatest impact.

Informal musical and social contact with them had a beneficial effect on the playing of almost every British musician who came in contact with these two American giants, but there was also a reverse benefit, as neither saxophonist (in Carter's case, clarinetist, pianist, and trumpeter as well) would have been able to spend as much concentrated playing time as a small-group soloist as they managed in Europe, had they stayed in their respective American big bands, limited to a few measures of compressed solo space in each arrangement. The chance to stretch out, night after night, developed the solo talents of both men, as well as those of their coterie of dedicated British hangers-on.

Hawkins was in Europe for the longer period, arriving in March 1934 and staying until July 1939. Carter first moved to Paris in 1935, but joined Henry Hall's BBC Dance Orchestra in March 1936 as an arranger, eventually returning to the United States in May 1938. Because Hawkins had been invited to the country by bandleader Jack Hylton, his work permit allowed him to appear in public with that group (and the sister orchestra led by Mrs. Jack Hylton), but Carter was not allowed to play publicly in Britain, except in after-hours informal settings. Otherwise he was allowed only to appear on recordings or to rehearse the BBC band, which he described as "a very good orchestra, with excellent musicians in there."[15] He recalled:

> I took them through the scores myself, to try to interpret the phrasing I had in mind. I was only on temporary work permits, and I had to leave periodically and apply for re-entry, and after a decent interval they would allow me in again. I was never refused, but it was always sort of limiting in time and restrictive in the conditions.

Carter made use of his time in continental Europe, between work permits, to play and record prolifically, sometimes taking British musicians with him. However, the one environment in which he was allowed to play openly in Britain itself was the after-hours clubs.

> I always played there when I had the time. I used to go to a club called the Nest and there was another one called the Shim-Sham. Not only was I sitting in with a lot of the local musicians, but I

was recording with them too, because I was allowed to make records. I made a series for British Vocalion, with players like Gerry Moore, Andy McDevitt, Ted Heath, and Albert Harris among others. One disc, which as far as I know was the first jazz disc in three–four time, which I must add was Leonard Feather's idea, was *Waltzin' the Blues*. It perhaps wasn't as revolutionary as it might have felt at the time, with people now doing seven–four and eleven–eight, but at the time it was kind of refreshing for a change.[16]

Unquestionably, Carter's regular day-to-day work with the musicians of the BBC's dance orchestra had a beneficial effect on their playing and ensemble discipline – Carter had already demonstrated his skills in this respect with the Fletcher Henderson Orchestra and McKinney's Cotton Pickers. Even more important was his work in the commerical recording studios with a wider circle of British players whose talents he nurtured and extended by example. Carter's effortless skill on all the reeds and trumpet, not to mention his occasional turns at the piano, made him a role model for almost all the musicians he played with, and, in addition to those mentioned by Carter himself, trumpeters Max Goldberg and Tommy McQuater, trombonist George Chisholm, and reed players Buddy Featherstonhaugh, Freddy Gardner, and E. O. Pogson all went on to become world-class soloists.

Several examples of Carter's London discs rank with those of his American studio bands, even if the most consistently impressive soloist is Carter himself, for example, taking both clarinet and alto saxophone solos on his March 1936 *Swingin' at Maida Vale*, although trumpeter Duncan Whyte and tenorist Featherstonhaugh are also fluent and distinctive, certainly no less assured than many a sideman on contemporary American swing record dates. Carter's most notable achievement on this and other sessions from the same period is the ensemble cohesion and dynamic control he obtains from the band, which plays his familiar loping melodic lines and dramatically slurred accents with much the same precision as he managed to elicit from McKinney's Cotton Pickers. The delicate opening of *Nightfall*, recorded the following month, uses the typical Carter devices of muted trumpets and trombones offset by hushed saxophones, ushering in first the leader's lower-register clarinet and then (unusually) his tenor saxophone. Again the ensemble playing, not least the muted brass punctuations behind the tenor solo, is exemplary.

In contrast to Carter, because he was not principally an arranger, nor a multi-instrumentalist who could demonstrate ideas to members of almost every section of a band, Coleman Hawkins exerted less influence on how musicians played together than on the way they went about playing extended solos. In the decade before his arrival in Britain he had been the major player to develop the solo voice of the tenor saxophone, through his many discs with Fletcher Henderson's orchestra. He had only made a handful of discs in his own right before leaving America, but his first British recordings find him setting the pattern for what would become his regular playing environment for much of the rest of his life, producing long, rhapsodic solos with great invention and drive accompanied only by a rhythm section. *Lady Be Good*, from November 1934, is typical, with workaday solos from his accompanists, but a truly inspired series of ideas from Hawkins himself, presaging the approach he would take on his famous disc of *Body and Soul* on his return to the United States four-and-a-half years later.

Both Hawkins and Carter made numerous successful recordings in Holland and France as well, in the periods between work permits, bringing musicians across Europe into contact with improvisation at its highest level.

In the later 1930s, once the British Musicians' Union and Ministry of Labour had introduced their restrictions on visiting American players, enthusiasts missed out on the opportunity to hear entire orchestras like that of Jimmie Lunceford, which came through on a return journey to the United States, but was prevented from playing. Exceptionally, Teddy Hill's band was allowed to spend five weeks in July and August 1937 in London, with subsequent appearances in Dublin and Manchester. It accompanied a singing and dancing show known variously as the *Cotton Club Revue* or *Harlem on Parade*, and the work permits stipulated that the band was to keep still, apart from those movements necessary to operate their instruments. With Dizzy Gillespie, saxophonist Russell Procope, and trombonist Dickie Wells in the line-up, the band was hailed on a visit to Paris just before its London engagement as the best to come to Europe since Ellington, but the British papers were less enthusiastic. What is certain is that the orchestra did have an influential effect on those local musicians who heard it, including the members of the house band at the Ritz Ballroom in Manchester where the Hill band came to relax by sitting in between their shows. Gillespie is recalled as playing "about the best trumpet ever to be heard in the Ritz tunnel."[17]

As war clouds gathered over Europe, some American soloists continued to visit. Art Tatum, whose 1938 visit was mainly confined to an exclusive

Soho nightclub, went almost unnoticed by fans and journalists alike, although he was interviewed by clarinetist and bandleader Rudolph Dunber, with a photograph appearing in *Rhythm* magazine. Fats Waller, on the other hand, toured the variety-theater circuit, from Scotland to the South Coast, and, as well as making some solo organ discs, corralled a band of English and West Indian musicians into playing on record, in a fair approximation of his New York studio groups. Waller made his most artistically adventurous sequence of solo recordings, his *London Suite*, while in Britain the following year. However, the outbreak of war curtailed his 1939 European tour.

One significant addition to the posters for touring acts in the summer of 1939 was the Quintet of the Hot Club of France, with Django Reinhardt and Stephane Grappelli, making one of its several visits to Britain, and proving that by the time World War II broke out, a potent influence on British jazz now hailed from across the English Channel, rather than beyond the Atlantic Ocean.

Not long before the outbreak of war, a number of musicians, who had formerly played in such established dance bands as the Ambrose Orchestra, formed the Heralds of Swing, a co-operative swing band, to work in London's Paradise Restaurant. As a ten-piece band, it proved too expensive to be a long-term proposition at the venue, and it had a somewhat checkered career in the months leading up to the war, which began in September 1939. However, several of its members enlisted in the RAF No. 1 Dance Band, which became known as the "Squadronaires," and which also became a highly proficient swing band, with Dixieland overtones, rather in the style of Bob Crosby's Orchestra. With soloists such as Tommy McQuater and George Chisholm, it produced some outstanding recordings, and paved the way for a post-war generation of British jazz musicians who tackled the music with a verve and lack of inhibition comparable to that of their American contemporaries.

## Germany

In a similar manner to Britain, Germany experienced African-American entertainers as a regular part of its theatrical and musical life from early in the twentieth century. The first high-profile event was in 1905, not long after *In Dahomey* had successfully toured in Britain, when Will Marion Cook brought a variety troupe called the "Memphis Students" to Berlin, where they appeared at the Schumann Circus after previously stopping off in London and Paris. The musicians included banjo players and saxophonists, as well as the virtuoso drummer, Buddy Gilmore, and there was novelty dancing and singing that emphasized syncopated rhythm and shuffle beats.[18]

In 1924, the African-American trumpeter Arthur Briggs brought his Savoy Syncopated Orchestra from Belgium to Vienna, where it worked at the Weinburg Bar. From 1926 to 1928, Briggs remained in German-speaking countries, using Berlin as his base for touring, and for recording more than 40 sides, with a personnel drawn from Belgium and Germany. But it was another theatrical presentation, *Chocolate Kiddies*, that brought the first fully fledged African-American jazz orchestra to Germany in 1925, namely Sam Wooding's band. The program was a revue with singers, dancers, and comedians, all accompanied by the band, playing charts by Wooding, including his own arrangements of compositions by Duke Ellington and Jo Trent that had been hastily written overnight for the show, just a few days before his departure for Europe. The band's immediate popularity with Berlin audiences led to a series of recordings, which were made in July 1925, just over a month after the band's opening at the Admiralspalast. A typical example, *Shanghai Shuffle*, is packed with strong solos and an arrangement that has a genuine sense of shape and form, each chorus contrasting with the last. Wooding told Chip Deffaa: "I arranged the music we played. That's what made it a novelty. . . . One strain would be maybe an augmented chord, another strain would be the octave and I treated each one differently."[19]

This is certainly true of this disc, one of the lively numbers that had local audiences stamping their feet and shouting "Bis! Bis!" – initially interpreted by the musicians as a derogatory term like "Beast!," but which they came to understand was the local way of asking for "More!" After an opening bugle call, Willie Lewis's baritone sax takes the opening melody with syncopated punctuations from the brass. Then Tommy Ladnier's powerful muted trumpet takes a dramatic solo, before an upward-moving saxophone figure ushers in some scored brass flares. A lower-register clarinet solo (by Garvin Bushell) has some growly vocal tone contrasting with a smooth clarinet trio, the orchestral device beloved of Don Redman and Fletcher Henderson, which is used very effectively here to provide upward glissandi in the powerful final choruses.

Such an arrangement, which was subtantially more energetic and uninhibited than Elizalde's discs of a year or two later in England, displays an ensemble every inch the equal of Fletcher Henderson's orchestra, and far more sure-footed and confident than the band with which Duke Ellington opened a little later at the Cotton Club in New York. When Wooding left the United States in 1925, he was secure in the knowledge that his band was as accomplished as any of the groups then playing in New York or Chicago. What is more, he recorded in Berlin four months before the first of Louis Armstrong's epoch-making Hot Five recordings in Chicago. It was to be Wooding's tragedy that when he eventually decided to return to the United States for good, fashions there had passed him by; a fate which was also to befall Noble Sissle. Nevertheless, during the time Wooding was based in Berlin, on and off until 1931 (his band traveling widely through Europe and lasting through two incarnations, each of which involved several changes of line-up), he gave Germany access to a hot jazz orchestra as dazzling as anything that could be heard in the large cities of the United States.

The revue (which also had regular changes of personnel, and was discarded once and for all after a season in Darmstadt during Wooding's second period in Europe, in the later 1920s) had links with Berlin's earliest experience of African-Americans, as the star performers were Rufus Greenlee and Thaddeus Drayton, whose act included banter in numerous European languages which they had acquired touring Europe in the years before World War I.

Off stage, Wooding's band dressed and looked the part of well-heeled international entertainers. A penchant for "dog-walking coats" was accompanied by ownership of several dogs, although the popularity of these pets declined after Sidney Bechet turned up in the middle of the night in Berlin with a Dobermann and challenged Garvin Bushell's Great Dane to a fight at four in the morning. The police were called to quash the affray.

Otherwise, trumpeter Doc Cheatham recalled that they were "treated like kings," and decked themselves out in the latest fashions, while clarinetist Garvin Bushell reveled in being a tourist, taking time out from the band's travels to visit the Roman remains in Pest (in Hungary) and the Viennese catacombs. Like all formally educated jazz players, Bushell had studied Mozart, and thoroughly enjoyed seeing an exhibition of Mozartian memorabilia in Vienna.[20] And yet, in many ways, a smartly attired troupe of African-American entertainers remained an exotic anomoly in 1920s Europe. Doc Cheatham recalled that on an overcrowded slow train from Turkey to Hamburg, whenever new passengers came on board and peered into the band's compartments, the musicians would "jump up and down and do a wild dance to scare them away." Superstitious and unfamiliar with such a sight, the other travelers gave Wooding's troupe a wide berth.[21]

Nevertheless, racial superstition and prejudice were rare experiences for the band in Europe, although in Berlin, during March 1926, there was one incident which proved a harbinger of the extreme right-wing attitudes that were subsequently to prevail in the 1930s as fascism gradually took over. Several members of the band were relaxing after hours in a bar when half a dozen students (some of whose faces were marked with dueling scars) came in and threatened the musicians, saying, "We're going to run the Schwarzes out tonight, we don't want you here." Only the presence of some ex-prizefighters among the musicians and dancers overcame the students' hostility and saw them off in the fracas that followed.[22]

Ironically, it was the reserved and cynical English who were most blasé about the band's actual performances, and Garvin Bushell attributed their poor reception on a visit to England to the fact that the band was: "too classy. . . . I think the British audience would have accepted a black orchestra doing comedy and slapstick, but we had a classy organisation, and Europe had rubbed off on us. So we didn't do well in London at all."[23] Wooding concurred that there were a few experiences in Europe of audiences who felt his musicians did not "know their place," but for the most part he found that European audiences were "crazy about jazz. And the Europeans liked the Negro's style of jazz better than they did Paul Whiteman's."[24]

This may well have been the case, especially in the Francophone and Hispanic countries where the band recorded, but in Germany public tastes were a little more complex, and overshadowed by developments in the political system. Just over two years after Wooding's first tour of Germany, an incident occurred that indicated the strong underlying racial and moral tensions within the wider German-speaking world. Josephine Baker was forced to return to the free and easy atmosphere of Berlin after she was abruptly expelled without a work permit from Vienna in Austria. "[She] will therefore not appear dressed only in a couple of bananas in that city, which boasts it is another Paris," reported the French columnist Clement Vautel.

> All the political parties, from the nationals and the Christian socialists to the socialists at last find themselves in accord about something: the black peril must be fought.
>
> Josephine Baker . . . having been engaged by the director of a Viennese music hall, all the parliamentary factions have demanded of Mr. Siepel, president of the council, to declare her undesirable. . . .Vienna, home of the opera and the waltz is anxious to keep out jazz.[25]

High unemployment and the exorbitant cost of admission were cited as reasons for her expulsion during a parliamentary debate on February 25, 1928, but Dr. Jerzabeck, leader of the clerical party, despite protesting he was not opposed to Baker on grounds of "color or nationality," made it clear that his main complaint was against "public posters all over Vienna showing the dancer attired in only a string of pearls and a few ostrich feathers 'like a Congo savage.'" Such an exotic "coffee and milk" physique, as another paper put it, was not considered suitable even for the privileged eyes of the bourgeoisie.[26] These hard-line Austrian attitudes would soon find a sympathetic echo throughout Germany, but not until the artistically liberal climate in Berlin had run its course and the forces of fascism took over.

Despite the continued presence of Wooding, Baker, and several significant African-Americans throughout the 1920s, the predominant early influence on German jazz musicians was undoubtedly that of white Americans, and as with Fred Elizalde's band in London, it was interaction between the visiting and local players that fostered a home-grown tradition. When violinist Alex Hyde's New York Jazz Orchestra, a large, white American jazz and dance band, arrived in Berlin in 1925, it was forced to recruit local replacements when its star trumpeter left to take a cure for alcoholism and its tuba player got caught in a diamond-smuggling racket. The after-hours scene in Berlin was already an international free-for-all centered on British saxophonist Billy Bartholomew, American bandleader Eddie Woods, and Canadian trumpeter Harry Brooks.[27]

Hyde cut several discs "mit seinem New Yorker Jazz Orchester," and the majority of these are best described as "hot dance music," with Hyde's occasionally tentative violin carrying the melody lines. Nevertheless, within the ranks of his American and German recruits were some impressive soloists, and there are strong cornet and trombone choruses; for example, on his April 1925 recording of *Shine*. When Hyde left to return to the United States, a German leader called Felix Lehmann, who used the stage name Fred Bird, took over his charts and most of the musicians, going on to win a golden saxophone in a jazz-band contest at the 1925 Leipzig Ausstellung (international exhibition). Many of these musicians subsequently went on to Poland, working for a dubious character called "Mr. Alexander," a Polish-American from Milwaukee who had been hounded out of the United States for bootlegging, but who ran the Pavillon Mascotte ballroom in Warsaw. The seeds of jazz were thus sown in Poland by American expatriates for a movement which later became a symbol of freedom during the Cold War years, when the free jazz of Krzyzstof

Komeda and Tomas Stanko broke through the restraints of the time, to travel first around Poland and then to Scandinavia.

The free-for-all Berlin jazz scene of the 1920s surreptitiously crept into the images of this city's nightlife that were vividly captured in the arts, for example through the writing of Christopher Isherwood and the graphic art of George Grosz. The very name of the music conjured up an image of exotic, yet decadent, entertainment, going back to the derivation of the word jazz itself. Also in the late 1920s, the Austrian composer Ernst Krenek incorporated the idea of an African-American saxophonist and violinist into the title role of his modernist opera *Jonny Spielt Auf* ("Johnny Strikes Up the Band") and for the Leipzig premiere in February 1927, true to Krenek's view of the jazz musican as an exotic figure, the role was played by an African-American. (In a significant example of the racial climate that prevailed at the time, for the New York premiere two years later, the white American baritone Michael Bohnen was obliged to play the role in blackface.[28]) Krenek's attempts to convey jazz through an onstage "jazz band" in the opera are something of a caricature, with repetitive rhythms and seventh chords as the main distinguishing features, but his philosophical questioning of the relationship between high art and popular culture sees jazz's qualities of primitivism and lack of inhibition as revitalizing art music, which is represented by the character of Max, a composer. In the final moments of the piece, Johnny is seen astride a station clock which transforms into an image of the world. As he stands on the North Pole, he begins a tune which signifies the entire world being caught up in a "Charleston-stamping" dance. The German critics universally praised this "scurrying, humorous work,"[29] which also brought railroad trains, radio sets, and police cars onto the operatic stage for the first time. Nevertheless, ominous undercurrents in German society emerged at the Munich premiere, where gas bombs were thrown on stage during Johnny's singing of a sequence of spirituals.

In Grosz's pictures there is a less high-minded depiction of jazz, and in works such as *Queen Bar* (1927) or *The Latest Hit* (1929), caucasian jazz bands perform for the wealthy upper-class clientèle of Berlin's nightclubs, with debauchery never far away. Grosz himself was an amateur banjoist who loved the tuba-led two-beat of early jazz rhythms (his son Marty, who grew up in America, subsequently became a virtuoso jazz banjo and guitar player), so his drawings are unusually accurate and atmospheric depictions of the jazz he enthused over: trumpets with plunger mutes are held high in the air, suggesting growling and other effects, while saxophonists shut their eyes and crouch low to the accompaniment of intense, bespectacled pianists. This kind of music – the direct descendent of the colorful, programmatic repertoire of the Original Dixieland Jazz Band – was played by the Weintraub Syncopators, Germany's first home-grown "hot" jazz band, formed in 1924, and which recorded from 1928 until it disbanded while on tour in 1937 in Australia – a place of safety for its Jewish personnel, including the band's leader Stefan Weintraub. Similar music was played by the house band of Electrola records in Berlin, the Goldene Sieben (Golden Seven), formed in 1930 to keep up a relentless supply of good-time discs. Their earliest Dixieland performances, by a front line of Kurt Hohenberger, trumpet, Erhard Krause, trombone, and Franz Thon, clarinet, were superseded by a big-band instrumentation, although these three musicians remained prominently featured in later recordings such as *St. Louis Blues* (November 1937).

The Goldene Sieben were formed, and worked, against a background of political turmoil in Germany. The country's economic crisis was accelerated by the aftershocks of the Wall Street crash in America, and in the first years of the 1930s there was a stand-off between the extreme left-wing elements and the right-wing national socialists, who eventually prevailed. When Adolf Hitler was proclaimed Chancellor of Germany in January 1933, and as his party's manifesto rapidly became law, the tide turned rapidly against foreign musicians who had been living and working in Germany. Many left, either in the run–up to Hitler's move to power, or in its aftermath. Those who stayed, like banjoist Michael Danzi (an American of Italian origin, with a German wife and child), had to be sponsored by a German national as "desirable foreigners."[30]

The immediate effect in 1933–4 was that leaders became "wary of using a non-German, but slowly they got enough courage to employ an *auslander*." For a year or two, foreigners continued to work relatively freely alongside local players. During this time, the *Reichsmusikkammer* made numerous pronouncements, a small number of which were actually beneficial to working musicians, including one that included the provision of days off for players who had hitherto worked seven days a week. Nevertheless, the general impression given by Nazi policies was to favor German indigenous forms of music over imported American styles.

From 1935 onwards, posters and newspaper articles began to denounce jazz, as *entartete* or "decadent" music, and Goebbels spoke in harsh, derogatory terms of *Americano nigger kike jungle musik*. It was not uncommon to find jazz denounced in the terms used by "Buschmann" in a 1938 paper:

"Impresarios who present swing dancing should be put out of business. Swing orchestras that play hot, scream on their instruments, stand up to solo and other cheap devices are going to disappear. Nigger music must disappear."[31]

Those remaining American, black, and Jewish musicians who were able to do so did their best to leave Germany and its territories before the ominous import of such statements could be put into effect. But, by a curious paradox, just as the public threats of the Nazi regime against the music became more vociferous, that same regime surreptitiously continued to condone jazz as a form of entertainment. Because jazz had become such an integral part of the club, cabaret, and variety scene in Berlin, it was tacitly allowed to continue at the very center of the Reich, and, at theaters such as the prestigious Scala in Berlin, American stars appeared until well into 1939, often arriving direct from Broadway, and they were backed by a local band that was well-versed in foxtrots and swing.

The American press carried stories that showed the uneasy climate in Berlin, and although the occasional African-American musician, like trombonist Herb Flemming, a veteran of James Reese Europe's and Sam Wooding's bands, who played there in the Club Sherbini up until July 1937, was praised for "the distinction of figuratively thumbing his nose at Adolf Hitler, Nazi dictator of Germany," it was clear that fewer and fewer international musicians wished to "flout the most rigid principle of Aryan supremacy laid down by Herr Hitler."[32] Flemming, however, is a curious case, having acquired what is generally regarded as a spurious Arab ancestry, feigned a Tunisian birthplace, and taken the name Nicolliah El-Michelle, in order to have his visa granted, and to avoid the country's overt prejudice against "nigger music." In the bizarre double standards of the day, he actually appeared as a bandleader in the 1936 film *Unter Heissen Himmel*, which starred Hans Albers and Lotte Lange.[33] Also, in spite of the propaganda against swing, some British musicians played in late-1930s Germany, including Jack Hylton and Henry Hall, whose band appeared in Berlin as late as January 1939, although with strict instructions to play nothing by any Jewish composer.

By 1937, however, the overall political climate throughout Germany had gradually eradicated jazz from its central position in popular music. Popular and well-established bandleaders, such as the Romanian James Kok, left the country, as did some founder-members of the Goldene Sieben, although Hohenberger continued to perform and record, and so did other leaders, such as Horst Winter. Nevertheless, in due course, through its oppressive actions, the Nazi regime ushered in a change in perception. Although jazz maintained a tenuous hold on Berlin cabarets and theaters until the very outbreak of war, and although the regime never actually imposed an outright ban on jazz, the music ceased to be a symbol of decadence. As the war began, it became a symbol of political rebellion, and acted as a rallying point for those who opposed the regime.

There had been energetic and enthusiastic groups of jazz-record collectors in early 1930s Germany, and in 1934 Francis Wolff (later a co-founder of Blue Note records in the United States) set up the Hot Club of Berlin. A year or two later the Hot Club of Frankfurt was established, and there remained a ready market for American jazz discs until war came. The catalogs of several American labels were distributed by local companies such as Elektrola and Telefunken, even though the names of musicians with overtly Jewish connections such as Jean Goldkette's were discreetly removed from the labels. Shortly before war broke out, Wolff escaped to the United States, another branch of his Jewish family successfully reaching Britain, but other knowledgeable German fans remained behind, some even occupying posts of some seniority in the military or civil regime, and secretly continuing their enthusiasm for American – and particularly African-American – jazz.

In the occupied territories, jazz was officially frowned upon; in many it became a subversive counter-culture, and remained so throughout occupied Europe until 1945, although musicians such as Ernst Landl in Austria, Stan Brenders in Belgium, and Ernst Van't Hoff in Holland continued careers of sorts. Brenders openly broadcast music by Jewish composers, but was not censured, and it seems as if in Francophone areas, generally the Nazis' attitude towards jazz was laxer. Certainly, as Mike Zwerin discovered when researching this cloudy area of musical history, in one instance a German officer (and pre-war jazz-record producer), Dietrich Schutz-Koehn, was encouraged by the authorities to broadcast jazz to occupied France from Nîmes. In Paris, the occupying authorities issued permits to those bands licensed to play in the nightclubs, and in spite of Goebbels's pronounce-ments, these included numerous jazz groups.[34]

Further east it was a different story, and numerous Jewish musicians, many of them well-known, were interned. The majority, even those who were allowed to play jazz for inmates and guards, such as the band of musicians from Poland and Czechoslovakia that played in a propaganda film about the camp at Theresienstadt, were killed. A few, such as the Czech trumpeter Eric Vogel, escaped – in his case en route to Dachau – and lived to tell the horrifying tale of his colleagues who were not so fortunate. As the Germans were exterminating dozens of talented musicians, in a bizarre paradox, which perhaps explains why jazz was never overtly banned, the Nazi propaganda machine itself undertook the broadcasting of locally produced arrangements by Lutz Templin of popular American jazz numbers, to try to ensnare listeners to its broadcasts. The words of the familiar songs were sung in English, but subtly amended, so that *Bye Bye, Blackbird* became *Bye Bye, Empire*. The healthy and vital jazz scene that had existed in 1920s Germany was to take a very long time to recover from the brutal regime of the Nazis.

# France

From the start of the 1920s, there were focal points for visiting African-American musicians in several of the principal cities of Europe, and these often combined a mutual interest in contemporary styles of music with the sense of community that sprang up among small groups of expatriates. Paris was perhaps the most active of all such European centers in the period up until 1939, and it regained this level of activity again after World War II.

During and after World War I, Paris played host to African-American entertainers, including the man who claimed to have brought jazz to France, the singer and dancer Charles Baker (1863–1928). His three-piece band played ragtime and jazz-related tunes up until the time he was partially paralyzed by a stroke, in 1923, and even before World War I, he had been a popular entertainer in the city. It is rumored that he performed *Alexander's Ragtime Band* before European royalty at the Hôtel l'Abbaye.[35]

One man, above all others, who took a central role in establishing the city's importance was the former drummer with Ciro's Club Coon Orchestra, Louis Mitchell. Having worked in London with Dan Kildare, and then taken his own Syncopating Sextette to Glasgow, he returned to the United States at the end of World War I and formed a new band called Mitchell's Jazz Kings. This group traveled to Paris around May 1919, and by early 1920 had opened at the Perroquet Cabaret in the Casino de Paris.

Mitchell was sponsored by a racehorse owner, Leon Volterra, who helped establish the band's long-term residency in Paris and encouraged them to record several sides in 1922–3. Before gambling and alcoholism ended his career, Mitchell became the hub of the milieu of African-American musicians in the city. "I was on the scene for only a short time, but everyone showed me acts of courtesy and goodwill," wrote clarinetist Rudolph Dunbar, a veteran of Will Vodery's Plantation Orchestra in New York, who came to Europe with the revue *Dixie to Broadway* in 1924. He continued:

> The small community of black musicians in Paris expressed a common identity of interest that automatically formed a union among themselves . . . and it was Louis Mitchell, pioneer among black Americans in Paris, whose indomitable enterprise paved the way for black musicians and entertainers.[36]

In early 1920s America, jazz was widely regarded as exotic, or slightly naughty, and its very name evoked thoughts of sexual innuendo. In Paris, by contrast, black musicians were chic. "During that epoch, black musicians were in vogue in Parisian life," wrote Dunbar. "Louis Mitchell appealed to the imagination, understanding and taste of the French people."

In addition to Mitchell, a number of other African-Americans based their careers in Paris during the pre-war period. One of the first to work there was trumpeter Arthur Briggs, although from 1924 until the start of the 1930s he spent most of his time in Austria and Germany, returning to France after working with Noble Sissle in 1931.

To a greater extent than in either Britain or Germany, both as members of touring bands and in the context of theatrical performances from cabaret to revue, African-Americans were adopted into the mainstream of cultural life in France. In particular, they appealed to the movements in French intellectual life that sprang up in the wake of the Great War. "The black revue came to symbolize postwar modernism," wrote Phyllis Rose, in her biography of Josephine Baker, whose *Revue Negre* opened in Paris in October 1925, backed by a jazz orchestra directed by pianist Claude Hopkins. It typified, in her words:

> the new Cubist sensibility which savored angles and fragments rather than curvilinear forms, juxtaposition rather than fluidity as a principle of coherence, frenetic energy rather than graceful lyricism. Isadora Duncan had refreshed European culture by bringing it the spirit of an Americanized Greece. Josephine Baker would refresh it by bringing the spirit of an Americanized Africa.[37]

In the 1920s and 1930s, revues and theatrical performances by African-Americans were presented in several parts of France as well as in Paris. Sam Wooding's orchestra and its associated revue appeared in France as it had done in Germany and Britain, and so did shows by Lucky Millinder and Wooding's former sideman Willie Lewis.

In the mid-1920s, it was the omnipresent Louis Mitchell who continued to act as go-between for many bands, Garvin Bushell crediting him, for instance, with first booking the Wooding orchestra into the Hotel Negresco in Nice, where it was often to play again. Other destinations for traveling revues were Monte Carlo and Biarritz. In the early 1930s, Millinder played at the Sporting Club d'Eté at Monte Carlo, in a vast theatrical entourage that also included Enric Madriguera's Latin American Orchestra and the Hungarian gipsy band of Bela de Racz.[38]

In due course, just as had happened in Britain and Germany, a growing number of local musicians became proficient jazz players, either in conjunction with Americans, or on their own. One of the most extraordinary examples of international cooperation was the predominantly French-based Gregor and His Gregorians. Few bands anywhere in the world had a more exotic lineage.

Gregor (Krikor Kelekian) was born in 1898 in what was then Constantinople, where his family perished in one of a series of massacres of itinerant Armenians. By 1915 he had not only become a proficient musician (specializing in vocals) but also was a remarkable dancer, and he toured the theaters of war-torn Europe, first with a Jamaican called Joe Frisco Bingham, and then with a girl called only "Loulou." Gregor and Loulou specialized in jazz dance, and after touring Italy, France, Holland, and Belgium, Gregor ended up taking over their accompanying orchestra – a band led by Eduardo Andreozzi, who had himself pioneered jazz band music in Brazil.[39]

In 1928 he briefly fronted English clarinetist Sid Phillips's band, before founding his own orchestra, which contained white Russians, French, and English players. This band played in Paris, toured Spain, and was featured at the smartest nightspots in Le Touquet and Nice. Its players included the outstanding French trumpeter Phillipe Brun, and jazz violinists Stephane Grappelli and Michel Warlop. In 1930 Gregor toured South America and stayed for two years in Argentina before returning to the scene of his former triumphs in France. He subsequently lived in Switzerland, Iran, Greece, the Lebanon, and Iraq, in all of which he ran theaters, dance halls, and occasional orchestras. His talent for finding bright young musicians and developing their careers earned him the title the "European Fletcher Henderson."

Philippe Brun also led his own groups, and appeared in the orchestra led by Ray Ventura, the Collegians, which was the best-known native French big band of the 1920s and 1930s. In addition to Brun, its soloists also included trumpeter Gus Deloff and saxophonist Alix Combelle (who made a significant contribution to discs by Benny Carter and Coleman Hawkins under the name of Hawkins' All Star Jam Band).

The most influential European jazz musician in 1930s France (who also recorded in Hawkins's band) was the Belgian-born gipsy guitarist Django Reinhardt. His daring guitar solos, haunting compositions, and stirring rhythm playing were sufficiently well-developed and mature to have the same ring of originality and innovation about them as the playing of such significant American musicians as Louis Armstrong and Sidney Bechet, even though Reinhardt owed as much of his sound to the traditions of European gipsy guitar playing as he did to jazz.

He acquired something of a legendary status very early in his career, first because he overcame the horrendous injuries of a caravan fire in 1928 that crippled his left hand, to become the supreme master of his instrument, and, second, because there was a paradox at the heart of his personality. At the same time as being an undoubted master of the guitar, with an easy charm that won him friends the world over, and a musical ear second to none, he was also illiterate, proud, and inconsiderate, and, at heart, an itinerant gipsy, who never came to terms with commercial success, was childlike in his handling of money, and repeatedly turned what might have been artistic triumphs into near disasters.[40]

The people into whose culture Django was born were "Manouches," predominantly French-speaking gipsies settled all over France and the Francophone areas of Belgium. In the two world wars this fluid, patchily documented, and largely untraceable community shrank rapidly: in the first war because they inhabited the area that became the fiercest zone of trench warfare, and in the second because of Nazi genocide. Nevertheless, the Manouche tradition was of immeasurable importance in creating Reinhardt's approach to jazz. In their study of the Francophone gipsy (Tsigane) tradition, François Billard and Alain Antonietto make the point that:

> In general, Tsiganes are sensitized to music while still very young, because of the role music plays in their everyday life, compared to the case in other societies. With them, no family event or rejoicing is without music – marriages, baptisms, celebrations.[41]

They go on to promote the idea that this total immersion in music, even despite the encroachment of modern diversions such as television, has produced a number of identifiable characteristics, most significantly a form of melancholy romantic expressivity, that are common to the entire tradition, and particularly to the twentieth-century dynasties of gipsy guitarists, the Reinhardts (Django, his brother Joseph, and son Babik), and other families such as the Ferrets (also known as Ferrés) and the Rosenbergs.

The different gipsy traditions that progressively arrived in France in the nineteenth century had collectively created the musical landscape of the Parisian subculture in which Reinhardt grew up. This began with the Zingari troupe in the 1840s, complete with Magyar costumes, and was followed by a progressive influx of Moldavian gipsies, who were gradually attaining a degree of freedom of movement in the nineteenth century after a past in which they had (from the fourteenth century) been the slaves (from which the word "slav" derives) of princes, boyars, and churchmen. By the mid-1860s, the first Transylvanian gipsies had arrived, bringing Bohemian and Romanian music with them, which again had a tradition of being performed in slavery.

The writer Alexandre Privat d'Anglemont (1815–59), who came from Guadeloupe in the French Antilles, and who became a member of the circle of Baudelaire and Dumas, made the point as early as 1854 that this had obvious parallels with the background of African-American slavery, in his description of an itinerant dark-skinned gipsy musician wandering the streets of Paris, playing either the mandolin or the single-stringed, long-necked fiddle known as a *gusle*:

> He is a gipsy of Wallachia, a Bohemian as we would say, born in Bucharest into the service of some Boyar. He is here in Paris to study, but he will return to his own land with French ideas, and hurrying to free his people. But what is freedom for a gipsy of Wallachia, any more than an American Negro, if it is not the right to do nothing? So he sets himself to wander the city, playing the gusle, and dancing all day long....[42]

There is, therefore, a shared background between Europe's first leading jazz musician and the African-Americans whose music he was to assimilate himself: a background of slavery and oppression. Also, they had in common a tradition of string-band playing, which I have already suggested was of great importance in the development of early jazz in America.

String playing was also the final element of gipsy influence on nineteenth-century Parisian music, through the work of the virtuoso violinists János Bihari, Mihály Barna, and Panna Czinka. These players were brilliant at extemporizing ornamental variations on any composition, in the manner of Paganini, but they also popularized the Hungarian *csárdás* and *verbunkos*, to concert-hall and vernacular audiences alike. The latter dance (originally symbolizing military recruitment), alternated slow passages with extremely rapid sections, and in French gipsy culture this approach spread to the *csárdás*, in due course leading to a slow introductory section and then to fast sections alternating between brisk and flat out. These dances, and their accompanying music with its improvised ornament, became staples of the Manouche string-band tradition, and would certainly have been regular components of the musical background of Reinhardt's childhood.

He and his guitarist brother Joseph were brought up by their mother in an encampment on the outskirts of Paris after World War I. Django had no formal education, learning most of what he knew by sneaking into cinemas and watching films, as well as playing billiards and poker like a demon in local bars, and acquiring a taste for gambling that never left him. He did not show much interest in music until he was twelve, when he begged for a guitar, and was eventually given a six-string guitar-banjo. To his family's astonishment, he mastered it within a few weeks, and before long he was accompanying his uncle in the seedier bars around the Porte de Clignancourt.

The same year (1921) Reinhardt started to play professionally with an accordionist called Guérino. From the waltzes and romances he later composed and played on unaccompanied guitar, it is clear that the French café music from his time with Guérino was also subtly absorbed into his style. Guérino specialized in playing a particularly seedy species of Parisian dive, the *bals-musettes*, which presented music to accompany the transactions of pimps, whores, and gangsters. Reinhardt's apprenticeship was in this atmosphere, in darkened clubs heavy with Gauloises and cheap scent.

Reinhardt graduated from *bals-musettes* to many other kinds of musical entertainment, sitting in with café groups, winning talent contests, and playing for dances of all sorts. His main fame came from the skill with which he played the popular American dance tunes of the day, which he learned at first hand from expatriate bands like Billy Arnold's, or from the African-American revues that came to town. In 1928, he made his first records (all of French café music, mainly with accordionist Jean Vaissade), and he received an offer from English bandleader Jack Hylton that looked set to make his name.

It was never to be. On November 2, 1928, Reinhardt accidentally ignited a collection of artificial flowers in his caravan. The resulting inferno left him with horrendous burns to his right leg and left hand. For some days it looked as if he would lose his leg, but it was saved, and he learned to play the guitar again, even though his third and fourth fingers were crippled, and his hand had to be dressed medically for almost eighteen months. Only willpower got him walking normally again, but with immense self-determination Reinhardt was back on the Paris scene as a musician by mid-1930.

During a period of traveling, Reinhardt met Louis Vola, a multi-instrumentalist who ended up employing him back in Paris, where he met a number of musicians who were to become his long-term colleagues, including bandleader André Ekyan and the violinist and pianist Stephane Grappelli. By now, Reinhardt's main work was playing American-style dance music (albeit with a French accent, on tunes such as Michel Warlop's *Presentation Stomp*) and French *chansons*, on which singers such as Jean and Germaine Sablon, Elaine De Creus, and Aimé Simon-Girard were accompanied by Reinhardt's mixture of jazz chording and Manouche ornamentation. (Jean Sablon's *Le Même Coup*, from April 1933, exemplifies these discs, and combines some remarkable playing behind the vocal with a brief but brilliant solo.)

In 1934, not long after an English tour with Ekyan, Grappelli and Reinhardt found themselves in Louis Vola's band again at the Hotel Claridge. In the interval they started duetting, and guitarist Roger Chaput and Vola himself, on bass, joined them. The resulting quartet of violin, two guitars, and bass, although having many similarities with African-American string bands, was unusual in European jazz at the time, and its sound appealed to the writer and producer Charles Delauney, who presented concerts on behalf of the Hot Club of France. Delauney, and his Hot Club colleague, Pierre Noury, found they were extremely popular, especially once Django's brother, Joseph Reinhardt, joined them on a second rhythm guitar.

It is important to point out that although both Reinhardt and Grappelli had heard recordings by the American duo of Venuti and Lang through a mutual friend and record collector, Emile Savitry, these American discs were not particularly well-known in France, and had none of the popularity they had acquired in England or Germany. Reinhardt and Grappelli may have assimilated some superficial aspects of their approach to ensemble playing from the Americans, who began recording together some years earlier in the late 1920s, but Grappelli was always at pains to point out that they "had nothing to learn from Eddie Lang."[43] In particular, Reinhardt's solo style, capitalizing on the nasal, metallic tone of the metal-stringed Selmer guitar, using bursts of percussive power, alternation between extended single lines and chordal phrases, and ornaments ranging from trills and tremolos to elaborate melodic variations, was altogether more fully developed and emotionally powerful than Lang's, carrying with it the full weight of Manouche tradition.

For the majority of its discs, the quintet settled into a regular format, typified by *Runnin' Wild*, from April 1937. Grappelli would play the opening melody fairly straightforwardly on violin, and then on the second chorus would add a modest level of variation, accompanied by bass, two rhythm guitars, and Reinhardt, also playing rhythm. Then, for the third and fourth choruses, Reinhardt would play solo, before ushering in Grappelli for a much freer improvised chorus, leading to a final "out" chorus reminiscent of a Dixieland band, where the rhythmic tension is stepped up by the double bass slapping a four–four rhythm, and behind Grappelli's solo line, Reinhardt adds tremolos, urgent punctuations, and heavily accented chords to the even chug of the other rhythm instruments.

For the most part, Grappelli's urbane violin was more fluent that Joe Venuti's, and his phrases tended to run across bar-lines for several measures in flowing melodic thought-patterns that were to be his trademark well into his final years in the 1990s. Reinhardt, however, generally produced playing of even more exceptional originality. On *Runnin' Wild*, he opens his solo in the middle register with some repeated octaves, only breaking into his familiar runs in the second half of the chorus. In his second run-through, his phrasing adopts question-and-answer routines, and in a long downward run of repeated note clusters he varies the place on which his heaviest accent falls on each repetition. His closing runs dash breezily through the harmonic structure of the tune, but he adds glancing allusions to augmented and dimished chords as he goes, constantly creating and releasing tension between his own implied harmonies and those of the written tune, played by the accompanying guitars. Structurally, tonally, rhythmically, and melodi-cally, this is playing of a high order, and across the quintet's overall output, in those examples of pieces where more than one take exist, Reinhardt demonstrates that although he consistently applies certain formulae, he plays quite differently on each. In this he has certain similarities to the stride and boogie-woogie pianists I have already discussed, whose improvisation involves placing familiar motifs in new settings. Reinhardt's motifs seem to derive equally from his own imagination, from his listening to jazz on record, and from the Manouche tradition.

The Manouche influence is strongest in solo pieces such as *Parfum* (April 1937), where such jazz devices as chordal passages and bent "blue" notes alternate with runs, rhythmic punctuations, and out-of-time interludes that have equally as much in common with flamenco. The mixture gets more complex on a piece like *St. Louis Blues* (September 1937), where Reinhardt plays solo, with just a single guitar and bass for accompaniment. Although the opening chorus has something in common with blues guitar, with long, bent notes and simple phrasing, the remainder of the piece interpolates numerous ideas from the gipsy tradition, including an apparent speeding up after the minor section, where the underlying harmonies continue at the original tempo, but for twelve measures the rhythm section marks eighth-notes rather than quarter-notes.

Within the small world of Parisian jazz, the quintet, which adopted the name of the Hot Club, was recognized by the mid-1930s as of unusually high quality in both its concerts and recordings, and Reinhardt began to mix on equal terms with visiting American jazz musicians. He formed a strong friendship with Coleman Hawkins, with whom he later recorded. The quintet itself made a steady stream of ever more impressive discs, but on many other Parisian record sessions, Reinhardt sat in with such visitors as Benny Carter, Bill Coleman, Dicky Wells, Rex Stewart, and Barney Bigard, proving himself to be a soloist of similar caliber. To them, he was a revelation, as Coleman, who was hired as a guest vocalist with the quintet, remembered:

> One of the guitarists was the greatest I had ever heard, because guitars in those days played mostly rhythm style. But this fellow took solos and had ideas and a technique that was out of this world . . . the solo guitarist was Django Reinhardt.[44]

Nevertheless, Reinhardt was restricted to playing rhythm guitar on some recordings on which Coleman appears on trumpet under Dicky Wells's leadership, but even his chordal playing commands the attention, almost as effectively as his soloing, and his sudden tremolos behind Coleman on *Sweet Sue* (July 7, 1937) are electrifying. The trumpeter's *Bill Coleman Blues*, made a few months later, is a spontaneous duet with Reinhardt, and shows the two-way flow of ideas that made Reinhardt's work genuinely inspirational. Among other American partnerships, he also jammed with Duke Ellington at a Paris club, cementing a friendship that would lead to a tour of the United States after World War II.

Like many European musicians, the quintet ignored the growing signs of war. Early in 1939, the group went to Scandinavia, unaware that visas were now required to pass through Germany. Given the heritage of most of the group, and the Third Reich's attitude to gipsies, it was lucky they were only briefly held up and questioned by the German authorities. When war was declared, the quintet was on what had become one of its regular visits to London. At the sound of the first air-raid siren, an event which, although it was a false alarm, turned out to be one of the few moments of drama in the so-called "phoney war" of the fall of 1939, Reinhardt panicked and set off for France, leaving not only Grappelli but also his guitar behind in London. The group was separated throughout the war, and although it was reunited afterwards, the old magic was not always recaptured as time went on, and fashions in music moved away from the swing era into bebop. Reinhardt was better equipped than the others to tackle modern jazz, his quick ear giving him an immediate response to the sounds of Dizzy Gillespie and Bud Powell, and George Shearing told me that he heard Reinhardt sit in on 52nd Street during his visit to New York in 1946, playing bebop tunes with the same ease as his swing repertoire. Nevertheless, even Reinhardt's immense genius was almost swept aside by changes in public taste and prevailing jazz fashion.

Before the German occupation of France, Reinhardt had carried on his normal life in Paris, playing hither and yon, and, like many Parisians, behaving as if there were not a war on. He fled before the German advance, but he then returned to Paris and began to make a living inside the German occupied zone. As a gipsy, he was certainly more likely to survive by taking a high-profile role as an entertainer, and he formed a new quintet, with the inexperienced young clarinetist Hubert Rostaing taking Grappelli's place. As an antidote to the cultural mores of the Nazis – and bearing out my point about the laxer attitude to jazz that the Germans took in their Francophone occupied countries – Parisians suddenly sought out swing, and the band became very popular.

Reinhardt became sufficiently famous that he was able to behave in a way that few other musicians, let alone gipsies, could during the occupation. In 1942, obviously having acquired the requisite travel documentation from the Nazi authorities, he went to Belgium with his band, and cut several records with local musicians as well, including two haunting sides on which he plays violin with a lyrical melancholy that suggests he had been playing the instrument all his life.

Right at the end of the war, the precariousness of his position finally dawning on him, Reinhardt tried to make his way to Switzerland. At Thonon, close to the border, he played regularly for mixed French and German audiences. He was arrested on the eve of his attempted escape to Switzerland, and only the fact that the local German commandant was a jazz fan saved his life. Once he had been set free, the locals thought he must be a collaborator. When he finally reached the border, he was not admitted. The Swiss, being neutral, were prepared to admit Jews and black people, but despite evidence of Nazi brutality to gipsies they would not admit Reinhardt. Dejectedly he made his way back to Paris, where he saw out the remainder of the war, for some of the time fronting a club named after him.

Reinhardt's most consistent playing was in the Quintet of the Hot Club of France, but his 1930s discs with American visitors, and a handful of his later recordings on electric guitar, are also indicative of his extraordinary talent. He was the figurehead of a school of gipsy-influenced guitar players that was still current across Europe at the start of the twenty-first century, of whom the most significant include Christian Escoudé, Bireli Lagrene, Boulu and Elios Ferré, Fapy Lafertin, and the Rosenberg family. He was also influential on many Americans. Fats Waller's regular guitarist Al Casey, for example, told me that in the mid-1930s he saw Reinhardt as a major influence, as important to his playing as Charlie Christian became at the end of that decade.[45] In the latter half of the twentieth century, Reinhardt continued to be an important influence in the United States, acknowledged by players as different as Charlie Byrd, Barney Kessell, and Joe Pass.

In Reinhardt's lifetime, the Argentinean guitarist Oscar Alemán had a very similar approach to the instrument. Alemán came to Europe in 1931, with a guitar duo called Los Lobos, specializing in tango, but with a hunger to learn jazz. His appetite whetted by hearing Don Dean in Brazil, he settled in Paris in 1932 and accompanied Josephine Baker and Freddy Taylor. He took Reinhardt's percussive approach and fluid phrasing back to South America when he returned there later, as demonstrated in his 1942 recording of *I Got Rhythm* (*Tengo Ritmo*) made in Buenos Aires.

In Europe during the 1930s several groups were established that looked to Reinhardt and the quintet for stylistic inspiration rather than to the United States. These included guitarist Marcel Mortier and the Quintette du Hot Club de Belgique, Sven Stiberg and the Svenska Hotkvintetten, Robert Normann in Norway, and Ingmar Englund with the Rytmi Swing Ensemble in Finland. Grappelli's influence as a soloist was also important and he is regarded as the father of a school of French jazz violinists that includes Jean-Luc Ponty, Didier Lockwood, and Dominique Pifarely.

## Elsewhere in Europe

In the 1920s, attitudes to jazz polarized in Sweden more dramatically than in any other European country. There was a backlash against what was described by a group of leading cultural personalities as the "infectious disease" of jazz, and they enlisted the support of the Swedish Musicians' Union in petitioning the government to prevent any importation of the music.[46] Despite this, there were numerous (and continual) local attempts to assimilate the sounds of ragtime and jazz, and, in due course, by 1930 the very same Musicians' Union that had been so hostile underwent a *volte face*, and began to promote "propaganda" concerts at which Swedish jazz was featured.

Musicians from Canada, the United States, Britain, and the other Scandinavian countries brought ragtime and Dixieland styles to Sweden in the early 1920s, but one of the first local bands to have any genuine jazz feeling was the Chrystal Band, led by pianist Helge Lindberg, whose trombonist Harry Hednoff played improvised solos with a swinging bravado on discs such as *He's the Hottest Man in Town* (recorded for Polyphon in January 1926).

Also in 1926, members of the Svenska Paramount-orkestern played on a transatlantic liner, which gave them access when they arrived in New York to such American players as Bix Beiderbecke and Joe Venuti. The band's violinist Folke "Göken" Andersson was a competent improviser, and solos such as his chorus on the 1928 discs *Det var i sommernattens elvte timma* and *Tambou* have a sense of structure and line that melds Venuti's approach with motifs that are clearly borrowed from Scandinavian fiddle music – a style which takes over completely on another disc, *Alla kvinnor ä' lika dana*. However, even on this folk-based tune, trumpeter Gösta "Smyget" Redlig leads the ensemble with the same jaunty brightness as Beiderbecke, and his solo playing owes much to the Davenport cornetist.

By the end of the 1920s, Sweden was beginning to produce some quantity of creditable local jazz musicians, notably in the band led by pianist Håken von Eichwald. By this time, in France jazz was chic, in Germany it had decadent overtones, and in Britain it was seen as having its natural home in dance venues like the Hammersmith Palais or on the music hall and theatrical circuit, where most visiting Americans played. Swedish musicians, however, trying to play jazz, trod a fine line between the idea on the one hand that their music was a form of comedy (such as the frenetic animal impressions on George Enders's hilarious *Hund och katt* from 1929), and on the other that it should be saccharine dance music. There was a similar perception in the other Scandinavian countries and in the Netherlands, where the growth of the music followed in the wake of Swedish developments.

In Sweden, von Eichwald's band recorded prolifically from 1930, with some creative arrangements and a growing confidence among its soloists. Most fascinating is the way it tackles material drawn from African-American bands in a style that owes more to white musicians such as Adrian Rollini and Bix Beiderbecke – a good example being the November 1932 recording of Cab Calloway's *Scat Song*, which has a Venuti-styled violin solo from Clarence Toresen and Bixian trumpet from Redlig and Åke Johanssen-Jangell.

Once jazz had lost its controversial status in Sweden and become part of the mainstream of 1930s entertainment, von Eichwald became known as Der Schwedische Jazzkönig (the Swedish Jazz King), and as well as playing at the fashionable Kaos nightclub in Stockholm, he toured and recorded in Germany, and also visited Switzerland and Czechoslovakia. The period's other significant leader was Arne Hülphers (who took over Von Eichwald's line-up in 1934), and in his best recordings he steered his orchestra towards a more African-American feel in its rhythm and solo playing, a good example being his version of Will Hudson's *Harlem Heat* (December 1934).[47]

By this point in the 1930s Swedish jazz had a number of parallels with Britain. First, local musicians were beginning to obtain and play arrangements by Ellington, whose orchestra's influence increased as that of the Beiderbecke/Whiteman school declined. Just as Billy Cotton made discs of Ellington charts, so too did the Swedish TOGO band, a semi-professional orchestra whose informal 1934 version of *Rockin' in Rhythm* shows considerable understanding of the Ellington style. Second, visiting Americans who spent time with local players exerted considerable influence in shaping their approach to jazz. Benny Carter's 1936 recordings with his Swedish All Stars and the Sonora Swing Band are not quite as polished as the discs he made with his long-term associates in London, but it is obvious that he encouraged a confidence among the soloists, in particular, trumpeter Thore Ehrlong, who bases his concept of phrasing on Armstrong and "Red"

Allen rather than his countrymen's usual taste for Beiderbecke.

In 1939, the African-American vocalist and trumpeter Valaida Snow, having made numerous discs in London, recorded in Scandinavia with Lulle Ellboj in Stockholm and Winstrup Olesen in Denmark, and she, too, demonstrated the degree to which a confident American soloist could add cohesion and confidence to European bands.

Denmark's jazz scene developed more or less in parallel with that in Sweden, and reed player Kai Ewans was the equivalent to von Eichwald and Hülphers, his orchestra backing Benny Carter and also playing some original arrangements by Kai Moller and Leo Mathiesen that accurately captured the American idiom of the late 1930s.

Jazz in Belgium was established roughly contemporaneously with Sweden and Denmark, and the country was visited by numerous African-American entertainers in the 1920s. Local musicians soon adopted some of the ideas of jazz. Notable among them was the Brussels-born pianist Clement Doucet, who spent time working for an organ-builder in the United States in the early 1920s, and got to know George Gershwin and his circle. On his return to Europe, in 1924, he began his lengthy recording career by cutting ragtime piano rolls in Paris, and then going on to record for French Columbia and Pathé, playing solos that were a mixture of ragtime, novelty piano, and jazz. He also participated in ensemble recordings with the French pianist and bandleader Jean Wiener. One of the first recordings ever made by an all-Belgian group of musicians is *Slippery Elm*, made in London during June 1927 by Charles Remue and his New Stompers Orchestra. Despite the slightly hesitant character of the leader's clarinet solo, the band has a cohesiveness and swing comparable to many contemporary American groups. Remue remained in London to work with the Savoy Orpheans after his band cut its recordings in Britain, but he subsequently returned to Brussels and joined the orchestra led by his former pianist, Stan Brenders. This band went on to become the national radio big band, and it was Brenders who backed Django Reinhardt on his visit to Belgium during the occupation.

Reinhardt also recorded with Fud Candrix, whose lengthy career as a big-band leader began in the mid-1930s, his main rivals being Jean Omer and Eddie Tower.

Although it is generally regarded to have recorded such pieces as Jelly Roll Morton's *Shreveport Stomp* in Berlin in 1926, Gregoire Nakchounian and His Russian North Star Orchestra, led by an Armenian clarinetist, was largely Dutch, and some discographers believe the recordings, made for the

Vox label, might actually have been cut in Amsterdam. The band is known to have cut a second session for Vox in Berlin in early 1927, but it indicates a healthy awareness of jazz among Dutch players from the mid-1920s. Certainly by 1929, when Adrian Rollini made a visit to Amsterdam, there was a strong contingent of local enthusiasts and players, organized by Max Goyarts, who seems to have played a similar role to that of Charles Delaunay in France.[48]

As in Britain, contests for amateur bands were organized in both Holland and Belgium, and the Dutch winners of the Brussels International Jazz Championship in the mid-1930s went on to record in 1936–7. The identity of the band is unclear, but the spoken introduction to their record of *Limehouse Blues* begins with the words: "Hey kid, d'you know where the Lumirex Mike Serenaders are playing?" This cryptic clue suggests the band was originally hired to promote the Lumirex Studio in The Hague. It recorded in the style of a Philadelphia small group like the Washboard Rhythm Kings, with heavy slapped string bass and straightforward swinging solos, but because its discs were issued on glass-based acetates, very few have survived.[49]

Like those musicians discussed so far who worked elsewhere in Europe, Dutch and Belgian musicians, amateur and professional, benefitted from the presence of experienced American players. Principal among them was pianist Freddy Johnson, who worked widely in Europe in the 1930s and 1940s, until he was arrested by the Nazis and eventually repatriated to the United States during World War II. He co-led a band with the Surinamese saxophonist Lex Van Spall, which was recorded at a session promoted by the Hot Club of Haarlem at the Casino Hamdorff in Laren, and demonstrated a lively and convincing grasp of swing.

The most accomplished of all the Low Countries' bands, however, was Het Ramblers Dansorkest, "The Ramblers," formed in 1926 by pianist Theo Uden Masman to play in an Amsterdam cabaret. It was a year or two later — certainly after the first convincing Swedish records — that the band began to play consistently high-quality jazz on disc, but by the late 1920s it was as well-established as that of von Eichwald, and traveling throughout Europe. It became the house orchestra of the VARA radio station, which widened the range of its repertoire, and jazz became just one element in its work as a popular dance orchestra, which continued until its eventual dissolution in 1964. Nevertheless, a recording like *Wabash Blues*, cut in The Hague during February 1935, and mainly featuring a small group from within its ranks, known as the "Swingin' Rascals," is a perfect example of why this band was such a good accompanying orchestra for Americans like Coleman Hawkins and Benny Carter. It could swing well, it had good soloists, and above all a real sense of being a band, with everyone working together in the rhythm to support the soloists, and arranged brass and reeds.

The development of jazz in Russia is more complex than in other parts of Europe, as the music emerged just as Russia was entering a period of violent upheaval. In the last tsarist days, prior to the revolution, there had been a general enthusiasm for ragtime and cake-walks, but under Bolshevism there was a conflict of ideological interest not unlike that which was later to exist in Germany. In principle, the country's new rulers disapproved of American popular music, since it was strongly identified with Western capitalist society. In practice, such music was ideally suited to the tastes of the great majority of the post-revolutionary population that was neither peasant nor nobility, and it continued to enjoy considerable popularity once the echoes of the civil war began to die away. The catalyst for inspiring the move from ragtime to jazz in the emergent Soviet Union was Louis Mitchell, whose Parisian group was the inspiration for Kurt Strobel's "Murphy Band," which he led in Estonia from 1919, and for the jazz band assembled by the poet and intellectual Valentin Parnakh in Moscow during October 1922.[50]

Parnakh's band appears to have played syncopated two-step and ragtime dances, with a minimum of improvisation (if any) and a maximum of eccentricity, in keeping with the idea that jazz was somehow bound up with the intellectual *avant-garde*, as part of which the group appeared in a play presented by the experimental director Vsevolod Meierhold in 1922. However, as time went on and jazz became better-established during the period of Lenin's New Economic Policy (N.E.P.), up until 1928, helped by the visits of Sidney Bechet (with Benny Peyton's Band) and Sam Wooding's orchestra, the music became less two-dimensional and more enmeshed in popular culture. However, as S. Frederick Starr suggests in his history of jazz in the Soviet Union, "for the next half century jazz in the U.S.S.R. was saddled with the image of decadence and abandon which all true Stalinists applied to the N.E.P. era as a whole."[51]

This image was at odds with Stalin's regime in Russia from 1929, as the N.E.P. was left behind and the Cultural Revolution began, and while some writers of the time were still keen to espouse the concept of jazz as a pure form of proletarian expression, a majority sided with such heavyweights as Maxim Gorky, who wrote derisively of its sound, or with the Association of Proletarian Musicians, who sought to have jazz banned, partly for xenophobic reasons and partly because the very message of individual freedom embodied in an improvised "people's music" was in conflict with the centralist, puritanical control of popular taste they sought to impose. However, the relaxation of the Cultural Revolution in 1932 re-established jazz to some degree, and many dance orchestras, billed as "jazz bands," appeared in fashionable Moscow hotels.

The degree to which any of these played what would be recognized elsewhere in the world as jazz is questionable, but the principal musician to work towards establishing a local style that included improvisation, spontaneity, workable arrangements, and a degree of swing was the pianist Alexander Tsfasman, whose first band was established to promote the products of the A.M.A. music publishing firm in 1928. He kept going through the Cultural Revolution, and became a major figure in the resurgence of jazz in the mid-1930s. Tsfasman had spent six years at the Moscow Conservatory, and his formal training helped him to create well-crafted charts for his band, which progressively grew from a six-piece Dixieland-style line-up, modeled on Benny Peyton's visiting group, to an eleven-piece band, plus an African-American tap-dancer. Despite the political climate of the time, Tsfasman espoused all things American (a country he never visited), and his dapper suits, fondness for gambling, and prima donna behavior were all designed to cock a snook at the drabness of an unimaginative regime. His discs are generally of American standard, and he was a master of contrasts, such as the transition on one of his early 1930s records, of Irving Berlin's *Always*, from a beautifully written introduction for strings to the main, rhythmic big-band arrangement.

His overt fondness for America and Americana brought him into disfavor in the late 1930s, and although he returned to lead a new band and entertain wartime troops behind the Russian front, his bandleading career was eventually ended by the state in 1947. He was recognized and honored after Stalin's death, but his contribution to jazz in the Soviet Union was over by the early 1940s. Nevertheless, in the fifteen years or so of his active career as a jazz musician, Tsfasman had proved that it was possible to assimilate a working knowledge of jazz mainly from recordings, and to use that as the basis for development quite independently from the United States.

Also active during the 1930s and, in his way, keeping the flame burning for jazz in the Soviet Union was Leonid Utesov. A man who had begun his entertainment career in the circus, he brought a passionate interest in circus clowns and theater together with his enthusiasm for jazz to create a hybrid of jazz and theatrical performance, which translates as "Thea-jazz." He modeled his act on that of Ted Lewis, but not the musical excellence of

Lewis's sidemen Jimmy Dorsey and Muggsy Spanier, who had made such an impression in Britain, rather the corny, jokey, top-hatted entertainer-clarinetist himself. Utesov's main musical achievement was to have presented a reasonably authentic and convincing form of jazz to a popular audience, while generally conveying to the regime the impression that he was satirizing this decadent form of American entertainment.

Certainly, Tsfasman and Utesov, together with a small coterie of Muscovite bandleaders, succeeded in bringing some aspects of genuine jazz to the Soviet Union, but by the late 1930s time was running out, and the demise of the music was accelerated by the formation of an unwieldy State Jazz Orchestra in late 1938.

Jazz was moribund until the alliance with the United States during World War II, following the German invasion, spawned a brief renaissance. Along with American vehicles, aid, and equipment came recordings, and – for those close to the front – broadcasts. Soviet bands obtained American arrangements, and there was a leap forward into the swing era for those in war-torn Russia.

Perhaps the most remarkable story is that of cornetist Eddie Rosner, a Polish Jew who ended up fronting the State Jazz Orchestra of Byelorussia during World War II. He had led a flourishing and famous big band featuring his own Harry James-styled solos, which was based in Germany and Poland before the war. When the Germans invaded Poland, he sought safety with the Russians. Instead of being shipped off to Stalin's camps with many fellow Poles, his band became the most accomplished Soviet jazz orchestra, a standard Rosner maintained even when some of his Polish sidemen left for the army and he replaced them with new musicians from the Baltic states. By the end of the war, Rosner, along with Utesov, who was leading the main State Jazz Orchestra, was a well-known musician, akin to a national hero. Within a year and a half, in the wake of yet another reversal by the Stalinist regime, jazz was outlawed once more, and in the decades that followed it became a music of resistance and rebellion.


## Further Afield

Jazz spread during the pre-war years to many parts of the world, but outside Europe the main developments were in South America and Asia. Argentina, in particular, was important, and I have already mentioned the contribution of guitarist Oscar Alemán. One notable pioneer of jazz in the country was Don Dean's band, which was modeled on the style of an American college band of the late 1920s. Its discs include some exceptional jazz violin and guitar solos, and the band's alto saxophonist had some of the mannerisms of the white Chicagoans. Don Dean McClusky was an American who spent some years living in Argentina and made a number of discs for the local branch of the Victor company. Discographers are still seeking the names of his band of mainly Buenos Aires musicians with a couple of Americans added.

Argentina was also the destination for Sam Wooding's orchestra on its 1927 return to the American continent from its first European tour. Wooding believed that he "opened up" Argentina to jazz, and it is certainly the case that his entire traveling revue would have been one of the most polished American acts to have appeared in the numerous cities the tour visited.[52]

Other Americans who made their mark in South America included saxophonist and trumpeter Frank "Big Boy" Goudie, who fled from Paris ahead of the German occupation to join a band at the Cabaret Mexico in Rio De Janeiro. His view was that Brazil had been underexposed to jazz, and that in 1940 a full American band "would be such a novelty they'd have to call the cops to keep the crowds away." Given the significant part that Brazil was to play in the development of jazz from the 1950s onwards, Goudie's observations suggest it had had little direct contact music with the music prior to 1940, and the leader of a local group of singers with whom he worked is quoted as saying: "The American white man has brought his prejudice to us; we need the colored man to bring us his talents."[53]

The American musician who will most be remembered for taking jazz to the Orient was pianist Teddy Weatherford. He first went east with Jack Carter's band in 1926, but chose not to return to the United States with his colleagues. Instead, he went on to lead a series of bands in Singapore, Manila, and Shanghai. It was from there that he was sent back, in 1934, to the United States to recruit an all-American band to play at a new Shanghai ballroom called the Canidrome. The owners had heard Duke Ellington's records and wanted a similar band. Weatherford sent Buck Clayton's Harlem Gentlemen, a collection of some of Los Angeles's best session players, led by the man who was later to become Count Basie's star trumpeter. "We didn't have anything in the first place, so we had nothing to lose," recalled Clayton. "Things were so cheap in China that fifty dollars stretched a long way compared to America."[54]

While Clayton took his band to China, where other expatriates were also employed, Teddy Weatherford went on to India, where he held down a long residency in Calcutta, also working in Bombay and in what was then Ceylon. He died of cholera in Calcutta in 1945, but not before he had cut several discs with a trio and big band. Among numerous examples of other early jazz recordings from the sub-continent, the discs by Jimmy Lequime's Grand Hotel Orchestra, which were recorded in Calcutta in 1926, stand out. This group had a core of Californian musicians who met up in India with their international colleagues from Russia, the Philippines, South Africa, and Austria. The band's work contains an early example of an Al Bowlly vocal, a precursor of the many sides he and pianist Monia Liter were to make after both moved to London. Lequime (who may have originally hailed from Canada) was a balanced trumpeter whose work combines invention and swing.

Perhaps the most high-profile jazz musician in the older styles of jazz to be popular in the Orient was Adulyadej Bhumibol, who played clarinet in the style of Benny Goodman, but who only ever recorded privately owing to the demands of his day job as King of Thailand.

# PART II

# From Swing to Bop

# CHAPTER 6

# Small Groups in Transition

## Swing Street

Soon up arose 52nd Street downtown. It had a long row of
joints, but more elaborate: the Three Deuces, the Onyx
Club, the Yacht Club, Leon and Eddie's, Jimmy Ryan's – a
good dozen of sizzling clubs.

Danny Barker, from *A Life in Jazz*

Two short blocks of midtown Manhattan, between Fifth and Seventh
Avenues, became the jazz capital of the world for just over a decade from
the mid-1930s. Known variously as "Swing Street" or the "street that never
slept," West 52nd Street was home to upwards of a dozen different clubs,
all of which became to some degree jazz legends. There were regular
changes of name, location, and ownership, but all these venues in the
basements of a row of crumbling brownstone houses offered the very best in
jazz in a proximity and profusion unmatched anywhere else in the world. By
the early 1940s, established stars like Lester Young and Coleman Hawkins
played cheek-by-jowl with a new generation of up-and-coming names like
Thelonious Monk, Max Roach, and Dizzy Gillespie, while even the noisiest
basement became stilled as Billie Holiday stepped up to the footlights and
sang her langorous ballads.

In the 1920s, a number of small speakeasies had opened up on West
52nd Street, while prohibition was still in force. Nowadays, with its densely
packed, high-rise buildings amid an area of big business, it is hard to imagine
a time when the section running west to Seventh Avenue was a couple of
blocks of down-at-heel brownstones mainly used for housing, as only one or

two isolated buildings survive from that era when Midtown Manhattan was on a more human scale. But beginning in the late twenties, exactly as had happened a little earlier in Harlem, the basements began one by one to be taken over as long, narrow clubs. The similarity of the buildings was such that all the clubs were fundamentally the same. There would be a coat check after you came down the few steps inside the front door, a bar running along the side of the room, a small stage straight ahead, and perhaps a kitchen out at the back, next to a cramped band room.[1]

One of the earliest speakeasies on the Street was the Onyx Club, at number 35, which first opened its doors in 1927. It was run by Joe Helbock, and patrons might be entertained by a pianist, such as Joe Sullivan, or a singing string band, such as the Spirits of Rhythm. When prohibition was finally repealed in December 1933, the Onyx set the standard for the new type of jazz club that would dominate 52nd Street. Early in 1934, Helbock moved over the road to number 72 and reopened as a full-scale nightclub, and before long his old premises had taken on a new identity as the Famous Door. Where there had been one club there were now two, and the Onyx had moved up-market by hiring Art Tatum as its main act, alongside the ever-popular Spirits of Rhythm.

Soon, two clubs became four, and so on, as the area's nightlife expanded apace, and, as was so often the case in the history of jazz, organized crime took a hand in making this happen, and in shifting the focus of jazz in New York to this district of Midtown. In the latter years of prohibition, as well as the venues I mentioned in Chapter 3, where the stride pianists held sway, or the large cabarets and dance halls where the big bands worked, a row of small clubs had been established on 133rd Street in the very core of Harlem. All of them began as speakeasies, and as 1934 dawned they made the transition to legitimate (or at least outwardly legitimate) clubs. They had slightly wild names like the Mad House, Mexico's and the Nest, as well as the more prosaic Tillie's and Jerry's. The majority of these uptown venues were owned by mobsters, the gangland bosses of New York, and as guitarist Danny Barker put it:

> It was common to see taxi cabs roll uptown loaded with the bosses and the help. They would come uptown after closing time for more good times. There, the bosses saw whites spending money like crazy after getting boozed up. Downtown those same wild spenders were tight-fisted and reserved. . . .[2]

Musicians like Barker tell of the scenes that went on in the after-hours Harlem clubs, where all would be quiet and peaceful until well after midnight when the first customers showed up. Waiters, musicians, and dancers would all be sitting around talking or reading, until at a sign from the doorman they would spring into action. The band would strike up, singers and dancers would appear from nowhere, strutting their stuff on a tiny stage or between the tables, while the waiters sang along with the band or rattled their trays noisily to create the sound of applause. From a somnolent doze, the club would become a hive of exotic activity in a matter of seconds.

After a while the same gangland bosses who had made uptown the fashionable after-hours place to be decided that they would become even better off if they could persuade the big spenders to part with their money downtown, without having to make the half-hour cab ride northwards into deepest Harlem. There were more people with money downtown, so why not create as many opportunities as possible for them to spend it?

The musicians who worked in the bands that provided entertainment for many Harlem clubs watched as the mob went into action to move the epicenter of jazz nightlife to 52nd Street. Not only were the new downtown clubs set up and equipped more lavishly than the Harlem "joints," but they hired big names to provide their entertainment. Eventually, in 1936, even the prestigious Cotton Club relocated downtown, to 200 West 48th Street, just four short blocks from "Swing Street." Hand-in-hand with the move southwards, a press campaign was being waged to dissuade casual visitors from making the trek to Harlem. "There appeared in the scandal newspaper columns in bold black print: 'Be careful going to Harlem. You risk being mugged, beaten and robbed,' " wrote Danny Barker.[3]

By 1935, the Onyx, the Famous Door, the Hickory House, the Yacht Club, Leon and Eddie's, Tony's, and the 21 Club were all in operation on 52nd Street. At this point in their history, these new clubs were mainly segregated, and it would not be until the end of the decade in 1939, when Barney Josephson opened his Café Society in Greenwich Village, that integration among audiences began in earnest. Nevertheless, from the outset, just as they employed African-American waiters and bar attendants, Helbock and a number of other club owners on 52nd Street presented mainly African-American musicians — a legacy of the kind of thinking that had brought big-spending crowds to Harlem's clubs, and which had also influenced record company policy in the 1920s and early 1930s. As music historian Scott DeVeaux put it:

Although they might prefer for social reasons to have their musical needs satisfied by musicians of their own race, white audiences before the swing era were more inclined to believe that black bands could authentically deliver the "hot stuff" and were ultimately more comfortable seeing blacks rather than whites engaged in such a subversive activity.[4]

Throughout the 1930s, the majority of 52nd Street clubs catered exclusively for white patrons, but most (especially those that employed mainly African-American musicians) would relax their segregation rules sufficiently to let a select few black people in, even if only to sit in the band room, the kitchen, or the cloakroom. Some formerly famous personalities, such as old-time pianists and blues singers who now found work hard to get, took to running the hat and coat checks, so they could be part of the new musical scene, one notable example being bluesman Cow Cow Davenport, who became washroom attendant at the Onyx. But, as pianist Sammy Price recalled:

> Some places on 52nd Street were kind of funny too. Like Leon and Eddie's and the 21 Club. [If you were black] you didn't even go that way on 52nd Street – the buck stopped in the middle of the block west of Sixth Avenue. But Jimmy Ryan's wasn't lily white, 'cause they had black musicians playing there and occasionally black people went in.[5]

In other words, Ryan's, at number 53, was the furthest east that African-Americans would feel able to enter a club as patrons, without hindrance.

By the time that more than half a dozen clubs were in operation on the street, most offering entertainment, a broadly similar musical policy started to emerge. There would be a small band – often just a quartet – with a famous leader, such as trumpeter Henry "Red" Allen or saxophonist Pete Brown. This band would play sets of about 50 minutes, and alternate with an intermission act, either a solo pianist or, in the better-off venues, a trio, such as that of Nat King Cole or guitarist Al Casey (who provided backing for singer Billie Holiday).

In the early days following Prohibition, there were several notable exceptions to the prevailing employment of African-American musicians, and among the first bands that appeared on the street were white groups that generally followed the Dixieland model of clarinet and trumpet with rhythm, most notably those led by trumpeters Wingy Manone and Louis

Prima. These bands had something in common with a band that worked at the Famous Door in 1935, the Mound City Blue Blowers with singer and kazoo player Red McKenzie, trumpeter Bunny Berigan, and guitarist Eddie Condon.[6] Some of the more Dixieland-orientated groups carried on into the middle to late 1930s. Manone, for example, continued to trade for several years on the success of his 1935 hit record *Isle of Capri*, and when Prima set off for Chicago and Los Angeles, his role was taken over by another white New Orleans trumpeter, Sharkey Bonano, who played on the street with his Sharks of Rhythm from 1936. But, for the most part, the stylistic divisions among the groups playing on the street gradually began to erode, and an informal swing approach started to coalesce. More and more African-American players were employed, and many of these musicians made their living by flitting from one club to another or from one band to another as the weeks went by, creating a stylistic homogeneity. Instead of the counterpoint of the traditional New Orleans front line, with clarinet and trumpet, and sometimes a tailgate trombone as well, trumpeters and saxophonists started to play short unison phrases, or "riffs," based on, or paraphrasing, the tune, and soon most numbers began and ended with little more than such a unison riff, opening up in the middle of the piece for lengthy displays of soloing.

One of the most prodigious soloists, and a catalyst for introducing this type of loose swing arrangement, was violinist Stuff Smith, who took his band into the Onyx Club in 1936. His trumpeter, Jonah Jones, made his reputation at the club for long, dramatic solos in an Armstrong-influenced style: "With Stuff I had all the solos I wanted," he recalled. "I'd be there blowing, and Stuff would be playing riffs on his violin, muttering into my ear 'One more, Jonah! One more!.' "[7]

This process, with Jones soloing as Smith plays ever more forceful riffs behind him, is brilliantly exemplified on Smith's comic patter disc *Knock Knock, Who's There?*, from August 1936.

As well as those resident bands like Smith's, whose job it was to create this kind of exhilarating, electrifying solo playing night after night in the clubs, an added ingredient of excitement came from big-band stars sitting in with the house band. Musicians like Roy Eldridge and Chu Berry, while they were working together, first in the 1935 big band of Teddy Hill and a year later with Fletcher Henderson's re-formed orchestra, would drop in on a club after their job in a ballroom or theater, and then suddenly march up onto the stage to indulge in furious solo battles with the resident group. "Roy would heat up a club," recalled Danny Barker, and the people would come down and hear them. . . . Chu Berry and Roy Eldridge would be in there with a rhythm section and they would light up the place. After they left the Savoy, playing with Teddy Hill, they would go down to the clubs – about five or ten joints.[8]

At first, these cutting contests were the preserve of Harlem, but as the focus of jazz in New York moved downtown, the practice soon spread to the street, and was to continue into the 1940s as newer styles of jazz emerged.

Whether played by a resident pianist or small group, or by such energetic sitters-in as Eldridge and Berry, the music of the 52nd Street clubs increasingly became the informal counterpart of big-band swing. Rhythmically and harmonically, it was identical to the kind of music played by the African-American big bands of Calloway, Lunceford, or Basie, or the white bands of Goodman and Dorsey, with a four-to-the-bar even pulse, and the twelve-, sixteen- and 32-measure structures of popular songs. In place of the arranged passages for massed reeds and brass there were simple "head" arrangements, and plenty more space for solos, but in just the same way that there was little radical stylistic development in big-band swing between, say, Goodman's first *Let's Dance* broadcasts in 1934 and the end of the decade, over the same period there was little fundamental change in the overall style of most swing small groups either, once their *modus operandi* had been established.

This long and relatively stable period, during which swing grew into a genuinely popular style, accounts to a great extent for the reason that the changes in jazz that were to take place in the 1940s were seen at the time as so radical and revolutionary. In the brisk development of the music from a few years before the O.D.J.B.'s 1917 discs until the early 1930s, jazz had evolved at a breathless pace, but in the second half of the 1930s, for almost the first time, there was a period of consolidation, just as the music reached its widest-ever public. In the big bands, this consolidation was largely a question of stylistic nuance, of the emergence of dominant methods of arranging – the transition from the work of pioneers like Don Redman, Benny Carter, and Fletcher Henderson to the newer styles of Sy Oliver and Eddie Durham, or Eddie Sauter and Mel Powell. In the small groups, it was more to do with the expansion of the improvised solo, from the few measures most players were allowed within a big band chart to the endless choruses of unfettered extemporization so beloved of such players as Roy Eldridge, Chu Berry, Stuff Smith, and Jonah Jones. How little the contextual framework for such soloing changed during the decade was commented on by Coleman Hawkins, who was absent from the United States during his European period from early 1934 to 1939. "Man, when I went away, they were playing those same changes. Nothing changed. Maybe a little faster, but they're playing them same changes."[9]

Hawkins was to become one of the catalysts in introducing the new ideas that entered jazz as the 1940s began. During the heyday of swing on the street, he was out of the country, but as we shall see, even during his absence he exercised an influence on shaping the climate in which the changes of the 1940s became possible.

The popularity of the new swing small groups was enhanced by radio broadcasts direct from some of the 52nd Street clubs, like the Onyx and the Yacht Club. Some of the most glorious music by pianist Fats Waller and his Rhythm exists in his 1938 "airshot" recordings from the Yacht Club, where the listener eavesdrops on his little band playing a live session with none of the constraints of studio recording. Of course, no sooner had the clubs started this kind of broadcast than the phonograph companies wanted to record the bands that played on air, repackaging their new-found freedom back into the three minutes or so of the 78 r.p.m. disc.

All the main record companies (and, later, a few small independent firms, such as Milt Gabler's 1938 offshoot of his Commodore record store) signed up the 52nd Street artists, and a string of semi-impromptu numbers came to be recorded, many of them with titles that sought to immortalize the best-known clubs. In 1935, Roy Eldridge cut one of the first such tunes, *Swingin' on that Famous Door*, with clarinetist Joe Marsala and the Delta Four. Not to be outdone, Wingy Manone (who had been the record company's adviser on Marsala's session) made a spirited version of *Swingin' at the Hickory House* the following year, in which his vocal extolled the virtues of 52nd Street in general, and that club in particular. Stuff Smith's vocal on *Onyx Club Spree*, from 1937, called his musicians together to "swing 'cos swing's so grand . . . to give a demonstration of a big old jam," and there were similar sentiments from the same session in *Onyx Club Stomp*. Other comparable discs are Chu Berry's *Forty-Six West Fifty-Two* (named for the Commodore jazz record store on the street) and Fats Waller's *Yacht Club Swing*, both cut in the fall of 1938.

Perhaps the most prolific label to record the street's musicians was Decca, whose talent scout J. Mayo Williams asked pianist Sammy Price to recruit studio backing bands for a whole series of jazz and blues recordings for their budget-priced "race" series. As well as recording jazz tunes with his own "Fly Cats" or "Texas Bluesicians," Price provided an impressive series of small groups to back singers like Sister Rosetta Tharpe, Bea Booze, Blue Lu Barker, and many more. Among his sidemen for these sessions were such significant soloists and ensemble players as Henry "Red" Allen, Buster Bailey, Benny Carter, Wellman Braud, and O'Neill Spencer, all of them experienced in the cream of the city's big bands as well as in the small groups of the street. On these discs, and a comparable number on which Lil Hardin Armstrong was pianist or organizer, it is possible to hear much of the sound of 52nd Street as it was every night of the week for several years, with a consistency of approach and a shared sense of how small-group jazz should be played.

In almost all memoirs and interviews dealing with musicians who worked on the street, there is a sense of wonder that such an array of talent should have appeared with such intensity in so small an area. Vibes player Milt Jackson, who first arrived well into the 1940s, was typical:

> Just before I came out of the services, I went to New York for the weekend on a pass, and I just ran around, stayed up for over 48 hours. All the musicians I'd always heard about and dreamed about, suddenly here they were, right here in the flesh and I just went completely nuts. In 52nd Street, in those two blocks, you could hear so many artists. It was unbelievable. You might catch Billie Holiday in the Onyx, go up the Street to the Three Deuces where Charlie Parker was playing with his group. Three doors away there was Coleman Hawkins, and Art Tatum was playing another club just up the Street. It was just remarkable and totally unbelievable.[10]

Hard on the heels of the clubs that opened in the first wave had come new ones. The Hickory House, the Downbeat, the Club Samoa, Kelly's Stable, the Flamingo, and the Spotlite were among those that were in business around the start of the 1940s.

As I have suggested, a few key musicians did a lot to establish the prevailing swing style on 52nd Street, and perhaps most important among them was trumpeter Roy Eldridge who, in addition to his habit of sitting in, led his own bands at the Famous Door in 1935, and Kelly's Stable in 1940. Born in Pittsburgh in 1911, into a musical family in which his elder brother Joe played saxophone and violin, Eldridge began his musical career on drums at the age of six. He graduated to bugle and then trumpet. Even as a child, he practiced for several hours a day, a habit he maintained until old age, his contemporaries marveling that he would put in several hours of solo exercises, even when he was playing a concert or club date in the evening.

As well as absorbing a good knowledge of sight-reading and harmony as he grew up, Eldridge did something quite unusual for a trumpeter – he used his brother's saxophone and clarinet exercise-books as the basis for his own practice. Whereas other brass players might have taken a simpler, more conventional, approach to learning each valve combination or lip position, Eldridge was attacking music designed to help saxophonists master the complex fingering of their instruments. As a result, he quickly developed an uncanny fluency and speed, as well as jumping easily from the highest to the lowest registers of his instrument. This was easy for a saxophonist, where operating one key shifts the pitch of the instrument by a whole octave, but much tougher for a brass player who has to use lip tension to achieve the same effect.

Eldridge's musical role-model during his teens was saxophonist Coleman Hawkins, and this is how Hawkins came to have an indirect influence, *in absentia*, on the music that developed on 52nd Street. Eldridge taught himself to play Hawkins's recorded sax solos on trumpet, especially the one from Fletcher Henderson's *Stampede* [CD track 4], which Eldridge turned into his own party piece. In the 1980s, Eldridge still acknowledged the importance of this: "I was always a real fan of his. I got my first job through learning his solo on Fletcher's record of *Stampede*, and I've still got records of his going way back to when he was doing the slap-tonguing."[11]

Although they were often to work together in the 1950s and 1960s, Eldridge did not meet Hawkins until the saxophonist returned from Europe in 1939. But prior to that meeting, in his wide-ranging work with the territory bands of Zach Whyte and Speed Webb, his subsequent playing with Charlie Johnson, Teddy Hill, and Fletcher Henderson, and with his own groups in New York and Chicago, Eldridge brought one aspect of Hawkins's influence to bear through his radically new way of approaching jazz trumpet.

It was, no doubt, unavoidable that one trumpeter above all others, Louis Armstrong, would also have an influence on Eldridge's style, so all-pervading was Armstrong's approach to the instrument. A recording like *Shoe Shine Boy*, from August 1936, which Eldridge cut with Henderson, has clear echoes of Armstrong in both the timing and sound of the vocal, and the firm on-the-beat phrasing and melodic simplification of the trumpet solo. His solo on Gene Krupa's *Let Me off Uptown* [CD track 15] punches out a series of high notes that are also very much in the Armstrong manner, but pushing at the upper end of the range, and they also have a more elastic sense of time – a quality Eldridge also brings to his vocal, where delaying or lingering on certain syllables propels him forward into the next phrase with added urgency. These vocal qualities are also obvious in his muted trumpet interjections to Billie Holiday's *God Bless the Child* **[CD track 9]**. By contrast, on Eldridge's more spectacular high-note and rapid-fire solos with Henderson, on such pieces as *Jangled Nerves* or *Riffin'*, there are clear affinities with the range, speed, and attack of Jabbo Smith, although Eldridge tended not to acknowledge Smith as an influence.

In his own mind, one of the most important trumpeters in shaping his ideas was Rex Stewart, Armstrong's successor in the Fletcher Henderson Orchestra, who at one point rehearsed at the Eldridge family home with a band led by Roy's elder brother Joe. Stewart's mixture of aggressive flair and rapid execution attracted Eldridge, and, reflecting on this, Stewart was later to write:

> I do accept the role of link between Louie and Roy Eldridge, as I first developed a style that Roy liked, and he told me that he had followed it. Then Roy developed another dimension of his own, which was faster and better than mine. [12]

Stewart, of course, was the other notable soloist on that famous disc of *Stampede*, from which Eldridge had learned Hawkins's solo by heart, and there is no reason to suppose he did not take the time and trouble to master the cornet solo as well.

This blend of influences is readily apparent on a disc Eldridge and Chu Berry made to commemorate their practice of turning up to play in after-hours clubs. *Sittin' In*, cut for Commodore in November 1938, opens with the two discussing where they will "go out and play some swing," and quickly launches into a fiery 32-measure solo from Eldridge. In the first sixteen, he leans back on the beat, leaving a short space before launching dramatically into his upper register, but in bars 16–24, he plays a repeated figure that is derived directly from Hawkins's saxophone style. This mixture of high-note bravura passages and extended phrases, some of which were built, like a Hawkins's solo, on repeated fingering patterns, is a distinct departure from Armstrong's manner of soloing. It is more fluid, almost subversive, and sacrifices much of Armstrong's innate sense of form, and of building gradually to a climax, for something more immediate – it bursts from the starting gate in a series of sprints, rather than running a steady race.

Through his recordings and live appearances, plus a long-running series of broadcasts in 1936–7 with his own band from Chicago, Eldridge was to be a dominant influence on trumpeters of the thirties and forties (in many ways as significant as Armstrong was on the twenties and early thirties). He was an inspiration to contemporaries like Charlie Shavers, who captured many of the nuances of his style, but he also did a lot to form the approach of younger players such as his eventual successor in Teddy Hill's band, the young Dizzy Gillespie, or the former territory-band player Howard McGhee, who joined the groups of Lionel Hampton and Andy Kirk in the early 1940s.

There is a danger, in singling out figures such as Eldridge to indicate the influence he had on musicians of his own generation and the one that followed, that other comparable trumpeters of the period are overlooked in favor of only identifying the new or the revolutionary. This is the pitfall of seeing jazz only in terms of a series of revolutionary steps, or what the French scholar Michel Laplace has called: "The false logic of a unique path that leads ineluctably from prehistoric caves to atonal ecstasy."[13] Certainly, both the big-band world and the 52nd Street clubs abounded with other trumpeters who – though less revolutionary than Eldridge – were major participants in consolidating the swing style. Cootie Williams perfected the muted growling of Bubber Miley, and, in addition to his playing with Ellington's orchestra, made many exemplary small-group discs. Bill Coleman, with Fats Waller's recording band and Teddy Hill's orchestra, brought an intense lyricism to his trumpet solos, a quality he shared with Buck Clayton's work for Count Basie and Billie Holiday. Henry "Red" Allen offered a different slant on the New Orleans approach of his colleague and friend Louis Armstrong, which alternated laid-back relaxation with frenzied attack, plus an oblique way of attacking notes, and tumbling, blurry phrases that were packed with excitement. Frankie Newton matched some of Allen's excitement with elements of the lyricism of Coleman and Clayton, whereas other musicians, such as Herman Autrey, sought to carry on the lineage of Armstrong with punchy solos on discs such as Fats Waller's 1936 *I'm Sorry I Made You Cry*. Another influence on Autrey was Oran "Hot Lips" Page, whose bluesy style had been honed in the territory bands of Walter Page and Bennie Moten.

Yet *consolidation* is very much what these players were about – refining approaches that had gradually evolved during the twenties and into the relative stability of the swing era. Eldridge, by contrast, introduced a dramatically new way of tackling trumpet improvisation by bringing a fresh element to the playing technique of his instrument, through mastering note patterns that had been worked out for the saxophone. Because I view jazz as a syncretic music, made up by bringing together disparate elements into a new whole, Eldridge's contribution is highly significant because it marks a change driven from *within jazz itself*, rather than an external influence, or one drawn from the musical sources that went to make up early jazz. This was also to be a crucial step in the development of the modern jazz of the 1940s, as Martin Williams pointed out: "The crucial thing about the bebop style is that its basis came from the resources of jazz itself, and it came about in much the same way that innovation had come about in the past."[14]

The other two principal swing musicians who instigated comparable changes from inside jazz were Coleman Hawkins and Lester Young, and the work of both saxophonists was to prompt many of the further developments into bebop.

During his absence in Europe, Hawkins had been mainly perceived in the United States in terms of what he had achieved before he left. There had been sporadic – and therefore somewhat unrepresentative – accounts of his European triumphs in the American trade press, such as *Metronome* and *Down Beat*, but his steady stream of British, French, Dutch, and Swiss recordings was, for the most part, hard to obtain in America, and only six out of a total of almost 50 discs had been reissued in American versions.[15]

It appears that his main rival for supremacy on the tenor saxophone, Lester Young, had made a point of hearing Hawkins's work on his Paris records, not least because, following his unhappy and short-lived experience of trying to follow Hawkins in the Henderson orchestra, Young had built a successful career for himself with Basie, and, through the championing of the likes of John Hammond, was widely regarded as New York's pre-eminent tenorist when Hawkins returned to America on the last day of July 1939. Within a week or two of his return, Hawkins took on Young in a tenor "battle," a re-run of an epic duel from Young's Kansas City days, and opinions were divided on who had triumphed – Billie Holiday weighing in to defend Young, when *Down Beat* suggested Hawkins was the victor.[16]

The contrast between their styles of playing precisely mirrored the ways in which each was to influence the next phase in jazz development: Hawkins emphasizing harmony, and Young tackling melody and rhythm.

In his investigation of the background to the modern jazz of the 1940s, Scott DeVeaux observes that, throughout the swing era, Hawkins was much concerned with the idea of *progress*. Being modern, up to the moment, fashionably dressed, impeccably turned out, were all obvious facets of

Hawkins's personality, but as an artist he underwent a major change during his European sojourn. As I have suggested in the previous chapter, he made the transition from sideman to star, and he moved from being billed by Henderson as the "World's Greatest Saxophonist," despite playing only a few featured choruses with the big band, to a position where he genuinely was able to stamp his authority, personality, and musicianship on every appearance. He dominated most of his European recordings by making himself the sole center of attention, and this allowed him to put his solo playing firmly in the spotlight. On public appearances, his colleagues remember him sitting at the bar or the back of a club drinking substantial quantities of brandy as he waited for his feature spot, but then moving center-stage when summoned, to present a dominating demonstration of his solo prowess.

DeVeaux suggests, convincingly, that by the time he returned from Europe, Hawkins had introduced several highly sophisticated harmonic ideas into his own playing as a means of enriching his solos, while his accompanists continued to provide a conventional harmonic setting of the kind that barely altered during his years abroad. Further, DeVeaux suggests that he had done so primarily because of his clear-cut notion that progress was important, and that: "in place of the romantic popular song – product – he offered process, a *way* of playing that privileged the virtuoso over the composer."[17]

In Hawkins's famous version of *Body and Soul* from October 11, 1939, there are plenty of examples of the way that Hawkins impressed his virtuosity on the harmonic structure of the piece to create something new. DeVeaux cites, among other things, his use of chromatic passing tones, of "half-step" movements from phrase to phrase, and also the use of substitute harmonies, replacing the chord the composer originally used with another. Hawkins often superimposes his own new harmony over the extant chording played by the rhythm section, and a device he employs in *Body and Soul* is the tritone substitution – using a variant of the dominant-seventh chord to resolve some of the harmonies in the piece in an unusual way, and often delaying such resolution of a chord until the last moment. Where he substitutes a harmony in this way, but retains the chords of the original accompaniment, he deliberately creates a kind of dissonance that was refreshingly new in jazz, and which only someone with Hawkins's erudite understanding of harmony would have introduced. This could be a hiding to nothing. As Scott DeVeaux points out, such harmonic specialization narrows the range of improvisational possibilities because "the tendency is always to fill in, to flesh out, to maintain the illusion of harmonic movement even where it is absent."[18] Yet Hawkins succeeds in avoiding this sterility through over-complication, because of the emotional meaning he manages to convey in his playing.

The recording of *Body and Soul* is nothing more nor less than a long rhapsodic tenor saxophone improvisation, with no lyric, a more-than-usually mobile underlying harmonic structure, and no arrangement; just a simple accompanying rhythm with occasional long-drawn-out notes from the other brass and reeds of Hawkins's nine-piece band. It is the antithesis of the hot Fletcher Henderson charts played by Goodman. It lacks the ornately arranged setting in which Shaw had positioned his slower solos, and, after setting off close to the original melody, it soon moves away from it, the tenor sound hardening from the soft, fluffy-edged opening chorus to a tougher, more impassioned tone as the piece reaches its climax. Indeed, with the exception of a few solo piano pieces, this was one of the first successful jazz records to consist solely of a lengthy, virtuoso improvisation by a single soloist.

The disc's commercial success was due, at least in part, to Hawkins's ability in Signifyin(g), to convey meaning, to create a "telling event," and in his own mind he was absolutely clear what this event was, as he explained to his band's vocalist, Thelma Carpenter: "You greet the song, then you slowly get closer to it, caressing it, kissing it, and finally making love to it."[19]

The passion, highly charged eroticism, and the way that the contour of his solo graphically parallels love-making, a sexual climax, and what Hawkins called the subsequent "satisfaction" undoubtedly helped this record to become a juke-box favorite and one of Hawkins's most enduring and popular discs. He had played the piece often during his long stay in Europe as a soloist, and he was to make it a consistent part of his repertoire. The young saxophonist Bob Wilber and his friend Denny Strong, making their first visit to 52nd Street as teenagers in the mid-1940s, some five years after Hawkins recorded the tune, witnessed him use it to open his act at Kelly's Stable:

> He picked up his tenor as one of the guys in the band asked, "Whadya wanna play, Bean?" In a deep mellifluous voice that sounded much like his huge saxophone tone, he replied, "*Body* – one, two." Denny and I sat there goggle-eyed, less than three feet away from the great man, as he went through his intricate improvisations on *Body and Soul*. We were in seventh heaven – he was one of our idols.[20]

Hawkins continued to specialize in this kind of ballad playing, and he brought the same mixture of technical proficiency, harmonic adventure, and erotically charged emotion to numerous other songs, such as *I'm Through with Love*, *What Is There to Say?*, *Someone to Watch Over Me*, or *It's the Talk of the Town*.

But there was another side to the innovations that Hawkins brought back to the United States from his long years of playing as a solo improviser in Europe, where he had developed the kind of harmonic flexibility and sure-footed chordal substitution displayed on *Body and Soul*; this was to incorporate his advanced harmonic thinking into pieces that were played at a far quicker tempo, and in which, in DeVeaux's words, he struck "an ingenious balance between the vertical dimension of harmony and the horizontal logic of the melodic line." This description develops an idea articulated by the composer and theorist George Russell that some musicians tend to think "vertically," in other words they think of chords as a vertical stack of notes, exactly as they appear on an individual note system in a score, and they attempt to arpeggiate the significant notes of each stack as they pass through the harmonic sequence of a piece; and other musicians prefer to think "horizontally," focusing mainly on the melodic line of a piece rather than its accompanying harmony.[21] Hawkins belongs to the former group, although his harmonic command was such that he could generally build interesting melodic ideas out of his exploration of harmony. As well as a far harsher attacking tone on his up-tempo playing, Hawkins packed his solos with complex, often dissonant ideas, in which his speed of thought and execution outstripped many of his rivals'. There is a brief glimpse of his authoritative, forceful playing at faster tempos in his guest appearance with Count Basie on *9.20 Special* **[CD track 14]**. This combination of rapidity and invention was to become a significant cornerstone for the reed players of the 1940s, just as Eldridge's extension of the range and complexity of trumpet lines was to influence the same generation of brass players.

I have already discussed the way that Count Basie exploited (and to some extent exaggerated) the contrasting sounds of his tenor soloists, the gruff Herschel Evans (a Hawkins-influenced player) and the lighter-sounding Lester Young; and this difference symbolizes the distinct influences of Hawkins and Young on solo saxophone playing as the 1930s led into the 1940s.

Because he was a member of Count Basie's orchestra until December 1940, Young was only an informal sitter-in on 52nd Street, but he became a bandleader there in his own right in February 1941, with a residency at

Kelly's Stable. Nevertheless, through his recordings with Basie, and, equally, his small-group sessions with Teddy Wilson and Billie Holiday, Young's alternative approach to the tenor saxophone was widely known, and he was voted into the number four position among tenor saxophonists in the *Down Beat* poll of December 1940. (He finally topped the poll in 1944, the year his career fell apart when he was inducted into the U.S. Army.)

No less well–turned out than Hawkins, Young complemented his immaculate pinstripe suits and fashionable shirts and ties with a few touches of eccentricity, not least his fondness for a "pork-pie" hat, and for a playing stance in which his saxophone jutted out at an unorthodox 45-degree angle. His unusual visual appearance was augmented by his extremely personal language, a bizarre mixture of profanity, nicknames, and "jive" talk, and all these elements together suggest that Young's entire approach to life, as well as his saxophone playing, was original and somewhat tangential.

Ironically, for two such urban sophisticates, both Hawkins and Young began their working lives in the territories, yet again underlining the importance to jazz of its early regional development. Hawkins, as we know, began with Jesse Stone's band before touring with Mamie Smith, and Young started in the family band led by his father, which was based during his childhood in New Orleans, but then relocated to Memphis and, later, Minneapolis. Soon after he entered his twenties, Young, who was born in 1909, was on the road with Walter Page, and after working in various other bands, he rejoined Page's Blue Devils for the years 1932–3, going on to work with Bennie Moten, George E. Lee, Count Basie, and, briefly, Fletcher Henderson. Whereas Hawkins forsook the touring vaudeville circuits early in his career to join Henderson in New York, Young spent most of his career before 1936 in areas where the blues was a dominant form of popular entertainment. Unlike the robust, harmonically exacting style of Hawkins, Young's was packed with subtle blues inflections, microtonal alterations of pitch (particularly his ability to alternate different fingerings to produce the same note, giving a contrasting nuance to each repetition of it), and a wistful sense of timing, together with an ability to emphasize certain notes with an accent or even a "honk" that mirrored the vocal characteristics of blues.

Nevertheless, his main instrumental influence was unorthodox for an African-American musician, and it came not from face-to-face contact, but from recordings by the white saxophonists Jimmy Dorsey and Frankie Trumbauer. Both these musicians played higher-pitched instruments than Young's tenor – Dorsey favoring the alto, and Trumbauer the intermediate instrument, the C-melody saxophone. Young borrowed Dorsey's fondness for the kinds of alternate fingering patterns that provided different timbral possibilities for sounding a note, and he modeled his airier tone on Trumbauer's instrument, saying: "I tried to get the sound of a C-melody on a tenor." Although close analysis shows that Young's actual phrasing owed relatively little to Trumbauer, the similarities of tone and of general structure in their solos are striking, and Young admired the way Trumbauer "always told a little story. . . . He'd play the melody first and then after that he'd play around the melody."[22]

This simple statement is revealing of the most fundamental difference between Young's approach to extended solo playing and Hawkins's. However brilliantly and rhapsodically Hawkins built his solos, such as on *Body and Soul*, he usually did so by moving away from the composer's original melody as quickly as was practical to do so, after milking it for the dramatic effect of his opening statements, and then relying almost totally on the harmonic framework of the piece. Young, however, was much more of a melodist, what George Russell would classify as a "horizontal" thinker, and he preferred to superimpose the logic of his melodic lines over an underlying chord structure, even when these chords were more complex than his melodic ideas. Indeed, numerous commentators, including Russell, Gunther Schuller, and Scott DeVeaux, have pointed out that, far from employing the kind of substitute harmonies beloved of Hawkins, Young sought to simplify or reduce the harmonic material in a tune, occupying a "single harmonic zone" or creating a kind of "harmonic stasis."[23]

Young's solo on *Lester Leaps In*, with Count Basie's Kansas City Seven **[CD track 10]**, includes numerous examples of his tendency to simplify; although to counterbalance the most minimal aspects of the solo there are several neatly executed runs, arpeggios, and fills, in which he moves airily round the tenor. For example, on the second chorus of the piece he begins his solo with a paraphrase of the simple riff that had formed the melodic statement of the piece. This is rapidly pared down even further to a repeated four-note pattern that Young plucks up from a passing phrase in Basie's economical piano accompaniment and re-uses as he moves into the second eight measures. After the middle section, he repeats a simple three-note motif in much the same way.

In the second chorus of his solo, the band somewhat messily begins a sequence of breaks, where the accompaniment drops out for alternate blocks of four measures. Here, in the passage after the middle eight, Young offers a textbook example of his habit of repeating a single note, played with alternating fingering patterns to alter its timbre. In one of the most detailed published studies of Young's playing, Lewis Porter has not only analyzed the solo on *Lester Leaps In* in some depth but has also identified the numerous formulae, or fragments of melodic material, that Young consistently used to construct his solos. Many jazz soloists – before and after Young – have relied on such formulae, but Young opened up the method by which many players of the 1940s would incorporate them as the building-blocks of their solos. Yet Young's aims in doing so were abundantly clear, as Porter confirms:

> This approach allowed Young considerable freedom in construct-ing his melodic lines, enabling him to concentrate on beauty and lyricism. Like many jazz performers of his generation, Young relied on his ear in choosing melodies to fit over the chord progression. If something sounded good it didn't matter that it agreed or disagreed with a literal interpretation of the chords. Music theory, of which Young and his peers knew little, could be a guide, but was certainly not law.[24]

By focusing primarily on the melodic direction of his playing, Young introduced dissonance in a very different way from Hawkins. Particularly, when he constructed a melody line by using formulaic patterns, it would not necessarily fit exactly with the underlying harmony, and could drift in and out of dissonance with what was being played by the rhythm section. However, the listener was deceived by hearing the internal logic of the line itself, and the passing dissonance added an exciting extra quality to Young's sound which was quickly spotted by the up-and-coming generation of the 1940s as an effect to be mastered and absorbed into their own playing. (Some of Young's favorite formulae derived as much from fingering patterns that fell neatly under the hand as from their melodic content, and this also became a trait of some bebop players.)

Another major benefit of Young's melodically driven approach to improvisation was that he tackled rhythm in a distinctly different way from Hawkins. Whereas Hawkins tended to construct rising and falling patterns of eighth notes, relying on harmonic complexity to provide interest, Young's solo on *Lester Leaps In* abounds with rhythmic variation. Some phrases enter exactly on the beat; others are delayed by an eighth note, or a quarter note. When a motif is repeated, it is often placed differently over the accompanying beat on each repetition, sometimes using a minute delay or anticipation. Furthermore, within his light, airy tone, he is still able to add weight or emphasis to certain notes, and he includes considerable timbral variety, by using substitute fingering, or the occasional honk. In other well-known examples of his solo playing, particularly his various recordings of *Honeysuckle Rose* with Basie, Young uses his characteristic formulae to set up complex cross-rhythms. Overall, Young's rhythmic diversity was far greater than that of Hawkins, because he was not impelled to reflect every passing harmonic nuance.

Between them, the work of these two saxophonists was highly significant in influencing their own generation and the one that came next. As with Eldridge, I have singled them out for their revolutionary contribution to their contemporaries' thinking about jazz, and there is the same danger of seeing saxophone playing from this period as more to do with change than consolidation. Just as it was for trumpeters, the 1930s was a period during which saxophonists in general drew many of the ideas of the previous decade together into a coherent style.

During the time that Hawkins was making his reputation as a tenorist with Fletcher Henderson, Prince Robinson was recording significant tenor saxophone solos with McKinney's Cotton Pickers, in a manner that, to some extent, transposed early jazz clarinet lines to the deeper instrument – not least because Robinson himself doubled effectively on clarinet. One of the first players to specialize on the tenor saxophone, and to develop, as Hawkins did, a style that was essentially independent of the clarinet was the white Chicagoan, Bud Freeman. There are obvious similarities in his playing to that of Hawkins – not least a forceful, occasionally gruff tone and an arpeggiated style. Freeman's phrasing tended to be more anticipatory, more ahead of the beat, than Hawkins's, and he liked to include long, repetitive patterns in his solos that were not so much complex harmonically as demanding in terms of intricate fingering patterns, speed of execution, and detailed ornamentation added to, basically, eighth-note or sixteenth-note phrases. His most famous feature, *The Eel*, which he first recorded in 1933 but cut in a definitive version with his own Summa Cum Laude Orchestra in July 1939, is a good example of this. It has a simple introduction and a chromatic bridge passage leading into a succession of twelve-bar blues choruses, over several of which Freeman superimposes a rugged solo, constructed of repeated formulaic phrases, but packed with rhythmic variation. There is, however, a danger in such reliance on repetitive patterns as the basis of improvisation, and when I played with Freeman in the 1970s during his extended stay in Britain, there was a constant danger that his solo on any up-tempo blues would unwittingly turn into *The Eel*.

I have already mentioned the close affinities between Herschel Evans and Coleman Hawkins, and there were also strong parallels between Hawkins's approach and the playing of Chu Berry and Ben Webster. Berry was, as I have suggested, the saxophone counterpart of Roy Eldridge, self-assured at the brightest of tempos, and breezily matching the speed and flow of his friend's ideas – both of them producing playing that was a vigorous, buoyant metaphor for a newly confident America clambering out of the Depression. In Gunther Schuller's memorable phrase, the two men operated on a "speedier wave length"[25] than many of their contemporaries, and certainly in the mid-1930s, when Hawkins was in Europe, Berry (who unashamedly acknowledged Hawk's influence) became the dominant figure amongst cutting-edge swing tenorists. His sparkling work on broadcasts with Teddy Hill (barely represented by his two recorded solos with the band), on his full-length features with Henderson and Calloway, and, above all, on the recorded jam sessions he led himself or participated in for the likes of Gene Krupa and Lionel Hampton, displayed his phenomenal speed of execution, accuracy of articulation, and ability to think on his feet. He lacked the intricate harmonic knowledge of Hawkins, but his use of occasional whole-tone runs and the sureness with which his ear guided him through the most complex accompanying harmonies gave his late-1930s work the sense of being equally modern and forward-looking. His public reputation was built on such beautifully balanced ballads as his Calloway features *Ghost of a Chance* and *Lonesome Nights*, both of which were suited to his fluffier tone, which was altogether less aggressive than that of Hawkins (although the former piece has striking similarities of structure and pacing with Hawkins's *Body and Soul*). But Berry's real forte remained his playing at speed (such as on Henderson's *Jangled Nerves*), and it was this that was most admired by his fellow musicians. His tragic death in October 1941 robbed jazz of a major solo voice.

At the time that Berry was killed in a motor accident, Webster was coming into his own as a major soloist with Duke Ellington, whom he had rejoined (following a brief stay with the band in the mid-1930s) the year before. Like Hawkins and Young, Webster's background was in the territories, and he had played with both Bennie Moten and Andy Kirk. His early solos have plenty in common with Hawkins, although they combine this with some of the innate bluesy qualities of the Midwest. Nevertheless, as late as January 1940, in his short solo with Teddy Wilson's big band on *711*, Webster's abrasive tone and arpeggiated lines could be those of Hawkins himself. As was often the case with soloists whom he encouraged, just as he had done with his earlier reed-playing recruits, Johnny Hodges and Barney Bigard, it was Duke Ellington who drew out Webster's potential and individuality, once the tenorist became a fixture in his orchestra later in 1940.

Webster was a stocky, compact individual with bulging eyes and a formidable temper. Ellington somehow harnessed this innate aggression, and bundled it together with the soft, sentimental side of the man that came out in his exquisite and sensitive ballad playing. Webster's unhurried approach to slow or medium-paced pieces is demonstrated by Ellington's 1941 *Just a-Settin' and a-Rockin'*, where his lazy statement of the theme is followed by a gloriously lyrical solo, played with a sensuous, warm, tone and floating over the underlying rhythm with an unparalleled sense of relaxation. What set apart Webster's up-tempo solos in Ellington's band from those of his contemporaries was that he somehow managed to build this warmth and unobtrusive laziness into his opening statements. In both *Conga Brava* and *Cottontail*, from 1940, he enters in this manner before building up in intensity and power, always with the slightly sinister feeling that violence might erupt at any moment. He learned from his section-mate, altoist Johnny Hodges, how to hold a single note for several beats – sometimes several measures – adding passion to it with a shake, a terminal vibrato, or by edging up to it in a minuscule glissando, and he alternated such lengthy notes with choppy up-tempo passages, in which he particularly favored brief chromatic downward runs, or repeating a phrase while simultaneously moving it up or down by a half-tone. Webster matured into one of the most distinctive saxophone voices in jazz during his time with Ellington, and he retained his pre-eminence for the rest of his career, right up until his death in Amsterdam, in 1973, following almost a ten-year exile in Europe.

At a time when jazz fashions changed around him, Webster remained constant: he was not to attempt to embrace the bebop movement as Hawkins did, nor was he to be overtaken by his own imitators as eventually happened to Young. Instead, from the moment he began leading his own small groups on 52nd Street, in 1944, he specialized in ballad playing, in developing his lazy, warm tone – at one extreme into little more than a slow, breathy throb, and at the other into a powerful passionate voice, full of human experience and emotion.

There were other swing-era saxophonists who, to a greater or lesser degree, developed the approach to the instrument initiated by Hawkins, and who, to some extent, remained in his shadow, without developing the individuality and unique voice that both Berry and Webster managed.

Tenorist and bandleader Charlie Barnet was one example – a competent player and occasional soloist, most famous for his version of Ray Noble's *Cherokee*, who added little to the tenor vocabulary. Nevertheless, he commissioned some stimulating arrangements for his band, and also made a point of integrating African-American musicians with his brass and reed sections a few months before Benny Goodman and Artie Shaw's better-known pioneering efforts at interracial bandleading. Other major tenorists with white bands who owed much to Hawkins include Vido Musso with Goodman and Tex Beneke with Glenn Miller's band.

There was, however, one school of tenorists who developed the Hawkins approach in a new direction by mixing his robust tone and arpeggiated phrasing with the soulfulness of the Southern blues. This was the large number of players who came from, or grew up in, Texas. Herschel Evans was one of the earliest of them to make a name, and his successor in the Basie orchestra, Buddy Tate was another. Tate was born in 1915, and he became the senior figure among such Texas contemporaries as Arnett Cobb (born 1918) and Illinois Jacquet (born in Louisiana in 1918, but raised in Houston). None of these players adopted the more advanced aspects of bebop harmony and rhythm, and all of them kept alive the basic virtues of the swing era – an attractive and popular blend of robust, melodic improvisation with the vocal tone and phrasing of the blues.

It is one of the most remarkable aspects of 52nd Street that even as the swing era came to an end and newer styles of music began to be heard in the clubs up and down the street, there was still room for the swing orthodoxy well into the middle to late 1940s. In 1944–5, for example, when the teenage Bob Wilber was commuting down from Scarsdale to hear what was on offer, on a typical night he heard saxophonist Joe Eldridge (Roy's brother) leading a swing trio with drummer Zutty Singleton, Billie Holiday with guitarist Al Casey and altoist Pete Brown, and the Coleman Hawkins band.

I have hinted at the ways in which the soloists who came into their own whether as bandleaders, sidemen, or sitters-in on 52nd Street were to influence the course of jazz, but the economic necessities of small clubs that could hold limited numbers of patrons also had an effect on redefining the nature of the ensemble. Only clubs like the Famous Door, which employed the entire Basie band, bucked the trend of alternating two small groups, or a quintet and a pianist. In the transition that took place on the street from the Dixieland model of the early days to the swing small groups of the mid-1930s to the mid-1940s, a new orthodoxy was established which subsequently became the basis of the first bebop ensembles.

Because I have focused on New York, and 52nd Street in particular, there is a danger of assuming that it is likely to be representative of what was going on elsewhere in the United States. But there are some striking parallels to what was going on during the 1930s in New York in other leading cities across the United States. I have already mentioned Roy Eldridge's broadcasts from Chicago, which were networked so that his seven- or eight-piece band was heard across large areas of the country, albeit after midnight. In 1941, Coleman Hawkins led a large band in the same city at Dave's Swingland (which later became the Rhumboogie Club), but by the following year he had scaled down to a septet at White's Emporium. So two of the major transitional influences on New York jazz spent considerable amounts of time in Chicago, even though, as a whole, the city had not regained the vibrant and intense jazz scene it had enjoyed in the 1920s.

The closest parallel to what went on in New York was in Los Angeles, where over approximately twenty years the Central Avenue area had become the capital both of the West Coast African-American community and of the Californian jazz world. Stretching from downtown Los Angeles to the southern suburb of Watts, Central had almost as many clubs as 52nd Street, but spread out over a far greater geographical area. Restrictive housing covenants had focused the African-American community along two sections of Central, from 3rd Street for about 60 blocks, where there was a white area, and then below that from 92nd Street to Watts. At the epicenter of the Avenue's social and musical life was the high-class Dunbar Hotel, where visiting stars like Duke Ellington and Ella Fitzgerald stayed. Close at hand was the Club Alabam where Curtis Mosby's band held sway, and there were numerous other clubs: the Downbeat, the Humming Bird, Joe's Basket Room, the Jungle Room, the Kentucky Club, the Last Word, Lovejoy's, the Plantation, and the Swing Club.[26]

Many of the musicians who had worked on 52nd Street moved west to play on Central Avenue, or came to Los Angeles for short residencies, before returning to the Street, creating a similar set of small swing groups to those in New York. Eighth Street, at its intersection with Central, was even something of a parallel for Harlem, as pianists like Art Tatum and Nat King Cole worked in its small collection of clubs, along with newer arrivals like Gerald Wiggins, who settled in Los Angeles after traveling west as a member of the Californian big band of Les Hite in 1942. Benny Carter also made the city his base that same year, using many Central Avenue alumni in his newly formed West Coast big band. There were frequent after-hours jam sessions at the clubs on the avenue, and also at the old black Musicians' Union building for local 767.

From 1941 to 1942, Lester Young co-led a band in Los Angeles with his brother Lee playing drums, and they worked at Billy Berg's club on Pico and La Cienega. Other acts that appeared there during their stay included the Spirits of Rhythm, Billie Holiday, and the comic duo of multi-instrumentalist Slim Gaillard and bassist Slam Stewart. In effect, this was 52nd Street in miniature, and Berg was to keep such a mixture when he relocated to Vine Street in Hollywood. Overall, the Los Angeles scene was as lively as any in the United States, and it closely mirrored New York's move to the orthodoxy of swing small groups, to the extent that when bebop began in earnest, it did so almost simultaneously on opposite sides of the continent.

## Swing in, Swing out: Changes to the Small Swing Ensemble

> In the end I had to give up the big band to stop the financial rot.
>
> Teddy Wilson, from *Teddy Wilson Talks Jazz*

So what was the new ensemble orthodoxy, and how did it take shape? By the end of the 1930s, there was cut-throat competition to succeed in the big-band world. In the wake of Gene Krupa and Harry James, numerous other ex-sidemen of Benny Goodman had set up their own orchestras. Bunny Berigan, Vido Musso, and Toots Mondello were all leading groups, as was Teddy Wilson, who had rashly financed his own big band on the strength of his earnings with Goodman. It was soon evident that one of the great ironies of the later years of the swing era was that the music largely developed by African-Americans became so dominated by white orchestras that such players as Wilson, Coleman Hawkins, and even, to some extent, the multi-talented Benny Carter, were all gradually squeezed out of being able to run successful big bands of their own. In the days when Jean Goldkette or Ben Pollack had been discouraged from recording too much hot music, and Henderson was being similarly steered away from his "pretty" repertoire, as far as recording companies and, in many cases, the managements of dance halls, clubs, and hotels were concerned, there had been a clear stylistic division between white and African-American bands, and a consequential rough-and-ready division of opportunity.

Following Goodman's success at playing a hotter brand of jazz, this distinction was clouded, and as the 1940s approached, many African-American bandleaders found themselves unable to compete with white bands, who were handled by white agencies, and their wares marketed by white-managed record companies. Even at the most basic practical level, the white groups did not have to deal with the privations of segregation, and virtually everything, from travel and accommodation to eating and using washrooms, was a good deal less difficult for such orchestras. Closer to home, for musicians based in New York, from the mid-1930s many white bands began to be presented at the (white-owned) theaters and clubs of Harlem, venues that had hitherto been the preserve of African-American musicians. At least one newspaper pondered why it was that the African-American bands displaced by these newcomers to the Apollo and similar venues were not offered "the chance to work in the big hotel spots downtown left by the white bands that came to Harlem."[27]

That having been said, and despite the conspicuous success of Harry James in particular, there were nevertheless several white bands that did not last the distance. Among the best-known, Jack Teagarden's progressively ran into debt, and Bunny Berigan broke up and re-formed his group more than once, before his premature death, prompted by alcoholism, in 1942, aged just 33.

At the same time, the best-established of the African-American bands fortunately remained afloat – Ellington, Calloway, Lunceford, and Basie. Although he had severed his links with Chicago's Grand Terrace after ten years, Earl Hines also survived as a big-band leader, helped by the popular success of his vocalist Billy Eckstine, who had a major hit in 1940 with *Jelly, Jelly*. Out in the West, Les Hite continued to thrive in Los Angeles, helped by his orchestra's residency at the New Cotton Club in Culver City, which was a solid enough foundation for him to undertake a national tour in 1942.

In the Midwest, those territory bands that had survived either carried on touring their provincial circuits and working out of their regional centers, or, like Andy Kirk, they relocated to New York. Kirk's move had been on the strength of a hit record, in his case the 1936 ballad sung by Pha Terrell, *Until the Real Thing Comes Along*, and from his band's new base he undertook arduous, but successful, touring. Kirk rivaled Lunceford for his willingness to take one-nighters at considerable distances from one another. Other African-American musicians attempted to cash in on the success of the big white bands by directly emulating them – a particularly ironic example being

Jimmie Noone, who formed a short-lived large group in 1939 comparable to that of Benny Goodman – the very clarinetist that Noone himself had influenced.

However, by 1940, press reports began to appear pointing out that job opportunities for African-American musicians were in sharp decline. One New York paper stated:

> The jobless musical tribe increases and you can see its swelling membership daily in front of the Lafayette Theater, Rhythm Club, and other favorite gathering spots of bandsmen. Many things contribute to the fact that the very persons responsible for the popularity of jazz and swing music are the ones to get the least out of it.[28]

Attempting to quantify this observation, under the heading "Negro Employment Down," *Billboard* ran a report suggesting that the number of jobs open to African-American musicians had declined over the previous three years by up to 30 percent by late 1940.[29] That year, both Coleman Hawkins and Teddy Wilson fronted their big bands at the short-lived Golden Gate Ballroom in Harlem, a venue that was eventually forced out of business by the competitive tactics (fair and unfair) of the Savoy. Soon both leaders were compelled by economic necessity to lead smaller groups, and Wilson, in particular, did so in order to pay off the horrific debts he had incurred trying to keep his big band going. "I decided to finance my own band and lost," he wrote, "because I had to pay the salaries and expenses of my men while not enough was coming in. The music world, like any business is a game of chance, and you have to run the risk of losing."[30]

Benny Carter, who had led a succession of large orchestras after his return from Europe, also cut down to a small band in 1941 before relaunching his career in the West, and during the long period that Wilson was fronting his sextet at the Café Society, in Greenwich Village, the small groups of Carter and Hawkins both worked for some time on 52nd Street.

Another well-known leader, Edgar Hayes, who had gone on from his days in the Blue Rhythm Band to create a big hit with his own orchestra's *Stardust*, broke up his popular big band in 1941, and moved to California as a soloist. His counterpart, pianist-leader Claude Hopkins, dissolved his orchestra in 1940, although he briefly put together another big band in 1941–2, before taking a wartime job in an aircraft factory. However, Hopkins was fortunate enough to be given the factory band to lead, and went on to form several other large ensembles of his own once his war work was over. Other well-established African-American big-band leaders were not so lucky, and some, such as Teddy Hill, gave up bandleading altogether.

Hill became the manager, in 1940, of an uptown club that presented music, called Minton's, which became one of a small number of after-hours hang-outs for performers, and which, indirectly, contributed further to the decline in employment prospects for his fellow musicians. The owner of the club, Henry Minton, had been the first black delegate to the New York branch of the American Federation of Musicians, Local 802, and, together with Hill, he welcomed performers from the world of black show-business to the venue, particularly on the traditionally quiet night of Monday, when, to drum up trade, musicians and dancers were offered a free supper, and there was open house for sitters-in on the bandstand. Musicians came along in considerable number, for the opportunity to jam, but as one local press report observed, this set a dangerous precedent:

> Only the pianist, the drummer and the sax player are on duty for the skimpy crowd in the place. Around 12 or 1 a.m., musicians start trickling in, bringing their horns or guitars with them. A lot of handshaking goes on among the visiting musicians and those working, and in the next few minutes the sax player is joined by three other saxophonists, maybe a clarinetist. A guitar player climbs on the stand. A bass fiddler starts plonking in the spot where there was no bass player before. ... The boss is an observing fellow. Four or five Monday nights like this in a row in which he gets free music via the "jam session" prompts him to lay off the drummer and the sax player, retaining only the pianist for that night, since musicians can always be relied upon to fill in.[31]

Not many of the sitters-in realized the effect their eager music making was having on regular employment. Nor was Minton's the only such club, where a small number of regular players was augmented by unpaid extras. Drummer Freddie Moore had led his trio at one of the first of them, Harlem's Victoria Café, in the mid-1930s, where his group with altoist Pete Brown and pianist Don Frye was often padded out with sitters-in. Among the better-known successors to this club was Clark Monroe's Uptown House, which opened a little before Minton's, in the late 1930s, and lasted until 1943, when it moved to 52nd Street. It was not even necessary for the "house band" there to be particularly well-seasoned musicians, as the owner could rely on a ready supply of more experienced players showing up to sit in, as I discovered from one of the club's former resident pianists, Gerald Wiggins, who told me:

> We felt we were just lucky to be playing somewhere. We weren't making any money. I was making three dollars a night up at Monroe's Uptown House, and that was a lot of money for me, because I was seventeen years old and had no real business being there in the first place.[32]

"Wig" remembers seeing the recently demobbed Norman Granz in the audience, watching the sitters-in there in the early 1940s, and believes that it was from witnessing the popularity of these occasions that Granz became one of the first entrepreneurs to realize how to make money out of organized jam sessions, which he went on to do in 1944 with his inaugural Jazz At The Philharmonic concerts. (In fairness, Eddie Condon began presenting public jam sessions somewhat earlier than Granz, starting at New York Town Hall in 1942, but these were deliberately less adversarial than Granz's popular jousts between high-profile soloists, which aimed to recapture the heat of the spontaneous cutting contest.)

In many jazz histories, Monroe's Uptown House and Minton's have taken on a symbolic importance for quite a different reason: because they are seen as the environment in which a new set of improvisational ideas emerged, ideas that in due course developed into bebop. In my view – for reasons that will become clear in the next chapter – this overstates the importance of these venues. Furthermore, the ensemble template on which many of the ideas of bebop were to develop was something that owed just as much to the regular groups that were working on 52nd Street, and principal among them was the tight-knit sextet established in 1937 at the Onyx Club by the former bassist with the Fletcher Henderson orchestra, John Kirby.

When Kirby first began to front the house band at the Onyx, with a line-up that included guitarist Teddy Bunn, altoist Pete Brown, and trumpeter Frankie Newton, his erstwhile Henderson colleagues expressed their incredulity that this diffident, somewhat retiring figure was "leader material."[33] It looked as if they would be proved right when the band's high-profile scat-singer, Leo Watson, as well as Bunn, Brown, and Newton all left in quick succession. But before coming to the Onyx, Kirby had spent a few months with Lucky Millinder, during which his ideas had coalesced about the kind of group he wanted to lead, and in order to implement his plan, he drafted in as replacements trumpeter Charlie Shavers, from Millinder's Blue Rhythm Orchestra, and altoist Russell Procope, from Teddy Hill's band. Together with three other former Millinder colleagues, clarinetist Buster Bailey, pianist Billy Kyle, and drummer O'Neil Spencer, this sextet of Kirby's settled into a remarkably long-lived line-up, which stayed intact until Spencer left, suffering from tuberculosis, in 1941. Over two-and-a-half years of the band's life were spent at the Onyx Club, allowing it to develop into a tight-knit organization, something that was also helped by the close personal bond amoung the players as a result of their previous work together in various big bands. Kirby also had an eye for visual presentation, and he dressed his line-up in identical white tail-suits, or the very latest double-breasted blazers and snappy ties, creating an impression of dapper uniformity which was, to some extent, reflected in the cool precision of the band's musical arrangements. Over the next five years, the band became extremely popular, through broadcasts and its recordings for several labels – Decca, Vocalion, Okeh, and Victor – which sold well.

Charlie Shavers had grown up close to the Savoy Ballroom, where he had absorbed much of Roy Eldridge's revolutionary style at first hand, but his move to Kirby drew him out as a player, even though during most of his time in the band he largely abandoned his flamboyant open horn in order to demonstrate his mastery of muted playing. Shavers was still only twenty years old when he joined Kirby, but he quickly proved to be the band's outstanding talent. In the big bands he had already worked for, such as Millinder's, or earlier with Frankie Fairfax and Tiny Bradshaw, he had tended to work in partnership with his close friend (in effect his foster-brother) Carl "Bama" Warwick, who was a fine lead trumpeter, which left Shavers to play less demanding section big-band parts and take occasional solos. With Kirby, Shavers had to do all the work, and he loved it. "John Kirby's was a fine small band and I did a lot of the arrangements. . . . This band of Kirby's was my favourite band . . . when we went on a date, we never had to take any music with us – we had all memorized the whole book."[34]

This was no mean feat. No other band of the period – large or small – was playing such intricate, tightly wrought arrangements as Kirby. Some critics, notably Gunther Schuller, have found these charts stifling and artificial, to the extent that they are "barely in the realm of jazz."[35] Certainly, some of the band's best-known pieces were relatively facile treatments of light classics, and, for many years afterwards, Shavers reckoned his most popular arrangement to be the band's version of Grieg's

*Anitra's Dance*. There were others such as Chopin's *Minute Waltz*, Donizetti's *Sextet* from *Lucia di Lammermoor*, and Tchaikowski's *Dance of the Sugar Plum Fairy* from *The Nutcracker*. Few of these swing versions of the classics have stood the test of time, but, for the most part, they avoid being pretentious or as ponderous as some of Paul Whiteman's nods in this direction, and in the overall output of the Kirby band they are accompanied by a great number of sparkling, brilliantly inventive, and witty original pieces. I suspect that, over time, Shavers's *Undecided* has substantially overtaken *Anitra's Dance* in popularity, and his *Pastel Blue* was a more subtle piece of work than either. Representative examples of the band's work include such originals as Shavers's and Kirby's *Close Shave*, or neat arrangements of current popular songs such as *It's Only a Paper Moon*.

These contrasted considerably with the more established manner of music-making on the street, such as the rough-and-ready jamming of Stuff Smith, or the simple head arrangements with pyrotechnic solos recorded by Chu Berry and Roy Eldridge or Hot Lips Page. Instead, Kirby set out his novel philosophy to a *Down Beat* correspondent as follows:

> For one thing, I believe that jazz, to be good, should be restrained and organized. For that reason, I don't believe in out-and-out jamming. The boys and I believe that the only way we can gain distinction, apart from our ability to improvise, is to develop a distinguishing ensemble style and to prove by arrangements and our ability to execute them that the band is musicianly and versatile. . . . I believe that symphonic pieces can be handled by a jazz combination in such a way that serious music lovers won't throw up their hands in despair. With a combination like the one we have, we can give a tasteful treatment to all these classical things, but with a big orthodox swing band it would be hard to avoid the hackneyed "swinging" of the classics.[36]

However, not least because of the emphasis Kirby himself gave to its versions of classical pieces, and, equally, because of his success in achieving a uniformity of style across its other work, the importance of his band as a transitional force in jazz has tended to be overlooked. Its ensemble voicings were to be widely imitated by the next generation of players – just a few bars of Dizzy Gillespie and Charlie Parker playing *Dizzy Atmosphere* or *Groovin' High* reveal obvious affinities with the timbre and voicings of the muted trumpet and alto of Shavers and Procope in the Kirby front line.

Furthermore, what Shavers's arrangements created was, as even Schuller grudgingly admits, "a way out from the polyphonic practices of the New Orleans past ... and the omnipresent call-and-response routines of the Henderson-orientated formulas."[37] But was this all? What grounds are there for thinking that Kirby's band was rather more important than simply being a relatively jazz-free ensemble playing a kind of lukewarm chamber music?

For a start, its rhythm section was subtly different from those of the majority of swing bands, large and small, because Kirby dispensed with a guitar. When Teddy Bunn left, early in the group's life, he was never replaced. This threw the onus of the band's pulse onto Kirby himself, who had already proved in such pieces as Fletcher Henderson's 1930 *Chinatown* that he was a buoyant, swinging bassist, but who had now developed his style to something that was subtler, more even-sounding, and less percussive than his New Orleans-derived slapped bass of the early 1930s.

The opening chorus of *Close Shave* (recorded in July 1941) is a good demonstration of this, as Kirby's solid bass line is supported by Spencer's brush work and occasional accents, leaving pianist Billy Kyle to add sporadic chords, and to answer the unison front-line melodic phrases with single-line right-hand figures of his own. With no explicit chordal statement on every beat (what guitarist Danny Barker used to call the "big fat chords" he was required to provide when he had played alongside Kyle and Spencer in the Millinder orchestra), the whole feeling of Kirby's rhythm section is more open than those of most other bands of the time. Kyle's solo, which arrives in the third chorus, has the front line supporting him, with backing riffs, but it is a perfect demonstration of his off-center, left-hand chording and arsenal of right-hand techniques that, as stated Chapter 3, avoid arriving at a chordal resolution, hence keeping an irresistible sense of momentum. The tightly controlled background, neat riffs of the arrangement, and *sotto voce* style of the ensemble only serve to throw the short instrumental solos into high relief, making them sound far more impressive and exciting than they would do in a less restrained setting.

Second, a number of the band's arrangements involved newly composed themes or riff patterns substituting for the original melody of a piece. This was not a new idea, and plenty of impromptu jam-session discs from the late 1930s involved minimal riffs cooked up on the spur of the moment over the chord sequence of such standards as *I Got Rhythm*. Obvious examples of this include Lionel Hampton's *Stompology* from April 1937, which drops the two bar tag at the end of the tune and replaces Gershwin's melody with a few simple phrases. Indeed, later the same month, *Rhythm, Rhythm*, by another

Hampton recording group (which included both John Kirby and Buster Bailey), uses the same chord sequence all over again, with nothing more than a simple paraphrase of the original tune by Johnny Hodges to introduce a string of solos. Several other swing-era bands did this kind of thing – particularly small groups such as Goodman's trios and quartets – but few bands introduced newly composed themes over existing chords in so comprehensive a manner as Kirby, pointing so firmly towards the way that modern jazz players of the 1940s would use the device.

The old jam-session favorite *Sweet Georgia Brown*, which Kirby recorded in May 1939, is a case in point. The first chorus has an entirely new melodic structure, played in unison by both alto and clarinet in their lower registers, creating a dramatic springboard for Shavers's muted trumpet to launch into the original tune for the second chorus. It was only one step away from this kind of rewriting to drop the original melody altogether, and claim the piece as a new tune, something which many bebop composers were to do in the following decade. (This particular disc of *Sweet Georgia Brown* is prescient regarding bebop in another respect, since the neatly executed front-line break during the piano solo consists of the main riff for Dizzy Gillespie's *Salt Peanuts*, which would eventually be one of the best-known examples of the new music. Equally, Thelonious Monk's famous bebop composition *Blue Monk* is derived from the ensemble riff in Kirby's *Pastel Blue*.)

Another of the Kirby band's novel variations on a well-known song comes in its disc of Irving Berlin's *Blue Skies*, from August 1939. Here, there is a distinctive downward-moving theme that introduces each eight-bar section of the second chorus, in which the contrasting front-line riff and the answering piano phrases completely alter the balance and feel of the tune to something quite different from Berlin's original.

Several of the newly written pieces by Shavers, Kyle, and Kirby recorded by the band use quite familiar chord sequences, but they include some interesting experiments with phrasing that also point to one of the hallmarks of bebop, which was to introduce phrases of varying length. Most swing-era riff tunes are constructed of patterns that neatly divide into four-measure sections, but a piece such as Shavers's *Comin' Back*, from the band's final Victor session in February 1942, uses a three-bar riff in its head section that is answered by a single measure from the piano – and this unevenness creates an unorthodox and attention-grabbing effect.

A third reason for taking seriously Kirby's influence on the jazz that followed is that the popularity and relative longevity of his group made it one of the best known on 52nd Street, and after its various lengthy runs at the Onyx, plus forays as far afield as Chicago and Los Angeles, it also appeared at several other clubs on the street including the Hickory House and the Famous Door.[38] In addition to its own recordings, it backed Kirby's wife, the singer Maxine Sullivan, on several of her discs, as well as playing on sixteen sides with the Ohio-born vocalist Una Mae Carlisle, a former protégée of Fats Waller. In all of these, its tight-knit urbane style predominated, and other groups up and down 52nd Street began to model not just their instrumentation, but also their overall approach on the Kirby pattern.

One example was Kirby's former altoist Pete Brown, whose "jump" style of playing was a major influence on Louis Jordan, but whose 1942 band at the Onyx Club with trumpeter Harvey Davis and tenorist "Pazuza" Simon was very similar in style to the Kirby sextet. Brown kept to this approach when he went into the studios for Leonard Feather in February 1942, to make four sides with the singers Helen Humes and Nora Lee King. For this he borrowed two members of the front line of another 52nd Street band that was playing in a similar style, led by Benny Carter. Carter's clarinetist Jimmy Hamilton, and his trumpeter Dizzy Gillespie, played tight, Kirby-inspired riffs alongside Brown on such titles as *Mound Bayou* and *Unlucky Woman*.

I will go into more detail about Gillespie in the next chapter, but his presence in Benny Carter's small group prompted critic Barry Ulanov to make specific comparisons with Kirby in *Metronome*:

> Commercially, Benny Carter's small crew might be the first to rival Kirby's in that outfit's almost one-band field. Its performances are not as slick as the latter's yet, nor are its books alive with the saleable novelties that mean so much to the Kirbys. But the material is all here.[39]

Carter became a staunch enthusiast for Gillespie's playing, and withstood criticism of his young trumpeter's eccentricities of style (both from the owners of the Famous Door and from the press) with fortitude. "I could see that Dizzy, when he was with me for several months, was groping for something. And he knew his music . . . I stood up for him."[40] Gillespie, for his part, having earlier played in the big bands of Teddy Hill and Cab Calloway, was using the experience of playing in a well-disciplined small group for several weeks to learn how this kind of ensemble functioned, and he was later to say that the sixteen weeks or so that he spent shoulder-to-shoulder with Benny Carter on 52nd Street was his best musical experience apart from his subsequent work with Charlie Parker.[41] There was, therefore, a direct connection between one of the principal architects of modern jazz and the swing groups of the Street.

Later, in the spring of 1944, when Gillespie himself had made the final transition from swing player to out-and-out bebopper, he spent a few weeks replacing his old friend Charlie Shavers in John Kirby's band at the Aquarium Club. His empathy with the group on recordings of the broadcasts they made is obvious, and he stays well inside the Shavers model, playing such characteristic Kirby arrangements as *Close Shave* and *Taking a Chance on Love*. However, on *Rose Room*, played as a head arrangement, with Buster Bailey stating the melody on clarinet to usher in a series of solos, Gillespie shows just how a fully fledged bebop solo could fit happily inside the Kirby style. This is a clear demonstration of the affinities of Kirby's format with the emergent approach to small-group jazz of Gillespie and his circle. However, by the time of these broadcasts with Kirby, Gillespie had already led his own prototype bebop group at the Onyx Club for around three months, from late 1943 to early 1944, and it was clear that a major change in jazz was afoot. With the arrival of Gillespie's small group on the street, a clear signal had been sent out that the long, stable predominance of swing as the universal jazz style was about to end.

# CHAPTER 7

# The Birth of Bebop

## A Psychological Shift

[There was] an unspoken policy, a psychological shift on the
part of the musicians that performers should create the
kind of music they wanted to play. If audiences liked it, so
much the better, but this was no longer the first priority.

Charles Fox, in Geoffrey Haydon and Dennis Marks,
*Repercussions: A Celebration of African-American Music*

So far, the subject of bebop, the modern jazz of the 1940s, has been
mentioned from time to time, but without much in the way of explanation
as to what it was, or how it differed from the jazz that had gone before it.
Whereas swing had largely been to do with consolidation, unifying
approaches to meter, chording, the voicing and arranging of melodies, and
ways of building improvised solos, the new movement involved changes not
just to those areas of unification, but also at a more fundamental level, to all
the underlying elements of music itself: melody, harmony, and rhythm.

First, in terms of melody, the practice I described in relation to John
Kirby's *Sweet Georgia Brown* became widespread, with new tunes being
superimposed on many a well-worn chord sequence, and completely
replacing the original. These fresh melodic lines were not modeled on the
simple riff patterns of the swing era, nor were they intended to set song
lyrics to music by obeying the normal rules of scansion. Instead, the new
melodies were jagged; full of dense, rapid figures, and uneven in phrase
length. In a number of cases, once the new melody became established, it
would be slightly re-harmonized, moving the whole thing a step or two

further away from the original chords.

At the same time, improvising soloists began to extend the length of their melodic lines, and to build these from asymmetrical phrases, so that they avoided the standard conventions of swing, and a straightforward division into units of four or eight measures. Phrases could also be of uneven length, in order to extend over the normal cadences that tend to be placed at the end of every four bars. This is a logical development of the devices used by Lester Young and Ben Webster to construct solos from strings or sequences of motific patterns, and in the hands of a young generation of virtuoso instrumentalists, the phrases became more intricate, and the harmonic thinking that underpinned their construction became more complex.

Second, substitute harmonies of the kind I have identified in the playing of Coleman Hawkins became increasingly common. In Art Tatum's solo piano work, for example, he would frequently reharmonize passages by adding passing chords, replacing others, and creating dissonant effects between his two hands. Chords that extended beyond the octave began to be more frequently employed, so that altered ninth, eleventh, and thirteenth chords began to be used, as well as the flattened fifth. In due course, it became common practice to replace whole sections of the harmonic accompaniment to a piece, usually with more complex chords than the composer's originals, and this idea spread from solo pianists or instrumentalists to entire ensembles. A good example of this is the way in which Dizzy Gillespie and Tadd Dameron reworked the "A" section to Vernon Duke's popular swing-era tune *I Can't Get Started* [CD track 12] to produce a more subtle series of underlying chords, a chromatically descending series of II–V pairings, complemented, in this case, by a newly composed shifting countermelody for the accompanying saxophone and trombone that adds a new sense of movement to the ballad.[1]

Third, the rhythmic backdrop became more complex, and instead of the evenly spread four–four chug of the guitar-driven swing rhythm section, with the drummer marking time on bass and snare drum, the responsibility for maintaining momentum moved, as it had begun to do in John Kirby's band, to the double bass and the ride cymbals, leaving the drummer free to introduce snare drum accents or "rimshots" that were no longer automatically placed on the second and fourth "off" beats of each measure. The drummer's bass drum, instead of marking the first and third "on" beats, or even, as Gene Krupa did, emphasizing a four–four pulse, might suddenly interject unexpected off-center accentuations (known, with ironic contemporaneous reference to World War II, as "dropping bombs") which often fell on the eighth and final beat of a two-measure phrase. Or, rather than isolated accents, the drummer might play a jagged series of emphatic notes, of the kind that earned drummer Kenny Clarke his onomatopoeic nickname "Klook-a-mop." And it was just such an attempt to render a musical sound into words that gave the new jazz itself a name – a piece with one of the abrupt, jagged melodies of the new music called *Bu-dee-daht*, which was at first corrupted into *Bu-re-bop*, later shortened to *re-bop* and then *bebop*.[2]

The bassist would play a "walking" part, developing the innovations of Walter Page with Basie, and Jimmy Blanton with Ellington, which had shifted bass lines away from the simple chordal arpeggios of Pops Foster and Wellman Braud to more flexible, mobile lines with melodic characteristics of their own, and the incorporation of passing notes to underline the more subtle harmonic changes in a piece.

The piano, too, would favor occasional chordal accents or accentuations, rather than underpinning each chord of every bar. This had the effect of generally loosening up the whole feeling of the rhythm section, and making its playing less predictable. Piano solos shifted from the two-handed, ragtime-based approach of stride to a newer, fleeter style, in which the right hand played long sinuous melodic lines while the left prodded an asymmetrical chordal accompaniment. Many of these devices were present in Art Tatum's playing, although his work co-existed with bebop's development rather than being directly absorbed into it. The polyrhythms found in the front-line interplay of early jazz gradually migrated to the rhythm section.[3]

As these various elements coalesced, a discernible new form of jazz developed. The principal musicians involved were trumpeters Dizzy Gillespie and Howard McGhee; saxophonists Don Byas, Budd Johnson, and Charlie Parker; pianists Tadd Dameron, Thelonious Monk, and Bud Powell; bassist Oscar Pettiford, and drummers Kenny Clarke and Max Roach. As I suggested in the previous chapter, the orthodox view is that the development of their new ideas took place in the after-hours clubs of Harlem, mainly Monroe's Uptown House and Minton's, in the early 1940s, where a group of young, technically advanced African-American musicians, who began by playing informal swing jam sessions, gradually developed an ever more complex system of playing. It was widely believed that this was done with the intention of keeping less adept musicians (predominantly, by implication, white swing players) from being able to keep up with them.

Autobiographical statements from some of the musicians involved tended to support this view, such as Dizzy Gillespie's often-quoted remark: "On afternoons before a session, Thelonious Monk and I began to work out some complex variations on chords and the like, and we used them at night to scare away the no-talent guys."[4]

Having analyzed Gillespie's career in some detail, the impression may be one of a more conscious process than was actually the case. Gillespie's earliest after-hours experiments (without Monk, who came to Minton's early in 1941) took place at Monroe's in 1939, and he was away on the road with Calloway for much of the next two years, and then with other leaders, including Ella Fitzgerald and Charlie Barnet. For four months at the end of 1941 and the start of 1942, he was working until the small hours at Kelly's Stable, with Benny Carter, and so his participation was limited to a few brief periods, certainly shorter than his remarks have generally been interpreted to suggest.[5]

Furthermore, a large number of the oral history accounts of Minton's confirm that on many — if not a majority of — occasions, there were distinguished swing stars sitting in; players like Artie Shaw, Benny Goodman, Lester Young, and Roy Eldridge, who were certainly not "no-talent" guys, but who were not all likely to have been acquainted with all of the harmonic innovations being developed by Monk and Gillespie. Indeed, as Mary Lou Williams recalled, speaking of the jam sessions there, "when Thelonious Monk first played at Minton's there were few musicians who could run changes with him."[6] The implication is that, for much of the time, Monk had to restrain himself in order to accommodate sitters-in. For example, as the house drummer Kenny Clarke wrote, when Benny Goodman showed up, "We used to just convert our style to coincide with his, so Benny played just the things he wanted to play. We did that for others, too."[7]

Informal recordings made (for the most part by an enthusiast named Jerry Newman) at Minton's and Clark Monroe's Uptown House, in 1941, reveal that what was being played was still recognizably swing. On these scratchy glimpses behind the scenes of the after-hours clubs, pianist Kenny Kersey, for example, uses occasional substitute harmonies, and adopts a flowing linear right-hand style, but his playing is still close to that of Billy Kyle. Drummer Kenny Clarke tends mainly to play in a straightforward swing manner, adding punctuations similar to those of his mentor Sid Catlett, and only moving occasionally towards the more fragmentary accents of bebop, while backing Charlie Christian's guitar solos. (As I said earlier,

Christian died too early for his own style to make the migration into bebop.) The most notable exception among these players is Dizzy Gillespie, whose trumpet solos over the chord sequence of *Exactly Like You*, on a lengthy version of a nameless piece Newman titled *Kerouac*, after the beat poet and habitué of the after-hours clubs, contain several devices that would be cornerstones of his future style, from the use of the flattened-fifth interval to phrasing that prefigures a fully fledged band riff he later employed in his composition *One Bass Hit*.[8]

However, in Gillespie's case there are just as convincing recorded examples of his future style in commercial discs made with Les Hite and Lucky Millinder in 1942, and even in aspects of some of his solos with Calloway from as early as 1939. So perhaps we should look further afield than the after-hours clubs of New York to see how and why bebop developed, not least because it was happening at a time when, as we have seen, firstly, high-profile jobs in the music business were shifting from African-American musicians to white players and, secondly, many African-American bandleaders were being forced to scale down to smaller groups. Thirdly, general racial tensions in Harlem were worsening, and there was an underlying fear of rioting; a fear which turned out to be justified in August 1943 when a young black soldier was shot in the shoulder by a policemen, triggering a night of street battles around 125th Street that ended with six fatalities. Against such a background, it would be easy to interpret bebop as a conscious revolution by African-American musicians, highly charged with the racial and political agenda of the time. But in just the same way as there is more to the early story of jazz than a simple migration from New Orleans to Chicago, so, too, is the story of bebop more complex than one of after-hours jamming leading to a widespread revolution.

For a start, most of the prime movers in the movement were musicians who, by 1942 or thereabouts, had played in, or were still members of, a wide range of big bands. Dizzy Gillespie had worked successively with Frankie Fairfax, Teddy Hill, Edgar Hayes, Cab Calloway, Ella Fitzgerald, Charlie Barnet, Les Hite, and Lucky Millinder. Charlie Parker had played in the Kansas City-based territory bands of George E. Lee and Jay McShann. Drummer Kenny Clarke had worked with Leroy Bradley and Roy Eldridge, then played in territory bands including the Jeter-Pillars Orchestra, and ended up in New York with Claude Hopkins, Edgar Hayes, and Teddy Hill. Bassist Oscar Pettiford had toured the territories in his family group, before joining Charlie Barnet's big band. Bud Powell was in the process of moving on from being a teenage prodigy in the Harlem stride style to becoming the pianist with the Cootie Williams Orchestra. As accomplished members of such bands, this is no ordinary group of rebels. It is hard to categorize them as Amiri Baraka has done as rebelling against the "tasteless commercialism" of swing,[9] when for the most part they had worked hard to become committed professional musicians within the world of the swing orchestras and, in most cases, reached the higher echelons of such bands.

As their new ideas about jazz began to develop, several of these musicians were out on the road, in many different regions of the United States. It is certainly the case that, during the period in 1943, when both Dizzy Gillespie and Charlie Parker were together in Earl Hines's orchestra, their radical approach became the talking point of jazz musicians everywhere they went. However, in the hot-house world of the big bands, which had similar channels of communication to those that helped spread the early message of jazz through the black show-business world of the early twentieth century, there is little doubt that the word was out on these particular musicians some years earlier, when they were with Calloway and McShann respectively.

What was it, then, that drew these musicians together? In his history of bebop, Scott DeVeaux proposes some answers. First, he suggests that, in view of the fact that bebop was predominantly (though not exclusively) an African-American development, it was "rooted deeply in the uncomfortable realities of race in America." He suggests that without the climate in which black musicians lived and worked in a separate and unequal world from their white counterparts, musicians "of such divergent talents and temperaments might not have found themselves forced into the same narrow space," albeit a space that, because of the demonstrable material success of some African-American swing bands, offered one of the few chances to overcome racial barriers.[10]

Second, he points out that this was a youthful alliance, that the majority of the bebop pioneers (Kenny Clarke excepted) were born between 1917 and 1924, putting all of them in their very early twenties during the formative years of their new music. They were all young and enthusiastic enough to want to make their own mark on the music, in the same way that earlier revolutionaries like Louis Armstrong and Duke Ellington had put their stamp on jazz in their twenties.

In my view, there is a third and more significant factor, to do with the sheer amount of music these young professional musicians played. We know already that bandleaders such as Artie Shaw and Harry James suffered physical collapses from the intensity of playing at a consistently high level during several shows a day to boisterous, demanding audiences at the height of the swing era. Although both these men carried the main burden of the solos with their respective orchestras, there is little doubt that their rank-and-file musicians were worked extremely hard as well, providing the right kind of enthusiastic, energetic background for their leaders. This level of workload transcended the color barrier. Just like their white counterparts, African-American orchestras played long hours in dance halls, theaters, and cabarets, and for those with recording contracts, their studio sessions had to be fitted in as well.

But for the ordinary sidemen, there was little opportunity to play lengthy improvised solos, as Shaw and James were able to do. Jonah Jones, for example, preferred to stay in the small clubs on 52nd Street for years, rather than join Cab Calloway (as he eventually did) because:

> I figured Cab's band wasn't the place for solos, because his show was so big. He had eleven boy singers and tap dancers, Bill Bailey, Pearl's brother, the Miller Brothers and Lois, it was wonderful! What a show, but there were no chances for trumpet solos.[11]

Before Jones joined Calloway, the band's main trumpet soloist was Dizzy Gillespie, but on record, from 1939 until 1941, Gillespie's contribution is mainly limited to a few bars on each disc, with only the occasional full-chorus solo. Even on the broadcasts that survive of the band's club dates, instrumental soloists played a subservient role to Calloway himself, and, as Jonah Jones suggests, in theaters there were all the additional singers and dancers to be featured as well.

Calloway's band, as we know from Chapter 4, used up a huge volume of new arrangements, but with the exception of a tiny number of more challenging pieces by Don Redman and Benny Carter, the rest tended to reinforce the structures and harmonies of the popular songs of the period. When he joined the band in 1939, aged 21, Gillespie was its youngest member. Although he was largely self-taught, he already had a formidable command of harmony, as he demonstrated in his own arrangements for the band, produced within a few months of his arrival, and containing some of the most advanced harmonic thinking in the band "book."

The older members of the line-up, particularly those few whose careers stretched back to the days of the Missourians, accepted a degree of boredom as a condition of working in the best-paid orchestra of the period. As the band's guitarist Danny Barker said:

> It was a very monotonous deal sitting on a stage playing one and a half hour stage shows four, five, sometimes six times a day, seven days a week for months and months at a time. Playing the same songs over and over under the hot stage lighting. When the stage show was over you went to the small crowded dressing room, always near the roof of the theater. You practiced, worked with your hobby, wrote letters. Many musicians could not take the daily routine, blew their tops and quit.[12]

Gillespie's reaction to the potential boredom of this daily routine was twofold. He went in for practical jokes, clowning around and horseplay, to the extent that Calloway described his antics as "a pain in the neck."[13] More importantly, as time went on, instead of continuing to create miniature replicas of his idol Roy Eldridge's way of playing, he used his few bars of solo space here and there to cram in as many of his new harmonic and melodic ideas as possible. The band's pianist, Bennie Payne, described how Gillespie would "just take off in double time." Danny Barker – trying to follow him by playing the right guitar chords – said "you had to listen because his new sounds kept you off balance until he came back in on time." Even Calloway himself admitted: "His improvisation . . . was just what he was thinking all that time, and he put it into his playing. And all those intricate changes he would make on his horn . . . nobody had ever heard anything like this before."[14]

Because Calloway was dismissive of Gillespie's music, urging him to "play what was written," and describing his trumpeter's new harmonic ideas as "Chinese music," perhaps too little attention has been paid to the other aspect of the remark I have quoted, namely that the music the trumpeter was playing was what "he was thinking all that time." The former head of B.B.C. classical music, Sir William Glock, used to have a saying that his head was always full of music, although the pity was that it was somebody else's. It seems to me a quite valid assumption that Gillespie's head was equally full of music, but in his case the majority of it was his own; new and original.

This view is supported by Gillespie's own account of his discovery of the potency of the flattened fifth: the A natural in an E flat major chord, in an arrangement by Rudy Powell for Edgar Hayes's band. "With the flatted fifth I really got turned on. And from that one phrase – just one bar – I started developing that passage and listening to it, and before you knew it I was trained like that. I was excited about the progression and used it everywhere."[15]

Gillespie's enthusiasm carried to other members of the Calloway band, and guitarist Danny Barker and bassist Milt Hinton would rehearse chord substitutions and bass lines with him in backstage dressing rooms on tour, or up on the roof of the Cotton Club. In the end, Barker dropped out once he had mastered chords that "would be correct with his extensions,"[16] but Hinton remained, impressed at Gillespie's extraordinary ability to hear altered chords, or to suggest creative bass lines. Hinton told me how Gillespie painstakingly explained to him how to employ the idea of the circle of fifths, often used by improvisers, and a device employed by John Kirby's band in its recording of *From A-flat to C*. Gillespie also showed him how to make the most basic chordal substitutions; for example, putting an A minor chord in place of a C major to emphasize the sixth of the C major scale and to create an effect of passing dissonance. It seems that from early in his career Gillespie had the ability to hear how he wanted all the instruments surrounding him to back up his own solos, and he developed into an outstanding teacher. "Dizzy was enlightening me about all these different changes," Hinton said, "the different combinations of sounds they made, and I just loved that."[17] It was only four years after these first experiments with Hinton that Gillespie was explaining to the young pianists George Wallington and Billy Taylor how he wanted them to voice the piano chords in his quintet on 52nd Street.

So it is fair to conclude that Gillespie had an exceptional ability to "hear" music in his head, a degree of perception that suggests an unusually well-developed cognitive sensibility. The same seems to be true of altoist Charlie Parker. Bandleader Jay McShann recalled hearing Parker for the first time in Kansas City as he passed by a club:

> I heard this sound, it was a different sound, so I was saying to myself, "Who is that blowing?" So I decided to go in and see who it was. After he'd finished blowing I walked over to him and said: "Man, where you from? I haven't met you, and I thought I'd met all the musicians in town."
>
> He said, "I'm from Kansas City, but I've been out of town. . . . with George Lee's band."
>
> I told him, I said, "Well you blow different from anybody else round here, and that's why I came in. I just wanted to see who it was."[18]

McShann recalled how when other musicians heard Parker play, they immediately knew that he was hearing and understanding music at a level way above most of them, a skill he had developed during his time on the road with George Lee's band, which he described as "woodshedding" – in other words the opportunity to put in long hours of practice through the night-after-night routine of a working band.

In my view, a significant result of this intense musical experience was that it developed the musical skills of those who had the ability to think in musical terms way beyond the normal. Only the youngest members of Calloway's orchestra – Gillespie and Hinton – reacted to their daily routine in this way, and in McShann's orchestra, Parker's ideas similarly inspired trumpeters Buddy Anderson and Orville Minor, whereas the remainder of the rank-and-file players made no such unusual development in either band. This was not something new to the start of the 1940s. Benny Carter, for instance, rapidly developed his exceptional abilities in the 1920s in Charlie Johnson's orchestra, but not many of his contemporaries developed his extraordinary all-round skills. But the difference is that in the 1940s, with the universality of swing, and a greater number of bands in existence, the opportunity was there for many more players to develop in this way than had previously been the case.

So is there – at least in part – a psychological explanation for the way the first bebop players developed out of the big swing orchestras? In the words of psychologist Glenn D. Wilson: "What musical training and experience contributes is a language-like system for coding and describing the auditory sensations that are basic to music. This assists with remembering, discussing and performing music."[19] It is quite plausible to think of the generation of young musicians who developed bebop as having developed this "language-like system" to an extraordinary degree, owing to the circumstances in which they had been required in the swing orchestras to play music for so many hours each day.

But if there was, at least in part, a psychological impetus to the creation of the ideas behind bebop, these ideas themselves challenged the psychological perceptions of the audience for the music. It was an audience conditioned by the relatively long and stable period in which swing had become the universal sound of jazz. For instance, the flattened-fifth interval that preoccupied Dizzy Gillespie appeared so novel because, since medieval times, musicians had avoided it. Referred to by church theorists as *diabolus in musica* ("the devil in music"), the flattened-fifth, the tritone interval between C and F sharp, had been studiously side-stepped in classical music, and hence in the forms of popular music that owed at least part of their harmonic language to Western art music. to the ears of music theorists, from medieval to Victorian times, the dissonance created by this interval that divided the scale exactly in two was unpalatable: to the beboppers its use invited a consonant resolution that made it both thrilling and attractive; to audiences (and indeed some other musicians) not used to hearing it, its use seemed hostile and threatening, an effect compounded by adding such additional dissonances as ninths, elevenths, and thirteenths. And, by changing the harmonic and rhythmic structure of the music as well as employing such *avant-garde* intervals in their melodic lines, the beboppers challenged what Berlyne has defined as the principle of "optimal uncertainty."[20] This is the point where a balance is struck between the predictable and the totally unpredictable, where an audience is equipped to comprehend the structure and form of a piece of music, but is equally capable of hypothesizing about what will come next. By simultaneously challenging melody, harmony, and rhythm, the beboppers pushed the level of uncertainty beyond the levels for which many listeners were prepared.

This business of building up an orthodoxy and then challenging it has been a principle in music throughout its history, and in writing of classical composers, Glenn D. Wilson observes: "in taking the complexity of music one step further than his predecessors, each composer depends on the cultural learning that has been contributed by previous composers."[21] Exactly the same is true of the bebop generation, except, as Charles Fox points out in the quote that opens this chapter, the bebop musicians themselves were making a psychological shift: they were aiming to create music that they wanted to play, rather than that which an existing audience wanted to hear.

## A Remarkable Partnership

Bird and Dizzy fit just like a hand and a glove. They sounded like one horn. If somebody could put one mouthpiece on two horns and play it at the same time, that's what they sounded like. Bird used to play with Red Rodney and Miles, but it was never like with Dizzy.

Ray Brown, in an interview with the author

The two figures who came to symbolize bebop more than any other musicians were Charlie Parker and Dizzy Gillespie. They were both largely self-taught, and although they did not meet until June 24, 1940, their musical ideas had developed independently along remarkably parallel lines, both of them exploring the kinds of melodic, harmonic, and rhythmic change I have described. They had very different personalities, which perhaps explains why their playing was so complementary, and would dovetail so closely after they first worked together in the Earl Hines Orchestra in 1943, and went on to play alongside one another in numerous small groups.

Gillespie was a natural showman, someone who easily assimilated the stagecraft, easy wit, and athletic mobility of the bandleaders for whom he worked, including Lucky Millinder, Tiny Bradshaw, and Cab Calloway. His sunny stage personality was combined with an eccentric line in clothing, and his pinstripe suits, beret, and horn-rimmed spectacles were complemented by a goatee beard – the whole effect giving fans of the new music a visual identity, a style of dress, and a behavioral code. In later years, his upward-pointing trumpet compounded his zany, hip image. Although he had something of a reputation as a firebrand in his youth, and carried a vicious-looking knife (he left both the Edgar Hayes and Cab Calloway bands in hot-blooded scuffles), Gillespie was to become a consummate professional. He cared about being prompt and well-prepared, and he took on many of his own attitudes as a leader from the disciplinarian manner in which Calloway treated his men off stage. He knew the value of writing down and organizing his musical ideas, and as well as learning to be a more than competent pianist, he became skilled with pencil and manuscript paper, also perceiving it as his mission to proselytize for the new music. He married Lorraine Willis during his time with Calloway, and they remained together until his death over half a century later. Despite the infidelities and separations incurred by a constant life on the road, his stable home life provided a bedrock for his career, and he was not drawn into the shady world of hard drugs and excess that became a major temptation for many of the young bebop musicians.

Parker, by contrast, was a mercurial, transient figure, whose instrumental genius contrasted with a chaotic lifestyle. Whereas Gillespie moved easily round the stage, Parker tended to stand stock-still, focusing all his mental and physical energy on his alto saxophone. Off stage, he had a ready charm, wide-ranging intellectual interests, and a Bohemian attitude that could make him delightful company when he was not too overcome by artificial stimulants. He had a formidable constitution which withstood a gargantuan intake of alcohol and narcotics, and his personal relationships were volatile and complex. But in the same way that a romantic, idealized image attached itself to the tragically short life of Bix Beiderbecke, the meteoric glitter of Parker's 34 years also turned him into a legendary figure.

Musically, the complementary nature of Parker and Gillespie was even more marked. Parker's playing was steeped in the blues of Kansas City, whereas despite his Southern background, Gillespie was never an instinctive blues musician. Gillespie's development of the Eldridge trumpet style and his painstakingly acquired academic knowledge of harmony combined with Parker's more instinctive approach. Gillespie described their "meeting of the minds" as follows:

> I know he had nothing to do with my playing the trumpet, and I think I was a little more advanced, harmonically, than he was. But rhythmically he was quite advanced, with setting up the phrase and how you got from one note to another. . . . Charlie Parker heard rhythms and rhythmic patterns differently, and after we started playing together, I began to play, rhythmically, more like him.[22]

So what was the background against which these two musicians came to develop such complementary ideas almost completely independently of one another, before their first meeting in Kansas City?

When John Birks Gillespie was born into the rural farming community of Cheraw, South Carolina, on October 21, 1917, his parents had already produced eight older children. Life in the country was hard, and although Dizzy's father – a bricklayer and local bandleader who regularly brutalized his children – introduced his son to music, Gillespie was largely self-taught, first on the trombone and later on trumpet. At fifteen, he won a place at the Laurinberg Institute, some 35 miles from Cheraw, where he played in the band. Although he was on a scholarship, Gillespie supported himself by working on the school farm, while also studying agriculture, and throughout his life he would tell interviewers about his knowledge of and love for farming.

Around mid-1935, Gillespie's widowed mother and his immediate family followed the great exodus from the Southern states and moved north. They settled in Philadelphia, and Gillespie found a job playing in the band of Frankie Fairfax. Fairfax's former pianist and arranger Bill Doggett had recently quit the band in a row over finances, but he became good friends with Gillespie, and taught him much about arranging and big-band voicing, which was to prompt his interest in harmony and composition. Quite by chance, the band itself was packed with musicians who went on to be jazz stars, including clarinetist Jimmy Hamilton, who went on to work alongside Gillespie in Benny Carter's band and later became a star of Ellington's orchestra, drummer Shadow Wilson, who worked with many significant bands, and, most importantly, trumpeter Charlie Shavers, who introduced Gillespie to the ideas and solos of Roy Eldridge. Soon, Gillespie (who was given his "Dizzy" nickname owing to his behavior in Fairfax's band) was playing a passable imitation of Eldridge, which is how he sounded in 1937 when he cut his first records in New York with Teddy Hill.

Hill had formerly employed Eldridge himself, and then his main soloist became Frankie Newton. When Hill was offered a European tour, Newton did not want to travel, and Gillespie took his place in time for the record date, a few days before the band sailed. It was a novel experience for the young trumpeter to come to Europe as part of a "name" band, and he lived it up, buying flashy European clothes and sampling the delights of London and Paris. It is in the written accounts of this visit that Gillespie's individuality as a soloist began to be mentioned by critics, summed up by the Parisian author Maurice Cullaz who recalled:

> He was already playing in a way that differentiated him from Roy Eldridge. He had a very varied and powerful style ... all the [local] trumpeters came and asked Dizzy to show them his trumpet and his embouchure, because he was easily playing two octaves above middle C, and everyone was fascinated with the apparent ease with which he played.[23]

Soloing was one thing, but at this early stage in his career Gillespie's ensemble work still left something to be desired. The group's first trumpeter, Bill Dillard, used the week-long Atlantic crossing to teach the young Gillespie some of the principles of big-band playing that he had never learned during his informal musical education.

This proved to be a major asset for Gillespie. He never lost his love for and sympathy towards the sound of a big band, and his major contributions to this genre through his own large ensembles are discussed both in the next chapter and in Chapter 15. When he joined Cab Calloway's Cotton Club Orchestra in 1939, this gave him further valuable big-band experience among some of the top musicians in the United States at the time, and both

with Calloway and in a freelance session with Lionel Hampton, Gillespie cut
the first records on which, rather than imitating Eldridge, his own individual
solo voice can clearly be heard to be developing – the majority of these
being made some time before he had met or heard Charlie Parker. I have
already mentioned Gillespie's composition for Calloway of *Pickin' the
Cabbage*, on which he plays a solo during the March 1940 recording, but that
piece is more important for the way it prefigures the structure and harmonic
language of some of his later writing, and his trumpet work is at its most
distinctive elsewhere in the band's recorded repertoire.

His earliest session with the band, in 1939, produced a pair of bravura
solos on *Pluckin' the Bass*, a piece which, as its name implies, was a vehicle for
Milt Hinton, but which, in each of two takes, has some dazzling playing
from Gillespie. The second, more confident solo shows many hallmarks of
his later style, from the burst into the high register towards the start, to a
device similar to Lester Young's habit of repeating a note with several
different tonal inflections, which Gillespie (a walking encyclopedia of
alternate trumpet fingerings) achieved by altering the combination of valves
for each repetition of the note. Among dozens of other solos, his best work
with Calloway includes the clearly sculpted line of his measured ballad
playing on *Topsy Turvy*, the tumbling downward runs of a broadcast
recording of *Limehouse Blues*, the athletic leaps between registers of *Bye Bye
Blues*, his haunting, harmonically daring playing over the chromatic chords of
*Cupid's Nightmare*, and a favorite triplet configuration that he was to use in
different ways throughout his career, but which first emerges in *Boo-Wah-
Boo-Wah*.

Although the final recordings Gillespie made with Calloway date from
after his meeting with Parker, there is no immediate sign that that encounter
had brought about a change in his playing. Despite telling interviewers that
his playing altered almost at once after he met Parker,[24] it took until after
the period when the two men played for Earl Hines in 1943 for the cross-
fertilization to become obvious, and for aspects of Parker's less-orthodox
rhythmic approach to become a regular feature of Gillespie's work. After
leaving Calloway as the result of an altercation in 1941, Gillespie recorded
with a couple of other big bands before joining Hines, and his 1942 solos on
Les Hite's *Jersey Bounce* and Lucky Millinder's *Little John Special* both show a
dramatic improvement in his range and speed in the upper register. These
were the last commercial discs Gillespie made before the start of the
recording ban in 1942, and, despite his already commanding presence, it
was going to be an altogether more confident and developed player who

re-emerged on disc in 1944, although a couple of informal recordings do exist that allow us to catch some rather foggy glimpses of his work during the ban, one being a hotel-room session with Parker, and the other a fragment of a broadcast by Gillespie's first fully fledged bebop quintet on 52nd Street.

During the period leading up to their work together with Hines, Charlie Parker was not as much in the public eye as Gillespie. Jay McShann's territory band was no less busy than Teddy Hill's or Cab Calloway's, but as the bulk of his work was in the Midwest and Southwest it did not bring him to the attention of the same kind of wide national audience. Apart from some radio transcription discs from Wichita in 1940 that were recorded for local network broadcasts and which were not issued as records at the time, it was not until April 1941, during a visit to Dallas, Texas, that the band cut its first commercial sides with Charlie Parker on alto saxophone, thus opening up the possibility of his work being widely heard far away from McShann's touring orbit.

Parker had been born on August 29, 1920, in Kansas City, Kansas, over the state line from its more illustrious namesake in Missouri, where the Pendergast regime held sway, and to which his family moved in 1927. Not long after this, Parker's father left home and did not return. Charles Parker Sr. had been a singer and dancer, and he drifted off into Kansas City low-life. The young Parker's musical education was haphazard, and when, in the early 1930s, he began to sit in with local bands, he revealed little of his future promise. He was, however, exposed to the area's rich musical life, and as well as hearing at first hand many of the musicians who played in the city's clubs, he began to practice regularly. Indeed, he told fellow saxophonist Buddy Collette that his lifelong nickname came from his habit of getting up at four or five in the morning (or indeed, staying up listening to music until that time) and then taking his alto to a nearby park where he would play, perhaps with a friend from Lincoln High School, from which Parker more or less dropped out in his mid-teens.

> Often they'd get high out there. The cops would drive by and wave at them. They allowed him to practice as long as it was far enough away from the residential area. That's where the nickname came. The people heard that little alto of his so often in the park that they started calling him "Bird."[25]

In 1936 he played for the winter season in the local band led by saxophonist Tommy Douglas, and this gave him the same kind of apprenticeship that

Gillespie had begun somewhat earlier with Frankie Fairfax. The following year Parker worked in the Ozarks in the territory band of George Lee, and as part of his assiduous practice regime during this time began to learn by heart the solos of Lester Young almost as soon as they were released on discs with Count Basie's band. This added to the development of his remarkable musical memory – indeed, he told Buddy Collette late in his life: "I can sing any solo on record that Lester has played."[26] (This statement is at least partly borne out by his playing on one of the McShann transcription discs from late 1940, where his solo on *Lady Be Good* is full of conscious echoes of Young's with Jones-Smith Incorporated.)

It was after that period with Lee that Jay McShann first heard Parker, and knew immediately that this was a player with a novel approach to his instrument and the music. Before long they were working together in a band with drummer Jesse Price and altoist Buster "Prof" Smith, who were both veterans of the territory bands. When Smith moved to New York, Parker followed him by way of Chicago, where musicians who heard him sitting in at jam sessions confirmed the originality of his sound. In New York, from 1938 to 1939, he seldom played anywhere at first except in after-hours jams. To make ends meet he took a job in the kitchens of a restaurant where Art Tatum was working, and during the drudgery of washing up he absorbed plenty of the pianist's ideas about harmonic substitutions, patterns of runs, and the integration of fast-tempo passages into slower pieces. Later, he found work playing in the house band at the Parisien, a taxi dime-a-dance hall where no tune lasted longer than a minute and the musicians would run through around 50 numbers in each set. Despite this being a kind of musical drudgery not far removed from washing up, there could hardly be a better way of getting to know the standard dance repertoire, and Parker assimilated the melodies and chord structures of hundreds of tunes, fragments of which would frequently turn up as quotes in his mature solo playing.

From this, and a subsequent engagement with a band in suburban Kew Gardens, Parker was in the same position as I have described for many swing-band musicians, playing a vast amount of music every day, the majority of it unchallenging and routine. He, too, reacted with a psychological shift in his approach, which apparently began at an all-night Harlem jam session on 139th Street, with a rhythm section led by guitarist Biddy Fleet, during which Parker became aware that he had arrived at a method of basing his solo lines on something altogether more challenging, and towards which he felt his playing had consistently been moving. He was to describe it as: "By using the higher intervals in a chord as a melody line and backing them with appropriately related changes, I could play the thing I'd been hearing."[27]

In effect, what Parker began to do was to adopt melodic lines that emphasized notes drawn from the upper triads of such extended chords as ninths, elevenths, and thirteenths, and to combine these with some of the dissonant intervals that were inherent in substitute chords such as augmented fourths and major sevenths. What a small number of other players had been accustomed to use in passing, Parker began to employ as a fundamental ingredient in his solos. He was also to use the same thinking in composing some of his jagged new melodies that were placed over the chords of familiar songs, so that, for example, when he came to create *Ornithology*, it was written over the chords of *How High the Moon*, and *Now's the Time* was built over a simple blues, both with a few "appropriately related changes" substituting here and there for the original harmonies.

The violent death of his estranged father abruptly brought Parker back to Kansas City, whereupon he joined Harlan Leonard's band. This was short-lived, as Parker (who was already addicted to drugs and alcohol) found it hard to show up on time, and he left after a few weeks. Then, in one of the first of many efforts to straighten himself out, he joined Jay McShann's band, and it was with this group that he spent the majority of his time from mid-1940 until the late summer of 1942. On his first three commercial recordings with McShann from April 1941, Parker did not achieve the same kind of dramatic impact as the older and more experienced Gillespie had done with Hill, Calloway, Hite, or Millinder. However, in the bouncing *Swingmatism*, Parker's individual approach to the alto – his clearly defined tone, articulation, and melodic sense are all apparent. Even more importantly, his strong blues feeling comes across in his backing to singer Walter Brown.

As it turned out, the fact that both types of material were recorded by the band was something of an accident. McShann wanted to make discs only of his popular up-tempo dance pieces, very much in the Moten/Basie manner, such as *Swingmatism*, but Decca wanted nothing but the blues, particularly since the band was being recorded on a field trip to Texas for the company's "race" label. Fortunately, even though he already employed a fine ballad vocalist, Al Hibbler, McShann had asked bluesman Walter Brown, whom he had heard singing at a Kansas City club, to come with the band to Texas, and they had taken the precaution of rehearsing a few pieces together, some with the rhythm section and some with the full band, including Parker's head arrangement of *Hootie Blues*. ("Hootie" was McShann's nickname, referring to an incident in which he became famously inebriated on local illegally distilled hooch.) "We had only one thing in mind, really," recalled McShann,

> which was recording all this other stuff that we had, which we liked. So we stayed in the studio down there for about two hours and a half and Dave Kapp told us: "Now you know we're running out of time, fellas. And what you all played I thought was okay; it was good, but I can't sell it." He said, "Can you play the blues?" I says, "Yeah!" So the first thing we played was *Confessin' the Blues*, which went on to be a really big seller in its time.[28]

This piece features Brown with just McShann and the rhythm section, who went on to round off the session as a piano trio on a couple of bluesy boogie tracks.

However, among the community of professional swing musicians, it was not the best-selling *Confessin' the Blues* that attracted attention, but its "B" side, the full-band version of *Hootie Blues*, which had a single chorus of Parker's alto between Brown's vocals. Hearing the disc in faraway Los Angeles, altoist Sonny Kriss observed: "Some musician I might never meet or hear again had discovered a new way through the blues progression."[29] By this point, Gillespie's contribution to the music had been to push forward the technical boundaries of the trumpet beyond those drawn by Roy Eldridge, in respect of its range and speed, and to attack the fundamental harmonic structure of jazz, by playing and composing pieces that incorporated difficult and unfamiliar chord structures, or involved breaking up the rhythm with new ostinato patterns. In contrast, this first significant blues solo by Parker showed that the essence of his talent was to find extraordinary levels of improvisational possibility in the simplest and best-known material. Indeed, the Parker scholar James Patrick has pointed out that the majority of the saxophonist's work from this point onwards is based on a relatively small core repertoire, of blues and 32-measure popular songs: "By restricting himself to a few harmonic sources, Parker was able to improvise over a few familiar patterns against which he constantly tested his ingenuity and powers of imagination."[30]

So here again is evidence of the complementary skills of Parker and Gillespie, and on Saturday February 14, 1942, when the Jay McShann band arrived in New York to open a short season opposite Lucky Millinder's band at the Savoy Ballroom, they had the opportunity to jam together on a regular basis for the first time.

Contrary to some accounts, notably Ross Russell's biography of Parker, Dizzy Gillespie had not yet joined Millinder, and at the time Parker arrived in town the trumpeter was between jobs, having just finished working with Benny Carter's small group and being about to open the following week at the Apollo with Fletcher Henderson. So, for a short while, he and Parker were finally able to get together at Minton's or the Uptown House for after-hours jamming, but as Gillespie pointed out on numerous occasions, the times they actually jammed together with any regularity apart from this were relatively infrequent.[31]

However, on this visit, instead of slipping into New York almost unseen and unheard, as Parker had done in the late 1930s, he became a talking point among musicians and members of the public alike. This was because, on its first night at the Savoy, McShann's band comprehensively "cut" Millinder's, as McShann recalled:

> Well, Lucky had a great band, and he was cuttin' everyone, and usually you'd be hounded right out of there. The two bands would play there for over five hours, turn and turn about. We'd take our break, and they had a place where we could go down and take a little taste, and then we'd come back and Lucky would go downstairs while we came back on the stand. Anyway, during the first part of the night we just played stock arrangements, pop tunes, that sort of stuff. Then about half way through the night Bird started asking the different cats in the band, "When are we going to get into our book?" So, finally, I said, "Okay, let's get into our own book of charts."
>
> Lucky had hired this little guy, a band boy, to keep an eye on us, and as soon as we started, this little guy went downstairs and he says to Lucky: "Lucky, you better come up and see what these cats are doin'!"
>
> Lucky says, "No, I'm not worried about them Western dogs, we're gonna run them all the way back to where they came from."
>
> Well, we'd only played a couple of those things when Lucky came back and did his next set. But the minute he'd gone downstairs again, that little band boy was after him saying: "Lucky, you'd better come back up here and see what these

Western dogs is doing now!"

So, in the end Lucky came up, and I think when we'd finished playing a full set with Bird and all, the house just broke out and panicked for about fifteen minutes. And we broke into Lucky's time because they couldn't get the house quiet. So finally Lucky came back on and by that time he'd only fifteen minutes of his own set left to play, and when he hit his last note, we fell right back in and the house went wild.[32]

Particularly on Parker's spectacular high-speed solo on Ray Noble's tune *Cherokee*, which was to become a long-term inspiration for him, he was playing consistently in a way that nobody in New York had heard from a saxophonist before. McShann recalled that, quite apart from what went on when Parker sat in at the after-hours clubs, most of the big-band saxophonists in New York turned up at the Savoy to check out this sensational new altoist, but they didn't want to be seen doing so by their colleagues, and they would skulk away to the darkest corners of the ballroom.

One would be in one corner, and as he was looking over at the band, he'd run into somebody else trying to hide in the same corner. "Oh man! What are you doin' here?" "Well, what are you doin' here?" All the cats was up there diggin' Bird, but they'd hide around corners.[33]

One musician who made a pilgrimage to the Savoy to hear Parker play his set piece *Cherokee* was Howard McGhee, who went with his colleagues from the Charlie Barnet band: "We all stood there with our mouths open because we had never heard anybody play a horn like that."[34]

After a few months, having been fired from the band during a trip to Detroit, Parker remained in New York when McShann went back to the Midwest. With all the temptations of the big city, the saxophonist's drug habit had slid out of control after almost a couple of years of holding himself together for his job in the band. He rejoined the house quartet at Monroe's Uptown House, playing for a share of the kitty, which just about kept him in food and stimulants. Later he moved to Minton's, where the regular rhythm section now included drummer Kenny Clarke and pianist Thelonious Monk, and according to Clarke it was during this period, in late 1942, that many of the new ideas of bebop began to come together between rhythm section and front-line players. Parker stayed in and around New York, jamming at these after-hours joints, before eventually joining Earl Hines's big band in January 1943.

The difference between the haphazard world of the jam session, with the unpredictability of who would turn up to blow, and uncertainty about what the prevailing style would be, compared to the day-in-day-out routine of a big band was considerable. So, too, was the financial security and reward involved. Following the urging of some of Parker's friends, including the trumpeter Benny Harris, who wanted to help the saxophonist find a regular job to get him out of the downward spiral of living off tips and a meager kitty to buy just enough food, drink, and drugs to survive, Hines was taken to hear Parker playing – by all accounts extremely impressively – at the Uptown House. Hines and his vocalist Billy Eckstine conspired to attract Parker to the band by telling him Gillespie had already agreed to join. Then, when they came through Philadelphia in late January, where Gillespie, having by this time finished his short stay with Millinder, was leading his own group at the Down Beat Club, they persuaded him to join the band, saying that Parker had already agreed to do so. It was the oldest trick in the world, but it worked, and for the first time Parker and Gillespie were playing regularly alongside each other in one of the leading big bands of the day.

With Hines, Parker did not play alto sax, but was hired to play tenor. Perhaps this explains why he returned to an assiduous practice routine, which he shared with Gillespie. Hines recalled:

> Time and time again, when we were playing theaters Dizzy used to go up in Charlie Parker's dressing room and read music out of his exercise book and Charlie Parker sometimes used to go down to Dizzy's and read music out of his exercise book. And these are the things that Dizzy and Charlie were playing . . . they had any number of long passages.[35]

This suggests that both men took one stage further the kind of practice routine I have mentioned in connection with Roy Eldridge, who worked his way through saxophone exercises and the solos of Coleman Hawkins on the trumpet. Doing so developed their ability to think and play as one, for no passage to be too difficult to be played in unison on trumpet and alto sax – but I also interpret it to mean that they worked out ideas in one another's manuscript books that were to be added to the Hines band's library of arrangements. Although Hines made it quite clear to interviewers that he did not much like the new music himself,[36] he did not stand in the way of his two most talented sidemen playing modernistic solos, and adding new pieces to his stock of charts, which included an early version of Gillespie's *A Night in Tunisia*, *Salt Peanuts*, and a ballad setting of *East of the Sun* for the band's new singer, Sarah Vaughan.

The Hines band has been dubbed the "incubator" of bebop, and, not least because of the sustained contact between Parker and Gillespie that it brought about, there are good reasons for recognizing its importance as a fertile breeding-ground for the new music. Several musicians who went on to become significant bebop players themselves encountered the partnership of Parker and Gillespie during this period with Hines. In March, Howard McGhee, for example, ended up jamming all night with them in Philadelphia. In April, they appeared in Washington where pianist Billy Taylor heard them for the first time. He told me:

> I knew Benny Harris, who was in Earl's trumpet section and who was vital in spreading the word about the changes Diz and Bird were making, and it was Benny who introduced us. . . . In fact, even before Benny introduced us, the word was out on Dizzy among musicians. "Here are some guys to watch in Earl's band: Dizzy and Charlie Parker."[37]

At a time when the American Federation of Musicians had imposed its recording ban, and no jazz discs were being made, the jungle telegraph that spread news of the innovations to be heard in Hines's orchestra should not be underestimated. Its ranks were packed with young, forward-looking players, including the trumpeters Shorty McConnell and Gail Brockman, who quickly caught on to much of what Parker and Gillespie were doing. Also, Benny Harris, who flitted through the brass section at various times, went on to be independently influential in the bebop movement, because he composed, or co-wrote, with Parker and Gillespie, several jagged bebop melodies that became favorite improvising vehicles, including *Little Benny* and *Lion's Den*.

The Hines orchestra was one of the most commercially successful African-American bands of the period, and owing to the hit records by its singer Billy Eckstine, made just before the ban was imposed, it had achieved the kind of cult status afforded to very few other groups. Indeed, when the best-selling of all its discs, *Jelly, Jelly*, was at the height of its popularity, in late 1942, Hines and Eckstine were mobbed in Philadelphia and Hines had his coat literally torn from his back by adoring female fans.[38] Prompted by Hines's own dazzling piano work, the band had a naturally extrovert style, demonstrated by such lively numbers as *Second Balcony Jump*, and although it was capable of supporting his more syrupy ballads, it also provided gritty backings for Billy Eckstine on the bluesier end of his repertoire, such as *Stormy Monday Blues*, a piece that became as enduring a hit as *Jelly, Jelly*. This level of success and popular acclaim allowed Parker and Gillespie to be heard in their brief solo appearances with Hines by a wide range of audiences, and after hours by a broad cross-section of interested and eager musicians – although behind the scenes there was already a battle to keep Parker away from drugs, or, at any rate, to control his intake to the extent that he remained capable of playing with the band.

Every movement in popular music seems to bring with it its preferred elixir. For the jazz pioneers who worked through Prohibition, bathtub gin and rotgut whisky exerted a powerful fascination, and hastened the end of many talented players, from Freddie Keppard to Bix Beiderbecke. Drugs, and particularly heroin, were to be the scourge of the bebop generation, and Parker's brilliant instrumental skills, which, in his early years, seemed to his followers not only undimmed but somewhat heightened by his drug use, were to have the unfortunate effect of leading many of those who hoped to emulate his inspired playing to try narcotics as well. A typical example from a few years later than the Hines period was altoist Frank Morgan, who was to get closer than almost anyone to Parker's playing style. "If Charlie can play that well, then that's what I'm gonna do," he told West Coast trumpeter Clora Bryant.[39] Hines's sidemen made efforts to control Parker's drug use, and curb his habits of sleeping through sets, or failing to turn up on time, but it was a losing battle, and despite his prodigious talent, much of the rest of his short career was to be an uneasy balance between the obligations of a professional musician and the half-life of the full-time drug addict.

Parker and Gillespie both left Hines in August 1943, along with Eckstine who intended to form a big band of his own. It took several months for this to happen, and in the interim, Parker moved to Washington and then home to Kansas City. Gillespie landed a short-term job in Duke Ellington's band in a New York theater, and in late October he opened at the Onyx club, leading a quintet that included bassist Oscar Pettiford. The other members came and went, with Thelonious Monk and Billy Taylor both deputizing on piano before the young Sicilian-born musician George Wallington became the band's permanent pianist. On drums, "Doc" West was soon replaced with Max Roach, and after a couple of weeks in which Lester Young played tenor, his place was taken first by Don Byas and then by Budd Johnson. From the one surviving fragment of a recording made by the quintet with Johnson, Wallington, Pettiford, and Roach, it is clear that Gillespie's band was the first fully fledged bebop band to appear on 52nd Street – indeed, the first anywhere in the world to appear at a regular nightclub, rather than an after-hours venue.

It had apparently been Gillespie's intention to use Bud Powell on piano and Charlie Parker on saxophone in this group, but Powell was on the road with Cootie Williams, and Parker had not organized a transfer of his union card from Kansas City to the New York local, and so was prevented from taking a regular job in the city. Nevertheless, the line-up that came to be recorded shows that Gillespie's little group was remarkably successful in consolidating all the changes that had been going on in jazz during the artificial silence of the recording ban. In the disc of the quintet's *Night in Tunisia*, Budd Johnson packs a series of Parker-like runs into his solo, and chooses intervals that emphasize his awareness of bebop harmonies. Gillespie himself produces a masterly solo, full of his dazzling corkscrew runs and buoyant upper register figures, and as Pettiford carries the underlying pulse, Roach stirs up the rhythm with rimshots, snare accents, and bass-drum punctuations, with Wallington stabbing occasional off-center chords.

Up until this point, there had been plenty of hints at how front-line soloists would tackle the new jazz, not least in the recordings of Gillespie and Parker with their respective big bands that were made before the ban. However, the missing link from discs prior to 1942 is the way in which the rhythm section would back up such soloists. All Gillespie's solos with Calloway, Hite, and Millinder were supported by a straightforward four-to-the-bar swing, in just the same way as Parker had been accompanied by McShann. In my view, the main change to emerge from the after-hours clubs like Minton's and Monroe's Uptown House is that they provided the opportunity for rhythm sections to work out how to accompany bebop. The constant playing and practice regimes of big bands on the road had given many musicians the chance to tackle new ideas about melody and harmony, and ways of incorporating these into solos and arrangements. Danny Barker, for example, recalled the way that Tadd Dameron was working out prototype bebop chording with Harlan Leonard's band in Kansas City during 1940.[40] Equally, Howard McGhee had become a featured soloist with Charlie Barnet in 1942, and then the following year with Andy Kirk, and he had tried his new solo ideas with both bands. But even though there had been some comparable isolated attempts by rhythm players to integrate the choppier, broken rhythms and unusual punctuations of bop into big bands – notably Kenny Clarke's playing with Teddy Hill's final line-up – these were generally unsuccessful. Instead, the after-hours clubs could and did offer drummers, pianists, and bassists the chance to work out a different approach, as they backed up an unending supply of soloists, and Gillespie's 1943–4 Onyx Club quintet was the moment this all came together in a regular working band.

By the end of the 1940s, a schism began to open up among musicians about the degree to which it was desirable for rhythm sections to break up the beat in this way. In 1949, Parker launched into print in the pages of *Down Beat* saying: "The beat in a bop band is with the music, against it, behind it. . . it pushes it, it helps it. Help is the big thing. It has no continuity of beat, no steady chug, chug."[41]

The following month, Gillespie retorted, by making the valid point that most audiences found this difficult to follow, and that in his own music he intended to reintroduce a more definite concept of a beat: "We'll use the same harmonics, but with a beat so that people will understand where the beat is."[42]

Indeed, in the early 1950s, Gillespie would systematically turn his back on the choppy broken rhythms of bebop, and in both his small groups and, big bands he worked on combining the harmonic and solo language of bebop with something much closer to a conventional swing rhythm. In parallel with this, the basis of much other 1950s jazz, including hard bop and soul-jazz, would be built around a return to a strongly defined beat, so that, in effect, one of the most vaunted bebop innovations turned out to be relatively short-lived. Nevertheless, the broken, punctuated, rhythmic approach pioneered by Roach, Pettiford, and Wallington was to be a major defining characteristic in much of the music to be recorded from 1944 until the end of the decade.

Much has been written about the significance of the jam session in jazz, and, in particular, to the development of bebop. From the earliest days of jazz, musicians had got together to jam: there were sparring matches, tests of instrumental skill, and long solos wringing the last drop of inspiration out of well-known chord sequences. In the swing era, there was an added incentive for those who played nothing but third or fourth brass or reed parts in a section to flex their improvisatory muscles. In most big bands, it was easy to get typecast, and almost never be offered a solo, as trumpeter

Doc Cheatham discovered when he made his name as a lead trumpeter for Sam Wooding, McKinney's Cotton Pickers, and Cab Calloway, rather than the subtle soloist he became in later years. For such musicians, the jam session was a safety valve, and a social interaction for those who traveled with different line-ups to meet one another and play together. But is it really the case that "the after hours jam session became an integral part of the aspiring musician's education," as Scott DeVeaux suggests? Is this not a romanticized view, particularly when, as in his description, it is couched in terms of "this ritual of competition ... deeply ingrained in African-American culture"?[43]

I remain skeptical about the degree to which the jamming at Minton's and Monroe's genuinely moved jazz forward, beyond consolidating the changes to the role of the rhythm section. Much more of the development that would subsequently become part of the universal vocabulary of jazz took place, it seems to me, in the regular working line-ups of bands on 52nd Street, beginning with Dizzy Gillespie's quintet, which played at the Onyx from October 1943 until March 1944, and then moved (with a couple of personnel changes) to the Yacht Club for another few weeks. (Also, despite various accounts that suggest this was a band co-led with Pettiford, it was always Gillespie's name that featured in the group's advertisements and press notices.[44])

Back in the winter of 1941–2, when Kenny Clarke had been working alongside Dizzy Gillespie in Benny Carter's band, there had been the chance for Clarke to find appropriate means of backing Gillespie's solos on a consistent repertoire, played night after night. And the discipline of playing in a regular small group was to force Gillespie to focus his own ideas into one or two choruses; to make every statement pithy, rather than rambling on as he might in an unfocused jam. If nothing else, it is certainly the case that, once again given the opportunity to work on a nightly basis with a consistent small-group line-up, Dizzy Gillespie moved modern jazz along significantly with his quintet at the Onyx, because it allowed him to consolidate a repertoire. At Pettiford's and Budd Johnson's insistence, many of the themes that Gillespie had been carrying around in his head were committed to paper as lead sheets, and this is when many of the tunes that would be recorded by Gillespie with diverse ensembles over the next eighteen months or so were written down, systematically, for the first time. As well as pieces like *Bu-dee-daht*, which indirectly gave its name to the genre, this core repertoire included Gillespie's *Woody 'n' You*, and both pieces ended up being recorded in early 1944, when the majority of

Gillespie's quintet went into the studios as part of a larger band, nominally fronted by Coleman Hawkins, for what is generally regarded to be the first commercial bebop record session.[45]

As 1944 began, and the dust began to settle in the A.F.M.'s long-running dispute with the record companies, a number of small independent firms were set up that quickly moved into action to get their discs on the market in advance of the majors. The Apollo label was one of these. It had been set up by Teddy Gottleib, who owned the Rainbow Music Shop in the very center of Harlem, on 125th Street, and on February 16 (followed up by a second session six days later), Gottleib recorded Hawkins leading a band of three trumpets, six saxophones, and rhythm. Up until the start of the recording ban, it was unlikely that any company would have taken the risk to record an upstart new style of jazz played by largely unknown players. But given the dearth of instrumental recordings brought about as a consequence of the A.F.M. action, almost any new ensemble discs might well have sold in 1944, even if they contained the new music of the beboppers. Gottleib hedged his bets, banking on the established name of Coleman Hawkins producing a paraphrase of his famous version of *Body and Soul* on a track called *Rainbow Mist*, which could be relied upon to be a safe seller. But he also recorded some far more modernistic fare, which accomplished two things: it allowed Hawkins to identify himself clearly with the younger players on the Street and their new sounds (he was to employ both Max Roach and Thelonious Monk in his own groups there), and it allowed those same younger players to be heard on record playing music much closer to the style that Gillespie's quintet was playing at the Onyx.

If Hawkins's name was needed to ensure the discs sold, the person behind the scenes who came up with the arrangements and organized the date was Dizzy Gillespie. Hawkins "wanted his coat to be pulled with this kind of music, and he wanted to be in first," recalled Budd Johnson.[46] But Max Roach confirmed the power behind the throne: "Dizzy was the straw boss. He did . . . most of the arranging on that date. He was the guy who organized the musicians and since I was the drummer in his band, of course, he called me in on the date."[47]

There are two key soloists on the three more modernistic tracks recorded by the band: Hawkins and Gillespie. Hawkins displays his knowledge of harmony by playing some stunningly intricate lines that reflect all the subtle reharmonizations of *I Got Rhythm* in *Bu-dee-daht*, just as pianist Clyde Hart demonstrates his competence at integrating the new harmonies into his playing. But in *Woody 'n' You* and *Disorder at the Border*, it is Gillespie who dominates the session, to the extent that in many musicians' minds these were *his* records, rather than Hawkins's. And the reason he is so effective is the way that *his* regular rhythm section alter their backing to accommodate his unpredictable style.

This was not small combo bebop of the type that would be more widely recorded later in 1944 and increasingly in 1945, but it did give some hints of Gillespie's abiding interest in integrating bop with larger ensemble forces, which he did during mid-1944, when he was reunited with Parker in Billy Eckstine's new orchestra.

In late March, Gillespie had moved from the Onyx to the nearby Yacht Club, following an altercation with the pugnacious Oscar Pettiford. With slightly changed personnel, including Leonard Gaskin on bass, his quintet was billed as "The Swingsational Dizzy Gillespie with Budd Johnson,"[48] and they worked opposite Billy Eckstine. This was a significant reunion, because although both Gillespie and Eckstine were soon to move on elsewhere, just over two weeks after opening together at the Yacht Club they made their first recordings with a prototype of the new big band that Eckstine intended to lead on a full-time basis.

Since leaving Hines, while Gillespie had been leading his own band on 52nd Street, Eckstine had worked mainly as a single act, playing clubs or theaters, where he was supported by house rhythm sections or specially assembled groups. But the catalyst in prompting him to form his own band was the imposition in 1944 of a new cabaret tax which took a 30 percent levy on nightclub earnings.[49] This tax was subsequently a factor in the decline of 52nd Street, but, for the time being, the clubs kept going. However, Eckstine's agent Billy Shaw felt that a big band playing theaters, dances, and shows for the many army bases that had been set up across the country would be less ruinous than continuing to book the singer as a single into clubs affected by the tax. On the band's first studio session, Eckstine and his prototype line-up, of which Gillespie was musical director, recorded a blatant attempt to cash in on the earlier success of *Jelly, Jelly*, called *Good Jelly Blues*, plus a version of *I Stay in the Mood for You* that combined Eckstine's vocal with a powerful, modernistic arrangement by Gillespie in which his trumpet soared dramatically over the final ensemble.

Today, recording a disc and then backing it up with a tour to maximize both box-office and record sales is a commonplace practice. In 1944 it was not such a well-known technique, but it worked to perfection, as the tiny Deluxe company which had issued Eckstine's discs could not keep up with demand. Following the recording ban, and exacerbated by wartime restrictions on the supply of shellac, the firm only had the raw materials to produce 20,000 copies of the disc each month, but they were besieged with over 72,000 initial orders. At the same time, with interest aroused by the disc, Billy Shaw took deposits from theaters willing to book the band in advance, and on June 9 it set off to play its first live date. Despite the constant ravages of the draft and occasional confusions over travel arrangements, there was plenty of work, and the core of the band's personnel eventually settled down, although it was never completely stable for more than a few weeks at a time. The line-up that Eckstine and Gillespie put together contained, in due course, the largest collection so far assembled of musicians interested in playing the new jazz, including Charlie Parker (who had returned from the Midwest to join the band); trumpeter Howard McGhee; saxophonists Budd Johnson, Dexter Gordon, Gene Ammons, and Leo Parker; trombonist Bennie Green (a veteran of Hines's orchestra for whom Gillespie had arranged a solo on *Night in Tunisia*); pianist John Malachi; bassist Tommy Potter; and drummer Art Blakey; with Sarah Vaughan as the band's additional vocalist.

Therein lies the importance of this orchestra. Through this pool of forward-looking, young, exuberant musicians it became a meeting-place for ideas, an opportunity to try out new thoughts about arrangements, and a traveling laboratory for bringing the after-hours experimentation of big-band musicians out of the dressing rooms and rehearsal halls, and putting it center-stage in the context of a large orchestra. When the band began, it had no "book" of arrangements, and Eckstine hurriedly put together a skeleton repertoire by borrowing a few numbers from Basie, and using some of the charts that Gillespie had written for the progressive white bandleader Boyd Raeburn. But, otherwise, there was a perfect opportunity to put together a library that reflected the new thinking in the band's line-up. "As we kept doing these one-nighters, we were constantly writing," recalled Eckstine. "*Blue 'n' Boogie* was a head arrangement. We were constantly sitting down everywhere we'd go and have a rehearsal and putting things together on these kind of things."[50]

There has been a constant tendency for jazz ensembles to get bigger at every phase in the music's history. I have pointed out the existence of large ensembles in the pre-1920 period, and discussed bands like King Oliver's gradually growing larger during the 1920s. Equally, Paul Whiteman's band ballooned into a vast leviathan, Ellington's Kentucky Club band expanded into a larger unit at the Cotton Club, and in the late 1930s and early 40s, swing small-group leaders like Coleman Hawkins, Teddy Wilson, and Roy

Eldridge all followed the trend towards increased line-ups, however briefly. Bebop was no exception, and Eckstine began a trend that I shall examine in more detail in the next chapter, but which took in the West Coast orchestras of Gerald Wilson and Roy Porter as well as Gillespie's various big bands, and those of Woody Herman and Stan Kenton.

To a large extent, this has to do with the point I made earlier about bebop being a music developed predominantly by big-band players. Eckstine's new line-up was living proof of this: the musicians included several veterans of the Hines and McShann bands, plus Dexter Gordon, who had arrived from Louis Armstrong's big band, Gene Ammons from the King Kolax group, and Art Blakey from Lucky Millinder's orchestra. Only Gillespie and Budd Johnson had acquired the experience of playing bebop night after night in a regular quintet setting, so it is important to note that at this very early point in its development, bebop was not just a style developed by former big-band players, but was a genuine big-band music in its own right.

Members of Eckstine's band looked back on it as a life-changing experience. Eckstine himself called it "the love thing." Blakey said: "We had a ball because we weren't interested in nothing else, just wanted to play some music." And Dexter Gordon remembered it as "*Très, très* exciting. . . . This band was so special because we felt we had a mission."[51] Because of the large number of musicians who subsequently came through its ranks, and because their associations stretched far beyond Eckstine's group into the depths of the big-band world and, indeed, into the local jazz scenes in many parts of the United States (Gordon, for example, being well connected in Los Angeles, Ammons in Chicago, and so on), Eckstine's band became a vitally important element in spreading the word among players themselves about the new ideas that were going on in jazz. For this reason, even critics such as Leonard Feather, who had not been particularly well-disposed towards the group to start with, was later to refer to it as "the legendary Billy Eckstine band."[52] Beyond the musicians' community, which kept in touch with the deeds of the band's various sidemen, Eckstine's orchestra also commanded plenty of attention in the press, particularly the African-American papers, which ran regular stories about the band's progress round the country on its travels. But in keeping with the ethos of the modern jazz musician, exemplified by Charlie Parker, the band also reflected the more sinister side of bebop culture, and the reed section, in particular, became seriously involved in narcotics, something that would shadow the careers of Dexter Gordon, Gene Ammons, and another new arrival, Sonny Stitt, for many years to come.

Whereas the Earl Hines band of 1943 made no recordings, Eckstine's group did venture into the studios again in late 1944, but amid numerous vocals, only a couple of tracks from its December 5 session reveal anything of the excitement and electric atmosphere remembered by its musicians. Also, the Deluxe company consistently managed to produce some of the worst sound quality of the period, but, through the murk, it is possible to make out the thrill of a tenor saxophone battle between Gene Ammons and Dexter Gordon, rounded off with a stratospheric final solo from Gillespie over the full band on a piece called *Blowing the Blues Away*. On the other jazz-orientated track, *Opus X*, the degree to which the band had altered the concept of the big-band rhythm section is apparent, with Art Blakey dictating the dynamic shape of the piece, breaking up the beat in the manner of Clarke or Roach, but integrating such swing-era devices as accented rimshots and snare-drum press rolls to underline the arrangement.

Listening to this music today, Blakey's playing seems a perfectly logical development from the swing drumming of musicians such as Chick Webb or Sid Catlett. As Eckstine himself observed:

> Kenny Clarke, Art Blakey and the best . . . they don't throw bombs unless they mean something. While the horns are taking a breath, the drummer fills up a gap. That's what bombs were for originally. In other words, they fill out the music, and maybe set up a pattern for you to think up something on. . . . If you ever listen to Diz humming something, he hums the drums and bass part and everything, because it all fits in with what he's doing.[53]

To musicians, the role of this style of rhythm section may have been obvious, but to the general public it was not. This band was the first popular dance band to play the new type of music on the usual touring circuit of theaters, dance halls, and clubs, and despite huge enthusiasm for Eckstine's popular singing, and the inclusion of other well-known singers and dancers on the bill, much of what his band played made no connection with his audiences. "It was still a dance-crazy public," recalled Eckstine, "and we were playing music that was a little bit too wild for them to dance to."[54]

The Eckstine orchestra was recorded again – both formally and on airshots – in 1945, but by then, first Parker and then Gillespie had both left, and for the time being shifted the focus of bebop development back to the small-group format. Nevertheless, before he finally broke up the band in

1947, Eckstine continued to hire the most forward-thinking musicians in jazz, starting with Fats Navarro, who took Gillespie's place, and, later, playing the same parts as the band toured to the West Coast, was a young Miles Davis.

## From the Three Deuces to Billy Berg's

> I was in seventh heaven, three times tripled over. Man, I was getting the best education. I was going to the best conservatory in the world, every single night for three solid weeks, and I loved every second and every minute.
>
> Milt Jackson, in an interview with Charles Fox

In the early months of 1945, Charlie Parker and Dizzy Gillespie both freelanced with various bands in and around New York. Parker broadcast with Cootie Williams from the Savoy, and Gillespie worked at the Apollo Theater and on records with Boyd Raeburn, for whom he was also writing arrangements. During this period, they also made a number of freelance discs – both separately and together – that mark the beginning of a phase in which small-group bebop was comprehensively defined on record, setting out a pattern that has lasted through into the twenty-first century as the fundamental language of "straightahead" jazz; in other words, jazz that continues to be based on chord changes and structures that are drawn – or not too far removed – from the popular song.

In September 1944, Parker had recorded with guitarist Tiny Grimes, but even his exemplary blues choruses on the best piece from this session, *Tiny's Tempo*, have a regular swing rhythm section, and despite the presence of pianist Clyde Hart, the supporting musicians are harmonically unadventurous. In January 1945, Parker and Gillespie were also both members of a bizarre session under Clyde Hart's leadership, mainly notable for the way in which the blues singer Rubberlegs Williams preserved for posterity his embarrassing descent into incoherence, after Parker had spiked his coffee with alcohol and benzedrine.

However, Gillespie's inaugural discs under his own name, a sextet session (which had Don Byas in place of Parker) from January 9, another on February 9 (with Dexter Gordon), and its successor (with Parker) from February 28, were to become the first great landmarks in the recording of the new music. On the same date as the first of these sessions, Oscar Pettiford also led an eighteen-piece studio band playing some head arrangements by Gillespie that included an expansion of one of the pieces that they had played regularly together in the Onyx club band the previous year. *Something for You* is based on *Max Is Making Wax*, and its adventurous brass voicings and blustery solos from Don Byas and Gillespie himself give a strong hint as to how the Eckstine band might have sounded blowing freely on just such a rapidly put-together chart, with lengthy solos over simple backing riffs building up a great sense of excitement and power.

Some of this big-band feeling carried over into Gillespie's own small-group session that followed on afterwards in the studio, and one of the pieces the sextet recorded, Tadd Dameron's medium-tempo *Good Bait*, was subsequently to have a long life as a cornerstone of Gillespie's repertoire in his various large ensembles. Dameron was, at this point, a close friend of Gillespie, and they had spent hours together clustered round the small piano in the trumpeter's apartment, working out some of the principles of bebop arranging. They had met while Dameron was in Harlan Leonard's orchestra, perhaps explaining why there is a bluesy Midwestern feel about *Good Bait* that mirrors some of the sound of Count Basie's Kansas City small groups, even down to Trummy Young's brilliantly accurate imitation of Basie's trombonist Dicky Wells. Only some of the ensemble voicings and a typically extrovert solo by Gillespie mark this out as different from a standard swing small group, but the same could not be said of *I Can't Get Started* **[CD track 12]**.

This disc has already been mentioned in respect of the reharmonization of the piece by Dameron and Gillespie, but it is equally important because of the way it took one of the most popular trumpet solo vehicles of the swing era and reworked it into a new harmonic and solo language. In August 1937, Bunny Berigan had made a celebrated recording of the tune, complete with a stately Armstrong-style series of opening statements, leading to a straightforward version of the theme itself, accompanied by Joe Lippman's arrangement for the saxophones of chording based on Vernon Duke's original harmonies. The piece ends with a stunning restatement of the theme in the trumpet's upper register, and a final high-note climax. Although it was well within the stylistic parameters of soloing pioneered by Armstrong, even down to the way the shape of the arrangement mirrors his numerous mid-1930s discs with Luis Russell, the topicality of the lyric and the beautifully burnished sound of Berigan's trumpet became indelibly stamped on the popular imagination. This *was* the song, in just the same way that Bing

1. Dan Kildare's Clef Club Orchestra: *(left to right)* Walter Kildare, Seth Jones, George Watters, Dan Kildare, Joseph Myers, John Ricks, Louis Mitchell. Members of the band recorded in London in 1916, and Mitchell subsequently became one of the pioneers of bringing jazz to France. (English Columbia Records publicity photograph)

2. Territory bandleader Jesse Stone in March 1997, with his wife Evelyn McGhee Stone. (Author's collection)

3. Jelly Roll Morton, holding forth outside the Rhythm Club. (Danny Barker)

4. Louis Armstrong with trombonist Tyree Glenn. (Mike Doyle/Symil Library)

5. Eubie Blake *(right)*, aged 99, with fellow pianist McCoy Tyner. (Randi Hultin)

6. Fats Waller in the early 1920s. (Author's collection)

7. The Duke Ellington Orchestra, in 1941, during the period of the "Blanton–Webster" band. Personnel *(left to right):* Juan Tizol, Sam Nanton, Lawrence Brown, Fred Guy, Johnny Hodges, Barney Bigard, Ellington, Ben Webster, Sonny Greer, Otto Hardwicke, Jimmy Blanton, Harry Carney, Wallace Jones, Rex Stewart, Ray Nance. (Claire P. Gordon)

8. Fletcher Henderson and alumni, 1942: *(left to right)* Henderson, Sid Catlett, Henry "Red" Allen, John Kirby, Benny Carter, Lawrence Lucie, Russell Procope, Buster Bailey. (Charles Peterson, courtesy of Don Peterson)

9. The Cab Calloway Cotton Club Orchestra, on the road playing in an impromptu theater, *circa* 1942. (The Cab Calloway Collection, Boston University)

10. Lester Young. (Nancy Miller Elliott)

11. Buck Clayton and John Hammond, at Clayton's 70th birthday party in 1981. (Nancy Miller Elliott)

12. The Benny Goodman Quartet, in a late reunion: *(left to right)* Teddy Wilson, Goodman, Gene Krupa, Lionel Hampton. (Teddy Wilson Collection)

13. Billie Holiday at the Park Lane Hotel, New York, 1939. (Charles Peterson, courtesy of Don Peterson)

14. John Kirby's sextet at the Onyx Club, March 24, 1938: *(left to right)* Russell Procope, Charlie Shavers, Buster Bailey, O'Neil Spencer (partially obscured), Maxine Sullivan, John Kirby. (Charles Peterson, courtesy of Don Peterson)

15. Dizzy Gillespie in his later years, complete with upswept horn and his cheek "pouches". (Peter Symes)

16. Charlie Parker and trumpeter Chet Baker, 1952. (Ray Avery)

17. Bud Powell. (Jan Persson)

18. Woody Herman. (Mike Doyle/Symil Library)

19. Pioneers of the New Orleans Revival (i): bassist Pops Foster, trumpeter Bunk Johnson, soprano saxophonist Sidney Bechet at the Savoy in Boston, 1945. (Charles Peterson, courtesy of Don Peterson)

20. Pioneers of the New Orleans Revival (ii): trumpeter Alvin Alcorn, bassist Ed Garland, trombonist Kid Ory. (Ray Avery)

21. Recording *Kind of Blue*, New York, April 1959. John Coltrane, Cannonball Adderley, Miles Davis, Bill Evans. (Don Hunstein/Sony)

22. Horace Silver, shortly after the Jazz Messengers period. (Ray Avery)

23. Shorty Rogers. (Peter Symes)

24. The Count Basie Orchestra, in a late incarnation of the "Old Testament" band during the 1940s, with Lester Young on tenor sax at the left of the reed section. (Ray Avery)

25. A pensive Charles Mingus in 1970, after his return to playing the previous year. (Jan Persson)

26. Ornette Coleman with his fusion band Prime Time in 1987. (Peter Symes)

27. Malachi Favors Maghoustus appearing complete with face paint and African costume during an Art Ensemble of Chicago concert, London, 1997. (Peter Symes)

28. Anthony Braxton. (Derek Drescher)

29. Herbie Hancock, 1997. (Derek Drescher)

30. An outstanding ambassador for jazz as world music, Abdullah Ibrahim, at London's Jazz Café, 1997. (Peter Symes)

31. Cassandra Wilson – looking forward from within the tradition. (Derek Drescher)

Crosby appropriated *I'm Dreaming of a White Christmas* in the 1942 film *Holiday Inn*.

So Gillespie's decision to rework it involved making a clear statement to the record-buying public that there was another way to tackle this piece. The most noticeable contrast with Berigan's treatment is Gillespie's freedom and mobility. Instead of chipping every note out of granite, Gillespie intersperses his grand statements of the theme with swift, darting phrases, almost as if he is offering a separate, ironic commentary on the main piece. This creates a sense of two distinct levels in his playing, helped by the use of some characteristic bebop intervals in his swifter asides. Together with the countermelody for saxophone and trombone and the new underlying harmonies, Gillespie succeeded brilliantly in producing a version of the piece that had no debt whatsoever to Berigan. This modern restatement of so well-known a swing standard, with its delicate balance between a sense of the original song and something new and exciting, all worked out at a daringly slow tempo, showed that the new movement in jazz could encompass the antithesis of the stereotypical fast-moving bebop tune, of which the other two pieces Gillespie recorded on the same day are good examples: *Salt Peanuts* and *Be Bop*.

The discs that most effectively carried the message of the new jazz to the world at large, however, were the sides made by Gillespie's sextet once Parker had joined the line-up, first on February 28, including *Groovin' High*, and at a subsequent session on May 11, that produced *Hot House* and a definitive version of *Salt Peanuts*. Although these discs were made for the tiny Guild label, they did receive a measure of international distribution. Together with a version of *Blue 'n' Boogie*, which featured Dexter Gordon, the records finally reached Europe towards the end of the year, and in the immediate aftermath of World War II they were seized on as demonstrating the massive changes that had taken place in jazz, of which record enthusiasts in Britain and France had been completely unaware. Undoubtedly, the isolation caused both by the war and by the A.F.M. ban gave European critics a clear view of a process that was less apparent to those who had been close to it throughout its development. This is why, within a few months of *Down Beat's* dismissive comments that Parker and Gillespie were "still too acrobatic and sensationalistic to be expressive in the sense of true swing,"[55] the French critic André Hodeir, in a detailed analytical article that included transcriptions of solos and considerable technical discussion of the harmonic and melodic advances he heard, brought an entirely different perspective to bear, praising "two black discs with red labels, in which is inscribed the future of African-American music."[56]

These performances stand apart from many swing record dates because, in an updated version of the John Kirby band's approach to arranging, Gillespie had given thought to the setting of the solos. For example, *Groovin' High* (which borrows the chords of the old popular song *Whispering* for its main theme) has a composed introduction, neatly worked-out modulations, choruses of varying lengths, and a half-tempo coda. (An earlier attempt to record the piece, with Dexter Gordon, which was not issued at the time, shows the degree to which Gillespie amended the shape of the performance to make a more balanced recording, and experimented with the contrast in tonality between his open horn, which he used originally, and the muted effects of the version eventually issued.) Similar care was applied to all the pieces. By introducing such variations in texture, this compensated for the residual swing feeling of the rhythm sections, where the drummers in the sextet, Cozy Cole and Sid Catlett respectively, had none of the ability to break up the beat that had already been demonstrated by Clarke, Blakey, or Roach. But with Clyde Hart's spare pianistic contributions to the February session and Al Haig's Bud Powell-inspired playing on the May tracks, together with the exceptional soloing of Parker and Gillespie, such shortcomings as there were in the rhythm were effectively overcome. (Hart died of tuberculosis within days of the February recordings, and the music lost one of its most skilled transitional figures to this scourge of the period. The disease had also been responsible for the deaths of Jimmy Blanton and Charlie Christian, both of whom had played similarly important roles in leading up to the transition from swing to bebop.)

Hodeir's description catches the raw excitement experienced by most of those who bought these sextet discs of hearing Parker and Gillespie's new approach to soloing for the first time. Of Parker he says:

> The manner in which this marvelous improviser treats the theme, ornamenting it without giving the impression of rambling, never overdoing it, and indeed, by contrast, brightening up his melodic phrases by the use of silences between them ... will ravish the listener and confound the critic.[57]

And of Gillespie:

> More powerful and sure than Armstrong, more rapid than Eldridge, he seems to laugh at difficulties ... he climbs into the

highest register with derisive ease, and his ample tone and heat
are something to marvel at.[58]

Early in March, between the two sextet recording sessions on which Parker
appeared, Gillespie formed a regular quintet line-up, and with it, he brought
bebop back to 52nd Street by opening at the Three Deuces. As well as
himself and Parker, the rest of the band were: Al Haig, piano; Curly Russell,
bass; and Stan Levey (later replaced by Max Roach), drums. The group
appeared there until July, when Gillespie put together his first big band,
which he intended to take out on the road.

The four-and-a-half months or so during which Parker and Gillespie
played alongside one another at the Three Deuces cemented their musical
relationship into one of the most exceptional partnerships in jazz. Whereas
Roy Eldridge and Chu Berry had triumphed with the thrill of the chase, the
Parker/Gillespie pairing added their superlative, almost telepathic,
ensemble skills to an equally exciting ability to play extended, dramatic
solos. When they appeared at a New York Town Hall concert on May 16,
*Metronome* critic Barry Ulanov wrote: "Dizzy and Charley [sic] played their
unison passages with fabulous precision, no easy achievement when your lips
and fingers are tangled up in mad running-triplet figures."[59]

Adding to the core repertoire that Gillespie had established with Budd
Johnson at the Onyx the previous winter, he and Parker now built a nucleus
of pieces that were to underpin their particular brand of bebop, and which
they not only trotted out at the Town Hall concert, but would return to
again and again in subsequent public appearances: *Be Bop*, *Blue 'n' Boogie*,
*Cherokee*, *Confirmation*, *Dizzy Atmosphere*, *Groovin' High*, *Night in Tunisia*, *Round
about Midnight*, *Salt Peanuts*, and *Shaw 'Nuff*.

Up until this point, the prime mover in bringing bebop to 52nd Street,
and thence to a wider public, had been Gillespie. He was the titular leader at
the Three Deuces, as he had been at the Onyx, he had consolidated a
repertoire, had thought about how to arrange and present the music on disc
under his own name and for other leaders, and had helped to develop the
abilities of those who played it with him; from pianists, to whom he
demonstrated chord voicings, to drummers, with whom he discussed the
finer points of rhythm. He genuinely did hear the entire arrangement of a
piece in his head, as Eckstine suggested. But many histories of jazz,
prompted by the perceptions in Ross Russell's biography of Parker, *Bird
Lives!*, have taken the view that Parker was the principal architect of defining
small group bebop.[60] And this is largely due to the idea that to create great

music it is important to live the "jazz life," in other words, the self-destructive, hedonistic, Bohemian lifestyle espoused by Parker. "Dizzy was verbal, witty, extroverted, sunny of disposition – everything Charlie was not," wrote Russell. "Dizzy was accessible to everyone. You did not elevate such a man to a hierarchy. Blowing musicians, who were in the position to know, all agreed that Parker was the fountainhead of the new music. The flow of musical ideas suggested mysterious, primal forces."[61]

Even today, the strength of those "mysterious, primal forces" is apparent from the power and conviction with which Parker's playing leaps from the grooves of the discs he recorded in 1945, helped by the clarity of his articulation and his plangent tone. But his talent was mainly to do with spur-of-the-moment instant creativity, albeit drawing upon some of the most sophisticated harmonic ideas to have been absorbed by any improvising musician up until that time. His partnership with Gillespie benefited not just from the trumpeter's ability to match many aspects of Parker's virtuoso playing, but also from the knack of placing that playing in a suitable framework or context. My perception of Gillespie is that he had an altogether more wide-ranging musical curiosity about the way such a context might be developed, and this led him to experiment with numerous possibilities for expanding and extending bebop – from moving forward the big-band ideas he had begun with Eckstine to experimenting with Afro-Cuban rhythms, and from further exploring the dissonant harmonies he had worked out with Thelonious Monk and Tadd Dameron to creating even more experimental charts with Gil Fuller, eventually leading to his early modal experiments with George Russell.

Gillespie was often to define bebop not so much as a "revolution" but an "evolution"[62] and in later life, when he had become a grand patriarchal figure in jazz, he could justifiably point to his own seminal role not just in one, but in several areas where jazz had evolved into a richer, more wide-ranging music, in the wake of his small-group playing with Parker. By contrast, Parker's contribution was less widely spread, limited both by his short life and the way in which he chose to live it. Nevertheless, the profound influence of his solo playing on generations of saxophonists, including the main revolutionary figures who followed him, such as John Coltrane and Ornette Coleman, should not be underestimated. I have sometimes been accused of overstating Gillespie's importance at the expense of Parker, but I could not disagree with one of my sternest critics in this respect, Francis Davis, when he says: "Unmatched among modernists as a blues player, Parker brought a human cry to bebop's experimentalism –

ultimately as crucial an element to the music's acceptance as Gillespie's showmanship."[63]

If Gillespie's easy stage manner, sense of humor, odd attire, and verbal skill made him the public face of bebop, Parker's playing knitted the music into the depths of the African-American experience, not least through his infallible sense of rhythm, and his ability to superimpose his advanced concept of time over a residual four-square beat. Furthermore, whether he was playing at a blisteringly fast tempo, or in his more reflective slower style, which foreshadowed many of the ideas of "cool" playing in the 1950s, the blues inflections in his work made many of his performances "telling events." In much the same way as Lester Young saw every solo as being a mini-narrative, so, too, did Parker, who said:

> Ever since I've heard music, I've always thought it should be very clean, very precise . . . as clean as possible, anyway . . . and more or less to the people, something they could understand, something that was beautiful . . . there's definitely stories and stories and stories that can be told in the musical idiom. . . . It can be very descriptive in all kinds of ways, you know, all walks of life.[64]

In the second half of 1945, after Gillespie had gone out on the road with his first big band, Charlie Parker became a bandleader himself, first working with a small combo at the Three Deuces, with Don Byas sharing the front line duties, and then (after an abortive attempt to move to the Downbeat Club) opening at the Spotlite, with Miles Davis and Dexter Gordon joining the group in place of Byas. Parker also made an appearance on a recording session led by one of his regular pianists on 52nd Street, Sir Charles Thompson. But in late November, at a time when he was once again rehearsing with Dizzy Gillespie to form a new quintet that was to appear on the Street and then travel to California, Parker made the first records under his own name. Although the session, for Savoy, was somewhat chaotic, it did produce one definitive example of Parker's ability to tell "stories and stories and stories" in his playing, in the form of the most dazzling individual solo he had yet recorded. The track was called *Koko*, and owing to the confusion surrounding the details of the session at which it was cut, it acquired legendary status, arousing much critical controversy as to who was actually playing alongside Parker.

The rest of the session featured four members of Parker's regular working band: the saxophonist himself, trumpeter Miles Davis, bassist Curly Russell, and drummer Max Roach. Apparently, the intention was to use Bud Powell on piano, but Powell had returned to his mother in Philadelphia, and instead a relatively obscure figure called Argonne Thornton (also known as Sadik Hakim) was at the keyboard, despite Savoy's labels and liner notes implying that Powell himself was actually present. Particularly backing Miles Davis, Hakim reveals himself as barely up to the task, but on *Koko*, Davis surrendered the trumpet chair to Dizzy Gillespie (whose presence was not credited by Savoy either) who also swiftly moved over to play piano behind Parker's outstanding solo. The piece was based on the chord sequence of *Cherokee* and, indeed, a fragment of an earlier take that survives confirms that Parker and Gillespie were recreating their standard 52nd Street interpretation of Ray Noble's tune. On the final, issued version of the piece, probably in order to accommodate as much solo playing from Parker as possible, but possibly also to avoid the danger of having to pay composer's royalties, the explicit *Cherokee* introduction is dropped, and there is a brief, arranged preamble including solo sections for Gillespie (on trumpet) and Parker, before Parker's two-chorus solo. Roach rounds things off, followed by a brief tag for alto and muted trumpet. Parker's solo itself is a masterly piece of work; a seamless flow of ideas, allusions, and little phrases that are caught, repeated, transposed, and tossed away as the next idea is taken up. His awareness of the jazz tradition surfaces, too, as he throws in a section of the classic New Orleans clarinet solo from *High Society*, always regarded as a difficult test piece for reed players, and here just thrown casually into the mix before the solo sweeps onwards. Unaware that it was Gillespie who was providing the prodding, urgent piano chording that supported Parker, the original sleeve-note writer John Mehegan added a query to his apt description of the piece:

> Bird's two choruses represent some of his greatest blowing. Like all great improvisers, Parker's choruses would build to an unbelievable cascade of pitch and time; as here, the second chorus is to me the perfect microcosm of Bird's genius. Why Diz didn't blow a chorus on this, I do not know. His interludes here are magnificent fantasies pulsating with harmonic inference.[65]

This outstanding performance apart, it seems a little overstating the case, as the Savoy Records' publicity was to do, that this was "the greatest recording session made in modern jazz history."[66] It did indeed produce this one gem, but otherwise its scattershot nature was a reflection of Parker's own personality – random, disorganized, but occasionally touching genius.

These same aspects of his character were to surface in an altogether more worrying way in the sextet that Dizzy Gillespie took to California to open at Billy Berg's in Hollywood for a two-month stay, starting on December 10, 1945. For a week or two beforehand, Gillespie fronted a quintet with Parker back at the Three Deuces, and from this experience Gillespie was well enough aware of Parker's unreliability as regards timing and showing up for the nightly session that he had booked vibes player Milt Jackson to travel with the group to Billy Berg's as an additional front-line musician, "so we always had five guys."[67] As is evident from his remarks quoted at the head of this section, Jackson regarded this opportunity to work every night alongside Parker and Gillespie as the chance of a lifetime, not realizing until later that he had been hired as a stopgap, should Parker fail to appear. Once the band actually opened at the club, the owner, Billy Berg himself, felt the line-up was not "heavy enough" so he subsequently also added Lucky Thompson on tenor sax. Replacing their 52nd Street counterparts, Bud Powell and Max Roach, the band had two young, white, musicians on piano and drums – Al Haig and Stan Levey, respectively – and Ray Brown on bass, who had only arrived in New York a matter of weeks before the sextet set off for the west.

On the journey out, Parker's erratic character and reliance on drugs became all too obvious to his colleagues. However, the few examples recorded by the sextet in California, mainly for radio broadcasts, show that when all its members were present and correct, this was an exceptional band by any standards, and the pieces they played include versions of *Dizzy Atmosphere* and *Groovin' High* that are substantially lengthier than the commercially recorded discs of the same tunes. This is the closest example we have to hearing how the partnership of Parker and Gillespie actually sounded on a live gig, during the heyday of their collaboration in the mid-1940s. In a more relaxed environment than trying to cram their performance into the playing time of a standard 78 r.p.m. disc in a recording studio, *Groovin' High* opens out by another two-and-a-half minutes. Instead of split choruses, the solos extend into one or more full choruses, and Gillespie, in particular, shows the way he integrated into his playing elements of the extrovert big-band showmanship of his apprentice-ship – particularly on the open-horn high notes and final flares of his dramatic solo.

The Parker–Gillespie partnership was to dissolve soon after these broadcast recordings were made, as Parker remained on the West Coast, shortly to suffer a breakdown from alcohol and drug abuse, whereas Gillespie and the other members of the band returned to New York, in due course to launch the most successful bebop big band of the decade, which is discussed in the next chapter. Although they would be reunited from time to time, in studios, on the concert platform, and occasionally during club sessions, January 1946 marked the end of the great collaboration between these architects of the new music.

The standard view of this West Coast trip by the Gillespie sextet is that it was the moment that bebop spread its wings from the confines of the Harlem after-hours clubs and 52nd Street, and traveled to other parts of North America. In his survey of West Coast jazz, Robert Gordon puts this position admirably: "Modern jazz burst upon the Los Angeles scene in the December of 1945, when trumpeter Dizzy Gillespie brought his all star sextet West from New York for an eight-week engagement at Billy Berg's Hollywood nightclub."[68]

The same account summarizes the other frequently held view of this event:

> [On] opening night ... the house was packed and the crowd wildly enthusiastic. ... The remainder of the engagement was all downhill. The musicians and hard-core cognoscenti who had formed the bulk of the opening-night crowd returned as and when they could, but there weren't enough of either successfully to support the band or the club. The mood ... ranged from indifference to outright hostility.

So this so-called landmark event was, apparently, nothing of the kind – just a short-lived flash in the pan that did little to make an impact on the well-heeled audiences of Hollywood, who knew how they liked their swing to sound, and were having none of this new upstart music, with its jagged ensembles, rapid-fire solos, and jumpy rhythms.

Except that the view presented by Gordon, which mirrored a wide range of other published sources, including Leonard Feather's widely distributed account of this "miserable" gig, where "hardly anyone in California understood or cared about bebop,"[69] turns out not to be entirely accurate.

In fact, the engagement was far more successful than such accounts suggest. There was already an informed audience for bebop out in California and, furthermore, very similar music had been featured at Billy Berg's before Parker and Gillespie arrived, and was still being played in the city's main jazz area, its own "52nd Street," namely Central Avenue. The catalyst had been Coleman Hawkins, who had followed his 1944 *Disorder at the Border* record session with Gillespie by fronting his own increasingly bebop-orientated group on 52nd Street in New York, which he had brought out West to play at Billy Berg's in February 1945.

Hawkins had employed Thelonious Monk as his pianist back in New York, and although Monk did not travel with the group, the line-up Hawkins brought to Los Angeles included Oscar Pettiford as well as McGhee. The recordings this band made for Capitol during its stay in California included such Monkish contributions to the repertoire as *Rifftide* and *Stuffy*, and on these McGhee shows the extent to which he had developed his own extension of the Eldridge style into a convincing bebop approach. But the reason this band did not excite the waves of publicity aroused by Parker and Gillespie was that Hawkins had established his name as a swing star. Leavened by a quantity of his familiar husky ballads, his sets could include plenty of new material without his audience being fully aware of what it was they were listening to. "California people knew about Coleman Hawkins," said McGhee,

> but they didn't have the slightest idea what the band was like. And so when they came they said "Oh Man! What a band! We haven't heard music like that ever!" So I guess Coleman was the one who opened up the West Coast as far as modern sounds in jazz.[70]

McGhee stayed on in California after Hawkins returned to New York, and drew round him a nucleus of musicians every bit as inspired by modern jazz as McGhee was himself. He found a gig on Central Avenue at the Downbeat Club, and recruited Vernon Biddle, piano; Bob Kesterson, bass; and Nat McFay, drums; with James King on tenor. He soon added another tenorist, Teddy Edwards, who had made his name locally, first in the visiting territory band of Ernie Fields and subsequently in the rhythm-and-blues orchestra of Roy Milton, based in Los Angeles. McGhee and Edwards formed a natural partnership, which was to be renewed many times over the following decades, and which once again emphasized the debt of the beboppers to the big-band tradition, with the tenorist swiftly becoming as solid and dependable a foil for McGhee as Hawkins had been. "When Hawk left and he [McGhee] decided to stay," recalled Edwards,

479

he couldn't find anybody who had the right combination of harmonic knowledge and speed. I had both. ... I had studied harmony before I wrote my first big band orchestrations for Ernie Fields, and the main thing I had to do with bebop was to learn the songs, and incorporate ideas like the flatted fifth. But the rest, I knew. ... At our first gig at the Downbeat, the drummer, McFay, couldn't really play the tempos, but I was really glad because soon afterwards, Roy Porter joined on drums and then we really got started.[71]

Porter had garnered his experience in New York while in the army reserves, and then on the road in the territory band of Milton Larkin, during which time he had heard Kenny Clarke's innovative drumming, plus many of the other new ideas coming into jazz in Harlem and on 52nd Street. He rolled much of what he had heard into his own style, and he was widely regarded as the first drummer to develop an authentic bebop approach in the West after settling in Los Angeles in 1944. Based on his experience across the country, Porter was sure that McGhee "was truly the 'bearer of gifts,' being the one who brought bebop to the West Coast." He went on: "When I went to work for Maggie [McGhee], the drummers in Los Angeles were just playing swing drums, rudiments, paradiddling and ratamacuing. They just weren't happening."[72]

The band worked mainly at the Downbeat, which became its home base, but it also played in Hollywood at Billy Berg's, at the Jade Palace, the Streets of Paris, and the Hi-de-ho Club, as well as traveling from time to time to San Francisco to play at the Backstage club. This gave it a strong local following for its new sounds, and, consequently, it made its first recording for Joe Bihari's Modern label, an offshoot of a local record store and juke-box business, in May 1945, and cut a further four sides for the Aladdin company in September, thereby documenting its work several months before Parker and Gillespie's arrival. Furthermore, the Downbeat had no problem attracting an audience for the new music, either from the local African-American community on Central Avenue, or from the visitors from elsewhere in Los Angeles who flocked to the area's plentiful clubs.

Trumpeter Clora Bryant had heard some of the after-hours players in New York when her all-girl band from Texas, the Prairie View Co-eds, had worked at the Apollo Theater in 1944, and so she had an idea of how bebop had developed in the East. The following year, her family settled in Los Angeles, and her brother took her to hear the music on Central Avenue.

"When I got here," she told me, as I met her at the former Dunbar Hotel, a short distance from where the Downbeat used to be located,

> I was amazed. I noticed how many jazz places there were, and my brother and I stayed into the night to hear the music. We joined the crowd of people spilling out on the street outside the Downbeat. Inside there was Howard McGhee, Teddy Edwards, Vernon Biddle, and Roy Porter. It seemed to me like the people really knew their music as far as bebop was concerned.[73]

In view of its freshness and apparent popularity, Clora Bryant resolved to find out more about the new music, buying records, listening to these musicians, and finding others who wanted to play in the style among her friends on Central, and her generation of students at UCLA where she had enrolled. (She was eventually to work occasionally alongside Charlie Parker herself, during his stay in California in 1946–7, and was certainly one of the few female trumpeters to share a quintet front line with him, if not the only one.)

In the same summer of 1945 that Bryant came to the city, the sixteen-year-old twin brothers Art and Addison Farmer came on vacation to Los Angeles and made their way to Central Avenue. Art noticed that – similar to 52nd Street – most of the clubs were modest in size, with a small stage big enough only for a sextet or quintet, and then the sound of McGhee's group drew the twins into the Downbeat.

> It was crowded so we just sort of walked in, stood around and stood up next to the wall. As far as I know, that was the first organized band out here that was really playing bebop. Dizzy and Bird hadn't come out here at that time. I think Dizzy had been out here with other bands, but he and Bird hadn't come out with the quintet yet. Certainly people were playing bebop. We were playing it; we were trying to play it before Dizzy and Bird got here. It just sounded good to me. I didn't have to ask myself, "Gee, what is this? Do I like it or don't I like it?" because my mind was completely open at the time.[74]

Farmer's observations are interesting for several reasons, not least because he was to become a masterly post-bop trumpeter himself, but particularly because he points out that McGhee's was an "organized" band. Just like

Gillespie's group at the Onyx from 1943 to 1944, or the Gillespie–Parker quintet at the Three Deuces in 1945, this was a regular working line-up with a properly worked-out repertoire of its own (much of which was recorded for posterity in 1945–6 for Modern, Aladdin, and particularly the Dial label, which was set up in 1946 by Ross Russell, Parker's erstwhile biographer and owner of the Tempo Record Store in Los Angeles). This reinforces my point that however useful the endless jamming in clubs like Minton's and Monroe's may have been in developing some of the underlying aspects of bebop, the real momentum in drawing the style together and making it the basis of the jazz language for the next half century took place in regular working line-ups, in which nightly experiment and development was possible among a consistent team of musicians. Nevertheless, a vital ingredient in the development of bebop seems to have been that in the main centers of its development there was a healthy relationship among the clubs where such regular line-ups could be heard, providing a model for those who wanted to emulate them, and other venues that encouraged after-hours jamming where such emulation could take place.

The fact that McGhee's band developed in the West, independently of New York, underlines the further point that bebop was a much wider phenomenon than simply a New York-based movement. However, like 52nd Street and New York's informal uptown haunts, Central Avenue had the same informal relationship among clubs with regular working line-ups such as McGhee's band at the Downbeat, and the dozens of informal after-hours jam sessions hosted at such other venues as the Elk's Club, Lovejoy's, or the Jungle Room. It was in those places that a new generation of Los Angeles musicians, such as Art Farmer, or the altoist Sonny Criss, began their attempts to emulate what McGhee's regular group was doing.

Several of the other main regional centers across the United States where bebop developed had a similar relationship between the opportunities to jam and formal clubs with regular bands – Kansas City for instance, where, in 1945, saxophonist William Green worked each night from 9 p.m. until 1 a.m. on 18th and Vine with the quartet of pianist and trumpeter Willie Rice, who welcomed would-be boppers into his home for jam sessions during the day.

> I started learning how to play bebop at that time . . . being exposed
> to Willie Rice who was a great trumpet player and also pianist.
> Oh, he really was responsible for my understanding. He had like
> an open house all day for musicians who wanted to come.[75]

In due course, Green was another experienced bebop player who arrived in Los Angeles to join its burgeoning modern jazz scene.

When Gillespie and Parker did finally arrive there, as I have said, their engagement at Berg's was much more successful than was generally thought to be the case. Their bassist Ray Brown confirmed to me that far from being fired from Berg's as some reports suggested, the band "finished out the engagement."[76] Equally, both Sonny Criss who was in the audience more than once, and Harry "The Hipster" Gibson who shared the bill with the Gillespie sextet and Slim Gaillard's group, confirmed that on most nights "the place was packed." Criss went on to point out that Berg's was an interracial club, and that the new music caught the atmosphere in this "groovy" venue that "embraced people from all walks of life."[77]

So by the end of 1945, bebop had arrived in the West by several routes, and it was being played not just by its two leading exponents from the East, but by a growing cross-section of local musicians as well. California was to continue to be an important area for the development of bebop, not least because of the contribution Charlie Parker made to the local scene after Gillespie and his band went home. Gillespie remained a significant influence from afar – young Californian pianist Hampton Hawes, prompted by his junior high school colleague Eric Dolphy, heard the first discs Gillespie made for Victor shortly after returning to New York, and found it "the hippest music I ever heard in my life. . . . I knew that was the way I wanted to go."[78] And the subsequent small-group discs Gillespie made for Musicraft would have a similar effect on many musicians across the land. But Gillespie's own goals shifted, and in 1946, at a time when the economics of big bands were problematic, he nevertheless decided to go ahead and form his own fully fledged bebop orchestra, a project that occupied him until 1950, and which is discussed in the next chapter.

Parker, by contrast, descended into a parlous state in early 1946, as his drug dependency worsened. He joined Howard McGhee's band in March, continuing to appear with the group between April and July, and to record for Ross Russell's burgeoning Dial label. However, after collapsing at a recording session on July 29, he ended up being imprisoned and then hospitalized at the Camarillo State Hospital, where he underwent almost six months of cold turkey treatment and rehabilitation. But before and after his collapse he played and recorded with many Los Angeles musicians, and he had a great effect in shaping local attitudes to jazz. Certainly players like altoist Sonny Criss and tenorist Wardell Gray benefited enormously from the regular contact they had with such an influential player.

## Bebop Piano

Bud's playing was so completely perfect and so highly
stylized in that idiom. He outbirded Bird and he outdizzied
Dizzy.

Al Haig, from Ira Gitler, Swing to Bop

So far I have dealt mainly with the two most visible figures in the bebop
movement, Charlie Parker and Dizzy Gillespie. However, as I hinted in
Chapter 3, the harmonic and technical revolution that went on in jazz-piano
playing in the early 1940s was every bit as important as the extension of
trumpet and saxophone technique spearheaded by Gillespie and Parker, and
an integral part of what Gillespie referred to as the "evolution" that was
going on in jazz. The most innovative pianist, in terms of introducing and
developing the harmonic ideas of bebop, was Thelonious Monk, who was a
member of the house band at Minton's from the very early 1940s.

Monk's largely self-taught technique included elements of stride (which
he would still occasionally demonstrate well into the 1970s) but it was in
many respects the antithesis of pianistic, and it is remarkable that a player
with quite such an unorthodox approach should have had such a big impact
on jazz piano. Monk played from the shoulder, in an intensely physical
manner, lifting his hands high at the end of each phrase and keeping his
fingers straight, rather than adopting the conventional practice of bending at
the joint below the knuckle. Watching his odd, crablike hand movements, it
is remarkable that he achieved the results he did, although the clear contours
of his melodies and the compositional sense of his improvised lines won out
over the more chaotic aspects of his physical relationship with the keyboard.
"He seems," wrote his biographer Laurent De Wilde, "to dominate the
keyboard with all his weight, as opposed to someone like Bill Evans or Glenn
Gould, who keep their foreheads practically glued to the keys."[79]

It was Monk's younger counterpart and friend, Bud Powell, who
developed a dazzling virtuoso technique that corralled many of Monk's
harmonic ideas into a bravura style that matched that of the pioneer bebop
saxophonists and trumpeters. In contrast to Monk's movements, some of
which seemed to have come straight off the building site, Powell had a
conventional classical stance, keeping his upper body still and focusing all his
power into his fingers, which sped over the keys at incredible speed. His
tendency to sit slightly sideways at the piano, with one leg splayed out,
served to draw his audience's attention to his nimble fingering, often

accompanied, Glenn Gould-like, by grunts and moans of concentration.

Monk, as we know from Dizzy Gillespie's comments, spent his free time during his Minton's period working out substitute harmonies, and the kitchen of his home in New York's San Juan Hill district, on 63rd Street, where he kept his piano, became a mecca for other musicians including not just Gillespie, but also Budd Johnson, Bud Powell, and, from 1944, Miles Davis, all of whom tried out new harmonic ideas in this informal setting. A major element of Monk's genius was to be aware of which notes of a chord needed to be sounded to make most effect, and that even the same group of notes, or their inversion, would have a completely different sound when pitched in a different register. As De Wilde (himself a pianist in the Monk tradition) explains:

> [Monk] taught the science of the maximum economy in the choice of the notes making up a chord. Why play three when two were enough? And that's another torture for whomever tries to reproduce Monk's music: you always think you're hearing more notes than he's actually playing.[80]

During his time at Minton's, Monk was also responsible for numerous compositions, several of which were based on extant chord sequences, but usually displaying his own jagged melodic sense. Nevertheless, partly because he worked uptown rather than at a more popular downtown location, and partly because of his somewhat eccentric character, Monk's own playing took a while to become widely heard or well-known. He worked on 52nd Street with Kenny Clarke late in 1942, but went back to Minton's before his return to the Street with Coleman Hawkins in 1944. Although Hawkins recorded a number of Monk's tunes and took on board his harmonic ideas, it was not until the pianist was taken up as a protégé of the Blue Note record producer Alfred Lion, in 1947, that his body of work began to be properly documented.

More than any of the other New York-based beboppers, Monk epitomized the psychological shift I discussed earlier. He sported eccentric hats and a fuzzy goatee, twirled around on stage during drum or bass solos, habitually moved in a kind of circular orbit through public spaces such as hotel lobbies or airport lounges, and was extremely reticent in talking about his work. In this respect he symbolized the idea of the 1940s modern jazz musician as an artist, as Ingrid Monson suggests:

Monk's reluctance to verbalize – to interviewers, musicians seeking instruction, and even friends and family members – provides further evidence that music was his true language. Monk spoke the unspeakable through music and took the listener to "another level" through his utterly original compositions and improvisation.[81]

Perhaps this uncompromising attitude was helped by the fact that he lived at home with his mother (his wife Nellie joining mother and son in the family apartment) and, therefore, had less imperative than many of his contemporaries to go out and earn a living. (Nevertheless, he was fairly uncommunicative with his own family. His son, the drummer T. S. Monk, once told me in a BBC interview that when he was first employed by his father, virtually no words passed between them, but that the pianist brought in the first tune they played at such a slow tempo it made him eliminate all the "flashy" elements in his drumming and focus on keeping time as best he could – a perfect example of Monk's preference to communicate in music rather than words, and, as T. S. confirmed, making his point in a way that could not be contradicted.)

Even if he was not widely known by the general public in the 1940s, Monk's impact on his fellow musicians was considerable, and as the saxophonist in Gillespie's Onyx Club quintet, Budd Johnson, observed, this took place very early in the decade: "I really heard Monk doin' this stuff before anybody. I don't think anybody else had the tunes. I really would put Monk before Diz in my knowledge."[82]

Unfortunately, because Monk came late to formal recording, his important influence was not as well reflected on disc in the same way as that of Parker or Gillespie came to be. Although Jerry Newman made a certain number of unofficial discs during the period that Monk was at Minton's, in 1941, the pianist on these cannot always be identified with total certainty, and in some instances was more probably Kenny Kersey. However, in an analysis of those pieces on which Monk is thought most likely to be present, Scott DeVeaux has identified several instances where his ideas were applied to the reshaping of popular songs, either by reharmonizing them or by producing a pared-down, simplified version of their melodies: "Monk had a well-known fondness for major and minor seconds, major and minor sevenths, minor ninths and tritones – intervals that he liked to present in an exposed, unadorned fashion."[83]

He goes on to suggest that Monk's affinity for the Tin Pan Alley repertoire, and the way he was consistently drawn to interpret certain standard songs from it throughout his career, had a considerable bearing on his originality as a composer, not least because his discoveries about harmony could be reapplied to his own compositions. DeVeaux produces an interesting hypothesis that demonstrates how this may apply to Monk's use of dissonant parallel minor ninths in his own *Ruby My Dear*, having discovered the effect through reharmonizing the standard *April in Paris*.

In any event, we can be sure that Monk was applying his own unusual approach to harmony on his arrangements for Coleman Hawkins's band which he joined in 1944. When the sextet toured to Canada, bassist Selwyn Warner described Monk as:

> Very bright, quiet and cool, but not eccentric. Monk did the arrangements for the band; so too did Benny Harris and Denzil Best. . . . The group played all kinds of interesting new things, but I never heard anyone in the group use the words bop or bebop; they were just thought of as new arrangements.[84]

In October 1944, Monk's playing was heard for the first time on a commercial recording when he took short solos on Hawkins's *Flyin' Hawk* and *On the Bean*, and his comping behind the tenor shows the degree to which his harmonic experimentation, both in his kitchen and on the bandstand at Minton's, had developed into an original piano style.

I have said already that, in my view, the primary importance of the after-hours clubs like Minton's was that this was where the concept of the bebop rhythm section was able to coalesce. Although there is evidence that Monk (through his intransigent personality) was the prime mover in making life difficult for sitters-in, even Kenny Clarke, who led the group there, defined this as a matter of professional competence, when he told Burt Korall: "There's no truth to the story that we purposely played weird things to keep musicians outside the clique off the stand. All we asked was that a musician be able to handle himself. When he got up on that stand he had to know."[85]

And *knowing* what one was about became particularly important as Monk and Clarke began experimenting with unusual accents – Monk's percussive piano and Clarke's bass drum often putting the emphasis on unusual beats, which could become a trap for the unwary. Equally, Monk's insistence on playing his own compositions with the quartet of himself, Joe Guy on trumpet, Clarke on drums, and bassist Nick Fenton would have been intimidating for those unable to hear the relatively straightforward sixteen-

or 32 bar structures that underpinned most of Monk's unconventionally harmonized new pieces. In Hawkins's band, judging by its recordings, there was a workable compromise between the more outlandish elements of Monk's playing and the swing antecedents of Hawk's saxophone style. Also, his tenure with this band gave Monk the same kind of opportunity as Gillespie had had, with Benny Carter or his own groups, to hone his skills in a more commercial environment, and Monk played for much of the second half of 1944 with Hawkins at the Downbeat club on 52nd Street, a booking that ran for some months after his debut on record.

Yet despite his position of influence, Monk did not start to consolidate his work until 1947. By then, having decided not to travel to California with Hawkins, he had spent time in the big bands of Lucky Millinder and Cootie Williams, and in 1946 had opened with Dizzy Gillespie's new orchestra at the Spotlite in New York, but he proved to be an erratic attendee, and his interpretation of big-band charts was quaintly original, so he seldom stayed long in a large-band setting, leaving Gillespie after a week or two. In the fullness of time, many of his own compositions were to become big-band pieces, and as early as 1944, Cootie Williams had recorded Monk's 'Round About Midnight. However, Monk's strengths as a player were always in a small group, as he proved when the Blue Note label opened up the door for him to begin recording on October 15, 1947.

*Humph*, the first of Monk's pieces to be recorded under his own name, has a skittish, downward-moving head arrangement, mirrored in the opening of his subsequent piano solo, and this close similarity between his themes and his manner of soloing was to be a consistent factor in his later output. He thought and composed pianistically, even if this was constrained by his unorthodox technique at the piano. Because it is based on *I Got Rhythm*, this piece has no structural oddities, but his other composition from the same date, *Thelonious*, has an extra two bars in the bridge and a two-bar tag, giving it an overall thirty-six measure form, and the sense of suspense, created by the chromatically descending horns of the opening, and by Monk's use of both silence and dissonance in his solo, is broken by the inclusion of some jaunty stride passages here and there.

In his second session, made by just a trio with Gene Ramey on bass and Art Blakey on drums, Monk reworked one of his Minton's favorites, Gershwin's *Nice Work If You Can Get It*, but more importantly, recorded four more of his own pieces. In their different ways they all show areas in which he influenced jazz piano, starting with the haunting ballad *Ruby My Dear*. This is a good example of a composition built around a simple phrase, in this case a four-note downward evocation of the syllables "Ru-by-my-dear," a technique that although it was not new to jazz, was quite distinct from setting an entire song lyric. It was a method of writing that would be taken up and developed eagerly by other pianists, notably Dave Brubeck, who has a fondness for using the names of colleagues as inspiration for such musical phrases, notably such polysyllabic fellow pianists as "Mar-i-an Mc-Part-land."

*Well You Needn't* was to be recorded by Miles Davis in the 1950s, but it shares its chords with Tadd Dameron's virtually contemporaneous *Dameronia*, and is a good example of a piece where Monk uses similar thematic material for the central eight-bar bridge section to that of the main theme, thereby creating a different effect between sections of the song from the conventional popular song notion that the bridge should be quite distinct. His other two pieces from this date were important because they were both identified with colleagues – *Off Minor* had earlier been recorded by Bud Powell, and *Introspection* had been arranged for Dizzy Gillespie's big band during Monk's short stay in the line-up the previous year, demonstrating the effect he had on a wider pool of musicians than those with whom he recorded.

His recording career, as with so much else about Monk, was not entirely straightforward. Alfred Lion arrived in the United States from Germany in the mid-1930s, and with his friend from the Hot Club of Berlin, Francis Wolff, who escaped the Nazi regime later in the decade, he had established Blue Note records in 1939, mainly by issuing boogie-woogie piano and traditional jazz. A hit record of Gershwin's *Summertime* by Sidney Bechet had helped keep the company afloat during the war, as had the assistance of the Commodore Record Shop's Milt Gabler, who not only found a job for Wolff and had helped distribute Blue Note product, but also was generous towards the company with his ration of shellac and his manufacturing deal at the unlikely source of the Scranton Button Factory, whose pressing equipment he adapted to make phonograph discs.[86]

Lion was a man of tremendous zeal and considerable knowledge, and as the war ended, and he was once again able to start making new recordings, he had the vision to realize that the music he loved by Bechet, James P. Johnson, Albert Ammons, and George Lewis had its contemporary counterpart in the new sounds of the beboppers. By appointing the swing tenorist and man-about-52nd Street Ike Quebec as his talent scout, he was able to tap into a source of new and interesting musicians, few of whom had other recording prospects, and Monk became one of his great passions.

Later in his professional life, Lion was to develop an equally passionate enthusiasm for two other pianists, continuing to demonstrate his perceptive ear for the unusual and his commitment to musicians whose commercial prospects were not immediately obvious. They were Herbie Nichols and Andrew Hill, who each shared with Monk a startlingly original approach to piano jazz and to composition. For all three of these pianists, Lion overcame his usually conservative instincts to make copious recordings of his favorites.

Even if they were slow to sell at the time, the seven sessions he organized for Monk between 1947 and 1952 are a valuable document of Monk's work, made close enough to the period when he was working out many of the precepts of bebop to demonstrate the importance of his influence. They also include the definitive versions of his most enduring compositions *Criss Cross*, *Evidence*, and *Misterioso*. Other important pieces he recorded during this time included *Eronel and Hornin' In*.

Monk then moved to Prestige for a couple of years, and from there to Riverside, where the producer Orrin Keepnews (who had met Monk socially through Lion, and had written enthusiastically about him in 1948 for *Record Changer* magazine) became his recording supervisor, and helped establish Monk as a major jazz star. The pianist's work is generally categorized by these recording contracts, since, owing to a couple of drugs charges, of which one was a trumped-up offense, his cabaret card, allowing him to perform in New York clubs, was withdrawn, and he worked erratically in the city in the mid-1950s. The Riverside period led to some exceptional recordings of more of Monk's compositions, including *Crepuscule with Nellie*, *Pannonica*, and *Brilliant Corners*. This last piece is particularly unorthodox, with a tripartite structure including both seven- and eight-measure sections that hover between different scalar patterns, and different tempi. It proved so complex to record that Keepnews, in a departure from his normal practice, eventually edited the issued version together from the 25 or so takes that were attempted by a quintet that included tenorist Sonny Rollins, altoist Ernie Henry, Oscar Pettiford, and Max Roach. As the Scottish critic Kenny Mathieson says: "the palpable sense of the musicians struggling to master the very artificial hair-raising complexities of the pianist's scheme is one of the primary sources of the music's enduring fascination."[87]

In the late 1950s, Monk formed a regular quartet (see Chapter 16 for a discussion of its work with John Coltrane on tenor saxophone), and for most of the 1960s, after moving to the Columbia label, both on record and in his regular tours and club appearances, he performed a repertoire largely based on his original compositions of the 1940s and 50s, with Charlie Rouse on tenor and a number of different bassists and drummers, among them Larry Gales, bass and Ben Riley, drums. He did add a small number of new pieces during this time, but the core of his repertoire had been established many years earlier. One example is the twelve-measure blues *Straight No Chaser* **[CD 2, track 3]** which he first recorded during his Blue Note period in 1951, and returned to again and again during the 1960s. Monk's piano introduction is a perfect instance of his marriage of a spiky uneven theme with unusually placed accents that deceive the ear as to where the beat should fall. This continues into the theme itself, which begins as a four-note motif placed just before the first beat of the first measure, and then reappears as a seven-note motif starting just before beat four, later returning to a four-note motif, and so on. The polyrhythmic nature of the theme is much simplified in the opening solo by Rouse, under which the rhythm section supplies a straightforward swing beat, although Ben Riley consistently varies his cymbal patterns and snare-drum accents. Behind the first chorus by the tenor is a characteristic Monk accompanimental maneuver; virtually a heterophonic treatment of the theme that dovetails with Rouse's line, before the piano drops out for the remainder of the saxophone solo. Monk's own solo which follows is full of his characteristic devices, from the first phrases that descend deep into the lower register of the keyboard to the brief restatements of part of the theme and then two sections built on repetition, first of short phrases and then of a single note.

After touring the world in the early 1970s with a cohort of bebop pioneers called the Giants of Jazz, Monk gradually withdrew from public life, and he ended his days as a recluse, in the New Jersey apartment of the Baroness Pannonica de Koenigswarter, his long-term patron and dedicatee of his composition *Pannonica*.

Bud Powell's career, by contrast, ended in 1965 in scuffling obscurity, brought about by his own recurrent bouts of mental illness, acute reactions to the effects of drugs and alcohol, and his decision to return to New York from the relative comfort and security of Paris, where he had been based permanently from March 1959 until the late summer of 1964. During that Parisian period, he both survived tuberculosis and overcame his dependence on anti-schizophrenic drugs. In the course of his stay there, although his playing lacked the speed and finesse of his work from the late forties and early fifties, he recorded an album in 1961 called *A Portrait of Thelonious* that was a poignant reminder of the closeness between these two revolutionary pianists at the time they were starting their careers.

Powell was born in New York, in 1924, into a musical family. His father had been a stride pianist and his younger brother, Richie, whose life was tragically snuffed out in a motor accident, became a promising post-bop pianist. Powell met Monk at Minton's around 1941–2, at a time when he was running with a group of young pianists that included Al Tinney and the erstwhile resident at the Uptown House, Gerald Wiggins. The three of them used to sit in wherever they could. Even when he was a teenager, Powell's mother was aware of his susceptibility to alcohol, and she tried to find responsible friends to act as "minders" to her wayward son. One of these was Al Tinney and another was Mary Lou Williams, who confirmed Powell's closeness to Monk:

> When Bud came to me for help and if he got a little bit out of line, I'd say: "I'll tell Monk." He'd say: "Don't do that, baby doll." He respected Monk, he was crazy about Monk. We were going to do three-piano things. The three of us rehearsed on one piano and that was so funny.[88]

It was Mary Lou Williams who also confirmed the close musical relationship between the two, and in a 1954 interview she underlined Powell's debt to Monk:

> I am forced to the conclusion that Monk influenced him as a kid. He idolises Monk and can interpret Monk's compositions better than anyone I know. And the two used to be inseparable. At the piano Bud still does a few things the way Monk would do them, although he has more technique.[89]

Powell's technique was obvious from his earliest days, and when he joined Cootie Williams's orchestra, at the age of nineteen, with Williams becoming his legal guardian until the age of twenty-one, Powell could often stop the show with his brilliance. Ray Brown, who later worked with Powell, remembered seeing him with the Williams band at the theater in Pittsburgh, and accompanying the stage acts so brilliantly that he outplayed the dancers he was supposed to be backing.[90] Through his work with Williams, Powell acquired a big-band apprenticeship of the kind that had led to the after-hours experiments of many of his contemporaries, and his 1944 discs with a small group drawn from the full-band line-up include several solos. *My Old Flame* and *Sweet Lorraine* both show Powell's indebtedness to Art Tatum, but the prophetic glimpses of his future style, on *Floogie Boo*, and on the double-time *I Don't Know*, are analogous to Parker's few solo choruses with Jay McShann.

A brutal beating about the head by police in Philadelphia, during a road tour with Williams in January 1945, was the trigger for many of Powell's subsequent difficulties. His injuries led to a long period in the hospital and persistent headaches and other mental problems for the remaining twenty years and seven months of his life. Nevertheless, he reappeared on the scene as a freelance pianist during the second half of 1945, and at the end of the year was, briefly, a member of Dizzy Gillespie's quintet at the Three Deuces on 52nd Street, which formed the nucleus of the band that traveled to Billy Berg's in Hollywood. Whatever the state of his mental and physical health, this was a high point in Powell's musical career, Gillespie commenting: "Bud Powell was the definitive pianist of the bebop era. He fitted in with us more than anybody else because of the fluidity of his phrasing. He played just like we did, more than anybody else."[91]

Unfortunately, Powell did not record with Gillespie and Parker at this point, and when the band set off for Berg's, he and Max Roach remained in New York, but it is possible to get a sense of how brilliantly Powell was playing around this time from a session made in January 1946, less than two months after Gillespie and Parker set off, which features Dexter Gordon.

During his time in the Eckstine orchestra, and playing on discs with Gillespie and Sir Charles Thompson during 1945, Gordon had pioneered playing bebop on tenor saxophone. His style incorporated some intrinsically rhythm-and-blues elements – deep bass-register honks, and repeated riff phrases – but his overall muscular approach was a remarkably successful attempt to forge a convincing way of tackling the new jazz on the larger horn. Powell was a perfect accompanist – sensitive and unobtrusive, but still including some original ideas about chord substitution on the ballad *I Can't Escape from You*, and displaying his debt to Tatum in the configuration of his runs in *Dexter Rides Again*. On the two up-tempo pieces from that January session, *Long Tall Dexter* and *Dexter Digs In*, the pianist produces solos, for the period, are startling for their fluency and harmonic complexity.

Several times in 1946, Powell was to produce similar demonstrations of his peerless speed and sophistication. He added fleet solos to discs by J. J. Johnson's Be-boppers in June, Sonny Stitt's Be-Bop Boys in August, and two all-star groups with Kenny Clarke in September. At this stage in his career, Powell combined his facility as a soloist with remarkable abilities as a band pianist. In later life, his forte became the trio of piano, bass, and drums, but in his 1946 band records he delineated what became the standard way of comping within a bebop small group, and this was so influential that most modern jazz pianists of the late 1940s based their approach on Powell's work in these significant sessions. There are similarities in Powell's playing – both as soloist and accompanist – with the slightly earlier recordings of Al Haig with Gillespie and Parker, but Haig was, to some extent, in awe of Powell (as the quotation at the head of this section suggests), and even though Powell later told the French interviewers Henri Renaud and Francis Paudras that Haig was his idea of "a perfect pianist,"[92] I nevertheless believe Powell to have been the primary model for this style of playing.

Three discs, in particular, reveal the comprehensive way that Powell had developed his approach from that of, say, Clyde Hart or Kenny Kersey, both of whom remained perched between the linear soloing of Earl Hines, the swing comping of Billy Kyle, and something more modernistic. First, on *Jay Bird*, from his session with trombonist J. J. Johnson (made by a quartet with whom Powell had appeared at the Spotlite on 52nd Street, plus altoist Cecil Payne), he accompanies the solos by leaving the bass line to Leonard Gaskin and playing stabbing, unevenly placed chords, each emphasizing changes to the underlying harmony. Occasionally (following Monk's example), he worries away repeatedly at a particularly dissonant chord like a terrier with a rag. And then, behind his own right-hand solo, built of a cascading line of single notes, he accompanies himself, using exactly the same type of stabbing occasional chording with his left hand, and throwing the clarity and logic of his melodic phrasing into sharp relief.

On Sonny Stitt's *Bebop in Pastel* (a theme composed by Powell, better known as *Bouncin' with Bud*) he demonstrates another characteristic device, interpolating pianistic comments on the head arrangement, including a brilliant upward run that occupies the last two measures before Kenny Dorham's trumpet solo. And whereas, by this point in 1946, neither Dorham nor altoist Stitt had yet developed the same easy fluency as Parker or Gillespie, Powell's own solo is simultaneously bursting with ideas and is a masterpiece of economy, his brisk phrasing having all the authority that his front-line colleagues lacked.

Finally, on *Webb City*, with Kenny Clarke's Be-Bop Boys, Powell trades choruses with one of the other young lions of the bebop movement, trumpeter Fats Navarro, who was beginning to develop his own extension of the Gillespie style. The piece is a quasi big-band arrangement by Powell and Gil Fuller, based loosely on *I Got Rhythm*, but in his two separate solos, there is no better demonstration of how Powell's rapid right-hand phrasing stood direct comparison with the linear improvisation of a front-line instrument.

Powell's stupendous keyboard abilities from this period were not to last long, because late in 1947 he was committed to the Creedmore Hospital with severe psychiatric problems, and his subsequent treatment, which involved electric shocks and dousing in ammoniac water, may well have permanently damaged his memory.[93] Although he regained some aspects of his former brilliance, he was never again so consistent, and much of his later work shows him agonizingly pitting himself against seemingly impossible obstacles of speed or dexterity. Nevertheless, before his committal he made one trio session, in early 1947, for the obscure DeLuxe label. The tracks almost vanished for good before they were issued, when the company went bust, but they were finally brought out by Teddy Reig's Roost imprint, and they include two pieces that are the epitome of Powell's contribution to bebop piano. The first is a blistering rendition of the old standard *Back Home Again in Indiana*, and the second is an original, based on the chords of Benny Harris's *Little Benny*, called *Bud's Bubble*.

Perhaps the well-known contour of *Indiana*, and Powell's startlingly original reinterpretation of it, make this the more extraordinary performance of the two, as well as the faster, being played at 88 measures per minute. The opening chorus has clear links to Tatum, not least in the way Powell integrates his left-hand chording with the melody, but from then on he embarks on three choruses of right-hand soloing supported by jabbing left-hand chords, combining a torrent of ideas with so precise a touch that every note stands out clearly. In the lines played by his right hand, he manages great variety in his phrase lengths, and also adds ornaments, in passing, to even his most helter-skelter ideas. His left-hand chords are minimal, but he shares Monk's ability to suggest a fuller chord than is actually sounded, with a particular fondness for including intervals of a major or minor second. The four-measure chordal passages which he then exchanges with Roach demonstrate that he was far from simply a "right-hand" player as some of his critics suggested, and he ends with a chorus that uses one of the new melodies that the 52nd Street beboppers had worked out to run over this well-known chord sequence.

From these landmark recordings (which were not issued until after his release from hospital and his subsequent return to playing) Powell's career went on to be a series of peaks and troughs, although he maintained two long-term associations with record companies, first with Blue Note, and, second, with Norman Granz's emergent stable of labels, such as Clef and Norgran, which eventually coalesced into Verve. His finest recordings were made for Blue Note, and these include a large number of his original compositions, including *Bouncin' with Bud* and *Dance of the Infidels*. Three discs stand out from this association: *Un Poco Loco*, a piece in Latin meter that exists in three takes, each of them more developed in complexity; *Parisian Thoroughfare*, which is a programmatic portrait of the city with which Powell was to be most identified (although he had never been there when he recorded the number in 1951); and the claustrophobic *Glass Enclosure*, regarded by many as a metaphor for Powell's life in mental institutions.

Powell's playing underwent something of a renaissance during his years in Europe, and he fronted a fine trio with drummer Kenny Clarke and Pierre Michelot on bass, the configuration being known in Paris as "les trois patrons" (the three bosses). Former American colleagues would occasionally drop in on the trio at their residencies at the Blue Note or Le Chat Qui Peche, and be amazed by what they heard. Lou Levy recalled a night at the Blue Note when:

> He was playing *The Best Thing for You* at a tempo you wouldn't believe. That thing is a roller-coaster of changes . . . and he did it like a loop-the-loop, chorus after chorus, with such strength. . . . He never ran out of gas. It was a night that I'll never forget! . . . the greatest jazz performance I ever been lucky enough to hear.[94]

The fact that his playing was able to flourish was remarkable, given that his Parisian sojourn was complicated by the way that his common-law wife, Altevia Edwards, known as Buttercup, attempted to help control his schizophrenic tendencies with large doses of a suppressant drug, which slowed his responses and must have made it physically impossible for him to achieve anything like a proper control over the keyboard. His friendship with the photographer and graphic designer Francis Paudras, who became his most devoted fan and biographer, led to a change in regime, and Powell was weaned off his drugs, and made an attempt to avoid alcohol as well. Just as his playing began to improve, he was diagnosed with tuberculosis and spent several months in a French sanitarium, recovering. However, by the end of his stay in Europe, he recovered much of his former power and drive as a pianist. A late reunion with Dexter Gordon and Powell's trio on the Blue Note album *Our Man in Paris*, from 1963, produced his best playing from the late years, particularly on a haunting version of *Stairway to the Stars*. There are further hints of his powers on a session recorded during a seaside vacation on the Normandy coast when he met up with Johnny Griffin, and both principals play with great gusto despite what must have been one of the worst pianos on the continent.

The few recordings Powell made after returning to New York are a tragic portrait of an artist in terminal decline, and his hesitant, heartrending attempt to play Gershwin's *Someone to Watch Over Me*, from one of his final sessions in late 1964, is one of the most poignant musical epitaphs in jazz.

Once again, I have focused on a period of great change in jazz, and singled out those musicians most responsible for it. But in the history of jazz in its first century, there was no more significant change than the advent of bebop, and the increase in harmonic and rhythmic complexity and sophistication this brought about. It is what the French historian and philosopher of science Michel Serres refers to as a "bifurcation" – a "fork in the road,"[95] and once musicians like Monk and Powell had selected which fork they would follow, there was to be no turning back as far as the development of jazz piano for the next few decades was concerned.

Powell's technical innovations in fingering, control, and speed were considerable, and it is significant that two of the pianists who were most successful in taking up what he had developed were white and classically trained. I have already mentioned Al Haig, but equally significant was Dodo Marmorosa, who was a devotee of Teddy Wilson and Art Tatum, and who went on to work in the big bands of Gene Krupa, Tommy Dorsey, and Artie Shaw. After settling in Los Angeles, he became part of the burgeoning bebop scene there, and made numerous recordings, both as the house pianist for the small Atomic record label, and for numerous other firms. His right-hand lines tended to be more spartan than those of Haig or Powell, and he added bluesy overtones to his phrasing on pieces such as a quartet version of *Smooth Sailing*, with tenorist Lucky Thompson, made in late 1946, which also demonstrated his assertive style of accompanying. There are fascinating glimpses in his playing of ideas that would develop as later aspects of bebop, not least the "locked hands" style developed by Milt Buckner and George Shearing, which is foreshadowed in a radio transcription disc of *Dodo's Bounce*, made in 1946. But two years later, having stacked up an impressive quantity of recordings, including sessions with Charlie Parker, Marmorosa fell ill and returned to his Pittsburgh home, from where he seldom ventured back into the spotlight, except for a brief return in the early 1960s.

By contrast, Haig's career was longer, and he enjoyed a lengthy association with Charlie Parker, both before and after the saxophonist's spell at the Camarillo State Hospital. Haig had studied piano at Oberlin College and added a knowledge of clarinet and saxophone while in a Coast Guard band stationed on Ellis Island, which may well have assisted his assimilation of the long, right-hand, horn-like lines he was to master so effectively. His full-blown interest in the new music followed in 1944, but in another example of the spread of ideas away from New York, his initiation into bebop came in Boston, through saxophonist Rudy Williams, a former member of the Savoy Sultans, who had formed a close friendship with Dizzy Gillespie at the Savoy and who remained closely in touch with the developments going on in the music nationwide. In Williams's band at the Top Hat in Boston, Haig assimilated many of the new ideas about chord substitution and reharmonization that were to become fundamental aspects of his playing, and he arrived in New York to work at the Elks Rendezvous in Harlem with altoist Tab Smith, in late 1944.

Haig is a paradoxical figure as regards the school of thought that interprets bebop as a musical mirror of the African-American militancy that had ignited into the 1943 street riots in Harlem (and similar events across the nation) and, indeed, which views the music as a uniquely New York-based cultural phenomenon, driven by the after-hours experimentation at the Uptown House and Minton's. This is the perception, summarized by Eric Lott, of "music [attempting] to resolve at the level of style what the militancy fought out in the streets: . . . [where] Harlem was a magic place, a refuge that lent young musicians, triply alien – migrant, Negro, occupationally suspect – the courage to conquer."[96] Having discovered the music in another city altogether, even when he arrived to work in Harlem, Haig seldom hung out in other uptown venues during his residency at the Elks club, but made a beeline for 52nd Street, where he eventually joined the band led by guitarist Tiny Grimes.

> It was while working at the Spotlite with Tiny that I met Charlie Parker. He used to come to the club occasionally and sit in, and subsequently asked me if I would like to join a group that was to include Dizzy, Max Roach, Tommy Potter and myself. We rehearsed and opened at the Three Deuces Club in 1945.[97]

Haig's long association with Parker and Gillespie stemmed from that initial gig at the Three Deuces, and even when the band re-formed, in the fall of 1945, with Bud Powell on piano, Haig was wooed back from Charlie Barnet's big band to rejoin them at Billy Berg's. Subsequently, he joined Gillespie's small group in New York, and was then reunited with Parker in a quintet with Miles Davis, after the saxophonist's return to the East in late 1947. Haig, along with drummer Stan Levey, who began his bebop career in

Gillespie's small group in Philadelphia, before the trumpeter joined Earl Hines, was one of the most significant white bebop musicians, and, through his close association with so many of the principal figures in the movement, is demonstrable proof that even in its formative period this music was not the unique preserve of African-American musicians. In later life, Haig occasionally sounded off about the fact that bebop was so often presented solely as an African-American revolution: "I think that crow jim certainly does exist . . . it's usually a discriminatory activity in reverse. Working with Dizzy and Bird we were honored by most white groups and beloved by colored people."[98]

Haig, it seems to me, exemplifies the idea of the psychological shift that was going on among musicians, and his exceptional technical skills as a pianist made him a welcome member of the inner circle of bebop innovators, who found him quickly able to adapt to and absorb new ideas. As well as refining Powell's linear technique into a smoother (if less emotionally charged) solo style, he was among the most effective accompanists in modern jazz, and as well as his exemplary backing to Charlie Parker, he recorded equally impressively with Stan Getz and Wardell Gray.

Among the other pianists associated with the early development of bebop, I have mentioned Tadd Dameron, although mainly in the context of his work as an arranger. He came into his own as a pianist in the late 1940s, transferring many of his compositional ideas to the piano, and in parallel to the stylish economy with which he voiced his charts, he had a similar flair for precise, pared-down solos. He led his own groups from 1948 until he was imprisoned for narcotics offenses in the mid-1950s.

Without doubt, the other most unusual pianist to have been caught up in the bebop movement in the middle-to-late 1940s was George Shearing. Not only is he one of the very few Europeans to have made an international reputation as a jazz pianist, but he is also blind, and he began his career in the all-blind dance band, led by Claude Bampton, in Britain, in the late 1930s, going on to lead his own groups and build a considerable name for himself as a soloist and broadcaster. Then, after a visit to the United States in 1946, and partly through the encouragement of his friend Leonard Feather, who had made a similar move, Shearing resolved to settle there the following year to develop his career, and to leave behind him the reputation he had built up in Britain, starting all over again in the tough musical environment of New York.

On his first short visit, Shearing experienced plenty of heady excitement at the richness of the musical life that abounded on 52nd Street, and he sat in everywhere he could, meeting many of his idols, including Art Tatum. (He had got to know Fats Waller in Britain in the late 1930s.) But in 1946, Shearing had yet to find his distinctive solo voice. He was masterly at imitating all styles of jazz piano, from the authentic Chicago boogie-woogie that he played on his early British discs like *Jump for Joy*, to the rippling swing of Teddy Wilson and the mercurial runs of Tatum. When he found bebop on 52nd Street, he knew he had discovered the roots of his future style, and in the discs he made on a swift return to Britain in 1948, like *Consternation* and *The Man from Minton's*, there were all the signs that he had brilliantly assimilated the vocabulary of modern jazz, and, particularly, the speed and fluency of Bud Powell. Sitting in on 52nd Street, and at Minton's, where he played with the swing drummer Sid Catlett, had brought greater power and confidence to his playing, but he felt there was still something missing.[99]

In 1949, he found what he was looking for – a combination of the "locked hands" chordal style that had been developed by pianist and organist Milt Buckner with the ensemble voicing of the quintet that he began to lead that year under his own name, after initially co-leading a small group with clarinetist Buddy DeFranco. This style was to be a distinct development of the bebop vocabulary, and it involved using parallel harmonies for each note of the melody in a three-note, right-hand chord, with the left hand doubling the melody an octave below. By shifting all the rhythmic momentum of his group to the bassist and drummer, Shearing could play melodic, chordal patterns across the beat, and this subsequently fueled his great interest in Latin rhythms, which he shared with Dizzy Gillespie. In his quintet, he doubled the notes of his "locked hand" melodies on guitar and vibraphone, creating an unusual, spacey texture which remained the foundation of his ensemble style into the twenty-first century.

John Lewis developed a similarly spacious style, and he incorporated (as did Shearing) a knowledge of classical counterpoint into his writing and playing, but his work will be discussed in the next chapter, following his association with the big bebop band led by Dizzy Gillespie. Before discussing the transfer of bebop ideas to larger bands – or, given the early importance of the Hines and Eckstine bands, *back* to larger bands – I shall briefly consider the final phase in which the early form of small-group bebop was consolidated, taking in the years up to the death of Charlie Parker in March 1955.

## Closing the Door on Bebop

Charlie Parker opened the door, showed the world, and
then he shut the door behind him.

Tony Scott, from Robert Reisner, *Bird: The Legend of Charlie Parker*

In the late 1940s and early 1950s, bebop spawned a number of other
developments in jazz. First among them was the move to large orchestras
spearheaded by Dizzy Gillespie, Gerald Wilson, and Roy Porter, among
others. But there was also a general move to simplify some of the
complexities of the style. On the one hand, there were attempts to adopt
less complex themes, such as *Blue Monk* or Milt Jackson's *Bag's Groove*. On
the other, there was the debate about the role of the rhythm section to
which I have alluded, regarding the *contretemps*, in *Down Beat*, between
Parker and Gillespie, from 1949, that had Bird defending the broken
rhythms and fragmentary patterns exemplified by Max Roach or Kenny
Clarke and Gillespie justifying his decision to put a recognizable beat back
into his playing.

Gillespie's move towards simpler rhythms initially led him to explore
rhythm and blues in his early 1950s small groups, and then to shift back
towards a modified version of the swing rhythm section, both in his long
association with Jazz At The Philharmonic, and in his 1950s big bands. As
the vogue for cool jazz began, initiated by pianist Lennie Tristano and
consolidated by Gil Evans and Miles Davis, every increase in sophistication
of the harmonic palette tended to be matched by a further simplification of
the accompanying rhythm. This trend found its zenith in the close
connections between the rhythmic approach of the West Coast bands of
Shorty Rogers and the 1930s swing of Basie's Kansas City Five or Seven.
And as Horace Silver and Art Blakey began to modify the small-group style
into something that incorporated blues and gospel sounds into the
repertoire, a blues-inflected backbeat became a cornerstone of the sub-
genres of hard bop and soul jazz.

All these are investigated in more detail in subsequent chapters, but
while each of these new developments was catching on, the original small-
group bebop style continued unabated. Indeed, in the same way that bars
and clubs throughout the world are still featuring Dixieland in the early
years of the twenty-first century, musicians in all parts of the globe still get
together regularly to jam on *Scrapple for the Apple*, *Parker's Mood*, or *Donna
Lee*, since bebop is an equally widespread phenomenon. Nevertheless, the

period in which the small-group style – defined by Parker and Gillespie, or Parker's subsequent front-line partners Miles Davis, Red Rodney, and Kenny Dorham – was at the cutting edge of the music, when bebop was a driving force in the development of jazz, came to an end in the mid-1950s, more or less at the time of Parker's premature death at the age of thirty-four.

Well before his final decline, however, Parker's most consistent and prolific period, in which he did much to define the way that small-group bebop would always be approached in future, dated from his return to the East in 1947 until his cabaret license was revoked in mid-1951. In the first couple of years after he got back to New York, he worked often on 52nd Street, starting with seasons in April, May, and August 1947 at the Three Deuces and returning there in March the following year. In July 1948, he moved into the Onyx for a short spell, but in September Parker moved to a new venue, a few blocks away on Broadway and 47th Street, called the Royal Roost. Although he did appear back at the Three Deuces in 1949, the majority of his New York nightclub appearances from late 1948 onwards were at the Royal Roost, the nearby Bop City, or a club just above 52nd Street on Broadway called Birdland. Named in Parker's honor, the last venue opened in December 1949, and he played there most frequently thereafter.

This new, larger, generation of Broadway clubs would be where bebop ultimately both found a regular home and where it gradually began the metamorphosis into the new styles that derived from it, but as a result of the intense activity in the smaller clubs of the street during 1947–8, by the likes of Parker, J. J. Johnson, and Fats Navarro, bebop had become known as "Fifty-second Street Jazz," in the common parlance of both musicians and critics. This was somewhat ironic, because the majority of the musicians who had worked on the street from the 1930s until around the start of 1947 were united not so much by bebop as by the *lingua franca* of swing. During the latter year the clarinetist Bob Wilber, who was studying in New York with Sidney Bechet, observed: "Bop was all the rage, and Ryan's was the only traditional jazz spot left on 52nd Street."[100] In his autobiography, Wilber recalls that it was also in September 1947 that the "split" between traditional and modern types of jazz arose in earnest.

This was fueled by critic Rudi Blesh who championed the older styles, and *Metronome* magazine's Barry Ulanov, for the more modern tastes. An artificial "war" between styles was set up, to be aired on radio in a series of "Bands for Bonds" broadcasts. This transformed into a vigorous debate in the music press, instigated by an article by Ulanov in the November 1947 *Metronome*, called "Moldy Figs vs. Moderns," and initiated a polarization in jazz that has continued ever since. Before long, many of the old-style swing and traditional jazz musicians were finding it hard to get work, and drifted off into other occupations, either staying in music as copyists or union delegates, or taking day jobs as bank guards or cab drivers. Yet, during the heyday of the street, all styles had happily co-existed, and the would-be beboppers sat on bandstands alongside the older generation of players, just as, up in Harlem, the stars of swing had been welcome sitters-in at Minton's or the Uptown House.

Even so, most of the main clubs on the street survived into the late 1940s. By that time, with the United States enmeshed in a period of post-war depression, there had been a sea-change in public taste. During the years that modern jazz had been growing up, swing had ceased to be America's most popular music, and, in a more generic sense, jazz itself ceased to be popular music. The new kinds of music to take hold were, first, the singing of popular vocalists like Frank Sinatra and Bing Crosby and, second, rhythm and blues. In due course, people looked for larger venues where they could dance to rhythm blues, and whereas, at the same time, many of the stars of modern jazz followed Parker's lead and moved to the larger, more spacious, clubs on Broadway, or further downtown, ironically, most of these discouraged dancers and packed in more customers by presenting "jazz for listening." Soon, 52nd Street began to lose its luster. Furthermore, it was progressively being overrun by girlie shows and strip joints, on the one hand, and drug dealers on the other. Fewer and fewer of the remaining clubs presented music, while outside on the street the police began to clamp down on both  the dealers, and their customers. "Marijuana was the main thing then," recalled clarinetist Tony Scott. "The bad element used to take advantage of out-of-towners, and soldiers and sailors. The police started to make some arrests and warnings were given, and things were made harder and harder on the club owners."[101]

The area had always looked dingy and unattractive by day, but as clubs began to close their doors for the last time, it lost its night-time fascination, and the public started to stay away.

The final nail in the coffin of the street as an area for music was when whole buildings began to be torn down and redeveloped. As a property boom took off in New York, landlords realized that they would make far more money by selling their land for redevelopment than by hanging on to the low rents from rows of old brownstone houses. Midtown was going high-rise, and the old street was an anachronism. Just two clubs – Jimmy Ryan's and the Hickory House – clung on for dear life until the 1960s, but then even they were unable to resist the tide of redevelopment. The Hickory House closed for good, but Ryan's hung on for another twenty years, in a new location a couple of blocks away on 54th Street. When it finally dimmed its lights for the last time, the greatest period in New York's history as the jazz capital of the world was over.

Charlie Parker's rehabilitation and the start of the stage in which he dominated small-group bebop began on the West Coast in early 1947, a few weeks before his return to New York. Released from the Camarillo, he resumed playing gigs in Los Angeles during February with a quartet including pianist Erroll Garner, bassist Red Callender, and an old colleague from 52nd Street, Harold "Doc" West on drums. The group recorded in the West for Ross Russell, who had sold his Tempo Music shop to put all his energies into Dial Records, and also into looking after Parker, who had been released into his care, and for whom he set about trying to arrange some bookings, first locally and then back in New York.

Next, Parker recorded with a larger group, including tenorist Wardell Gray, and, particularly on the chase choruses of *Carvin' the Bird*, Gray illustrates how his own phrasing had been influenced by Parker (the other dominant influence on his work being Lester Young). Gray was to be one of the major bebop innovators on the tenor saxophone, until his death in mysterious circumstances in Las Vegas, in 1955. Trumpeter Howard McGhee, on the same session, demonstrates the facility with which, compared with his playing in 1945, he, too, had absorbed Parker's phrasing and timing, notably where he picks up from Parker's solos by repeating the saxophonist's last phrase, however complex.

At a time when Gillespie was pouring all his energies into his large orchestra, Parker's focus on small-group jazz was to affect players of virtually every instrument. It is possible that the whole course of this period of jazz history would have been different, had Parker's return East led to him successfully rejoining Gillespie, to become a member of his 1947 big band. As it was, because the altoist had swiftly regressed to his use of drugs and alcohol within days of his release from the Camarillo, he was well under their influence when he sat in with Gillespie's orchestra, on April 8, 1947, at the Savoy Ballroom. He soloed adequately enough, but would not play the written parts, and kept falling asleep on the bandstand. All thoughts Gillespie might have had of hiring him evaporated, and Parker was compelled once more to start leading his own quintet at the Three Deuces, a band that included Miles Davis and Max Roach, with bassist Tommy Potter and pianist Duke Jordan. Davis, as it turned out, also played briefly in Gillespie's trumpet section, but he opted to return to the Street with Parker.[102]

As Parker's fellow altoist Phil Woods said, recalling the months that followed his return to the Three Deuces: "I was in New York in 1947; it was impossible to be in that milieu – especially if you were an alto player – and not be touched by Bird. . . . We're all a result of all the people we've ever heard . . . but Bird was the Beethoven of our time."[103]

Parker's reputation spread both by word of mouth to those with access to the club, and through his increasing number of recordings. Among the musicians' community, of which Woods and other players such as Tony Scott or saxophonist Jimmy Heath were a part, there was also the opportunity to jam with the master at the Three Deuces. In the first weeks of the quintet's residency there, Parker often invited numerous fellow musicians to sit in with the band on the later sets. Apparently, this caused some resentment from his regular sidemen, notably Miles Davis and Max Roach, who had both made some personal sacrifices to play with Parker, rather than in Gillespie's big band. So to try to appease his band members, Parker resorted to the same technique that Monk and Clarke used to use at Minton's, as singer Dave Lambert recalled:

> Sometimes when I went to hear Bird, he'd be on the stand with a group of about four men, and there'd be another four or five waiting to sit in and jam. Bird was never discourteous to a musician. He never told them verbally to get off the stand; instead he called a number – *All The Things You Are* in the key of E – and start off *pow* at a ridiculous tempo and in a tough key and the guys would walk off the stand. . . . The musicians just petered off, and the men were separated from the boys.[104]

This, of course, simply intensified the awe in which Parker was held by those around him. So, too, did his attitude to audiences. Whereas Gillespie had a good line in witty banter, dressed the part of an entertainer with his berets and glasses, and was supported by a stream of press releases, photos, cartoons, and articles from the Billy Shaw office, to capitalize on his public image, Parker chose to take a different tack, something that was intricately bound up with the whole psychological shift in bebop. Rather than adopt the mannerisms of African-American show-business, as Gillespie did, Parker either sidestepped them or satirized them in a series of private in-jokes. Sets opened with an ironic stock remark about the "enormous" expense the club had gone to to present the quintet, and finished with a list of names. Enthusiastic cheers or clapping would be put down with "ordinary applause will suffice," but often there would be no announcements at all, at least during the sets themselves. As Ian Carr puts it in his biography of Miles Davis:

> Parker was rejecting the idea of the black musician as entertainer; he wanted his music to be taken on its own merits, to speak for itself . . . he was readjusting the whole relationship of performing artist and audience. . . . He had to flout the tenets of the white society that dominated American life because it demanded that.[105]

In taking this line, Parker put clear water between himself and Gillespie. In Gillespie's stage demeanor from this period, as preserved in his 1946 film *Jivin' in Bebop*, he moves, dances, and conducts the band with all the mannerisms of his old swing-era bosses Cab Calloway and Lucky Millinder. By contrast, accounts of Parker's appearances at Harlem's Apollo Theater made much of the contrast between the old-style big bands, with their elaborate costumes and presentation, and Parker's more spartan approach: "Yard simply walked to the microphone, announced the number, tapped his foot three times, and detonated a musical powder keg."[106]

Such stage manners were to be taken to even greater extremes by Miles Davis, but it was Parker who began this public reappraisal of performance values, to deflect all focus from the performers, and concentrate solely on the music. Because he wanted to focus on improvisation above all, this put immense strain on him as an artist. His recourse to alcohol and heroin was at least partly the consequence of consistently testing his own improvisational capacity to the limit.

So what were the innovations by which he defined the genre? Scholars have transcribed many of his recorded solos from 1947 to 1951, which yield extraordinary results when they are analyzed, in terms of their variety and complexity. These include not just his commercial recordings for Dial, Savoy, and (later) Verve, but also the work of his dedicated fan Dean Benedetti, who made dozens of on-site recordings of Parker at several clubs including the Hi-de-ho in Los Angeles early in 1947, and, subsequently, at the Three Deuces and Onyx clubs on 52nd Street.

The first aspect of Parker's mature style was his speed. Even since his

1945 discs with Gillespie, he seemed to have increased his ability to play phrases that crammed in several notes a second. And those notes were precisely placed as these phrases combined together into long, seamless lines. This technique, a kind of musical patchwork, has the technical name of *cento* in musicology, and Thomas Owens has identified over 100 of the different motifs that Parker most commonly used in constructing his solos, but which he unfailingly stitched together in new and different ways for each individual performance.[107] Second, in addition to this store of his own commonly used motifs, he was supremely adept at the incorporation of quotations into his solos, taking a common jazz musicians' practice and elevating it into an art form, with a vast frame of thematic reference that took in not only all the Tin Pan Alley repertoire of his days in the Parisien Dance Hall, but also the works of several classical composers, including nineteenth-century figures such as Wagner and contemporary figures such as Stravinsky. Third, he continued to develop his harmonic sophistication, and managed to create lines that were coherent, with an internal logic of their own, but which used all manner of complex harmonic devices, not only the extended chords and substitutions discussed earlier, but also anticipating or hanging on to various chords in a sequence to create a dramatic contrast with their normal placing in his accompaniment.[108] Finally, his extraordinary rhythmic sense created unprecedented variety in his solos. Some of the most exceptional of these devices have been identified and analyzed by James Patrick,[109] but equally instructive is Miles Davis's comment about actually playing alongside Parker during 1947–8:

> Bird used to play forty different styles. He was never content to remain the same. I remember how at times he used to turn the rhythm section around. Like we'd be playing the blues, and Bird would start on the eleventh bar, and as the rhythm section stayed where they were and Bird played where he was, it sounded as if the rhythm section was on one and three instead of two and four. Every time that would happen, Max Roach used to scream at Duke Jordan not to follow Bird, but to stay where he was. Then, eventually it came round again as Bird had planned and we were together again.[110]

This period of Davis's work with Parker brought the young trumpeter from East St. Louis to national attention for the first time. He had made a few discs with Parker in 1945–6, but the second stint of their collaboration shows the beginning of the emergence of his own distinctive jazz voice. His discs show him gradually shedding the dominant influence of Gillespie, and playing more to his own strengths – a more restricted range, less speed, and a reflective beauty of phrasing and tone that was an effective counterpart to Parker's torrents of notes and hard, biting sound. Davis attributed some of his tone and style to Freddie Webster, a former member of the Earl Hines orchestra, who spent part of 1946 in Gillespie's big band, before his death, aged 31, in 1947. Certainly in Davis's first session as a leader, in which he led a version of Parker's quintet in which the saxophonist made a rapid adjustment to playing tenor sax, rather than his usual alto, and with John Lewis on piano, Davis produced several examples of the way in which his playing was beginning to contrast with, rather than parallel, Parker's. Most effective is a cool, reflective solo on *Milestones* (not related to his subsequent, more famous tune of the same name), which prefigures Davis's work a couple of years later with his nonet.

Davis and Roach quit Parker's band suddenly in December 1948, after a display of particularly childish behavior by their leader made them feel both humiliated and betrayed by a man they looked up to as a musical idol. Parker first replaced Davis with Kenny Dorham and later with the white trumpeter Red Rodney.

McKinley "Kenny" Dorham had been in the trumpet section of Gillespie's big band, but his playing with Parker's quintet was mainly an interesting hybrid between the styles of Gillespie and Davis. He had much of Gillespie's range and facility (both skills that Davis had not developed to the same degree) but his timing and tone were clearly influenced by Davis's more reflective style. In May 1949, a couple of days before the quintet traveled to the Paris International Jazz Festival, he recorded four tracks for Norman Granz with Parker's regular working line-up, which, by then, included Al Haig, Tommy Potter, and Max Roach, on which he negotiates the tricky head arrangements with ease, and produces solos on two tunes (both, confusingly, called *Passport*, although they are quite different) that display his hybrid style to perfection, including his habit of phrasing slightly behind the beat. In the mid-1950s, Dorham would go on to be one of the architects of "hard bop," with Art Blakey and others, but during his time with Parker, although he was an accomplished foil for the saxophonist, he had not yet developed his own distinctive voice.

The same was to some extent true of Red Rodney (born Robert Rodney Chudnick), whose early admiration for Harry James had given him a powerful, wide-ranging technique, which had been developed by informal contact with Gillespie at Philadelphia's Down Beat club. He is one of the earliest examples of Gillespie's talent for identifying and developing younger brass players, and it was Gillespie who first brought him to the Three Deuces and introduced him to Parker. Rodney's career was soon blighted by heroin addiction which, despite Parker's blandishments, he took up in emulation of the saxophonist. But after a checkered life in which he survived long-term narcotics problems, imprisonment, and a bizarre episode as a confidence trickster and fraudster, which culminated in a military payroll heist, and a slow rehabilitation, he emerged in the 1970s as a powerful and authentic bebop star, playing to the potential he showed but never quite realized in the early 1950s with Parker. As a mature player who had experienced an exceptional degree of involvement in both the high and low life, he packed emotional power in his playing. As a young man, on such discs as the celebrated 1951 *Swedish Schnapps*, with Parker, his timing was nervous and jumpy, and between a number of brilliantly and clearly executed ideas were patches of waffling, makeweight phrases. Nevertheless, there was a daring about his playing that indicated the unorthodox talent for improvisation that he would later bring to his life as well as his music.

Because he survived his addiction and criminal phase, however, Rodney's accounts of his time with Parker are significant, with the added benefit of hindsight. He was sure, for example, that despite the way in which so many of Parker's recorded solos stand up to academic analysis, they were the intuitive product of an exceptional ear. "I have no way of proving that except my own experience with him," he told Gene Lees. "A lot of people say, 'No no, he knew, he was very knowledgeable.' I don't think so. Dizzy, yes. Not Bird. At that time I was very harmonically very unaware of how things went, I was using my ears to hear everything."[111]

Equally, he was able to discuss the reasons why so many of the bebop generation followed Parker's lead and became addicted to heroin:

> When I listened to that genius night after night, being young and immature . . . I must have thought, "If I crossed over that line, with drugs, could I play like that?" Drugs were heavily involved in that part of jazz music. It wasn't the swing players who were using junk. It was the new bebop generation that did that. I was one of the last. I saw all those people doing that. I watched Bird and I knew what he did. You want a sense of belonging. You want to be like the others. And so I tried it.[112]

Despite Parker's fury that Rodney had done as he did, not as he said, they shared their addiction for the remainder of Rodney's three years with the band.

Earlier, Rodney had played a significant part in two of the bebop big bands that developed in parallel with Gillespie's: the Claude Thornhill Orchestra and the Woody Herman band, and when he left Herman, in 1949, to become Parker's trumpeter, he ended up being an influential figure, even if his own playing was still developing. By his own account, he, Davis, Dorham, and Fats Navarro were the most-in-demand bebop trumpeters on 52nd Street in its final phase.

Navarro himself was not a regular member of Parker's band, although his playing with the saxophonist on a small number of airshots and informal recordings suggests he was a more mature talent than Davis, Dorham, or Rodney. He had been aged just twenty when he joined Andy Kirk's orchestra, and he had then replaced Gillespie with Eckstine. Between leaving Eckstine, in late 1946, and his death from tuberculosis and heroin addiction, in July 1950, he made numerous small-group recordings, showing a style that incorporated many of Parker's rhythmic and motific ideas into Gillespie's overall approach to the trumpet. His tone was rounder than Gillespie's and, particularly in his recordings with various-sized groups led by Tadd Dameron, Navarro was a model for the playing of Clifford Brown in the early 1950s.

After losing his cabaret card in 1951, Parker's career became a round of touring to places where he was able to work without the restrictions imposed on him in New York. He was an occasional, if unreliable, member of Jazz At The Philharmonic, and he also toured as a guest star with Stan Kenton. He achieved most popular fame through his "Parker with Strings" project, in which he and his rhythm section toured and recorded with a smallish string section.

From time to time, in television studios, on special gala concerts, or billed alongside one another at Birdland, he was reunited with Gillespie, and the most famous of these reunions took place at Toronto's Massey Hall on May 15, 1953. In a line-up with Bud Powell, Charles Mingus on bass, and Max Roach on drums, whose efforts were recorded by Mingus and later reissued on his own Debut label, there is a chance to hear the last high point of small-group bebop as it was defined by Parker and Gillespie. In performances of *Wee*, *Hot House*, *A Night in Tunisia*, *All the Things You Are*, and *Perdido*, the quintet produced perfect exemplars of all the characteristics I have described in this chapter, from Roach's choppy rhythms to Powell's astringent chording; from his glittering piano runs to Parker's dazzling solos, packed with quotes and allusions, and topped by Gillespie's ability to coalesce this demanding music into a form that was greeted not just with enthusiasm but also with near-hysterical acclaim by the audience.

The remainder of Parker's life lasted less than two years, and he died (as Monk was later to do) in the care of the Baroness Pannonica de Koenigswarter, to whose midtown hotel suite he had made his way when he felt ill on setting out for a gig in Boston. But after his death, the Parker legend continued. His improvisational genius had changed jazz forever, and the heights to which he developed the art of the jazz solo during the late 1940s were not to be surpassed for many years.

CHAPTER 8

# Big-Band Bebop

## Dizzy Gillespie's Orchestra and the West Coast Bands

> A big band is different from working with a small band. I
> have an expertise in playing in the cracks, aside from playing
> solos, playing in between what the band is doing and along
> with the section. I like that kind of stuff, and I'm pretty
> good in front of a big band. I move a lot, and I conduct all
> right.
>
> Dizzy Gillespie, in an interview with Charles Fox

Because bebop was largely born out of the big bands, and also because its
early message was spread by the large orchestras of Earl Hines and Billy
Eckstine, there was little doubt that it would in due course be taken up as a
genuine form of big-band music in its own right.

Neither of those bands I have mentioned was entirely committed to the
new music. Hines was prepared to let Parker and Gillespie add a few
arrangements to his book, and to let them – plus the likes of Benny Harris,
Budd Johnson, or Bennie Green – take a modernistic solo here and there,
but he soon reverted to a more conservative approach, even adding a string
section for a while. Eckstine's enthusiasm for bebop, and his inclusion of a
cadre of talented sidemen as well as a growing body of modernistic
arrangements, was tempered by the commercial imperative to follow up his
hit vocals like *Jelly Jelly* and *Good Jelly Blues* with more of the same, plus a
smattering of familiar ballads such as *A Cottage for Sale* or *Prisoner of Love*.

During 1944, while he had been musical director of Eckstine's
orchestra, Gillespie had come to an understanding with the band's agent,

Billy Shaw, that if he did well, Shaw would back him in setting up his own big band. And in July 1945, Shaw was as good as his word, and booked Gillespie's new big band out on the road as part of a touring package called "Hepsations of 1945." With a certain degree of naiveté, Gillespie began trying to rehearse his sections by getting them to sit in with him at after-hours joints, when he had finished his nightly stint with Parker at the Three Deuces, but having recruited an old colleague from Les Hite's orchestra, arranger Gil Fuller, to help him prepare the band, he saw sense and booked proper rehearsals at a 52nd Street studio. The partnership of Gillespie and Fuller was to prove a potent one, and it built on the shared platform of experience in arranging this music that the trumpeter had gained around his piano at home with Tadd Dameron, and that Fuller had acquired in writing for bands of various sizes. Fuller worked up full-band charts based on those pieces of Gillespie's core repertoire that he and Budd Johnson had notated back in 1944 at the Onyx, and on Sunday, July 8, what the press called the "terrific sizzle band" set off on the road.

For almost two months, the band trawled through the Southern states via Virginia and the Carolinas to Florida, and then through Georgia, Alabama, Louisiana, and Texas into the Midwest, before arriving at the McKinley Theater in the Bronx in late August. It played a mixture of armories, dance halls, auditoriums, and theaters, but, for the most part, at all these venues the uncompromising modernism of Gillespie's raucous eighteen-piece band was presented in the context of an old-fashioned variety package alongside the Nicholas Brothers dancers, the comedians Patterson and Jackson, and dancer Lovey Lane. It fared best in the big urban theaters which it reached at the end of the tour, including the Regal, Chicago, and the Paradise, Detroit, but the visit to the South was a salutary experience for Gillespie. "We didn't fare too well on that tour," he recalled. "It was a big show that went down South, but they weren't ready for us. They were just ready for the blues down there."[1]

Billy Shaw's posters and handouts all proclaimed that there would be "an evening of dancing to a great new band," but in reality few of the rural Southern audiences presented with this new music could work out how to dance to it at all. They might, as Gillespie's comments suggest, have more happily taken on board the nascent style of rhythm and blues, which was taking off the same year in the newly launched West Coast bands of musicians such as Roy Milton and Johnny Otis, but they could not cope with the lightning tempos and bristling section-work of a bebop orchestra. Although Gillespie claimed "I could dance to it. I could dance my ass off to it. They could've too, if they had tried,"[2] the reality was that the psychological shift that had gone on in terms of small-group bebop applied to this big band as well. The "Hepsations of 1945" was a landmark; the moment that big-band jazz formally ceased to be synonymous with African-American social dancing. And in due course Gillespie admitted as much: "Our style of playing, generally, was geared for people just sitting and listening to music."[3]

The tour was Gillespie's baptism of fire as a bandleader. He was dealing with a constantly shifting personnel: some of his musicians were taken by the draft, others decided not to tour the South, there were constant problems with transportation, and, on top of all that, Max Roach underwent a cold-turkey treatment for heroin addiction while the band was on the road. The lack of enthusiasm of the Southern crowds did not alter Gillespie's resolve to play big-band bebop, nor did it lead him to shed all the trappings of African-American show-business, as his subsequent bands often traveled with a panoply of singers, dancers, and comedians, but it did lead him and Billy Shaw to think long and hard about how to relaunch the band more effectively. They eventually did so in the late spring of 1946, once Gillespie had returned to New York from Billy Berg's and built up a core audience for his new small group at a new 52nd Street club, run by Clarke Monroe, called the Spotlite.

In the meantime, however, there was another extremely successful attempt to launch big-band modern jazz out on the West Coast, and before 1945 was out, the orchestra led in Los Angeles by trumpeter Gerald Wilson had made several remarkably effective recordings, including the first version of *Groovin' High* to be cut by a large band, in a brash, forward-looking setting scored by Wilson himself.

Gerald Wilson is one of the most accomplished and overlooked figures in jazz history. He was born in the South in 1918 at Shelby, Mississippi, but he spent his teenage years in Detroit, where he not only became an accomplished trumpeter, but acquired a good working knowledge of harmony. He first met Gillespie in 1938, when the Edgar Hayes Orchestra came to Detroit, and they spent many evenings together during the several weeks of the Hayes band's residency there. In 1939, when Wilson replaced Sy Oliver in Jimmie Lunceford's band, Gillespie took the young trumpeter under his wing in New York and showed him around. Wilson told me:

> It was a time when many of us were searching for new things to say, musically. I had just begun to start writing when I joined

Jimmie. However, my first arrangements for the Lunceford band itself were not done until a few months after I joined. But I was lucky and in early 1940 the first of my pieces was recorded by the band. And then they recorded another one in 1941. I was putting to use things I had learned in school, and picked up from playing, and I used these ideas in my first recorded chart which was called *Hi Spook!* I didn't title it by the way – Jimmie honored a radio club in Seattle, Washington that came on at midnight and was supposed to be a ghost club. It was accepted very well in the world of orchestral jazz because it used some things that would now be recognized as integral to big-band writing, but were not in use at that time harmonically and rhythmically. The flat five had evolved in the very early days of bebop, and Duke had already introduced the sharp nine to orchestral jazz, in pieces like his *Carnegie Blues*. I should say that using chords like this in an arrangement is quite a different thing from improvisers landing on such a chord in the course of a solo, and although Ellington introduced several of these ideas, he didn't really pursue them. In my case I was experimenting with writing as many as six parts, in order to use some of these complex chords simultaneously. In *Hi Spook!* I used the minor ninth, just as we use it today, and just as the beboppers used it, and I was using thirteenths and augmented elevenths (which of course, equate to flat fives).[4]

In the context of Lunceford's earlier work written by Sy Oliver, *Hi Spook!* is dramatically different. It takes the high-energy sound of a piece like *Lunceford Special*, and reframes it into a harmonic context that is blatantly modern in outlook. Another equally novel Wilson composition and arrangement for Lunceford, *Yard Dog Mazurka*, was to become the basis of Stan Kenton's *Intermission Riff*. As I have pointed out in Chapter 4, Lunceford's band was technically equipped to play almost anything put in front of it, and, just as Gillespie had Calloway's band work its way through the advanced voicings of *Paradiddle* and *Pickin' the Cabbage*, Wilson had Lunceford's orchestra trying out several of his equally advanced harmonic ideas – not simply in the handful of his charts they recorded, but in numerous others that were absorbed into the band's regular book for dances and concerts.

When Lunceford toured to California in 1942, Wilson decided to stay put in the sunshine, and he joined Les Hite's orchestra not long after Gillespie had left it. Before forming his own band, he briefly saw military service in the Great Lakes Navy band, alongside Clark Terry and other modern-minded players, and then as a civilian he played in Benny Carter's West Coast orchestra, which in the mid-1940s was packed with musicians who were absorbing the new ideas of bebop, including trombonist J. J. Johnson. Wilson appeared as a freelance on several of Carter's 1945 recordings, but late the previous year he had formed his own first band, with the intention initially of backing singer Herb Jeffries. He took his new line-up into both the Plantation and the Downbeat on Central Avenue. His musicians included the trombonist Melba Liston, whose early arrangements for the group show much of the secure grasp of modern jazz arranging she was later to display as a member of Dizzy Gillespie's 1950s orchestras.

So, at the same time that Teddy Edwards and Howard McGhee were playing small-group bebop on the Avenue, well ahead of Parker and Gillespie's arrival, Wilson was playing big-band jazz which was developing many of the advanced harmonic ideas he had tried out with Lunceford. He cut numerous discs for the local Excelsior label and for Black and White records, and along with the swing bands of Benny Carter, Wilbert Baranco, and Jimmy Mundy, he recorded for the AFRS "Jubilee" radio show. As discographer Chris Sheridan observes in terms of these broadcasts, Wilson's "boppish" band is "more thoroughly modern – despite the swing-styled rhythm section – than any of the others."[5]

On Wilson's 1945 disc of *Groovin' High*, Hobart Dotson's high-note trumpet and Eddie "Lockjaw" Davis's tenor solos are an uneasy compromise between the rapidity of bebop and the clichés of swing, but the ensemble writing is consistently adventurous; although some of the saxophone harmonies have a sour timbre, as a consequence of very close scoring, this is offset by the brilliance of the brass writing, with punchy, off-center chords jostling with harmonized melodic phrasing that is brashly extrovert at the start and finish of the piece. The dynamics are brilliantly contained in the saxes' stealthy *sotto voce* entry under the piano solo, and in many ways the entire piece is a more rounded example of the modern big-band arranger's craft than the work of Tadd Dameron or Gil Fuller on many of Gillespie's own early discs, the difference being that Gillespie's own soloing, and that of his star tenorist James Moody, was so firmly inside the bebop idiom and so brilliantly charismatic that they compensated for any shortcomings in the writing. Nevertheless, Wilson's 1945 and early 1946 discs, including a riotous *Cruisin' with Cab*, show that bebop was being played in large-band form within months of Parker and Gillespie's sextet discs, and well before Gillespie's own orchestra started to record.

Wilson might have continued to make an impact in the 1940s, not least because of such accomplished recordings as his reflective, evocative piece called *Dissonance in Blues*, from 1947, which featured Red Callendar's exceptional bass playing, but despite a burgeoning national career, his band was short-lived. One reason it is not better known today is that, according to saxophonist Teddy Edwards, although the boom times in the Los Angeles docks and shipyards drew all kinds of people to California, the notable exception in the mid-1940s was any nationally known jazz writers.

> A lot of things were not documented that should have been. But there was no jazz magazine as such out here, and there were only two newspaper writers, one for the *California Eagle* and the other for the *Los Angeles Sentinel*, who ever printed anything at all about our music.[6]

Yet, briefly, Wilson's band became known way beyond the confines of the West Coast. After a lengthy booking in Salt Lake City, it was hugely successful at the Apollo in New York, where it first played in 1946, and at the El Grotto in Chicago, where it appeared after a short season in Pittsburgh, before moving into one of the country's top clubs, the Rivreia in St. Louis, where it played opposite Ella Fitzgerald. And there, in late 1947, Wilson broke up his band. "I had hit the top too soon," he wrote. "I was not even near where I wanted to be as a musician, and I knew this. . . . I made up my mind that I was going to disband and return to Los Angeles and I did just that."[7]

Wilson subsequently worked in the trumpet sections of the Count Basie and Dizzy Gillespie bands, while he underwent a long period of study as an arranger with Benny Carter, among others, and when he finally returned to bandleading in the 1960s he was no less adventurous than he had been first time out. His discs for Pacific Jazz, made between 1961 and 1969, are landmarks in modern jazz arranging and he encompassed many of the prevailing styles of that period from modal writing to Latin jazz, and from Third Stream to fusion, with the same skill and penetrating compositional intelligence he had brought to his first bebop orchestra.

Wilson's point, in his interview with me, that big-band bebop was entirely different from small-group improvisation, because the arranger was predetermining harmonies that an improvising soloist was likely only to alight upon in passing, is a significant one. It underlines, I believe, why the big-band format held such a continual fascination for Dizzy Gillespie, notwithstanding the fact that his entire professional apprenticeship was served in some of the leading orchestras in the United States, to the extent that the big band was his natural home. In one oral history account after another, Gillespie's colleagues tell of his skills as a teacher and mentor — showing pianists voicings, helping drummers solve difficult rhythmic problems, jotting down ostinato patterns for his bassists, and confirming the point I made earlier that he heard entire performances in his head.[8]

So when he opened back in New York at the Spotlite club, in March 1946, it was with the intention of augmenting his sextet into a big band as soon as possible. For the time being, he retained Al Haig, Stan Levey, Milt Jackson, and Ray Brown, and added Leo Parker on baritone and alto, but at the outset he said to Jackson and Brown: "I'm gonna get a big band. It's gonna be different, but if you guys want to stay, you're welcome."[9] The sextet worked opposite Coleman Hawkins, and although Gillespie was on the verge of signing a new contract with the small independent Musicraft label, Leonard Feather, by now a champion of the new music after his initial opposition, produced a set of 78 r.p.m. discs for Victor that combined four sides apiece by Gillespie and Hawkins into a boxed "album" called *New Fifty-Second Street Jazz*. The popular success of these discs did little harm to Gillespie's reputation at the Spotlite, and in late April he was eventually able to enlarge his band to a full-sized orchestra of seventeen pieces. "Dizzy's second attempt to run a big band seems certain to be more successful than his first," wrote Leonard Feather. "Clark Monroe's Spotlite Club has squeezed the 17 men into its limited space, giving them a good chance to whip the ensembles into shape."[10]

At first Monk played piano, but he was soon replaced by John Lewis, an army friend of Kenny Clarke who had returned from war service to take over the drum chair. James Moody came into the line-up after being demobilized from the Air Force band in which Gillespie had been impressed with his playing the previous year, and, over the course of a few weeks, the big band settled into its run at the club. At the same time, Gillespie was starting to make a new series of small-group discs for Musicraft in which the altoist Sonny Stitt did an uncanny job of recreating the sound of Charlie Parker. Stitt also led the section at the Spotlite and it takes no more than a few moments of hearing the band's airshots to reveal that it had a raw power and aggression that had been heard in no other big band in jazz up until that point, including Wilson's West Coast ensemble.

The writing, by Tadd Dameron, Gil Fuller, John Lewis, and Gillespie himself, plus themes contributed by band members such as Ray Brown, was crammed with new ideas, but the thing that really stood out about the band was not what it played but how it played. "To be in that little club, the Spotlite, with its low ceiling and hear the band play *Things to Come*," wrote critic Ira Gitler, "it would take your head off. Incredible. Definitely one of the most exciting experiences you could ever have."[11]

And many other eyewitnesses (or ear-witnesses) have described this ebullient energy which captured the mood of the players. As Ray Brown recalled: "You can't wait to get up, you can't wait to get to the bandstand, you can't wait to play. . . . The music is new, it's exciting, and we all know that somehow this music is beginning to catch on."[12]

The band worked at the Spotlite until a week into July, by which time the entire orchestra had had virtually three months to coalesce into a tight-knit unit. Judging by the recordings it made before leaving New York for its first series of one-nighters and theater dates around the country, Gillespie and Fuller had made a good job of transferring many of the elements of bebop to larger forces. The British critic Jack Cooke perfectly summed up, in a 1969 article, what it was about this band that was so exceptional:

> The performances of the group . . . remain the most articulate and valuable extensions of big band thinking for many years, the last attempts within a conventional format to push the concepts of orchestral techniques into line with solo techniques.[13]

Gillespie's first big-band discs demonstrate this thinking. Whereas Gerald Wilson's approach was essentially that of an established – if experimental – big swing-band arranger, adopting the harmonic innovations of bebop into his regular method of writing for large bands, Fuller and Gillespie were trying something much more ambitious, which was to transfer the mobile freedom of the bebop small group to larger forces. Howard Johnson, the band's alto saxophonist, who was never a soloist of comparable class to his section-mates Sonny Stitt or James Moody, was empowered by the writing to play with something approaching the same freedom as his improvising colleagues: "I was playing first chair alto," he wrote, "playing what somebody had written, and I more or less had to get into the spirit of what they were doing."[14] The skill with which the sections interpreted the charts as if they were improvising them as bebop solo lines is immediately obvious in Tadd Dameron's *Our Delight*, a medium-tempo piece in which Gillespie's solo trumpet and Moody's tenor interweave with long, loping lines from the brass and reed sections. But the *pièce-de-résistance* from these recordings (and from the airshots from the Spotlite itself) is Gil Fuller's breakneck *Things to Come*. It would be hard to imagine dancing to this helter-skelter arrangement, which sets off at a gallop, and where the fluency of Gillespie's trumpet, Stitt's alto, and Milt Jackson's athletic vibes solo is matched by the high-speed precision of the brass and reed playing, whipped along by Clarke's irregularly accented drumming, and rounded off by an extraordinary glissando played by the entire band. As a collective artistic achievement, this is one of the great highlights of the bebop era.

To those who were attuned to what this remarkable band was trying to achieve, the contrasting writing styles of Dameron and Fuller were at the heart of the Gillespie orchestra's musical appeal. Dameron's beautifully crafted arrangements retained his Midwestern experience, and were predominantly melodic, with hummable tunes and a preponderance of medium tempi, of which *Stay On It* and *Cool Breeze* are good examples. Fuller's tended more towards the jagged lines of bop solos, to extremes of tempo, and even his treatment of Ray Brown's melodic fragment that constituted the main subject of *Ray's Idea* was more complex than Dameron's best themes such as *Our Delight* or *Good Bait*.

In mid-1947, following the success of Gillespie's earlier small-group album, Victor signed a contract to record his full orchestra, and in moving from the small Musicraft company, the band's work took on all the benefits of major record label distribution and marketing. There was also a constant stream of marketing material emanating from Billy Shaw's office, intended to help attendances at the band's live appearances by keeping Gillespie's zany bebop image in the public eye. Shaw focused on what became a cult of modernism, on "hep" language, and on clothing and accessories. At some of the band's concerts, audiences were encouraged to appear with spectacles, berets, and goatees that emulated Gillespie's, and as mail-order advertise-ments started to tout bebop garb, cartoons and placards appeared with the legend "bebop spoken here." The zenith of this marketing blitz was a feature in *Time* magazine that showed Benny Carter and Gillespie running through the ridiculous movements of a "bebop greeting."[15]

In today's marketing-driven world, this kind of activity may seem perfectly natural, but it was innovative and unusual in the 1940s, and certainly an original approach to selling adventurous music that was, in terms of the easy listening of the swing era, much more difficult to appreciate. Nevertheless, bound up with this novel marketing strategy were several tried-and-tested ideas, starting with the fact that, as I suggested in the last chapter, the cult of modernism was a thin veneer over the timeworn practices of the African-American variety stage. Gillespie's clothes, language, and antics might seem to be a long way removed from the mugging stage persona of Louis Armstrong, who was seen by some modernists as an "Uncle Tom," to the extent that Gillespie publicly sought to distance himself from him, not least by claiming Eldridge, rather than Armstrong, as his major influence. However, to those such as Charlie Parker who were challenging the old stage mannerisms of African-American show-business in a far more radical way, the parallels were all too obvious. Miles Davis, Parker's trumpeter, who spurned such behavior, wrote:

> As much as I love Dizzy and loved Louis "Satchmo" Armstrong, I always hated the way they used to laugh and grin for the audiences. I know why they did it – to make money and because they were entertainers as well as trumpet players.[16]

I have little doubt that if Gillespie had not adopted such an engaging stage persona, and been so well-versed in the African-American show-business mores of the time, his band would not have survived through a period of dramatic decline in large orchestras, as it did successfully until 1950. As it was, chastened by the experience of his "Hepsations of 1945" tour, but aware that he needed to win over more conservative provincial audiences in order to make a living away from the big cities of New York and Chicago, he trod a fine line between presenting uncompromisingly modern music to a large public and retaining his links with the entertainment traditions. His press billings from the period chart this tricky course, so that, on the one hand, a 1946 tour with Ella Fitzgerald and "her throbbing, vibrant and electrifying swing voice" had "the merry mad genius of music, Dizzy Gillespie" appearing along with "a bright and happy summertime stage show [with] Freddie and Flo comedy capers and Ralph Brown,"[17] and on the other, there were genuine attempts to introduce "jazz for listening" to the club and cabaret circuit. By late 1947, for instance, at the Club El-Sino in Detroit, Gillespie was packaging his club act as a "concert." The advertisements read:

> This concert is the first of its kind to be offered by any night club in the country. . . . Up until now this presentation was enjoyed only by patrons at Carnegie Hall, Cornell University and Symphony Hall in Boston.[18]

However, to make such concerts and his Victor recordings palatable to a general public that was still getting used to the idea of a full-sized, brash, dissonant bebop orchestra, Gillespie included a large number of comic scat-singing numbers into his repertoire. He shared these with Kenneth Hagood and, later, Joe Carroll, superimposing "bebop" syllables over the kinds of lines played by improvising horns – indeed, despite the limitations of his vocal range, Gillespie's singing was a direct mirror of his approach on trumpet. Hence *Oop-Pop-A-Da*, *Ool-Ya-Koo*, *Cool Breeze*, and *Jump Did-Le-Ba*, for example (plus, towards the end of the band's life, comic turns such as *Hey Pete, Let's Eat Mo' Meat!*) were neatly integrated with Fuller's contemporary charts, Dameron's enticing voicings, and other modernistic arrangements from Gerald Wilson, Linton Garner, Pete Rugolo, and Mary Lou Williams.

One other reason for the presence of so many vocals was the exhausting technical demands which the high-voltage arrangements made on the brass players. "After about half an hour," Ray Brown remembered, "you'd look over at the trumpet section, and everybody's lip's hanging down, looking like some ground meat."[19] As a result, in addition to featuring plenty of vocals in each set, Gillespie took to handing over a few numbers to the rhythm section of Brown, John Lewis, Milt Jackson, and Kenny Clarke. This measure, born out of expediency, was ultimately to lead to the birth of the Modern Jazz Quartet, which was none other than the Gillespie band's rhythm section by another name. The MJQ (initially the "Milt Jackson Quartet" and later known by the "Modern Jazz" tag) did not come into being as a formal entity until 1951, but the essence of its sound, with the bluesy phrasing of Jackson's vibraharp pitted against the classical clarity of Lewis's piano, began at the Spotlite in 1946. By early 1947 it was being billed separately as an act in its own right, appearing at Smalls's Paradise, in Harlem, during one of the big band's lay-offs as "The Atomics of Modern Music."

The Modern Jazz Quartet was one almost accidental by-product of Gillespie's big band, but the band had another very significant impact on jazz, beyond the degree to which it swiftly became the most successful attempt of all to transfer bebop from the small groups of 52nd Street to a full-sized jazz orchestra. This was the creation of Afro-Cuban jazz, and it came about through Gillespie's decision to incorporate the Cuban percussionist Chano Pozo into his rhythm section. Pozo (born Luciano Pozo y Gonzales, in Havana, in 1915) made his debut at a Carnegie Hall concert on September 29, 1947, which became the moment when Gillespie's long-held interest in ways of combining Latin and Cuban rhythms with bebop came fully to fruition.

Back in his Calloway days, Gillespie's interest in this had been aroused by his fellow trumpeter Mario Bauza, who had not only had a hand in persuading Calloway to record pieces like *Chili Con Conga*, but also had many connections with New York's Cuban community through his own background in Havana. In the 1930s, Bauza had introduced Gillespie to musicians such as the flautist Albert Socarras, which whetted Gillespie's interest in sitting in with Latin groups, and by 1947, Bauza himself had spent some years playing in the Cuban band led in New York by Machito. By this time the jazz orchestras of Woody Herman and Charlie Barnet had experimented with some aspects of Cuban rhythm, mainly in pieces such as Herman's *Bijou* or Barnet's *New Redskin Rumba*, but no-one had yet undertaken a more full-scale integration of Cuban rhythms with modern jazz. So it was to Bauza that Gillespie turned when he started looking for a suitable Latin percussionist to add to his own big band line-up. "Mario Bauza cut me into Chano Pozo," he recalled. "Chano Pozo couldn't even speak English. He was just staying round New York, working Russian theaters, behind dancers, and things like that."[20]

Gillespie was enthusiastic about the idea of adding layers of polyrhythms to his band, so in addition to some of the overtly Cuban-influenced numbers he brought into the repertoire for his new percussionist, he was quite content for Pozo to play along with the band on its normal bebop arrangements. This caused quite a few problems for the regular rhythm section – Ray Brown, for instance, saying: "This guy's doing all this while we're just trying to swing straight out, and it seemed to inhibit us."[21] Such tensions aside, the fourteen months or so that Pozo spent in the band, before he was murdered in a drug-related incident in Harlem, made a dramatic difference to big-band jazz, and their work together was a powerful influence not only on all Gillespie's subsequent orchestras, but also on many other bands, most notably that of Stan Kenton.

By far the most impressive piece that Pozo played with Gillespie was not the perennial *Manteca*, which Gillespie retained in his repertoire for the rest of his playing life after first recording it in December 1947, but *Cubana Be/ Cubana Bop*, recorded earlier the same month, and written for Pozo's first appearance with the band back in September at Carnegie Hall. The basic theme for this extended number, which originally stretched over two sides of a 78 r.p.m. disc, came from Pozo, but it was expanded and orchestrated by the composer George Russell who, by this time, had already begun his lifetime fascination with using scales, based on modes, as the basis of improvisation. Instead of a conventional chord sequence, the piece is constructed on a scale which Russell defined as "B flat auxiliary diminished."[22] After a dramatic introduction from Pozo's congas and Joe Harris's drums, the whole orchestra moves, in a sinister way, up and down this scale, which is then used to underpin the harmonies of a simple and beautiful theme that is played by Gillespie's solo trumpet. After a series of exchanges between Gillespie and the congas, Pozo starts a sequence of chanting which is answered by a shout-back from the other members of the band. In concert, starting with the second performance of the piece at Boston's Symphony Hall, Pozo used to come center-stage for this, wearing African costume. This sequence is followed by the entire band piling in massed chords on the same modal scale that introduced the piece.

*Cubana Be/Cubana Bop* is important because it is one of the first modal compositions in jazz, prefiguring a style of improvisation that took another ten years to become widely adopted, following the examples of Miles Davis, John Coltrane, and George Russell himself. It also anticipated the movement towards all things African, exemplified by Pozo's costume and chanting, which surfaced not only in Gillespie's own 1960s work and dress, but also in the work of musicians as varied as Ahmed Abdul-Malik, Ornette Coleman, and Randy Weston.

This aspect of internationalism — the incorporation of consciously African elements into the presentation of music that was already combining Cuban rhythms with those of bebop — was one of the most prominent aspects of the band's playing when it became the first bebop big band to tour to Europe, with a trip to Scandinavia, Belgium, and France in 1948. Recordings of its concerts in Stockholm and at the Salle Pleyel in Paris (where the band played its first set without music because the charts had been delayed en route from the North) reveal its spectacular ensemble strength and its buoyant ability to combine Kenny Clarke's dramatic drumming with Pozo's dazzling conga rhythms to support Gillespie's solos, at a time when he was playing better than he had done at any point in his career. "It affected the consciousness of all musicians," wrote Maurice Cullaz, who remembered Gillespie's 1937 appearance with Teddy Hill and was on hand again to witness this new group.

> I think most of today's French jazz musicians who were at the concert discovered their vocation for jazz then and there, and particularly for bebop. They'd already had contacts with the music via discs and Voice of America broadcasts, but I believe it was at this [Salle Pleyel] concert that the music really clicked for them.[23]

Later, several of Gillespie's musicians, including trumpeter Benny Bailey, drummer Kenny Clarke, and tenorist James Moody (who had actually left the orchestra before its tour) relocated to continental Europe, where they acted as mentors to a generation of enthusiastic local jazz musicians, anxious to learn bebop at first hand. They paved the way for a long post-war traffic between France, Holland and Scandinavia (in particular), and the United States, in which other musicians such as Nathan Davis, Kenny Drew, Dexter Gordon, Oscar Pettiford, Bud Powell, Hal Singer, and Ben Webster became temporary European residents.

The 1948 big-band tour was the first of many in which Gillespie himself became an ambassador of jazz to the rest of the world, a role that he fulfilled admirably for the U.S. State Department in the 1950s, and thereafter on his own account for the rest of his life. Also in 1948, Louis Armstrong brought his All Stars to Europe to play at the Nice Festival, and, in due course, Gillespie naturally assumed the role of international father figure of jazz which Armstrong had made his own since the 1930s.

However, when Gillespie returned to the United States from that first European tour, there were clear signs that the big-band era was coming rapidly to a close. Many leaders who were far better established than he was were forced to scale down to small groups as Cab Calloway did, or quit leading altogether. I have already suggested how Billy Shaw's marketing skills had helped the band to survive from 1946 to 1948, at a tricky time for large ensembles, but Gillespie's problems were compounded by the fact that he no longer made much pretence of playing for dancing. In Europe he had been most successful playing in large concert halls, which were sold out for several days running. But in America the idea of the jazz concert was still in its infancy. Press reports, for example, of Gillespie's appearances for Gene Norman at the Hollywood Bowl and Pasadena Civic Auditorium, make it clear that the local disc jockey had only recently "introduced the jazz concert medium to southern California,"[24] and although the Gillespie band performed at some of the nation's major halls, in Boston, New York, and (for Norman) in Los Angeles, such events would not keep a band working at a time when the provincial circuit was still built largely around the touring variety promotions that had gone on since the early days of the century. Even the new rhythm and blues bands, such as that of Johnny Otis, toured as part of a package with singers, dancers, and comedians, and played a fair proportion of dances.

After its European trip the band's New York base became the Royal Roost, the "Metropolitan Bopera House," which was its ideal environment;

a large club with more space than the Spotlite and (as the *New York Times* reported) "no dance floor, no lavish review, just tables and the shattering blasts of twenty-odd musicians."[25] But no band could survive on one club alone, with sporadic weeks in theaters that would hire such a progressive-sounding group and strings of one-nighters linking the longer residencies. Reports in the trade press revealed that, compared to Gillespie's successes of 1946–7, audiences were falling away, and slowly but surely the end came in sight for this pioneering bebop big band. He kept going through 1949, and some of the musicians who passed through his ranks were evidence of his ability to spot and employ the very brightest talents, including trumpeter Willie Cook, trombonist J. J. Johnson, and saxophonists Yusef Lateef, Jimmy Heath, John Coltrane, and Paul Gonsalves. By the middle of 1950 he gave up the struggle because, as *Down Beat* reported, "He's got possibly the best band he ever had, and it looks as if he'll be breaking it up any day. Because he can't get work."[26] Gillespie returned to fronting a big band in the mid-1950s, but, as discussed in Chapter Fifteen, by that time a major change had gone on in the big band world.

Gillespie's 1946–50 big band was without doubt responsible for spreading the message of bebop every bit as effectively across the United States as the small groups of Charlie Parker. Even Parker's appearances in the touring Jazz At The Philharmonic packages, and with his string ensemble, lacked Gillespie's consistency of recorded output, high-profile concert appearances, and the innovative combination of adventurous writing with the uncharted territory of Afro-Cuban jazz. Furthermore, just as Parker had hit his creative peak in the late 1940s, Gillespie's own, miraculous playing was faster, higher, and more accurate and inventive than that of any trumpeter in any form of music up until that point. "He was a harmonic and technical genius," said his trumpet section-mate, Benny Bailey.

> For us in the brass section of that 1948 big band, he was the guy to look up to. When I talked to other trumpeters like Fats Navarro and Kenny Dorham, they felt far, far beneath Dizzy, actually. Because Diz was doing everything with the horn and harmonically that you could possibly do.[27]

But whereas it was one thing for musicians in many parts of the country to put together a quintet or a sextet and to emulate the playing of Parker as best they could, it was quite another to assemble an entire bebop big band, and so there were not many musicians able directly to follow Gillespie's example, however high profile. In due course, the innovations of this pioneering big band filtered through into the work of many of the larger bands that were formed in the 1950s, but its effects in the late 1940s were limited to a handful of high-profile white ensembles which are discussed in the next section, and just one or two African-American groups.

Of these the most important were the band led by saxophonist Jimmy Heath in Philadelphia (which did not record, but became a feeder organization for Gillespie's own group) and the West Coast orchestra of drummer Roy Porter. The first of these is discussed in Chapter 16 in terms of its importance to the careers of Heath, John Coltrane, and other significant Philadelphia musicians. Porter's Seventeen Beboppers, by contrast, had no direct connections with Gillespie's band, but it is exceptional both because it made an independent attempt to interpret bebop in a big-band form, and because of the remarkable caliber of the soloists it produced. Porter himself had not only played with Howard McGhee and Teddy Edwards, but had been Charlie Parker's drummer on several sessions for the Dial label. In essence, Porter's band grew out of a rehearsal band – in other words an informal group that met on a regular basis to play through charts in semi-public rehearsals, which in its case were held in a restaurant close to the intersection of Vernon and Central Avenues called the Chicken Shack, and later at the Club Alabam on Central itself, where Curtis Mosby's swing orchestra used to play in the 1930s and early 1940s. However, Joe Howard, Robert Ross, and Jimmy Knepper,the band's arrangers, were all experimenting in taking forward the language of large-band bebop; Howard by constant harmonic exploration and Ross by writing what Porter called "intricate passages for each section to play."[28] Furthermore, the band's reputation spread quickly in the local area to the extent that it played often in the clubs of Central Avenue or out-of-town areas such as Bakersfield.

Through the efforts of local disc jockeys it came to be recorded, and it made around nine sides for the Savoy label, which include the first solo appearances of altoist Eric Dolphy, who was to make a huge impact on the jazz of the late 1950s and early 1960s, with both John Coltrane and Charles Mingus, as well as with his own groups. Porter's other sidemen included trumpeter Art Farmer and trombonist Jimmy Knepper, as well as "Sweetpea" Robinson, another remarkable alto saxophonist, whose promising career ended abruptly when his wife shot him dead.

The band's career almost ended equally abruptly when Porter, Art Farmer, and saxophonist Clyde Dunn were injured in an automobile accident in New Mexico while on route to the start of the band's first national tour in 1949. Although the band re-formed, and recorded a few sides for the local Knockout label (whose master discs were subsequently destroyed), Porter was also unable to keep a large band going in the economics of the time, and in mid-1950 he eventually broke up the orchestra and left for Oakland to join the bebop small group led by Sonny Criss, thus drawing to an end the early stage in the development of African-American big-band bebop.

## From Krupa to Kenton

> Gene embraced anything new. Nothing frightened him. And
> he had what was really the first white name bebop band.
>> Red Rodney, in Gene Lees, *Cats of Any Color*

Although the African-American bands of Wilson, Gillespie, and Porter very much took the lead in transferring the ideas of bebop to larger forces, white musicians had been active in the new jazz from the outset. Stan Levey had first worked with Gillespie at the Down Beat in Philadelphia, in 1942, and he went on to play with him frequently on 52nd Street and in California. George Wallington had been a member of Gillespie's Onyx Club quintet, and pianists Al Haig and Dodo Marmorosa were also prominent among the first beboppers to record. In the world of small groups, there was, therefore, a degree of integration from the moment that the new jazz coalesced into a recognizable form, and emerged from the big-band dressing-rooms and after-hours clubs. What mainly characterized the small-group bebop musicians was their ability to handle the music's complexities, rather than any question of race or background.

However, despite the pioneering efforts of Benny Goodman, Charlie Barnet, Artie Shaw, and a number of other white bandleaders to introduce African-American soloists into their groups, there was still a long way to go in the mid-1940s before big bands would become fully integrated as they are today. For the most part, such high-profile white bands employed individual black soloists among a largely white line-up, just as, on the other side of the divide, Roy Porter, for example, hired trombonist Jimmy Knepper: "I wasn't that particular, frankly, about white boys being in the band," he wrote, "because I wanted to keep a loose, swinging feeling. But when he played he sounded so good that I jokingly asked him if his mother or father were black."[29]

As a consequence of this degree of segregation between white and African-American orchestras, the move towards bebop happened more or less separately among white bands, and it followed in the wake of the pioneering efforts of Eckstine, Gillespie's 1945 Hepsations Orchestra, and the first Gerald Wilson band. In the early 1940s, one or two white orchestras, notably those of Boyd Raeburn, Jimmy Dorsey, and Woody Herman, had commissioned arrangements from Gillespie, but these were generally played as if they were conventional swing charts, without the entire orchestra taking on the spirit of the music in the way Howard Johnson felt empowered to do with Gillespie's own band. Indeed, Gillespie himself discussed this in terms of his occasional gigs and recording dates with white orchestras:

> Touring with Charlie Barnet, I discovered some of the differences between working with 'white' and 'colored' bands. In the different black bands, you had to play differently, because every 'colored' band played, or phrased, its own unique way. So you had to adjust yourself to many peculiar styles of playing. In the white bands I worked with, Charlie Barnet and Boyd Raeburn, everything was more standardized, and a musician didn't have to change too much as he moved from one band to another.[30]

Ironically, as the quotation at the head of this section suggests, one of the very first white groups to embrace the new style more wholeheartedly was led by a man who is generally thought of as the epitome of the swing era – drummer Gene Krupa.

Yet by the mid-1940s, Krupa's career had suffered some severe ups and downs, and when he began to hire musicians and arrangers with an interest in bebop, he was working hard to regain his former reputation and status. In 1941 he had separated from his wife Ethel, and he had attracted plenty of press attention after a much-publicized affair with the film star Lana Turner (who was also one of the ex-wives of Artie Shaw). Then, his popular vocalist Anita O'Day left in early 1943, but within a month or two of her departure, Krupa was forced to break up his band; he was sent to jail on May 18 for "contributing to the delinquency of a minor" when his teenage band boy was arrested trying to dispose of some marijuana on Krupa's instructions.[31]

After his release, following a brief return to Benny Goodman and a stint with Tommy Dorsey, Krupa re-formed his band; as a consequence of the draft having made many experienced players unavailable, he ended up hiring a new line-up of relative unknowns. After a short-lived brush with a string section and some somewhat sloppy arrangements, this shook down to a firmly jazz-orientated group, that included several young, experimentally minded musicians. In early 1946, his personnel included trumpeter Red Rodney, saxophonists Charles Kennedy and Charlie Ventura (who later led a group billed as "bop for the people"), and staff arranger Gerry Mulligan.

Mulligan was born in 1927, but his extraordinary talents as an arranger surfaced during his teenage years, and he was already writing for Johnny Warrington's band at the age of seventeen. In 1945, he made a conventional swing arrangement of *How High the Moon* for bandleader Elliott Lawrence, in whose saxophone section he played. But the following year he thoroughly overhauled the chart for Krupa, acknowledging his growing awareness of bebop by introducing Charlie Parker's *Ornithology*, which was written over the same chords, as a theme for the saxophone section in the second chorus. Overall, the recording of this piece remains recognizably the work of a swing band, but an extremely forward-looking one, with the harmonic ingenuity of Mulligan's writing for the saxes matched by the fluent boppish solo trumpet of Red Rodney.

In Mulligan's most accomplished chart for Krupa, *Disc Jockey Jump*, recorded in January 1947, there are signs that the reed section was beginning to be able to handle playing long, linear melodies of a bebop character with the kind of fluency redolent of spontaneous improvisation that Gillespie's saxophones were managing under Sonny Stitt or Howard Johnson's leadership. Krupa's own playing remains irredeemably rooted in swing, with a snare solo redolent of Chick Webb, but he handles the abrupt drum accents of the chart itself with aplomb, and effectively underpins some solos that are also moving in a convincing bebop direction, notably from altoist Charles Kennedy and trumpeter Don Fagerquist. More importantly than the quality of the individual solos, there are elements in the writing here that would be influential on many other arrangers, particularly those who worked for Woody Herman and Stan Kenton, whose bands I shall come on to discuss. Mulligan's deft use of muted trumpets in unison with the alto saxes for the main opening and closing themes was also later to become a hallmark of writers like Ernie Wilkins and Neal Hefti in their charts for the 1950s Basie band.

Krupa was not beyond adopting a little of Dizzy Gillespie's marketing hype for his own purposes, and as well as recording the medium-tempo bounce *Calling Dr. Gillespie* (which had a Dizzy-styled trumpet solo feature for Fagerquist or Rodney), he occasionally dressed the entire band in berets and dark glasses to create an image of his musicians being more fully fledged beboppers than was apparent from their actual playing.[32] Overall, his presentation was slick and professional, and individual touches, such as music stands made from drum shells, gave his band a memorable public image, helped further when Anita O'Day returned to the fold. She had spent the intervening period with Stan Kenton's up-and-coming band, but produced the following unforgettable account of the differences between the two bands: "Stanley was a gentleman, but working with him was like wearing a tight girdle. Working with Gene made you feel relaxed as if you were lounging around in an old kimono."[33]

The proof of her remarks can be found in the combination of relaxation and powerful jazz feeling that comes across in the surviving recordings of Krupa's band on live appearances and broadcasts. These qualities are uppermost in its most convincing bebop performance of all: a February 1946 broadcast from Hollywood of Mulligan's *Bird House* – an ingenious chart that strings together its main theme from fragments of Charlie Parker solos. (Parker was, of course, in Hollywood at the same time, and Red Rodney maintains that the opportunity to hear Parker and Gillespie at Billy Berg's was one of the reasons he agreed to make the West Coast tour with Krupa's band.[34] No doubt all the members of Krupa's entourage who had not already encountered Parker on 52nd Street did so during their stint in Los Angeles.) Bearing in mind Martin Williams's point I quoted earlier, that bebop was developed from the resources of jazz itself, *Bird House* must surely be one of the earliest examples of a piece that uses elements of bebop solos as its main building-blocks.

While Krupa was playing, broadcasting, and recording on the West Coast in 1946, Woody Herman's First Herd was playing in the East and Midwest, working the big hotels and clubs in New York and Chicago. If I have so far overlooked Herman in my survey of the swing bands, it is because his work from the middle-to-late 1940s eclipses anything he did in the 1930s, after taking over most of Isham Jones's band to form the basis for his own first orchestra in 1936. Herman, who was born in Milwaukee in 1913, was always a talented clarinetist and saxophonist, but he came into his own as a soloist in the early 1940s, particularly on clarinet, on which he combined the fluency of Jimmie Noone or Barney Bigard with occasional use of the rasping, edgy, vocal tone of another New Orleans musician, Edmond Hall. Then, after adding a series of exceptional players to his line-up, including bassist Chubby Jackson, guitarist Billy Bauer, drummer Buddy

Rich, and then Dave Tough, trombonist Bill Harris, tenorist Flip Phillips, and the arrangers Ralph Burns and Neal Hefti (who also played in the trumpet section), he gradually transformed his band into one of the most polished and technically brilliant of all. He was featured on the cover of *Metronome* in December 1945 and January 1946, won best band of 1945 in both the *Metronome* and *Down Beat* polls, and *Newsweek* summed up his career to date by saying: "Herman and his outfit have put almost nine years of hard work into building a band which is commercial and at the same time sticks to Woody's concept of jazz and swing."[35]

But a few months into 1946 this concept had changed radically with, on the one hand, a collaboration with Stravinsky, who wrote his *Ebony Concerto* for the band, and, on the other, the arrival of bebop into the repertoire, first of Herman's "band-within-a-band," the Woodchoppers, and then into his full orchestra.

In his biography of Herman, Gene Lees, who knew the bandleader well, has tried to pick apart the web of myth and marketing hype that surrounded the Stravinsky composition, and, in particular, the story that the composer had become interested in writing a jazz piece after hearing Herman's band playing numbers such as the twelve-bar blues *Caldonia* or the light-hearted *Goosey Gander*. This apparently convinced Stravinsky that "Woody's musicians would be the best media for performing his works in the proper spirit and interpretation." According to Columbia's publicists, this would bring about "one of the most extraordinary unions of two schools of musical thought – jazz and 'modern.'"[36]

To capitalize on Herman's extraordinary success of 1945, with discs such as *Apple Honey*, *Caldonia*, *Laura*, and *North West Passage*, it made sense to try a new angle, and "modernism" seemed a good bet. So the publicists hyped the idea that Stravinsky was so bowled over by hearing the band that he "donated" the piece (and rehearsed it with the band) as a Christmas present for Herman. Lees sees this as "fabrication – record company hokum at its worst," and he suggests that the piece more probably arose out of a stratagem cooked up between Herman's attorney and a representative of Stravinsky's publishing house, who saw potential in it for both their clients. Even if Stravinsky did actually go through with the formal motions of presenting the score to Herman as a gift, money almost certainly changed hands in some considerable quantity.

Few composers from the world of classical music more perfectly suited the image of modernism than the Russian emigré who had written the *Rite of Spring*, and whose interest in African-American music went right back to

1918, when he composed his *Ragtime for Eleven Instruments*. Despite the fact that Stravinsky was among the composers who had already added to the voluminous symphonic jazz library of the by now extremely unfashionable Paul Whiteman Orchestra, with his *Scherzo à la russe* of 1944, the general perception of him at the time his new work for Herman was announced to the world was as one of the icons of modern music. What is also clear is that while he liked some of the superficial characteristics of jazz, the timbres of muted brass and saxophones, the martial rhythms of snare-drum rolls, and abrupt, syncopated accents, these did not add up to a coherent jazz vocabulary, and they were effects grafted on to his own very distinctive compositional language. *Ebony Concerto* is an atmospheric piece of program music, full of clichés of modernism, but ultimately neither convincing jazz nor a particularly good example of Stravinsky. Herman's musicians, used to the band's outstanding rhythm section, were disorientated when they discovered that Stravinsky had not written in a way that used this great strength of the band at all, and that its components were used separately, as they might be in a classical orchestra, with no coherent relationship to one another or to an underlying jazz rhythm. The *Ebony Concerto* is, more than anything, a sizable white elephant.

Nevertheless, the piece did Herman's reputation no harm at all, and it strengthened the modernist aspirations of his own arrangers – notably Ralph Burns who had shown, in his chart of *Bijou*, just how several elements of Stravinsky's compositional language could be used to make a highly effective jazz composition, full of what Burns called "grunts and cheeps and everything."[37]

The aspect of modernism that arrived in the band in the person of trumpeter Shorty Rogers, who joined in late 1945, just in time to take part in Stravinsky's rehearsals for *Ebony Concerto*, was ultimately to have a far more significant effect on the Herman Herd's long-term future, by progressively introducing the sounds of bebop. Born Milton Rajonsky in 1924, Rogers was a student during his teens at the High School of Music and Art in New York; from the age of eighteen he played in Will Bradley's band, and then moved to the small combo led on 52nd Street by vibes player and xylophonist Red Norvo. He was, as a result, present on the Street just at the time that the first experiments in bebop were taking place. After a short spell in the army, he took Conte Candoli's place in Herman's trumpet section – on the very day Candoli was drafted to the self-same army camp Rogers had just left.

Rogers had been a bandsman during his military service, and like many aspiring arrangers he found this an ideal place to try out his skills:

> I took *The Man I Love*, a George Gershwin tune, and I just found some chords. And they were all whole notes. Just the simplest thing you could do, but a sustained background to the melody. And I wrote it out for five saxes. It was an army band so there were musicians round all the time. You could yell: "I need a few guys! Come over here and we'll try something out!" I'd copied the parts and I counted off, and to my complete amazement it sounded okay. I couldn't believe it. It's such a great feeling to put something on paper, and that moment, when you hear people breathe into it, it comes to life, and you hear something coming to your ears – it's just the most wonderful, rewarding feeling. So I got hooked real bad then.[38]

At first, he had little opportunity to try out his skills, because Herman was well-staffed with more than competent arrangers. But in May 1946, the band was in Chicago for a couple of weeks, and Columbia suggested to Herman that he make an entire album (a set of 78 r.p.m. discs) by his small group the Woodchoppers. Shorty Rogers takes up the story:

> He went and talked it over with Red Norvo, who was in the band, and said: "Do you think we could get it together?" And Red said, "Yeah. Shorty's here. We can do a few of the tunes that we did with the 52nd Street group." So Woody invited me to do the album and I think I wrote the majority of the numbers – Red Norvo and I collaborated on some of them, but that was the first thing that was recorded I did for Woody's band.[39]

Some months earlier in 1945, Norvo had led a studio jam session in which Charlie Parker and Dizzy Gillespie had played alongside swing-era players such as Teddy Wilson, and there is something of the same transitional feeling about the Woodchoppers sides on which he appears with Herman and Rogers. Nevertheless, Rogers's writing on *Igor* and *Fan It* shows an awareness of many of the harmonic innovations of bop – not least the series of descending chords at the end of the latter – and despite a resolutely swing-styled rhythm section anchored by bassist Chubby Jackson (who would later be another pioneer of bringing bop to Europe around the same time as Gillespie) there are some convincing solos in the bop idiom from guitarist Billy Bauer, tenorist Flip Phillips, and Rogers himself.

In another few months, Rogers began to write for the entire band, and *Back Talk*, his first big-band chart, has the same transitional feeling about it as the small-group sides, but it has some very clear pointers to the future. The most successful aspect of the piece is that it harnesses the band's incredible energy and power. Second only to the Gillespie Orchestra, the 1946 Herman band conveys an astonishing vigor in its recordings – the savage power of the brass, the serpentine precision of the reeds, and the pounding rhythm section, which was propelled by the drumming of Don Lamond, had many of the ingredients of bebop. *Back Talk* uses the bop device of creating a new melody over extant chords – in this case the sequence of *I've Found a New Baby* – and Rogers's section writing of the final choruses, in which Flip Phillips exchanges four-bar sections with the entire band before Herman's clarinet soars over the whole ensemble, rivals the writing of Gil Fuller for excitement, though remaining somewhat less adventurous harmonically.

At the end of 1946, Herman broke up his band, which had by no means yet become a bebop orchestra, but which had showed more potential than most comparable white groups for successfully becoming one. Around the same time several other leaders took cuts in their fees, or gave up their bands as well. The principal reason was economic. Bands had hiked their fees in the boom times of the end of the war and its immediate aftermath, but as recession bit there was less money in the economy, and the average gate takings at the nation's dance halls and theaters were not keeping pace with the demands of the bandleaders, nor the salary expectations of their sidemen. The vogue for popular singers and for rhythm and blues was also splitting the interests of what audience there was. A few beleaguered bandleaders blamed bebop – if not the leading figures in the new music, then their myriad hangers-on for the decline. An embittered Charlie Barnet, for example, who had never previously been completely antipathetic to bebop, and had been a great champion of transitional African-American players such as Howard McGhee, thundered:

> Outside of the top exponents of the music like Charlie Parker and Dizzy Gillespie, the boppers were a bunch of fumblers who were obviously incapable of handling the new idiom. ... This effectively delivered the death blow to the big bands as we had known them.[40]

Despite the prognoses of gloom from such former rivals, after opting for semi-retirement and sporadic recordings as a soloist, Herman re-formed an orchestra on the West Coast in the early fall of 1947, with the specific intention of packing it with players proficient in the new music. This was the same year as Benny Goodman's short-lived venture into leading a bebop-orientated line-up with Fats Navarro and Wardell Gray among his recruits, but whereas Goodman's foray into modernism was a temporary blip in an otherwise straightforwardly swing-orientated career, Herman's new band was to become one of the most celebrated and innovative line-ups in jazz history.

"I felt," said Herman, when he was asked about his decision to regroup, "I had to do something productive that I really liked."[41] And the distinctive idea that he "really liked" came from a Los Angeles band, led by trumpeter Tommy Di Carlo at Pete Pontrelli's Spanish Ballroom, that featured a line-up which included four tenor saxophones: Stan Getz, Jimmy Giuffre, Zoot Sims, and Herbie Steward. (Both Getz and the band's other trumpeter, Gene Roland, were veterans of the Stan Kenton orchestra back East.)

Giuffre and Roland wrote the arrangements for this unorthodox instrumentation. Although Count Basie had pioneered the idea of using two tenor saxophones battling with one another as soloists, and reinforcing one another in the ensemble texture of his reed section, there was an entirely different tonal quality about four tenors playing together, which Jimmy Giuffre perceptively defined as "like syrup."[42] In Di Carlo's band, this was combined with the fact that all four tenorists were technically advanced, to the extent that they rivaled most altoists in terms of speed and upper-register range. This sound, it seemed to Herman, would give his new orchestra a character quite different from his earlier band. Furthermore, Getz, who had worked with Benny Goodman as well as with Kenton, and had begun to combine the light, fluffy sound of Lester Young with the harmonic depth and rapidity of Charlie Parker, had been playing in a rehearsal band with Shorty Rogers, who was rapidly developing his own knowledge of bebop. This rehearsal group had tried out some of its arrangements on the public under the leadership of saxophonist Butch Stone, and it was clear to all who heard them that the combination of Rogers's steadily more modernistic writing and Getz's unique tone and approach to the tenor was a potent combination.

Herman hired Sims, Steward, and Getz to join his new line-up, plus a baritone player from Boston called Serge Chaloff. With his own alto saxophone (or that of another player who joined the ranks, called Sam Marowitz) melding with the section, this gave him a range of possibilities, since Steward doubled on alto, allowing Herman to opt for two altos, two tenors, and baritone; or alto, three tenors, and baritone. Jimmy Giuffre was not forgotten either, and Herman commissioned him to take on some of the arranging for the new band along with Rogers and Ralph Burns. The combination of bebop charts and the distinctive sound of its four new saxophonists became the defining elements of the Second Herd, and it has been known ever since as the "Four Brothers" band after Jimmy Giuffre's composition of that name, which it recorded in December 1947 **[CD track 17]**.

The main melody line of *Four Brothers* is carried by Getz, with Chaloff shadowing him an octave below, and the other two tenors sandwiched in between, with the brass adding occasional stabbing chords. The theme has many of the trademarks of a Lester Young solo, in both its lightness of timbre and lyrical phrasing, and the same spirit pervades the solos which follow in quick succession from Sims, Chaloff, Steward, and finally Getz, who plays well up into the alto range with the purity of tone that was to be his hallmark throughout his career. The harmonized coda and individual solo tags once again marked out the four distinctive saxophone voices of the new band, which, owing principally to the dynamic drumming of Don Lamond, had lost nothing of the energetic spark of its predecessor.

Before long, other arrangers were imitating this new approach to big-band voicing, but Herman's strong suit was that from the outset his other arrangers adapted the sound created by Giuffre to very different kinds of setting, so that, for instance, Shorty Rogers's up-tempo *Keen and Peachy* (a contrafact of *Fine and Dandy*) kept enough ingredients of the same formula to be identifiably the work of the same band, but had plenty of characteristics of its own. It emulated *Four Brothers* in the voicing of the opening theme by the saxes, before expanding into a full-band piece which, although originally based on a spontaneous head arrangement, rivaled Gil Fuller's writing for excitement and vigor in the version that was finally recorded. Rogers told me that many of the band's best-loved pieces evolved from taking standard chord sequences like this, and letting each of the sections work out a riff of its own before combining them into a powerhouse blend. In many of his charts he skillfully pooled such impromptu ideas with composed themes of his own. The feel of this number, however, is unquestionably bebop, and the difference between this incarnation of Herman's band and its 1946 counterpart is marked by the completeness of its stylistic shift to embrace the new jazz. Even as through-composed a piece as the final section of Ralph Burns's *Summer Sequence* (the other three movements of which had been recorded by the First Herd) managed to harness the "Four Brothers" sound in its closing ensembles, and contains a delicately poised, lyrical solo by Getz, with unmistakable bebop inflections. As Jimmy Giuffre pointed out, the way in which his template for the three tenors and baritone was used – both collectively and as individual solo voices – became the secret of the band's sound, and its success: "It was the right timing, the right soloists – a beautiful band with crisp brass sounds. It was a road map for the future. I was really inspired in combining Lester Young and bebop in that piece."[43]

The band put Herman's principal soloists on the map as well – Getz had not found the right setting for his translucent sound before, in the bands of Kenton or Goodman; Sims excelled in the rough-and-tumble competition among the tenorists; and Chaloff rapidly became one of the leading baritone soloists in jazz. In the trombones, Earl Swope's robust sound was a fitting replacement for Bill Harris, and the trumpets were packed with talent, including the high-note specialist Ernie Royal.

The last weeks of 1947 saw the band engaged in frantic recording activity as 1948 was to begin with yet another A.F.M. recording ban, and for most of the following year the only sound documents that chart the band's exceptional progress are taken from its regular broadcasts. Nevertheless, such a prolonged absence from commercial recording undoubtedly harmed the Herman band's chances of getting established across the country, and its initial popularity was not sustained. Its efforts have become far more widely appreciated in posterity than they were at the time, and the discs it did manage to make either side of the ban have seldom been out of print during the five decades that followed. During 1948, as evidenced by the glimpses of his work from airshots, Getz matured into one of the major solo voices in jazz, and shortly before the year end, when the band was finally able to return to the studios, he recorded his masterly solo on Burns's ballad *Early Autumn*. This gave him sufficient reputation to launch his solo career. He led his own groups from this point onwards, and was to be a major influence on the "cool" school of players in the 1950s.

Herman's Second Herd continued to be the leading white bebop band for the rest of the decade. Its bop repertoire was continually extended, and as well as playing, Herman adapted his characteristic vocals to take in bop scatting – much as Gillespie had done – on pieces like Shorty Rogers's *Lemon Drop*, with Rogers and vibes player Terry Gibbs joining in some close-harmony fun on the intricate nonsense lyrics. Furthermore, he managed to find excellent replacements for his tenorists when Steward and Getz left, bringing in Al Cohn and Jimmy Giuffre as well as Gene Ammons, an

African-American veteran of Billy Eckstine's band, at various times. During the period Ammons was in the sax section, there were two other African-American musicians in the line-up, Oscar Pettiford and Ernie Royal, and it was a symptom of the times when the band arrived in Washington, D.C., the capital of the land of the free, that the Loew's Capitol Theater would not let them play with the Herd, as it had contracted an "all-white" band.

Herman seethed, but he was in no position to make too much of a stand, because he was under serious pressure to keep the band going. Although the cognoscenti liked and appreciated his new sound, his old fans who wanted to hear his old hits *Apple Honey* or *Blue Flame* were not turning up to hear the new-style repertoire, or buying his discs in sufficient numbers. He lost as much as $175,000 dollars in the first year (interestingly, by comparison, Milt Jackson believed that Gillespie had also lost well over $100,000 in his first year with the big band).[44] Herman was also fighting factionalism in his ranks, owing to the fact that – in keeping with the ethos of the new music – his line-up included several heroin addicts. Continuing financial losses, and, despite much critical acclaim and the move from Columbia to Capitol, consistently falling record sales finally sealed the fate of the "Four Brothers" band in late 1949. In the same year Goodman broke up, and by February 1950, even Count Basie had been forced to scale down to an octet for the first time since 1936. Basie hired baritone player Serge Chaloff from the wreckage of Herman's band and subsequently added tenorist Wardell Gray, alongside clarinetist Buddy De Franco and trumpeter Clark Terry, to create his first overtly bebop-influenced band. Shorty Rogers, however, went in a very different direction, to the one other white band that had experimented with bebop and Afro-Cuban jazz, and which was still in business – the giant orchestra of pianist Stan Kenton. He told me:

> The Four Brothers band broke up in December of '49. Wichita Falls, Texas, was our last gig. Everyone went to their home, be it New York or wherever, and just scattered. I went back to Los Angeles, but Shelly [Manne] and Buddy Childers were in Woody's band at this time, and they had been called to join the upcoming Stan Kenton Innovations Orchestra. Buddy spoke to Stan and said, "Shorty's available." Shelly spoke for me, and arranger Pete Rugolo spoke for me, and then Buddy spoke for me again and again, so finally, Stan said, "OK. Let's get him on the band."[45]

Pianist Stan Kenton had been born in Wichita in 1911, and was as full of energy as he was with pretentious ambition. His tireless work at writing, leading, and promoting his work had actually led to a couple of brief periods of retirement, the second inspiring an interest in psychoanalysis as enthusiastic as his interest in music. When he formed the 43-piece "Innovations In Modern Music Orchestra" which Rogers joined, it was to be a grandiose venture – with strings and orchestral woodwind – that eclipsed even Paul Whiteman's most otiose schemes of the 1920s, but which produced nothing as worthwhile or long-lasting as *Rhapsody in Blue*.

I have seldom read a better description of Kenton's tangential relationship to the main course of jazz history than the one written by the British critic Jim Burns in 1969. He said:

> As the years roll on, Kenton will be seen more and more as having been rather like a man living in the middle of a lake. He could still get to the mainland for his supplies (the products of what was happening there) but once back on the rock he tended to live his own life. It was influenced by what he had taken from the mainland but he nevertheless set his own pace and worked out his own way of doing things. [46]

One reason that Kenton's work stands apart from that of many other big bands of the 1940s is that he was based on the West Coast. After beginning his recording career for Decca, he soon transferred to the new Capitol label, a musician-run business based in Los Angeles, and, in contrast to the relative obscurity of the African-American Californian bands led by Gerald Wilson and Roy Porter, Kenton established a high profile for himself, not least by regular broadcasts on the Bob Hope show, on which he was resident bandleader in 1943.

Paradoxically, though, whereas Wilson and Porter were connected to the world of African-American music by their own experiences in orchestras like Lunceford's or Larkin's, and through the vibrant Central Avenue scene, where almost every major performer of note in the world of black show-business arrived at some time or another in the 1940s, Kenton's world was a more isolated one. To be sure, bands like Goodman's or Krupa's came to Los Angeles to play a season from time to time, or to work in a movie, but they were connected to the world of New York, Chicago, and the East. Kenton was always something of an exotic visitor to the East, even during those periods in 1942, 1944, 1945, and the winter of 1947–8, when his band was working on that side of the country for various spells of time. So, in Burns's metaphor, California was Kenton's rock, and he and his numerous arrangers built up their corpus of work there with a degree of independence from what was going on elsewhere. Furthermore, although Kenton's own writing at first drew most conspicuously on Duke Ellington's work and that of the Lunceford orchestra, this body of work was extremely diverse. There was, as Ted Gioia has pointed out, not so much a "Kenton sound" as a number of "Kenton sounds" that existed simultaneously,[47] and were as varied as the group of writers he employed to supplement his own charts.

Chief among his writers was the Sicilian-born Pete Rugolo, who was the band's full-time arranger from 1945 to 1949, and whose work covered as diverse a range of interests as Kenton's own. Rugolo was quick to absorb the harmonic language of bebop, if not its rhythmic implications, but he was also interested in numerous other ideas, and the main bebop qualities in his mid-1940s arrangements tend to come from the band's impressive array of soloists rather than the charts themselves. His *Unison Riff* of October 22, 1947 is a typical example, where spectacular trumpet and alto solos (the latter by a more than usually in-form Art Pepper) are sprinkled into a relatively swing-orientated arrangement which has none of the fluent boppish section writing or playing apparent from the Gillespie orchestra or Herman's contemporaneous band, and the massive chords piled on at the end serve to accentuate, not integrate, the distinct roles of orchestra and soloists.

Kenton has remained a controversial figure, adored by a factional band of hard-core supporters, but more generally viewed as an anomaly in jazz history at best or entirely overlooked at worst. Consequently, there are few surveys of Rugolo's writing for Kenton and of the range of compositional ideas – many of them drawn from contemporary classical music – he tried out. In the best of them, Max Harrison has drawn attention to his consistent use of motifs as compositional building-blocks, his investigations of contrast between tiny two-note or three-note phrases and lengthy solos in works such as *Abstraction*, and the cross-rhythms and textural explorations of *Fugue for Rhythm Section*. And there were other equally interesting avenues of musical adventure in the music of the band's other regular arrangers Bob Graettinger and Bill Holman.[48]

One of Kenton's first attempts at playing an out-and-out bebop arrangement was *How High the Moon*, recorded in December 1947, although this was largely written not by Rugolo but by Woody Herman's trumpeter-arranger Neal Hefti. (Hefti had been almost as significant in determining the

Herman band's bebop orientation as Shorty Rogers, and his unison chorus for the trumpets in Herman's *Caldonia* was, he said, based on hearing Dizzy Gillespie play these melodic figures on 52nd Street with Benny Carter in 1942,[49] but his more important contribution to jazz arranging was his work for Count Basie's 1950s orchestra, discussed in Chapter 15.) The outstanding moment in the rather raggedly played chart of *How High the Moon*, with June Christy's attempts to scat a bop vocal, is a translucent alto solo by Art Pepper, who was to become one of the defining solo voices in the band, and who had comprehensively absorbed the improvisational vocabulary of Charlie Parker, while retaining a comparable lightness on alto sax to that of Lester Young on tenor.

In what was already a large orchestra in the late 1940s, Pepper was not featured by Kenton as often as his talents deserved. "Art didn't have the chance to be exposed with the band as much as he might have been," recalled June Christy. "[It] is a tendency of Stan's. He likes the full, big band sound, and he's reluctant, really, to let anyone be the star."[50] Christy also made it clear that Kenton was not always aware of when the band was playing at its best – his manic lifestyle and complex artistic ambitions sometimes occluded his judgment, and more than once the band would reach its peak when he was off checking box-office takings or doing promotional work away from the bandstand. This remained true when his 1940s band transmogrified into the Innovations Orchestra, and a line-up full of some of the country's most original and modern-styled soloists was harnessed alongside orchestral woodwind and strings. Some of his musicians, such as altoist Bud Shank, remained grateful to Kenton for getting him to explore numerous woodwind instruments beyond those he was already playing, and he became one of the leading flautists in jazz (his mid-1950s recordings on flute with tenorist Bob Cooper playing oboe are a direct consequence of the instrumental versatility Kenton demanded of his sidemen, and remain extremely attractive performances); others found their solo opportunities declined with little commensurate reward.

In the Innovations band, many of the threads Kenton had been working on previously were pulled together, not least his own version of Afro-Cuban jazz. To me – paradoxically, given the size of his band – his efforts have always seemed lightweight in comparison to the wholehearted commitment of Gillespie and Pozo, but Kenton did start working on harnessing Cuban rhythms the same year as Gillespie, in 1947, and (although I suspect some element of influence from Gillespie crept into his later Afro-Cuban pieces) he always claimed that his original inspiration was independent. According to Kenton, it stemmed from the work of a Cuban band led by Noro Morales at the Embassy Club in New York and, subsequently, from hearing Machito (in whose band Gillespie's old mentor Mario Bauza was playing).[51] Certainly, Kenton had recorded Pete Rugolo's *Machito* in the spring of 1947, but his later pieces, such as *Cuban Carnival* or *Peanut Vendor* (a huge hit based on a sanitized Latin rhythm), were made three months after Chano Pozo's well-publicized debut with Gillespie in September of that year.

Kenton's Innovations Orchestra of 1950 continued to include some Cuban or Latin-influenced material, but in retrospect by far its most interesting work involved the comprehensive adoption of bebop ideas into its charts and style of playing. This again had a lot to do with the arrival of Shorty Rogers, who was able to bring with him the writing expertise he had gathered with Herman. His first chart was produced within a few days of the band getting together:

> We started rehearsing every day in January of 1950 with the strings and French horns and quite an ambitious group of musicians. So Stan said, "Shorty, I want you to write an original for the band. Just write whatever you want. If you wanna use strings it's fine; if you don't wanna use them, don't use them." So I wrote this one original. It had no title on it when I brought it in, but Stan and everyone liked it, so it went in the program as we traveled round. He'd call it *An Expression from Rogers*, but when we got back to Los Angeles to record it, one of the A. and R. men from Capitol said, "Let's change the name to *Jolly Rogers*!" and that became the title of it.[52]

The piece uses the kind of flowing bebop-inspired lines that Rogers had already made part of his vocabulary, and the cool qualities in his own solo trumpet playing contrast with the dramatic high-note excursions of Maynard Ferguson in the closing ensembles. Although Rogers left the band after eighteen months, both during his remaining time in the trumpet section and afterwards he continued to write pieces for the band that highlighted its individual soloists, including the eponymous *Art Pepper* and *Maynard Ferguson*, plus *Coop's Solo* (for Bob Cooper). These are by no means the only bebop-inspired numbers played by Kenton in the 1950s, but they are among the best, and they also stand as the link between the white big bands of the 1940s that successfully absorbed the new music, and the cool West Coast movement of which Rogers was to be a key figure (along with Krupa's former arranger Gerry Mulligan) from 1951 onwards, and which is discussed in Chapter 14.

Art Pepper was the outstanding soloist of the Kenton orchestra from 1946 until 1951, and despite spending much of the 1950s in jail as the consequence of his addiction to heroin, he, too, became a colleague of Rogers in the new West Coast movement. Kenton, meanwhile, continued to inhabit his rock in the lake, and although he was forced to scale down his Innovations band by shedding most of his woodwind and string sections, he continued to play what has become known as "progressive" jazz. This built on some of the Western art music compositional ideas Rugolo had used in the late 1940s, and explored dissonance, aspects of serialism, and atonal playing, not only in Rugolo's scores, but, particularly, in some of the more ambitious pieces by Bob Graettinger and Bill Holman. In due course, this led towards the so-called "Third Stream" movement of the 1950s.

Although bebop would continue to underpin most harmonic and improvisational thinking throughout the 1950s, the days of the "pure" bebop orchestra barely lasted into that decade. Big-band rhythm sections turned away from the fragmented rhythms and uneven accents of Max Roach or Kenny Clarke, and returned to a modified form of swing, in which a four–four pulse contained the accents and bombs of the bebop innovators in a more controlled way. And composers and arrangers, as Kenton's so conspicuously were to do, began to treat bebop as a stylistic resource that was just one of a number of compositional options, but by no means the only or the dominant way of writing for larger forces as the 1950s went on.

CHAPTER 9

# Dissemination

## The A.F.M. Recording Ban of 1942

The strike not only created a vacuum between jazz musicians
and listeners; more important, it eliminated a major source
of communication among jazz players themselves: the
phono-recording that served as text and teacher to the jazz
community.

H. Wiley Hitchcock, from *Music in the United States*

The recording ban that was introduced by the A.F.M. on August 1, 1942
was more than a stylistic watershed, in which its beginning marked the end
of the swing era and its end the emergence on record of modern jazz. As we
know, much of the development of bebop carried on regardless of the ban,
and the new stylistic tenets were spread via the old show-business conduits
of communication, depending less on the phonograph record to spread ideas
than on touring big bands and word of mouth while the ban was in force.
However, from the time of Coleman Hawkins's discs made in the spring of
1944, the growth of bebop became more rapid, with the aid of recordings
that could be studied in detail. And just as players of almost every
instrument had pored over Louis Armstrong's discs in the 1920s to learn
every nuance of his solos, a new generation of trumpeters listened to Dizzy
Gillespie on *Disorder at the Border*, while rhythm sections tried to emulate the
new rhythmic approach of Clyde Hart, Oscar Pettiford, and Max Roach.

But the ban had another, far less obvious, effect: it accelerated the pace
of technological change, not least because the not-for-profit V-Disc program
authorized during the ban by the United States War Department to provide

current recordings for its armed forces, introduced the idea of 12-inch unbreakable vinyl 78 r.p.m. discs with a six-and-a-half minute playing time, thereby breaking the 25-year orthodoxy of the three-and-a-half minute disc as the standard format for jazz.

The start of the movement towards extended playing times went hand-in-glove with a restructuring of the entertainment industry, of which jazz was still a major component in the early 1940s. This restructuring had begun with the dispute in 1941 between ASCAP and the broadcasters about radio royalties to composers, discussed in Chapter 4. As a consequence of that dispute, the work of composers of country and blues songs, represented by BMI, became far more widely heard on the United States network radio stations, tilting the balance of the entertainment industry towards singers as never before. The A.F.M. dispute was to have a similar effect, although that was not the intention of the musicians' union, any more than ASCAP had intended to open the door for a rival group of composers to be heard on radio instead of its own members.

The basic case of the A.F.M. was that new technology, in the form of talking pictures and broadcasting – and particularly the broadcasting of phonograph records – was eroding the job prospects of its members. It made the point that the arrival of the talkies, for example, had cut the jobs of 20,000 members of the A.F.M. who had previously played accompaniments to silent movies, and that the more widespread broadcasting of phonograph discs would have exactly the same effect on those musicians hitherto employed to play live on air.[1] And so, led by the powerful head of its Chicago local, James C. Petrillo, the union demanded a levy from the record companies in the form of a royalty payment on each disc sold. The eventual settlement did succeed in getting a minuscule percentage of sales income paid to a union fund for out-of-work musicians, but even though the A.F.M. managed to achieve almost total solidarity from its members in supporting its boycott of making instrumental discs, singers remained able to record, and – coming hard on the heels of the publishers' dispute – recorded and broadcast entertainment was irrevocably altered in favor of vocal performance.

In terms of jazz, as far as the stylistic watershed brought about by the ban was concerned, several of the ingredients of bebop were present before it took place, in the recordings I have mentioned by, for example, Gillespie with Calloway, Hite, and Millinder, or Parker with McShann. But when recording activity resumed soon after Decca and Blue Note became the first companies to settle with the union in September 1943, those ingredients were far more obviously and consistently present in such prototypical bebop performances as the Coleman Hawkins session I referred to above. By that date, there had also already been a significant number of technical innovations that would fundamentally alter the relationship between jazz and recording.

As I said, up until 1942, the 78 r.p.m. disc was the dominant medium for commercial recording, usually in 10-inch format with approximately a three-minute playing time, but also, for many classical and a tiny number of selected jazz releases, in a 12-inch format which allowed over a minute of extra time. Before the ban, there had been experimental long-play discs running at $33\frac{1}{3}$ r.p.m., some used for studio back-up or safety copies of 78 r.p.m. discs, and there had also been the early development of 16-inch long-play discs designed for radio transcription broadcasts, but none of these was for direct sale to the public. V-Discs – even though they were not for sale, but for mass distribution to the forces – opened up the possibility of longer playing times becoming generally available for the first time.

All these formats were based on the principle of musicians recording straight to disc – in other words the sounds they made being captured by an electromechanical system and transferred straight to a wax disc, which formed the basis of the manufacturing master. But alternative techniques were beginning to appear that allowed, first, far longer performances to be recorded, and, second, the possibility of amending or altering a master without having to repeat an entire performance. From the late 1930s, wire recording, which used a form of magnetic technique, was being used to preserve live radio broadcasts, and the capture of one of the most sophisticated such devices, a German AEG Magnetophon, by Allied forces in 1944 led ultimately to the development of the Ampex tape recorder three years later. The technological landscape altered irrevocably at this point, and opened up the possibility of recording efficiently complete sets or lengthy works. This would obviate the technical limitations of, say, Goodman's 1938 Carnegie Hall concert or Ellington's 1943 *Black, Brown and Beige*, both which spanned several 78 r.p.m. acetate masters, with considerable variation in quality between different discs. As the possibilities grew for longer performances to be recorded, musicians began to think in terms of making discs that were no longer bound by the constraint of the three-and-a-half-minute playing time, opening up both composition and improvisation.

But had there been just such a link between the means of dissemination and music in the early years of jazz?

During the first 40 years or so of jazz history, live performance itself had ceased to be the sole means by which most forms of popular music were disseminated. In the late nineteenth century, the first medium to challenge performance was sheet music. Popular songs were printed cheaply and distributed in great number in many countries of the world, particularly from the Tin Pan Alley district of New York (a nickname applied to an area of Broadway which, originally centered on East 14th Street and Union Square, later moved uptown to East 28th Street, and finally, in the inter-war period, centered on the Brill Building at around 50th Street) where most music publishers were based. The first great period of Tin Pan Alley activity was in the 1890s, and it remained a major force into the 1950s. But sheet music as a medium of communication presupposed a musically literate consumer. The biggest change to underpin the transition of popular music in the first half of the twentieth century from the old concept of performer and audience to something that involved a far wider public was the development of mechanical, and then electrical, means for reproducing performance, and before moving on to the period of rapid change that followed the A.F.M. ban of 1942, I shall briefly recap on the major developments as they affected jazz up until that point.

## The Player Piano

> Some time since, the QRS company announced the addition of a special department through which the characteristic music of the Negro race would be made available for the player piano and recorded by artists of their own people, thus insuring accurate interpretations.
>
> Advertisement in the *Chicago Defender*, August 18, 1923

The pneumatically operated piano was patented by Edwin Scott Votey (1856–1931) in 1897. It consists of a conventional piano, in which is built a mechanism that operates the keys to correspond with perforations in a paper roll. Air drawn through the holes by suction (from a vacuum created by treadles) operates valves, which, in turn, force down the keys. Skilled operators and sophisticated developments in the cutting of rolls and the corresponding playback machinery allowed the device to be developed into the "reproducing piano," which became a far better means than early sound recording to recreate the finer points of performances by great pianists. But at a humbler domestic level, this piano, which did not require a competent pianist to play it, became a principal source of home entertainment, and in the space of two years in the early 1920s, nearly half a million instruments were manufactured.

Piano rolls were cut by leading concert pianists (including Paderewski, Rachmaninoff, and Artur Rubinstein), but, as the quote at the head of this section suggests, they were also made by major performers in the emerging styles of ragtime and jazz, helping to distribute these forms to a wide public. Many pianists learned the finer points of technique by slowing down a piano roll and working out how to finger the more daunting passages. Advertisements in the African-American press from the mid-1920s show the use of sophisticated modern mail-order marketing methods to create and sustain a public for piano rolls by popular artists.[2] The QRS Company promoted performances by several African-American "composer-pianists," thereby hoping also to push up sales of sheet music to hopefuls aspiring to emulate them. Principal among the composers promoted in this way were J. Lawrence Cook, Clarence Williams, James P. Johnson, and Fats Waller.

The piano roll and player piano gradually declined as a source of home entertainment. The instruments themselves were space-consuming and costly, and they required an operator to pedal the mechanism and operate the speed and volume controls. Furthermore, a degree of skill was required to overcome the mechanistic character of playback and recreate even the simplest nuances of live performance. Nevertheless, in the rare instances where an exceptional operator is able to bring to life a reproducing roll cut by a pianist at a time when phonograph recordings of pianos were still inconsistent, the results can be remarkable. For example, Michael Montgomery's painstaking recreations of Fats Waller's piano-roll performances for the Biograph record label show that Waller was a far more dazzlingly accomplished pianist in the early 1920s than he appeared to be on disc, notably in his 1924 roll *A New Kind of Man*, with a staggeringly difficult set of chords in the left hand that change on every beat, and Montgomery also offers a tantalizing glimpse as to how the master-and-pupil team of Waller and James P. Johnson sounded playing a duet, on the 1926 *If I Could Be With You One Hour Tonight*. Although they recorded together on disc in the Louisiana Sugar Babes, with Waller playing organ, this is the only chance to hear the two Harlem masters going through their show-stopping piano routine from the revue *Keep Shufflin'*, with a mixture of formulaic stride decoration and a thrilling tempo change towards the end that is genuinely exciting, despite the limitations of the medium.

549

As recording on disc in the mid-1920s began to give an increasingly faithful sound reproduction, the gramophone supplanted the player piano in terms of home entertainment, not least because it did not involve so great an investment in machinery or the operator's time. Before moving on to sound recording itself, we should look briefly at the music-box industry. Flourishing briefly in Europe in the years before World War I, Swiss- and German-made disc and cylinder music boxes disseminated an enormous quantity of music in the emergent ragtime tradition. The popular rag, *At a Georgia Camp Meeting*, was available in more than 25 different mechanical music-box versions, which did not involve a human "performer" at all. With a variety of chime sounds these discs managed to capture something of the jaunty syncopation of ragtime through the craftsmanship with which the discs or cylinders that operated the notes were made. As a consequence, American music was heard across Europe by the most unlikely means.[3]

On the other hand, as sound recording came into existence as a potent market force, this statistic pales into insignificance compared with the availability of sound recordings of this same song by Kerry Mills. The main manufacturing centers of disc and cylinder recordings between 1892 and 1921 were the United States, Britain, and Germany. Between them, during that period, these different centers produced 26 disc, and eleven cylinder, recordings of *At a Georgia Camp Meeting*. An equally popular song, *Alexander's Ragtime Band*, by Irving Berlin, appeared in at least 44 disc recordings and two cylinders, compared with fifteen mechanical music-box versions.

## Sound Recording

> The music had to be played into a long tin horn which was
> connected at its narrow end to a steel needle that cut
> grooves in a revolving disc made of beeswax. The vibrating
> sounds were transformed onto the disc in the shape of wavy
> lines.
>
> Rudi Blesh, from *Combo USA*

It is hard to appreciate how large the sound recording industry became within a very few years. Thomas Alva Edison (1847–1931) patented his cylinder recording device in 1877, and disc recorders were patented in 1886 by Alexander Graham Bell and others. By 1904 the Gramophone Company had 120,000 sides in its catalog, and even medium-sized companies, such as Favourite of Hanover, had more than 20,000 issued sides from well over three times that number of master recordings.

As the twentieth century progressed, sound recording techniques developed rapidly, cylinders were largely abandoned, and the earliest hill-and-dale vertical cut discs were supplanted by those with grooves cut laterally. The first records were made acoustically: sound gathered by a "horn" was transmitted direct to a mechanical disc-cutting device, as described in the quotation above by Rudi Blesh. The results were variable, and recording engineers were reluctant to record full sets of drums as sudden loud noises caused the cutting needle to jump out of its groove, so many bands used wood blocks or cymbals rather than full drum sets during the acoustic recording era. (Examples include the Original Dixieland Jazz Band **[CD track 1]** and King Oliver's Creole Jazz Band **[CD track 3]** although on the latter, Baby Dodds's snare drum syncopations can be clearly heard.)

Stories are legion of early jazz bands having to adjust their playing techniques to acoustic studio recording. Even starting a performance off with a tap of the leader's foot was a problem, and the Original Dixieland Jazz Band, for example, was forced to replace Nick La Rocca's heavy footfalls with a red light as the signal to begin.[4] Musicians were also forced to line up in a different way from their normal appearance on stage, to try to achieve a balance on the recording that approximated to their usual sound. King Oliver's band, for example, suffers from giving both the clarinet and trombone undue prominence, but according to several eyewitnesses, this had to do with the difficulties of balancing the robust cornet of Louis Armstrong with the less forthright playing of Oliver himself. It is, perhaps, something of a miracle that so many of their cornet breaks are so perfectly together, given Armstrong's recollection that "Joe would be right in the horn blowing and I would be standing back in the door playing second trumpet [sic]."[5] Some scholars of recording history have called this story into doubt, but in his history of the Gennett label, even Rick Kennedy, one of the most skeptical commentators, acknowledges:

> Oliver and the rhythm section crowded close to the acoustic horns while Johnny Dodds, Armstrong and Dutrey stood further back. . . . The more romantic image will always be of a shy, still undiscovered Armstrong, cast off into a far corner of Gennett's stark studio, blowing his horn with Herculean power.[6]

A further ingredient of early recording was that the studio temperature was kept extremely high, to provide the optimum conditions for the wax discs on which the recordings were cut. Even in the harsh Indiana winters, the temperature in the Gennett studio was "80 to 85 degrees,"[7] to keep the wax sufficiently soft to take the cutting equipment properly. Sometimes, however, things got too warm for comfort. Trumpeter Doc Cheatham recalled a session in Barcelona, Spain, during the 1920s, when Sam Wooding's band made a series of records during its second long European tour:

> It was so hot that the wax began to melt as we were recording. So they had to put ice on top of the wax while we recorded to prevent it from melting. Because of this, we stayed there a long time. We ended up being there just about all day trying to record.[8]

There were other odd experiments to make the best of acoustic recording, and to minimize some of the problems of transferring a live, improvised music to the studio. Trying to muffle the incessantly tapping foot of Jelly Roll Morton was one such problem that preoccupied many of the engineers who recorded his early classics.

The advent of electrical recording in 1925 led to greatly increased fidelity, and some of the results from the late 1920s until the end of the 78-r.p.m. era in the 1940s are little short of miraculous in their quality. Even so, some of the practices of the acoustic era persisted, particularly the unwillingness of engineers to record drums. At Gene Krupa's first session for the McKenzie-Condon Chicagoans in 1927, he intended to use all his drums. Cornetist Jimmy McPartland recalled:

> We came into the studio there and Gene set up his bass drum, tom-toms, the whole set. Then we made a take to see how it sounded, and immediately the recording manager, Mr. Ring, ran out saying, "You can't use all those drums; throw those drums out; just use sticks, cymbals, wood blocks and so forth." After some protests they finally worked the thing out by laying down rugs that took up the vibration. . . . So they let Gene play the drums, and he beat the heck out of them all the way through the set, which was fine for us because it gave us a good solid background.[9]

Gradually and – it seems – reluctantly, recording engineers allowed drummers into the studio, thereby finally allowing recorded jazz to sound more like the music that was actually being played out in the clubs, theaters, and cabarets. One apocryphal story relating to the slow admission of the drum set to recorded jazz was the amazement expressed by American musicians on reaching Europe, and finding that bands there who had learned jazz from recordings had studiously recreated the clopping wood blocks and restrained cymbal crashes as the basis for their rhythm sections.[10]

Even so, there was reluctance on the part of engineers to let bands set up for recordings as they would normally. Louder instruments were set to one side or surrounded by baffles. Fats Waller's drummer Harry Dial told me how he had to convince Victor's recording director Eli Oberstein that he had sufficiently controlled technique to be allowed to play as an integral part of the band on the first discs made by Waller's Rhythm:

> Not only was I using the bass drum, I had the whole kit. . . . I did it without padding or anything, and so that I could be picked up sufficiently, Oberstein set me on a platform right in the center of the band. That's the way we recorded. Usually they put the drummer away in the corner. Away in another city I used to call it.[11]

Putting drummers in corners and bassists behind screens could cause problems for a rhythm section trying to integrate its sound. There were even more problems for a band that used a large instrument such as a pipe organ. Again, Fats Waller's band was one of the first to try to tackle this, particularly the inherent time lag caused by the sound of Victor's massive pipe organ at its Camden, New Jersey, studios reaching the microphone later than that of a jazz ensemble placed closer to it. In his 1928 date with the Louisiana Sugar Babes, he relied on Jabbo Smith's cornet or Garvin Bushell's clarinet to provide jazz rhythm and timing, adding little more than a soft chordal backdrop from the organ, as he also did for the more rhythmically assertive piano of James P. Johnson. Bushell recalled Waller's console being "about a city block"[12] away from the other musicians. In his later Camden recordings from the mid-1930s, Waller tended to put the bass, guitar, and drums of his rhythm near the microphone, to create drive and momentum, while he provided a more coloristic backdrop at the organ, in sharp contrast to the driving rhythm of his piano playing. He later found the ideal compromise in the crisp, rhythmic qualities of the Hammond organ, which he could integrate fully with his band, both on disc and in concert.

Perhaps one of the more bizarre experiments in early electrical recording was when Bessie Smith cut a session for Columbia on the very day its new system had been installed on May 5, 1925, with a contingent from Fletcher Henderson's band. Concerned that the studio was too resonant for the sensitive new electric microphone, the engineers suspended a fabric tent from the studio ceiling to dampen its acoustics. With spectacular results, the tent collapsed as the second take of *Yellow Dog Blues* came to an end, smothering the musicians with heavy fabric. Judging by the booming sound of the bass register of Fletcher Henderson's piano on her next session (without the tent) of *Soft Pedal Blues* from May 14, perhaps the engineers had a point about the unsuitability of the studio acoustics.[13]

The record industry reached a high point before the Wall Street crash of 1929, when United States domestic output reached sales of more than 100 million discs per annum (it fell to six million in 1932). I have already suggested how recorded performances influenced the playing style and development of jazz musicians in a way that had previously been impossible. Musicians outside America, for example, learned to emulate the styles of influential players entirely from recordings. Furthermore, recording allowed some forms of folk art, such as the country blues, to reach a huge international market on a scale never before possible for an extremely localized development. And, as I have said in Chapter 4, field recordings benefited not just folk and blues singers, but many of the territory bands.

Technically, the period from 1925 to 1942 was dominated by electrically recorded 78 r.p.m. discs, and appeared to enter the same period of relative calm as jazz itself did during the swing era, with few technical developments, apart from gradual and consistent improvements in quality, both on the full-price labels and on their budget "race records" counterparts. There was, however, one technical innovation at the start of the 1930s that was only properly discovered in 1981 – the first stereo recordings.

These came about as part of an ongoing process to extend playing time beyond the normal limits of a 78 r.p.m. disc, but without sacrificing the huge advances in quality that had been made in the 1920s. An English inventor called Noel Pemberton-Billing had returned to the early vertical-cut process in 1922 to produce discs that had a 20-minute running time, but they were never produced commercially. Edison perfected the first microgroove disc in 1926, the so-called Diamond Disc, but it did not catch on, any more than Columbia and Hit-of-the-week's "minimicrogroove" 78s from 1932. However, Victor's engineers worked on maintaining the groove size of a conventional 78 r.p.m. disc and slowing down the running speed to 33⅓ r.p.m., which produced a playing time of between ten and fifteen minutes.

The resulting discs were called "program transcriptions," and were marketed at only a few cents more than the regular 78 r.p.m. discs, along with a special turntable. Despite some serious up-market promotion, this series was not a commercial success, and the resulting discs are, for the most part, extremely rare today. However, not least to fit in with the smart art deco covers and gold labels of such a prestige product, several of Victor's most high-profile artists made discs for this series, including Duke Ellington, the jewel in their jazz roster, who recorded two short sets of three numbers apiece in February 1932. It was not until 1981 that the collectors Steven Lasker and Brad Kay discovered that apparently different versions of both sets existed: *Mood Indigo*, *Hot and Bothered* and *Creole Love Call*, and *East St. Louis Toodle-Oo*, *Lots o' Fingers*, and *Black and Tan Fantasy*. It turned out that Victor's engineers had used two separate microphones and two independent cutting tables to produce simultaneous recordings of the same performances, even though, in 1932, there was no available technology to synchronize playback. The results were issued in 1985, and give a vivid stereo impression of the Ellington orchestra, in which it is even possible to hear the soloists coming forward for their respective turns and then returning to their places in the sections. It turns out that although the playback technology for stereophonic sound would not be developed for approximately another two decades, both HMV's engineers in Britain and Victor's engineers in the United States had been experimenting with stereo recording since 1929, and that many more stereo masters exist, although these are mainly of classical performances, including Elgar conducting his own *Cockaigne* overture with the BBC Symphony Orchestra.[14]

Efforts to record and produce longer-playing discs continued after the failure of the Victor "program transcription" series. I have already mentioned the large diameter 33⅓ discs produced for radio transcriptions, which were not commercially available, and the way in which recordable acetate discs could be used in series to record long pieces or concert sets. The way forward finally became clear at the end of the A.F.M. recording ban of 1948, following which the 78 r.p.m. standard gave way to two new microgroove standards: the 45 r.p.m. discs developed by RCA Victor and the 33⅓ r.p.m. long-playing records developed by Columbia.

The former had two formats: a single with a similar playing time to its

78 r.p.m. predecessor of three-and-a-half minutes, or an "extended play" version with smaller grooves and up to seven minutes a side. In its "single" form, the 45 r.p.m. disc continued to be responsible for shaping thousands of popular-music performances to fit this prescribed length, just as the 78 had done before it. In shaping the development of popular music, the recording standards setters made a major contribution to the abiding musical form of the twentieth century by adopting these formats. Despite the decline of jazz as a truly popular form in its own right after the swing era many jazz musicians continued to record and issue "singles" well into the 1960s and beyond. However, far more importantly for jazz, the long-playing record, combined with the advent of tape recording, made an entirely different contribution. Single, $33\frac{1}{3}$ r.p.m. discs could now supplant "albums" of several 78 r.p.m. discs, such as the Dizzy Gillespie/Coleman Hawkins "New Fifty-Second Street Jazz" collection discussed in Chapter 8. And finally, it gave musicians a medium for extended composition or improvisation, combined, before long, with stereophonic sound, to the extent that in the forthcoming chapters, many of the most significant recordings lie well outside the constraints of time that applied to all but a handful of the discs made prior to 1942.

The final major change that applied to jazz recordings after the A.F.M. ban is that the stranglehold of the three major companies – Columbia, Victor, and Decca – was broken. Three new major labels were founded in the years between the 1942 and 1948 A.F.M. bans: Capitol, MGM, and Mercury. Furthermore, although many of the little companies that sprang up in 1944–5 did not survive, a number of smaller independents did carry on, and Commodore (established in 1938), Blue Note (1939), and Atlantic (1947) are among those that shaped the course of jazz through the clarity of their artistic vision. Others, such as Jazz Man, Climax, and American Music were in the forefront of the revival of older styles of jazz discussed in Chapter 11. This interest in retrospective styles of jazz was, to a large extent, initiated by record collectors and enthusiasts, and this was fueled by another major change that occurred during the early 1940s, when the major companies began to issue their back-catalog material in a fairly systematic way.

Because jazz had always been treated by the companies as popular music and, therefore, pretty much ephemeral, only the very best-selling sides remained in catalog, and a host of potentially saleable older items by artists from Louis Armstrong and King Oliver onwards had been let out of print. But following his innovative attempts to record unfashionable styles of traditional jazz for Decca in 1939, in the album *Chicago Jazz*, the producer George Avakian initiated a reissue program for Columbia in 1940. There were more such efforts as the decade continued, including John Steiner's reissue of parts of the Paramount catalog, and Orrin Keepnews and Bill Grauer's first attempts to reissue material under the imprint of their *Record Changer* magazine, which developed (in the early 1950s) into RCA Victor's "Label X" reissue series of material by Johnny Dodds, Jelly Roll Morton, and other figures of the classic jazz era.

## Radio Broadcasting

> I heard McKinney's Cotton Pickers on a cat's whisker set, in a radio broadcast from the Graystone Ballroom in Detroit. I knew then and there that this was the band I wanted to play with.
>
> Doc Cheatham, in an interview with the author

Although the first known broadcast of music took place as early as 1906, when a recording of Handel's *Largo* was played on the air from Brant Rock, Massachusetts, broadcasting did not play a major role as a force in the development of popular music until the start of the 1920s, when the first commercial stations KDKA in Pittsburgh and WWJ in Detroit were established.[15] From 1922, hillbilly music came to be performed over the air from stations in Atlanta, Georgia, but we know from the experience of Jesse Stone that the sounds of the territory bands had begun to be heard on local radio in the Midwest a little earlier.

At around the time Stone was broadcasting from St. Joseph, Missouri, the white Kansas City dance band, another Midwestern group, led by drummer Carleton Coon and pianist Joe Sanders, became one of the first jazz-orientated ensembles in the world to aim at the radio audience as its main public. As the Coon-Sanders Novelty Orchestra, it began broadcasting in 1921, leading on to a series of regular late-night programs from December 1922. Within a short time, the group became known as the Coon-Sanders Nighthawks, playing fairly gentle, undemanding, lightly syncopated music – almost a precursor of "smooth jazz" – and through its nightly sessions relayed from the Plantation Grill of the Muehlebach Hotel, it became the best-known white jazz orchestra in the Midwest. Its request programs were so popular that Western Union installed a tickertape machine to transmit listeners' dedications direct to the stage at the hotel.[16] The band subsequently moved to Chicago, opening at the Blackhawk in 1926. By the late 1920s, its counterpart in the territories was the African-American Alphonso Trent Orchestra, which was heard from the Adolphus Hotel in Dallas every night on the WFAA station, and which became far better known through radio than as a result of its sporadic ventures into the recording studio.

If the Midwest and Southwest had a slight headstart in broadcasting jazz, New York was not far behind. Ethel Waters is known to have sung on radio with Fletcher Henderson in 1922, and two years later the full Henderson band's sets at the Roseland Ballroom in New York started to be broadcast as live "remote" relays over station WHN, beginning a lengthy tradition of such stations eavesdropping on club or dance-hall sets for regular transmissions. I have already discussed the importance of the late 1920s relays from the Cotton Club in establishing the careers of both Duke Ellington and Cab Calloway, and many other musicians went on to benefit from such broadcasts of their regular appearances, including McKinney's Cotton Pickers from the Graystone in Detroit, and because at this stage all broadcasts were on medium- or long-wave frequencies, in good conditions they could be heard many hundreds of miles away from the transmitter. For example, Doc Cheatham, as mentioned in the quote at the start of this section, heard McKinney's band as he was on the road with Marion Hardy between New York and Chicago.

In the United States, the rapid development of broadcasting was a consequence of the commercial structure of the industry where (unlike in most European countries in which a single company, often state-owned, operated a monopoly control) large networks were established to broadcast an individual program through a number of connected stations over a wide area. These networks competed for listeners, and the two major groups – the National Broadcasting Company (NBC) and Columbia Phonograph Broadcasting System (CBS) – had the financial resources to mount quite spectacular performances for radio. These concerns were established in 1926 and 1927 respectively, and at the same time the development of "sponsored" radio, in which manufacturing companies paid for musical or variety programs as a means to advertise their products, began. One of the earliest bands to undertake such shows was that of Paul Whiteman, who began by treating the radio as welcome extra revenue for himself and his sidemen, and squeezed the broadcasts into his normal schedule. When he appeared on the *Old Gold* show in the 1920s, he was also playing from 7 p.m. to 3 a.m. every night at New York's fashionable Paradise Restaurant. From the late 1920s, Whiteman went on to appear in numerous radio programs, often with his band as the centerpiece of a larger entertainment. During the year 2000, the musicologist Denise Lanctot reconstructed one of Whiteman's typical broadcasts from the Biltmore Hotel, under the name *Radio Rhapsodies*, which included all the trimmings: vocalists, dancers, musical advertisements, a detective serial, and copious sound effects, and it was in this context that many of Whiteman's more jazz-orientated pieces, along with such aberrations as his syncopated version of Liszt's *Liebestraum*, first reached a large section of his public.[17] Radio became an increasingly important aspect of his career, and, in later life, he spent some years as a music director for ABC.

Although the record industry collapsed for a few years in the wake of the 1929 Wall Street crash, radio did not, but kept going and growing; as well as relays from clubs and cabarets, the networks continued to mount large-scale studio shows, of a similar pattern to Whiteman's Biltmore program described above. Having broadcast regularly during 1928–9 from the Savoy in London, with Fred Elizalde, multi-instrumentalist Adrian Rollini returned to New York at the onset of the Depression and picked up where he left off in the American studios. By 1932 he was doing seven radio shows a week, using all his instruments, including bass saxophone on the *Norman Claudier Show*, piano on *Forty Flying Fingers*, and percussion on the *James Melton Show*. He was first call to play vibraphone on Studebaker commercials, and, on top of that, ran his own nightclub, Adrian's Tap Room, where he played every night with the house band. Such a versatile musician could work virtually non-stop on the New York stations that fed the various networks. By the 1930s, the operation of the networks was sufficiently advanced that some shows co-ordinated relays from more than one area of the country. This sometimes led to confusion, particularly if an announcer and band were unable to hear each other, but it also led to such shows as the NBC's *Bandstand*, which had a roving format, and picked up performances from many different parts of the country on each week's program. Because of the different time zones in the United States, bands sometimes performed the same show twice, a couple of hours apart, to be heard at peak hours on Eastern and Pacific time respectively. Many musicians recounted stories of how the second shows were generally better, as the material became familiar, and liquid refreshments between sets helped the bands to relax!

The musicians who worked in the radio studios developed their own camaraderie and arrived at a code of behavior built around what became an almost intuitive sense of time, conditioned by the position of the second hand on the studio clock. Whatever went on in rehearsal or between broadcasts was replaced by sobriety and professional musicianship while actually on air. But this also gave rise to some of the worst of all musicians' practical jokes, where the subject of the joke would be bound by the same protocol of silence. Paul Whiteman was the object of several ruses cooked up by his band members, but one of the most celebrated incidents involved another leader, and occurred during one of the Studebaker shows on which Adrian Rollini appeared with his younger saxophonist brother, Art. The band was conducted by society bandleader Richard Himber. Unknown to him, the musicians had advanced the studio clock by five minutes, so when he raised his baton as the sweep-hand came up to the hour, the men held their instruments ready: "Himber gave a downbeat. Nobody played," remembered Art. "He turned an unhealthy pallor and gave another downbeat. Still no response. He was desperate now, but the men broke out laughing, and Himber realised he had been tricked."[18]

Studio orchestras were, for the most part, white during the early days of radio broadcasting, and the industry only began seriously to integrate its studio orchestras after World War II.[19] However, in the 1920s and 1930s, African-American musicians constituted a high percentage of those performing on live relays from clubs and theaters, and a small number became individual radio stars. Because of the fall-off in the record industry, radio's importance as the means to promote popular performers – both African-American and white – expanded dramatically during the Depression. The period saw continued growth in the number of radio receivers from the seven million or so that were in operation in 1927, not least because of the invention of the automobile radio, and the potential audience for both the main networks increased substantially. As a result, many popular musicians turned to radio to continue their careers, and jazz artists were no exception. Fats Waller, for example, made more than fifteen recording sessions (including 54 separate "takes") during the calendar year 1929. So severe was the cutback in the recording industry following the Wall Street crash that he entered the recording studio only six times in the next four and a half years.

Instead, Waller began broadcasting regularly. He started on *Paramount on Parade*, in 1930, moved on to *Radio Roundup* in 1931, and, after a short visit to Paris, began appearing on WLW in Cincinnati, where his weekly show, *Fats Waller's Rhythm Club*, reached a radio audience in the Midwest many times bigger than the average sales of one of his earlier records. He also played on a late night program called *Moon River*, on which he performed standard and romantic songs on the organ.

Waller adapted his nightclub act for the microphone, and his penchant for satirical vocals and risqué patter dates from his work on the *Rhythm Club*, where, along with announcer Paul Stewart and a singing group called the Southern Suns, he appeared as a stern deacon, warning against the perils of the "Devil's music," before undergoing a weekly conversion to the joys of swing. Through networking, Waller's show came to be heard in many parts of the United States, and when he returned to New York in 1934 and resumed his recording career, he had become a nationally known star as a vocalist and humorist.[20]

Waller's experience was shared by many other performers. I have already discussed the significant role that radio played in establishing Ellington and Calloway, and in launching the careers of Benny Goodman and Count Basie, the former through his *Let's Dance* program being heard nationally, and the latter as a result of John Hammond hearing an experimental short wave broadcast from the Reno Club on station W9XBY.[21] Basie's band went on to make numerous "remote" broadcasts from the Savoy in New York and from various other parts of the country, and a number of these have survived in the form of acetate recordings. Goodman, along with most of the big white swing bands, became a mainstay of the sponsored network shows. *Let's Dance* had been financed by the National Biscuit Company, but one of the biggest of all commercial sponsors was the tobacco industry, and Goodman went on to appear on *Camel Caravan*, on which the Dorsey brothers also later worked, before transferring their affections to Raleigh tobacco.

Goodman's female singers, among them Helen Ward, Helen Forrest, Peggy Lee, and Martha Tilton, all owed much of their success to radio, in addition to those discs by the band on which they were featured, and Ward, in particular, is associated with projecting the "girl-next-door" image to her listeners. I will go on to discuss jazz singers in more detail in the next chapter, but it is important to mention the significance of radio in the career of Bing Crosby. Although he was never quite an out-and-out jazz singer, there were many elements of jazz in his work, and he often sought a jazz context for his songs. His style of crooning depended on the use of a microphone, into which he sang at a volume and with a degree of informality that would have been impossible in live unamplified performance. Radio suited him as a medium, just as the phonograph record did, and from his earliest broadcasts with Paul Whiteman in the 1920s to the years after his debut in his own right in 1931, which popularized his theme *Where the Blue of the Night*, he exemplified how to create a symbiotic relationship among his radio work, recordings, and the sales of sheet music, to maximize the popularity of all three.

Disc jockeys, such as Martin Block, Al Jarvis, and, later, Gene Norman, built their careers on the playing of phonograph records over the air, although they were also all ardent champions of live music, Block introducing several broadcast concerts including one by a memorable band that included both Louis Armstrong and Fats Waller; Jarvis helping to promote many bands in the West; and Norman setting up his ambitious concert series in and around Los Angeles that, in due course, produced some of the finest work by bands as different as those of Dizzy Gillespie and Louis Armstrong in the late 1940s and early 1950s.

In addition to being heard by the American public, Armstrong and Ellington both reached a large audience through occasional broadcasts while on their visits to Britain during the 1930s, although the BBC's attitude to jazz was somewhat ambivalent. There were occasional series of American relays known as *America Dances* or *Swing Music from America* from 1935, as well as rebroadcasts of the French series *Swing That Music* in 1937. Such programs ended in September 1939 with the outbreak of war, and the music was not regularly established again on its networks until the advent of the weekly *Radio Rhythm Club*, with a live studio band, in 1940. However, even if British and European listeners lacked the regular contact with the live jazz scene enjoyed by their American counterparts, it was in London, on September 30, 1938, that Fats Waller made one of the world's first television jazz broadcasts for the BBC. The earliest experiments with television broadcasting began in 1928, but it was not until the late 1930s that the new medium took off on both sides of the Atlantic. In Britain there was just the BBC's single channel, but by 1940, in the United States there were 23 stations in operation, and this number grew rapidly after World War II, ushering in a new medium for jazz performance that would become as significant as the long-playing record and the advent of magnetic tape.

In terms of radio broadcasting, the war led to the setting up of the Armed Forces Radio Service, a United States government-inspired phenomenon as important to jazz as the development of the V-Disc. The Special Service Division of the War Department established a special network to broadcast to American troops at overseas bases. To fulfill the musical needs of the network it produced complete radio broadcasts by many jazz musicians, on 16-inch transcription discs. A number of different shows were made that included jazz, such as *Spotlight Bands* and *G.I. Jive*, but most important was the *Jubilee* series, mainly devoted to African-American bands, which began in 1942 and carried on throughout the A.F.M. recording ban, thereby preserving the sound of many groups that were otherwise only patchily recorded. Examples include the West Coast orchestras of Benny Carter, Gerald Wilson, and Wilbert Baranco, but also the sextet that Dizzy Gillespie and Charlie Parker brought to Billy Berg's in 1945–6. Many of these shows were compered by Ernie "Bubbles" Whitman, who specialized in what now seems an excruciating form of banter, but which has served to preserve the otherwise unrecorded voices of many musicians during their brief exchanges between numbers. The series ran until 1950, and encompassed a wide stylistic range from the swing orchestras of Count Basie and Lionel Hampton to the bebop big band of Dizzy Gillespie. Duke Ellington was featured frequently, and was also the subject of his own AFRS series, *A Date with the Duke*, which included 79 transcriptions from the mid-1940s.

For the most part, for the first 25 years, the radio broadcasting of jazz was regarded by broadcasters and musicians alike as part of the business of entertainment, but in 1947 ideology entered the frame, and the critic and historian Rudi Blesh began his long-running *This Is Jazz* show, which sought to recreate an earlier form of New Orleans jazz. Blesh believed passionately in traditional jazz, and that the music had somehow taken a wrong turning, not simply with bebop, but years before with the advent of swing. He assembled a band of veteran players to prove his point, although with some quaint idiosyncrasies, such as employing Chicagoans Wild Bill Davison, Muggsy Spanier, or Marty Marsala on trumpet, saying: "One of my basic ideas is always to use a white trumpeter against a Negroid rhythm section."[22]

Although much of the music on *This Is Jazz* was spirited and fun, the pedagogical aura of Blesh's ideas hung over many of the broadcasts both in his stilted announcements and in his views about repertoire, so that finally clarinetist Albert Nicholas was stung into strong criticism of him in *Down Beat*, calling him an "aggressive, egotistical balloon-bomb."[23] No doubt there were just such egotistical figures in the world of more commercial broadcasting, but Nicholas accused Blesh of encouraging his colleagues to play "like Uncle Toms of the worst sort," and drew up his battle lines to resist Blesh's ideological position. I will go on to consider the "revival" of New Orleans jazz in more detail in Chapter 11, but this series marked the start of broadcasting where such an agenda lay behind the programing, with the style and content of the music dictated by aesthetic concerns rather than commercial ones. Jazz radio broadcasting in the second half of the century would never be quite the same again.

## Jazz on Film

> I don't remember whether we were actually shown in the picture or heard on the sound track. We may even have been left on the cutting-room floors for all I know.
>
> Marshal Royal, from *Jazz Survivor*

It may seem bizarre, but jazz began its involvement with film almost a decade before the first sound movies. Despite the absence of the music itself from the end product, the use of the word jazz and brief shots of musicians in action conveyed everything that was risqué about the reputation of the music in its earliest days. Just as "Stein's Band From Dixie" found that the word added a frisson of daring to their raucous ragtime, so the producers of silent films found that they could communicate the atmosphere of low life through images of bands, or titles such as *Jazz and Jailbirds* or the *Jazz Bandits*, both of which were pre-1920 pictures.

Some musicians appeared in cameo shots in early Hollywood movies, one of the first being the Los Angeles band Wood Wilson's Syncopators, who showed up in a 1916 short called *Penny Dance*.[24] Other West Coast groups, such as Kid Ory's band of New Orleans expatriates, made similar appearances, but, in addition, Ory's band, along with a number of others, including the Black and Tan Orchestra, were often brought to the Hollywood lots to play atmospheric background music to put the actors in the right mood for playing nightclub and similar scenes. These bands did not appear on screen, and there is no record of what they played.[25] Overall, the silent movies served largely to create a visual jazz stereotype of fast-living recklessness – epitomized in such pieces as *Children of Jazz* (1923) – which was just the first in a long series of stereotypes that have dogged the relationship of jazz and film. A key issue, once the talking picture had been invented, became the representation of race in jazz, with a polarity far more acute than in the record business.

Although the record industry was entirely white-owned and managed until 1921, with the advent of Black Swan and similar African-American ventures, complete African-American bands had been recorded before the 1920s, including those of James Reese Europe and W. C. Handy; after Perry Bradford's efforts in getting blues singers and jazz accompanists recorded, in the wake of Mamie Smith's debut for Okeh in 1920, the industry, as a whole, began increasingly to invest in African-American acts. As we know, there were also various integrated recording sessions from the mid-1920s.

The world of the movies was more complex, but the first moves to create an African-American film industry predated those of the recording business, and had taken place in 1913, when William Foster, a writer for the *Chicago Defender*, founded the Foster Photoplay Company in Chicago. From that point onwards, Chicago became the center for African-American film-making, and, over time, other companies were established. Their ethos was expressed by Luther J. Pollard, founder of the Ebony Film Corporation, when he said in 1917:

> We proved to the public that colored players can put over good comedy without any of that crap shooting, chicken stealing, razor display, watermelon eating stuff that colored people generally have been a little disgusted at seeing.[26]

Such a philosophy was at odds with the output of Hollywood and its white production companies who succeeded in reinforcing virtually all the stereotypes Pollard lists, as well as rigidly enforcing a policy of non-integration on screen during the first decade or more of the talkies. In addition, films aimed at the general (white and African-American) audience by the major production houses were seldom straightforward about the portrayal of jazz. Some films were designed so that appearances on screen by African-American musicians could be cut out for showings to certain audiences.[27] Sometimes, white musicians mimed to soundtracks played by African-Americans (occasionally the reverse occurred), and where scenes concerning jazz were integrated with broader plot-lines, even the most distinguished black musicians tended to be reduced to eye-rolling stereotypes in menial jobs. (This continued for decades: Fats Waller, for example, played an elevator operator in the 1935 film *King of Burlesque*, Louis Armstrong was a street cleaner in *Every Day's a Holiday* (1938), and, several years later, Billie Holiday was cast as a maid in the 1946 picture *New Orleans*. In view of such performances, it is small wonder that many of the bebop generation followed the examples of Charlie Parker and Miles Davis in deliberately dissociating themselves from any kind of stage demeanor that might be identified with such old-style show-business stereotypes.)

Such problems of stereotyping began with *The Jazz Singer*, the very first synchronized sound movie, in 1927, which was, despite its title, not about jazz at all, and which had Al Jolson run through his blackface stage act: a survivor of the performance traditions of the nineteenth century. In the public mind, it cemented "jazz" together with this blackface image, and it did no services at all to the accurate depiction of the music as it was experienced by listeners to live bands, black or white, or to recordings. (The subsequent biopic about Jolson, *The Jolson Story*, made in 1946, does the music even fewer favors and suggests, as Krin Gabbard has pointed out, that "whites are more accomplished than blacks in the performance of jazz. . . . Jolson is portrayed as a visionary who understood the appeal that 'jazz' could have for a large white audience."[28]) In 1930, Paul Whiteman's film *King of Jazz* appeared, and it had some similarities with *The Jazz Singer*, principally that it was also not really about jazz, although to the public it reinforced Whiteman's image, however erroneously, as the pre-eminent figure in the music. Whereas *The Jazz Singer* took a heavily made-up Lithuanian-born Jewish entertainer and misrepresented him as a singer of jazz, *King of Jazz* elevated the rotund figure of Whiteman to a throne he had usurped.

Although I have underlined Whiteman's importance to the craft of arranging at the start of the 1920s, and believe he was genuinely important in the early development of big-band jazz, by the time he made this movie he was no longer either making the running in the development of the music, or including much out-and-out jazz in his repertoire. Nevertheless, the film is significant in one respect, which is that it presents a number of the most important popular entertainers of the day in a series of set pieces, the most lavish of which is a treatment of Gershwin's *Rhapsody in Blue*, creating the overall effect of a variety show transformed to film, and using cinematic effects that would be impossible on a stage.

The first movies to get close to portraying jazz in a way that both involved African-American musicians and presented convincing jazz performances by them were two films made in 1929 by Dudley Murphy. Bessie Smith starred in the first, a short piece built around *St. Louis Blues*, and even if the plot and exaggerated acting is redolent of an olio sketch from a contemporary revue, Smith's charisma and presence still imbues her performance with moments of spine-tingling power, as she sings, backed (on screen) by a band featuring James P. Johnson and several members of Fletcher Henderson's orchestra. Murphy's second film, *Black and Tan*, features Duke Ellington's orchestra and the dancer Fredi Washington. Although it runs just short of nineteen minutes, it packs in shots of Ellington rehearsing with trumpeter Arthur Whetsol, dance sequences by the Five Hot Shots, members of the Cotton Club chorus line, and a powerful performance of the title piece (*Black and Tan Fantasy*) by the full band with the Hall Johnson choir.

The flimsy plot introduces yet more of the cinematic stereotypes of jazz – a composer-pianist (Ellington) who has fallen behind with the rent, a salt-of-the-earth dancer (Washington) who has found a club where the pianist's band can play and at which she will dance (despite a fatal heart condition), and, finally, the devil-may-care dancing of the chorus. Yet Murphy's direction is imaginative, and from kaleidoscopic views of the dancers – intended to replicate the stricken Washington's blurred vision – to an underfloor view of her own final dance of death, he invests the short with plenty of cinematic originality, to the extent that *Billboard* reviewed it as "artistic, beautifully done, [and] well played."[29]

This was the first of many films in which Ellington and his band appeared, and, for the most part, unlike various other African-American jazz stars of the period, he managed to present himself and his band with dignity and some resemblance of their stage appearance and sound. In *Check and Double Check* (1930) his band became the first African-American group to appear in a feature film that otherwise featured an all-white cast. (Well, almost all-white, in that the stars "Amos" and "Andy" were the white actors Freedon F. Gosden and Charles F. Corell, who played in blackface and whose nationally syndicated radio show, sponsored by Pepsodent toothpaste, went out nightly at 7 p.m. on the East Coast, and had made them nationally famous.) Although the Ellington band is seen and heard playing *East St. Louis Toodle-Oo* and *Old Man Blues*, the film also exemplifies the knots that Hollywood could tie itself in over racial issues. First, the producers thought that the more light-skinned members of the band were not "black" enough, and insisted that Barney Bigard, among others, played in blackface make-up. Second, for a vocal on *Three Little Words*, in which Ellington's trumpet section is seen apparently singing the words into large megaphones, the producers dubbed onto the soundtrack a recording of the song made by the white singing trio the Rhythm Boys, with Bing Crosby. The majority of Ellington scholars now believe that the band accompanying the vocal is an all-white orchestra as well, recorded and dubbed onto the film some time after Ellington had left Hollywood, having played a farewell West Coast concert at the Shrine Auditorium on August 29, 1930, to return to New York.[30]

It was almost three years later that Ellington's band made its next "short" film – a nine-minute, single-reel affair called *Bundle of Blues*, which was part of a long series from Paramount known as "One Reel Acts and Band Shorts," and was designed to be shown as a curtain-raiser to a main feature. In due course, this series was to be a valuable document of many bands of the era, but in 1933 it represented something of a first for Ellington, as very few other African-American bands had so far made such films, and unlike those who had, such as Noble Sissle and Elmer Snowden, who were seen in the context of vaudeville acts, or Louis Armstrong, who was dressed in a leopard-skin for his short *Rhapsody in Black and Blue* to play *I'll Be Glad When You're Dead You Rascal You*, Ellington presented his band as it would appear on stage. This was also the case when he returned to Hollywood to appear in the feature film *Murder at the Vanities*, and his band appears in Gus Andrews' Café (the fictional café of the film) in the context of a revue (in which the musicians are seen on a lavish stage set surrounded by a chorus line, even though this starts with the band in eighteenth-century dress and ends with them being mown down by a symphonic conductor with a machine-gun!). A few weeks before his departure to China with his own orchestra, trumpeter Buck Clayton was married on the set of this film, with Ellington acting as master of ceremonies.

Clayton had played in the orchestra of Charlie Echols, which was well-known around Los Angeles, and by the time of this film he was playing in a group led by Earl Dancer (Ethel Waters's husband) that played casual jobs on film sets for various movies. This band, and several others, substantially increased its regular income by working in movies, and there are many documented film appearances by Mutt Carey, Les Hite, and Curtis Mosby's groups, as well as the territory band of Speed Webb, which spent some time in Hollywood. Saxophonist Marshal Royal estimated that on top of a basic wage of $55 per week for playing with Hite at the New Cotton Club in Culver City, he augmented his average weekly salary to well over $100 through his occasional film appearances, and the band's screen credits included *Taxi* (1932), *Cabin in the Cotton* (1932), and *Sing, Sinner, Sing* (1933).[31]

Well-known Hollywood bands such as Hite's were hired for short scenes and cameos in the mainstream output of the Hollywood studios, but what of the African-American film industry?

By the early 1930s, its pre-eminent figure was the novelist, publisher, and film director Oscar Micheaux. A former Pullman porter from Metropolis, Illinois, Micheaux had tried his hand at farming in South

Dakota, and, after losing his land to mounting debts during the drought of 1915, went on to recount his experiences in a novel, *The Homesteader*, which he published and distributed himself – his diligent efforts turning it into something of a cult best-seller. When he was approached by the Johnson Brothers – who made films for African-American audiences – about turning his work into a film, he insisted on directing it himself. When they refused, he set up his own production company and went on to make his novel into the first full-length, all-black feature film. He ended up directing over 40 more movies, all but two of them made in Chicago.[32]

One of the ones he made in New York (where he was welcomed into Harlem Renaissance society, and became a popular local figure) was the 1932 picture *The Girl from Chicago*, starring Grace Smith and Carl Mahon. Micheaux's methods were simple, low budget, and to the point. He could often only afford one take of any scene, and he had to get everything right first time; when he wanted a band, he did what anyone needing a group in Harlem would do – he dropped in at the Rhythm Club. There he met Danny Barker, who recalled:

> The guy came up and said, "Say, fellows, I'm looking for a band."
> "For what?"
> He said, "We're making a movie down the street. A colored movie. We don't have much money, but we want five guys to come over and play. Just about two minutes. Might take about twenty minutes to set y'all up. But just play one tune. I'll pay y'all five dollars apiece."[33]

The band, with two other well-known musicians – Ward Pinkett and Geechie Fields, alongside Barker – played *St. Louis Blues*, and the musicians were paid off. To his surprise Barker saw the picture as one of the movies showing at the Howard Theater in Washington when he worked there with Lucky Millinder a year or two later, and he heard from relatives and friends that it had played in black theaters in many parts of the United States. Micheaux's methods included securing advance bookings from black theaters to help finance his films, selling the idea by using still photographs of his chosen actors. But he managed to create a body of work that naturally rolled jazz (along with other forms of African-American music, with notable appearances by Paul Robeson) into a cinematic view of the world that ran counter to the methods of Hollywood.

In terms of Hollywood's mainstream output, two genres of film involving jazz were prevalent in the 1930s. First (following in the wake of *Check and Double Check*), there were more pictures that aimed to transfer well-known radio stars to the big screen. The *Big Broadcast* series began in 1932 with a mixture of white and African-American stars, from Bing Crosby and George Burns to the entire Cab Calloway Orchestra, and later additions to the series included the dancers Bill "Bojangles" Robinson and the Nicholas Brothers (1936) and Benny Goodman's band (1937). These were made for Paramount, and the rival Republic concern launched a competing series under the "Hit Parade" title in 1937, featuring Ellington. These movies, that strung together a sequence of star acts, pointed towards a number of films that were to be made the following decade, notably *Cabin in the Sky* (1942) and *Stormy Weather* (1943), which incorporated a range of African-American performers in short cameo performances thinly linked by a plot of no consequence, a tradition directly descended from stage shows such as *Shuffle Along* or *Keep Shufflin'*.

The second genre arose during the swing era and produced vehicles for big bands such as those of Benny Goodman and Glenn Miller to play a sizable selection of their hit numbers during the course of the action. *Hollywood Hotel* (1937), by the former, includes the first screen appearance of Goodman's racially integrated quartet, and Miller's band ran through most of its best-known repertoire in *Sun Valley Serenade* (1941) and *Orchestra Wives* (1942). Both Goodman's and Miller's lives became the subject of later "biopics," in which actors (Steve Allen and James Stewart, respectively) played the musicians concerned, and although Hollywood went to some lengths to acknowledge Goodman's involvement with African-American musicians and to depict the formation of his trio and quartet, there are still bizarre fabrications, such as Lionel Hampton being portrayed (by himself) as a waiter, rather than the high-profile West Coast star he was when Goodman added him to the small group.

Numerous swing bands appeared in films in the period leading up to and during World War II, and movies offer an opportunity to see and hear bands who were unable to make commercial discs during the A.F.M. ban. As well as full-length wartime pictures, numerous bands also made a type of film widespread in the early 1940s and known as "soundies." These short films were the forerunners of today's rock videos. They were made to run on a film juke-box called a Mills Panorama, which played the picture onto a screen when a customer inserted a dime, and over 1000 such short films were produced from 1941 to 1947.

Established entertainers, such as Louis Armstrong, Cab Calloway, Duke

Ellington, and Fats Waller, all made soundies, but these films also helped to launch the careers of the next generation of popular performers, including the rhythm-and-blues singer Louis Jordan. As well as instrumental or vocal technique, and a command of studio recording practice, performers now had to concentrate on playing to the camera. The soundies, and the emergence of television immediately after the war, began to lead musicians away from the traditional skills of live performance on stage, although many soundies represent a fascinating crossroads, where the traditional stagecraft of the variety show coalesces with more subtle ways of playing to the camera, and also the filmcraft of the various directors involved. Few better examples of this exist than the range of ways in which Fats Waller is presented in his four soundies from 1941. *Ain't Misbehavin'* and *Honeysuckle Rose* are the most television-like, with straightforward performances by the band, plus a group of dancers in *Honeysuckle Rose*. *Your Feet's Too Big* comes straight out of the stage-variety-show genre, with some comic dancing by a man wearing impossibly over-sized shoes, whereas *The Joint is Jumpin'* is genuinely cinematic with a true-to-life recreation of the mayhem of a Harlem rent party.

Perhaps the most paradoxical movie of the mid-1940s is Dizzy Gillespie's full-length *Jivin' in Bebop*. Made in 1946 by the independent Alexander company, it uses the most old-fashioned techniques to present the most modern of music. It captures accurately the power and excitement of Gillespie's bebop big band, but it does so by filming a theatrical performance that still relies (as Gillespie's touring act did) on presenting the band as it would appear at, say, the Apollo Theater in Harlem. In direct contrast, the most cinematic and modernistic treatment of jazz on film, from the decade of the recording bans, is firmly rooted in the swing era, in Gjon Mili's *Jammin' the Blues*, a 1944 short that involves a group featuring Lester Young, Harry "Sweets" Edison, and Illinois Jacquet, and which perfectly captures the romance, excitement, and swing of African-American jazz at its informal best.

# CHAPTER 10

# Jazz Singing to 1950

The dilemma of jazz singing can be expressed as a paradox:
all jazz derives from vocal music, but all jazz singing is
derived from instrumental music.

Joachim E. Berendt, from *The Book of Jazz*

In 1926, André Schaeffner published his observations about the way in which
African-American jazz instrumentalists became "les imitatrices de la voix,"
and in Chapters 1 and 2 I discussed the way in which, on recordings made
the year before, Louis Armstrong's cornet playing formed just such a
counterpart to the blues singing of Bessie Smith. His instrumental work, and
that of other players such as trombonist Charlie Green, assimilated elements
of the timbre, tone, and emotional power of the classic female blues singers,
and used them to enrich the improvisational language of jazz. But if one
accepts Joachim Berendt's paradox, expressed above, it is also the case that,
at about the same time, singers began to take on some of the new rhythmic
and melodic freedom being developed by instrumentalists.

There were several distinct ingredients that went into creating an
approach to singing that was undeniably a form of jazz, rather than a jazz-
inflected form of blues or vaudeville. These included wordless singing that
emulated instrumental tone or color; somewhat more rhythmic wordless
singing that used nonsense "scat" syllables; actual vocal imitation of
instruments; and amending the rhythm and melodic line of both a song tune
and its lyrics in the way that, for example, a lead trumpeter might choose to
re-shape a jazz melody. All these things first came together most
convincingly in the singing of Louis Armstrong, who was to some extent
the living embodiment of Berendt's paradox – a cornetist influenced by

singers who then applied his newly developed instrumental style to his own singing. But various of the individual components I have set out surfaced in the work of other musicians a little earlier than on Armstrong's first vocal records from February 1926.

The first significant jazz singers were female; women who had much in common with the "classic" blues singers, but who brought a more "instrumental" approach to their work, and principal among them was Ethel Waters, whom I have already mentioned. Her recording career started in 1921, and she combined a great sense of drama in delivering her lyrics with subtle alterations in timing and rhythm. Not long after her earliest records, she toured with clarinetist Garvin Bushell, who described her as a syncopating jazz singer, "influenced by the horns she'd heard,"[1] and this comes across on some of the records she made within the next couple of years. She was hugely influential, and more recent singers, as different as Jimmy Rushing and Cleo Laine, have acknowledged the degree to which they learned from her.[2] In the 1920s, she was one of the first vocalists to milk the words of a song for dramatic content in a way that was far more overtly theatrical than the emotional punch with which Ma Rainey or Bessie Smith packed their lyrics. Her 1925 hit *Go Back Where You Stayed Last Night* was one such example, and its impact, compared to songs by those other singers, was vividly described by another female vocalist of the period, Edith North Johnson:

> She was really attractive, slender and sang in such an expressive way. I always thought she was one of the better singers that we had because she knew what to emphasize and what not to emphasize. I just thought when she sang, "Go back to where you stayed last night!" she meant, "Go on back there! Everything is over! Go back there where you were stayin' las' night! Git back there, go on!" – I thought she was real good. If you sing, well that's all right and people enjoy it. But if you don't have no personality with your singing, your singing is enjoyed but you are soon forgotten.[3]

Waters was a sophisticated urban stylist, able in equal measure to inject irony, *double entendre*, and refinement into a song, and in this respect her peers included, at the refined end, revue artists like Elizabeth Welch and Adelaide Hall, and, at the more robust end, more bluesy singers such as Alberta Hunter. Aside from these last-named individuals, who developed very much in parallel with Waters, many other female African-American singers of the 1920s based their approaches directly on hers, including her early use of "scat" syllables. One notable early example of wordless "scat" singing is Edith Wilson's vocal on *Dixie Blues* of 1922, which prefigures Duke Ellington's later use of the female voice in an instrumental role.

Waters and her peers were very effectively described by the critic Henry Pleasants as "cake-walkin' babies" rather than "classic" blues singers, to make the point that the majority of their songs were drawn from the vaudeville tradition, rather than the blues.[4] In his comprehensive survey of jazz singing, Will Friedwald sees this aspect of their output as "moving further and further away from indigenous black style and becoming increasingly albino."[5] In my view this misses the important ingredient of Signifyin(g) in their work. Never mind that some of the song forms and lyrics owed their provenance to Tin Pan Alley – the knowing irony with which they were delivered, and the subtleties brought to the words, generally serve to "tell a story" at several different levels. This applies to most of Ethel Waters's output from the very early 1920s, but it is particularly true of a select number of her contemporaries, those singers who traveled to Europe from the mid-1920s onwards to perform for predominantly Caucasian audiences. Friedwald suggests that they "polished up the rougher aspects of the black tradition so much that they were actually acceptable to white society," but I see their work as ineffably cool, absolutely central to the African-American tradition, and full of its inbuilt and knowing sophistication.

To take a couple of examples, Adelaide Hall's *Too Darn Fickle*, recorded in London in 1931, begins with a little light scatting and then moves into a clear and unadorned delivery of the verse, but as she moves into the chorus, lingering on some words such as "exclusively," and emphasizing occasional phrases – "Why that could never be!" – with shifts of pitch, we suddenly realize that it is Hall herself who is being fickle – her vocal is a mirror of coquettishness, and as she criticizes her lover she runs through a whole gamut of feminine wiles that suggests her own fickleness and changeability. It is an extraordinarily accomplished performance, and as well as obvious improvisation in the form of scat-singing and of shifting the pitch and timing of the melody, it actually uses the delivery of the lyrics, the alteration in their meaning, as a form of improvisation. Like its counterpart from the same recording date – Fats Waller and Andy Razaf's song *Doin' What I Please* – it mixes African-American cool with a streak of feminist independence.

This point becomes clearer when Hall's version of the latter song is compared with one by a male singer; and how she adds to, and makes more complex, its insouciant hedonism. When Don Redman sang his version of Andy Razaf's unisex lyrics to *Doin' What I Please*, on a disc made the year after Hall's, the song describes a suave sophisticated man-about-town (the kind of character who features in Danny Barker's portrait of the well-known Harlem Renaissance figure Henry Saparo, the "playboy of Miss [Alelia] Walker . . . [a] good-looking, immaculately dressed man sometimes carrying a guitar case"[6]). Redman's half-closed eyes and laconic delivery epitomize someone who has "romances like a dog has fleas," who can "outsmart all these other smarties . . . [and] get my satisfaction steppin' out."[7] But transfer this to a woman, and it suddenly encapsulates all sorts of issues about female independence and sexual license. For any female singer, in 1931, to sing,

> I'm living independently,
> and from now on I vow,
> I'm free and single,
> my conscience is at ease,
> I'm free to mingle,
> doin' what I please,[8]

was one thing, for that singer to be an African-American woman was another, and demonstrates an attitude and a musical statement of freedom of choice that was altogether more interesting than "polishing up the rougher elements of the black tradition."

This disc was made some years after Hall first became an influential singer, but some of the same sentiments surface in the very earliest recordings of Alberta Hunter, made almost a decade before. Hunter was also to work mainly in Europe for almost ten years from 1927, but she had made a number of significant discs by the time she left the United States. Like Hall she experimented with the nuances of delivery (or at least she tried to do so as much as early acoustic recording technology would allow), and she also introduced the microtonal flattening of certain pitches, borrowed directly from the blues, in a piece such as *Gonna Have You, Ain't Gonna Leave You Alone*, recorded with Eubie Blake at the same 1922 session as she cut her own extremely commercially successful composition *Down Hearted Blues*.[9]

Hunter was already a veteran of the recording studios by the time she made several discs with the Red Onion Jazz Babies in a line-up that included Louis Armstrong, in 1924, and, through working with her, he gained, therefore, direct experience of this more theatrical style of diction and presentation, in contrast to his recordings made the following year with Bessie Smith.

I have mentioned that Ethel Waters and Edith Wilson included elements of nonsense syllables or "scat" singing in their work some time before Louis Armstrong's vocal debut on record, and another important early scat singer was the white vaudevillean Cliff Edwards, who worked under the name "Ukulele Ike" and is today best remembered for providing the voice of Jiminy Cricket in Walt Disney's 1940 cartoon film *Pinocchio*. Back in the 1920s, on his first recording, *Old Fashioned Love*, made for Pathé in 1923, he demonstrated a good command of scat phrases, which he then developed into the ability to improvise complete choruses as early as 1924. It is likely that some degree of scat singing had formed a part of Edwards's act as early as 1919–20, when tuba player Joe Tarto toured the variety circuit with him in a Dixieland band,[10] but he is mainly known to jazz-record collectors for the numerous discs he made in 1925–6 with Red Nichols, which, together with his solo records, brought him to widespread attention as a jazz-influenced singer. (At least they did so in the short term, because Edwards was an unstable character who made and lost his reputation – and his fortune – as an entertainer several times.)

When Louis Armstrong came to record *Heebie Jeebies* in 1926, he apparently dropped the sheet on which the lyrics were written so that he was forced to make up some nonsense words. He wrote:

> I did not want to stop and spoil the record which was moving along so wonderfully. So when I dropped the paper I immediately turned back into the horn and started to Scatting. . . . Just as nothing had happened.[11]

As a consequence, he opened the song with its normal lyric, and returned to conventional language at the end, but in between he created a completely wordless vocal, where varied syllables and an extraordinary range of timbres replicate some of his instrumental techniques. He was not doing anything particularly novel – simply falling back on what was, within the world of vaudeville and theater, already a fairly well-known manner of singing, employed by African-American and white musicians alike. Indeed, he had used scat before on record himself, on Fletcher Henderson's *Everybody Loves My Baby*, perhaps having subconscious recourse to an old New Orleans manner of singing (which, according to Jelly Roll Morton in his Library of Congress recordings, goes back to the turn-of-the-century vocals of Joe Sims of Vicksburg, Mississippi, who influenced many Crescent City musicians). However, Armstrong's originality as a scat singer – and, in due course, as an overall jazz singer – comes from the way in which he employed his rich musical imagination to create phrasing and melodic lines every bit as inventive as those he played on the cornet.

He does so on *Heebie Jeebies* despite the most plodding accompaniment from his Hot Five – the rhythm section of banjoist Johnny St. Cyr and pianist Lil Hardin Armstrong. His voice already has its familiar gravely rasp, but, as Gunther Schuller says: "In his singing we can hear all the nuances, inflections and natural ease of his trumpet playing, including even the bends and scoops, vibratos and shakes."[12]

I think Schuller may be overstating the case to continue by saying that Armstrong "added a new school or technique of singing to Western music, notwithstanding the fact that its orientation is completely African in origin." It would be more accurate to say that Armstrong refined a technique that was already in use, not only on record, but also in vaudeville and variety, and that although it had obvious African overtones, by the time of the *Heebie Jeebies* record date in February 1926, scat-singing had been taken up and developed by white entertainers as well.

However, a small number of further recordings serve to illustrate other aspects of jazz singing as it began to be developed by Armstrong and his contemporaries during the second half of the 1920s.

To start with, there are some key discs that illustrate the voice acting in direct emulation of an instrument. Adelaide Hall demonstrated through her wordless vocal on Duke Ellington's October 26, 1927, recording of *Creole Love Call* just how perfectly she could match the instrumental style of Bubber Miley, and the growls and moans of his plunger-muted horn. She creates a kind of abstraction of Bessie Smith's style of singing, with the words removed and the tonal and timbral qualities thrown into sharp relief, albeit filtered via the medium of Miley's instrumental approach. Hall's father was a professor of music in Brooklyn, and she grew up as a singer with a well-trained ear. She began her professional life as a chorus dancer in Lew Leslie's revues, but was promoted to leading lady after the premature death of Florence Mills, finding herself both singing and dancing opposite such show-business heavyweights as Bill "Bojangles" Robinson. She was, therefore, quite a star in her own right when a chance encounter with Ellington led to her recording with his band. She recalled:

I was touring with a show closing the first half of the bill, and

Duke and his boys were opening the second half. One night . . . I think we were in Toronto . . . I stood at the side of the stage to listen to Duke's music and he played this new number, and I started to hum. Duke heard me and he walked over and said, "We're going to make a record together with you doing that," and I said, "But I don't really know what I was doing," and he told me not to worry but just to do it.[13]

On her opening chorus of *The Blues I Love to Hear*, made at the same session as *Creole Love Call*, she mixes scat and lyrics. Then she offers a half-sung, half-spoken commentary on the subsequent instrumental chorus that is a verbal equivalent to the kind of "playing in the windows" Armstrong had done with Bessie Smith, and she rounds off the piece with a curious chorus that begins by being wordless, and then repeats the sentence "That's the blues I love to hear" over the final four bars of the main sequence and its subsequent tag. She closes with an unmistakable impression of Louis Armstrong, as he had sounded on *Heebie Jeebies*, which by this time had become a modestly successful hit. Hall was one of the first musicians to imitate Armstrong's vocal style on record, an early example of a process examined in detail by Hugues Panassié, and which he summed up as it applied to trumpeters and vocalists alike as "a veritable orgy of imitation."[14]

When Armstrong came to record *Hotter than That*, in December 1927, he repaid Hall's compliment and adopted the kind of entirely wordless singing that she had produced for Duke Ellington. He scatted his way through a duet with guitarist Lonnie Johnson, where, after a complete chorus of vocal accompanied by guitar, the two men exchange phrases during a musical conversation of the highest order. In the same way that there is a sense of tremendous freedom in Hall's ethereal vocal on *Creole Love Call*, unfettered by lyric or written melody line, there is much the same here, with Armstrong using his voice exactly as he might have done his cornet, but by now actually reveling in the particular qualities of his vocal sound as a contrast to that of his instrument. Yet, as if to underline the fundamental similarities of his vocal and instrumental improvising, on the one hand Armstrong recreates the sound of a cornet "rip" into the upper register in his vocal,[15] and on the other, after a spectacular cornet solo, Armstrong ends the disc by trading phrases with Johnson again, only this time using his horn instead of his voice.

Duke Ellington employed Johnson in a very similar way on his recording of *The Mooche*, from October 1928, when singer Baby Cox exchanged musical phrases with the guitarist, but by this time Armstrong had already produced perhaps the most brilliant example of his wordless singing on an exceptional disc that is also a *tour-de-force* of his brass playing, *West End Blues* **[CD track 7]**.

I have already discussed the way that this recording symbolizes a major alteration in the direction of jazz, and how it broke irrevocably with the collective improvisation of Armstrong's precursors such as the O.D.J.B. Not only did it change the balance of the collective front line, but Armstrong's sung duet with Jimmy Strong's clarinet, a high tenor-voiced series of imaginative obbligato ornaments behind the clarinet's melody line, put the human voice on an equal footing with the other instruments in the band as an improvisatory force.

In 1929, with the success of Armstrong's appearances in the revue *Connie's Hot Chocolates* in New York, in which he turned Fats Waller and Andy Razaf's song *Ain't Misbehavin'* into a hit, and launched his career as a singer and entertainer as well as trumpeter, he went on to take the lead in developing the art of producing jazz interpretations of popular song. But before considering that, it is worth tracing a separate line of development that builds on his wordless singing of the 1920s, and runs through scat and instrumental imitation to the frenetic bebop vocals of Dizzy Gillespie and Joe Carroll in the 1940s.

Throughout the two decades or so involved, there is a major sense of continuity in the use of wordless vocals in the work of Duke Ellington, who, having used the device in 1927 with Adelaide Hall, went on involving the voice as part of his orchestral palette well into the 1940s. After the period of his records with Hall and Baby Cox, Ellington's regular vocalist from 1931 until 1942 was Ivie Anderson, and on her recording debut with the band, *It Don't Mean a Thing if It Ain't Got That Swing* **[CD track 13]**, from February 1932, she shows two sides to her use of scat-singing, opening with low, moody phrases, and then (after a conventional vocal with lyrics) producing a lively series of scatted phrases over the closing ensembles. As time went on, Anderson developed into a sensuous ballad singer who combined blues sensibility with her fondness for wringing meaning out of songs, often pitched in her lower register, but when called upon she produced vocal solos that fitted the instrumental texture of the orchestra and its soloists. As a consequence of her scatting and improvisational ability, Anderson's singing of words had more instrumental qualities about it than many of her contemporaries. The very best example of this is *I Got It Bad and That Ain't Good* (from the show *Jump for Joy*, recorded in June 1941), in which she created a perfect vocal counterpart to the langorous alto saxophone of Johnny Hodges. Although she delivered the lyric with uncommon delicacy and clarity, she mirrored Hodges's habit of scooping up to his longer notes from a quarter of a tone or so below their actual pitch, and she invested phrases of the lyric such as "Friday rolls around" with all the qualities of Hodges's instrumental style.

Once Anderson had left Ellington to return to her former home base of Central Avenue in Los Angeles, and open her Chicken Shack restaurant and club, her place was taken by, amongst others, the classically trained Kay Davis, who produced some dazzling examples of wordless singing including the remarkable *Transblucency* (1946), which features her high soprano voice floating over the orchestral ensemble, and she also appeared on a remake of *Creole Love Call* (1949). In Chapter 4, I mentioned Ellington's extended suite *Black, Brown and Beige*; the vocal version of the blues that it contains, initially performed in concert by Betty Roché, and, subsequently, commercially recorded by Joya Sherrill, is another demonstration of Ellington's continued interest in using the voice as an instrumental effect.

But if individual vocalists using scat and wordless singing techniques were integrated into Ellington's palette of orchestral colors, there were other singers who employed these devices more independently. In Paul Whiteman's orchestra, his vocal trio the Rhythm Boys (Harry Barris, Bing Crosby, and Al Rinker) had a stylistic range that encompassed everything from slow, close-harmony ballad singing to up-tempo scat. And, because they were a vocal group, they could behave almost as if they were an independent section of the orchestra. On the 1928 *From Monday On*, for instance – augmented by Jack Fulton, Charles Gaylord, and Austin Young – they ran through several aspects of their stylistic range, from slow opening barbershop harmonies to a rapid scat chorus that follows, and then backing Bing Crosby's singing of the lyric itself with the kind of snappy riffs usually produced by a brass or reed section. Just as Whiteman's brass take some of their jazz feeling from Bix Beiderbecke's splendid solo on this number, so, too, do the vocalists, with Crosby singing across the beat and timing some of his phrases on a longer meter, echoing the cornetist's phrasing. However, neither the Rhythm Boys nor their female counterparts of the period – the Boswell Sisters – ever managed the kind of abstract, quasi-instrumental sounds of Ellington's best vocalists. This came to be achieved – initially with stunning success, and then a rather predictable monotony – by the Mills Brothers, who began recording in 1931.

As well as close-harmony singing of words and scat syllables, the brothers – Harry, John, Herbert, and Donald – accompanied only by John Mills's guitar, created uncannily accurate vocal impressions of jazz instruments, to the extent that, at their best, they are almost indistinguishable from an instrumental ensemble. On some of their early records, they accompany Crosby, but their work can be heard most clearly on the discs on which they sing just as a quartet. Comparison of their different recordings of the same song suggests that they had worked out their harmonies and solos, and learned their arrangements – so there was little actual improvisation involved, but their ability to transfer the timing and phrasing of jazz instrumentalists into a purely vocal art was extraordinary. When their earliest discs arrived in England, the *Melody Maker* commented that "everyone swears the tuba is played by Adrian Rollini,"[16] but in fact there was no tuba – only the bass singing voice of John Mills, who produced an incredibly convincing imitation of the bass horn. Their first few recordings included two versions of *Tiger Rag*, and on the second of these Harry produces a simulation of a cornet solo that borrows much of its timing and phrasing wholesale from Louis Armstrong. Here, then, is a further extension of Berendt's paradox – a singer directly imitating a trumpeter imitating a singer.

The Mills Brothers' act, and certainly their recording technique, depended on the way in which they used the microphone. Neither John's tuba impressions nor Harry's trumpet sounds would have been so effective were it not for the way they worked quite close to the mike. Indeed, one recurring aspect of their early recordings is the general lightness of touch that they had vocally, allowing the recording process itself to do some of their work for them in successfully achieving their "instrumental" sounds. Although they had begun as a conventional close-harmony singing group, working vaudeville theaters in their home state of Ohio, and blending the white barbershop harmonies of groups like the Rhythm Boys with the secular equivalent of the African-American gospel quartets of the Southern states, they refined their "instrumental" act during a ten-month season in the late 1920s on station WLW in Cincinnati. When they arrived in New York in 1930 and began recording for Brunswick the following year, their discs carried the legend: "No musical instruments or mechanical devices used on this recording other than one guitar."[17] Before long, they had a number of imitators, including the Three Peppers, the Four Blackbirds, and the Four Southern Singers, but few of them managed the natural sense of time and the balanced jazz phrasing that, despite the degree of carefully learned arrangement involved, marked out the Mills Brothers' best efforts.

One of their earliest discs was a version of *Nobody's Sweetheart*, which bears comparison with another version of the same song recorded the following year by the 52nd Street string band and vocal group the Spirits of Rhythm. Whereas the Mills Brothers' version is a highly accurate impersonation of jazz, the Spirits of Rhythm disc is undoubtedly that of an improvising jazz ensemble, both instrumentally and vocally. Furthermore, the Spirits contained one maverick but highly original improviser in the shape of its vocalist Leo Watson, who also played a kind of small guitar called a tiple. Watson's forte was to sing long improvised scat solos, that mingled nonsense syllables, instrumental impressions, and actual words into what Laurence Koch accurately dubs a "stream-of-consciousness" style.[18] *Nobody's Sweetheart* has just such a vocal, as well as some brilliant close-harmony passages from the other members of the group, the tiple-playing and singing brothers Wilbur and Douglas Daniels, supported by the driving guitar of Teddy Bunn and the homemade percussion of Virgil Scoggins.

There was another comparable group from around the same period called the Cats and the Fiddle, which was built around the guitar of Tiny Grimes in much the same way as the Spirits of Rhythm was anchored by Bunn, but despite some clever close-harmony passages in their ensemble singing, the Cats lacked the vocal innovations of Watson.

Watson also dabbled as a drummer and trombonist, but his forte was as a singer, and in his act, according to reports of his long residencies at New York's Onyx Club, he took instrumental imitation to the extent of miming the actions of players: "[He] moved his arm in and out, just like a trombonist (Benny Morton was his idol), improvising one elaborate scat chorus after another."[19]

It is the elaboration of his vocals that is the most astonishing thing about Watson. He seems to have had a talent for baroque, almost surreal, ornamentation, that eventually took him away from 52nd Street, and onto the bigger stages of the white swing orchestras, where he became a featured vocalist, first with Artie Shaw, in 1937, and then, the following year, with Gene Krupa. Ironically, his restriction to one or two choruses per piece gave him only limited moments to shine with these bands, compared to the freedom of his performances with the Spirits of Rhythm, both at the Onyx Club and on record. Nevertheless, his discs with Krupa demonstrate the range of his innovations, from the straightforward lyric of *Jeepers Creepers*, with its altered melody and craftily repeated phrases, to the whirlwind scat of *Nagasaki*. He also lingers over the repeated tag line of *Tutti-Frutti*, which has much in common with the verbal surrealism of Slim Gaillard, a singer and multi-instrumentalist who had recorded this same tune just a few weeks earlier, and who subsequently recorded with Watson himself in the 1940s.

Gaillard combined much of Watson's verbal invention with the hepster's language pioneered by Cab Calloway. I shall come on to discuss the other aspects of Calloway's work shortly, but from the early 1930s he was an important contributor to the development of wordless singing, not simply by finding endless ways of delivering his catch-phrase "Hi-de-hi," but through integrating scat, lyrics, and instrumental interludes into clever pieces such as *The Scat Song* (December 1933). Calloway used his nonsense lines as a way of drawing his audience into a performance, and he described the process as follows:

> When the band was swinging and the feeling got right, I'd start to
> hi-de-ho. You know, singing:
>     "Hi-de-hi-de-hi-de-ho."
> Then the band would answer:
> "Hi-de-hi-de-hi-de-ho."
> Then I'd sing back again:
> "Wha-de-do-de-way-de-ho."
> And the band would swing and sing:
> "Wha-de-do-de-way-de-ho."
> When it really got to feeling good, I'd holler for the audience
> to join in.
>     "Wah-de-wah-de-wah-de-doo," I'd sing.
>     "Wah-de-wah-de-wah-de-doo," the band and the audience
> would holler back. By now the place is jumping.[20]

Calloway's inventive use of nonsense syllables and his ability to enthuse an audience to sing such gobbledygook along with him gave rise to a whole imaginary language, which he published into a "dictionary" in the late 1930s.[21] It also included some of the words associated with his low-life characters Minnie The Moocher and Smoky Joe, and thus it made coy references to the secret language of drugs – the world of reefers, muggles, and vipers – but the entire enterprise consolidated the idea of the "hepster" or "hipster" speaking in jive talk, an image Calloway was keen to project in his singing. (Mezz Mezzrow's glossary of "jive" in his autobiography *Really the Blues*, published in 1946, is a more fully blown attempt to translate the language used by those Harlem characters to whom Mezzrow "pushed his gauge," and the scent of marijuana hangs over such statements as: "Jive, I found out, is not only a strange linguistic mixture of dream and deed . . . it's a whole new attitude to life."[22])

I have already suggested that in his low-life songs in *Minnie the Moocher* vein, Calloway's use of language constituted a complex form of Signifyin(g) in which different meanings were conveyed to different groups of listeners. But for the most part his "hepster's" language in song was rather different. As the French linguist Jean-Paul Levet says in his study of jazz argot, the majority of the words Calloway employed were not in general use among African-American musicians, and therefore Calloway's, and subsequently Gaillard's, "hep" vocabulary "means nothing, because its usage was exclusive to them."[23] Nevertheless, both singers clearly communicated effectively to their audiences by using baloney, and both, like Leo Watson, used words themselves as an improvisatory device. Calloway projected irrepressible bonhomie, and his energetic delivery drew audiences into the slipstream of his rapidfire delivery. Gaillard, by contrast, was decidedly more surreal, and his songs based on food (*Avocado Seed Soup Symphony* or *Matzoh Balls*), machines (*Cement Mixer*), or plain nonsense (*Flat Foot Floogie*) are masterpieces of the language he devised and referred to as "vout," many sentences having the phrases "a-reeney" or "o-rooney" added to several words.

For quite such a high-profile figure, parts of Gaillard's life remain mysterious, and other aspects of it, although true, seem fantastically improbable. He was born in 1916, and most early reference sources suggest this event took place in Detroit. But when he came to make his film autobiography for British television, after settling in London in the 1980s, Gaillard revealed not only that he had been born in Cuba, but also that his father, who was a ship's steward, took him to sea as a small boy and accidentally abandoned him on the island of Crete. The obvious Hispanic overtones in his sung-nonsense language may well go back to his early childhood, and his talent for words dates from the necessity of making himself understood in Crete until the time he was picked up six months later.

Gaillard had an innate musical talent. He played guitar well and with considerable jazz feeling. He was a competent pianist and his party trick was to play fast passages using the backs of his fingers, something that he was still doing in his seventies, when I played in a supporting band to him at the Breda Festival in Holland. As a younger man, he perfected another miracle of physical co-ordination, in an act that combined tap-dancing and playing the guitar simultaneously, and throughout his life he had a quick and surreal wit that was all the better for mixing his well-worn gags with the unexpected. I still remember someone from a table near the stage being halfway to the bar to order a vodka and peanut butter for Slim before they realized it was a put-on.

Gaillard arrived in New York in 1937, and after winning a radio talent show, he formed a duo with bassist Slam Stewart. The two of them then began a long-running radio show for station WNEW. Their 1938 recording as "Slim and Slam" of *Flat Foot Floogie* was a hit, leading to a whole series of further discs in which standards such as *Chinatown* were gradually squeezed out by ever more surreal and humorous numbers, including *Laughin' in Rhythm*. (For his part, Slam Stewart was no less an influential figure on the vocal side of jazz than Gaillard. Stewart specialized in taking bowed solos on the bass, with which he sang along in unison. In terms of Berendt's paradox, this unified the two roles of singer and instrumentalist, and Stewart's scatted syllables can be seen as a key to the thought processes behind his bowed bass lines. This technique of singing in unison, or at a regular harmonic interval, with an instrumental line seems to have been one that was particularly popular among string players, and other bassists, notably Major Holley in the United States and Coleridge Goode in Britain, followed Stewart's example, a style which Stewart claimed he developed from hearing violinist Ray Perry. Over time, other instrumentalists began to deploy the technique, and in the post-war period, such musicians as guitarist George Benson and flautist Roland Kirk integrated their played and vocal lines.)

After his success on radio in the East, in due course Gaillard ended up in Los Angeles, demonstrating his talents on screen in such films as *Star Spangled Rhythm* and *Hellzapoppin!* (both made in 1942), and earning himself the nickname "Dark Gable." His brand of surreal vocals and witty stage act made him a favorite at Los Angeles nightclubs, and he was working at Billy Berg's in Hollywood when Charlie Parker and Dizzy Gillespie came in to play opposite him. During their stay on the West Coast, Parker and Gillespie recorded with Gaillard, adding the unmistakable sounds of bebop to a remake of *Flat Foot Floogie*, plus other sides including *Poppity Pop* and *Slim's Jam*. Although there was apparently a certain amount of animosity between Gillespie and Gaillard at the time, arising out of some minor incident at Billy Berg's, not only did much of Gaillard's brand of vocal and surreal humor metamorphose into Gillespie's earliest scat vocals with his big band from 1946, but also it seems that the collaboration between Gaillard and the beboppers may, unwittingly, have led to a ban on the new jazz on Los Angeles radio when station KMPC stopped playing it. A report in *Time* decried the music as "hot jazz overheated, with overdone lyrics full of bawdiness, references to narcotics and double talk," and this certainly seems to sum up Gaillard's collaboration with Parker and Gillespie.[24]

The other influence on the bebop scatting that Gillespie, and his band vocalists Kenny Hagood and Joe Carroll, performed from the mid-1940s was singer Babs Gonzales. He was a larger-than-life personality who formed a vocal trio called Three Bips and a Bop with pianist Tadd Dameron and guitarist Pee Wee Tinney. They recorded a number of Dameron's pieces in vocal arrangements, starting by making *Oop-Pop-A-Da* for Blue Note in 1947, which went on to be a commercial success for Dizzy Gillespie, when he made his own version of the piece that same year. Gonzales, who had a surprisingly light tenor voice, went on to record under his own name for Capitol, and his 1949 *Professor Bop* shows his engaging method of singing a conventional lyric with emphasis on the more unusual bebop intervals, to which he adds moments of scat. Nevertheless, compared to the free-flowing singing of Gillespie and Carroll, it is a surprisingly mannered performance, and it lacks the fluidity with which Gillespie transferred his trumpet style to his voice, or the vocal gymnastics of Sarah Vaughan, the first female singer to make a convincing job of singing bebop. Sarah Vaughan, however, belongs to a rather different jazz-singing tradition, and this can also be traced back to Louis Armstrong, through the side of his work that involved bringing jazz pitching, phrasing, timbre, and timing to conventional lyrics, and which fully developed after his 1929 hit with *Ain't Misbehavin'*.

The summer of 1929 was a turning point in Armstrong's career. He had finally moved away from Chicago, which had been his base since leaving Fletcher Henderson, and relocated to New York, where he opened in the revue *Hot Chocolates*, in June 1929, playing in the production both during matinees and evenings at the Hudson Theater on Broadway, and later every night at Connie's Inn in Harlem. Initially, Armstrong's part in the show was to sing and play *Ain't Misbehavin'* from the orchestra pit, and the *New York Times* drew attention to "its rendition between the acts by an unnamed member of the orchestra," calling it "a highlight of the premier."[25] Before long, Armstrong was out of the pit and on stage, sharing top billing with the show's co-composer Fats Waller and its female star Edith Wilson. As the run went on, his fame and reputation grew among the New York theater-goers, first the well-heeled white audiences catered for by both the Hudson and Connie's, and then with the African-American public, who flocked to hear him at the Lafayette Theater in Harlem, where he was also booked to appear as a variety artist during the run of *Hot Chocolates*, fronting his former

Chicagoan orchestra led by violinist Carroll Dickerson. It was with this group that he recorded *Ain't Misbehavin'* on July 19, 1929, and although the disc became a considerable success for him, only a few months afterwards he severed ties with these long-term musical associates, and, under the direction of his manager Tommy Rockwell, reinvented himself as a popular entertainer with a rather different set of backing musicians.

Nevertheless, the disc is very much the template for the dozens of recordings Armstrong made with big-band accompaniment during the 1930s, as I described in Chapter 4 in the section concerning his work with Luis Russell. But that discussion did not dwell on his singing, and *Ain't Misbehavin'* is an outstanding example of Armstrong's ability – unrivaled in the 1920s – to bring jazz sensibility to a popular-song lyric.

The theme is introduced on the disc by Armstrong's muted horn, before the middle eight is taken by Dickerson's stilted violin, followed by some syrupy phrasing from the reeds, but, if nothing else, this creates the impression of a song drawn from a show – of footlights and greasepaint. When Armstrong starts to sing, he paraphrases the melody from the outset, and he ends each of the first and second eight-measure sections of the song with a semi-scatted vocal break that mirrors his approach to playing breaks on the trumpet. Early in the vocal, it is clear that he is going to be somewhat economical with Razaf's lyric, losing the odd word or phrase here and there but without destroying its overall sense. The phrase "I'm happy on the shelf" is sung like a downward-moving trumpet figure, with an additional "babe" tagged on to the end, to balance it musically. His first break loses the last two words, "for you," from the written lyric, and he replaces these with an urgent improvised figure built on the words "Oh, baby, love you; really . . . love you."[26] Overall, the effect is rather as if Armstrong is both singer and backing instrumentalist, using the power of his voice and his imagination to convey both roles, and in the process – just as the likes of Adelaide Hall, Alberta Hunter, and Ethel Waters did – making the words themselves part of his improvisatory material.

Whereas Armstrong had done some scatting, and simultaneously had made minor alterations to the lyrics of the songs he had recorded in Chicago with his Hot Five and Seven, few of these from *Georgia Grind* and *Heebie Jeebies*, in February 1926, until his move to New York were particularly important as songs – indeed there are just five exceptions: *You Made Me Love You* (1926), *Squeeze Me, Basin Street Blues, St. James Infirmary* (all 1928), and *I Can't Give You Anything But Love* (1929). Yet, in these, as Bruce Crowther and Mike Pinfold point out in their survey of jazz singing, however far

Armstrong strayed from the written song: "Usually there remained some vestige of the original words. For Armstrong, scat remained a vocal tool to be used sparingly to enhance an interpretation and create something special and identifiably his own."[27]

Nevertheless, *Ain't Misbehavin'*, with its fine balance between the underlying song and Armstrong's verbal and musical additions, was the song that cemented his transition from brilliant trumpeter and instrumentalist to popular singer, and it is highly significant that in his first recording of it he took such remarkable liberties with the lyric and melody line without sacrificing the song's underlying content and meaning. Reports suggest that he had been doing a little of this kind of singing at the Sunset in Chicago, in 1927–8, but it was his move to New York, and Rockwell's decision to encourage him to perform recognizable popular songs rather than his own jazz originals, that achieved the twin effects of boosting Armstrong's career way beyond jazz circles and defining his hugely influential style of jazz singing.

Rockwell recognized that the kind of act Armstrong did in front of his big band at the Lafayette (expanding his solo features in *Hot Chocolates* into a fully fledged set) would be the way forward, and that any recordings that came in the wake of *Ain't Misbehavin'* would be perfect fodder for the nation's juke-boxes, a new craze that grew rapidly as the 1930s began. So in the six months that followed Armstrong's stage and recording success with *Ain't Misbehavin'*, he went on to record the first of a whole string of recognizable standards: *Black and Blue* (also from *Hot Chocolates*), *Some of these Days*, *When You're Smiling*, *After You've Gone*, *I Ain't Got Nobody*, and *St. Louis Blues*. To all of these he applied his unique blend of phrasing and improvisational approach, and by 1931, when he cut two versions of *Stardust*, his contrasting vocal treatment on each disc shows the degree of improvisational invention he brought to his singing. Through tackling this material he ended up influencing other vocalists and instrumentalists alike.

Danny Barker tells the vivid story of how Armstrong affected a group of half a dozen or so trumpeters he met when he arrived in New York in 1930:

> They had been listening to Armstrong records on the jukebox and discussing and arguing about Louis's singing. Ward Pinkett had convinced them that to get the sound of Armstrong's voice they should all catch colds. ... I am sure that Louis Armstrong has never had a fan that worshipped him more than Ward Pinkett; all his talk was Armstrong. He was forever singing Louis's vocals,

and he would get so carried away by Louis's music that he would sit by the jukebox in joints in Harlem with his horn in his lap and cry in admiration of Louis.[28]

Pinkett was just one of the many trumpeters who adopted Armstrong's style both as a player and as a vocalist. Although each brought an individual spin to the Armstrong approach, his influence is unmistakable on a generation of trumpeters/singers, ranging from white New Orleans players, like Wingy Manone and Louis Prima, to such African-American swing stars as Roy Eldridge, Jonah Jones, Ray Nance, Hot Lips Page, and Rex Stewart. Other musicians took matters further and actually produced convincing impressions of Armstrong – any visitor to New Orleans's Bourbon Street in the 1970s and 1980s will have heard the All Stars' one-time drummer Freddie Kohlman singing like Armstrong, with both the Dukes of Dixieland and his own band, and there were many other equally effective imitators in towns and cities much further from Armstrong's birthplace. As the Kansas City vocalist Jimmy Rushing put it, "If I ever get stuck when I'm singing I drop right back on Pops's [Armstrong's] style – it's the basic way of jazz singing and you can't get away from it."[29]

Throughout the 1930s and well into the 1940s, Armstrong's template for jazz singing was almost universal among African-American musicians. Virtually every record session he made from 1929 until the recording ban in 1942 produced one or two gems of popular songs, including several that became uniquely associated with him, such as (in chronological order) *When You're Smiling, Confessin' (That I Love You), Just a Gigolo, Them There Eyes, That's My Home, Sleepy Time Down South, Old Man Mose, Thanks a Million, I'm Putting All My Eggs in One Basket, Eventide, Swing that Music, It's Wonderful, Shadrack,* and *Jeepers Creepers.* His style was absorbed and developed into the work of the other two great vocalists of the period, Cab Calloway and Fats Waller, and it also had much to do with defining the timing and phrasing of Bing Crosby.

However, partly because of the route his career took after leaving Paul Whiteman in 1930, making popular discs, broadcasting, and acting in films, as he became more and more of an all-American icon, Crosby tended to remain a jazz-influenced singer, rather than a true improvising jazz musician. As stated in the last chapter, his principal importance to jazz singers, as well as demonstrating how to combine jazz timing with a sense of relaxation and ease of delivery, was in microphone technique. His assimilation of white and African-American vocal techniques into his characteristic "crooning" involved a radical rethink of how a singer delivered a song, and his breath control, subtle ornamentation of his lines, and habit of singing on consonants were all tailored to the microphone.

Perhaps the main exception to the Armstrong style among out-and-out jazz musicians was his old friend and frequent recording colleague, trumpeter Henry "Red" Allen. Their New Orleans patrimony gave the men a common musical background, but just as Allen's blurry attack as an instrumentalist, his occasionally hurried phrasing, and consistently surprising leaps between registers contrasted increasingly with the clean attack and sculpted phrasing of Armstrong's trumpeting, so too did Allen's singing diverge from the Armstrong template. Allen's gasping vocal on *Who Stole the Lock?* with Jack Bland's Rhythmakers from October 1932, hanging back on each phrase and then-trying-to-cram-in-as-many-words-as-possible-in-the-time-remaining, could hardly be a greater contrast to the secure, relaxed ease of Armstrong's confident singing, and it is perhaps a little unfair of Gunther Schuller to have condemned this and Allen's numerous vocal sides for Vocalion as "neither original nor plagiaristic enough" to have been as successful as Armstrong.[30]

One other instrumentalist associated with Armstrong created as individual and distinct a singing style as Allen, and that was trombonist Jack Teagarden, who was one of the first significant white jazz singers. Not only did Teagarden demonstrate a technical skill on the trombone that advanced way beyond that of Miff Mole or Fletcher Henderson's Jimmy Harrison, but also his Southern upbringing had given him the equally influential experiences of some formal musical education (from his mother) and the spontaneous singing of African-American revivalist worship meetings. His sense of timing allowed him to lean back on the beat and appear to deliver his vocal lines very late, but without any sense of rush. His penchant was for medium ballads such as *I've Got a Right to Sing the Blues*, *Stars Fell on Alabama*, and *A Hundred Years from Today*, and his mellow, warm-toned delivery of these, with a modicum of alteration of the melody line, and considerable liberties with time, epitomized his style. Later, as a member of Armstrong's All Stars, he sang many duets with Armstrong, demonstrating the contrast between his relaxed, lazy delivery and the innately jazzier sound of Armstrong.

I have already pointed out the direct connection between Cab Calloway's *St. Louis Blues*, from his very first session in 1930, and Armstrong's disc of the same piece made the previous year. As a scat singer and progenitor of "jive," Calloway drew heavily on Armstrong's work as well, but in other respects he was an equally inventive and original singer.

Calloway was the first African-American singer to front a nationally famous band. This threw his vocals into the spotlight in a way that was quite different from other singers who were not bandleaders, or from those who were predominantly instrumentalists. He did not have the trumpeting genius of Armstrong or the pounding stride piano of Fats Waller to fall back on. Although his discs are packed with the well-crafted arrangements and instrumental solos I have already discussed, and although at Chu Berry's insistence, he eventually began to record a proportion of purely instrumental numbers, the vast majority focus on Calloway, just as his surviving broadcasts from the Meadowbrook Inn in New Jersey or the Club Zanzibar in New York show how he dominated his band's live sets, loudly urging on his musicians, even during instrumentals.

As Gunther Schuller has pointed out, Calloway had an exceptional vocal range, and combined this with a pure, powerful voice and remarkably clear diction.[31] When, in later life, he appeared as Sportin' Life in Gershwin's *Porgy and Bess* (a role modeled on Cab himself), the operatic critics who reviewed his performances praised the way his voice and personality were rolled into one larger-than-life stage presence. For example, Lord Harewood, the editor of Kobbé's opera guide, wrote:

> Cab Calloway . . . as the super spiv Sportin' Life was playing for the first time a role some of whose aspects were derived from a style of singing he himself had invented. His voice is big, though hardly operatic in quality, his self-confidence and authority are boundless, and his personality seemed ubiquitous by the end of the evening. Someone said of him that he was giving not so much a performance as his backing to the show.[32]

And the critic Elizabeth Forbes, who was at the same London opening of *Porgy and Bess*, at the Stoll Theatre, Kingsway, in October 1952, told me:

> He was electrifying. When he was on stage, you looked at nobody else, even if he wasn't singing, speaking, or doing anything. Because he had such superb diction, you could hear every single word that he sang, and consequently really enjoyed his role. He has remained in my memory as by far the best singer in the show, and when you recall that he was appearing opposite Leontyne Price, that was quite some feat.[33]

This mixture of stage presence, vocal power, and projection was developed early in the 1930s by Calloway as the heart of his act. He rolled into his singing an astonishing range of allusion, from Armstrong's timing, scatting, and phrasing, to a far wider range of influences, that encompassed Jewish cantors, country blues singers, and fast-talking, streetwise low-life characters. As a random example, consider, for instance, his vocal on *Nagasaki*, recorded in July 1935.

Compared with Leo Watson's far more instrumental approach to scatting on this same piece, Calloway uses the written lyric as his launch pad, and builds scat phrases from syllables of the song title, including "Oh de-sag, Oh de-wack"; he adds in other Japanese-sounding syllables such as "fuji"; he interpolates a reference to "ol' Satchmo," followed by a swift impression of Armstrong; he puts in street-corner speech as spoken dialog: "ought to go down Nagasaki!," "Them cat's'll mug you!," and then follows this with a fully scatted chorus, before urging his band to "swing it you dogs!"

The sheer variety and invention of this vocal – which is typical of dozens of others – is denser, more complex, and delivered with more panache than virtually any other singer of the period. Couple that to Calloway's long-running series of songs about "Minnie, the Moocher," and the levels of meaning he packs into the majority of them, and his status as leader of the highest-earning African-American band of the 1930s, and as a huge star in his own right, is fully explicable and justified.

In this latter series of songs, mainly in minor keys, sung at a medium-slow tempo, and about the "roughest, toughest frail" with "a heart as big as a whale," Calloway made each a Signifyin(g) event – with the coded references to "kicking the gong around" (opium or, less frequently, cocaine addiction) and the trance-like actions of Minnie and Smoky Joe. As he sings of them dreaming of "a million dollars worth of nickels and dimes – she sat and counted them all a million times," he is communicating a set of very different ideas to an African-American audience aware of Harlem low-life than to his white listeners – only some of whom would spot the full meaning behind the lyrics. In the original *Minnie the Moocher* song, Calloway's storytelling diction is precise, and not a word of the tale is missed, but he also adds Hebrew-style cantoral chanting, high-pitched shrieks, and scatting which is answered by the enthusiastic shout-back of his band. The same held for the series of sequels to the original: *Minnie the Moocher's Wedding Day*, *Smoky Joe*, *Kicking the Gong Around*, and *The Ghost of Smoky Joe*, amongst others.[34]

This style of performance clearly made a lasting impression on some of his sidemen – Illinois Jacquet, his one-time tenorist, for example, was still singing *Minnie the Moocher* and doing a passable impression of Calloway's scat routine in 1996, some 50 years after he left the band. Others were less impressed – going through this routine night after night added to the boredom of his bandsmen, and to break the monotony, Doc Cheatham remembered that when Cab sang "The curtain parted," the band would invariably answer back "and Minnie farted!"[35]

As well as his "Minnie" series of songs, the rest of Calloway's work can be divided into songs with overtly sexual *double* (or occasionally *seule*) *entendres* (including *Aw, You Dog!* and *Six or Seven Times*), scat vehicles that trade on his "hi-de-ho" routine (such as *Hi-de-ho Man*, and *Hi-de-ho Romeo*), jive songs (like *Jumpin' Jive* or the *Scat Song*), and, finally, straightforward songs of the kind sung by most other singers. Owing to Irving Mills's policy of getting his copyright works and publications recorded by as many bands as possible, several of the "Minnie" series were also cut by the Mills Blue Rhythm Band with the far less effective George Morton as vocalist. O'Neil Spencer, the same band's drummer, was the indifferent singer on its version of the risqué Harold Arlen/Ted Koehler number *Trickeration*, which received a particularly vigorous and definitive performance from Calloway and his orchestra. Just as Calloway used a vast range of allusion within his vocals, so his overall stylistic range as a singer was extremely broad. This was also combined with a voice so powerful that on several discs he can clearly be heard pulling back from the microphone for his loudest, highest notes, so as not to distort the recording.

It was hard, therefore, for others to imitate him, and the majority of singers steered clear of his specialties, unless compelled to perform or record them by Irving Mills. However, some aspects of his style, from his jive-talk to his high-register, shrill wails, were absorbed by other singers such as Billy Banks, whose 1932 *Mean Old Bed Bug Blues* has very similar phrasing and delivery to Calloway on such songs as *Aw, You Dog!*

There has always been something of a mystery as to the identity of the second, falsetto, vocalist on *Mean Old Bed Bug Blues*, but there is an established school of thought that suggests it is the work of Banks's pianist, Fats Waller. I have never been entirely convinced about this, preferring to believe the band's trumpeter, Henry "Red" Allen, who recalled that it was Banks himself, demonstrating his skill as a female impersonator, but it is certainly true that once he had begun to sing, both on radio and as a guest with Ted Lewis's orchestra (in March 1931), Waller's vocals became a mainstay of his performances.

Unlike Armstrong, who brought his improvisational genius to even the most tawdry material, or Calloway who scatted, shrieked, and danced on the most inane numbers, Waller found it irresistible to lampoon his material. As Morroe Berger commented, in one of the first articles to assess Waller's skills as a vocalist rather than as a pianist:

> Waller went at this music differently. Although he improvised on it superbly, he couldn't resist making fun of the lifeless lyrics when he came to the vocal choruses. His ingenuity in demolishing the pathetic pretensions of these verses constitutes an art form in itself.[36]

Much as I have shown how Adelaide Hall used the subtleties of her delivery to add an entirely different layer of meaning to *Too Darn Fickle*, Berger points out that Waller put himself outside the normal position of the vocalist in many of his songs. Instead of singing *to* the object of the song, or *about* the object, Waller distances himself altogether. Consequently, he delivers the lyric simultaneously with a stream of amendments to the written words, commentary on them (both spoken and sung), and a range of exaggerated performance styles from mock-operatic baritones to girlish falsettos, and from stentorian seriousness to mocking humor. If Armstrong managed, in *Ain't Misbehavin'*, to be both singer and instrumentalist in his vocal, in much of his output Waller manages simultaneously to combine the roles of performer and critic of the song.

Much of Waller's skill was purely verbal – a quick punning wit, and the ability to interpose deflating bursts of normality into the most schmaltzy lyrics. Some of his routines were worked out – he had favorite comic interpolations that could be used at almost any point in almost any song, and favorite adjectives, such as the use of "Arabian" to mean fine and exotic – but Berger's analysis of dozens of his recordings shows the extent to which Waller applied his spur-of-the-moment wit to create focused and apposite comic material on song lyrics he can only have confronted for the first time when he got to the recording studio.[37] As we know from his sidemen, these visits to the record company were fairly impromptu affairs. His drummer Harry Dial recalled:

> When we went in the studio we had no idea what we were going to make. We made them four tunes and all we had seen was piano parts. We knew them piano parts, everyone had piano parts. A lot

of people don't believe we didn't have full arrangements, especially when you consider a number like *Serenade for a Wealthy Widow*. We didn't have no arrangement, and the horns didn't have no lead sheet. The other guys used the piano part and Fats, Al [Casey, the guitarist], and the bass player had to transpose. Fats would run through everything first. He ran through 'cos he vocalized on everything. He was phenomenal. He'd sit down, never having heard a composition and play it. He'd play it and then he'd sing it like he'd been doing it for six months.[38]

So, in the light of Dial's comments, we can view Waller's talent as a form of jazz improvisation – the spur-of-the-moment harnessing of verbal skills, together with his formidable musical talent to create memorable and funny interpretations of songs that, in many cases, would otherwise have been completely forgotten.

Overall, Waller recorded several hundred vocals, mostly on workaday Tin Pan Alley tunes, and in them, as Berger says, he "took a music based upon black culture (but at a distance from it) and reinvigorated these 'white' tunes with black language, humor, and point of view."[39] Where there were questions of dubious taste in the original song, such as what would now be regarded as racist lyrics, Waller was merciless. He lampooned *Darktown Strutters' Ball* by shouting, "Ah Sepiatown! ... look at my little bronzed body," but he was equally tough on what were normally sacrosanct forms for African-American entertainers, including the blues, introducing his *Original B Flat Blues* as "the woozy-woozy, bluesy-woozy, woozy blues." For Waller, the unsophisticated content of most vocal blues was fair game for satire, every bit as much as the vapid lyrics of *I Love to Whistle*, or the many other lightweight tunes Victor gave him to record.

Berger makes the point that Waller's use of black speech patterns was more a question of pronunciation and intonation rather than syntax and diction, and that to some extent his use of musicians' language and jive-talk was as much a put-on as his occasional exaggerated British accent, or elaborately rolled "r"s. The complex layers of meaning in Waller's vocals suggest that he, too, is Signifyin(g) in much of his work. There are obvious examples of creating a dramatic "telling event," such as the rent party in *The Joint Is Jumpin'*, both on disc and in "soundie" form, but there are also dozens of more subtle moments where, as Berger says, "Waller was an insider to the white fans who enjoyed [his] amusing confidences, yet he remained an outsider, for he obviously was not impressed with jive except for show-business purposes, and he even kidded jive talk itself."[40]

It was, for example, an entirely Wallerish amendment to the lyric of *I'm Crazy 'bout My Baby* to add a translation in standard English: "I'm exasperated about my offspring, my offspring's exasperated about me."

Much as Calloway developed "series" of numbers that became uniquely his, so, too, did Waller, and most famous were his repetitive patter-songs, such as *Your Feet's Too Big*, its sequel, *Your Socks Don't Match*, and *Twenty-four Robbers*, or the children's chant *Shortnin' Bread*. Ironically, despite his tendency to lampoon anything remotely romantic, his most popular vocals (and certainly the most frequently requested on radio for decades after his death) were light romantic numbers, in which he kept the fooling around to a minimum, such as *I'm Gonna Sit Right Down and Write Myself a Letter* or *My Very Good Friend the Milkman*. These come into the category that a 1938 *Melody Maker* article pointedly described as "mildly irresponsible," rather than "riotous,"[41] but it is perhaps in the riotous category that Waller made his most distinctive contribution, and most riotous of all is his 1935 *Twelfth Street Rag*. In a perceptive analysis of the piece, Humphrey Lyttelton has drawn attention to Waller's extraordinary ability to fuse his verbal fun and games with the musical content of the song, at the same time as turning in a powerhouse piano solo and some thunderous, rocking ensemble playing.

In particular, there is a device that Waller used sparingly, but which had great effect; which was to declaim the lyrics in an entirely different rhythm from the natural sound and sense of the words. As Lyttelton describes it: "Fats uses the words as written, but distributes them in a rhythmic pattern against shifting guitar figures to produce what, for all the sense the words impart, could be described as an effective scat chorus."[42]

Later in the same piece, as his instrumentalists take their solos, Waller produces a description, and verbal sound effects, of a riotous party, but as Lyttelton observes, even a phrase like "Waiter, get some hot dogs ready!" exactly matches the rhythm of trumpeter Herman Autrey's solo. Finally, Waller simply shouts "Yeah!" in answer to each of Autrey's phrases, making himself a third member of the front line along with Autrey and clarinetist Rudy Powell. Not even Calloway could shed inhibition as a vocalist, as Waller could, and produce such an extrovert impression of his musical personality. Waller's genius as a jazz vocalist was to find ways of improvising that moved in entirely different directions from his skills as a pianist. Other singers, such as Bob Howard and Putney Dandridge, tried to emulate his style, but none had his inspired mixture of improvisational skill and humor.

However, one type of song Waller began to record involved a rather different vocal style from all his others. These were pieces of "jump" music – prototype rhythm and blues – in which Waller's vocals were answered by a shout-back from his band, including such titles as *Hold Tight* and *Stop Pretending*. These differed from Calloway's dramatic call-and-response routines because they tended to be built on twelve-bar blues structures or similar sixteen-bar patterns, and prefigured the bluesy vocal style of Louis Jordan and later West Coast singers like Roy Milton and Joe Liggins.

Jordan had been an alto saxophonist and occasional vocalist with the big band of Chick Webb, but before he launched his own Tympany Five, in 1938, his recordings as a singer and saxophonist only hinted at his talent, and he was generally viewed as what John Hammond called a "comedian saxophonist."[43] Despite his comic stage presence, ready grin, and brilliant delivery of amusing songs, Jordan was the antithesis of Waller's spur-of-the-moment invention, and, as his biographer John Chilton revealed, he was a perfectionist obsessive, who endlessly rehearsed the "spontaneous" sound of his band and worked hard to make his alto or baritone sax vignettes as flawless as possible. (His devotion to practice was such that he would not even get up from his chair to open the window, calling for his wife to do this as he continued playing.) Interestingly, in view of earlier observations about the John Kirby band and its influence on the prototype bebop musicians, Jordan also took the Kirby sextet as his model, but although he replicated aspects of its brilliant precision and neat riff-based sound, he used this as the launch pad for his own extrovert vocals and alto solos. "Generally," he said, "a black artist at that time would either stick to the blues or do pop. I did everything."[44]

At the end of the 1930s, for the first two years after he launched his own band, "doing everything" actually diluted Jordan's commercial appeal. He did not have an identifiable style (as Waller did), nor familiar subject matter (as Calloway had). It took him until September 1940 to find the ideal format for his tightly drilled small group, when he made *A Chicken Ain't Nothin' But a Bird* (a piece that Calloway also recorded a matter of weeks later). In Jordan's version of the tune, he introduced an underlying shuffle rhythm, a trick that New Orleans trumpeter and vocalist Louis Prima had introduced on 52nd Street some years before, but which in Jordan's case provided the ideal bouncy underlay for his vocals. Many of the medium-tempo tunes he recorded over his next sessions, in 1941–2, were built over a similar, easy eight-to-the-measure shuffle.

Jordan excelled at this kind of comic-patter song, but he went on, in 1941, to make a big hit with a conventional blues built on a simple, straightforward twelve-measure sequence, with four beats to the bar – *I'm Gonna Move to the Outskirts of Town*. In due course Jordan moved further towards this kind of performance, and throughout the 1940s (between the recording bans) he produced a string of discs, from comic vehicles like *Five Guys Named Moe* to blues features like *Caldonia*, that pointed the way to rhythm and blues, a direction also followed by his one-time mentor Jesse Stone, who had worked with Jordan in a New York show called *Striver's Row* in 1941, but whose association with him went back to Chick Webb days. Stone told me:

> I was writing shows for the Apollo and other theaters and I had a seven-piece band of my own at the Renaissance Ballroom in New York. I knew Louis Jordan because he was playing in Chick's band as third saxophone player, and Chick got me in to rehearse his band and write some things for it. Louis came over to me and told me he wanted to sing, and could I ask Chick if I could make some arrangements for him to sing on. So I went and talked to Chick about it, and he said "Sure!" So I made a couple of arrangements for him, and the first night he did the tunes, I was there, to check on it. He broke up the house, they applauded him so much, but he didn't have a third tune to play. Anyway, after that, Chick wouldn't call those tunes any more, and I said to Louis, "Man, you're a threat! You should quit his band and get a band of your own and do that style of singing." At first he didn't want to leave a high profile band like Chick's; when he finally did, I turned over some of the members of my Renaissance Ballroom band to him, when he formed his first Tympany Five group at a little club [the Elks Rendezvous] on Lenox Avenue.[45]

Stone remained in touch with Jordan as a guiding light during the first years of his own band, known as the Tympany Five, and there are clear signs of a common approach in Stone's own rhythm-and-blues songs cut a decade or so later under the pseudonym Charles Calhoun.

However, another reason for Jordan's departure from Webb's band, in 1938, apart from the urging and advice of such mentors as Stone and the singer/trombonist "Snub" Mosley, was his complex relationship with the band's main vocalist, Ella Fitzgerald. Jordan had recorded some vocals with her, and he was also attracted to her, starting an affair by giving her presents and attention with an ardor that was not so keenly reciprocated. This was at a time when she was increasingly taking the limelight as the band's main singer, and sensing the danger of their relationship, Webb reckoned that she and the band would be better off without Jordan, despite his considerable skills as an instrumentalist. It proved to be the making of Jordan, and it was also the making of Fitzgerald, who ended up taking over Webb's band herself when the diminutive drummer died in June 1939.

As I suggested at the start of this chapter, women played a more significant role in the development of jazz singing than in any other area of early jazz, and after the initial efforts of Ethel Waters, Alberta Hunter, Adelaide Hall, and others, a new generation of major female singers emerged in the 1930s, of whom Ella Fitzgerald was one of the two principals, the other being Billie Holiday.

Fitzgerald's is one of those archetypal rags-to-riches stories in jazz – the more poignant in her case as it turns out to be true. She was more or less living on the streets when she won a talent contest at Harlem's Apollo Theater on November 21, 1934. After a few false starts, in the spring of 1935 she joined Chick Webb's orchestra as his female singer, mainly through the insistence of his now-forgotten male crooner Charles Linton.[46] Within a short time Fitzgerald became the focus of almost all Webb's recordings, appearing on 60 percent of the discs he made after she joined him in the spring of 1935 until his death.

On record, her earliest discs are not particularly special. Her first minor hit, *Sing Me a Swing Song (and Let Me Dance)*, made in June 1936, reveals little of the extraordinary range, melodic fluidity, and precise diction she was to develop. For much of the song she stays within a very narrow range, apart from a brief paraphrase of *Comin' Through the Rye*, and she has a curiously nasal tone, compared with the very clear and sweet sound of her later work. A better hint of her future qualities can be heard in the first discs she made under her own name five months later with a small group drawn from Webb's band, in particular, the ballad *My Last Affair*. Here, her timing, range, and choice of notes suggest a maturity far beyond her eighteen years. In particular, the way she hangs on to certain notes, adds subtle ornaments, and takes all the demanding intervals of the melody in her stride with perfect intonation, shows a very different approach to singing from the rough-and-ready sound of many of her contemporary male vocalists. She lacks the dramatic, actressy, nuances of Adelaide Hall or Alberta Hunter, but her musicality, and the confidence with which she inhabits the lyric and makes it sound a completely natural extension of her voice, is something new in jazz.

Webb had actually hired her to sing up-tempo numbers with his band, as a contrast to the tenor ballads of Linton, but it soon became obvious that she had an extraordinary ability as a ballad singer, coupled with a remarkable memory for tunes and lyrics. As time went on, she delivered songs with growing confidence and clarity, so that a ballad such as *This Time It's Real*, cut eighteen months or so after *My Last Affair*, is an altogether more assured and purposeful effort. Fitzgerald went on to perfect this aspect of her craft in a series of "Songbook" albums made for Norman Granz in the 1950s, in each of which she focused on the works of a particular composer or songwriter, including George Gershwin, Cole Porter, Harold Arlen, and Rodgers and Hart. When I heard her in person for the first time, in 1976, it was her continuing ability to sing these standard songs with conviction and vocal perfection that was most remarkable about her, and as the British critic Benny Green said, her "perfect intonation, natural ear for harmony, vast vocal range and purity of tone helped to make Ella's versions of these beautifully witty, gay, sad, lovingly wrought songs the definitive versions."[47]

However, even if her sublime interpretations of ballads eventually became the most celebrated and enduring aspect of Fitzgerald's art, she initially made her reputation in Harlem, and on the more widely spread juke-boxes of the late 1930s, with her more up-tempo numbers with Webb. Press reports of her singing with Webb at the Savoy Ballroom report that "when Ella sang, she had the whole crowd rocking with her."[48] In May 1938, she recorded her first hit record, a modified children's song called *A-Tisket, A-Tasket*, and this illustrates her more up-tempo style. The opening verses are rather plodding, with Fitzgerald almost running out of breath at one point, but from the minute the tune returns in a minor key, and Fitzgerald follows this with a series of inventive phrases that are answered by a band shout-back, she starts to improvise a new vocal line, and to play around with the rhythm just as a jazz instrumentalist would. She was the first female singer in jazz to master this instrumental quality of the voice to a level comparable to that of Louis Armstrong.

This hit record put Fitzgerald on the map, and she rapidly became the leading female jazz vocalist in the United States. At one point, six months before Webb's death, no fewer than four of her discs had become best-sellers, and these spanned her whole stylistic range.

One disc in particular, among those she made with Webb, demonstrates the way her more up-tempo singing skills would develop: a version of Trummy Young and Sy Oliver's *Tain't What You Do*, cut in February 1939. For most of the piece, Fitzgerald takes the same role as Young on his own recording with Lunceford – she sings and the band answers back. But for the final chorus there is an abrupt reversal – the band sings the main melody and Fitzgerald is left free to extemporize around the chorus of male voices. After a slightly hesitant start, she is soon producing a fine, sinuous line of brilliantly inventive scat. It is one of the earliest examples of her using her voice as a pure, wordless instrument, just as Adelaide Hall and Ivie Anderson had done with Ellington, but Fitzgerald surpassed them both. There had been hints of this talent a little earlier, and *You'll Have to Swing It*, *Organ Grinder's Swing*, and *Dipsy Doodle* all contain examples of her scat-singing, but in the case of *Tain't What You Do*, what stands out is the way she phrases, both above the other voices and over the accompanying rhythm. (Perhaps it is prophetic that the massed chorus ends with a shout of "Rebop!") This disc hints at her future skills and extraordinary freedom as a scat singer. With her astonishingly quick ear, a mind that allowed her to commit songs to memory rapidly, and a gift for mimicry, she was to become the outstanding scat singer in jazz.

In the opinion of her biographer, Stuart Nicholson, the turning point in the development of Fitzgerald's scat-singing came in October 1945, when she recorded a version of *Flyin' Home*, although this was not released until 1947. Her vocal line includes some phrasing culled from bebop, not least in the form of imitation or quotes, although her underlying natural style always remained within the harmonic boundaries of swing. As *Down Beat* said at the time: "Not only is her intonation perfect, her instrumental conception magnificent, the rhythmic effect climactic, but she tosses in some sly digs at Dizzy, Babs, Slam, Hamp, Leo Watson and others by singing variations on their better known ideas."[49]

Between making this disc and its release, she became a regular performer in Norman Granz's Jazz At The Philharmonic concerts (discussed in the next chapter), and perfected an act where, generally supported by a trio with pianist Hank Jones (or sometimes Raymond Tunia), she would run through the gamut of vocal techniques, from delicately balanced interpretations of ballads, with perfect diction and utter respect for the composer's conception, to free-for-all scatting, where she held her own against an array of the most formidable instrumental soloists in jazz. First in Granz's concert packages, and subsequently as a "single" artist with her own trio, appearing at the world's clubs, concert halls, and festivals, this was to be Fitzgerald's natural habitat, and she continued to appear with her trio until well into the 1990s, occasionally returning to the big-band format with Count Basie's band.

Basie's had also been one of the two orchestras with whom Billie

Holiday sang early in her career, the other being Artie Shaw's. However, like Fitzgerald, her natural forte was also the setting of a small group, either the seven- or eight-piece bands of Teddy Wilson or Eddie Heywood, with whom she recorded, or just a pianist or piano trio for her club and concert appearances. Like Fitzgerald, Holiday had a tough childhood, and she also began recording in her teens, first on a session that John Hammond organized with Benny Goodman, and then, as she entered her twenties, with Teddy Wilson's band. Unlike Fitzgerald, Holiday imposed her own distinctive musical personality on every song she sang. She seldom sang the written melody, and often changed the words, becoming a consummate improviser with both form and content.

Although the man she believed to be her father, and whose name she took, Clarence Holiday, was a jazz musician who had played with Fletcher Henderson, he never lived at home, and Holiday was mainly brought up by her mother, in a somewhat hand-to-mouth existence. At around the age of twelve, while her mother was running a small restaurant in Baltimore, Holiday herself worked in a "sporting house" (at this stage running errands for the madame, although after a history of abuse she ended up being drawn into prostitution), and there she heard Louis Armstrong's *West End Blues*, which made an indelible impression on her. "I heard a record by, as we call him, Pops, and it was called *West End Blues*, and he sang 'Ooh be doo,' and I would wonder why he didn't sing any words and he had this most beautiful feeling."[50] She went on to make clear that Armstrong was her main influence as she developed into a singer, and his timing and phrasing linger close to the surface in many of her subsequent recordings. There were other influences, too, and at various times she referred to Bessie Smith, Ethel Waters, and the Russian-born Jewish singer Sophie Tucker, who had once performed in blackface as a "coon shouter" and went on to be known as the "last of the Red Hot Mamas," as having made an impression on her.

Yet, in spite of all these influences, the most noticeable thing about Holiday is her complete originality. Her voice had a distinctive timbre, tinged with melancholy, and she managed simultaneously to sound both girlish and worldly-wise. Even her very first disc from 1933, *Your Mother's Son-in-law*, has these qualities, although for much of it a somewhat nervous teenage Holiday is shouting out the lyric for all she is worth over the boisterous Benny Goodman band. Her voice already has an emotional "catch" in it, and her phrasing glides across the beat, much as Armstrong's did.

By the time she was back in the studio with Wilson in 1935, her confidence had grown, and her characteristic approach was fully formed. On *What a Little Moonlight Can Do* she phrases like a saxophonist or trumpeter, easing through the melody in the most minimal, understated way. Despite treating the words with far less respect than Ella Fitzgerald would usually have done (except in her scatting mode), Holiday manages to communicate a knowing sense of fun, a clear idea of *exactly* what a little moonlight can do, and the combination of her interpretation of the lyric and her innately jazzy timing is irresistible. On this piece she is accompanied by a band that includes Roy Eldridge, Benny Goodman, and Ben Webster. Later, starting in January 1937, Wilson's sidemen often included members of the recently arrived Count Basie band, and Holiday forged a particularly strong musical partnership with tenorist Lester Young, whose light, airy solos and relaxed timing were a perfect counterpart to her voice. In this series of sessions organized by Teddy Wilson, his choice of musicians, skeleton arrangements, and exquisitely tasteful accompaniments led to the creation of a string of recorded masterpieces that, ironically, had no counterpart outside the studios. Apart from a short season at the Café Society and a few isolated gigs, Wilson seldom played for Holiday in public, but in the studio, surrounded by the cream of New York's swing players, they consistently made magic.

She made a different kind of magic appearing at Barney Josephson's Café Society Downtown, a Sheridan Square nightclub at the northern fringes of Greenwich Village that catered for integrated audiences from the outset, and identified itself with the liberal, Bohemian crowd. Holiday would sing three or four songs in each one-hour set, with a band initially led by trumpeter Frankie Newton. (When she was off stage, she was kept well away from her audience. Sometimes she took a cab ride up to Central Park between sets; other times she remained backstage. When she was backed at the club a little later by Eddie Heywood's band, Holiday asked trumpeter Doc Cheatham to sit outside her dressing-room and smoke his pungent pipe tobacco, in order to obscure the distinctive whiff of marijuana emanating from under her door.)

Unlike the hustle and bustle of some 52nd Street clubs, from her earliest appearances at Café Society, Josephson had his waiters control the noise of the crowd when Holiday was singing:

> I used to wonder at how quiet – for a nightclub – it was when I sang. I found out later that the waiters made a habit of going up to the noisiest characters and saying, "Miss Holiday is afraid you

aren't enjoying yourself, pay up and go." Well, that was news to me.[51]

A former shoe salesman, Josephson had firm ideas about how he would present the musicians who appeared at his club. Although John Hammond was involved in raising finance to run the Café Society and in suggesting who might play there, it was Josephson who put blues singer Josh White on a high stool and had him sing his protest songs, and it was Josephson who encouraged Holiday to sing a protest song of her own, *Strange Fruit*, written by a Jewish high-school teacher, Abel Meeropol, under the name Lewis Allan. The song was a graphic account of a Southern lynching, and Josephson knew how to make every performance a memorable event that would get both his club and his star singer talked about:

> I made her do it as her last number, and no matter how thunderous the applause, she had orders from me not to return for even a bow. I wanted the song to sink in, especially since it closed every show. The room was completely blacked out, service stopped, at the bar, everywhere . . . and everything was dark except for a little pin spot on her face. That was it. When she sang *Strange Fruit*, she never moved. . . . The tears never interfered with her voice, but the tears would come and just knock everybody in that house out.[52]

The song added a dimension to Holiday. As her biographer Donald Clarke suggests, this turned her from a very individual jazz singer into a *chanteuse*, someone who tells graphic and moving stories in song. Not long after she added the piece to her repertoire, her photograph appeared in *Time* magazine, and she cultivated her image as a dramatic figure dressed in white with a gardenia in her hair. In due course she took the politically sensitive subject-matter of *Strange Fruit* to most of the venues at which she sang, from the stage of the Apollo Theater to clubs across the United States, and it also became a hit record (despite being banned by many radio stations) when she recorded it in April 1939 for Milt Gabler's Commodore label, backed with the blues *Fine and Mellow*.

*Strange Fruit* was quite unlike any other jazz song of its time, and, indeed, was the first song to confront the question of race in such a direct way. Andy Razaf and Fats Waller's *Black and Blue* was the first high-profile protest song from the time Louis Armstrong recorded it in July 1929, and

Ethel Waters had made a stage success out of Irving Berlin's *Supper Time* (a piece recorded by Artie Shaw's white vocalist Helen Forrest), which includes a reference to lynching, but Holiday's song was of a different order. Its subtle, ironic lyrics were delivered in an equally subtle way, with a perfect balance between dignity, pain, and poignancy. In his study of the piece and its effect on the social and musical climate of the age, David Margolick suggests that it had a profound effect on the racial politics of jazz. Certainly its bleak, uncompromising message was at odds with the light, frothy love songs at which Holiday had hitherto excelled, and which were the normal fare for female singers in the swing era.[53]

Several of the most ardent musical campaigners for civil rights claimed inspiration from the song, Charles Mingus saying, "That's when I changed my idea of a song telling a story. That music is here to tell the white world the wrongs they done in race." Norman Granz was inspired to begin his campaign to desegregate the jazz audience after hearing of Holiday's experiences at Hollywood's Trouville Club, where, in a supreme irony, her black friends were prevented from being admitted to hear her perform the song. Max Roach, who went on to record such polemical pieces as his *Freedom Now!* suite, said: "She made a statement that we all felt as black folks. No-one was speaking out. She became one of the fighters. . . . She became a voice of black people and they loved this woman."[54] There was, perhaps, more of a political revolution inherent in this single song than all the bebop movement of the following decade.

However, not all Holiday's live performances included *Strange Fruit*, and, particularly as she grew older, she performed it less often, preferring to end her shows with a lighter piece such as her blues *Fine and Mellow*. This and a small number of other pieces were to become the core of her repertoire until her death, aged 44, in July 1959. Among this cluster of favorites, *God Bless the Child* **[CD track 9]** has a neat balance between her frothier songs of a woman wronged in love and the deeper gravitas of *Strange Fruit*. Her delivery, timbre, and phrasing show her unique approach to jazz singing – not least the rueful wail of "Money – you've got lots of friends," with which she enters the middle eight bars, trailing off her phrases like a saxophonist, and pitching slightly below the true note to create her distinctive melancholy, plaintive sound. In the years that followed many singers would fall under her influence, from Peggy Lee to Abbey Lincoln, and, more recently, Dee Dee Bridgewater.

There were many other successful female singers of the swing era, from the "canaries" of the white swing bands, such as Mildred Bailey, Helen

Forrest, Helen Ward, Martha Tilton, Mary-Ann McCall, and Lee Wiley, to such African-Americans as Una-Mae Carlisle, June Richmond, and Maxine Sullivan. Yet few of these made the same kind of innovative contribution as Fitzgerald and Holiday. It took until the 1940s for two singers to emerge who would make a similarly important impact on the development of jazz.

The first of these was Dinah Washington, whose gospel-tinged, powerful voice was a forerunner of the soul movement of the 1950s, and who became extremely successful in the pop world herself, until her premature death from an overdose of sleeping pills in 1963. She made several solo recordings on the West Coast in the early to mid-1940s in which she was paired with such accompanists as saxophonist Lucky Thompson and vibes player Milt Jackson, and she also sang for a period with Lionel Hampton's band, in both instances displaying her strong, clear approach to blues and ballads alike.

The second was Sarah Vaughan, whom I have already mentioned. She had been second pianist and vocalist with Earl Hines's 1943 big band at the time it included both Dizzy Gillespie and Charlie Parker. She went on to sing for Billy Eckstine, and made discs with Parker and Gillespie's small groups, including a version of *Lover Man*, made in 1945. By developing her craft as a singer as one of the bebop generation, and also because she was a pianist, Vaughan assimilated the harmonic and melodic aspects of bebop before any other female singer, although it took until the end of the 1940s and a record contract with Columbia for her to display the degree to which she had absorbed these. Nevertheless, even in some of her earliest discs she used her voice as an instrument more fully than even Fitzgerald, some critics believing that she abandoned any sense of lyrics altogether in pursuit of the musical demands of a song, thereby stretching Berendt's paradox to the limit.

# CHAPTER 11

# The New Orleans Revival and Mainstream Jazz

## Not So Much a Revival, More a Way of Life

> Within weeks of joining the [Bob Crosby] band, Haggart was producing scores that were highly original creations, which cleverly captured the spirit of the so-called "Golden Age of Jazz" of a decade earlier, but presented it as a contemporary sound.
>
> John Chilton, from *Stomp Off, Let's Go!*

During the relative stability of the swing era, there were several forces bubbling away under the surface of jazz. I have already looked at the main one, the emergence of bebop, which was the most forward-looking of the changes to emerge in the 1940s, but at the same time the forces of conservatism were at work, looking back at the days of King Oliver, Jelly Roll Morton, and the young Louis Armstrong as a "Golden Age," and seeking to recapture the gutsy excitement of 1920s "classic" jazz. Later in this chapter I will be looking at a new movement – the "revival," that sprang up in the late 1930s, driven mainly by record enthusiasts and collectors – to rediscover and record some of the pioneers of jazz. But a handful of bands kept the older styles of jazz alive in their work throughout the 1930s, or returned to those styles in preference to playing swing. I have mentioned 52nd Street groups such as those of Wingy Manone and Sharkey Bonano, as well as Glenn Miller's Dixieland arrangements for the Dorsey Brothers, but the most high-profile white swing band of the 1930s that made Dixieland a major element of its repertoire, in both big-band and small-group form, was the orchestra led by Bob Crosby.

607

Crosby came to front his orchestra on account of the demise of Ben Pollack's band. Pollack, as we know from Chapter 4, had three outstanding qualities – he was (until he largely gave up playing to focus on leading) an accomplished drummer; he had an uncanny ability for spotting talent; and he worked hard to establish his band as a leading society entertainment troupe, balancing the sweeter end of his repertoire with a fair proportion of jazz, so that when the Depression sliced into the entertainment world in 1929, his band kept working, almost as if nothing had happened. From 1925, in California, and subsequently in Chicago and New York, Pollack had recruited some marvelous players, especially from the up-and-coming Chicago generation a little younger than his own. Benny Goodman, Jimmy McPartland, Jack Teagarden, and Glenn Miller were among his sidemen.

Yet Pollack's blind spot became all too obvious as the 1930s began, when he courted and then married a former star of the *Ziegfield Follies*, singer Doris Robbins. In the company of Pollack's excellent band, which, by then, included reedmen Gil Rodin, Matty Matlock, and Eddie Miller; guitarist Nappy Lamare; and drummer Ray Bauduc (the last three from New Orleans, who imported the genuine flavor of the Crescent City into their playing), Robbins was second-rate, especially when she embarked on love-lorn duets with Pollack which left both band and audience squirming with embarrassment.

Sooner or later it became obvious to his musicians that Pollack was no longer booking his band on the best engagements, unless Robbins was included and given top billing, and before long, instead of being constantly in demand, the band began to experience periods of unemployment, entirely through Pollack's capricious behavior. Things came to a head in late 1934, after a date at Frank Sebastian's New Cotton Club at Culver City in California. The band piled up their music on Pollack's doorstep and retreated to the East Coast, staging a collective walk out that left Pollack without a band for the first time in nearly a decade. He soon recruited a new line-up which included Harry James, among others, but his band never regained the heights it had once enjoyed.

Things went rather better for his ex-sidemen. After landing a record deal and starting to get regular work in New York, saxophonist Gil Rodin – who had been instrumental in the walk out from Pollack, and worked to keep the band together – sought the assistance of the Rockwell and O'Keefe Agency in finding a new leader, and, before long, the band had agreed to take on Bing Crosby's younger brother Bob, who had been having an unhappy time as vocalist for Tommy Dorsey. The Bob Crosby Orchestra opened at the Roseland Ballroom in New York, in June 1935. Along with the star sidemen from Pollack's band already mentioned, two of the band's future chief arrangers were in the ranks: saxophonist Deane Kincaide and bassist Bob Haggart, who, together with Matlock, put together a new book of charts for the group.

In recruiting these three, Rodin had managed to find a uniquely complementary group of talents. Kincaide, whose arrangements were the most modern and swing-styled, left fairly early in the band's life, but Haggart and Matlock (who often vacated the clarinet chair for periods of time to concentrate on writing rather than playing) created the group's unique brand of big-band Dixieland, by featuring the strong New Orleans-style reed solos of Eddie Miller (or occasionally Matlock himself), plus the trumpet of Yank Lawson and the trombone of Joe Harris within each arrangement. These players were encouraged to play together in a Dixieland manner, backed by long notes or riffs from the other band members, creating the effect of hot small-group jazz within the massed forces of a big band.

On the road and during their residencies, the band, slowly but surely, began to build a public for its more overtly jazz-styled performances, which occupied a larger-than-normal proportion of its sets. Yet this was not immediately reflected in its recorded output, partly because (like Pollack's earlier version of the line-up) it reflected the received industry wisdom that white bands were not "hot" jazz bands in the same way as their African-American counterparts, but partly also because, although it kept very busy in the recording studios, its first discs included a run of syrupy ballads for Crosby, often with violins added to the robust-sounding ensembles. Its first session did contain Johnny Mercer's *The Dixieland Band*, arranged by Deane Kincaide, but the other tracks included *Flowers for Madame* and *In a Little Gypsy Tea Room*, sung by Crosby. All the signs were that it would continue to record material that was not representative of its normal programs, because the Decca company were unsure of how its brand of Dixieland would sell. Fortunately, in a tale familiar from many bands who had something new and different to offer, but were not allowed to play it on disc, a trade-off was arranged, and in return for backing the singer Connee Boswell, in April 1936, the band got to cut two of Bob Haggart's most characteristic charts, *Muskrat Ramble* and *Dixieland Shuffle*. From that point on, a regular sprinkling of similar, buoyant, hard-driving Dixieland pieces found their way onto disc alongside the endless ballads for Crosby or sessions with other singers, including the young Judy Garland.

As the 1930s wore on, the team of trumpet, trombone, clarinet, and tenor began to be featured, not only as a spotlighted group within arrangements for the whole band, but also as a group in its own right, which came to the front of the stage, accompanied by the rhythm section, as a popular aspect of the band's live concerts and club dates.

This element of the group's live performances was formalized into a band with a name during a benefit concert for pianist Joe Sullivan on April 18, 1937. The whole event was broadcast, and at one point the announcer mentions that the group featured will be "The Bob Cats" and the name stuck. (According to John Chilton, who has written the standard account of Crosby's band, the name was coined by the writer and enthusiast, Helen Oakley Dance.) The little "band-within-a-band" epitomized the whole essence of Crosby's orchestra. It never lost the sense of an impromptu jam session, and by featuring the main solo players as a small group, its hard-swinging Dixieland style crystalized into one of the finest small bands in jazz history.

In his monograph, Chilton quotes review after review pointing out how the large amount of solo space allocated to the main players, and the driving rhythm section, made this one of the most consistently jazz-orientated of all the white bands of the 1930s. In terms of consistency, it was better, even, for much of the time, than the contemporary Benny Goodman Orchestra, because of its authentic old-style jazz feeling.[1]

Many critics feel this was the result of Ray Bauduc's presence in the rhythm team, with his characteristic New Orleans drumming. His snare drum press rolls, two-to-the-bar bass drum, and off-beat patterns on his Chinese cymbals were an inspiration that had also driven along many a freelance studio band led by fellow New Orleanians Wingy Manone and Louis Prima. But Bauduc was not the only star; he fitted well with guitarist Nappy Lamare and the string bass of Bob Haggart, leaving pianist Bob Zurke room for his stride and boogie-woogie features and solos. Haggart's self-taught bass style was propulsive. He used to describe his unorthodox fingering in terms of "sausages," but this did not stop him from being one of the most sensitive and swinging bassists of the 1930s. He might have been a star on many other instruments as he had a talent for making music out of almost anything, but he put this to good use in his many compositions and arrangements, instinctively knowing how to write the best voicings and parts for all the instruments of the band.

In 1938, the Crosby group was joined by New Orleans clarinetist Irving Fazola, and although he was not the most cultured of men (comments from his fellow musicians recall his insatiable appetite for food, drink, and women, and his habits of swearing and breaking wind), he produced some of the most delicate and beautiful examples of the Crescent City's clarinet style. His solo feature, *Spain*, from February 1940, captures his limpid tone and the way his tender clarinet contrasted with the robust backing of the small group. "Faz" played alongside a number of different lead trumpeters, including Yank Lawson and Billy Butterfield, but consistently created the same kind of hot, small-group jazz in the Bob Cats, whoever was his partner. Another feature of the small band was the moment when Bob Haggart and Ray Bauduc would play together, and their famous duet on *Big Noise from Winnetka*, in which Bauduc played with his drumsticks on the strings of the bass while Haggart whistled the theme, arose as they played a warm-up set for an audience before a broadcast, becoming a regularly requested part of the band's "act."

Crosby's band survived the moment in 1938 when Yank Lawson and Charlie Spivak set off to join Tommy Dorsey, as the book of charts was strong enough to be equally effective with different musicians playing the main roles. Billy Butterfield happily took the lion's share of the solos that had previously fallen to Lawson. In due course the band also survived Fazola's departure (he was replaced by Matlock for a while, and then by the up-and-coming Hank d'Amico), and the incumbency of several other lead trumpeters including the Chicago veteran Muggsy Spanier.

By 1939, Crosby's band was making very good money, and as a co-operative venture, it made many of its musicians comfortably off. It had landed the coveted weekly radio show *Camel Caravan*, which it took over from Benny Goodman, and as well as breaking house records during an extended run at Chicago's Blackhawk Restaurant, it broke through to a national audience.

Musicians came and went, including pianist Bob Zurke, who left in an ill-fated venture to run his own band. Fortunately he was replaced by Benny Goodman's former pianist Jess Stacy, who proved ideal for the band. As the 1940s dawned, the band appeared in a movie (*Let's Make Music*) and went on touring and recording. Crosby was based on the West Coast in the early 1940s and his orchestra continued to work after war had broken out, playing ballrooms and appearing in films. However, in due course its members began to be drafted, or – in the case of two vital sidemen, Ray Bauduc and Gil Rodin – to enlist before they were drafted. A final tour was arranged for late 1942, and they set out to make as much money as possible for the co-operative before the band finally folded.

Crosby himself had decided to follow his brother into the world of movies, and signed a film contract for 1943, but he did do a brief tour early in the year with those of his sidemen who had not been drafted. This was the last genuine appearance of the Crosby band. For eight years the band had continued to keep the sounds of collectively improvised Dixieland alive, with compositions such as Haggart's *South Rampart Street Parade*, or his ballad *What's New?*, to add new standards to the corpus of traditional jazz that stood comparison with the classic works of Oliver and Morton. In his new pieces, among which were also *Dogtown Blues* and *My Inspiration*, as well as his fresh take on classic numbers such as *Savoy Blues*, Haggart's voicings were contemporary enough to feel in tune with the swing era, but the overall sense of the music was still that of the polyphonic ensembles of the "classic" jazz period. This was also the feeling perpetuated in the Crosby band's many reunions, and also in much of the work Haggart subsequently did in partnership with Yank Lawson, in a series of jointly led bands, for many years.

I mentioned that Chicagoan cornetist Muggsy Spanier joined the Crosby band in 1940, but the year before, he had been involved in a venture of his own which was a more conscious effort to return to the jazz of the past than the Crosby Orchestra's determination to keep Dixieland alive and revitalized. Spanier's 1939 Ragtime Band did, it is true, play a number of new compositions, but it is best remembered for returning to the classic repertoire of the 1920s, which Spanier had played himself as a member of the generation of young white Chicagoans who learned at first hand from Oliver and Armstrong. Spanier had been quite extensively recorded in the 1920s, so in some respects his band was an early example of the "revival," of self-consciously returning to the style he had demonstrated on his discs with the Bucktown Five (1924), the Stomp Six (1925), McKenzie and Condon's Boys, the Chicago Rhythm Kings, and the Jungle Kings (all 1928).

Early in 1929 Spanier had joined the large orchestra led by clarinetist Ted Lewis, who could hardly be called a jazz musician. He was a vaudeville entertainer in the old-fashioned sense, who played a little, sang a little, joked a little, and somehow crept into the public's imagination in a way that kept him working and successful during the Depression. He hired several good jazz musicians, however, and a handful of his discs have some sprightly jazz moments amid the corny songs and routines that make up the majority. There were also opportunities to travel, and, as mentioned in Chapter 5, Spanier came to Europe with Lewis in 1930, spending time in London (during which he recorded for bassist Spike Hughes, although the results were never issued).

Squeezed into a shiny silk uniform, and backing the top-hatted Lewis's routines, Spanier began to lead the life of a typical big-band sideman. There were occasional freelance recordings and club dates, he tried his hand at marriage in what turned out to be a short-lived disaster, and he increasingly joined fellow bandsmen, like his friend the trombonist George Brunis, in drinking sessions.

Nothing much changed in 1936, when Spanier transferred to the big band which Ben Pollack formed after the majority of his original band left to set up the Crosby Orchestra. He continued to drink and to contribute as much jazz to the band's concerts and records as circumstances would allow. In New Orleans, in 1938, after suffering a shake-up in a minor car accident, Spanier collapsed with a perforated ulcer. He almost failed to survive his admission to hospital, and it was the skill and care of Dr. Alton Ochsner that revived him. Ochsner later wrote to Spanier's second wife that "he had every complication a person could develop."[2]

Friends were aghast at the cornetist's condition, although they rallied round, and Ted Lewis contributed a generous check towards the hospital expenses. Nobody seriously thought a man who had been so ill would make the kind of recovery that would allow him to resume the grueling late nights and constant traveling of a jazz musician. Only Dr. Ochsner believed his tough patient had it in him to return to playing, and ensured that, for much of the year Spanier took to recover at the Touro Infirmary, his cornet was near at hand. Spanier was later to pay tribute to his medical team in two compositions, *Oh, Dr. Ochsner!* and *Relaxin' at the Touro*.

By April 1939, well over twelve months after his initial collapse, Spanier was ready to resume his career, and he chose to take his first steps as a leader in his own right, doing what he knew he could do best: playing the driving, powerful, small-group jazz he had learned as a young man. When Muggsy Spanier's Ragtime Band opened on April 29, it was just over a year since King Oliver had died, in obscurity, in Savannah, Georgia. His tunes formed a key part of the Ragtimers' programs, in the bizarrely decorated Panther Room at Chicago's Sherman Hotel, where the band played amid leopard-skin curtains, chairs, and wall decorations.

The band spent the first part of its career in Chicago, playing opposite some of jazz's greatest names during the months at the Panther Room. From the outset, it established a brassy, cohesive ensemble sound, and a driving four-to-the-measure beat that was infectious, and communicated easily and directly to its audience. It was consistently successful, playing for tea dances, and occasionally in the hotel's Old Town Room, and Spanier reported to the

*Melody Maker*: "There hasn't been a band like this in town since the days of Teschemacher."[3] It made its first recordings in Chicago, and played various conventions and theaters, including taking part in a "Battle of Swing" with Fats Waller's group at the Regal.

It then moved to New York in October, where it played at Nick's club in Greenwich Village. Spanier's achievement was to prove that old-style jazz could be a sell-out attraction at a major club in each of America's two main cities, and the sales of his eight records on Victor's Bluebird label – the individual sides becoming known to collectors as the "great sixteen" – grew around the world as the years went by. The cohesive power of the band's sound was in no small measure due to the close bond of experience between Spanier, clarinetist Rod Cless, and trombonist George Brunis, helped in the band's latter stages by the addition of pianist Joe Bushkin to the line-up. Other members of the band came and went, but despite changes of personnel and the absence of a guitar from all but the first records, the tight ensemble sound of Muggsy Spanier's Ragtimers became one of the most distinctive and immediately recognizable in jazz.

On a piece such as *Big Butter and Egg Man*, Spanier steered clear of emulating Louis Armstrong, instead preferring to remain in the middle range of the cornet and focusing on rhythmic drive, much as he had done in the 1920s. On this piece George Brunis urges the cornetist on with shouts of encouragement during a final solo that moves each phrase further and further upwards, showing that he and Spanier had learned a thing or two from Ted Lewis about how to add a sense of theater to their discs, and there are similar contributions from Brunis on *Dinah*, including a vocal and a dramatic tempo change. Comparison of alternate takes recorded by the Ragtime Band shows that its routines were fairly fully worked out, even though Rod Cless reported that the band "were all fakers and could handle the acts without orchestrations,"[4] and despite its overall archaic approach it followed Crosby's lead in adapting some swing-era ideas, such as the long-note backing from the other front-line instruments behind individual solos, thereby retaining a sense of the full-ensemble texture.

Despite its name, the band played little actual ragtime – the only recorded example is *Eccentric Rag*, complete with all its multi-part structure and solo breaks, although the band's urgent tempo is considerably faster than the stately pace advocated by Joplin for the performance of this type of music. Nevertheless, the band revived and repopularized several classics from the 1920s, including *At the Jazz Band Ball*, *Dippermouth Blues*, *Livery Stable Blues*, and *Riverboat Shuffle*.

At the end of 1939 the band broke up, and Spanier returned to Ted Lewis before joining Crosby. Despite his success, he had found it hard to get his band re-booked anywhere except a club like Nick's, which tended to feature the older styles of jazz, and, furthermore, Victor showed no interest in recording more sides, despite encouraging sales figures. Spanier went on briefly to lead a big band, and then reverted to Dixieland small groups for the rest of his life, although none of these had the same impact as his Ragtime Band.

Virtually all Spanier's musicians had played in swing orchestras of one kind or another – Brunis and Spanier with Lewis, Cless in a commercial dance band at Chicago's Silhouette Club, bassist Bob Casey in the NBC studio band, pianist Joe Bushkin with Bunny Berigan, and tenorist Nick Caiazza with Joe Haymes. They viewed the Ragtime Band as a collective reaction against swing – the opportunity to play loose-limbed, predominantly improvised jazz, around a core of head arrangements. And it was a similar reaction to the restrictive straitjacket of playing stock big-band charts that led trumpeter Lu Watters to form his Yerba Buena Jazz Band at almost the same time, over on the West Coast, in San Francisco. His clarinetist, Bob Helm, who initially played in Watters's large swing orchestra at Sweet's Ballroom, told me how their new band evolved out of after-hours jams at the Big Bear Tavern:

> Some of the swing arrangements got pretty boring and repetitive to play four or five times a night, and six nights a week. So all of us jazz musicians were sort of confined to playing these charts in the seven ballrooms in the Bay Area, or the few clubs and theaters in town. In order for us to blow, or to let off steam, somebody discovered this place in a canyon over the Berkeley Hills, obscure enough so you didn't have a lot of other musicians all dropping in, playing in different styles. We used to gather there after two in the morning, when the nightclubs in town had closed, and blow off steam. If they had enough people, the owners would keep the bar open, and have a barbecue, so it became a gathering place for jazz musicians. It was Lu and [trombonist] Turk [Murphy] and I who started the Yerba Buena Band there. The 1939 World's Fair was in progress, and as we were rehearsing, I remember we talked about how great it would be to be able to play all jazz, and not have to play any pop tunes, apart from maybe a condescension to the pop tunes of the day here and there, and if the worst came

to the worst maybe a waltz or a polka, in order to hold down a job, but primarily, the music would be jazz music of the kind we liked. The old two, three, or four strain tunes that would not pall if you had to play 'em, two or three times a night.[5]

It took until late in 1940 for Lu Watters to find a place for his new eight-piece band to play in a more public setting, at the Dawn Club, in the Union Square district of San Francisco, where the city's Hot Music Society held its monthly meetings. But in contrast to the informal swing jam sessions that had been the norm there in 1939 and 1940, Watters had firm ideas about the approach of his new group, which featured himself and Bob Scobey in a two-trumpet line-up redolent of Oliver's Creole Jazz Band:

> I wanted to adhere to the early Chicago style of King Oliver and Louis Armstrong and to extend it creatively while remaining inside the traditions laid down. . . . King Oliver, for instance . . . had such melodic impact. People think a great melody is one that is easy to remember, the "hummable" type. Well, that quality is important, but a great melody needs a little more than that; a little complexity, just enough intellectual content to make it surprising.[6]

This marked out Watters's approach from that of the Crosby band or Spanier. Whereas the former embodied a continuation of a tradition, and the latter a reversion to his own earlier work, Watters went in for a conscious, intellectualized recreation of what African-American musicians had been playing in 1920s Chicago. In due course, there would be other bands around the world who followed more or less exactly the same thinking, such as George Webb and Humphrey Lyttelton in Britain, or Graeme Bell in Australia, but Watters was the first to do this; and alongside his somewhat lumbering arrangements of classic Armstrong Hot Five pieces, such as *Muskrat Ramble* and the *Irish Black Bottom*, Watters gradually added a number of originals in comparable style: *Terrible Blues*, *Big Bear Stomp*, *Emperor Norton's Hunch*, and *Annie Street Rock*.

The band really came together musically at the Dawn Club, coalescing there from an after-hours jam-session group into a regular line-up that specialized in Watters's characteristic repertoire. Bob Helm remembered that there was one problem they had not anticipated:

> The audience was enthusiastic, but they didn't know the names of
> any of the tunes, so we had to make a flash-board on the
> bandstand, and for each piece we'd put up "foxtrot," or "waltz,"
> and the name of the tune and its composer. We noticed that that
> got some favorable response, so in due course we did what
> classical string quartets do — we handed out the program at the
> door for all the five sets for the evening.[7]

Photographs of the band at the Dawn Club show not only the little
blackboard with the tune titles on it, but also the band's very unorthodox
way of lining up, with the rhythm section in front and the two trumpets,
trombone, clarinet, and tuba playing over the heads of banjo, drums, and
piano. I asked Bob Helm why they took to doing this:

> The rhythm section had a tendency to get lethargic on slow tunes,
> which had a terrible effect on us as a front line, and we thought,
> "Perhaps they're not hearing what we're trying to do in the front
> line, so let's put the rhythm section in front and the horns in
> back, or over their heads," and it did help . . . with both the
> lethargy on slow tunes and the fact they tended to speed up on the
> fast ones.[8]

In due course Helm left the Yerba Buena after a row over the rhythm
section's tendency to drag, but during the time he was in the band, and
when he returned to the fold at the end of the war, the main rhythmic
momentum came, as he suggested, from the boisterous front line, its big
brassy sound carrying all before it, and making up for the shortcomings in
the rhythm section. This was to be something of a feature of the West Coast
revivalists, and when various members of Watters's line-up went on to form
their own bands – notably trumpeter Bob Scobey, trombonist Turk Murphy,
and Helm himself – they retained this feeling that it was the collective front
line – not the piano, banjo, tuba, and drums – that was the rhythmic
powerhouse of their line-ups. Indeed, Murphy played for some years with a
drumless rhythm section, relying on banjo, piano, and tuba (or occasionally
double bass) to support the rhythmic vigor of his front line.

Although all Watters's records have a rather refreshing feeling of
amateurism about them, the majority of his musicians were well-seasoned
professionals who had, like Spanier's sidemen, played in a variety of swing
groups. They played their music this way out of choice, its rough edges and

collective improvisation cocking a snook at the precision riffs and slick section work of the swing bands. And it struck a chord with some high-profile record producers, Nesuhi Ertegun and Norman Granz both recording Watters, and Columbia's George Avakian making several sessions with Turk Murphy.

These bands gave rise to a long-lived local tradition which was kept alive well into the 1980s at a succession of San Francisco venues, starting with the Italian Village and moving on to Watters's club, Hambone Kelly's, and Murphy's Earthquake McGoon's bar.[9] A mythology grew up around the clubs, particularly McGoon's, which at one stage featured the added attraction of one of the country's biggest collections of magic tricks, belonging to an illusionist called Carter the Great. Murphy fueled the legend of himself and his music as that of rough, tough, rugged, hard-drinking types, but he, in particular, turned out to be a skilled arranger with a remarkable degree of subtlety and invention, in contrast to his deliberately perpetuated public image. His work for George Avakian included what might be regarded as a very early example of a "concept album," devoted to the works of Jelly Roll Morton, and on a piece such as *Mister Jelly Lord*, which Turk Murphy's Jazz Band recorded for Columbia on September 14, 1953, the subtlety of Turk Murphy's arrangement stands out. It is faithful to the spirit of Morton, but the chord voicings for the front line, particularly towards the end, suggest an imaginative and unusual ear. His skills were not lost on those who heard his work, and Murphy was in due course responsible for some very well-known arrangements indeed – not least the famous Louis Armstrong All Stars version of *Mack the Knife*, from 1955.

In 1943, starting with occasional Sunday afternoon jazz sessions in July, at the "Chamber Jazz Room" on Golden Gate Avenue, and culminating in a formal concert at San Francisco's Geary Theater, Turk Murphy was involved in the "Hot Seven," led by veteran New Orleans trumpeter Bunk Johnson, and made up of Murphy, clarinetist Ellis Horne, and other Lu Watters sidemen. This group (which scored highly in a "battle of bands" against the local swing sextet led by the now-forgotten Saunders King), and the resulting recordings it made, was one of the first instances of younger white revivalists joining forces with father figures of the music, and it came about as a consequence of the movement I mentioned earlier, initiated by record collectors and amateur historians, to rediscover and record the "pioneers" of jazz.

## Burgundy Street Blues

> King Bolden and myself were the first men that began
> playing jazz in the city of dear old New Orleans and his band
> had the whole of New Orleans real crazy and running wild
> behind it. Now that was all you could hear in New Orleans,
> that King Bolden's band, and I was with him.
>
> Bunk Johnson, in a letter to researcher and author<br>Bill Russell in 1939

Even in 1939, the idea of record collectors and jazz enthusiasts bringing together their favorite musicians to make records was not a new idea. As discussed in Chapter 5, the English bass player Spike Hughes had crossed the Atlantic in 1933 to assemble a "dream" big band of New York's finest black jazz instrumentalists to play his compositions and arrangements. He was followed two years later by another British bandleader, Ray Noble, who assembled a similar all-star collection of white players.

Both Hughes and Noble, however, were working leaders, playing music of the age with the finest American musicians available. By contrast, when the French author and collector Hugues Panassié arrived in the United States, in late 1938, he not only assembled a "dream" band, but in doing so, he deliberately attempted to recreate an earlier period from jazz history by seeking out trumpeter Tommy Ladnier, a veteran of Fletcher Henderson's and Sam Wooding's bands, reuniting him with Sidney Bechet. At the start of the decade, Bechet and Ladnier together had cut some splendid examples of New Orleans-style jazz, and Panassié hoped to rekindle some of the spirit of those earlier discs, at a time when musical fashion was focused away from the classic forms of early jazz.

By December 1938, Ladnier's lip was in poor shape, and his playing was a shadow of its former self, leaving him unable to recapture his fiery style from his days with Henderson, or which he had displayed in a masterly *Maple Leaf Rag* with Bechet's Feetwarmers in 1932. Yet some of the sides he and Bechet made for Panassié, like *Royal Garden Blues* and the plaintive *If You See Me Comin'*, can properly be described as the very first jazz revival discs. In the late 1930s, a number of players who had made their names in the 1920s were still actively recording for the major companies, even though the best such records, by Jelly Roll Morton or Bechet (with his regular Victor recording group), sounded anachronistic to many listeners. Apart from one session that he organized for Frankie Newton, James P. Johnson, and an all-star swing band, Panassié went even further against the prevailing fashion and sought to reunite instrumentalists of an earlier generation whose work he already knew from record. But what happened next, spurred on by the publication of the book *Jazzmen*, edited by Frederick Ramsey Jr. and Charles E. Smith, was the start of a movement to record legendary players, many of whom had never before been heard on disc.

In 1939, jazz itself was still only about a quarter of a century old, so musicians who had been young tigers at the start of the 1920s were still for the most part in middle age and able to play. The record collector, violinist, and *avant-garde* percussionist Bill Russell, who wrote two chapters of *Jazzmen*, struck up correspondence with many jazz pioneers. He admired the drumming of Baby Dodds, he traveled to hear Jelly Roll Morton in the flesh, and from his Pittsburgh home, he and Frederick Ramsey finally made contact with Bunk Johnson, a legendary, but shadowy, figure.

Johnson's replies, full of hubris and self-aggrandisement, formed the basis of Russell's chapters in the book, creating a somewhat spurious portrait of Bolden, but in the process enthusing a small coterie of Russell's fellow collectors to retrieve Johnson from the obscure plantations of New Iberia where, toothless and retired from music, he drove a truck for a rice mill. If you believed Johnson's own accounts, he was born in December 1879 in New Orleans, and was therefore around to witness the dawn of jazz. Subsequent researchers have come to the conclusion that Bunk was ten years younger, giving the lie to most of his claims to have been a pioneer member of Buddy Bolden's band, but equally never disproving that he was indeed the man whom Sidney Bechet, Zutty Singleton, and Lee Collins remembered hearing in New Orleans when they were growing up.[10] One fact never in doubt was his talent as a storyteller, particularly concerning himself.

Johnson cajoled a group of enthusiasts into subscribing for a local dentist (Dr. Leonard Bechet, Sidney's brother) to make him a set of false teeth so that he could play again. He only ever used his new teeth to play, his gums having hardened for most everyday purposes, and the dentures actually hurt him if they were left in for any period of time. For the rest of his life, Johnson was forever leaving the teeth behind in bars or on buses or trains.

His embouchure newly equipped, he made some tentative test recordings at his home for the field-recordist Mary Karoley, and by mid-1942, two sets of enthusiasts had made separate plans to record him properly, playing once more with a band and bringing the Bolden era magically to life once more. Dave Stuart, who ran the Jazz Man record store in Los Angeles, came to New Iberia with a couple of enthusiastic friends, while the second collection of fans consisted of Bill Russell himself and Gene Williams, a young writer who published the magazine *Jazz Information*. When they all arrived in Louisiana in mid-1942, they worked together to set up the inaugural date for Johnson on Dave Stuart's Jazz Man record label, an offshoot of his shop.

The band was recruited by the hit-or-miss method of driving from bar to bar or club to club in New Orleans, seeking out players who had been recommended to Russell by word of mouth. In fact, very few of those originally mentioned were located, or – once they had been found – agreed to play. Then Johnson recalled a clarinetist who had been alongside him a few years earlier at a dance, when bandleader Evan Thomas was violently murdered. The clarinetist was called George Lewis, and he was a friend of Jim Robinson, the trombonist who had appeared on Sam Morgan's famous 1920s recordings, and who had also played on a solitary session by the trumpeter Kid Rena in 1940. Before long, together with Robinson and Lewis, the team had recruited bassist Austin Young (uncle of Lester Young) and pianist Walter Decou. When they eventually gathered to record at Grunewald's music store, the band was filled out with banjo player Lawrence Marrero and drummer Ernest Rogers.

Nine full sides were cut on June 11, 1942, and eventually issued along with discs of Bunk reminiscing. "Bunk himself was breathtakingly good," wrote Gene Williams. "He remembered accurately the old tunes he wanted to record and taught the younger men, when necessary, some of their parts. He played the lead straight and then took off effortlessly on endless beautiful variations."[11]

Gene Williams then brought a broadly similar line-up (with three replacements: trombonist Albert Warner, bassist Chester Zardis, and drummer Edgar Mosley) into the San Jacinto Hall on October 2 to make a further fourteen sides. To the enthusiasts who had "discovered" Johnson these were vitally important documents, establishing a direct connection to Bolden, the "first man of jazz." On both occasions, Johnson fueled the myth and the sense of his connection with the past by opting to play some unusual pieces from the dim recesses of his memory, negotiating complex ragtime pieces with ease (and much more confidence than his fellow musicians), while also throwing in a few popular songs of the day. Gene Williams recalled:

> The performances are arranged the way Bunk wanted them, few
> solos, emphasizing the creative strength of the old-style New

Orleans ensemble. Bunk's thrilling lead and Lewis's busy variations, led the band through the fine melodies in a way that will make many jazz enthusiasts furious at the circumstances which deprived us until now, of so much great music.[12]

The fury of some jazz enthusiasts was countered by the incredulity of others who, bred on the smooth sounds of the swing era, could scarcely believe that anyone would want to bother with Bunk's apparently far more primitive approach. In the midst of this, Bunk's supporters pointed to a *Down Beat* feature on Bunk, in which his claims to have helped teach Louis Armstrong were apparently confirmed by Satchmo himself, who said: "What a man! Just to hear him talk sends me. I used to hear him in Frankie Dusen's Eagle Band in 1911. Did that band swing! How I used to follow him around. He could play funeral marches that made me cry."[13] The search for a figurehead of the revival movement was over: Bunk Johnson was its self-appointed living link with history.

"Up in San Francisco, Bunk was a legend, he could do no wrong," wrote Kid Ory's clarinetist Joe Darensbourg, concerning Johnson's trip to California to work with Turk Murphy, the year after his recording debut. Darensbourg, a sophisticated Creole musician, was piqued that a drunkard with "no chops" and exaggerated tales of how he had "taught that gatemouth sonofabitch Louis Armstrong" should command so much attention.[14] In the West, as well as his recordings with Murphy, Johnson recorded discs demonstrating "Bolden's style," and his success helped to convince a group of enthusiasts, among whom, once again, were Gene Williams and Bill Russell, that he should be brought to New York to take his chance in the jazz capital of the world.

In 1943 and 1944, Russell was occupied making numerous further recordings in New Orleans, where, by focusing on non-union players, he avoided the problems of the A.F.M. ban. He launched his American Music record label in the process, and he also worked with Blue Note's director Alfred Lion to issue some remarkable discs by Johnson's clarinetist George Lewis on the Climax label, with some fiery trumpeting from Avery "Kid" Howard, another Crescent City pioneer, notably on a dramatic version of *Climax Rag*, which gave its name to the imprint. In May 1945, Russell also made the first documentary recordings of a New Orleans Brass Band, in a specially assembled group led by Johnson. Finally, Russell went to New York, later that summer, to work with Gene Williams on bringing their "discovery" to the city.

Bunk Johnson's subsequent arrival at a down-at-heel Second Avenue ballroom called the Stuyvesant Casino was greatly hyped, but even so those who backed him lost money. Tensions emerged rapidly between Johnson and drummer Baby Dodds, and, later, with George Lewis, who suffered excruciating dental problems. Yet somehow the band held together, and despite a growing waywardness, Johnson displayed some shreds of loyalty to Bill Russell and Gene Williams, who had done so much to relaunch his career, by seeing out the engagement, despite frequent drunken benders and an elastic sense of time-keeping. His discs for Victor and Decca, which were made during the course of his New York visit, put Johnson's vigorous brand of homespun revivalism onto major record labels that spread his work far more widely than Jazz Man, Jazz Information, or Russell's tiny independent American Music company had managed.

Of his Decca sides, *Tishomingo Blues* stands out for some forceful playing by Johnson, the plaintive clarinet of Lewis, and a solo by pianist Alton Purnell that uses a decidedly superior instrument to one provided for his Victor appearances. Nevertheless, the Victor sessions, which produced eight sides, had a greater impact round the world, and musicians in various lands, inspired by the rising trot of *One Sweet Letter from You*, or the moving, heartfelt *Franklin Street Blues*, began to play in a way that emulated the band's collective ensembles, with relatively few solos. This approach offered a radically different take on "New Orleans jazz" from the 1920s discs of Oliver, Morton, and Armstrong, or the more sophisticated revivalism of Sidney Bechet. Johnson's angular, gently syncopated lead, with its sense of ragtime, and Lewis's loping arpeggiated ornaments, punctuated by Robinson's brash tailgate trombone, had quite a different sound from any earlier recordings, and there is strong argument in retrospect for saying that, contrary to the claims of Bill Russell or Gene Williams, this was not a "revival" of a previous style so much as a new form of traditional jazz that was very much of its time.

In the 1980s, in the wake of research into Johnson's life by Donald Marquis and Lawrence Gushee, that put forward the theory of Johnson having been born later than he admitted, thereby discrediting his claimed association with Bolden, critics tended to devalue his trumpeting as well, such as J. R. Taylor, who wrote "conclusions about the earliest jazz trumpet styles must be drawn cautiously from his recorded work, for his best solos and ensemble lead parts resemble those of Louis Armstrong, by whom they may have been influenced."[15]

This is an extraordinary observation, first because Armstrong himself made it extremely clear that in some respects Johnson influenced *him*, and second because a comparison of the common repertoire that the men put on record displays virtually no direct connections between Johnson's playing and Armstrong's. Armstrong wrote that although Johnson did not "teach" him in a formal sense, he absorbed the old man's sound, as he "would sit in front of that horn . . . in the days of the honky tonks." Overall, however, he felt that Johnson mainly affected his tone rather than his phrasing: "Bunk didn't offer nothing but tone. He didn't have the get-up-and-go that Oliver did: he didn't create a phrase that stays with you."[16]

Johnson's lead and solos on those pieces where Armstrong had already cut well-known versions, such as his 1944 American Music versions of *St. Louis Blues* and *Dippermouth Blues*, are immediately recognizable as Johnson. Compared to Armstrong he occupies a more limited range, he phrases behind the beat, and he articulates his notes in less fluid phrasing, retaining the simple syncopation and detached, slightly staccato delivery of ragtime. He relies on diminished chords to a greater degree, and he generally plays melodic adornments to the original tune rather than the complete re-composition preferred by Armstrong.

Pianist Don Ewell, who occasionally replaced Purnell at the Stuyvesant, and later had a trio with Johnson, told me when we worked together in the 1980s that he thought this very melodic style of Johnson's was "a form of contemporary folk music," and others who heard his band during its New York run have tended to agree, including Bechet's pupil Bob Wilber.[17] However, at the time, this was not a perception that was widely voiced, and Johnson's music became a key element in the polarization of ancient and modern forms of jazz in New York, and, later, throughout the world. Critics, led on the one hand by dyed-in-the-wool traditionalist Rudi Blesh, and on the other by *Metronome* magazine's Barry Ulanov, took sides in the debate discussed in Chapter 7, which was characterized by Leonard Feather as being between the true lovers of jazz (modernists) and reactionary "moldy figges."

It is a supreme irony that, despite his typecast role in this debate, Bunk Johnson himself always wanted to record with more swing-orientated musicians. Both his farewell to the West Coast, sessions featuring his "V-Disc Veterans," with Wade Whaley and Floyd O'Brien; and his so-called "Last Testament Band," his final New York recordings, found him in the company of swing players. The latter session – even though it focused on the ragtime repertoire – included trombonist Ed Cuffee and clarinetist Garvin Bushell, as well as New Orleans compatriots Wellman Braud and Danny

Barker, all of whom were, by then, veterans of the big bands. This was the generation of men whose stylistic background made it hardest for them to find regular work in the years that followed, but they would surely have identified with Bunk as he diligently bought the latest sheet music to play the current hits at the Stuyvesant, sharing his sense of mystification that Gene Williams and the other critics only wanted him to play tunes from the 1920s and before. Many of these players would have gone along and joined in on the nights that Bunk went uptown from the Stuyvesant to sit in on 52nd Street with the swing players of the day.

Johnson's "last testament" session came from his final visit to the North in 1947, and he died back in New Iberia two years later, his stream of letters gradually changing from optimism to despondency and, finally, becoming requests for help and money, after he lost the use of his left arm in a stroke. The privately recorded "last testament" masters were not issued until almost three years after his death, when George Avakian brought them out on Columbia.

Nevertheless, Johnson's influence – mainly on account of his Decca and Victor sessions, but also on over 100 other sides recorded for various smaller labels – would continue to be felt for many years after his death. His former sideman George Lewis went on to be a figurehead of the "revival" of New Orleans jazz, and toured and recorded widely in the 1950s and 1960s. Among the bands that Lewis played with as a soloist in his late-flowering international career was that of Ken Colyer in England. Colyer's band had its origins in the Crane River Jazz Band, formed in March 1949, before Johnson's death, and its second cornetist Sonny Morris told me how its stylistic orientation had been determined from the outset, when Colyer arrived to join the nascent band, with a wind-up gramophone and a pile of the Victor 78s by Bunk Johnson, announcing: "This is what we should be playing."[18]

In addition to inspiring Colyer and other musicians in various parts of the world, the "revival" movement involved the rediscovery of numerous other American pioneers who were encouraged to "recreate" earlier styles of jazz. During the years that Bunk Johnson was driving a truck, one of the greatest names in 1920s classic jazz, whose playing adorned many a disc by Louis Armstrong and King Oliver, had settled in California to breed chickens. Trombonist Kid Ory was always a wily businessman, had been a pioneer of African-American jazz on the West Coast, and took to farming to counter the effects of the Depression. Throughout the 1930s, he kept his hand in as an occasional musician, still playing trombone from time to time, or taking some gigs on double bass. At almost the same time as Johnson was being brought before the microphone in Louisiana by Dave Stuart and Gene Williams, Ory took up his trombone professionally again to play with Barney Bigard, and in 1944 his career restarted in earnest when he appeared on the Orson Welles TV show in Los Angeles, though for years afterwards, as he moved into larger houses and better neighborhoods, he generally kept an incubator and a run full of chickens.

Billed as a legend of jazz and surrounded by other pioneers including, briefly, clarinetist Jimmie Noone, Ory played the role to the maximum. He had never forsaken music as thoroughly as Johnson had, and had rapidly progressed from playing at a rough joint called the Tip Toe Inn to working all round the Los Angeles area, as well as recording, first for Nesuhi Ertegun and Dave Stuart's Crescent label; then for an enthusiastic physician, Doc Exner, who ran another small-scale record label; and, eventually, for Decca and Columbia. With Mutt Carey's punchy, staccato trumpet lead almost unchanged since their first discs together in 1921, Ory recorded a cross-section of Dixieland standards such as *High Society* and *Ballin' the Jack*, but his best work came on his own up-tempo compositions, such as *Muskrat Ramble* and *The Girls Go Crazy*, or his quaint, long-remembered songs in Creole *patois*, such as *Blanche Touquatoux* or *C'est l'autre can-can*. Ory's transition to success was also helped when Barney Bigard helped him to collect thousands of dollars' worth of unpaid royalties for songs he had written in the 1920s. His fame spread on the West Coast and beyond with a series of broadcasts for the AFRS in the late '40s from Hollywood's Beverly Cavern, and several more radio shows in the early 1950s from San Francisco's Club Hangover. He recorded consistently from 1944 until the early 1960s, with his largest volume of material on the Good Time Jazz and Verve labels.

The Kid Ory band was brilliantly marketed by Good Time Jazz in the mid-1950s, who even included recipes for Creole food on the LP sleeves, and with its old stagers like pioneer bassist Ed Garland, trumpeter Alvin Alcorn, drummer Ram Hall, and guitarist Bud Scott, the band had an immediately identifiable sound that survived numerous minor changes of personnel. Ory could be difficult when drunk, but he was a stickler for rehearsal and discipline, and the little arranged tags that appeared in his tunes behind solos or to mark the ends of choruses were testimony to his hard work. Ory first took his band overseas for a European tour in 1956, and three years later he followed in the wake of George Lewis by undertaking another international visit. Lewis brought his band of New Orleans veterans to Europe in January 1959, aged 58, but when Ory followed between September and November of that year, he was already over 70.

The publicity surrounding Lewis made much of his frail stature and long-term health problems, but he generally played powerfully and in a manner highly charged with emotion, helped by the inclusion in his repertoire of hymns, spirituals, and his poignant *Burgundy Street Blues*. Ory, by contrast, appeared quite vigorous, but his own playing had declined somewhat from the early days of the revival in the 1940s, and was a minimalist skeleton of his pioneering work on 1920s discs with Morton and Armstrong. It was memorably described by British critic Max Jones as having "the finesse of a shipyard riveter."[19] Nevertheless, his touring band, with Henry "Red" Allen on trumpet, had all the hallmarks of a well-drilled Ory ensemble, from its neatly arranged tags to Alton Redd's heavy off-beat drum accents (a stylistic device he claimed Ory insisted upon).

Allen made no concessions to revivalism, and he played with Ory exactly as he would have done with his own sextet at the Metropole in New York: fizzing solos, packed with new ideas, jostling with elements of how a New Orleans lead horn had been played when he was growing up. Allen's larger-than-life stage presence, and his habits of playing one-handed while reaching out to the audience, or pointing skywards, were at odds with the aura of sincerity and down-home charm exuded by such revivalists as George Lewis, and were more in keeping with the stage mannerisms of Louis Armstrong, who had returned to leading a Dixieland-style group of his own, the All Stars, in 1947.

Armstrong's decision to scale down from a big band was forced by the same economic circumstances as the demise of other large orchestras in the wake of World War II. His return to a traditional format was fueled, to some extent, by revivalism, by the critical success of a small group including Ory and Barney Bigard, with which he had played in the 1946 film *New Orleans*, and, particularly, by the enthusiasm of the New York promoter Ernie Anderson, who persuaded Armstrong's manager, Joe Glaser, that the trumpeter could make a far more lucrative living touring with a six-piece band than with an entire orchestra that often played for as little as $350 per night. Anderson made his point by giving Glaser $1000 to keep the big band at home and secure Armstrong's services for the first "All Stars" concert at New York Town Hall.[20] In the wake of this, Armstrong's line-up was firmly established, with Jack Teagarden on trombone, Barney Bigard on clarinet, Dick Cary (soon replaced by Earl Hines) on piano, Arvell Shaw on bass, and Sid Catlett on drums. This band's first extended residency at Billy Berg's club, later in 1947, was, in its way, an even more significant landmark for traditional jazz than the month that Charlie Parker and Dizzy Gillespie had spent there in 1945–6 had been for bebop. In the years that followed, the line-up remained relatively stable, having a slow turnover, with clarinetists Edmond Hall, Joe Darensbourg, Buster Bailey, and Joe Muranyi passing through the ranks, along with trombonists Trummy Young and Tyree Glenn, pianist Billy Kyle, bassists Milt Hinton and Mort Herbert, and drummers Barrett Deems, Cozy Cole, and Danny Barcelona, among others.

Kid Ory apparently turned down the chance to become the All Stars' first trombonist on financial grounds, but he continued to lead his own band until 1966, when he finally retired for the second time. The Armstrong All Stars continued until shortly before the trumpeter's death in 1971. In most biographies of Armstrong, the 24 years he spent fronting the All Stars tend to be glossed over and treated as an afterthought, compared to his hugely influential work of the 1920s and 1930s. Yet this is a little unbalanced. The All Stars, playing virtually every night of the year, and touring incessantly, brought traditional jazz to a huge international audience round the world, and Armstrong lived up fully to his sobriquet "Ambassador Satch." If, on the one hand, he courted public acclaim and fortune by singing such lightweight pieces as *Hello Dolly*, *Wonderful World*, or *All the Time in the World*, then, on the other, virtually all the music made by the All Stars was worthy of note – not just the recreations of his early repertoire in his recording project for Milt Gabler, the "Musical Autobiography," but also albums such as *Satch Plays Fats* or *Satch Plays W. C. Handy*, in which he produced some of the most brilliant playing of his career. The mature Armstrong was as formidable a player as the young tiger of the 1920s, and the difference was admirably summed up by Humphrey Lyttelton, who heard the All Stars playing at Nice, France, in 1948:

> I was particularly struck by the almost puritanical simplicity of his playing: all the old trappings and ornaments which were such familiar characteristics of his earlier phases have been swept away . . . and there was left a music which, with its purity and serenity, brought us perhaps nearer the fountainhead of his genius than we have ever been before.[21]

From the earliest All Stars sessions, these qualities are apparent, and a concert recorded with the original personnel of the band at Boston's Symphony Hall on November 30, 1947, includes some spectacular examples both of Armstrong's soloing and of the relaxed, yet driving, support of his sidemen, among which an extended version of *Muskrat Ramble* (described by saxophonist and critic Loren Schoenberg as "in many ways the definitive Armstrong All Stars performance"[22]) demonstrates the accuracy of Lyttelton's observations, in terms of both Armstrong's vital ensemble lead and his inspired solo. Some aspects of his programs were repetitive, but so what, if he played *Indiana* or *Sleepy Time Down South* every night and the first few notes alone could produce the same spine-tingling effect at each performance?

With such a high-profile figure as Armstrong involved once again in the earlier styles of jazz, Dixieland, or traditional, jazz enjoyed an upsurge in popularity during the 1950s and 1960s. Internationally, some musicians were drawn to Armstrong's manner of doing things, and emulated his approach. Such players ranged from those like Lyttelton himself, who was a figurehead of British revivalism during the 1950s, and whose playing tended to derive from Armstrong's earlier styles, to Irakli de Davrichewy in France, who convincingly recreated the sound of the trumpeter's playing with his All Stars.

However, the most popular forms of music to come out of the traditional revival did not follow Armstrong, Allen, or Ory so much as the more rugged sounds of Bunk Johnson and George Lewis. This was largely to do with the fact that in New Orleans itself, various other pioneers emerged in their wake, and began to be celebrated by enthusiasts as part of a burgeoning tradition, particularly after art dealer Larry Borenstein opened his former art gallery in New Orleans's St. Peter Street as a jazz venue under the name Preservation Hall, in 1961.[23] From the 1940s onwards, prodigal sons of New Orleans who had left in the 1920s returned to some sort of local celebrity, starting with trumpeter Herb Morand (a member of the Harlem Hamfats in the 1930s), who joined the George Lewis band for a year or two before his death in 1952.

More high-profile was Punch Miller, at one stage in the 1920s a rival to Armstrong, who cut a small number of greatly underrated revivalist records for Savoy, in December 1947 in New York, with Edmond Hall, Jimmy Archey, and Ralph Sutton, including his masterpiece *I Just Can't Help Myself*. After his return to his home town, he made some powerfully emotional blues recordings in New Orleans, including *Corrine Blues* from a 1960 session for Grayson Mills's Icon label, which also produced a flamboyant *Exactly Like You* that hinted at Miller's former prowess. Other high-profile figures who returned to the city included swing trombonist Preston Jackson and guitarist Danny Barker.

Through Preservation Hall and Bill Russell's continued recording activities for American Music, followed in due course by Riverside's Living Legends series, many other figures in the musical life of New Orleans came to be heard by a wide public, including trumpeters Andy Anderson, Peter Bocage, John Brunious, Ernie Cagnoletti, Kid Sheik Cola, Kid Howard, Percy Humphrey, Dede Pierce, and Kid Thomas Valentine; trombonists Homer and Wendell Eugene, Earl Humphrey, Frog Joseph, Louis Nelson, Eddie Summers, "Showboy" Thomas, and Albert Warner; clarinetists Milé and Paul Barnes, Albert Burbank, John Casimir, Louis Cottrell, Israel Gorman, Willie Humphrey, and Joe "Cornbread" Thomas; saxophonists Harold Dejan, Captain John Handy, Emanuel Paul, and Reuben Roddy; pianists Sweet Emma Barrett, Charlie Hamilton, Joe James, Jeannette Kimball, Sing Miller, Billie Pierce, Joe Robichaux, and Dave "Fat Man" Williams; banjoists George Guesnon, Narvin Kimball, "Father Al" Lewis, Lawrence Marrero, and Emanuel Sayles; bassists Joe Butler, Sylvester Handy, Louis James, Papa John Joseph, Alcide "Slow Drag" Pavageau, James Prevost, and Chester Zardis; and drummers Louis and Paul Barbarin, Alex Bigard, Cié Frasier, Sammy Penn, Joe Watkins, and Alfred Williams.

The advent of Preservation Hall provided a venue for many of these musicians to play regularly, and their simple, unadorned music carries a formidable emotional punch that only partially transfers to record. Kid Thomas, for example, could whip up his band into a rhythmic frenzy with his staccato, stabbing trumpet phrases on a piece like *Kid Thomas Boogie Woogie*, and he seemed completely unaffected by the influence of Armstrong or Oliver. He led a group continually from 1930 to the 1980s, and maintained his fiercely independent approach throughout.

The range of the city's clarinetists perhaps best demonstrates the breadth of musical talent uncovered by the revival, and its depth. At one extreme were raw, self-taught talents like Milé Barnes or Israel Gorman, whose direct blues playing was no mere imitation of the voice but a passionate channeling of primitive expression through their instruments, whereas the delicate, well-schooled fluency of Louis Cottrell was full of suave Creole sophistication. Somewhere in the middle came Albert Burbank, whose well-cultivated technique was combined with a strongly emotive style, in which the old pull between uptown and downtown elements was finely balanced.

In 1952, British trumpeter Ken Colyer, who had joined the merchant navy in order to earn his passage to America, jumped ship in Mobile, traveled to New Orleans, and became the first of the European revivalists to sit in and record with the city's musicians. Only non-union players would record with him, and he ended up making a 10-inch LP with a six-piece band that included clarinetist Milé Barnes and Buddy Bolden's one-time bassist Albert Glenny. After he returned to Britain, Colyer joined a new band assembled by trombonist Chris Barber, and, inspired by the romantic elements of the story of his visit to the Crescent City, a movement fell into place behind him. Within a couple of years, his personnel had included not only Barber but also clarinetists Monty Sunshine and Acker Bilk, all of whom went on to be prime movers in the 1960s vogue for "trad" jazz, a simplified form of New Orleans jazz that broke through to the European pop market.

Barber, as well as making lightweight "trad" records such as the children's song *Bobbie Shaftoe* or the ragtimey *Whistlin' Rufus*, began bringing American jazz and blues musicians to Britain, and introducing the subjects of his personal enthusiasm to a large public. Between the 1950s and the 1970s, his band toured with a wide variety of players from country bluesmen, such as Sonny Terry and Brownie McGhee, to the sophisticated jumping alto and vocals of Louis Jordan, and from the gospel singing of Sister Rosetta Tharpe and Alex Bradford to the Ellingtonian timbres of Ray Nance. Other high-profile guests included New Orleans trumpeter Alvin Alcorn, trombonist Trummy Young, and the MJQ's pianist John Lewis.

The drummer Barry Martyn, Barber's more fundamentalist counter-part, specialized in touring only with New Orleans musicians themselves, and starting with Kid Sheik Cola, in 1963, he brought an impressive array of such players to Europe, including George Lewis, Kid Thomas, Percy Humphrey, Louis Nelson, and Captain John Handy. Martyn's efforts were paralleled by Gerhard "Doggy" Hund and the White Eagle Band in Germany, "Papa" Arne-Bue Jensen in Denmark, Gérard Tarquin and the Haricots Rouges in France, and Yoshio Toyama in Japan. In due course Martyn himself went on to lead a band on the West Coast of the United States called the "Legends of Jazz," made up of former sidemen of the Kid Ory and George Lewis bands.

The revivalism initiated by record enthusiasts became a huge international movement over time, and helped to keep alive archaic styles of jazz that might otherwise have withered on the vine. With the benefit of hindsight, it seems to me that, ultimately, the same became true of swing or "mainstream" jazz, and that, to start with, this was largely due to the efforts of the concert promoter and entrepreneur Norman Granz.

## Jazz At The Philharmonic and "Mainstream" Jazz

> Everything that was rotten in contemporary jazz was to be
> found in this musical catastrophe. Here it was in a nutshell –
> the depths, the very caricature of post-war small band
> swing. It showed what happens when all the cheap and banal
> tricks of trivial, facile musicians are paraded for the benefit
> of the lowest class of swing enthusiasts.
>
> D. Leon Wolff, in *Down Beat*, November 18, 1946

Few people in the jazz world have been ambivalent about Jazz At The
Philharmonic. The competitive spirit of the staged jam session – warts and
all – is either appealing or not; you either love it or loathe it. The same
applies to the wider ethos of Norman Granz's Clef, Mercury, Norgran, and
Verve recordings, which presented the concerts themselves on disc, or
recreated in the studio such key ingredients of JATP as lengthy jams on the
blues, battling "chase" choruses between key instrumentalists, and medleys
of ballads. From the mid-1940s until 1957, when he ceased touring his
shows in the United States, and for a further ten years in Europe and Japan,
Granz's concert packages kept the spirit of the swing era alive, and he also
introduced jazz to thousands of people the world over.

From the time of his very first Jazz At The Philharmonic event, in 1944,
Granz also became a pioneering figure in terms of the marketing of jazz, and
this is every bit as important as his contribution to the music itself. He not
only sold his concert events brilliantly, but he also was one of the first
people to realize the sales potential of "live" recordings, and of the
importance of selling a brand name and an image in tandem with the music
itself. The combined success of his discs and concerts, featuring the biggest
names in jazz, ultimately gave him a degree of political clout that allowed
him to take on bigotry and racism and make genuinely important moves for
the integration of audiences, as well as taking a firm stand against segregation
in restaurants, hotels, and transportation across the United States.

However, Granz's achievements, his success as a record and concert
producer, and as a social reformer, should not occlude the fact that his
musical policy was essentially conservative. It idealized a golden age of
swing, when titanic figures did battle on their instruments in the ranks of big
bands, or in after-hours sessions, and Granz sought to recreate a sense of
that excitement for a vast concert-hall audience who preferred to see their
idols in the relative comfort of such a setting, as opposed to smoky clubs or

outdated ballrooms. His very first event, on July 2, 1944, featured such big names as saxophonist Illinois Jacquet, pianist Nat "King" Cole, and guitarist Les Paul; and, by the following year, Billie Holiday, Coleman Hawkins, Willie Smith, and Charlie Ventura were among the other famous musicians who had appeared in his all-star line-ups in Los Angeles. Invariably the soloists took successive choruses on the blues, or well-worn standards, and performed appropriate features – Hawkins, for example, would play *Body and Soul* with only pianist Milt Raskin in support.

In 1946, when Granz began to tour his package shows across the United States, he hired a similarly high-profile cast, as trumpeter Buck Clayton recalled:

> Every night was something that everybody had been waiting for, to see Coleman Hawkins and Lester Young battle it out. We would begin with all of us playing with the rhythm section. Hawk would blow his own beautiful solo and bring down the house, then it would be my turn to get into it. After me came Lester with his own unique style of playing which was totally different from Hawk.[24]

Such concerts were not breaking much new ground musically, but they delivered legendary figures in jazz to the listening public, doing the very thing that had made them legends in the first place. Arguably, such swing musicians as Hawkins and Young might well have found it difficult to get work of a comparable level of visibility and reward at a time when the modernism versus "moldy figges" debate was squeezing many other swing players out of the musical employment market altogether. Granz knew that he could trade on the fame that his soloists had built up in the 1930s and 1940s; he also knew that the public expected to hear Hawkins play *Body and Soul*, or Young play *Lester Leaps In*, when they came to his events. Such cannily managed conservatism meant that even such figureheads of 1940s modernism as Charlie Parker and Dizzy Gillespie played with swing-orientated rhythm sections when they performed for JATP, both men accommodating the rhythmic aspects of their bebop approach to the kind of setting in which they had come of age as players.

In due course, Granz extended his ambitions beyond the shores of the United States, recognizing that there was a global market for his vision of jazz, and tapping into a huge international public. Also, over time, Granz created a style of management for his concerts, and for the stable of individual artists whom he booked, including Ella Fitzgerald and Oscar Peterson, that was as pace-setting for the post-war era as that of Irving Mills had been for the 1920s and 1930s. He put advertising to work in a way that had never been seen before in the jazz world, and did not stint on his promotional budgets, realizing that spending on one activity, such as concerts, would bring a measurable marginal benefit to his record business, particularly if his records encapsulated aspects of his concert programs. He understood the importance of strong design, and his disc labels, LP sleeves, and panel advertisements stand out from others of the late 1940s and early 1950s by virtue of their unified appearance, including the clever use of his logo, a powerful line-drawn motif of a trumpeter. In the jazz world at that time, such effective linking of the worlds of visual design and music was rivaled only by the spartan Bauhaus images adopted by Alfred Lion at Blue Note, involving Frank Wolff's monochrome photography and Reid Miles's innovative graphics. Granz's album covers, mostly drawn by David Stone Martin, but the odd one by Merle Shore, were every bit as distinctive. His accompanying liner notes consistently made the case for jazz that "swings ... [and] is both exciting and enjoyable."[25]

Granz's first JATP concert promotion was motivated by his social and ethical concerns, when a group of Mexican detainees were sent to San Quentin Prison as suspects in a killing – a number of suspects that seemed more than reasonable to many in the arts and film world of Los Angeles, who detected a racial motive in the imprisonment, and formed the "Sleepy Lagoon Defense Committee" to campaign for their release. Granz, who had already tried his hand at promoting jazz in clubs, organized a concert at Philharmonic Hall to raise funds for the campaign, and the proceedings were recorded by the Armed Forces Radio Service (AFRS). Guitarist Les Paul was still in uniform, and working for the AFRS, when he was invited to appear on the bill for this inaugural JATP event – ending up jamming on stage with Nat "King" Cole, where he sensed something rather special was taking place:

> I looked into that audience and I saw them standing on their seats. I said, "Wow." But we were busy doing our thing. We sensed there was a reaction. We could hear a roar going up and we knew we had something going. But Nat and I were busy outwitting each other. When it reached a climax, I saw hats up in the air – they were screaming and hollering.[26]

In such a heavily charged atmosphere, with an audience at the same kind of fever pitch as Benny Goodman's Paramount Theater crowds from the 1930s, the musicians felt the temptation to "grandstand" – to play more and more outrageously, and the soloist who fell most naturally into this role, to the extent that his blustery ballad playing is often overlooked because of his propensity for crowd-pleasing honks and squeals, was tenorist Illinois Jacquet. He told me he had started to play in this way as a member of Cab Calloway's orchestra, trying to find something entertaining for the crowds with which to follow Calloway's "Hi-de-ho" routines.

> That got me started, but when I got to play on this concert, Nat "King" Cole on piano, Les Paul, Lee Young on drums, J. J. Johnson, Jack McVea – we had a jam session. The place was packed. We had the kind of audience that was glad to see this, and whatever I did it was okay. If I'd stopped and whistled it would've been okay, 'cos once you hit 'em and you go 'em, you gotta know how to hold 'em. So I started playing like that then to please the audience.[27]

Jacquet's solo on *The Blues: Part Two* became a benchmark for the vulgar, crowd-pleasing side of JATP concerts, provoking a frenzied audience reaction with his tendency to substitute freak effects, high notes, and noise for a controlled flow of ideas. Although there are many great moments in the recorded legacy of JATP, there is an almost equal number of vapid chase choruses, with soloists vying to play louder, higher, and faster than one another – all of which may have been very exciting in a concert hall at the time, but make for extremely tedious listening today.

Nevertheless, when Granz first set about trying to issue the results of his concerts, the idea of the recorded live performance was in its infancy, and he had to overcome considerable opposition to the idea from the industry itself. As with so much of Granz's career, the outcome of his efforts, and its importance to the way jazz was subsequently recorded and presented, vastly outweighs the shortcomings of some of his concert recordings. He saw the potential for issuing discs as soon as he heard the transcriptions of the July 1944 concert, recorded by the AFRS.

> I thought of it not as a recording session but as a documentary of an event as it happened with no doctoring. I wanted to capture the spontaneity of a jam session on record. When I heard those

discs, I realized you could never get that in a studio where you get a controlled performance.[28]

There had been such documentary recordings made before, but few had been commercially issued. The landmark concerts of the 1930s and 1940s, discussed earlier, had yet to appear, as it was not until 1950 that Benny Goodman's 1938 Carnegie Hall concert was finally released, and Ellington's 1943 performance, from the same venue, of *Black, Brown and Beige* first surfaced in its entirety in the 1960s on an Italian bootleg LP, with the "official" version not appearing from Prestige until the 1970s. Although Eddie Condon's jam sessions at New York Town Hall were inaugurated in 1942, they were not commercially recorded at the time, and the eventually released sides were mainly from amateur recordings of live broadcasts of the concerts.

Curiously, Granz's idea had been most successfully pre-empted in Britain, where, despite the wartime conditions, the *Melody Maker* and No. 1 Rhythm Club had actually organized the "First English Public Jam Session" at EMI's Abbey Road Studios in November 1941. At this event, several all-star musicians appeared before an invited audience in the large studio where Sir Edward Elgar had made his celebrated 1930s recordings; the results, featuring such players as trumpeters Kenny Baker and Dave Wilkins, plus saxophonists Carl Barriteau and Buddy Featherstonhaugh, were issued by HMV, splitting the extended performances of *Tea for Two* and *St. Louis Blues* into separate parts for issue on successive sides of 78 r.p.m. discs, just as Granz was eventually to divide up the earliest of his issues in the pre-LP era.

It seems that this British venture made little or no impact on the American market, least of all on the West Coast where Granz was based, and that the major record companies in the United States were unaware of what their principal European counterpart was doing. Granz unsuccessfully approached Columbia, Decca, and RCA with his JATP masters, all of them turning him down on account of "mistakes, crowd noise, and musicians shouting."[29] Eventually Moe Asch of the independent Disc Records agreed to issue the material, and in 1947, *Jazz At The Philharmonic Vol. 1* was finally released, starting the series rolling with extracts from a February 1945 concert. Granz disliked Asch's distribution arrangements (through which he lost control of the masters), and, subsequently, he released the concert recordings himself, starting in June 1947 on the Mercury/Clef label.

Whatever the jazz critics of the period thought, Granz's formula was extremely successful with the public. "We started touring, packing auditoriums all over the United States," recalled Jacquet. "Everywhere we'd go, even Carnegie Hall, the packages began to get bigger and bigger. There's Ella Fitzgerald, Gene Krupa, Buddy Rich, Dizzy Gillespie. . . ."[30] Granz worked tirelessly to ensure the success of his concerts, and once he started to tour his package shows around the United States, he put enormous energy into promotion, going to each port of call ahead of time and ensuring the local disc jockeys had JATP records, that the African-American and white newspapers carried suitable publicity stories, and so on. Also, ahead of the twice-yearly, six-week touring season, Granz had his own grueling agenda:

> I had to go out three months ahead of each tour to do the physical work – the ordering of tickets and the advertising, and laying out the things that you need. It's true I would have local people in some cities, but I always wanted to oversee things and be sure that conditions were right.[31]

The conditions extended to his strongly held views that his troupe should play for racially mixed audiences, and that his musicians should be treated royally, to the best hotel and travel arrangements possible. This offered a considerable contrast for many of them to the way they had been obliged to go about things in the past. Dizzy Gillespie, for example, had played odd concerts with Granz in New York in the 1940s, but began touring with the package in 1954. There was a marked difference between his experience on the road with the "Hepsations of 1945," and with his subsequent big band, staying in all-black hotels and areas, and suffering considerable privations on the road, and what Granz was now able to offer, as Gillespie recalled:

> Jazz At The Philharmonic was "the élite." Norman Granz hired the best musicians and made them fight one another on stage musically. He paid them top money, and they traveled first class. He was the first one for whom musicians always traveled that way, lived in the best hotels, and so on, and he was the first one to insist that we played in Texas to a non-segregated audience.[32]

It was not just Texas where the barriers were broken down, and Granz began to use his increasingly important commercial muscle to coerce promoters in several states to go along with his principles of integrated audiences, just as he encouraged hoteliers to accept his star musicians, be they white or black. Granz deserves great credit for his stance – the more so because, as he pointed out in a long interview with Nat Hentoff that covered his attitude to political and social matters in detail:

> With Jazz at the Philharmonic, I could play anywhere I wanted ... so that I could have stayed out of the South forever, and the issues never would have arisen to the degree that they did. So I could keep playing the Northern cities, and there I wouldn't have had the opposition that I had in the South for desegregating a concert hall. ... So in that sense I deliberately chose to go down South, because I *did* want to ... effect some kind of a precedent.[33]

From taking on hoteliers to pulling his entire package out of a hall where the management would not agree to his demands, Granz earned the lasting respect of his musicians. When trumped-up charges by local police led to some members of his cast, including Ella Fitzgerald, being unfairly arrested in Houston, Granz spent $2000 clearing their names.[34]

Through this and other actions that challenged needless shows of authority, racial discrimination, or just the downright pointless or unfair, Granz had a radical impact on the climate for jazz in the 1940s and 1950s. He also became a major catalyst in establishing internationally what the English critic Stanley Dance called "mainstream" – the kind of swing-playing that survived into the 1950s and which absorbed much of the more accessible elements of bebop harmony and melodic improvisation. By mixing players like Parker, Gillespie, J. J. Johnson, and Kai Winding together with swing-era giants like Young and Hawkins, and, particularly, through his studio-based record sessions that pitted such soloists against one another – or where they backed Billie Holiday, Ella Fitzgerald, or Sarah Vaughan – Granz helped heal some of the more damaging aspects of the "modern" versus "trad" split of the 1940s.

Certainly the musicians whom he relied on to provide support for his soloists saw it this way. His principal accompanist in the studio and on JATP for many years was Oscar Peterson, who told me:

> I cherish those days, because they did a lot for me in the way of developing my playing, with all those wonderful great musicians – Coleman Hawkins, Dizzy, Roy, Benny Carter. It was a great training ground and I still appreciate what they gave me. ... Right at the start when I was standing in the wings watching Hank

Jones playing for Ella Fitzgerald, I learned a lot about the art of accompaniment. And when it came to my turn to provide it, I had already understood that everybody needs the right sort of accompaniment, that everyone wants – and needs – something different. Pres [Lester Young], for example, wanted a kind of loose, floating time; Dizzy wanted a more "sock-it-to-me" kind of feeling, plus he also wanted his own particular sets of chords for some songs, and I had to satisfy that. Roy "Speedy" Eldridge was always ready for battle … then I think what was beautiful about the ballad sets that followed was that we weren't just playing one tune – each soloist picked something different so there'd be a change of color from player to player. Bill Harris might play *The Nearness of You*, Coleman Hawkins might play *Body and Soul* – but oftentimes each would play another feature, and following that kind of color change, from artist to artist, where you play a chorus of this and then a chorus of that, it always kept us on our toes musically, about what was going on.[35]

Peterson fluently accommodated the full range of styles of the JATP soloists, and although other rhythm sections toured with the entourage – from the Modern Jazz Quartet to Dizzy Gillespie's entire quintet, and from Gene Krupa's trio to various ad hoc aggregations, Peterson's trio, plus Buddy Rich, Louie Bellson, or J. C. Heard on drums, were by far the most frequently heard.

The impact of Jazz At The Philharmonic was also to be felt on the growing movement for jazz festivals that sprang up after World War II. Starting with the first Nice Festival in France, in 1948, and followed by the Paris Festival the following year, the first big American festival began at Newport, Rhode Island, in 1954. This event borrowed many of its ideas about the presentation of jazz from Granz's touring concert packages, and the same was true of many of those that followed in its wake, including Monterey from 1958, where jam sessions between star soloists, a succession of big names from the swing era, and different artists appearing with the same rhythm section all featured in the mix at one point or another.

But during the period that Granz's packages toured the world, jazz itself was not standing still. There were new changes going on, new styles emerging, as bebop was consolidated into various movements that took its tenets in different directions. In JATP events, bebop was reabsorbed into the mainstream, Dizzy Gillespie's trumpet battling with swing-era giants like

Charlie Shavers on well-known standards or the blues, rather than tangling with Charlie Parker's alto on intricate new compositions. Elsewhere, bebop ideas launched two parallel movements, at opposite ends of the stylistic spectrum: on the one hand, the aggressive, gospel-tinged sounds of soul jazz and hard bop, and on the other, the gentle, impressionistic sounds of "cool" jazz, of whom the first high-profile progenitor was Charlie Parker's one-time front-line partner, Miles Davis.

# PART III

# Consolidation of Bebop

CHAPTER 12

# Early Miles Davis

> With the single exception of Louis Armstrong . . . there has been no series of recordings in jazz history that has the impact of the Miles Davis Quintet and Sextet records, nor the later albums with Gil Evans and the large band. . . . Seen against the backdrop of all jazz, it is a great achievement; seen against the backdrop of contemporary music as a whole, it is even greater.
>
> Ralph J. Gleason, quoted in Jack Chambers: *Milestones I*

Miles Davis remains one of the most chameleon-like figures in jazz. Few other musicians so constantly reinvented themselves throughout their careers with such conviction and success, to the extent that almost all periods of his work have strong advocates, who will claim that *this* is the "real" Miles Davis. Traditionally, historians have focused on three distinct areas of Davis's work, where his music had far-reaching effects on the overall course of jazz and its development. These are his *Birth of the Cool* nonet sessions from 1949, in which he, Gil Evans, Gerry Mulligan, John Lewis, and Johnny Carisi pioneered a new way of writing for medium-sized forces; his subsequent orchestral collaborations with Evans, including *Sketches of Spain* and the *Porgy and Bess* suite; and his pioneering of modal jazz in his sextet of 1958–60, which recorded *Kind of Blue*.

Yet he deserves equal attention for his 1960s quintet with Herbie Hancock, Ron Carter, Tony Williams, and Wayne Shorter, which explored new relationships between rhythm section and soloist, including a radical reassessment of the role of time signatures and their relationship to the harmonies of jazz; for the free-form experiments of the 1970s which launched jazz-rock fusion through such albums as *In a Silent Way*; and for his sequence of remarkably innovative and creative funk-fusion bands from the 1980s.

I will consider the period from the 1960s quintet onwards in Chapter 20, but here I will be focusing mainly on Davis's significance as the dominant player in the jazz of the 1950s, up to and including *Kind of Blue*, in what I have called the "consolidation" of bebop – finding new directions in which to move forward from the innovations of the 1940s. Davis was particularly well placed to do this, because of his close affinity with Charlie Parker, and I have already pointed out the way his approach to trumpet diverged from that of Gillespie as his recording association with Parker progressed, notably from the time of *Milestones*, cut in August 1947.

Whereas Gillespie's playing in the mid-1940s was all about dashing drama, exploiting the full range of the instrument, and his technical innovations in speed and mobility, Davis was beginning to have the confidence to display poise, balance, and coolness. He did not end his phrases with the terminal vibrato beloved of swing players in the post-Armstrong tradition; he did not rush to the extremes of the horn, preferring to stay in its middle range and playing more considered phrases; and his Harmon-muted lead and solo playing had a growing sense of space about them. Comparing the different takes of *Milestones*, Davis's solo is quite similar from one to another. It has compositional elements about it: a neatly repeated and transposed phrase early in the first eight measures, and a similar figure at the start of the middle eight is identical; and as well as these thematic ideas, Davis has just as assured an overall approach on each solo.

Parker, it seems, disliked Davis's sound on the open horn and encouraged him to use the mute, and this, in particular, encouraged Davis to step back from the dominant Gillespie influence on bebop trumpet playing and to draw more heavily on the brass traditions of his home area, St. Louis, as Clark Terry, another significant trumpeter from the same region, told me:

> They got along beautiful – except Bird didn't like Miles's sound. If you remember from their earliest recordings, Miles always had a mute in. Every time he played something open, Bird would say to him: "Put the mute in, man! Put the damn mute in!" He just didn't like Miles's sound. So Miles started to use the mute. Concerning that Harmon mute, many people think Miles was the one who started that particular tradition, but that was a pretty

well-known thing in St. Louis. Everybody used to do that. Some of them just used the stem with the little cup on the end, making a "wa-wa-wa" sound. Others took the stem out, but the use of that mute was indigenous to the St. Louis jazz sound.[1]

But Davis had taken more than his use of the mute from his local tradition. There was a proud and independent dynasty of trumpeters in the town, from whom young players could learn, starting with flamboyant territory-band pioneers such as Charlie Creath "the King of Cornet," whose tone was said to be so glorious that the faint-hearted would swoon at its sound, and running down through such lyrical players as Levi Madison, who starred with the Original St. Louis Crackerjacks in the mid-1930s, making a handful of records with the band, and being widely regarded as having what Clark Terry described as "the most beautiful sound of anyone in the area."[2] Other creators of the "St. Louis sound" included the great parade trumpeter Leonard "Ham" Davis (who played his lead parts one-handed), Walter "Crack" Stanley, George Hudson, and Baby James – pioneer members of a line which extended right down via swing-era players such as Irving "Mouse" Randolph and Joe Thomas to more recent stars such as Clark Terry and Lester Bowie.

Terry himself was to become a significant influence on Miles Davis, but it was Davis's teacher, Elwood Buchanan, who was the young man's direct link to the trumpet traditions of his local area. Discussing his pupils over a glass of beer, some time in the late 1930s, Buchanan told Terry that in his opinion there was only one problem with Davis:

> He said, "He likes to shake them notes." Because when I first heard Miles as a young skinny boy, he loved to play with a big vibrato – he was very fond of Harry James, who was his idol there for a while. But "Buke" didn't like that – he would take a ruler, and he'd hit Miles across the hand if he shook his long notes, saying: "Stop that! You're gonna shake enough when you get old!" So this contributed to Miles's very straight tone, plus the fact that Buchanan had studied with Joe Gustat, who was first trumpet in the St. Louis Symphony. Gustat insisted on all of his players using a very thin curlicue-type mouthpiece with a deep, bucket type of cup. Miles learned about this, and over time he grew so fond of these mouthpieces he had me looking for them! They were called Heim mouthpieces, and I used to hustle up a

Heim for him whenever I visited a new music store. This kind of very deep mouthpiece gives you a great tone, but makes it very difficult to get up high. Later when I played alongside Cat Anderson in the Ellington band, who had a phenomenal high range, he used the opposite kind of mouthpiece – it just looked like a dent with a pinhole in it . . . but if Miles had gone for more range, and a shallower mouthpiece, he wouldn't have had that pure tone, that beautiful sound, that he did have.[3]

With Davis's early instruction on how to produce a clear, vibratoless tone came lessons in reading music and plenty of opportunity to play jazz within the thriving musical community of the St. Louis region. Davis's father was a dentist with strong opinions about the importance of education (his own father having been a successful book-keeper who elevated the family from poverty to the black middle class), and the young trumpeter was prevented by his parents from accepting the offers he received to go on the road with various bands that passed through town, encouraging him to remain in school. He did, however, take the odd trip away from the area during vacations, and he also sat in with many of the bands that came to town, including spending a week or two alongside Dizzy Gillespie and Charlie Parker in the Billy Eckstine orchestra when another trumpeter was taken ill.

This direct contact with Parker and Gillespie was important, and so too was the degree to which local musicians, keeping their ears to the ground for new records, new soloists, new bands, and new ideas, filtered these through to Davis. Yet there are strong grounds for believing, as Clark Terry suggests, that much of Davis's subsequent originality, his own "new" sound, arose from his prolonged exposure to an independent local St. Louis tradition that is not as well-represented on record, or in previous accounts of jazz history, as are the sounds of New York and Chicago. If Davis had gone off on the road with Tiny Bradshaw, Earl Hines, Jimmie Lunceford, or any of the others who offered him work, then he might have become just another trumpeter, schooled among the pool of swing players who criss-crossed the country in such bands, but without the non-conformist attitude instilled in him by the independent-minded players of southern Illinois and Missouri.

At the age of eighteen, and already an experienced band trumpeter, Davis enrolled at the Juilliard School of Music in Manhattan. He did not last long there, leaving within a year, but for that period he split his time between formal studies and practice, and hanging out on 52nd Street, where he eventually ended up sitting in with Coleman Hawkins, then being hired for a few weeks by another saxophonist, Eddie "Lockjaw" Davis, and eventually joining Charlie Parker's quintet at the Three Deuces after Dizzy Gillespie had set off on his 1945 Hepsations tour. Davis had renewed his friendship with Parker from the days of the Eckstine band, and the two men roomed together briefly. Parker consistently encouraged the young trumpeter, and could clearly see his potential, which is only partially apparent from the recordings they made together, as discussed in Chapter 7. As well as *Milestones*, there are glimpses of Davis's future sound on some of their other discs. The somewhat hesitant open-horned solo on *Now's the Time*, from the *Koko* session of November 26, 1945, is one example, and it has been picked up by various listeners as the earliest evidence of Davis's originality, Red Rodney, for instance, commenting, "It was a new sound . . . it was a young guy that didn't play the trumpet very well, but had discovered a whole new way of treating it and playing it."[4]

Significantly, the longer Davis's association with Parker continued, and particularly when it was renewed after the saxophonist's period in the Camarillo Sanitarium, their recorded work increasingly demonstrated their dissimilar qualities. As Ian Carr puts it in his biography of Davis:

> Instead of sparks being created by the competition of two virtuoso horns, as had been the case when Dizzy was in the band, Parker was looking for the dynamism of contrast. His own gargantuan abilities would be offset against the understatement and lyricism of Miles's horn.[5]

It was these two qualities that marked out Davis's work as he slowly established his independence from Parker during the second half of 1948, prior to leaving the quintet for good. Although he continued to broadcast and make records with Bird (despite another A.F.M. recording ban) Davis was beginning to pursue a new direction of his own. This came about through his contacts with a group of musicians who had been part of the society big band led by Claude Thornhill, and centered around that group's former arranger Gil Evans.

Whereas Parker and Gillespie had explored new ideas about harmony, speed, and rhythm, Evans, together with saxophonists Gerry Mulligan and Lee Konitz, plus trumpeter Johnny Carisi, was more concerned with tone and texture. Their ideas did not necessarily have all their roots in the jazz tradition. Evans – the key figure in this group – had discovered his interest in the classical impressionist composers, Ravel and Debussy, not long after coming to New York, around 1941, to join Thornhill, having hitherto written for his own band in California.

Thin, gaunt, ascetic in character, Evans was a self-taught arranger and composer who had his mind firmly focused on music, even though his tiny apartment on West 55th Street was something of a chaotic open house and increasingly bustled with the comings and goings of his fellow musicians. In 1983, he told British jazz critic Charles Fox:

> I had no classical background – all I knew was jazz and popular music . . . by the time I got to New York I was interested in impressionism and its harmonic language, because up until that time I only had the regular pop and jazz language from Fletcher and Duke. I went to the public library . . . [and] I used to take the scores and copy the whole scores . . . transpose it all just to learn it. And I got my harmonic language from Debussy and Ravel and Manuel De Falla and all the impressionists. So I got a chance to use that language with Claude Thornhill . . . meanwhile bebop arrived and I started writing some of *those* things, but he didn't want that kind of a band, though every band had to play *some* jazz, of course.[6]

In his early days with Thornhill, Evans built on the somewhat unorthodox sound that the pianist-leader had created for himself. Evans was always quick to acknowledge that it was Thornhill who first brought French horns into the big-band line-up, and who started to use the tuba as an additional tone color in the brass section, rather than to hold down a bass line, and Evans's early charts for the band show him exploring these possibilities. The fusion of impressionist voicings with bebop that Evans mentioned surfaced in the pieces he wrote for Thornhill immediately after World War II – arrangements of *Anthropology*, *Donna Lee*, and *Yardbird Suite*. Of these, *Donna Lee*, from November 1947, has an aggressive, almost Kentonish, flavor about it. After Thornhill's opening piano solo, Evans sets a segment of Charlie Parker's recording of the piece for muted trumpets doubled by the saxophones, catching the flavor of a bebop small group, but then, after trombone and alto solos, he throws in some brilliant brass-section writing that exploits Thornhill's unusual instrumentation. Overall, the arrangement is rather disjointed – a series of effects strung together with solos in between – whereas the medium-paced *Yardbird Suite* is more unified. On that, after some impressionistic comings and goings by Thornhill at the keyboard, the full ensemble voicings of the opening theme (reduced to the reed section only in the middle eight) hint at Evans's future economical style, and Konitz's clear-toned alto leaps from the ensemble as it was to do on subsequent Evans arrangements.

What the Thornhill sides lacked, even with Lee Konitz in his reed section, was a truly distinctive and fresh solo voice to balance the subtlety and complexity of Evans's scoring – the very thing that Davis's trumpet was now set to become. Evans left Thornhill in 1948 as the recording ban bit, and the band's work dried up. Soon, the friends and former colleagues that met in his apartment were experimenting to see if they could transfer the ethereal impressionist sounds Evans had achieved in his big-band writing to a smaller group. Evans described what went on:

> I lived right close to 52nd Street. I rented this room, and I left the door open for two years. I left it open literally so people just came down. . . . I had a piano, record-player, an early recorder that made acetates . . . plus a wild interest. We'd get together and discuss chords and that, and that's how I got together with Miles Davis. . . . The thing that Miles Davis and I had in common was the appreciation of a certain kind of sound. . . . So we figured out a way to get that sound that I had with Claude Thornhill into a small combination. Just six horns, to cover the whole harmonic range.[7]

There is little doubt that Evans, Mulligan, and Johnny Carisi would have come close to achieving the sound they were after in any case, had Davis not become part of their circle, but he landed a booking for their putative nine-piece band at the Royal Roost Club in September 1948, and this proved the catalyst the musicians needed to organize their thoughts into a repertoire that could be played in the club. Yet Davis did more than simply find a gig (and, subsequently, a recording contract) for the music – his playing was, as Mulligan explained, at the very core of how they ended up conceptualizing the music:

> Thinking of Miles as the lead voice affected the way we all wrote for the band. Stylistically, Miles was the perfect choice. It's hard to imagine other trumpet players having the same effect on the ensemble. If we'd had a trumpet player that had a more

conventional open sound, it wouldn't have had the same impact on the ensemble. Miles's melodic approach and lead voice was a particular influence on the ultimate sound of the ensemble.[8]

Each arranger – including John Lewis, who had recently left Dizzy Gillespie's big band after its tour to Europe in early 1948, and who apparently posted his arrangements from Paris where he had stayed on after Gillespie's concerts there[9] – approached writing for the nonet from a slightly different standpoint, but they were all following Evans's lead. Some recordings that survive from the Royal Roost gig, some time before the nonet made any commercial discs, suggest the band had a slightly more florid style at first than its eventual crisp, economical sound, as Evans sought to establish a template for its charts. One example of this is Evans's score for *Why Do I Love You?* and it owes a lot to his Thornhill days with a whimsical opening flourish complete with trills, and a final full-band chorus that has all the parts moving against one another in a kind of poised slow motion. Nevertheless, Evans produced a fullness of sound with just nine players comparable to that which he had achieved with the entire Thornhill Orchestra, justifying Davis's comment that he "can use four instruments where other arrangers need eight."[10]

John Lewis produced one of the more fascinating scores to be recorded by the group once it went into the studios for Capitol, and his version of Denzil Best's *Move*, from January 21, 1949, places a cameo of a small bebop group into a larger band setting. Davis and Lee Konitz act out the Parker/ Gillespie roles of a conventional bebop front line, their efforts set in a feather bed of tonal effects from the other horns, with some sustained harmonies and punctuational flurries at the ends of phrases. Lewis also uses the baritone saxophone and tuba to create some downward-moving figures together, and these are what give this setting the characteristic Evans sound. Lewis's own composition *Rouge*, recorded at the group's second studio session with the composer on piano, uses the full instrumentation more or less throughout, apart from a fluttering, rapid solo from Konitz and a more measured response from Davis, but it mainly uses long, extended passages of ensemble, as well as a neatly used fanfare device that opens the piece and recurs throughout it. Just as in *Move*, where Lewis experimented with putting a bebop *small* band into a larger setting, *Rouge* experiments with scaling down the sound of a bebop *big* band to fit the nonet.

In complete contrast to Lewis's pieces, Mulligan's *Venus de Milo* has a neat little theme which hints at the spare, open sound that Mulligan was to achieve in his own "piano-less" quartet a little later, and Davis's vibrato-less, open-horned, balanced solo also prefigures the sound of Chet Baker with Mulligan's groups, not least because of its juxtaposition with Mulligan's own baritone solo which creates an aural association between Davis's clean trumpet sound and the large horn.

If Mulligan's writing hinted at the spartan simplicity he was to achieve in the 1950s, Carisi's was, contrastingly, more complex, the rapidly moving part-writing of *Israel*'s opening being followed by a knotty theme with rhythmic shifts and plenty of twists and turns, a sense of which continues behind the solos with the erratic punctuation of John Lewis's piano. But the masterpiece of the twelve commercial sides recorded by the band is Gil Evans's *Boplicity*, with its long, subtly harmonized version of a theme written and led by Davis, followed by a great variety of textures behind Mulligan and Davis's solos, over the very basic and simple rhythmic backdrop of Nelson Boyd's walking bass and Kenny Clarke's understated brushwork. The piece sounds modernistic, sophisticated, and a world away from the frenetic dash of 52nd Street bebop. This number, above all others recorded by the nonet, was to point the way for the "cool" jazz movement of the 1950s, and to earn the eventual 1954 album that collected all the band's twelve sides the title "Birth of the Cool." It was also a harbinger for the later collaborations of Evans and Davis, which involved setting the trumpeter's solos amid large jazz-orchestral forces.

Davis himself was later dismissive of *Boplicity*. Although he praised Evans as his "favorite writer," he told Nat Hentoff that the piece wasn't played often because "the top line isn't interesting. The harmonization is, but not the tune itself."[11]

But at the time Davis made the third and final studio date for the Capitol "Birth of the Cool" sessions in 1950, his life had undergone a major change. From having been a teetotal, non-smoking youth, who had not been drawn into the many temptations of drugs and alcohol on offer during his tenure with Charlie Parker, he became addicted to heroin. Although the period from 1950 to 1953 – the year that he finally put himself through a cold-turkey cure – produced some occasionally impressive recordings, and a few notable concert appearances, Davis – his mind often dwelling on finding the money for his next hit of heroin, and no longer coolly focused on his music – failed to build on the immense promise of the nonet discs.

In 1954, there began to be signs that he was returning to the level of creativity and promise he had shown in 1949, but during the intervening years, when others of his Birth of the Cool associates such as Lee Konitz,

Gerry Mulligan, and John Lewis were exploring further the territory that Davis and Evans had opened up, Davis himself returned to the setting of a conventional bebop combo. During these fallow years he made several discs for Prestige, plus a couple of significant sessions for Blue Note. A number of these recordings reflect what was to be a recurring factor in all stages of Davis's career, namely the fact that even during his addiction, his ear was towards the music being made by a younger generation with innovative ideas, and with whom he formed new associations. In this case his principal new partner was tenor saxophonist Sonny Rollins.

Rollins was only four years younger than Davis, and he had also had an early start in music, taking up the saxophone, at the age of eleven, in 1941. In junior high school in New York, his remarkable progress was observed by another saxophonist – two years younger still – Jackie McLean, who eventually joined him in the Miles Davis band:

> Sonny was . . . eons ahead of me in music. He started playing much earlier – and when I got my horn at fourteen, he was already the king of the neighborhood. He used to play like Coleman Hawkins on the alto. Everybody knew who he was. He'd go up on the stage at junior high and play for the assembly. He was ahead of me in school.[12]

At this time, in the mid-1940s, McLean recalled that over in the Bronx, there was an even more accomplished teenage saxophonist, Andy Kirk Jr., son of the celebrated territory bandleader, who was already developing beyond the ideas of Charlie Parker.

> He was the most celebrated young sax player – Sonny Stitt and Bird used to sit in the room and hear him practice. Sonny playing like Hawk wasn't like what Andy was doing, which was more connected to Bud and Bird. But then Sonny went away, he went upstate and nobody saw him for nine months, until one day I was sitting in my house and the doorbell rang – it was Andy: "Sonny's back."
>
> I said, "So What?"
>
> He said, "You should hear him, he's ridiculous. You know who hired him? Miles. I went out to Brooklyn last night and heard him, and he's incredible."
>
> That night I went out to Brooklyn, and as I came out of [the]

subway and started walking towards the club, I heard this sax. I thought it was Bird, but as I got through the door, I saw it was Sonny. And what he was doing bowled me over. He had made a complete transformation. Like a metamorphosis to a butterfly. Everyone on stage was mesmerized, including Miles.[13]

This rapid development capitulated Andy Kirk Jr. into a profound depression, and as Rollins overtook him stylistically, and in terms of fresh ideas, Kirk began a terminal slide into heroin addiction, to the lasting sadness of his father. In contrast, Rollins's prowess brought him plenty of work and acclaim. In particular, Bud Powell had been intending to use McLean, his young protégé, on his first Blue Note record date in 1948, with Fats Navarro, but after he ran through the music with Rollins, there was no doubt that he, not the younger McLean, should play on the disc. Other musicians thought similarly highly of Rollins, and he played with several cutting-edge players in New York, from Thelonious Monk to Charlie Parker; but in 1949, following the Brooklyn gigs recalled by McLean, he began playing regularly with Miles Davis – the start of an association that lasted, on and off, until 1957. Davis, according to McLean, had a hard time holding a regular line-up together during his drug-addicted years of the early 1950s, but he tried to use Rollins wherever possible. Rollins gave Davis a comparable counterpart to Parker – a muscular, active, heavyweight saxophonist whose profusion of ideas and rapid-fire technique could offset the pure tone and sparse phrasing of Davis's trumpet.

In 1951, Bud Powell made up for overlooking McLean on his own discs by recommending him to Davis as an additional front-line voice. During Powell's mental illness, McLean had looked after him, taken him to gigs, attempted to keep him away from alcohol, and generally become extremely close to him. In return, Powell had fostered the development of the young altoist, who combined something of Charlie Parker's speed with a sharp-edged, acidic tone, and was beginning to have an authentic and original saxophone voice of his own.

One day, after [I] had been playing with Bud a lot, he called me and said, "Miles just came by the house, and I told him you're coming down to sit in with him. So go down to Birdland and sit in with him – tonight."

I said, "Tonight?"

He said, "Yeah, tonight."

So I went down that night. My name was on the door, and I walked up and looked at Miles on the stage, and Gene Ammons – who was playing saxophone on the date – rolled his eyes at me, as if to say "What's this kid doin' here?"

He was a big, cruel-looking dude if he wanted to be. He was really a nice guy, I learned after that, but that very first night, I looked up at the stage and got real worried about going up there with Miles, whom I idolized. Anyway, I went up and sat in. Miles said afterwards, "Come by my house. Give me a call." And he wrote his address on a matchbook. He went on, "Come tomorrow. You write music?"

I said, "Yeah. I gotta couple o'tunes."

He said, "Right, bring them!"

I said, "I don't have them written, but I can show them to you."

So I went out to see him the next day. He had a job that weekend in Newark, and Sonny was in his band. It was Sonny Rollins, Art Blakey, Walter Bishop, and Percy Heath. I went and played that first job after rehearsing some things at his house that I could play – stuff that wasn't too hard. Plus, I had four or five things of mine. I taught him the song *Dig* that I had written on *Sweet Georgia Brown*. So that was how I joined him because of Bud, and I spent three-and-a-half years with him off and on.

During that time, Sonny kept himself to himself. He was much more mature than me and saw me as a silly kid until I started using drugs – and then the whole attitude changed. I thought I had to do that to be accepted into the hierarchy. Everybody idolized Sonny, he just destroyed other sax players. Everybody began to try to play like him; people like Hank Mobley and others from out West. I was in a fortunate place being in Miles's band next to Sonny, even though they bruised me from night to night. They just mauled me. I was between the two of them. Miles would play, Sonny would stand at the side of the stage, so that behind Miles's great solo, I would have to go and play. I'd only been playing four years – which was a short period to have arrived at a mature voice. When I finished, Sonny would walk out – building some great image of stone in sound. I just tried to stay and hold myself together musically, but it was a bad time because all of us were getting high – Miles and everyone.[14]

McLean nearly died of his habit, and subsequently became an ardent anti-drugs campaigner. Later, Rollins also kicked heroin in similar fashion to Davis, but the front-line partnership of Davis, McLean, and Rollins produced some creditable recordings in 1951, notwithstanding their collective reliance on the drug, and a piece like the aforementioned *Dig* shows Rollins constructing just such a stone ediface, before Davis's intricate, introspective solo and McLean's Parkerish, extrovert sound. One aspect of Davis's work that Prestige could now capture was his ability to develop ideas over several choruses, as he began making LP recordings for them that gave him a vastly extended performance time for each piece.

There were shortcomings, however, not least the fact that promoters fought shy of employing a man who was known to be a junkie, and the band worked sporadically. This led to problems in the studio even after Davis had kicked his habit, and Horace Silver, who played piano on several of Davis's recordings from 1954, told me that because of his erratic working pattern, Davis often came to the studio with his lip in poor shape, and they would only be able to make one – or at most two – takes of each number.[15] This was responsible for the sense of hurried informality and the limitations in his range on sessions such as the quartet sides Davis made for Blue Note in March 1954.

However, in the record dates that followed that Blue Note date – during the first half of 1954 – there are clear signs of a resurgence in Davis's career. He was playing a higher proportion of new and original compositions, establishing a core repertoire for his live appearances. He worked consistently with Silver, bassist Percy Heath, and drummer Kenny Clarke (although the latter two were concurrently in the MJQ), who provided a propulsive but unfussy backdrop for the front-line soloists; a markedly simpler approach than the complex rhythmic patterns of 1940s small-group bebop. In April, with tenorist Lucky Thompson and trombonist J. J. Johnson, he produced a perfect example of extended soloing over the relaxed, yet driving, support of this rhythm section, on a thirteen-minute track called *Walkin'*. The tune itself has a checkered history, having been written by Jimmy Mundy, copyrighted by Richard Carpenter, and originally recorded as *Gravy* by Gene Ammons. But the tune scarcely counts once Davis's unison arrangement of the theme, with its obviously accentuated flattened fifths, has given way to a series of blues choruses. Although Davis opens with a long solo, his art is at its most sublime in the two further choruses he takes near the end, where his playing is pared-down and unfussy, yet is the very essence of the bluesy, melodic trumpet tradition of

St. Louis. (Few of his early solos have such striking similarities, in phrasing and approach, to the blues playing of his mentor Clark Terry.) He plays this second solo after the atmosphere has been heightened by Lucky Thompson over several choruses on tenor – a masterpiece that almost failed to be recorded when producer Bob Weinstock began to get worried about the length of the track: "When we were making the tune I showed Lucky the stopwatch. He played way past the time, but I didn't stop the take, so we got one of the greatest tenor solos in history. The tune, the whole performance is my favorite of all the things I made."[16]

On a set of slightly less extended quintet numbers with Sonny Rollins and the same rhythm team, made a couple of months later, Davis signaled that he was in touch with all the major directions in which bebop was developing in the 1950s. *Doxy*, with the gospel feel of its opening ensemble, and the voicing of the trumpet and tenor in the head arrangement, presaged the soul-jazz movement in which the group's pianist Horace Silver would go on to make his reputation – his own spare solo perfectly balancing secular blues and sacred influences with an underlying sense of bebop harmony. Rollins's *Airegin* demonstrated the kind of high-speed, aggressive, hard-bop playing that Silver would also go on to develop with Art Blakey. But most significant is Davis's playing on *Oleo*, another Rollins composition, on which the trumpeter produced his first extended recorded solo with a harmon mute, in the style that would be a major characteristic of his own playing not just in the immediate post-bop period, but for most of the next 40 years. Although this was to be the most easily imitable aspect of his work, it is worth recalling that, in Clark Terry's opinion, it had its origins in Davis's exposure to the St. Louis brass-playing tradition. Both this muted sound and its clear-toned, open counterpart were to form the aural identity of the mature Miles Davis, however many times he reinvented the context in which he worked.

In the mid-1950s that context was occasionally decided by others, particularly Bob Weinstock, who followed the successful quintet recordings with Rollins by teaming Davis on disc with Percy Heath, Milt Jackson, and Thelonious Monk in late 1954. Reports of tension between Monk and Davis, which arose when the pianist was asked to lay out and let the trumpeter play "strollers" with just bass and drums, heightened the creative energy of this session. The trumpeter's career then suffered an involuntary hiatus when he was imprisoned in the spring of 1955 by his girlfriend Irene Birth for failing to pay support to his children. Consequently, he had no regular group on his release, and for his next major appearance, he was presented at the Newport

Jazz Festival with a pick-up band. (This turbulence in Davis's personal life seems to have spurred him on artistically. Other traumas, from a beating he received from police outside Birdland to accidents in his expensive Italian cars, seemed only to stoke up his creative fires still further.) Davis's playing at Newport was at an extremely high level, and won him many plaudits from crowd and critics alike; it had the additional benefit of being directly responsible for changing the course of his career. Not only did he get the opportunity to establish a regular line-up, but also to sign for a major record company. This was because producer George Avakian, at Columbia, had heard his festival set, and had contracted him to the label.

This event alone signals that there had been a major change in the commercial environment for jazz since the big-band era. By the mid-1950s, although it was no longer the dominant form of commercial entertainment, a modest amount of jazz was still running parallel with other, newly ascendant forms of popular music in the activities of the major record labels. Otherwise, it was increasingly a minority or specialist taste, catered for by smaller independent companies like Prestige or Blue Note. From around the time of the decline of the swing bands, in the late 1940s, individual record producers wielded a growing amount of influence in record companies. The importance of popular vocalists, whose recorded output had to be carefully steered and marketed, was partly responsible for this, but so too was a changing pattern in entertainment, where recordings and radio played an even bigger role than they had before the war. George Avakian himself had moved from being an enthusiast, who had begun in the marginal roles of managing Columbia's jazz reissues and producing Chicagoan Dixieland revival discs, to a position of considerable power. (At the other end of the spectrum, for example, he was to become a champion of the experimental music of John Cage, and by issuing his work on Columbia, taking a major role in establishing Cage as an influence on the pop world of the 1960s and 1970s.) He told me:

> Miles was something of an odd figure at the time, but I got to know him pretty well. He was fun to hang out with – a very pleasant guy, contrary to some of the stories about him and the reputation he got later on. When he got off junk, which I was convinced he had, having heard him over many Monday nights at Birdland, albeit without a regular group – nor indeed a manager – he'd come over to me and say, "Hey, George, I want to record with you." Of course he knew that Columbia could do more for

him at the time than any other label that he'd recorded for. I saw he was getting straightened out, and he'd keep on bugging me, but he had a long time to go on his Prestige contract. So Miles, who was a smart guy, came up with an idea that was, I think, unique in record company contracts at that time. He said, "Why don't you get permission from Bob Weinstock at Prestige to record me now, but agree that you won't put the recordings out until my contract with Prestige expires? And his theory was that Weinstock would like that, because once Columbia had him on the label and started spending its promotional budget, it would also result in much bigger sales for Miles's Prestige catalog.

Well, then I heard him play at Newport; he just did a walk-on with Monk, Zoot Sims, Gerry Mulligan, Connie Kay, and Percy Heath. The second piece they played was *Round Midnight*, and it was a spellbinding performance. My brother was listening with me, and he said, "Why don't you go ahead and sign him, because somebody else will after tonight, because already the buzz is going round, 'Miles is back!'"

The following week I worked out the details of how we'd be able to record him at Columbia, although they were concerned he was a former drug addict, might go back on the stuff and die before they'd had a chance to sell any discs. I told them Miles was straight, and so good he was going to be another Dizzy Gillespie.[17]

Avakian prevailed, and although Columbia's main concern was that the $4000 advance Davis wanted was a big risk for an ex-junkie, the company went ahead with the contract. Within a few weeks Avakian got a call from Davis saying that he had formed a new quintet and was ready to record. The line-up was entirely different from his 1954 groups, and involved the drummer Philly Joe Jones (who had been a running-mate of Davis's during the height of his drug addiction), pianist Red Garland, bassist Paul Chambers, and – in place of Sonny Rollins, who had abruptly decided to leave town – a young tenorist who had previously been a member of Dizzy Gillespie's big band and sextet, John Coltrane.

The most striking difference between Davis's earlier work and this new band was the approach of its rhythm section, and particularly the axis between Garland and Jones, who had worked with him during June in a quartet session for Prestige. In the new group, there was firm evidence that

Davis was striking out in a quite different direction from the soul-jazz and hard bop of Horace Silver and Art Blakey. Jones's aggressive drumming, emphasizing the off-beat, and underpinned by Chambers's metronomic and meticulously accurate bass, was paired with one of the most elegant pianists of the period. Garland was not a particularly assertive or percussive player, and there is a light, bright feeling about his playing. Consequently, as well as providing an insistent drive, the rhythm section developed a sense of space in its work, creating room for Davis's spare solos and the more intense playing of Coltrane.

Its major influence was that of the trio of pianist Ahmad Jamal, a player who combines moments of great power with passages of quiet reflection. Davis recognized Jamal's influence on Garland, and encouraged the similarities, saying: "Listen to the way Jamal uses space. He lets it go so that you can feel the rhythm section and the rhythm section can feel you. It's not crowded."[18] Jamal's critics, including the late Martin Williams, tended not to see beyond what they regarded as the "chic and shallow"[19] elements of his work. However, Williams perceptively argued that Jamal's instrument was as much the audience as his trio. What Williams dismissed as bombast – playing at the quietest level, and then opening up for some dramatic chording – actually served another purpose: willing the audience to concentrate. When I reviewed Jamal's trio in performance at the Regattabar in Cambridge, Massachusetts, in 1995, I wrote: "All that accompanied the quieter passages was the tapping of well-shod feet on the deep carpet – not a murmur of conversation, not a clink of a glass, as listeners fell under his spell."[20]

It was exactly this same factor in his work that had attracted Davis 40 years earlier, and Davis – continuing, as he had done with Parker, to avoid announcements or in any way being seen to act the entertainer – began to use group dynamics as Jamal did, in order to compel his audience's attention. This also created a suitable atmosphere for the intensity of his own solos or those of Coltrane. This phase in the development of the saxophonist's playing is discussed in more detail in Chapter 16, but his earliest recordings with Davis, made for Columbia under the deal with Avakian, before the end of the Prestige contract, show that he was continuing in Davis's succession of heavyweight front-line partners. Their relationship was accurately summed up by Peter Watrous:

> Though deeply rooted in bop, the two horn players took idiosyncratic approaches to its language, Miles by distilling the essence of a phrase into a few notes, Coltrane by cramming

bushels of them into a small harmonic space.[21]

The band first recorded for Avakian in October 1955, but the first examples of its playing to be released appeared the following April and dated from November, under Davis's old Prestige contract. To satisfy the terms of that arrangement, for the most part the band simply went into the studios and played – and was recorded "as live." The results capture an engaging blend of spontaneity and control that mirrored the group's live appearances, not least its mastery of ballads. Although the quintet was occasionally blown apart by disagreements between Davis and its members, and only spent around half the time between 1955 and 1957 actually working consistently, it was the anchor of his professional life during the period, and it coalesced into a formidable ensemble. Even after Coltrane left in 1957 to sort out his life and his drug dependence, and was briefly replaced by, first, Sonny Rollins and then Cannonball Adderley, before rejoining to turn the group into a sextet, this small band remained at the center of Davis's work, and it became the most influential ensemble of the period for the future of jazz.

Although its outstanding influence was musical, it also soon reached the point where it had the pulling power and sales potential to bring about quantum changes in the business of playing jazz for a living. Davis held out against playing for 40 minutes in every hour at a club, preferring to play three or, preferably, two longer sets, and he also took a stand against the prevailing fee structure for concerts, in which a second house in the same venue used to earn the musicians only 50 percent of the fee of the first. Davis saw to it that he was paid the same for both.[22]

The Prestige albums made by the band, before it got into the stride of the Columbia relationship in late 1956, were issued over quite a long period, Bob Weinstock cannily exploiting the material well after the remaining months on his contract had expired. Called *Cookin'*, *Relaxin'*, *Workin'*, and *Steamin'*, these, together with the earliest Columbia album *Round about Midnight*, contain a number of well-known popular songs. Built around Davis's Harmon-muted lead, Philly Joe Jones's heavy drum accents, and the contrasting elegance and flurry of Garland and Coltrane, this body of recorded work marks the last period in his work when Davis would rely entirely on the conventional manner of improvising all his pieces over chord sequences based on song forms. (A curiously abstract, semi-modal, version of the traditional number *Sweet Sue*, made during this period by the quintet for a Leonard Bernstein album illustrating styles of improvisation, shows just how far Davis could develop ideas that *were* based on such conventional structures. It never refers to the theme, and the closing moments between Davis and Coltrane is much more about spontaneous interaction than it is about the old concept of collective improvisation.)

Although some of the quintet's numbers such as *All of You*, *If I Were a Bell*, and *My Funny Valentine* remained in Davis's repertoire for another ten years, not only did his interpretation and manner of improvising on them open out over time to find other improvisational methods than simply running over and over the same chords – such as vamps, drones, and repeated ostinatos – but also by the late 1950s he was supplementing these numbers with pieces that were built entirely on modes (or scalar patterns) rather than chord sequences.

Furthermore, in 1955–6, the close rapport among the members of the quintet, Davis's encouragement of spaciousness in the rhythm, while never sacrificing drive, and, above all, the searching qualities of his own playing, brought a new level of emotional depth into jazz. On a par with Armstrong's inventive response to Bessie Smith's heartfelt blues, or Parker's fusion of the Kansas City blues with the harmonic and melodic rapidity of bebop, Davis explored what his biographer Ian Carr describes as "the quality of profound, and sometimes painful, introspection."[23]

Nevertheless, his canny use of familiar themes, however inventively or introspectively they were treated, built up his popularity with the general listening public, and, coupled with the effect of Columbia's promotion, Davis began to break through to a huge international audience. This was helped immeasurably by the other major recording project that Avakian initiated, soon after the start of Davis's new contract, which was to reunite him in the studio with Gil Evans. Avakian recalled:

> With Prestige recording Miles, I figured there would be so many albums by the quintet coming out, we'd got to do something different. I proposed that we make that "something different" an expansion of the nine-piece group which had been a commercial failure on Capitol, although artistically very influential. My idea grew into a band of nineteen pieces and Gil Evans. It came about because I'd been recording Gunther Schuller, who I really thought had something unusual to say with his approach to jazz, and we planned an album called *Music for Brass*. Gunther had written a classical composition of his own with that title, and he had then commissioned John Lewis and Jimmy Giuffre and J. J.

Johnson to write more pieces for the same instrumentation to make up the album. Gunther, who knew what was going on with Columbia and Miles, said, "There are trumpet and flugelhorn solos on two of these pieces. Would Miles come in and play as a guest?" And Miles agreed. He'd never recorded on flugelhorn before, but it didn't phase him. And that was the inspiration for what became *Miles Ahead*. The idea was to feature just Miles as a soloist with a large ensemble – it'd be very different, and I said to him I want you and Gil . . . to make one of the compositions a piece called *Miles Ahead*, so that the theme, the cover, the whole promotion would be tied in with the idea of Miles being way, way ahead of the pack. And that was the way we would operate with the second album.[24]

The resulting album was not only the publicist's triumph that Avakian had planned, but it was also a major artistic triumph for Davis and Evans, adding another dimension to the trumpeter's work by effectively placing him as the flugelhorn soloist in an album-length concerto, albeit one constructed of several different compositions, and melded into a whole by Evans's subtle pencil and by the deft splicing of the best takes into the finally released album. *Three Little Feelings*, by John Lewis, and J. J. Johnson's *Jazz Suite for Brass*, both written for Schuller's project, were precursors of this extremely productive reunion with Evans.

Even when he was arranging the work of other composers (and those whose work was involved in *Miles Ahead* included Dave Brubeck, Johnny Carisi, Ahmad Jamal, and Kurt Weill), Evans arranged with a sense of improvisation, more often than not creating a recomposition of the original. This is equally striking on his next collaboration with Davis, a 1958 suite based on George Gershwin's music for *Porgy and Bess*. A piece as well-known as *I Wants to Stay Here (I Loves You Porgy)* sets Davis's opening statement in a newly conceived bubbling foment of reeds, with an ostinato countermelody running underneath, and after a fully orchestrated melodic section, the same mood of shifting, brooding uncertainty continues in the accompanying orchestral parts. Davis himself largely improvises on material that had little to do with the original structure of the song. As he told Nat Hentoff:

We only used two chords for all of that . . . when Gil wrote the arrangement for *I Loves You Porgy*, he only wrote a scale for me to play. No chords. And that other passage with two chords gives you a lot more freedom and space to hear things.[25]

The *Porgy and Bess* suite was another commercial triumph, cementing Davis's stature as an internationally renowned musician, and bringing him a level of earnings far beyond that of most post-bop jazz musicians. Its success was later repeated in further collaborations with Evans, including *Sketches of Spain*. But, equally importantly for the development of small group jazz, Davis's comments about the basis for his improvisations were consistent with what he had been doing for some time in his quintet – both in his regular band and in a line-up assembled in France during December 1957 to play at the Club St. Germain and also to provide the music for Louis Malle's film *L'Ascenseur pour l'échafaud*.

For the film, Davis, tenorist Barney Wilen, and a French rhythm section improvised the soundtrack during a single overnight session in the studio, as rushes of the film were projected for them. There were ten sections of music, but each was based on minimal preparation, agreement on a key or tonal center, and a tempo. This experience was a turning point for Davis, as Ian Carr observes: "For perhaps the first time, it became clear to him that it was possible to create absorbing music with neither formally written themes nor any real harmonic movement."[26]

It was also a turning point for jazz. Within a relatively short period, musicians would be experimenting with the idea of playing without boundaries – of totally "free" improvisation. This development is discussed in Chapters 16 to 18, but whereas much of that music was perceived as "difficult," Davis's remained accessible to his audience, and the 10-inch LP disc of his improvised works for Malle's film became a popular album.

The music he developed over the next year or so with his American band built on this turning point, and involved a collaboration with another Evans – this time the pianist Bill Evans. On one occasion Evans shared his philosophy of music with the writer Gene Lees, and what he said chimes exactly with the mood of the moment when he joined Miles Davis's sextet:

> Jazz is not a what, it is a how. If it were a what, it would be static, never growing. The how is that the music comes from the moment, it is spontaneous, it exists in the time it is created. And anyone who makes music according to this method conveys to me an element that makes his music jazz.[27]

Combining this philosophy with Davis's recent experimentation into creating complex music out of very little – the simplified harmonic structure of modes, or of alternation between two basic chords – the conditions came about that gave rise both to the next pioneering phase in Davis's music and, ultimately, to his most celebrated album of all: *Kind of Blue*.

Prior to working with Bill Evans, on his return from Paris, Davis had put together a sextet, adding John Coltrane back into the line-up of Cannonball Adderley, Red Garland, Paul Chambers, and Philly Joe Jones. This band recorded together in April 1958, including a piece called *Milestones*, which was not the old number of the same name Davis cut with Charlie Parker, but a new piece based entirely on a modal structure. Whereas some of the impromptu improvisations Davis had produced for Louis Malle's film were modally based, none had the kind of catchy melody and clear structure of *Milestones*. Because *Milestones* has a bridge passage, it offers a contrast between two harmonic backdrops and behaves more like a conventional chord sequence than some modal compositions, but it offered the sextet a new opportunity. As Davis explained to Nat Hentoff: "You can go on forever. You don't have to worry about changes and you can do more with the line. It becomes a challenge to see how melodically inventive you are."[28]

Davis, Coltrane, and Adderley, whose bluesy and exciting alto playing was a perfect counterpart to the other two horns, became able to stretch out and play long solos that drew on their inner resources in a new way, with no help from a rapidly changing chord structure to give them "licks" to fall back on. When Garland left the band, his place was taken by Bill Evans, and, at that point, virtually all the pieces fell into place for the sextet to develop its exploration of modal improvisation further, a process completed when drummer Jimmy Cobb was drafted in to replace Philly Joe Jones.

Bill Evans was a former pupil of the modal innovator George Russell, whose work with Dizzy Gillespie was discussed in Chapter 8; he was also classically trained and possessed a commanding piano technique. In the history of jazz piano, the withdrawn, pallid, bespectacled Evans was to go on, during the 1960s, to become one of its greatest innovators, bringing a sense of introspective exploration to almost every piece he touched, and leading some of the most searching trios in the history of the music. But in 1958, with just one album behind him, he joined the Davis band as a virtual unknown.

Bringing an introverted, understated pianist to his line-up may have chimed with Davis's perception that less is more, but Evans had some problems over being the only white member of the band, and also with his bandmembers, who felt held back by the pianist's approach. Evans could often rise to the occasion and produce highly charged, rhythmic solos, but this was not his main forte, and after a frenetic seven months he left the sextet in November 1958, to be replaced by Dizzy Gillespie's then pianist Wynton Kelly, who was an intuitive accompanist, and of whom Cannonball Adderley noted that he "plays with the soloist all the time ... he even anticipates your direction."[29]

Evans, however, was called back by Davis to rejoin the sextet for the recording of *Kind of Blue*, and although there is unresolved speculation as to exactly who wrote what, the label crediting Davis with all the compositions on the session, and Evans claiming a role in *Flamenco Sketches* and *Blue in Green*, his contribution to the whole ethos of the recording is beyond doubt. He played on all the tracks except the blues *Freddie Freeloader*, on which Kelly produces a *tour-de-force* solo.

*Kind of Blue* became an iconic album. It was a record that demonstrated the complete transition of recorded jazz, from isolated single tracks on 78 r.p.m. singles to entire LPs with a musically related content throughout. Every track demonstrated Davis's ability to throw out the old and complacent in jazz and to build even the simplest blues from a new starting point. The single piece that draws everything together from Davis's late 1950s work and points the way for the future is *So What* **[CD track 19]**. The piece has an overt 32-measure structure, although this is built on sixteen bars in an initial Dorian mode, and this is followed by a second a half-step up, before the original returns. The bass pattern, played by Paul Chambers, is – in a reversal of normal practice – the theme, with the horns answering in a call-and-response pattern, and the mix of bass riff and simple, catchy horn line is instantly memorable. Davis's initial solo on open trumpet, a simple melodic statement of such power that George Russell later orchestrated it as a theme in its own right, has all the hallmarks of his clear, light sound, helped by the simplicity of the underlying mode, and it demonstrates forcibly that modal improvisation was no mere experiment, but that he had drawn it fully into the mainstream of the improviser's vocabulary. It also demonstrates Davis's mastery of timing – phrasing behind the beat when it suits him – and, overall, taking huge liberties with time.

Coltrane and Adderley both produced characteristic solos, Adderley's simply transferring his usual blues-tinged bustle to a new harmonic environment, and Coltrane's showing a focused absorption in the intricate harmonic possibilities opened up by the spartan backdrop – from stark, slowly declaimed phrases to bristling little runs that dart all over in scalar patterns. The long-term effect of this kind of modal thinking on Coltrane is discussed in Chapter 16, but the other major sound of innovation on this track is Evans's solo. It illustrates dramatically his personal introspection, but the complexity of his chording becomes more and more apparent on each listening, as does his use of unorthodox intervals, including jarring, dissonant seconds.

In a decade – from his work with Charlie Parker to *Kind of Blue* – Miles Davis had investigated most of the possibilities for jazz opened up by bebop – from cool jazz to soul-jazz and hard bop – but this album is the clearest illustration possible that much of the jazz played after 1960 would abandon almost all the most obvious attributes of the "revolution" of the 1940s. Complex chord sequences were being replaced by the most basic modal structures; choppy polyrhythms were being replaced by simple ostinatos or a straightforward, gentle swing; and the pyrotechnic soloing of Parker, Gillespie, Navarro, and Brown was being replaced by understatement and introverted intensity. *Kind of Blue* forms a bridge from the immediate post-bop era to Davis's later experiments, leading in due course to fusion. But before that, Davis briefly dallied with other movements, and these are investigated in the next chapter.

# CHAPTER 13

# Hard Bop and Soul-Jazz

Guidelines to musical composition:

A. Melodic Beauty
B. Meaningful Simplicity
C. Harmonic Beauty
D. Rhythm
E. Environmental, Hereditary, Regional, and Spiritual
   Influences.

Horace Silver, from liner notes to *Serenade to a Soul Sister*
(Blue Note 84277)

When Miles Davis cut his quintet session of June 29, 1954, with Sonny Rollins, Horace Silver, Percy Heath, and Kenny Clarke, the resulting tracks, *Doxy*, Airegin, and *Oleo*, showed not only something of Davis's own future direction, but also of the other new movement in post-bebop jazz of the time, which became known as "hard bop." The year 1954 was the one in which the various ingredients that defined this sub-genre of bebop came together as a recognizable form; in which aggressive brass and saxophone solos, using all the harmonic and melodic ingredients of bebop, began to be set in a highly accessible framework of catchy riff-based melodies, over a gospel-tinged rhythm, buoyed up with the backbeat inflections of rhythm and blues.

There had been signs of this development a little earlier in the decade. On the demise of his big band in 1950, Dizzy Gillespie had formed a quasi-rhythm-and-blues band to play on his newly launched Dee Gee record label, making discs such as *We Love to Boogie*, *School Days*, *The Bluest Blues*, and *Oo-shoo-be-doo-be*. These are among his least distinguished records, and only occasional numbers from his 1951 output, such as *Tin Tin Deo*, with the young John Coltrane on tenor, or the wildly swinging, two-part *The Champ*, with Art Blakey's infectiously rhythmic drums, hint at Gillespie's future development; his mid-1950s big band on the one hand, and his role as a Jazz At The Philharmonic soloist on the other. Partly because Blakey's robust drumming lacked a suitable counterpart – Gillespie either used vibist Milt Jackson on piano, or comped himself behind Jackson's vibes solos – the more rhythm-and-blues-tinged efforts seem unbalanced, having neither the modified swing style of a JATP rhythm team nor the choppier bebop of a 1940s small group.

Yet it is significant that Blakey was a part of Gillespie's experiments in this direction as his drumming was to be a major element in developing hard bop. In August 1953, he was a member of a studio line-up with trumpeter Clifford Brown that pointed in this direction, and numbers like *Cherokee* or *Hymn of the Orient* rely for their infectious swing on Blakey's off-beat hi-hat accents, the latter track, particularly, prefiguring Blakey's groups from later in the decade. The direct and hard-swinging approach of this rhythm section, with John Lewis and Percy Heath alongside Blakey, contrasts to Brown's other sessions for the Blue Note label from 1953, where Philly Joe Jones and Kenny Clarke, respectively, play more complex parts that hark back to the earlier days of bebop drumming.

On a live session with Brown from the following year, cut on February 21, 1954, at Birdland, Blakey is a little more overbearing – perhaps because he was cast in the role of leader – but the pianist for this session is Horace Silver, and his prodding, bluesy piano dovetails ideally with Blakey's drums. On pieces such as *Wee Dot*, this rhythm section prompts Brown into some magnificent playing, an example of the interaction which is also part of the prototypical approach of hard bop, spurring on the seamless flow of his ideas, his clear articulation, his dazzling display in all registers, and the way he blends with altoist Lou Donaldson on the head sections. The rhythm section is the ideal combination of Silver's *desiderata*, "meaningful simplicity" and "rhythm," and for pieces such as Brown's exploration of the ballad *Once in a While*, "melodic and harmonic beauty" are added to the mix as well.

Brown's total technical command of the trumpet made him a very different kind of player from Miles Davis, and whereas he could produce a comparable beauty of tone in the middle register, he had far fuller control of the extremes of his range, and he was masterful at speed. His work in Art Blakey's band at Birdland includes plenty of evidence that he was the most complete trumpet virtuoso to emerge in jazz in the wake of Dizzy Gillespie (who had encouraged him to keep playing after he was badly injured in a road accident and had to spend months recovering).

Stylistically, the playing of this Birdland quintet is still in transition – it harks back, from time to time, to the frenetic small-group 52nd Street bebop of the 1940s, but, frequently, Blakey and Silver pare down their supporting roles to something approaching the generally more popular and populist style of their slightly later soul-tinged work.

Over the months that followed, Brown's own work developed in parallel with that of Blakey and Silver, and later in 1954 he formed a quintet with drummer Max Roach that took a broadly similar tack, most noticeably in the way that Roach also reduced the complexity of his accompaniment, so that on much of the band's work, exemplified by Brown's composition *Joy Spring*, recorded on August 6, 1954, his sparse off-beat is comparable to Blakey's and makes a marked contrast to the cross-rhythms and fills of his 1940s work with Parker and Gillespie. The Clifford Brown/Max Roach Quintet made a series of outstanding discs, first with Harold Land on tenor, and then Sonny Rollins, but the band was shortlived, as both Brown and the group's pianist Richie Powell (younger brother of Bud) were killed in a motor crash on June 26, 1956.

Aside from Art Blakey, the other main catalyst in hard bop was Horace Silver, who grew up in Norwalk, Connecticut, where he was born in 1928. By 1950–1 his trio had become the rhythm section for the quartet led by Stan Getz, with whom he made several recordings. At this stage, he sounded like a competent bebop pianist, with occasional overtones of Bud Powell, and he was also a tidy accompanist for Getz's feathery tenor playing. After leaving Getz, Silver decided to move to New York, although as with so many musicians who moved there, his career was then put on hold while he spent the necessary six months earning the right to transfer to Local 802. He was only allowed to work one night a week in the city, but because he had saved some money during his time with Getz, and because he had landed a gig across the river, in New Jersey, which he was able to play without prejudicing his Union transfer, and which earned him $30 per weekend, he was not only able to survive but also began to make his name around the New York area.

"When I got my card," he told me, "I knocked around playing with a lotta different groups. Name bands, no-name bands. Floor shows. Dances."[1] Silver lived, during this period, in the Bronx, and while he was there he met altoist Lou Donaldson through Arthur Woods, a mutual friend and amateur musician who tried to play alto, but whose main work was in films. "He knew all the cats, and hung out with Bird," recalled Silver.[2] Having been introduced to Donaldson by Woods, Silver jammed with him at an uptown rehearsal studio called Nuby's, and through trying to extend their mutual understanding of bebop they became friendly, first playing gigs together and, eventually, with bassist Gene Ramey and drummer Art Taylor, ending up on Donaldson's first record session for Blue Note. The group's normal drummer was Art Blakey, who did not make that date, but who was booked when Donaldson planned to return to the studio on October 9, 1952. For some reason, now long forgotten, Donaldson canceled this date three days before it was due to take place, but Alfred Lion called Silver and asked him if he would take it on with Ramey and Blakey as a trio session.

"It was an opportunity, and I had plenty of tunes written," remembered Silver, and he pulled these together during the customary rehearsal that Lion subsidized before the making of any Blue Note session.[3] The numbers they cut included a piece called *Safari* that had an insistent Latin left-hand pattern comparable to Powell's *Un Poco Loco*, which gives way to one of the trademarks of Silver's playing in which his left hand grumbles along playing repeated notes, alternating notes, or repeated chords. It is a slightly muddy but entirely original approach to how a pianist might accompany right-hand bebop improvisations, but when I asked him how he came to develop it he had no explanation: "My left-hand thing, that's something that came to me very unconsciously. I can't tell why. I just started playing like that and it happened. All of a sudden – I didn't consciously program it to do that."[4]

On his first and second sessions, Silver played a few standards including *Thou Swell* and *Prelude to a Kiss*, indicating the breadth of his listening interests, but he also, as he said, brought in a number of original compositions. The key to his original contribution to jazz, to the creation of "hard bop," comes from his ability to craft witty, catchy themes, and to combine these with the increasingly blues and gospel-tinged elements in his solo playing. He had started writing when he was only fourteen or fifteen years old, and by the time of his first recordings had amassed a pile of playable pieces that demonstrated his knack of composing tunes. But, just as with his left-hand patterns, he was at a loss to explain how he came to write pieces such as *Horacescope* or the unusually structured *Ecorah*, a piece that wends its way through numerous blues choruses before finally arriving at its 32-measure theme:

Most of my music comes by telepathy, it comes to me in my

sleep, and I get up and write down what I hear. I try to write melodies that'll catch on, are simple to play, and simple to understand. I try to write the kind of music that, when I play a new tune, has the kind of simplicity and depth that people will go home singing, and carry with them.[5]

By the time of his trio sessions, Silver was working as an occasional relief pianist at clubs around New York, including Birdland and the Café Bohemia, and as well as his compositional talent, he was making more and more of a name for himself on account of his bluesy soloing.

When Miles Davis hired him for recordings, in 1954, it was because he wanted Silver's playing to take the band to "a more funky kind of blues,"[6] using the word that Silver himself had added to the title of one of his most bluesy compositions from his third trio record date in November 1953, *Opus De Funk*. "It was," said Silver, "a word that was floating round then. People were playing funky. I didn't see myself as a funky guy. I played that way, but I hadn't been dubbed 'funky' yet."[7] But the term itself swiftly came to symbolize what hard bop was all about.

"Funk" was originally an African-American term for body odor, and particularly those odors relating to sexual activity. Some musicians such as trumpeter and composer Quincy Jones, who was also to make a name for himself as a writer and player of funk tunes, were not keen on having the term used about their work: "The word 'funky' always embarrasses me," he wrote. "For me, it means a form of sincerity. But it's extremely difficult to define . . . I prefer to say 'soulful.' " And Dizzy Gillespie, Jones's colleague of the mid-1950s, said: "it reasserted the primacy of rhythm and blues in our music and made you get funky with sweat to play it. . . . Hard bop, with its more earthy, churchy sound, drew a lot of new black fans to our music."[8]

So where had this bluesy, gospely tinge come from in a player who had grown up in the New England state of Connecticut? I asked Silver to explain:

> That Gospel feel? Well, it's both a "yes" and "no" in terms of my background. I didn't go to Black churches as a kid, because my dad was Portuguese, so I went to Catholic school and church. But my mother was a Methodist and I would occasionally go to her church and dig the singing there. But I think the real thing that brought it into my music was that my Grandmother lived a block

away from a storefront sanctified church. Sometimes when I'd pass by, they'd be swinging, so I'd stop and listen. They'd have tambourines, drums, a sax, maybe a trombone, and I fell in love with that kind of music.[9]

During the course of 1954, Silver played on several discs with Miles Davis, as discussed in the last chapter, that brought his "funky kind of blues" to considerable critical attention, but it was the quintet with whom he next recorded under his own name, in November 1954 and February 1955, that cemented his reputation as one of the progenitors of a new style of bebop.

In the wake of his recordings with Davis and Clifford Brown, Silver's increasingly blues-inflected playing could be heard regularly in late 1954 at Minton's, in Harlem, where he was leading his own quartet, with tenorist Hank Mobley, bassist Doug Watkins, and drummer Arthur Edgehill. Prior to joining Silver, Mobley had been a member of the touring rhythm-and-blues band led by Paul Gayten between 1949 and 1951, acquiring plenty of experience in playing blues to audiences in all parts of the United States. After freelancing around New York he then worked with Dizzy Gillespie's small band, as well as appearing on some of the trumpeter's big-band studio dates. This background made him an ideal foil for Silver – well-versed in the harmonic language of bebop, but equally experienced in the raunchier, more direct sounds of rhythm and blues. To this was added a personal philosophy that made him a particularly subtle and effective player, having taken on board the advice of his pianist uncle, Dave Mobley: "If you're with somebody who plays loud, you play soft. If somebody plays fast, you play slow. If you try to play the same thing they're playing, you're in trouble."[10]

Mobley was a productive composer and, between them, he and Silver wrote a lot of the repertoire they played at Minton's. To my mind, many of the stories concerning Minton's club's importance in the early days of bebop (about which I was skeptical in Chapter 7) actually gained currency during this period in the 1950s, when it presented a series of small modern-jazz groups that were, in their way, quite innovative and which upheld a musical policy consistent with the idea that the club had spawned bebop. This was enhanced by the fact that visitors would hear impressive sitters-in – Silver's band being no exception, as it was joined frequently by trumpeter Kenny Dorham and Art Blakey. From their jamming together in Harlem it was a short step to this band appearing on Silver's next recording date:

I had done three or four trio recordings for Blue Note, and they asked me to do another one. So I said I'd like to use some horns, and Alfred Lion said, "Yeah, okay." I used Kenny Dorham, Hank Mobley, Doug Watkins, Art Blakey, and myself. So we rehearsed and did one 10-inch album. He liked it and then we did another – and those two included tunes like *Doodlin'*, *The Preacher*, *Room 608*, and as a result of doing those two albums together, we got together, the musicians that is, and said, "Hey, we sound pretty good together, we gel. We ought to keep this going." So that's what started the Jazz Messengers.[11]

The name had come from Blakey, who had led his seventeen-piece Messengers in the late 1940s, and had revived the name for an earlier Blue Note session. This new version of the band was a cooperative, although its first quintet discs appeared under Silver's name, and it remained together for two years from the spring of 1955, until Blakey finally took over the leadership. At its heart was the rhythmic relationship between Silver's funky, bluesy timing and Blakey's forthright drumming, his tremendous press roll hauling players from one chorus to the next with unfettered power. Equally, his drum solos included passages where he used his hand or elbow to alter the tunings of his tom-tom heads, the resulting "talking drum" sounds mirroring the experiences of West Africa that he had absorbed during an extended stay there, after Billy Eckstine's big band had broken up in 1947. With Watkins's elegantly simple bass lines, the Messengers were anchored by this rhythmic ebb and flow between Blakey and Silver, who told me:

> We weren't trying to do nothing but just cook, swing, make it happen. We called Art "Little Dynamo," he had so much drive, power, swing. When you played with him you had to match up to him. You had to play strong when you played with Art Blakey. When I played with Kenny Clarke, I had to change the whole thing around, because he was softer and a little more delicate. But Art was loud – robust, you know? Primitive. You had to match up so as not so sound like a weakling or a fool.[12]

And with the arrival of that cooperative band, the Jazz Messengers, Blue Note had found the core of musicians who would make the label the natural home of hard bop. Ironically, the piece that did most to spread the message of the style, Silver's *The Preacher*, was almost dropped from the recording because Alfred Lion considered it too "old timey."[13] Fortunately, Silver's enthusiasm prevailed and the number was recorded and issued, creating something of a template for other musicians who wanted to play in the style. As David H. Rosenthal points out in his study of hard bop, pieces like this and *Doodlin'* had "barely a nod to bebop's vocabulary," but just as Silver and Blakey began to be criticized for playing "simplified" bebop, they also began to break through to a mass audience. At a time when jazz itself was less and less a mainstream form of popular music, it seemed foolhardy to chide musicians who were succeeding in keeping it in the public eye. The Messengers' fusion of late 1940s bebop with the vocabulary of early "gutbucket" jazz, plus gospel and rhythm and blues went down well in black neighborhoods, and became popular juke-box fare. This led Blakey to underline the populist element in his music in a *Down Beat* interview, saying, "When we do get our message across, those heads and feet do move."[14]

One important element in the success of the earliest Messengers recordings, in addition to the purely musical ingredients, was the extraordinarily high technical standards of the recordings themselves, which also had a lot to do with establishing the sound of hard bop in the public imagination.

Up until January 1953, virtually all Blue Note's sessions had been recorded at WOR studios in New York, but then Alfred Lion started to use a new engineer, over the river in New Jersey. His name was Rudy Van Gelder, and the clarity and presence of his recordings set new standards in jazz, ultimately influencing the sound of almost all the main labels recording the music in the 1950s and 1960s. In 1997, I visited him at his present studio in New Jersey, while researching a radio series about Blue Note, and I asked him how he had managed to get such exceptional results – particularly as his first efforts were not done in a purpose-built studio at all:

> I had been recording as a hobby in my parents' home in Hackensack, New Jersey . . . and I had recorded a small band for another company, on which the leader was Gil Melle. Alfred Lion had heard this record that I made and he purchased it, and [in time] he wanted to do another one of Gil, so he went to the engineer who had been working for him and said he wanted to make a record that sounded like that. And the engineer listened and to it and said, "I can't get that sound, go to the fellow who did it." He did. That's how I met Alfred and it went on from there. . . . The house was a one-floor building in a U-shape and

the central part of the 'U' was the living-room, which became the studio – it really wasn't a studio as such, it was still a living-room, but it had a small control-room, with a glass window between it and the living-room. It had a fairly high ceiling for a home, and there were hallways leading off, little alcoves, to give it space, so acoustically it was larger than the apparent size of the room and it had a really nice sound."[15]

At first, in the early 1950s, Rudy Van Gelder recorded in between stints at his day job as an optometrist, and as his reputation grew, in his "spare" time he did an increasing amount of work for New York's independent jazz labels. "Savoy recorded on Fridays, Prestige on Saturdays and Blue Note on Sundays," Hank Mobley told author John Litweiler.[16] This may have suited the record companies, but not all the musicians who turned up to work in the Van Gelder's living room were quite so sure – saxophonist Johnny Griffin, for example: "The studio was at his house, in the living room. He'd say, 'Oh! Don't bring them hamburgers in my living room! Don't spill the drinks on the rug!' We'd drive him crazy – can you imagine all of us jazz musicians in his house?"[17]

Despite the occasional tensions between the lackadaisical behavior of musicians and the formality of the Van Gelder household, the results achieved in the Hackensack living-room were first rate. But, to my ears, there is a distinct difference between the high quality of clarity and sound that was achieved for Blue Note, and what seems to me a less consistent and brilliant result for other labels, and when I discussed this with tenor saxophonist, arranger, and producer Bob Belden, he told me that this was all down to the role of the producer of the session, and his ability to interact with the engineer.

Every engineer has a basic "sound" and will know his room or studio, but you have to tell him where the perspectives are – where the drums sit, where the bass sits, where the panning is. You have to let him [the engineer] know how you want it. You might want a brighter cymbal sound, you might want a real exciting trumpet sound, playing close to the mike, so you hear the air and the spit. Or some people want it further back, so that you can hear the room in the sound. These things are the difference between Bob Weinstock [of Prestige] going and making a date, and Alfred Lion [of Blue Note]. Prestige was almost Rudy Van

Gelder producing, as far as the sound was concerned, and you can hear the difference. Alfred, for instance, would like the bass a certain way ... [he] was able to pull out a certain kind of perspective.[18]

In addition to the technical end of things in the studio, Lion, guided by his talent-scout, Ike Quebec, organized virtually everything about his sessions so that he would get the best possible results. Not only did he provide refreshment for his players, with a buffet and drinks laid on before recording began, but also he generally insisted on a prior rehearsal, which he and his business partner Frank Wolff would attend. The musicians were paid for the rehearsal, and this ensured that more thought went into the resulting album than would happen with an *ad hoc* session, and also that problems could be ironed out well before the band reached the studio. For some of his musicians, there was often another benefit of the rehearsals that has been less well publicized. Quebec was an excellent swing tenor saxophonist, and was also briefly Lion's chauffeur, as well as a shadowy figure on the fringe of the 52nd Street drugs world, and this had some bearing on the way sessions were run. Stories are legion from the period of record dates for other companies being held up while addicted musicians sorted out their supply of narcotics – some of Bob Weinstock's dates with Miles Davis being typical – but this was seldom a problem with Blue Note. According to Jonah Jones, a former colleague of Quebec's in the Cab Calloway Orchestra, Quebec had been free of drugs during his big-band days, but had become a user by the time Jones came to record with a swing band for Blue Note. Quebec persuaded Lion that the company should have paid rehearsals, not least because it was an attractive option for those addicted musicians who constantly needed funds to fuel their habit. At the most cynical level, it bought their loyalty. I suspect Lion was not particularly aware of this, nor that occasionally it was more than drinks and snacks that was provided for his players prior to their Sunday studio sessions, but it is certainly the case that there were many heroin users on the Blue Note roster, and the frequency with which some of them recorded had more to do with the need to buy narcotics than a consistent flow of creative ideas. Hank Mobley has gone on record as admitting that his plentiful recordings of the period were to generate the money for drugs, but in a 1973 *Down Beat* interview he also provided a marvelous eyewitness account of a Blue Note recording session, even though it was generally Frank Wolff, not Alfred Lion, who wandered round taking photographs:

If we had a date Sunday, I'd rehearse the band Tuesday and Thursday in a New York studio. . . . We'd be making a tape, and sometimes my horn might squeak, and Frank Wolff would say, "Hank Mobley! You squeaked! You squeaked!" – and the whole band would crack up. We couldn't get back to the tune. And old Alfred Lion would be walking around, [snap] "Mmmm!" [snap] – "Ooh!" [snap] – "Now vait a minute, it don't sving, it don't sving!" So we'd stop and laugh, then come back and slow it down just a bit. Then he'd say, [snap, snap] – "Fine, fine dot really svings, ja!"[19]

Attending the rehearsals, getting to know the players, joking and photographing, Lion and Wolff struck up an unusually close rapport with many of their artists, which often led to excellent results. The kind of enthusiast-managed independent record label represented by Blue Note was entirely different from the pre-war style of recording, and its work, and that of Prestige, Savoy, and – a little later – Riverside, captured the emergence of hard bop on record. As I have indicated, Lion's results tended to outshine the others in this particular genre (although individual discs by Sonny Rollins and Miles Davis from their Prestige contracts are also outstanding). Rudy Van Gelder explained why Lion's results were of such a consistently high quality:

He would come in with a very clear idea of what the finished product would be. He had rehearsed the music, he had heard the music, he knew the musicians both personally and musically, and there was nothing he didn't know about what was going to happen when he came to the studio. Bob Weinstock for Prestige was just the opposite: everything was very loose, he relied on the musicians to do what they felt they wanted to do, and he let them do it on their own, he wasn't too critical about performances, and he created a very relaxed, totally different attitude. [Lion and Wolff] were there being fairly intense, they wanted to strive for as close to perfection as they could whereas with Weinstock it was a question of "Let's have fun, let's play the blues and get some nice things goin' ," . . . and you can hear that in the records. [Alfred] was with me in the control room all the time. . . . He left it to me when it was going well and I was doing what he wanted. But if it deviated from that I would hear from him instantly. . . .

> One of the good things about Alfred was that I understood what he wanted, instinctively, I knew the kind of sound he was after and I was able to deliver it for him. And if something really went wrong, and he didn't know why, he'd say, "Rudy, go out and fix it!" and that's what I could and did do for him.[20]

Van Gelder's sound was a vital ingredient of the first Messengers sessions, and it is as essential a part of pieces like *Doodlin'* and *Room 608* as Blakey's propulsive drumming or Silver's catchy melodies and funky piano. The theme of *Doodlin'*, in major seconds, and the alternation between a gospel groove and straightahead swing of *The Preacher* were captured in the kind of balance that has been sought after by most hard-bop combos ever since – even Horace Silver's late-1990s quintets seeking a similar instrumental balance and ensemble sound, albeit on much more contemporary compositions by the leader.

Both Silver and Blakey were to enjoy long recording associations with Blue Note, even though various incarnations of the Messengers over the next 35 years or so would also record for a number of different companies. At the heart of Blakey's relationship with Blue Note was the fact that he became another of Alfred Lion's passions – just as Thelonious Monk had been. The Blue Note discographer and reissue producer Michael Cuscuna summed up the relationship as follows:

> When Ike Quebec first introduced Alfred to Art Blakey, Alfred said he would just go anywhere to hear him. He followed Art Blakey round New York for the next seven or eight years, he'd go hear him back a burlesque show if that's what he happened to be doing. Art struck a chord in him, like he's done for a lot of us. It filled the bill – the passion, the drama, the dynamics of the way Art Blakey plays drums and causes music to be shaped fit Alfred like a glove. . . . He truly typifies the Blue Note sound.[21]

And, looking back to the first session he recorded with Blakey in 1947, Lion himself acknowledged the power of the relationship in a speech in 1986 to mark the relaunching of the Blue Note label by EMI under the stewardship of Bruce Lundvall by saying: "In the late 1940s I joined Art Blakey and the Messengers as one of his little 'messengers.' He sent me out to preach the good gospel of jazz which I did for him all over the world for 30 years."[22]

The next Blue Note session to involve the Jazz Messengers, after the two

678

debut 10-inch LPs by Horace Silver, presented some very special problems for Rudy Van Gelder, as Lion had decided to capture the subjects of his enthusiasm not in the safety of the Hackensack living room, but in a live session at a club. This was not the first live session to be issued – the 1954 date with Clifford Brown, for example, predated it. But Van Gelder's challenge was to capture an established band sound, already familiar to listeners from his studio recordings, amid the teeming excitement of the Café Bohemia on Barrow Street in Greenwich Village. The results are a triumph – combining Van Gelder's extraordinary clarity of sound with the electric atmosphere of a live gig and the distinctive aural character of the Jazz Messengers. This is one of the first really effective live location recordings of a band in the history of jazz, where the results are comparable to those that might be achieved in a studio, but Van Gelder found it was far from easy to achieve them. He told me:

> As I listen to it now, I understand what everybody likes about it, but at the time I couldn't see it. Today there are huge trucks parked outside with their diesel engines idling and monster cables going into the club, but I used to insist if I was doing a remote I'd go in there with one of my machines and put it on one of the tables, right off the side of the stage and I did that at the Vanguard and other clubs as well. Club owners were universally unhappy about that, because it was money they could not make from me sitting at that table. The waiters, waitresses, and owners didn't like me, but that's the way I did it. I sat there with pair of headphones, and Alfred on one side of me, and the machine in front of me, and that was it. I had to seek out a pair of headphones with good isolation so I could sort out what I was getting from the sounds in the club, so I'd end up next day with my ears ringing because it was so loud ... it was really a nightmare.[23]

This session by the Jazz Messengers, live at the Café Bohemia in 1955, includes some remarkable moments, and a far more spontaneous feel than the well-organized studio recordings. What is more spine-tingling than the instant that Kenny Dorham launches off into a beautifully articulated solo on the *52nd Street Theme*? He is accompanied by just Doug Watkins's bass and some extrovert drum accents from Blakey, before a snare drum roll brings in Horace Silver and some stabbing piano chording. Combined with the studio sessions, this recording by the band defined the emergent moments of hard bop.

Before long, Art Blakey was to take over the leadership of the Messengers, and soon almost all the other members of the group were recording for Blue Note under their own names. Mobley and Dorham had both cut sessions in 1955 that used other members of the cooperative quintet, and on these discs the Blakey–Silver axis remained dominant, as it did, for example, on Mobley's recordings as late as 1957, with almost the complete original Messengers line-up involved, apart from Art Farmer playing trumpet in place of Dorham.

In April 1956, the Jazz Messengers were signed by George Avakian at Columbia, who was aiming to add to the label's bebop roster, following his contract with Miles Davis. By this time, Donald Byrd had taken Kenny Dorham's place in the line-up, but Silver was still in the rhythm section, and pieces such as *Nica's Dream* [CD track 18] are among the final numbers he cut with the band. It has all the hallmarks of Silver's compositional approach – a Hispanic rhythm under the first sixteen-measure theme, which is repeated before a repeated eight-measure sequence in a swing rhythm, returning to the first theme for a final sixteen measures. Even the solos are constructed over this 64-bar structure with its alternation of time in the center, but because the theme itself is catchy and memorable, and because Blakey's drumming neatly and simply underpins both aspects of its rhythmic structure, the piece remains approachable rather than daunting. After fluent solos from Mobley and Byrd – Mobley's underlining his subtly understated style, and Byrd's, at this stage, still somewhat reliant on the approach of Dorham, although neatly returning to elements of the theme here and there – Horace Silver's piano solo demonstrates his gospel-tinged style, from the opening trill to the right-hand phrasing in his opening chorus. On the Hispanic sections of the piece, Silver adopts his characteristic left-hand style – a constant grumbling behind his clearly articulated right-hand lines.

Silver made his last recordings with the Jazz Messengers in May 1956, before leaving the band. Late in the year, he cut an album under his own name with a studio line-up featuring trumpeter Donald Byrd, Mobley, Watkins, and drummer Louis Hayes. The disc was called *Six Pieces of Silver*, and one of the half-dozen compositions was a six–eight, Latin-tinged piece called *Señor Blues* which had a simple, stabbing riff theme running over a piano ostinato. Byrd's full-toned solo proved that – in contrast to his rather more tentative playing with the Messengers – another distinctive and characterful player had arrived on the hard-bop scene, and Silver showed he had discovered a rich vein of invention drawn from his own part-Portuguese heritage that would later surface again in some of his other compositions such as *Song for My Father* and *Cape Verdean Blues*.

*Señor Blues* became a hit, and Silver found himself being urged by Miles Davis's booking agent, Jack Whittemore, to form a band of his own. Eventually, despite not being keen on the pressures of bandleading, Silver formed a quintet, taking with him Mobley and Watkins from the original Jazz Messengers and adding Art Farmer on trumpet, and, first, Art Taylor and then Louis Hayes on drums. From the time he made his next disc for Blue Note, *The Stylings of Silver*, in May 1957, he gradually ceased to be a sideman on discs by other players, as he had been for Miles Davis and Sonny Rollins, and focused on leading his own groups, which he has continued to do ever since.

There was a contrast between his work ethic and that of Blakey. Blakey liked to develop his bands on the road, using the experience of nightly performance to refine and rework the repertoire his groups played. At best, this method paid off for him, and even members of his line-ups 30 years later went through the same experience: "You'd write a song and think it would sound a certain way, and take it to the band," remembered tenorist Jean Toussaint, who was in the Messengers in the 1980s.

> And when Art played it you'd say "Is that my tune?" Without saying "This should go here," he'd rearrange it. I learned so much from him about presentation, dynamics, how to build. He'd hold the audience's attention. Once he'd got the audience tuned in, he'd keep them.[24]

However, if his line-up was going through personnel changes, or was not working consistently, this method fell down, and as Blakey admitted to Art Taylor: "I've done a lot of recording which was rushed, and I'm not the type of musician who can rush and play things like I want. I have regretted most of the recordings I made when I heard them. . . . Most of my recordings were just hurry, hurry."[25] Silver, by contrast, rehearsed constantly. When he assembled his longest-lived line-up, from 1958 to 1964, with trumpeter Blue Mitchell and tenorist Junior Cook, he worked not only with the band on its overall sound, but also with each musician. Mitchell remembered: "Horace took a lot of time rehearsing the band and the players individually, especially me on a lot of things that were new to me . . . how to govern your solos, and just the way he set his music up – his presentation was so marvelous."[26]

The result was a band that ingeniously cross-fertilized the funky blues-based Southern tradition with bebop, plus a hint of the pianist's own

Portuguese heritage, and Silver's immaculately presented pieces, such as *Juicy Lucy*, *Sister Sadie*, *Peace*, *Blowin' the Blues Away*, and *Strollin'*, all became extremely popular, many of them being issued as single 45 r.p.m. discs for the juke-box and broadcast markets. His next line-ups involved trumpeters Carmell Jones and then Woody Shaw, plus tenorist Joe Henderson, who were with the band in the mid-1960s, and, later still, tenorist Stanley Turrentine and trumpeter Charles Tolliver, who were in the 1968 quintet that produced the enduring *Serenade to a Soul Sister*. By the 1970s, Silver was beginning to experiment with fusion, but he returned to the hard-bop format again in the 1990s.

In 1957, after Silver's departure from the Jazz Messengers, Blakey assembled a new line-up. For a while he used trumpeter Bill Hardman and altoist Jackie McLean, who was later replaced by tenorist Johnny Griffin. Blakey switched from label to label, from major to specialist, and back again, with many of the characteristics of "hurry, hurry" about his work. Even an Atlantic session with Thelonious Monk on piano is somewhat patchy. But in 1958 he returned to the stability of the Blue Note company, with its built-in rehearsal time, and a line-up of the Jazz Messengers that was beginning to be fully bedded-in through the kind of work on the road with which Blakey liked to fine-tune his repertoire. On October 30, 1958 he cut *Moanin'*, featuring trumpeter Lee Morgan and tenorist Benny Golson. This kind of slow, groove-based number was to become a Blakey trademark – as much his aural signature as the Cape Verdean Portuguese tinge in Silver's music was to become his. And the success of *Moanin'* led to a great revival in Blakey's fortunes, as his tenorist Benny Golson recalled:

> That particular album really gave Art a shot in the arm. It was epochal for him, because he changed from one thing, and moved on to something else. And it really started to get good for him, which was great. Because when I joined the band, he had never been to Europe, it had been a while since he had recorded, and things didn't happen that should have been happening. I helped him to organize some things and get a direction for the band, and after I left, he just kept right on going, Wayne Shorter took my place, and they just kept moving ahead.[27]

Golson, in many respects, took the role that Silver had occupied – composing a large amount of material for the band and also rehearsing and directing the group. For much of his subsequent career, Blakey continued to employ just such a musical director, following on, as Golson recalled, with Wayne Shorter. This produced an ideal balance between Blakey's instinctive talent and his ability to hear ways of developing a piece as it was played regularly, with a more structured organizing imagination. Golson, himself, wrote a number of pieces that would be in the band's repertoire for many years to come, including *Blues March*, as well as more unusual and relatively short-lived numbers, such as the *Drum Thunder Suite*. In due course, Golson went on to be equally celebrated as a composer (for pieces such as the poignant *I Remember Clifford*) and as a tenorist. He co-led the Jazztet with West Coast trumpeter Art Farmer, which united hard bop with a somewhat "cooler" style.

*Moanin'*, however, was written not by Golson, but by the band's pianist Bobby Timmons, and it typified, as several of Silver's tunes had done, the kind of number that, issued in single form, would cross over to the lucrative juke-box market. One aspect of the piece that made it so effective, as well as the powerhouse soloing of Lee Morgan — a former member of Dizzy Gillespie's big band — was the extraordinary rapport that developed between Morgan and Golson in their ensemble or riff playing. This was almost as telepathic as that which had existed between Parker and Gillespie, as Golson told me:

> On our first trip to Europe, as we came off stage in Paris, a fellow called Bruce Wright, who was an attorney and friend of the band, said, "How do you and Lee manage to play together like one person?" I said, "I don't know — I've never thought about it." Well, then I *did* think about it, and we went on and played some more, and I listened as we were playing, and it seemed to me it was like a composite man, playing the two instruments. We'd never rehearsed and said, "We're going to do it this way," or "We're going to do it that way." It just happened. I can't explain it. Maybe we just thought alike or something. I don't think anybody else ever played *Moanin'* quite the way we did, where the articulation, everything, between the horns was exactly the same. I never had the same experience with any other trumpet player, not even Art Farmer. We'd always speak about it beforehand, but Lee and I, we never spoke about it.[28]

As Benny Golson said, from the date of this recording, in late 1958, Art Blakey's career took off. Trumpeter Freddie Hubbard eventually took Lee Morgan's place, pianist Bobby Timmons gave way to Cedar Walton, and the new line-up began recording in late 1961. By now Blakey's style had become more established from the days when Horace Silver had described him as the "Little Dynamo," so I asked Cedar Walton to outline what it felt like to play alongside Blakey on pieces such as his own composition *Mosaic*:

> He had a real powerful presence, but for a piano player it was just heavenly. But because he had this power, you had to watch yourself in terms of blending in the rhythm section. Art was so great with cues, dynamics, and so on, and he drove the band from the rear. He drove us like that, but he was actually very sympathetic and sensitive, but as a piano player I was a bit meek before I met him. He developed my "radar," because he'd leave holes and cracks for you to get in and out, and I developed a keen sense of that. He left spaces with some sensitivity for a pianist, because he'd been a pianist himself before he moved over to drums, after hearing Erroll Garner and deciding he'd be better playing drums![29]

Both Lee Morgan and Freddie Hubbard developed the art of hard-bop trumpet playing during their time with the Jazz Messengers. Morgan's opening solo on a piece like Bobby Timmons's *Dat Dere*, from March 6, 1960, exemplifies most aspects of his style – from the neat restraint with which he negotiates the tricky main theme to the way he edges into his solo, playing stark phrases slightly behind the beat, before throwing in the kind of soaring upper-register figure that he had culled from his time with Dizzy Gillespie. He then worries a short motif through several registers, before alternating trills with clear high notes, and after some more staccato phrasing he employs the half-valve position, one of his favorite devices, which gives the effect of squeezing his notes. All through, he continues to phrase behind the beat, keeping to the accessible, bluesy style of the Messengers, however complex the ideas he is wrestling with in his solo lines.

Complexity was an even more essential ingredient of Hubbard's playing, and it developed in tandem with the growing passion and intensity of Wayne Shorter's tenor solos. The piece I mentioned earlier, Walton's *Mosaic*, offers an opportunity to compare Hubbard's playing with Morgan's. After a squawking, intense solo from Shorter, Hubbard takes a brief solo of his own, but unlike Morgan's playing it is tightly phrased, right on top of the beat, creating a sense of urgency that is the antithesis of Morgan's ability to retain a funk feeling in his work, whatever the tempo. Hubbard favors choppy little phrases that are punched out with a pugnacious passion, and his leaps into the higher register retain the same punchy feeling.

Strangely, the best opportunity to compare these archetypal hard-bop trumpeters, Morgan and Hubbard, comes not from a regular date at recording engineer Rudy Van Gelder's New Jersey studio, nor from a session by Art Blakey and the Jazz Messengers, but from a live set recorded in 1965 by Blue Note at a Brooklyn club called Cookers, which came about almost by chance, as the drummer on the date, Pete LaRoca, remembered:

> I think Freddie's wife belonged to some sort of society, who actually put the gig together, got the club and all that. It was a sort of club like Smalls' [Paradise in Harlem], mainly a restaurant-cum-ballroom, and they'd put tables and chairs where the dance hall was. "Just Us" was the name of her social club, and they had the idea of booking Freddie and Lee at the same time. Which was probably guaranteed to be something of a draw. To hear the two of them together was not that common a situation, so it was a very popular thing.[30]

Hearing Freddie Hubbard and Lee Morgan sparring with one another on a piece such as *Walkin'*, from that session known as "Night of the Cookers," after the venue where it was recorded, demonstrates the kinds of difference between their respective styles that I have outlined above. But by 1965, as far as the general public was concerned, Lee Morgan had become hard bop's most famous trumpeter, on account of his tune *The Sidewinder*, which had become a major hit, the album reaching number 25 on the *Billboard* charts. Like so many of the most famous pieces in popular music, this track, which was to become the epitome of the 1960s Blue Note sound, just as Silver's *The Preacher* had been that of the 1950s, came about by chance, at a session just before Christmas in 1963, according to Morgan's bassist Bob Cranshaw:

> That record date was really very funny. We'd done everything that were going to record. Lee Morgan left to go to the men's room and he stayed for twenty minutes or more. He was gone. But he was in there writing *Sidewinder*. Evidently, Alfred and Frank wanted something with a kinda nice groove to it. They were always talking about "groove" and we didn't have a groove on the album. So twenty minutes later Lee came out with this tune. I remember [pianist] Barry Harris saying I wanna be on a hit, and never thinking that this tune would be it, that it would

start a whole kind of revolution. We never thought about it. We'd heard Horace Silver things, which were always kinda funky and groovy, but we never thought this tune would turn out to be what came out. I played a pickup of *dum-de-dum-doom*, but we played the tune so long with the solos that when we came ready to go out I had forgotten it, because there was nothing written down for the bass part. So, I forgot the pickup, and when we finished all the solos, all I could do was laugh. We had to stop, and Lee had to sing to me what I had played, so I could pick it up again. Then we punched in the last outchorus.[31]

Lee Morgan's *The Sidewinder* became Blue Note's best-seller of the period. The single could be heard on juke-boxes in all parts of the United States, and it was, according to the hard-bop historian David H. Rosenthal, one of the most influential of discs in establishing "the pervasiveness of jazz in the ghetto [which was] seen in the work of many R and B musicians formed during the 1960s."[32] Funk, soul-jazz, and the Lee Morgan "groove" were to be formative influences on Kool and the Gang; Earth, Wind and Fire; and The Crusaders; as well as on the mid-to-late 1960s work of jazz-soul cross-over artists like Ray Charles. But with *The Sidewinder*, as Michael Cuscuna told me, came a phenomenon that acted almost as a stranglehold on the music's development – certainly in terms of the Blue Note label, and, in due course, on its equally "groove"-orientated competitors, Prestige and (to some extent) Riverside:

> The title cut absolutely took off and it got on the pop charts. The song was used on car commercials and it was just everywhere. So pressure came from all the independent distributors that were carrying Alfred Lion's records to "Give me another one of them." What you then saw was that each disc by all the hard bop guys, Blue Mitchell, Hank Mobley, and so on, would have a lead-off cut that would be in the groove with a funky riff theme, preferably with an apostrophe in the title.[33]

In terms of the Blue Note label, whether the pressure came from the independent distributors Cuscuna mentioned, or whether, in fact, it arose from the relentless discipline with which Alfred Lion applied his own aesthetics to each session and, using a selection of bands drawn from a relatively small group of musicians, tried to repeat his success, a sameness and a predictability began to creep into his output. This happened notwithstanding the brilliance of Rudy Van Gelder's sound, the combination of neatly written hard-bop themes with marketable groove rhythms, plus the incorporation of Frank Wolff's moody photographs in Reid Miles's elegant Bauhaus-inspired designs. Gradually, each new release came to sound and look very similar to the last one. Lee Morgan's discs, for example, went on to include *The Joker*, *The Rumproller*, and *The Gigolo*, all emulating *The Sidewinder*.

In the world of jazz education during the period, with its focus on big-band playing, up-and-coming musicians like Bob Belden actually overlooked much of Blue Note's output at first, partly because it tended to feature the archetypal hard-bop quintet format, but also because of the stereotyping brought about by *The Sidewinder*. But browsing through his local record store, he discovered that there were still treasures to be found, and that some of the hard-bop quintets of this mid-to-late 1960s period were truly exceptional:

> *In and Out* – by Joe Henderson – that took me over. That record was just amazing. Even if you weren't that hip to jazz, that would draw you in. . . . The way Kenny Dorham and Joe Henderson played. When I bought that record I was at a music school that taught precision and ensemble playing, and they tended to put down small-group sessions as not being challenging to the ensemble, but with this record – the way Kenny and Joe played together was a model of perfection. They breathed together, their pitch and phrasing was perfect, and when you realized that, it brought you into the subtle nature of a lot of this music.[34]

Henderson had gathered much of his style from playing soul-jazz with the organist Brother Jack McDuff, and he combined the bluesy style that such work demanded with a harmonic knowledge and swiftness of execution that compared to that of Sonny Rollins. He was, as I mentioned earlier, a significant member of Horace Silver's 1960s groups, but his own band, with Kenny Dorham, became extremely influential, as did his later work with pianist Herbie Hancock.

Sonny Rollins has been somewhat sidelined so far in this chapter, although from the time of his work with Clifford Brown and Max Roach, in 1956, he was an important figure in the world of hard bop. In an extraordinary burst of creativity in 1956, he made a series of albums for Prestige that captured his dazzlingly proficient playing and his seemingly inexhaustible fund of improvisatory ideas. Whereas Silver and Blakey had explored the connections of blues, gospel, and Portuguese music with jazz, Rollins chose to look at, among other areas, his Caribbean connections, and produced such memorable, calypso-based compositions as *St. Thomas*, which he recorded with Max Roach on his album *Saxophone Colossus*, perhaps the finest of his 1956 output.

He also explored waltz-time in a piece such as *Valse Hot*, but his most enduring contribution to 1950s jazz was in pioneering a new form of small-group instrumentation that is now commonplace but which was then hailed as revolutionary. Because he found very few pianists to be compatible with his ideas and style, he formed a trio of tenor saxophone, bass, and drums, and this freed his imagination in a most positive way. Starting with an album called *Way Out West*, in 1957, but also exemplified in location recordings by his new group made at the Village Vanguard club, Rollins took old, and frequently well-worn, tunes and worked over them in ever lengthier performances. He took a break from performing between 1959 and 1961, although he was often to be found practicing in public, on New York's Williamsburg Bridge, demonstrating the underlying irony that he was both accessible and withdrawn at the same time – factors that have continued to be a part of his music.

Rollins's replacement in the Miles Davis band, altoist Cannonball Adderley, was also to become a leading figure at the soul-jazz end of hard bop, but his impact was felt somewhat later than many other musicians in the movement, owing to the fact that his first quintet, jointly led with his cornetist brother, Nat, lasted for only a few months in 1956, and did not re-form until late in 1959 (the intervening period being the time that Cannonball spent with Davis). A series of discs for Riverside, made from 1959 onwards, show the blues-influenced character of the Adderley brothers' band, and although Cannonball himself possessed a remarkable and fluent technique, his most effective work was as a blues player, and it was epitomized by his first hit *This Here*, a soul-waltz by Bobby Timmons, recorded live in an eleven-minute version at only the band's second concert after it was re-formed in 1959. Louis Hayes's powerful drumming places an accented back beat on the second of every group of three beats, and underpins a lengthy solo from Cannonball that neatly embeds bebop licks into a rhythm-and-blues styled solo. This formula would continue to work effectively for the altoist until his sudden death, aged 46, in 1975, and other gospel-tinged hits for the group included the 1966 *Mercy, Mercy, Mercy*, written by the band's Austrian pianist, Joe Zawinul.

Nat Adderley's career lasted far longer, until health problems curtailed his ability to travel in the late 1990s, and he contributed some lasting standards to the soul-jazz movement, as both a composer and player, including *Work Song* (1960, with guitarist Wes Montgomery) and *Jive Samba* (1962).

I mentioned the organist Brother Jack McDuff in connection with Joe Henderson, and he was just one of a large number of jazz organists who came to prominence in the 1950s, playing the Hammond organ, and embracing soul-jazz. The majority of these players recorded either for Blue Note or Prestige, and both labels tapped into a vernacular tradition in Philadelphia. The town was, as Jimmy McGriff expressed it to me, "organ city,"[35] and others who worked or came from there included Shirley Scott, Richard "Groove" Holmes (from nearby Camden, New Jersey), and the doyen of the city's players, Jimmy Smith.

Smith became the kind of enthusiasm for Blue Note's Frank Wolff that Art Blakey had been for the same company's Alfred Lion, and Smith made numerous discs for the label that caught his robust style of blues mixed with churchy gospel sounds. Among them, as well as the explicit link of its title, his 1958 disc *The Sermon* – an extended twenty-minute jam – is probably the finest example of his style of gospely soul-blues. It has solos from several Blue Note regulars including the little-known saxophonist Tina Brooks, a twenty-year-old Lee Morgan, and a hard-edged Lou Donaldson, and it shows how an organ trio (Hammond, guitar, and drums) could form the basis of an extended bluesy jam session. Smith's driving, powerful style has continued to be a vital force in jazz ever since, and is probably the only element of the hard-bop revolution to have remained current and popular for almost half a century.

Hard bop itself began to feel something of a spent force by the early 1970s, and even though Art Blakey and Horace Silver continued to play in the style for many years afterwards, the days of their music becoming hit records were over. Several of the movement's key musicians had begun to dabble in rock fusion – a natural direction, given the obvious affinities between the style and rhythm and blues – and others seemed unable to break the stranglehold of *The Sidewinder*. The moment that hard bop came to an end as a vital force in jazz was when Lee Morgan was shot dead by his jealous mistress at Slug's club on New York's Lower East Side, on February 19, 1972, aged just 33. With his death, not only had the music lost the creator of *The Sidewinder*, but it also had lost its most identifiable solo voice, and a man whose public persona as a moody, arrogant hipster personified the raunchy, bluesy aspects of this offshoot of bebop.

# CHAPTER 14

# Cool Jazz and the West Coast Movement

> As far as the "birth of the cool" is concerned, I think Lennie
> [Tristano] is much more responsible than the Miles dates.
> It's hard to say it's unemotional, because it's not exactly
> that, but there was a coolness about his whole approach in
> terms of the dynamic level.
>
> Gerry Mulligan, quoted in Ira Gitler: *Swing to Bop*

If the hard bop of Clifford Brown, Horace Silver, and Art Blakey was one direction in which bebop developed during the 1950s, then the other – cool jazz – was its antithesis. In place of the brisk solos of Brown, Lee Morgan, Hank Mobley, or Sonny Rollins, and their bluesy, funky, backdrop, came ensemble precision, cerebral rigor, and a tonal approach that eschewed human, vocalized, instrumental sounds for a vibratoless, controlled lightness, exemplified by, for example, the open horn of Miles Davis in his nonet recordings and the clear-toned alto of Lee Konitz.

The starting point for "cool" jazz goes back well beyond the Davis nonet, or the arrangements of Gil Evans for Claude Thornhill, discussed in Chapter 12. It begins with the airy tenor saxophone playing of Lester Young, or his white counterparts Frankie Trumbauer and Jimmy Dorsey, who combined formidable technique with a smooth tone, and who deliberately sought another approach to their playing from the idea of being "imitatrices de la voix." There was a link to these 1920s reed players and Thornhill's band in the person of reed player Danny Polo, who was in the band for much of the late 1940s but had been in Jean Goldkette's group 20 years earlier. This line of development had continued with the playing of Stan Getz, who, after the period of his work covered in Chapter 8, had

690

moved on to front a quartet. From 1951 this included Horace Silver, but the previous year, Getz recorded during May, for the Roost label, with Al Haig (piano), Tommy Potter (bass), and Roy Haynes (drums), demonstrating his feathery tone even on up-tempo pieces such as his own *Sweetie Pie* or *Hershey Bar*. On these he appeared occasionally to be playing alto sax, such was his ability to produce sweetness of tone and evenness of feeling in the tenor's highest register.

There is a similar lightness and airiness about the contemporaneous playing of Lee Konitz, although he was, of course, an altoist. As I mentioned earlier, Konitz had been a member of the Claude Thornhill Orchestra, and his association with Gerry Mulligan and arranger Gil Evans dated from that time. But before that, and independently of his subsequent work with Miles Davis in the nonet, Konitz played regularly with his mentor, the blind Chicagoan pianist Lennie Tristano, throughout the mid-to-late 1940s, and he continued to do so into the beginning of the following decade. In 1949, Tristano cut the first session for producer Bob Weinstock's "New" label (later to become Prestige), and the success of his disc *Subconscious-Lee* (which featured Konitz) paved the way for Weinstock to undertake more recording of this style of cool, detached jazz, including sessions by Getz.

Well before he recorded for Weinstock, Tristano's work had already received attention as a result of his first discs on the Keynote label, and even before he left Chicago, in the mid-1940s, he had begun to gain a reputation as a teacher and proselytizer, numbering not only Konitz among his pupils, but also guitarist Billy Bauer and composer Bill Russo. Once he had settled in New York, Tristano consolidated his reputation as a pianist, playing with, among others, Charlie Parker and Dizzy Gillespie on Barry Ulanov's radio programs, that pitted the modernists against Rudi Blesh's traditionalists, proving that he had complete technical command of complex right-hand bebop lines, as well as producing some highly effective and exciting "locked hands" phrasing, notably on the group's recorded broadcast of *Hot House*. He was voted "Musician of the Year" by *Metronome* in 1947, but the same year he wrote a feature in the magazine called "What's Wrong with the Beboppers?," railing against bebop, and the musical imitation it had created, particularly what he called "these little monkey men of music" who were "steal[ing] note for note the phrases of the new master of the idiom, John Birks 'Dizzy' Gillespie. Their endless repetition of those phrases makes living in their midst like fighting one's way through a nightmare in which bebop pours out of the walls, the heavens and the coffeepot." In reaction to this somewhat William Burroughs-like view of bebop's conformity, he subsequently wrote a follow-up piece ("What's Right with the Beboppers?") that prefigured many of the ideas that would become current in jazz in the late 1950s, not least as a consequence of his own experiments. These included "cool, light and soft" qualities, and "a more subtle beat which becomes more pronounced by implication. At this low volume level, many interesting and complex accents may be introduced effectively. ... The skillful use of scales fosters the evolution of many more ideas than does the use of arpeggios."[1]

In many ways this second article was a rallying call for what became "cool" jazz, and over the next few years, despite an eclectic range of enthusiasms that took in the work of Chu Berry and Roy Eldridge, Tristano continued both his individual line of experimentation and the teaching he had begun in Chicago, thereby becoming one of the first major figures in this new sphere of the music. Bauer and Konitz followed him to New York, and learned and played alongside him, as did a new pupil, tenorist Warne Marsh. These musicians were to become the core of Tristano's working band in the early 1950s, along with bassist Arnold Fishkin and drummer Shelly Manne, and all but Marsh appeared on *Subconscious-Lee*. Part of the piece's atmosphere comes from the precise unison with which Konitz's alto and Bauer's guitar, using a single-string technique, play the head theme together, creating a spacy texture beneath the saxophone lead. Equally, Tristano's neat, precise, yet probing, piano is just as important to the overall feel of the piece. However, his single-mindedness was something of a problem for Bob Weinstock, supervising his very first recording session:

> The first session gave me a rude awakening into what recording was. Lennie was a perfectionist and he wanted to make take after take. I had a great ear for what was good and what was bad. I was ready to blow my top but I didn't. I went to Shelly Manne and asked him what was going on. He told me not to worry and said they're going to get tired. He was right and they didn't take much longer.[2]

The focus with which Tristano pursued perfection in the studio was a hallmark of his work at the keyboard. He mastered the art of playing in a different time signature in each hand, and took this way beyond the conventional accomplishments of being able to superimpose, say, three beats over four, by grouping his rhythms in patterns of five, nine, or, occasionally, eleven. His chording could be harmonically adventurous, although he tended generally to stay within bebop harmonies, preferring to explore time signatures, the rhythmic possibilities for melodic development, and lines built on scalar patterns. Often his accompanying rhythm section was encouraged simply to maintain a regular, even pulse, with none of the normal accents of the bop or hard-bop styles, while Tristano overlayed long, linear solos that contained many subtle nuances of variation in time and rhythm. His exceptional ear allowed him to remember and transcribe the most complex music, and he once confounded the trumpeter Sonny Berman with a part that Berman pronounced unplayable, only to be told it was one of his own solos that Tristano had written down during a broadcast.[3]

He conveyed much of his skill to his pupils, whom he encouraged to sing recorded solos by the likes of Charlie Parker and Fats Navarro, but also to think about the meaning, or feeling, of what they were singing. "He based his approach on having you learn to improvise and how to express feeling spontaneously," wrote one pupil, Lennie Popkin.[4] And, in a defense of his more unorthodox experiments, some of which, such as the discs *Intuition* and *Digression* from May 1949, were progenitors of the freely improvised atonal jazz more usually associated with Ornette Coleman or John Coltrane in his *Ascension* period, Tristano himself stressed the importance of emotional content in his music: "It would be useless for me to play something I don't feel ... I wouldn't be doing anything."[5]

I suspect his early experiments in free jazz would not have been possible had not Tristano surrounded himself with like-minded musicians, a community of players who, through studying with him, came intuitively to share his approach, much as Charles Mingus did for many years in the 1960s and 1970s with his Jazz Workshop, or the Brazilian Hermeto Pascoal did with his ensemble in the 1980s and 1990s. Certainly, the extraordinary cohesion with which Tristano's sextet played his intricate compositions was due to an affinity among the musicians that went beyond the normal. Between 1949 and 1951, when he founded a school of music at Flushing, Long Island, Tristano's influence grew as he attracted a wider circle of pupils, and, in due course, the members of his band took on pupils as well. Among them were several British players who worked on transatlantic liners, such as the *Queen Mary*, and who came into New York to jam on 52nd Street and to learn about modern jazz at first hand. Bassist Peter Ind was one of them:

> To hear this sound with the two saxes ... it was really something. ... What drew me to that music was not so much the validity of the line but more this marvellous sound — with Billy Bauer on

guitar and the two horns, the way it all blended in. . . . It was only later that I began to appreciate more the musical subtleties of it. . . . Every trip I'd get the bass off the boat and we'd go up to Long Island Railroad and out to Flushing and take a lesson and of course, this was one of the highlights of the trip. . . . There was a tenor player called Grey Allard who was studying with Warne, Ronnie [Ball] and I were studying with Lennie, Bruce Turner studied with Lee and quite a few others, like an alto player called Dougie Fordyce, who was also studying with Lennie for quite a while.[6]

So what were Tristano's methods? What did these young English players take away with them? Peter Ind believed that the pianist inculcated a distrust of the superficial, and helped him to learn how to follow his musical ideas through on his instrument, to create a musical line, and have the musicianship to avoid resorting to cliché.

It was the start of a new awareness. I realised for the first time that to be a thorough musician, one had to do all the simple things really thoroughly, and Lennie started us all off on scales. What I learned from doing scales slowly, and with feeling, has been a mainstay of my playing.[7]

Crouched in the tiny practice room on F-deck of the *Queen Mary*, rolling and pitching in the Atlantic gales, his bass squeezed between a bulkhead and the propeller shaft, and with his ear close to the fingerboard to hear what he was playing above the vibrating roar of the liner's hidden depths, Ind worked on all Tristano's exercises and scalar patterns between each visit to Flushing. In due course, Ind went on to record with Tristano's trio in 1951 and 1955, proving that the pianist's ideas had influenced and drawn into his circle, at the very highest level, musicians from beyond the United States.

It was not just pupils and members of his close circle of musicians who admired Tristano's mixture of intellectual rigor and focused, if often introspective, playing. The composer Aaron Copland, for instance, told *Down Beat*: "I like his sense of harmonic freedom and his ability to write a piece on one expressive thing without being dull. It seems like real composition to me, not happenstance."[8] Whereas Copland viewed Tristano's work objectively, from outside the jazz world itself, pianist Bill Evans was an equal enthusiast from inside jazz, with what was ultimately perceived to be a very similar sense of pianistic and compositional intensity. He observed:

> Lennie Tristano's early records impressed me tremendously. Tunes like *Tautology*, *Marshmallow*, and *Fishin' Around*. I heard the fellows in his group building their lines with a design and general structure that was different from anything I'd ever heard in jazz. I think I was impressed by Lee [Konitz] and Warne [Marsh] more than by Lennie, although he was probably the germinal influence.[9]

Profound and significant as his influence was to be, on cool jazz, on the lyrical introspection of Evans, and, in the 1960s, on the dawn of the free-jazz movement, Tristano became less and less visible as the 1950s went on. Although he continued to teach, he gradually withdrew into a secluded world from which he only occasionally emerged for a recording or sporadic gigs at New York's Half Note club. After 1968 he gave up public appearances altogether, and he died, aged only 59, in 1978.

Konitz, Marsh, and Bauer continued to play the urbane, controlled, and detached style associated with Tristano's sextet, although Konitz combined this for a period in the 1960s with a revived interest in the areas of free improvisation he first explored in Tristano's 1949 recordings. Konitz is the member of Tristano's circle who has remained the most influential, having been directly involved in Miles Davis's *Birth of the Cool* album, and then working on several projects with Gerry Mulligan over the years, before embarking on a long career as an international soloist. His clear, vibratoless, alto style influenced numerous other saxophonists, principally Art Pepper and Bud Shank, who became prime movers in the West Coast "cool" school.

Whereas Tristano's influence, and that of his circle, was most keenly felt during the late 1940s and 1950s, his fellow pianist John Lewis remained a significant and influential figure in jazz right up until his death in 2001. Like Konitz and Mulligan, Lewis was a key figure on the Davis *Birth of the Cool* sessions, first as a composer/arranger and then as a pianist, but his interest in composing went back much further, to the time he traveled to Europe in 1948 as a member of Dizzy Gillespie's big band. He told me that one major impetus for him as both a writer and teacher was to avoid the effects of seasickness on their rough January crossing:

> To try and take the fellows' minds off the voyage, I did do some

teaching on the boat, but the main teacher for all of us in that band was Dizzy. He dictated the notes for many of the pieces we recorded and the way we would play them. I started writing music seriously when I was in his band, beginning with something I'd written even earlier which I turned into *Two Bass Hit* for bassist Ray Brown, who I thought was a player made in heaven, because he carried on the great innovations of Jimmy Blanton with Duke Ellington a few years before.[10]

As I mentioned, the Modern Jazz Quartet, in which Lewis arrived at a quintessentially "cool" sound, grew out of the Gillespie big band's rhythm section, but the quartet did not take shape as an entity in its own right until 1951–2. Before that, Lewis wrote and played for the Miles Davis nonet. His arrangements of *Move* and *Rouge* were discussed in Chapter 12, but in Lewis's own mind, as well as experimenting with upsizing or downsizing the kinds of forces for whom he had previously written, he saw this album as the opportunity to explore his major preoccupation with Western classical music – the contrapuntal writing of the baroque era:

> What I was trying to do there was to find new ways to use the instrumentation of his nonet which included tuba and French horn. Especially the tuba, because the musician involved, Bill Barber, was, and still is, a remarkable player. So I tried to use the possibilities these instruments offered in a polyphonic way, so you'll hear a couple of melodies going on simultaneously with contrasting instrumental colours in my pieces for that group.[11]

Every bit as much as Tristano's interest in superimposing different time signatures over a basic jazz pulse, Lewis's preoccupation with writing two or more parts that moved contrapuntally against one another was to be a significant aspect of cool jazz, where the transition from composed parts in the opening of a piece to improvised lines as it developed became smooth and almost imperceptible. He had this in common, for example, with some elements of Gerry Mulligan's writing for the Davis nonet, and Mulligan took the idea further with the interplay between his baritone and the trumpet of Chet Baker in his early West Coast quartet. Above all, there was comparable interaction between Lewis's sparse, minimalist piano and the fuller vibraharp lines of Milt Jackson in the MJQ, as Jackson explained:

> The people . . . couldn't tell the part that was improvised and the part that wasn't. Because the group eventually became so tight-knit, it got so we could breathe together . . . one knew when the other was going to breathe, and after you've rehearsed three or four times a day, four or five times a week, for the better part of some twenty years, you get like that. It just becomes a natural thing. I can guess what color shirt he's going to come walking in the room with. . . . I was with the Modern Jazz Quartet more years than I was married.[12]

Jackson had grown up a multi-instrumentalist in Detroit, singing and playing guitar, and also playing piano and vibraharp (a larger-scale version of the vibraphone), on which he eventually specialized. By slowing down the electrically rotated vanes in his vibes, he produced a more soulful, throbbing tone than earlier players of the instrument, and his facility allowed him to play lines of comparable complexity to those of Dizzy Gillespie and of Charlie Parker, with whom he had traveled to the West in 1945–6. His instinctive jazz talents made him a perfect foil for the more studied, cerebral approach of Lewis, particularly on those pieces where the pianist introduced his classical ideas of counterpoint. I asked Lewis where his interest in this style of music had come from:

> My fascination with polyphony and European music began very early, while I was having classical piano lessons, and also playing all kinds of music with my cousins as a child in a family band. My most wonderful discovery from that time was when I first heard Bach. Albuquerque, New Mexico, where I grew up, had a surprising amount of music, and I had access to much of it, as well as a large number of visiting musicians. I remember Paderewski coming to play there on one of his final United States tours.[13]

From his schooldays until the time of his death, Lewis retained an abiding interest in the classical tradition, and in performing material that brought this together with jazz. In the 1950s and 1960s, he became a prime mover in what his long-term colleague Gunther Schuller named "Third Stream" territory – music that lies between the two traditions – both at the summer schools in Lenox, Massachusetts, where he and Schuller taught, and also in the formation of Orchestra U.S.A. from 1962 to 1965. Subsequently he worked with critic Gary Giddins and Roberta Swann on the American Jazz

Orchestra, which also had Third-Stream ambitions. (Interestingly, Tristano's former pupil William Russo became another leading light in this genre.)

Early in the life of the Modern Jazz Quartet, which had finally settled into its long-term personnel of Lewis, Milt Jackson, bassist Percy Heath, and drummer Connie Kay, at the close of 1954, having previously had Ray Brown on bass and Kenny Clarke on drums, Lewis made clear his intention of bringing his music into the concert hall, and away from the saloons where so much jazz was performed. Wearing tuxedos and behaving like classical performers drew the attention of audiences to the group's intimate and delicate playing, and to the compositional nature of much of its work – "elevating it," as Jackson put it, "into a classic realm." This realm involved a remarkable control of dynamics, and a mutual awareness in performance that led to the quartet's music being dubbed "chamber jazz." Very few other small ensembles, apart from the trio of Ahmad Jamal mentioned in Chapter 12, have consistently made dynamic contrast so significant an element of live performance.

The importance of the classical tradition to Lewis was nowhere more apparent than in his solo playing, a career that began in earnest between 1974 and 1981 when the MJQ was temporarily out of action, and revived after the group finally broke up in 1994 with the death of its drummer Connie Kay. In his unaccompanied work, he always found a place for genuine baroque music alongside his own latter-day experiments in counterpoint. The two extremes can be found in his solo recordings – a 1984 set of his interpretations of Bach's 48 preludes and fugues on the one hand, and a bluesy, yet elegant, all-out jazz recital from 1990, issued as *The Private Concert*, on the other.

Another parallel between Lewis's jazz career and his classical interests was his ability to write programmatic pieces that depicted a place, an incident, or an event in music, just as a classical composer might do. This was not particularly common in jazz – the main other writer of such pieces being Duke Ellington. And, like Ellington, Lewis constantly revisited his compositions as time went on, often finding new meaning in works he had written decades before. For example, he was inspired, from the 1940s onwards, by his visits to France, writing several compositions, such as *Concorde*, *Vendome*, and *Versailles*, which became staples of the MJQ repertoire. One such composition to which he liked to return, and was still finding a source of inspiration at the time of his last solo album, *Evolution*, made two years before his death, is *Afternoon in Paris*. Shortly before his eightieth birthday he told me:

I originally recorded it in the early fifties with Sonny Rollins and J. J. Johnson. That was a kind of jam session, with everyone just blowing on the tune, and I've come back many times since to explore the tune in more detail. Another older piece I've [often] come back to, with French connections, is my composition *Django*, which I wrote back in the 1950s, not long after his death. He [Django Reinhardt] was the first European jazz musician to make an impact on me, and I had first heard his playing in 1944 or '45 during the war, when I was in Rouen, in France. A buddy and I were on a pass, and we'd gone into a small bar. There was a juke box there, and we put on a recording he'd made as a duo with trumpeter Bill Coleman. I thought it was some of the most incredible playing I had ever heard, and I got to meet him later on, when he came to New York, where he was invited by Duke Ellington. I was playing on 52nd Street with Dizzy ... and Django would come and stay with us all night long. I still miss him – not least because all his life he was a continuously developing musician, always developing, and never stuck in one period or style.[14]

Lewis's piece *Django*, first recorded by the MJQ in December 1954 with its original drummer Kenny Clarke still in the line-up, became one of the best-known pieces by the group, and it was particularly successful because it struck a balance between the composed and the improvised. It begins with the piano playing spread chords behind Jackson's rather tentative statement of the melody, but Jackson picks up the pace and the mood in the second chorus by launching directly into an improvised chorus, as Lewis continues to hint at the underlying melody. One of the tensions in the MJQ that led to its break up from 1974, for several years, was that Jackson felt it was "getting too far over to the contrapuntal,"[15] and that it was restricting his ability, in particular, to stretch out on long solos. This feeling was accentuated by the group's work on film scores or ballets, where his improvisatory role was severely restricted. For the ballet *Comedy*, for example, the group's first collaboration with a dance company in 1962, Jackson recalled: "The first ballet we did? There was really a challenge ... because jazz is always a certain amount of improvisation, [but] the first time I played a whole ballet script for the dancers and all, every note I played was written. There was no improvisation whatsoever."[16]

When the group got the balance between composition and improvisation right, as it did, for example, on many of its earliest recordings, the results were compelling. A piece such as *Ralph's New Blues*, cut for Prestige at the group's first session in 1955 with drummer Connie Kay, has a modally based theme written round a short motif of Jackson's, but superimposed over a blues sequence. The motif is treated fugally by bass, piano, and vibes in the opening choruses, before the number opens up for improvisation. The tensions of the theme pulling between F minor and A flat major are enhanced by the underlying blues harmonies, and even when Jackson begins his plaintive series of blues choruses, Lewis continues to state the motif in his accompaniment. This idea of keeping a composed motif running throughout a number or using it to underpin a solo became an MJQ trademark, and is best demonstrated in Lewis's brilliant – almost minimalist – countermelody to Gershwin's *Summertime*, recorded by the group in a collection of pieces from *Porgy and Bess* under its long-standing contract with Atlantic records in 1964. The results are cool and sophisticated, and caught on with the public, making the group one of the best-known jazz ensembles in the world.

There were parallels in John Lewis's interest in the classics with the early career of pianist Dave Brubeck, who was a music major at the College of the Pacific at Stockton, California, and who went on to study during his army service with the serialist Arnold Schoenberg, and, subsequently, at Mills College with the French composer Darius Milhaud. Back in the 1920s, Milhaud had traveled to Harlem to hear jazz at first hand, sounds that he incorporated into his 1923 ballet *La Création du monde*, but his importance for Brubeck was not so much to do with his innate sympathy for, and interest in, jazz, as in supplying him with ideas from the classical world that could readily be transplanted into the pianist's regular evening jobs playing jazz around the Bay Area. Brubeck summarized the importance of his studies as follows:

> I absorbed, almost through osmosis, from all my teachers, which is the real reason why you study. . . . I found I had the ability to do something most students don't have. When I learned something, I could use it that day or that night. I found that if we were in counterpoint and we were going over two-part inventions, well, that night my piano playing would be two lines. Or if somebody had mentioned Darius Milhaud using two tonalities, on the job that night, *I'd* be using two tonalities.[17]

Evidence of this ability to include bitonal – or indeed polytonal – characteristics into his playing can be heard in Brubeck's earliest trio recordings from September 1949, where his version of *Blue Moon* includes a solo chorus that runs through a series of tonal centers, and, indeed, elsewhere in the piece the main theme constantly seems to be trying to escape into a different key, only for Brubeck to haul it back time and time again. Brubeck's trio was the rhythm section of an experimental octet he had first formed in 1946, and which explored some of the same territory as Tristano and Gil Evans. The Bay Area disc jockey Jimmy Lyons heard the octet – "The Eight" – and persuaded NBC to broadcast its rhythm section on his regular show *Lyon's Busy*, which led to the trio getting a long-term residency at the Burma Lounge in Oakland, where Brubeck's small-group style coalesced. The Treasury Department then sponsored the radio show, bringing Brubeck's work to a bigger audience, and opening up the opportunities for the band to perform up and down the West Coast and to travel to Chicago.

By the very early 1950s, his trio discs (and one session by the octet) on the fledgling Fantasy label had established Brubeck as a leading and individual voice in jazz piano. A swimming accident, and his subsequent convalescence, led to the break-up of his first trio, but launched the solo career of his drummer and vibes player Cal Tjader. However, in 1951 Brubeck returned to the studios and the club circuit, leading a quartet with altoist Paul Desmond, a former member of The Eight, and possessor of a highly distinctive solo style. The group remained together until 1967, and its finest incarnation included drummer Joe Morello (who joined in 1956) and bassist Eugene Wright (from 1958).

Desmond's purity of sound and his ability to create a memorable melody line out of relatively few notes are the most enduring aspects of his style, and which have led him to be seen as a key figure in cool jazz. Although he was to tell Brubeck that he was influenced by the swing era "jump" altoist Pete Brown,[18] the main characteristic of Desmond's playing in the 1950s was that he steadfastly tried to avoid adopting the mannerisms of Charlie Parker. Like Lee Konitz, this involved developing an entirely different tone, with almost no vibrato. He told Gene Lees:

> I was starting out, and every saxophone player, and alto players
> especially, and every musician for that matter, was suddenly
> turned around and stunned by Charlie Parker. And many of them
> tried to adapt what he was doing, which meant they could only

become copies with varying degrees of effectiveness. ... I practically put ear muffs and blinders on to avoid falling into that quicksand, because I knew it would be the finish for me.[19]

In particular, Brubeck and Desmond shared an affinity for playing ballads, for creating new melodies over the original harmonic structure that had a compositional quality of their own. Brubeck made the point that in any carefully chosen melodic line, Desmond's mind was probably working no less rapidly than Parker's, but that he played only one sixteenth of the number of notes in order to do so:

> There are so few guys that can play with the purity Paul had, but when I hear them ... people who can develop a theme and not play a million notes, but rather choice notes, I think we were right. ... Paul was picking those notes with a great combination of intellect and concern for the purity of his sound and he wasn't out to dazzle anyone.[20]

Together, Brubeck and Desmond became extremely popular on the college circuit – indeed several of their early 1950s albums were made before ecstatic student audiences at Oberlin and Pacific colleges and the universities of Ohio and Michigan. In the early 1950s, the quartet played a great number of standards, but in due course, an increasing proportion of Brubeck's originals came into the repertoire, including his famous composition *The Duke*, which was originally called "The Duke meets Darius Milhaud," because of its juxtaposition of compositional ideas: while using an Ellingtonian style of melody with allusions to his duets with bassist Jimmy Blanton, it runs through a twelve-tone row in its opening section and then moves on to a polytonal passage in the bridge.

Brubeck also began experimenting with time signatures. In Chapter 5, I mentioned Benny Carter's 1930s experiments in three–four time, and the same decade Fats Waller had recorded his *Jitterbug Waltz*. But such experiments were few, and in the late 1950s virtually all jazz was still being played in four–four meter. Even Lennie Tristano's complex time structures were generally offset against a regular four-square pulse, and the idea of jazz being played in more complex meters was novel. By 1959 the climate was changing, and I mentioned, for example, Bobby Timmons's waltz-time *This Here*, which was recorded by Cannonball Adderley. The same year, Brubeck took experiments with time a whole stage further, with the album *Time Out*, in which every piece had a different time signature. (This encouraged his detractors, many of them musicians envious of his success, to question his ability to "swing" in four–four – something his ample body of subsequent work disproves, with its driving, natural rhythm.)

By far the most famous of the pieces included on the album was *Take Five* [**CD 2, track 1**], which was also released in slightly truncated form as a single that became a million-seller for the quartet. The piece arose because drummer Joe Morello had been experimenting in five–four rhythms, and he and Paul Desmond began working on a piece "to close a show with a drum solo. It was a good vehicle for me because I was very comfortable in that time signature."[21] Desmond had come up with two themes that fitted over a three-plus-two-beat ostinato, and Brubeck suggested he make the second the bridge to the first, playing the themes in his characteristically sparse manner, and thereby creating the first widely known jazz piece with a five–four time signature.

"It's hard to believe," said Brubeck, a couple of decades later, "that *Take Five* was something the average musician could not play. Now any studio guys could probably play it without any problem. High-school kids don't even think twice about it now."[22] The irony is that for all the perceived problems musicians had with the piece in 1959, apart from the mental gear-change needed to think and play in five beats to the bar instead of four, *Take Five* is extremely simple – its complexity coming entirely from Desmond's deceptively straightforward-sounding solo. Brubeck's piano keeps a constant pattern running under the A section of the tune, and even during the bridge section he continues to hint at the shape of this motif, albeit on different chords, before returning to the pattern for the repeat of the first section. Under Desmond's solo, which follows, Brubeck continues to play the A-section pattern, with no variation on the underlying chords whatever – paralleling the modal playing of Miles Davis from the same year – and this figure remains a constant presence throughout the remainder of the piece, even to the extent of continuing under the drum solo, just as a minimalist composer builds a piece from a tiny repeated fragment.

The *Time Out* album had a number of other pieces in unusual meter, including *Blue Rondo à la Turk*, in nine–eight, and *Unsquare Dance* in seven–four. The close musical affinity among the members of the quartet and Morello's rhythmic flexibility allowed the band to take such pieces in their stride, and over the years that followed, more and more groups observed the quartet's example and adopted unorthodox time signatures, although Brubeck continued to make the running during the 1960s, with pieces such as *It's a Raggy Waltz*, *Waltz Limp*, and *Eleven Four*. The quartet's sound, with Desmond's clear, beautiful alto tone and Brubeck's often sparse accompaniments, became an identifying characteristic of cool jazz, although Brubeck's occasional forays into sequences of harsh, jagged chording and his consistent ability to coax swing and momentum out of even the most arcane time signature gave the group great versatility, and in much of its work it transcended the "cool" label. However, after breaking up his original line-up in 1967, Brubeck then chose to work into the early 1970s in a new quartet with Gerry Mulligan, which to many audiences simply served to underline his cool credentials.

Back at the time of *Birth of the Cool*, Mulligan had toyed with varied time signatures himself, interpolating brief passages of three–four into his chart for *Jeru* on the Davis album. His other work from the 1949–50 period was more conventional bebop fare, and his recordings with tenorist Brew Moore, trombonist Kai Winding, and pianist George Wallington are straightforward, if highly arranged bop charts, with ordinary "blowing" solos, rather than an outgrowth of the low-key instrumental approach and intricate ensemble voicings of the Miles Davis/Gil Evans group. There were more explicit links with the latter, however, in Mulligan's tentette, which recorded for Prestige in the fall of 1951. He used two baritone saxophones (his own and that of Max McElroy), which gave the group comparable depth to that of tuba and baritone; Allen Eager played a light-toned tenor that evoked some of the atmosphere of Lee Konitz's playing, while Ollie Wilson's valve trombone hinted at the french horn sound in the Davis group. Mulligan's arranging for this group mirrored several of the *Birth of the Cool* ideas, not least the fugal interplay at the start of *Funhouse*. However, in late 1952, Mulligan left New York and headed for California, where, after a brief period as a staff arranger for Stan Kenton, he became the leader of a new quartet that was to become a major contributing factor in the development of cool jazz.

Some commentators have seen the quartet as a sidestep in Mulligan's long-term progression as a big-band arranger, such as his biographer Jerome Klinkowitz, who wrote, "Mulligan's heart was always in big band writing, and ... the 1952 quartet appears as more of an aberration than a logical point in Mulligan's development."[23] However, in terms of his path to national fame, his growth as an instrumentalist, and his consolidation of many of the ideas from *Birth of the Cool*, his "pianoless" quartet, with trumpeter Chet Baker, was to be the most important stage in his entire musical career. It came about through one of those coincidental sets of circumstances that put him in the right place at the right time. The place was the Haig Club on Wilshire Boulevard in Los Angeles, a small venue that seated fewer than a hundred listeners. Together with Howard Rumsey's Lighthouse Club on Hermosa Beach, where Mulligan was a frequent sitter-in, of which more later, this was one of the very few venues in the Los Angeles area that countenanced any form of modern jazz. "It was all Dixieland territory then," wrote french horn player John Graas. "The club owners in Hollywood and Los Angeles wouldn't hear of anything but Dixieland."[24] The resident band at the Haig club was the vibes, guitar, and bass trio led by Red Norvo, and although the club owned a piano, it was stored during sets by this group. Mulligan persuaded the owner that he could keep the instrument off-stage, and that he would bring in a quartet of baritone, trumpet, bass, and drums to play on Mondays, the Norvo group's night off. The idea had begun to germinate in his head when he was doing some recording with a conventional rhythm section, but the pianist (Jimmy Rowles) failed to show up, and he cut three sides with just bass and drums. With the addition of Chet Baker – whom Mulligan had met at local jam sessions – on trumpet, the group acquired its distinctive sound.

Baker modeled his open-horn playing on that of Miles Davis – clear, vibratoless, and remaining predominantly in the middle register. The interplay between his trumpet and Mulligan's baritone immediately evoked the *Birth of the Cool*, as did the lightness of the rhythm section which was unhampered by a chordal instrument. The group might have remained an interesting local curiosity, but for the fact that the Haig Club employed a former record company artist and repertoire manager, Richard Bock, as its publicist. Not only did Bock encourage Mulligan to record (indeed it was he who had supervised the informal session with just baritone, bass, and drums), but he also formed his own record company to issue the results. Just as Lennie Tristano's *Subconscious-Lee* had launched what eventually became Bob Weinstock's Prestige label, so the Mulligan Quartet's single of *Bernie's Tune*, backed by *Lullaby of the Leaves*, became an almost immediate success for Dick Bock's new imprint, Pacific Jazz. Pacific was to focus on presenting West Coast modern jazz, and Baker was to become one of its principal artists, giving the label a focus and direction that centered on cool jazz.

The quartet was only together for a year. Both Mulligan and Baker were, despite their clean-cut appearances, heroin addicts. In due course it was Baker, with his matinée-idol looks and neat features, whose life was ravaged and destroyed by the drug, whereas Mulligan kicked his habit in the mid-

1950s by going "cold turkey." However, in an ironic reversal of their later lives, it was, initially, Mulligan who was arrested and imprisoned for three months, hence breaking up the group. He subsequently re-formed a quartet that originally had either Bob Brookmeyer on trombone or Jon Eardley on trumpet in place of Baker, and, later, Art Farmer on trumpet. The group with Brookmeyer toured to France in 1954, and by the following year Mulligan had returned to New York. However, in California, in late 1954, and then back in the East, he occasionally expanded his line-up to a sextet, with Brookmeyer, Eardley, and tenorist Zoot Sims, but the quintessential drumless sound of both his mid-to-late 1950s quartet and sextet owed its origins to the 1952–3 group with Baker.

Part of its success was that Mulligan largely recorded extremely well-known standard songs. Examples include *Lullaby of the Leaves*, *My Funny Valentine*, *Frenesi*, and *The Lady Is a Tramp*. His refreshing approach to playing such familiar material caught the public imagination, and not only did the quartet attract far more listeners than could be accommodated at the Haig, but its discs, for both Pacific Jazz and the Bay Area-based Fantasy label, also sold extremely well. Among the latter was *Carioca*, a Latin-tinged piece that perfectly demonstrates the template Mulligan used for constructing his neatly crafted quartet arrangements. Chico Hamilton's Latin percussion begins the track, with an ostinato-bass figure from Carson Smith accompanying the harmonized melody for trumpet and baritone. The second chorus begins with a downward fugal flourish – baritone and trumpet chasing one another through their range, before the rhythm section shifts into a walking four–four, and Mulligan takes a solo. Behind Baker's subsequent chorus, Mulligan provides some dense harmonic filling-in, eventually subtly reverting to a riff based on the tune's opening figure, before the two horns play a close-harmony coda.

The blend between arrangement and improvisation is directly comparable to that of the Modern Jazz Quartet, and there was another parallel, in that Milt Jackson and Chet Baker were both slow at reading music. Jackson learned how to do this during the formative years of the MJQ, having relied on his exceptional ear to busk his way through arrangements with Dizzy Gillespie, but there was always a strong element of the instinctive about his playing. When he joined Mulligan, Baker could read, but he was more of a "speller" than a fluent sight-reader. He consequently ended up playing an intuitive, more completely improvised part compared to that of Mulligan, just as Jackson's extemporary lines were counterbalanced by John Lewis's more controlled, cerebral piano. The proof of this comes in *Line for Lyons*, one of the quartet's originals, where Baker starts out by playing the melody line, under which Mulligan weaves a second, intricately harmonized part behind him, and exactly the same happens during the trumpet solo, where Mulligan sketches out the harmonic movement of the piece with his judicious choice of backing notes. Significantly, Baker does not play comparable backing harmonies to Mulligan's solo (something he does on only a few of the group's discs), and in the closing ensemble Mulligan consistently indicates the thematic material with which baritone and trumpet play tag over the final chorus, relying on the trumpeter's quick ear to pick up the phrases he has to follow.

Mulligan was well aware of Baker's strengths and weaknesses in this regard, telling Gene Lees:

> It's not a question of whether [Chet] couldn't read chords or anything like that. It's that he didn't care. He had one of the quickest connections between mind, hand, and chops that I have ever encountered. He really played by ear, and he could play intricate progressions.[25]

The intricacy, not only of the progressions over which Baker's solos were based, but also of the structure of the solos themselves, was remarkable. It was more than usually apparent from the group's recordings, because this was a band that almost never raised its voice. Everything was delivered in a calm and controlled way, so that even an up-tempo swinger such as *Bark for Barksdale* was delivered *mezzo forte*, with the loudest sounds coming from Hamilton's occasional bass-drum punctuations. On this piece, Baker's agile and fluent solo contains some extraordinarily rapid runs, figures of a speed and complexity more usually associated with such flamboyant players as Dizzy Gillespie, but, in his understated way, Baker negotiates them with ease, bringing to mind another of Mulligan's comments about him: "He had incredible facility. Remarkable. So it's obvious that at some point in his life, Chet Baker practiced a lot. It's all well and good to be able to do that. You're not born able to do that. You're maybe born with a facility to learn quickly."[26]

Through his work with Mulligan's quartet, and his own subsequent quartet recordings for Pacific Jazz (with a conventional piano, bass, and drums rhythm section), Baker was one of the defining voices of what became identified as the West Coast school of "cool" players. He also sang, in moody, level tones that matched his relaxed style of trumpet playing, and he became a frequent poll-winner, as well as working briefly with Charlie Parker on the saxophonist's latter-day visits to California. His recordings from the mid-1950s, in a variety of line-ups in California, also included work with altoist Art Pepper, and tenorist and arranger Jack Monterose.

Before its enforced break-up, the original Mulligan Quartet itself made an explicit link with *Birth of the Cool* in January 1953, by recording several pieces with Lee Konitz's alto added to the line-up.

There was a somewhat unexpected side-effect of the Mulligan Quartet's discs, in that, later in the decade, they apparently exerted a profound influence over the bossa nova craze. In 1950s Brazil, American jazz records were not easy to come by, but the exception seems to have been Bock's Pacific Jazz label, and the quartet's suave, elegant sides were much admired by Antonio Carlos Jobim and João Gilberto in creating their own distinctive brand of restrained excitement. Indeed, according to Gene Lees, Jobim's one-time lyricist, Mulligan was one of the first American players Jobim met after his Carnegie Hall debut, and they remained lifelong friends.[27]

After his return to New York, Mulligan continued a long career, both as one of the most distinctive and accomplished soloists on the baritone, in large and small settings, and as composer, arranger, and bandleader of a series of experimental large groups. He was just as much an individual with pencil and manuscript paper as he was in making the weighty and unwieldy baritone saxophone sound feather-light and flexible. From his 1949 arrangements on *Birth of the Cool* to the 1960s charts he produced for his own Concert Jazz Band, he always had a knack of creating dazzling instrumental effects with smaller-than-normal forces, just as his inventive settings managed to make his quartets (with or without piano) take on some qualities of a larger orchestra.

I mentioned that Mulligan had jammed from time to time at a club called the Lighthouse, and this Hermosa Beach venue on the southern part of the Los Angeles coastline became the focal point for another group of musicians who fueled the vogue for cool jazz. Predominantly white, and mainly recent members of such big bands as those of Woody Herman or Stan Kenton, they were drawn both towards experimenting with many of the new ideas currently emerging from bebop under the overall "cool" banner, and also towards a club whose very purpose was to provide a venue for musicians who were keen to come off the road and settle down playing modern jazz. The Lighthouse was a bar that had seen better days, and was revived by Howard Rumsey, a former Kenton bassist, who talked the owner John Levine into trying out jam sessions as a way of reviving his trade. The doors opened on May 29, 1949, and, to start with, only offered live music at weekends, with Rumsey playing discs during the week. But before long there was music on five nights out of every seven.

By 1951, trumpeter Shorty Rogers had become a regular there, and he told me in 1991 that his experience was typical of many of the circle of players who worked at the club:

> It was my opportunity to stay in Los Angeles, live at home with my family, and get off the road. There was so little work going in Los Angeles, I couldn't really make it there, but the club gave me a steady job playing jazz every night. And for me, that alone would have been enough. Except that it went much further than that. The place had a kind of family atmosphere, and it became a very special time of my life – something to cherish. As time goes on it becomes more apparent to me how valid the music was, because the whole bunch of guys down there working included Shelly Manne, Milt Bernhardt, Art Pepper, and Hampton Hawes. It was at 30 Pier Avenue, and just a few doors west of there you're on the beach. Go out and walk a few feet further on and you're in the Pacific Ocean. So it was very much a beach place. On Sundays, which became the big marathon all-day session there, from two in the afternoon 'til two in the morning, the prices were very inexpensive. People could come in and have a beer for 25 cents. People would hear the music and come in off the beach around 2.15 in their bathing suits. Sometimes I'd look up off the bandstand and see the same guy sitting there with the same beer – been there all day long! But amongst the people in bathing suits there'd be people in dress suits, people from Hollywood, from the movie community. The mixture was wonderful and the one thing they all had in common was an enjoyment of jazz and the fun of being there. And this rubbed off on the musicians. We were part of it, and they were part of it.[28]

He and altoist Bud Shank have both recalled how many people they subsequently met in their travels around the world who first heard them as one of the "fat sweaty bodies, covered in sand, falling off the bar stools at the Lighthouse."[29] But the club was also put on the map when Contemporary Records signed a deal with Rumsey in 1952, and began to record the house band, creating a series of mementos of the way the music sounded for those who visited, and also spreading those sounds to the outside world. In the first few discs, Rogers, plus tenorists Jimmy Giuffre and Bob Cooper, was featured, plus Bernhardt and Manne. Ironically, because live recordings were still problematical, as we know from Rudy Van Gelder's experiences on the other side of the continent at the Café Bohemia, many of the discs purporting to represent the club's atmosphere were no such thing, as Rogers recalled: "Although there was [later] a lot of live recording done at the club, those first recordings were done in a studio. From time to time, someone'd yell or something, to get a little of that Lighthouse atmosphere in there."[30]

Although that environment was important to both the visiting public and the musicians, what was really extraordinary about the Lighthouse was the degree to which it became a learning organization for those who played there. In Bud Shank's view, "It was a place of learning, of experiment, of creativity, of study, and amongst all the funny and crazy things that went on, it offered a structure, a framework for creativity that will probably never be equalled again."[31]

So what did go on? And what was so exceptional about it? To start with, Rumsey's choice of musicians created a character about the house band that seemed to remain constant, even if the personnel changed. Rogers told me that whichever of its regulars, Frank Patchen, Hampton Hawes, Pete Jolly, or Marty Paich was on piano, the "flavor" of the band continued unaltered. Through the mammoth weekly jam session, not only did the house musicians end up playing the equivalent hours to an extra week of normal gigs at the club, and hence develop an exceptionally close rapport with one another, but word got out about this among both the studio musicians and visiting bands, so that there was a constant interaction between the regulars and a stimulating stream of visitors. Rogers singled out trumpeter Maynard Ferguson and Gerry Mulligan as particularly memorable contributors, and both of them were to record in Rogers's various projects from the period.

Most important, however, was the fact that so many of the house band were writing prolifically, at the same time as studying arranging and composition. Rogers and Giuffre were working with Dr. Wesley La Violette, for two hours a week, and then applying what they learned to writing new charts – in some instances up to three a day. Frank Patchen was also a student of La Violette, and Bud Shank and some of the other band members studied with Rogers (already, as we know, an established talent from his work with Woody Herman and Stan Kenton). From Rogers's account of his studies, some striking parallels emerge with the thinking of John Lewis:

There was an influx of new material coming in like an avalanche. It never quit. Working with pencil and paper like that was a fun thing; to be able to write something and think "Hey! We can go to work tonight and hear it!" Not having to wait years to hear your work was great, and it fed back into our lessons. The basis of our study was the study of counterpoint. I used it some. Jimmy used it more than me. We looked at the old masters: Bach, Beethoven, Mozart. Some of the things we wrote had a baroque flavor, but once that part ended we just went into a lot of blowing![32]

As well as studying the music of the past, Rogers encouraged his circle to listen to as many examples of great recorded jazz as possible, and, in addition to Charlie Parker solos, he was particularly keen on the Count Basie small-group repertoire, which, he told me, had a major influence on his writing, with its mixture of lightness, swing, and robust strength. The same discs also had a profound effect on Jimmy Giuffre, whose brittle clarinet tone owed a lot to Lester Young's work with Basie on that instrument. Bud Shank recalled Rogers encouraging him to go out with his colleagues in the band and hear as many jazz discs as they could get hold of in the listening booths of Los Angeles record shops, throughout the mid-1950s.

In Rogers's own case, the facility he developed as a composer led him into a long and lucrative career writing for Hollywood films and television shows, and more or less abandoning jazz as a player, arranger, and bandleader from the 1960s until the early 1980s. However, for a short period in the 1950s – having used the Lighthouse and his continuing role as a Kenton arranger as a springboard – he became a significant bandleader in his own right, making a series of significant discs with his "Giants," in ensembles of every size from a big band to a nonet, as well as in the band's everyday working configuration as a quintet.

Rogers's first album under his own name was made while he was still on Kenton's staff as an arranger. Called *Modern Sounds*, it was the brainchild of disc jockey Gene Norman, who had got to know Rogers in his Woody Herman days. "He called me up and said, 'Let's do an album,'" recalled Rogers. "He produced it himself, and I think he had to shop it around a bit, but Capitol bought it, and I admired him for taking a chance on us."[33] Because the octet on the album included a french horn and tuba, its obvious parallels with Davis's *Birth of the Cool* nonet have been seized upon by numerous critics over the years who have been unnecessarily harsh on it, seeing it as derivative, but lacking in the ensemble density and experimental voicings of Gil Evans, Johnny Carisi, John Lewis, and Gerry Mulligan. If, as Max Harrison suggests,[34] it is not listened to in comparison with those writers at all, but is heard as a quantum leap forward in Rogers's arranging skills, from his work with Herman small groups in the late 1940s, then it demonstrates that he had plenty of ideas, but that these came from a different direction altogether. The octet's instrumental similarities with the Davis group produced little direct effect on Rogers's writing style, which focused on transferring some of the devices he had used with Kenton to smaller forces – the feathery opening section to tenorist Bob Cooper's feature *Coop's Solo*, which Rogers wrote just a month or so before *Modern Sounds*, is a clue, as is the way part of the up-tempo section of the same tenor solo was scored, not improvised, to interact with the ensemble voicings behind it.

More importantly, the Davis approach had scant impact on Rogers's natural *playing* style, which on a piece such as the blues *Popo* combines all the drive and excitement expected of a Herman small group with a beautifully written chart. A four-measure scored interlude separates the light-toned, but extrovert, solos of Art Pepper on alto and Jimmy Giuffre on tenor, and there are some throaty ensemble chords using the saxes, french horn, and tuba behind Rogers's own first solo chorus. This trumpet solo is impressive, and shows Rogers remaining in the middle range of Davis or Baker, but deliberately picking up thematic ideas from his score, and also playing around with some striking chord substitutions, particularly in the fifth and sixth measures of his second chorus. What really confirms Harrison's observation that this has less to do with the Davis nonet material than the Herman tradition is the rhythm-section playing. Hampton Hawes's prodding, joyous piano is a constant spur for the soloists, and he in turn is egged on by the forceful drumming of Shelly Manne, who also adds some vocal encouragement for the soloists. This has all the bounce and drive of Manne's late-1940s work in the Herman band alongside Chubby Jackson, and, coupled with the tonality of the saxes, which echo the lightness of Getz or Cohn, the connection becomes more obvious with each hearing.

Rogers's small groups, from a little later in the 1950s, became far more self-consciously cool – notably his series of blues pieces starting in 1955 with *Martians Go Home* (a piece of graffiti in the men's room at Zardi's Club that was immortalized here, and in a long sequence of subsequent "Martian" song titles). Here, his own playing, and that of Jimmy Giuffre on clarinet, is deliberately to do with playing fewer, better-chosen notes – a move almost certainly inspired by the teaching of Dr. La Violette, every bit as much as by the influence of other "cool" players.

However, the album that forever linked Rogers's name to the cool movement was something of a misnomer. It was not a small-group session at all, but a full, big-band recording made for Victor in 1953, and issued under the name *Cool and Crazy*. Surrounded by clever publicity and hype, it became one of a series of RCA discs whose covers presented Rogers in bizarre costumes and settings – about which he had mixed feelings:

> I don't usually walk around with a space helmet on! But that album came about because a man called Jack Lewis had helped on the production of *Modern Sounds*, and he went to RCA and suggested they record me. They said, "We don't know about that, but we have this great title for an album that we want to get made, *Cool and Crazy*, but we don't know who to make it with." Jack spoke on my behalf, and it wound up being me.[35]

Cool it may not all have been, nor particularly crazy, but it was Rogers's most daring and experimental writing to date. His big band was largely populated by members of the Stan Kenton Orchestra, plus a core of Lighthouse regulars, and like the *Modern Sounds* octet, was anchored by the propulsive drumming of Manne, this time supplemented by Curtis Counce on bass and Marty Paich on piano. The brass section included the high-note specialist Maynard Ferguson, and there is a punchy, forthright quality about its playing that gives it a vigorous, if somewhat slimmed-down, flavor of the contemporaneous Kenton sound. Only the solos – notably from the reed section of Art Pepper, Bud Shank, Jimmy Giuffre, and Bob Cooper – retain the lightness and control associated with cool, but again, this is more a question of playing in the Herman "Four Brothers" tradition than emulating the style of Lee Konitz or Gerry Mulligan.

However, Rogers's writing encompassed several of the ideas to which I have referred in passing, as part of the work of other members of the "cool" movement. On *Cool and Crazy* he explored irregular ostinati in the memorably named *Tales of an African Lobster* (one of a series of outlandish titles that were largely the product of Shelly Manne's penchant for puns and word-play), and he piled on more and more timbral density on *Infinity Promenade*. By the time of *I'm Gonna Go Fishin'* in 1962 he was also exploring bitonality, and he had collaborated with trumpeter Harry "Sweets" Edison on remaking a number of titles associated with the Count Basie band that took a somewhat different tack from Basie's own development, as discussed in the next chapter.

Unfortunately, few of Rogers's compositions for the Giants or his studio orchestra were played by anyone else, so his work was not taken up on a very wide scale, and remained something of a West Coast curiosity. Only Art Pepper, who recorded a session for Pacific Jazz in 1957, produced different readings of such Rogers charts as *Bunny* and *Popo*. It took until the early 1990s, and the re-formation of the Lighthouse All Stars, for an international audience to hear this music again, when Rogers, Shank, Cooper, and several other former colleagues, who had given up their Hollywood studio jobs, once more went on the road, and breathed new life into the arrangements. But in his new writing for this latter-day group, Rogers was far less experimental than he had been in the 1950s. During the period of his studies with La Violette, he had written not only for the Lighthouse band and his own Giants, but also for other leaders including vibes player Teddy Charles, and for an unorthodox trio led by Shelly Manne that featured just drums, Giuffre's reeds, and Rogers himself on trumpet. As well as *Three in a Row*, which was based on serial techniques, this group began to explore free-form ideas in pieces such as *Abstract No. 1*.

In his substantial body of work recorded for Atlantic and Victor under his own name, Rogers was one of the most significant figures in the West Coast jazz of the 1950s. At a time when Central Avenue in Los Angeles was winding down, its clubs were closing, and its players spreading to other cities and other areas, the focus on the Lighthouse and newer clubs such as Zardi's changed the emphasis in the city from the older, continuous African-American tradition to a newer style more associated with white players. I have suggested some reasons, above, why this movement has been bracketed with "cool" jazz, but another reason, apparent from surveying Rogers's output over the entire decade, is its extraordinary breadth of timbral and tonal color. Not only did Rogers himself begin to use the deep-toned flugelhorn for much of his work from the mid-1950s onwards, but by working with musicians who were experienced in the instrumental doubling required by Kenton, or by studio bands, he had a huge range of reed sounds available, and his sections not only included all the saxophones, but also tenor and alto flutes, plus the occasional, less orthodox woodwind. In John Graas he had a long-term colleague who brought the french horn into his line-ups as a solo instrument as well as an ensemble timbre, and some of his early bands included the tragically short-lived Frank Rosolino, who pushed the technical boundaries of the trombone higher and faster than most players before him.

This coloristic variety is the abiding influence of Rogers and his circle, as well as proving that there were different areas of the classical tradition that could be explored creatively in jazz. In a parallel movement, arising out of the decline of Central Avenue, one other band made its name in the mid-1950s, exploring timbre and color in a manner that linked in to the cool school. This was the quintet led by drummer Chico Hamilton, after his early work with Mulligan's "drumless" quartet, and it sought a novel sound through the unorthodox instrumentation of reeds, guitar, cello, bass, and drums.

The band arose when Hamilton was playing drums for singer Lena Horne and discovered Fred Katz, her pianist, was also a cellist. Together with Mulligan's former bassist Carson Smith, guitarist Jim Hall, and reed player Buddy Collette, the group went into another beach bar, a short distance from the Lighthouse, called Strollers. Despite the indifference and incomprehension of the regulars, it took off, notably after the local radio station, KFOX, began doing live relays from the club, and at this point Katz abandoned the original idea of doubling on piano, owing to a bandstand as cramped as the one at the Haig, which made it easier for him to stick to cello. The band became a by-word for "chamber jazz" – a West Coast equivalent of the MJQ or latter-day Mulligan quartets – but, as time went by, it began to experiment with an idea pioneered by Tristano in the late 1940s: completely free improvisation. Buddy Collette recalled:

> Fifty percent of the time, we'd just play, improvise, not even discussing what we would play. Somebody would start a line and that line would continue with answers, fugue statements, recapitulations, and those kinds of things. The ideas would move around and come back at you like an echo. It might have begun with just a look, and before we knew it, all our minds would be locked into one. We'd frequently get requests for certain pieces, but couldn't play them again for any amount of money. They were one-time only pieces, that depended on what . . . we felt at that moment.[36]

This idea of free improvisation – demonstrated on the band's 1955 recording, *Free Form* – was one that would be explored in another Los Angeles club, the Hillcrest, just a couple of years later, with the first experiments of Ornette Coleman, discussed in Chapter 17. But the Hamilton group's great public triumphs came from a rather different aspect of their work, which was daring to play quietly. Most famous of these pieces was Buddy Collette's *Blue Sands*, an exercise in semi-free mood music, based on a flute exercise. It was the band's performance of this, stilling a huge crowd of several thousands at the 1956 Newport Jazz Festival before generating wild applause, that paved the way for Duke Ellington's celebrated *Diminuendo and Crescendo in Blue*, and everywhere the piece was played, its quiet focus produced a similar *coup-de-théâtre*. Other members of Hamilton's line-up learned from this approach, and quiet restraint became a hallmark of the playing of guitarist Jim Hall and saxophonist Charles Lloyd (who, along with Eric Dolphy, followed Collette into the band). At the 2000 Chicago Jazz Festival I watched Lloyd playing *The Water is Wide* – a gospelish, quiet ballad – in front of a crowd of 8000, and using exactly the same technique of restraint and calm to still them into listening hard and then applauding rapturously. The abiding lesson of the cool school is, perhaps, that to say something worth saying softly is more effective than shouting at the top of your voice.

CHAPTER 15

# Big Bands in Transition

> The new band didn't have the stars in it that the other band
> had, but the band was jumping, and every one of those
> soloists was taking care of business.
>
> Count Basie, from *Good Morning Blues*

The standard instrumentation of the swing-era big band survived beyond the collapse of the majority of the great orchestras in the late 1940s. In a small number of cases, notably Duke Ellington and (apart from a year in the early 1950s) Count Basie, the original orchestras themselves continued. Other bands that survived the period include that of Woody Herman who re-formed a number of times, but nevertheless maintained some kind of continuity. Stan Kenton's giant orchestra swelled to its most unwieldy size at the very moment that most other leaders were disbanding, but, thereafter, fell back to a succession of more conventional groups, even if these were still referred to in the press as being "progressive." In contrast, other leaders like Benny Goodman and Artie Shaw re-formed their bands sporadically, but with considerable stylistic jumps between line-ups. Shaw's last regular group was his 1953–4 Gramercy Five, but he led studio groups in 1955 and 1968. He conducted a "tribute band" in the 1980s. Goodman led a far more consistent series of big bands and small groups until the 1980s. Harry James led a Basie-styled band in Las Vegas for many years, and his swing era counterparts Buddy Rich and Maynard Ferguson also led large groups for several decades.

Nevertheless, even though some bands managed to survive the period from around 1946 to 1955, by the mid-1950s the jazz big-band style had changed irrevocably, and not even the leaders who fronted their groups right

717

through this period sounded the same at the end of it as they had done at the beginning. The two orchestras that had most to do with this transformation were those of Dizzy Gillespie and Count Basie, who experimented with the delicate balance between ensemble style, soloists, and – most significantly – the arrangements their bands played.

At first glance, the bebop big band that Gillespie led first in 1945, and then from 1946 to 1949, before regrouping, first in the studios and then on the road in the mid-1950s, seems to have little in common with Basie's blues-drenched Kansas City style group. But closer examination shows that they shared arrangers, initially Tadd Dameron, later Buster Harding, perhaps most notably the underrated Ernie Wilkins, and also Quincy Jones. Furthermore, Basie ultimately supplied Gillespie with the solution to the main problem that beset his 1940s efforts to transfer bebop to the forces of a big band. This was the inability of many audiences to perceive a basic, simple beat in the choppy, broken rhythms that accompanied Gillespie's earliest large-band arrangements. Throughout the period 1946–50, his band sounded very different from most of the surviving swing orchestras, and it is little wonder that, from the time of his 1945 "Hepsations" tour onwards, audiences away from the urban heartbeat of New York tended to be puzzled by a rhythmic approach that seemed hard to dance to. Nevertheless, in New York itself, other leaders, including Boyd Raeburn, Jimmy Dorsey, and Woody Herman, were impressed, and commissioned arrangements from Gillespie that adopted his rhythmic and harmonic innovations in a big-band context. By example, by commissioning new material from like-minded writers, and by disseminating his ideas to this broader cross-section of players, Gillespie contributed to an irrevocable change in the art of big-band writing, pushing the technical demands on those who played his music in terms of both speed and range.

The changes are easily discernible in the bulk of the arrangements Gillespie's own band played, mainly by Tadd Dameron, Gil Fuller, and Gillespie himself, which had dramatic, high-speed figures for the brass and saxophones that emulated the improvised lines of bebop small groups.

Nevertheless, by the mid-1940s, some arrangements were already common to Gillespie's and Basie's bands, although the stylistic traffic was at that point very much from Gillespie to Basie. The common link was Tadd Dameron, who, after learning his craft in Kansas City with Harlan Leonard's band, a rival to Basie's orchestra, had subsequently honed his arranging skills in New York alongside Gillespie, absorbing bebop harmony. Around the time that Gillespie's big band was heard regularly at the Spotlite, in 1946,

Gillespie and Dameron parted company, apparently because Gillespie was reluctant to pay Dameron for arrangements that they had, in essence, worked out together.[1] However, Dameron, who shared Basie's ability to pare away unnecessary detail, was a masterly "dearth writer" as saxophonist Benny Golson put it,[2] and he sold several charts to Basie. He wrote medium-tempo pieces that fitted the Count's Kansas City groove, and which offset vamps played by the trombones and rhythm with clear, clean lines for the other horns.

There is a considerable contrast in the way 1940s Gillespie and Basie bands both played some of his arrangements, notably *Stay On It* and *Good Bait*. In Basie's band, the inexorable four-square rhythm of the leader, Freddie Green on guitar, Walter Page on bass, and Jo Jones on drums had changed little from the 1930s, and only the presence of soloists like trombonist J. J. Johnson hinted at the bebop potential in the compositions. Gillespie's band, by contrast, added layers of complexity to Dameron's writing, through the way the charts were interpreted. His December 1947 recording of *Good Bait* adds Latin rhythms over Dameron's four-square beat; the beat is anticipated in the brass section's punctuations to the theme, and these are picked up by the drummer, Joe Harris, who also drops in off-center accents to complement Gillespie's solo over the ensemble.

This complexity of approach made the Gillespie band exciting, innovative, and completely unlike any other big band of the period. I made the point earlier about its rhythmic density, and it is worth re-examining one or two discs already mentioned that exemplify this. Take, for example, *Things to Come*, written by Gillespie and Fuller, which, on its original 1946 recording, is played at a breakneck tempo, with Kenny Clarke's drums adding punctuations that underline the contours of the jagged melody lines, rather than on the second and forth beats of each measure, as a swing drummer might. Another example is the uneven opening to *Oop-pop-a-da* (1947). In the same piece, Clarke turns the beat around behind the trumpet solo, and the brass riffs cut across the beat under the tenor solo.

With the advent of Gillespie's first Afro-Cuban experiments (also in 1947), where Chano Pozo's uncompromising congas pull against the jazz beat of the rest of the rhythm section, the band made a deliberate attempt to explore polyrhythmic textures, and even after Pozo's untimely death, Gillespie sought out substitute conga players to maintain this rhythmic density. Ironically, as seen in Chapter 7, it was Charlie Parker who initiated the first critical discussion of this problem in the pages of *Down Beat* during September 1949. Parker's keen ear, attuned to the ebbing and flowing of rhythm, and the breakneck exchange of ideas in bebop small groups, detected a problem in Gillespie's efforts to transfer this to larger forces.

What he heard was a discernible deterioration in Gillespie's own playing: "A big band slows anybody down, because you don't get a chance to play enough." And he saw Gillespie's attempts to transfer the rhythmic mobility of bebop small groups to larger forces as the culprit. To Parker, this was unlikely to work in a large band: "the beat in a bop band is with the music, against it, behind it . . . it pushes it, it helps it. Help is the big thing. It has no continuity of beat, no steady chug-chug."[3]

While confused would-be dancers might argue that Gillespie had all too successfully transferred the fluid beat and unorthodox rhythmic accents of bebop to a large-band setting, and that the band was producing anything but a straightforward chug-chug, Gillespie himself admitted that the results were not right. Parker had correctly identified a flaw in this experimental big-band form. However, whereas Parker's solution was to urge Gillespie to give up the folly of big-band leadership and return to small groups, Gillespie's visionary ear was cocked towards a solution. In his riposte to Parker, in the following month's issue, he wrote: "We'll use the same harmonics, but with a beat, so people will understand where the beat is."

Within a year, Gillespie had been forced by economics to disband, but when he regrouped in the early 1950s, his new bands had a much more conventional swing beat, despite the occasional bebop accent, or the incorporation of Afro-Cuban rhythms. The model for this came directly from Count Basie, and dates from 1953, when Gillespie toured alongside the Basie band. Within a year, Gillespie had recorded a set of big-band charts by Buster Harding, who was one of Basie's principal arrangers (including yet another shared arrangement, *Hob Nail Special*), and Gillespie went on to make more discs the following year using arrangements by Basie's other arrangers, Ernie Wilkins and Quincy Jones.

Why should this be the case? For what reason would an established bebop musician who had created a major innovation in big-band writing and playing want to absorb ideas from a stride pianist a generation older, who had cut his teeth in territory bands and after-hours clubs in Kansas City?

The answer lies in the fact that the leaders faced the same problem. They wanted to make a large band swing like a small one, and since the mid-1930s, Basie had succeeded in doing this by paring away detail rather than adding it. If anything, his 1950s band involved even more paring away than his earlier one, with a greater contrast between the sparseness of his rhythm section and the fullness of the reed or brass sections, as well as extra discipline in the way his sections played their parts and interacted with one another.

Despite a coming and going of personnel, owing to the war, to the draft, and to economic fluctuations, Basie's late-1940s band had remained stylistically similar to his 1930s group. For the most part, it played many of the same charts by pioneer Basie members, like Harry Edison and Buck Clayton, and its approach was still rooted in riffs and blues. Even when more modern-sounding soloists were involved such as Clark Terry or Paul Gonsalves (both later to become long-term Ellingtonians), they were subordinate to the overall Basie sound.

When his big band was forced to break up, between January 1950 and May 1951, Basie scaled down to a septet and then, for the majority of the time, an octet. In the front line were Terry, clarinetist Buddy De Franco, tenorist Charlie Rouse, or Wardell Gray, and baritone saxophonist Serge Chaloff. Originally the rhythm section was only Basie, bassist Jimmy Lewis, and drummer Gus Johnson. But, as Clark Terry recalled, "We just looked up one day and Freddie Green was there with his guitar. He just re-hired himself."[4] It was this small group that marks the transition between one distinct era in Basie's big-band sound and the next, since all the soloists were conversant with bebop, and when they were not playing impromptu "head" arrangements, they were playing pieces by bop-orientated composers, such as Neal Hefti, who composed *Neal's Deal* and *Bluebird Blues* for their first recording.

In due course, through his 1957 arrangements for the *Atomic Mr. Basie* album, Hefti would be regarded as the main architect of the "new" Basie sound. His voicings, which included flutes alongside muted trumpets, were unusual, and Basie's unerring gift for stripping arrangements down to their essentials and selecting the right tempo (such as the daringly slow *Li'l Darlin*, from October 1957) were certainly significant factors in redesigning the big-band palette. Hefti had been a trumpeter in the Woody Herman band, and he had been an admirer of Gillespie's playing in 52nd Street clubs. His stock-in-trade was long sinuous brass lines (which owed a lot to Gillespie's solos) and unusually voiced ensembles which sat easily over the four-square Basie rhythm section, enlivened by occasional punctuations from drummer Gus Johnson or his successor Sonny Payne.

To most musicians in the band, however, Ernie Wilkins, a childhood friend of Clark Terry, was an equally significant factor in re-engineering its sound. Because Wilkins actually sat in the saxophone section, as he was later to do with Gillespie, he really understood the mechanics of making the band swing, whilst tackling more ambitious material in terms of harmony and structure. Wilkins transferred the simplicity of Basie's octet to the forces of the big band. Then it became a question of interpretation. Trombonist Grover Mitchell (who played in Basie's original orchestra and, at the start of the twenty-first century, leads the posthumous Basie band) said:

> Basie would say to arrangers: "Be who you are, don't try to imitate other writers, or try to write 'the Basie way.' Write well, and we'll take care of the playing." Nevertheless, Ernie Wilkins made a great contribution to the way in which the band approached playing arrangements. He was a craftsman, a hammer-and-nails writer, but his impact on the band was as significant as that of Sy Oliver on the Lunceford band during the swing era.[5]

Mitchell's point is important. Once the arranger had set the framework for a band, it was then up to the band to add the characteristics that endowed the piece with that particular group's personality. When the Basie band played charts by Ernie Wilkins or Quincy Jones, it played to its strengths: ensemble discipline and contrasting dynamics, providing a robust framework for its soloists, including trumpeters Joe Newman and Thad Jones, trombonists Al Grey and Benny Powell, and saxophonists Eddie "Lockjaw" Davis, Frank Wess, and Frank Foster. Drummer Louis Bellson, who spent a number of short periods with the band, told me: "Wilkins, Jones, and Neal Hefti were perfect swing writers. As Harry James said, 'Hefti wrote the greatest rests in the world – leaving plenty of space.' And the charts by all three more or less played themselves."[6]

By contrast, when the Gillespie Orchestra played music by these writers, there was a dramatic difference in sound. Partly, this was due to the way in which Gillespie's own solo role dominated each performance. From the 1940s onwards, he took the lion's share of solos in his band, and so an arrangement like Jones's *Jessica's Day*, recorded by Gillespie in May 1956 and by Basie in January 1959, is, in the former, virtually a solo vehicle for Gillespie, whereas it is treated far more orchestrally by Basie, having solos from trumpet, alto, and tenor, plus a flute–bass duet in the introduction.

Not only did the two bands offer a contrast in playing similar material, but the Gillespie band also behaved very differently on stage – when trombonist Al Grey left Gillespie in the middle of this period to join Basie, he was promptly reprimanded for talking to the other musicians during a

show (which was commonplace practice with Gillespie), and he also found
he had almost no solos. With Dizzy, he recalled:

> I had solos galore. But when I moved to Basie, nothing. I spoke to
> Basie, and he said, "I know you want to play, but you wait. You
> just got here." And it wasn't until I blew up at him after our tour
> of England that he commissioned Thad Jones to write pieces for
> me, like *H.R.H.*[7]

The freer, more easy-going atmosphere of Gillespie's band was coupled with
a formidable energy, similar to that of his mid-1940s bands; so much so that
at one level it is impossible to conceive the contemporary Basie band tearing
into a piece like *Dizzy's Blues*, recorded at Newport in 1957. Gillespie had
also transported this energy to the Middle East and to South America, on
tours sponsored by the U.S. State Department, and, in the process, being
one of the first official "jazz ambassadors" for his country. Yet what Gillespie
took from Basie during this period was a simplification of his rhythm section
and charts that had similar long-flowing bebop lines and dramatic contrasts
of dynamics, and which created a workable, popular, fusion of the bebop
innovations of the 1940s with the hard-driving swing and power of the big-
band tradition. (It is an instructive contrast to examine Tadd Dameron's
nonet recordings from 1953, with Clifford Brown on trumpet and Philly Joe
Jones on drums, where he achieves a small-group feel with medium-sized
forces, and occupies territory that is midway between the Gillespie and Basie
big bands, on numbers such as *Dial "B" for Beauty* or the up-tempo *Philly
J. J.*)

I mentioned the changed role of the rhythm section in Duke Ellington's
band, which settled in the mid-1950s into a four-year period during which
the entire personnel of the group remained remarkably stable. The
orchestra's renaissance is generally regarded to have taken place following its

Virtually all subsequent big-band developments grew out of the kinds of
changes pioneered by Basie and Gillespie, from the way in which Ellington
gave greater prominence to his mid-1950s rhythm section, with Sam
Woodyard on drums and Jimmy Woode on bass, to the writing and
arranging of newcomers like Toshiko Akiyoshi. Basie and Gillespie set so
much of the agenda for the big band in the second half of the twentieth
century that without them, even an innovator like Sun Ra, who
deconstructed earlier notions of section writing, and how the ensemble
works together, would have had no rules to break.

appearance at the 1956 Newport Jazz Festival, where it made its remarkable recording of *Diminuendo and Crescendo in Blue*, comprising two brief compositions linked by 27 choruses of blues improvisation by tenorist Paul Gonsalves. This famous recording (which was re-released in 1999 in a new, technically miraculous version, in which Columbia's mono master tapes were mixed into genuine stereo by combining them with the simultaneous recording originally made by Voice of America) exemplifies the degree to which the Ellington rhythm section was moving in a parallel direction to those of Basie and Gillespie, by simplifying what it did, and by creating what producer George Avakian referred to in his liner notes as "a triumph of the good old rocking (R & B if you will) blues beat which has been too often missing in jazz."[8]

After a period in which the band had been without its key soloist Johnny Hodges, had had a succession of indifferent drummers (apart from a short spell by Louie Bellson), and was on the receiving end of negative criticism from many quarters, this concert was Ellington's moment to prove his critics wrong. Reunited with Hodges (who played magnificently in other parts of the concert), and with Sam Woodyard firmly ensconced on drums, he had a point to prove, and as Avakian said in the same notes: "Within an hour, reporters and critics were buzzing about it. By next morning, it was generally conceded to have been one of the most exciting performances any of them had ever heard."

Although Avakian did not continue as Ellington's producer after a studio session on the Monday after Newport to recreate some of the music played at the concert, the job subsequently going to Irv Townsend, Avakian's decision to sign the band to such a major label as Columbia might be seen as prescient, given the band's subsequent triumphs. He gave me this account of the events that led up to the festival appearance – the first time the band had appeared at the Newport event, which was then in its third year:

> I had just signed Duke and thought, "Let's do something spectacular. Let's record Duke and other Columbia artists at Newport," which was something nobody had ever done. There had never been a formal major label recording at a jazz festival. So I called Duke and I asked him if he had something that he could do as an exciting first performance there, so that we can record the premiere and call it, say, the *Newport Jazz Festival Suite*. He said, "Billy Strayhorn and I always have something – we'll put something together." He called the musicians together just before

they went up on stage for that set, telling them, "Look, we've all worked very hard on the suite and George has stuck his neck out for us and we just have one shot to record it. But don't fret about any mistakes. Billy Strayhorn is gonna check as we play and see where any patches have to be made, and we're going into the studio the day after tomorrow to fix up patches." Now that wasn't going to be easy, I knew, but it was the only way we were going to get away with it because we knew, Duke and I, that there were going to be mistakes. And after that he said, "Let's just relax and have a good time. Let's play something we haven't played in a long time. Let's play *Diminuendo and Crescendo*." And the guys started looking at each other, some of them puzzled, and Gonsalves spoke up and said, "We don't know that." And Duke said, "Sure you do, we played it umpteen months ago or something. It's just the blues. We change keys, you come on and take a solo, and then I'll take you out and that's the end of it."[9]

In fact, as Ellington scholar Eddie Lambert discovered, Ellington had been using *Diminuendo and Crescendo* on and off for almost twenty years. At Randall's Island, in New York, in 1938, it had raised the crowd to fever pitch, and Gonsalves himself had first recorded a version of the interlude between the two sections in June 1951. A *Melody Maker* review of the band's performance at the Pasadena Civic Auditorium in 1953 commented on the saxophonist's "seemingly unending succession of choruses that must have lasted quite five minutes and duly aroused the fans as intended."[10] So even if Gonsalves was momentarily thrown by his leader's suggestion, and had not played the piece for three years, it was actually something he had been called upon to do previously, and Ellington must have had a shrewd idea how it would go down with the crowd, not least after his band had worked its way through the pitfalls of an entirely new suite that was hardly finished in time for the concert.

The audience and critical reaction to the band's performance is not in doubt. Avakian's brilliantly evocative account, as presented in his notes to the recording, has entered jazz folklore, and the figure of a platinum blonde woman in a dark dress dancing to the band and inciting the crowd is as powerful as his image of Basie's drummer Jo Jones urging on the rhythm section by beating a rolled-up newspaper on the stage. Not mentioned in his account is the fact that the band had been offstage for three hours between sets (four key members of the line-up were missing for the early evening appearance) and that the musicians did not appreciate being made to wait in a cold tent. In his essay on the piece, reissue producer Phil Schaap suggests that one reason for the band's exceptional performance was its pent-up anger at being kept waiting (quite apart from being potentially upstaged by the Chico Hamilton Quintet – see Chapter 14).[11]

I've always been skeptical about the degree to which Jo Jones actually influenced the events at Newport. Sam Woodyard's simple but effective beat was to become such a feature of the 1950s band, particularly when he locked on to Jimmy Woode's bass, that the musicians hardly seem to have needed the catalyst of the presence of another drummer to spur them on at Newport. Jimmy Woode confirmed this, when he told me:

> He was on the side, slightly in front, because the stage was a little elevated, and he had a newspaper, but the band was into it. We really didn't need much egging on. Of course it was inspiring to see him there, enjoying himself, having a ball. He was just as knocked out as we were, because it was so infectious to the public, to the whole scene. Ellington couldn't stop the band, George Wein was trying to stop the band, but the band refused to stop! It was just one of those rare moments in jazz history that happened, and now that I listen to it in retrospect, it was far too short![12]

With this kind of location recording in its infancy, and the fact that Voice of America's microphones for the broadcast, Columbia's mikes, and those of the public address system were all jostling for the musicians' attention, the commercial recording of this landmark performance came off worst at the time, with Gonsalves blowing heartily into the wrong microphone. Avakian told me it took three weeks of work with the primitive equalizers of the day to raise the levels on Gonsalves's solo sufficiently for it to be issued. The *Newport Festival Suite* was largely re-recorded in the studio, and festival atmosphere dubbed on to it, for the issued version of the *Ellington at Newport* album, which became the band's best-selling disc from 1956, until it was superseded in 1999 by the new version combining the Voice of America feed with the Columbia tapes.

If nothing else, the original issue of the Newport concert shows that not only was recording technology beginning to advance dramatically during the tape era, but also that producers who were now used to the deft application of the razor-blade to create "perfect" studio performances by splicing

726

together takes now felt confident enough to transfer this thinking to live events. In due course, such manipulation of an art form that still included a large component of improvisation (in this case 27 choruses of it!) was to prompt a considerable ethical debate, which surfaced again in the 1990s, with so much 1950s material being re-examined as it was reissued on CD. The late-1990s attitude at Columbia was to produce as complete a documentary account of what took place at the Festival itself, complete with the odd clinker by the band in playing through a new work, and this reflects a growing movement towards "documentation" by record companies, largely prompted by the pioneering philosophy of Michael Cuscuna at Blue Note and his own Mosaic company. But where should this start and finish in respect of those pieces from the mid-1950s when tape editing was still in its infancy?

In 1997, Blue Note issued its "Ultimate" version of John Coltrane's *Blue Train* album, in which the famous cut of the title track was revealed to contain the piano solo (by Kenny Drew) from a different take that was for the first time presented in its entirety. When I spoke to him about it, Rudy Van Gelder, the session's original engineer, described this new issue as a "desecration,"[13] because he, Coltrane, and producer Alfred Lion had worked hard, back in 1957, to create the best possible version of the piece for release, and he felt their efforts in producing the finest artistic result and a balanced album were now being undone. The same applies to the 1990s Mosaic reissues of *Buck Clayton's Jam Sessions* from the same period – a series of studio-based loose-knit jams, intended to recapture the informal after-hours atmosphere of 1930s Kansas City. When these discs were originally issued, notably the 1953 pairing of the *Huckle Buck* and *Robbins' Nest*, they were constructed from numerous takes, which Mosaic restored to their original form. Interestingly, the original producer here was also George Avakian, who frankly described at the time how he had created the issued version of *Robbins' Nest* by inserting solos from one take by trumpeter Joe Newman and Clayton himself, together with a trombone duet between Henderson Chambers and Urbie Green, into a completely different take, to create what he felt was the best result for commercial issue. The artistic effect was of a well-balanced session, with plenty of vigorous exchange of ideas between the soloists, but that was not what actually happened, as Avakian made clear:

> The final placement of this particular Green–Chambers duet may result in a misconception by keen-eared fans. . . . It appears when

listening to *Robbins' Nest* that an idea with which Henderson Chambers toys several times in his solo (seventh chorus) is derived from the startling D-flat with which Urbie Green begins the duet near the beginning of the record. Actually, if you stop to think about the splices, Chambers played his solo first, and later on (both in his solo in the ninth chorus . . . and in the duet in the fifteenth chorus) Urbie has already found that the idea has taken root in his subconscious. The D-flat came along fifteen minutes later, during take 2![14]

The ethics of this began to be hotly debated at the time, but a reasoned argument in defense of Avakian's methods was put forward in 1957 by British trumpeter Humphrey Lyttelton, who wrote:

> The more general objection to the juggling of tapes after a session is that it makes for artificial perfection at the expense of realism. . . . But is any record realistic? There are shortcomings in the actual process of recording which make a certain amount of faking necessary. . . . It is the end product which counts, and as long as there is no artistic dishonesty, no mechanical counterfeiting of the music, I can see no reason why tape surgery should not be used to achieve a more realistic recording than would otherwise be obtained.[15]

This is a useful insight into the thinking of the time – rather than the occasionally judgmental attitude of commentators almost half a century later who question the wisdom of such editing, in what was still viewed, in the major companies at least, as very much a branch of the popular entertainment industry. It is ironic that Ellington, the man at the center of the art-versus-entertainment debate in the 1920s and 1930s, should once again be at the center of so similar a debate concerning his 1950s work.

Ellington's band and those of Basie, Kenton, and Herman continued to be the principal large jazz orchestras of the late 1950s, Gillespie having been forced to disband again in 1957, although he re-formed his group several times between then and the mid-1960s (and was regularly leading big bands again in the late 1980s and early 1990s). The artificial spontaneity of his 1956 Newport disc notwithstanding, Ellington's next major projects for Columbia were albums that were very much crafted as complete works of art, with a long gestation period, and assembled from the pick of a very large number of recorded takes. While his band was out on the road, frequently performing the *Newport Festival Suite* (and reprising *Diminuendo and Crescendo in Blue* at a Fairfield Connecticut concert), Ellington was working on the music for *A Drum Is a Woman*, and his Shakespearean suite *Such Sweet Thunder*. Both were created from several recording sessions, and the story behind the former is extraordinarily complex, as it was a dramatic piece with a choir and spoken narration by Ellington at his most verbally ornate. It was performed complete as a light-hearted entertainment built around the history of jazz, for a television show.

To confuse matters, two versions of the recorded suite were issued, one accidentally duplicating a track at the expense of another, one movement was omitted altogether from both LPs, but surfaced on a separate EP disc, and the television broadcast was mimed to various different takes of the music, some as issued and some not. As Ole J. Nielsen says in his definitive Ducal discography, the extraordinary range of variations created from tape splicing, the running together of different takes, and the different issues in disc and film format would be beyond the scope of any normal reference book.[16] From the mid-1950s onwards, therefore, even the creation of Ellington's major works was going to involve a close collaboration with his record producers, and there was plenty of opportunity for rogue versions of his work to make their way into the marketplace. This was a problem that would afflict many other performers over the coming decades, but Ellington's *Newport* and *Drum Is a Woman* experiences were early high-profile examples.

*Such Sweet Thunder* was less controversial as a recording, and it was a more orthodox piece for the band with no added singers, narrators, or harps. It very much marked out the direction of the formal development of Ellington and his music over the years to come, with one foot in the traditional, yet showing he had an ear cocked to current thinking – movements such as his waltz *Lady Mac* proving that he, too, was in tune with the late-1950s experiments with time signatures. Simultaneously with these formal works, the band was almost continually recorded on its live appearances, and dozens of informal discs, legitimate and bootleg, catalog Ellington's regular work as a dance band, concert orchestra, recitalist, television performer, and mobile test-bed for his big ideas, with movements of suites – recent and forthcoming – showing up in his concert and dance programs, as captured by the amateur and professional microphones of the era.

From the time of his Newport appearance until late in his life,

Ellington's own piano playing was at a high point. He could still occasionally fall back on earlier stride-based and ragtime-based styles, but for the most part he settled for a highly distinctive, somewhat angular style, characterized by rippling, running figures which he used as introductory passages or punctuations. His angular, percussive style is brilliantly demonstrated by his trio version of *Searching (Pleading for Love)* **[CD 2, track 4]** that was made for an album called *Piano in the Foreground*. His sparse, simple playing is full of rhythmic momentum, and it is clear how he could act as a rhythmic catalyst for his full orchestra.

For the most part, Ellington's writing from the mid-1950s continued lines of exploration he had mapped out many years earlier. He frequently adapted themes, motifs, or entire sections of earlier pieces, and set them in new contexts, but his band's overall approach, his visionary use of orchestral texture and color, and his ability to feature and draw exceptional performances from his team of distinctive soloists remained consistent throughout. In all this, he remained isolated from the currents of fashion in jazz. He barely nodded in the direction of bebop and pursued a completely individual direction that nevertheless appeared current and fresh to his listeners. The transition of his band in the 1950s was from being the victim of economic circumstance, out of critical favor, to once again being seen as a national institution.

There were, however, other currents of transition among big bands that began in this decade, and continued through into the 1960s. They were the exploration of new areas of timbre and tone of Gil Evans (both in his studio sessions for Miles Davis and in his own work); the related experiments in harmony, using modal systems, of George Russell; the breakdown of writing for conventional brass and reed sections in the work of Sun Ra; and the experiments in time signatures of Don Ellis (which took place in the 1960s). Few of these musicians managed to maintain regular big bands, with the exception of Sun Ra, who spent much of the 1950s leading his group in various locations in Chicago. Ellis played as a sideman with numerous bands, but did not establish his own regular line-up until the mid-1960s.

Gil Evans had spent the first half of the 1950s, after *Birth of the Cool*, in relative obscurity, doing some arrangements for film and television, and creating one album for singer Helen Merrill that gave him the reputation as expensive on studio time, as he liked to rehearse meticulously to achieve the best possible results. The release of *Miles Ahead* altered perceptions of him, and he began to be perceived as a writer of rare vision and originality. And once again, George Avakian, the man who seems to be at the center of this chapter, gave him the chance to prove it, with the first recording for a full-sized fourteen-piece band under Evans's own name. (Evans had made one other session for Bob Weinstock with a ten-piece group, but this lacked the resources of a full big band.) Avakian had left Columbia in 1958, and said, "one of the first things I wanted to do was record with Gil again,"[17] so he set up a session for Dick Bock's Pacific Jazz label that put Cannonball Adderley in the role of principal soloist in a selection of old jazz standards in fresh arrangements by Evans, the whole thing being called *New Bottle, Old Wine*.

Ironically, the session was something of a paradox – Evans the perfectionist honed his collection of session players into a cohesive sound in conditions that were the complete reverse of his preferred surroundings:

> We did that whole album in nine hours with no rehearsal. It came off in a dumb-assed studio that you could hardly hear the bass or anything, it was outrageous. But when I hear it now . . . it sounds good to me. . . . A masterpiece is just a successful experiment. You never hear of the unsuccessful ones.[18]

The rushed time and unsuitable conditions did not hinder this from being "a successful experiment." Evans excelled himself, and in Max Harrison's words, "the lines of these scores are chiselled with a cool and reasoned accuracy that never tones down the luminous glow of of his orchestral writing."[19] One immediately obvious element is a sense of humor which is almost completely absent from Evans's work with Miles Davis. The lumbering tuba is given the Louis Armstrong melody on *Struttin' with Some Barbecue*, Art Blakey's brushes whisk and whirl their way through the theme of Charlie Parker's *Bird Feathers*, and the corny ending to *King Porter Stomp* is played deadpan.

Proof of the effect of the Gillespie–Basie axis, even on Evans's work, comes in the central section of this album: a sonorous treatment of a piece Gillespie had played and recorded since the 1940s, Monk's *Round Midnight* (the opening redolent of *Will o' the Wisp*, in Evans's score for Miles Davis), and, particularly, a brilliantly original version of Gillespie and Chano Pozo's *Manteca*. The dreamlike atmosphere of the opening of this latter piece is underpinned by the insistent ostinato of the original, which then breaks out at high volume for the full orchestra, but in due course the Afro-Cuban feel is abandoned in favor of solos over a regular swing beat. This serves to focus the imagination on the extraordinarily accomplished section writing behind

Adderley's alto solo. The entire album demonstrates Evans's links to the jazz tradition, through the choice of material, and his radical sense of re-orchestration, which makes it very much a case of "new wine" in old bottles.

He was to repeat this format with some equally dazzling writing in a follow-up disc called *Great Jazz Standards*, featuring trumpeter John Coles as his main soloist, but also including contributions from soprano saxophonist Steve Lacy and veteran reed player Budd Johnson, on orchestrations of pieces as wide-ranging as Bix Beiderbecke's *Davenport Blues* and Clifford Brown's *Joy Spring*.

From these late-1950s experiments, it still took Evans a number of further collaborations with Davis and several years to establish a band of his own, but when he did, he proved that his thinking was as original as ever. He applied his unorthodox voicings to material as wide-ranging as songs by Jimi Hendrix and compositions by Charles Mingus. But his principal importance in the 1950s and 1960s was to continue to expand the orchestral palette in ways that complemented the work of Duke Ellington, and his subsequent albums, such as *Out of the Cool*, picked up and developed many of the ideas that appeared in his own first discs from the late 1950s.

George Russell, by contrast, did front a regular small group in the 1950s and early 1960s, but was only occasionally able to expand this to a larger band. I have mentioned Russell in passing several times, in connection with Dizzy Gillespie in creating the modal introduction to *Cubana Be / Cubana Bop*, and in relation to his influence on Miles Davis in exploring modes as a means of improvisation. His *Lydian Chromatic Concept of Tonal Organization*, published in 1953, was one of the first formal theoretical works to have been produced by a jazz musician (he was an experienced jazz drummer, pianist, and arranger), and it became widely adopted around the world. He told me:

> Toru Takemitsu, the Japanese composer, translated the first edition into Japanese when it first came out, and it was published in Japan well before I'd done the first revision in 1959. He told me it was one of the two most revealing books on music ever published, along with Messiaen's *Technique de mon langage musical*. But there were just as many enthusiasts for it among the jazz community, such as Art Farmer, or John Lewis who used to stop by when I was writing it, holed up in a little hotel room on 24th Street in New York, across from the RCA studios. He [Lewis]

could see how convinced I was that the theory had grown out of jazz, and he encouraged me to persevere and keep doing it. Other people like Roland Kirk enthused over it, but he'd actually learned it wrongly – he never got it right, but what he played sounded great anyway![20]

His own mid-1950s "Jazz Workshop" sextet grew out of a rehearsal band made up of musicians who were interested in his concept, including Farmer and pianist Bill Evans (for whom he was commissioned, in 1957, to write the orchestral suite *All About Rosie*, which has become something of a standard). The Workshop period allowed Russell specifically to develop his theories in connection with jazz, and he articulated the principle which most closely allied his work to that of Gil Evans in the original notes to the first (and only) album by his Workshop sextet.

> Because the best written jazz sounds improvised, it may be concluded that the best of our jazz composers, down the years, have: (1) embraced the instrumental improvisation that jazz is so noted for, (2) captured the vitality of its strongest improvisers and (3) proceeded to improvise, with greater and greater subtlety, jazz compositions that sound as fresh and uninhibited as a compelling solo by an inspired jazz soloist. . . . A jazz writer is an improviser too. Given a set of musical facts (just as a soloist is given a sequence of chords) he can, in the same way that the soloist improvises upon chords, improvise upon these musical facts pertaining to his composition, and produce a swinging, logical, vital-sounding piece of new music.[21]

The ideas explored in the Workshop set are all vital, and encompass almost all the areas in which jazz musicians were experimenting in the 1950s – *Ye Hypocrite, Ye Beelzebub* uses a six–four meter in an opening modal section, and then moves into a chord sequence that runs forwards for nine-and-a-half measures, before reversing, running backwards, and finishing off by reverting to its original direction. *Jack's Blues* explores dissonance with a theme built in seconds; *Night Sound* is chromatic, with a constantly shifting tonal center; and *Round Johnny Rondo*, as its name suggests, explores dissonance in a canonical or contrapuntal framework. *Fellow Delegates* uses chromatic drums (a device employed at the same time by Sun Ra) while the relatively straightforward *Ezz-thetic* re-examines a piece recorded in the early 1950s by Lee Konitz and others.

Perhaps Russell's attempts to improvise with pencil and paper would not have been so brilliantly successful were it not for the caliber of his musicians, but Art Farmer and Bill Evans, in particular, brought just the kind of incisive edge to his group that he sought to achieve in his writing. In spring 1960 the group was expanded into a studio big band to explore more of Russell's ideas in the three-part *Chromatic Universe* and *The Lydiot* — the start of occasional big-band sessions that explored ideas ranging from polytonality to modes. He worked on a theory of "tonal gravity" in stacking tonal centers on top of one another, and in later pieces, such as *Vertical Form VI*, he followed his conviction that there ought to be a system of "rhythmic gravity" also:

> One can stack tempos at varying speeds and rates into a kind of structure similar to an architect building a skyscraper. You then deal with more than one feeling simultaneously. In my work, this is a key piece of that kind of thinking, even though large sections of it are straightahead, but it actually goes back to Charles Ives who was the father of this kind of music.[22]

In the 1960s, after leading a small group in New York, Russell taught in Scandinavia, where much of his work was recorded, and he formed a band that moved into rock fusion territory, in which forward-looking European soloists such as saxophonist Jan Garbarek and guitarist Terje Rypdal rubbed shoulders with American expatriate experimentalists such as Don Cherry. In 1969, Russell returned to the United States, to teach at the New England Conservatory, along with his old colleague Gunther Schuller, with whom he had worked in John Lewis's Lenox Summer Schools in the 1950s. In the 1980s, after various short-lived big bands, he formed his Living Time Orchestra, which combines American and European musicians, but it is not a band like the posthumous Gil Evans Orchestra that is bound to a specific period in his repertoire, such as his best-known piece *All About Rosie*. "Funnily enough, the Living Time Orchestra has almost never, if ever, played it, because it is not a 'retrospective' orchestra," Russell told me. "But it's done every year at the New England Conservatory, where it's now considered something of a 'must play' for all my young students."[23]

Russell's importance as a catalyst for ideas in the United States and Europe has been seriously underestimated by earlier historians, and the new thinking he introduced into big-band composing and arranging, from the late 1950s, set in motion much further exploration of almost all the concepts covered above.

Sun Ra's band grew out of a rehearsal band in Chicago during the 1950s, but it explored new territory in a far more outrageous fashion than Evans or Russell. Dressing in outlandish costumes and claiming a link to Saturn, Ra was a forerunner of many of the ideas of the AACM, discussed in Chapter 18. Some of the older Chicago musicians involved in that movement had occasionally sat in with the former Fletcher Henderson Orchestra pianist, or at any rate swelled the crowds at his sparsely attended gigs. However, in his 1950s work he anticipated some of their concepts of free jazz, particularly the establishing of a mood through interactive improvisation, rather than composed prescription, but he was also signaling a new approach to big-band voicings by breaking down the traditional idea of sections and section writing. When he came to reinterpret some of the classic 1920s and 1930s material associated with Henderson, he did not re-orchestrate it with the skilled precision used by Gil Evans on the *Old Wine* album, but relied instead on something closer to the collective memory exercises with which *avant-garde* European experimentalists such as Cornelius Cardew and the Scratch Orchestra tried to recreate the great works of the classical canon.

In his own music of the mid-1950s, recorded in Chicago, he showed his penchant for added percussion, and (as I mentioned earlier) sometimes included tuned drum solos, such as in his jaunty blues *Call for All Demons*, recorded in 1956. Ra's aesthetic was to "educate" his audience and players by looking towards tomorrow. But beneath the hyperbole, the talk of space and a new future, are some key tenets of what he introduced to jazz. On his *Sun Song* album, from 1957, he approached free-jazz ideas in some of the tracks, the idea of trying to portray the idea of simple chord changes being complex (in *Fall off the Log*) and of polytonality in the title track itself. These were all ideas that would continue to be explored in his work, but, increasingly, he looked at ways of developing the route he had begun in pieces like *Call for All Demons*, combining atonal, often microtonally improvised, solos over complex and conventional rhythmic backdrops.

Conventional rhythmic backdrops were not the forte of trumpeter Don Ellis. At the start of the 1960s, in a series of small groups with pianist Jaki Byard, he worked on serial and atonal ideas, but although he flirted briefly with ideas of totally free improvisation, he later moved away from that, preferring to establish a formal structure against whose boundaries he could push. Although there were to be experiments with electric trumpets and fusion instruments before his brief career was snuffed out by heart trouble in 1978, Ellis became the master of exploring time signatures. His mid-1960s big band worked in a series of clubs in and around Los Angeles, and after breaking through to a wider public at the Monterey Festival, with a series of pieces built on extraordinarily complex time signatures, he went on to show how such music could be played with verve and swing. This period of his experimentation reached its height in *Live in Three-and-Two-Thirds-over-Four Time*, recorded for Pacific Jazz, with radical re-readings of everything from *Freedom Jazz Dance* to the old potboiler beloved of Dixieland bands, *Bill Bailey*.

The 1950s and early 1960s saw the creation of a new common approach to commercial big bands, headed by Basie and Gillespie, which was followed by most leaders, and which gave a new backdrop for experiment. If this decade had seen the consolidation of bebop into hard bop on the one hand and cool jazz on the other, with a comparable orthodoxy established for large ensembles, what was to come in the 1960s was a breaking down of that order, but also the establishing of some new paradigms. On the one hand, John Coltrane set new standards for instrumental improvisation, and, on the other, Charles Mingus re-examined the relationship between composer and improviser.

# PART IV
# New Jazz

CHAPTER 16

# Coltrane and Mingus

## John Coltrane

The man's playing is in essence lyrical – even when he is at
his most demoniacally complex.

Nat Hentoff, *Hi-Fi/Stereo Review*, May 1963

Because of the breadth of his work, his technical innovations as an
instrumentalist, and the stimulating combination of discipline and
experiment he brought to the groups he led, John Coltrane became the
most influential saxophonist on the jazz of the last four decades of the
twentieth century, overtaking Charlie Parker as a universal role model.
Coltrane's career began substantially earlier than that of Ornette Coleman,
the other dominant innovator in jazz saxophone playing of the 1960s, whose
work is discussed in the next chapter, but his lasting contribution to the
development of jazz straddles Coleman's. Although Coleman outlived him,
and continued to develop the free jazz ideas he first explored in the late
1950s into the twenty-first century, Coltrane passed through a free stage
around 1965 that drew heavily on Coleman's work, and then moved beyond
it.

He extended the possibilities of both speed and range on the tenor. He
combined a spiritual intensity most obvious in his ballad playing (in which he
also spearheaded a revival of the soprano saxophone) with a charismatic
ability to express great emotional power and passion, often through rapidly
executed cascades of notes, which the critic and author Ira Gitler memorably
termed "sheets of sound." He developed the exploration of modes as a
vehicle for improvisation, moving from such early work with Miles Davis on

*Milestones*, via his own gold disc of *My Favorite Things*, into the extended sophistication of his own *Impressions*. He created a distinctive raw tone on tenor, and, having demonstrated his ability to articulate complex ideas throughout the entire range of the instrument, added a panoply of additional effects which he incorporated into his improvisational language, including vocal tones, multiphonics, honks, squeals, and high, shrieking harmonics. He also stretched the average length of an improvisation, not only on disc, with such tests of stamina as the dozens of choruses in his fifteen-minute solo on the blues sequence *Chasin' the Trane*, but also in hundreds of unrecorded club and concert sets, where a single number by his quartet might last three-quarters of an hour or more. Elements of his style are to be found in the work of subsequent players as different as Michael Brecker and Courtney Pine.

The all-pervasive aspects of Coltrane's influence mentioned so far can be found in his work from 1957 to 1965, which is universally held to be his most important period and which I shall discuss further, but there is also a strong case for re-examining his later output after the turning point of the June 1965 *Ascension* album, in which he pushed the boundaries of collective free improvisation further than anyone else in the decade. In both issued versions of that disc, apart from a brief, repeated five-note motif used as introduction and bridge between solos, he abandoned most elements of form that had been retained by Ornette Coleman and, although his own contribution was perhaps more firmly harmonically anchored than was realized at the time, took the concept of a large, anarchic free-jazz ensemble about as far as it could go. In the wake of this disc, many of the movements that followed, in North America at any rate, such as the AACM or Art Ensemble of Chicago, returned to some kinds of formal structure, albeit not necessarily to ones that had prevailed in jazz before.

Historically, therefore, *Ascension* is significant precisely because it became a landmark – if not an outpost – of collective free playing. It did not inspire widespread imitation in quite the same way that Coltrane's earlier work had done, because it shed many of the elements that had hitherto been part of the definition of jazz: improvisations based on chord sequences, on underlying harmony, or on melody, and which employed a rhythmic sense of swing. But its power, collective passion, and primal screaming qualities nevertheless had formative roles in the subsequent *avant-garde*. In Europe, musicians like Willem Breuker, Evan Parker, and Peter Brötzmann, and in the United States John Zorn, all have common ground with Coltrane's work during and after *Ascension*.

In 1965, in the short term, because of Coltrane's already established importance as a soloist and innovator, the free phase of his mid-1960s work did much to legitimize the playing of those other musicians whom he brought into projects such as *Ascension* or *Kulu Se Mama*, including Archie Shepp, Pharoah Sanders, Marion Brown, John Tchicai, and Rashied Ali. Not all commentators have seen this as a positive step, and one reason why this music needs to be re-assessed is the prevalence of the position adopted by such critics as Doug Ramsey, who wrote: "[He] was often surrounded by sidemen who were not qualified to be in his company. His music had virtually become pure energy. For the most part it was impenetrable."[1]

The degree to which late Coltrane is "impenetrable" depends largely on whether the listener is seeking an obvious connection to what had gone on in jazz up until that point. If preconceptions about harmony, melody, and swing are suspended, and the music is approached in its own terms, it becomes a series of profound, impressive, and frequently uncomfortable statements. Up until that point, Coltrane had, in Francis Davis's words, "been the magic figure of consensus – the man in whose music recent tradition and the urge to explore further reached a workable truce."[2] In 1965, the truce broke down. In the music that followed *Ascension*, Coltrane progressively withdrew from the idea of a large, improvising collective, and explored other avenues of free playing that were linked to his spiritual and religious concerns, principally a sense of color and texture.

Coltrane's links to the "recent jazz tradition" were impeccable. His career began in the bebop era, when he joined Dizzy Gillespie's late-1940s big band alongside a number of fellow musicians from the Philadelphia area who were in thrall to the innovations of Parker and Gillespie. However, he made virtually no records during this period, and none that show he was anything other than competent in bebop or in rhythm and blues. He took until the mid-1950s to find his feet as a soloist, a process which began slowly during his first period in Miles Davis's quintet. Later, after a break in 1957 to kick a growing drug habit, he played with Thelonious Monk, and then returned to Davis, before focusing on leading his own groups for the last six years or so of his life, which was cruelly cut short by liver cancer in 1967.

Coltrane was a slow starter as a distinctive jazz voice, given the major figure he was to become. Whereas contemporaries like Sonny Rollins made an impact extremely early in the 1950s, it took almost a decade longer – until shortly after his thirtieth birthday – for Coltrane to cement his individual contribution to jazz. When he did so, he managed to make difficult and complex ideas accessible to a large audience, so that in the wake of approachable hit records such as *My Favorite Things* or *Greensleeves*, or in his collections of ballads from 1962 to 1963, he carried a substantial public with him right through to the visionary, spiritually inspired work of his final years, such as his duets with drummer Rashied Ali on *Interstellar Space*.

Although Coltrane led a relatively stable quartet from 1961 to 1965, his work of the 1960s is characterized by a remarkable rate of change, a development so swift as to have left even some of his most devoted followers puzzled and confused. Nevertheless, his record-buying public remained loyal, not least because, as the writer Gary Giddins, a college student during Coltrane's final years and a keen collector of every new album as it appeared, said: "If it was by Coltrane, you had to take it seriously."[3] But among critics, many of whom seemed to feel they had some proprietorial rights over him, the climate was less certain. As Don DeMichael put it in a *Down Beat* article: "By the time most critics had caught up with Coltrane, the tenor saxophonist had gone on to another way of playing."[4] The rapidity of this change, and Coltrane's openness to ideas that were unacceptable to several of his more voluble critics, led to considerable controversy.

Those who admired his succinct mastery of ballads were aghast at his increasingly extended solos, and live sets occupied by just one high-speed number. Others who marveled at his technical accuracy and precision were appalled by the honks and falsetto squeals he introduced into some mid-1960s solos. His creative partnership with Eric Dolphy was dismissed in *Down Beat* as "gobbledegook." His collective improvisations *Olé* and *Ascension* were treated like the emperor's new clothes.

Whereas most listeners seemed able to come to terms with Coltrane's work up to and including his final recordings for Atlantic in 1961, the debate began in earnest with his subsequent move to the Impulse label, and with a stepping-up of the pace of development in his recorded output. Nevertheless, underlying it was a slower, entirely consistent, and evolutionary development in Coltrane's own playing that in my view links even his most experimental and exploratory recordings back to his 1959 piece *Giant Steps*.

One common thread that runs through Coltrane's entire musical life was his strong link to Philadelphia, to where he moved from his native North Carolina shortly before his seventeenth birthday. He frequently returned there for periods of reflection, or recuperation, and in almost all phases of his career, he drew on the city's fertile pool of creative talent to find his closest musical colleagues. From his early days with Jimmy Heath and Dizzy

Gillespie to his famous quartet with McCoy Tyner and Jimmy Garrison, and from his *avant-garde* experiments with Archie Shepp to his final work with Rashied Ali, they all had Philadelphia connections.

It was there in his late 'teens that he began to focus his attention seriously on the saxophone (initially the alto and subsequently the tenor) and where he made the first of the many musical contacts that were to continue throughout his life. These included firm friendships with several fellow saxophonists, including Bill Barron, Benny Golson, and, a little later, Jimmy Heath. After military service in a Navy band, and then playing in various rhythm and blues groups, including those of King Kolax and Eddie "Cleanhead" Vinson, towards the end of the 1940s Coltrane ended up in the big band of the local trumpeter Cal Massey. With Massey's band, and in a similar line-up fronted by Jimmy Heath, Coltrane was able to focus on playing bebop.

He and Heath worked obsessively to master the phrasing and speed of Charlie Parker, a practice regimen that continued when both men joined Gillespie's band in 1949. Heath was nicknamed "Little Bird" for his prowess, but he acknowledged that Coltrane possessed comparable skill at replicating the style of Parker and others. Jimmy Heath told me:

> I had enough nerve to think I could have a band copying Dizzy Gillespie's arrangements, plus other arrangements from local writers. I was fortunate because with [trumpeter] Johnny Coles, [saxophonists] Benny Golson, and John Coltrane, and Nelson Boyd who was playing bass, I had some real good guys. . . . John and I did a lot of things together, including dating girls, but we practiced, we transcribed, we had serious discussions about our predecessors, because Coltrane was very interested in what our predecessors had done, as I was, because we saw this music as basically a continuum. We have to have one foot in the past and one in the future, as Dizzy said. Then we worked together in Dizzy's big band. That was a school every day.[5]

When Gillespie's big band broke up in 1950, Coltrane and Heath remained with the trumpeter's small group, until Heath's own narcotic problems grew unmanageable. On record, Coltrane's solo playing from that period is restricted to little more than an unrepresentative boogie-woogie with Gillespie's sextet, but in person, he was already capable of making an impact. When the group was on the road and played near Jefferson City,

Missouri, where Ira Gitler was in college, Gitler, who was at that stage an aspiring alto saxophonist himself, heard it.

> Dizzy was coming to play a dance. My friend who was a piano player and I went over there, and afterwards there was a little barbecue joint where some of the locals played. Jimmy Heath and Coltrane were the two saxophonists with Dizzy at that time, and they sat in. I remember in retrospect hearing Coltrane playing alto, and he was quite into the Bird thing.[6]

In 1958, Gitler himself talked to Coltrane about that period: "What I didn't know with Diz was that what I had to do was really express myself," Coltrane remembered.

> I was playing clichés and trying to learn tunes that were hip, so I could play with the guys that played them. Earlier, when I had first heard Bird, I wanted to be identified with him . . . to be consumed by him. But underneath I really wanted to be myself. You can only play so much of another man.[7]

Between his work with Gillespie in 1950–1 and his debut with Miles Davis in 1955, Coltrane played in the bands of Earl Bostic and Johnny Hodges. However, his playing continued to mature in a direction that owed little to either of those well-established saxophonists, save for the technical advice he received from Bostic in tone production, fingering, and breath control. This was not least because, even though in the early 1950s he was addicted to both heroin and alcohol, he kept up his relentless practice regime, thereby extending his instrumental command well beyond mere imitation of Parker.

In due course, and after he eventually rid himself of dependence on alcohol and hard drugs, Coltrane's practicing itself became an addiction, to the extent that even when he had become the leading saxophone virtuoso in jazz during the 1960s, he would rush backstage to practice between sets, or ignore visitors to his home for hours at a time as he completed his exercises.

However, Coltrane had yet to establish his pre-eminence during the plentiful recordings he made with Davis from October 1955 to late 1956, and in these his playing is clearly at a crossroads, having progressed beyond Parker to absorb a range of additional influences that extend from Dexter Gordon to Lester Young, but not yet having wrapped them into a convincing individual style.

On the sessions made under Davis's newly signed contract for Columbia, painstakingly produced by George Avakian, Coltrane strives for an evenness of approach. However, even the most poised of his solos, such as his chorus on *Budo* from the quintet's first studio date, conceals a potpourri of influences beneath the surface. As mentioned in Chapter 12, to complete the terms of his previous contract with Prestige, Davis was contemporaneously obliged to make a further set of discs for that label; to get these out of the way, he recorded the material for several albums "as live" in lengthy single takes. On these, Coltrane's tendency for uneven playing is even more apparent, and, as his biographer Brian Priestley put it:

> On adjacent numbers or even during the same solo, he can change from directionless faltering to articulate passion; and all within a style that leans heavily on Dexter Gordon and perhaps on Sonny Rollins also, but seems to be aiming fitfully for the glittering precision of Parker or even of a pianist like Tatum or Bud Powell.[8]

Because the Davis Quintet of the mid-1950s was nudging at the boundaries of jazz in so many different places, Coltrane's unevenness of style is just one of a number of noticeable characteristics that were commented on at the time, but which did not stand in the way of the group's exceptional influence on the jazz of the period. Against Philly Joe Jones's strident drumming, well-forward in the mix on recordings and equally dominant on live gigs, plus Red Garland's spacey piano and Paul Chambers's economical bass lines, as stylistically schizophrenic a tenor solo as, say, that on *It Could Happen to You* from the Prestige album *Relaxin'* does not sound particularly extraordinary. Yet it remains an unconsolidated collection of apparently random thoughts.

Overall, not least because of Chambers's unhurried two-beat accompaniment, this solo retains the gentle feel of a ballad, and occasionally there are delicate and beautiful phrases that mirror the original melody or are startlingly creative contrafacts of it. But in between, Coltrane includes fragmented forays into Parkerish phrasing, none of them seen through; there is the occasional quote, including a moment of *Them There Eyes* which is itself unresolved, and some clumsily un-swinging phrases, as squarely on the beat as the work of an unpracticed novice.

It took a return home to Philadelphia, and ridding himself of his drug habit in the early months of 1957, for Coltrane to draw these diffuse elements together, and so to create a consistent, definitive style that he could rely on producing in any circumstances. Although his playing continued to evolve, what he arrived at in 1957–8 became the basis of his subsequent all-pervasive influence as a saxophonist.

The public first became aware of this when Coltrane returned to New York and embarked on a prolific series of recordings under his own name, mainly for Prestige, but also including the somewhat atypical yet highly influential *Blue Train* for Blue Note, which put Coltrane amid Alfred Lion's repertory company of hard-bop players including trumpeter Lee Morgan and pianist Kenny Drew. *Blue Train* displayed some aspects of Coltrane's new-found confidence and consistency of direction; it also showed an increasingly obvious mastery of harmony, but it was in his numerous dates for Bob Weinstock at Prestige that these elements were more fully documented on disc. More importantly at the time, both in terms of Coltrane's view of his musical development and because a handful of recordings of its performances survives, he appeared at the Five Spot in a quartet with Thelonious Monk. The group's exceptional playing drew even the most hardened of critics to hear the band again and again. Ira Gitler recalled:

> I was there an average of three times a week, when the Monk Quartet was playing – that's how good it was. It was always an intense experience. They threw themselves into the music, they had quite a wide repertoire, and there was the excitement of the new combination of Coltrane and Monk that carried through. It was an emotional experience. Trane had started back with his individual recordings at Prestige . . . and that's when he started doing those extended strings of notes for which I came up with the name "sheets of sound." In the Monk group, those multi-note runs fit perfectly with Monk's music, which you can hear on the live recording of *Trinkle Tinkle*. The sixty-fourth notes . . . he was doing created extraordinary textures.[9]

Although the tapes of the quartet at the Five Spot were amateur recordings from Coltrane's first wife Naima's collection, finally issued in their entirety in the 1990s complete with boxy, low-fidelity sound and poor balance, the music they contain is of extraordinary quality, and, as Gitler says, *Trinkle Tinkle* in particular is a remarkable demonstration of Coltrane's new technique. It also offers a comparison with a studio version of the tune cut for Orrin Keepnews's Jazzland label – one of just three properly recorded pieces by this Monk group. In both discs, the rapidity of Coltrane's phrasing and his dazzling runs, which contain so skillful a choice of notes as to convey an impression of constantly shifting reactions to the underlying chord structure, combine into what Gitler called a "residual harmonic effect," a series of diffuse melodic patterns whose collective abstraction moves far beyond the elements from which they are constructed. The studio recording is magisterial, and of a completely different order from Coltrane's 1955–6 discs with Davis. The live recording, however, is a living portrait of an artist in transition. The startling and extended tenor solo ruthlessly wrings out the wet towel of Monk's knotty little melody in as many harmonic ways as possible. It is as if we can hear actually taking place the very process of technical enrichment Coltrane himself described as having learned from Monk. In Coltrane's own words:

> I felt I learned from him in every way. Through the senses, theoretically, technically. I would talk to Monk about musical problems, and he would sit at the piano and show me the answers just by playing them. I could watch him play and find out the things I wanted to know. Also I could see a lot of things that I didn't know about at all.[10]

The "things" that he learned included a concept of multiphonics – of sounding more than one note simultaneously and, just as importantly, of *appearing* to sound more than one note simultaneously. This was drawn from Monk's genius for implying rather than actually sounding notes. In one interview, Coltrane talked at length about Monk's chord voicing, and how, even when he left the minor third out of a chord, it would retain its minor characteristics.[11]

On the Prestige albums Coltrane made under his own name during his tenure with Monk, there are several examples of his high speed virtuoso playing, of the ability he learned from Monk of implying harmony, and of the dazzling command of harmonic nuance at high speed that informed his choice of notes in his "sheets of sound." At slower tempos, there is also a growing sense of conviction, of "rightness," about the form and shape of his ballad solos. A piece like *Violets for Your Furs* from the Prestige album *Coltrane*, recorded in May 1957, has the same sense of predetermination I have noted earlier in the best solos by Armstrong, Parker, or Gillespie, and which is generally the hallmark of the most distinguished soloists in jazz.

This creation of perfectly shaped solos, so right that they sounded composed, coincided with a growth of Coltrane's own confidence in his abilities, which was something noticed by the man who engineered many of his recording sessions, Rudy Van Gelder:

> When it came to making decisions about what were the good takes, or whether this thing was being successfully recorded, he knew when it was right. He had a command of his own music and he knew what he wanted, to the extent that he could say "That's a good take." That's not always possible, and I admire the musicians who can do that. Sometimes they want to go home and listen to this thing for a month or they can't tell which take is a good one, or they want to do it over again. They'll try it, learn it, peak out, and keep going making take after take to see if they could do better. But he had a way of knowing when it was right.[12]

Most of Coltrane's biographers concur that hand-in-glove with kicking hard drugs and alcohol, he underwent a deepening of his already strong religious convictions in 1957, which seems to have underpinned his growing self-confidence as a musician. Even so, he was to undergo a further period of growth, in which he matured from having asserted himself as a major voice to becoming the pre-eminent saxophonist in contemporary jazz, and this came about through his return to Miles Davis's band in 1958.

This time, Coltrane found himself sharing front-line duties not just with Davis, but also with altoist Cannonball Adderley. At first, the band still had the rhythm section with whom Coltrane had worked previously, bassist Paul Chambers, pianist Red Garland, and drummer Philly Joe Jones, but the narcotic problems of the latter two led to their replacement by first Bill Evans and then Wynton Kelly on piano, and by Jimmy Cobb on drums. However, the old rhythm section was still on hand when the group recorded *Milestones* in April 1958. This disc – apparently the result of a chaotic studio session – was a landmark, not simply because it demonstrated Coltrane's quantum leap forward as a soloist since his earlier work with Davis, but because the title track adopted George Russell's ideas about using modes as a basis for improvisation, rather than chord sequences. It was not by any means the first modal jazz record (Gillespie's *Cubana-Be/Cubana-Bop*, also partly inspired – and arranged – by Russell, probably deserves that honor) but it had a dramatic impact on the way that much jazz improvisation would develop thereafter, and paved the way for Davis's subsequent *Kind of Blue* album, which forever defined the genre of modal jazz.

I have already discussed the importance of *Kind of Blue* in terms of Davis's work, and this stage in Coltrane's development is exemplified by *So What* from that disc, on which he takes the first of the two saxophone solos **[CD track 19]**. For Coltrane, the most important lesson was one that he was to apply somewhat later in the sessions he made under his own name – to pare down his accompaniment to the simplest level, and focus on using his solos to encapsulate his own increasingly complex harmonic ideas. In doing so, he was also able to capitalize on two compatible but distinct ways of improvising within Davis's band – focusing either on developing melodic material, or on developing harmonic material.

Coltrane was a thoughtful and articulate man, precise in setting out his views to careful and considerate interviewers, and he summed up exactly what he took from this period of work with Davis, whom he considered as significant a mentor as Monk:

> He was moving . . . to the use of fewer and fewer chord changes in songs. He used tunes with free-flowing lines and chordal direction. This approach allowed the soloist the choice of playing chordally (vertically) or melodically (horizontally). In fact, due to the direct and free-flowing lines in this music, I found it easy to apply the harmonic ideas that I had. I could stack up chords – say on a $C_7$, I sometimes superimposed an $Eb_7$, up to an F[sharp]$_7$, down to an F. That way I could play three chords on one. But on the other hand if I wanted to I could play melodically.[13]

It took some time for these ideas to percolate into the sessions Coltrane made under his own name during his final period with Davis. In January 1959, he moved from Prestige to Atlantic, and so began to enjoy major-label exposure of his own, at a time when he was still appearing on discs with Davis for Columbia. Because his own recording sessions involved many of his own compositions, his writing style underwent adaptation as he took into account Davis's methods of improvising "vertically" or "horizontally," but it was not until he left the trumpeter's group after a European tour in 1960, and became a full-time bandleader himself, that he began consistently to use a comparably potent mix of simple settings for complex ideas.

This is not to suggest that the question of finding the right setting for his playing was unimportant to Coltrane. Indeed, quite the reverse is true, as he thought hard about the sound of his rhythm sections, and in many of his own compositions specified precisely what he wanted the piano, bass, and drums to be doing. His discs from 1959 to 1961 chart his attempts to find the right kind of support, both in terms of what his players were asked to do, and also in terms of the selection of individual musicians.

I asked Coltrane's biographer Lewis Porter what best exemplified this process at work, and he suggested the three recordings of *Like Sonny*, made between March 1959 and September 1960. He said:

> This piece gives a very good idea of the attention to detail that Coltrane brought to composition. It changes each time he records it, which he ended up doing three times. Each time it has a different "feel." So, for example, the first time, on what is known as the first *Giant Steps* session, from March 26, 1959, with Cedar Walton on piano, he has piano and bass playing in unison, and the whole thing has a kind of Afro-Latin feel. Then, the next time he records it, which was originally issued on the *Coltrane Jazz* album [recorded with Wynton Kelly on piano, on December 2, 1959], it's got a very soft Latin feeling, almost a bossa nova feel to it. One thing a lot of people don't realize is that Coltrane was hip to Latin music very early on, and a bossa nova feel in late 1959 was way ahead of the game. Then he records it again in his one beautiful and not so well-known session for Roulette in 1960, with Billy Higgins on drums, which has a different, relaxed sound . . . not a repetitive rhythm so much as a loose, floating quality that *suggests* a Latin feel. And in all these three very different recordings of the same tune, he's always thinking, what should the bass be doing? What should the piano or drums be doing?[14]

The majority of Coltrane's own recordings dating from his last period with Davis share this kind of concern, and in the surviving holographs of his compositions, several have fully worked-out bass parts, for example, that reinforce Coltrane's integrated view of composition and recording.

His most influential, and perhaps his best-known, composition from the period up until 1961 predated his move towards more open settings, however fully worked out. This was *Giant Steps*, from 1959, which was the antithesis of simplicity. Despite being no more than a compact sixteen measures in length, it is an extraordinarily dense and complete composition in terms of the interlocking of its melodic and harmonic content. The shifting chords – two contrasting eight-bar sections, the first using root movements in thirds and the second a series of ii-V-I progressions – work in tandem with a tune that appears to be moving up and down at the same time – almost the qualities of an M. C. Escher picture, as Pat Metheny once memorably expressed it.[15] The perpetual motion of the chord sequence gave Coltrane endless opportunities to demonstrate his ability to superimpose over it rapidly moving harmonic ideas, and he chose to do so largely by building his solo choruses on a series of four-note pentatonic patterns.

It took Coltrane a couple of recording sessions, with two different rhythm sections, to arrive at a version he was happy to see released, and despite the disastrous fire at Atlantic's vaults, which destroyed many of the company's alternate masters, the process of its creation on disc is largely preserved. The key to it, as I discovered from the pianist on the originally issued version Tommy Flanagan, was the speed at which the piece was to be played:

> We were neighbors. I lived on 101st Street, and John lived on 103rd Street, and I knew him from seeing him with Miles. . . . I used to go by his house and there was always a session going on there because he couldn't stop playing. He played a little piano himself, and he had a piano in his apartment. I used to go by, and sometimes play some of his tunes with him that he was going to use on recording dates. One day, he wanted to do this tune *Giant Steps*. It was a little more irregular than usual, and I guess that's why he brought it by to me, because normally nobody prepares you for a record date like that, for just one tune. He said, "You won't have any problems with this." I played the chord progressions, and there was nothing too bad about that – it seemed like they were a little out of order, but anyway, when I got to the date, I had no idea that the *tempo* was going to be as fast as it was. I did what I could to keep my head above water![16]

On the issued take, for his solo, Flanagan uses rapid right-hand single-note phrases of the type developed by Bud Powell, but although he acquits himself well, it is clearly a piece that would be hard going for any pianist, given the mixture of harmonic complexity and rapid tempo. On another of the surviving takes, he plays a chordal solo, focusing on the tune's shifting harmonies. Cedar Walton, who was on an earlier session at which Coltrane first recorded the tune, avoided taking a piano solo altogether.

*Giant Steps* was not the only such complex tune that Coltrane developed at this stage: other pieces such as *Countdown*, *Exotica*, and *Fifth House* have similarly dense chord progressions. The sheer technical challenge of this group of numbers has made them into test pieces for saxophonists everywhere, and, in Lewis Porter's words, "required fare in jazz education programs."[17] But while aspiring saxophonists (not to mention would-be rhythm sections) still work out on these chords in the twenty-first century, Coltrane himself soon recognized that this was a passing stage in his development, and, as he was to do several times in the 1960s, he moved on. He confirmed to British author Val Wilmer that this was largely due to Miles Davis's infuence:

> At the time I left Miles, I was trying to add a lot of sequences to my solo work, putting chords to the things I was playing, and using things I could play a little more music on. It was before I had my own group that I had the rhythm section playing these sequences forward, I made *Giant Steps* with some other guys and carried the idea on into my band. But it was hard to make some things swing with the rhythm section playing those chords, and Miles advised me to abandon the idea of the rhythm section playing those sequences, and to do it only myself.[18]

This perception underpinned the musical philosophy of Coltrane's eventual regular quartet with McCoy Tyner, Jimmy Garrison, and Elvin Jones. Coltrane's most memorable creations with that group are almost all based on relatively simple harmonic platforms – such as the modal setting for the well-known contour of the song *My Favorite Things* (which this quartet reinterpreted several times after Coltrane's original recording with Steve Davis on bass), the blues sequence of *Chasin' the Trane*, or the tiny motifs that underpin *A Love Supreme*.

The success of such pieces is central to Coltrane's enduring influence and his importance to jazz in the last decades of the twentieth century. In all of them, his complex solos were not simply masterful harmonically and technically but they also conveyed powerful emotion, often with a hint of vulnerability. Simplifying the role of his rhythm section allowed Coltrane to use his own prodigious technique to express ideas and feelings, and not just to be an end in itself.

Furthermore, because the material on which he built his most complex improvisations could be easily assimilated and was comprehensible to an audience, then whatever layers of harmonic complexity he added in his solos, or however Jones's surging drums fragmented the meter into polyrhythms, much of what he did would remain accessible.

Despite the fact that listeners at the time were not always aware of it, and because Coltrane's fascination with altering his musical environment suggested the outwardly fast and furious rate of change in his work already mentioned, this relationship between his complex solos and the comparative simplicity of their setting actually continued well after the break-up of the quartet, throughout his more abstract recordings and his forays into free jazz and the "new thing," from 1965 to 1967. Coltrane's own solos in many of these apparently free performances were still built on his harmonization of relatively simple melodic fragments, or of some discernible element of underlying form. Even when he added vocal tones, high register shrieks, and other sounds derived from the improvisational language of saxophonist colleagues like Archie Shepp or Pharoah Sanders, he seldom forsook the use of phrases built on recognizable harmonic variation. This defines the essential difference between Coltrane and Ornette Coleman.

Coleman was above all a supreme melodist, but, as I shall point out in the next chapter, he was quite happy if the harmonization of even his most memorable melodies altered on each performance. Equally, Coleman functioned best with a clear underlying beat – either the walking bass and conventional timekeeping of Charlie Haden and Billy Higgins in his original quartet, or the jazz-rock flavor of Prime Time. By contrast, Coltrane's melodies were not always so clear cut, and he could function with a less sharply defined sense of rhythm. He was fascinated, for example, by the coloristic drum style of Rashied Ali, which replaced Elvin Jones's metrical approach. His harmony came from within, as Archie Shepp explained to me, in connection with the *Ascension* album of 1965: "John always liked to know where he was. Even when he was playing free, he liked to be able to refer to harmonies he was familiar with."[19]

A similar view is taken by Coltrane's son Ravi, himself a saxophonist, who became well-versed in almost every aspect of his late father's 1960s period by analyzing and cataloging his tape collection, which included dozens of unissued items and informal practice sessions. Not only did Ravi hear this firm command of structure in his father's playing, whatever the context, but he could also pin down where much of the structure came from:

> I hear *Giant Steps* in many of his 1965–6 recordings. In many of his solos he used that progression in major thirds, and the idea of dominants setting up a resolve. It's not there so much in his work with the quartet in 1962–4, but it came back very strongly in 1965–7.[20]

Indeed, Coltrane himself was quite candid in 1962 with the French interviewer Benoit Quersin in identifying the effect that *Giant Steps* had had on his work:

> Some things I could have used in . . . *Giant Steps* . . . I could have probably taken . . . and applied to something else and they might have taken up a few bars and that [would] have been it. But at that time I was obsessed with the thing and it was all I had in my mind, because it was my first step into playing some extended chord structures. . . . That was the first . . . record I made with them in there. And since then I've done it, but it hasn't been so obvious because I've learned to do it as part of something and not as a whole.[21]

So *Giant Steps* can be seen as the beacon that shone forward over Coltrane's most influential work of the 1960s and the freer playing that followed. Continuing to use ideas from his solos on the sequence, he worked to simplify the structure, though not the texture, of his accompaniment. Even when he eventually discarded the harmonic clarity of McCoy Tyner and the metrical precision of Elvin Jones for his final quartet with Alice Coltrane on piano and Rashied Ali on drums, he continued to explore aspects of the *Giant Steps* sequence in his playing.

Important as *Giant Steps* was, however, Coltrane's 1960s work is unlikely to have been able to develop as it did, were it not for the exceptionally intuitive ensemble he achieved with Tyner, Garrison, and Jones. This flexible and sympathetic group of colleagues accompanied Coltrane's rise to cult status in the early 1960s, and was crucial in creating the body of work through which he subsequently had most influence on the course of jazz. The recordings of this quartet, in both studio and live performance contexts, document the period of greatest change in Coltrane's work – to the extent that such change is often discussed in terms of his evolution from album to album. Furthermore, just as, from the 1940s, Alfred Lion at Blue Note and, from the 1950s, Norman Granz at Verve (and its predecessors) had used design and presentational style as prerequisites of the overall concept of each disc issued, so Impulse continued the tradition in the 1960s. Gary Giddins suggests:

> A lot of things are involved here, including the way the Impulse records looked. The orange spine, the handsomely packaged

gatefold covers, the boast on the back of every one that this is "The New Wave in Jazz," the nature of the liner notes, which usually gave each one a political cast. . . . The records moved so quickly, from a place where you knew what Coltrane was doing to a place where you had to concentrate to follow him.[22]

As the series went on, critical lines were drawn under each release as, one by one, hitherto enthusiastic jazz writers baled out. Ira Gitler, staunch supporter of Coltrane's late-1950s work, found the extended solos from the 1961 live sets recorded at the Village Vanguard such as *Chasin' the Trane* went on for too long, calling them "a treadmill to the Kingdom of Boredom." John S. Wilson found the *Ballads* album "unimpressive" in his *Down Beat* review. Joe Goldberg, writing in *Hi-Fi/Stereo Review*, disliked the "embarrassingly open and fervent" religious manner that accompanied *A Love Supreme*, and so it continued, until the quartet itself changed personnel in 1965.

For the most part, such critical reaction was focused directly on the music, but among the public at large – perhaps, as Giddins suggests, fueled by the overtly political message of the packaging – Coltrane's music came to symbolize much of the African-American unrest of the time. It was possible to read signs of racial protest and of the growing movement for identity with all things African into the expanded forces of his Impulse debut album *Africa/Brass*, or into the gritty, angry solo triumph of *Chasin' the Trane*. Yet Coltrane himself protested this was not the case, and that his playing was not an overt statement of political anger. ("If it is interpreted as anger, it is taken wrong."[23]) Even his one direct political statement, the tune *Alabama*, written in the wake of the 1963 bomb atrocity in Birmingham, is more meditative than overtly angry. Certainly he never publicly adopted the radical political stance of his new thing colleagues such as Archie Shepp, or of the Chicagoan revolutionaries of the AACM. Nevertheless, through the shrewd presentation of his work by producers Creed Taylor and Bob Thiele, the hard-edged music of Coltrane's quartet became synonymous with this period of protest.

The first of the "classic" line-up to have become a regular member of the quartet, once Coltrane eventually left Miles Davis, was McCoy Tyner. The two men first met at a time the saxophonist was at home in Philadelphia, during his 1957 withdrawal from drug addiction. Tyner remembered:

I used to sit on the porch of his mother's house and talk to him. Then he went back with Miles in the late 50s, but we made a verbal commitment that I would go join his band whenever he formed it. It took him a long time. Whenever he wanted to leave Miles, Miles coaxed him to stay. Then Benny Golson, who was also from Philadelphia, offered me a trip to San Francisco, so I went there for three weeks with Benny and Curtis Fuller. . . . When we got back he said, "Art Farmer and I are going to form a band. Would you like to be a part of it?"

I said, "Of course, but I promised Coltrane whenever he left Miles that I would join his band."

He said, "Okay."

So I stayed with them about six or seven months, and made that record, *Meet the Jazztet*, which I liked, but my heart was in playing with John. Shortly after I first met John, he played one of my songs, *Chronic Blues*. And then once I joined the band he allowed me to do a few more little things. I wrote *Greensleeves*, of course not the original piece, because that's public domain, but I wrote John's arrangement of *Greensleeves*. And he was very generous that way in allowing all of us to develop.[24]

As already mentioned, *Greensleeves* – of which Tyner's version dated from the quartet's first Impulse session in December 1961 – was conceived as a popular follow-up to Coltrane's highly successful recording of *My Favorite Things* on Atlantic. This had featured Tyner and Jones with Steve Davis on bass, and after being released as a 45 r.p.m. single it sold in sufficient numbers to earn a gold disc. The sound was refreshingly new and original, and its mass popularity did much to distance Coltrane from his work with Miles Davis.

On both discs Coltrane played soprano saxophone, which he used to create an ethereal floating quality in his ballad playing, ideally suited to the predominantly modal backdrop in waltz-time created by Tyner, and (on *My Favorite Things*) the repeated pedal notes of Davis's bass line.

The popularity of these discs, combined with Coltrane's appealing sound on soprano, had a lot to do with reviving the instrument, and bringing it into regular use in contemporary styles of jazz, rather than remaining a bastion of traditionalism in the wake of Sidney Bechet. According to Coltrane himself, the freedom with which he found he could play over the entire range of the soprano had an effect on his tenor playing:

I hadn't always played all over it, because I was playing certain ideas which just went in certain ranges, octaves. But by playing on soprano . . . it soon got so that when I went on tenor, I found myself doing the same thing. It caused the change or the willingness to change and just try to play as much of the instrument as possible.[25]

Arguably, this further liberation of Coltrane's tenor playing had every bit as much to do with the presence of Tyner in his group as it did with his work on soprano. Tyner's ability to sense exactly the right level of support, when to supply dense chording, when to play very little, and – most important – when not to play at all opened up considerable opportunities for the saxophonist. It also created the environment in which drummer Elvin Jones, the next member of the group to join, could create a rhythmic dialog with Coltrane.

Jones was an exceptionally talented drummer, and the youngest of three Jones brothers (Hank and Thad were his seniors) who had made their mark on the Detroit jazz scene before finding national fame. His early playing experience gave him a thorough grounding in swing and bebop styles, but his speciality was in creating a dense maelstrom of polyrhythms. This did not always make it easy for pianists and bassists who worked with him; his home town compatriot Tommy Flanagan (who often worked in a trio setting with Jones) told me that alongside him on the bandstand, you always had to listen intently to hear the "one," the downbeat, because Jones was so adept at moving the emphasis around.

As Coltrane pared down the harmonic backdrop to his work, Jones and Tyner between them supplied an increasing rhythmic density, underpinned on bass by first Steve Davis, then Reggie Workman, and finally the quartet's long-serving bassist Jimmy Garrison. What they achieved was not – despite Coltrane's fondness for his own practice regime – the result of rehearsal. Everything was worked out in public on the bandstand during the group's packed calendar of engagements and its long club tenures at the Half Note. From the time he joined, Tyner remembered no more than half a dozen formal rehearsals, and that may be an overstatement. Jones agreed:

We never had a rehearsal, for anything. Everything that we did, all the compositions we played – John would start by playing an outline of what we were gonna do, the new composition for that evening. Sometimes we'd play it for a week, because we worked

757

practically every day for years. After that time, he only had to begin an idea and all of us would immediately pick up the thread of it.[26]

Nevertheless, the group's work was not entirely spontaneous, and underlying it there were, of course, sketched chord sequences, hastily jotted ideas, and more fully worked out compositions, but they were all tried out for real in performance.

Pinning down the contribution of Jimmy Garrison, the fourth member of the group, in how they achieved this is less straightforward than describing the playing of Tyner or Jones. In his work with Ornette Coleman from 1960, Garrison had demonstrated his ability to imply a harmonic sequence in a chordless rhythm section, and he was so impressive in this context that Coltrane recruited him. Jones described Garrison's arrival as "the turning point" in the creation of the quartet, saying "his aggressiveness, his attitude towards the instrument gave us all a lift."[27] For a further insight, I spoke to Roy Haynes, the man who briefly replaced Jones in 1963. Haynes said:

> When Garrison would stop playing, when it was just the drums and John Coltrane, you could tell that Garrison wasn't there. You could feel it when he came in. He wasn't the loudest bass player, but he had a great feel. I don't think he really got a lot of the credit he deserved as a bass player. He had something that you could feel inside you, in your body, on the bandstand, as you were listening to him.[28]

This is well demonstrated in *Dear Old Stockholm*, from April 29, 1963, one of the discs Haynes made with the quartet, where the piano drops out, and there is an interchange between drums and tenor in which the bass participates – clarifying exactly the "feel" described by Haynes. From the same session, *After the Rain* shows an early example of Coltrane playing almost an entire ballad out of tempo, with Tyner, Garrison, and Haynes supplying texture rather than time. When Jones rejoined, this textural element continued to be important.

From 1961 to 1965, this quartet was a group every bit as influential as the Armstrong Hot Five, the Parker/Gillespie Quintet, Miles Davis's various bands, and Ornette Coleman's original quartet. Its body of work consolidated Coltrane's genius and his position of influence. Its studio work contains everything from poised ballads and modally based hit records to intense, high-speed interplay, with Coltrane's powerful horn at its center. Its live recordings capture the trance-like passionate intensity of Coltrane's club work – memorably described by Eric Nisenson:

> Roiling arpeggios alternating with moments of intense lyricism often accentuated by saxophone cries and wails ... Coltrane eventually was almost completely bent over forward, his face flushed, and at one point saliva poured out of the side of his mouth. He seemed to be not in this world.[29]

The quartet also pioneered two further aspects of Coltrane's importance to jazz history: his experiments with extended form, and his incorporation of spiritual ideas into his work. These are inextricably linked, not just overtly in such pieces as the four-part *A Love Supreme*, but in the motivation for Coltrane's own lengthy improvisations. He told several interviewers that his work was a search, a process of "continual looking," and his song titles, liner notes, and general conversation reflected his interests in religion, in astrology, and in the boundaries of human experience. His drug addictions of the 1950s behind him, he nevertheless experimented with LSD in the 1960s to investigate its effects in opening up new areas of consciousness, new aspects of "continual looking."

In my view, it was this process of searching that led Coltrane to embrace the free jazz movement. From the early 1960s he had been impressed by Ornette Coleman's work, and had recorded an album with the three other members of Coleman's quartet, Don Cherry, Charlie Haden, and Ed Backwell. He was a frequent attendee at the Five Spot while Coleman played there in 1960–1, and he knew most of the participants of Coleman's 1960s double quartet album *Free Jazz*. Although I believe this disc was something of a blind alley in Coleman's own development, as discussed in the next chapter, it undoubtedly influenced many of his circle, and that included Coltrane.

In *Africa/Brass*, his very first recording for Impulse, in 1961, Coltrane produced music that had several things in common with *Free Jazz* (including the presence of both Freddie Hubbard and Eric Dolphy from Coleman's line-up). The title track was in extended form, for a larger than usual ensemble, which experimented with collectively improvised backgrounds. When he came to make *Ascension* some years later, many of the same elements reappeared. In addition, *Ascension* exploited a curious duality, which extended Coleman's idea of the double quartet in a very literal-minded way. Each instrumental voice (with the exception of piano and drums) was doubled, and the soloists were deliberately encouraged to display contrasting characteristics. Rashied Ali told me that he had been invited to play drums on the disc alongside Jones but had declined – suggesting that Coltrane had originally planned to double the percussion as well.

As Coltrane told Frank Kofsky, when he brought Rashied into the line-up alongside Jones, he had also intended to double the percussion with his regular group:

> I figured I could do two things: I could have a band that played like the way we used to play, and a band that was going in the direction that the one I have now is going in – I could combine these two, with these two concepts going.[30]

Such duality became a regular feature of Coltrane's touring band in late 1965, with two drummers and the additional saxophone of Pharoah Sanders joining him in the front line, until Jones finally left and Rashied Ali continued as sole percussionist. Yet there was duality of a different sort going on at a far deeper level as well.

It was obvious to listeners to a piece like *Welcome*, a luminous ballad recorded by his classic quartet in June 1965, that Coltrane's playing could achieve a serene, prayer-like quality. It was hard to equate this quality with the anarchic sounds of *Ascension*, made just eighteen days later. With two takes of just over half an hour apiece, and a free-form eleven-piece collective playing simultaneously between each extended solo, this seemed to be the antithesis of the densely focused, spiritual intesity of the regular quartet. Yet to Coltrane, the two radically different styles of music were simply different aspects of his own search, of "continual looking," so he allowed the ensemble of *Ascension* to function in much the same way as he functioned himself in the context of the regular quartet. As Archie Shepp put it: "The idea is similar to what action painters do, in that it creates various surfaces of color which push into each other, creating tensions and counter tensions and various fields of energy."[31] The description is as valid of Coltrane's own playing as it is of the entire ensemble on *Ascension*. The point is even more clearly made in Coltrane's last extended suite to be recorded – the five-part *Meditations*, cut at the end of 1965, where Coltrane sought to combine the motif-based compositional elements of *A Love Supreme* with a smaller-scale version of the ensemble freedom of *Ascension*.

Coltrane's final period was cut short by the onset of his fatal illness. His playing had always relied on his prodigious energy level, and with the onset of cancer this went into rapid decline. Rashied Ali told me how shocked he was to see Coltrane playing from a chair in some of their final concerts together.

His last period extended the coloristic ideas that stemmed from *Ascension*, and involved Alice Coltrane's abstract piano and Rashied Ali's percussive backdrop. This group's 1966 Japanese concerts are the most dramatic illustration of its ability to provide shifting colors and textures behind Coltrane's lengthy, impassioned solos, which for the most part build from tiny, repetitive phrases to demonic convolution. This music is not easy to assimilate or assess; it has never become part of the *lingua franca* of contemporary jazz in the same way as his playing from 1957 to 1965. Yet it repays detailed investigation, not least as the final resolution of Coltrane's exploration of his *Giant Steps* ideas.

Perhaps the most fruitful route by which to approach the last period is from the album *Stellar Regions*, a posthumously released collection of material by his very last regularly working ensemble. These pieces are all relatively short and concise, and I am grateful to Ravi Coltrane for suggesting this way into his father's final work. He told me:

> In much of his last period, the palette is so broad, there was so much happening, that I was listening to the music without really hearing what was going on. But through *Stellar Regions* I gained a series of associations I could use while listening to the other music from the time. I think when you are listening to some of his longer solos you eventually just bale out, your brain shuts down after twenty minutes or so through the sheer overload of ideas. But these tunes are all four or five minutes, which was very uncommon in my father's work. Listening to them honed my ear to what was going on in the group with Rashied and my Ma, and when I went back to his other discs from the time, I found I was able to focus in better on what was going on, in even the broadest palettes.[32]

## Charles Mingus

> Here's Charles Mingus, standard issue thumbnail sketch. A
> fat, bristling, light-skinned black guy who busted people on
> the bandstand, who stopped his shows midstream if a cash
> register rang or a fan or a musician said or did something
> that set him off. If he was set off enough, he yelled at or
> lectured or swung on or pulled a blade on the offender, like
> he was the 240-pound wrath of Zeus.
>
> Gene Santoro, from *Myself When I Am Real*

Whereas John Coltrane was the outstanding jazz instrumentalist of the
1960s, Charles Mingus was its outstanding composer – building on his
considerable achievements of the middle-to-late 1950s. He was an outsize
personality as well – a stocky, powerful-looking man, and on stage he had a
charismatic presence, although he was often at the center of controversy and
rows. I first heard him perform at the New Orleans Jazz and Heritage
Festival in 1976, where fortunately there were no rows. He played a
magnificent solo set lasting over an hour; his intense concentration and sheer
force of musical ideas held a vast, bustling tent almost silent as he played
both on double bass and on piano. Much of that set was a long exploration of
the Vernon Duke standard *I Can't Get Started* – one of the pieces that
fascinated Mingus, and from which he seemed constantly able to squeeze
new ideas.[33] Later, playing a set with his quintet of the time and performing
his own music, he went a long way to proving that he was, after Duke
Ellington, the most prolific and versatile composer in jazz.

Not every audience in every venue saw that pensive, creative side of
Mingus at work. Mingus viewed himself as an outsider, and all too often he
behaved as one. His frequently stated anti-establishment views, and the kind
of behavior as caricatured above by Gene Santoro, often tended to obscure
the creative genius of his finest work. However, starting from his childhood
in Los Angeles, the reasons mounted as to why he should feel excluded: he
could count European, African, and Asian blood in his lineage, and his
schoolmates taunted him as a "yellow nigger." His father (an ex-soldier) had
"passed" for white, but Mingus's complexion precluded this; however, it
also prevented his acceptance by many of his African-American
contemporaries, thereby effectively excluding him from the two main
social groups in the district of Los Angeles in which he was raised. He
recalled: "I just found myself with the Japanese, the Greeks, the Italians and

Mexicans, and a few more guys like me."[34]

He carried this sense of social isolation into both his education and his music. Despite an unusually high IQ, he performed abysmally in school; as an instrumentalist, a false start on trombone having led him to become a cellist, he was essentially self-taught, so that, even in the area in which he was to excel, he did not at first learn to read music fluently, and relied instead on his exceptional musical ear.

The quality of his ear was readily apparent to saxophonist Buddy Collette, one of Mingus's lifelong friends who, when he was fourteen and Mingus was just thirteen, coerced the young cellist into trading in his cello for a double bass. By the following week, Mingus was playing a Saturday night dance with Collette's band. Collette said:

> The things he did that first night on the bass showed that he had real ability. It's amazing to hear somebody with musical talent. . . . Mingus's notes that first gig were not right – not that he didn't have good ears. It's just that he didn't know where the notes were . . . but his time was good. . . . All of a sudden there was a feeling and a choice of rhythm patterns right from the beginning that told me this was someone special.[35]

Collette and a small circle of musical acquaintants, including the trombonist Britt Woodman, recognized immediately that Mingus was outstandingly talented, and took his musical education in hand. Collette introduced him to Red Callender, a prominent bassist in Los Angeles who had worked with many high profile musicians including Louis Armstrong. Callender became a teacher and mentor for Mingus, who in due course ended up briefly playing in Armstrong's big band himself. Mingus also went on to study with Herman Rheinschagen, a former bassist with the New York Philharmonic.

In addition to intensive musical practice, Mingus improved his personal confidence through self-defense training and weight lifting, and allied himself firmly with the local African-American community, making what his biographer Brian Priestley describes as "a conscious choice to be an underdog rather than an outcast."[36]

Mingus became a prominent figure on the Los Angeles jazz scene during the height of Central Avenue's importance as the center of local activity, described in Chapter 6. While they were still teenagers, to the amusement of other passengers, he and Collette would jam on the Red line streetcar that wound its way via Central from Watts in the south to downtown Los Angeles in the north; they also took part in the rich world of after-hours playing that was on offer. Also, Mingus – along with many other promising musicians of his generation – studied with trumpeter Lloyd Reese, a key figure in the musical community of Central Avenue, who taught at the old black Musicians' Union building in the heart of the area's clubs.

Much of the pre-war world of African-American entertainment rubbed off on Mingus, both from playing gigs around Los Angeles with veterans like Kid Ory and Barney Bigard, and from his subsequent period in Armstrong's big band. Just as Charlie Parker and Miles Davis were to do on the East Coast, he rejected the eye-rolling, mugging stage persona of such older entertainers, nevertheless simultaneously acquiring a knowledge of and respect for the sounds they made: "our" music, as he called it. This was to resurface in a significant proportion of his later work as a composer and performer, which contains a dramatic balance between material drawn directly from both the African-American vaudeville tradition (songs like *Eat That Chicken*, or his parody of a 1920s dance routine on *Cocktails for Two*) and the uncompromisingly modern improvisations of musicians like saxophonist Eric Dolphy (another Central Avenue alumnus). Mingus was also to draw the sounds of gospel music and the church into his jazz vocabulary, just as he was to assimilate the compositional language of Duke Ellington, whose band made a huge impact on his own as a young man. Initially, however, his career was more of a player than of a composer.

Mingus appeared on the scene at the right moment to build on the innovations in double bass playing that had been pioneered by Milt Hinton, Jimmy Blanton, and Oscar Pettiford, and which were being taken forward by other musicians of his own generation such as Ray Brown. He instinctively understood the harmonic innovations of bebop, although these played a more significant role in his own playing after 1950, but to start with, by combining his own ideas with the technical approaches to ensemble and solo playing learnt from Callender, he became both a melodic and an artful constructor of bass lines, and a soloist of distinction. In between his work with the "name" bands of Armstrong (in 1943) and Lionel Hampton (1947–8), in which he began to prove his credentials at a national level, he worked with Collette in a cooperative octet called the Stars of Swing. When the group opened at the Downbeat on Central Avenue, its leadership was almost hijacked by tenorist Lucky Thompson, but the members of the band had established, through long hours of rehearsal at Mingus's house, a set of new compositions and a novel approach to dynamics, so Thompson was forced to back down in the collective interest, eventually being replaced by Teddy Edwards. Several members of the group recorded under "Baron" Mingus's leadership, and the results are comparable to a forward-looking Ellington small group of the period, unusually rich in color and texture. (A particularly Ellingtonian aspect of Mingus's highly atmospheric recording from May 1946 of *Pipe Dream* comes from Britt Woodman's eloquent trombone solo – much in the style of Lawrence Brown, whose place he was to take in the Ellington band in February 1951.)

Pianist Gerald Wiggins was working close at hand to the Downbeat, and he described Mingus at that time:

> Mingus was a hothead, he was ready to fight for anything. He was a bit erratic, but he had so many things going on in his mind. He wanted to do it all – write, compose, play bass – and if it was possible to do all those things at the same time he would have done it. [37]

The Stars of Swing did not last, but its discs helped to cement Mingus's local reputation, and his opportunity to make a national name arrived in Los Angeles in 1947 with Lionel Hampton's orchestra. The vibraphonist was looking for a second bassist to play alongside Joe Comfort in his line-up, and take solos – something Mingus was well-equipped to do. The young bassist also brought an arrangement of his own *Mingus Fingers* to the band, which Hampton recorded in November 1947. There was something of an altercation over payment, as Gladys Hampton (Lionel's wife and manager) tended not to pay such inexperienced arrangers for one-off pieces of work. After Mingus left, taking the parts for his chart with him, he recorded the piece again with his old friend Buddy Collette back in Los Angeles. Collette recalled:

> Those sessions were done for Dolphin's of Hollywood. We did *Mingus Fingers* and *These Foolish Things*. Dolphin didn't pay you any money, but he was recording everybody. Nobody, none of the big companies like Capitol, were taking any interest in jazz, but this man started recording jazz. His discs got played on the radio and that helped you get a name. [38]

The playing on this chamber jazz disc is sufficiently unusual to make the point immediately as to why radio play would have boosted Mingus's reputation. After a chromatic introduction from Collette's clarinet, he and Mingus play the head of *Mingus Fingers* in unison, showing Mingus's clear articulation. His subsequent unaccompanied bass chorus makes light of the chordal structure of the piece, in a solo that very much builds on the style established in the early 1940s by Oscar Pettiford. What is unique about it is Mingus's singing sense of melody – it is clear this is a bassist with no hidebound concept of his role as simply that of anchoring the rhythm section, and with a formidable ability to attack his notes with precision and power.

He was fortunate to be able to develop this side of his playing by becoming part of a group that was designed to show off the bass to the full. In 1950, he joined a trio with guitarist Tal Farlow and vibraphonist Red Norvo (precursor of the line-up that played opposite Gerry Mulligan at the Haig), and their lightweight, open sound was the perfect setting for his playing. He was with the group only until 1951, but in that brief time, the trio began to be featured in jazz polls, and they made several discs. In them are plenty of details that pick up on the small-group innovations in *Mingus Fingers*, including Mingus playing high-note solos while Farlow accompanied him by producing bass lines on the guitar.

Not since Jimmy Blanton had a bassist generated the kind of press attention that Mingus attracted. Ralph J. Gleason's *Down Beat* review of the trio, late in Mingus's tenure, was typical:

> Musicians and public share one opinion regarding Charlie – he's the greatest bass player they have ever seen. Smiling and happy, playing unbelievable things with apparent ease, Charlie after all these months with the beautiful Norvo trio still knocks out Red and Tal every night. . . . Charlie Mingus is not only one of the most impressive of the contemporary musicians, but one of the most impressive thinkers about music that jazz has produced.[39]

One reason in particular for Gleason's interest in Mingus was that the bassist had written him a lengthy letter, setting out his beliefs, which Gleason went on to publish. In it are many ideas that Mingus had already explored both in his life and in his work – for example, the question of the difference between jazz and classical music, and the respective abilities of such musicians to swing. But most important is a statement – almost a mission statement – that linked Mingus's philosophy directly to that of Ellington: "True jazz is an art, and as with all the arts, is the individual's means of expressing his deepest and innermost feelings and emotions."[40]

In the mid-to-late 1950s, Mingus was to move further and further towards the position where his music would get fully to grips with those deep feelings and emotions, and to do so, he drew on the full breadth of the jazz tradition. He was not a narrowly restricted bebop player, any more than he was merely an adventurous swing player: he was already showing signs of his genuine originality. His friends Buddy Collette and Britt Woodman both commented that if there was a different way to do something normal and straightforward, Mingus would probably find it. Except, that is, in actually getting down to the business of writing music. On his return to Los Angeles from a road tour with Les Hite in the 1940s, Woodman had been staggered to observe how Mingus had developed as a musician, not just as a bassist, but as a pianist and composer, and he immediately made the very telling comparison to Ellington: "His writing was similar. He had Duke in mind. See, the thing was, Mingus was so natural, what he heard, he could write."[41]

After leaving Norvo, with whom he had traveled quite extensively, Mingus settled in New York. Once there, he built on his reputation as an innovative and versatile bassist, and he began playing at the highest level with musicians including Bud Powell, Billy Taylor, and (briefly) Duke Ellington. His short stay in the Ellington Orchestra was ended in typically hot-headed fashion, through an altercation with trombonist Juan Tizol, the first of many high profile scuffles from Mingus's East Coast career. In the mid-1950s, Mingus and drummer Max Roach co-formed a record company, called Debut, which preserved much of Mingus's work from this period, including the famous 1953 Massey Hall concert with Charlie Parker and Dizzy Gillespie, discussed in Chapter 7.

Perhaps because of the long hours that he, Collette, and the Woodmans had spent jamming at Mingus's house in Los Angeles, he was drawn to the idea of writing and playing in a workshop setting. Other composers with whom he joined forces included Teo Macero and Teddy Charles, but this first stab at a Jazz Composers' Workshop did not give Mingus quite the forum he wanted for composition and improvisation. So, in 1955, he began his own Jazz Workshop, assembling a like-minded collection of individuals (many of them having West Coast connections, including trombonist Jimmy Knepper and saxophonist Eric Dolphy from Los Angeles, and altoist John Handy, who had worked for years in San Francisco).

There are parallels here with the work of Gil Evans and his "salon" during the *Birth of the Cool* period, and also with the Jazz Workshop group of

George Russell. But whereas Evans was interested in developing his very individual style of orchestration and arrangement, and Russell was experimenting with his modal theories, Mingus was aiming higher – to create a body of work that would genuinely explore the whole gamut of human emotion.

The workshop was to be his preferred method of evolving his compositions over the following years. In order to communicate ideas that did not translate easily to paper, he liked to sing or dictate the parts each musician was to play, so that they *heard* rather than *read* the music. (There are, however, stories of how his regular pianist Jaki Byard surreptitiously jotted down the parts so that the band could remember them later.) As he composed, Mingus increasingly used the piano, eventually playing the instrument in his live performances.

In the ten years from 1955, Mingus established two constants in his work: a set of related pieces that changed gradually from performance to performance, and the pool of players mentioned above, who specialized in interpreting his ideas. Consequently, a composition like *Fables of Faubus* (written in 1959 and reworked in 1964) was also developed into *Original Faubus Fables* (1960) and *New Fables* (1964). Over time, this and numerous other pieces mutated, just as improvising musicians might alter their approaches to playing a solo.

One of the pieces that altered over time was Mingus's *Haitian Fight Song* (later called *II B. S.*). His comments on the 1957 recording made for Atlantic (some two years after first writing the piece) are illuminating about why this and so many of his performances were packed with meaning – becoming Signifyin(g) events for their audience:

> [It] could just as well be called *Afro-American Fight Song*. It has a folk spirit, the kind of folk music I've always heard anyway. It has some of the old church feeling too. I was raised a Methodist but there was a Holiness Church on the corner and some of the feeling of their music, which was wilder, got into our music. There's a moaning feeling in those church modes. . . . My solo in it is a deeply concentrated one. I can't play it right unless I'm thinking about prejudice and hate and persecution and how unfair it is. There's sadness and cries in it, but also determination. And it usually ends with me feeling, "I told them! I hope somebody heard me!"[42]

On this recording, originally issued on his album *The Clown*, as he was to do in the majority of his groups in the later 1950s through to the 1960s, Mingus used drummer Dannie Richmond, with whom he developed an exceptionally flexible rhythmic platform for his soloists. Bass and drums moved the beat around, making abrupt transitions into double or triple time, or sometimes dropping out altogether. In this piece, after an introductory section for solo bass, Mingus introduces a five-note ostinato pattern that underpins the main theme statement and its various repetitions. Trombone and alto are joined in the opening section by shouts and wails, before the trombone takes off into a solo. Underpinning this, Mingus and Richmond run through several ideas – alluding to the ostinato, then frantically doubling the tempo, before playing a series of stops that emphasize the first three beats of each measure, then returning to a swing tempo. This series of basic accompanimental ideas is used for both piano and alto solos, but varies the sequence in which they are introduced, so creating the impression that the piece is a more complex construction than it appears. Mingus's bass solo is suitably harsh and angry to express the feelings he described, but it also runs through the same basic variations in pattern and speed that are used behind the other soloists.

On other pieces with this "folk spirit" or gospel feel, Mingus and Richmond ring the rhythmic changes even more dramatically, governed by the sense that the beat itself is a movable element, and that they could break down old swing era or bebop concepts of a constant, unvarying pulse, yet without losing a sense of being directly connected to the entire African-American music tradition. Whereas a musician like Don Ellis (who occasionally collaborated with Mingus) was to experiment with unorthodox time signatures, Mingus and Richmond proved that it was possible to create immense flexibility, a sense of ebb and flow, inside a conventional time signature. On *Wednesday Night Prayer Meeting*, with a larger Jazz Workshop band, from the 1959 album *Blues and Roots* they create a six–eight pulse into which pianist Horace Parlan feeds in and out, sometimes playing with and sometimes against them; at other times they stop playing, leaving the brass and reeds to continue with just handclaps or shouts for accompaniment.

In contrast to the cool of Miles Davis, or, contemporaneously, the reductions by John Coltrane of the harmonic complexity of his accompaniments, Mingus's backings are extrovert, both rhythmically and harmonically dense, and driven by a sense of ensemble in which all the players are equal – there is no sense (as there sometimes is with Coltrane) that the band consists of a star soloist being backed by a mere rhythm section.

769

Against this kind of varied setting, in much the same way as Ellington had done, Mingus created music that would exploit the musical personalities of his musicians: the jagged saxophone and bass clarinet of Eric Dolphy, the sparring saxes of John Handy and Booker Ervin, the gospel-tinged reeds of Roland Kirk, the rounded trombones of Jimmy Knepper and Britt Woodman, and the witty, eclectic piano of Jaki Byard.

For much of the second half of the 1950s, Mingus recorded for the Atlantic label, to whom Coltrane was also signed at the end of the decade. Briefly, these two musicians, who were responsible for shaping so much of the music of the years that followed were marketed alongside one another. Today, Atlantic's continuing reputation rests largely on its innovative and exemplary jazz catalog of that period, which was also to include Ornette Coleman. But in the eyes of Ahmet Ertegun, its then chief executive, this music was something of an indulgence compared to his own mission to keep signing hit rhythm and blues records. Looking back at those days, during the celebrations of his company's fiftieth birthday in 1998, he told me:

> They were all signed by my elder brother Nesuhi, who died in 1989. I didn't have time to get too involved . . . when they were recording for us, I was simply trying to keep the company alive. We were undercapitalized, at risk from distributors who paid late, and depended on the product for the following month to keep us going. I loved jazz, but it didn't sell that quickly, although over the years that followed, my brother's sessions sold a lot more copies than the overnight hits I got into.[43]

Mingus's *Blues and Roots* session, recorded for Atlantic in February 1959, took several months to appear, a delay explained by Ertegun's frank exposition of the company's financial health. In April, during the gap between recording it and seeing it released, Mingus signed with Columbia, and, although the original concept was a disc of Jelly Roll Morton pieces updated in his own style, instead he made one of his most consistently brilliant albums. Displaying the entire range of his compositional interests, and the degree to which he was in tune with the spirit of the times while simultaneously going his own way, *Mingus Ah Um* was not just a brilliant pun – it was a landmark in his career.

*Better Git It in Your Soul* was a six–eight gospel piece that far outdid *Wednesday Night Prayer Meeting* in intensity and feeling, with shouts, handclaps, speaking in tongues, and a range of other musical impressions.

(As Gene Santoro points out, this number was in stiff competition with the Adderley Brothers' *This Here*, described in Chapter 13, which became a hit when released as an eleven minute single.[44]) *Jelly Roll* (the only link with the original concept of the album) was a revision of his earlier *Jelly Roll Soul* and looked backwards to New Orleans and forwards towards some elements of free jazz. But the most enduring piece was a long, slow lament, *Goodbye Pork Pie Hat* **[CD track 20]**.

From the sinuous, weaving opening, with the combined tenors of John Handy and Booker Ervin, to Handy's exquisite, mournful solo, the piece is a masterpiece of combined restraint and feeling. In it, despite the slow tempo, are many hallmarks of the workshop's approach. The wide open beat of Mingus and Richmond, with Mingus occasionally offering a commentary on the solo rather than a bass line, Horace Parlan placing the occasional chordal accent in the most unexpected place, and Handy's own playing, which includes a section in gospel-like flutter-tonguing, all add up to the most moving tribute to Lester Young, the wearer of the hat in question, who had died a couple of months before the recording. The theme itself is what sticks in the mind, and it is only after repeated hearings that one realizes that almost the entire second half of the piece is a scored reading of the theme – Mingus's ideal blend of the composed and the improvised, with the join almost impossible to discern in the emotion of the performance.

As the new decade began, Mingus entered his period of greatest creativity with a series of outstanding compositions, including another series of musical laments, this time for Eric Dolphy, who died in Berlin in June 1964, shortly after taking part in a European tour with Mingus. *Praying with Eric* led to a whole series of evolutionary *Meditations*. He also produced what many commentators believe to be his greatest sustained work with the eleven-piece workshop of 1963, *The Black Saint and the Sinner Lady*, which has the widest mix of eclectic influences found in any of his recordings. But despite this high level of musical creativity, his own life was in turmoil. He found it impossible to resist taking on the establishment – setting up rival free concerts outside the Newport Festival, launching another new independent record label of his own, and organizing performances that were often an uncomfortable mix of rehearsal and performance, of which his 1962 New York Town Hall event was the most spectacular disaster. By the mid-1960s, he faced financial ruin, and was suffering from unstable mental health.

His career was put on hold until 1969, when he began once more to tour and perform, and soon afterwards a Guggenheim fellowship gave him a degree of stability and public recognition. In the early 1970s, he made his most successful big band recordings. Until 1977, with the onset of Lou Gehrig's disease (amyotrophic lateral sclerosis), a form of muscular paralysis, he toured and recorded quite regularly with his quintet. After his paralysis took hold in earnest, he supervised a final big-band recording of his music, and wrote themes for a collaborative project with singer Joni Mitchell, although the recorded large-band sections of this work were not included in the final album. He died in January 1979.

Mingus was a transitional figure in jazz history. By working collectively and dictating his compositions, he drew strong parallels with the free jazz movement, which began at the start of the 1960s. Yet he never lost a sense of compositional form, and remained fascinated by one of the biggest central issues in jazz – the boundary between composition and improvisation. His early experience with the likes of Louis Armstrong and Lionel Hampton gave him a strong sense of continuity and tradition, and it is perhaps fitting that his final recorded bass solo should have been on an album with Hampton. However, his own bands were at their best when tradition became just one of the elements that he fused into performance, adding a wider range of effects and ideas, including vocal tones, voice, and poetry, than any jazz bandleader before him.

The strength of his themes and compositional frameworks for improvisation have given rise to several movements that perpetuate his music and keep it alive into the twenty-first century. These began with the Mingus Dynasty bands of the early 1980s, which involved several of his former sidemen, and have continued with the Mingus Big Band, which has played regularly in New York and around the world since 1991. Gunther Schuller has frequently supervised performances of some of Mingus's large-scale orchestral works. Since his death, his compositions have continued to be recorded, and have been performed by musicians as different (and unexpected) as the British traditionalist Chris Barber and the former rock guitarist with The Police, Andy Summers, thereby proving something of his universal appeal and the durability of his writing.

CHAPTER 17

# Free Jazz: Ornette Coleman and the "New Thing"

## Ornette Coleman

> You could tell whenever the band was playing, because the
> audience would be outside on the sidewalk, and then
> when the intermission came, they'd go into the club for
> a drink.
>
> Paul Bley, describing the debut of Ornette Coleman at the
> Hillcrest Club, Los Angeles, in 1958[1]

When a musician comes along who is so revolutionary as to question everything that has happened in jazz, and who turns it on its head without losing touch with its traditions, then the development of the music reaches another of what Michel Serres, the French philosopher of science, calls "bifurcations" – forks in the road. It is not always clear which direction will turn out to be the main highway in the future, and sometimes even a brightly lit, well-directed route will suddenly peter out into little more than a dusty footpath. When saxophonist Ornette Coleman joined pianist Paul Bley's band in Los Angeles, his ten year search for the right setting for his own innovative ideas came to an end, and he had the first public platform for his compositions and solo playing. With so extreme an audience reaction to its new sounds, Bley's group lasted less than a month, but it set in motion a train of events that launched Coleman's career as the most significant jazz innovator of the last 40 years of the twentieth century, and opened up a viable broad highway on which what would become known as "free jazz" was to develop. From Bley's line-up grew Coleman's own quartet with trumpeter Don Cherry, bassist Charlie Haden, and drummer Billy Higgins,

773

which systematically set about exploring the idea of improvising without chord changes, whilst retaining the rhythmic impetus, the "swing," of jazz. Coleman's principal innovation was to redirect the basis of jazz improvisation from the harmonic to the melodic.

In the list of jazz innovators, Coleman belongs alongside Armstrong, Parker, Gillespie, Davis, and Coltrane. A softly spoken, gentle man, he has a passionate, vocal intensity in his playing that connects directly back to the African-American race consciousness described by Henry F. Gilbert in 1917, and which owes much to his upbringing in the deeply segregated town of Fort Worth, Texas in the 1930s and 1940s. During this period, it was still believed that to touch the head of a black man brought good luck, and Southern whites would think nothing of walking up to even the best dressed black citizen, lifting his hat, and rubbing his forehead. Coleman's music is rooted in the soulful blues, country fiddling, and rhythmic dancing that were his community's natural defenses against such entrenched indignities. He also has a restless, questing mind that produces melodic ideas at a prolific rate – "Ornette can write ten tunes in ten minutes," Dewey Redman, his friend from schooldays, told me – and yet he has the objectivity, the detachment from the mainstream, and the sheer doggedness to follow through his ideas that are the marks of genius. Some of his staunchest supporters, including composer Gunther Schuller, have described this sense of purpose as almost a kind of dyslexia, a way of processing musical and other ideas that interprets written words and music in a startlingly different fashion from most of us. Yet, despite the fact that, during the last decade of the twentieth century, he received numerous honorary degrees and the 1994 MacArthur Foundation "genius" award, and in 1997 experienced revivals in Japan, Paris, and New York of his major orchestral piece *Skies of America*, his music has still not broken through to the kind of universal popular acceptance enjoyed by his near contemporary, Sonny Rollins.

Rollins continued to pack concert halls throughout the 1990s by demonstrating that he still played bebop superbly, with an inexhaustible fund of invention. But by changing the way we listen to jazz, and redefining ideas about collective improvisation, Coleman achieved something more, something less tangible, and, because of its very radicalism, something that divided his listeners into either staunch enthusiasts or those who just did not get it, despite the fact that his revolutionary ideas were first widely heard in the 1950s.

For example, *Down Beat*'s John McDonough, who hated the double quartet album *Free Jazz* when it first came out in 1960, was still railing against it in the magazine over 30 years later: "jazz had never produced a music in which fakes could move so easily and undetected among real musicians."[2] By contrast, Gunther Schuller, Coleman's principal apologist, takes the opposite view: "it is precisely because Mr. Coleman was not 'handicapped' by conventional music education that he has been able to make his unique contribution to contemporary music."[3] Even for a man of Schuller's acute ear, Coleman's music presents problems. It is not easy to analyze it in the normal way, since phrases of a melody change length within performances, and underlying harmonies shift erratically. With typical candor, Coleman himself once said: "I would prefer it if musicians would play my tunes with different changes as they take a new chorus, so there'd be all the more variety in the performance."[4]

Any conversation with Coleman about his work is likely to focus on his theory of "Harmolodics" – an attempt to draw together his insights about music, language, dance, and theories of time and relativity. He is quick to say Harmolodics is "not a style but a philosophy," but for an apparently general philosophy it seems bogged down in minutiae about how one tone relates to another. And some of it flatly contradicts normal understanding. Coleman says:

> There's a theory I have, that if you write a C, then if you put a different clef sign in front of it, it changes to four other notes, depending on whether it's a bass, tenor, alto, or treble clef. If you hear another note, you can substitute that one for the original, since the idea of the melody is already set.[5]

This is a complicated way of describing transposition, a device that puts his melodic lines together in a kind of organum or simple polyphony. Analysts of Coleman's work, and some of his staunchest supporters including established composers and theorists in their own right such as Gunther Schuller and George Russell, have tended largely to disregard his theoretical ideas, and instead to focus on his extraordinary instinctive genius for melody and for creating immediately identifiable improvisations on his main instrument, the alto saxophone. His plangent tone, his use of microtonal intervals, and his repeated phrases (which are constructed, at least in part, to lie under the fingers in a mechanical way, fitting saxophone fingering patterns, and consequently having an internal motific logic quite distinct from their harmonic environment) are obvious aids to such immediate identification. His tendency to worry at a phrase like a terrier, extending the structure of a composition to accommodate his worrying until the bone is well and truly shaken, is another. So, too, is his scratchy but passionate violin playing, with its echoes of the country hoedown, or his wild, ballistic trumpet, which confounds many an orthodox practitioner with its uncanny ability to create seemingly impossible effects.

Rather as he relates to music in an instinctive way, Coleman has used language to create illustrative figures of speech to explain his work. In one giant, Confucian metaphor, in a conversation with me, he compared what he does to the difference between words and language:

> You can make up words. But when you put them together into language, you have to have someone to understand them. Going back to the dawn of words, God said: "Let there be light," and light came. Before language, words had power, something to do with making things exist. But put words in the context of a language and they mean something else. I was in Italy once, playing violin, and someone shouted at me, a man who was really moved, screaming "Molto bene, molto bene." It meant "Good," but I didn't know the language and I thought it sounded negative, and he meant "Stop!". So you see, there's an example today of where words are not the same thing as language.[6]

This image typifies a way of thinking that Coleman has developed after years of his music being misunderstood by those unwilling even to recognize that his musical "words" do need a language of their own to set them in context.

His career began in Fort Worth, in the late 1940s, where he adopted the local musical *lingua franca*, and played with several local rhythm-and-blues bands. He started his career in high school, playing initially in imitation of Louis Jordan, and then of Charlie Parker. Interestingly, he was at school with two musicians who worked with him for long periods in later life, saxophonist Dewey Redman and drummer Charles Moffett.

Moffett first worked with him in a band called the Jam Jivers, with Warnell Goodley on trumpet and Prince Lasha on reeds. Then Coleman joined Red Connors, a local rhythm and blues player, before going on to work with the touring blues groups of Silas Green, Clarence Samuel, and Pee Wee Crayton. The legend goes that Coleman taught himself to read music and to finger the saxophone (initially the alto, and later the tenor), and in so doing incorporated some basic errors into his understanding of musical theory. He figured that A, rather than C, was the home note of the basic scale, relying on the alphabet rather than the piano keyboard, and the habits he learned then stayed with him.

> In Texas I originally got an alto. But the tenor was very popular, and after I got one and started playing it, everyone started dancing. I was playing in a club, with gambling and girls – all very illegal in the late 1940s. So when the Texas Rangers would come to break up the gambling and chop up the tables, all the guys would grab the girls and dance so they couldn't be arrested. One day, one of the girls didn't want to dance, and she stabbed a guy and killed him. I didn't want to play in this club – which was called Upstairs – if my music was going to influence events like that. I went home and told my mother, and she said: "What do you expect? D'you think they're going to pay you for your soul?" I thought, "My soul?" I hadn't thought of that. So in due course – although it took me three years – I went back to playing the alto.[7]

This is a slightly attenuated version of events, but at its heart is the reason for his return to the alto and his subsequent discovery of his musical "soul."

Coleman's ideas and attitudes marked him out from the start as an individual. His interest in bebop caused him problems with audiences and employers when he introduced modern jazz ideas into his rhythm-and-blues performances, and his long-haired, bearded, hippy appearance caused him further problems with the racist Southern authorities as well as with the public. At one point in the late 1940s, he was savagely beaten up while on the road in Louisiana, and was forced to spend time recuperating with the Lastie family, one of New Orleans's musical dynasties; his attackers had thrown his tenor saxophone down the street, and this marks the moment when he finally returned to specializing on alto. Later he suffered the indignity of bebop musicians he admired putting down their instruments and walking away when he tried to sit in with them. Nevertheless, he persevered, not only in developing a formidable alto technique while doing a succession of menial jobs in Los Angeles where he settled, but also in starting to write a voluminous repertoire of original music. His written notation is fluent but unorthodox, and does not always seek to resolve niceties such as exact pitch and precise rhythms. Coleman says:

> I write music that sounds like inspirational ideas. A melody may have structures that express themselves at other levels, not just a

single line of music, but I also express a musical philosophy that if I'm playing with someone else and they can do better, they have the right to change it.[8]

This approach to music goes back to a moment of Damascus-like conversion in his life every bit as revelatory as the moment in 1939 when Charlie Parker was reputed to have been playing *Cherokee* with Biddy Fleet and worked out how to use the upper partials of the underlying chords to construct the melodies he'd been hearing in his head:

> After three years or so in Los Angeles, learning how to play bebop, I realized I didn't have to transpose to be with the piano. I found I could use notes in a way that was equal to using chords, but if I used notes as chords without them being chords, I was no longer restricted to doing sequences. At first I tried to understand how it would work in terms of writing music. That's to say I started by improvising, and then took it into writing. I found that this idea doesn't allow you to compose in sequences, so I use "movement" as another word to describe each new melody.[9]

The underlying point is the crux of Ornette's importance to jazz improvisation. If you abandon chord sequences as the basis for improvisation, and use melodic fragments instead, and if you play those fragments at whatever length, pitch, and speed feel right, even if the underlying pulse never changes, you then have the essence of what he began to explore in earnest in the mid-1950s in Los Angeles during informal sessions with trumpeter Don Cherry, drummer Billy Higgins, pianist Walter Norris, and bassist Don Payne.

What Coleman had arrived at in isolation was what many of the West Coast *avant-garde* had been searching for, and in due course, Coleman found fellow musicians who were sympathetic to his ideas. Among them was a man who would become his long-term collaborator, bassist Charlie Haden, who recalled:

> It was my night off from my regular gig, and I went to an after hours jam session based around Gerry Mulligan's band at a place called the Haig. The room was jam-packed, and you couldn't even walk in there, but a man came up on stage, took out a plastic alto sax, and began to play. And the room lit up for me. I'd never

heard anything so brilliant, because I'd gone to a lot of jam
sessions myself and been hearing a way in which I could play
without using chord structures, but staying on a certain part of
the tune, or staying in a mode, or even creating an entirely new
structure. Whenever I tried it, people would get upset, but here I
heard somebody actually doing all that. It really startled me, but
almost as soon as he started to play, they asked him to stop.[10]

The obscure figure, long-haired and bearded, with his plastic alto, slipped
away through the crowds, and it took Haden a few days to track Coleman
down. They jammed together, and ended up playing for two days and a
night at Coleman's apartment. Two things remain in Haden's mind about
that experience. First, that every surface was covered in music, indicating
Coleman's prolific capacity for composition, and second, that during one of
these pieces where the initial statement of the theme was coupled with a
particularly intricate harmonic sequence, Coleman said: "First you play it
like this, then you make up your own chords."[11]

Those who heard him at that time, including the MJQ's pianist John
Lewis, knew that Coleman's 1958 debut recording *Something Else!* was
taking jazz in a new direction. Lewis was particularly fascinated, not only by
the originality of the compositions, but also by Coleman's use of melodic
motifs from the whole spectrum of his playing experience:

Ornette would play fairly randomly with phrases you'd never
heard before, but inserted with that were phrases you knew very
well, from old standards or folk songs, and it reminded me of
James Joyce's use of literature, or Dylan Thomas's. To me it was
a delight, something really new in jazz.[12]

Soon after Haden and Coleman had met, Paul Bley invited Coleman and
Cherry to join his band, which already included Haden and Higgins. Bley
shared John Lewis's perception of Ornette's unique improvisational talent,
but he was also able to identify immediately what it was about Coleman's
music that was so innovative: "It didn't take me more than a second to
realize that this was the missing link between playing totally free, without
any givens, and playing bebop, with steady changes and steady time."[13]

In due course, after a much-talked-about debut at the 1959 Lenox
Summer School of Jazz in Massachusetts by Coleman and Cherry, the two of
them, plus Higgins and Haden, moved east at the instigation of Lewis and

Percy Heath. By the time the quartet arrived in New York, Coleman had recorded four albums under his own name, three of which had by this stage been issued, and had done plenty to excite expectations about his work.

*Something Else!, the first album, and Tomorrow Is the Question*, the second (both recorded for Contemporary), chart the saxophonist's emergence from the conventions of bebop to the point at which his own innovations became the central point of his music. The former, with pianist Walter Norris, is the last occasion that Coleman employed a pianist in his own groups until Dave Bryant joined his fusion band Prime Time in the 1980s. (Coleman's discs with Paul Bley were made under Bley's leadership.) By working with just bass and drums thereafter, Coleman was able to open up the harmonic framework for his improvisations far more flexibly. On both his early albums, he shows the originality of his compositions – several of these have forms that do not fall into the usual popular song structure of twelve-, sixteen-, or 32-measure sections, and, for example in a piece like *The Sphinx*, he also alternates tempi and mood between different parts of the number. The process of documenting his original ideas was underway.

By the time of *The Shape of Jazz to Come* and *Change of the Century*, his next two West Coast recordings for Atlantic, made with Cherry, Haden, and Higgins in the spring and late summer of 1959 respectively, Coleman had achieved a perfect balance between his ideas and the ability of his fellow musicians to execute them. He and Cherry mingled their melodic lines with the same intuitive understanding of a Parker and Gillespie or a Lee Morgan and Wayne Shorter; Haden's consistently inventive bass lines and Higgins's rhythmic drive retained a clear connection with the jazz tradition. On these two discs, recorded on the West Coast in the same year that Miles Davis, Bill Evans, and John Coltrane were exploring modes as a basis for improvisation in *Kind of Blue*, Coleman proved there was another route forward.

Virtually all Coleman's new compositions had a clear and instantly memorable theme, from the plaintive wail of *Lonely Woman* to the blues of *Ramblin'* or lilting Latin swing of *Una Muy Bonita*. In almost all the performances on the two albums, it is clear that there is a very direct connection between the contour and melodic content of each theme and the improvisations that surround it, but added to this was, first, Coleman's idea that the tonal center of a phrase could shift according to individual notes in the melody line, and, second, the principle he articulated in his conversation with me: "if I'm playing with someone else and they can do better, they have the right to change it."[14]

It was this absolute belief in the spontaneous principle of improvisation that set Coleman apart from his contemporaries – notably Mingus – in so marked a fashion. As his biographer Peter Niklas Wilson put it: "The nature of improvisation, in Coleman's view, is incompatible with predetermined patterns, be they harmonic, rhythmic or structural; the pre-existent form should not determine the improvised line, the improvisation should instead *create* the form."[15] In due course, Coleman was to find other ways of making this point explicit. For example, he was to record the title track of his 1987 disc *In All Languages* with both his original quartet and his fusion band Prime Time, showing radically different treatments of the same initial melodic material in different settings. And with his 1996 acoustic quartet he recorded two versions of the album *Sound Museum*, in which on sister issues titled *Three Women* and *Hidden Man*, substantially the same repertoire is presented in sharply contrasting performances.

Until the fall of 1959 when Coleman's quartet arrived in Manhattan to play at the Five Spot, initially for a couple of weeks but extended as a result of his success to over two months, the radicalism of his approach to improvisation had not been immediately apparent to all those who heard his records. At the club it took a very short while indeed for him to make clear to all those who heard him in person just how radical he was. The band was loud, it was atonal, in the sense that he and Cherry both made liberal use of microtonal pitches, and its approach to Coleman's core repertoire altered constantly from night to night. Above it all was the plaintive sound of his own alto saxophone, mingling aggressive and uncompromising modernism with the deep emotional power of blues phrasing and timbre.

Behind the band's first New York appearances had been month upon month of prior informal rehearsal at Ornette's home, or – in the four weeks before the band was fired – during the afternoons before their work with Bley, at the Hillcrest Club in Los Angeles. As a consequence they played with a sense of ensemble seldom achieved by even the most regularly working bands. George Russell went to hear them several times, and he told me:

> They had their own mysterious way of communicating, and doing things in a group. There was no kind of signal or apparent preparation before things they did. Ornette would just stick the horn in his mouth and without even a nod, blow. And everybody would instantly play the same melody. In the audience, you'd look for a signal or a count-off or something, but none of that took place. That's how tight his group was.[16]

Charlie Haden agreed, saying: "We were very intuitive of each other, and we felt the same way about music. . . . There was no such thing as counting off a tempo, there was just beginning to play."[17] The controversy aroused by the quartet's residency at the Five Spot, in Cooper Square on the edge of the seedy Bowery district, extended to fellow musicians, critics, intellectuals, and the general public. The entrenched attitude of New York's own modern jazz players, who felt that it was still necessary to "pay one's dues" by working one's way up through the Big Apple's musical echelons in time-honored fashion, made them predictably hostile – not only had these upstarts arrived from the West and moved straight into a high-profile venue where Monk, Coltrane, and Cecil Taylor had played, but also they were threatening the city's whole system of musical values. In Paul Bley's memorable phrase, "Ornette struck fear into the heart of the average world-famous jazzman walking the streets of New York, because nothing would be the same again."[18]

Stories abound of the antagonism of the likes of Roy Eldridge, Miles Davis, and Max Roach, and, according to Coleman's old friend Dewey Redman, this did not change much in the following years. He recalls being in a festival dressing room with Dexter Gordon and Sonny Stitt, both of whom, as they arrived, had studiously ignored Coleman (in whose band Redman was playing in the late 1960s). Only after hearing Coleman's lengthy practice routine, which was a devastatingly accurate representation of Charlie Parker's playing, and which impressed everyone who heard it, could these lions of the jazz circuit bring themselves to drop in and pass the time of day with Coleman.[19] Even musicians who felt themselves to be in sympathy with Coleman's ideas were not always wholehearted in their praise – Mingus, for example, wrote in *Down Beat*: "It's like organized disorganization, or playing wrong right."[20] Only a select group of musicians whose own orientation was constantly to push at the boundaries of jazz were consistently supportive: notably Jimmy Giuffre, John Lewis, George Russell, and Gunther Schuller (who, as I have hinted above, in his capacity as a critic and historian was to become the foremost analyst of Coleman's early work).

Among other critics and intellectuals, reactions ranged from outright hostility to warm enthusiasm. The conservative faction of Stanley Dance, George Hoefer, and *Down Beat*'s George Crater were dismissive. But Whitney Balliett, John Tynan, and (principally) Martin Williams were enthusiastic, and did much to get Coleman's music established. Yet it was the English social historian Eric Hobsbawm who pointed out that at the Five

Spot the crowd was made up of young white intellectuals, and that Coleman's music would not go down well in front of the uptown African-American audiences of Harlem clubs like the legendary Smalls's Paradise. Over the next three decades, Coleman would do much to change this, first by basing himself in the consciously community-based environment of his Artists' House in SoHo (a loft with performance space), and eventually locating his Harmolodic recording and publishing business in the heart of Harlem, near 125th Street Station. But in 1960–2 – at a time when the political freedom movement had barely stretched its wings – he had not acquired a secure following in the African-American community, and although he was invited to a small number of festivals and played short residencies at clubs elsewhere in the United States, he also became a victim of the precarious nature of his own success. The band was regularly re-booked at the Five Spot, surviving there even after narcotic problems removed first Higgins and then Haden from the line-up. The Atlantic albums sold well, but the band was not being commensurately well-paid by the club. In due course, in an effort to earn comparable amounts to other cutting-edge musicians of the time (many of whom were less lionized), Coleman increased his fees and his work dried up.

This led to an extraordinary period of retreat and reappraisal by Coleman, and to the production of a voluminous output of new compositions, in many of which he examined the internal structures and tonality that underpinned his characteristically memorable melody lines. He was not to return to the format of his original quartet for some time, but he was to use these months away from the limelight to develop a number of other ideas that had originally surfaced in 1960–2, before the December 1962 Town Hall appearance, his last public concert for two-and-a-half years. These were, first, larger ensembles following on from his *Free Jazz* album; second, experiments in classical performance and serialism first begun with Gunther Schuller; and, third, the new timbres and tonal possibilities of a trio formed in 1962 with his childhood friend drummer Charles Moffett, plus bassist David Izenson.

The double quartet of his 1960 album *Free Jazz* may have given his music a name, but in many ways it was a cul-de-sac in his own work, despite proving immensely influential on other musicians who were to record extended free-form works for large ensemble, such as John Coltrane's 1965 *Ascension*. Haden, for example, felt that bassist Scott LaFaro, trumpeter Freddie Hubbard, and bass clarinetist Eric Dolphy, who were added for the *Free Jazz* recording alongside Coleman's regular quartet and their additional drummer Ed Blackwell, were not in sympathy with Coleman's principles of improvisation; while most commentators would feel it was stretching a point to call LaFaro "a traditional jazz player," Haden's description of him as such was designed to underlie the point that LaFaro and Hubbard were still essentially conventional bebop players who had not absorbed Coleman's ideas.[21] Coleman, on the other hand, perceived something quite different in what many of his contemporaries heard as the anarchic sounds of eight musicians playing an extended, spontaneous collective piece, albeit one in which there was far more of a discernible sense of jazz rhythm than in, say, Coltrane's *Ascension*. It triggered much of his thinking about large ensembles that would later surface in Prime Time: "if anyone can learn anything through repetition, regardless of how advanced it is, if it can be repeated you can learn it. So imagine how it must be for someone that hasn't learned anything and doesn't have to repeat it, and only has to learn about himself."[22] Coleman saw *Free Jazz* as epitomizing liberation from preconception, and its absence of formal structure or harmony as allowing musicians who were normally restricted by their training to discover more about themselves.

It was Coleman's own independence from preconception and formal training that drew Gunther Schuller to his music. They had first met at Lenox, where Schuller had introduced Coleman to many aspects of jazz history, and Coleman, in return, had impressed Schuller with the "unfettered imagination of his melodic world." Throughout the late 1950s, Schuller had been experimenting with what he dubbed "Third Stream" music – drawing together his own disparate interests to create what he termed "a style in which attempts were made to fuse basic elements of jazz and Western art music – the two mainstreams joining to form a 'third stream.'"[23] In Coleman, he heard a musician who could take his Third Stream experiments a whole stage further on. Schuller recalled:

> I had been a twelve-tone composer for a long time before that, since the late 1940s, and as a composer and someone involved in jazz in a variety of ways, I was always somewhat disappointed that the harmonic language of jazz, and even of bebop with all of its eleventh chords and flatted fifths, was still basically the language that Debussy, Ravel, Schoenberg, and Szymanowski had used from 50 or 60 years earlier. Being an atonal twelve-tone composer, I was hoping that some players would come along who could operate in such a context. My work with the Modern Jazz

Quartet, for example, all through those years, was difficult because John Lewis and Milt Jackson were always basically tonal improvisers. Their work was based on chord changes – the jazz language. So I was looking for someone free enough, either aurally or in technical knowledge, to be able to operate in an atonal context, and lo and behold that is what happened with Ornette Coleman.

I don't mean by that that he necessarily understood anything about twelve-tone technique, but somehow I knew that if I gave Ornette the twelve-tone row on which my piece *Abstractions* is based, and I could introduce it to him in such a way that he learned it by ear, he could then improvise with this material in the sort of fragmented, pointillistic, melodic fashion that he had achieved by this time. He was something of a godsend to me because he understood my language and I understood his language, so we could improvise and compose together.[24]

Schuller's *Abstractions*, a four-minute miniature, recorded in December 1960, is the first of a series of works in which Coleman became increasingly involved with Western art music, and it is as effective in the ensemble sections (where his alto combines spontaneously with Schuller's scored passages for string quartet, two basses, guitar, and drums) as in the improvised bridge section for solo saxophone. From this start, Coleman went on to produce several works of his own, notably his wind quintet, premiered in Britain on his return to public performance in 1965, and his extended 1972 orchestral suite *Skies of America*.

Every movement of the piece displays the union between Coleman's developing concept of Harmolodics and the approaches he had developed to ensemble improvisation during the previous decade and a half. In particular, *The Artist in America* **[CD 2, track 9]** shows this combination at work. The string writing is based mainly on a long theme, the harmony of which is created by positioning the notes in the same place on the stave, but prefacing them with a different clef – hence the violins are in the treble, the violas in the alto, the cellos in the tenor, and the basses in the bass clef. The subsequent movement of these lines against each another creates what I referred to earlier as the "organum" effect, except for those moments when the upper strings make skittering runs behind Coleman's alto, in periodic explosions of activity that interrupt the main melodic flow. His playing is superimposed on the orchestra – effectively a different block of sound in the composition, whose third element is the pitting of two drummers against one another. On one stereo channel he employs an orchestral tympanist who improvises with great panache, and on the other, a jazz drummer who mainly marks a conventional swing beat, in a strange role-reversal between normal expectations of their functions.

If such pieces by Coleman failed to go as far as Schuller's in exploring serialism, or unorthodox structure, and if they were somewhat restricted by the simplistic polyphonic nature of Coleman's compositional approach, they nevertheless went a long way towards solving the major problem that confronted Third Stream musicians every bit as much as more jazz-based composers such as Mingus, namely the effective integration of improvisation with composed structures. In this Coleman has been singularly successful throughout his career, returning to the symphony orchestra plus improvising jazz group genre again in his soundtrack collaboration with composer Howard Shore for the film *Naked Lunch* in 1992, and in subsequent live concerts accompanying projections of the film in 2000 and 2001. After viewing the 2001 London performance, I wrote:

> Music, moving image and the sense of occasion came together to make this an exceptional event, Ornette's plangent sax figures occasionally cutting through the action, but equally successfully conjuring up that nether land between what William Burroughs called "cocaine bebop" and the mysterious Moroccan sounds of Joujouka.[25]

More about the Moroccan connection shortly, but in the soundtrack Coleman fused a number of his own trio compositions with Shore's orchestral scores, which mirrored Coleman's own writing by leaving room open for the saxophonist's trio to improvise.

Among his other Third Stream works, the wind quintet which Coleman composed during his absence from the stage in the early 1960s was not, however, the most long-lasting of the consequences of his period of retirement. That was unquestionably his adoption of the violin and trumpet as additional instruments – on both of which he was entirely self-taught, and therefore approached according to his own principles of having no preconceptions. Ironically, his decision to take up the violin was itself enshrined in a Third Stream composition by George Russell, who recalled:

> He came by my house in the early '60s, when I was living on Bank

Street in the Village. Morton Feldman, John Cage and Gil Evans all lived on the same block. Ornette visited in a state of great excitement – he'd just bought a violin. He'd never played it in his life, but he picked it up and started playing anyway. "Let's try some things," he said. It was the baptism of his violin, and I had the good sense to record what turned into about 30 minutes of music. Years later, I found the tape, and I thought I'd try to make something of it. The recording was horrible, in some places I could barely make out what he was doing, but at the centre of it was a thing like a hoe-down. I took that as the main idea, and I worked away on it until I had *Dialogue with Ornette*, which I wrote for symphony orchestra.[26]

Coleman's ability to catch the nuances of the country hoedown as effectively as some of the *avant-garde* string effects of Schuller's *Abstractions* in his violin playing was a piece of musical synthesis every bit as clever and accomplished as the Joycean qualitites of his alto saxophone playing already noted by John Lewis. On a piece like *Snowflakes and Sunshine*, recorded in 1965 by his trio at the Golden Circle Club in Stockholm, Coleman's opening violin solo has elements of both these influences, coupled with passion and intensity that match any of his work on alto saxophone from 1959 to 1960. On the same piece he displays his trumpet style, which is equally passionate, but far less anchored in aural traditions. It is primal, wailing, and deeply personal. When George Russell was asked what he heard in this type of playing he said, simply, "Ornette, that's what."

This was Coleman's principal achievement in his return to performance – to remain true to his own sound, whatever instrument he played and in whatever context. In the last three decades of the twentieth century he was to prove this over and over again, by putting himself in playing circumstances where his individual musical voice always remains startlingly clear, whether the background is funk, ethnic music, or even just a duet with another player.

Some commentators, like Schuller, see this consistency as a fundamental lack of change in Coleman's own playing. By using the same fingering patterns, altered pitches, and highly melodic approach to improvisation (still centered on his idea of soloing without relying on chord changes) as he had adopted in the late 1950s, argues Schuller, his alto saxophone voice is hardly likely to have altered much over time. But this takes no account of Coleman's restless imagination, or his ability to transfer his unique voice, his qualities of intensity, to entirely different instruments and settings. Part of the reason for the continuity of his individual voice is that he has always retained an intellectual clarity about his work and his own role within it, whether in an individual, group, or orchestral context.

This was strengthened in 1972–3 when he spent time in Morocco with a group of former court instrumentalists, originally of Persian origin, who had for generations devoted themselves to music within a Sufi mystic tradition – the Master Musicians of Joujouka. In their traditional ethnic ensembles of shawms and drums, Coleman found a different view of the ensemble from anything he had encountered before in jazz, or in Western art music. The ensemble itself was the end goal, the aim of its players. Unlike a jazz group, which is always the coming together of a collection of individual improvisers, the Master Musicians suppressed their individual egos to the collective sound. Coleman himself played alongside them and the experience shaped his subsequent fusion ensemble Prime Time, which for much of its life has had two guitars, two basses, and two drummers. Denardo Coleman, his son, has often been one of the drummers; he said that the ensemble principle of Prime Time is that because there are two of everything, then "everyone can have the lead, and nobody can have the lead."[27] In other words, the collective ensemble is as significant a part of the sound as the individual voices within it. This articulated in a satisfactory way many of the ideas Coleman had been working towards in *Free Jazz*, in his symphonic works, and in his regular small bands; from his trio with David Izenson on bass and Charles Moffett on drums to his later groups which reunited him with Dewey Redman, Charlie Haden, and Ed Blackwell.

Prime Time began in the mid-1970s, and continued throughout the latter part of the twentieth century to provide Coleman with a platform that presented his playing in a rock or funk context. Yet it retained many of his ideas about freedom of execution and from preconception, so that in due course it earned the tag "free fusion." It also gradually reintroduced a fuller harmonic context to his small-group work, first through guitars and then through the addition of keyboards. There was a similarly full harmonic depth to Coleman's acclaimed collaboration with guitarist Pat Metheny in 1985, *Song X*.

Plenty of other interviewers had been told, as I was, that Coleman found he did not need to transpose to be "with" the piano, so the most critical amongst them formed the view that after his early experiments with Paul Bley and Walter Norris he stopped using a piano because he could not keep in tune with it. Yet all these critics were confounded: first, by the way he used other instruments, from the double-stopped *arco* bass of David Izenzon to full string sections, and from the Prime Time guitars of Charles Ellerbee and Bern Nix to the Grateful Dead's Jerry Garcia, as substitutes for the piano's harmonic function, and, ultimately, when he introduced pianist Dave Bryant into the line-up of Prime Time. In the 1990s, he drew Geri Allen into his acoustic quartet; his most vital late 1990s work was his duo with yet another pianist, Joachim Kuhn.

Coleman's own reasons for using the piano sparingly over the years are very simple:

> Most jazz pianists play in a "pop" style – that's to say, they play chords as you would do for a singer. And, without sounding degrading, they're always put in the situation to be support. None of the pianists I use play like that. Dave Bryant plays the way he conceives Harmolodic music, fitting in with two guitars, two basses, and two drummers. And Joachim Kuhn plays in a style that's almost orchestral in the way he improvises. With him the chordal structure is there, but much freer than in a set sequence – it's almost a new format.[28]

Kuhn's trance-like improvisational state can be terrifying in its intensity, and Coleman thrives on this, because it fits in with his philosophy of music-making: "The word improvise is supposed to mean something that's not there that you bring there," he says. "In jazz, it's when a person can change his will and thought at the moment he wants to do it. The same twelve notes support all kinds of different performances – there must be something in those twelve notes that lets each individual be free."[29]

This is the legacy of his extraordinary and dominant contribution to jazz history. Throughout the twentieth century, many jazz musicians paid lip service to improvisation, and then, either by written composition or by playing formulaic solos that were largely worked out in advance, sought to submerge the true business of improvising. Throughout his career, this has never applied to Coleman, and in addition to rethinking *how* to improvise by freeing himself from chords, and reworking the relationships between soloist and ensemble in a variety of ways, he has never abandoned the fundamental principle of freedom from preconception: "Most jazz musicians follow maps to improvise. I prefer musicians who are seeking something freer, easier, more enjoyable. The main thing that makes towards music perfection is the will to make it better instantly."[30]

Such tenets have been taken up with enthusiasm by those who have worked closely with Coleman at almost every stage of his career. The next section looks in detail at a number of other musicians who sought freedom from preconception and an equally unfettered collective framework for improvising.

## Free Jazz: The Followers of Coltrane and Coleman

> Trane was very sensitive to the generation that followed him, to younger players like myself and some of the guys he used on the *Ascension* record. Including people like Freddie Hubbard. Always had his ear to the ground for new ideas. He was one of the very first people to latch onto the importance of Albert Ayler and his sound. He did more to glorify and expand the implications of Albert's sound than perhaps even Albert, because fortunately Trane lived long enough to do that.[31]
>
> Archie Shepp, in an interview with the author

Between the double quartet of Ornette Coleman on his 1960 album *Free Jazz* and John Coltrane's *Ascension* in 1965, musicians in several parts of the United States began to examine ways in which new improvisational ground could be broken by dispensing with many of the elements that had hitherto been part of the music's structure. There would be no need to rely on chordal instruments such as the piano or guitar, the double bass did not have to supply a continual pulse or underlying harmony, and drummers could play intricate polyrhythms, or move toward coloristic shadings rather than "keeping time" as earlier jazz drummers had done. Melodies, or fragments of melodies, were introduced fleetingly by one soloist, picked up and developed by another, or replaced by a new idea. As a consequence of the work of Coleman and his circle of musicians, who began such explorations, and those such as Coltrane, who took the ideas up and went further with them, jazz could be defined no longer in terms of improvised solos over a repeated chord sequence, of variations on a familiar melody, of relying on a pre-set arrangement, or of creating a sense of swing using a "rhythm section" and a "front line." Instead, those characteristics became elements in a much broader concept of improvisation.

I have already quoted Paul Bley's view that when he first heard Ornette Coleman, he recognized a "missing link" between chordally based jazz and a totally free manner of ensemble playing. He went on to say:

> A little earlier than when I met Ornette in 1958, I had sent for trumpeter Herbie Spanier from Toronto to come and play totally free improvisations with me. But those didn't involve steady time, and they also involved a lack of harmony, a lack of chord changes, and so on, and in a way we had skipped a stage, so to speak, and we were looking forward to 1964 and Albert Ayler.[32]

Coleman, by contrast, retained a rhythm section playing "time" – indeed, around the time they started working with him, Charlie Haden and Billy Higgins had occasionally played entire sets as a duo, with just bass and drums but without ever sacrificing a recognizable jazz beat. Throughout the period of his first quartet, and even, to some extent, in his subsequent trio with Charles Moffett and David Izenzon, Coleman retained that sense of beat, and he mainly succeeded in influencing a generation of jazz musicians because his own improvisations were (and would continue to be) intensely melodic. Many were atonal – not conforming to conventional ideas of pitch and harmony – but they were both logical and memorable, and would still be built over structures that had a recognizable connection with popular song form, even if the number of measures fluctuated and the space for soloing was extremely variable.

When the Coleman Quartet was appearing at the Five Spot, in 1960, John Coltrane was frequently in the audience. As Charlie Haden told Neil Tesser: "Coltrane was in the club every night, hanging out; he would usually sit at the same table and listen to every note we played. . . . He was very, very serious, and determined to put what he learned from Ornette into his own music."[33] The degree to which he did this was not immediately apparent, because an album that he recorded in 1960 with the other three-quarters of Coleman's quartet, trumpeter Don Cherry, bassist Haden, and drummer Ed Blackwell, fell victim to Atlantic's policy of bringing out its discs very slowly, so *The Avant Garde* did not appear until 1966, by which time free jazz had evolved much further.

On the two tracks on which this line-up appears (three others have the MJQ's Percy Heath on bass), Coltrane attempts to meld his modally based style of improvising with the walking bass of Haden and the loose New Orleans beat of Blackwell. The attempts are not entirely successful, even in an intense soprano solo on *The Blessing*, that whirls like a dervish through a scale-like pattern. The other members of the quartet respond interestingly to Coltrane, not least because they abandon Coleman's use of microtones – Cherry, in particular, plays, for the most part, precisely in tune, and delivers virtually straightforward bebop solos, even on his own *Cherryco*. So, clearly, in 1960, Coltrane was not only some distance away from the freedom he would attain in mid-decade, but he also acted as a restraining influence on those who had already discovered and explored the "missing link."

To arrive at a convincing approach to free jazz himself, Coltrane went on to absorb two other major sets of influences. The first was a far less conventional approach to his own instrument, with the vocal timbres, extensions of range, and freak effects adopted by the likes of Pharoah Sanders, Archie Shepp, and, above all, Albert Ayler; the second was the complete abandoning of the kind of metrical and melodic structure that lay behind Coleman's work, an approach being pioneered by pianist Cecil Taylor.

Taylor is the common link between these players. Both Ayler and Shepp spent time in his quartet in the early 1960s, which was the very stage in his development when Taylor's playing – on record, at any rate – shed the last vestiges of single note melodic lines or fragments, and moved wholeheartedly into dense textural playing, with percussive note clusters and a completely atonal approach.

Taylor had undergone a conventional conservatory training; he was well-versed both in classical piano and in the jazz styles prevalent around Boston, where he studied. He knew his way round the recorded jazz piano tradition, but his major influence in the early 1950s was Horace Silver, a player who in some respects paralleled Thelonious Monk, in that his technique was unorthodox, yet he poured his personality and his feelings into his playing. In a conversation with A. B. Spellman, Taylor compared Silver's total commitment to his music to that of the soul singer James Brown, as part of "the genuine tradition of a people," and Spellman went on to say that, in Taylor's view: "Kneeling while screaming and ripping off his shirt is not merely a part of James Brown's showmanship, it is an essential part of the communication of the highly emotional songs that James Brown sings, and if he moves the audience, that technique is sound."[34]

Taylor's playing was often to become the pianistic equivalent of ripping off his shirt – a percussive, totally involving, release of energy that would leave him and his audience drained. There was an almost balletic quality about his movements at the keyboard – indeed, he once said that he tried "to imitate on the piano the leaps in space a dancer makes."[35] At the same time, he was keen to exploit the percussive qualities of the piano, and to the British journalist Valerie Wilmer, who once described him as playing "88 tuned drums" rather than piano keys, he said, "We in black music think of the piano as a percussive instrument: we beat the keyboard, we get inside the instrument."[36] The question of cultural origins of the music, and the identification of Taylor's all-out approach with African-American culture, in a decade that was increasingly involved in protest and questions of black identity, was to become a significant element in the free jazz movement.

By 1956, when he brought his first quartet into the Five Spot in New York, and became the first *avant-garde* player to put the Cooper Square club on the map, Taylor had already shed many of the conventional ideas about form. "Form is possibility," he was to write,[37] and he viewed the form of his music as something quite separate from the popular song formats that had defined much jazz up to that point. Huge, sweeping performances, lasting between 20 minutes and two hours, were far from inchoate, and took on what Nat Hentoff called "an immense, intense, organic unity."[38] Such lengthy numbers, running counter to the normal practice in the nightclubs where he played, sometimes even caused him problems in the usually tolerant atmosphere of the Five Spot, but Taylor was unabashed. He had a keen intellectual perception of where form and order derived from in his music, saying:

> There is no music without order — if that music comes from a man's innards. But that order is not necessarily related to any single criterion of what order should be as imposed from the outside. Whether that criterion is the song form or what some critic thinks jazz should be. This is not a question then of "freedom" versus "nonfreedom," but rather it is a question of recognizing different ideas and expressions of order."[39]

In the late 1950s and early 1960s, when Archie Shepp was in the group, Taylor was still writing out elements of his pieces, but with altoist Jimmy Lyons, his successor, charts gave way to something freer and less structured, as Lyons recalled:

> He has scales, patterns, and tunes that he uses, and the soloist is supposed to use those things. But you can take it out. If you go into your own thing, Cecil will follow you there. But you have to

know where the tune is supposed to go, and if you take it there another way than the way Cecil outlined it, then that's cool with Cecil. That's the main thing I've learned with Cecil, the music has to come from within and not from any charts."[40]

So, by the time of his mid-1960s discs for Blue Note, Taylor was producing pieces that were almost entirely free of written music, his "scales, patterns, and tunes" being dictated just as Mingus dictated his. Taylor, however, did not work all that frequently. After his first triumphs at the Five Spot, even his appearances there trailed off, and when he won a *Down Beat* "new star" award in 1962 he was scuffling for work. In America, with the exception of a few bands such as the MJQ, who had taken their music out of nightclubs and saloons, a jazz audience wanted, for the most part, to go out and enjoy itself. The degree of commitment Taylor required from his audience did not sit happily with the social mores of those whose money kept the clubs afloat. The social, community-based movements, discussed in the next chapter, which ultimately did a lot to develop such an audience, were still in their infancy.

It was different in Europe. As Ornette Coleman was subsequently to do after his return to playing in 1965, with a triumphant concert in England that ranks among his finest work with his trio, Taylor headed for Europe, and in 1962 toured Scandinavia. He found European audiences tolerant, enthusiastic, knowledgeable, and interested in his music. Although he used prepared piano techniques, and one or two other devices that had become *de rigueur* both with the American followers of John Cage and with the European *avant-garde*, Taylor always viewed his music as distinctly African-American, but this European tour went to prove that, if nothing else, there was a different attitude towards his work there, and that this attitude was equally receptive to the European classical *avant-garde* and to its improvising jazz-related equivalent. Jimmy Lyons and Taylor's drummer Sonny Murray both believed that the six months of consistent work that the group undertook on the continent was the best thing that ever happened to them, and Taylor himself said:

In some of those small towns you have small concert halls or auditoriums that are acoustically perfect. You have instruments, I'm talking about pianos, that are excellent. You have an audience that comes there prepared to be moved.[41]

On his return, Taylor had very little work, but continued to generate critical approval for his few appearances and occasional LPs, including his uncompromising Blue Note album *Conquistador*, on which each side was occupied by a single extended performance by a sextet that included several of his regular collaborators: trumpeter Bill Dixon, altoist Jimmy Lyons, bassists Henry Grimes and Alan Silva, with Andrew Cyrille on drums. Taylor's sporadic working pattern continued into the 1970s, when he began an international career as a soloist. One outstanding example of this, which contrasts his playing to an equally iconoclastic figure, who remained within the harmonic and rhythmic traditions of jazz, was a 1977 Carnegie Hall concert with Mary Lou Williams, even though the event was more successful as the sum of its parts – the efforts of the two pianists to find common ground for playing together being the least rewarding element. Taylor also toured with a band from time to time, but in the late 1970s began to specialize in working in duo with percussionists, starting with Tony Williams on his album *Joy of Flying*. Later percussion partners included Max Roach and the South African drummer Louis Moholo.

Tenorist Albert Ayler worked with Taylor in Copenhagen in 1962, and he was no stranger to Europe, having played in army bands a few years earlier, and jammed in various cities, including Paris (as recalled by Roscoe Mitchell in Chapter 4). Between leaving the army and joining Taylor, he played bebop in Scandinavia, but he also began to record his own music. Ayler had worked as a young man in rhythm and blues bands (as Ornette Coleman had done) and, as we know from Roscoe Mitchell's account, he was taking liberties with the blues in his army days: "At one of those sessions he was playing the blues. After the first few choruses he really started to stretch the boundaries."[42]

Although his first discs from Scandinavia are less disturbing and less frighteningly abstract than some of his later American work, they show the same huge sound recalled by Mitchell, and the use of pitches that fall between the notes of the conventional scale, but these are more than conventional "blue notes." Like Ornette Coleman, Ayler used microtonality as part of his improvisational vocabulary, and he demonstrated this most effectively in a similar formation to Coleman, without piano, and supported by just bass and drums. This was the setting for his most exceptional performance of a piece he worked through and reworked many times, *Ghosts*.

At times Ayler shows little obvious connection to what had gone on in jazz before – the most memorable aspects of his playing are its timbral qualities, its deep sound, his wide vibrato, and his use of honks and squeals. But he also built his pieces round simple, folk-like melodies (*Ghosts* is one of these) and his way of interpreting them, his exploration of timbre, and the interaction with the other musicians (such as bassist Gary Peacock and drummer Sunny Murray) prefigure several currents in jazz that became stronger in the late 1960s and early 1970s, from the unusual timbres that became central to the work of the Chicago AACM musicians (discussed in the next chapter) to the noise-based playing of the European *avant garde* saxophonist Peter Brötzmann. In his final years, before his death in mysterious circumstances at the age of 34, when his body was found in New York's East River, Ayler passed through phases of playing more formally composed works, and then performing in a rhythm and blues setting.

The blues was a constant factor in the work of Archie Shepp, although as a published poet and playwright, he was perhaps equally interested in the verbal expressivity of the form as its musical framework. In latter years, looking, and occasionally sounding, like a lightweight Ben Webster, Shepp has re-explored the mainstream and bebop repertoire with a broad, buttery tenor tone, and a stark, but fluid, sound on soprano saxophone. The 1960s radical child can, nevertheless, be seen very much as the father of this particular man, and from his apprenticeship in Philadelphia with Cal Massey and other local musicians who also shaped Coltrane's playing, to his own earliest recorded work at the start of the 1960s, Shepp always had a penchant for the romantic ballad repertoire, which was counterbalanced by the extreme radicalism of his poetry and other literary work.

In the period leading up to his collaboration with Coltrane, he played with Cecil Taylor, with trumpeter Bill Dixon, in the New York Contemporary Five with Don Cherry and saxophonist John Tchicai, and in his own groups with trombonist Roswell Rudd. Of all those players, it was Cecil Taylor who made the greatest impression on Shepp: "Cecil influenced my thinking very much when I came to New York, not least because he was very articulate, well read, and intelligent."[43] But if Taylor encouraged his radical side to shine through, it was Coltrane who helped him to connect this with the traditions of African-American music. Shepp says:

> What accounts for the greatness of certain musicians is their ability to synthesize, to cull, from the things that went before, and the things going on around them, and then to project these into a future idea, as he did with *Ascension*. Coltrane was, notwithstand-

ing Ornette's abilities, much more conscious of what he was about. He insisted on the blues as an essential referent – both from an intellectual standpoint but also from the soul. Coltrane opened many doors. . . . For me, Trane's influence was not only musical but personal. I haven't found a player today that's gone beyond where he got to. For example, he really introduced the concept of extended works. Mingus had done it earlier for ensembles, but Trane was the first saxophone soloist to use long-form improvisations to explore harmonic and melodic ideas in more depth.[44]

To Shepp, Coltrane's example of emphasizing the spiritual qualities in his music, whether the fundamental values of the African-American Christian church or a more mystical spirituality, was extremely important, as was Coltrane's decision in the 1960s to work with him, John Tchicai, Pharoah Sanders, and other young musicians. This was, he felt, both a means of them learning from Coltrane, just as earlier generations had learned from Dizzy Gillespie or Monk, and also of Coltrane absorbing some of their new ideas into his own work, the process, as he put it, of "synthesis" or "culling." Here again, just as in the very earliest days of the music, is evidence of the degree to which jazz has continued to be a syncretic music.

Coltrane acted as a mentor for Shepp, helping him sign a record deal with Impulse, and sharing the 1965 album *The New Thing at Newport*, so that, on the original LP, the Coltrane Quartet was on one side, and Shepp's band with vibes player Bobby Hutcherson was on the other. What is noticeable about this comparison, in retrospect, is how much more starkly modern Coltrane's work is than that of Shepp, whose words, rather than his music, carry the radicalism. But because of the power of his words, and because he always related his musical actions of the time to the black radical movement, he was perceived as the most overtly political of Coltrane's circle. Late in 1965, he took on the readership of *Down Beat*, whom he perceived as mainly white and middle class, saying: "I play about the death of me by you. I exult in the life of me in spite of you."[45]

Shepp's political stance was to be echoed across the country, and I will discuss the musical and political organizations that sprang up in the 1960s to foster African-American music in the next chapter. But nobody involved in the cutting-edge jazz of the 1960s could be unaware of the political climate in which race had become a major issue. Drummer Rashied Ali explained to me how the period was viewed from within Coltrane's group of associates:

Those were trying times in the 60s. We had the civil rights thing going on, we had King, we had Malcolm, we had the Panthers. There was so much diversity happening. People were screaming for their rights and wanting to be equal, be free. And naturally, the music reflects that whole period . . . that whole time definitely influenced the way we played. I think that's where that really free form came into it. Everybody wanted to get away from the rigid thing, away from what was happening before; they wanted to relate to what was happening now, and I'm sure that music came out of that whole thing.[46]

Despite the radical African-Americanism of his writings, and the feeling expressed by Rashied Ali that free jazz was bound up with political protest, one of Shepp's frequent collaborators in the mid-1960s was Roswell Rudd, a white trombonist. At first glance, he seems an incongruous figure to be part of one of the iconic free jazz ensembles, but he brought several distinctive elements to the music.

First, together with saxophonist Steve Lacy, he had spent time studying in detail the music of Thelonious Monk, and had learned a lot about Monk's approach to structure and ensemble playing. Second, he had become a close friend and colleague of the innovative pianist Herbie Nichols, who – despite little commercial success – had experimented with the form and structure of jazz compositions, in addition to writing the enduring standard *Lady Sings the Blues*. One of Nichols's characteristic habits, in his job as a saloon pianist in Greenwich Village, was to interpolate into his playing witty and observant musical comments on people as they came into the club, and Rudd had become fascinated by this idea of instantaneous musical commentary on events going on around him as he played. Third, he was also fascinated by world music, at a time when this was not the object of interest that it has become today. He worked with the ethnomusicologist Alan Lomax (the same man who had recorded Jelly Roll Morton's reminiscences for the Library of Congress) as the archivist for his collection of field recordings of music from all over the globe. Rudd told me: "Listening to these recordings out of context have a way of opening you up; you tend to find more similarities between the various styles than differences."[47]

Bringing these various elements into Shepp's groups would have been important enough on their own, but Rudd had actually cut his teeth on a very different type of jazz altogether, and I was genuinely surprised by his explanation of what he considered the main ingredient he brought to the mid-1960s free jazz of players like Shepp or drummer Milford Graves:

> I have to say it was Dixieland that led me to free. It was really the
> only kind of music I knew inside out apart from the marching
> band music I grew up with as a kid. Compared to most bop,
> Dixieland is very free. Bop is an extremely disciplined music, but
> there was a lotta stuff in the kind of Dixieland I played that was
> really wide open. I loved the fact that if you played one of
> instruments in a band you had a part to play. You'd learn what to
> do from masters who played the traditional trombone or clarinet
> roles in creating the texture of the music. Once you had your
> part, you had a stepping stone for your improvisation. I loved the
> way that Dixieland musicians improvised collectively. So in free
> jazz, I was coming from that a lot of the time. The strange thing
> was, I got to New York City and started playing with people my
> own age who were used to bop or Billy Strayhorn, and just as I
> learned from them, they got something from me. Horn players in
> that bebop genre were used to just playing a head, then series of
> solos. But when someone was playing a solo and I would start to
> come in and play at same time, they'd look at each other and say,
> "Well! What do you know?" But I had been doing that all along.
> It was a trade-off for getting acquainted to newer developments: I
> was bringing an older thing into it and a third thing was coming
> off of that.[48]

Rudd played in Shepp's band on a remarkable session recorded for Impulse
at the Both/And Club in San Francisco, in 1966, and as well as including
some of Herbie Nichols's music in the program, the band displays Shepp at
the height of his free phase, including recitations and piano playing in an
eclectic and challenging set.

Shepp was to continue as a major innovative figure in free jazz for
another decade or so, but thereafter he gradually moved away from the
radical freedom of the 1960s, preferring, as mentioned, to focus on the Ben
Websterish side of his playing, or on the blues, which he sings with
conviction. He has been particularly active in duo settings, notably with
pianist Horace Parlan, but also in appearing in concert with other pianists
including Andrew Hill. When I asked him why he had abandoned the kind of
free music that was still being played in the 1990s by Rashied Ali, Rudd, and
several of his other former collaborators, he referred me back to his view

that everything he had done with Coltrane had related to the blues:

> I moved further and further away from that kind of free music. I
> was beginning not to enjoy it. It was too cerebral for me, too
> intellectual, and the blues referents seemed to be neutralized, for
> the sake of playing notes that were different or doing things that
> surprised the audience.[49]

The blues had also been an early influence on the third of this trio of
saxophonists who had an impact on Coltrane, Pharoah Sanders. He had
played in various rhythm and blues bands in California, before coming to
New York in 1962. Sanders's main innovation in the decade's free jazz was
his shrieking extensions of the upper range of the tenor, and long, jagged
runs that passed through a series of microtonal notes; his influence on
Coltrane can be heard in both versions of *Ascension*, and in their subsequent
formal and informal collaborations, where, gradually, many similar
techniques found their way into Coltrane's playing.

I said earlier that Europe was helpful in establishing the careers of Cecil
Taylor, Albert Ayler, and Ornette Coleman, and it was to play a similarly
important role in Archie Shepp's music, to the extent that many of his
recordings since the 1960s have been made there. For the most part – with
the exception of Coleman, who has always been rapturously received in
Britain, and who recorded several of his major works in London – Britain
has not been so consistent a platform for American free jazz as continental
Europe, most notably France and Scandinavia. Indeed, so hostile was the
reaction to Coltrane's one and only British tour in 1961 that he never
returned. Sharing a bill with one of Dizzy Gillespie's most energetic
quintets, British critics unanimously put down Coltrane's group with Eric
Dolphy, and Bob Dawbarn's *Melody Maker* review was typical, criticizing the
group's hour-long set as "belonging more to the realms of higher
mathematics than music," with the band "all apparently playing in different
tempos and frequently in different time signatures."[50]

There was a hostile reaction from much of the British critical
establishment to anything post-bop, and indeed, from some quarters, such
as Henry Pleasants and Philip Larkin, to bebop itself.[51] But this was not
shared by musicians, and in the 1960s, Britain developed a strikingly wide
panorama of free jazz players who were, in many respects, the major link
between, on the one hand, the work of Coltrane, Taylor, and Coleman and,
on the other, the classical *avant-garde*. A group such as the improvising

ensemble AMM, for example, combined such jazz players as drummer Eddie Prevost and saxophonist Lou Gare with members of the Scratch Orchestra, Cornelius Cardew, and Chris Hobbs, who came entirely from a classical background and were leading members of the British new music movement, involved with the work of Cage, Stockhausen, Christian Wolff, and LaMonte Young. Mixing conventional instruments, amplified cellos, and home-made string instruments with everything from coffee tins to electric cocktail mixers, AMM was, as Cardew put it, "searching for sound." He went on to say:

> This proliferation of sound sources in such a confined space [the London School of Economics music room] produced a situation where it was often impossible to tell who was producing which sounds – or rather which portions of the single room-filling deluge of sound. In this phase the playing changed: as individuals we were absorbed into a composite activity in which solo playing and any kind of virtuosity were relatively insignificant.[52]

Several British ensembles explored this idea of the ensemble as a composite entity, notably the work of drummer John Stevens and his Spontaneous Music Ensemble, whereas, at the other pole, players such as the guitarist Derek Bailey and saxophonist Evan Parker explored the possibilities for sustained solo improvisation. In some respects, Stevens's group started out on similar lines to Ornette Coleman's trio, with saxophonist Trevor Watts taking a similar role to his American counterpart, but, over time, British groups have substantially diverged from the American model.

The saxophone trio SOS experimented with using tape loops behind the playing of its three soloists, John Surman, Mike Osborne, and Alan Skidmore. The trio Iskra 1903, with trombonist Paul Rutherford, bassist Barry Guy, and guitarist Derek Bailey, went a long way towards abandoning rhythmic structures in favor of the exploration of timbre. But the most original British approach to free jazz of the period came from the Jamaican saxophonist Joe Harriott, whose albums such as *Abstract*, from 1960, explored a number of ideas which became the titles of pieces – including *Tonal*, *Pictures*, *Shadows*, and the more overtly melodic *Calypso Sketches* – in a free context, but without sacrificing the sweet lyricism of Harriott's sound, or the equally mellifluous flugelhorn tone of his collaborator Shake Keane.

Bailey, through a succession of annual events in London known as "Company" weeks, created an informal series of ensemble settings in which collective playing was explored. Similar large-scale free ensembles have been put together by Paul Rutherford, whose Iskrastra is an eighteen-piece band, similar to the ensemble Centipede, led by Keith Tippett. Many British free jazz players of the 1960s were involved in the orchestra led by pianist and composer Mike Westbrook, in whose works such as *Marching Song* (1969) and *Metropolis* (1971) very freely played solo and ensemble passages contrast with Westbrook's formal, almost Ellingtonian, sense of orchestral color and form.

Virtually all these figures have continued to be involved in the European free jazz scene, and some, such as Trevor Watts's Moiré Ensemble, and the trio of Evan Parker, Barry Guy, and Paul Lytton, have achieved considerable international fame. John Surman's work has involved collaborations with several leading European free jazz players, including the German trombonist Albert Mangelsdorff, but by the 1980s, he had moved from free jazz to a variety of more formal contexts.

Mangelsdorff, who was a leading proponent of multiphonics, the technique of creating two or more notes simultaneously, became one of a number of leading free jazz musicians in Germany, of whom others included the pianist Joachim Kuhn, the trumpeter Manfred Schoof, and the pianist Alex Von Schlippenbach, founder of the long-lived Globe Unity Orchestra.

However, one vital element in developing the individual tradition of free jazz that has grown up in Europe has been the constant interaction between American free jazz players and their European counterparts. In the late 1960s, a new generation of such Americans arrived, spawned mainly by the various politically motivated organizations that had grown up in urban America during the decade of protest. The impact of the members of the AACM, BAG, and similar groups was to be just as significant in finding new directions for free jazz as the pioneering European work of Albert Ayler, Cecil Taylor, and Ornette Coleman.

CHAPTER 18

# Politicization: The AACM and Other Organizations

> Chicago can be so invisible to the rest of the world. In the
> U.S. we just fly over it from one coast to the other coast.
> There's not much national media that comes out of Chicago,
> or at least there wasn't in the 60s and 70s, and it could have
> just died on the vine, this whole AACM movement.
>
> Howard Mandel, in an interview with the author[1]

On May 8, 1965, a new kind of musical revolution began in Chicago, when Muhal Richard Abrams started the Association for the Advancement of Creative Musicians, otherwise known as the AACM. At a time of great social change and unrest, this organization provided a focal point for the city's musicians to come together and develop an entirely new way forward for jazz. Through the groups that emerged from the organization, such as the Art Ensemble of Chicago, and a number of passionate advocates for this music, both critics and record producers, far from withering on the vine, in due course it came to international attention.

So far, I have examined the way in which the 1960s *avant-garde* developed from the experiments in free jazz of Ornette Coleman and John Coltrane. The *Ascension* album by Coltrane was made the year that the AACM came together, and most of the figures I have examined so far were either directly connected with that disc – Archie Shepp, John Tchicai, and Pharoah Sanders – or they were playing in a manner that related to some aspect of it, from Albert Ayler's humanized vocal tones to Cecil Taylor's deconstruction of conventional form. By and large, even though they hailed from different parts of the country, the *avant-garde* connected with Coltrane and Coleman was a New York-based movement. In the mid-1960s,

Coleman's Artists' House project was an attempt to bring his music into the local community, which failed, not just because of local opposition in the downtown Manhattan area where he chose to locate, but because it did not fully draw the community into the collective act of music-making. But Abrams in Chicago, and like-minded individuals in other urban centers, notably St. Louis and Los Angeles, created an *avant-garde* movement that succeeded in making far more successful connections with the local population, and also built on the political climate of the time to unite the African-American community in a positive, creative way.

The AACM succeeded musically because, on the one hand, it took the freedom of *Ascension* as a starting point and looked for new avenues to explore, and, on the other, it conducted that exploration by extending and building on a strong, local, self-contained tradition. I discussed the question of the degree to which *Ascension* was a jumping-off point with critic Gary Giddins, who said:

> It put free jazz to a whole different level, of just how free it could be. I remember once comparing it to a black on black canvas or a white on white canvas – after you paint a canvas that's completely white and hang it up in a museum, you've gone as far as you can go ... what are you going to put on it? That's what happened with the *avant-garde*: Coltrane got to the white canvas with *Ascension*, and after that in Chicago you had guys like Lester Bowie and Muhal Richard Abrams who came out of free jazz but were playing a whole different way – they were using melody, they were using rhythm-and-blues rhythms, using whatever they wanted. Coltrane had given us a new canvas and we could begin on that again.[2]

It was, to a large degree, because the Chicagoan musical community was relatively isolated, small, and self-contained, that the ways of decorating that brand new canvas developed as they did. The first moves had happened back around 1960–1, when Muhal Richard Abrams began organizing concerts with his Experimental Band, and collected around him a number of kindred spirits: his colleague Phil Koran, pianist Jodie Christian, and drummer Steve McCall. Under Abrams's guidance, musicians of an experimental frame of mind rehearsed with one another under the collective umbrella organization of his orchestra. Saxophonist Roscoe Mitchell, who had been in the army, and then worked briefly with Coltrane, giving him both an insider's and an outsider's perspective, put the local scene in context for me:

One big difference is, when you got places like New York and L.A., you gotta lot of musicians there that are doing a lot of jobs, and the one thing I've enjoyed about Chicago is that you're absolutely able to get musicians together to rehearse on a consistent basis, so you can like look at long-range things. What it's resulted in, it's given us musicians and instrumentations that we can create pieces with, that no-one else can even have.[3]

By the start of the 1960s, Chicago was no longer the creative center for jazz it had been in the 1920s, and the decline I discussed earlier had slowly but surely continued. During the 1930s, a few individuals such as Earl Hines had hung on and made a career there, but many others were forced to move or leave music altogether. Since World War II, the musical life of the city had remained on a downward spiral, and what jazz activity there was was limited to a few clubs. The Bee Hive, the main bebop club, closed in 1956. Some that continued, like Joe Segal's Jazz Showcase, which was at various locations, including the Pershing Lounge, presented acts from out-of-town like Dizzy Gillespie, John Coltrane, and Sonny Rollins, and in the 1960s Miles Davis made a series of famous appearances at the Plugged Nickel Club on North Wells Street. Other venues such as Bill and Ruth Reinhardt's Jazz Limited on East Grand Avenue survived from 1947 to 1974 featuring mainly traditional and Dixieland jazz. New music played by local players was mainly restricted to the social life of the African-American community on the South Side.

Even so, in the period after World War II, several innovators of national importance had continued to come to Chicago and to be heard by the city's musicians – especially by such locals as tenor saxophonist Fred Anderson, who were half a generation or so older than those who started the AACM. Anderson told me:

I got a chance to see Charlie Parker several times. In fact, I heard him the last time he was in Chicago. I got a chance to see Lester Young and other people like that. So I kinda pieced the music together in my head through those guys – but they were so advanced. I thought I had to do a lot of work, so I used to study all the time, work on my scales and chords, and try to figure out how they was done – a lot of those things. And I tried to listen to the music at the same time. And then after I got to the point where I was pretty good technically, I could hear their music.

805

And from there on I got the idea of how to put a lot of things together. I never did copy anything. . . . I did it another way. . . . I was listening not for what they were playing but how they were getting there. . . . I didn't really realize that I was creating a style. I kept on playing and studying. I used to write down a lot of exercises. Finally, I decided I would stop writing 'em and start playing 'em.[4]

Fred Anderson was one of the Chicagoan players who successfully began to develop a new and individual jazz voice during the 1950s. He was rather endearingly described by record producer Chuck Nessa as one of jazz's "great meanderers,"[5] with a style that produced long, rambling solos of great intensity and moments of beauty.

Anderson, and many of the other Chicagoan musicians who were interested in exploring *avant-garde* ideas, had direct contact with one of jazz's great iconoclasts, who was based in the city right through the 1950s: Sun Ra. Sun Ra's music from this period has already been discussed in terms of his innovations in big-band writing and arranging, but, as saxophonist Von Freeman told me, the Chicago version of Ra's Arkestra was where plenty of the improvisational ideas that were to go into the AACM, particularly those concerning large ensembles, first got tried out:

Sun Ra was doing that long before some of those guys were even born. . . . I used to play with him and people would laugh. He played in a couple of places round town. One of them was called Transitions. We used to play in that club and it would be more of us than there was audience. Then we worked in a club called Dreamland on 63rd Street, where he would play once a week. And there'd be no audience. But that didn't phase him, because he had his own thing, his own vision, and eventually he had the last laugh.[6]

Following on from Sun Ra's influence, the scene was set for a new type of music to take hold in Chicago; but the problem was that there was almost nowhere for this to happen. Times were so hard for some of the innovative young musicians that pianist Jodie Christian was actually playing regular sessions in a beauty parlor, while the other club where locals played – McKee's Lounge on 63rd Street – was often closed. On top of that, the

African-American community in Chicago was only too well aware of the strained political climate.

This was the period when the city was under the administration of Mayor Daley, which took a manipulative and cynical view of racial politics. There were several African-American aldermen on Daley's city council, but for the most part their positions were sinecures – the consequence of working as political hacks, doing door-to-door canvassing and the like for the Democrats. They held little actual political power in a city that was deeply segregated, and where the actions of the big corporations and banks were unscrupulous concerning the property market. Through the way that developments, loans, and planning were handled, the city became more, rather than less, segregated, with white families encouraged to sell up cheaply in mixed neighborhoods, only for their properties to be resold expensively to incoming black families, thereby creating a deeply divided community.

Author John Litweiler has studied Chicago's music of this period in his book *The Freedom Principle*, and he remembers the tense background of local politics, where once again housing, as it had been in the 1920s, was becoming a social tinderbox:

> When you walked across the street, you knew which was the black neighborhood and which was the white neighborhood, because the white neighborhoods were getting the city services. I think only now [2000], let's say in the last 20 or 30 years, do you see a lot of freedom of movement between communities. There were riots. Especially after Martin Luther King was assassinated. ... I live on the South Side myself, and a couple of blocks from home the National Guard with their tanks were all set up in the park.[7]

As it turned out, the riots were few and far between; and, rather than taking to the streets, the musicians in the community, motivated by pianist Muhal Richard Abrams, found this climate of social unrest was the very catalyst they needed to go out and create their own opportunities to perform, to make music that would have a unifying influence. Abrams wrote to several key musicians, asking them to join a new association to advance their artistic work – the AACM. Forming such an organization, with a long title represented by an acronym, was very much in the spirit of the times, emulating the four key civil rights and proto-black power movements of the mid-1960s – the NAACP, SNCC, SCLC, and CORE. The first of these, the National Association for the Advancement of Colored People, had pursued the perpetrators of racism through the courts. The Student Nonviolent Coordinating Committee organized such events as the sit-ins at segregated restaurants in North Carolina. The Southern Christian Leadership Conference arose from Martin Luther King's actions to boycott the bussing of students in Birmingham, Alabama. The Congress of Racial Equality was a Chicagoan organization, to which many AACM members already belonged. Saxophonist Joseph Jarman explained the thinking behind the AACM, and its specifically artistic agenda:

> There was tremendous anxiety in the political climate at the time because there was protest against the Vietnamese war, there were protests against the political activities in the Southern United States, protests against the flower generation in the North, there were political protests against the government. So it was a very exciting, nervous period. Of course *within* each community it was very calm and relaxed. We had experienced a view of union. And that's how the letter [from Abrams] came about, because we were experiencing unity in the various communities. The intent of the whole idea was to allow us the opportunity to perform; but to perform with dignity, with pride, without humiliation, without limitation. Alongside Muhal Richard Abrams there was also Phil Koran. They were the two main forces. And there was a list of activities and a list of goals giving us the responsibility to do what we wanted to do, and approximately just a month after that meeting we had our first AACM concert. We had rented a place, set up the seats, people came in, sat down, musicians came in and performed. There were no interruptions, nothing; it was just enjoy the music and thank you very much. It was extraordinary to have this kind of feeling and this kind of opportunity, because there was so much conflict outside. It was impossible to get a job playing this kind of music in one of the local clubs.[8]

All of a sudden, young musicians like Joseph Jarman found a direction in their lives – and this came not only from the newly formed AACM, but also from the players half a generation older, who had survived the rough times in Chicago's musical life, like Fred Anderson. Once a week, during 1965, Jarman would take a 45-minute train ride outside the city to Evanston,

Illinois, where Anderson then lived, for a music lesson, although Anderson preferred to think of this as "just playing together," rather than any form of formal tuition. Subsequently, Jarman began to perform publicly with Anderson, and was nominally the leader of their group, but he has always acknowledged Anderson as taking an equal share in shaping their music, and of his overall importance to the approach of the AACM musicians. A piece like *Adam's Rib*, on Jarman's 1966 album *Song for*, shows the collaboration at work, in music that creates a sense of compositional form by integrating long, scored passages with free-form improvising.

Among the musicians on this disc by Jarman were several members of Muhal Richard Abrams's Experimental Band. This band never actually recorded under its own name, but since 1961 it had consistently been a focus for Jarman's own generation of young players, many of whom attended Wilson Junior College. Abrams encouraged them to challenge almost all their prior assumptions about music, so that those new listeners who heard the band unawares were in for a shock. Howard Mandel has written at length about the band, and he recalls in his book *Future Jazz* how out-of-town pianist Don Pullen reacted when he went to hear it for the first time:

> The first time I heard Muhal's big band . . . I thought everybody in it was crazy! Honest to God, it was the most shocking and surprising thing I'd ever heard, and I started to go home. But then I sat there thinking: "These cats are not kidding." Muhal had charts and music for them to play – even more amazing. When they hit the first notes, I thought, "Wait a minute, they're going to start over." But they didn't – they kept going![9]

Mandel himself often heard the Experimental Band during the mid-1960s, and shared this sense of the unexpected – of a band sounding so wrong that it created a rightness of its own. He recalled the unusual spread of notes, the unorthodox way the musicians played together, the unusual combinations of instruments, with strings and voices added to the mix, all creating a musical landscape that distantly resembled other jazz of the period, but had entirely different color.

This was largely due to Abrams, who had a conventional background accompanying bebop and rhythm-and-blues players, as well as the inventor and saxophonist Eddie Harris, but who had worked out a personal philosophy that encouraged musicians to develop their own individual voices, to have the courage to play the unexpected, and to discard rules about what they should or should not play. The lack of recordings by the Experimental Band makes it difficult to relate descriptions such as Mandel's or Pullen's to any kind of sound documents. The closest we can get is in a piece such as Jarman's *Song for Christopher*, made by a ten-piece group drawn from the Experimental Band, on his album *As If It Were the Seasons*. Delicate flute and bell sounds are superseded by the vast energetic ensemble of the entire group, but from which detailed moments, featuring the flute, trombone, or other individual soloists consistently emerge. It has a totally different sound from pieces like Coleman's *Free Jazz* or Coltrane's *Ascension*; a sound best described as retaining a sense of delicacy even in the midst of cacophony. To try to get closer to understanding this approach, I asked Howard Mandel if, from the perspective of someone who had listened to the Experimental Band itself during the 1960s, he could characterize the differences between its work and the prevalent New York approach to the *avant-garde* at the same time:

> The New York school was all about strong statements, trying to blow things apart, by musicians who were frustrated with the limitations of music. The Chicago school said, "We have heard what you do and we're totally in love with it. We are going to start at the point where you have blown the old conventions apart." They saw a whole universe of sound that was not beholden to the club scene. You did not have to play it the way Coltrane was obliged to play at the Village Vanguard where there was an audience that was drinking, and buying tickets for individual sets. The AACM was mostly not playing in taverns; they were mostly playing concerts. They had no commercial imperative – they didn't seem to care if they were attracting audiences or not. They had a coterie, a core audience that would show up, and which was big enough to bring in some door money. Beyond that they weren't thinking about making records, or making any sort of deal. It was parochial, it was Chicago – they didn't expect it.[10]

Before the actual formation of the AACM, various other small groups sprang up that shared the philosophy of Abrams, but performed independently of the Experimental Band. One of the earliest to be established was the Roscoe Mitchell Quartet, which came together in 1963, with drummer Alvin

Fielder, trumpeter Fred Barry, bassist Malachi Favors Maghoustus, and Mitchell himself on assorted saxophones and percussion.[11] Most of Mitchell's associates were connected with Wilson Junior College, and there was a pool of young musicians there who began to share his open-minded approach to music, many of whom, such as Henry Threadgill and Joseph Jarman, went on to make their own individual mark on the city's music.

Mitchell had, as we know from his remarks quoted earlier about his time in the army, previously played bebop in a Jazz Messengers style band. On leaving the service, he had become fascinated by John Coltrane, and particularly the middle-to-late-period modal playing of pieces like *Out of this World*, from the *Coltrane* album, on Impulse. After meeting and rehearsing with Abrams, he began to combine aspects of Coltrane's bleak sound and modal feeling with a distinctive and individual approach of his own. He was no longer interested in blowing over chord changes the way he had done in his army band. Neither did he necessarily wish to abandon chord changes altogether, like Coleman. He began to explore ideas that nobody in the New York School had done, beginning with very small sounds: tinkling bells, shakers and scrapers, unusual cymbals, and so on. He found he could use the contrast between these quiet, unusual timbres and the full sound of saxophone, trumpet, and drums to convey a combination of ideas and emotions not always present in jazz: irony, lyricism, and sarcasm. The contrasts in his work are summed up by his often quoted maxim that "fifty percent of music is silence."[12]

Furthermore, he did not accommodate his ideas in conventional song-form structures, as Coleman had done in many of his quartet pieces from 1959 to 1962. Mitchell developed a range of options, from multi-part pieces like his *Little Suite*, to extended, single compositions, such as the title track of his first album *Sound*. And, in such works, as Howard Mandel points out, he used the new sounds he had explored as a central element of his conception: "Playing from a microtonal, microsonic level, there are little sounds played with little instruments, and these are not just used as an introduction; they pervade the entire structure of the piece, and can come back at any time, depending on the composer's will."[13]

The title track of *Sound*, recorded by Mitchell in 1965, demonstrates the bell and percussion sounds which were to become hallmarks of his work. Elsewhere on the album his sextet plays his *Little Suite* with Lester Bowie, his newly arrived trumpeter from St. Louis, playing harmonica — or, as it is thought of in Chicago, the "blues harp." The very use of the instrument and its timbre create both associations with the blues tradition and a very different timbral quality from most free jazz of the period. The title of the piece refers to his "little instruments" and not long after the time this recording was made, Mitchell and his quartet were carting round a couple of tons of gongs, bells, chimes, drums, and shakers, not to mention his forest of saxophones, and other woodwinds such as recorders.

In the twenty-first century, Mitchell still adheres to the principle of playing several instruments, and when I discussed this with him, he referred me back to the big bands of the 1920s, to photographs of orchestras like Fletcher Henderson's or King Oliver's Dixie Syncopators, with each reed player sitting behind an array of instruments. In his view, just as was the case for them, each instrument will have a specific role at some point in one of his compositions, and that still applies to his latter-day band, the Note Factory. For his set at the 2000 Chicago Jazz Festival, he was still surrounded by a jungle of saxophones and percussion.

One noteworthy aspect of his percussion is that he does not employ the kinds of conventional instruments that can be bought in a music shop. He told me:

> In a lot of places where you might have just a wing-nut on top of a cymbal, you can go round to the old used stores, and get these old brass candleholders. They have the same thread, and they fit, and this kind of thing allows me to refine my percussion instruments. ... You practically have to crawl into my set of instruments now to get at them. I think that out of Chicago there was a group of musicians that approached percussion from a melodic standpoint of view.[14]

There may have been no original intention among the AACM musicians to document or record their work, let alone to make commercial discs, but things changed when Mitchell's first album, *Sound*, was cut for Delmark – the recording subsidiary of a famous Chicago store called the Jazz Record Mart, run by blues and traditional-jazz enthusiast Bob Koester. Scraping together the money for session after session, by the mid-1960s Koester had single-handedly documented an entire cross-section of the vibrant Chicago blues scene, from Magic Sam and J. B. Hutto to Johnny B. Moore and Junior Wells. And he had a similar mission to record traditional jazz players like Art Hodes, Albert Nicholas, and Barney Bigard. I am not sure he had ever intended to start documenting the AACM, but that is what he ended up doing, thanks to a young man working in his record shop called Chuck Nessa, who talked Koester into letting him produce three sessions by musicians he had heard at AACM concerts on the South Side:

> I had just heard them in concert and said, "Damn!" and although I didn't understand at first what they were doing, I knew that they did. There was just this confidence in the way they went about doing things. This was not crap, this was the real thing. And so it was on the strength of that instinct that I moved forward and had a real crash course. By the time we got into the recording studio, a month or six weeks after I first heard them, I'd been to rehearsals, hung out with the guys, and got a feel for what was going on. In those days it was a big deal, and there were arguments about whether what Coltrane was doing was legitimate or not, and everybody seemed to be afraid of being tricked into buying some bogus music. After Coltrane, was Ayler a faker? And then here comes this, but there was just no doubt in my mind.[15]

In due course, Nessa left the record store and went on to make further recordings of the Mitchell Quartet or, as it soon became, the Roscoe Mitchell Art Ensemble, on his own newly founded label. As it turned out, the first disc he made was with just a trio, as drummer Philip Wilson, who had by this time joined the group, got an offer to go on the road with the Paul Butterfield Blues Band, and left Chicago. Wilson did record some further sessions, under either Lester Bowie's or Mitchell's leadership, and, in due course, this group of musicians, sometimes with Wilson, and at others with Thurman Barker or Robert Crowder on drums, coalesced into a regular line-up, which became pretty much self-sufficient in pursuing its musical aims. On two early trips to the West Coast, armed with copies of its latest LP, the group had no concert schedule arranged, but set about improvising one on arrival. Borrowing a Mill Valley House from blues musician Nick Gravenitis, a friend of Mitchell's, they camped out, played gigs in storefronts and public places, sold some discs and generally proved that they could survive playing their unusual blend of music. On their second trip, just Mitchell, Bowie, and Favors headed west with a camper-van full of instruments and Bowie's motorcycle, but again they improvised their survival.

In 1969, the same three musicians, plus saxophonist Joseph Jarman, traveled to Europe to play in Paris. In the United States this band was still called Roscoe Mitchell's Art Ensemble, but in a press interview shortly after the band arrived in France it was dubbed the "Art Ensemble of Chicago" and the name stuck. By this time, the band had already taken its music not just to the West Coast, but had played most major Eastern cities in North America. The decision to travel to Europe came as a consequence of the wanderlust of their trumpeter Lester Bowie, who even sold his furniture to finance the trip. And in a shared effort to survive, Mitchell stepped down as leader, and the group became a cooperative. Once it got to Paris, the band quickly settled into a period of astonishing productivity, recording fifteen albums and two film soundtracks in the two-and-a-half years its members were in France.

Initially, there were culture-shocks for the band members, from the ferocious Parisian traffic to the sidewalk café culture, but if the members of the Art Ensemble had never seen anything quite like Paris, it was also clear that Paris had never seen anything quite like the Art Ensemble. This is because, even before the band went to France, as well as decking out the stage with several cases full of unusual percussion instruments, its members had adopted face paints, bizarre headgear, and outlandish costumes. Howard Mandel suggested to me some of the reasons for this:

> Joseph Jarman has talked to me about the face paint. This was not war paint as it has sometimes been described, but rather a mask. A mask would give a sense of ritualization to the performance, and put the musicians on a different path, making it clear that they were performing, as opposed to just having come off the sidewalk and gone on stage. So it was a way of preparing themselves for a special state of mind that allowed them to be creative.[16]

In fact the prime mover for the face paint and costumes was bassist Malachi Favors Maghoustus, who had seen an African ballet troupe, and was convinced that he had to add the costumes, masks, and paints to his music. "Since it was in my ancestry, I felt it belonged, so that's why I got the paint and stuff," he told me.[17] At first he took quite a ribbing from the others in the band, but once Jarman had decided to apply paint as well, the band got behind the idea, and added distinctive costumes – from Bowie's white surgeon's coat to African robes for Jarman and Favors, and collective bizarre masks and hats. With a few strokes of paint, an Art Ensemble concert had moved from a musical event to performance art.

Consequently, the Art Ensemble of Chicago now made a considerable visual impression on stage – but in some of its Parisian pieces like *Rock Out*, with Jarman on guitar, Favors on electric bass, and Mitchell and Bowie sharing the percussion duties, the band created a considerable aural impression as well, with a sound that was extraordinarily different from those made by most *avant-garde* jazz groups that stayed with the conventional bebop instrumentation. And, during the stay in Paris, the quartet added to its range by bringing in an additional musician – percussionist Don Moye.

In the early days of the group, as demonstrated on the discs made for Chuck Nessa, Philip Wilson had been a very sympathetic drummer, extracting what Mitchell called "melodic" tones from the drums. After Wilson accepted the offer to go off with Paul Butterfield, the remaining members of the Art Ensemble had directed more of their energies into percussion, and for a time managed without a dedicated percussionist or drummer, although all of them had their respective "little instruments." Before leaving the United States, they had met Moye at concerts in an artists' complex in Detroit, and when they got to Paris, he had already arrived in the city. His vast range of drum styles, absorbing everything from rhythm and blues or soul backbeats to rock-inflected rhythms, plus conventional jazz styles and a range of ethnic approaches to drumming, fitted the diverse musical approach of Mitchell so well that Moye ended up joining the band.

Moye himself found the comparable eclecticism of the Art Ensemble very stimulating:

> What I heard was the broad range of styles that they had. I didn't associate that necessarily with a particular movement; I didn't necessarily associate what they were doing, say, with Trane, but I was attracted to their diversity, the range of styles. We used to have a thing every day called the hot twenty. We'd play different songs, anything you'd hear on the radio, classical music. Then another time at one of their concerts I heard them playing *Tiger Rag* – Lester, Roscoe, and Philip – and the piece evolved from something free into an official, correct ragtime version, and then it went on somewhere else. So I said this is something I could really get into. The music defies labeling.[18]

The degree to which Moye's presence helped the group to broaden its range, to exaggerate the comic and the satirical, as well as the noble and the anguished, was immediately apparent when the band returned to Chicago. In a live album of their first concert after returning, issued, once again, on the Delmark label, the music flows from piece to piece in a continuous set that follows the music from one mood to another, one tempo to another, and one configuration of instruments to another. A piece like the gently humorous *Checkmate*, included in that set, also shows the way in which the band had absorbed parts of the traditional jazz and swing repertoire into its playing, echoing the moment when Moye heard *Tiger Rag*, and it is significant that another Chicagoan, saxophonist Henry Threadgill, was simultaneously experimenting along very similar lines with Scott Joplin ragtime compositions played by his trio Air.

In many concerts, Joseph Jarman and Roscoe Mitchell played, to some extent, straight men to the puckish, humorous trumpet of Lester Bowie. Despite this obvious humor, their irreverent and wide-ranging repertoire, and the starkly free elements elsewhere in their work, the Art Ensemble members had found themselves warmly welcomed by the generation of expatriate African-American bebop players who lived in Paris, and perhaps this explained part of the obvious assimilation of older styles into their sound. When Joseph Jarman looked back at the Paris days, he remembered:

> As soon as we got there we met one of my great heroes, Johnny Griffin, and Kenny Clarke. Kenny sat me down and gave me a music lesson, just telling me some historic things. Yes, we were in the last era of that particular view of things, they gave us everything we needed, everything we wanted, it was extra-ordinary.[19]

Just as Paris had been a Mecca for African-Americans of the bebop era, from Griffin and Clarke to others like Bud Powell and Hal Singer, in 1969–72 it once again acted as a magnet for musicians of the free-jazz era. Many of the players who had participated in a Pan-African music festival in Algiers, in July 1969, traveled on to Paris at the invitation of photographer Jacques Bisceglia and sometime record producer Claude Delcloo, who both worked for the radical arts magazine *Actuel*. A second planned festival, which also involved various rock bands, was planned for Paris in October, but actually took place in Amougie in Belgium after the Parisian Police discouraged the organizers from holding it in the French capital. Between the two events, a great concentration of free-jazz musicians remained in Paris and, at Delcloo's encouragement, recorded for the BYG company, creating a snapshot of this stage in the *avant-garde*. Among them were Archie Shepp,

Jimmy Lyons, Andrew Cyrille, and another coterie of musicians from the AACM.

This second group of Chicagoans who recorded in Paris was the trio of violinist Leroy Jenkins, trumpeter Leo Smith, and saxophonist Anthony Braxton. Needless to say, like the Art Ensemble, they all played copious other instruments as well, but their unusual combination of alto sax, trumpet, and violin was – for me at least – the most fascinating. Braxton was a more than usually brilliant instrumentalist, someone who had a unique sound on alto sax, and a formidable control, which allowed him to master most other reed instruments as well, plus piano. He has told many interviewers that his early inspiration was altoist Paul Desmond and even though there are few direct echoes of Desmond's sound in Braxton's playing, this is an example of a "hidden" influence, where Desmond's tone and speed of thought exerted a subtle and constant pull in the background. A jazz influence may not necessarily be obvious to be important. He told me he had benefited immensely from the AACM's philosophy of trying simultaneously to evolve the music, evolve a better relationship between the musicians and the community, and adopt an intellectual position where each individual could use music to explore his or her own connection with reality. It had been a vital stage in his own musical development, although by the time the trio got to France he was beginning to move on.[20] But the music he produced with Jenkins and Smith in Paris was very varied – just as much so as the Art Ensemble's – and it also used silence and space, which was something I discussed with violinist Leroy Jenkins.

> Actually, that's part of the music itself, space. We all use it. It's part of this style of music that we do. Space is very important, because there's so much rhythm in between space and playing. There's so much you can play with. That's why I do it, although at the other extreme, in my compositions I try to crowd in as much as I possibly can. I do use space a lot when I play, but not so much in my writing.[21]

This creative use of space is particularly apparent on the trio's disc *Silence*, released by Black Lion from the group's Paris period, where Braxton's flute and Jenkins's tentative violin shadow one another on a long, sinuous theme with occasional clarion calls from Leo Smith's trumpet. With no rhythm instruments, except when one of the trio has occasional recourse to percussion, the group was moving away from the explicit statement of time, and exploring a different kind of interaction in which the instruments became timbral forces. This was in marked contrast to the Art Ensemble, which, although playing very freely, used Moye's extraordinary rhythmic control to move in and out of a whole range of time signatures.

Since his first recording with Muhal Richard Abrams in 1967, on *Levels and Degrees of Light*, Braxton has seen recordings as a consistent documentation of his music. It means, as he says, that if future critics speculate on, for example, the way his work relates to *Ascension*, he can demonstrate exactly where it does or does not, and how it changed over time:

> I can talk to you about what happened. I can tell you how I started with it, and how I proceeded with it, like it or not. It's evolved in a consistent way, and I can show how it's related to other things. . . . Whatever the merits or demerits of my work, I was always trying to do something.[22]

And so *Three Compositions of the New Jazz*, his first trio recording with Smith and Jenkins, carries his own remarks with it on what they were trying to achieve with their collective exploration of space and silence: "We're dealing with textures now," he wrote, "individual worlds of textures. We're working towards a feeling of *one* – the complete freedom of individuals in tune with each other, complementing each other."[23]

Even on this first album, Braxton demonstrated an approach that had plenty in common with the 1960s classical *avant-garde* world of composers such as John Cage, or the pioneer minimalist LaMonte Young. For a start, the record sleeve included reproductions of his graphic scores for the pieces it contained – the titles are the diagrams themselves, and the performances are conceived with the aleatory, or chance-based, approach of Cage and his school in mind. There were similar diagrams on his next disc from 1969, the double album *For Alto*, the first such extended record of solo saxophone improvisation in jazz history.

On this, although some aspects of his saxophone technique resemble that of Roscoe Mitchell or of Chicago's other jazz revolutionaries of the period, Braxton's solo work was clearly striking out in a different direction. As *Down Beat* said at the time, the 24-year-old's "solo vocabulary of multiphonics, pointillistic intervals, and scalar lyricism was already in place."[24]

As it turns out, Braxton's theory of self-documentation becomes more complex once the timing of the release of his various discs is taken into account – those that did not appear close to the time of recording perhaps not making their influence felt until his career had moved on several steps. Although *For Alto* was actually recorded in 1969, before he left for France, it did not appear for almost two years, by which time Braxton, having been less rapturously received in Paris than the Art Ensemble, had moved on to New York to play with an Italian free-improvisation group Musica Elettronica Viva, and, subsequently, with Chick Corea in Circle. He continued with his fellow members of Circle – bassist Dave Holland and drummer Barry Altschul – after Corea quit the quartet, adding trumpeter Kenny Wheeler or trombonist George Lewis (another Chicagoan) to the line-up. As the 1970s and 1980s moved on, Braxton worked in a bewildering variety of contexts, from Derek Bailey's Company in London to the Globe Unity Orchestra in Germany, and from his own quartets with pianist Marilyn Crispell to vast orchestral forces for his composed works.

The scope of Braxton's work and the connections in it to the music of American and European experimental composers from the classical domain have troubled some critics, who have looked for obvious connections with jazz, and this is not helped by Braxton's use of the obscure language of academia in discussing much of his output. However, just like the Art Ensemble, there are moments in his work when he has consciously explored the jazz tradition – his thought-provoking *Charlie Parker Project*, from 1993, for example, or the various groups in which he explores jazz standards at the piano – but his overall oeuvre, his numbered and well-documented compositions exploring Ghost Trance Music, aspects of minimalism, of chance (driven by a Wheel of Fortune), of puppetry, of theater, video, and cinema, make it uncategorizable except in its own terms. Braxton's music may not all be about jazz, but his restless, exploratory imagination is, and his improvisatory and instrumental talents are remarkable. His range of interests confounds stereotypes, and he is genuinely stung by accusations that his music is in some way not wholeheartedly African-American, to the extent that he has tried to distance himself from attempts to categorize his work:

> I used to say I was a jazz musician, and all jazz musicians said, "No, you're not." So I thought about it, and said, "Wait a minute, if I say that I'm a classical musician, then I can do whatever I want *including* play jazz! If I say I'm a jazz musician, then I have to play jazz 'correctly.'" All this is part of what the jazz world has become. . . . An attempt to enshrine blackness and jazz exoticism and confine it within one definition-space runs

contrary to the total progression of the music. . . . Remember
now, I'm called the "white Negro." Nobody wants to use those
terms, but I'm supposed to be the embodiment of that which has
not been black, when in fact I never gave one inch of my beliefs
or experiences. What is this notion that you can corral blackness?
That's a marketplace notion.[25]

Perhaps one reason why Braxton's music has exercised critics so much in
terms of its conformity (or lack of it) to African-American stereotypes is to
do with the political origins of the AACM and its connection to
organizations that were advancing the African-American cause in the
1960s. Yet, well-documented and linear as Braxton's development has been,
its strikingly different direction was all part of Muhal Richard Abrams's
concept of diversity within the AACM – something that few of its members
lost as they moved on into new phases of their careers.

But if the distinguishing feature of the Chicago revolutionaries was their
very diversity, how is it possible to assess their collective contribution to
jazz? One thing that has become very clear to me in exploring their music is
that each of the AACM's major soloists was investigating new kinds of
source material to link into the free jazz of the time. For example, if one
takes four very different soloists, and the ideas they fed into their music,
these range from Braxton's investigation of texture, of jazz freed from time,
and notated graphically, to the spiritual inspiration of Kalaparusha Maurice
McIntyre, to the jazz saxophone tradition that inspired Fred Anderson, and
even further back to the formal ragtime of Scott Joplin and its effect on
Henry Threadgill.

In the late 1960s, McIntyre frequently played alongside Braxton in
Chicago, and was described by Braxton as "the most important tenor
saxophonist since Coltrane."[26] Whereas Braxton's music looked outwards
towards European contemporary composition, McIntyre's focused intensely
inwards: on his own inner spirituality, and on very specific aspects of the
local saxophone tradition – both the Chicago blues and the new jazz of his
regular colleagues Roscoe Mitchell and Fred Anderson. McIntyre actually
recorded Chicagoan rhythm and blues with J. B. Hutto and the Hawks, his
raw tenor energy cutting through the sound of the band in his various solos
on the band's *Hawksquad* album. But this is little preparation for the
powerful emotions of his album *Humility in the Light of the Creator*, the high
point of his short career, but a glimpse of the religious passion he could
create in his playing.

I have mentioned Henry Threadgill's exploration of Joplin's music, but he is another example of a musician open to a huge range of influences, and interested – in the best Abrams manner – in finding ways of interpreting them in his own playing. Threadgill began recording with Abrams himself back in the 1960s, but soon made his own mark. In due course, with Air, playing off the bass of Fred Hopkins and drums of Steve McCall, who, like Philip Wilson, was a very "melodic" player, Threadgill put a contemporary spin on pieces like the *Ragtime Dance*, but most of the music they played was his own, much of it laboriously written out, note for note, and thereby, like Braxton, confounding the conventional idea of jazz – particularly free jazz – as being an entirely improvised music.[27]

In some ways his latter-day discs with bands like his Very Very Circus seem to me to be looking back, too, but in this case to the Experimental Band of 1960s Chicago. In much the same way as the original AACM was about community music-making, Threadgill has kept his contacts with his audience alive, but he has not necessarily sought the conventional jazz listener. In 1993, one Very Very Circus tour took in schools, prisons, truck-stops, and coffee houses as well as more traditional venues.[28]

The 35th anniversary of the AACM, in 2000, was an opportunity to reflect on the degree to which it had been successful in the community-based side of its work. The Association was well-represented on the city's Jazz Festival that fall, with many thousands of people turning out for Roscoe Mitchell and the Note Factory – one aspect of his musical life that Mitchell has followed quite independently of the Art Ensemble of Chicago – as well as for a memorial concert to Lester Bowie, who had died in November 1999. There were fringe events involving many other AACM alumni, including Joseph Jarman, but there were also independent community-based celebrations in which younger musicians played, having been encouraged by the kind of mentors that Abrams himself had been in the 1960s.[29] In Joseph Jarman's view, this keeps alive the spirit of the AACM which started in 1960s Chicago:

> In the very beginning, there was an AACM music school, and some of the people that are very well-known now began as little kids in that music school. And it's been passed on. One of my greatest pleasures was . . . at the 35th anniversary festival, fifteen kids between the ages of eight and sixteen came on the stage at the Museum of Contemporary Art. It brought tears to my eyes because I had forgotten that we – many, many years ago – were

taught by volunteers too . . . and that was a very important part of
the philosophy: to be able to pass it on. To encourage younger
people, to give them the energy, strength, and power to have
creative lives.[30]

The AACM's success in passing on its philosophy to younger players is, at
least in part, due to the fact that while some of its founders, like Muhal
Richard Abrams, Anthony Braxton, Henry Threadgill, and Jarman himself,
no longer live in Chicago, there is a constituency of senior figures in the
organization who made it very much their business to remain in the city and
keep what they had started alive. These are musicians like Fred Anderson,
Jodie Christian, Malachi Thompson, and Ari Brown. At the time of the 2000
festival, all of them were playing regularly at Fred Anderson's club, the
Velvet Lounge, which has provided a long-term platform for AACM
members to keep working in their home town, as Ari Brown explained to
me:

> A musician like Fred is of the temperament that asks, "What's
> goin' on?" He's been a steadfast innovator and protector of the
> traditions of the music for a long time. I remember Fred back in
> the sixties, and his energies haven't ceased. The Transitions club
> back then reminds me of Fred Anderson's place today because
> there you could play whatever you wanted. You knew you had a
> receptive audience. If you were a musician who was on the
> cutting edge, or trying to do something creative, it's one of the
> best vehicles for you to do your thing.[31]

Ari Brown's music, some of it built round his ability to play alto and soprano
sax simultaneously, in deliberate emulation of multi-instrumentalist Roland
Kirk, is the kind of material that continued to be played well into the
twenty-first century at Fred Anderson's Velvet Lounge five nights a week.

Another musician who played there regularly with his Africa Brass is
trumpeter Malachi Thompson. He also still leads his original band from the
1960s, Freebop, which is yet another example of AACM diversity in that, as
its name suggests, it took the formal structures of bebop as a starting point
for free improvisation. Thompson left Chicago with the first wave of AACM
departures, but when he returned in the 1990s, after recovering from a
serious illness, he threw all his energies into community music. He has been
composer-in-residence for one of the big South Side arts schemes, and in the

late 1990s wrote the music for a show that involved many young players, singers, and dancers, about the vital life on Chicago's 47th Street which was at the center of the South Side jazz world in the years before the AACM was formed. His work, and that of other contemporary Chicagoans like Ari Brown, Jodie Christian, Kahil El Zabar, and those members of the Art Ensemble, Don Moye and Malachi Favors, who still live in the city, has ensured the continuation of the aims of the AACM, to promote performance, innovation, and dignity for the city's black musicians.

Quite early in the life of the Art Ensemble, its members decided to limit the amount the band toured and recorded – in order to keep separate musical careers going, but also to avoid staleness and repetition in their playing. Another way in which they did this was to enter enthusiastically into projects that linked their music with that of other cultures, an idea that fitted neatly with the AACM's ideas about pluralism which drew in many forms of musical inspiration. This has ranged from the African music of the singers Amabutho, to explorations of Jamaican ska, reggae, and calypso rhythms, recorded on the Art Ensemble's *Coming Home Jamaica* album, which was one of Lester Bowie's last recordings with the band, and a typical example of his impish humor. Chapter 19 considers further the ways in which such world music influences became part of jazz.

Bowie's own musical career, which, like Mitchell, he continued independently of the Art Ensemble, took in a vast stylistic range, again consistent with the AACM philosophy. His Brass Fantasy repertoire encompassed everything from James Brown to the Spice Girls, his organ ensemble used blues and funk as starting points, and his playing with the all-star group, the Leaders, put him in standard post-bop territory. Through all this, he remained a distinctive trumpeter himself, perhaps not widely enough recognized for the degree to which he developed the jazz expressivity of the instrument, notably through his characteristic use of half-valved, vocalized moans and slurs, which punctuated his more orthodox solos.

I have taken the AACM as a paradigm for the growth of a vital new jazz movement from within a local community, but there were several other regional centers in the United States where the same thing happened. Perhaps most significant, in that it had close links with the AACM, but also produced a significant number of high-profile musicians, was the Black Artists' Group – or BAG – in St. Louis.

This was formed a few years after the AACM, in 1968, and saxophonist Oliver Lake, one of its key members, told me that it emerged out of an informal jam-session atmosphere in the city. In the mid-1960s, several of the more experimentally minded musicians used to gather in Forest Park to play outdoors in the summer near the Art Museum there, and in the winter they would play at one another's houses. But the impetus to begin a more formally organized group came from what had been going on in Chicago. Lake recalled:

> I was one of the founder members of the Black Artists' Group along with Julius Hemphill and Floyd LeFlore and some poets and writers. There was a bunch of us got together all the time. Then I made a trip to Chicago to see Lester Bowie, who'd started playing with the AACM, and with what became the Art Ensemble. I went and saw him and listened to what was going on, and went to some meetings of the AACM, headed by Muhal. A lot of those guys became good friends, as I was very impressed with their organization. But back in St. Louis, we weren't formally organized, we just got together on our own in our houses and did things. After I'd been to Chicago and saw how they were presenting themselves, creating an audience for music which was very experimental, I came back and got all my friends together, and said, "Why don't we become a branch of the AACM?" Hemphill said, "Wait a minute. We hang out with a lotta poets and dancers, and they're part of our group, so why don't we form our own organization?" That was really the seed that started BAG.[32]

The multimedia nature of BAG was its most distinctive difference from most other community-based experimental organizations in African-American arts. But in terms of jazz, it developed the early careers of such musicians as Hamiet Bluiett, Joseph Bowie (Lester's brother), Bakaida Carroll, and Bobo Shaw, as well as Lake, Hemphill, and LeFlore. At its height, in 1969–70, BAG had over 50 musicians, dancers, and poets, all under the one roof, doing concerts and other performances, as well as teaching and fundraising. This work across several genres became a distinctive characteristic in the music of many ex-BAG musicians in the years that followed. For example, Oliver Lake created such pieces as his one-man poetry and jazz show *The Matador of 1st and 1st*, his string ensemble *Movements Turns and Switches*, and a vast multimedia piece premiered in Montclair, New Jersey, in 1999, *Broken in Parts*. He also led a reggae band in the 1980s called Jump Up, demonstrating his openness to a totally different genre of music from that in which he had made his original reputation. Julius Hemphill, as well as writing for saxophone ensembles and his big band, produced music for dance troupes. And Hemphill, Lake, and Bluiett, along with the Californian David Murray, became members of the World Saxophone Quartet, a group as innovative in its way as the Art Ensemble of Chicago.

In much the same way as the Art Ensemble and Braxton had traveled to France in 1969, Lake and a contingent of BAG members went there in 1972, after a rift in the organization among various artistic factions in St. Louis (which signaled the end of BAG in its original configuration). But just as it had been for the Art Ensemble, Paris became a unifying experience for the BAG musicians. Lake recalled:

> We'd played just about everywhere in that tri-state area round St. Louis and we were saying to each other, "Let's break out of this circle." Lester Bowie had come back from Paris, and he visited St. Louis and talked about the great reception received by the Art Ensemble. So he said, "Why don't you go check it out?" Paris happened to be the spot where they had stopped, so we thought, "Why not go and base ourselves there as well?" They gave us all their contacts, and we piggybacked on what they had done. We stayed there approximately two years.[33]

The BAG group, which also included Carroll and Joseph Bowie, did not go in for face paints and outlandish costumes, but it did mirror another aspect of the Art Ensemble, as every musician doubled on several instruments.

BAG and the AACM both grew up in cities where there had been a flourishing jazz scene in the 1920s, but a slow decline since. At this point, there was no such large-scale movement in New Orleans – the other city where that had been the case – as the traditional revival, begun in the 1940s, had borne fruit in the 1960s with the launch of Preservation Hall, and there were countless opportunities for musicians to work in the older styles. Pianist Ellis Marsalis, for example, subdued his natural bebop instincts to play Dixieland along Bourbon Street, with "Papa" Albert French, and former bebop experimenters such as trumpeter Thomas Jefferson and drummer Freddie Kohlman reverted to doing impressions of Louis Armstrong in tourist hot spots such as the Maison Bourbon or the Paddock Lounge. Equally, the local rhythm-and-blues movement, headed by Fats Domino and Allen Toussaint, had created another vibrant tradition and an equivalent number of chances to find work. There was, however, a concerted effort to involve younger musicians in playing jazz; there are parallels with the community-based music of Chicago and St. Louis in ventures such as the Fairview Brass Band, on the one hand, founded by Danny Barker to keep the street parade tradition alive (in which the young Wynton Marsalis gained his first marching band experience), and, on the other, in the teaching of clarinetist Alvin Batiste and trumpeter Kidd Jordan, who fostered a more experimental approach. In due course, their innovations, and those of Ellis Marsalis, led to the establishment of the New Orleans Academy of Creative Arts, or NOCA, which has performed a very similar community function to that of the informal AACM school.

But for a direct, politically inspired parallel to the AACM or BAG, one has to look west, to Los Angeles. This is where Ornette Coleman's first quartet had coalesced, and there continued to be a line of free-jazz development from the approach begun by Coleman through the work of such players as trumpeter Bobby Bradford and saxophonist John Carter.

However, a musically quite distinct and more overtly political approach was taken by the Pan-Afrikan Peoples Arkestra of pianist Horace Tapscott. A former big-band trombonist, Tapscott recognized that the African-American community in Los Angeles lacked its own cultural activities. With the end of restrictive housing covenants and the decline of Central Avenue, there was no longer a focal point for the community, and so in 1961 he set out to create one, in a remarkably similar manner to Muhal Richard Abrams. He told Steven Isoardi:

> Music gets people's attention and brings people together. It's a focal point. I felt that having an arkestra that had a message to give, playing original music, dances and poetry, would give us an opportunity to open up all the areas in our culture that had been stopped. ... We wanted to preserve the black arts in the community. We wanted an aggregation that put all this music – this music that came from the blues, and from the churches, but even then from the same source, from the same scales – into one place.[34]

Tapscott sought out players who were individuals, not part of the studio community, but who shared his sense of musical exploration. In due course, he formed the Underground Musicians' Association, the UGMA, and this became a far more overtly political organization than either BAG or the AACM, discussing racial and other issues in an open manner. In terms of its musical development, after playing in one another's houses, the Arkestra moved, as BAG had done, outdoors, and appeared regularly in South Park on 51st Street and Avalon Boulevard. In 1963, it took on a house, and this acted as a focal group for the teaching and drama activities as well as music. From the mid-1960s, several musicians who later moved to become associated with the East Coast free-jazz movement passed through the ranks of the Arkestra, including Arthur Blythe, Azar Lawrence, David Murray, and the brothers Butch and Wilber Morris.

The UGMA also focused its attention on the Watts area, particularly in the period from 1963 to 1964, when the district began to attract increasing numbers of artists, writers, and poets. In 1965, the band was playing on 103rd Street at the very time the shooting incident that triggered the infamous riots took place in Will Rogers Park. Tapscott and the members of the band remained at the center of the community during the insurrection, but out of anger came the same kind of unifying attitude that Jarman noted in Chicago. As Tapscott later wrote: "We settled down a lot of people into thinking again, instead of destroying, by playing, talking, by just being there."[35]

The resulting music grew out of what the writer Stanley Crouch called "the layover of fervor that had come into the black community following the Watts riot of 1965, when the August sky filled with smoke and flame and it really seemed that race war would spread through the whole state."[36] In the aftermath, funding was forthcoming for many of the activities that had begun in Watts before the riots, which helped to build them up again afterwards, creating an atmosphere memorably described by Crouch as "those years of dashikis and black leather jackets, of afros as large as woolly igloos, of a romanticized Africa, of revolutionary hot talk, and of interest in Eastern religions."[37] Tapscott deliberately focused his efforts on the community, recording mainly for his own Nimbus record label, and writing prolifically for local events and performances. However, a small number of his pieces were recorded by Bob Thiele for wider distribution, and show an approach quite distinct from that of the Art Ensemble or BAG. A piece such as *The Giant Is Awakened* is built around a repeated set of piano chordal figures, with Arthur Blythe's wailing saxophone superimposing a plaintive roar above it. There is a dense rhythmic background, created by two bassists and the complex drumming of Everett Brown Jr. The piece demonstrates the degree to which Tapscott's music is very much ensemble-based, with the role of the individual or soloist subsumed into the overall group sound, something very much in keeping with his political and community ideals.

The work of this community of *avant-garde* musicians was to have a profound effect on the new jazz of the 1980s and 1990s through the move east by Murray, Butch Morris, and Blythe. In Murray's collaboration with the World Saxophone Quartet he forged a link between West Coast experimentalism and the music of BAG; and in Morris's theories of "conduction," developing ideas of directing free-jazz performances by gesture, originally tried out by Ornette Coleman's drummer Charles Moffett, despite the paradox of a "free" ensemble being "directed," his ensembles spread to include traditional Japanese instruments, turntables, and other exotica, mirroring the Chicagoans' fascination with unusual instruments and tone colors.

The politicization of jazz in the United States had its counterparts elsewhere in the world. South African jazz is discussed in the next chapter, but perhaps the most telling parallel to the music so far discussed here is the Eastern European scene. In much the same way as African-American musicians used music as an organizing social force, representing a powerful collective reaction to the conditions in Chicago and Los Angeles, to oppression, to the police brutality of Watts, and to racism in general, musicians in the Eastern Bloc saw jazz as a unifying metaphor for those oppressed by the political system there. German pianist Joachim Kuhn told me:

> I remember the moment I first heard Ornette Coleman's music. Somebody in a bar told me his name, saying that this was the new man who plays without chord changes. I was very much interested, very much attracted, because at that time East Germany, where I lived, was not a free country. But this kind of expression – free expression – that is what jazz really meant.[38]

It was because it dispensed with convention that free jazz became such a vital symbol of freedom in Eastern Europe. Jazz without rules, but which acted as a uniting force, became a metaphor for life, but it was also a passport out of the East to play and perform. It was possible to play this subversive music, but, simultaneously, to be celebrated for doing so by the very authorities at whom it cocked a snook.

Perhaps the best illustration of this comes in the career of the Polish trumpeter Tomas Stanko, who played music that was at first inspired by bootleg recordings of Chet Baker and Miles Davis, smuggled into Poland, or heard illicitly on Voice of America broadcasts. With other players, such as saxophonist (later violinist) Zbigniew Siefert and the composer Krzysztof Komeda, Stanko played music that combined great lyricism and beauty both with elements of the abstract expressionism of his country's visual arts and with others drawn from free jazz, although like Ornette Coleman he seldom lost contact with an underlying jazz beat or sense of time. His music took him out of Poland, and at a time when travel was difficult he appeared in Czechoslovakia, Yugoslavia, and Scandinavia. Subsequently, Stanko has developed a truly international career, but his emergence onto the international stage in the 1960s was a remarkable parallel to the way that American musicians turned the political and social events of the decade to their musical advantage.

CHAPTER 19

# Jazz as World Music

"World music" to me has at least two meanings. First of all
the regular meaning – a music composed of ethnic elements
from various parts of the world. But on the other hand,
American pop music is the real world music. It's
everywhere in the world and everybody listens to it whether
they like it or not. . . . There is no pure musical mind
anymore which has known one source and stayed with that.
Jan Garbarek, from *Jan Garbarek: Deep Song*, by Michael Tucker

So far I have consistently advanced the argument that jazz itself is a kind of
world music: a syncretic mixture of African and European influences that
came together in the United States, and then spread back outwards to the
rest of the world. In one sense, because jazz was so much of a universal form
of popular music in the middle of the twentieth century, it fits Jan
Garbarek's definition of world music being "American pop music,"
becoming omnipresent during the swing era, and spread by recordings and
broadcasts, although it did not hold on to that position of universal
dominance in the second half of the century. In Chapter 5 it was seen how
jazz moved around the world in the years prior to World War II, and since
the end of the war, jazz has been a much more fully international music. Not
only have American musicians extended their influence to all parts of the
world, but there has also been just as significant a set of influences flowing in
the other direction, with the traditional musics of Europe, Africa, Asia, and
South America being absorbed into both North American jazz, and the jazz
of many other countries as well.

The last few chapters have examined the careers of some of the

American musicians who settled in Europe for various lengths of time, from the bebop generation of Kenny Clarke and Bud Powell, to the early free-jazz players like Cecil Taylor and Albert Ayler; and their successors, such as the Art Ensemble of Chicago. All these musicians interacted with the local population, playing, recording, and spreading ideas. Yet this is not a new phenomenon in jazz. Many of the Creole players who were pioneers of the music in the early twentieth century drew on a very wide range of musical influences. For example, in the late 1930s, Sidney Bechet and Zutty Singleton collaborated with trumpeter Kenneth Roane and pianist Willie "The Lion" Smith in recording a set of *meringués* – dances from the Dominican Republic. Many dances from the Caribbean – and particularly the French Antilles – were included in Bechet's repertoire during his period in France in the 1950s. Thus, Bechet was a musician who both absorbed other musics into his own, and then, in his sojourn in Europe, communicated these ideas on to a new generation in a new country. Half a century later, French bands such as Les Haricots Rouges still include Caribbean Creole and Antillean dances in their repertoire.

Musicians like Bechet and Singleton were well aware of the New Orleans Creole heritage. The French language was still spoken on the streets as they grew up, and plenty of people had family links to the earlier period when the city was governed by the Spanish. Jelly Roll Morton, for example, recorded illustrations of what he called the "Spanish tinge" in such pieces from his Library of Congress recordings as *La Poloma*.

This was a piece where he said that, by bringing in a little jazz feeling, he could "change the color from red to blue."[1] And Morton's metaphor might just as well be applied to other early jazz where African-American interpretations of music from other regions turned from red to blue by mixing in the soulful sounds of jazz and the blues. For example, in 1930 Duke Ellington recorded a piece based on a Samoan dance called *Maori*. It was little more than a novelty dance, but, nevertheless, it showed a jazz orchestra actively incorporating unusual source material into its work. Ellington also occasionally incorporated unusual instruments, and certainly on a piece such as *Accordion Joe*, made in 1930 with soloist Joe Cornell, there was a definite traditional-music feel to the arrangement, rather than the sense that Cornell was simply transferring jazz-piano ideas to the free-reed instrument.

In the 1930s, the use of traditional instruments in jazz was, however, something of a novelty. It took the determined efforts of a number of jazz musicians in the 1960s and 1970s to start exploring the instrumental resources of world music more fully and incorporating them into jazz. One of the first pioneers among Americans was Yusef Lateef, who, as well as playing a robust style of tenor sax, recorded on oboe, argol, and shehnai. Then, after his work in Ornette Coleman's quartet, Don Cherry, in particular, became a pivotal figure in using non-Western instruments in jazz. Another was the Brazilian percussionist Nana Vasconcelos. To accompany his singing into an echo-and-delay unit, he uses one of the world's oldest instruments, the berimbau, a kind of musical bow with a wire string stretched on a stick with a gourd resonator; the string is hit with another stick. By the 1980s, in Cherry's various bands, or in the trio Codona, with Cherry and Collin Walcott, Vasconcelos was using a huge collection of traditional percussion instruments, including pots, gourds, shakers, rattles, and various types of drum. When I asked him where he acquired them he said, "Most of them I make myself. If I ask somebody to make them with the particular sound that I want, then they don't really know how. But I can work to get the sound I want. My inspiration is a mixture of sounds from nature, and of the simple instruments used by children."[2]

In Don Cherry's band, Nu, Vasconcelos had to blend his panoply of Brazilian percussion instruments into the sound of Ed Blackwell's drum set. This question of the integration of two different approaches to percussion is at the heart of the incorporation not just of the timbres of ethnic instruments into jazz, but also of the authentic rhythmic use to which they are put. Chapter 8 mentioned Ray Brown's apprehension about the Afro-Cuban drumming of Chano Pozo with Dizzy Gillespie, back in the 1940s, but in the wake of Pozo and Gillespie's innovations, jazz rhythm sections began to be more open to different rhythmic input. George Shearing, for example, incorporated *clave* rhythms into his quintet repertoire, and Stan Getz worked with Jobim and Gilberto on bringing the bossa nova into bebop. I asked conga drummer Don Alias, one musician who has brought Latin drumming into several jazz contexts, whether the integration of ethnic rhythms was now an easier matter than it had been for Chano Pozo. He feels it is down to the openness and sensitivity of the jazz drummer for it to work out successfully:

> A drummer would see you coming through the door of a club with the conga drum and cower at the very idea of you sitting in. But I had a tactic to help me get "in" with any band's regular drummer. I'd wait to hear whether they were familiar with what you might call the language of drums before I even tried to sit in. If they were – we'd get along fine.[3]

Perhaps the most high-profile integration of folk and traditional music with jazz has come from Latin America and the Caribbean. Brazil has been a particularly fertile area for this, not just with the bossa novas of Jobim and Getz, but also with the more revolutionary sounds of Airto Moreira and the singer Flora Purim, notably in their collaborations with Miles Davis and their own band Fourth World. Most influential of all in the last twenty years of the twentieth century has been the multi-instrumentalist and composer Hermeto Pascoal, who also recorded with Davis, but who has subsequently taken his own group of musicians on several world tours, demonstrating a closeness and unity of purpose that has been achieved by communal living and the intense study of music. His long, loping melodic lines, his unique sense of orchestral color, and his vital sense of humor have made him a hugely influential figure, particularly on those young European musicians who have joined in his big-band tours in Britain and on the continent.

In the wake of Chano Pozo, Cuban music has also been similarly important in terms of its cross-fertilization with jazz, and the links between Cuban musicians and their American counterparts were maintained by the efforts of Dizzy Gillespie, among others, during the long political stand-off between the countries since the 1960s. Gillespie introduced several Cubans, including the trumpeter Arturo Sandoval, to international audiences, and his lead has subsequently been followed by other players such as trumpeter Roy Hargrove, whose *Crisol* project of the mid-1990s involved other members of the significant Cuban band Irakere, to which Sandoval formerly belonged, along with the influential pianist Chucho Valdés.

Along with musicians like Nana Vasconcelos, Don Alias, and Airto Moreira, who brought an array of Latin American percussion instruments into jazz, musicians from the Indian subcontinent such as Trilok Gurtu have integrated traditional instruments with the conventional drum kit, although Gurtu sets up his kit quite unlike a Western drummer, squatting behind his drums on a slightly raised dais, with the instruments ranged around him in a semi-circle. Having worked to achieve a big, full, snare-drum sound, he tried to obtain a much deeper than normal tone from his bass drum, bringing ideas about traditional tuning to the Western kit, and taking similar care over the tone of the cymbals which he would be integrating with his other instruments, ancient and modern. Among his Indian percussion, he uses unorthodox, larger-than-normal tablas to counterbalance the power of the Western kit.

Indian percussion – and other traditional instruments – have become consistent ingredients in many jazz groups from different parts of the globe, so it is fitting that any survey of world traditions and jazz begins with the music of India.

# India

You do not have to be Indian to play Indian music and to do it very well.

John Mayer, from the notes to *Ragatal* by Indo-Jazz Fusions

One of the first bands to investigate the cross-currents between Indian music and jazz was Indo-Jazz Fusions, a double quartet set up in Britain in the 1960s by the Indian violinist John Mayer and altoist Joe Harriott, just a year or two before the Beatles began their association with Ravi Shankar. It also included members of Harriott's free-jazz group, notably trumpeter Kenny Wheeler, bassist Coleridge Goode, and pianist Pat Smythe, who played alongside Indian musicians Diwan Motihar on sitar, Viram Jasani on tamboura, and Keshav Sathe on tabla.

To some extent, the earliest examples of the band's work were call-and-response: the Indian musicians would play something built around a traditional scale, and the Western musicians would answer with an improvised section built on some of the same scalar patterns or melodic fragments, but gradually Mayer managed to effect a more complete integration. When I was working with him on annotating a recent album by his latest edition of the band, he explained the fundamentally different structure of Indian music, but one which, in many ways, first became fully accessible to jazz in the 1960s, the decade when moves became widespread by jazz musicians to subsume into their playing concepts of modal improvisation and of different types of rhythmic sophistication:

Indian music is basically built around a linear technique. There's no harmony in a Western sense, just one extended melodic line accompanied by a drone. The absence of harmony is compensated for by very complex rhythms. As I found out more about Western music, I realized there are similarities with the techniques of serialism. In serialism, you are dealing with an atonal sequence, and in ragas, the Indian scale system, you are dealing with a tonal sequence, but one which goes up one way and down another, what's called the *aroha-avaroha*.[4]

834

In jazz terms, the end result of some of Mayer's music is to create something of a synthesis between the organum-like approach of Ornette Coleman's classical compositions, and the modal basis of Coltrane's improvisations. Several pieces in the Indo-Jazz Fusions repertoire are created through the stratification of voices, layering one on top of another, but only ever using the notes of the raga to achieve this. It has the effect of providing a harmonic structure, but only using the notes of the ragas themselves. Other pieces were newly composed by Mayer, and adopted ideas from ragas, or, in one or two cases, superimposed two different ragas on one another. But the improviser has to think harder than usual when the raga is unusually constructed. One of Mayer's compositions, *Chhota Mitha*, is an example, as Mayer explained:

> It is based on a raga [the raga sohini], but an unusual one that doesn't include the fifth note of the scale — what in Western music we'd call the dominant. This sets quite a different challenge for the improvising player, because they have to work within an unfamiliar scale, and even the underlying drones are different, changing the character of the sound.[5]

Indian scales are just one element of Indian music that has cross-fertilized with jazz. In Mayer's original band the use of Indian instruments was relatively unusual, although his sitar player, Diwan Motihar, also recorded with jazz pianist and composer Irene Schweitzer, in Europe. However, with the revival of interest in the instrument through the work of the Beatles and Ravi Shankar, the sitar eventually became one of the most evocative sounds of the late 1960s.

The original Indo-Jazz Fusions broke up in 1973, following the premature death of Joe Harriott, and Mayer did not re-form the band until the 1990s, but shortly before the end of the first incarnation of the ensemble, a group came together in the United States that took up where Mayer left off in exploring Indian rhythms and instruments. The band was Oregon, and one of its most charismatic members was the multi-instrumentalist Collin Walcott. He developed a command of several Indian instruments, including sitar, tabla, and traditional percussion, and worked with the iconoclastic American clarinetist Tony Scott in some of his earliest attempts to fuse jazz and Eastern music, as well as playing sitar for Miles Davis's 1972 album *On the Corner*.

Oregon was a band of multi-instrumentalists, but its most characteristic sounds were the saxophone playing of Paul McCandless, the acoustic guitar of Ralph Towner, and the bass instruments of Glen Moore, blended with Walcott's percussion and sitar. Walcott was killed in a car crash in Germany in 1984, while he was on tour with Don Cherry and native North American saxophonist Jim Pepper; his successor in Oregon was the Indian percussionist Trilok Gurtu. Gurtu's combination of Western and Indian instruments into his drum kit has already been discussed; he combines his mastery of percussion with a form of unorthodox singing that uses the very rapid syllables of the South Indian Karnatic tradition. It is a consonant-heavy, highly rhythmic sound – something which Gurtu would frequently turn into a dialog with guitarist John McLaughlin in his 1980s groups, and has continued to use in his own latter-day bands such as the Crazy Saints. Despite coming from a long-established tradition, it also sounds completely contemporary. As Gurtu says: "If a rapper hears this, he won't know it's coming from India."[6]

Trilok Gurtu studied tabla with Ahmed Jan Thirakwa, and he also learned a lot about Indian music from his mother, the singer Shobha Gurtu. Both he and his mother recorded with Don Cherry, of whom he said: "With Cherry I never played anything in AABA song form. I'm Indian, so why play American music? What statement would that be making?"[7] After this, Gurtu went on to record with many of the pioneering names who brought world music and jazz together, including McLaughlin, Norwegian saxophonist Jan Garbarek, and Nana Vasconcelos. His own bands have had various degrees of jazz involvement, but his most high-profile jazz-orientated group was his mid-1990s Crazy Saints, with saxophonist Bill Evans, violinist Mark Feldman, and the French keyboard player Andy Emler. He has also had the experience of seeing his 1980s efforts at fusing jazz and Indian music form the basis of new music in the twenty-first century, as young British Asian musicians have sampled his work; and in the music of the Asian Dub Foundation, Talvin Singh, and Nitin Sawnhey, many of the insistent percussion sounds were originally his.

John McLaughlin, of course, had a long history by the time he recorded with Gurtu of exploring the connections between Indian music and jazz. In the 1970s he founded Shakti, with tabla player Zakir Hussain, and their partnership has been periodically revived, allowing McLaughlin to explore a more contemplative, acoustic kind of jazz than the high-energy fusion discussed in the next chapter.

## Africa

> There was no space for *anybody* to do *anything* in South
> Africa. We [had] to come over . . . we were tired of it. I was
> working with Chris McGregor and Chris McGregor's a
> white cat. We were not supposed to play together; we were
> not supposed to be on the same bandstand with Chris; we
> were not supposed to play for white people. . . . I was
> supposed to play places where my *mother* wouldn't be
> allowed to come in and hear me play. And they wouldn't
> only refuse her to come to my concerts, they would also
> beat her up maybe.
>
> Louis Moholo, interviewed by Richard Scott in *The Wire*, no. 85,
> March 1991

In some respects, the big band known as Chris McGregor's Brotherhood of
Breath, which was in action from the late 1960s, was parallel to Indo-Jazz
Fusions. It was made up of South African musicians like McGregor himself,
Mongezi Feza, Dudu Pukwana, Harry Miller, and Louis Moholo, and British
players such as Malcolm Griffiths, Nick Evans, Mike Osborne, John Surman,
and Alan Skidmore; it brought together the joyous sounds of South Africa
with some of the best post-bop players in Britain. But whereas Indo-Jazz
Fusions was born out of experiment, the Brotherhood of Breath came about
as a consequence of the political regime in South Africa, and was one of a
number of bands in which that country's most talented musicians worked in
exile as a consequence of the dread hand of apartheid. The anger and
resentment created by the regime fueled a particularly rich vein of music,
and in the time-honored way in which music became a creative channel for
those who wished to protest – much as was happening in Chicago, St. Louis,
and Los Angeles – the 1960s was the decade when Africa once again made a
direct impact on jazz.

Because of the way that so much African music was syncretized into jazz,
the image of the continent has always been a significant one in the United
States. Early American jazz musicians frequently tried to create impressions
of Africa in their music, and well-known examples include several from
Ellington's "jungle" period, and Bechet's compositions such as *Jungle Drums*
from 1938, or the exotic landscape of his *Egyptian Fantasy* from 1941. But in
the most comprehensive survey of pieces that develop the African metaphor
in title or content, Norman C. Weinstein has shown that it was a far more

deep-rooted and more persistent theme than has often been supposed, ranging from early rags, such as Eubie Blake's 1899 *Sounds of Africa* (which became *Charleston Rag*), to a considerable number of 1920s jazz numbers, by both African-American and white bands.[8]

In the 1940s and 1950s, numerous American musicians looked to Africa for inspiration, but it was John Coltrane, in 1961, who made one of the most profound statements about what Africa stood for among jazz musicians in the United States. His visionary piece *Africa* produced some of his most exalted playing, and was a powerful influence over other musicians of the time. However, his work leading up to this piece has again been examined by Norman C. Weinstein, who sees a growing interest in the saxophonist's use of African ornamentation from 1957 to 1959, leading to the programmatic evocation of the continent in several works of the *Africa* period, which he sees being consolidated in what he calls Coltrane's "African Spiritual Music" of his final years.[9]

Most importantly, Coltrane had been influential in creating a climate of Afro-centrism among American jazz musicians that was in place when the diaspora of South African musicians began in the early 1960s. It may seem extraordinary, but the first-ever complete band of black South African musicians to make a record had only done so less than two years earlier than Coltrane's *Africa*.

That band was the Jazz Epistles: Abdullah Ibrahim on piano, Jonas Gwangwa on trombone, Kippie Moeketsie on alto, Johnny Gertze on bass, and Makaya Ntshoko on drums, plus trumpeter Hugh Masekela, who told me:

> We were only able to do one album. Not very many were pressed and it soon sold out. Then Sharpeville happened, and gatherings of more than ten people were declared illegal. We had to break up the band. We were only three months old as a band, and we were just about to undertake our first national tour. All the shows were sold out, but it never happened. It was a great disappointment for us.[10]

Pieces like *Dollar's Moods* and *Carol's Drive* from that early album, which was only re-released for the first time as a CD as recently as 1999, reveal a band that mingled many aspects of hard bop with the clear thematic ideas that both Abdullah Ibrahim (then known as Dollar Brand) and Hugh Masekela were to develop in their subsequent international careers. Underlying it all was the infectious beat of Gertze and Ntshoko. However, the real inspiration behind the band, according to Masekela, was its saxophonist:

> Kippie Moeketsie was our mentor, our teacher. We were very lucky, Jonas and I, in particular, because he took us under his wing – I guess in the same way that Charlie Parker did for Miles. We learned an awful lot from him, and he was a hell of an activist. One of the most important things he taught us as musicians was to be truthful, that in music you'd better stick to what you believe. . . . He showed us how to absorb tradition and pass it on, not just in our music at the time, but to the next generation. He was into classical music, too, he played all the classical clarinet concertos, he was open to all kinds of music, but above all he passed on the values of the traditional South African life. There's no opportunity to get that now except by passing it on through the generations – whatever you get, treat it with respect, and then pass it on.[11]

This tradition of mentoring, of passing on musical and social values from one generation to the next, was a major aspect of the new jazz of the 1960s. It was vital to the musical traditions of India – both John Mayer and Trilok Gurtu stressed how important it had been for them – and it had direct parallels in the thinking of Muhal Richard Abrams, Oliver Lake, Julius Hemphill, and Horace Tapscott.

Masekela left South Africa in 1961, and moved to the United States, where he made a considerable reputation over the next ten years or so, playing his blend of bop and South African township music. Of the other Epistles, the most high-profile was Abdullah Ibrahim, who moved to Zurich in 1962, where his trio accompanied his wife, the singer Sathima Bea Benjamin. There they were heard and recorded by Duke Ellington on a European visit in 1963, and Ellington was instrumental in getting Ibrahim booked for the Newport Festival and recognized as an international talent. He toured with numerous American musicians at this point, including Don Cherry, who again showed his enthusiasm and interest in the fusion of non-American forms of music with jazz.

At the time of his playing with the Jazz Epistles, Ibrahim showed obvious affinities with Thelonious Monk in his playing, and he was also fascinated by the music of Ellington. He returned briefly to South Africa in 1976, the year of the Soweto riots, and after that time there was growing evidence of

African content in his compositions and his approach to playing. As a composer, he favors simple, repetitive, hymn-like melodies, and tends to set up a gentle ostinato or a sequence of hymnal chords to produce a slow build-up during a performance. In his ensembles, such as his small jazz group Ekaya, he tends to dictate his themes to his musicians, as Mingus or Tapscott did, and he described his method of building elaborate numbers out of the very simplest material, and the different directions in which this can develop, as follows:

> Within the music, you inject a formula for a specific purpose, having in mind a specific effect. So, depending on what, how and who is involved, you use specific formulas. In some instances you have what seems a very basic formula, and, in another situation, you will use what seems to be very eloquent language, but it's the same information. [12]

In contrast to Masekela and Ibrahim, who moved from South Africa to the United States, a number of musicians came to Britain, partly because of its former Commonwealth connections with the country, but partly also because of the growing interest in free jazz and new music there. As drummer Louis Moholo, who came to London with Chris McGregor, said:

> I was away from South Africa and away from the chains. I just wanted to be free, totally free, even in music. Free to shake away all the slavery . . . being boxed into places – one, two, three, four – and being told you must come in after four. I was just a rebel, completely a rebel. And of course there were people like Evan Parker, whom I saw also as a rebel. From then on I just played free, I met John Tchicai, Steve Lacy, Peter Brötzmann. Me and John Stevens were actually the first drummers to play free music in Britain. [13]

The band with whom Moholo came to London in 1964, via France and Switzerland, was McGregor's Blue Notes. It was a sextet that included several outstanding players, from the radical altoist and composer Dudu Pukwana to the lyrical trumpeter Mongezi Feza, plus the powerful bassist Johnny Dyani. The band was an extraordinarily tight-knit group, although that did not preclude it playing very freely, and most of its members went on to join McGregor's Anglo-South African big band, the Brotherhood of

Breath, mentioned earlier. McGregor himself was the only white member of the group, but he had defied the rules of apartheid to continue playing with the other musicians in South Africa, and he was a compositional and organizing force in the band after its move to Europe. Lack of funding and the growing individual careers of its members led McGregor to move to France in 1974, where he was based until his death in 1990. Like almost all the Blue Notes, except Moholo, he died young, but his "wild bunch who could take you to the heights," as Valerie Wilmer called the Brotherhood,[14] made a huge impact on European jazz and British jazz in particular. In addition to the first generation of British players mentioned earlier, who worked with the Brotherhood of Breath, McGregor acted as a mentor for several younger instrumentalists, notably the trombonist Annie Whitehead, who has continued to reinterpret South African themes and rhythms in her work.

Back in South Africa, during the period of apartheid, jazz continued to be played within the black community. One musician who stayed there, and has since encouraged a new generation of musicians, is Pops Mahomed.

> You know, in those days when apartheid was beginning, the music was very restricted, and we didn't get to hear much music from abroad except for what was on the pop charts. I think one of my main influences was Cliff Richard and the Shadows. On the other hand we had bands coming out to us from Johannesburg. I lived east of there, and we had Abdullah Ibrahim, the Manhattan Brothers, Maria Makeba that used to come. And when they played in my social center in my town, they used to play in a style that still had links back to Glenn Miller, Count Basie, and the big bands. Also, pennywhistle music had a big influence on the start of township jazz, because when they started listening to musicians like Benny Carter and Charlie Parker, local players would started to practice those styles on pennywhistle. The instrument was so soft, they would practice on that, and then eventually transfer their ideas to saxophone to start imitating the Americans. Because of the influence of the pennywhistle, the sound they produced was a bit different, and that was one of the main ingredients of Kwela music or township jazz. On the other hand, we had shibeens in the townships, which were strictly illegal at the time, and we had people coming in from Zimbabwe, and they used traditional instruments, and in the shibeens they would link up with the jazz

musicians coming out from Johannesburg, which was like the New York of South Africa. It was a privilege for local musicians to be jamming with these people. So the fusion of these sounds was a very beautiful thing that happened in the shibeens, and the sad thing is it was never recorded, because it never happened in the recording studios at the time.[15]

In the years since the end of apartheid, Pops Mahomed and members of the band Barungwa recreated some of the sounds of one of those shibeens on disc. But during the years that the policy was in force, black African musicians were banned from playing for white audiences, and if the police found white listeners in a black club, it would lose its license. So the only way that township jazz came to be heard by the rest of the world until the 1990s was through musicians who went into exile, such as Abdullah Ibrahim, or the District Six (in London).

In the 1990s, there seemed to be a sudden explosion of this music onto the world stage as many musicians who had hitherto not been heard outside South Africa were recorded for the first time. Since then, the forces of modernism and commercialism have swept through the country, and the music that was so firm a rallying point for the black community during the years of oppression is no longer a natural direction for young musicians to take. But, as a player who specializes on traditional instruments, from didgeridoos to lammellaphones, and integrating them with jazz, I wondered how Pops Mahomed saw the future for the fusion of jazz and South African music.

> I could slowly see traditional hardcore music dying from the face of this earth. It's very limited on radio stations in South Africa, because they're now employing young DJs who are into hip-hop and trance, and drum 'n' bass. They don't feel it's appropriate to be playing our music, because it's not cool. So, because of that, we had a problem of educating our DJs about their cultural roots. I have been workshopping with some of the DJs to try and make them identify who they are, and realize how important the township music was for their survival. But you can't blame them, because since the end of apartheid, you have this great influence of the West coming in through TV, and radio stations just blasting away rap and hip-hop, and the audience believing this is the latest thing and it's cool.[16]

Through the work of Pops Mahomed and Darius Brubeck (the son of Dave), who has run the jazz department at the University of Natal in Durban as a multiracial workshop for many years, the South African jazz that burgeoned during the apartheid era has continued to develop, and players who kept the music alive, such as bassist Victor Ntoni, drummer Lulu Gontsana, and saxophonist Barney Rachabane, have brought their sounds to an international public. Perhaps the brightest hope was the brilliant young pianist Moses Molelekwa, until he was tragically found hanged in 2001 at the age of 27. He had mapped out a way forward for jazz in his country, mingling his strikingly original playing and compositions with the new urban form of *kwaito* music. When the record producer Robert Trunz first heard the piano playing of Molelekwa in 1993, cutting through a fourteen-piece big band at Johannesburg's Market Precinct, he described it as "a waterfall tumbling over a high ledge and covering the ground below with a carpet of bubbles."[17] His individual touch, lyrical phrasing, and incorporation of traditional rhythms gave him a highly distinctive style, and made him the musical heir to Abdullah Ibrahim. Molelekwa was also a catalyst in producing discs by other young musicians.

His career is a good example of how musicians growing up during the apartheid era were drawn to jazz as a unifying force in a troubled community. He was raised in Thembisa, and his parents introduced him to jazz records by Monk and Coltrane, before encouraging him to attend weekend classes at the Federated Union of Black Arts Academy in nearby Johannesburg, where he later became a prizewinning, full-time student. In his late teens he was already playing with his country's finest musicians, including Miriam Makeba, Thembi Mtshali, and Jonas Gwangwa. When trumpeter Hugh Masekela returned from the United States to South Africa, in 1988, he invited Molelekwa to join his international touring band, the first of many overseas trips which later included work with Julian Bahula and Dorothy Masuka.

Molelekwa's own groups, Brotherhood and Umbongo, won first prizes in the early 1990s in the Music of Africa Competition, an event sponsored by a gin-distilling company to promote the best talent to emerge during the years of oppression. A couple of award-winning albums launched Molelekwa's international career, and at the time of his death he was working on another album of his own music as well as producing material by several *kwaito* bands.

His death has left a huge void in his country's young jazz scene, but Hugh Masekela, the man who kick-started Molelekwa's career, intends to put his belief about passing ideas on to the next generation into practice, and since returning to South Africa has continued to seek out new talent, which he is able to bring to wider attention through the international reputation he gained during the apartheid era. His old colleague, Abdullah Ibrahim, takes a similar view, and continues to tour and record with a vibrant mixture of American and South African players.

## Europe and Russia

> I haven't got any special grounding in folk music. I play the old melodies in a quite untypical way. The purists may have their doubts, but it was absolutely necessary for me to play the music in my own way . . . to play the music in the traditional way, I would have had to practise for ever, without necessarily managing it.
>
> Jan Garbarek, from *Jan Garbarek: Deep Song*, by Michael Tucker

There are two main ways that European folk music has been brought into jazz: the first is where traditional melodies have been arranged and absorbed into jazz; the second is where traditional and jazz musicians play alongside one another, and, just like the Indo-Jazz project, it was in the 1960s that this type of experiment took off. The scholar Joachim Ernst Berendt commissioned a set of pieces from pianist George Grunz that brought a Swiss pipe-and-drum band onto the same stage as his jazz group. In numbers like *Change of Air*, recorded in Basel in 1967, Grunz, bassist Jimmy Woode, and drummer Daniel Humair played alongside the pipe-and-drum bands of Alfred Sacher and George Matthys, combining traditional Alpine music with jazz.

And a more recent example of this kind of fusion also came from the Alps during the 1990s, this time over the border in Austria, with the Alpine Aspects band, led by Viennese saxophonist Wolfgang Pushnig, which combined a group of improvising jazz musicians with the brass band Amstetter Musikanten. In pieces such as his *Root March*, Pushnig bases the melodic content of his own solos on the traditional themes played by the brass.

The way that jazz musicians have absorbed such European folk themes into their work, as a source of melodic inspiration, has been particularly important in Scandinavia. In the opinion of Norwegian singer Karin Krog, this had a lot to do with a particular American saxophonist: "Well, I think we have to go back to the 1950s, when Stan Getz visited Sweden and recorded a tune called *Ack Varmeland du Skona*, which is a Swedish folk tune from Varmeland, and it became quite internationally renowned."[18]

Getz's tune became world famous as *Dear Old Stockholm*, and was subsequently widely recorded by musicians all over the world, but perhaps most influentially by Miles Davis, apart from Getz's own version. Getz lived in Sweden for a period, and the musicians with whom he worked followed his example and absorbed folk melodies into their work. The distinctive, simple, melodic character of such tunes, and their minor, slightly bluesy feel, made them natural tools for players such as Nils Lindberg and Arne Domnerus. During the 1960s and 1970s, Norwegian musicians also picked up on using folk music, and both bassist Arild Andersen and saxophonist Jan Garbarek used Norwegian traditional music as the basis for improvisation, as did larger ensembles such as the Brazz Brothers.

Garbarek's range is far wider, of course, and he has experimented with playing alongside musicians from many parts of the world, bringing the distinctive, slightly bleak tone he developed during his early period with George Russell's bands to a variety of collaborations. But, to some extent, this kind of magpie selection – a little from the Middle East, something else from Norway, and his inclusion of early vocal music by the Hilliard Ensemble on his album *Officium* – can seem superficial, rather like Paul Simon's attempts to bring world influences into several of his projects, beginning with his *Graceland* album. At his best, and most distinctive, and working with predominantly European source material, Garbarek has proved that it is possible to create convincing jazz with scant reference to the African-American tradition. Most of his work appears on the ECM record label, run from Munich by Manfred Eicher, which has specialized in distributing music by jazz musicians from outside the United States, together with that of a number of open-minded Americans, such as Keith Jarrett, Chick Corea, and Gary Burton.

In Denmark the presence of several long-term resident American musicians has produced a very thorough exploration of local folk sources. Just as Stan Getz's presence in Sweden inspired many local musicians to look again at their own store of melodies in the 1950s, so the expatriate American pianist Kenny Drew was a similar catalyst a decade later in Denmark. In 1966 he recorded as a duo with bassist Niels-Henning Ørsted Pedersen, exploring such numbers as the old Danish song *Det var en lørdag aften* ("Once a Saturday Night").

More recently, the singer Karin Krog, and British saxophonist John Surman, have turned their attention to Nordic folk melody, and – also as a duo – arranged several folk songs collected by the ethnomusicologist Anders Heyerdahl. Thanks to collectors like him, and others like L. M. Lindeman and O. M. Sandvik – who cataloged volumes of Hardanger fiddle music, and the dances of the Gudbrandsal, Østerdal, and Røros regions – there's a vast amount of similar material available, a lot of which lends itself to jazz treatment. So in a strange kind of parallel, at the same time that folk-song collectors such as Henry F. Gilbert were transcribing the songs of African-Americans, a comparable group of folklorists were doing the same in Europe, ultimately providing source material that would be interpreted by the musical heirs of both traditions.

In the former Soviet Union, rather a different set of conditions prevailed. From the end of World War II, the society was a closed one, and many of the cumbersome formal structures imposed by the state, and discussed in Chapter 5, remained in place right up until the end of the 1980s. However, particularly in the field of piano playing, there was a strong connection between the world of the classical academic conservatory and that of jazz, with musicians trained to an extraordinary level as classical pianists applying their talents to jazz.

One of the first jazz pianists to make an impression on the music world there was the Moldavian-born Leonid Chizhik, who graduated from the Gorky M. I. Glinka State Conservatory in 1970. He is generally credited as being the first Russian pianist to give recitals of improvised music in the Soviet Union, at a time when the state, as a matter of course, frowned upon such potentially dissident activity, despite allowing occasional U.S. State Department-sponsored visitors, like Benny Goodman or Dave Brubeck, to perform for what was clearly a sizeable – if generally somewhat covert – audience. Also, a number of European jazz bands were invited to perform at Soviet summer festivals, keeping another supply of jazz ideas coming into the country. However, although Chizhik's playing, from stride piano through to freer forms, was well-known within the U.S.S.R., and quite widely recorded in the 1970s and 1980s, virtually none of his work has been available in the West.

That is not the case with his contemporary, Sergei Kuryokhin, who died, aged 42, in 1996. He believed passionately that the suppression by the state of improvised music and jazz should act as a major source of inspiration, and his series of multimedia "Pop Mechanics" projects, documented in the West by Leo Feighin's label, Leo Records, were an extraordinary mix of parody, satire, and protest. As a solo pianist, he had acquired an in-depth knowledge of the Russian performance tradition, and he put this to good use by frequent allusions to it in creating his own individual style of jazz improvisation. As a way of understanding his methods, a piece such as *Blue Rondo à la Russ* (a tribute to Dave Brubeck), on his 1991 disc *Some Combination of Fingers and Passion*, shows how he could assimilate familiar material from a well-known jazz influence into a new composition.

One musician with whom Kuryokhin worked, the saxophonist Vladimir Chekasin, is the link between such assimilative compositions and the complete masters of the art of musical collage in Russian jazz – the Ganelin Trio, led by pianist Vyacheslav Ganelin, until his self-imposed exile to Israel broke up the group in 1987. Ganelin's trio (of which the third member was drummer Vladimir Tarasov) produced extraordinary music, full of wide-open spaces, simple, edgy rhythms, and free-form improvisation of a wildness not often found in American or Western European playing. A starting point in approaching the Ganelin Trio's work is their interpretation of the familiar, such as the spacious and extraordinary version of Kurt Weill's *Mack the Knife*, found on their album *Con Affetto*, recorded in Moscow in 1983.

This features a tinkling, repetitive cymbal beat, and phrases from Chekasin's saxophone that occasionally recall Charlie Parker, before setting off on an abstract version of the theme, using multiphonics and a range of other devices. Underpinning it all is Ganelin's piano, with plenteous allusions to several different pages in the story of classical and jazz pianism. Having heard the group's interpretations of such material it becomes easier to fathom what is going on in their celebrated, but initially daunting, set pieces such as the extended *Ancora Da Capo*, many of them recorded at the 1980 Berlin Jazz Tage.

Ganelin's training was somewhat different from the other musicians' mentioned so far, as he attended the conservatory in Vilnius, in Lithuania. In the early 1970s, he began playing free jazz wherever possible, and for the most part this meant festivals. The trio appeared, for example, for several consecutive years, at the Autumn Rhythms Festival in Leningrad, a curious event at which no foreign musicians were allowed to play. The group's appearances there led, in due course, to events outside the U.S.S.R., and while these remained few and far between, Ganelin's trio was the first major exponent of contemporary Soviet jazz to be heard in the West.

Following this, the group's records gradually appeared in the West, and its members played at various non-Soviet venues, eventually making their way to the 1986 JVC Festival in New York. In those pre-*perestroika* years, another link between East and West was being forged by the Anglo-Russian pianist Vladimir Miller, who subsequently went on to form the Moscow Composers' Orchestra, which has collected together numerous instrumentalists from those who saw jazz as a unifying medium for artistic action and aesthetic protest during the Cold War. For a major London Concert in 1996, performing a piece called *Let Peresky Dream*, Miller managed to include the Ganelin Trio's former drummer Vladimir Tarasov among his musicians.

During the Soviet era, there was another course open to those who wanted to play jazz, which was to institutionalize the subversive or dissident aspect of the music, rather than identify with it. One of the most high-profile musicians to take this approach was the pianist Igor Bril. A decade or so older than Ganelin and Kuryokhin, he moved through a series of official appointments, starting with the All-Russian Society for Guest Performances in the 1960s, and moving on to the Experimental Studio for Improvised Music, eventually, in 1984, becoming head of the light music department of the Gnessins State Musical and Pedagogical Institute in Moscow. Although Bril has recorded consistently, and composed a substantial body of work, little of it has successfully made the journey to the West.

His contemporary, Nikolai Levinovsky, has had rather wider exposure in the West, at least through the medium of live performance, as he made numerous tours of Europe and the Indian subcontinent with his band Allegro, playing largely original music, much of which has been recorded for the Russian Melodya label, but which is not easily available outside Russia.

That classical conservatory tradition is apparent in the playing of Olga Konkova, a younger Russian pianist who was one of the first students from her country to gain a place at Boston's Berklee School of Music in the early 1990s. There is a quality in her attack, her touch, and her phrasing that immediately indicates that she tackles the keyboard quite differently from the majority of her American or European counterparts. Konkova attended the Russian Academy of Music in Moscow, but her specialist education began a lot earlier:

> In Russia, if you want to be a musician, you start when you're five or six. And then you have to go through music school – the minimum is usually about eight years, and then there's an audition to your music college. There'll be four years more study there, and then there's another audition to your conservatory or university, where the degree course is another four years. To start

with, I focused on the classical repertoire — Bach, Mozart, Beethoven and Chopin — but of course that's how it is for everybody. We have a very strong performance tradition, going back to Anton Rubinstein and beyond, and my teacher was always talking in terms of old masters when she was teaching me how to play. We were trying to learn how Rachmaninov or Prokofiev approached their own music, because they were fantastic piano players; Shostakovich, too, who was my own favourite.[19]

Konkova's interest in jazz began when she heard a bootleg tape of Miles Davis; a fuzzy, fifth- or sixth-generation copy of his playing from the 1960s, but she found it utterly fascinating. She had been studying composition, and discovering jazz gave her an opportunity to combine her studies in composition and performance to create music in which these things were going on together. This highly technical and compositional approach to her playing has developed over the years, and on her 1999 album *From Her Point of View*, Konkova comprehensively reworks Gershwin's *Summertime* into a bravura solo piece, reharmonizing sections of it and giving it a very pianistic treatment, as she does with another standard, *On Green Dolphin Street*. Now settled in the West, Konkova demonstrates the integration into jazz of a tradition very different from the folk musics adopted by some of her other European counterparts.

849

# CHAPTER 20

# Jazz Fusions

## Origins of Jazz-Rock

> What we failed to recognize was that the whole point of
> rock "n" roll depended on its lack of subtlety.
>
> George Melly, in *Revolt into Style*

In looking at the long-term work of politically and socially motivated
organizations such as the AACM, or of the cultural cross-currents between
jazz and world music, I have already discussed areas of jazz to the very end of
the twentieth century. Previous histories, where they have surveyed these
areas at all, have tended to do so as a kind of sideshow to the dominance,
during the 1970s and 1980s, of jazz-rock. So all-pervasive was this genre in
the 1980s that many commentators prophesied an end to acoustic jazz, and
the death of styles that related to bebop, hard bop, and mainstream jazz, in
which there was any clear-cut connection with jazz's past.

In the 1990s this balance changed. Many of the musicians who had been
deeply involved with jazz-rock returned to an acoustic setting, or, in some
instances, appeared for the first time without the trappings of a rock rhythm
section. In parallel with the growth of a conscious conservatism that sought
to rediscover and re-evaluate the jazz tradition, many other players took the
acoustic jazz of the late 1960s as a jumping-off point, and took their music
on in new directions, in which rock was often an ingredient, but not the sole
*modus operandi*. Musicians like Andrew Hill, who had been at the forefront of
experiment in the 1960s, but who had been largely overlooked for the two
decades that jazz-rock was at its height, re-emerged with major-label record
contracts and new ideas for the millennium.

Jazz-rock has not, of course, gone away, any more than has its immensely popular, anodyne derivative, "smooth jazz," but it can now be seen as a phenomenon that grew in the late 1960s, peaked in the 1970s and 1980s, and was superseded, on the one hand, by the resurgence of acoustic-based styles, plus a return to many of the concepts of the post-bop jazz rhythm section, and, on the other, by a new postmodern form of experiment in which rock, along with many other genres of music, from Klezmer to hip-hop, became just one source for mining ideas and samples.

When jazz-rock began, it was an attempt to escape the conventions of the jazz rhythm section, but by taking a different route from that of free jazz, which had focused on coloristic percussion and absence of meter. It went in the opposite direction, abandoning the loose interaction of jazz rhythm playing for the taut, tightly controlled, on-the-beat sounds of rock. The presence (or absence) of a clearly discernible beat in jazz had been an issue since the late 1940s, with the *Down Beat* debate, referred to earlier, between Charlie Parker and Dizzy Gillespie. With the onset of free jazz, the disappearance of melody, and the erosion of beat, not to mention its political affiliations with movements that drew attention to the deficiencies of the "Land of the Free," a large proportion of the record-buying, dance-going public in the United States turned their backs on jazz. The same was true in Europe, and with the upswing of rock in the mid-1960s, plus the international popularity of groups such as the Beatles, the process was accelerated. By the same token, many of those involved with jazz in the early 1960s turned their backs on rock. The British jazz singer and critic George Melly wrote: "To us in the jazz world it seemed a meaningless simplification of the blues with all the poetry removed, and the emphasis on white, and by definition, inferior, performers."[1]

At the same time a new generation of instruments arrived, driven by the explosion of interest in rock, and these were seized on by jazz musicians, eager to explore their potential for new sounds. In addition to the Hammond organ, there were new keyboards, ranging from the first widely available electric pianos to various synthesizers. The bass guitar could be used to create more incisive rhythmic patterns than the double bass, and to compete with a rhythm section involving electric guitar, electric bass, and amplified keyboards, front lines were not only amplified, but began to use effects units as well.

The first moves towards jazz-rock began not in the United States but in Britain, in the same musical melting-pot of rhythm and blues, traditional jazz, skiffle, and bebop, from which the "British invasion" rock groups of the

1960s emerged. The pivotal figure was the guitarist, singer, and sometime radio compere Alexis Korner, who founded his band Blues Incorporated in 1962, with singer Cyril Davies. Several future rock stars flitted through his personnel, or were regular sitters-in with the band, including vocalist Mick Jagger, bassist Jack Bruce, and drummers Charlie Watts and Ginger Baker. But the key innovation in Korner's band was that over a straightforward rhythm-and-blues beat, with simple harmonies, he added a hard-bop saxophone section, usually of Dick Heckstall-Smith and Art Themen, but sometimes with multi-instrumentalist Graham Bond on alto as well.

Although other significant British modern jazz musicians, including bassist Spike Heatley and drummer Phil Seamen, sometimes worked in the line-up, its rhythm section, by and large, adhered to the simple, raw energy of rhythm and blues, keeping the accompanying harmonies uncomplicated, and leaving the saxophonists to add a layer of modern-jazz sophistication. As the writer Mark C. Gridley points out, "the rhythmic properties of Coltrane's lines were found far more compatible with rock accompaniment than were bop lines,"[2] and this is exactly the effect that Korner achieved in 1962–3.

Soon afterwards, Graham Bond formed his own band, which became known as the Graham Bond Organization, which briefly included guitarist John McLaughlin as well as Jack Bruce and Ginger Baker. To those who heard the band live, this group often featured long jazz improvisations in a framework that veered closer towards out-and-out rock music. This was the direction in which Bruce and Baker moved, after Bruce had played alongside guitarist Eric Clapton in another band that fused Chicago urban blues with a hard-bop sax section, John Mayall's Bluesbreakers. In June 1966, Baker, Bruce, and Clapton formed Cream. Jack Bruce recalled:

> Eric . . . had this reputation, and having played with him a couple of times I knew he was good. But it was more Ginger's idea, this band Cream. He asked Eric to form a band, but Eric said, "Jack's going to be the singer in it." The first gig was the Twisted Wheel, Manchester, and then we played the Windsor Jazz Festival. People immediately caught on to what we were doing. We already had a very large fan base, and people expected much more than we could deliver at the time, because we had no material. I was trying to write some originals, but the rest of what we did was standard blues.[3]

It is significant that their earliest appearances were in a jazz context, and certainly in 1966 Bruce and Baker still thought of themselves as jazz musicians.[4] Also, despite the fact that Cream was marketed as a rock band, and worked mainly in the United States, reviewers still connected the band's growing tendency to play long instrumental solos with jazz. According to Bruce, this sort of extended soloing was not part of the act to start with, but came in gradually as the band toured America.

> The long solos came later when we played at the Fillmore, and everybody was so laid back and stoned they said, "Keep playing!" so we just started improvising. And that became our albatross. . . . They were extremely ecstatic moments, when each of us would just take off on long things, sometimes entirely on our own. It wasn't like jamming – it was transcendental music. The one or two things recorded don't come near the really good nights. We were really two bands, because when we did the album *Wheels of Fire*, we made one LP in the studio and the second live. In the studio we had four tracks or even eight tracks, and we could overdub ourselves, but on stage there were just the three of us, so we decided just to play really loud, and get away with it.[5]

As well as playing loudly, Cream was demonstrating that jazz had numerous ideas that it could bring to rock – from Baker's polyrhythmic drumming to Bruce's highly inventive bass playing, which mixed the conventional repetitive patterns of rock with passages of melodic improvisation. Labels became hard to apply to the band's work, and it is clear, in retrospect, that while it was to be a formative influence on the whole hard-rock movement, Cream was also to have an immense impact on jazz – notably on bands such as Tony Williams's Lifetime, in which Bruce pitted his bass lines against a master jazz drummer no less inventive than Baker. All three members of Cream have tended to dodge the issue of trying to classify what they did in the band's brief life before it broke up in October 1968, Bruce himself saying wryly: "I think you could easily argue that Cream was a jazz band with Eric being Ornette Coleman without knowing it. . . . I was writing the songs, so I was trying to apply free-jazz rules to pop songs, with some success."[6]

These "rules" involved the repetition of riffs – of which his *Sunshine of Your Love* is perhaps the best-known – that then opened up into a simple vamp for long-drawn-out improvisations. By and large, Cream did not cycle its way through 32-measure songs, but adopted different structures that involved the simple "hook" of a catchy rock theme being combined with the opportunity for open solos. This was to be a central idea in jazz-rock – albeit one, as Bruce says, that came from jazz in the first place.

Before long, other British bands were experimenting in similar territory, and in the summer of 1968, drummer Jon Hiseman formed what most people regard as the first out-and-out British jazz-rock band: Colosseum. Hiseman points out that in 1960s Britain, musicians found it quite difficult to make a full-time living playing jazz, which is why several players such as Heckstall-Smith, Themen, and Alan Skidmore had turned to improvising on blues sequences in the bands of Graham Bond and John Mayall, which were ultimately far more commercially successful than most jazz groups.

In contrast to those blues-based concerns, in Colosseum Hiseman set out, *ab initio*, to play jazz, using far more complex chord sequences, but within the context of a recognizable rock rhythm that audiences would find familiar from Bond and Mayall's music. He recalled:

> The blues wasn't interesting to me, and I wanted to take it much further than that. After two and a half years we recorded Mike Gibbs's *Tanglewood 63*, which is a reworking of a big-band jazz arrangement for five instrumentalists and three voices.[7]

Gibbs, from what was then Rhodesia, was soon to become an influential figure in American jazz-rock, through his work at the Berklee School of Music in Boston, and his collaborations there with vibes player Gary Burton, which included *Throb*, cut by Burton's quartet in the United States.

In Britain, another jazz-rock group, formed in 1969, that was to gain a worldwide reputation with tours to the United States and, for a time, a recording contract with Capitol, was Ian Carr's Nucleus, which consisted mainly of players who had been playing in free-jazz or post-bebop styles. Carr himself came from the North East of England, and started off as a bebop trumpeter in an influential band called the EmCee Five, but had also worked occasionally with rhythm-and-blues singer Eric Burdon and the Animals. Then, for much of the 1960s he had co-led one of Britain's most innovative jazz small groups with saxophonist Don Rendell. His new colleagues – oboist/keyboard player Karl Jenkins and drummer John Marshall – had played with the experimental composer Graham Collier. Carr saw the migration to jazz-rock as a definite move by the musicians themselves towards a more formal type of structure:

We'd all been playing free jazz in the 1960s. For a long time it was quite interesting, but then we really needed to have the disciplines of sequences and tonality. And the most interesting way to do it was, if you have a slow pulse, you can subdivide the pulse and get all kinds of different time signatures within it. . . . One thing we did soon after forming the group was to get our own P.A. system and to get an electric piano, so that we could always control the sounds that we made, and we could always rely on the piano being in tune. But once you get those sounds and equipment you start using them for different effects. Through them, I found new ways of making the music breathe. And with free jazz, composition had been relegated to the sidelines. But when jazz-rock came in, composition was brought back on an equal basis with improvisation.[8]

Carr demonstrated this in his own extended compositions for the album *Solar Plexus*, which was a commission from the English Arts Council for an augmented line-up, in which rock bass lines and repeated motifs combined with some exceptional free-jazz solo playing from Carr's fellow trumpeters Kenny Wheeler and Harry Beckett. Nucleus was extremely creative in a short period, producing its first three albums within the space of 1970 alone. These early attempts were not heard in America at the time, but were only released in Britain. Furthermore, the band's first disc *Elastic Rock* was made before the British release of *In a Silent Way*, the seminal American jazz-rock album by Miles Davis.

Davis's move into the territory in which he would make the running for almost another two decades came at the end of the period in which Britain set the pace for the development of jazz-rock. Although bands such as Soft Machine (which was an intriguing fusion of free jazz, minimalism, and rock, and which went through numerous incarnations of personnel, in which each of these three different influences had the upper hand by turns) became internationally popular, the main momentum of the 1970s was to come from the United States. That is not to say, however, that British musicians did not make an impact on jazz-rock in America. Three English players, who became part of the circle of Miles Davis, each represented one of the three areas I have just listed: bassist Dave Holland emerged from the London free-jazz scene; guitarist John McLaughlin from a mixed background of free jazz and rock-inflected rhythm-and-blues bands; and cellist/arranger Paul Buckmaster, who came from London's experimental classical scene, going on to work with Davis on his album *On the Corner*, before following a subsequent career in rock, in which he played with the Third Ear Band and arranged for Elton John.

## Miles Davis and Jazz-Rock

> All of a sudden jazz became passé, something dead you
> put under a glass in the museum and study. All of a sudden
> rock 'n' roll was in the forefront of the media.
>
> Miles Davis, in *Miles: The Autobiography*

In the period after *Kind of Blue*, Miles Davis's band underwent some major changes. By September 1964 he had assembled a new quintet that was beginning to explore yet more uncharted territory with his customary panache. The rhythm section of pianist Herbie Hancock, bassist Ron Carter, and drummer Tony Williams began to tackle time in a different way from any of his earlier bands, and, in particular, the young and flamboyant Williams would often enter into musical dialog with Davis's trumpet, breaking down the traditional concept of the rhythm section. In Wayne Shorter, Davis not only had a passionate, technically advanced tenorist who took the band in a different direction from Coltrane, but he also had a composer of skill and ability, who had already proved his credentials as Art Blakey's music director in the Jazz Messengers.

To start with, the band was playing a high proportion of standards in its repertoire, although changing many of them almost beyond recognition. In nearly eight hours of music recorded by the quintet at Chicago's Plugged Nickel Club in 1965, there is an opportunity to study how this particular group changed its approach to what was essentially the same set-list from one house to the next over a couple of nights. It is always a mistake in the study of jazz to assume that a particular recording of a piece by a band is typical of the way the piece was always approached. This set of discs is the proof of that. On pieces such as *My Funny Valentine* and *Stella By Starlight*, Davis produces radically different readings at each performance, as he and Shorter deconstruct the melody, substituting some melodic passages of their own, but also fragmenting the composer's melodic line completely. Carter was still providing them with a basis of time and harmony, but Williams overlaid this with constantly shifting, dense textures. These are particularly apparent on two contrasting takes of *Agitation*, on one of which Davis plays a shimmering succession of runs that dart all over his horn, in parallel with the rapidly changing drum rhythms. Elsewhere, Hancock often lays out behind solos, leaving just bass and drums to open up the texture under Davis or Shorter.

In the more measured conditions of the studio, discs such as *E.S.P.* or *Miles Smiles* show the processes the band used in more clarity, as if under a microscope, and the group's use of a simple five-note passage as the basis of *Footprints*, on the latter album, shows how loose its approach had become, compared to the similarly constructed *So What?*, from *Kind of Blue*. I asked Dave Holland to assess this quintet which he was to join at the end of the decade:

> I would say that Tony Williams was the focal point for the band's rhythmic development. If you discuss this with Herbie, he speaks of Tony as being a very important influence on him, as to how he approached rhythm – it really changed his approach to how to use the piano rhythmically. When you look at that band . . . the key thing is the synthesis of all those people: Wayne's compositions that gave them a vehicle to do the things that they did, Ron Carter's approach to rhythm and harmony that reworked a lot of the songs from a bass point of view, Herbie's approach to comping, and his search for alternatives to the traditional way of using the piano, and of course Miles's way of bringing these together and making them cohesive. The sum of the elements became much more than the individual parts. . . . It's something that influenced generations of players, including myself, and I waited in London for each record to come out, to put it on the turntable and figure out what the heck was happening.[9]

In four years, the quintet mutated from a band that was playing in an acoustic manner, that could be identified with Davis's earlier groups with Coltrane, to something quite different. It passed through a phase in which apparently quite free sections alternated with conventional head arrangements, or in which there were constant shifts of time and pace, such as Hancock's *Madness*, from June 1967. It also played pieces that adapted Ornette Coleman's technique of playing in time, using a regular meter, but abandoning chord changes, leaving Hancock and Carter free to suggest harmonies for the soloists – an effect which came to be known as "time, no changes."

In 1968, although retaining the same players, Davis began radically to alter the sound of the band, and eventually arrived at an approach which had begun to include some elements of jazz-rock. This is exemplified in pieces such as *Stuff*, recorded almost a year later than *Madness*, with Hancock on electric piano, Carter on electric bass, and Williams creating dramatic variations on a rock-influenced beat. This piece has plenty in common with the early sound of Ian Carr's Nucleus, particularly in the way Davis and Shorter phrase the long, riff-based theme together over almost six minutes of accompaniment from the rhythm section, before the trumpeter launches into a solo. By this point in the 1960s, Davis had already perceived that the use of a rock beat would hold the attention of his public, however abstract some of the solos played over such a background became.

In the period after the break-up of this quintet, during which Chick Corea replaced Hancock, Holland replaced Carter, Jack DeJohnette replaced Williams, and, for some recordings, keyboard player Joe Zawinul and guitarist John McLaughlin were added, Davis's music entered a fluid phase. Holland recalled that this was a time when Davis was, at one level, experimenting with chromaticism as a basis for improvisation, and at another, continuing to explore aspects of rock.

There were many elements of rock on the 1969 albums *In a Silent Way* and *Bitches Brew*, but equally, a piece such as *Sanctuary* **[CD 2, track 5]**, from the latter, has a fluid, floating beginning, before a firm jazz-rock pulse is set up, eventually reverting to the fluid accompaniment at the end. Davis's melodic, haunting solo on this track was easily accessible to his earlier listeners, but some of the material his band played in the period from 1969 to 1972 was simply puzzling to his audience. His long sequence of material recorded at the Fillmore East in New York, over four nights in 1970, created fluid, occasionally cacophonous, albums in which Keith Jarrett and Chick Corea were both playing keyboards, and Airto Moreira and Jack DeJohnette were playing percussion, and the results were extremely uneven, "seesaw-ing," as his biographer Ian Carr puts it, "between the abstract and the concrete."[10] But Davis was evolving a new way of working, analogous to the rock industry itself, where large amounts of material were recorded and then edited on tape into albums that could be issued. With producer Teo Macero, he worked to construct albums out of isolated recordings of grooves and vibes that felt right, by melding them into contiguous pieces.

Ironically, Holland and Corea left because they felt the group was not going far enough in the "free" direction, and they moved on to form Circle, with Anthony Braxton and Barry Altschul (discussed in Chapter 18). Jarrett, Zawinul, and the new intake of musicians, including rock bassist Michael Henderson, gave the Davis band more of a rock focus; this was added to by the presence of John McLaughlin for the track *Right Off*, from the 1970 *Jack Johnson* album, which he described as "just a boogie,"[11] but which showed the possibilities for Davis to play as a soloist over a solid rock-cum-rhythm-and-blues basis. Henderson had worked with soul musicians such as Aretha Franklin and Stevie Wonder, and, unlike Holland, who was constantly experimenting with the role of the bass (as Jack Bruce had been doing in Cream), Henderson was prepared to lay down repetitive bass patterns, just as any rock or soul musician would.

A major influence on Davis at this point was the rock guitarist Jimi Hendrix, with whom he had shared the bill at the 1970 Isle of Wight Festival, and who was experimenting with long-drawn-out improvisations similar to those of Cream, but with the added use of electronic distortion and other effects. Hendrix's powerful riff-based ensemble playing and his inventive, lengthy solos attracted not only Davis, but also Gil Evans (who continued to arrange Hendrix material for his big band well into the 1980s), and there were plans to record together, which were stalled by Hendrix's accidental death in September 1970.

Nevertheless, in the British guitarist John McLaughlin, Davis had found a soloist who combined Hendrix's raw power and aggression with a formidable jazz technique, and a background that encompassed rhythm and blues and free jazz. (McLaughlin's 1969 album *Extrapolation*, recorded in Britain with saxophonist John Surman and drummer Tony Oxley, is a masterpiece of European free jazz of the period.) McLaughlin was not a member of Davis's regular touring band, but he worked on several of the albums recorded from 1969 onwards, some of his most powerful and astringent playing being heard on the 1970 disc *Live-Evil*, where he joined the band as a guest on some live dates.

Gradually, Davis was moving towards a wider concept of fusion, in which not just jazz-rock and free influences would coalesce in his work, but also an altogether broader range of music, from sitar drones to various types of world-music percussion, was featured. With the 1972 album *On the Corner*, he worked with Buckmaster, who had demonstrated some of his tape-based pieces to Davis, and wrote the basis of several of the numbers on the disc. However, in the studio Davis and his musicians altered the ideas, as Buckmaster says: "they played them more or less accurately to begin with and transformed them in the Stockhausen sense – making them more unrecognizable until they became something else."[12]

Davis was arriving at the approach that would be the basis of his work over the last stage of his life. Although there would be long periods of absence through ill health, the principles of *On the Corner*, in which he, the other horns, and chordal instruments soloed and interacted over a rock-based "sound stream" accompaniment, were to become a constant. He also began to play his trumpet through an effects unit, which allowed him to create wa-wa effects as he played. This went hand-in-glove with a change in the trumpeter's orientation towards his audience. He had hitherto sold large quantities of discs – from his collaborations with Gil Evans to *Kind of Blue* – to an enthusiastic white record-buying public. He had not targeted the African-American audience, but he now pronounced that he aimed to be "accepted by black audiences on the same terms as the Temptations."[13]

His concept of the "soundstream" meant that his accompaniment became a *melange* of different tempi, rhythms, and sounds, and he directed this on stage, not always playing a lot himself, and mapping out ideas at the keyboard. In the studio, the process was more mysterious. Davis, and his producer, Teo Macero, would construct the issued albums from a range of material, often resulting from spontaneously convened gatherings that Davis called to record an idea or sound that intrigued him at the time. Only a musician with his sales potential could corral musicians and engineering teams together on such an *ad hoc* basis, but as saxophonist David Liebman recalls:

> You didn't go into the studio with the idea that a definite record would come out of this or that session . . . there was usually no warning. The road manager would call and give the time to report. Most often the next day in the morning. . . . Seemingly the red light (for recording) was always on at a Miles session and there were no run throughs, sound checks, or announcements of takes. Often with Miles beginning something at the organ, things would slowly begin with the band kind of falling together, waiting for him to point at you for a solo.[14]

A track such as *Rated X*, from September 1972, shows precisely this process in operation, with Davis's organ setting out a few harmonic pointers for passages of rhythm playing of varying intensity. From time to time, Davis would emerge over the soundstream to play some of his familiar open-toned trumpet, or in his new wa-wa style. But for those who had idolized his trumpeting, and who had felt rewarded by the sheer amount he had played with the Shorter Hancock Carter Williams group of the 1960s, the new band was not always rewarding in concert. A London appearance in 1973, at the Rainbow, predominantly a rock venue, drew mixed reviews:

> Miles has grasped with his usual unerring judgement how to succeed with the wider audience he now aims at. The emphasis is on visuals, and Miles himself, wearing beautiful clothes and looking wonderful for a man of forty-seven, is visuals epitomized. He's managed to whip up his line-up of saxophone, guitarist, bassist (and an electric sitar player inaudible on the night), drummer and conga player into an exciting swirling rhythmic unit, as recognizable as a Miles Davis "sound" as were the quintets with Coltrane and Shorter. . . . The amazing and heart-breaking crunch lies in the fact that Miles himself hardly plays at all; he just spits a strangled "beep" into the action every couple of minutes and we're left with an efficient backdrop with nothing to back up.[15]

Davis was absent from the stage, largely through illness, from 1975 until 1980, and when he returned, there was a more conscious "pop" feel to his work. In 1980–1, with saxophonist Bill Evans (no relation to the pianist), guitarist Mike Stern, bassist Marcus Miller, and drummer Al Foster, Davis began finding ways of rectifying the kinds of criticism leveled at him in the review above, and, gradually, many of the earlier aspects of his trumpet playing were reintegrated with his rock backdrop. There was the occasional ballad or standard, and – as his lip and stamina returned – shades of his former lengthy soloing. Albums such as *The Man With the Horn* and *We Want Miles* showed him finding the definitive style of his final decade. For the most part, his line-ups drew on new up-and-coming players who were making their names on the New York scene, or who, like guitarist John Scofield, who succeeded Stern, had come through jazz education at institutions such as Berklee. Scofield, with John McLaughlin briefly back in the band, was featured prominently on Davis's final Columbia album from 1985, *You're Under Arrest*, in which Davis's links with the pop world are underlined by treatments of numbers by Cyndi Lauper and Michael Jackson.

In the majority of his last albums for Warner Brothers, Davis continued with the kinds of methods of creating albums he had begun in the early 1970s. For *Amandla*, his 1988–9 album, he was reunited with Don Alias, the percussionist from the *Bitches Brew* period, but whereas in the late 1960s and early 1970s Alias remembered Davis as a man he hung out with, who was good company and "one of the cats," the Davis of the late 80s was a more remote figure. He did not even attend some of the studio sessions, and Alias told me:

> The camaraderie of the earlier sessions was gone, and I don't think this was just because I was working with a lot of younger generation musicians like Marcus Miller or Omar Hakim. It was more to do with the way Miles worked. He more or less let me do what I liked. He'd call me up on the phone before I went into the studio and say, "Don, I want you to layer what you did," – or "Make it sound like five thousand drummers are playing."[16]

In his final years Davis also participated in two large-scale orchestral recordings, one, with Palle Mikkelborg, creating some splendid new music, and the other, just months before his death in 1991, looking back with Quincy Jones at the high points of his work with Gil Evans. These were outside the normal run of his later work, which continued in jazz-rock vein. Because of his high-volume sales, the large number of extremely good and influential musicians who passed through his ranks, and his own restless energy during the periods when he was in good health and working regularly, Davis is the dominant figure in jazz-rock. Few of the developments in fusion would have taken place without his input, and it is significant that many of the most influential jazz-rock bands of the 1970s and 1980s are composed of his former sidemen. One of them, John Scofield, summed up for me why Davis was so influential on his generation:

> The idea of playing electric backbeat music is something I might not have followed up on very much, if I hadn't played with Miles. Because that got me into that world. It was his influence that got me doing that. With Miles, I felt we never really got on record what we did in concert. We'd take off in a way that just wasn't captured on record. I think Miles's idea of playing is what you might call "funky" jazz, using elements of pop music in jazz, and those rhythms and that instrumentation is only coming into fruition right now [2001] – and it's happening with bands like Medeski, Martin, and Wood. It took a minute, after his death. There was a lot of bad fusion, and people got sick of it and it went

away. But I like the way this new generation is tackling it. In a way, it's like punk rock, that first came out in Britain and America in the early 70s, went away and resurfaced with Kurt Cobain. I think it's gone that way with fusion.[17]

## Fusion in the Wake of Miles Davis

Jazz makes use of a broader range of musical tools – from the simple to the complex. The pop thing has fewer tools at its disposal. It doesn't need them. It's about editing. Being concise. Saying concise things.

Herbie Hancock[18]

Partly because Miles Davis attracted musicians who shared his interest in jazz-rock, in the period from 1968 to 1975, and partly because Davis himself was so influential, the majority of the most significant jazz-rock bands of the period were associated with the trumpeter. The first musicians to leave the Davis quintet of the 1960s were pianist Herbie Hancock and drummer Tony Williams, and each was to become a leading figure in the fusion world. It was Williams who had first invited British guitarist John McLaughlin to the United States to join his trio Lifetime, with organist Larry Young. (Bassist Jack Bruce joined them the following year.) And it was because McLaughlin owed his first allegiance to Williams that he refused to accept Miles Davis's repeated offers to join the trumpeter's band.

Lifetime was both innovative and influential, but, at the time, not as successful commercially as it deserved to be. In the world of fusion a record deal was everything, and the trio's first disc, *Emergency!*, for the up-and-coming Polydor label, was poorly mixed and less well distributed than it might have been had it appeared on one of the other major labels. The group broke up in 1971, and whereas neither Williams nor Young managed such musical heights again in their careers, it acted as a launch-pad for McLaughlin. His work with Lifetime, and as a guest on Davis's albums, had brought his intense guitar playing to the American public, and this had been helped by appearances on albums with other musicians including Wayne Shorter, as well as a couple more discs of his own.

In July 1971, McLaughlin put together his Mahavishnu Orchestra, its name suggested by his guru Sri Chinmoy, and comprising an unorthodox line-up with McLaughlin himself and violinist Jerry Goodman backed by keyboard player Jan Hammer, bassist Rick Laird, and drummer Billy Cobham. The band was loud, powerful, and aggressive, using many of the techniques of distortion and high volume associated with Hendrix, and, equally, it changed meter, texture, and tempo with staggering aplomb. The band's opening album, *The Inner Mounting Flame*, demonstrated all these ingredients, and among its most varied tracks is *Meeting of the Spirits* **[CD 2, track 6]**, which includes several shifts of gear. The piece also displays some of the other key elements of the Mahavishnu Orchestra, the blending of McLaughlin's guitar lines with those of Goodman's violin, the extraordinary variety in Cobham's drumming, and the ebb and flow of the music, which keeps reaching, dropping back from, and regaining a scorching intensity. There are obvious similarities with Cream, not least in the way Cobham takes the rhythmic density of Ginger Baker's jazz-based approach to drumming to a new level of complexity and sophistication, but also in the sheer power of the music.

Internal wrangles caused this group to break up after a couple of years. Then McLaughlin formed a new Mahavishnu Orchestra, with French virtuoso violinist Jean-Luc Ponty, but this was also a relatively short-lived band, and also broke up with a certain degree of rancor. By mid-1974, he started working with the acoustic, Indian-influenced band Shakti, and by this time he had also appeared on tour and as a recording guest with Carlos Santana. McLaughlin's influence would continue to be felt through his periodic returns to fusion, through the long-term popularity of his first Mahavishnu recordings, and through the activities of his former colleagues who carried on in similar vein: Billy Cobham, with a band that included the young Brecker Brothers, and Jean-Luc Ponty, reactivating his solo career with *Upon the Wings of Music* (1975).

Whereas the departure of Tony Williams from the Miles Davis band had led him directly to Lifetime, from where McLaughlin had founded Mahavishnu, Herbie Hancock's direction was somewhat different. At first he led a sextet that picked up some of the reins of the independent recording career he had enjoyed at Blue Note throughout the 1960s and during his tenure with Davis, and which was in keeping with that label's hard-bop policy. The band, which featured trumpeter Johnny Coles and tenorist Joe Henderson, had a softer, more melodic approach than Davis's band during the last months that Hancock was with it, before he was ousted by Chick Corea. The sumptuous arrangement of *I Have a Dream*, from his album *The Prisoner*, featuring flutes and ensemble passages redolent of Gil Evans, and played by an augmented version of his sextet, shows little of a future direction that would move towards funk and pop. But buried in the Blue Note vaults was an unissued session that hinted at another course for Hancock: a rhythm-and-blues set, made in 1966, that included a track called *Don't Even Go There*, with cornetist Melvin Lastie and tenorist Stanley Turrentine. This was very much of its time, not unlike the funk-crossover discs made by altoist Lou Donaldson (also featuring Lastie), but it showed that Hancock had a firm grasp of the rhythm-and-blues idiom.

After a couple of albums for Blue Note, Hancock's fortunes changed, as his subsequent collaborator Bob Belden wrote: "Warner Brothers made an offer that Herbie couldn't refuse; he was given a sizable increase in funds for recording and the music was to be treated like a pop act."[19] Ironically, apart from the addition of electronic instruments, Hancock's short stay with Warner, his so-called *Mwandishi* period, after the Swahili names he and the band took, had little in common with pop music. His band was an inappropriate opener for the pop acts that it toured with, and it failed to pull in a sizable audience in its own right. In 1973, Hancock broke up the band and set about creating a different group, that would reflect his listening to musicians such as Sly and the Family Stone or James Brown. "Instead of getting jazz cats who knew how to play funk, I got funk cats who knew how to play jazz," he said.[20]

Up until that point, he was to say, he had talked a lot about openness in music, but had not necessarily practiced what he preached.

> I started to realize that I drew lines myself. One thing was, I loved hearing Sly Stone. If he would have said, "Come and sit in," I would have done it. But, for me to actually do that, it was no-no-no-no. It was like, "I'll do that on your stage in your setting, but in my setting I don't want to do that." . . . Anyway, I decided that I wanted to try it myself. I looked at it from a lot of different angles. I said, "You might lose all this audience you've gained up to this point, and you might even gain a new one." But I said, "I have no choice, I have to do it."[21]

With reed player Bernie Maupin, from his earlier band, and a new rhythm section of "funk cats," Hancock moved to Columbia, Davis's label, and recorded the seminal jazz-funk album of the 1970s, *Headhunters*. The album, and *Chameleon*, a single from it, sold voluminously, earning a gold disc and, in due course, a platinum disc, a rarity for any jazz artist, and particularly one whose hit record was not a vocal, but an instrumental. The radical difference in Hancock's approach from his earlier work, using the kind of repetitive rhythms familiar from Sly Stone's work, is exemplified by his composition *Watermelon Man* **[CD 2, track 7]**. The piece had been recorded before, in a hard-bop version by Hancock himself, and transformed into a hit by the Latin bandleader Mongo Santamaria, so the basic source material would have been familiar to his audience, allowing Hancock to take considerable liberties with his own song.

The scene is set by a mixture of panpipes and percussionist Bill Summers blowing over the top of a beer bottle, to create a kind of crazily offset pipe-organ feeling, under which a slow funk groove creeps in on bass and drums. Between them, Hancock and Maupin construct the elements of the well-known theme, neither actually stating it explicitly, but allowing the listener to put it together.

Hancock's band went on to be spectacularly successful, and in the 1980s and early 1990s, he continued to make funk and pop records, as well as returning to acoustic jazz in 1977 with the band VSOP, which put Freddie Hubbard (and later Wallace Roney) together with Wayne Shorter and the former Miles Davis rhythm section of himself, Williams, and Carter. He also recorded with the young New Orleans trumpeter Wynton Marsalis, and toured in duo with his old Davis colleagues; first, pianist Chick Corea, and later, once again, Wayne Shorter; and there were more Davis connections when he arranged the music for Bertrand Tavernier's film *Round Midnight*, which featured Shorter, plus John McLaughlin as a bop guitarist. In the late 1990s, in the wake of an album called *The New Standard* – which produced jazz interpretations of rock and pop pieces by musicians as varied as Prince, Kurt Cobain, and Stevie Wonder – Hancock toured with an all-star band of jazz-rock musicians including John Scofield and Michael Brecker, and his old Miles Davis colleagues, Dave Holland, Jack DeJohnette, and Don Alias. This was an extraordinarily successful weaving together of the jazz-rock and acoustic jazz sides of his career into a new whole.

Wayne Shorter did not leave Davis until somewhat later than Williams and Hancock. He had evolved into a remarkably original saxophonist in the Davis quintet, and he had also, as Dave Holland pointed out above, written a substantial amount of material for the group. In 1970, he formed a new band Weather Report with the Austrian keyboard player Joe Zawinul, who had also appeared on Davis recordings, and had made his mark as a composer with *Mercy, Mercy, Mercy*, which he had written for the Adderley Brothers, whilst a member of Cannonball's quintet.

Weather Report was, in its way, as defining a part of the 1970s jazz-rock movement as Hancock's Headhunters band. Whereas McLaughlin and Williams had been drawn to the power and freewheeling solos of heavy rock, and Hancock had been influenced by the funk of James Brown and Sly Stone, Weather Report took a more compositional approach, going back to what Ian Carr referred to as "the disciplines of sequences and tonality." However, viewed as an entity, the quality of the compositions the group played is decidedly uneven. Over the course of fifteen albums or so, beginning with *Weather Report* and ending, in 1986, with *This Is This*, the band subsumed Shorter's remarkable solo talents into a largely unremarkable ensemble sound, from which various members of the group would occasionally emerge for vacuous solo displays.

To start with, the band grew naturally out of the Davis style, and Wayne Shorter was still a solo voice to be reckoned with on pieces such as *Euridice*, from its debut album. The real commercial breakthrough for the group took another seven years, by which time the band had gone through three bassists – Miroslav Vitous, Andrew White, and Alphonso Johnson – and a succession of drummers. The catalyst was the arrival in the ranks of another bassist Jaco Pastorius, who had replaced Johnson during the making of the *Black Market* album. Pastorius was a virtuoso electric bassist, with a warm sound on the fretless Fender bass, and an ability both to play the kind of rapid solo lines and chordal passages one might expect of a regular guitarist, together with urgent, propulsive funk bass lines, which he had honed into a fine art from several months on the road with a band led by the white soul singer Wayne Cochrane. Joe Zawinul described his impact on Weather Report:

> Jaco was in a space all of his own. He was so different from all the other bass players of that time. He had that magical thing about him, the same kind of thing Jimi Hendrix had. He was an electrifying performer and a great musician. And he was really responsible for bringing white kids to our concerts. Before Jaco came along we were perceived as a kind of esoteric jazz group. We had been popular on college campuses, but after Jaco joined the band, we started selling out big concert halls everywhere.[22]

It is Pastorius who starts *Birdland* **[CD 2, track 8]**, the band's best-known track, from the first full album he made with the band – *Heavy Weather*. The main features of the piece, apart from its two themes, is the interplay between Zawinul's variety of keyboard tones and Pastorius's bass, the whole thing being underpinned by an urgent, insistent, underlying rhythm. Shorter's contribution is mainly to the ensemble, as well as a short solo passage before the second theme emerges, and a brief return later over some tumbling downward figures from Zawinul. The overall impression is of intense business, of frantic activity that is obviously leading somewhere but never quite arriving – this is jazz robbed of space for improvisation, with what solos there are being crammed in and around the bustling repetitive patterns. In live events, the band featured lengthy solos by its members, but despite settings of great richness and density, the problem was inherent in the shallowness of the compositions – as Richard Cook put it, "there's nothing to expend virtuosity on."[23]

This did not deter Pastorius, in particular, and one typical account of his playing describes how he "took a 25-minute bass solo, and, at its conclusion, got down on his knees in a single spotlight and prayed to the still-humming Fender."[24] Pastorius left the band in 1982, drifting into the largely self-destructive downward spiral of his last years, dying after a brawl in a Florida club in 1987. The band moved into a period with little creative energy, although both Zawinul and Shorter have revived their careers since – Zawinul with a continuation of his jazz-rock and fusion ideas in his Syndicate, and Shorter in a succession of projects that have allowed him once again to work with compositional and improvisatory freedom.

When Chick Corea left the Davis band, his first moves were towards free jazz. Then, in 1971, he founded the band that brought him international fame in his own right, Return to Forever. To start with, this was a gentle Latin-orientated group, with Brazilian singer Flora Purim and her husband, percussionist Airto Moreira, at the core of its sound, but it gradually became a fully fledged rock-fusion group. Gone were the airiness and grace of early albums such as *Light as a Feather*, and in their place came the powerful guitar riffs of Bill Connors and thudding drumming of Lenny White. A number of other powerful fusion players came through the ranks of Return to Forever, and although it broke up in 1980, there have been occasional reunions; Corea then continued his interest in high-wattage keyboard playing in his Elektric Band, a trio with bassist John Patitucci and drummer Dave Weckl. However, like Hancock, he returned to acoustic jazz in the late 1970s, and, as well as playing duets with Hancock, or vibes player Gary Burton, he has also led an outstanding series of conventional piano, bass, and drums trios.

Of the musicians who worked with Miles Davis after his return to playing in the 1980s, several went on to have independent careers in jazz fusion, from saxophonist Bill Evans to guitarists Mike Stern and John

Scofield. Stern has kept abreast of developments in jazz in the 1980s and 1990s, and has recorded with some of the New York downtown experimentalists such as Bill Frisell, whereas in the late 1990s, as he suggested in the comments quoted earlier, Scofield has begun to work with a new generation of funk-orientated players, creating a direct link between the fusion of Miles Davis and the jazz-rock of the twenty-first century.

The seeds of Scofield's interest in the funkier side of jazz were sown early, and as a student at Berklee College of Music in Boston he came into contact with Gary Burton, one of the early experimenters in cross-over, whose 1970s bands included a string of high-profile guitarists: Sam Browne, Gerry Hahn, Mick Goodrick, and Pat Metheny. Scofield said:

> As a guitarist, Gary Burton's groups had been a huge influence on me, through discs like his *Duster* record in the late sixties, and his band was one I used to go hear. While I was at Berklee, I heard he was coming there to teach, and I could hardly believe it. My room-mates at the time were a bassist and a drummer, and after he arrived at the college, Gary used to come by and jam with us every evening as he waited for the traffic to ease up so he could drive home. So we played with him day in, day out, and that was my real music education. He ended up being a mentor to me and a bunch of other guys who were around in the early seventies.[25]

After his period with Davis, Scofield recorded a string of albums under his own name for the Blue Note label, most characterized by his open, spacey tone, and a relaxed mingling of rock figures and rhythms with workable jazz compositions. He toured widely, and built up a strong following in Europe, where he worked in a variety of contexts, including being featured in classical compositions by the young British composer Mark-Anthony Turnage. But in 1997 he recorded a funk album, *A Go-Go*, with the trio Medeski, Martin, and Wood, representatives of the new generation of players he referred to, who have a strong following among college age kids.

> They're part of this phenomenon in the States ... called jam bands, which is young rock bands playing for dancing, but they improvise as well. In many ways, Medeski, Martin, and Wood are the kings of the jam-band scene. So after working with them on *A Go-Go*, I started to be invited to play on a few jam-band festivals, and met some of the musicians from a jam band called Deep

Banana Blackout. They're an incredible funk band, and they play old-school meters or James Brown funk, which is right up my alley, and so from that group drummer Eric Kalb with bassist Dave Livolsi and percussionist Johnny Durkin came and played with me, and recorded on my subsequent album, *Bump*. On that, I wanted to play some different types of tune, so I asked drummer Kenny Wolleson and bassist Tony Scherr, two jazz musicians who play in the downtown scene in New York City . . . in the group called Sex Mob, and they [create] some rock and general grooves.[26]

## From Jazz-Rock to "Smooth Jazz"

By the time I hit New York, I think I was nineteen years old, it was a time when a group of musicians from my generation had kind of crossed barriers in various ways. And we started to mix jazz and R & B, and of course, that eventually became what we now . . . refer to as fusion.

Michael Brecker[27]

The name of Gary Burton has come up several times so far in this chapter, as one of the figures who, quite independently of Miles Davis, began to explore jazz-rock. Burton was a teenage prodigy, and he was financed through the Berklee School of Music on the back of his RCA record contract, signed before he was twenty. His first discs were actually made in a country-music style during a vacation in Nashville, but he began to record seriously in the 1960s, demonstrating his originality as a vibraphone player who took a pianistic, chordal view of his instrument (and using four mallets to show the degree to which he took a non-liner view of his playing). Early in the 1960s he met Michael Gibbs, a fellow-student at Berklee, and he was frequently to record Gibbs's music, although mainly after he formed his first full-time quartet in 1967, having by then cut his teeth professionally in the bands of George Shearing and Stan Getz.

The Burton quartet with Larry Coryell on guitar and Steve Swallow on electric and acoustic bass tackled a number of rock-orientated pieces, and the light, but forceful sound of this group, and its successors which included the guitarist Pat Metheny, prefigured much of the fusion movement. So, too, did the pieces that Gibbs wrote, not only for Burton, but also for his own groups, which he organized after moving to Britain in 1965. Colosseum's version of *Tanglewood 63* has already been mentioned, and Gibbs's other major piece from this era was *Family Joy, Oh Boy!*

Drummer Billy Cobham also started playing jazz-rock in the late 1960s, before his occasional recordings with Miles Davis or his work with John McLaughlin, and one of the first groups he led included the trumpeter Randy Brecker and his saxophonist brother Michael. Together, and independently, the brothers were to become two of the most influential jazz-rock players of the period from the 1970s onwards. They were both extremely accomplished musicians, and were in demand for all kinds of session work, among which were Randy's recordings with the rock band Blood, Sweat and Tears, which featured a "horn section." Playing with Cobham on the Columbia album by the group Dreams cemented their reputations, and they ended up producing, playing on, and musically directing sessions for a broad cross-section of bands, from jazz to rock, during the early 1970s.

After working together in Dreams, between 1970 and 1972, Michael and Randy formed the Brecker Brothers group in 1974, which became one of New York's leading fusion bands. It played a range of neatly written pieces by both brothers, that got the balance between composition and improvisation more or less right. Michael Brecker, in particular, developed into a tenorist of spectacular ability, combining a technique to rival that of John Coltrane with a fund of inventive ideas. Albums such as *Don't Stop the Music* (1976) and *Straphangin'* (1979) exemplify the tight jazz-rock sound of the Brothers' band.

Both of them have led significant solo careers, and Michael, in particular; he set up the group Steps, subsequently known as Steps Ahead, with the vibes player Mike Mainieri, which created a lighter jazz-rock style. However, from 1987, after making his first eponymously titled solo album, Michael Brecker increasingly moved away from jazz-rock, specializing in his coruscating tenor style, saying: "I had spent two or three years with my brother Randy, and the Brecker Brothers was quite an electric group. I had toured with Paul Simon. This was a chance for me to get back into more of an acoustic playing format, which I had been craving."[28] The saxophonist David Sanborn, who had a comparable career as a session player and with a succession of jazz-rock cross-over records, also began making acoustic jazz albums in the early 1990s.

During the years that the Brecker Brothers was getting established, in the 1970s, guitarist Pat Metheny left Gary Burton and formed his own group, which had a heavy emphasis on jazz-rock. The focus was on his virtuoso guitar playing, and on pieces written by, or with, his keyboard player Lyle Mays. Metheny's albums sold strongly; in addition to outside projects, such as a series of trios with such players as bassists Dave Holland or Charlie Haden, and drummers Roy Haynes and Jack DeJohnette, his own band kept up an impressive workload, playing up to 300 dates a year from the mid-1970s until 1994.[29] Metheny's range of jazz interests, his virtuosity, and prolific energy mean that although much of his output is very accessible, he has remained a jazz musician through and through, from his first band album, the *Pat Metheny Group*, for ECM in 1978, until the present.

By contrast, his exact contemporary Earl Klugh, despite recordings with George Benson, another cross-over guitarist, and with Return to Forever, has specialized in lightweight, undemanding discs, in which his acoustic guitar solos are set over a simple repetitive rock backing. Klugh is one of the progenitors of so-called "smooth jazz," which has become so widespread in broadcasting and the record industry that it is what passes for jazz altogether in the minds of many listeners. So, too, was the music of saxophonist Grover Washington Jr., whose discs such as *Winelight* sold in colossal numbers, and appeared on pop, jazz, and rhythm-and-blues charts. The most anodyne performer in this field is the saxophonist Kenny G. (Kenneth Gorelick), whose albums frequently succeed in the United States pop charts, but whose simple, melodic alto and soprano playing, underpinned by predictable rock rhythms, is the antithesis of improvisation, collective interaction, swing, soul, or heart.

CHAPTER 21

# Postmodern Jazz

> Without argument, without appeal to any body of opinion,
> the vast reorganization in our circumstances has quietly,
> while we were looking the other way, dismantled anything
> resembling a tradition.
>
> John Wain, from Professing Poetry[1]

Up until the 1970s, the story of jazz is a straightforward narrative. It is one in which there may be changes of emphasis, or national outlook, or definition. It may be viewed in a way that avoids the establishing of a canonical framework of artists and works, by looking at the social, commercial, or intellectual aspects of that narrative, but there is a clear sense of development, of the music moving forward. At some points, such as the 1920s "Jazz Age," the music has epitomized the flavor of a time, just as the "swing era" did in the 1930s to 1940s. At others, such as the period of social unrest in the 1960s, the music has reacted to the spirit of the age, its players seeking freedom in music as a metaphor for freedom in society.

But in one fell swoop, all that changed, with the birth of the "information age." The quotation above comes from the inaugural lecture by John Wain as Oxford Professor of Poetry, given in December 1973. I sat in the Sheldonian Theatre on an extremely hard wooden bench and listened to him deliver these words, together with a number of observations on the tradition of poetry, but I realized at the time that what he was saying applied just as much to jazz as it did to literature. Most jazz historians have subscribed to the view of tradition set out in T. S. Eliot's essay, *Tradition and the Individual Talent*. In it, he says,

Tradition cannot be inherited, and if you want it you must obtain it by great labour. It involves, in the first place, the historical sense . . . and a historical sense involves a perception, not only of the pastness of the past, but of its presence.[2]

The awareness of the "presence" of the tradition of the past has shaped the playing of musicians throughout jazz. Dizzy Gillespie conceived his playing as the result of a kind of relay race in which the baton had been passed from Louis Armstrong to Roy Eldridge to him, and although we may argue that perhaps other players such as Jabbo Smith or Henry "Red" Allen were allowed to carry the baton for a while before handing it on to Eldridge, it is a broadly accurate perception, and one that Gillespie demonstrated in his recording *Pops Confessin'*, which, albeit intended as a parody, shows the degree to which he had mastered the older trumpeter's style.

But new technology was to change all that. The days when musicians learned at the knees of older players, served their apprenticeships in big bands, participated in after-hours jam sessions, congregated in dressing rooms for impromptu opportunities to play, have all largely gone. (The closest parallel is the world of the student or youth big band, which has become the launch pad for many successful careers in Europe and the United States.) The decade in which this transition took place was the 1970s. I dwelt at some length in the previous chapter on the importance of Miles Davis in nurturing jazz-rock, and it seems to me significant that it was his circle of musicians from 1968 to 1972 who went out and developed a range of approaches to this style of music after first experimenting with Davis. He opened their minds to the possibility and empowered all of them to follow his methods for developing the genre. They were one of the last coteries of musicians to be part of the continuous tradition of development.

Furthermore, the 1970s saw the end of the era when a musician could think about belonging to "a band," a single musical organization, to the exclusion of other groups. From that decade onwards, a jazz musician's life became increasingly fragmented, often working with several groups at around the same time, wherever the work came from, or taking (as the Brecker Brothers did) copious amounts of studio work. This became obvious to Barry Kernfeld, the editor of the *New Grove Dictionary of Jazz*, when compiling accounts of musicians' lives for the second edition of the book, and noticing, as he dealt with a greater number of biographies of those active in the late twentieth century, how the pattern of describing a career in terms of single affiliations to a band or leader broke down comprehensively in the fifteen years or so following the 1970s.[3]

What supplanted the continuous tradition is what Mauriac called "le musée imaginaire," the virtual availability, in recorded form, of the entire recorded history of the music. Of course musicians did use recordings to learn their craft, from very early in the days of jazz. I have recounted tales of players avidly studying the latest discs by their heroes or heroines as they appeared, to understand every nuance of that player's style. But whether this was taking place in 1920s Chicago, where Jimmy McPartland and his friends clustered round the phonograph to hear Bix Beiderbecke and the Wolverines, or whether it was Dave Holland in London puzzling over the 1960s Miles Davis quintet, what they were learning was *current*, it was *now*, it was fashionable, it was at the cutting edge.

Instead, with the burgeoning reissue industry, and, more recently, the second wave of reissues engendered by the arrival of the compact disc, today's player is confronted by a bewildering array of material. As Wain put it in his lecture, today's musician:

> only has to walk to the record-shop on the corner to be deluged with the sounds of every civilization, every epoch, every corner of the earth, with no one of them "predominant" ... in the feverishly mushrooming jungle created by the total availability of all styles.[4]

It is therefore possible for a musician to embark on a career at the beginning of the twenty-first century and choose to assimilate elements from almost any style in the history of jazz as a starting point. Furthermore, the burgeoning number of educational institutions around the world that teach jazz will help such a musician develop several of those styles – with a particular emphasis on the change-related playing of hard bop, or the section discipline of a Kenton-era big band. But whereas that is comparatively easy, it is far harder for a musician to remain part of a tradition with any kind of continuous development.

There are a few exceptions. Some are accidents of geography and history; and principal among them is New Orleans. It was easy in the late twentieth century for jazz musicians to find work there, playing Dixieland in the bars and taverns of Bourbon Street, entertaining the conferences and conventions. As well as the young players who are educated at NOCA or Loyola University, there are still family brass bands, like Doc Paulin's, or the Mardi Gras Indian marching societies, the latter passing on not just traditional songs, but also a secret language into the bargain.

These family or community-based organizations are, however, exceptions, and to see many of the city's other brass bands out on the street is a little like going to a French Quarter version of Disneyland – the groups contain players who would rather be playing bebop, or Latin jazz, or almost anything else, working their way through the old marches. Meanwhile, in Preservation Hall, a dwindling number of old timers play alongside European or Japanese copyists, attempting to recapture the rough and ready music, not so much of the 1920s, but the 1960s revival. Yet fighting to be heard above the endless repetitions of *The Saints* is a discernible contemporary tradition. At a venue such as the Snug Harbor on Frenchman's Street are bands such as Astral Project, taking a new spin on post-bop jazz with the funky New Orleans street beat of drummer Johnny Vidacovich combined with the hard-edged saxophone of Tony Dagradi and the guitar of Steve Masakowski. Or, experimenting with time signatures but building on the city's traditional drum style is Jason Marsalis, with a quintet including bassist Roland Guerin who has looked again at the slap bass techniques that were being used by some of the city's oldest musicians, to try to incorporate them into a contemporary improvisational language. Equally, trumpeter Nicholas Payton, son of one of the city's leading bassists, has begun taking the Dixieland music he heard as a child and reinterpreting it in a contemporary style, tearing up old warhorses such as *Li'l Liza Jane* as if they were hard-bop originals:

> I had to deal with that music, because I grew up with it, but I needed to do something different. Two years on [from starting the band] we're introducing a larger number of original compositions that are freer in rhythm and harmony, but without losing sight of lyricism and a sense of swing.[5]

Alongside indigenous musicians, such as Payton, Guerin, and Marsalis, a community of out-of-town players has been drawn to the city, to become part of its continuing tradition, just as musicians from all over the United States made their way to Chicago in the 1920s for similar reasons. One example of a pianist who has moved to New Orleans from St. Louis is Peter Martin, former accompanist to singer Betty Carter, and one-time member of saxophonist Joshua Redman's band. He told me:

> The city's music still has an identifiable character. There's an

organic flow between the musicians. Beyond just liveliness, the music is a line passed from person to person across the generations, like no other place I've been. Although it's the birthplace of jazz, musicians don't treat it as a museum – it's a living thing . . . the quality of their musicianship is amazing.[6]

The most high-profile proselytizer for the New Orleans tradition is, of course, Wynton Marsalis, older brother of Jason, and a player who had the benefit not only of his father's links with the Crescent City's past, but also experience of playing with Art Blakey's Jazz Messengers, which had its own traditions to uphold.

Yet I was surprised to discover that Marsalis himself was not all that interested in the local tradition while he was actually growing up. I wondered, for example, whether he had absorbed at first hand the Armstrong-influenced styles of older players such as Thomas Jefferson:

It was there but I didn't like it. I never listened to Thomas Jefferson . . . Teddy Riley was the one I knew the most, who was of a younger generation than Thomas Jefferson or Alvin Alcorn and other great old New Orleans trumpeters. I never really respected that way of playing, so that's why I can understand when people can't "hear" that style. I thought it was all tied to the minstrel show and Uncle Tomming and that stuff. I liked Freddy Hubbard and the modern players, playing a funk beat and "sus" chords, and not playing triads. That music is very triadic, and all full of quarter notes. In the seventies, the younger generation were all playing funk tunes and playing fast, and to hear somebody playing the melody on *Way Down Yonder in New Orleans* was considered to be extremely corny. What turned me around was when I started to understand that those sus chords and the things we were trying to play would not allow us a deep development. In order for us to develop, it was necessary for us to be jazz musicians and not be so fad orientated. Deep down I liked the New Orleans style. I just wouldn't allow myself to like it because it wasn't socially acceptable.[7]

Greatly to his credit, Marsalis stood back from the hard bop he had played with Blakey and with Herbie Hancock, and began his own exploration of the jazz tradition. But instead of starting with the jazz he had grown up with, and was part of, he worked his way backwards from bebop, and, as Richard Cook put it:

> If his first bands sounded like oblique descendents of the already-oblique Miles Davis groups of the early 60s, that shell was soon shucked in favour of Mingusian ensembles, Ellingtonian voicings, New Orleans survivals that could embrace Jelly Roll Morton and Joe Oliver. It looked able to spread in any direction but always *within jazz*.[8]

What Marsalis has done, in addition to conducting this exploration, is to document his journey. And through his own outreach work he has reached the point where he has taken on the role of mentor himself for players whom he first heard as young students, but who have now graduated to become professional musicians. Some, such as bassist Rodney Whitaker and trumpeter Seneca Black, have ended up playing alongside Marsalis in the Lincoln Center Jazz Orchestra.

The competence with which he has worked back into the tradition is obvious from many of his recordings, not least his epic Pulitzer Prize-winning opera *Blood on the Fields*, in which the section *Freedom Is in the Trying* **[CD 2, track 13]** echoes the sounds of the New Orleans music of the streets that Marsalis was worried might not be "socially acceptable" for him to like, when he was a boy.

Creating an itinerary as he has done, through the recorded tradition, but supplemented by first-hand contact with many of the players who helped develop the music by bringing them to New York's Lincoln Center to work with the band, is not only spreading the message about jazz to Marsalis's growing public around the world, but also helping to build a core of musicians who can regard themselves as part of a continuous tradition. Shortly before his death in the spring of 2001, for example, John Lewis conducted an evening of his compositions at the Lincoln Center, which he had rehearsed and developed with the band. Through this kind of event, and by mixing a large proportion of new music, his own or that of other members of his band such as the trombonist Wycliffe Gordon, Marsalis attempts to avoid falling into the pitfalls of sterility that can dog jazz "repertory" projects. His counterpart at Carnegie Hall, trumpeter Jon Faddis, himself a protégé of Dizzy Gillespie, does much the same, commissioning a high proportion of new arrangements for the band to play.

However, the New Orleans connection does exemplify two very

different ways of tackling the jazz tradition. On the one hand, players like Peter Martin, Nicholas Payton, and Jason Marsalis are attempting to move an extant and continuous local tradition forward, to take from a living link with the past what they need to move their own music onwards. On the other, Wynton Marsalis and the Lincoln Center band are digging back into the tradition, trying to keep an approach to music alive that is rapidly losing such living links with the past. I think much of the jazz scene at the start of the twenty-first century can be looked at in precisely these terms – of those who are looking forward and those who are looking back. And in that first category I include those experimentalists who are starting from a new basis altogether, but who still have links with jazz through improvisation, composition, or those elusive qualities of heart, soul, and swing. To conclude this history, and suggest that this is a way of approaching the continuing narrative story of jazz, these categories are summarized briefly.

## In the Tradition: Looking Back

When I play I don't have to think myself back to another era. It just comes out this way.

Harry Allen[9]

It was in the 1970s that word started going round the jazz scene of a young American tenorist, born in 1954, who was not taking a post-Coltrane approach to his instrument, but focusing instead on the swing-based approach of Ben Webster and Lester Young. His name was Scott Hamilton, and he swiftly became the figurehead of a movement that took the late swing era as a jumping-off point for developing his style. He worked in the latter-day bands of Benny Goodman, and also recorded with a number of saxophonists who had made their names in the swing era itself – from Flip Phillips to Buddy Tate – before joining George Wein's touring band known as the Newport Festival All Stars.

Hamilton became a role model for a number of other players, proving that it was possible to reinvestigate older styles and find something new to say. His contemporary, cornetist Warren Vaché also worked with Goodman and Wein, but he epitomized a route into the music that was followed by several more players in this vein. He had studied music in college, and he had taken lessons with older musicians (in his case, the trumpeter Pee Wee

Erwin) to embed himself more firmly in the tradition. Furthermore, his father was a musician, jazz educator, and author, and so there was a family interest in the swing style. His younger brother, reed player Allen Vaché, took a similar course into traditional and mainstream jazz.

Tenorist Harry Allen, born almost a decade later than Hamilton, was also the son of a musician and studied at Rutgers University, with its well-known jazz department, and he, too, became well-known for playing in a swing-era style. In his remarks, and those of Hamilton, there was often a young fogey-ism, a defensive reaction to questions as to why their instrumental talents were applied to reinvestigating the past, to mining chord sequences that have been worked over thousands of times before, to staying within a framework that had begun to feel dated in the 1940s. Allen's answer that, "swing just sounded like more fun than anything else. There's always something fresh to do,"[10] seemed to be dodging the issue.

But guitarist John Pizzarelli, the son of swing-era guitarist Bucky Pizzarelli, takes a different view. The music may be well-worn within the jazz community, but performing swing-era material for a young audience is introducing it to that listenership for the first time. He says:

> A lot of people ask me the same question: "Swing jazz is swing jazz, so what are you going to do with it?" My answer is that I want to find a sound within the style. I try not to think of it as finite. Maybe there's a group of instruments I could put together or some way of using a band that would make people say, "Gee! That's something new." I really like playing this style and I'd like to find some way of giving it broad appeal.[11]

His answer has been to add the vocal repertoire of Nat King Cole (plus a number of songs in comparable style) to the material he plays with his trio and occasional big band. Not all his results have avoided the sentimental or the well-worn, but his improvisational abilities on the seven-string acoustic guitar are exceptional, and he is a formidable duetist, notably in a series of albums with his father that take in an eclectic range of the guitar tradition. His vocal style compares to that of Harry Connick Jr., who has put his piano playing and singing in the context of a big band that employs many of the New Orleans musicians who are part of the living tradition I mentioned earlier.

It is, of course, a fallacious argument to suggest that because musicians like Hamilton and Allen have selected swing from "le musée imaginaire" their work is any less "valid" than that of those who have chosen, say, hard bop or free jazz. But their work does not have the sense of adventure or excitement that has generally been associated with the cutting edge of jazz, or with the playing of those who are looking forward from within the tradition rather than backwards.

The same applies to singers, and, in particular, to the question of repertoire. This is something that applies, especially, to the work of Diana Krall. She has not been short of mentors, and both Ray Brown and the late Jimmy Rowles guided and developed both her playing and her singing in the years that led up to her position of international stardom. Studying with Rowles, she says, made sense of how she should go about singing which, at music college, had been tied up with all sorts of issues to do with operatic range and choral singing:

> [With Rowles] it was sinking in that it's not your voice, not whether you have an operatic voice or not, but what you do with it that counts. If you want to sing you should sing. I was still pretty much a kid when I went to study with him, and I'd spend every day at his house and I'm still getting to grips with things he taught me. The beauty of the music for a start. Jimmy Rowles was not flashy, but he was incredibly complex harmonically in his knowledge, which extended from music in general to Debussy and Ravel in particular. The way he played and sang was very, very subtle, and the beauty of the music came through in the way he played and sang songs like *Poor Butterfly*, *Nature Boy* or *How Deep is the Ocean*. Those things sunk in while I was there, but I'm still processing that, and coming to terms with his whole artistry.[12]

Perhaps it is the very power and depth of Jimmy Rowles as an influence that has made Diana Krall look over her shoulder into the musical past for inspiration, rather than the present. She makes a dramatic contrast, for instance, from her one-time school classmate, trumpeter Ingrid Jensen, who followed a very similar route from the same high-school band to today's New York scene. But whereas Jensen works on her own compositions, and plays with cutting-edge colleagues like Dwayne Burno and Bill Stewart, as well as having a musical agenda that is to do with advancing the cause of female instrumentalists in jazz, Krall still plays standards, generally in a setting that mimics the instrumentation and genre of Nat King Cole's trio. She is on the defensive about this:

I am a storyteller, and I play the piano, which is the most challenging thing for me at the moment, and always has been. Singing's a challenge too. But as far as compositions go, I feel like I'm studying my Shakespeare, and I'm not ready to write and direct my own play yet. I'm studying songs from Jerome Kern to Joni Mitchell, and there's a lot of music there – it's not an excuse, but I'm not ready to write. And I'm fulfilled by performing standards – I don't see too many people singing songs any more.[13]

Given the plethora of newly released albums each year by singers tackling the great American songbook, it seems that plenty of other singers are equally fulfilled by performing standards. But what is missing from this approach is what I have felt to be an essential element of jazz – and particularly jazz singing – throughout its history: the *frisson* of daring, the challenge of making a new song work, of inhabiting a lyric for the first time and personalizing it. Krall's conservatism makes an interesting contrast with the energetic scatting of her Chicagoan contemporary Kurt Elling, who has developed extremes of speed and syllabic control in his singing that explore entirely fresh territory.

The contrast in attitudes is exemplified in Britain between two singers who are also very much contemporaries, with a similar media profile, and each supported by a large, independent record company of comparable size: Claire Martin and Stacey Kent. Martin began to sing original compositions – her own, or those of the musicians she worked with, from the time of her 1992 debut. Not all of these worked, particularly some of her attempts to portray the life of the twenty-first-century urban girl in song, but with every album there was a sense of trying something new, of progression in terms of accompaniment, content, rhythm, and so forth, yet with enough of the familiar to retain her audience. Kent, by contrast, has stuck to the standard repertoire, and to a broadly consistent, swing-based setting. She tackles her music superbly, and her counter to charges that the daring and danger are missing is that she believes it is possible to focus instead on interpreting the content of a lyric, using a different level of improvisatory imagination to "become the person" in the lyric:

Standards are a perfect blend of poetry and melody and music and I can sing them, feel them, deliver them my own way, being myself, and telling someone else's story, and/or my own story, at the same time.[14]

There is much to be got out of a lyric, and a song, but it strikes me that the imperative throughout jazz history has been to mingle that investigation of the tradition with something new and original. No better example exists of the determination to do this than that of Oscar Peterson. I annotated several of his albums during the 1990s, a decade when he suffered a number of health problems, but worked hard to conquer them, returning to perform and record as soon as he was able. In the case of every disc, he recorded at least one new composition, and modified his approach to older pieces at the same time. The members of his quartet have told me often about his relentless drive to write and record his latest ideas, and he demonstrates perfectly my contention that one should use the tradition to look forward, rather than back.

## In the Tradition: Looking Forward

In a retrospective situation, everyone can play the notes and stuff, but they don't have the magic, because they've become so homogeneous that something's lost. In our day, we would play, and then the technique would come to fit whatever we wanted to play. But today they develop the technique first, and then play in a kind of chronological isolation. They haven't had direct contact with the masters, and that's where the magic is missing, because although you can get a lot of stuff academically, the real feeling, the feeling that creates the magic, has to be taught to you. That's where you learn the stuff that's not written, the tones, the colours, the things you can do, and that's what we got from contact with the masters.

Andrew Hill[15]

The feeling of "magic" described by Andrew Hill is bound up in the elusive definition of jazz, and it is a quality that he has sought to find in his playing from the 1960s to the start of the twenty-first century, often by ruthlessly abandoning the past. The bands with which he revived his career for Blue Note in the 1980s were set aside, and in the 1990s he moved through several stages, including a free-form trio with Reggie Workman and Pheeroan Ak Laff, ending up with a sextet at the end of the decade with which he recorded a whole set of new material for his album *Dusk*. Yet even in that album it is possible to recognize qualities that were present in his early work, the tones and colors he describes.

Hill exemplifies the concept of looking forward from within the tradition. As a boy he was taught by Earl Hines, whom he met while doing a newsround in Chicago. He became one of the most iconoclastic and inventive musicians on the Blue Note label in the 1960s, and on his return in the 1980s, became a mentor in his turn to young players such as altoist Greg Osby. Osby was one of a generation of players (including the equally inventive saxophonist Steve Coleman) who came out of the urban M-Base movement, an exciting aggregation of musicians who explored rap, hip-hop, and other urban grooves in their playing. In his late-1980s work with Hill, he also began to embrace the tradition, and his late 1990s projects, including *Banned in New York*, have combined his acoustic hard-bop approach with some of the openness and innovation he acquired from Hill. In Osby's circle of players in and around the New York scene, the connection with Hill has been significant, and the pianist Jason Moran (who plays in Osby's quartet) has produced a vital and absorbing composition called *Retrospect*, by playing Hill's piece *Smokestack* backwards. He discovered the effect through working with a turntable to sample the disc, and – bizarre as it might sound – inverting the composition has created an entirely new musical contour, yet the piece still has audible connections with Hill's approach.

I have picked out this very tangible example of a connection with the tradition, but it goes to show how a modicum of ingenuity can provide new quarry for the improviser.

Another example is where a regular working band consciously looks back to tackle the recorded legacy of the past. In 2000, trumpeter Dave Douglas recorded an album inspired by the music of Mary Lou Williams. As well as taking material she recorded and reinterpreting it, Douglas wrote originals which he felt continued Williams's exploratory approach to jazz:

> There are some pieces ... that go pretty far out in the experimental department. That's who I am as a composer. But I also think it's fair to say that Mary did her own exploring, and her own trailblazing in terms of new sounds. So one of my new tunes, *Multiples* was inspired directly by her piece *Zoning*. And then there's her *A Fungus Amungus*, a very *avant-garde* piano solo she recorded in 1963, which would be easy to transform into today's language. But in re-recording her early work like *Mary's Idea* or

*Waltz Boogie*, it's not my goal to take these beautiful pieces of music and turn them into some kind of downtown New York postmodern extravaganza. I am coming at all her music with a lot of respect. So, the more adventurous sounds you'll hear on this record are on my pieces inspired by her, rather than her pieces interpreted by the sextet.[16]

Douglas has also investigated Balkan music in his Tiny Bell Trio, and unorthodox instrumentation in his group Charms of the Night Sky with accordion and violin, but the general direction of his music has been to mix experimentation with traditions of which he is a part.

Douglas has frequently been associated with the experimental New York downtown scene, working with a group of musicians that includes saxophonists John Zorn and Tim Berne, guitarist Bill Frisell, and a number of other iconoclastic figures who work regularly at the Knitting Factory and other downtown Manhattan venues. Zorn has had a particularly wide-ranging (and well-documented) career, but just as Douglas has drawn in Balkan and European folk influences into some of his work, Zorn has connected with different ethnic traditions, notably Jewish music, and drawn this into jazz. His unorthodox instruments, duck calls, gun effects, and the like are also extending the boundaries, by introducing the elements of shock and surprise, but, for all that, Zorn has worked in many areas of the tradition, and has a clear view of how his music relates to the continuity of jazz.

The same is true of saxophonist David Murray, whom I have already mentioned in connection with the World Saxophone Quartet, and who was also associated with the Knitting Factory during a number of years when the club was the base for his experimental big band. Murray has extended the playing technique of both the tenor sax and bass clarinet (his two main instruments) by developing their upper range and combining a formidable speed with continuous breathing, to create seemingly endless torrents of sound. His extension of instrumental technique has been matched by a bewildering variety of ensembles, most of which are to do with the balance of playing "inside" and "outside" – in other words, between structured and free improvisation. At his most successful, he has managed to bring many of the most exciting and challenging aspects of free jazz into a setting that is not daunting for general audiences, and by working with musicians in many parts of the world, has taken his approach to new listeners and new musicians, who find him a singularly inspiring figure. The same could be said of a number of other figures, including saxophonist Joe Lovano, who encompasses a particularly broad stylist range, or trumpeter Tom Harrell, who has produced a strip of inventive compositions for his playing in a style that combines elements of free jazz and hard bop.

David Murray and Greg Osby are examples of saxophonists who have worked from within the tradition to find new improvisational territory. This is not an easy thing to do after the all-pervading influence of John Coltrane, but several saxophonists have begun to chart territory that does not necessarily use Coltrane as a jumping-off point. There are certainly Coltrane echoes in the playing of Branford Marsalis **[CD 2, track 12]** but he is one of a number of players who have gone back to the work of Sonny Rollins as an alternative approach, both in terms of his use of melodic material in improvising solos, and also in the instrumentation of his groups. (Marsalis has also gone further than most jazz musicians into hip-hop and rap territory with his band Buckshot Lefonque, an area also being covered in Britain by Courtney Pine in his work with DJs.)

Another player who has taken the Rollins approach to the saxophone as a starting point is Joshua Redman, and his commercial success allowed him the relatively scarce luxury of keeping a regular working band together for much of the 1990s. This has clear benefits – and shows the degree to which such consistency is absent from the work of many of his colleagues, where the possibility to work on ideas as a band tends to be project-based, rather than a continual process. As a consequence of working over several years with a consistent group of colleagues, Redman has taken a new approach to the idea of extended composition, and in his 2001 suite, *Passage of Time*, he has produced a continuous, hour-long piece. It breaks down into eight movements, but the music moves inexorably on from one to the next without pause, and there is a strong sense of harmonic and thematic connection among them. As the title suggests, there are games with time – the movement *Our Minuet*, for example, is in five, not three, beats to the bar – and the whole piece experiments with the way we perceive time and meter. The rapport with which this is played demonstrates the benefits of long periods of working together.

There have been experiments with time in the playing of several pianists. Benny Green, for example, the official protégé of Oscar Peterson, has produced compositions in which contrasting sections of meter work into one another, and he has experimented in some of his trios with the idea of collective acceleration or deceleration – not an easy thing to achieve with a group that only plays together occasionally. And there is a similar sense of temporal experiment in the trio of Brad Mehldau, where he has worked to develop an ensemble rapport with bassist Larry Grenadier and drummer Jorge Rossy.

In criticizing those singers who remain beached within the standard repertoire, I had also in mind examples of others who are very definitely not, but who remain within the tradition looking out. The best example of this – for several decades – has been Abbey Lincoln, who has consistently addressed in her lyrics those issues of the day that concern her. Whether these are addressed to unborn children or remonstrating with the mothers of today for the way we treat youngsters in society, Lincoln's lyrics are matched by a pithy delivery. She has a clear view of why she tackles the subjects she does:

> There's lots more to life than the relationship between a man and a woman. If you're privileged to be up there on stage, you ought to have something to say. I'm thankful the industry affords me a way of life in which I can be an artist, be an observer and a reporter, leave messages for our children – and so that's what I do.[17]

Other singers have taken a similar approach, and, most notably, Cassandra Wilson has tackled unusual themes, while simultaneously working in challenging musical environments. I could single out numerous other examples, but the point is that a creative approach to the tradition, to take advantage of what it has to offer, is more in keeping with the long history of jazz than to move in the direction of the repertory movement and simply recreate a past that is no longer part of an everyday social, political, economic, and musical context. The last words, which sum up this philosophy, belong to John Wain, who suggests that the availability of the tradition still has room for new soil and new roots:

> No one starts from a more favoured position than anyone else, no one is closer to or further away from the centre than anyone else; no one . . . is in fashion or out of fashion.[18]

# Notes

## Introduction

[1] Early examples of histories include Henry Osgood: *So This Is Jazz* (Boston, 1926) and Robert Goffin: *Aux frontières du jazz* (Paris, 1932). However, the real movement of jazz histories began in the 1930s with Hugues Panassié: *Hot Jazz* (translated from *Le Jazz hot*, Paris, Correa, 1934, by Lyle and Eleanor Dowling) (London, Cassell, 1936). The first attempt at oral history was by Frederick Ramsey Jr. and Charles Edward Smith: *Jazzmen: The Story of Hot Jazz Told in the Lives of the Men Who Created It* (New York, Harcourt, Brace and Company, 1939). This was followed by Rudi Blesh: *Shining Trumpets* (London, Cassell, 1949) (first published in the United States in 1946) and Marshall Stearns: *The Story of Jazz* (New York, Oxford University Press, 1956).

[2] Hugues Panassié: *op. cit.*

[3] Rudi Blesh: *op. cit.*

[4] Krister Malm: "Ethical concerns and new directions: the music industry," in Helen Myers (ed.): *Ethnomusicology: An Introduction* (London, Macmillan, 1992).

[5] A number of scholars of popular music, including Philip Tagg and Peter Van de Merwe, have initiated a debate about the possible antecedents of jazz in Western music, but all the examples I single out are undeniably present in African music.

[6] Melville Herskovits: *The Anthropometry of the American Negro* (New York, Columbia University Press, 1930). A summary of the subsequent debate is in Paul Oliver: *Savannah Syncopators* (London, Studio Vista, 1970).

[7] Paul Oliver: *Songsters and Saints* (Cambridge, Cambridge University Press, 1984) covers this in detail.

[8] Gunther Schuller: *Early Jazz: Its Roots and Musical Development* (New York, Oxford University Press, 1968) offers a chapter describing in detail the intrinsically African elements of rhythm, harmony, melody, form, timbre, and improvisation in early jazz.

[9] Paul Oliver: *Savannah Syncopators* (London, Studio Vista, 1970).

[10] See examples in Lowell H. Schreyer: "The banjo in ragtime," in John Edward Hasse (ed.): *Ragtime: Its History, Composers and Music* (London, Macmillan, 1985), 56.

[11] Henry F. Gilbert: *Musical Quarterly*, 1917, 577ff.

[12] These include the lives of Clyde E. Bernhardt, Garvin Bushell, Joe Darensbourg, Sammy Price, Marshal Royal, and Rex Stewart.

[13] "F. A. Barasso, a smart showman, organized in 1907 the first circuit in the United States for the employment of Negro actors. His brother, A. Barasso, inspired the organization of the T.O.B.A. circuit in 1909, which gave employment to colored actors in forty houses all over the United States. This, more than anything else, encouraged the investment of large capital in the building of colored theaters all over the country." – George E. Lee: *Beale Street: Where the Blues Began* (New York, Robert O. Ballou, 1934).

[14] Sammy Price: *What Do They Want?* (ed. Caroline Richmond) (Oxford, Bayou Press, 1989).

[15] For example, in one week in February 1911, the *New York Age* lists a couple of dozen vaudeville acts and their whereabouts, including: Saparo and Jones at the Bowdoin Square Theater, Boston; The Five Music Spillers at the Colonial Theater, Erie, P.A; the Dixie Serenaders at the Music Hall, Lewiston, Maine; and so on (not to mention King and Bailey "at the Hippodrome, Brighton, England," *New York Age*, February 9, 1911).

[16] Samuel B. Charters and Leonard Kunstadt: *Jazz: A History of the New York Scene* (2nd. edn.) (New York, Da Capo, 1981).

[17] Katherine E. Longyear: "Henry F. Gilbert," in H. Wiley Hitchcock and Stanley Sadie (eds.): *The New Grove Dictionary of American Music* (London, Macmillan, 1986); Claire McGlinchee: "American literature in American music," *Musical Quarterly* (1945), 31, 112.

[18] Frank Tirro: *Jazz: A History* (2nd. edn.) (New York, Norton, 1993): "Jazz . . . was first performed by Black Americans newly released from bondage who expressed their God-given talents and their beliefs about freedom, identity and art through their music. Jazz is still a profound manifestation of freedom, talent, achievement and identity" (p. xviii).

# Chapter 1

[1] Author's interview with Jesse Stone, March 9, 1997.

[2] Adolphus "Doc" Cheatham: *I Guess I'll Get the Papers and Go Home* (ed. Alyn Shipton) (London and Washington, Cassell, 1995).

[3] Alyn Shipton: *Groovin' High: The Life of Dizzy Gillespie* (New York, Oxford University Press, 1999).

[4] Pleasant "Cousin Joe" Joseph: *Cousin Joe: Blues from New Orleans* (Chicago, University of Chicago Press, 1987) (corroborated by interviews with the author at Ascona Festa New Orleans Music Symposium, 1988).

[5] Reprinted in Paul Oliver: *Story of the Blues* (London, Barrie and Rockliffe, 1969).

[6] Grace King: *New Orleans: The Place and the People* (New York, Macmillan, 1895).

[7] *Ibid.*

[8] Danny Barker: *Buddy Bolden and the Last Days of Storyville* (ed: Alyn Shipton) (London, Cassell, 1998).

[9] Julio Finn: *The Bluesman: The Musical Heritage of Black Men and Women in the Americas*

(London, Quartet, 1986) gives a useful chronicle of the place of voodoo in the development of African American music. See also Eileen Southern: *Music of the Black Americans: A History* (3rd. edn.) (New York, Norton, 1997).

[10] Reprinted in Rex Harris: *Jazz* (Harmondsworth, Penguin, 1952).

[11] Alan Lomax: *Mister Jelly Roll: The Fortunes of Jelly Roll Morton, New Orleans Creole and "Inventor of Jazz"* (rev. edn.) (New York, Pantheon, 1993).

[12] Samuel B. Charters IV: *Jazz. New Orleans 1885–1963: An Index to the Negro Musicians of New Orleans* (rev. edn.) (New York, Oak Books, 1963).

[13] Eileen Southern: *op. cit.*; Lydia Parrish: *Slave Songs of the Georgia Sea Islands* (New York, Creative Age Press, Inc., 1942) (quoting N. G. J. Ballanta, suggests that the "Negroes in the United States" employ a pitch system of seventeen gradations within the octave).

[14] Richard Alan Waterman: "African influence on the music of the Americas," in Sol Tax (ed.): *Acculturation in the Americas* (Chicago, University of Chicago Press, 1952). Quoted in Paul Oliver: *Savannah Syncopators* (London, Studio Vista, 1970).

[15] Stan Hugill: "Shanty," in Stanley Sadie (ed.): *The New Grove Dictionary of Music and Musicians* (London, Macmillan, 1981). Lydia Parrish: *op. cit.* mentions that it was common practice, as reported by the slaver Captain Canot, for "men, women, girls and boys" to be allowed on deck "to unite in African melodies," but it is equally likely that they heard the songs of the crew, both at work and at leisure in the forecastle.

[16] Charles Joyner: *Down by the Riverside: A South Carolina Slave Community* (Urbana, University of Illinois Press, 1984). He states that the language was adopted by African-Americans who hailed from a widespread area of West Africa, and whose familial tongues included Fante, Ga, Kikongo, Kimbundu, Makinda, Twi, Ewe, Ibo, and Yoruba. Elements of all these found their way into the new language, although earlier sources have suggested a more restricted provenance. The Carolina Low Country (Society for the Preservation of Spirituals) (New York, Macmillan, 1931) links the Gullah of the Carolinas specifically to Angola, but Lydia Parrish *op. cit.*, p. 41, suggests a wider West African provenance.

[17] Howard Rye and Tim Brooks: *Visiting Firemen 16: Dan Kildare* (Storyville 1996/7, Chigwell, 1997) was the first published attempt to reassess these valuable sound documents. The recordings are available on *The Earliest Black String Bands, Vol. 1: Dan Kildare* (Document 5622).

[18] Lowell H. Schreyer: "The banjo in ragtime," and Frank J. Gillis: "Hot rhythm in piano ragtime," in John Edward Hasse (ed.): *Ragtime: Its History, Composers and Music* (London, Macmillan, 1985).

[19] Author's interview with Blue Lu Barker for BBC Radio, May 1997.

[20] Paul Oliver: *Songsters and Saints* (Cambridge, Cambridge University Press, 1984).

[21] Alan Lomax: *op.cit*

[22] Samuel B. Charters IV: *op.cit.*

[23] Danny Barker: *A Life in Jazz* (ed. Alyn Shipton) (London, Macmillan, 1986).

[24] Joe Darensbourg: *Telling It Like It Is* (ed. Peter Vacher) (London, Macmillan, 1987).

[25] Gunther Schuller: *Early Jazz: Its Roots and Musical Development* (New York, Oxford University Press, 1968).

[26] "Will Marion Cook on negro music," *New York Age*, September 21, 1918.

[27] *New York Age*, May 9, 1912.

[28] Barney Bigard: *With Louis and the Duke* (ed. Barry Martyn) (London, Macmillan, 1985).

[29] *New York Age*, October 27, 1910; *New York Age*, September 9, 1912.

[30] *New York Age*, September 21, 1918.

[31] *New York Age*, May 17, 1919. Subsequent billings for Carnegie Hall from the issue of July 27, 1919.

[32] "Making music for the army," *New York Age*, January 4, 1919.

[33] Edward A. Berlin: *King of Ragtime: Scott Joplin and His Era* (New York, Oxford University Press, 1994).

[34] W. W. Kenilworth: "Demoralizing rag time music." *Musical Courier* 46 (May 28, 1913), 22, quoted in Edward A. Berlin: *op. cit.*

[35] Rex Stewart: *Boy Meets Horn* (ed. Claire P. Gordon) (Oxford, Bayou Press, 1991).

[36] Rainer E. Lotz: "*The musical spillers*." Privately published paper (August 1992).

[37] Edward A. Berlin: *op. cit.*

[38] Rex Stewart: *op. cit.*

[39] *Baltimore Afro-American*, December 8, 1917.

[40] Paul Oliver: "That certain feeling: blues and jazz . . . in 1890?" *Popular Music* (1991), 10 (1), 11.

[41] Eileen Southern: *op.cit.* p. 338 discusses this.

[42] W. C. Handy: "How I came to write the 'Memphis Blues,'" *New York Age*, December 7, 1916. (Dates of publication are from the worklist in Eileen Southern: "W. C. Handy," in H. Wiley Hitchcock and Stanley Sadie (eds.): *The New Grove Dictionary of American Music* (London, Macmillan, 1986.))

[43] *Ibid.*

[44] Attention to the words of the blues has been the focus of several significant books by Robert Macleod, Paul Oliver, Jeff Todd Titon, and Guido Van Rijn.

[45] She certainly did not sell the "million" copies suggested by Perry Bradford and numerous other sources. In his researches for the fourth edition of Godrich and Dixon's *Blues and Gospel Records*, Howard Rye ascertained that Bessie Smith's *Downhearted Blues/ Gulf Coast Blues*, Columbia's best-selling blues record of all, prior to 1929, managed a total of just 276,796 units. It is improbable that Okeh, for whom Mamie Smith recorded, was any more successful.

[46] "Quality corporation books Mamie Smith," *New York Age*, November 13, 1920.

[47] Garvin Bushell (as told to Mark Tucker): *Jazz from the Beginning* (Oxford, Bayou Press, 1988).

[48] *Ibid.*

[49] Adolphus "Doc" Cheatham: *I Guess I'll Get the Papers and Go Home* (ed. Alyn Shipton) (London and Washington, Cassell, 1995).

[50] Garvin Bushell: *op. cit.*

[51] Perry Bradford: *Born with the Blues: Perry Bradford's Own Story* (New York, Oak Publications, 1965).

[52] Sophie Tucker: *Some of These Days* (New York, Hammond, 1948).

[53] Black Swan was preceded by Broome, as an African-American-owned label, and also by the obscure See Bee, but there is little information about these, and Black Swan was certainly the first such label to make any impression upon the market.

[54] Other African-American musicians did make recordings with some jazz content prior to

Ory, and not in the role of accompanists – the reed improvisations of Wilber Sweatman, in 1917, are the first examples of a recorded jazz solo, and the orchestras of W. C. Handy and Ford Dabney have a few jazz elements in what are otherwise orchestral ragtime discs.

[55] I have discussed the origin of this term with Paul Oliver, who ascribes its coinage to Rudi Blesh's jazz criticism of the 1940s.

[56] Thomas L. Riis: *More Than Just Minstrel Shows: The Rise of Black Musical Theater at the Turn of the Century* (I.S.A.M. Monographs no. 33: Brooklyn, Institute for Studies in American Music, 1992).

[57] *Ibid.*

[58] Derrick Stewart-Baxter: *Ma Rainey and the Classic Blues Singers* (London, Studio Vista, 1970).

[59] *Ibid.*

[60] Richard K. Spottswood: "Country classic and vaudeville women and the blues," in Lawrence Cohn: *Nothing But the Blues* (New York, Abbeville Press, 1993).

[61] Derrick Stewart-Baxter: *op. cit.*

[62] Teddy Wilson: *Teddy Wilson Talks Jazz* (ed. Arie Ligthart and Humphrey Van Loo) (London, Cassell, 1996).

[63] Bud Freeman: *Crazeology: The Autobiography of a Chicago Jazzman* (ed. Robert Wolf) (Oxford, Bayou Press, 1989).

[64] Danny Barker: *A Life in Jazz* (ed. Alyn Shipton) (London, Macmillan, 1986).

[65] Art Hodes: *Hot Man* (ed. Chadwick Hansen) (Oxford, Bayou Press, 1992).

[66] "Luckey Roberts supplies Prince of Wales w. records," *Baltimore Afro-American*, July 23, 1927.

[67] *New York Age*, February 7, 1920.

[68] Tom Davin: "Conversations with James P. Johnson," reprinted in John Edward Hasse: *Ragtime: Its History, Composers and Music* (London, Macmillan, 1985).

[69] *Ibid.*

[70] *Ibid.*

[71] *New York Age*, January 21, 1922.

[72] *New York Age*, January 28, 1922.

[73] Edward Brooks: *The Bessie Smith Companion* (2nd. edn.) (Oxford, Bayou Press, 1989).

[74] *New York Age*, July 1, 1922.

[75] Garvin Bushell: *op. cit.*

[76] *Pittsburgh Courier*, January 21, 1928.

[77] Chip Deffaa: *Voices of the Jazz Age* (Oxford, Bayou Press, 1990).

[78] Sammy Price: *What Do They Want?* (ed. Caroline Richmond) (Oxford, Bayou Press, 1989).

[79] Quoted in Lucien Malson: "Schaeffner 1926: Un premier livre sur le jazz et les racines africaines," *Revue de musicologie* (1982), 68, 1–2 (a volume in homage to André Schaeffner, titled Les Fantaisies du voyageur), subsequently reprinted in *Des Musiques du jazz* (Paris, Editions Parentheses, 1983).

[80] Quoted in William J. Schafer: *Brass Bands and New Orleans Jazz* (Baton Rouge, Louisiana State University Press, 1977).

[81] Harry Dial: *All This Jazz about Jazz* (Chigwell, Storyville, 1984).

[82] Ramsey, quoted in William J. Schafer: *op. cit.*

[83] Sammy Price: *op. cit.*

[84] Buck Clayton: *Buck Clayton's Jazz World* (ed. Nancy Miller Elliott) (Oxford, Bayou Press, 1989).

[85] *Ibid.*

[86] Joe Darensbourg: *op. cit.*

[87] Austin M. Sonnier: *Willie Geary "Bunk" Johnson* (New York, Crescendo, 1977).

[88] Bill Coleman: *Trumpet Story* (London, Macmillan, 1990).

[89] Rex Stewart: *op. cit*

[90] Joe Darensbourg: *op. cit.*

[91] William J. Schafer: *op. cit.*

[92] *Ibid.*

[93] John Chilton: *A Jazz Nursery: The Story of the Jenkins Orphanage Bands* (London, Bloomsbury Book Shop, 1980).

# Chapter 2

[1] Grace King: *New Orleans: The Place and the People* (New York, Macmillan, 1895).

[2] Chapters 1 to 3 of Nat Shapiro and Nat Hentoff: *Hear Me Talkin' to Ya* (Harmondsworth, Penguin, 1962) contain several such suggestions from musicians.

[3] Roy Carew: "The New Orleans legend," *The Jazz Reprints*, 1 (3) (Southsea, UK, 1963).

[4] Larry Gara: *The Baby Dodds Story* (Baton Rouge, Louisiana State University Press, 1992).

[5] Danny Barker: *A Life in Jazz* (ed. Alyn Shipton) (London, Macmillan, 1986).

[6] Roy Carew: *op. cit.*

[7] Samuel B. Charters IV: *Jazz. New Orleans 1885–1963: An Index to the Negro Musicians of New Orleans* (rev. edn.) (New York, Oak Books, 1963).

[8] Roy Carew: *op. cit.*

[9] Lee Collins: *Oh, Didn't He Ramble: The Life Story of Lee Collins as Told to Mary Collins* (ed. Frank Gillis and John Miner) (2nd. edn.) (Oxford, Bayou Press, 1989).

[10] Roy Carew: *op. cit.*

[11] Paul Whiteman (and Mary Margaret McBride): *Jazz* (New York, J. H. Sears, 1926).

[12] Autograph letter from Benson, reproduced in Danny Barker: *Buddy Bolden and the Last Days of Storyville* (ed. Alyn Shipton) (London, Cassell, 1998).

[13] Donald M. Marquis: *Finding Buddy Bolden* (Goshen, IA, Pinchpenny Press, 1978).

[14] Alan Lomax: *Mister Jelly Lord: The Fortunes of Jelly Roll Morton: New Orleans Creole and Inventor of Jazz* (rev. edn.) (New York, Pantheon, 1993).

[15] *Ibid.*, and Danny Barker: *A Life in Jazz* (ed. Alyn Shipton) (London, Macmillan, 1986).

[16] Cy Chain: "Bud Scott," *The Jazz Reprints*, 1 (3) (Southsea, UK, 1963).

[17] Roy Carew: *op. cit.*

[18] Danny Barker: *A Life in Jazz* (London, Macmillan, 1986).

[19] Larry Gara: *op. cit.*

[20] Lee Collins: *op. cit.*

[21] Barney Bigard: *With Louis and the Duke* (ed. Barry Martyn) (London, Macmillan, 1985).

[22] Alan Lomax: *op. cit.*

[23] Roy Carew: *op. cit.*

[24] Alan Lomax: *op. cit.*

[25] Bunk Johnson, interviewed by Bill Russell, May 7, 1943, San Francisco, and issued on "Early Bunk 1942–43," (American Music Unissued Series, Dan VC 7022).

[26] Louis Armstrong: *Louis Armstrong in His Own Words* (ed. Thomas Brothers) (New York, Oxford University Press, 1999).

[27] Tom Davin: "Conversations with James P. Johnson," reprinted in John Edward Hasse: *Ragtime: Its History, Composers and Music* (London, Macmillan, 1985).

[28] Gunther Schuller: "Rags, the classics and jazz," in John Edward Hasse: *op. cit.*

[29] Gunther Schuller: "Morton, Jelly Roll," in Barry Kernfeld (ed.) *The New Grove Dictionary of Jazz* (London, Macmillan, 1988); "The first great composer," Ch. 4 in *Early Jazz: Its Roots and Musical Development* (New York, Oxford University Press, 1968).

[30] Author's interview with Jesse Stone, March 9, 1997.

[31] John G. Heinz: "The world's greatest manipulator: recollections of Sam Davis," *Storyville*, 149 (March 1992), 180. Between periods of working the District in New Orleans, Davis played at the Charles Theater, Beaumont, Texas, and the Silver King in Houston around 1900, traveled with the A. H. Brown Carnival, and toured vaudeville with Drake and Walker. He roomed with Morton in Chicago, Dallas, and Detroit, where Morton apparently eloped with the female owner of their "rooming house."

[32] James Dapogny: "Jelly Roll Morton and ragtime," in John Edward Hasse: *op. cit.*

[33] *Ibid.*

[34] Andy Kirk: *Twenty Years on Wheels* (ed. Amy Lee) (Oxford, Bayou Press, 1989); Joe Darensbourg: *Telling It Like It Is* (ed. Peter Vacher) (London, Macmillan, 1987); Marshal Royal: *Jazz Survivor* (ed. Claire P. Gordon) (London, Cassell, 1996).

[35] Rex Stewart: *Boy Meets Horn* (ed. Claire P. Gordon) (Oxford, Bayou Press, 1991).

[36] Danny Barker: *A Life in Jazz* (ed. Alyn Shipton) (London, Macmillan, 1986).

[37] Pekka Gronow and Ilpo Saunio: *An International History of the Recording Industry* (trans. Christopher Moseley) (London, Cassell, 1998).

[38] For many years this was thought to have been 1922, but Floyd Levin's researches into the Nordskog recording company prove Ory's dics to have been cut in 1921. See Floyd Levin: "Kid Ory's legendary Nordskog/Sunshine recordings," *New Orleans Music*, 2 (4) (April 1991), 16.

[39] Frank Kofsky: *Black Music, White Business* (New York, Pathfinder, 1998).

[40] Johnny St. Cyr, quoted in Alan Lomax: *op. cit.*

[41] Danny Barker: *Buddy Bolden and the Last Days of Storyville* (ed. Alyn Shipton) (London, Cassell, 1998).

[42] *Down Beat*, January 1, 1941, quoted in John Chilton: *Sidney Bechet: The Wizard of Jazz* (London, Macmillan, 1987).

[43] William Howland Kenney: *Chicago Jazz: A Cultural History 1904–1930* (New York, Oxford University Press, 1993).

[44] *Ibid.*

[45] Nick LaRocca, interviewed in Brian Rust: "Grateful for the warning" *Storyville*, 9 (February–March 1967), 25.

[46] Rudi Blesh: liner notes to "*The Original Dixieland Jazz Band*" (RCA RD 7919, 1968); Pekka Gronow and Ilpo Saunio: *op. cit.*

[47] F. T. Vreeland: "More about 'jazz'" from the *Sunday Sun*, reprinted in the *New York Age*,

November 8, 1917.

[48] See note 45.

[49] "A letter from Bix," *Storyville*, 9 (February–March 1967).

[50] James T. Maher and Rudi Blesh, quoted in Richard M. Sudhalter: *Lost Chords* (New York, Oxford University Press, 1999).

[51] Mezz Mezzrow and Bernard Wolfe: *Really the Blues* (New York, Random House, 1946).

[52] Interview with Frederick Ramsey Jr.: *Down Beat*, December 15, 1940.

[53] George Bacquet's notes for a lecture given to New Orleans Jazz Club, April 17, 1948, reprinted in Alan Barrell: "B is for . . . Bacquet," *Footnote*, 17 (3) (February–March 1986).

[54] *Ibid.*, and Samuel B. Charters and Leonard Kunstadt: *Jazz: A History of the New York Scene* (2nd. edn.) (New York, Da Capo, 1981).

[55] Tom Stoddart: *Jazz on the Barbary Coast* (2nd. edn.) (Berkeley, CA, Heyday Books, 1998).

[56] *Ibid.*

[57] *Ibid.*

[58] From an autograph memoir by Fate Marable, reprinted in Wilma Dobie: "Remembering Fate Marable," *Storyville*, 38 (December 1971).

[59] Paul Vandervoort II: "The king of riverboat jazz," *Jazz Journal*, 23 (8) (August 1970).

[60] Dobie: *op. cit.*; Gara: *op. cit.*; Vandervoort: *op. cit.*; Harry Dial: *All This Jazz about Jazz* (Chigwell, Storyville, 1984).

[61] Louis Armstrong: *op. cit.*

[62] Larry Gara: *op. cit.*

[63] Harry Dial: *op. cit.*

[64] Data from 1940 census: Chicago population 3,396,808; immigrants 672,705; negroes 277,731.

[65] Bud Freeman: *Crazeology: The Autobiography of a Chicago Jazzman* (ed. Robert Wolf) (Oxford, Bayou Press, 1989).

[66] William Howland Kenney: *op. cit.*

[67] Personnel details from Laurie Wright: *King Oliver* (Chigwell, Storyville, 1987).

[68] The story of Oliver's "Harmon" mute is in *Down Beat*, March 1, 1940.

[69] Bud Freeman: *op. cit.*

[70] Larry Gara: *op. cit.*

[71] Louis Armstrong: *op. cit.*

[72] *Ibid.*

[73] *Chicago Defender*, August 18, 1923, and September 1, 1923; *New York Clipper*, September 14, 1923.

[74] *Chicago Defender*, October 6, 1923.

[75] Dating from James Dapogny: *Ferdinand Jelly Roll Morton: The Collected Piano Music* (Washington, Smithsonian Institution, 1982).

[76] The parts for *High Society* and *Oh, Didn't He Ramble* have now been published in William Russell: *Jelly Roll Morton Scrapbook* (Copenhagen, JazzMedia APS, 1999).

[77] The commercial affiliation between publisher and label is recounted in Rick Kennedy: *Jelly Roll, Bix and Hoagy: Gennett Studios and the Birth of Recorded Jazz* (Bloomington, Indiana University Press, 1994).

[78] James Dapogny: *op. cit.*

[79] Nat Shapiro and Nat Hentoff: *op. cit.*

[80] *Ibid.*

[81] "The melodic instruments of the classic jazz band, frequently clarinet, cornet and trombone ... comprised the portion of the improvising jazz ensemble that was primarily melodic and syncopated." Frank Tirro: *Jazz: A History* (New York, Norton, 1993); Rudi Blesh's concept of the polyphonic "stomp pattern" in the front line, articulated in *Shining Trumpets*, is similar.

[82] Rick Kennedy: *op. cit.*

[83] Gunther Schuller: *Early Jazz: Its Roots and Musical Development* (New York, Oxford University Press, 1968).

[84] *Pittsburgh Courier*, April 16, 1927.

[85] James Dapogny: *op. cit.*

[86] *Pittsburgh Courier*, May 7, 1927.

[87] Gunther Schuller's *Early Jazz* has a full analysis of several of the Red Hot Pepper pieces.

[88] Gunther Schuller: "Morton, Jelly Roll," in Barry Kernfeld: *op. cit.*

[89] Samuel B. Charters and Leonard Kunstadt: *op. cit.*

[90] Richard Hadlock: *Jazz Masters of the Twenties* (New York, Macmillan, 1965). Further illuminating discussion of this disc is to be found in Edward Brooks: *The Bessie Smith Companion* (2nd. edn.) (Oxford, Bayou Press, 1989) and Humphrey Lyttelton: *The Best of Jazz (i): Basin Street to Harlem* (Harmondsworth, Penguin, 1978).

[91] Ernst-Alexandre Ansermet: "Bechet and jazz visit Europe," reprinted in Andrew Clark: *Riffs and Choruses* (London, Continuum, 2001).

[92] Samuel B. Charters and Leonard Kunstadt: *op. cit.*

[93] "Bessie Smith to play south during fall," *Pittsburgh Courier*, September 12, 1925; "Blues queen goes big at New Lincoln," *ibid.*, March 22, 1924; "Bessie Smith to appear at Star next week," *ibid.*; "Bessie Smith, nationally known singer of 'blues' is stabbed by highwayman," *Pittsburgh Courier*, March 7, 1925.

[94] Columbia catalog, reproduced in Samuel B. Charters and Leonard Kunstadt: *op. cit.*

[95] Louis Armstrong: *Swing That Music* (New York, Da Capo, 1993).

[96] *Pittsburgh Courier*, August 29, 1925.

[97] Louis Armstrong: *Louis Armstrong in His Own Words* (ed. Thomas Brothers) (New York, Oxford University Press, 1999).

[98] Rex Stewart: *op. cit.*

[99] Max Jones and John Chilton: *Louis: The Louis Armstrong Story 1900–1971* (London, Quartet, 1971).

[100] Louis Armstrong: *Louis Armstrong in His Own Words* (ed. Thomas Brothers) (New York, Oxford University Press, 1999).

[101] Adolphus "Doc" Cheatham: *I Guess I'll Get the Papers and Go Home* (ed. Alyn Shipton) (London and Washington, Cassell, 1995).

[102] Louis Armstrong: *Swing That Music* (New York, Da Capo, 1993).

[103] Louis Armstrong: *Louis Armstrong in His Own Words* (ed. Thomas Brothers) (New York, Oxford University Press, 1999). The Okeh executive was E. A. Fearn, head of the Consolidated Talking Machine Company that distributed Okeh discs.

[104] *Ibid.*

[105] Hugues Panassié: *Hot Jazz* (translated from *Le Jazz hot*, Paris, Correa, 1934, by Lyle and Eleanor Dowling) (London, Cassell, 1936).

[106] Rudi Blesh: *Shining Trumpets* (London, Cassell, 1949).

[107] Biographical details from John Chilton: *Who's Who of Jazz* (5th. edn.) (London, Macmillan, 1989); Samuel B. Charters and Leonard Kunstadt: *op. cit.*

[108] The definitive account of this phenomenon is in Horst H. Lange: *The Fabulous Fives* (2nd. edn.) (Chigwell, Storyville, 1978).

[109] *New York Age*, November 8, 1917.

[110] Richard Hadlock: *op. cit.*

[111] "Joe Tarto," in Chip Deffaa: *Voices of the Jazz Age* (Oxford, Bayou Press, 1990).

[112] Albert McCarthy: *Big Band Jazz* (London, Barrie and Jenkins, 1974).

[113] Bud Freeman: *op. cit.*

[114] Richard Hadlock: *op. cit.*

[115] Gunther Schuller: *Early Jazz: Its Roots and Musical Development* (New York, Oxford University Press, 1968).

[116] Eddie Condon: *We Called It Music* (2nd. edn.) (Westport, CT, Greenwood Press, 1970).

[117] Richard M. Sudhalter, Philip R. Evans, and William Dean-Myatt: *Bix. Man and Legend: The Life of Bix Beiderbecke* (London, Quartet, 1974).

[118] Ralph Berton from an article in *Harper's* (November 1958), quoted in Richard Hadlock: *op. cit.*

[119] "Jimmy McPartland," in Max Jones: *Talking Jazz* (London, Macmillan, 1987).

[120] Nat Shapiro and Nat Hentoff: *op. cit.*

[121] "The pioneer: Bill Challis," in Gene Lees: *Arranging the Score* (London, Continuum, 2000).

[122] *Ibid.*

[123] For a brief history of the violin in jazz, see Matt Glaser and Alyn Shipton: "Violin," in Barry Kernfeld (ed.): *op. cit.*

[124] Arthur Rollini: *Thirty Years with the Big Bands* (Oxford, Bayou Press, 1989).

[125] Richard Hadlock: *op. cit.*

[126] Eddie Condon: *op. cit.*

[127] *Ibid.*

[128] "Jimmy McPartland," in Max Jones: *op. cit.*

[129] William Howland Kenney: *op. cit.*

[130] Barney Bigard: *op. cit.*

[131] William Howland Kenney: *op. cit.*

[132] Adolphus "Doc" Cheatham: *op. cit.*

[133] Gunther Schuller: *Early Jazz: Its Roots and Musical Development* (New York, Oxford University Press, 1968).

[134] Chip Deffaa: *op. cit.*

[135] Danny Barker: *A Life in Jazz* (ed. Alyn Shipton) (London, Macmillan, 1986).

# Chapter 3

[1] Figures from Cynthia Adams Hoover: "Piano," in H. Wiley Hitchcock and Stanley

Sadie (eds.): *The New Grove Dictionary of American Music* (London, Macmillan, 1986).

[2] Tom Davin: "Conversations with James P. Johnson," in John Edward Hasse: *Ragtime: Its History, Composers and Music* (London, Macmillan, 1985).

[3] John R. T. Davies: "Eubie Blake: his life and times," *Storyville*, 6 (August–September. 1966), 19.

[4] Eubie Blake, interviewed by Marian McPartland for *Piano Jazz*, NPR, December 15, 1979.

[5] Rudi Blesh: *Combo USA* (Philadelphia, Chilton Book Co., 1971).

[6] Mark Tucker: *Ellington: The Early Years* (Oxford, Bayou Press, 1991).

[7] Willie "The Lion" Smith (with George Hoefer): *Music on My Mind* (New York, Da Capo, 1978).

[8] Mark Tucker: *op. cit.*

[9] Eubie Blake, interviewed by Marian McPartland for *Piano Jazz*, NPR, December 15, 1979.

[10] Tom Davin: *op. cit.*

[11] Scott E. Brown: *James P. Johnson: A Case of Mistaken Identity* (Metuchen, N.J., Scarecrow, 1986).

[12] James P. Johnson confirmed that this range of music was being played from early in the twentieth century in and around New York and, undoubtedly, New York players brought these influences with them to Atlantic City, in the same way as players from elsewhere (see Tom Davin: *op. cit.*).

[13] Garvin Bushell (as told to Mark Tucker): *Jazz from the Beginning* (Oxford, Bayou Press, 1988).

[14] "Eubie Blake . . . is musical genius," *Pittsburgh Courier*, January 13, 1934.

[15] Scott E. Brown: *op. cit.*

[16] Nat Hentoff: "Harlem piano," (liner notes to *Luckey and The Lion*, Good Time Jazz, S10035, 1960).

[17] Willie "The Lion" Smith (with George Hoefer): *op. cit.*

[18] Rudolf Fisher: "The Caucasian storms Harlem," *The American Mercury*, 11 (1927), reprinted in Robert Walser: *Keeping Time: Readings in Jazz History* (New York, Oxford University Press, 1999).

[19] Henry A. Francis. "Musical attributes of Fats Waller the pianist," in Laurie Wright (ed.): *Fats in Fact* (Chigwell, Storyville, 1992).

[20] "Fats Waller," in Humphrey Lyttelton: *The Best of Jazz (ii): Enter the Giants* (London, Robson Books, 1981).

[21] Alyn Shipton: *Fats Waller: His Life and Times* (New York, Universe, 1988).

[22] Scott E. Brown: *op. cit.*

[23] *Baltimore Afro-American*, August 5, 1939.

[24] Teddy Wilson: *Teddy Wilson Talks Jazz* (ed. Arie Ligthart and Humphrey Van Loo) (London and New York, Cassell, 1996).

[25] *Ibid.*

[26] *Ibid.*

[27] Alyn Shipton: *Groovin' High: The Life of Dizzy Gillespie* (New York, Oxford University Press, 1999).

[28] James Lester: *Too Marvelous for Words: The Life and Genius of Art Tatum* (New York,

Oxford University Press, 1994).

[29] Teddy Wilson (with Arie Ligthart and Humphrey Van Loo): *op. cit.*, 1996; Alyn Shipton: *Groovin' High: The Life of Dizzy Gillespie* (New York, Oxford University Press, 1999).

[30] Felicity Howlett, quoted in James Lester: *op. cit.*

[31] Raymond Horricks: *These Jazzmen of Our Time* (London, Gollancz, 1959).

[32] Teddy Wilson: *op. cit.*

[33] Alan Groves and Alyn Shipton: *The Glass Enclosure: The Life of Bud Powell* (Oxford, Bayou Press, 1993).

[34] Billy Kyle: "Piano style," *Rhythm* (July 1939), 114; further information in Howard Rye: *Finishing up a Date* (liner notes to Collectors Items 020).

[35] *Ibid.*

[36] Ed Kirkeby: *Ain't Misbehavin': The Story of Fats Waller* (New York, Dodd Mead, 1966). Kirkeby relates the previous titles of this piece on p. 141.

[37] *Baltimore Afro-American*, August 5, 1939.

[38] Paul Oliver: *Conversation with the Blues* (London, Cassell, 1965).

[39] Peter Silvester: *A Left Hand Like God: A Study of Boogie Woogie* (London, Quartet, 1988).

[40] Danny Barker: *A Life in Jazz* (ed. Alyn Shipton) (London, Macmillan, 1986). Vaughan's playing can be heard with the Mississippi Jook Band on Document DOCD 5105.

[41] Danny Barker: "The horses: boogity, boogity, boogity, boogity." Unpublished manuscript in his papers for *A Life in Jazz*.

[42] Roy Carew: "Of this and that and Jelly Roll," *Jazz Journal*, X (xii) (December 1957).

[43] Paul Oliver: *op. cit.*

[44] Danny Barker: *A Life in Jazz* (ed. Alyn Shipton) (London, Macmillan, 1986).

[45] Samuel A. Floyd Jr.: "Ring shout! literary studies, historical studies and black music inquiry," *Black Music Research Journal*, 11 (2) (Fall 1991), reprinted in Robert Walser: *Keeping Time: Readings in Jazz History* (New York, Oxford University Press, 1999).

[46] Stanley Crouch: "Big train" (liner notes to *Lincoln Center Jazz Orchestra: Big Train*, Columbia CK 69860, 1998).

[47] Danny Barker: *A Life in Jazz* (ed. Alyn Shipton) (London, Macmillan, 1986).

[48] William Russell: "Boogie woogie," in Frederick Ramsey Jr. and Charles Edward Smith (eds.): *Jazzmen: The Story of Hot Jazz Told in the Lives of the Men Who Created It* (New York, Harcourt, Brace and Company, 1939).

[49] Art Hodes: *Barrelhouse Boogie* (liner notes to Bluebird ND 88334, 1989).

[50] *Ibid.*

[51] Gunther Schuller: *The Swing Era* (New York, Oxford University Press, 1989).

[52] Sammy Price: *What Do They Want?* (ed. Caroline Richmond) (Oxford, Bayou Press, 1989).

[53] Lewis A. Erenberg: *Swingin' the Dream: Big Band Jazz and the Rebirth of American Culture* (Chicago, University of Chicago Press, 1998).

# Chapter 4

[1] Arthur Rollini: *Thirty Years with the Big Bands* (Oxford, Bayou Press, 1989).

[2] Paul Whiteman (and Mary Margaret McBride): *Jazz* (New York, J. H. Sears, 1926).

NOTES

[3] Hugues Panassié: *Hot Jazz* (translated from *Le Jazz hot*, Paris, Correa, 1934, by Lyle and Eleanor Dowling) (London, Cassell, 1936).

[4] Albert McCarthy: *The Dance Band Era. The Dancing Decades from Ragtime to Swing: 1910–1950* (London, Spring Books, 1971).

[5] Frank Tirro: *Jazz: A History* (2nd. edn.) (New York, W. W. Norton, 1993).

[6] Barry Ulanov: *A History of Jazz in America* (London, Hutchinson, 1959).

[7] Rudi Blesh: *Shining Trumpets* (London, Cassell, 1949).

[8] Paul Whiteman: *op. cit.*

[9] *Chicago Examiner*, May 18, 1915, reprinted in *Storyville*, 137, 200.

[10] Paul Whiteman: *op. cit.*

[11] "Whiteman will play at Savoy," *New York Amsterdam News*, September 13, 1933.

[12] Paul Whiteman: *op. cit.*

[13] This period is aptly summarized in Chapter 7 of James Lincoln Collier: *Jazz: The American Theme Song* (New York, Oxford University Press, 1993).

[14] Writers' Program of the Works Progress Administration in Northern California: *San Francisco: The Bay and Its Cities* (New York, Hastings House, 1940). This is the source of all W.P.A. quotes given below, and sections are reprinted in Tom Stoddard: *Jazz on the Barbary Coast* (2nd. edn.) (Berkeley, CA Heyday Books, 1998).

[15] James Lincoln Collier: *op. cit.* Details of other saxophone groups from Wally Horwood: *Adolphe Sax 1814–1894: His Life and Legacy* (Baldock, Herts., Egon, 1983).

[16] Al Rose and Edmond Souchon: *New Orleans Jazz: A Family Album* (3rd. edn.) (Baton Rouge, Louisiana State University, 1984).

[17] "Interview with George Morrison," in Gunther Schuller: *Early Jazz: Its Roots and Musical Development* (New York, Oxford University Press, 1968).

[18] Paul Whiteman: *op. cit.*

[19] Paul Whiteman: *op. cit.*

[20] Ronald M. Radano: "Vernon Castle," in H. Wiley Hitchcock and Stanley Sadie (eds.): *The New Grove Dictionary of American Music* (London, Macmillan, 1986).

[21] Figures from Pekka Gronow and Ilpo Saunio: *An International History of the Recording Industry* (trans. Christopher Moseley) (London, Cassell, 1998). More exaggerated claims appear in Paul Whiteman: *Records for the Millions* (New York, Hermitage Press, 1948), in which Whiteman confesses that "I was torn between my symphonic training and a desire to present novel treatments of jazz music. To get new effects I increased my band from nine to twenty men within the first three years after it was organized."

[22] Roger Pryor Dodge: "Negro jazz," *The Dancing Times* (London, October 1929), reprinted in *Hot Jazz and Jazz Dance. Roger Pryor Dodge: Collected Writings 1929–1964* (New York, Oxford University Press, 1995).

[23] *Ibid.*

[24] Gilbert Seldes: *Seven Lively Arts* (New York, Harper, 1924).

[25] "Paul Whiteman," in Max Harrison (ed.): *A Jazz Retrospect* (Newton Abbot, Devon, David and Charles, 1976).

[26] *Ibid.*

[27] Paul Whiteman: (and Mary Margaret McBride): *Jazz* (New York, J. H. Sears, 1926).

[28] Roger Pryor Dodge: *op. cit.*

[29] Max Harrison: *op. cit.*

30 Interview with Michael Tilson Thomas for BBC World Service Meridian documentary *Rhapsody in Blue at 75*, transmitted February 13, 1999, presented by the author.

31 Richard Crawford: "George Gershwin," in H. Wiley Hitchcock and Stanley Sadie: *op. cit.*

32 Max Harrison: *op. cit.*

33 Author's interview with Jesse Stone, March 9, 1997.

34 Gunther Schuller: *Early Jazz: Its Roots and Musical Development* (New York, Oxford University Press, 1968).

35 Author's interview with Bill Doggett, April 30, 1996.

36 Claude and Jean-Pierre Battesini: "Jesse Stone: entretien du 18 May 1994," *Bulletin du Hot Club de France*, 440, 441, 442 (1995); 444 (1996) (author's translation).

37 Gunther Schuller in *Early Jazz* dates Stone's band as lasting from 1923 to 1929, but my own interviews with Stone, and those of the Battesinis, suggest that he was leading his own band from around 1918, and was not consistently a leader himself through the mid-1920s, working for other leaders including George E. Lee. I have accepted his dating as the basis for his importance in this chapter.

38 Author's interview with Jesse Stone, March 9, 1997.

39 Gunther Schuller: *op. cit.*

40 Claude and Jean-Pierre Battesini: *op. cit.*

41 Author's interview with Jesse Stone, March 9, 1997.

42 Author's interview with Jesse Stone, March 9, 1997.

43 Author's interview with Buddy Tate, February 22, 1997.

44 Gunther Schuller: *op. cit.*

45 Adolphus "Doc" Cheatham: *I Guess I'll Get the Papers and Go Home* (ed. Alyn Shipton) (London and Washington, Cassell, 1995).

46 Claude and Jean-Pierre Battesini: *op. cit.*

47 Andy Kirk: *Twenty Years on Wheels* (ed. Amy Lee) (Oxford, Bayou Press, 1989).

48 *Ibid.*

49 "Alberta Hunter, Ethel Waters, Clara Smith, Fletcher Henderson and other stars to sing for new corporation," *Pittsburgh Courier*, October 13, 1923.

50 Feather, quoted in Albert McCarthy: *Big Band Jazz* (London, Barrie and Jenkins, 1974).

51 Gunther Schuller: *op. cit.*

52 Albert McCarthy: *Big Band Jazz* (London, Barrie and Jenkins, 1974); Nat Shapiro and Nat Hentoff: *Hear Me Talkin' to Ya* (Harmondsworth, Penguin, 1962).

53 Danny Barker: *A Life in Jazz* (ed. Alyn Shipton) (London, Macmillan, 1986).

54 Bill Coleman: *Trumpet Story* (London, Macmillan, 1990).

55 Garvin Bushell, quoted in Richard Hadlock: *Jazz Masters of the Twenties* (New York, Macmillan, 1965).

56 Gunther Schuller: *op. cit.*

57 Edith Wilson and revue billed in "Theatrical jottings," *New York Age*, January 25, 1924 and April 5, 1924.

58 John Chilton: *Song of the Hawk* (London, Quartet, 1990).

59 Kathy J. Ogren: *The Jazz Revolution: Twenties America and the Meaning of Jazz* (New York, Oxford University Press, 1989).

60 Rex Stewart: *Boy Meets Horn* (ed. Claire P. Gordon) (Oxford, Bayou Press, 1991).

[61] "Fletcher Henderson's Band scores at the Lafayette this week," *New York Age*, January 21, 1928.

[62] "Creole Revels scores hit at the Lafayette," *New York Age*, May 12, 1928; "Fess Williams and his jazz joy boys are presenting 'Cheyenne Days,' assisted by some hones'-to-goodness 'Injuns' including the only tap-dancing Indian on the stage . . .," *Baltimore Afro-American*, September 8, 1928.

[63] Kathy J. Ogren: *op. cit.*

[64] Rex Stewart: *op. cit.*

[65] *New York Age*, April 4, 1925.

[66] Rex Stewart: *op. cit.*

[67] Rex Stewart: *Jazz Masters of the Thirties* (New York, Macmillan, 1972).

[68] Gene Lees: *Arranging the Score* (London, Continuum, 2000).

[69] Gunther Schuller: *op. cit.*

[70] Benny Waters: *The Key to a Jazzy Life* (Toulouse, Les Arts Graphiques, 1985).

[71] Benny Carter, interviewed by Charles Fox for BBC Radio, December 27, 1977.

[72] *Ibid.*

[73] *Ibid.*

[74] Rex Stewart: *Boy Meets Horn* (ed.Claire P. Gordon) (Oxford, Bayou Press, 1991).

[75] Pictures in Danny Barker: *Buddy Bolden and the Last Days of Storyville* (ed. Alyn Shipton) (London, Cassell, 1998); Al Rose and Edmond Souchon: *New Orleans Jazz; A Family Album* (3rd. edn.) (Baton Rouge, Louisiana State University, 1984).

[76] Danny Barker: *A Life in Jazz* (ed. Alyn Shipton) (London, Macmillan, 1986).

[77] Chip Deffaa, interview with Bill Challis, quoted in Chip Deffaa: *Voices of the Jazz Age* (Oxford, Bayou Press, 1990).

[78] Author's conversation with Wild Bill Davison, December 1987.

[79] Richard M. Sudhalter, Philip R. Evans, and William Dean-Myatt: *Bix. Man and Legend: The Life of Bix Beiderbecke* (London, Quartet, 1974).

[80] Richard M. Sudhalter: *Lost Chords* (New York, Oxford University Press, 1999).

[81] Gene Lees: "Cincinnatus afternoon: Spiegle Willcox," in *Waiting for Dizzy* (New York, Oxford University Press, 1991).

[82] Artie Shaw, quoted in Chip Deffaa: *op. cit.*

[83] Nat Shapiro and Nat Hentoff: *op. cit.*

[84] Max Jones: "Albert Nicholas," in *Talking Jazz* (London, Macmillan, 1987).

[85] John Chilton: *Ride Red Ride* (London, Cassell, 1999).

[86] "The great King Menelik. . . .," *Chicago Defender*, February 2, 1929.

[87] Philip Larkin: "The hottest record ever made," in *All What Jazz* (London, Faber, 1970).

[88] Author's conversation with Snub Mosley, October 23, 1978.

[89] Examples include "Luis Russell Band on long dance tour," *Pittsburgh Courier*, July 27, 1935; "Luis Russell and Ted Smith at the Savoy," *Pittsburgh Courier*, August 3, 1935.

[90] Ellington's handwritten notes for his autobiography, quoted in Stuart Nicholson: *Reminiscing in Tempo: A Portrait of Duke Ellington* (London, Sidgwick and Jackson, 1999).

[91] Mark Tucker: *Ellington: The Early Years* (Oxford, Bayou Press, 1991).

[92] Mills, from a *Down Beat* interview, quoted in Mark Tucker: *op. cit.*

[93] *Chicago Defender*, April 16, 1927.

[94] Mark Tucker: *op. cit.*

[95] *Variety*, December 7, 1927.

[96] *Variety*, February 17, 1926.

[97] Kathy J. Ogren: *op. cit.*

[98] *Variety*, October 24, 1928.

[99] *New York Amsterdam News*, August 30, 1930.

[100] Irving Mills, quoted in Stuart Nicholson: *op. cit.*

[101] Advertisement for Black and Tan's opening run, reproduced in Klaus Stratemann: *Duke Ellington: Day by Day and Film by Film* (Copenhagen, JazzMedia APS, 1992).

[102] *Chicago Tribune* advertisement, February 13, 1931, and transcript of Mills's speech from *Pictorial Magazine* no. 837, reproduced in Klaus Stratemann: *op. cit.*

[103] Ellington is, in the sense of "la politique des auteurs," an *auteur*, within the description I have quoted in the text, from Krin Gabbard. "The Jazz canon and its consequences," in his *Jazz Among the Discourses* (Durham, N.C., Duke University Press, 1995).

[104] Ellington, in a Danish Radio "Faces of Jazz" broadcast, published in Stuart Nicholson: *op. cit.*

[105] Jed Rasula: "The medium of memory: the seductive menace of records in jazz history," in Krin Gabbard: *op. cit.*

[106] Andre Hodeir and Gunther Schuller: "Duke Ellington," in Barry Kernfeld (ed.): *The New Grove Dictionary of Jazz* (London, Macmillan, 1988).

[107] Gunther Schuller: *op. cit.*

[108] Garvin Bushell: (as told by Mark Tucker): *Jazz from the Beginning* (Oxford, Bayou Press, 1988).

[109] Rex Stewart: *Boy Meets Horn* (ed. Claire P. Gordon) (Oxford, Bayou Press, 1991).

[110] Carter Harman interview with Ellington, 1964, quoted in Stuart Nicholson: *op. cit.*

[111] John Chilton: *Sidney Bechet: The Wizard of Jazz* (London, Macmillan, 1987).

[112] Ralph Ellison: "Homage to Duke Ellington on his birthday (1969)," reprinted in Mark Tucker: *The Duke Ellington Reader* (New York, Oxford University Press, 1993).

[113] R. D. Darrell: "Black Beauty," reprinted in Mark Tucker: *The Duke Ellington Reader* (New York, Oxford University Press, 1993).

[114] All quotations in the foregoing paragraph from material in Mark Tucker: *The Duke Ellington Reader* (New York, Oxford University Press, 1993).

[115] Rex Stewart: *op. cit.*

[116] Hugues Panassié: "Duke Ellington at the Salle Pleyel," in Mark Tucker: *The Duke Ellington Reader* (New York, Oxford University Press, 1993).

[117] Rex Stewart: *Boy Meets Horn* (ed. Claire P. Gordon) (Oxford, Bayou Press, 1981).

[118] Ellington, quoted by Barry Ulanov in Eddie Lambert: *A Listener's Guide to Duke Ellington* (Latham, MD, Scarecrow Press, 1999).

[119] *Baltimore Afro-American*, March 4, 1939, and "Ellington draws $10,000 for Regal Theater," *New York Amsterdam News*, March 16, 1940.

[120] Ellington, quoted in Nat Shapiro and Nat Hentoff: *op. cit.*

[121] John Briggs's review from *New York Post*, quoted in Mark Tucker: *The Duke Ellington Reader* (New York, Oxford University Press, 1993).

[122] Typical examples include J. Bradford Robinson in his essay "Swing," in Barry Kernfeld (ed.): *op. cit.*, which suggests the style "originated around 1930 when New Orleans jazz was in decline."

[123] Garvin Bushell (as told to Mark Tucker): *op. cit.*

[124] Albert McCarthy: *Big Band Jazz* (London, Barrie and Jenkins, 1974).

[125] Calloway, quoted in Samuel B. Charters and Leonard Kunstadt: *Jazz: A History of the New York Scene* (2nd. edn.) (New York, Da Capo, 1981).

[126] Author's interview with Milt Hinton, March 23, 1993.

[127] Adolphus "Doc" Cheatham: *op. cit.*

[128] Alyn Shipton: *Groovin' High: The life of Dizzy Gillespie* (New York, Oxford University Press, 1999); the notes on pp. 370–1 discuss these charts in more detail.

[129] Gunther Schuller: *Early Jazz: Its Roots and Musical Development* (New York, Oxford University Press, 1968).

[130] Danny Barker: *A Life in Jazz* (ed. Alyn Shipton) (London, Macmillan, 1986).

[131] Author's interview with Milt Hinton, March 23, 1993.

[132] Author's interview with Harry Dial, October 24, 1986.

[133] Garvin Bushell (as told to Mark Tucker): *op. cit.*

[134] *New York Age* billings, May 16, 1931; June 20, 1931, September 5, 1931; *Baltimore Afro-American*, October 17, 1931.

[135] "Colored band of 13 men plus leader (Baron Lee) and four specialty entertainers," *Variety*, May 9, 1933; and other contemporary billings from *Pittsburgh Courier* and *New York Age*.

[136] Danny Barker: *op.cit.*

[137] "Sharecroppers," *New York Amsterdam News*, November 17, 1936.

[138] John Hammond (with Irving Townsend): *John Hammond on the Record* (New York, Ridge Press, 1977).

[139] "Baron Lee out of Blue Rhythm Band," *Variety*, May 13, 1933.

[140] "Blue rhythm," *Variety*, 27 February 1935.

[141] Danny Barker: *A Life in Jazz* (ed. Alyn Shipton) (London, Macmillan, 1986).

[142] *Variety*, October 27, 1937.

[143] Stanley Dance: "The Return of Sy Oliver," *Jazz Journal*, XXIII/9 (September 1970), 2.

[144] Andy Kirk: *Twenty Years on Wheels* (ed. Amy Lee) (Oxford, Bayou Press, 1989).

[145] Wilcox interview with Stanley Dance, quoted in Albert McCarthy: *Big Band Jazz* (London, Barrie and Jenkins, 1974).

[146] *Ibid.*

[147] Max Jones: *op. cit.*

[148] Stanley Dance: "The return of Sy Oliver," *Jazz Journal*, XXIII/9 (September 1970), 2.

[149] Max Jones: *op. cit.*

[150] *Ibid.*

[151] Ian Crosbie: "Jimmie Lunceford message from Memphis, Part 2," *Jazz Journal*, XXV/2 (February 1972), 26.

[152] G. T. Simon: *The Big Bands* (4th. edn.) (New York, Schirmer, 1981).

[153] Count Basie, interviewed by Charles Fox for BBC Radio, November 7, 1975.

[154] *Ibid.*

[155] Chris Sheridan: *Count Basie: A Bio-Discography* (Westport CT, Greenwood, 1986).

[156] Jay McShann, interviewed by Charles Fox for BBC Radio 3, February 8, 1980.

[157] Buck Clayton: *Buck Clayton's Jazz World* (ed. Nancy Miller Elliott) (Oxford, Bayou Press, 1989).

[158] Earl Hines, interviewed by Charles Fox for BBC Radio 3 (no date).

[159] Buck Clayton: *op.cit.*

[160] Buddy Tate, in conversation with John Chilton, reprinted in Chilton: *Song of the Hawk* (London, Quartet, 1990).

[161] Author's interview with Louie Bellson, July 13, 1999.

[162] "Count Basie at Howard," *Baltimore Afro-American*, April 24, 1937; "Count Basie Ork. at Apollo," *New York Amsterdam News*, June 5, 1937.

[163] Count Basie, interviewed by Charles Fox for BBC Radio, November 7, 1975.

[164] John Chilton: *Song of the Hawk* (London, Quartet, 1990).

[165] Author's interview with Bill Dillard, March 24, 1993.

[166] Harry Dial: *All This Jazz about Jazz* (Chigwell, Storyville, 1984).

[167] *Ibid.*

[168] For a fuller account of the consolidation of minor labels, see Pekka Gronow and Ilpo Saunio: *op. cit.* See also "Paramount," in Barry Kernfeld (ed.): *op. cit.*

[169] "Jimmy McPartland," in Max Jones: *op. cit.*

[170] *Ibid.*

[171] Gunther Schuller: *The Swing Era* (New York, Oxford University Press, 1989).

[172] "Glenn was making arrangements, as well as playing, and Fud Livingston also arranged. Both were terrific. That band really swung," from "Jimmy McPartland," in Max Jones: *op. cit.*

[173] Richard B. Sudhalter: "The jazz age: New York in the twenties" (liner note to Bluebird ND 83136, 1991).

[174] James Lincoln Collier: *Benny Goodman and the Swing Era* (New York, Oxford University Press, 1989) opts for Murphy; Brian Rust: *Jazz Records 1897–1942* (5th. edn.) (Chigwell, Storyville, 1983) opts for Kincaide.

[175] Ross Firestone: *Swing, Swing, Swing: The Life and Times of Benny Goodman* (New York, W. W. Norton, 1993).

[176] The disc, which involves the Big Band of Toulouse, France, is *Bob Wilber: Fletcher Henderson's Unrecorded Arrangements for Benny Goodman* (Arbors ARCD 19229, 1999).

[177] "Helen Ward," obituary, *The Times*, London, May 15, 1998.

[178] Lewis A. Erenberg: *Swingin' the Dream: Big Band Jazz and the Rebirth of American Culture* (Chicago, University of Chicago Press, 1998).

[179] James Lincoln Collier: *Benny Goodman and the Swing Era* (New York, Oxford University Press, 1989).

[180] James Dugan and John Hammond: "From spirituals to swing," reprinted in Robert Walser: *Keeping Time – Readings in Jazz History* (New York, Oxford University Press, 1999).

[181] Krin Gabbard (ed.): *Jammin' at the Margins: Jazz and the American Cinema* (Chicago, University of Chicago Press, 1996).

[182] Lewis A. Erenberg: *op. cit.*

[183] Ross Firestone: *op. cit.*

[184] James Dugan and John Hammond: *op. cit.*

[185] Arthur Rollini: *op. cit.*

[186] Teddy Wilson: *Teddy Wilson Talks Jazz* (ed. Arie Ligthart and Humphrey Van Loo) (London, Cassell, 1996).

[187] *Ibid.*

[188] Information on Christian from Collier: *Benny Goodman and the Swing Era* (New York, Oxford University Press, 1989). Firestone: *op. cit.*, and also from Dave Gelly "Charlie Christian," in Charles Alexander: *Masters of Jazz Guitar* (London, Balafon Books, 1999).

[189] Bud Freeman: *Crazeology; The Autobiography of a Chicago Jazzman* (ed. Robert Wolf) (Oxford, Bayou Press, 1989).

[190] Max Kaminsky: *My Life in Jazz* (London, Andre Deutsch, 1965).

[191] " 'Dorsey Brothers missed golden opportunity' says Hammond," *Down Beat*, July 1935.

[192] Bill Crow: *Jazz Anecdotes* (New York, Oxford University Press, 1990).

[193] Max Jones: *Talking Jazz* (London, Macmillan, 1987).

[194] Gunther Schuller: *op. cit.*

[195] Shaw liner notes, quoted in John White: *Artie Shaw; Non-stop Flight* (Hull, Eastnote, 1998).

[196] Gunther Schuller: *op. cit.*

[197] This is not to say that his original rhythm section was deficient; drummer Sammy Weiss, who had been Gene Krupa's predecessor with Goodman at the Billy Rose Music Hall, was a fiery and dramatic swing drummer. However, the earlier group's discs were not so consistent as those with Leeman.

[198] *Down Beat*, September 1938, quoted in John Chilton: *Billie's Blues* (London, Quartet, 1975).

[199] *Metronome*, May 1938; Hammond's *Down Beat* piece, quoted in Ross Firestone: *op. cit.*; final *Down Beat* excerpt from John White: *op. cit.*

[200] *Time*, January 23, 1939.

[201] John White: *op. cit.* There is a useful discussion of the degree to which Shaw improvised his solos, often with such an innate sense of form that some commentators believed they were composed, in Gene Lees: *Meet Me at Jim and Andy's: Jazz Musicians and Their World* (New York, Oxford University Press, 1988).

[202] Artie Shaw: *The Trouble with Cinderella: An Outline of Identity* (2nd. edn.) (New York, Da Capo, 1979).

[203] Lewis A. Erenberg: *op. cit.*

[204] Marshal Royal: *Jazz Survivor* (ed. Claire P. Gordon) (London, Cassell, 1996).

[205] Author's interview with Roscoe Mitchell, September 2, 2000.

[206] Peter J. Levinson: *Trumpet Blues: The Life of Harry James* (New York, Oxford University Press, 2000).

[207] *Ibid.*

[208] "Teagarden 'Broke' but happy," *Down Beat*, March 1, 1940.

[209] For more information on International Sweethearts Of Rhythm see Sally Placksin: *Jazz Women: 1900 to the Present* (London, Pluto Press, 1982)  and on Benson, see Lucy O'Brien: *She-Bop* (London, Penguin, 1995).

[210] Albert McCarthy: *Big Band Jazz* (London, Barrie and Jenkins, 1974).

[211] Gene Lees: *Meet Me at Jim and Andy's: Jazz Musicians and Their World* (New York, Oxford University Press, 1988).

# Chapter 5

1 "In Dahomey," in Kurt Gänzl: *The Encyclopedia of Musical Theatre* (Vol. 1) (Oxford, Blackwell, 1994).

2 Vodery, reported in *New York Age*, January 4, 1919; Europe details from his obituary, *New York Age*, May 17, 1919.

3 "Ted Heath," in John Chilton: *Who's Who of British Jazz* (London, Cassell, 1997).

4 Jeffrey P. Green: "Edmund Thornton Jenkins," in Barry Kernfeld (ed.): *The New Grove Dictionary of Jazz* (London, Macmillan, 1988). See also his book *Edmund Thornton Jenkins: The Life and Times of an American Black Composer, 1894–1926* (Westport, CT, Greenwood Press, 1982).

5 John Chilton: *Sidney Bechet: The Wizard of Jazz* (London, Macmillan, 1987).

6 Howard Rye: "The Plantation Revues," in *Storyville*, 133 (March 1988), 4.

7 Harry Gold: *Gold Doubloons and Pieces of Eight: The Autobiography of Harry Gold* (ed. R. Cotterrell) (London, Northway, 2000).

8 Arthur Rollini: *Thirty Years with the Big Bands* (Oxford, Bayou Press, 1989).

9 Jim Godbolt: *A History of Jazz in Britain, 1919–50* (London, Quartet, 1984).

10 "When I started gigging in 1950 I worked with veteran musicians who still talked excitedly about hearing Jimmy Dorsey live in 1930." John Chilton, letter to the author, December 2000.

11 Leslie Thompson, interviewed by Olga and Kevin Wright: "My face is my fortune," *Storyville*, 83 (June/July 1979).

12 Adolphus "Doc" Cheatham: *I Guess I'll Get the Papers and Go Home* (ed. Alyn Shipton) (London and Washington, Cassell, 1995).

13 Leslie Thompson: *op. cit.*

14 *Ibid.*

15 Benny Carter, interviewed by Charles Fox for BBC Radio, December 1977.

16 *Ibid.*

17 Alyn Shipton: *Groovin' High: The Life of Dizzy Gillespie* (New York, Oxford University Press, 1999).

18 Eileen Southern: *Music of the Black Americans: A History* (3rd. edn.) (New York, Norton, 1997).

19 "Sam Wooding," in Chip Deffaa: *Voices of the Jazz Age* (Oxford, Bayou Press, 1990); more information about Ellington and Trent's contribution to *Chocolate Kiddies* is in Mark Tucker: *Ellington: The Early Years* (Oxford, Bayou Press, 1991).

20 Garvin Bushell (as told to Mark Tucker): *Jazz from the Beginning* (Oxford, Bayou Press, 1988).

21 Adolphus "Doc" Cheatham: *op. cit.*

22 Garvin Bushell: *op. cit.*

23 *Ibid.*

24 "Sam Wooding," in Chip Deffaa: *op. cit.*

25 Vautel's comments reported in *Baltimore Afro-American*, March 3, 1928.

26 *New York Age*, March 3, 1928; *Baltimore Afro-American*, March 3, 1928.

27 Michael Danzi: "With Alex Hyde to Germany," in *American Musician in Germany, 1924–1939, as Told to Rainer Lotz* (Schmitten, Ruecker, 1986).

[28] Report of U.S. premiere in *New York Age*, January 26, 1929.

[29] German reviews summarized in *New York Age*, January 26, 1929.

[30] Michael Danzi: *op. cit.*

[31] Mike Zwerin: *Swing under the Nazis: Jazz as a Metaphor for Freedom* (New York, Cooper Square Press, 2000).

[32] "Worked with White Star right under Hitler's nose," *New York Amsterdam News*, July 17, 1937.

[33] Frank Driggs: "Herb Flemming," *Storyville*, 69 (February/March 1977), 84.

[34] Mike Zwerin: *op. cit.*

[35] "Charles Baker took jazz to Paris," obituary, *Baltimore Afro-American* April 7, 1928; Baker claimed to have performed before Grand Duke Alexander of Russia, although it is more probable that this was King Alexander I of the Serbs, Croats, and Slovenes, who was in Paris in 1915 during the period of his exiled government in Corfu.

[36] Rudolph Dunbar: *Triumph and Tragedy* (Oxford, Bayou Press, forthcoming).

[37] Phyllis Rose: *Jazz Cleopatra: Josephine Baker in Her Time* (New York, Doubleday, 1989).

[38] "'Lucky' Millinder plays Monte Carlo,"*Chicago Defender*, June 24, 1933; "Lucky Millinder a real hit in Monte Carlo," *Chicago Defender*, October 7, 1933.

[39] "Gregor," in P. Carles, A. Clergeat, and J.-L. Comolli: *Dictionnaire du jazz* (Paris, Laffont, 1988).

[40] The standard biography is Charles Delaunay: *Django Reinhardt* (trans. Michael James) (2nd. edn.) (London, Cassell, 1981); most of the information in this section is drawn from it.

[41] François Billard and Alain Antonietto: "De la virtuosité Tsigane ...," in François Billard: *Django Reinhardt: Un géant sur son nuage* (Paris, Lieu Commun, 1993) (author's translation).

[42] d'Anglemont, quoted in François Billard and Alain Antonietto: *op. cit.*

[43] Geoffrey Smith: *Stephane Grappelli: A Biography* (London, Michael Joseph/Pavilion, 1987); François Billard: *op. cit.*

[44] Bill Coleman: *Trumpet Story* (London, Macmillan, 1990).

[45] Author's interview with Al Casey for BBC Radio, November 22, 1998.

[46] Jan Bruér and Bengt Nyquist: "Varning For Jazz" (trans. Gregory David Pastic) (liner notes to *Svensk Jazzhistoria*, 1) (Swedish Jazz 1899–1930, Caprice 22037, 1998).

[47] Most of this information is based on Jan Bruér and Bengt Nyquist: "Hot-epoken," (trans. Jan Bruér and Lars Westin) (liner notes to *Svensk Jazzhistoria*, 2) (Swedish Jazz 1931–1936, Caprice 22038, 1998), this and the first volume cited above contain all the significant recordings referred to in the text.

[48] Rollini's visit was covered in the fall 1977 issue of *Dr. Jazz* magazine, and is summarized in Arthur Rollini: *Thirty Years with the Big Bands* (Oxford, Bayou Press, 1989).

[49] Information and contemporary Belgian press cuttings from John R. T. Davies. The disc is included in the Marshall Cavendish Jazz Greats series, 80, "Jazz international," with annotations by the author.

[50] S. Frederick Starr: *Red and Hot: The Fate of Jazz in the Soviet Union* (New York, Oxford University Press, 1983).

[51] *Ibid.*

[52] "Sam Wooding," in Chip Deffaa: *op. cit.*

53 "Brazil: a country without swing," *Baltimore Afro-American*, July 13, 1940.

54 Buck Clayton: *Buck Clayton's Jazz World* (ed. Nancy Miller Elliott) (Oxford, Bayou Press 1989).

# Chapter 6

1 "You went down a few steps and into this long, low basement room that held maybe 60 to 70 people, with a small stage at the end, and that's what most of the clubs on the Street were like." (Pianist Billy Taylor describing the Onyx, interview with the author, October 31, 1996.)

2 Danny Barker: *A Life in Jazz* (ed. Alyn Shipton) (London, Macmillan, 1986).

3 *Ibid.*

4 Scott DeVeaux: *The Birth of Bebop: A Social and Musical History* (Berkeley, University of California Press, 1997).

5 Sammy Price: *What Do They Want?* (ed. Caroline Richmond) (Oxford, Bayou Press, 1989).

6 Eddie Condon: *We Called It Music* (2nd. edn.) (Westport, CT, Greenwood Press, 1970).

7 Author's interview with Jonah Jones, May 25, 1995.

8 Danny Barker: *op. cit.*

9 Scott DeVeaux: *op. cit.*

10 Milt Jackson, interviewed by Charles Fox for BBC Radio, May 6, 1976.

11 Eldridge interview with John Chilton, reprinted in John Chilton: *Song of the Hawk* (London, Quartet, 1990).

12 Rex Stewart: *Boy Meets Horn* (ed. Claire P. Gordon) (Oxford, Bayou Press, 1991).

13 "Georges Paczynski n'abord pas le jazz selon cette optique (particularités des timbres et du rhythme), mais selon la fausse logique commune de nos jours d'un chemin unique qui mène inéluctablement des grottes préhistoriques à l'extase atonale. Cette idéologie et la découpe par périodes révolues (pré-bop) réduit ces genres majeurs (jazz traditionnel, mainstream) à lettre morte." Michel Laplace: "Une histoire de la batterie," *Jazz Dixie/Swing du ragtime au big band*, 18 (February 1998) 7–16.

14 Martin Williams: *The Jazz Tradition* (2nd. edn.) (New York, Oxford University Press, 1993).

15 John Chilton: *op. cit.*

16 "Les Young wasn't carved – Holiday," *Down Beat*, October 15, 1939.

17 Scott DeVeaux: *op. cit.*

18 *Ibid.*

19 *Ibid.*

20 Bob Wilber (assisted by Derek Webster): *Music Was Not Enough* (Oxford, Bayou Press, 1989). The evidence of Hawkins's fondness for the piece is in John Chilton: *op. cit.*

21 George Russell: *The Lydian Chromatic Concept of Tonal Organization for Improvisation* (New York, Concept Publishing, 1959).

22 Lewis Porter: *Lester Young* (London, Macmillan, 1985).

23 Scott DeVeaux: *op. cit.*

24 Lewis Porter: *op. cit.*

[25] Gunther Schuller: *The Swing Era* (New York, Oxford University Press, 1989).

[26] Club details from author's interviews with Gerald Wiggins, November 19, 2000, and Teddy Edwards, November 22, 2000, as well as Clora Bryant *et al.*: *Central Avenue Sounds: Jazz in Los Angeles* (Berkeley, University of California Press, 1998).

[27] *New York Amsterdam News*, December 30, 1939.

[28] *New York Amsterdam News*, November 16, 1940.

[29] *Billboard*, November 23, 1940.

[30] Teddy Wilson: *Teddy Wilson Talks Jazz* (ed. Arie Ligthart and Humphrey Van Loo) (London, Cassell, 1996).

[31] *New York Amsterdam News*, November 16, 1940.

[32] Author's interview with Gerald Wiggins, November 19, 2000.

[33] Rex Stewart: *Jazz Masters of the Thirties* (New York, Macmillan, 1972).

[34] Sinclair Traill: "Charlie Shavers," *Jazz Journal* xxiii (5) (May 1970), 8.

[35] Gunther Schuller: *op. cit.*

[36] *Down Beat*, December 15, 1939.

[37] Gunther Schuller: *op. cit.*

[38] Daniel Nevers: "Les plus grand des petits orchestres," (liner notes to *The Complete Una Mae Carlisle and John Kirby*, RCA Jazz Tribune (France) NL 89484, 1986). Other information from Ian Crosbie: "The biggest little band," *Jazz Journal*, xxv (3) (March 1972), 26.

[39] *Metronome*, January 1942, 11 and 47.

[40] Morroe Berger, Edward Berger, and James Patrick: *Benny Carter: A Life in American Music* (Metuchen, N.J., Scarecrow Press, 1982).

[41] Alyn Shipton: *Groovin' High: The Life of Dizzy Gillespie* (New York, Oxford University Press, 1999).

# Chapter 7

[1] Steven Strunk: "Harmony," in Barry Kernfeld (ed.): *The New Grove Dictionary of Jazz* (London, Macmillan, 1988) notates and analyzes Gillespie's and Dameron's substitute harmonies in this piece.

[2] Alyn Shipton: *Groovin' High: The Life of Dizzy Gillespie* (New York, Oxford University Press, 1999); Barry Ulanov: *A History of Jazz in America* (London, Hutchinson, 1959).

[3] Thomas Owens: *Bebop: The Music and the Players* (New York, Oxford University Press, 1995) charts the stylistic development from swing to bebop in detail in Chapters 1 and 2.

[4] Nat Shapiro and Nat Hentoff: *Hear Me Talkin' to Ya* (Harmondsworth, Penguin, 1962).

[5] Alyn Shipton: *op. cit.*

[6] Nat Shapiro and Nat Hentoff: *op. cit.*

[7] *Ibid.*

[8] Alyn Shipton: *op.cit.*; for analysis of several of the solos on Newman's recordings, including Gillespie's *Kerouac*, see Jonathan Finkelman: "Charlie Christian, bebop, and the recordings at Mintons," in Edward Berger, David Cayer, Dan Morgenstern, and Lewis Porter (eds.): *Annual Review of Jazz Studies*, 6 (Metuchen, N.J., Scarecrow Press, 1993), 196.

[9] LeRoi Jones (Amiri Baraka): *Blues People: Negro Music in White America* (New York, William Morrow, 1963).

[10] Scott DeVeaux: *The Birth of Bebop: A Social and Musical History* (Berkeley, University of California Press, 1997).

[11] Author's interview with Jonah Jones, May 25, 1995.

[12] Danny Barker: *Buddy Bolden and the Last Days of Storyville* (ed. Alyn Shipton) (London, Cassell, 1998).

[13] Cab Calloway (with Bryant Rollins): *Of Minnie the Moocher and Me* (New York, Thomas Y. Crowell, 1976).

[14] Payne and Calloway quotes from *ibid.*; Barker quote from Danny Barker: *A Life in Jazz* (ed. Alyn Shipton) (London, Macmillan, 1986).

[15] Dizzy Gillespie and Al Fraser: *Dizzy: To Be or Not to Bop* (London, Quartet, 1980).

[16] Danny Barker: *A Life in Jazz* (ed. Alyn Shipton) (London, Macmillan, 1986).

[17] Author's interview with Milt Hinton, March 23, 1993.

[18] Jay McShann, interviewed by Charles Fox for BBC Radio 3, February 8, 1980.

[19] Glenn D. Wilson: *Psychology for Performing Artists* (London, Jessica Kingsley, 1994).

[20] D. E. Berlyne: *Aesthetics and Psychobiology* (New York, Appleton Century Crofts, 1971).

[21] Glenn D. Wilson: *op. cit.*

[22] Dizzy Gillespie and Al Fraser: *op. cit.*

[23] Laurent Clarke and Franck Verdun: *Dizzy Atmosphere* (Arles, Actes Sud, 1990).

[24] "In about a month's time I was playing like Charlie Parker." Gene Lees: *Waiting For Dizzy* (New York, Oxford University Press, 1991).

[25] Buddy Collete (with Steven Isoardi): *Jazz Generations: A Life in American Music and Society* (London, Continuum, 2000).

[26] *Ibid.*

[27] Michael Levin and John S. Wilson: "No bop roots in jazz: Parker," *Down Beat*, September 9, 1949; quote attributed directly to Parker in Nat Shapiro and Nat Hentoff: *op. cit.*; also quoted in Brian Priestley: "Charlie Parker," in Dave Gelly: *Masters of the Jazz Saxophone: The Story of the Players and Their Music* (London, Balaphon, 2000). However, Scott DeVeaux: *op. cit.* gives a little background to this moment of "epiphany" and shares my view that this moment came to symbolize a process Parker had been working through for some time.

[28] Jay McShann, interviewed by Charles Fox for BBC Radio 3, February 8, 1980.

[29] Ross Russell: *Bird Lives! The High Life and Hard Times of Charlie "Yardbird" Parker* (London, Quartet, 1973).

[30] James Patrick: "Parker, Charlie," in Barry Kernfeld (ed.): *op. cit.*

[31] Alyn Shipton: *op. cit.*

[32] Jay McShann, interviewed by Charles Fox for BBC Radio 3, February 8, 1980.

[33] *Ibid.*

[34] Scott DeVeaux: *op. cit.*

[35] Earl Hines, interviewed by Roy Plomley for BBC Radio, May 30, 1980.

[36] *Ibid.*, transcribed in Alyn Shipton: *op. cit.*

[37] Author's interview with Billy Taylor, October 31, 1996.

[38] *Chicago Defender*, November 28, 1942.

[39] Author's interview with Clora Bryant, November 19, 2000.

[40] Danny Barker: *A Life in Jazz* (ed. Alyn Shipton) (London, Macmillan, 1986).

[41] Michael Levin and John S. Wilson: *op. cit.*

[42] John S. Wilson: "Bird wrong; bop must get a beat: Diz," *Down Beat*, October 7, 1949.

[43] Scott DeVeaux: *op. cit.*

[44] "Gillespie it was agreed would be co-leader, but his name didn't even appear on the bill," Scott DeVeaux: *op. cit.* But it is clearly billed as Gillespie's band in various sources including: *New York Amsterdam News,* December 11, 1943; *The Jazz Record*, 15, December 1943.

[45] A dated analysis of the claims made for this session to be the first bebop recording date is in Scott DeVeaux: *op.cit.*

[46] John Chilton: *Song of the Hawk* (London, Quartet, 1990).

[47] Max Roach, interviewed by Charles Fox for BBC Radio, for "Drum beats," December 1989–January 1990.

[48] *New York Age*, March 25, 1944.

[49] Ted Yates: "Billy Eckstine, singer and orchestra leader being mentioned for Hollywood," *New York Age*, 2, September 2, 1944.

[50] Ira Gitler: *Swing to Bop: An Oral History of the Transition in Jazz in the 1940s* (New York, Oxford University Press, 1985).

[51] All quotes from Alyn Shipton: *op. cit.*

[52] Ira Gitler: *op. cit.*

[53] "Billy Eckstine," in Max Jones: *Talking Jazz* (London, Macmillan, 1987).

[54] *Ibid.*

[55] *Down Beat*, December 10, 1945.

[56] André Hodeir: "Vers un renouveau de la musique de jazz?," *Jazz hot*, 7 (May–June 1946).

[57] *Ibid.*

[58] *Ibid.*

[59] Barry Ulanov: "Dizzy dazzles for an hour: rest of concert drags," *Metronome*, June 1946, reprinted in Ken Vail: *Bird's Diary: The Life of Charlie Parker 1945–1955* (Chessington, Castle Communications, 1996).

[60] James Lincoln Collier: *The Making of Jazz* (London, Macmillan, 1981) is typical: "Ross Russell's *Bird Lives* . . . is one of a tiny number of truly first-rate jazz books, and I am depending on it for the facts of Parker's life." Equally, in Mark C. Gridley: *Jazz Styles: History and Analysis* (2nd. edn.) (Englewood Cliffs, Prentice-Hall, 1985) is the observation: "the musican who contributed mostly to the development of bop was alto saxophonist Charlie Parker."

[61] Ross Russell: *op. cit.*

[62] Dizzy Gillespie and Al Fraser: *op. cit.*

[63] Francis Davis: "Dizzy atmosphere" (review of Alyn Shipton: *op.cit.*), *New York Times Book Review*, August 8, 1999.

[64] Charlie Parker, interviewed by John McLellan for a Boston radio broadcast, January 1954, transcribed in Ken Vail: *op. cit.*

[65] John Mehegan: "The Charlie Parker story: the greatest recording session made in modern jazz history in its entirety" (liner notes to Savoy MG 12079).

[66] *Ibid.*

[67] Art Taylor: *Notes and Tones* (2nd. edn.) (New York, Da Capo, 1993).

[68] Robert Gordon: *Jazz West Coast* (London, Quartet, 1990).

[69] Leonard Feather: *From Satchmo to Miles* (London, Quartet, 1974).

[70] John Chilton: *op.cit.*

[71] Author's interview with Teddy Edwards, November 21, 2000.

[72] Roy Porter: *There and Back* (ed. David Keller) (Oxford, Bayou Press, 1991).

[73] Author's interview with Clora Bryant November 19, 2000.

[74] "Art Farmer," in Clora Bryant *et al.*: *Central Avenue Sounds: Jazz in Los Angeles* (Berkeley, University of California Press, 1998).

[75] "William Green," in Clora Bryant *et al.*: *op. cit.*

[76] Author's interview with Ray Brown, April 11, 1996.

[77] Gibson, quoted in Ted Gioia: *West Coast Jazz* (New York, Oxford University Press, 1992); Criss is quoted in Bob Porter and Mark Gardner: "The California cats," *Jazz Monthly* (April 1968).

[78] Art Taylor: *op. cit.*

[79] Laurent De Wilde: *Monk* (trans. Jonathan Dickinson) (New York, Marlowe, 1998).

[80] *Ibid.*

[81] Ingrid Monson: "Monk meets SNCC," in Mark Tucker (ed.): *New Perspectives on Thelonious Monk* (Chicago, *Black Music Research Journal*, 19 (2), 1999).

[82] Ira Gitler: *op. cit.*

[83] Scott DeVeaux: "Monk and popular song," in Mark Tucker (ed.): *op.cit.*

[84] John Chilton: *op. cit.*

[85] *Down Beat*, December 5, 1963.

[86] Author's interview with Gabler, May 16, 1997.

[87] "Thelonious Monk," in Kenny Mathieson: *Giant Steps: Bebop and the Creators of Modern Jazz 1945–65* (Edinburgh, Payback Press, 1999).

[88] Alan Groves and Alyn Shipton: *The Glass Enclosure: The Life of Bud Powell* (Oxford, Bayou Press, 1993).

[89] Max Jones: *op. cit.*

[90] Author's interview with Ray Brown April 11, 1996; full transcript of this portion of the interview in Alyn Shipton: *op. cit.*

[91] Alan Groves and Alyn Shipton: *op.cit.*

[92] *Ibid.* Transcript of an interview included on Elektra Musician E1 60030, originally assumed to have been recorded in May 1963, but which I have redated to May 1964 in the discography included in *The Glass Enclosure*.

[93] *Ibid.*

[94] Gene Lees: "The good gray fox, part one" (Ojai, California), *Jazzletter*, 9 (November 1990), 2.

[95] Michel Serres (ed.): *A History of Scientific Thought: Elements of a History of Science* (Oxford, Blackwell, 1995).

[96] Eric Lott: "Bebop's politics of style," in Krin Gabbard (ed.): *Jazz Among the Discourses* (Durham, N.C., Duke University Press, 1995).

[97] Mark Gardner: "Al Haig talks to Mark Gardner," *Jazz Monthly*, 186 (August 1970), 4.

[98] *Ibid.*

[99] Author's interview with George Shearing, September 1, 1999.

[100] Bob Wilber (assisted by Derek Webster): *Music Was Not Enough* (Oxford, Bayou Press, 1989).

[101] The move to larger clubs and the "listening only" policy of the Royal Roost is discussed in "Bop: skee, ree or be, it's still got to swing," *New York Times*, December 5, 1948. Scott quoted in Jack Chambers: *Milestones 1: The Music and Times of Miles Davis to 1960* (Toronto, University of Toronto Press, 1983).

[102] Dating from Ken Vail: *op. cit.*; Ken Vail: *Dizzy Gillespie: The Bebop Years 1937–1952* (Cambridge, Vail Publishing, 2000). Vail's research corresponds with mine for *Groovin' High*, namely that Parker's sitting in with Gillespie took place at the Savoy, but the suggestion is made that it was at the McKinley Theater in the Bronx, in Ian Carr: *Miles Davis: The Definitive Biography* (London, HarperCollins, 1998).

[103] Thomas Owens: *op. cit.*

[104] Jack Chambers: *op. cit.*

[105] Ian Carr: *op. cit.*

[106] August Blume, quoted in Jack Chambers: *op. cit.*

[107] Thomas Owens: *Charlie Parker: Techniques of Improvisation, ii* (Dissertation, UCLA, 1974), summarized in Thomas Owens: *op. cit.*

[108] James Patrick: "Charlie Parker and the harmonic sources of bebop composition," *Journal of Jazz Studies*, 2 (2) (1975), 3; James Patrick: "Charlie Parker," in Barry Kernfeld (ed.): *op. cit.*

[109] James Patrick: "Charlie Parker," in *ibid.*

[110] *Esquire*, March 1959, quoted in Ian Carr: *op. cit.*

[111] Gene Lees: "The nine lives of Red Rodney," in Gene Lees: *Cats of Any Color: Jazz Black and White* (New York, Oxford University Press, 1994).

[112] *Ibid.*

# Chapter 8

[1] Dizzy Gillespie, interviewed by Charles Fox, January 3, 1977.

[2] Dizzy Gillespie and Al Fraser: *Dizzy: To Be or Not to Bop* (London, Quartet, 1980).

[3] *Ibid.*

[4] Author's interview with Gerald Wilson, March 18, 2000.

[5] Chris Sheridan: *Groovin' High in L.A. 1946* (liner notes to Hep CD 15, 1992).

[6] Author's interview with Teddy Edwards, November 21, 2000.

[7] "Gerald Wilson," in Clora Bryant *et al.*: *Central Avenue Sounds: Jazz in Los Angeles* (Berkeley, University of California Press, 1998).

[8] See Alyn Shipton: *Groovin' High: The Life of Dizzy Gillespie* (New York, Oxford University Press, 1999) passim.

[9] Author's interview with Ray Brown, April 11, 1996.

[10] Feather press cutting (unattributed), reprinted in Ken Vail: *Dizzy Gillespie: The Bebop Years 1937–1952* (Cambridge, Vail Publishing, 2000).

[11] *Jazz Times* (October 1992), p. 27.

[12] Author's interview with Ray Brown, April 11, 1996.

[13] Jack Cooke: "Sixteen men stone dead," *Jazz Monthly*, 175, (September 1969), pp. 2ff.

[14] Stanley Dance: *The World of Swing* (New York, Scribner, 1974).

[15] *Time*, October 11, 1948.

[16] Miles Davis (with Quincy Troupe): *Miles: The Autobiography* (New York, Simon and Schuster, 1989).

[17] Handbill from Regal Theater, Chicago, July 19, 1946, reproduced in Ken Vail: *op. cit.*

[18] Handbill from Club El-Sino, Detroit, November 21, 1947, reproduced in Ken Vail: *op. cit.*

[19] Author's interview with Ray Brown, April 11, 1996.

[20] Dizzy Gillespie, interviewed by Charles Fox, August 31, 1976.

[21] Author's interview with Ray Brown, April 11, 1996.

[22] George Russell, interviewed by Ian Carr, June 29, 1992.

[23] Laurent Clarke and Franck Verdun: *Dizzy Atmosphere* (Arles, Actes Sud, 1990).

[24] "Dizzy Gillespie to appear at Pasadena Auditorium, July 19," *Down Beat*, July 1948, reproduced in Ken Vail: *op. cit.*

[25] *New York Times*, December 5, 1948.

[26] Jack Tracy: "Gillespie's crew great again, but may break up," *Down Beat*, June 16, 1950.

[27] Author's interview with Benny Bailey, April 27, 1993.

[28] Roy Porter: *There and Back* (ed. David Keller) (Oxford, Bayou Press, 1991).

[29] *Ibid.*

[30] Dizzy Gillespie and Al Fraser: *op.cit.*

[31] Bruce Crowther: *Gene Krupa* (New York, Universe, 1988).

[32] Joop Visser: *The Gene Krupa Story* (liner notes to 4CD set Properbox 1, 1998).

[33] Anita O'Day (with George Eells): *High Times, Hard Times* (New York, Putnam, 1981).

[34] Gene Lees: "The nine lives of Red Rodney," in *Cats of Any Color: Jazz Black and White* (New York, Oxford University Press, 1994).

[35] "Woody's blues heaven," *Newsweek*, December 31, 1945.

[36] Gene Lees: *Leader of the Band: The Life of Woody Herman* (New York, Oxford University Press, 1995).

[37] *Ibid.*

[38] Author's interview with Shorty Rogers, November 23, 1991.

[39] *Ibid.*

[40] Charlie Barnet (with Stanley Dance): *Those Swinging Years: The Autobiography of Charlie Barnet* (Baton Rouge, Louisiana State University Press, 1984).

[41] Robert C. Kriebel: *Blue Flame: Woody Herman's Life in Music* (West Lafayette, IA, Purdue University Press, 1995).

[42] Donald L. Maggin: *Stan Getz: A Life in Jazz* (New York, William Morrow, 1996).

[43] Robert C. Kriebel: *op. cit.*

[44] *Ibid.*, for Herman losses. Gillespie losses discussed in Alyn Shipton: *op.cit.*

[45] Author's interview with Shorty Rogers, November 23, 1991.

[46] Jim Burns: "Stan the man," *Jazz Monthly*, 176, (October 1969), pp. 22–4.

[47] Ted Gioia: *West Coast Jazz* (New York, Oxford University Press, 1992).

[48] Max Harrison: "Stan Kenton," in Max Harrison, Eric Thacker, and Stuart Nicholson (eds.): *The Essential Jazz Records*, Vol. 2 (London, Mansell, 2000).

[49] Alyn Shipton: *op. cit.*

[50] Art and Laurie Pepper: *Straight Life: The Story of Art Pepper* (New York, Schirmer Books, 1979).

[51] Kenton, interviewed by Brian Priestley for BBC Radio, March 1975.

[52] Author's interview with Shorty Rogers, November 23, 1991.

# Chapter 9

[1] Pekka Gronow and Ilpo Saunio: *An International History of the Recording Industry* (trans. Christopher Moseley) (London, Cassell, 1998); H. Wiley Hitchcock: "James C. Petrillo," in H. Wiley Hitchcock and Stanley Sadie (eds.): *The New Grove Dictionary of American Music* (London, Macmillan, 1986).

[2] These are discussed in Alyn Shipton: *Fats Waller: His Life and Times* (New York, Universe, 1988).

[3] Statistics and information about music boxes from Rainer Lotz: "Ragtime in Europe," from Alyn Shipton (ed.): *Ragtime and Early Jazz, Ascona Festival Symposium* (Arcegno, Switzerland, 1987).

[4] H. O. Brunn: *The Story of the Original Dixieland Jazz Band* (New York, Da Capo, 1986).

[5] Louis Armstrong: *Louis Armstrong in His Own Words* (ed. Thomas Brothers) (New York, Oxford University Press, 1999).

[6] Rick Kennedy: *Jelly Roll, Bix and Hoagy: Gennett Studios and the Birth of Recorded Jazz* (Bloomington, Indiana University Press, 1994).

[7] *Ibid.*

[8] Adolphus "Doc" Cheatham: *I Guess I'll Get the Papers and Go Home* (ed. Alyn Shipton) (London and Washington, Cassell, 1995).

[9] Bill Crow: *Jazz Anecdotes* (New York, Oxford University Press, 1990).

[10] *Ibid.*

[11] Author's interview with Harry Dial, October 24, 1986.

[12] Garvin Bushell (as told to Mark Tucker): *Jazz from the Beginning* (Oxford, Bayou Press, 1988).

[13] Edward Brooks: *The Bessie Smith Companion* (2nd. edn.) (Oxford, Bayou Press, 1989) Chris Albertson: *Bessie* (New York, Stein and Day, 1972).

[14] Brad Kay: "The 1932 band in true stereo," in Duke Ellington: *Reflections in Ellington* (liner notes to Everybody's EV 3005, 1985).

[15] Nathan W. Pearson Jr.: *Goin' to Kansas City* (London, Macmillan, 1988); "Broadcasting," in H. Wiley Hitchcock and Stanley Sadie (eds.): *op.cit.*

[16] John Chilton: *Who's Who of Jazz* (5th. edn.) (London, Macmillan, 1989); Coon-Sanders: Nighthawks (liner notes to RCA RD 7697).

[17] Denise Lanctot, Alyn Shipton, and others: *Radio Rhapsodies* (London, City of London Sinfonia, 2000) (program for UK tour of reconstructed Whiteman radio concert).

[18] Arthur Rollini: *Thirty Years with the Big Bands* (Oxford, Bayou Press, 1989).

[19] Buddy Collete (with Steven Isoardi): *Jazz Generations: A Life in American Music and Society* (London, Continuum, 2000) has an account of the integration of the musicians' unions and studios in Los Angeles in the 1950s.

[20] Alyn Shipton: *Fats Waller: His Life and Times* (New York, Universe, 1988).

[21] Ross Russell: *Jazz Style in Kansas City and the Southwest* (Berkeley, University of California Press, 1973).

[22] John Chilton: *Sidney Bechet: The Wizard of Jazz* (London, Macmillan, 1987).

[23] *Ibid.*, quoting *Down Beat*, October 8, 1947.

[24] Frank Driggs and Harris Lewine: *Black Beauty, White Heat: A Pictorial History of Classic Jazz, 1920–1950* (New York, William Morrow, 1982).

[25] Clora Bryant *et al.*: *Central Avenue Sounds: Jazz in Los Angeles* (Berkeley, University of California Press, 1988).

[26] Arnie Bernstein: *Hollywood on Lake Michigan: 100 Years of Chicago and the Movies* (Chicago, Lake Claremont Press, 1998).

[27] Ernie Smith: "Films," in Barry Kernfeld (ed.): *The New Grove Dictionary of Jazz* (London, Macmillan, 1988).

[28] Krin Gabbard: "Questions of influence in the white jazz biopic," in K. Gabbard (ed.): *Jammin' at the Margins: Jazz and the American Cinema* (Chicago, University of Chicago Press, 1996).

[29] *Billboard*, November 9, 1929.

[30] Klaus Stratemann: *Duke Ellington: Day by Day and Film by Film* (Copenhagen, JazzMedia APS, 1992).

[31] Details from *ibid.*; Buck Clayton: *Buck Clayton's Jazz World* (ed. Nancy Miller Elliott) (Oxford, Bayou Press, 1989); and Marshal Royal: *Jazz Survivor* (ed. Claire P. Gordon) (London, Cassell, 1996).

[32] S. W. Garlington: "Oscar Micheaux, producer, dies," *New York Amsterdam News*, April 7, 1951.

[33] Danny Barker: *A Life in Jazz* (ed. Alyn Shipton) (London, Macmillan, 1986).

# Chapter 10

[1] Garvin Bushell (as told to Mark Tucker): *Jazz from the Beginning* (Oxford, Bayou Press, 1988).

[2] Will Friedwald: *Jazz Singing: America's Great Voices from Bessie Smith to Bebop and Beyond* (London, Quartet, 1991); author's interview with Dame Cleo Laine, January 21, 1999.

[3] Paul Oliver: *Conversation with the Blues* (London, Cassell, 1965).

[4] Henry Pleasants: "Ethel Waters," in Barry Kernfeld (ed.): *The New Grove Dictionary of Jazz* (London, Macmillan, 1988).

[5] Will Friedwald: *op. cit.*

[6] Danny Barker: *A Life in Jazz* (ed. Alyn Shipton) (London, Macmillan, 1986).

[7] Andy Razaf and Fats Waller: *Doin' What I Please* (New York, J. R. Lafleur; London, Belwin Mills Music Ltd., 1931) (portion of lyric to verse 2).

[8] *Ibid.*

[9] Dating from R. M. W. Dixon and J. Godrich: *Blues and Gospel Records 1902–1943* (3rd. edn.) (Chigwell, Storyville, 1982).

[10] Chip Deffaa: *Voices of the Jazz Age* (Oxford, Bayou Press, 1990).

[11] Louis Armstrong: *Louis Armstrong in His Own Words* (ed. Thomas Brothers) (New York, Oxford University Press, 1999).

[12] Gunther Schuller: *Early Jazz: Its Roots and Musical Development* (New York, Oxford University Press, 1968).

[13] Chris Ellis: "Adelaide Hall: the singing blackbird," *Storyville*, 31, October 1, 1970, 8.

[14] Hugues Panassié: *Hot Jazz* (translated from *Le Jazz hot*, Paris, Correa, 1934, by Lyle and

Eleanor Dowling) (London, Cassell, 1936). A notable example of this orgy of imitation is Ethel Waters' version of *I Can't Give You Anything But Love*, recorded with Duke Ellington.

[15] J. Bradford Robinson: "Scat singing," in Barry Kernfeld (ed.): *op. cit.* includes a transcription of the parts of Armstrong's vocal that replicate brass technique.

[16] *Melody Maker* quote from 1932, reprinted in Geoff Milne: *The Mills Brothers from the Beginning, Vol. 1* ( liner notes to JSP 1099).

[17] *Ibid.*

[18] Laurence Koch: "Leo Watson," in Barry Kernfeld (ed.): *op. cit.*

[19] Charles Fox, quoted in Max Jones: *The Spirits of Rhythm 1933–34* (liner notes to JSP 1088).

[20] Cab Calloway (with Bryant Rollins): *Of Minnie the Moocher and Me* (New York, Thomas Y. Crowell, 1976).

[21] Cab Calloway: *The New Cab Calloway's Cat-ologue* (New York, Calloway, 1938); Cab Calloway: *The New Cab Calloway's Hepster's Dictionary: Language of Jive* (New York, Calloway, 1944).

[22] Mezz Mezzrow and Bernard Wolfe: *Really the Blues* (New York, Random House, 1946). There is a fuller account of jive in Bill Milkowski: *Swing It! An Annotated History of Jive* (New York, Billboard Books, 2001).

[23] Jean-Paul Levet: *Talking That Talk: Le Langage du blues et du jazz* (Hatier, Paris, 1992).

[24] Alyn Shipton: *Groovin' High: The Life of Dizzy Gillespie* (New York, Oxford University Press, 1999).

[25] *New York Times*, June 21, 1929.

[26] Armstrong's extemporized vocal on matrix 402534B, July 19, 1929, based on Fats Waller, Andy Razaf, and Harry Brooks: *Ain't Misbehavin'* (New York, Mills Music Inc., 1929).

[27] Bruce Crowther and Mike Pinfold: *Singing Jazz* (London, Blandford Press, 1997).

[28] Danny Barker: *op. cit.*

[29] Bruce Crowther and Mike Pinfold: *op. cit.*

[30] Gunther Schuller: *The Swing Era* (New York, Oxford University Press, 1989).

[31] *Ibid.*

[32] The Earl of Harewood: "Porgy and Bess: the work and its performance," *Opera*, November 1950, 710ff.

[33] Author's interview with Elizabeth Forbes, June 9, 1995.

[34] James Popa: *Cab Calloway and His Orchestra, 1925–1958* (2nd. edn), revised by Charles Garrod, (Zephyr Hills, FL., Joyce Record Club, 1987).

[35] Illinois Jacquet performed this song at the 1996 Brecon Festival. Adolphus "Doc" Cheatham: *I Guess I'll Get the Papers and Go Home* (ed. Alyn Shipton) (London and Washington, Cassell, 1995).

[36] Morroe Berger: "Fats Waller: the outside insider," *Journal of Jazz Studies*, 1, October 1, 1973, 3.

[37] *Ibid.*

[38] Author's interview with Harry Dial, October 24, 1986.

[39] Morroe Berger: *op. cit.*

[40] *Ibid.*

[41] *Melody Maker*, July 30, 1938.

[42] Humphrey Lyttelton: *The Best of Jazz (ii): Enter the Giants* (London, Robson Books, 1981).

[43] *Down Beat*, November 1937, reprinted in John Chilton: *Let the Good Times Roll: The Story of Louis Jordan and His Music* (London, Quartet, 1992).

[44] John Chilton: *op cit.*

[45] Author's interview with Jesse Stone, March 9, 1997.

[46] Stuart Nicholson: *Ella Fitzgerald* (London, Gollancz, 1993).

[47] Green, quoted in Digby Fairweather: "Ella Fitzgerald," in Ian Carr, Digby Fairweather, and Brian Priestley (eds.): *Jazz: The Rough Guide* (2nd. edn.) London, Rough Guides, 2000).

[48] Stuart Nicholson: *op. cit.*

[49] *Down Beat*, July 2, 1947.

[50] *Metronome*, February 1957, 24, reprinted in Stuart Nicholson: *Billie Holiday* (London, Gollancz, 1995).

[51] Donald Clarke: *Wishing on the Moon: The Life and Times of Billie Holiday* (London, Viking, 1994).

[52] *Ibid.*

[53] David Margolick: *Strange Fruit: Billie Holiday, Café Society and an Early Cry for Civil Rights* (Edinburgh, Payback Press, 2001).

[54] All three examples from *ibid.*

# Chapter 11

[1] John Chilton: *Stomp Off, Let's Go! The Story of Bob Crosby's Bob Cats and Big Band* (London, Jazz Book Service, 1983).

[2] Bert Whyatt: *Muggsy Spanier: The Lonesome Road* (New Orleans, Jazzology Press, 1995).

[3] *Melody Maker*, July 1, 1939.

[4] Whyatt: *op. cit.*

[5] Author's interview with Bob Helm, March 16, 1999.

[6] John Buchanan: *Emperor Norton's Hunch: The Story of Lu Watters' Yerba Buena Jazz Band* (Middle Dural, NSW, Australia, Hambledon Productions, 1996).

[7] Author's interview with Bob Helm, March 16, 1999.

[8] *Ibid.*

[9] Jim Goggin and Peter Clute: *The Great Jazz Revival* (San Rafael, CA, Donna Ewald, 1994).

[10] Christopher Hillman: *Bunk Johnson* (Tunbridge Wells, Kent, Spellmount, 1988).

[11] Eugene Williams: "Bunk Johnson's jazz band" (liner notes to "Jazz Information" discs, reprinted on Melodisc MLP 12–112).

[12] *Ibid.*

[13] Park Breck: "This isn't Bunk, Bunk taught Louis," *Down Beat*, June 1939.

[14] Joe Darensbourg: *Telling It Like It Is* (ed. Peter Vacher) (London, Macmillan, 1987).

[15] J. R. Taylor: "Bunk Johnson," in Barry Kernfeld (ed.): *The New Grove Dictionary of Jazz* (London, Macmillan, 1988).

[16] Louis Armstrong: *Louis Armstrong in His Own Words* (ed. Thomas Brothers) (New York,

Oxford University Press, 1999).

[17] Author's conversation with Don Ewell, September 18, 1980; Bob Wilber's paper at 1986 Ascona Festival symposium, "The Revival."

[18] Author's interview with Sonny Morris, August 1999.

[19] John Chilton: *Ride Red Ride* (London, Cassell, 1999).

[20] Anderson's full account of this is in Max Jones and John Chilton: *Louis: The Louis Armstrong Story 1900–1971* (London, Quartet, 1971).

[21] *Ibid.*

[22] Loren Schoenberg: "Louis Armstrong: highlights from his American Decca years" (liner notes to GRP 26382, 1994).

[23] The full story of the hall and its emergence is in William Carter: *Preservation Hall* (2nd. edn.) (London, Cassell, 1999).

[24] Buck Clayton: *Buck Clayton's Jazz World* (ed. Nancy Miller Elliott) (Oxford, Bayou Press, 1989).

[25] Granz's liner notes to JATP Vol. 7, quoted in Keith Shadwick: "Growing up with JATP," in Peter Pullman (ed.): *The Complete Jazz At The Philharmonic on Verve 1944–49* (liner booklet, Verve 314 523 893–2, (1998).

[26] John McDonough: "An introduction to JATP," in Peter Pullman (ed.): *op. cit.*

[27] Author's interview with Illinois Jacquet, July 11, 1992.

[28] John McDonough: *op. cit.*

[29] *Ibid.*

[30] Author's interview with Illinois Jacquet, July 11, 1992.

[31] Norman Granz, interviewed by Nat Hentoff in Peter Pullman (ed.): *op. cit.*

[32] Dizzy Gillespie, interviewed for "Norman's Conquests," a history of JATP broadcast on BBC Radio, April–June 1994.

[33] Norman Granz, interviewed by Nat Hentoff in Peter Pullman (ed.): *op. cit.*

[34] Alyn Shipton: *Groovin' High: The Life of Gillespie* (New York, Oxford University Press, 1999).

[35] Author's interview with Oscar Peterson, November 25, 1998.

# Chapter 12

[1] Author's interview with Clark Terry, October 8, 2000.

[2] *Ibid.*

[3] *Ibid.*

[4] Ian Carr: *Miles Davis: The Definitive Biography* (London, HarperCollins, 1998).

[5] *Ibid.*

[6] Gil Evans, interviewed by Charles Fox for BBC Radio, 1983, included on Gil Evans 75th Birthday Concert (BBC Jazz Legends CD 7007–2).

[7] *Ibid.*

[8] Gerry Mulligan, interviewed by Charles Fox for BBC Radio and reprinted in Ian Carr: *op. cit.*

[9] *Ibid.*

[10] Jack Chambers: *Milestones 1: The Music and Times of Miles Davis to 1960* (Toronto, University of Toronto Press, 1983).

[11] Nat Hentoff: "Miles: a trumpeter in the midst of a big comeback makes a very frank appraisal of today's scene," *Down Beat*, November 2, 1955.

[12] Author's interview with Jackie McLean, November 22, 1999.

[13] *Ibid.*

[14] *Ibid.*

[15] Author's interview with Horace Silver, March 19, 2000.

[16] Bob Porter: "Record man," in *The Prestige Records Story* (liner notes to Prestige 4PRCD 4426–2).

[17] Author's interview with George Avakian, February 24, 1999.

[18] Jack Chambers: *op. cit.*

[19] *Ibid.*

[20] Alyn Shipton: "Ahmad Jamal: reflections of a classic American musician," *Jazz Times*, June 1995.

[21] Peter Watrous: "John Coltrane: a life supreme," *Musician*, July 1987.

[22] Jack Chambers: *op. cit.*

[23] Ian Carr: *op. cit.*

[24] Author's interview with George Avakian, February 24, 1999.

[25] Jack Chambers: *op. cit.*

[26] Ian Carr: *op. cit.*

[27] Gene Lees: *Meet Me at Jim and Andy's: Jazz Musicians and Their World* (New York, Oxford University Press, 1988).

[28] Jack Chambers: *op. cit.*

[29] Ashley Kahn: *Kind of Blue: The Making of the Miles Davis Masterpiece* (London, Granta, 2000).

# Chapter 13

[1] Author's interview with Horace Silver, March 19, 2000.

[2] *Ibid.*

[3] Zan Stewart: "Horace Silver retrospective" (liner notes to Blue Note 7243 4 95576 3 8, 1999).

[4] Author's interview with Horace Silver, March 19, 2000.

[5] *Ibid.*

[6] Miles Davis (with Quincy Troupe): *Miles: The Autobiography* (New York, Simon and Schuster, 1989).

[7] Zan Stewart: *op. cit.*

[8] Jean-Paul Levet: "Funky," in *Talking That Talk*: *Le Langage du blues et du jazz* (Hatier, Paris, 1992).

[9] Author's interview with Horace Silver, March 19, 2000.

[10] Bob Blumenthal: "The complete Blue Note Hank Mobley fifties sessions" (liner notes to Mosaic MD 6–181).

[11] Author's interview with Horace Silver, March 19, 2000.

[12] *Ibid.*

[13] David H. Rosenthal: *Hard Bop: Jazz and Black Music 1955–1965* (New York, Oxford University Press, 1992).

[14] "Jazz Messengers blazing a spirited trail," *Down Beat*, 1956, quoted in Rosenthal: *op. cit.*

[15] Author's interview with Rudy Van Gelder, May 18, 1997.

[16] Bob Blumenthal: *op. cit.*

[17] Author's interview with Johnny Griffin, April 5, 1997.

[18] Author's interview with Bob Belden, May 16, 1997.

[19] John Litweiler interview with Hank Mobley, *Down Beat*, March 29, 1973.

[20] Author's interview with Rudy Van Gelder, May 18, 1997.

[21] Author's interview with Michael Cuscuna, May 16, 1997.

[22] Tape of Lion's speech supplied courtesy of Tom Evered, Blue Note Records.

[23] Author's interview with Rudy Van Gelder, May 18, 1997.

[24] Alyn Shipton: "Art Blakey and the Jazz Messengers, live at Ronnie Scott's Club, London, 1985" (liner notes to *BBC Jazz Legends* CD 7003–2, 2000).

[25] Art Taylor: *Notes and Tones* (2nd. edn.). (New York, Da Capo, 1993).

[26] Zan Stewart: *op. cit.*

[27] Author's interview with Benny Golson, April 2, 1996.

[28] *Ibid.*

[29] Author's interview with Cedar Walton, June 22, 1995.

[30] Author's interview with Pete LaRoca Sims, May 16, 1997.

[31] Author's interview with Bob Cranshaw, May 16, 1997.

[32] David H. Rosenthal: *op. cit.*

[33] Author's interview with Michael Cuscuna, May 16, 1997.

[34] Author's interview with Bob Belden, May 16, 1997.

[35] Author's interview with Jimmy McGriff, January 22, 1994.

# Chapter 14

[1] Both articles reprinted in Barry Ulanov: *A History of Jazz in America* (London, Hutchinson, 1959).

[2] Bob Porter: "Record man," in *The Prestige Records Story* (liner notes to Prestige 4PRCD 4426–2).

[3] Ira Gitler: *Swing to Bop: An Oral History of the Transition in Jazz in the 1940s* (New York, Oxford University Press, 1985).

[4] *Ibid.*

[5] John S. Wilson: "Lennie Tristano: watered down bop destroying jazz," *Down Beat*, October 6, 1950.

[6] "Peter Ind talks to Mark Gardner," *Jazz Monthly*, 180 (February 1970), 9ff.

[7] *Ibid.*

[8] Don Gold: "Aaron Copland: the well-known American composer finds virtues and flaws in jazz," *Down Beat*, May 1, 1958.

[9] Don Nelson: "Bill Evans," *Down Beat*, September 1, 1960.

[10] Alyn Shipton: "Never knowingly underplayed: John Lewis, a jazz legend in every department," *Piano*, 8 (5), September 2000, 23.

[11] *Ibid.*

[12] Milt Jackson, interviewed by Charles Fox for BBC Radio, May 6, 1976.

[13] Alyn Shipton: *op. cit.*, 23.

[14] *Ibid.*

[15] Milt Jackson, interviewed by Charles Fox for BBC Radio, May 6, 1976.

[16] *Ibid.*

[17] Ralph Gleason: "Dave Brubeck: 'They said I was too far out,'" *Down Beat*, August 8, 1957.

[18] Len Lyons: "Dave Brubeck," in Len Lyons: *The Great Jazz Pianists* (New York, Da Capo, 1983).

[19] Gene Lees: *Meet Me at Jim and Andy's: Jazz Musicians and Their World* (New York, Oxford University Press, 1988).

[20] Len Lyons: *op. cit.*

[21] John Swenson: "Take Five – one hit," in *Jazz: The Definitive Performances* (liner notes to Columbia/Epic/Legacy JZK 65807, 1999).

[22] Len Lyons: *op. cit.*

[23] Jerome Klinkowitz: *Listen. Gerry Mulligan: An Aural Narrative in Jazz* (New York, Schirmer, 1991).

[24] Alyn Shipton: "To the Lighthouse," *Jazz FM Magazine*, 11 (1992), 32ff.

[25] Gene Lees: *Arranging the Score* (London, Continuum, 2000).

[26] *Ibid.*

[27] *Ibid.*

[28] Alyn Shipton: "To the Lighthouse," *Jazz FM Magazine*, 11 (1992), 32ff.

[29] *Ibid.*

[30] *Ibid.*

[31] *Ibid.*

[32] *Ibid.*

[33] Author's interview with Shorty Rogers, November 23, 1991.

[34] Max Harrison, Eric Thacker, and Stuart Nicholson: *The Essential Jazz Records, Vol. 2* (London, Mansell, 2000).

[35] Author's interview with Shorty Rogers, November 23, 1991.

[36] Buddy Collete (with Steven Isoardi): *Jazz Generations: A Life in American Music and Society* (London, Continuum, 2000).

# Chapter 15

[1] Alyn Shipton: *Groovin' High: The Life of Dizzy Gillespie* (New York, Oxford University Press, 1999).

[2] *Ibid.*

[3] *Down Beat*, September 1949.

[4] Clark Terry, interviewed by Charles Fox for BBC Radio, April 1976.

[5] Author's interview with Grover Mitchell, September 21, 1999.

[6] Author's interview with Louis Bellson, July 13, 1999.

[7] Author's interview with Al Grey, October 29, 1999.

[8] George Avakian: "Ellington at Newport" (liner notes to Columbia CL 934, 1956), reprinted in Mark Tucker: *The Duke Ellington Reader* (New York, Oxford University

Press, 1993).

[9] Author's interview with George Avakian, February 24, 1999.

[10] Eddie Lambert: *A Listener's Guide to Duke Ellington* (Latham, MD, Scarecrow Press, 1999); *Melody Maker*, April 18, 1953, 3.

[11] Phil Schaap: "Ellington at Newport (Complete)" (liner notes to Columbia C2K 64932, 1999).

[12] Author's interview with Jimmy Woode, November 2, 1992.

[13] Author's interview with Rudy Van Gelder, May 18, 1997.

[14] George Avakian: "A Buck Clayton jam session" (liner notes to Columbia CL 546, 1955), quoted in Humphrey Lyttelton: *Second Chorus* (London, MacGibbon and Kee, 1958).

[15] *Ibid.*

[16] Ole J. Nielsen: *Jazz Records 1942–80: A Discography. Vol. 6: Duke Ellington* (Copenhagen, JazzMedia APS, n.d.).

[17] Gene Lees: *Gene Lees: Arranging the Score* (London, Continuum, 2000).

[18] *Ibid.*

[19] Max Harrison, Eric Thacker, and Stuart Nicholson: *The Essential Jazz Records, Vol. 2* (London, Mansell, 2000).

[20] Alyn Shipton: "Play what you mean," (interview with George Russell) *Jazzwise*, 10 (March 1998), 8.

[21] George Russell: "The jazz workshop" (liner notes to Koch CD 7850, 1957).

[22] Alyn Shipton: "Play what you mean," (interview with George Russell) *Jazzwise*, 10 (March 1998), 8.

[23] *Ibid.*

# Chapter 16

[1] Doug Ramsey: Liner notes to *John Coltrane: The Prestige Recordings*.

[2] Francis Davis: "Take the Coltrane," *Village Voice*, February 18, 1992.

[3] Author's interview with Gary Giddins, May 9, 2000.

[4] Don DeMichael: "John Coltrane and Eric Dolphy answer the jazz critics," *Down Beat*, April 12, 1962.

[5] Author's interview with Jimmy Heath, November 17, 1999.

[6] Author's interview with Ira Gitler, May 8, 2000.

[7] Ira Gitler: "Trane on the track," *Down Beat*, October 16, 1958.

[8] Brian Priestley: *John Coltrane* (London, Apollo Press, 1987).

[9] Author's interview with Ira Gitler, May 8, 2000.

[10] John Coltrane and Don DeMichael: "Coltrane on Coltrane," *Down Beat*, September 29, 1960, quoted in Eric Nisenson: *Ascension: John Coltrane and His Quest* (New York, St Martin's Press, 1993).

[11] August Blume: "An interview with John Coltrane," *Jazz Review*, January 1959.

[12] Interview with Rudy Van Gelder, included in the multimedia section of *The Ultimate Blue Train* (Blue Note).

[13] John Coltrane and Don DeMichael: *op. cit.*

[14] Author's interview with Lewis Porter, May 7, 2000; for further details, see Lewis

Porter: *John Coltrane: His Life and Music* (Ann Arbor, University of Michigan Press, 1998).

[15] Author's interview with Pat Metheny, February 21, 2000.

[16] Author's interview with Tommy Flanagan, December 4, 1999.

[17] Lewis Porter: "John Coltrane: the Atlantic years," in *The Heavyweight Champion* (liner notes to Rhino R2 71984, 1995).

[18] Val Wilmer: "Conversation with Coltrane," *Jazz Journal*, January 1962.

[19] Author's interview with Archie Shepp, April 13, 2000.

[20] Author's interview with Ravi Coltrane, May 8, 2000.

[21] Benoit Quersin: "La Passe dangereuse," *Jazz Magazine*, January 1963; transcribed and republished in English by Carl Woideck in Carl Woideck: *The John Coltrane Companion: Five Decades of Commentary* (New York, Schirmer, 1998).

[22] Author's interview with Gary Giddins, May 9, 2000.

[23] Ira Gitler: *op. cit.*; pushed hard on the subject by Frank Kofsky, in "John Coltrane: an interview," (originally published in *Black Nationalism and the Revolution in Music*, and republished in Carl Woideck: *op. cit.*) Coltrane says: "In music I make or have tried to make a conscious attempt to change what I've found."

[24] Author's interview with McCoy Tyner, March 1998.

[25] Frank Kofsky: *op. cit.*

[26] Elvin Jones interview from the BBC Radio sound archive.

[27] Ian Carr: "Jimmy Garrison," in Ian Carr, Digby Fairweather, and Brian Priestley: *Jazz: The Rough Guide* (2nd. edn.) (London, Rough Guides, 2000).

[28] Author's interview with Roy Haynes, May 8, 2000.

[29] Eric Nisenson: *op. cit.*

[30] Frank Kofsky: *op. cit.*

[31] Archie Shepp, quoted in liner notes to *Ascension*.

[32] Author's interview with Ravi Coltrane, May 8, 2000.

[33] Part of that performance on solo piano has been issued as *Themes for a Movie* (Flying Fish FF 099).

[34] Brian Priestley: *Mingus: A Critical Biography* (London, Quartet, 1982).

[35] Buddy Collete (with Steven Isoardi): *Jazz Generations: A Life in American Music and Society* (London, Continuum, 2000).

[36] Brian Priestley: *Mingus: A Critical Biography* (London, Quartet, 1982).

[37] Author's interview with Gerald Wiggins, November 19, 2000.

[38] Author's interview with Buddy Collette, March 19, 2000.

[39] Ralph J. Gleason: "Charlie Mingus: a thinking musician," *Down Beat*, June 1, 1951.

[40] *Ibid.*

[41] "Britt Woodman," in Clora Bryant *et al.* (eds.): *Central Avenue Sounds: Jazz in Los Angeles* (Berkeley, University of California Press, 1998).

[42] Mingus, quoted in Nat Hentoff: "The clown" (liner notes to Atlantic 1260, 1957).

[43] Alyn Shipton: "How the stars got into the Atlantic groove" (interview with Ahmet Ertegun), *The Times*, September 17, 1998.

[44] Gene Santoro: *Myself When I Am Real: The Life and Music of Charles Mingus* (New York, Oxford University Press, 2000).

# Chapter 17

[1] Author's interview with Paul Bley, February 21, 2000.

[2] "Pro and con," *Down Beat*, January 1992, 30–1, reprinted in Robert Walser: *Keeping Time: Readings in Jazz History* (New York, Oxford University Press, 1999).

[3] Gunther Schuller: "Ornette Coleman's compositions," in Gunther Schuller: *Musings. The Musical Worlds of Gunther Schuller: A Collection of His Writings* (New York, Oxford University Press, 1986).

[4] *Ibid.*

[5] Author's interview with Ornette Coleman, Paris, July 1997.

[6] *Ibid.*

[7] *Ibid.*

[8] *Ibid.*

[9] *Ibid.*

[10] Author's interview with Charlie Haden, February 20, 2000.

[11] *Ibid.*

[12] Author's interview with John Lewis, December 8, 1999.

[13] Author's interview with Paul Bley, February 21, 2000.

[14] Author's interview with Ornette Coleman, Paris, July 1997.

[15] Peter Niklas Wilson: *Ornette Coleman: His Life and Music* (Berkeley, CA, Berkeley Hills Books, 1999).

[16] Author's interview with George Russell, February 19, 2000.

[17] Author's interview with Charlie Haden, February 20, 2000.

[18] Author's interview with Paul Bley, February 21, 2000.

[19] Author's interview with Dewey Redman, February 22, 2000.

[20] *Down Beat*, 26 May, 1960.

[21] Author's interview with Charlie Haden, February 20, 2000.

[22] Author's interview with Ornette Coleman, Paris, July 1997.

[23] Gunther Schuller: "Third Stream," in Barry Kernfeld (ed.): *The New Grove Dictionary of Jazz* (London, Macmillan, 1988).

[24] Author's interview with Gunther Schuller, March 10, 2000.

[25] Alyn Shipton: "Ornette Coleman at the Barbican Hall, London," *Jazzwise*, 42 (May 2001).

[26] Alyn Shipton: "Play what you mean," (interview with George Russell) *Jazzwise* 8 (March 1998).

[27] Author's interview with Denardo Coleman, February 21, 2000.

[28] Author's interview with Ornette Coleman, Paris, July 1997.

[29] *Ibid.*

[30] *Ibid.*

[31] Author's interview with Archie Shepp, April 13, 2000.

[32] Author's interview with Paul Bley, February 21, 2000.

[33] Neil Tesser: "The avant garde" (liner notes to Rhino R2 79892, 2000).

[34] A. B. Spellman: *Four Lives in the Bebop Business* (New York, Limelight, 1985).

[35] Bill Dobbins: "Cecil Taylor," in Barry Kernfeld (ed.): *op. cit.*

[36] Valerie Wilmer: *As Serious As Your Life* (London, Quartet, 1977).

[37] Cecil Taylor: "Unit structures" (liner notes to Blue Note 84327, 1966).

[38] Nat Hentoff: liner notes to Cecil Taylor: "Conquistador" (Blue Note 84260, 1966).

[39] *Ibid.*

[40] A. B. Spellman: *op. cit.*

[41] *Ibid.*

[42] Author's interview with Roscoe Mitchell, September 2, 2000.

[43] Author's interview with Archie Shepp, April 13, 2000.

[44] *Ibid.*

[45] Shepp's *Down Beat* text quoted in Ian Carr: "Archie Shepp," in Ian Carr, Digby Fairweather, and Brian Priestley (eds.): *Jazz: The Rough Guide* (2nd. edn.) (London, Rough Guides, 2000).

[46] Author's interview with Rashied Ali, May 7, 2000.

[47] Author's interview with Roswell Rudd, October 29, 1996.

[48] *Ibid.*

[49] Author's interview with Archie Shepp, April 13, 2000.

[50] Bob Dawbarn: "What happened? Gillespie–Coltrane tour," *Melody Maker*, November 18, 1961.

[51] Ronald Atkins: "Burbles and squeaks: reflections on the British avant-garde," in Roger Cotterrell (ed.): *Jazz Now* (London, Quartet, 1976).

[52] Cornelius Cardew: "The Crypt – 12 June 1968" (liner notes to Matchbox Records, 1968).

# Chapter 18

[1] Author's interview with Howard Mandel, September 5, 2000.

[2] Author's interview with Gary Giddins, May 9, 2000.

[3] Author's interview with Roscoe Mitchell, September 2, 2000.

[4] Author's interview with Fred Anderson, September 3, 2000.

[5] Author's interview with Chuck Nessa, September 2, 2000.

[6] Author's interview with Von Freeman, February 26, 1999.

[7] Author's interview with John Litweiler, September 3, 2000.

[8] Author's interview with Joseph Jarman, September 3, 2000.

[9] Howard Mandel: *Future Jazz* (New York, Oxford University Press, 1999).

[10] Author's interview with Howard Mandel, September 5, 2000.

[11] Lincoln T. Beauchamp Jr.: *Art Ensemble of Chicago: Great Black Music Ancient to the Future* (Chicago, Art Ensemble Publishing Co., 1998).

[12] Author's interview with Roscoe Mitchell, September 2, 2000.

[13] Author's interview with Howard Mandel, September 5, 2000.

[14] Author's interview with Roscoe Mitchell, September 2, 2000.

[15] Author's interview with Chuck Nessa, September 2, 2000.

[16] Author's interview with Howard Mandel, September 5, 2000.

[17] Author's interview with Malachi Favors, September 2, 2000.

[18] Author's interview with Famadou Don Moye, September 2, 2000.

[19] Author's interview with Joseph Jarman, September 3, 2000.

[20] Author's interview with Anthony Braxton, June 20, 1994.

[21] Author's interview with Leroy Jenkins, November 22, 1999.

[22] John Corbett: "Anthony Braxton: of science and Sinatra," *Down Beat*, April 1994.

[23] John Litweiler: "Anthony Braxton: three compositions of the new jazz" (liner notes to Delmark DD415, 1968).

[24] *Down Beat* review of Braxton, quoted in liner notes to Anthony Braxton: *For Alto* (Delmark DE 420, 1969).

[25] John Corbett: *op. cit.*

[26] John Litweiler: *op. cit.*

[27] "That music is written, down to the drum parts. There's nothing vague about it." Threadgill, quoted in Howard Mandel: *op. cit.*

[28] Howard Mandel: *op. cit.*

[29] Alyn Shipton: "Windy City Blowin'," *The Times*, September 11, 2000.

[30] Author's interview with Joseph Jarman, September 3, 2000.

[31] Author's interview with Ari Brown, February 26, 1999.

[32] Author's interview with Oliver Lake, February 1998.

[33] *Ibid.*

[34] Horace Tapscott: *Songs of the Unsung: The Musical and Social Journey of Horace Tapscott* (ed. Steven Isoardi) (Durham, N.C., Duke University Press, 2001).

[35] *Ibid.*

[36] Stanley Crouch: *West Coast Hot* (liner notes to Novus BD 83 107, 1991).

[37] *Ibid.*

[38] Author's interview with Joachim Kuhn, July 1997.

# Chapter 19

[1] Jelly Roll Morton: "La Poloma," in *The Library of Congress Recordings* (Affinity AFS 1010–3).

[2] Author's interview with Nana Vasconcelos, May 28, 1995.

[3] Alyn Shipton: "Ay, ay, ay, ay, ay conga," (interview with Don Alias) *The Times*, January 14, 2000.

[4] Alyn Shipton: "Ragathal: John Mayer's Indo-jazz fusions" (liner notes to Nimbus NI 5569, 1998).

[5] *Ibid.*

[6] Author's interview with Trilok Gurtu, February 4, 2000.

[7] *Ibid.*

[8] Norman C. Weinstein: *Night in Tunisia: Imaginings of Africa in Jazz* (New York, Limelight, 1993).

[9] *Ibid.*

[10] Author's interview with Hugh Masekela, May 4, 2000.

[11] *Ibid.*

[12] Brian Priestley: "Cape crusader," (interview with Abdullah Ibrahim) *Wire*, 88 (June 1991), 16ff.

[13] Richard Scott: "Call me Mr Drums," (interview with Louis Moholo) *Wire*, 85 (March 1991), 34ff.

[14] Valerie Wilmer: "Chris McGregor: 1936–1990," *Wire*, 77 (July 1990), 28.

[15] Author's interview with Pops Mahomed, May 24, 1998.

[16] *Ibid.*

[17] Robert Trunz: *Finding One's Self* (liner notes to B and W 053, 1994).

[18] Karin Krog, interviewed by John Surman for BBC Radio 3, broadcast in December 2000.

[19] Alyn Shipton: "Feeling the beatnik," *Piano*, 8 (5) (September/October 2000), 36.

# Chapter 20

[1] George Melly: *Revolt into Style: The Pop Arts in Britain* (Harmondsworth, Penguin, 1970).

[2] Mark C. Gridley: "Jazz-rock," in Barry Kernfeld (ed.): *The New Grove Dictionary of Jazz* (London, Macmillan, 1988).

[3] Jack Bruce, interviewed by Barbara Thompson for BBC Radio, September 2000.

[4] Stuart Nicholson: *Jazz Rock: A History* (Edinburgh, Canongate, 1998).

[5] Jack Bruce, interviewed by Barbara Thompson for BBC Radio, September 2000.

[6] *Ibid.*

[7] Jon Hiseman, interviewed by Barbara Thompson for BBC Radio, September 2000.

[8] Ian Carr, interviewed by Barbara Thompson for BBC Radio, September 2000; author's interview with Ian Carr, June 26, 2000.

[9] Author's interview with Dave Holland, November 1997.

[10] Ian Carr: *Miles Davis: The Definitive Biography* (London, HarperCollins, 1998).

[11] *Ibid.*

[12] *Ibid.*

[13] *Ibid.*

[14] David Liebman: "Get up with it" (liner notes to reissue Columbia C2K 63970, 2000).

[15] Ron Brown: "Miles at the Rainbow," *Jazz Journal*, 26 (9) (September 1993), 19.

[16] Author's interview with Don Alias, December 4, 1999.

[17] Author's interview with John Scofield, January 30, 2001.

[18] Nick Coleman: "Rockit and see: Herbie Hancock," *The Wire*, 31 (September 1986), 27ff.

[19] Bob Belden: "Herbie Hancock: the complete Blue Note sixties sessions" (liner notes to Blue Note B2BN7243 4 95569 2 8, 1998). Belden co-arranged much of Hancock's *The New Standard* album for Verve.

[20] Stuart Nicholson: *op. cit.*

[21] Josef Woodard: "Herbie Hancock and Quincy Jones," *Down Beat*, January 1990.

[22] Bill Milkowski: *Jaco: The Extraordinary and Tragic Life of Jaco Pastorius* (San Francisco, Miller Freeman, 1995).

[23] Nick Coleman and Richard Cook: "Weather Report: a forecast history," *The Wire*, 32 (October 1986), 33.

[24] *Ibid.*

[25] Author's interview with John Scofield, February 24, 2000.

[26] *Ibid.*

[27] Eric Nemeyer: "Man of the times: an interview with Michael Brecker," *Jazz Improv*, 2 (2) (1999), 103ff.

[28] *Ibid.*

[29] Alyn Shipton: "Hit the road, Pat," (interview with Pat Metheny) *The Times*, April 4, 2000.

# Chapter 21

[1] John Wain: "Four to one at Ladbroke's," from John Wain: *Professing Poetry* (London, Macmillan, 1977).

[2] T. S. Eliot: "Tradition and the individual talent" (1919), quoted in John Wain: *op. cit.*

[3] Barry Kernfeld: "Jazz research through the eyes of Grove" (paper given at Leeds International Jazz Education Conference, April 6 and 7, 2001).

[4] John Wain: *op. cit.*

[5] Alyn Shipton: "Cool heat in the big easy," *The Times*, February 25, 1998.

[6] *Ibid.*

[7] Author's interview with Wynton Marsalis, February 9, 2001.

[8] Richard Cook: "American majesty" (interview with Wynton Marsalis), *The Wire*, 113 (July 1993), 42.

[9] Dave Gelly: "Harry Allen," *Jazz, the Magazine*, 20 (1993), 20.

[10] *Ibid.*

[11] Dave Gelly: "John Pizzarelli," *Jazz, the Magazine*, 20 (1993), 9.

[12] Alyn Shipton: "The awakening" (interview with Diana Krall), *Jazzwise*, 23 (June 1993), 16.

[13] *Ibid.*

[14] Bruce Crowther and Mike Pinfold: *Singing Jazz* (London, Blandford Press, 1997).

[15] Author's interview with Andrew Hill, April 28, 2000.

[16] Author's interview with Dave Douglas, February 21, 2000.

[17] Author's interview with Abbey Lincoln, February 24, 1999.

[18] John Wain: *op. cit.*

# Bibliography

Chris Albertson: *Bessie* (New York, Stein and Day, 1972).

Charles Alexander: *Masters of Jazz Guitar* (London, Balafon Books, 1999).

Louis Armstrong: *Louis Armstrong in His Own Words* (ed. Thomas Brothers) (New York, Oxford University Press, 1999).

Louis Armstrong: *Swing That Music* (New York, Da Capo, 1993).

Dorothy Baker: *Young Man with a Horn* (Boston, Houghton Mifflin, 1938).

Danny Barker: *Buddy Bolden and the Last Days of Storyville* (ed. Alyn Shipton) (London, Cassell, 1998).

Danny Barker: *A Life in Jazz* (ed. Alyn Shipton) (London, Macmillan, 1986).

Charlie Barnet (with Stanley Dance): *Those Swinging Years: The Autobiography of Charlie Barnet* (Baton Rouge, Louisiana State University Press, 1984).

Count Basie: *Good Morning Blues: The Autobiography of Count Basie as Told to Albert Murray* (London, Heinemann, 1986).

Lincoln T. Beauchamp, Jr.: *Art Ensemble of Chicago: Great Black Music Ancient to the Future* (Chicago, Art Ensemble Publishing Co., 1998).

Joachim E. Berendt: *The Book of Jazz from New Orleans to Jazz Rock and Beyond* (trans. H. and B. Bredigkeit with Dan Morgenstern) (London, Granada, 1983)

Edward Berger, David Cayer, Dan Morgenstern, and Lewis Porter (eds.): *Annual Review Of Jazz Studies, Vol.6* (Methuchen, NJ, Scarecrow Press, 1993).

Morroe Berger, Edward Berger, and James Patrick: *Benny Carter: A Life in American Music* (Metuchen, N.J., Scarecrow Press, 1982).

Edward A. Berlin: *King of Ragtime: Scott Joplin and His Era* (New York, Oxford University Press, 1994).

D. E. Berlyne: *Aesthetics and Psychobiology* (New York, Appleton Century Crofts, 1971).

Arnie Bernstein: *Hollywood on Lake Michigan: 100 Years of Chicago and the Movies* (Chicago, Lake Claremont Press, 1998).

Barney Bigard: *With Louis and the Duke* (ed. Barry Martyn) (London, Macmillan, 1985).

François Billard: *Django Reinhardt: Un géant sur son nuage* (Paris, Lieu Commun, 1993).

Rudi Blesh: *Combo USA* (Philadelphia, Chilton Book Co., 1971).

Rudi Blesh: *Shining Trumpets* (London, Cassell, 1949).

Perry Bradford: *Born with the Blues: Perry Bradford's Own Story* (New York, Oak Publications, 1965).

Edward Brooks: *The Bessie Smith Companion* (2nd. edn.) (Oxford, Bayou Press, 1989).

Scott E. Brown: *James P. Johnson: A Case of Mistaken Identity* (Metuchen, N.J., Scarecrow, 1986).

H. O. Brunn: *The Story of the Original Dixieland Jazz Band* (New York, Da Capo, 1986).

Clora Bryant *et al.*: *Central Avenue Sounds: Jazz in Los Angeles* (Berkeley, University of California Press, 1998).

John Buchanan: *Emperor Norton's Hunch: The Story of Lu Watters' Yerba Buena Jazz Band* (Middle Dural, NSW, Australia, Hambledon Productions, 1996).

Garvin Bushell (as told to Mark Tucker): *Jazz from the Beginning* (Oxford, Bayou Press, 1988).

Cab Calloway: *The New Cab Calloway's Cat-ologue* (New York, Calloway, 1938).

Cab Calloway: *The New Cab Calloway's Hepster's Dictionary: Language of Jive* (New York, Calloway, 1944).

Cab Calloway (with Bryant Rollins): *Of Minnie the Moocher and Me* (New York, Thomas Y. Crowell, 1976).

P. Carles, A. Clergeat, and J.-L. Comolli: *Dictionnaire du jazz* (Paris, Laffont, 1988).

Ian Carr: *Miles Davis: The Definitive Biography* (London, HarperCollins, 1998).

Ian Carr, Digby Fairweather, and Brian Priestley: *Jazz: The Rough Guide* (2nd. edn.) (London, Rough Guides, 2000).

William Carter: *Preservation Hall* (2nd. edn.) (London, Cassell, 1999).

Jack Chambers: *Milestones 1: The Music and Times of Miles Davis to 1960* (Toronto, University of Toronto Press, 1983).

Samuel B. Charters IV: *Jazz. New Orleans 1885–1963: An Index to The Negro Musicians of New Orleans* (rev. edn.) (New York, Oak Books, 1963).

Samuel B. Charters and Leonard Kunstadt: *Jazz: A History of the New York Scene* (2nd. edn.) (New York, Da Capo, 1981).

Adolphus "Doc" Cheatham: *I Guess I'll Get the Papers and Go Home* (ed. Alyn Shipton) (London and Washington, Cassell, 1995).

John Chilton: *Billie's Blues* (London, Quartet, 1975).

John Chilton: *A Jazz Nursery: The Story of the Jenkins Orphanage Bands* (London, Bloomsbury Book Shop, 1980).

John Chilton: *Let the Good Times Roll: The Story of Louis Jordan and His Music* (London, Quartet, 1992).

John Chilton: *Ride Red Ride* (London, Cassell, 1999).

John Chilton: *Sidney Bechet: The Wizard of Jazz* (London, Macmillan, 1987).

John Chilton: *Song of the Hawk* (London, Quartet, 1990).

John Chilton: *Stomp Off, Let's Go! The Story of Bob Crosby's Bob Cats and Big Band* (London, Jazz Book Service, 1983).

John Chilton: *Who's Who of British Jazz* (London, Cassell, 1997).

John Chilton: *Who's Who of Jazz* (5th. edn.) (London, Macmillan, 1989).

Andrew Clark: *Riffs and Choruses* (London, Continuum, 2001).

Donald Clarke: *Wishing on the Moon: The Life and Times of Billie Holiday* (London, Viking, 1994).

Laurent Clarke and Franck Verdun: *Dizzy Atmosphere* (Arles, Actes Sud, 1990).

Buck Clayton: *Buck Clayton's Jazz World* (ed. Nancy Miller Elliott) (Oxford, Bayou Press, 1989).

Lawrence Cohn: *Nothing But the Blues* (New York, Abbeville Press, 1993).

Bill Coleman: *Trumpet Story* (London, Macmillan, 1990).

Buddy Collete (with Steven Isoardi): *Jazz Generations: A Life in American Music and Society* (London, Continuum, 2000).

James Lincoln Collier: *Benny Goodman and the Swing Era* (New York, Oxford University Press, 1989).

James Lincoln Collier: *Jazz: The American Theme Song* (New York, Oxford University Press, 1993).

James Lincoln Collier: *The Making of Jazz* (London, Macmillan, 1981).

Lee Collins: *Oh, Didn't He Ramble: The Life Story of Lee Collins as Told to Mary Collins* (ed. Frank Gillis and John Miner) (2nd. edn.) (Oxford, Bayou Press, 1989).

Eddie Condon: *We Called It Music* (2nd. edn.) (Westport, CT, Greenwood Press, 1970).

Roger Cotterrell: *Jazz Now* (London, Quartet, 1976).

Bill Crow: *Jazz Anecdotes* (New York, Oxford University Press, 1990).

Bruce Crowther: *Gene Krupa* (New York, Universe, 1988).

Bruce Crowther and Mike Pinfold: *Singing Jazz* (London, Blandford Press, 1997).

Stanley Dance: *The World of Swing* (New York, Scribner, 1974).

Michael Danzi: *American Musician in Germany, 1924–1939, as Told to Rainer Lotz* (Schmitten, Ruecker, 1986).

James Dapogny: *Ferdinand Jelly Roll Morton: The Collected Piano Music* (Washington, Smithsonian Institution, 1982).

Joe Darensbourg: *Telling It Like It Is* (ed. Peter Vacher) (London, Macmillan, 1987).

Miles Davis (with Quincy Troupe): *Miles: The Autobiography* (New York, Simon and Schuster, 1989).

Chip Deffaa: *Voices of the Jazz Age* (Oxford, Bayou Press, 1990).

Charles Delaunay: *Django Reinhardt* (trans. Michael James) (2nd. edn.) (London, Cassell, 1981).

Scott DeVeaux: *The Birth of Bebop: A Social and Musical History* (Berkeley, University of California Press, 1997).

Laurent De Wilde: *Monk* (trans. Jonathan Dickinson) (New York, Marlowe, 1998).

Harry Dial: *All This Jazz about Jazz* (Chigwell, Storyville, 1984).

R. M. W. Dixon and J. Godrich: *Blues and Gospel Records 1902–1943* (3rd. edn.) (Chigwell, Storyville, 1982).

Roger Pryor Dodge: *Hot Jazz and Jazz Dance. Roger Pryor Dodge: Collected Writings 1929–1964* (New York, Oxford University Press, 1995).

Frank Driggs and Harris Lewine: *Black Beauty, White Heat: A Pictorial History of Classic Jazz, 1920–1950* (New York, William Morrow, 1982).

Rudolph Dunbar: *Triumph and Tragedy* (Oxford, Bayou Press, forthcoming).

Lewis A. Erenberg: *Swingin' the Dream: Big Band Jazz and the Rebirth of American Culture* (Chicago, University of Chicago Press, 1998).

Leonard Feather: *From Satchmo to Miles* (London, Quartet, 1974).

Julio Finn: *The Bluesman: The Musical Heritage of Black Men and Women in the Americas* (London, Quartet, 1986).

Ross Firestone: *Swing, Swing, Swing: The Life and Times of Benny Goodman* (New York, W. W. Norton, 1993).

Bud Freeman: *Crazeology: The Autobiography of a Chicago Jazzman* (ed. Robert Wolf) (Oxford, Bayou Press, 1989).

Will Friedwald: *Jazz Singing: America's Great Voices from Bessie Smith to Bebop and Beyond* (London, Quartet, 1991).

Krin Gabbard: *Jammin' at the Margins: Jazz and the American Cinema* (Chicago, University of Chicago Press, 1996).

Krin Gabbard (ed.): *Jazz Among the Discourses* (Durham, N.C., Duke University Press, 1995).

Kurt Gänzl: *The Encyclopedia of Musical Theatre* (Oxford, Blackwell, 1994).

Larry Gara: *The Baby Dodds Story* (Baton Rouge, Louisiana State University Press, 1992).

Dave Gelly: *Masters of the Jazz Saxophone: The Story of the Players and Their Music* (London, Balaphon, 2000).

Dizzy Gillespie and Al Fraser: *Dizzy: To Be or Not to Bop* (London, Quartet, 1980).

Ted Gioia: *West Coast Jazz* (New York, Oxford University Press, 1992).

Ira Gitler: *Swing to Bop: An Oral History of the Transition in Jazz in the 1940s* (New York, Oxford University Press, 1985).

Jim Godbolt: *A History of Jazz in Britain, 1919–50* (London, Quartet, 1984).

Robert Goffin: *Aux frontières du jazz* (Paris, n.p., 1932).

Jim Goggin and Peter Clute: *The Great Jazz Revival* (San Rafael, CA, Donna Ewald, 1994).

Harry Gold: *Gold Doubloons and Pieces of Eight: The Autobiography of Harry Gold* (ed. R. Cotterrell) (London, Northway, 2000).

Robert Gordon: *Jazz West Coast* (London, Quartet, 1990).

Jeffrey P. Green: *Edmund Thornton Jenkins: The Life and Times of an American Black Composer, 1894–1926* (Westport, CT, Greenwood Press, 1982).

Mark C. Gridley: *Jazz Styles: History and Analysis* (2nd. edn.) (Englewood Cliffs, NJ, Prentice-Hall, 1985).

Pekka Gronow and Ilpo Saunio: *An International History of the Recording Industry* (trans. Christopher Moseley) (London, Cassell, 1998).

Alan Groves and Alyn Shipton: *The Glass Enclosure: The Life of Bud Powell* (Oxford, Bayou Press, 1993).

Richard Hadlock: *Jazz Masters of the Twenties* (New York, Macmillan, 1965).

John Hammond (with Irving Townsend): *John Hammond on the Record* (New York, Ridge Press, 1977).

Rex Harris: *Jazz* (Harmondsworth, Penguin, 1952).

Max Harrison: *A Jazz Retrospect* (Newton Abbot, David and Charles, 1976).

Max Harrison, Eric Thacker, and Stuart Nicholson: *The Essential Jazz Records, Vol. 2* (London, Mansell, 2000).

John Edward Hasse: *Ragtime: Its History, Composers and Music* (London, Macmillan, 1985).

Geoffrey Haydon and Dennis Marks (eds.): *Repercussions: A Celebration of African-*

*American Music* (London, Channel Four Books/Century, 1985).

Melville Herskovits: *The Anthropometry of the American Negro* (New York, Columbia University Press, 1930).

Christopher Hillman: *Bunk Johnson* (Tunbridge Wells, Spellmount, 1988).

H. Wiley Hitchcock: *Music in the United States: A Historical Introduction* (3rd. edn.) (Englewood Cliffs, NJ, Prentice-Hall, 1988).

H. Wiley Hitchcock and Stanley Sadie (eds.): *The New Grove Dictionary of American Music* (London, Macmillan, 1986).

Art Hodes: *Hot Man* (ed. Chadwick Hansen) (Oxford, Bayou Press, 1992).

Raymond Horricks: *These Jazzmen of Our Time* (London, Gollancz, 1959).

Wally Horwood: *Adolphe Sax 1814–1894: His Life and Legacy* (Baldock, Herts, Egon, 1983).

LeRoi Jones (Amiri Baraka): *Blues People: Negro Music in White America* (New York, William Morrow, 1963).

Max Jones: *Talking Jazz* (London, Macmillan, 1987).

Max Jones and John Chilton: *Louis: The Louis Armstrong Story 1900–1971* (London, Quartet, 1971).

Pleasant "Cousin Joe" Joseph: *Cousin Joe: Blues from New Orleans* (Chicago, University of Chicago Press, 1987).

Charles Joyner: *Down by the Riverside: A South Carolina Slave Community* (Urbana, University of Illinois Press, 1984).

Ashley Kahn: *Kind of Blue: The Making of the Miles Davis Masterpiece* (London, Granta, 2000).

Max Kaminsky: *My Life in Jazz* (London, Andre Deutsch, 1965).

Rick Kennedy: *Jelly Roll, Bix and Hoagy: Gennett Studios and the Birth of Recorded Jazz* (Bloomington, Indiana University Press, 1994).

William Howland Kenney: *Chicago Jazz: A Cultural History 1904–1930* (New York, Oxford University Press, 1993).

Barry Kernfeld (ed.): *The New Grove Dictionary of Jazz* (London, Macmillan, 1988).

Grace King: *New Orleans: The Place and the People* (New York, Macmillan, 1895).

Andy Kirk: *Twenty Years on Wheels* (ed. Amy Lee) (Oxford, Bayou Press, 1989).

Ed Kirkeby: *Ain't Misbehavin': The Story of Fats Waller* (New York, Dodd Mead, 1966).

Jerome Klinkowitz: *Listen. Gerry Mulligan: An Aural Narrative in Jazz* (New York, Schirmer, 1991).

Frank Kofsky: *Black Music, White Business* (New York, Pathfinder, 1998).

Robert C. Kriebel: *Blue Flame: Woody Herman's Life in Music* (West Lafayette, IA, Purdue University Press, 1995).

Eddie Lambert: *A Listener's Guide to Duke Ellington* (Latham, MD, Scarecrow Press, 1999).

Denise Lanctot, Alyn Shipton, and others: *Radio Rhapsodies* (London, City of London Sinfonia, 2000).

Horst H. Lange: *The Fabulous Fives* (2nd. edn.) (Chigwell, Storyville, 1978).

Philip Larkin: *All What Jazz* (London, Faber, 1970).

George E. Lee: *Beale Street: Where the Blues Began* (New York, Robert O. Ballou, 1934).

Gene Lees: *Arranging the Score* (London, Continuum, 2000).

Gene Lees: *Cats of Any Color: Jazz Black and White* (New York, Oxford University Press, 1994).

Gene Lees: *Leader of the Band: The Life of Woody Herman* (New York, Oxford University Press, 1995).

Gene Lees: *Meet Me at Jim and Andy's: Jazz Musicians and Their World* (New York, Oxford University Press, 1988).

Gene Lees: *Waiting for Dizzy* (New York, Oxford University Press, 1991).

James Lester: *Too Marvelous for Words: The Life and Genius of Art Tatum* (New York, Oxford University Press, 1994).

Jean-Paul Levet: *Talking That Talk: Le Langage du blues et du jazz* (Hatier, Paris, 1992).

Peter J. Levinson: *Trumpet Blues: The Life of Harry James* (New York, Oxford University Press, 2000).

John Litweiler: *The Freedom Principle: Jazz after 1958* (New York, Da Capo, 1990).

Alan Lomax: *Mister Jelly Roll. The Fortunes of Jelly Roll Morton: New Orleans Creole and "Inventor of Jazz"* (rev. edn.) (New York, Pantheon, 1993).

Len Lyons: *The Great Jazz Pianists* (New York, Da Capo, 1983).

Humphrey Lyttelton: *The Best of Jazz (i): Basin Street to Harlem* (Harmondsworth, Penguin, 1978).

Humphrey Lyttelton: *The Best of Jazz (ii): Enter the Giants* (London, Robson Books, 1981).

Humphrey Lyttelton: *Second Chorus* (London, MacGibbon and Kee, 1958).

Albert McCarthy: *Big Band Jazz* (London, Barrie and Jenkins, 1974).

Albert McCarthy: *The Dance Band Era. The Dancing Decades from Ragtime to Swing: 1910–1950* (London, Spring Books, 1971).

Donald L. Maggin: *Stan Getz: A Life in Jazz* (New York, William Morrow, 1996).

Howard Mandel: *Future Jazz* (New York, Oxford University Press, 1999).

David Margolick: *Strange Fruit: Billie Holiday, Café Society and an Early Cry for Civil Rights* (Edinburgh, Payback Press, 2001).

Donald M. Marquis: *Finding Buddy Bolden* (Goshen, IA, Pinchpenny Press, 1978).

Kenny Mathieson: *Giant Steps: Bebop and the Creators of Modern Jazz 1945–65* (Edinburgh, Payback Press, 1999).

George Melly: *Revolt into Style: The Pop Arts in Britain* (Harmondsworth, Penguin, 1970).

Mezz Mezzrow and Bernard Wolfe: *Really the Blues* (New York, Random House, 1946).

Bill Milkowski: *Jaco: The Extraordinary and Tragic Life of Jaco Pastorius* (San Francisco, Miller Freeman, 1995).

Bill Milkowski: *Swing It! An Annotated History of Jive* (New York, Billboard Books, 2001).

Charles Mingus: *Beneath the Underdog* (ed. Nel King) (London, Weidenfeld and Nicolson, 1971).

Helen Myers (ed.): *Ethnomusicology: An Introduction* (London, Macmillan, 1992).

Stuart Nicholson: *Billie Holiday* (London, Gollancz, 1995).

Stuart Nicholson: *Ella Fitzgerald* (London, Gollancz, 1993).

Stuart Nicholson: *Jazz Rock: A History* (Edinburgh, Canongate, 1998).

Stuart Nicholson: *Reminiscing in Tempo: A Portrait of Duke Ellington* (London, Sidgwick and Jackson, 1999).

Ole J. Nielsen: *Jazz Records 1942–80: A Discography. Vol 6: Duke Ellington* (Copenhagen, JazzMedia APS, n.d.).

Eric Nisenson: *Ascension: John Coltrane and His Quest* (New York, St Martin's Press, 1993).

Lucy O'Brien: *She-Bop* (London, Penguin, 1995).

Anita O'Day (with George Eells): *High Times, Hard Times* (New York, Putnam, 1981).

Kathy J. Ogren: *The Jazz Revolution: Twenties America and the Meaning of Jazz* (New York, Oxford University Press, 1989).

Paul Oliver: *Conversation with the Blues* (London, Cassell, 1965).

Paul Oliver: *Savannah Syncopators* (London, Studio Vista, 1970).

Paul Oliver: *Songsters and Saints* (Cambridge, Cambridge University Press, 1984).

Paul Oliver: *Story of the Blues* (London, Barrie and Rockliffe, 1969).

Henry Osgood: *So This Is Jazz* (Boston, Little, Brown and Company, 1926).

Thomas Owens: *Bebop: The Music and the Players* (New York, Oxford University Press, 1995).

Hugues Panassié: *Hot Jazz (trans. from Le Jazz hot,* Paris, Correa, 1934, by Lyle and Eleanor Dowling) (London, Cassell, 1936).

Lydia Parrish: *Slave Songs of the Georgia Sea Islands* (New York, Creative Age Press, Inc., 1942).

Nathan W. Pearson Jr.: *Goin' to Kansas City* (London, Macmillan, 1988).

Art and Laurie Pepper: *Straight Life: The Story of Art Pepper* (New York, Schirmer Books, 1979).

Sally Placksin: *Jazz Women: 1900 to the Present* (London, Pluto Press, 1982).

James Popa: *Cab Calloway and His Orchestra 1925–1958* (rev. by Charles Garrod) (2nd. edn.) (Zephyr Hills, FL, Joyce Record Club, 1987).

Lewis Porter: *John Coltrane: His Life and Music* (Ann Arbor, University of Michigan Press, 1998).

Lewis Porter: *Lester Young* (London, Macmillan, 1985).

Roy Porter: *There and Back* (ed. David Keller) (Oxford, Bayou Press, 1991).

Sammy Price: *What Do They Want?* (ed. Caroline Richmond) (Oxford, Bayou Press, 1989).

Brian Priestley: *John Coltrane* (London, Apollo Press, 1987).

Brian Priestley: *Mingus: A Critical Biography* (London, Quartet, 1982).

Frederic Ramsey Jr. and Charles Edward Smith (ed.): *Jazzmen: The Story of Hot Jazz Told in the Lives of the Men Who Created It* (New York, Harcourt, Brace and Company, 1939).

Andy Razaf and Fats Waller: *Doin' What I Please* (New York, J.R. Lafleur; London, Belwin Mills Music Ltd., 1931).

Robert Reisner: *Bird: The Legend of Charlie Parker* (London, Quartet, 1962).

Thomas L. Riis: *More Than Just Minstrel Shows: The Rise of Black Musical Theater at the Turn of the Century* (I.S.A.M. Monographs no. 33) (Brooklyn, Institute for Studies in American Music, 1992).

Arthur Rollini: *Thirty Years with the Big Bands* (Oxford, Bayou Press, 1989).

Al Rose and Edmond Souchon: *New Orleans Jazz: A Family Album* (3rd. edn.) (Baton

Rouge, Louisiana State University Press, 1984).

Phyllis Rose: *Jazz Cleopatra: Josephine Baker in Her Time* (New York, Doubleday, 1989).

David H. Rosenthal: *Hard Bop: Jazz and Black Music 1955–1965* (New York, Oxford University Press, 1992).

Marshal Royal: *Jazz Survivor* (ed. Claire P. Gordon) (London, Cassell, 1996).

George Russell: *The Lydian Chromatic Concept of Tonal Organization for Improvisation* (New York, Concept Publishing, 1959).

Ross Russell: *Bird Lives! The High Life and Hard Times of Charlie "Yardbird" Parker* (London, Quartet, 1973).

Ross Russell: *Jazz Style in Kansas City and the Southwest* (Berkeley, University of California Press, 1973).

William Russell: *Jelly Roll Morton Scrapbook* (Copenhagen, JazzMedia APS, 1999).

Brian Rust: *Jazz Records 1897–1942* (5th. edn.) (Chigwell, Storyville, 1983).

Stanley Sadie (ed.): *The New Grove Dictionary of Music and Musicians* (London, Macmillan, 1981).

Gene Santoro: *Myself When I Am Real: The Life and Music of Charles Mingus* (New York, Oxford University Press, 2000).

William J. Schafer: *Brass Bands and New Orleans Jazz* (Baton Rouge, Louisiana State University Press, 1977).

Gunther Schuller: *Early Jazz: Its Roots and Musical Development* (New York, Oxford University Press, 1968).

Gunther Schuller: *Musings. The Musical Worlds of Gunther Schuller: A Collection of His Writings* (New York, Oxford University Press, 1986).

Gunther Schuller: *The Swing Era* (New York, Oxford University Press, 1989).

Gilbert Seldes: *Seven Lively Arts* (New York, Harper, 1924).

Michel Serres (ed.): *A History of Scientific Thought: Elements of a History of Science* (Oxford, Blackwell, 1995).

Nat Shapiro and Nat Hentoff: *Hear Me Talkin' to Ya* (Harmondsworth, Penguin, 1962).

Artie Shaw: *The Trouble with Cinderella: An Outline of Identity* (2nd. edn.) (New York, Da Capo, 1979).

Chris Sheridan: *Count Basie: A Bio-Discography* (Westport, CT, Greenwood, 1986).

Alyn Shipton: *Fats Waller: His Life and Times* (New York, Universe, 1988).

Alyn Shipton: *Groovin' High: The Life of Dizzy Gillespie* (New York, Oxford University Press, 1999).

Alyn Shipton (ed.): *Ragtime and Early Jazz: Ascona Festival Symposium* (Arcegno, Switzerland, 1987).

Peter Silvester: *A Left Hand Like God: A Study of Boogie Woogie* (London, Quartet, 1988).

G.T. Simon: *The Big Bands* (4th. edn.) (New York, Schirmer, 1981).

Geoffrey Smith: *Stephane Grappelli: A Biography* (London, Michael Joseph/Pavilion, 1987).

Willie "The Lion" Smith (with George Hoefer): *Music on My Mind* (New York, Da Capo, 1978).

Austin M. Sonnier: *Willie Geary "Bunk" Johnson* (New York, Crescendo, 1977).

Eileen Southern: *Music of the Black Americans: A History* (3rd. edn.) (New York, Norton, 1997).

A. B. Spellman: *Four Lives in the Bebop Business* (New York, Limelight, 1985).

S. Frederick Starr: *Red and Hot: The Fate of Jazz in the Soviet Union* (New York, Oxford University Press, 1983).

Marshall Stearns: *The Story of Jazz* (New York, Oxford University Press, 1956).

Rex Stewart: *Boy Meets Horn* (ed. Claire P. Gordon) (Oxford, Bayou Press, 1991).

Rex Stewart: *Jazz Masters of the Thirties* (New York, Macmillan, 1972).

Derrick Stewart-Baxter: *Ma Rainey and the Classic Blues Singers* (London, Studio Vista, 1970).

Tom Stoddart: *Jazz on the Barbary Coast* (2nd. edn.) (Berkeley, Heyday Books, 1998).

Klaus Stratemann: *Duke Ellington: Day by Day and Film by Film* (Copenhagen, JazzMedia APS, 1992).

Richard M. Sudhalter: *Lost Chords* (New York, Oxford University Press, 1999).

Richard M. Sudhalter, Philip R. Evans, and William Dean-Myatt: *Bix. Man and Legend: The Life of Bix Beiderbecke* (London, Quartet, 1974).

Horace Tapscott: *Songs of the Unsung: The Musical and Social Journey of Horace Tapscott* (ed. Steven Isoardi) (Durham, N.C., Duke University Press, 2001).

Art Taylor: *Notes and Tones* (2nd. edn.) (New York, Da Capo, 1993).

Frank Tirro: *Jazz: A History* (2nd. edn.) (New York, W. W. Norton, 1993).

Mark Tucker: *The Duke Ellington Reader* (New York, Oxford University Press, 1993).

Mark Tucker: *Ellington: The Early Years* (Oxford, Bayou Press, 1991).

Michael Tucker: *Jan Garbarek: Deep Song* (Hull, East Note, 1998).

Sophie Tucker: *Some of These Days* (New York, Hammond, 1948).

Barry Ulanov: *A History of Jazz in America* (London, Hutchinson, 1959).

Ken Vail: *Bird's Diary: The Life of Charlie Parker 1945–1955* (Chessington, Castle Communications, 1996).

Ken Vail: *Dizzy Gillespie: The Bebop Years 1937–1952* (Cambridge, Vail Publishing, 2000).

John Wain: *Professing Poetry* (London, Macmillan, 1977).

Fats Waller, Andy Razaf, and Harry Brooks: *Ain't Misbehavin'* (New York, Mills Music Inc., 1929).

Robert Walser: *Keeping Time: Readings In Jazz History* (New York, Oxford University Press, 1999).

Benny Waters: *The Key to a Jazzy Life* (Toulouse, Les Arts Graphiques, 1985).

Norman C. Weinstein: *Night in Tunisia: Imaginings of Africa in Jazz* (New York, Limelight, 1993).

John White: *Artie Shaw: Non-Stop Flight* (Hull, Eastnote, 1998).

Paul Whiteman: *Records for the Millions* (New York, Hermitage Press, 1948).

Paul Whiteman (and Mary Margaret McBride): *Jazz* (New York, J. H. Sears, 1926).

Bert Whyatt: *Muggsy Spanier: The Lonesome Road* (New Orleans, Jazzology Press, 1995).

Bob Wilber (assisted by Derek Webster): *Music Was Not Enough* (Oxford, Bayou Press, 1989).

Martin Williams: *The Jazz Tradition* (2nd. edn.) (New York, Oxford University Press, 1993).

Valerie Wilmer: *As Serious as Your Life* (London, Quartet, 1977).

Glenn D. Wilson: *Psychology for Performing Artists* (London, Jessica Kingsley, 1994).

# BIBLIOGRAPHY

Peter Niklas Wilson: *Ornette Coleman: His Life and Music* (Berkeley, CA, Berkeley Hills Books, 1999).

Teddy Wilson: *Teddy Wilson Talks Jazz* (ed. Arie Ligthart and Humphrey Van Loo) (London, Cassell, 1996).

Carl Woideck: *The John Coltrane Companion: Five Decades of Commentary* (New York, Schirmer, 1998).

Laurie Wright: *Fats in Fact* (Chigwell, Storyville, 1992).

Laurie Wright: *King Oliver* (Chigwell, Storyville, 1987).

Writers' Program of the Works Progress Administration in Northern California: *San Francisco: The Bay and Its Cities* (New York, Hastings House, 1940).

Mike Zwerin: *Swing under the Nazis: Jazz as a Metaphor for Freedom* (New York, Cooper Square Press, 2000).

# General Index

Figures in **bold** indicate major references or sections. Bands with a different name from their bandleader are indexed by that name as a main heading. Venues are listed by name as main entries; and also as page references for the subheadings of "venues" and "clubs" under individual place names, and as page references for the subheadings of individual place names under "clubs" and "venues."

957

# Index of Titles

This index includes the principal song titles, albums and shows discussed in the text, where they are all italicized, as they are here.